Microsoft
Visual Basic .NET
Comprehensive Concepts and Techniques

Gary B. Shelly
Thomas J. Cashman
Jeffrey J. Quasney

THOMSON
COURSE TECHNOLOGY

COURSE TECHNOLOGY
25 THOMSON PLACE
BOSTON MA 02210

SHELLY
CASHMAN
SERIES®

Australia • Canada • Denmark • Japan • Mexico • New Zealand • Philippines • Puerto Rico • Singapore
South Africa • Spain • United Kingdom • United States

Microsoft
Visual Basic .NET
Comprehensive Concepts and Techniques

THOMSON
COURSE TECHNOLOGY

Microsoft Visual Basic .NET
Comprehensive Concepts and Techniques
Gary B. Shelly
Thomas J. Cashman
Jeffrey J. Quasney

Managing Editor:
Cheryl Ouellette

Development Editor:
Lisa Strite

Marketing Manager:
Katie McAllister

Senior Product Manager:
Alexandra Arnold

Product Manager:
Erin Runyon

Associate Product Manager:
Reed Cotter

Editorial Assistant:
Emilie Perreault

Print Buyer:
Denise Powers

Director of Production:
Becky Herrington

Production Manager:
Doug Cowley

Design:
Betty Hopkins
Doug Cowley

Copy Editors:
Rich Hansberger
Ginny Harvey
Lori Silfen

Proofreader:
Nancy Lamm

Illustrators:
Kellee LaVars
Andrew Bartel

Cover Design:
Michelle French

Signing Representative:
Cheryl Ouellette

Compositors:
Jeanne Black
Betty Hopkins

Printer:
Banta Company

ISBN-13: 978-0-7895-6549-5
ISBN-10: 0-7895-6549-8

Microsoft Visual Basic .NET Comprehensive Concepts and Techniques

Contents

CHAPTER 3

Building an Application in the Visual Basic .NET Environment

CHAPTER 6

Repetition and Multiple Forms

CHAPTER 7

Using Menus, Common Dialogs, Procedures, Functions, and Arrays

CHAPTER 10

Accessing Databases
with ADO.NET, Handling Exceptions,
and Printing

APPENDIX A

Flowcharting, Pseudocode, and the Unified Modeling Language (UML)

APPENDIX B

Changing Screen Resolution and the IDE Layout

APPENDIX C

Visual Basic .NET Common Control Summary

APPENDIX D

General Forms of Common Visual Basic .NET Statements, Data Types, and Naming Conventions

APPENDIX E

The .NET Framework Class Library Overview

APPENDIX F

ASCII Character Codes

Preface

The Shelly Cashman Series® offers the finest textbooks in computer education. We are proud that our previous *Microsoft Visual Basic* books have been so well received by instructors and students. The *Microsoft Visual Basic .NET* books continue with the innovation, quality, and reliability found in the previous editions. In particular, a new step-by-step pedagogy has been integrated with an in-depth discussion of programming concepts and techniques. In addition, the end-of-chapter exercises are enhanced with critical-thinking problems.

Visual Basic .NET is the most significant upgrade since the introduction of Visual Basic. Some of the major enhancements to Visual Basic .NET include: (1) an easier-to-use integrated development environment (IDE); (2) support for Web Forms and XML Web services; (3) Windows Forms that provide a clear, object-oriented, extensible set of classes that enable you to develop rich Windows applications; (4) project templates that allow you easily to create various types of Windows and Web applications and controls; (5) new features that incorporate resources such as message queues, event logs, and performance counters into applications; and (6) new debugging features.

In our *Visual Basic. NET* books, you will find an educationally sound and easy-to-follow pedagogy that combines a step-by-step approach with corresponding screens. The Other Ways and Tip features offer in-depth suggestions about alternative ways to complete a task and programming techniques. Every programming chapter builds an application from start to finish, following a disciplined development cycle defined in Chapter 1. The Shelly Cashman Series *Microsoft Visual Basic .NET* books will make your programming class exciting and dynamic and one that your students will remember as one of their better educational experiences.

Objectives of This Textbook

Microsoft Visual Basic .NET: Comprehensive Concepts and Techniques is intended for a three-credit course that introduces students to the correct way to design and write programs using Visual Basic .NET. No experience with a computer is assumed, and no mathematics beyond the high school freshman level is required. The objectives of this book are:

- To teach the fundamentals of the Microsoft Visual Basic .NET programming language
- To focus on proper class design and class programming to provide students with a strong introduction to object-oriented design and programming techniques
- To emphasize the development cycle as a means of creating applications
- To illustrate well-written and readable programs using a disciplined coding style, including documentation and indentation standards
- To demonstrate how to implement logic involving sequence, selection, and repetition using Visual Basic .NET
- To introduce the new ADO.NET technologies
- To present new .NET application types, including Web applications and Web services
- To show proper error and exception handling using Try…Catch…Finally statements
- To use practical problems to illustrate application-building techniques
- To encourage independent study and help those who are working alone in a distance education environment

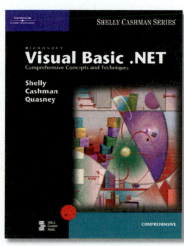

The Shelly Cashman Approach

Features of the Shelly Cashman Series *Microsoft Visual Basic .NET* books include:

- **Building Applications**   Each programming chapter builds a complete application using the six phases of the development cycle: (1) analyze requirements; (2) design solution; (3) validate design; (4) implement design; (5) test solution; and (6) document solution.

- **Step-by-Step, Screen-by-Screen Methodology**   Each of the tasks required to build an application within a chapter is identified using a step-by-step, screen-by-screen methodology. Students have the option of learning Visual Basic .NET by reading the book without the use of a computer or by following the steps on a computer and building a chapter application from start to finish.

- **More Than Just Step-By-Step**   This book offers extended but clear discussions of programming concepts. Important Visual Basic. NET design and programming tips are interspersed throughout the chapters. When a Visual Basic .NET statement is introduced, one or more tables follow showing the general form of the statement and the various options available. With in-depth appendices on the Visual Basic .NET common controls, general forms of statements and naming conventions and .NET Framework class library, the book can be used as a Visual Basic .NET reference manual.

- **Tip Boxes**   Tip boxes are used throughout the text to emphasize the correct way to design and write programs.

- **Other Ways Boxes**   Visual Basic .NET provides a variety of ways to carry out a given task. The Other Ways boxes displayed at the end of many of the step-by-step sequences specify the other ways to do the task completed in the steps. Thus, the steps and the Other Ways box make a comprehensive reference unit.

Organization of This Textbook

Microsoft Visual Basic .NET: Comprehensive Concepts and Techniques provides detailed instruction on how to use Visual Basic .NET. The material is divided into twelve chapters and six appendices as follows:

Chapter 1 – An Introduction to Visual Basic .NET and Program Design   Chapter 1 provides an overview of the capabilities of Visual Basic .NET, application development, program development methodology, program design tools, object-oriented design and object-oriented programming, and the .NET architecture.

Chapter 2 – The Visual Basic .NET Integrated Development Environment   Chapter 2 introduces students to the major elements of the Visual Basic .NET integrated development environment. Students modify the Take-Home Pay Calculator. The modifications consist of changing a property of a control and changing code. Topics include starting Visual Basic .NET; customizing the development environment; opening a project; running a project; setting a property on a control; modifying code; saving a project; printing a form and code; and accessing and using the Visual Basic .NET Help system.

Chapter 3 – Building an Application in the Visual Basic .NET Environment   Chapter 3 introduces students to the process of building a complete application in the Visual Basic .NET environment. The chapter begins with a requirements document for the State Tax Computation application and shows the process of proper design and analysis of the program. Topics include designing a Visual Basic .NET application; changing form properties; adding controls to a form; moving and resizing controls; changing properties of controls; writing code for an event procedure; commenting code; and using the assignment statement.

Chapter 4 – Working with Variables, Constants, Data Types, and Expressions   Chapter 4 presents students with the fundamental concepts of programming, including variables, constants, data types, and expressions. The chapter introduces two new controls in the development of the Automobile Loan Calculator. Topics include proper alignment and sizing of controls; setting a default button on a form; locking controls on a form; coding a form Load event; declaring variables and constants; using data types properly; using arithmetic expressions; understanding operator precedence; converting data types; and using intrinsic functions.

Chapter 5 – Decision Making   Chapter 5 provides an overview of the fundamental concepts involved with decision making in programming, including If…Then…Else and Select Case structures. The chapter introduces the ComboBox control and the ability to interact with the user through message boxes. Topics include coding an If…Then…Else statement; coding a Select Case statement; using a message box; using string concatenation; using relational operators in code; and using logical operators in code.

Chapter 6 – Repetition and Multiple Forms   Chapter 6 presents the fundamental programming concepts involved with repetition structures, including Do While, Do Until, For…Next, For Each…Next, and While…End While loops. The chapter introduces two new controls in the development of the Today's Sales Check application. Topics include adding additional forms to a project; changing the default icon of a form; anchoring controls to a form; working with Collections; coding a Do Until loop; coding a Do While loop; coding a For…Next and a For Each…Next loop, coding concatenation operators; coding keyboard events; working with multiple code windows; and specifying the Startup object for a project.

Chapter 7 – Using Menus, Common Dialogs, Procedures, Functions, and Arrays   Chapter 7 provides an overview of several advanced Windows controls and the use of arrays in programming. The chapter introduces five new controls in the development of the Know Your Dogs Quiz application. Topics include adding a main menu and a shortcut menu to forms; using common dialog boxes to interact with the user; using one-dimensional and multidimensional arrays; using collections of controls to access properties and methods in code; writing a function procedure; writing a sub procedure; creating enhanced message boxes to interact with the user; and writing code to pass arguments to procedures.

Chapter 8 – Debugging, Creating Executable Files, and Distributing a Windows Application   Chapter 8 provides a detailed introduction to the rich set of debugging tools available in Visual Basic .NET. After the enhanced Today's Sales Check application is debugged, an executable file is created for the application, and a Windows setup project is created for distributing the application to users. Topics include finding syntax errors during design time; finding run-time and logic errors during run time; setting breakpoints; executing one statement at a time by stepping; setting the next statement to execute; evaluating variables using DataTips, the QuickWatch window, and the Watch window; using the Autos, Locals, and Me windows to examine variables and objects; using the Command window to execute commands; creating an executable file; and creating a setup program to distribute a Windows application.

Chapter 9 – Designing, Creating, and Using a Class   Chapter 9 provides an overview of class design and the fundamental programming concepts involved in creation and use of a class in code. This chapter and the remaining chapters in the book develop a Compensation Review system for a human resources department. Chapter 9 introduces class design using the UML; creating an Employee class in code; and then creating a constructor, properties, and methods for the class. The Employee class that is developed in the chapter is used throughout the remaining chapters in the book. Topics include understanding when to create a class while designing a solution; designing a class using the UML; creating a new class; creating a class constructor, property, and method; creating a new class using inheritance; and using a class in a program.

Chapter 10 – Accessing Databases with ADO.NET, Handling Exceptions, and Printing   Chapter 10 presents the fundamental programming concepts involved with database access, structured exception handling, and printing. The chapter introduces three new controls and discusses the use of Crystal Reports in applications. An additional class that encapsulates database access code is added to the class library created in Chapter 9. Topics include using the MonthCalendar control; using the PrintDialog and PrintDocument controls; writing code in a class; understanding database connections and ADO.NET; understanding exception handling by the CLR; coding a Try…Catch…Finally statement to handle exceptions; reading records from a database using SQL; and understanding the functionality and major components of Crystal Reports.

Chapter 11 – Creating Web Applications and Writing Data to a Database   Chapter 11 introduces students to the development of Web applications and delves further into database concepts, including writing data to a database using SQL. The chapter introduces students to the process of building Web applications for the Compensation Review system in the Visual Basic .NET environment and using HTML controls and Web controls to build the user interface. Topics include creating a public procedure in a module; using optional parameters in a procedure; using the SQL UPDATE statement to update records in a database; starting a new Web application; understanding Web forms and Web applications; using HTML controls and Web controls in a Web application; and viewing the HTML code for a Web form.

Chapter 12 – Creating Console Applications, Understanding XML, and Creating Web Services   Chapter 12 provides an overview of XML and Web services, introduces Console applications, and presents text file input and output techniques. The chapter completes the Compensation Review system programming by creating output files that can be obtained by an outside payroll vendor. Topics include starting a new Console application; using command-line parameters for a Console application; creating and writing to comma-delimited and tab-delimited files; creating and writing to an XML file; starting a new Web service application; reading an XML file in code; using a Web service in an application; and debugging Console and Web services applications.

Appendices   This book concludes with six appendices. Appendix A covers program design tools, including flowcharting and the Unified Modeling Language (UML). Appendix B demonstrates how to take full advantage of the .NET IDE by setting the proper screen resolution and arranging windows to maximize productivity. Appendix C summarizes the common controls used in the book, along with common properties, methods, and events for those controls. Appendix D summarizes the Visual Basic .NET statements and naming conventions for data types and controls introduced in the book. Appendix E provides an overview of several common classes in the .NET Framework class library that a beginning programmer will find useful. Appendix F provides students with an ASCII chart.

End-of-Chapter Activities

A notable strength of the Shelly Cashman Series *Microsoft Visual Basic .NET* books is the extensive student activities at the end of each chapter. Well-structured student activities can make the difference between students merely participating in a class and students retaining the information they learn. The end-of-chapter activities in the *Visual Basic .NET* books are detailed below.

- **What You Should Know**   This table gives a listing of the tasks completed in the chapter in order of presentation, together with the page numbers on which the step-by-step, screen-by-screen explanations appear. This section provides a perfect study review for students.

- **Key Terms**   This list of the key terms found in the chapter, together with the page numbers on which the terms are defined, aids students in mastering the chapter material.

- **Homework Assignments**   The homework assignments are divided into three sections: Label the Figure, Short Answer, and Learn It Online. The Label the Figure section, in the chapters where it applies, involves a figure and callouts that students fill in. The Short Answer section includes fill-in-the-blank and short essay questions. The Learn It Online section is comprised of Web-based exercises that include chapter reinforcement (true/false, multiple choice, and short answer), practice tests, learning games, and Web exercises that require students to extend their learning beyond the material covered in the book.

- **Debugging Assignment**   This exercise requires students to open an application with errors from the Visual Basic .NET Data Disk that accompanies the book and debug it. Students may obtain a copy of the Visual Basic .NET Data Disk by following the instructions on page xviv in the preface of this book.

- **Programming Assignments**   An average of ten programming assignments per chapter require students to apply the knowledge gained in the chapter to build applications on a computer. The initial programming assignments step students through building the application and are accompanied by screens showing the desired interface. Later assignments state only the problem, allowing students to create on their own.

Shelly Cashman Series Instructor Resources

The two categories of ancillary material that accompany this textbook are Instructor Resources (ISBN 0-7895-6679-6) and Online Content. These ancillaries are available to adopters through your Course Technology representative or by calling one of the following telephone numbers: Colleges and Universities, 1-800-648-7450; High Schools, 1-800-824-5179; Private Career Colleges, 1-800-347-7707; Canada, 1-800-268-2222; Corporations with IT Training Centers, 1-800-648-7450; and Government Agencies, Health-Care Organizations, and Correctional Facilities, 1-800-477-3692.

Instructor Resources CD-ROM

The Instructor Resources for this textbook include both teaching and testing aids. The contents of the Instructor Resources CD-ROM are listed below.

- **Instructor's Manual**   The Instructor's Manual consists of Microsoft Word files that include lecture notes, solutions to laboratory assignments, and a large test bank. The files allow you to modify the lecture notes or generate quizzes and exams from the test bank using your own word processing software. Where appropriate, solutions to laboratory assignments are embedded as icons.

- **Figures in the Book**   Illustrations for every screen in the textbook are available. Use this ancillary to create a slide show from the illustrations for lectures or to print transparencies for use in lecture with an overhead projector.

- **ExamView**   ExamView is a state-of-the-art test builder that is easy to use. ExamView enables you quickly to create printed tests, Internet tests, and computer (LAN-based) tests. You can enter your own test questions or use the test bank that accompanies ExamView. The test bank is the same as the one described in the Instructor's Manual section.

- **Lecture Success System**   This ancillary, which consists of intermediate files that correspond to certain figures in the book, allows you to step through the creation of an application in a chapter during lecture without entering large amounts of data.

- **Instructor's Lab Solutions**   Solutions and required files for all the chapter projects, Debugging Assignments, and Programming Assignments at the end of each chapter are available.

- **Student Files**   Most of the projects created in this book do not use files supplied by the authors. In the few instances, however, where students are instructed to open a project to complete a task, the files are supplied.

- **Course Syllabus**   Any instructor who has been assigned a course at the last minute knows how difficult it is to come up with a course syllabus. For this reason, sample syllabi are included that can be customized easily to a course.

- **Chapter Reinforcement** True/false, multiple choice, and short answer questions help students gain confidence.

- **Interactive Labs** Eighteen completely updated, hands-on Interactive Labs that take students from ten to fifteen minutes each to step through help solidify and reinforce mouse and keyboard usage and computer concepts. Student assessment is available.

- **PowerPoint Presentation** PowerPoint Presentation is a multimedia lecture presentation system that provides PowerPoint slides for each chapter. Presentations are based on the chapters' objectives. Use this presentation system to present well-organized lectures that are both interesting and knowledge-based. PowerPoint Presentation provides consistent coverage at schools that use multiple lecturers in their programming courses.

Online Content

If you use Blackboard or WebCT, the test bank for this book is free in a simple, ready-to-use format. Visit the Instructor Resource Center for this textbook at course.com to download the test bank, or contact your local sales representative for details.

Acknowledgments

The Shelly Cashman Series would not be the leading computer education series without the contributions of outstanding publishing professionals. First, and foremost, among them is Becky Herrington, director of production and designer. She is the heart and soul of the Shelly Cashman Series, and it is only through her leadership, dedication, and tireless efforts that superior products are made possible.

Under Becky's direction, the following individuals made significant contributions to these books: Doug Cowley, production manager; Ken Russo, senior Web and graphic designer; Doug Cowley and Betty Hopkins, interior designers; Michelle French, cover designer; Kellee LaVars and Andrew Bartel, interior illustrators; Betty Hopkins and Jeanne Black, QuarkXPress compositors; Lisa Strite, developmental editor; Ginny Harvey, Richard Hansberger, and Lori Silfen, copy editors; Nancy Lamm, proofreader; and Cristina Haley, indexer.

Special thanks to Dr. John Maniotes of Purdue University for his contribution to the mechanical man exercise in Chapter 1, the mechanical mouse exercise in Appendix A, and the first section of Appendix A.

Finally, we would like to thank Kristen Duerr, senior vice president and publisher; Cheryl Ouellette, managing editor; Jim Quasney, series consulting editor; Alexandra Arnold, senior product manager; Erin Runyon, product manager; Katie McAllister, marketing manager; Reed Cotter, associate product manager; and Emilie Perreault, editorial assistant.

Gary B. Shelly
Thomas J. Cashman
Jeffrey J. Quasney

Shelly Cashman Series — Traditionally Bound Textbooks

The Shelly Cashman Series presents the following computer subjects in a variety of traditionally bound textbooks. For more information, see your Course Technology representative or call 1-800-648-7450. For Shelly Cashman Series information, visit Shelly Cashman Series at course.com/shellycashman.

COMPUTERS	
Computers	Discovering Computers 2004: A Gateway to Information, Web Enhanced, Complete Edition
	Discovering Computers 2004: A Gateway to Information, Web Enhanced, Introductory Edition
	Discovering Computers 2004: A Gateway to Information, Web Enhanced, Brief Edition
	Teachers Discovering Computers: Integrating Technology in the Classroom 2e
	Exploring Computers: A Record of Discovery 4e
	Study Guide for Discovering Computers 2004: A Gateway to Information, Web Enhanced
	Essential Introduction to Computers 5e (40-page)
WINDOWS APPLICATIONS	
Microsoft Office	Microsoft Office XP: Essential Concepts and Techniques (5 projects)[1]
	Microsoft Office XP: Brief Concepts and Techniques (9 projects)[1]
	Microsoft Office XP: Introductory Concepts and Techniques, Windows XP Edition, Course One (15 projects)
	Microsoft Office XP: Introductory Concepts and Techniques, Enhanced Edition, Course One (15 projects)[1]
	Microsoft Office XP: Advanced Concepts and Techniques, Course Two (11 projects)
	Microsoft Office XP: Post Advanced Concepts and Techniques, Course Three (11 projects)
	Microsoft Office 2000: Essential Concepts and Techniques (5 projects)
	Microsoft Office 2000: Brief Concepts and Techniques (9 projects)
	Microsoft Office 2000: Introductory Concepts and Techniques, Enhanced Edition (15 projects)
	Microsoft Office 2000: Advanced Concepts and Techniques (11 projects)
	Microsoft Office 2000: Post Advanced Concepts and Techniques (11 projects)
Integration	Integrating Microsoft Office XP Applications and the World Wide Web: Essential Concepts and Techniques
PIM	Microsoft Outlook 2002: Essential Concepts and Techniques
Microsoft Works	Microsoft Works 6: Complete Concepts and Techniques[2] • Microsoft Works 2000: Complete Concepts and Techniques[2]
Microsoft Windows	Microsoft Windows XP: Complete Concepts and Techniques[3]
	Microsoft Windows XP: Brief Concepts and Techniques
	Microsoft Windows 2000: Complete Concepts and Techniques (6 projects)[3]
	Microsoft Windows 2000: Brief Concepts and Techniques (2 projects)
	Microsoft Windows 98: Essential Concepts and Techniques (2 projects)
	Microsoft Windows 98: Complete Concepts and Techniques (6 projects)[3]
	Introduction to Microsoft Windows NT Workstation 4
Word Processing	Microsoft Word 2002[3] • Microsoft Word 2000[3]
Spreadsheets	Microsoft Excel 2002[3] • Microsoft Excel 2000[3]
Database	Microsoft Access 2002[3] • Microsoft Access 2000[3]
Presentation Graphics	Microsoft PowerPoint 2002[3] • Microsoft PowerPoint 2000[3]
Desktop Publishing	Microsoft Publisher 2002[2] • Microsoft Publisher 2000[2]
PROGRAMMING	
Programming	Microsoft Visual Basic .NET: Complete Concepts and Techniques[3] • Microsoft Visual Basic 6: Complete Concepts and Techniques[2] • Programming in QBasic • Java Programming 2e: Complete Concepts and Techniques[2] • Structured COBOL Programming 2e
INTERNET	
Browser	Microsoft Internet Explorer 6: Introductory Concepts and Techniques • Microsoft Internet Explorer 5: An Introduction • Netscape Navigator 6: An Introduction
Web Page Creation and Design	Web Design: Introductory Concepts and Techniques • HTML: Complete Concepts and Techniques 2e[3] • Microsoft FrontPage 2002: Essential Concepts and Techniques • Microsoft FrontPage 2002[3] • Microsoft FrontPage 2000[2] • JavaScript: Complete Concepts and Techniques 2e[2] • Macromedia Dreamweaver MX: Complete Concepts and Techniques[3]
SYSTEMS ANALYSIS	
Systems Analysis	Systems Analysis and Design 5e
DATA COMMUNICATIONS	
Data Communications	Business Data Communications: Introductory Concepts and Techniques 4e

[1]Available running under Windows XP or running under Windows 2000
[2]Also available as an Introductory Edition, which is a shortened version of the complete book
[3]Also available as an Introductory Edition, which is a shortened version of the complete book and also as a Comprehensive Edition, which is an extended version of the complete book

To the Student Getting the Most Out of Your Book

Welcome to *Microsoft Visual Basic. NET: Comprehensive Concepts and Techniques.* You can save yourself a lot of time and gain a better understanding of Visual Basic .NET if you spend a few minutes reviewing the figures and callouts in this section.

1 Each Chapter Builds an Application

Each programming chapter builds a complete application, which is carefully described and shown in the first figure of the chapter.

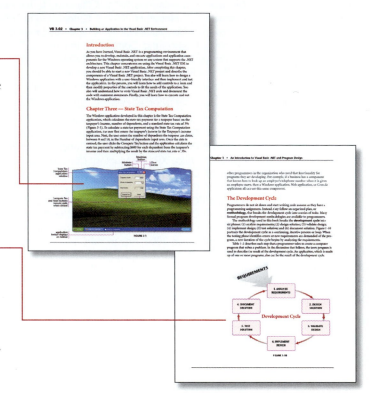

2 Consistent Presentation

The authors use a disciplined approach to building all chapter applications using the six phases of the development cycle. By the end of the course, you will be building applications using this methodology by habit.

3 Pedagogy

Chapter applications are built using a step-by-step, screen-by-screen approach. This pedagogy allows you to build the application on a computer as you read the chapter. Generally, each step is followed by an italic explanation that indicates the result of the step.

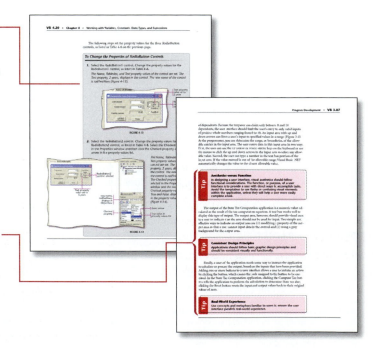

4 More Than Just Step-By-Step

This book offers extended but clear discussions of programming concepts. Important Visual Basic. NET design and programming Tips are interspersed throughout the chapters.

5 Review

After successfully stepping through the chapter, a section titled What You Should Know lists the Visual Basic .NET tasks with which you should be familiar in the order they are presented in the chapter.

6 Test Preparation

The Key Terms section lists the bold terms in the chapter you should know for test purposes.

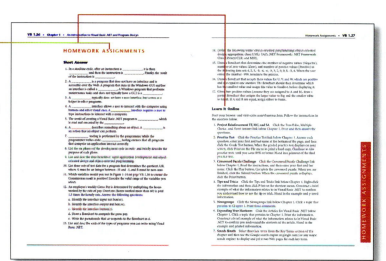

7 Reinforcement and Extension

The Short Answer exercises are the traditional pencil-and-paper exercises. The Learn It Online exercises are Web-based. Some of these Web-based exercises, such as the Practice Test and Crossword Puzzle Challenge, are for reinforcement. Others take you beyond the Visual Basic .NET topics covered in the chapter.

8 In the Lab

If you really want to learn how to program in Visual Basic .NET, then you must design, program, and debug applications using Visual Basic .NET. Every programming chapter includes a Debugging Assignment and several carefully developed Programming Assignments.

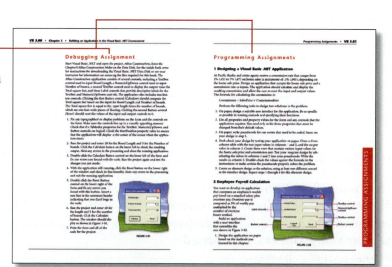

Visual Studio .NET Professional 60-Day Trial Edition

A copy of the complete version of the Microsoft Visual Studio .NET Professional 60-Day trial edition on DVD, which includes Microsoft Visual Basic .NET, can be found on the inside back cover of this book. When you activate the software, you will receive a license that allows you to use the software for 60 days. Course Technology and Microsoft provide no product support for this trial edition. When the trial period ends, you can purchase a copy of Microsoft Visual Studio .NET or Microsoft Visual Basic .NET, or uninstall the trial edition and reinstall your previous version.

Installation Recommendations
To complete the programming assignments in this book, visit scsite.com/vsinstall for recommendations on to how to install the 60-Day trial edition or any edition of Visual Studio .NET or Visual Basic .NET.

Minimum System Requirements

The minimum system requirements are a Pentium II-class processor, 450 MHz; Windows XP Professional (160 MB RAM) or Windows XP Home (96 MB RAM) or Windows 2003 Server (160 MB RAM) or Windows 2000 Server (192 MB RAM) or Windows 2000 Professional (96 MB RAM); 3.5 GB on installation drive and 500 MB on system drive; DVD-ROM drive; Super VGA 1024 x 768 or higher resolution monitor; mouse or compatible pointing device; and an Internet connection for activation.

Data Disk Download Instructions

A few of the exercises in this book require that you begin by opening a data file from a Data Disk. The following steps show you how to download the Data Disk from the World Wide Web.

1 Insert a formatted floppy disk in drive A. Start your browser and then enter the URL **scsite.com**.

2 When the SCSITE.COM page displays, scroll down and perform <u>one</u> of the following procedures: (a) *Browse by Subject area:* Click the subject category to which your book belongs. When the category list expands, click the title of your textbook. When the Textbook page displays, scroll down to the Data Files area and then click one of the links below Data Files for Students. Follow the instructions beginning with step 3 below. (b) *Support area:* Click Download Instructions. Follow the instructions on the screen.

3 When the File Download dialog box displays, click the Save button.

4 When the Save As dialog box displays, select a folder on your hard disk to download the file to. Write down the folder name listed in the Save in box and the file name listed in the File name text box for use in step 6, and then click the Save button.

5 When a dialog box displays indicating the download is complete, click the OK button. Close your browser.

6 Open Windows Explorer and display the contents of the folder to which you downloaded the file. Double-click the downloaded file name on the right side of the Windows Explorer window.

7 When the WinZip Self-Extractor dialog box displays, type **a:** in the Unzip To Folder text box, and then click the Unzip button.

8 When the WinZip Self-Extractor displays the number of files unzipped, click the OK button. Click the Close button in the WinZip Self-Extractor dialog box. Close Windows Explorer.

9 Remove the floppy disk from drive A and label it Shelly Cashman Data Disk. You now are ready to insert the Data Disk and open the required files.

1

An Introduction to Visual Basic .NET and Program Design

Objectives

You will have
mastered the material in
this chapter when you can:

- Describe Visual Basic .NET
- Describe the Visual Basic programming language
- Describe programs, programming, applications, and program development
- Identify each of the phases in the development cycle
- Define an algorithm
- Define objects, attributes, and methods
- Explain object-oriented programming (OOP) and object-oriented design (OOD)
- Describe rapid application development (RAD)
- Identify the key components of .NET

Introduction

Before a computer can produce a desired result, it must have a step-by-step series of instructions that tells it exactly what to do. The step-by-step series of instructions is called a **program**. The process of writing the sets of instructions for the computer to follow is called **programming**. **Programmers**, also called **software developers**, design and write programs. An **application** is a collection of one or more programs that is designed to complete a specific task, such as word processing or accounting. The process of using a programming language or programming environment to build software applications is called **program development**.

Microsoft Visual Basic .NET encompasses a set of tools and technologies that helps developers build programs quickly. Visual Basic .NET's user-friendly programming environment, along with the relative simplicity of its programming language, allows individuals with little programming experience to create a wide range of programs.

This chapter concentrates on the many uses of Visual Basic .NET and how Visual Basic .NET can help you develop programs. The chapter first covers the types of programs that you create using Visual Basic .NET and then covers the fundamental program design concepts and tools used to design a program logically to solve a problem. You also will learn about .NET and the technologies involved in Visual Basic .NET programs.

What Is Microsoft Visual Basic .NET?

Microsoft Visual Basic .NET is a programming environment that allows you to build programs for the Windows operating system or any operating system that supports Microsoft's .NET architecture. **.NET** (pronounced *dot net*) encompasses a series of technologies that allows almost any type of program to run in a common environment, which is discussed in more detail later in the chapter. Visual Basic .NET is the seventh version of Microsoft's Visual Basic programming environment. By adding .NET to the name, Visual Basic, Microsoft indicates Visual Basic's tight integration with Microsoft's .NET initiative. You often will see Visual Basic .NET referred to with the abbreviation, VB .NET. Visual Basic .NET is based on the **Visual Basic programming language**, which evolved from BASIC (Beginner's All-purpose Symbolic Instruction Code).

The Visual Basic .NET programming environment allows you to create programs for the Windows operating system and the Web. Figure 1-1 illustrates the types of programs you can create with Visual Basic .NET. A **Windows application** (Figure 1-1a) is a program with a graphical user interface that runs in the Windows environment. A **Web application** (Figure 1-1b) is a program that a user accesses through a Web browser. **Console applications** (Figure 1-1c) run in a text environment such as the Windows MS-DOS prompt or Command Prompt interface. **Components** (Figure 1-1d) are programs that serve as helpers or prebuilt pieces of other programs. A **Web service** (Figure 1-1e) is a program that receives a request for information from another program over the Web and returns data to the requesting program. A **Windows service** (Figure 1-1f) performs maintenance or data-gathering tasks without requiring user intervention.

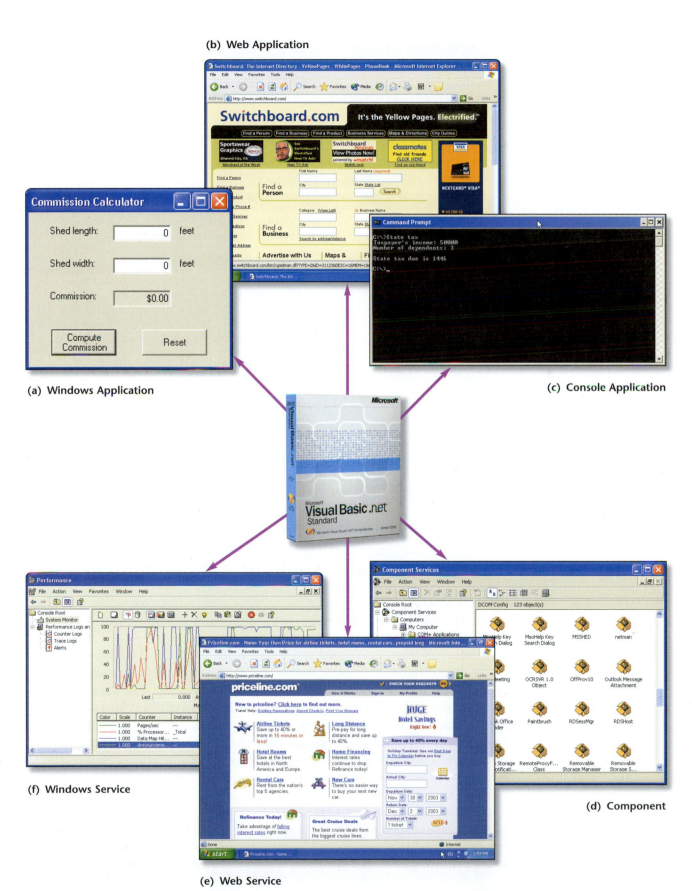

(b) **Web Application**

(a) **Windows Application**

(c) **Console Application**

(f) **Windows Service**

(d) **Component**

(e) **Web Service**

FIGURE 1-1

As shown in Table 1-1, Visual Basic .NET is available in a stand-alone edition, Visual Basic .NET Standard. It also is packaged in several editions of **Microsoft Visual Studio .NET**, which is a comprehensive set of programming languages and tools for building Windows applications, Web applications, and other programs and services. The edition of Visual Studio .NET or Visual Basic .NET most appropriate for you depends on the programming tasks you want to accomplish.

Table 1-1   Editions of Visual Basic .NET

EDITION	TYPICAL USE
Visual Basic .NET Standard	Hobbyist or small corporation with a small software development team
Visual Studio .NET Professional	Software developer, small or mid-sized corporation
Visual Studio .NET Academic	Student learning or instructor teaching Visual Basic .NET in an academic environment; includes everything in Visual Studio .NET Professional, plus additional samples and tools for creating classroom and lab materials
Visual Studio .NET Enterprise Developer (VSED)	Large corporation developing complex applications that interact with other systems and many data sources; includes everything in Visual Studio .NET Professional, plus additional tools to support larger development teams
Visual Studio .NET Enterprise Architect (VSEA)	Large corporation designing large applications; includes everything in Visual Studio .NET Enterprise Developer, plus additional tools for designing large applications

Programming and Application Development

When a program starts to run, its instructions are placed into the computer's memory, and the program is called a **stored program**. Memory also stores any data that the instructions process or manipulate.

Once the program is stored, the first instruction is located and sent to the control unit (**fetched**) where it is translated into a form the computer can understand (**decoded**), and then carried out (**executed**) (Figure 1-2). The result of the instruction is placed in memory (**stored**). Then, the next instruction is fetched, decoded, and executed, and the results are stored again in memory. This process, called a **machine cycle**, continues under the direction of the operating system, instruction by instruction, until the program is completed or until the computer is instructed to halt.

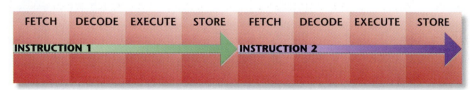

FIGURE 1-2

Programming also is referred to as **coding**, because the instructions written by a computer programmer are called computer code, or **code** (Figure 1-3).

```
[Design] Form1.vb

Form1                                    ▼   (Declarations)                              ▼

  1  Public Class Form1
  2      Inherits System.Windows.Forms.Form
  3
  4      Windows Form Designer generated code
136      ' Chapter 3:     State Tax Computation
137      ' Programmer:    J. Quasney
138      ' Date:          September 2, 2003
139      ' Purpose:       This project calculates state income tax due based
140      '                on income level and number of dependents.
141      Private Sub btnCompute_Click(ByVal sender As System.Object, ByVal e As System.EventArgs) Handles btnCompute.Clic
142          ' Calculate tax and display the result in the txtTaxDue text box
143          txtTaxDue.Text = 0.03 * (txtIncome.Text - 600 * nudDependents.Value)
144      End Sub
145
146      Private Sub btnReset_Click(ByVal sender As System.Object, ByVal e As System.EventArgs) Handles btnReset.Click
147          ' Set all input and output display values to 0
148          txtIncome.Text = "0"
149          nudDependents.Value = 0
150          txtTaxDue.Text = "0"
151      End Sub
152  End Class
153
```

FIGURE 1-3

The process of using a programming language or programming environment to build an application made up of one or more programs is called **application development**. An application tells a computer how to accept instructions and data from the user and how to produce information in response to those instructions. Most computer users do not code the programs that make up the applications they use for common business and personal purposes, such as word processing and spreadsheet applications, or Web browsers. Instead, they purchase the applications from software vendors or stores that sell computer products. These purchased programs often are referred to as **application software packages**.

Application Types

As shown in Figure 1-1 (on page VB 1.03), Visual Basic .NET allows you to develop different types of applications. Some programs you write will require an application that has a user interface, including Web and Windows applications, while other programs such as services and components will not. This section describes the types of applications you can develop in more detail.

Windows Applications

Visual Basic .NET allows developers to create Windows applications with a graphical user interface as shown in Figure 1-4 on the next page. The Windows graphical user interface (GUI) provides visual cues such as menus, buttons, and icons that allow a user to enter data and instructions into the computer.

Both Windows applications and Console applications, which are discussed on the next page, are called stand-alone applications. A **stand-alone application** is an application that does not require other applications or data sources to run in the operating system.

FIGURE 1-4

Web Applications

Web browsers provide another environment for Visual Basic .NET programs. Visual Basic .NET can be used to create complete Web sites and pages that run in almost any Web browser on any operating system. When you create and run a Web page using Visual Basic .NET, the program code is converted into standard Hypertext Markup Language (HTML). **Hypertext Markup Language** (**HTML**) is the Web authoring language that uses a set of special instructions called tags or markups to define the structure and layout of a Web document and specify how the page is displayed in a browser. The resulting application is called a Web application (Figure 1-5). The principles of Web page design are similar to those of Windows applications with a graphical user interface. Typically, developers work with a more limited set of buttons, menus, and other graphical interface objects when building Web pages than they would when building a Windows application.

FIGURE 1-5

Console Applications

Visual Basic .NET can be used to create Console applications that run within the Windows command prompt environment. While working with a **command prompt interface**, a user enters data and instructions into a computer by typing keywords or pressing keys on the keyboard. Figure 1-6 shows an example of a program running in a command prompt environment. The text, C:\>, is a prompt that tells the user that the application is awaiting a command from the user.

FIGURE 1-6

Windows Services

Unlike Console, Windows, and Web applications, some programs — such as services — do not require any user interaction at all. A **service** is a program that runs in an operating system and performs such tasks as maintenance, information gathering, security, and notification but requires no user interaction. Figure 1-7 shows a view of data gathered by a Windows service that monitors the computer system's performance. A Windows service often begins when Windows is started, and performs maintenance or data gathering tasks in the background while Windows is running.

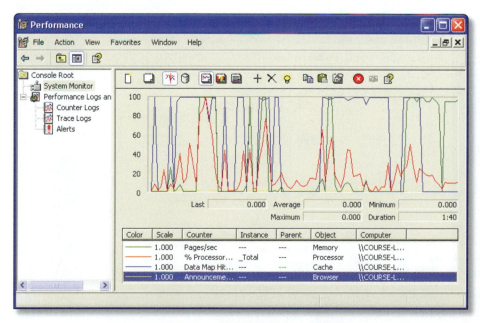

FIGURE 1-7

Visual Basic .NET allows you to create Windows services. For example, you can create a Windows service that sends an administrator an e-mail each time a user prints a document consisting of more than one hundred pages. The user will not see the Windows service running in the Windows GUI. As long as the Windows service is running on the user's computer, the service will monitor any request to print and check the page count, regardless of which application sends the request to print.

Web Services

Web services are a relatively new type of program that can be created using Visual Basic .NET. A Web service is a program that provides information to another program over the Web, but does not have a user interface. The information provided usually is specific and well defined. For example, an airline may create a Web service for programmers not associated with the airline who are developing travel-related Web applications. The airline's Web service may accept departure and arrival dates, departure and arrival cities, and the number of tickets being purchased as inputs (Figure 1-8). Based on this information, the Web service then sends a flight schedule back as output to the Web application. Once the Web application receives data from the airline's Web service, that data can be formatted for display on a Web page or used in any other way required by the programmers. A user does not provide data directly to a Web service; rather, data is sent in an electronic format from the Web application to the Web service and back again over the Internet. Web services developed in Visual Basic .NET rely on specific guidelines that determine how the input and output data should be formatted so that it can be sent electronically.

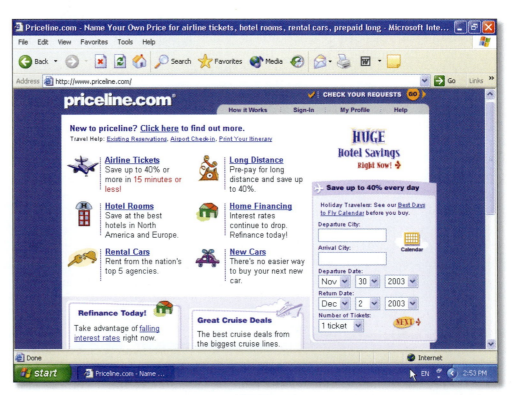

FIGURE 1-8

Components

Visual Basic .NET can create components for other programs to use (Figure 1-9). A component functions as a prebuilt program that can be used by other programs or applications to complete a task or process. Components usually have a programmatic interface, rather than a user interface. A **programmatic interface** defines the method in which other programs or applications should send and receive data from a component. A component works behind the scenes. Figure 1-9 shows the Windows Component Services Manager, which allows Windows users to view and control the components that the Windows operating system uses as part of its normal operations.

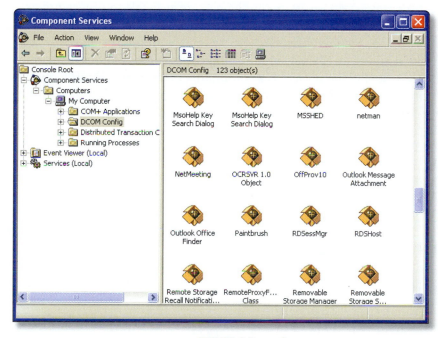

FIGURE 1-9

Components provide the benefit of **reusability**, which means they can be reused over and over by many programs developed by different programmers. Having reusable components means that companies can spend less time and money developing new programs, thus making components valuable to businesses. For example, a programmer first can develop an inventory component that knows how to get information about each product the company has in inventory. The development team then can use this inventory component in several applications to get information about a product in inventory. An accounting application, for example, can use the component to complete an end-of-month report. Another application used to create a catalog for the company's products can use the component to gather information about the product.

Windows services, Web services, and components are programs that do not have a user interface. Data is sent to the program and then data is returned or an action is performed by the program. Alternatively, the program can monitor the computer or operating system for a particular event to occur before performing an action. Often, common business functionality is programmed into a component, Web service, or Windows service, so that it can be made available to any other programmers in the organization who need that functionality for programs they are developing. For example, if a business has a component that knows how to look up an employee's telephone number when it is given an employee name, then a Windows application, Web application, or Console application all can use this same component.

The Development Cycle

Programmers do not sit down and start writing code as soon as they have a programming assignment. Instead, they follow an organized plan, or **methodology**, that breaks the development cycle into a series of tasks. Many formal program development methodologies are available to programmers.

The methodology used in this book breaks the **development cycle** into six phases: (1) analyze requirements; (2) design solution; (3) validate design; (4) implement design; (5) test solution; and (6) document solution. Figure 1-10 portrays the development cycle as a continuing, iterative process or loop. When the testing phase identifies errors or new requirements are demanded of the program, a new iteration of the cycle begins by analyzing the requirements.

Table 1-2 describes each step that a programmer takes to create a computer program that solves a problem. In the discussion that follows, the term program is used to describe the result of the development cycle. An application, which is made up of one or more programs, also can be the result of the development cycle.

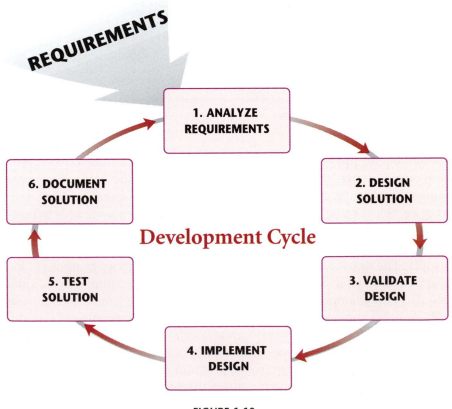

FIGURE 1-10

Table 1-2   The Development Cycle

	PHASE	DESCRIPTION
1	Analyze requirements	Verify that the requirements are complete, and translate user requirements into technical requirements, including descriptions of the program's inputs, processing, outputs, and interface.
2	Design solution	Develop a detailed, logical plan using a tool such as pseudocode, flowcharts, or class diagrams to group the program's activities into modules; devise a method of solution or algorithm for each module; and test the solution algorithms. Design the user interface for the application, including input areas, output areas, and other necessary elements.
3	Validate design	Step through the solution design with test data. Receive confirmation from the user that the design solves the problem in a satisfactory manner.
4	Implement design	Translate the design into a program using a programming language or programming environment by creating the user interface and writing code; include internal documentation, or comments, which are notes within the code that explain the purpose of code statements.
5	Test solution	Test the program, finding and correcting errors (debugging) until it is error free and contains enough safeguards to ensure the desired results.
6	Document solution	Review and, if necessary, revise internal documentation; and formalize and complete end-user (external) documentation.

Program requirements drive the development cycle. **Requirements** are supplied by the program's users or a representative of the users, and are presented in a **requirements document**. **Users** present a requirements document to programmers when they believe a particular problem can be solved by a program. A requirements document lists the functions and features that the program must provide for its users. Requirements include a statement of purpose for the requested program (also called a problem definition), the equations the program must use, and an explanation of how the program should respond to user interaction. Requirements may specify that a new program be developed or they may specify updates to an existing program. In addition, requirements indicate how the program will be made available to users or other programmers; for example, the requirements might specify that a stand-alone Windows application must be developed for the program, or they might specify that the program must function as a Windows or Web service.

An example of a requirements document is shown in Figure 1-11 on the next page. The document specifies the requirements for a new program that must be made available to users as both a Web application and a Windows application. The program's main purpose is to allow sales people inside and outside a company to calculate a commission on the sale of storage sheds.

REQUEST FOR NEW APPLICATION

Date submitted:	August 1, 2004
Submitted by:	Margaret Stevens
Purpose:	Inside and outside sales representatives request a quick method of verifying the correct commission they should receive on storage sheds that the company builds and they sell.
Application title:	Commission Calculator

Algorithms:	Commission is based on the square footage of the storage shed sold. The sales person knows the length and width of the shed. If the number of square feet is less than 200, then the commission is 7% of the total sales price. Otherwise, the commission is 11%. This year, prices are $5.00 per square foot.
	
	Calculations can be summarized as follows:
	
	SquareFeet = Length × Width
	TotalPrice = SquareFeet × $5.00
	
	If SquareFeet is less than 200:
	    Commission = TotalPrice × 7%
	Otherwise:
	    Commission = TotalPrice × 11%

Notes:	1) The outside sales force requires a Web interface for the program. Inside sales people do not have Web access and a Windows application is required for inside sales people. 2) Sales associates are accustomed to the following terminology: *Shed length, Shed width,* and *Commission.* 3) The application should allow the user to enter values for the length and width of the shed. 4) Due to state regulations, we do not make sheds whose length or width is greater than 30 feet. 5) The application should also allow the user to reset all values on the screen to zero (0) so that another calculation can be performed. 6) The calculation of commission should be designated by the term, Compute Commission. The resetting of the values should be designated by the term, Reset.

Approvals

Approval Status:	X	Approved
		Rejected
Approved by:	Randall Washington	
Date:	August 4, 2004	
Assigned to:	J. Quasney, Programmer	

FIGURE 1-11

Analyze Requirements — Phase 1

The first step in analyzing requirements is to verify that the requirements are complete and provide all the necessary information to solve the problem. If the statement of purpose is vague or unclear, or an equation is incorrect or incomplete, the programmer must request that the requirements document be revised to address these issues. Second, the programmer should make an initial determination that it is possible to solve the problem using a program.

In order to make sure that the problem can be solved, the programmer lists the input and output data required for the program. After doing so, the programmer determines whether the input data is available to the programmer for testing purposes. Next, the programmer ensures that the information provided explains how to convert the input data into output data so that a solution, or **algorithm**, can be developed. In other words, the requirements must clearly state the rules that govern how to convert the input into output.

The requirements must state how the user will interact with the program, which includes requirements that specify whether the program must be made available in an application with a user interface such as a Windows or Web application, or whether the program will be part of a service or component. The requirements may include terminology that the user is familiar with and, therefore, must be included in the user interface. The requirements help the programmer determine which technologies to use when designing a solution to the problem. For larger problems, the analysis also should include an initial breakdown of the problem into smaller problems so that programmers can develop solutions gradually and in smaller, more manageable pieces.

The requirements for the Commission Calculator shown in Figure 1-11 specify the input data that should be entered by the user and the equation that must be used to calculate the output data. The requirements also explain how users will interact with the program, including the rules that govern valid and invalid input data entered by the user. The end result of the analyze requirements phase is that both the user and the programmer must agree in writing that the requirements for the program are clear and complete. At this point, the programmer can begin to design a solution and the user can begin designing tests to verify that the solution satisfies the program's requirements.

Design Solution — Phase 2

When you **design** the solution, you develop a logical model that illustrates the sequence of steps you will take to solve the problem. Programmers use object diagrams, flowcharts, pseudocode, and storyboards to outline the logic of the program.

Often programs can be broken in to smaller pieces, called **objects**, which represent a real person, place, event, or transaction. Object-oriented design is an approach to program design that identifies how objects must interact with each other in order to solve a problem. The end product of object-oriented design is an object model. An **object model** illustrates the attributes and methods of an object. The **attributes** of an object are values that determine, for example, the appearance of an object. The **methods** of an object are instructions that the object uses to manipulate values, generate outputs, or perform actions. Attributes and methods together comprise an object. Objects often are individual programs themselves that can be reused by other programs.

The Commission Calculator requires that users access the program using one of two methods: a Web application and a Windows application. Rather than creating two completely separate applications for these two types of users, the algorithm used to solve the problem should be programmed only once. By centralizing the program logic for the two application types, maintenance of the program is easier and the logic only needs to be programmed once, rather than twice. The algorithm can be placed in an object. The Commission object has two attributes that correspond to the inputs, length and width. The object requires one method, getCommission(), that tells the object how to manipulate the input values and generate the required output. The getCommission() method performs the calculation after the attributes, length and width, are sent to the object by the program. Figure 1-12 shows a diagram of the Commission object using a standard diagramming technique that illustrates the methods and attributes of an object.

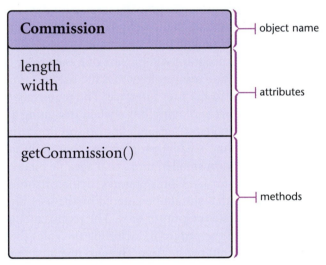

Commission — object name

length
width — attributes

getCommission() — methods

FIGURE 1-12

Programmers often create a diagram or picture called a **flowchart** that graphically represents the logic used to develop an algorithm. Table 1-3 shows a standard set of flowchart symbols used to represent various steps or operations in a program's logic. When you draw a complete flowchart, you must begin with a terminal symbol that is then connected by a flowline to the first logical step in the solution to the problem. Most of the time, each step required to solve a problem is represented by a separate symbol. Appendix A includes a more detailed discussion of how to develop flowcharts and diagram objects.

Table 1-3   Flowcharting Symbols and Their Meanings

SYMBOL	NAME	MEANING
	Process Symbol	Represents the process of executing a defined operation or group of operations that results in a change in value, form, or location of information; also functions as the default symbol when no other symbol is available
	Input/Output (I/O) Symbol	Represents an I/O function, which makes data available for processing (input) or for displaying (output) processed information
left to right / right to left / top to bottom / bottom to top	**Flowline Symbol**	Represents the sequence of available information and executable operations; lines connect other symbols, and arrowheads are mandatory only for right-to-left and bottom-to-top flow
	Annotation Symbol	Represents the addition of descriptive information, comments, or explanatory notes as clarification; vertical lines and broken lines may be placed on the left, as shown, or on the right
	Decision Symbol	Represents a decision that determines which of a number of alternative paths is to be followed
	Terminal Symbol	Represents the beginning, the end, or a point of interruption or delay in a program
	Connector Symbol	Represents any entry from, or exit to, another part of the flowchart; also serves as an off-page connector
	Predefined Process Symbol	Represents a named process consisting of one or more operations or program steps that are specified elsewhere

The next step in designing a solution is to develop the algorithm that represents the getCommission() method (Figure 1-12) of the Commission object. Figure 1-13 on the next page shows a flowchart that represents the algorithm used by the getCommission() method of the Commission object to calculate the correct commission. The flowchart includes a **control structure**, which is a portion of a program that allows the programmer to specify that code will be executed only if a condition is met. The control structure in the flowchart, for instance, illustrates how the program decides which commission rate to use based on the total number of square feet.

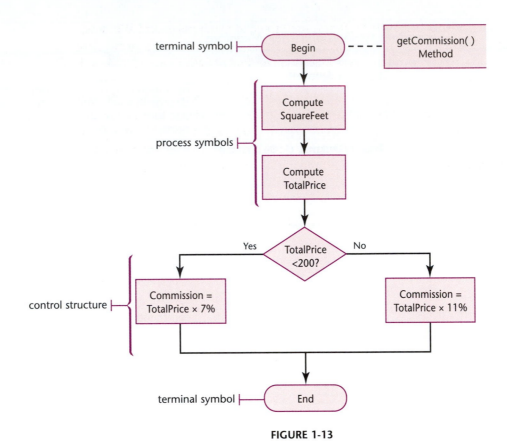

FIGURE 1-13

Programmers also use pseudocode to develop the logic of an algorithm for a program. **Pseudocode** expresses the step-by-step instructions using keywords, and depicts logical groupings or structures using indentation. Figure 1-14 shows the pseudocode for the getCommission() method of the Commission object. The pseudocode is not program code, but an English representation of how the code should be written. The pseudocode serves as an intermediary step between the requirements and the final program code. It allows the programmer to check the logic before proceeding to write code.

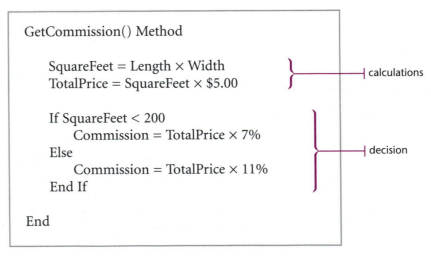

FIGURE 1-14

Because Visual Basic .NET often is used to create Web pages and Windows applications with graphical user interfaces, programmers may create a **storyboard**, or hand-drawn sketch, of how the application window or Web page will look and where the objects will be placed in the window or on the form. A storyboard also can serve as a reference for the logical names of these objects as you code your program.

The Commission Calculator application may use a similar user interface for both a Windows application and a Web application, as shown in the storyboard in Figure 1-15. Although these interfaces must be programmed separately, the user interface is similar and the same storyboard is useful for both.

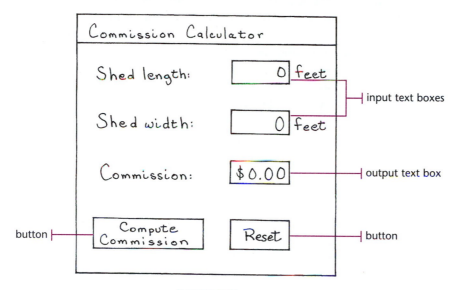

FIGURE 1-15

The end result of designing a solution includes technical documentation that explains how the program will meet the requirements. Any documents that relate to the design of the user interface should be made available to the user, who must validate that the design is correct and that the program's **usability**, which is a measure of a user's ability to interact with a program in a reasonable and intuitive manner, is acceptable.

Many programmers use combinations and variations of these program design tools. Your instructor or supervisor may prefer one type of design tool to another, and you will probably find one or two more useful than others as you develop your own programming style. In addition, companies often have written standards that specify the tools that must be used to design programs.

Validate Design — Phase 3

Both the programmer and the user must **validate**, or check, the program design. The programmer steps through the solution with test data to verify that the solution meets the requirements. The user also must agree that the design solves the problem put forth in the requirements. The validation of the design is the user's last chance to make certain that all of the requirements necessary were included in the initial requirements document. By comparing the program design with the original requirements, both the programmer and the user can validate that the solution is correct and satisfactory.

In the Commission Calculator application, the design can be validated by using a test case for input data and then stepping the test data through both the equation written in the requirements document and the algorithm presented in the program design. The results can be compared to be sure that they match.

Implement Design — Phase 4

The **implementation** of the design includes writing the code that translates the design into a program and, if necessary, creating the user interface. Coding also includes internal documentation, or **comments**, which are notes within the code that explain the purpose of the code. When programmers write the code and create the interface, their job includes testing the code as they write it. Related code that performs a specific task or function should be tested for correctness during the programming process. This type of testing is known as **unit testing**.

Based on the flowchart in Figure 1-13 on page VB 1.16 and the pseudocode in Figure 1-14 on page VB 1.16, Figure 1-16 shows some of the code necessary to implement the getCommission() method for the Commission Calculator application. Figure 1-17 shows the user interface developed for the Windows application from the original design illustrated in Figure 1-15 on the previous page.

```
5      Public Function getCommission() As Double
6          Dim dblSquareFeet, dblTotalPrice As Double
7          Dim Commission As Double
8
9          ' calculate the total number of square feet and the total price
10         ' based on the total number of square feet (square feet x $5.00)
11         dblSquareFeet = length * width
12         dblTotalPrice = dblSquareFeet * 5.0
13
14         ' if the number of square feet is less than 200, use the lower
15         ' commission rate
16         If dblSquareFeet < 200.0 Then
17             Commission = dblTotalPrice * 0.07
18         Else
19             Commission = dblTotalPrice * 0.11
20         End If
21
22         Return Commission
23     End Function
```

FIGURE 1-16

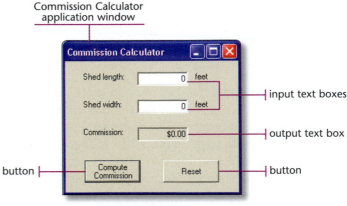

FIGURE 1-17

Test Solution — Phase 5

The purpose of **testing** is to verify that the program meets the requirements from the user's point of view. The program should perform its assigned function correctly under all normal circumstances. If the program includes a user interface, testing should ensure that the user interface also meets requirements. For larger projects, a test plan typically is developed at the same time that the requirements are agreed upon at the end of the analyze requirements phase. A **test plan** consists of a collection of test cases. **Test cases** are individual scenarios that include input data and expected output data and that are designed to ensure that the program solves a particular problem indicated in the program requirements.

If several programs or components comprise a finished application, then testing must ensure that all programs and components interact correctly. This is called **integration testing**.

The end result of testing the solution includes documentation of any problems with the application. If the user accepts the program as complete and correct, then the user documents this fact and the program may be put to use. If the testing results are unsatisfactory, then the results are documented and returned to the programmer. The resolution of the problems revealed during testing begins a new iteration of the development cycle, with the outstanding issues serving as requirements.

The Commission Calculator application requires testing to ensure that all possible cases of valid input data cause the program to calculate the correct result every time. The application must not allow the user to enter values disallowed by the requirements, such as a length or width greater than 30 feet. Test cases also should include input data that would result in the number of square feet being greater than 200 and less than 200. Based upon the requirements, the value of 200 for square feet is called a boundary value. **Boundary values** are values that cause a certain rule to become effective. Test cases include the testing of exact boundary values because common logic and programming mistakes occur when boundary values are reached in a problem.

Figure 1-18 shows the Commission Calculator application in the Windows environment being tested with input values of 10 feet and 20 feet for the length and width, respectively, of a shed. These input values result in an area of 200 square feet for the shed. Per the requirements, the correct commission should be calculated by multiplying the total sales price by 11%, which results in a commission of $110.00.

$$(200 \times \$5.00) \times 11\% = \$110.00$$

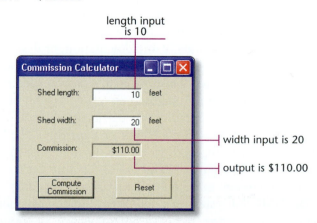

length input is 10

width input is 20

output is $110.00

FIGURE 1-18

Document Solution — Phase 6

The final phase in the development cycle is to document the completed solution. The **documentation** for a completed programming project includes the requirements documents, program design documents, user interface documents, and documentation of the code. The code should be archived electronically so that it can be accessed in the event that a programmer must fix an error in the code or use the code for other purposes.

In the Commission Calculator project, final documentation consists of all documents generated during the development cycle. This also includes electronic archiving and printing the program code and design. The complete set of documents for the project includes the requirements document, approval of requirements by the user and programmer, program design documents, test cases, program code, and hard-copy proof that the test cases were completed successfully.

Object-Oriented Programming and Object-Oriented Design

Object-oriented programming and object-oriented design represent a recent methodology of program development. **Object-oriented programming** (**OOP**) is an approach to programming and application development in which the data and the code that operates on the data are packaged into a single unit called an object. **Object-oriented design** (**OOD**) represents the logical plan of a program as a set of interactions among objects and operations. The benefit is that programs developed using an object-oriented approach are easier to develop and maintain.

Objects

As you have learned, an object is anything real or abstract, about which you store both data and operations that manipulate the data. Each object has its own set of characteristics and behaviors, known as attributes and methods. Examples of objects are an invoice, an organization, a computer screen used to interact with a computer program, an airplane, or an employee. Parts of the Windows graphical user interface, such as windows, buttons, and text boxes, are also objects. An object may be composed of other objects, which in turn may contain other objects. For example, a window object may contain text box, check box, and button objects. **Aggregation** is the term used to describe the concept of an object being composed of other objects.

A **class** is the programmatic implementation, or description, of an object. A class is what you use to describe an object in programming terms. Once an object and its behaviors are described in a class, you can create an instance of that class in your program. Whereas a class defines a set of objects, an **instance** is a programmatic representation of a particular object.

Just as flowcharts describe the logic of algorithms, the **Unified Modeling Language** (**UML**), examples of which are shown earlier in Figure 1-12 on page VB 1.14 and later in Figure 1-20 on page 1.22, provides a standardized model for object-oriented design to depict or diagram concepts graphically for design purposes. The UML is a system of symbols used to describe object behaviors and interaction, and to represent how a system behaves or should behave. The UML is a relatively new language, having been developed in the 1990s from a number of object-oriented design tools. You will learn more about representing a program design using the UML later in this book. Appendix A includes an introduction to the use of the UML. Figure 1-12 on page VB 1.14 is an example of a type of UML diagram that shows the attributes and methods for an object.

Rapid Application Development

Rapid application development (**RAD**) refers to the use of prebuilt objects to make program and application development much faster. Using prebuilt objects is faster because you use existing objects rather than creating new ones yourself. The result is shorter development cycles, easier maintenance, and the ability to reuse objects for other projects. One of the major premises on which industry implementation of OOP is built is greater reusability of code.

As shown in Table 1-4, the adoption of an object-oriented approach to programming and program design has two primary benefits. First, using OOP means that not all members of a development team need to be proficient in an object-oriented programming language such as Visual Basic .NET, Visual C# .NET, Delphi, Java, or C++. Second, OOP provides a more practical and economical approach to programming because the task of creating objects can be separated from the task of assembling objects into applications. Some programmers can focus on creating objects while other developers leverage their knowledge of business processes to assemble applications using OOD and OOP methods and tools.

Table 1-4   Benefits of Object-Oriented Design and Programming

BENEFIT	EXPLANATION
Reusability	Classes are designed so they can be reused in many systems or so they can be used in the creation of other classes.
Stability	Classes are designed for frequent reuse and become stable over time.
Easier design	The programmer looks at objects as a black box and is not concerned with the details inside the object.
Faster design	Applications can be created from existing objects.

As you have learned, Visual Basic .NET allows you to build applications that use the Windows graphical user interface. The elements that comprise the graphical user interface are all objects. For example, a button you click in an application is an instance of a button class. An attribute of the button might be the text or icon that appears on the button face. A method of the button might be the action that is initiated when you click the button.

In Visual Basic .NET, a graphical object such as a button that is used to build the user interface is called a **control**. Controls have properties such as color or width. As well, controls have **events**, which are actions or occurrences, such as clicking a button or opening a new application window that a program can respond or react to. Events cause methods to execute in controls. When an event occurs, a message is sent to a method in the control that can be programmed to perform some task or function. A control also can have methods that are not events and are used to set or get properties. For example, a button may have a setColor() method that sets the color of the button that the user sees. The background on which the controls are drawn is called a **form**. When the application executes in the Windows environment, forms become windows. Forms are just another type of control, and they have properties, events, and methods as do other controls, such as buttons. Figure 1-19 shows a Visual Basic .NET application running in the Windows environment and the various controls used to build the graphical user interface. A partial UML diagram for a button control is shown in Figure 1-20.

FIGURE 1-19

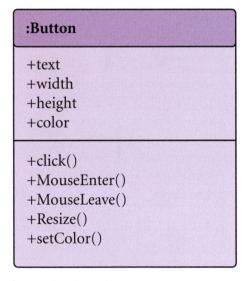

FIGURE 1-20

What Is .NET?

Microsoft announced its .NET initiative in 2000. As previously mentioned, .NET encompasses a series of technologies that allows almost any type of application to run in a common environment. Visual Studio .NET, which includes Visual Basic .NET, is the first major set of tools available that allow for applications to be created for .NET. The common environment in which applications created for .NET run is known as the **.NET Framework** (Figure 1-21).

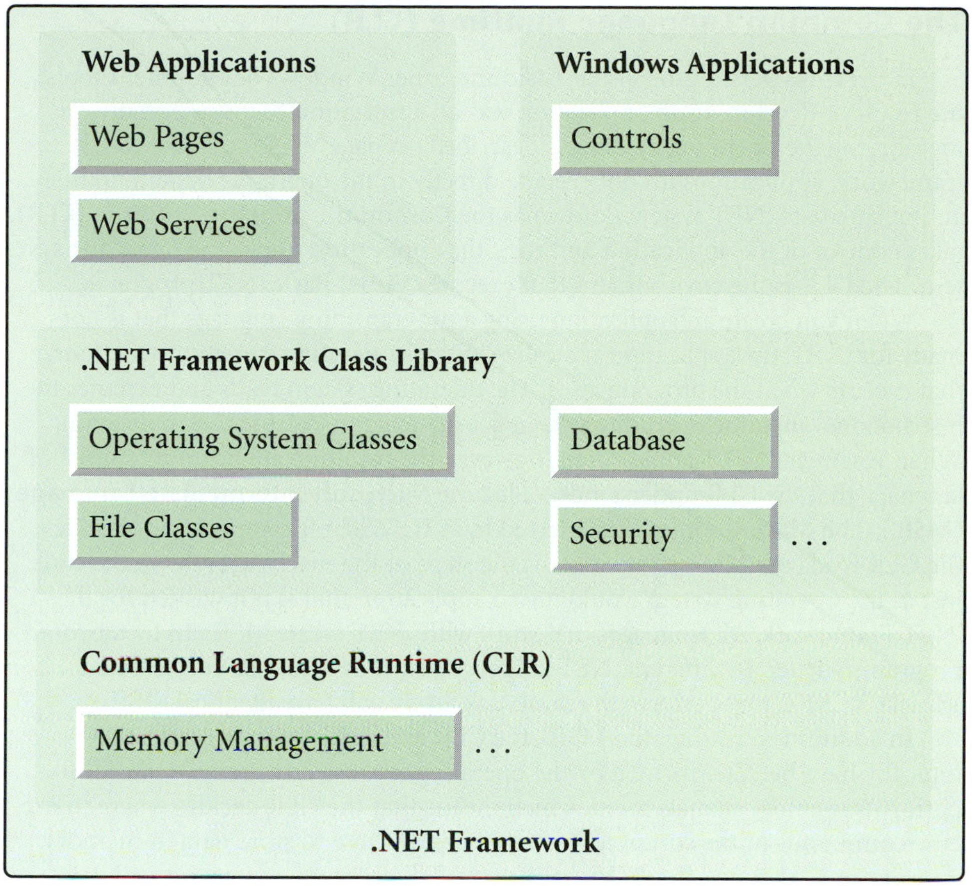

Web Applications

Web Pages

Web Services

Windows Applications

Controls

.NET Framework Class Library

Operating System Classes

File Classes

Database

Security . . .

Common Language Runtime (CLR)

Memory Management . . .

.NET Framework

FIGURE 1-21

The .NET Framework provides a programmer with a rich set of classes, known as the **.NET Framework class library**, which can be used to build applications. The class library offers two significant benefits to programmers. First, the class library provides commonly used classes that you do not have to spend time creating yourself. You can use these classes in your own programs. Second, it ensures that all programmers have access to the same common classes, thereby making code more understandable and reusable.

For these reasons and others, the .NET Framework is very powerful. First, it allows programmers using almost any .NET-enabled programming language to write applications and components (classes) that can be made available to others. In the past, programs written for the same operating system using different languages or technologies could not interact easily with each other. Second, the .NET Framework class library is full featured and extensible. The libraries provide almost any class that a programmer needs to interact with the operating system and other systems, such as databases and networks. In the past, programmers wrote complex code when working with other systems. Finally, the libraries provide an object view of the operating system and other systems. For example, a file in the operating system can be accessed through the library and the file will look like an object to the programmer. The file may have methods, such as readFile(), and attributes, such as fileSize.

The Common Language Runtime (CLR)

In previous versions of Visual Basic and other Windows development tools, the result of developing an application was an application that was executed in memory by the operating system, as described on page VB 1.04. In the .NET framework, applications do not execute directly in the operating system. Rather, an intermediate .NET system, known as the **Common Language Runtime** (**CLR**), takes control of the application and runs the application under the operating system. The CLR is the environment that executes Visual Basic .NET programs.

When you create an application using a programming language that is not made for .NET, the application typically contains operating system instructions that execute when the program runs. The operating system reads and executes the instructions when the operating system is instructed to execute the application. When you create .NET applications, however, the resulting applications consist of language that the CLR understands, called the **Microsoft Intermediate Language** (**MSIL**). The MSIL is sometimes referred to as IL. When the application executes, the CLR reads the MSIL and performs the steps of the machine cycle on the code, just as the operating system would for an application that is not written for the .NET Framework. All languages that work with .NET create MSIL. In fact, two programs written in different .NET languages, such as Visual Basic .NET and Visual C# .NET, that perform the same task, likely will have identical MSIL.

In addition to reading the MSIL, the CLR appropriates many tasks that typically have been performed by the operating system. For example, the CLR performs memory management, which means that the CLR decides where to execute commands in the computer's memory and where to store data in memory.

Figure 1-22 shows how a Visual Basic .NET program relates to the .NET Framework. The diagram illustrates the association between a Visual Basic .NET program, the MSIL that is created from the program, the CLR, and the Windows operating system.

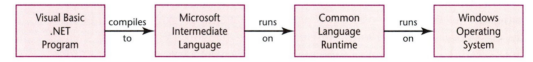

FIGURE 1-22

Visual Basic .NET Windows applications still are considered stand-alone applications, even though they require the CLR to operate. One benefit of the CLR is that a version of the CLR can be created for different operating systems. Therefore, you only need to create a .NET application once and it could run on several operating systems. In the past, creating one application to run on multiple operating systems was a very difficult undertaking. Visual Basic .NET allows you to create with relative ease programs that can run on many different types of systems.

Chapter Summary

This chapter provided an overview of application development, object-oriented design and object-oriented programming, and the Visual Basic .NET software development system. This overview has provided a context within which you can better understand the concepts and technologies involved in the chapters that follow. You also learned the fundamentals of program development, including the process and some of the tools used to assist in the process. Finally, you learned that Visual Basic .NET is a powerful programming environment that allows you to build complex object-based programs, including Console applications, Windows applications, Web applications, components, Windows services, and Web services.

Key Terms

aggregation *(VB 1.20)*
algorithm *(VB 1.13)*
application *(VB 1.02)*
application development *(VB 1.05)*
application software packages *(VB 1.05)*
attributes *(VB 1.13)*
boundary values *(VB 1.19)*
class *(VB 1.20)*
code *(VB 1.05)*
coding *(VB 1.05)*
command prompt interface *(VB 1.07)*
comments *(VB 1.18)*
Common Language Runtime (CLR) *(VB 1.24)*
components *(VB 1.02)*
Console applications *(VB 1.02)*
control *(VB 1.21)*
control structure *(VB 1.15)*
decoded *(VB 1.04)*
design *(VB 1.13)*
development cycle *(VB 1.10)*
documentation *(VB 1.20)*
events *(VB 1.21)*
executed *(VB 1.04)*
fetched *(VB 1.04)*
flowchart *(VB 1.14)*
form *(VB 1.22)*
Hypertext Markup Language (HTML) *(VB 1.06)*
implementation *(VB 1.18)*
instance *(VB 1.20)*
integration testing *(VB 1.19)*
machine cycle *(VB 1.04)*
methodology *(VB 1.10)*
methods *(VB 1.13)*
Microsoft Intermediate Language (MSIL) *(VB 1.24)*
Microsoft Visual Basic .NET *(VB 1.02)*
Microsoft Visual Studio .NET *(VB 1.04)*
.NET *(VB 1.02)*

.NET Framework *(VB 1.22)*
.NET Framework class library *(VB 1.23)*
object model *(VB 1.13)*
objects *(VB 1.13)*
object-oriented design (OOD) *(VB 1.20)*
object-oriented programming (OOP) *(VB 1.20)*
program *(VB 1.02)*
program development *(VB 1.02)*
programmatic interface *(VB 1.09)*
programmers *(VB 1.02)*
programming *(VB 1.02)*
pseudocode *(VB 1.16)*
rapid application development (RAD) *(VB 1.21)*
requirements *(VB 1.11)*
requirements document *(VB 1.11)*
reusability *(VB 1.09)*
service *(VB 1.07)*
software developers *(VB 1.02)*
stand-alone application *(VB 1.05)*
stored *(VB 1.04)*
stored program *(VB 1.04)*
storyboard *(VB 1.17)*
test cases *(VB 1.19)*
test plan *(VB 1.19)*
testing *(VB 1.19)*
Unified Modeling Language (UML) *(VB 1.20)*
unit testing *(VB 1.18)*
usability *(VB 1.17)*
users *(VB 1.11)*
validate *(VB 1.17)*
Visual Basic programming language *(VB 1.02)*
Windows application *(VB 1.02)*
Web application *(VB 1.02)*
Web service *(VB 1.02)*
Windows service *(VB 1.02)*

HOMEWORK ASSIGNMENTS

Short Answer

1. In a machine cycle, after an instruction is _____, it is then _____ and then the instruction is _____. Finally, the result of the instruction is _____.

2. A _____ is a program that does not have an interface and is accessible over the Web. A program that runs in the Windows GUI and has an interface is called a _____. A Windows program that performs maintenance tasks and does not typically have a GUI is a _____.

3. A _____ typically does not have a user interface, but serves as a helper to other programs.

4. A _____ interface allows a user to interact with the computer using buttons and other visual cues. A _____ interface requires a user to type instructions to interact with a computer.

5. The result of creating a Visual Basic .NET program is _____, which is read and executed by the _____.

6. A _____ describes something about an object. A _____ is an action that an object can perform.

7. _____ testing is performed by the programmer while the programmer writes code. _____ testing ensures that all programs that comprise an application interact correctly.

8. List the six phases of the development cycle in order and briefly describe the purpose of each phase.

9. List and describe four benefits of rapid application development and object-oriented design and object-oriented programming.

10. List three sets of test data for a program that determines the quotient A/B, where A must be an integer between -10 and -1, and B must be non-zero.

11. Which variables would you test in Figure 1-14 on page VB 1.16 to ensure the Commission result is positive? Describe the valid range of the variables you select.

12. An employee's weekly Gross Pay is determined by multiplying the hours worked by the rate of pay. Overtime (hours worked more than 40) is paid 1.5 times the hourly rate. Answer the following questions:

    a. Identify the interface input text box(es).

    b. Identify the interface output text box(es).

    c. Identify the interface button(s).

    d. Draw a flowchart to compute the gross pay.

    e. Write the pseudocode that corresponds to the flowchart in d.

13. List and describe each of the types of programs you can write using Visual Basic .NET.

14. Define the following terms: object-oriented programming; object-oriented design; aggregation; class; UML; RAD; .NET Framework; .NET Framework Class Library; CLR; and MSIL.

15. Draw a flowchart that determines the number of negative values (Negative), number of zero values (Zero), and number of positive values (Positive) in the following data set; 4, 2, 3, -9, -4, -6, -8, 3, 2, 0, 0, 8, -3, 4. When the user enters the number -999, terminate the process.

16. Draw a flowchart that accepts three values for U, V, and W, which are positive and not equal to one another. The flowchart should then determine which has the smallest value and assign this value to Smallest, before displaying it.

17. Given two positive-values (assume they are assigned to A and B), draw a partial flowchart that assigns the larger value to Big and the smaller value to Small. If A and B are equal, assign either to Same.

Learn It Online

Start your browser and visit scsite.com/vbnet/exs. Follow the instructions in the exercises below.

1. **Chapter Reinforcement TF, MC, and SA**   Click the True/False, Multiple Choice, and Short Answer link below Chapter 1. Print and then answer the questions.

2. **Practice Test**   Click the Practice Test link below Chapter 1. Answer each question, enter your first and last name at the bottom of the page, and then click the Grade Test button. When the graded practice test displays on your screen, click Print on the File menu to print a hard copy. Continue to take practice tests until you score 80% or better. Hand in a printout of the final practice test.

3. **Crossword Puzzle Challenge**   Click the Crossword Puzzle Challenge link below Chapter 1. Read the instructions, and then enter your first and last name. Click the Play button. Complete the crossword puzzle. When you are finished, click the Submit button. When the crossword puzzle redisplays, click the Print button.

4. **Tips and Tricks**   Click the Tips and Tricks link below Chapter 1. Right-click the information and then click Print on the shortcut menu. Construct a brief example of what the information relates to in Visual Basic .NET to confirm you understand how to use the tip or trick. Hand in the example and printed information.

5. **Newsgroups**   Click the Newsgroups link below Chapter 1. Click a topic that pertains to Chapter 1. Print three comments.

6. **Expanding Your Horizons**   Click the Articles for Visual Basic .NET below Chapter 1. Click a topic that pertains to Chapter 1. Print the information. Construct a brief example of what the information relates to in Visual Basic .NET to confirm you understand the contents of the article. Hand in the example and printed information.

7. **Search Sleuth**   Select three key terms from the Key Terms section of this chapter and then use the Google search engine at google.com (or any major search engine) to display and print two Web pages for each key term.

PROGRAMMING ASSIGNMENTS

1 Analyzing Requirements

Review the requirements document in Figure 1-23 and then answer the questions.

REQUEST FOR NEW APPLICATION

Date submitted:	September 13, 2004
Submitted by:	Anthony Normington
Purpose:	Phone representatives often receive phone calls from field engineers who are ordering refills for customer's cylindrical distilled water tanks that we refill. The phone representatives need to be able to convert the measurements into a reorder size in gallons.
Application title:	Water Volume Calculator
Algorithms:	The tanks may have a radius from 10 to 20 feet. The field engineer measures how far down the water level is from the top of the tank and also notes the tank's radius. Support engineers must calculate how many gallons of distilled water to send to the customer to fill the tank. If a shipment is over a certain number of gallons, the phone representative must be told by the application to notify a manager about a large shipment. Calculations can be summarized as follows: CubicFeet = 3.1416 x Radius^2 x Depth Gallons = CubicFeet x 7.47 If Gallons over certain amount then Notify user to inform manager of large shipment
Notes:	1) The application should allow the user to enter values for the radius and height down to the water level (depth). 2) The end user should not be able to enter a depth greater than the maximum depth of tank that we support. 3) The application should also allow the user to reset all values on the screen to zero (0) so that another calculation can be performed. 4) In the near future, we want to allow customers to access this calculation remotely. Customers would build their own applications and remotely access the calculation on our Web server.

Approvals

Approval Status:	X	Approved
		Rejected
Approved by:	Andrew Philips	
Date:	September 15, 2004	
Assigned to:	J. Quasney, Programmer	

FIGURE 1-23

1. List at least three relevant requirements missing from the requirements document that are necessary to design a complete application. Use these new requirements when completing the remaining tasks.

2. What are the types of programs that must be created in order to meet the requirements?

3. List the inputs and outputs necessary to solve the problem.

4. Design three sets of test data and step the test data through the algorithm listed in the requirements in order to obtain the expected output of the problem.

Assignments 2 through 7 involve solving problems using pseudocode, flowcharts, and object diagrams. For additional information about these topics, see Appendix A.

2 Writing Pseudocode

Write pseudocode to describe the logic illustrated by the flowchart shown in Figure 1-24.

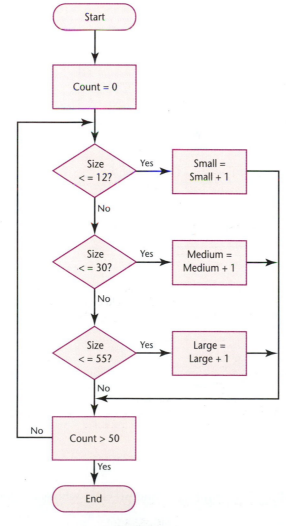

FIGURE 1-24

3 Understanding Flowcharts

A flowchart representation of part of a cardiovascular disease risk assessment is shown in Figure 1-25. The higher the point total, the greater the risk. In the spaces provided, write the point total for the following six people.

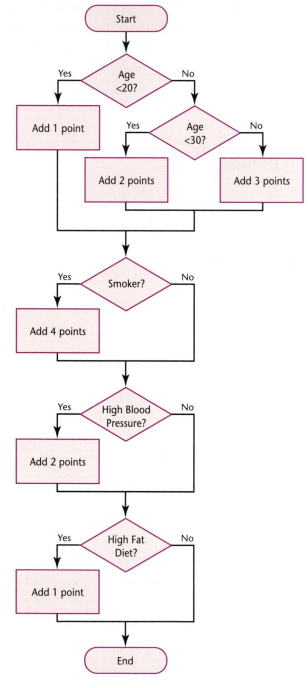

FIGURE 1-25

1. A 25-year-old smoker with high blood pressure who eats a low-fat diet.

_____

2. A 35-year-old nonsmoker with normal blood pressure who eats a low-fat diet.
   _____

3. A 20-year-old nonsmoker with high blood pressure who eats a high-fat diet.
   _____

4. A 45-year-old smoker with high blood pressure who eats a high-fat diet.
   _____

5. A 61-year-old nonsmoker with high blood pressure who eats a high-fat diet.
   _____

6. A 16-year-old nonsmoker with normal blood pressure who eats a high-fat diet. _____

4 Drawing a Partial Flowchart

Draw a partial flowchart to calculate the commission paid to a salesperson. The salesperson receives a 14% commission if his or her sales exceed $40,000. The commission is 9% if sales are less than or equal to $40,000, but greater than $25,000. Sales less than or equal to $25,000 earn a commission of 7%.

5 Creating a Flowchart

Draw one flowchart that enables the mechanical man to complete the Phase 1 and Phase 2 movements efficiently, as illustrated in Figure 1-26.

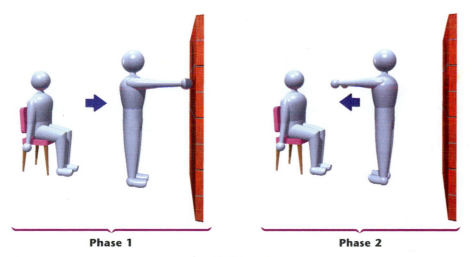

Phase 1   **Phase 2**

FIGURE 1-26

The mechanical man possesses the following properties:

1. He is restricted to a limited set of operations.
2. He is event-driven (doing nothing unless given a specific instruction).
3. He must carry out instructions one at a time.
4. He understands the following instructions:
   a. Physical movement:
      (1) Stand
      (2) Sit

(continued)

5 Creating a Flowchart *(continued)*

    (3) Take one step forward
    (4) Raise arms straight ahead
    (5) Lower arms to sides
    (6) Turn right (90 degrees without taking a step)

  b. Arithmetic:
    (1) Add one to a running total
    (2) Subtract one from a running total
    (3) Store a total (any number of totals can be stored)

  c. Logic:
  The mechanical man can decide what instruction he will carry out next on the basis of answers to the following questions:
    (1) Arithmetic results
      (a) Is the result positive?
      (b) Is the result negative?
      (c) Is the result zero?
      (d) Is the result equal to a predetermined amount?
    (2) Physical status
      (a) Are the raised arms touching anything?

6 Creating Object Diagrams

Identify the relevant objects in the mechanical man problem. Draw an object diagram for each one. List all the possible values of each of the attributes you identify.

7 Creating a High-Level Class Diagram

Pick any class of objects that interests you (for example, clothes, musical instruments, physical fitness equipment, etc.). Create a class diagram showing at least four levels of subclasses and superclasses. For each subclass, identify several attributes inherited from each of its superclasses.

8 Designing a User Interface

Based on your previous experience with Windows applications, draw a picture of a user interface for an application that will convert any amount of U.S. dollars into the equivalent amount in an international currency. The currencies should include Euro, Yen, Pounds, and Canadian dollars. Describe the events and methods (the exact exchange rates and calculations are not necessary). Referring to the user interface you designed, what mistakes could a user make? What will your application do in response to those mistakes?

9 Identifying Events and Methods

Start any software application available to you. On your own paper, briefly describe what the application generally allows the user to do. Identify five specific events in the application and their corresponding methods (operations). Write your name on the paper and hand it in to your instructor.

2

The Visual Basic .NET Integrated Development Environment

Objectives

You will have mastered the material in this chapter when you can:

- Start Visual Basic .NET
- Customize the Visual Basic .NET integrated development environment
- Open a Visual Basic .NET project
- Describe the basic components of the Visual Basic .NET integrated development environment
- Run a Visual Basic .NET project
- Set a property on a control
- Navigate the code window
- Modify code in an existing project
- Save a Visual Basic .NET project
- Print a Visual Basic .NET project's forms and code
- Use Visual Basic .NET Help
- Quit Visual Basic .NET

Introduction

This chapter concentrates on the Visual Basic .NET environment in which you work when you develop a Visual Basic .NET project. A **project** is a collection of code and other files that usually encompasses one program. This chapter explains how to modify an existing Visual Basic .NET program and then test the changes made to the program. After completing this chapter, you should be able to start Visual Basic .NET, describe the components of the Visual Basic .NET environment, and run a project from within the Visual Basic .NET environment. You will learn how to modify properties and existing code in a Visual Basic .NET program, and then save the changes you have made. Finally, you will understand how to document a Visual Basic .NET project and use the Visual Basic .NET Help tools.

Chapter Two — Calculating Take-Home Pay

In this chapter, you will open and modify the program in the Take-home pay calculator project, which is a Windows application. The application is a tool used by a company's human resources department when interviewing job candidates. When job candidates are told a yearly salary amount, they often ask what their weekly take-home pay will be based on that yearly salary. The Take-Home Pay Calculator application allows the human resources employee to make that calculation quickly.

To use the Take-Home Pay Calculator application, the user enters in a yearly salary, the percentage that the employee wants to contribute to his or her retirement plan, and selects which insurance plan the employee will use. As the information is entered, the application automatically updates the weekly pay amount displayed on the screen. The application makes the calculation by dividing the yearly salary amount by 52 to find the gross weekly pay amount. The application then deducts taxes, retirement account contributions, and insurance payments from the gross weekly pay amount to determine the net weekly take-home pay. The application deducts 6.2% for Social Security tax, 1.45% for Medicare tax, 2.5% for state tax, 18% for federal tax, $20 per pay period for individual insurance, and $30 per pay period for family insurance.

Recently, the company has moved to a biweekly pay schedule, which means the company distributes paychecks every other week rather than every week. This chapter shows the changes required to modify the Take-Home Pay Calculator application to calculate the net biweekly take-home pay based on a yearly salary amount.

Figure 2-1a shows the application before modifications. Figure 2-1b shows the application after modifications. As you can see from the two figures, the label, Weekly take-home pay, is changed to Biweekly take-home pay. Also, the resulting take-home pay that the application calculates is different for the two versions of the application. The biweekly take-home pay amount is twice the weekly take-home pay amount given the same salary, retirement plan contribution rate, and insurance plan contributions.

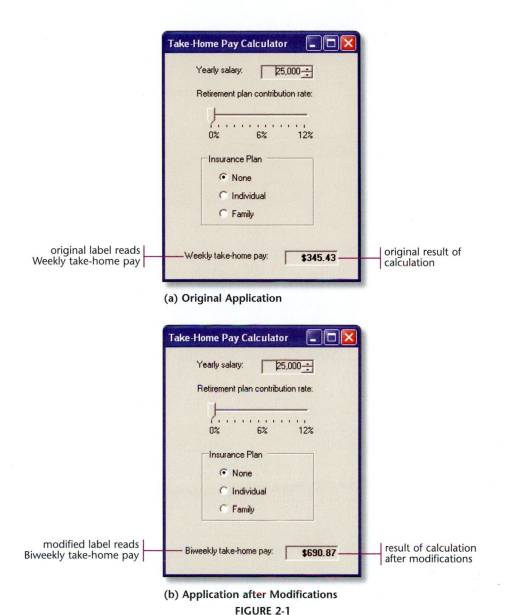

original label reads
Weekly take-home pay

original result of
calculation

(a) Original Application

modified label reads
Biweekly take-home pay

result of calculation
after modifications

(b) Application after Modifications

FIGURE 2-1

Starting and Customizing Visual Basic .NET

You typically develop and modify Visual Basic .NET applications in the integrated development environment. The **integrated development environment** (**IDE**) is part of the Visual Basic .NET application and contains the windows and toolbars that allow you to develop Visual Basic .NET applications and components. Many programmers find it convenient to display as many of the windows and toolbars as possible while working in the Visual Basic .NET IDE. Professional software programmers typically work in as high a resolution as their computer will allow in order to display many of these tools at all times. Some work with multiple monitors attached to the same computer in order to see as much information as possible.

When working on a project in Visual Basic .NET, you should set your computer monitor to as high a resolution as you can tolerate, so that you can display multiple windows and toolbars. The screens shown in this book use a 1024 × 768 resolution. For instructions on how to change the resolution on your computer, see Appendix B on page VB B.01.

> ### Tip
>
> **Resolution**
> When working with Visual Basic .NET, set your computer monitor to at least 1024 × 768 resolution or as high a resolution as you can tolerate.

As described, the Visual Basic .NET IDE contains the windows and toolbars that allow you to develop Visual Basic .NET applications and components. Visual Basic .NET records the size and location of these windows and toolbars when you close a project, so that the IDE displays the same configuration each time you start Visual Basic .NET.

If you are a student working in a computer lab, the IDE may look completely different every time you start Visual Basic .NET in the lab, which can be disorienting if you are new to Visual Basic .NET. To help solve that problem, Visual Basic .NET includes several profiles that customize the environment in which you work. In Visual Basic .NET, a **profile** is used to store personalized settings that define the layout of windows in the Visual Basic .NET IDE, keyboard shortcuts that apply, the default filter to use when searching for help, and other options. Once you choose a profile, Visual Basic .NET remembers it for the next time you use Visual Basic .NET on that computer.

As your proficiency in Visual Basic .NET improves, you can choose a different profile or modify the profile you are using already to change the settings for any existing projects and apply these settings when starting a new project. Each time you sit down at a computer in the lab, you should make sure to check the profile and modify it as described on the next several pages.

The following steps start Visual Basic .NET and customize the Visual Basic .NET environment.

To Start and Customize Visual Basic .NET

1. Click the Start button on the taskbar and then point to All Programs on the Start menu.
2. Point to Microsoft Visual Studio .NET on the All Programs submenu.
3. Point to Microsoft Visual Studio .NET on the Microsoft Visual Studio .NET submenu.

   The Microsoft Visual Studio .NET submenu displays (Figure 2-2). Microsoft Visual Studio .NET is highlighted.

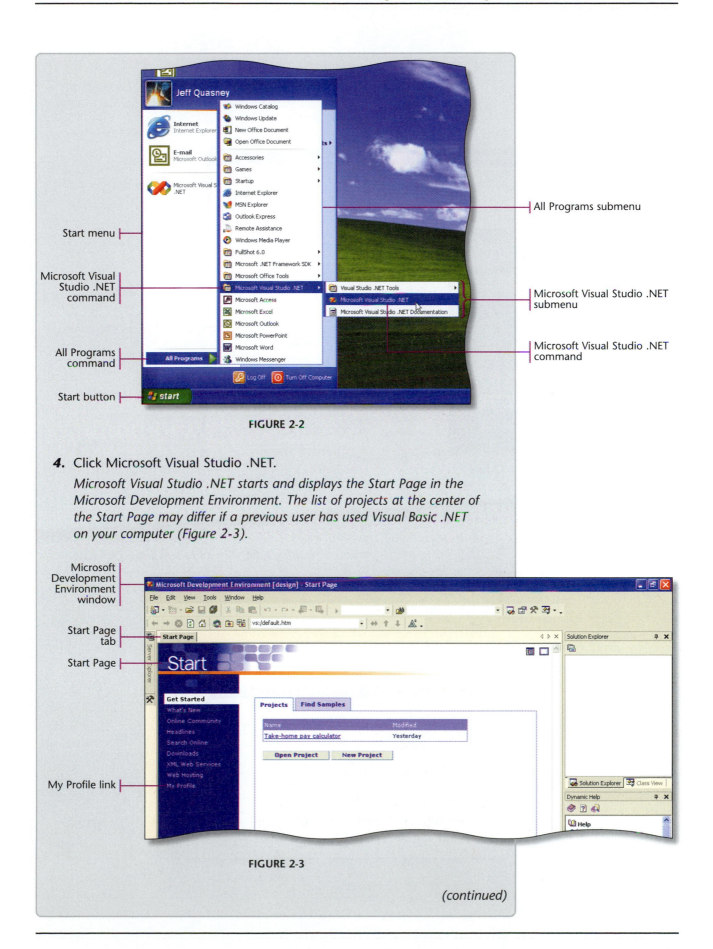

FIGURE 2-2

4. Click Microsoft Visual Studio .NET.

Microsoft Visual Studio .NET starts and displays the Start Page in the Microsoft Development Environment. The list of projects at the center of the Start Page may differ if a previous user has used Visual Basic .NET on your computer (Figure 2-3).

FIGURE 2-3

(continued)

5. Click the My Profile link on the left side of the Start Page.

The Start Page displays My Profile information (Figure 2-4). The selections made for the personalized settings may differ if a previous user has modified the selections.

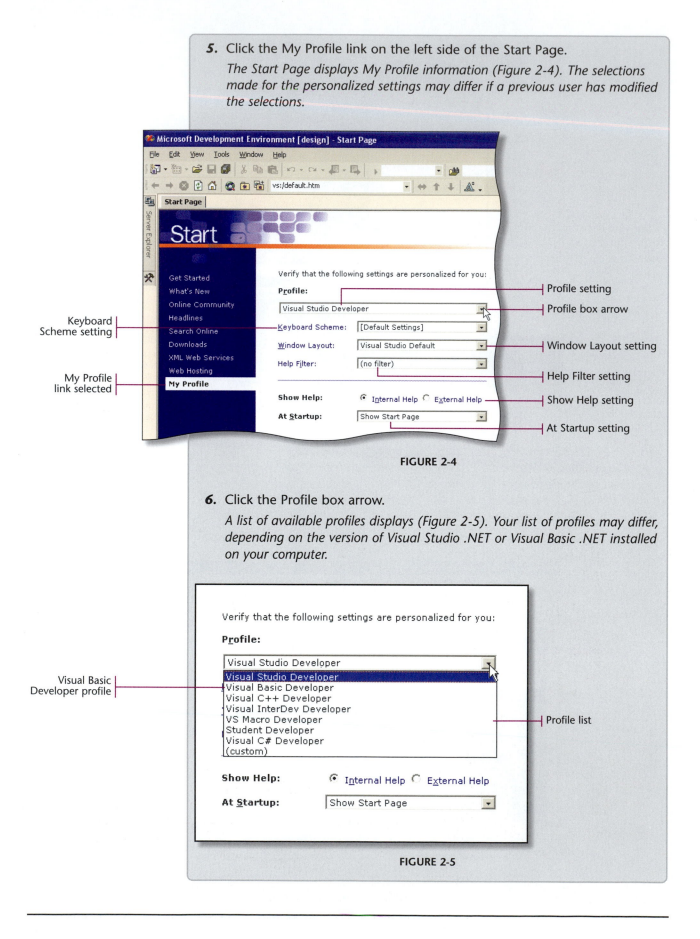

FIGURE 2-4

6. Click the Profile box arrow.

A list of available profiles displays (Figure 2-5). Your list of profiles may differ, depending on the version of Visual Studio .NET or Visual Basic .NET installed on your computer.

FIGURE 2-5

7. Click Visual Basic Developer in the Profile list.

The Profile changes to Visual Basic Developer. The Keyboard Scheme and Window Layout change to Visual Basic 6 and the Help Filter changes to Visual Basic (Figure 2-6). The Toolbox window displays with a push pin icon pointed down to indicate that the Toolbox window is pinned to the left side of the screen and will display until closed.

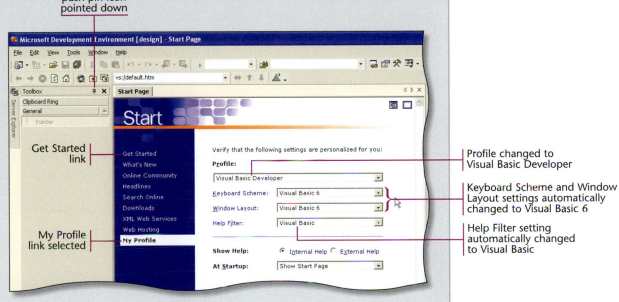

FIGURE 2-6

8. Click the Get Started link on the left side of the Start Page.

The Get Started information displays on the Start Page tab, and the Projects tab is selected. The Toolbox window remains pinned to the left side of the screen. The list of recently modified projects may differ if a previous user has modified Visual Basic .NET projects on this computer (Figure 2-7).

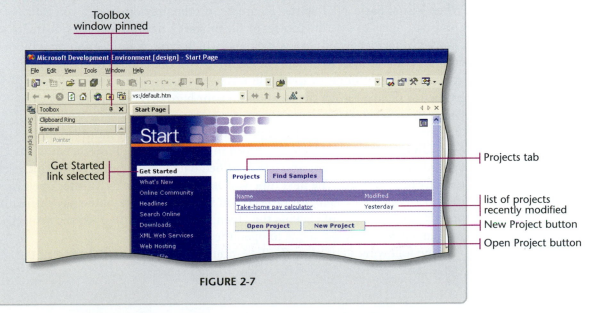

FIGURE 2-7

As discussed in Chapter 1, Visual Basic .NET is part of several editions of Visual Studio .NET. When you use Visual Basic .NET, you access Visual Basic .NET through Visual Studio .NET. Therefore, when you start Visual Basic .NET, the commands on the Windows Start menu are labeled as Visual Studio .NET.

You can experiment with other profiles and settings in the My Profile view of the Start Page (Figure 2-6 on the previous page) to see the changes to the development environment. Be sure to write down or remember the original settings before making any changes so that you can change them back if you do not like them. The Window Layout and Help Filter settings change the development environment most significantly. Setting the Window Layout to Visual Basic 6, for example, customizes the screen to display the Toolbox window automatically because Visual Basic developers typically use the Toolbox often. Setting the Help Filter to Visual Basic filters the large quantity of information in the Help system to focus on information most useful to a Visual Basic developer. Changing this setting reduces the time needed to navigate the Help system, which is discussed later in this chapter.

The Show Help setting determines whether Visual Basic .NET looks for Help files on your computer's hard drive, DVD-ROM drive, and CD-ROM drive, or on the Web. The At Startup setting (Figure 2-6) tells Visual Basic .NET what tab or page to display in the main work area when you start Visual Basic .NET.

Profile

In the My Profile view on the Start Page, select the Visual Basic Developer profile if you want to display the Toolbox window and limit the contents of Help to those topics relating to Visual Basic .NET, rather than all of the products associated with Visual Studio .NET.

Opening an Existing Project

When Visual Basic .NET starts (Figure 2-7 on the previous page), you can choose to open an existing project or file or start a new project. When you choose to start a new project, you choose which type of application or Windows component you want to create. For example, you can choose to create a Web application or a Windows application. When you choose to open an existing project or file, you select the location on your hard drive or floppy disk drive where the project or file is stored.

You also can open an existing project you have recently modified in the Get Started view of the Start Page. As shown in Figure 2-7, the Projects tab of the Get Started view lists the name and last modified date for any projects on which you recently have worked. The next time you start Visual Basic .NET after opening the Take-home pay calculator project, you will see the Take-home pay calculator project listed. Instead of clicking the Open Project button to open the project, you can click the project name to open the project.

The following steps open the Take-home pay calculator project from the Data Disk.

To Open an Existing Project

1. Insert the Data Disk in drive A. See the preface of this book for instructions for downloading the Data Disk or see your instructor for information about accessing the files required in this book.

2. Click the Open Project button.

3. If necessary, click the Look in box arrow and then click 3½ Floppy (A:).

   Visual Basic .NET displays the Open Project dialog box. The names of folders on the Data Disk in drive A display in the Open Project dialog box (Figure 2-8).

Open Project dialog box   3½ Floppy (A:) selected   Look in box arrow

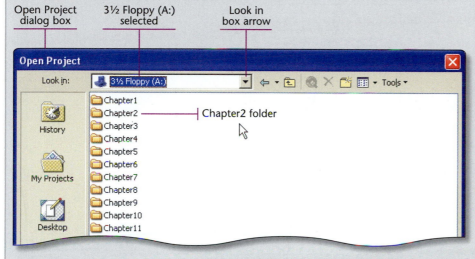

FIGURE 2-8

4. Double-click the Chapter2 folder.

   Chapter2 becomes the current folder in the Look in box. The Take-home pay calculator folder in the Chapter2 folder displays in the Open Project dialog box (Figure 2-9).

Chapter 2 current folder in Look in box

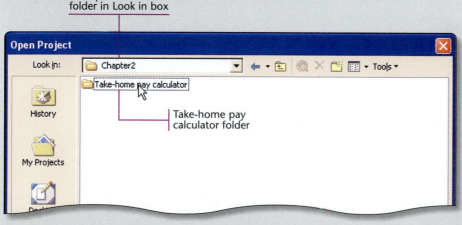

FIGURE 2-9

(continued)

5. Double-click the Take-home pay calculator folder.

6. If necessary, click the Take-home pay calculator solution file (Take-home pay calculator.sln).

Take-home pay calculator becomes the current folder in the Look in box. The Take-home pay calculator solution file and folder display in the dialog box (Figure 2-10).

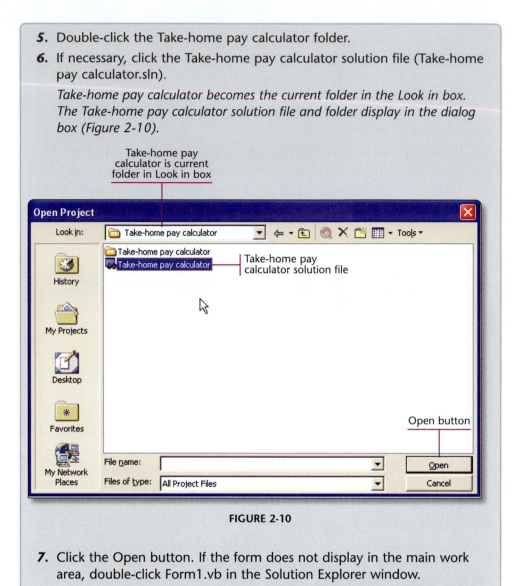

FIGURE 2-10

7. Click the Open button. If the form does not display in the main work area, double-click Form1.vb in the Solution Explorer window.

The Take-home pay calculator project opens in the Visual Basic .NET environment. The visual design of the Take-home pay calculator form displays on the Form1.vb [Design] tab in the main work area. The Solution Explorer window at the top right of the screen displays information about the project (Figure 2-11).

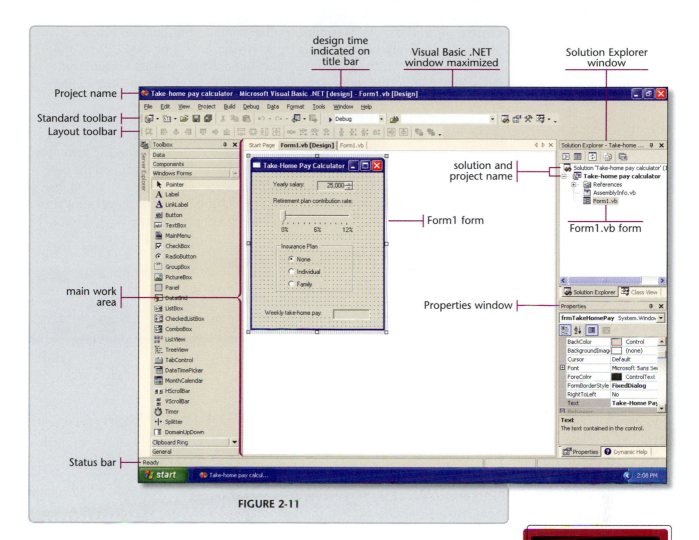

FIGURE 2-11

Visual Basic .NET opens the project as shown in Figure 2-11. When you first open a project, Visual Basic .NET enters a mode in the IDE called design time. When the IDE is in **design time**, you can make modifications to the forms and code of any program. When the IDE is in design time, the word, [design], displays on the title bar of the Visual Basic .NET window.

Exploring the Visual Basic .NET Integrated Development Environment

The Visual Basic .NET integrated development environment consists of several toolbar and window areas. Depending on the task you are performing and the options you choose, other toolbars and windows will display or replace the components shown in Figure 2-11.

Menu Bar and Toolbars

The **menu bar** displays the Visual Basic .NET menu names, each of which represents a list of commands that allow you to create, edit, save, print, test, and run a Visual Basic .NET application or component, as well as access many other essential commands. The **Standard toolbar** contains buttons that execute commonly used commands such as Open Project, Save, Cut, Copy, Paste, and others (Figure 2-12). The **Layout toolbar** contains buttons that execute commonly used formatting commands such as Align to Grid, Size to Grid, Center Horizontally, Center Vertically, and others (Figure 2-13).

The Standard and Layout toolbars allow you to perform common tasks more quickly than when using menus. For example, to save your work, you can click the Save button on the Standard toolbar instead of clicking File on the menu bar and then clicking Save on the File menu. Each button has a picture on the button face to help identify the button's function. Also, when you move the mouse pointer over a button or box, the name of the button or box displays below it in a **ScreenTip**. Each of the buttons is explained in detail when used in the steps.

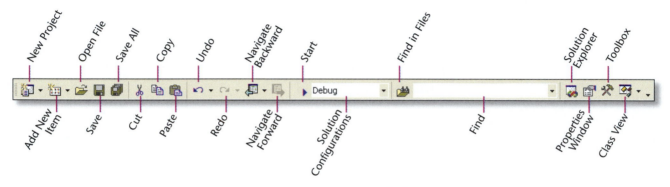

FIGURE 2-12

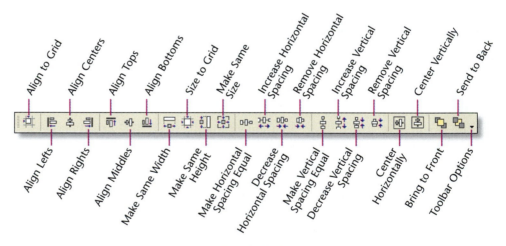

FIGURE 2-13

Visual Basic .NET contains several other toolbars to help you perform your work. If you right-click any toolbar in the Visual Basic .NET IDE, a shortcut menu displays that lists all the available toolbars in Visual Basic .NET. Figure 2-14 shows the toolbar shortcut menu. A check mark next to a toolbar name indicates that the toolbar currently is displaying in the IDE. The last menu command, Customize, allows you to change the toolbars to fit your own needs by adding, deleting, and modifying toolbar buttons. It also allows you to create new custom toolbars.

Toolbars

Right-click any toolbar in the Visual Basic .NET IDE to display a shortcut menu that lists all the available toolbars.

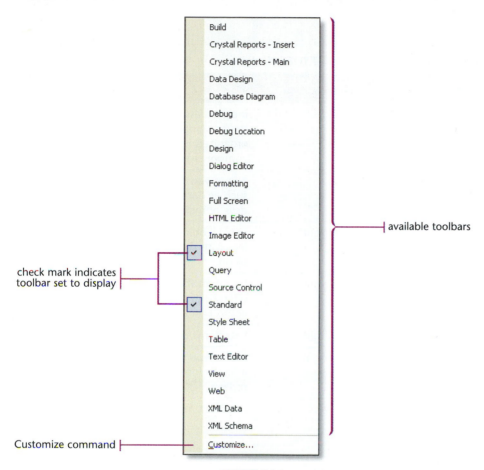

check mark indicates
toolbar set to display

available toolbars

Customize command

FIGURE 2-14

Status Bar

The **status bar**, which is located above the Windows taskbar at the bottom of the Visual Basic .NET window, displays information about the current state of the Visual Basic .NET IDE (Figure 2-11 on page VB 2.11). Mode indicators, such as Ready and Building, display on the status bar and specify the current mode of Visual Basic .NET. When the mode is **Ready**, Visual Basic .NET is waiting for you to perform a task. The status bar also presents information about the location of the insertion point and the progress of current tasks.

Status indicators on the status bar, such as INS or OVR, can be double-clicked to turn certain keys or modes on or off. Double-clicking the OVR status indicator, for example, changes Visual Basic .NET from **Insert** mode, which inserts characters as you type, to **Overtype** mode, which replaces existing characters as you type. You also can press the INSERT key on the keyboard to change the status between Overtype and Insert mode.

Windows

As you perform tasks in the IDE, Visual Basic .NET automatically opens different windows to help you complete the task. You also can open a window manually by clicking commands on the Other Windows submenu of the View menu. Table 2-1 shows a summary of the windows available in the Visual Basic .NET IDE.

Table 2-1   Visual Basic .NET IDE Windows

WINDOW NAME	DEFAULT SCREEN LOCATION	FUNCTION
Toolbox	Left	Includes assortment of tools available for designing forms and a user interface; organized into tabs containing related components, controls, or code
Server Explorer	Left	Allows you to view and manage servers, such as database servers, available during development
Solution Explorer	Upper right	Lists all objects in a solution, including files with program code, references, and so on
Properties	Lower right	List of attributes of object currently selected in the main work area, such as a control on a form
Class View	Upper right	Lists items that make up a class
Resource View	Upper right	Allows you to view resources, or external information, that are included in the project
Output	Main work area	Displays program output during execution
Help Content	Upper right	Displays table of contents for the Help system
Help Index	Upper right	Displays index of the Help system
Dynamic Help	Lower right	Displays Help topics for item selected in the environment
Autos	Lower left	Used during debugging; displays information about variables for the line of code executing
Locals	Lower left	Used during debugging; displays information about variables in the current procedure
Watch	Lower left	Used during debugging; displays information about variables that you have asked to be watched during run time
This	Lower left	Used during debugging; displays information about the current method

Table 2-1   Visual Basic .NET IDE Windows (continued)

WINDOW NAME	DEFAULT SCREEN LOCATION	FUNCTION
Call Stack	Lower right	Used during debugging; displays information about the history of what has been executed
Breakpoints	Lower right	Lists all breakpoints that you have set for the current project
Threads	Lower right	Displays information about all threads created by the currently running program
Command Window	Bottom	Allows a Visual Basic .NET statement to be run in real time
Immediate	Lower right	Allows code to be analyzed as it runs
Find Results	Main work area	Displays results of searches run
Document Outline	Left	Used to show the elements of the Web page when designing Web pages in Visual Basic .NET
Object Browser	Main work area	Allows you to examine and learn about the structure of objects, including properties and methods of objects
Running Documents	Upper left	Used for debugging applications that use Web pages
Task List	Bottom	Displays a list of tasks maintained for a project
Macro Explorer	Upper right	Allows you to select and run macros that you have available to use in the Visual Basic .NET environment

Each of the windows will be discussed in detail when they are introduced in this book.

The Components of a Visual Basic .NET Solution

When a project is opened, Visual Basic .NET opens the project within a solution, as shown in Figure 2-11 on page VB 2.11. A **solution** is a grouping of projects and related files. Solutions can contain one project, such as the Take-home pay calculator project, or many related projects, data files, graphic files, and any other files that relate to the programming task at hand.

You work on one solution at a time in Visual Basic .NET. You can, however, run multiple instances of Visual Basic .NET at the same time on the same computer in order to work on multiple solutions. This approach can be useful when working on related solutions or project, or copying elements of one project to another.

Copying across Projects
To copy elements in one project to another project, open each project in a separate instance of Visual Basic .NET and then use the Copy and Paste commands.

Projects, such as the Take-home pay calculator project, are individual programs and are always created within solutions. Projects within solutions may be programmed in different languages within the .NET architecture. Each individual project is written in one programming language, such as Visual Basic .NET or Visual C++ .NET.

A project can include several components, including files and other objects. When you start a new project to build a Windows application, Visual Basic .NET creates at least three files with the project: References, AssemblyInfo.vb, and a default form. As shown in Figure 2-15, each of these three files displays in a tree view below the project name in the Solution Explorer window. A **tree view** is a hierarchical list of items. Groups of items in the list can be collapsed or expanded by clicking plus (+) or minus (–) signs next to the group.

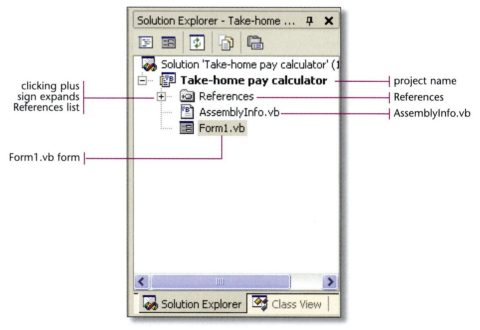

FIGURE 2-15

The first file, **References**, provides a tree view of .NET classes that are needed in the application. By default, five .NET classes are included in a new Windows application. The second file, **AssemblyInfo.vb**, is a file of code that includes information for the Visual Basic .NET compiler. This information uniquely identifies the project to the CLR. Visual Basic .NET provides the References and AssemblyInfo.vb file for a Windows application project, but you probably will never need to modify or view these files.

The third file is a default Windows form, Form1.vb. The Form1.vb file contains the information about the Take-home pay calculator form that displays in the main work area shown in Figure 2-11 on page VB 2.11. Form1.vb is highlighted in the Solution Explorer window to indicate that the form currently is active in the main work area. The Properties window is populated with information about the form that displays in the main work area. Most of this chapter concentrates on the modification of this third item, Form1.vb.

When you open a project file as shown in Figure 2-10 on page VB 2.10, you only need to open the project file. The project file knows where to locate the References, AssemblyInfo.vb file, the default form, Form1.vb, and any additional files needed for the program.

Running a Project

You can run projects within the Visual Basic .NET IDE in order to test the functionality of programs that you develop. When you **run** a project, the project is loaded into memory and the program code is executed by the .NET architecture. By running your projects often during the development phase, you can check for any problems, or **bugs**, that you may have introduced into your code inadvertently. You also can verify that the user interface displays as anticipated, to ensure that the user interface is understandable and easy to use.

Running a Project

Run your projects often during the development phase to check for any bugs that may have been introduced inadvertently.

When you run a project, the IDE enters a mode called **run time**. When run time begins, the IDE changes significantly, closing some windows and opening others. The functionality of these new windows will be discussed in later chapters.

An application is the version of your Windows application project that you distribute to end users. When users run your application, they will not need to use the Visual Basic .NET IDE. The distribution of applications to users will be discussed in a later chapter.

The steps on the following pages run the Take-Home Pay Calculator application from within the Visual Basic .NET IDE. Sample data values test the functionality and validity of the application.

To Run a Project

1. Click the Start button on the Standard toolbar.

As the application starts, Visual Basic .NET opens the Output window and displays informational messages that scroll by in the Output window. The Autos and Call Stack windows then display at the bottom of the IDE, on top of the Output window. The Toolbox and Properties windows are closed. The word, [design], on the Visual Basic .NET title bar changes to [run]. The application window displays, and the Yearly salary box is selected and ready for input. The application button displays on the Windows taskbar (Figure 2-16). The design view of the form continues to display in the background. The Weekly take-home pay result is $345.43 based on the default values for Yearly salary, the Retirement plan contribution rate, and the Insurance Plan.

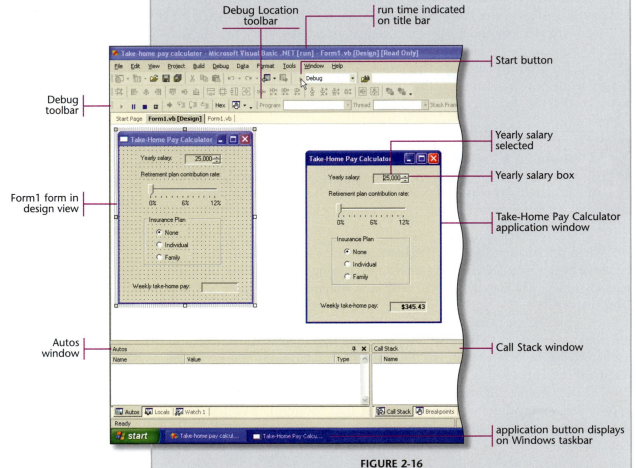

FIGURE 2-16

2. Click the Yearly salary box up arrow, until the number 42,000 displays.

The Take-Home Pay Calculator application window displays, with the Yearly salary set to 42,000 (Figure 2-17). When the Yearly salary value is changed, the value in the Weekly take-home pay text box automatically updates to $580.33.

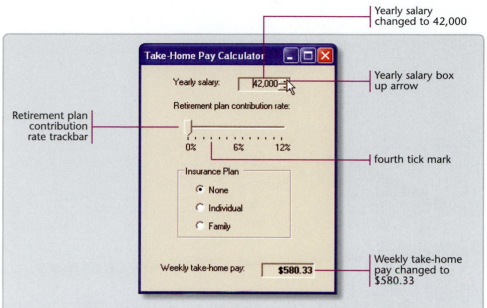

Yearly salary
changed to 42,000

Yearly salary box
up arrow

Retirement plan
contribution
rate trackbar

fourth tick mark

Weekly take-home
pay changed to
$580.33

FIGURE 2-17

3. Drag the Retirement plan contribution rate trackbar to the fourth tick
   mark, which represents 3%.

   *The Retirement plan contribution rate trackbar moves to the fourth tick
   mark to indicate a retirement plan contribution rate of 3%. The value in
   the Weekly take-home pay text box automatically updates to $556.10 as
   the contribution rate changes (Figure 2-18).*

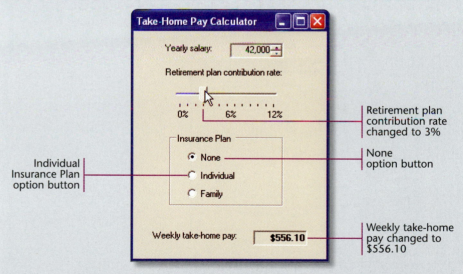

Retirement plan
contribution rate
changed to 3%

None
option button

Individual
Insurance Plan
option button

Weekly take-home
pay changed to
$556.10

FIGURE 2-18

4. Click Individual in the Insurance Plan area.

   *The Individual option button is selected, and the None option button is
   no longer selected. The value in the Weekly take-home pay text box updates
   to $536.10 to reflect the deduction taken based on the change in the
   Insurance Plan option (Figure 2-19 on the next page).*

(continued)

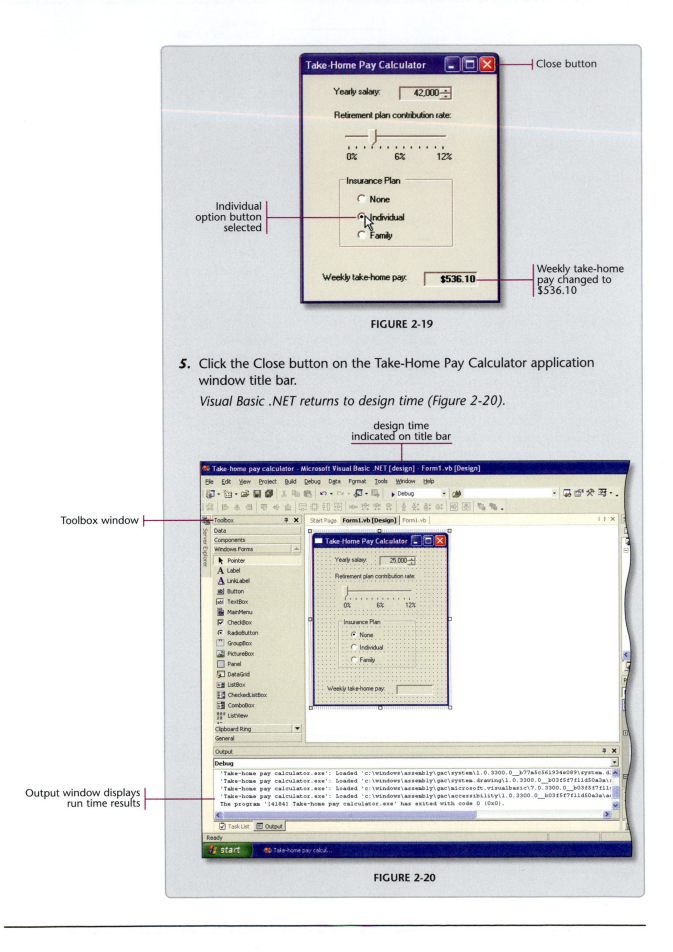

FIGURE 2-19

5. Click the Close button on the Take-Home Pay Calculator application window title bar.

Visual Basic .NET returns to design time (Figure 2-20).

FIGURE 2-20

You can click the Start button to run the application again and then use different data values for the yearly salary and retirement plan contribution rate, and select a different insurance plan option. You do not need to close and then restart the application each time you want to perform another calculation.

As just mentioned, running your projects allows you to check for bugs introduced into your code and verify that the project displays and behaves correctly. Running a project also enables you to learn about the program before you make modifications to it.

Modifying an Existing Project

One of the main tasks a programmer faces involves modifying a project rather than creating a new project. A programmer has three main tasks to consider in the implement design phase when modifying an existing project. First, the programmer gathers information about the existing program and the desired modification requirements. Second, the programmer modifies the user interface and the code in the project. Finally, the programmer unit tests the changes to ensure that they address the requirements and do not create additional problems, or bugs, in the program.

The modification requirements for the Take-Home Pay Calculator application call for a change from a weekly pay frequency to a biweekly pay frequency. This change means that the application must calculate biweekly take-home pay based on 26 pay periods in a year rather than 52. Making this modification requires two changes to the project. First, the text, Weekly take-home pay:, must be changed to the text, Biweekly take-home pay:. The text is displayed on the form using a **Label control**, which is a Visual Basic .NET control used to display text information on a Windows form. Figure 2-21 shows three Label controls in the application.

The second change involves modifying the project code that calculates the take-home pay based on 26 biweekly payments rather than 52 weekly payments.

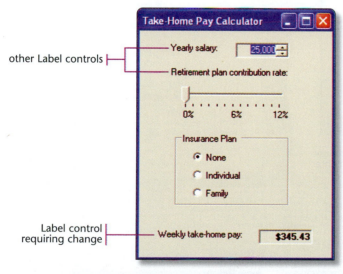

FIGURE 2-21

Modifying a Property of a Control

To make changes to an object on a user interface, such as a control, you click the item and then change the values of its properties in the Properties window. Changing a property's value is known as setting a property. A **property** is a characteristic or attribute of an object, such as its background color or the text that it displays. As described in Table 2-1 on pages VB 2.14 and VB 2.15, the **Properties window** lists the attributes for the object currently selected in the main work area.

The Properties window includes an Object box and a Properties list. The **Object box** in the Properties window displays the name of the currently selected object or control. The **Properties list** displays the set of properties and current value of the properties for the object or control named in the Object box.

The following steps use the Properties window to modify the Text property of the Label control.

To Modify the Text Property of a Label Control

1. **Click the Weekly take-home pay: Label control on the Form1 form in the main work area.**

   The mouse pointer changes to a double two-headed arrow. A shaded outline and handles display around the selected Label control. The control's name (Label6) displays in the Object box of the Properties window. The Properties list displays the set of properties and values for the Label control (Figure 2-22).

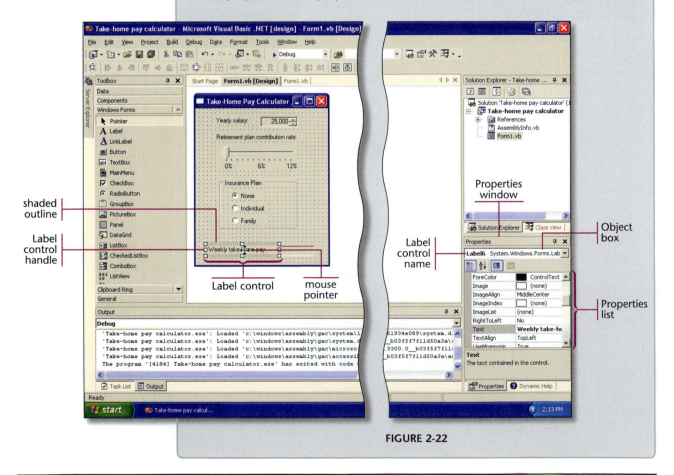

FIGURE 2-22

2. Scroll the Properties list until the Text property is visible.

3. Double-click the Text property. The Text property is the word Text in the left column of the Property list.

The Text property is highlighted in the Properties list (Figure 2-23). The Text property value is selected. A description of the Text property displays at the bottom of the Properties window.

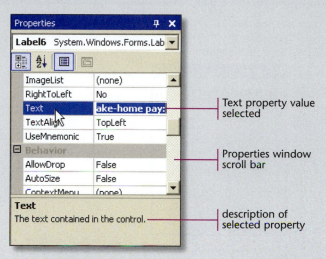

FIGURE 2-23

4. Type `Biweekly take-home pay:` and do not press the ENTER key.

The value of the Text property changes to Biweekly take-home pay: (Figure 2-24). You can correct mistakes made while typing by using the BACKSPACE key or the DELETE key. The Label control on the form still displays the original Text property value.

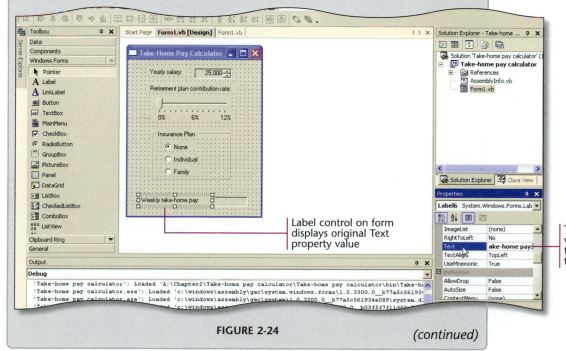

FIGURE 2-24

(continued)

5. Press the ENTER key.

The new Text property value displays on the Label control on the form (Figure 2-25).

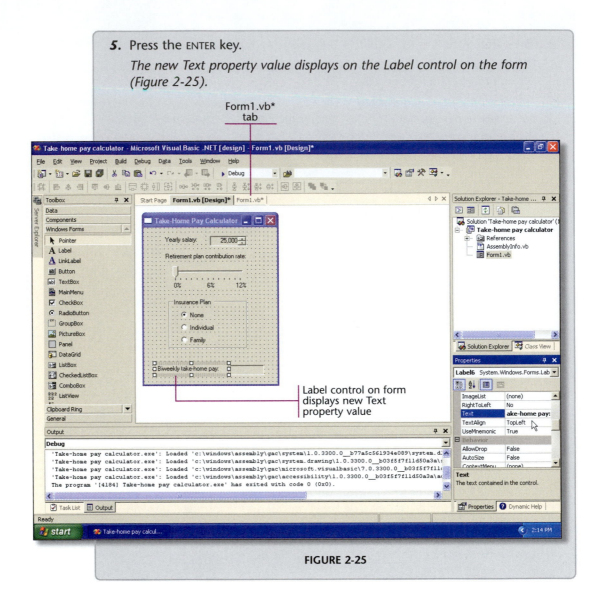

FIGURE 2-25

As shown in the Properties window in Figure 2-23 on the previous page, the Text property is just one of many properties for the Label control. The Properties window allows you to modify the value for any of these properties to change the appearance and functions of a control on a form. This same basic procedure is used for setting most of the properties of any type of control or object on a form during design time. Chapter 3 will discuss properties in more detail.

The Label control on the form now displays the text, Biweekly take-home pay, meaning the first change to update the application is complete. Next, you must modify the code that calculates the take-home pay in order to calculate take-home pay based on 26 biweekly payments rather than 52 weekly payments.

Navigating the Code Window

When you are designing the user interface of a Windows application, such as a form with controls, the main work area of the Visual Basic .NET environment contains a visual representation of the form that the user interacts with at run time. As shown in Figure 2-25, the word, [Design], on the Form1.vb [Design]* tab indicates that this view of the form is a visual representation of the user interface design.

Navigating to the Code Window

To display the design view of a form, click the tab in the main work area with the name of the form and the word, [Design], next to it. To display the code associated with a form, click the tab in the main work area with the name of the form on it.

Designing the user interface, however, is just one aspect of Visual Basic .NET programming. You also must program the actions that execute during run time. When you are programming, or coding, the main work area of the Visual Basic .NET environment displays the **code window**, which provides an area where you can view and edit code.

The code window includes an Object box and a Procedure box at the top of the window. The **Object box** of the code window (Figure 2-26 on the next page) includes a list of all of the individual forms, controls, and classes included in a project. The individual forms, controls, and classes included in a project are all objects. When you want to write or view code for a particular object in a project, you can navigate to the code by selecting it in the Object box. The **Procedure box** allows you to select individual procedures, or pieces of code, that are associated with the object currently selected in the Object box.

Writing or Viewing Code

To write or view the code associated with an object, select the object in the Object box in the code window and then select a procedure in the Procedure box.

The steps on the next page demonstrate how to navigate the code window.

To Navigate the Code Window

1. Click the Form1.vb* tab at the top of the main work area. If the Form1.vb tab does not display above the main work area, click View on the menu bar and then click Code.

The code window opens in the main work area. The name of the current form displays in the Object box in the code window. Lines of code previously entered display in the code window. The insertion point displays before the first character of the first line of code (Figure 2-26).

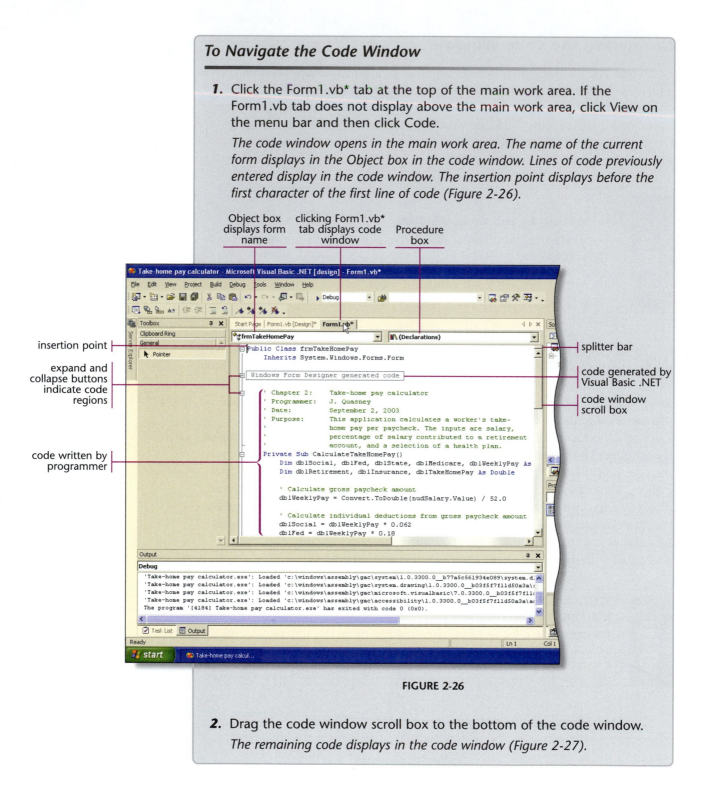

FIGURE 2-26

2. Drag the code window scroll box to the bottom of the code window.

The remaining code displays in the code window (Figure 2-27).

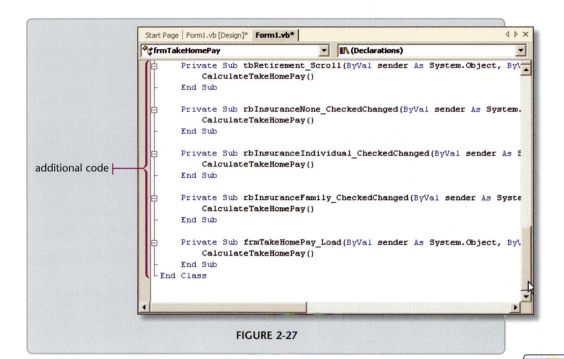

additional code

```
Start Page | Form1.vb [Design]* | Form1.vb*                              ◁ ▷ ×
frmTakeHomePay                        ▼   (Declarations)                    ▼
       Private Sub tbRetirement_Scroll(ByVal sender As System.Object, ByV
           CalculateTakeHomePay()
       End Sub

       Private Sub rbInsuranceNone_CheckedChanged(ByVal sender As System.
           CalculateTakeHomePay()
       End Sub

       Private Sub rbInsuranceIndividual_CheckedChanged(ByVal sender As S
           CalculateTakeHomePay()
       End Sub

       Private Sub rbInsuranceFamily_CheckedChanged(ByVal sender As Syste
           CalculateTakeHomePay()
       End Sub

       Private Sub frmTakeHomePay_Load(ByVal sender As System.Object, ByV
           CalculateTakeHomePay()
       End Sub
   End Class
```

FIGURE 2-27

OTHER WAYS

1. Press ALT+V, C
2. Press F7

As shown in Figure 2-26, Visual Basic .NET displays some words in the code in color. Most of the colored words are keywords. **Keywords** are words that have special meaning within Visual Basic .NET and provide a vocabulary for the Visual Basic .NET language. Some of the keywords shown in color in the code window include Public, Class, Private, Sub, and Dim.

Collapse and expand buttons on the left side of the code window indicate code regions. A **code region** is a group of related lines of code. Visual Basic .NET automatically knows how and when to create these regions as you create your code. Visual Basic .NET also allows you to define your own code regions. Code regions are collapsible and expandable, so that you can collapse or hide large sections of code so they do not clutter the work area.

The code window shown in Figure 2-26 displays four code regions. The plus sign (+) next to the second region indicates that this code is collapsed. The boxed-in text next to the plus sign indicates that this code was written automatically by Visual Basic .NET. The minus sign (−) next to the third region indicates that this code is expanded. The code that begins the third code region was written by a programmer and includes useful notations about the authorship and purpose of the code.

If you need to work with multiple sections of code at the same time, the **splitter bar** allows you to create two or more windows within the code window. You can drag the splitter bar vertically to create or remove additional code windows.

Modifying Code in the Code Window

The code window functions as a text editor for writing code statements. You can use the keyboard and/or a mouse to navigate, select, and modify code within the code window just as you would modify text with a text editor such as WordPad.

The following steps modify the code so that the application calculates take-home pay based on 26 biweekly payments rather than 52 weekly payments.

To Modify Code in the Code Window

1. Drag the code window scroll box up until the code displays in the code window as shown in Figure 2-28.

The fourth code region, which includes the code for the CalculateTakeHomePay procedure, displays in the code window (Figure 2-28). The code requiring the change is the sixth code line of the fourth code region. This line of code currently is set to calculate gross weekly pay by dividing the yearly salary by 52.0.

CalculateTakeHomePay
procedure

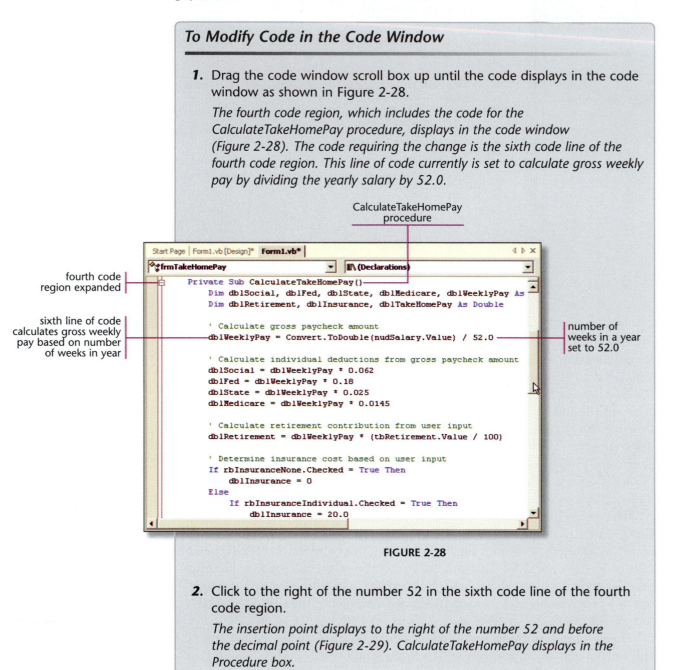

fourth code
region expanded

sixth line of code
calculates gross weekly
pay based on number
of weeks in year

number of
weeks in a year
set to 52.0

FIGURE 2-28

2. Click to the right of the number 52 in the sixth code line of the fourth code region.

The insertion point displays to the right of the number 52 and before the decimal point (Figure 2-29). CalculateTakeHomePay displays in the Procedure box.

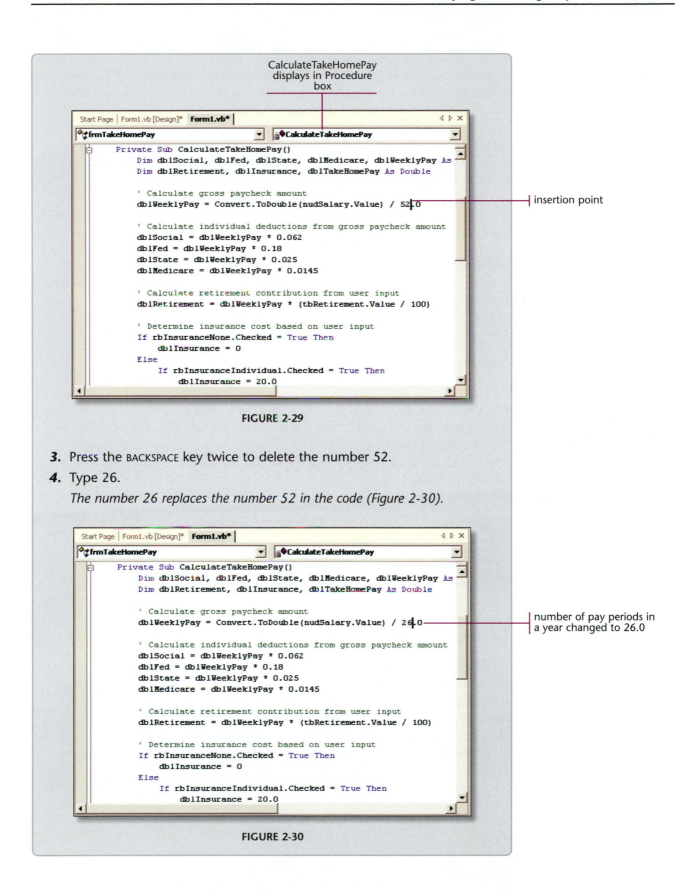

FIGURE 2-29

3. Press the BACKSPACE key twice to delete the number 52.

4. Type 26.

The number 26 replaces the number 52 in the code (Figure 2-30).

FIGURE 2-30

As shown in Figure 2-30 on the previous page, when you click a line of code in a code region, the Procedure box displays the current location of the insertion point. By watching the Object box and the Procedure box, you always know where you are writing or viewing code.

The preceding steps modified the number of weeks the Take-Home Pay Calculator uses to calculate take-home pay. The code change tells Visual Basic .NET to divide the yearly salary by 26.0, instead of 52.0, to calculate a gross pay amount for a biweekly pay period.

When you change the value from 52.0 to 26.0, be sure to use the decimal representation of these numbers to ensure the application correctly calculates the values. Chapter 4 will discuss the use of decimal representation in more detail.

The modifications to the existing project are now complete. The Text property value for the Label control is modified to display the text, Biweekly take-home pay:, and the code that calculates take-home pay is modified to base take-home pay on 26 biweekly payments. With the changes complete, the project should be saved and then run, so you can test the changes.

Saving and Running a Project

Before starting a new Visual Basic .NET project or quitting Visual Basic .NET, you should save your work. You also should save your project periodically while you are working on it and before you run it for the first time. Visual Basic .NET will save your project automatically when you run it. During the process of developing a project, however, you should err on the side of caution and save your work often.

Saving Changes
You should save your work periodically while you are working on a project and again before you run the project for the first time.

Saving a Project

Visual Basic .NET projects are saved as a set of files. For example, one of the files used extensively in the Take-home pay calculator project is the Form1.vb file, which is indicated on the tab in the main work area (Figure 2-31). The Form1.vb file contains the information that displays in both the Form1.vb [Design] window and the Form1.vb code window. Other files saved with a project contain information about the type of project and other options that are saved with the project.

The following steps save the Take-home pay calculator project on the Data Disk in drive A.

To Save a Project

1. Click the Form1.vb [Design]* tab.
2. Click the Save All button on the Standard toolbar.

   The asterisks next to Form1.vb [Design] on the window title bar and the main work area tab no longer display, indicating that the project has been saved (Figure 2-31). Because the project was opened from the Data Disk in drive A, Visual Basic .NET automatically saves the project on the Data Disk in drive A.

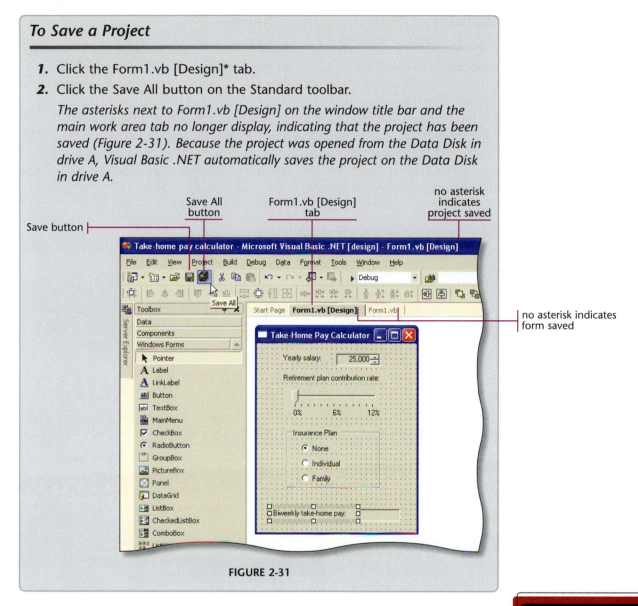

FIGURE 2-31

Clicking the **Save All button** saves all files associated with a project. You can click the **Save button** to save only the current file you are working on in the main work area. Using the Save button is practical if you are modifying an individual file that is part of a much larger project. If you want to save your work with a different file name or in a different folder or on a different drive, click the **Save Selected Items As command** on the File menu.

OTHER WAYS

1. Press ALT+F, L

Saving Projects and Files
If you are changing one file in a large project, then use the Save button to save the individual file rather than the Save All button, which saves all project files whether or not they were changed.

Running a Project to Test Changes

Once the project is saved, you should run the project to test that your changes have not introduced new bugs or caused problems with the functionality of the program or introduced invalid code. You also should test changes frequently as you are working on a project. If you have several changes to make to a program, for instance, it is important to test each change individually, so you easily can identify which change introduced a new problem into the project.

To test the changes in a project, run the project using the same steps used to run the project earlier in the chapter. The following steps run the project and test the changes made to the project.

To Run a Project to Test Changes

1. Click the Start button on the Standard toolbar.

The word, [design], on the Visual Basic .NET title bar changes to [run] as Visual Basic .NET enters run time. The Take-Home Pay Calculator application window displays in the center of the screen and the insertion point displays in the Yearly salary box (Figure 2-32). The design view of the form continues to display in the background.

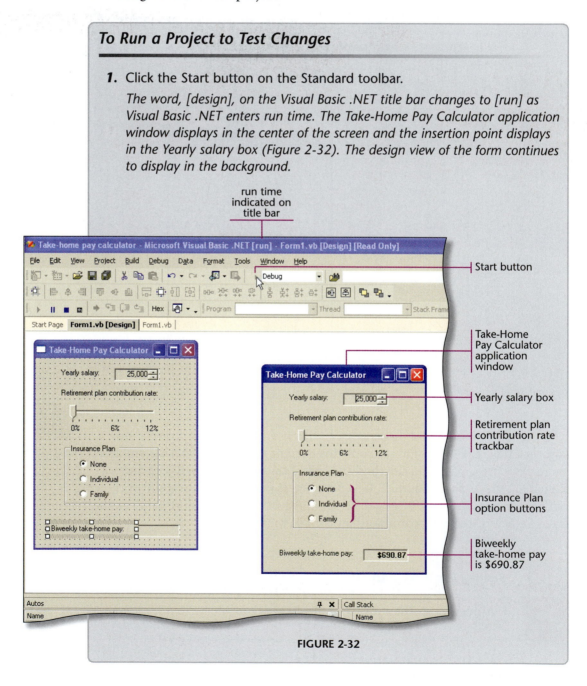

run time
indicated on
title bar

Start button

Take-Home
Pay Calculator
application
window

Yearly salary box

Retirement plan
contribution rate
trackbar

Insurance Plan
option buttons

Biweekly
take-home pay
is $690.87

FIGURE 2-32

2. Click the Yearly salary box up arrow until the number 42,000 displays.

3. Drag the Retirement plan contribution rate trackbar to the fourth tick mark, which represents 3%.

4. Click Individual in the Insurance Plan area.

The values of the controls change. The new Biweekly take-home pay text box updates to $1,092.19, to reflect the calculations based on selected values and a biweekly pay period (Figure 2-33).

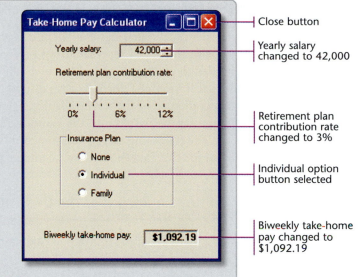

Close button

Yearly salary changed to 42,000

Retirement plan contribution rate changed to 3%

Individual option button selected

Biweekly take-home pay changed to $1,092.19

FIGURE 2-33

5. Click the Close button on the Take-Home Pay Calculator application window title bar.

The same values entered earlier in this chapter (Figure 2-19 on page VB 2.20) now produce a different result. Try entering various values for the three inputs to further test the project. See the deductions listed on page VB 2.02 if you want to check a calculation by hand.

If your program does not run as expected, check the changed code and the changed property to make sure they match the specifications in this chapter. For example, you may have misspelled a change in a property or put the wrong number in the code window. The process of making your code work as expected is known as **debugging**. Continue debugging the application by changing the Text property of the label or the code and then running the project to test that it operates as expected.

Testing Changes

Run a project often as you are modifying it to test changes, and verify that they have been applied correctly.

Documenting an Application

Documenting an application refers to producing a record of the design and code used to create an application. Documentation can be electronic or printed. A printed record, also called a **hard-copy output**, can make it easier to check your program or refine it. Often, project requirements dictate that you archive a hard-copy output of an application's code and user interface to share with a client or other developers.

Documenting the User Interface Design of a Form

Because Visual Basic .NET does not include functionality that allows you to print the visual representation of a form, you must use other Windows capabilities to print a record of the user interface. One easy way to print a copy of a Visual Basic .NET form in design mode is to use Windows' built-in ability to take a picture of the screen display. After the screen display picture is taken, the image can be pasted into the Windows Paint application and then printed.

The following steps print a record of the user interface design of the Form1 form for the Take-home pay calculator project.

To Print a Record of the User Interface Design of a Form

1. With the Take-home pay calculator project open in design time, press the PRINT SCREEN key.

Windows copies an image of the screen, as shown in Figure 2-34. The image is copied on the Windows Clipboard.

design time
indicated on
title bar

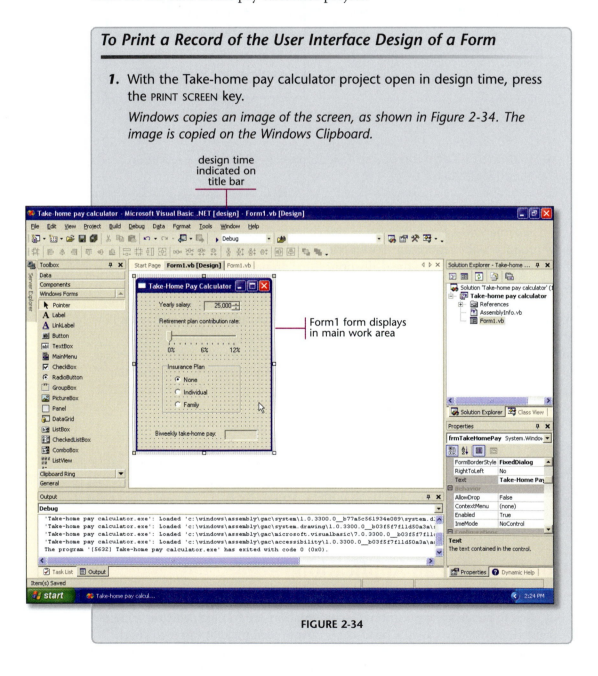

Form1 form displays
in main work area

FIGURE 2-34

2. Click the Start button on the Windows taskbar and then point to All Programs on the Start menu.

3. Point to Accessories on the All Programs submenu, and then point to Paint on the Accessories submenu.

The Accessories submenu displays, and the Paint command is highlighted (Figure 2-35).

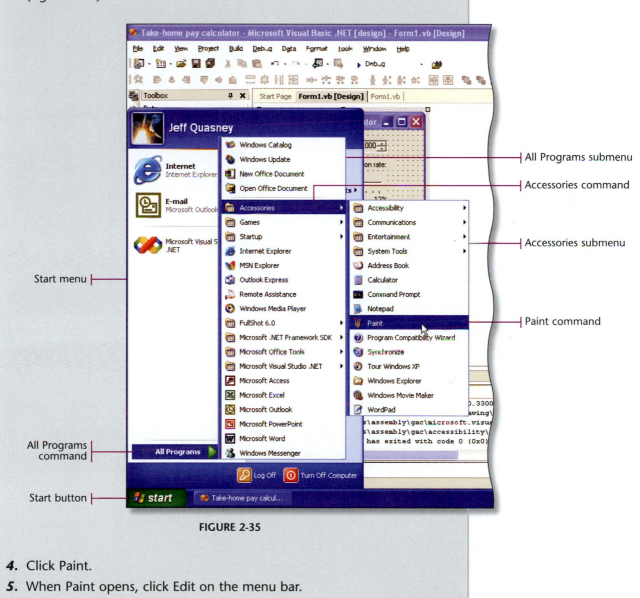

FIGURE 2-35

4. Click Paint.

5. When Paint opens, click Edit on the menu bar.

(continued)

6. Point to Paste on the Edit menu.

Paint starts and displays a blank picture area in the Paint window. The Paste command is highlighted on the Edit menu (Figure 2-36).

Paint
window

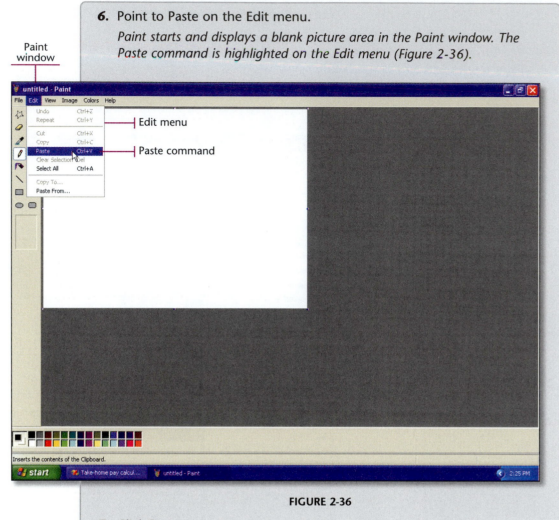

Edit menu

Paste command

FIGURE 2-36

7. Click Paste.

The screen image that was copied onto the Windows Clipboard is pasted into the picture area in the Paint window (Figure 2-37).

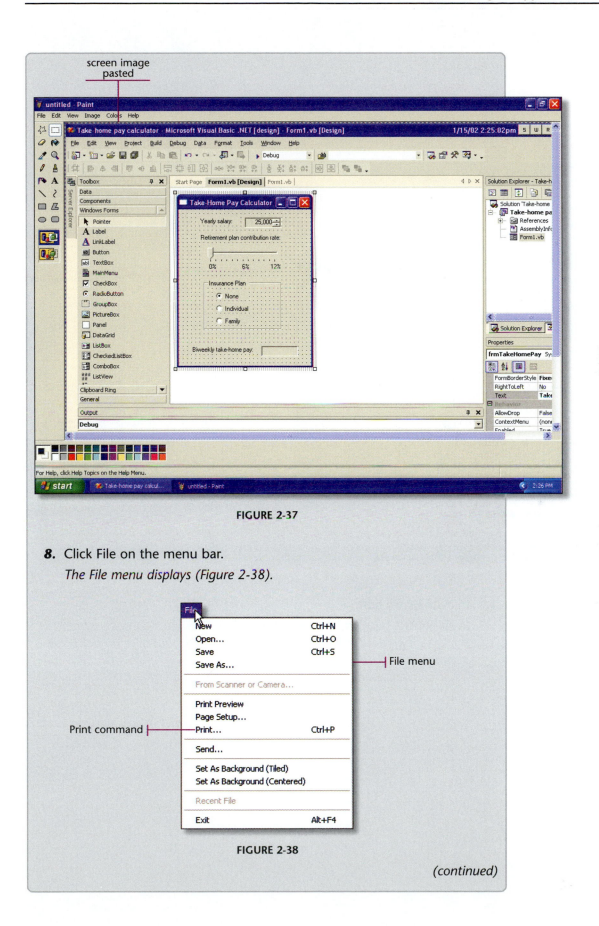

screen image
pasted

FIGURE 2-37

8. Click File on the menu bar.

The File menu displays (Figure 2-38).

File menu

Print command

FIGURE 2-38

(continued)

9. Click Print on the File menu.

The Print dialog box displays (Figure 2-39). The available printers in the Select Printer area will differ, depending on the printers installed on your computer.

Print dialog box

Close button

Print button

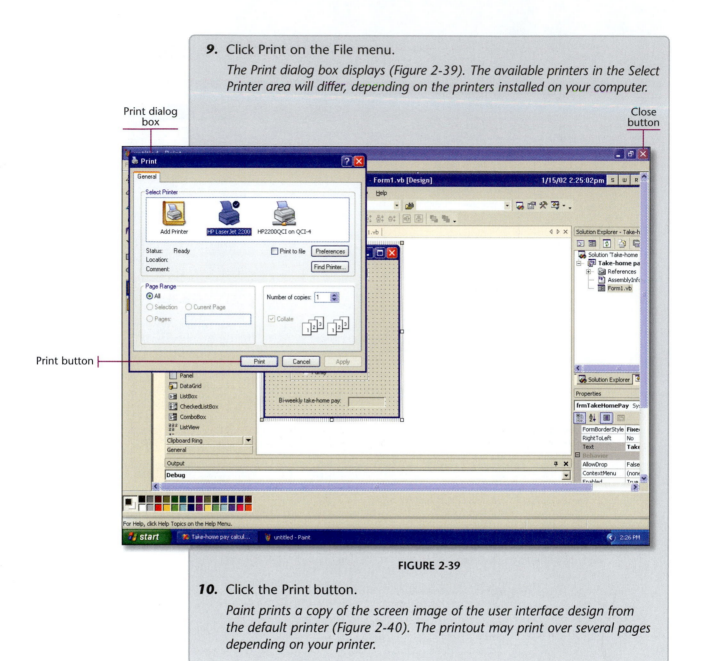

FIGURE 2-39

10. Click the Print button.

Paint prints a copy of the screen image of the user interface design from the default printer (Figure 2-40). The printout may print over several pages depending on your printer.

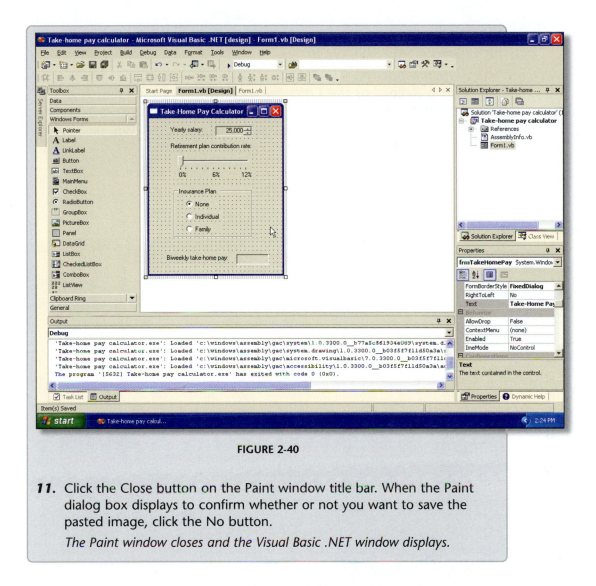

FIGURE 2-40

11. Click the Close button on the Paint window title bar. When the Paint dialog box displays to confirm whether or not you want to save the pasted image, click the No button.

The Paint window closes and the Visual Basic .NET window displays.

In addition to pasting the copied screen image from the Windows Clipboard into Paint, you also can paste the screen images into programs such as Microsoft Word or Microsoft PowerPoint. Additionally, you can save an electronic version of the screen in Paint by using the Save As command on the File menu in the Paint program.

Screen capture programs also allow you to capture a screen image and then create a printed record of a form's user interface design. Some of these programs allow you to capture only a specific rectangular area of the screen. You may need to experiment with your printer and the printer settings in order to obtain optimal results for printing a form's user interface design.

Documenting Code for a Form

Visual Basic .NET does include functionality that allows you to print a hard copy of the code used in a project. The **Print command** is available on the File menu when the active window contains printable items, such as code, help topics, Web pages, or other printable output. To print the form code, you first must display the code in the code window in the main work area.

The following steps print a record of the code in the Form1 form of the Take-home pay calculator project.

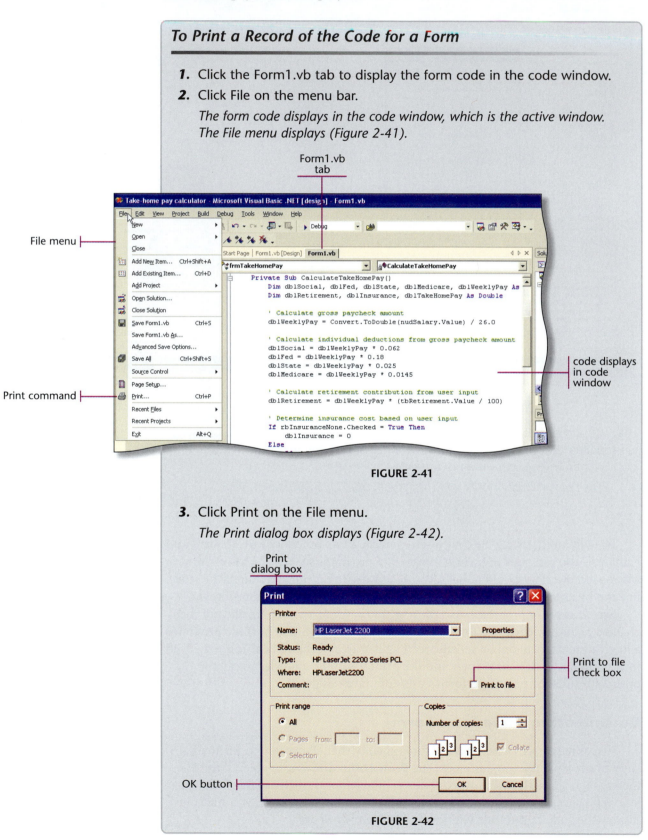

To Print a Record of the Code for a Form

1. Click the Form1.vb tab to display the form code in the code window.

2. Click File on the menu bar.

The form code displays in the code window, which is the active window. The File menu displays (Figure 2-41).

FIGURE 2-41

3. Click Print on the File menu.

The Print dialog box displays (Figure 2-42).

FIGURE 2-42

4. Click the OK button.

Visual Basic .NET prints a copy of the form code from the default printer. Continuation markers print to indicate that a line of code was too long to fit the width of the printed page (Figure 2-43).

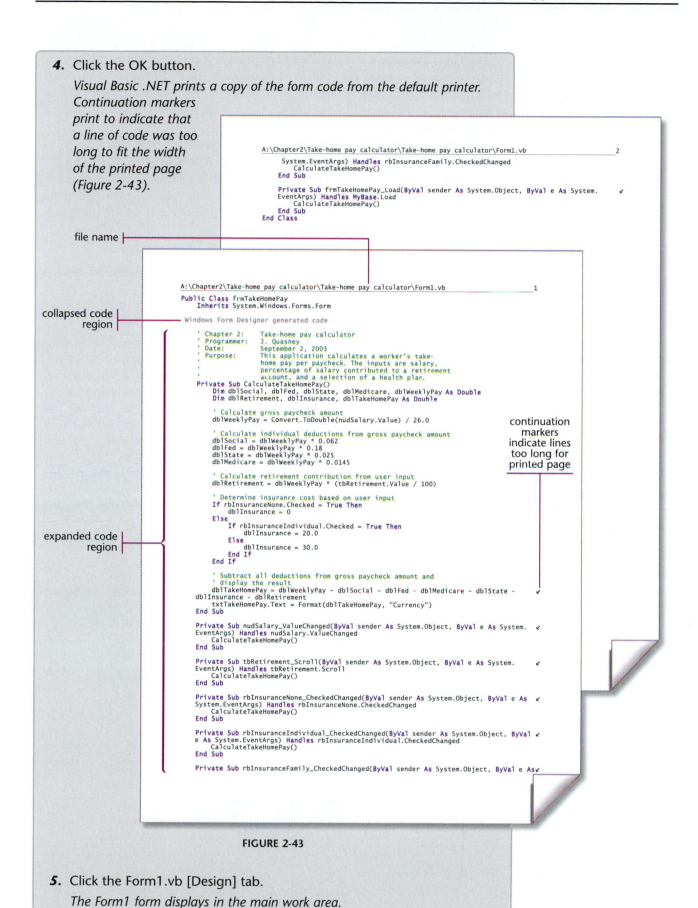

file name

collapsed code region

expanded code region

continuation markers indicate lines too long for printed page

FIGURE 2-43

5. Click the Form1.vb [Design] tab.

The Form1 form displays in the main work area.

The Print dialog box also allows you to print a selection from the active window or specific pages from the active window. If the Print to file check box is selected in the Print dialog box, the print output is sent to the file specified in the Print To File dialog box that displays after you click the OK button in the Print dialog box.

The printed page shown in Figure 2-43 on the previous page contains continuation markers on the right side of the page. **Continuation markers** indicate that a line of code was too long to print on one line and is continued on the next line. The printout does not distinguish code regions or print code in any collapsed code regions; it does, however, print descriptions of any collapsed code regions.

The changes to the Take-Home Pay Calculator application now are complete.

Visual Basic .NET Help

The Visual Basic .NET IDE includes an extensive Help system. Visual Basic .NET **Help** contains documents, examples, articles, and other information about the Visual Basic .NET language and environment to assist you in using Visual Basic .NET. While working in the Visual Basic .NET IDE, you can access Help in a number of ways.

Navigating the Visual Basic .NET Help System

As shown in Figure 2-44, the Help menu in the Visual Basic .NET IDE includes a number of commands you can use to access Help.

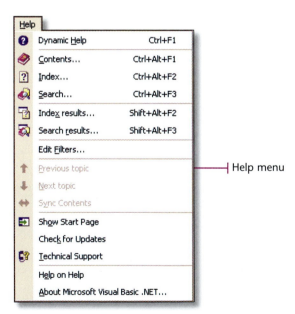

FIGURE 2-44

Table 2-2 summarizes the Help menu commands and where each command displays the Help information by default. Many of these Help menu commands also can be accessed using tabs on windows in the IDE.

Table 2-2   Help Menu Commands

MENU COMMANDS	DEFAULT DISPLAY AREA	ACTION
Dynamic Help	Lower right	Displays the Dynamic Help window
Contents	Upper right	Displays a tree view of all Help topics
Index	Upper right	Displays an alphabetical list of all Help items
Search	Upper right	Displays a search form that allows you to find topics by entering keywords
Index results	Bottom	Displays a list of Help articles related to an item that is clicked in the Index window
Search results	Bottom	Displays a list of Help articles generated from completing a search using the Search window
Edit Filters	Main work area	Allows a user to customize Help results by specifying filter criteria for all Help searches and results
Previous topic	Main work area	Allows a user to navigate to a Help article that previously displayed in the main work area
Next topic	Main work area	Allows a user to navigate to the next topic in the Search results or Index results
Sync Contents	Main work area	Causes the Contents window to navigate to the item currently being accessed in the Help system
Show Start Page	Main work area	Displays the initial Visual Basic .NET Start Page
Check for Updates	New window	Attempts to connect to Microsoft's Web site to check for new updates to the Visual Basic .NET application
Technical Support	Main work area	Displays links with contact information for Microsoft technical support
Help on Help	Main work area	Displays information on how to get the most out of using the Help system
About Microsoft Visual Basic .NET	New window	Displays copyright information, Visual Basic .NET licensing information, and system information

Depending on how Visual Basic .NET was installed on your computer, you may be required to insert one of the Visual Basic .NET CD-ROMs or DVD-ROMs when you need to access Help. If this is the case, you will need to locate the specific CD-ROM or DVD-ROM and insert it. It always is a good habit to keep the Visual Basic .NET CD-ROM or DVD-ROM in your CD-ROM or DVD-ROM drive while you are using Visual Basic .NET.

Contents, Index, and Search Windows

The Contents, Index, and Search Help menu commands display content from the Visual Basic .NET Help system. The **Contents window** shown in Figure 2-45 displays a listing of Help topics arranged much like a table of contents in a book. Expand and collapse buttons allow topics and subtopics to be displayed or hidden from view. Double-clicking any topic without a collapse or expand button displays the Help topic on a tab in the main work area.

>
>
> ### When to Use the Contents Window
> Use the Contents window for help as you would the table of contents at the front of a book or when you know the general category of the topic in question.

Help topic
displays on tab in
main work area

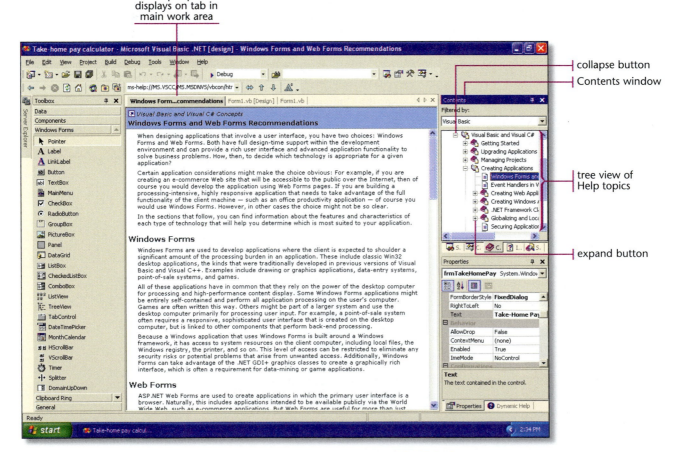

collapse button

Contents window

tree view of
Help topics

expand button

FIGURE 2-45

The **Index window** provides a navigational aid similar to a book index. Topics are listed alphabetically, and subtopics display below main topics. You also can type a topic in the Look for box to display a list of items related to that topic in the Index window. Figure 2-46 shows the Visual Basic .NET IDE. After clicking Index on the Help menu, typing Textbox in the Look for box, and then double-clicking TextBox control (Windows Forms), the topic is selected in the list in the Index window and the information displays on the tab in the main work area.

When to Use the Index Window
Use the Index window for help as you would the index in a book.

TextBox Control
topic displays on tab
in main work area

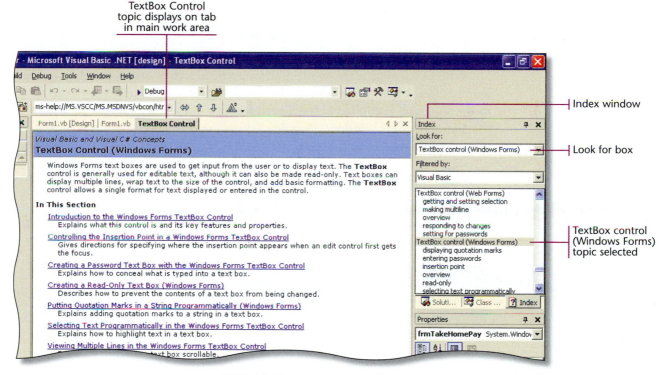

FIGURE 2-46

The **Search window** allows you to search the Visual Basic .NET Help system for a specific term or phrase. Figure 2-47 on the next page shows the IDE after clicking the Search command on the Help menu and then entering the search term, label control, in the Look for box.

When to Use the Search Window
Use the Search window for help when you know the word or phrase, or the first few letters of the word or phrase you want to look up.

Search window

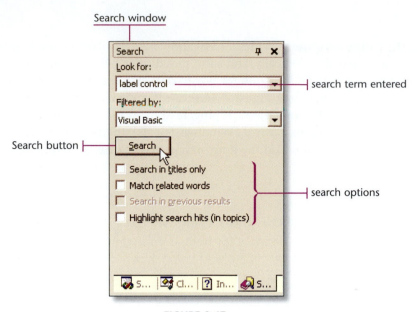

FIGURE 2-47

When a user clicks the Search button in the Search window, the Help system searches for Help topics related to the search term. Once it locates topics related to the search term entered in the Search window, it then displays the results in the **Search Results window**. Double-clicking the first topic in the Search Results window displays the Help topic in the main work area, as shown in Figure 2-48.

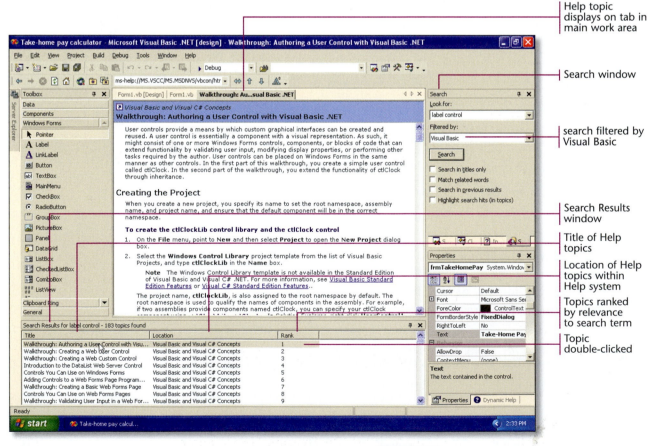

FIGURE 2-48

Dynamic Help Window

In Visual Basic .NET, **Dynamic Help** displays help for whatever task or window you are working with in the IDE. As you navigate in the IDE, open new windows, or select items on a form, Dynamic Help automatically updates itself with relevant information. By default, the Dynamic Help window displays in the same window area as the Properties window. You can access Dynamic Help either by clicking the Dynamic Help tab next to the Properties tab in the Properties window or by selecting Dynamic Help on the Help menu.

Figure 2-49 shows the Dynamic Help topics that display when the Retirement plan contribution rate TrackBar control is selected on the Form1 form in the main work area. To view a Help topic displaying in the Dynamic Help window, double-click the topic in the Dynamic Help window. The Help topic will display on a new tab in the main work area.

> **Tip**
>
> **When to Use the Dynamic Help Window**
> Use the Dynamic Help window to learn more about the item selected in the main work area.

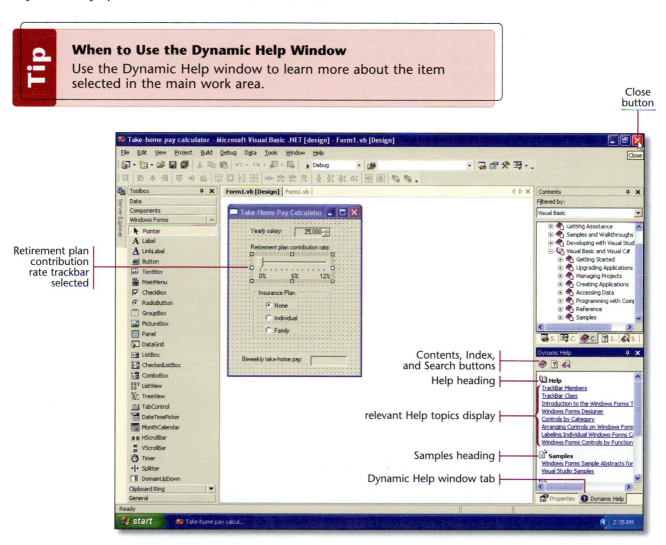

FIGURE 2-49

By clicking the headings within the Dynamic Help window, such as Help or Samples, you can collapse or expand the topic list. The Dynamic Help window also contains Contents, Index, and Search buttons on its toolbar. Clicking the

Contents, Index, or Search button will open the corresponding Help window in the upper right of the IDE.

Context-Sensitive Help

In addition to the types of Help accessed via the Help menu, you also can access Help in many areas of the Visual Basic .NET IDE by pressing the F1 key. This feature, called **context-sensitive help**, is available for most areas of the Visual Basic .NET IDE. For example, to get help about the Solution Explorer window, you would click the Solution Explorer window title bar and then press the F1 key. The Help topic about the Solution Explorer window then displays on a tab in the main work area. To close the Help tab, right-click the tab and then click Hide on the shortcut menu.

Hiding Help Windows
To hide a Help window, right-click the tab of the window and then click Hide on the shortcut menu.

Quitting Visual Basic .NET

When you have completed working with Visual Basic .NET, you should quit the Visual Basic .NET system to conserve memory for other Windows applications. Perform the following step to quit Visual Basic .NET.

To Quit Visual Basic .NET

1. Click the Visual Basic .NET Close button on the right side of the title bar (Figure 2-49 on the previous page).

If you made changes to the project since the last time it was saved, Visual Basic .NET displays the Microsoft Visual Basic .NET dialog box. If you click the Yes button, you can resave your project and quit. If you click the No button, you will quit without saving changes. Clicking the Cancel button will close the dialog box.

OTHER WAYS

1. Press ALT+F, X

Chapter Summary

In this chapter, you learned the fundamentals of using the Visual Basic .NET integrated development environment (IDE). You learned how to start Visual Basic .NET and then open and run a Visual Basic .NET project. You learned how to modify the properties of a control and modify code in a project. After you modified the project, you learned how to save and then test your changes. You also learned how to document an application by printing a record of the user interface design and code for a form. Finally, you learned how to access Help information about Visual Basic .NET using the Help system.

What You Should Know

Having completed this chapter, you now should be able to perform the tasks shown in Table 2-3.

Table 2-3 Chapter 2 What You Should Know

TASK NUMBER	TASK	PAGE
1	Start and Customize Visual Basic .NET	VB 2.04
2	Open an Existing Project	VB 2.09
3	Run a Project	VB 2.18
4	Modify the Text Property of a Label Control	VB 2.22
5	Navigate the Code Window	VB 2.26
6	Modify Code in the Code Window	VB 2.28
7	Save a Project	VB 2.31
8	Run a Project to Test Changes	VB 2.32
9	Print a Record of the User Interface Design of a Form	VB 2.34
10	Print a Record of the Code for a Form	VB 2.40
11	Quit Visual Basic .NET	VB 2.48

Key Terms

AssemblyInfo.vb *(VB 2.16)*
bugs *(VB 2.17)*
code region *(VB 2.27)*
code window *(VB 2.25)*
Contents window *(VB 2.44)*
context-sensitive help *(VB 2.48)*
continuation markers *(VB 2.42)*
debugging *(VB 2.33)*
design time *(VB 2.11)*
documenting an application *(VB 2.33)*
Dynamic Help *(VB 2.47)*
hard-copy output *(VB 2.33)*
Help *(VB 2.42)*
Index window *(VB 2.45)*
Insert *(VB 2.13)*
integrated development environment (IDE) *(VB 2.03)*
keywords *(VB 2.27)*
Label control *(VB 2.21)*
Layout toolbar *(VB 2.12)*
menu bar *(VB 2.11)*
Object box (Properties window) *(VB 2.22)*
Object box (code window) *(VB 2.25)*
Overtype *(VB 2.13)*

Print command *(VB 2.39)*
Procedure box *(VB 2.25)*
profile *(VB 2.04)*
project *(VB 2.02)*
property *(VB 2.22)*
Properties list *(VB 2.22)*
Properties window *(VB 2.22)*
Ready *(VB 2.13)*
References *(VB 2.16)*
run *(VB 2.17)*
run time *(VB 2.17)*
Save button *(VB 2.31)*
Save All button *(VB 2.31)*
Save Selected Items As command *(VB 2.31)*
Search window *(VB 2.45)*
Search Results window *(VB 2.46)*
ScreenTip *(VB 2.12)*
solution *(VB 2.15)*
splitter bar *(VB 2.27)*
Standard toolbar *(VB 2.12)*
status bar *(VB 2.13)*
tree view *(VB 2.16)*

Homework Assignments

Label the Figure

Identify the 18 Visual Basic .NET components shown in Figure 2-50.

1. _____
2. _____
3. _____
4. _____
5. _____
6. _____
7. _____
8. _____
9. _____

10. _____
11. _____
12. _____
13. _____
14. _____
15. _____
16. _____
17. _____
18. _____

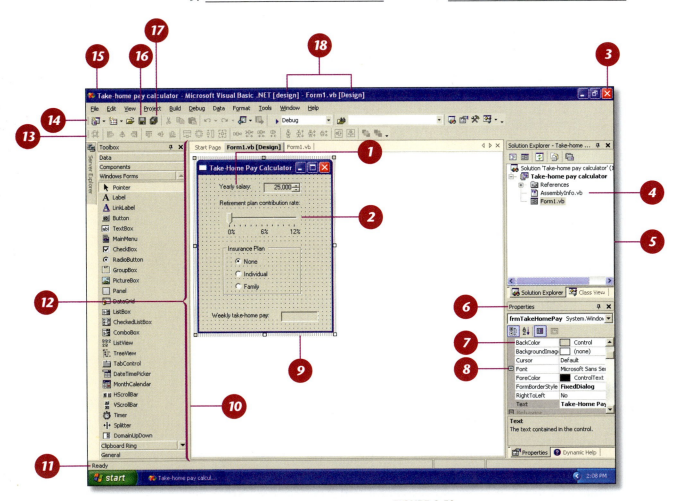

FIGURE 2-50

Short Answer

1. Which of the following Visual Basic .NET settings can you change through the My Profile link?

   a. At Startup   d. mouse scheme   g. default drive

   b. monitor   e. Window Layout   h. default browser

   c. Keyboard Scheme   f. Help Filter

2. The Solution Explorer window displays a _____ of the files that make up an application. The Properties window displays a list of the _____ of the _____ on the form.

3. When you first open a project, the IDE enters a mode called _____ time. When you run a project, the IDE enters a mode called _____ time.

4. List five items that may display on the status bar.

5. Fill in the default location and function for each of the IDE windows in Table 2-4

Table 2-4	Visual Basic .NET IDE Windows	
WINDOW NAME	**DEFAULT SCREEN LOCATION**	**FUNCTION**
Class View		
Help Content		
Properties		
Solution Explorer		
Toolbox		

6. Define the following terms: Solution, References, bugs, design time, run time.

7. List the labels on the Take-Home Pay Calculator application window in Figure 2-33 on page VB 2.33.

8. Briefly explain how you print a form and the code in Visual Basic .NET.

9. List the corresponding Help function keys for context-sensitive help, dynamic help, contents, index, search, index results, and search results.

10. Explain the purpose of the collapse and expand buttons in the code window.

11. Use Help to define the function of the following buttons on the Standard toolbar shown in Figure 2-12 on page VB 2.12: New Project, Add New Item, Navigate Backward, Navigate Forward, Start, Solution Explorer, Properties Window, Toolbox, and Class View.

12. What other ways can you use to display the code window?

HOMEWORK ASSIGNMENTS

13. Explain the difference between clicking the Save button and clicking the Save All button on the Standard toolbar.

14. What is the purpose of the tabs at the top of the main work area?

15. If a project is made up of three forms, then how many items will display below the name of the project in the Solution Explorer window?

16. Explain what the asterisk means that follows the tab name Form1.vb [Design]*.

17. Define the term property and list five examples of the properties of a Label control.

18. What is the function of the Save Selected Items As command on the File menu?

19. Briefly summarize when you would use the following Help menu commands: Contents, Index, and Search.

20. What is Dynamic Help?

Learn It Online

Start your browser and visit scsite.com/vbnet/exs. Follow the instructions in the exercises below.

1. **Chapter Reinforcement TF, MC, and SA**   Click the True/False, Multiple Choice, and Short Answer link below Chapter 2. Print and then answer the questions.

2. **Practice Test**   Click the Practice Test link below Chapter 2. Answer each question, enter your first and last name at the bottom of the page, and then click the Grade Test button. When the graded practice test displays on your screen, click Print on the File menu to print a hard copy. Continue to take practice tests until you score 80% or better. Hand in a printout of the final practice test.

3. **Crossword Puzzle Challenge**   Click the Crossword Puzzle Challenge link below Chapter 2. Read the instructions, and then enter your first and last name. Click the Play button. Work the crossword puzzle. When you are finished, click the Submit button. When the crossword puzzle redisplays, click the Print button.

4. **Tips and Tricks**   Click the Tips and Tricks link below Chapter 2. Click a topic that pertains to Chapter 2. Right-click the information and then click Print on the shortcut menu. Construct a brief example of what the information relates to in Visual Basic .NET to confirm you understand how to use the tip or trick. Hand in the example and printed information.

5. **Newsgroups**   Click the Newsgroups link below Chapter 2. Click a topic that pertains to Chapter 2. Print three comments.

6. **Expanding Your Horizons**   Click the Articles for Visual Basic .NET below Chapter 2. Click a topic that pertains to Chapter 2. Print the information. Construct a brief example of what the information relates to in Visual Basic .NET to confirm you understand the contents of the article. Hand in the example and printed information.

7. **Search Sleuth**   Select three key terms from the Key Terms section of this chapter and then use the Google search engine at google.com (or any major search engine) to display and print two Web pages for each key term.

Debugging Assignment

Start Visual Basic .NET and open the project, Greenling Realty, from the Chapter2\
Greenling Realty folder on the Data Disk. See the preface of this book for instructions for downloading the Data Disk or see your instructor for information about accessing the files required in this book. The project consists of one form that calculates commission on home sales for real estate agents. When a home is sold, Greenling Realty and the agent receive a total commission percentage from 1% to 6%, depending on the sale. The total commission percentage is input using the trackbar on the form. Greenling Realty receives 1.5% of the total commission percentage; the agent receives the rest. If the home sale price is at or above $300,000, then the agent receives an additional 20% commission.

The Greenling Realty project contains bugs in the user interface design and in the program code. Follow the steps below to debug the project.

1. Fix the spelling error in the Home Price Label control. The Label control currently reads Hose Price. Select the Label control and then modify the Text property value in the Properties window to make this change.

2. The Commission Rate TrackBar control currently is labeled with a rate of 0%. This label should read 1%. Select the Trackbar control and then modify the Text property value in the Properties window to make this change.

3. The Agent's Commission label contains a typographical error and currently reads Agen Commission. Select the Label control and then modify the Text property value in the Properties window to make this change.

4. Click Code on the View menu. Find the line of code that determines whether to give the 20% bonus. This line of code currently is checking for a limit of 30000, not 300000. Correct this error and return to the form design window.

5. Save the project and then run the project to test for any bugs. Use 350000 for a home sale price and 5% for the commission. The application should display as shown in Figure 2-51, with an Agent's Commission of $14,700.00.

FIGURE 2-51

6. Document the user interface design of the form using the PRINT SCREEN key on the keyboard and print it using the Windows Paint application. Document the form code by printing the code for the Form1.vb form. Circle the lines of code you modified on the code printout.

Programming Assignments

1 Opening and Modifying a Visual Basic .NET Project

Start Visual Basic .NET and open the project, Take-home pay calculator, from the Chapter2 folder on the Data Disk. See the preface of this book for instructions for downloading the Data Disk or see your instructor for information about accessing the files required in this book. The Take-home pay calculator project must be modified because the company is moving to a monthly pay period and increasing the percentage of gross pay that employees can contribute to the retirement plan to 14%. Figure 2-52 shows the Take-Home Pay Calculator application after the changes have been made to the user interface and code.

1. Click the 6% Label control. Change the Text property value from 6% to 7% in the Properties window.

2. Click the 12% Label control. Change the Text property value from 12% to 14% in the Properties window.

3. Click the Biweekly take-home pay Label control. Change the Text property value to Monthly take-home pay: in the Properties window.

4. Click the Retirement plan contribution rate TrackBar control. Change the Maximum property value from 12 to 14.

5. Click the Form1.vb tab to display the code window. Find the line of code that divides the yearly salary by 26.0. Change 26.0 to 12.0 to indicate a monthly pay period.

6. Use the Save All button on the Standard toolbar to save your changes.

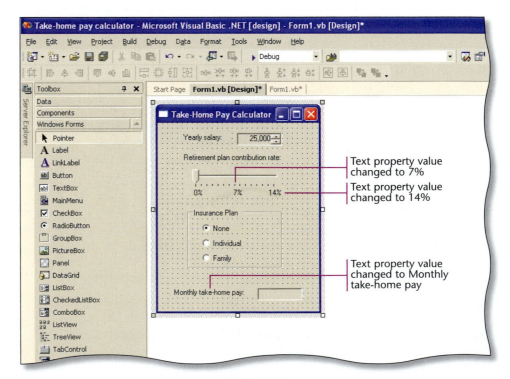

FIGURE 2-52

7. Click the Form1.vb [Design] tab. Run the application. Use relevant test data to verify that the modifications made to the project are correct. Use the modified application to determine the monthly take-home pay for each data set: (a) 30,000 yearly salary; 14% contribution to retirement plan; and the Family insurance plan; (b) 45,000 yearly salary; 13% contribution to retirement plan; and the Individual insurance plan. The monthly take-home pay for (a) is $1,416.25 and for (b) is $2,186.88.

8. Document the application by pressing the PRINT SCREEN key to capture a screen image of the form's user interface design and then print it using Paint. Use the Print command on the File menu to print the code for the form, Form1.vb.

2 Profit Margin Calculation

As an analyst for Ergo Office Chairs, you have been asked to update a simple profit margin calculator used by the accounting department. The application accepts a current inventory amount for a specific item, a unit cost for the item, and a margin used in pricing the item. The result produced is the total profit that can be expected from the total number of items in inventory. The application currently accepts a margin ranging from 20% to 40%. The president of the company has recently announced that all products must have a 30% to 45% margin. Additionally, the application currently limits the number of items on hand in inventory to 50. New requirements dictate that this inventory limit be increased to 75.

Perform the tasks on the next page to update the application as shown in Figure 2-53.

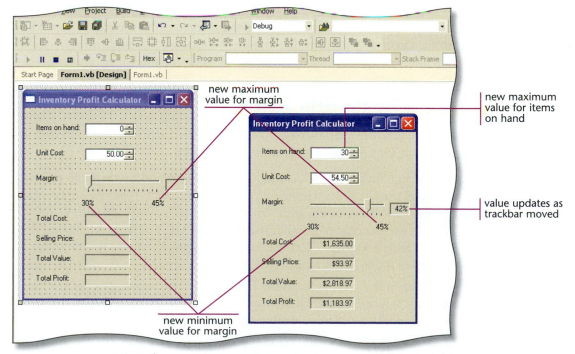

FIGURE 2-53

(continued)

2 Profit Margin Calculation *(continued)*

1. Start Visual Basic .NET and open the project, Ergo Office Chairs, from the Chapter2\Ergo Office Chairs folder on the Data Disk.

2. Click the 20% Label control. Change the Text property value from 20% to 30%.

3. Click the 40% Label control. Change the Text property value from 40% to 45%.

4. Click the Margin TrackBar control. Change the Minimum property value from 20 to 30. Change the Maximum property value from 40 to 45.

5. Click the Items on hand ListBox control. Change the Maximum property value from 50 to 75.

6. Navigate to the code window. Find the line of code that reads Private Sub CalculateTotalProfit(). Above this line, type the following line of code, substituting your own name and correct date where appropriate:

```
' Updated by: J. Quasney                    September 8, 2004
```

7. Locate the line of code that begins with Private Sub tbMarginScroll. Immediately below this line, type the following line of code:

```
txtMargin.Text = Convert.ToString(tbMargin.Value) & "%"
```

This line of code appends a percentage symbol to the value of the Margin TrackBar control and assigns the result to the Margin TextBox control next to the trackbar.

8. Save the project and then run the project to make certain no errors exist. If any errors are encountered, correct them, and save the project again. Run the project and enter the values shown in Figure 2-53 on the previous page. Verify that the results of your project match those shown in the figure.

9. Document the user interface design of the form using the PRINT SCREEN key on the keyboard and print it using the Windows Paint application. Document the form code by printing the code for the Form1.vb form.

3 Navigating the Help System

Perform the following tasks using a computer. After each step, use the Print command on the File menu to print the Help topic.

1. Start Visual Basic .NET. Click the Contents command on the Help menu. Navigate the Contents window through the following topic hierarchy: Visual Studio .NET; Developing with Visual Studio .NET; Working with Code, HTML, and Resource Files; Editing Code, HTML, and Text; Managing the Code Editor and View. Click the topic, Managing the Code Editor and View, to display the topic on a tab in the main work area.

2. Click the Index command on the Help menu. Type open project in the Look for box. Double-click the topic, Open Project dialog box, to display the topic on a tab in the main work area.

3. Click the Search command on the Help menu. Type trackbar in the Look for box and then click the Search button. Double-click the first result in the Search Results window to display the topic on a tab in the main work area (Figure 2-54).

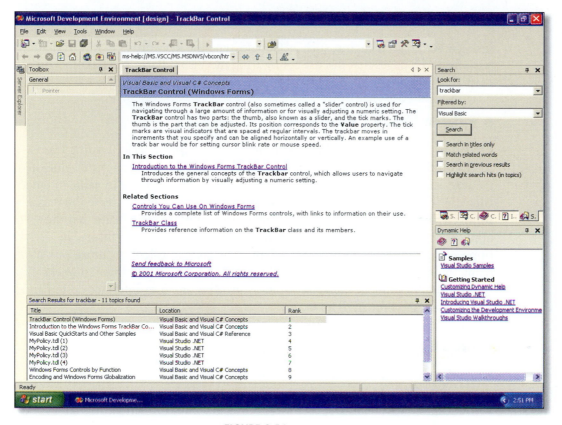

FIGURE 2-54

4. Use one of the methods discussed in this chapter to navigate to the Visual Basic Walkthroughs Help topic. Use the Print command on the File menu to print the Help topic. Scroll down through the topic and click the Creating a Simple Windows Form link. Print this topic.

5. Navigate to the Search window by clicking the Search tab at the bottom of the right Help window. Type Start Page in the Look for box. Click the Search in titles only check box. Click the Highlight search hits (in topics) check box. Click the Search button. When the results display in the Search Results window, double-click the Start Page topic to display the topic on a tab in the main work area.

4 Finding Help on the Visual Basic .NET Environment

Open Visual Basic .NET. While on the Start Page, navigate to the following two Help topics in the Dynamic Help window: Customizing the Development Environment and Visual Basic Sample Abstracts. Read and print each of the Help topics. Click the Help on Help command on the Help menu and then print the topic. Using the Help system, learn about the Microsoft Document Explorer and how to use it. Print the Help topics.

PROGRAMMING ASSIGNMENTS

5 Searching the Web

Using a Web search engine, such as Google, type the keywords VB.NET and IDE. Visit five Web pages that discuss configuring the Visual Basic .NET IDE. Print each Web page.

6 Future Value Calculation

Open the project, Jacks Trading Cards, from the Chapter2\Jacks Trading Cards folder on the Data Disk. The application calculates the possible future value of trading cards sold at Jack's Trading Cards based on the increase in value to date. Increase the maximum beginning price value from 25 to 50. Increase the maximum current price from 50 to 100. Change the interface to indicate that the application now calculates a future value result for 1 year in the future, as opposed to 6 months in the future. Change the code to calculate future value using the number 52 for the number of weeks (1 year), rather than 26 weeks (6 months). Document the application by printing the user interface design and the code for the Form1.vb form.

7 Modifying a User Interface

Open the project, Marias Gift Shop, from the Chapter2\Marias Gift Shop folder on the Data Disk. Maria uses this application to calculate how much a savings account or Certificate of Deposit (CD) at various banks might earn. Maria requests that you make a few changes to the application. She requests that rates vary from 2% to 7% (Text property value of the Label control), that the rate default to 5% rather than 2% (Value property of the TrackBar control), and that the principal default to 1000 rather than 0 (Text property value of the TextBox control). She would also like the result to display as currency (change Fixed to Currency in the code). Document the application by printing the user interface design and the code for the Form1.vb form.

8 Navigating the Start Page

The Visual Basic .NET Start Page contains several links on the left side of the page. Explore several of the items on the Start Page, such as What's New, Online Community, Headlines, and Downloads. These pages are Web pages maintained by Microsoft that display on the Start Page. Navigate the pages and print at least five different pages using the Print command on the File menu.

9 Visual Basic .NET Sample Applications

Visual Basic .NET includes two complete applications as samples. You will find many references to these samples in the Help system. The samples are called Duwamish and Fitch and Mather. Locate information about the Duwamish sample and print the Help page that shows a UML Sequence Diagram for creating a new customer account in the Duwamish Account Management system.

C H A P T E R

3

Building an Application in the Visual Basic .NET Environment

Objectives

You will have
mastered the material in
this chapter when you can:

- Design a Visual Basic .NET application
- Start a new Visual Basic .NET project
- Change the size of a form
- Change the property values of a form
- Add controls to a form
- Move and resize controls on a form
- Use the Label, TextBox, NumericUpDown, and Button controls
- Change the property values of controls
- Change the Name property to rename a control
- Write the code for a Click event procedure
- Display line numbers in the code window
- Use control properties in a method
- Document code with a comment header and comment statements

Introduction

As you have learned, Visual Basic .NET is a programming environment that allows you to develop, maintain, and execute applications and application components for the Windows operating system or any system that supports the .NET architecture. This chapter concentrates on using the Visual Basic .NET IDE to develop a new Visual Basic .NET application. After completing this chapter, you should be able to start a new Visual Basic .NET project and describe the components of a Visual Basic .NET project. You also will learn how to design a Windows application with a user-friendly interface and then implement and test the application. In the process, you will learn how to add controls to a form and then modify properties of the controls to fit the needs of the application. You also will understand how to write Visual Basic .NET code and document the code with comment statements. Finally, you will learn how to execute and test the Windows application.

Chapter Three — State Tax Computation

The Windows application developed in this chapter is the State Tax Computation application, which calculates the state tax payment for a taxpayer based on the taxpayer's income, number of dependents, and a standard state tax rate of 3% (Figure 3-1). To calculate a state tax payment using the State Tax Computation application, the user first enters the taxpayer's income in the Taxpayer's income input area. Next, the user enters the number of dependents the taxpayer can claim, between 0 and 10, in the Number of dependents input area. Once the data is entered, the user clicks the Compute Tax button and the application calculates the state tax payment by subtracting $600 for each dependent from the taxpayer's income and then multiplying the result by the standard state tax rate of 3%.

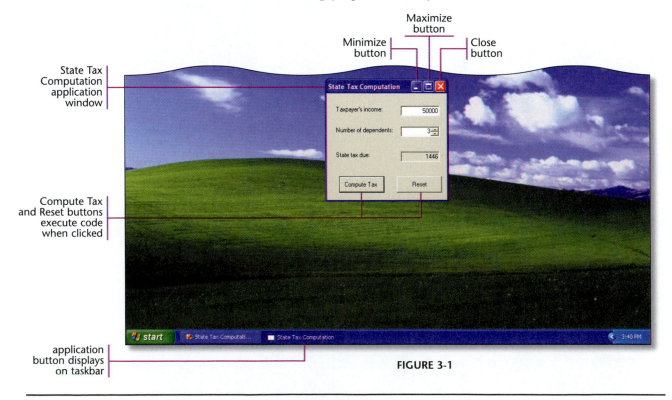

FIGURE 3-1

The calculation used by the State Tax Computation application to determine the state tax payment is represented by the following equation:

State Tax = 0.03 × (Income − (600 × Dependents))

The equation first multiplies the number of dependents (Dependents) by $600 and then subtracts the result of this calculation from the taxpayer's income in dollars (Income). The application then multiplies the result of that calculation by 0.03 (3%), to determine the state tax payment due (State Tax). After completing the calculation and determining the state tax payment, the application displays the state tax in the State tax due output area. When the user clicks the Reset button, the State Tax Computation application resets the input and output areas to their original values of 0.

As shown in Figure 3-1, the State Tax Computation application includes several of the common features of Windows applications. The application, for instance, occupies a window that the user can move on the desktop. The application window includes buttons that allow a user to minimize, maximize, or close the window. The application window also includes two buttons — the Compute Tax and Reset buttons — that a user can click to instruct the application to execute the code assigned to the button. Figure 3-2 shows the code the application executes when a user clicks the Compute Tax or Reset button.

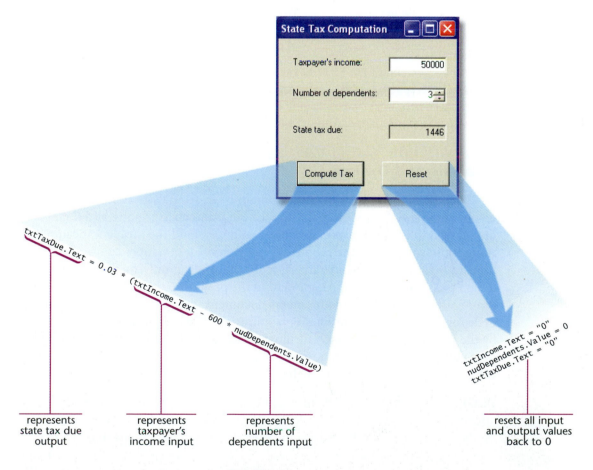

FIGURE 3-2

Program Development

As you learned in Chapter 1, the tasks involved in developing an application follow the series of six iterative phases outlined in the development cycle. The development cycle for the State Tax Computation application consists of tasks that correspond to the six phases, as shown in   .

Table 3-1   State Tax Computation Application Development Tasks

DEVELOPMENT PHASE	TASK NUMBER	TASK NAME	TASK
Analyze requirements	1	Analyze problem	Analyze the state tax computation problem.
Design solution	2	Design interface	Design the user interface for the application, including input areas, output areas, and form controls.
	3	Design program	Design the logic for the code and write pseudocode.
Validate design	4	Validate design	Prove that the solution produces correct results for the state tax computation program.
Implement design	5	Develop interface	Add user interface elements, such as input areas, output areas, and Button controls on a form.
	6	Write code	Write code to add event procedures for the buttons; add comment statements in code.
Test solution	7	Test	Test the application.
	8	Debug	Fix any problems with the application.
Document solution	9	Document	Print the program.

Analysis and Design

The first two phases in the development cycle — analysis and design — involve analyzing the problem the application is intended to solve and then designing a solution. Analysis is required to understand the problem the application should solve. Once the problem is understood, a developer can work with users to design a user-friendly interface for the application. The final stage of the design phase is to design the logic behind the program.

Figure 3-3 shows the requirements document that initiates the development cycle for the State Tax Computation application. The design requirements listed by the user are specific enough to allow for the development cycle to begin. The document specifies the reason for the request, the algorithm used to make the calculation, and the terminology that the user should see in the interface.

PROBLEM ANALYSIS   The problem that the State Tax Computation application should solve is the calculation of state tax due for a taxpayer based on the taxpayer's income, number of dependents, and a standard state tax rate

REQUEST FOR NEW APPLICATION

Date submitted:	August 28, 2003
Submitted by:	Jan Davies
Purpose:	The Personnel department often is asked to do a quick computation of a customer's state tax. Employees would save time and provide more accurate information if they had a stand-alone application at their disposal to perform the calculation.
Application title:	State Tax Computation
Algorithms:	State tax is computed as follows: *State Tax = 0.03 x (Income – (600 x Dependents))*
Notes:	1) Support personnel are accustomed to the following terminology: *Taxpayer's income* for Income in the above algorithm, *Number of dependents* for Dependents in the above algorithm, *State tax due* for State Tax in the above algorithm. 2) The application should allow the user to enter values for Taxpayer's income and Number of dependents, so that State tax due can be computed. 3) Because the taxpayer can only claim between zero and ten dependents, the application should limit the user's entry to only valid inputs of positive whole numbers ranging from zero to ten. 4) The application should also allow the user to reset all values on the screen to zero (0) so that another calculation can be performed. 5) The computation should be designated by the term, Compute. The reset of the values should be designated by the term, Reset.

Approvals

Approval Status:	X	Approved
		Rejected
Approved by:	Jessie Simms	
Date:	September 2, 2003	
Assigned to:	J. Quasney, Programmer	

FIGURE 3-3

of 3%. To complete the calculation and generate results, or output, for the user, the State Tax Computation application requires the user to input two values: Taxpayer's income and Number of dependents.

As you have learned, the application uses the equation

State Tax = 0.03 × (Income – (600 × Dependents))

to calculate the state tax payment due by a taxpayer. The equation requires two inputs to complete one calculation and generate one output. The first input, Taxpayer's income, is represented by Income in the equation. The second input, Number of dependents, is represented by Dependents in the equation. The application uses these inputs to calculate, or process, the output, State tax due, which is represented by State Tax in the equation. Each element of the equation corresponds to an element in the code that displays below the Compute Tax button in Figure 3-2 on page VB 3.03.

As indicated in the requirements document, the application also must provide a way to reset input and output values back to 0, so that a user can calculate the state tax payment due for another taxpayer. To reset these values, the application uses the equations

Income = 0
Dependents = 0
State Tax = 0

to tell the application to set the inputs — Taxpayer's income (Income) and Number of dependents (Dependents) — and the output — State tax due (State Tax) — back to the original values of 0. Each element of the equation corresponds to an element in the code that displays below the Reset button in Figure 3-2 on page VB 3.03.

INTERFACE DESIGN Once you have analyzed the problem and understand the needs, the next step is to design the user interface (Table 3-1 on page VB 3.04). A **user interface** (**UI**) is the way that a program accepts data and instructions from the user and presents results. A **graphical user interface** (**GUI**) provides visual cues such as a menu, a button, or a small picture, called an icon, to help the user enter data and give instructions to the computer. Many programmers design a user interface by creating hand drawings that show the various interface elements and how they will display to a user. Figure 3-4 shows an example of a hand drawing created during interface design for the State Tax Computation application. The title of the application and the text that displays in the input and output labels are specified in the requirements document (Figure 3-3 on the previous page).

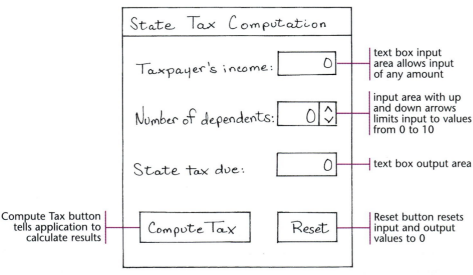

FIGURE 3-4

When designing a user interface in Visual Basic .NET, you must consider the inputs, processing, and outputs of data required by an application and then choose appropriate controls. In this application, the first input is the taxpayer's income amount. Because the taxpayer's income can be any amount, the user interface must allow the user to enter any number for the taxpayer's income. As shown in Figure 3-4, an input area with a text box is best for this kind of input, because it allows the user to enter any amount. The second input is the number of dependents. Because the taxpayer can claim only between 0 and 10 dependents, the user interface should limit the user's entry to only valid inputs of positive whole numbers ranging from 0 to 10. An input area with up and down arrows can limit a user's input to specified values in a range (Figure 3-4). As the programmer, you can determine the range, or boundaries, of the allowable entries in the input area. The user enters data in this input area in two ways. First, the user can use the UP ARROW or DOWN ARROW keys on the keyboard or use the mouse to click the up and down arrows in the input area to select any allowable value. Second, the user can type a number in the text box portion of the input area. If the value entered is out of the allowable range, Visual Basic .NET automatically changes the value to the closest allowable value.

Aesthetics versus Function

In designing a user interface, visual aesthetics should follow functional considerations. The function, or purpose, of a user interface is to provide a user with direct ways to accomplish tasks. Avoid the temptation to use flashy or confusing visual elements within the application, unless they will help a user more easily complete a task.

The output of the State Tax Computation application is a numeric value calculated as the result of the tax computation equation. A text box works well to display this type of output. The output area, however, should provide visual cues to a user to indicate that the area should not be used for input. Two simple and effective ways to indicate an output area are (1) modifying a property of the output area so that a user cannot input data in the control and (2) using a gray background for the output area.

Consistent Design Principles

Applications should follow basic graphic design principles and should be consistent visually and functionally.

Finally, a user of the application needs some way to instruct the application to calculate or process the output, based on the inputs that have been provided. Adding one or more buttons to a user interface allows a user to initiate an action by clicking the button, which causes the code assigned to the button to be executed. In the State Tax Computation application, clicking the Compute Tax button tells the application to perform the calculation to determine State tax due; clicking the Reset button resets the input and output values back to their original values of zero.

Real-World Experience

Use concepts and metaphors familiar to users to ensure the user interface parallels real-world experience.

PROGRAM DESIGN   Once you have designed the interface, the next step is to design a program that creates the desired results. The two program tasks include (1) calculating the state tax payment due using the equation,

$$\text{State Tax} = 0.03 \times (\text{Income} - (600 \times \text{Dependents}))$$

and (2) resetting the input and output values back to 0, so the user can perform the calculation again using different input values. The user can execute these tasks by clicking the corresponding button on the user interface.

One way to design the program code to execute these two tasks is to use pseudocode. Figure 3-5 shows the pseudocode used to design the procedures needed to execute the two program tasks. The pseudocode is not Visual Basic .NET code, but rather an English description of how the code should behave. For small programming projects, you can write pseudocode by hand along with a logic diagram. The pseudocode for the algorithm comes from the requirements document (Figure 3-3 on page VB 3.05).

```
ComputeTax Button Click Event
        Tax = .03 X (Income – 600 X Dependents)
End

Reset Button Click Event
        Income = 0
        Dependents = 0
        TaxDue = 0
End
```

FIGURE 3-5

Having analyzed the problem, designed the interface, and designed the program, the analysis and design of the application is complete. As shown in Table 3-1 on page VB 3.04, the next task in the development cycle is to develop the user interface of the application using Visual Basic .NET. Before you can begin developing the user interface, you first must start Visual Basic .NET and start a new project.

Starting a New Project

As you have learned, a project is a collection of code and other files that usually encompasses one application or class. When you start Visual Basic .NET, you can choose to open an existing project or start a new project. When you choose to start a new project, you can choose which type of application or Windows component you want to create.

Visual Basic .NET allows you to select from a number of different project types and templates so you can develop many different types of applications. The State Tax Computation application is a Windows application with a Windows user interface for user input and output display. The application is based on the Windows Application template provided by Visual Basic .NET. The following steps start Visual Basic .NET and start a new project using the Windows Application template.

To Start a New Visual Basic .NET Project

1. Insert the Data Disk in drive A. See the preface of this book for instructions for downloading the Data Disk or see your instructor for information about accessing the files required in this book.

2. Start Visual Basic .NET. When the Start Page displays, click the New Project button on the Start Page.

The New Project dialog box displays. By default, the Visual Basic Projects project type and Windows Application template are selected. A default project name and location display in the Name box and Location box. The default location may differ on your computer (Figure 3-6).

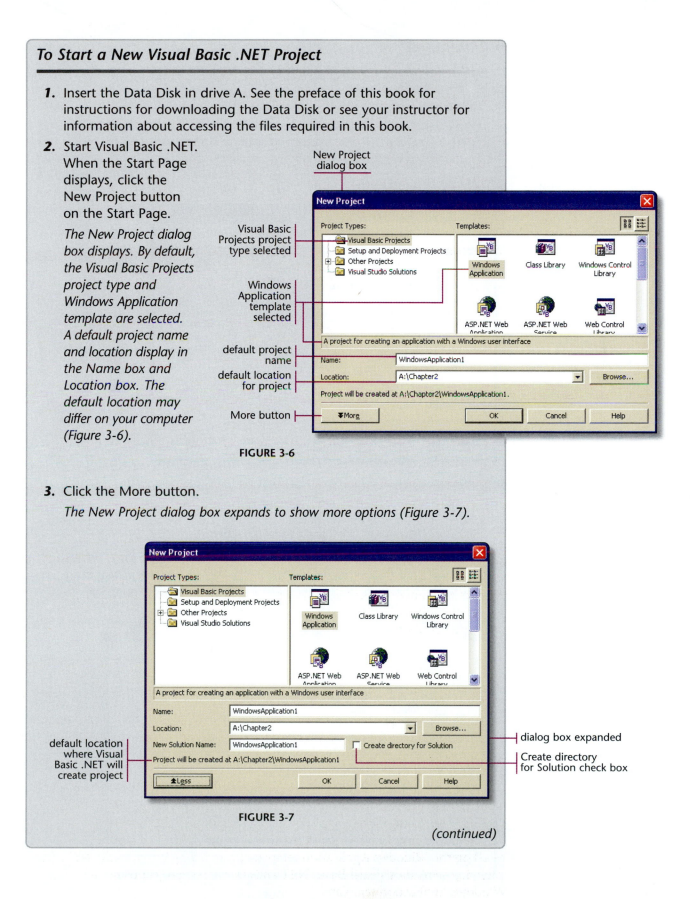

FIGURE 3-6

3. Click the More button.

The New Project dialog box expands to show more options (Figure 3-7).

FIGURE 3-7

(continued)

4. Click the Create directory for Solution check box. Double-click the text, WindowsApplication1, in the Name box. Type State Tax Computation in the Name box.

The Create directory for Solution check box is checked, so Visual Basic .NET will create a subdirectory with the same name as the project when the project is created. The new project and solution names display in the Name box and the New Solution Name box, respectively. The message below the New Solution Name box displays the new project name and location (Figure 3-8).

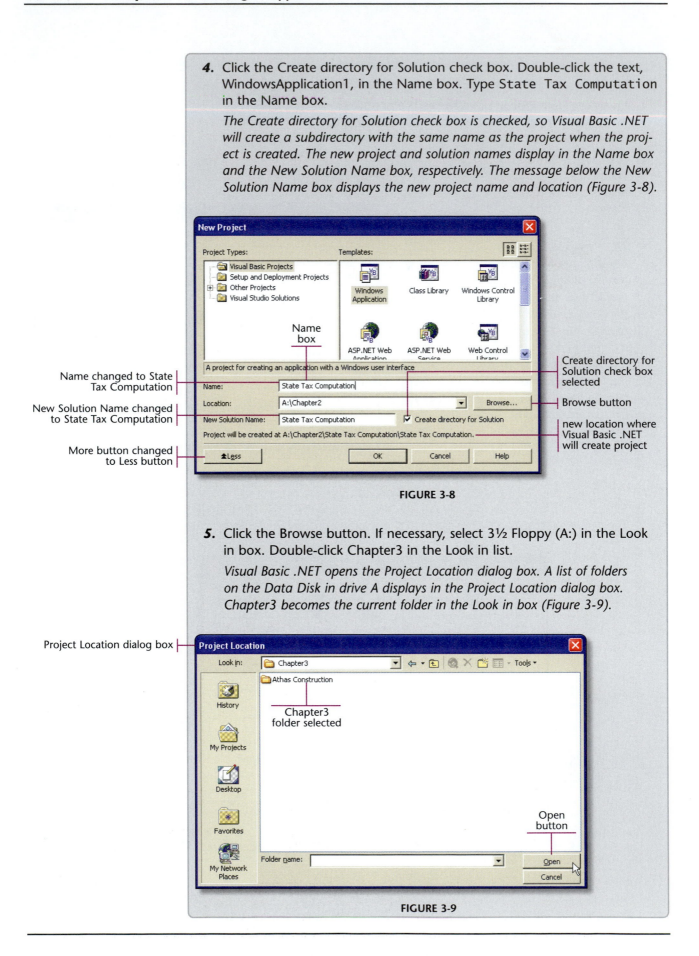

Name changed to State Tax Computation

New Solution Name changed to State Tax Computation

More button changed to Less button

Create directory for Solution check box selected

Browse button

new location where Visual Basic .NET will create project

FIGURE 3-8

5. Click the Browse button. If necessary, select 3½ Floppy (A:) in the Look in box. Double-click Chapter3 in the Look in list.

Visual Basic .NET opens the Project Location dialog box. A list of folders on the Data Disk in drive A displays in the Project Location dialog box. Chapter3 becomes the current folder in the Look in box (Figure 3-9).

Project Location dialog box

Chapter3 folder selected

Open button

FIGURE 3-9

6. Click the Open button.

The Location box and the message below the New Solution Name box change to display the Chapter3 folder as the location where Visual Basic .NET will create the project (Figure 3-10).

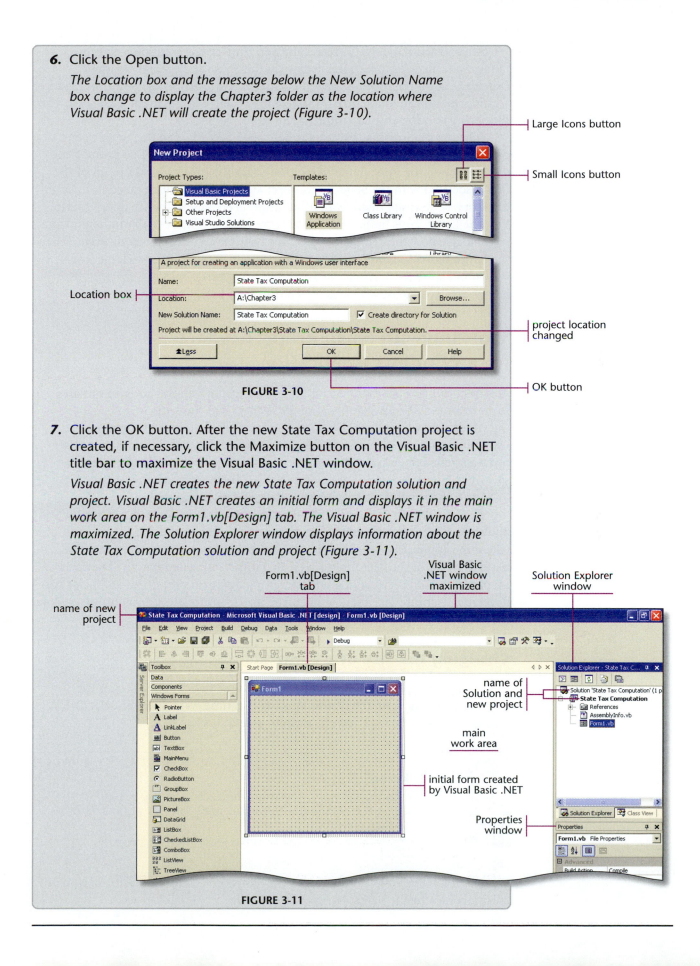

FIGURE 3-10

7. Click the OK button. After the new State Tax Computation project is created, if necessary, click the Maximize button on the Visual Basic .NET title bar to maximize the Visual Basic .NET window.

Visual Basic .NET creates the new State Tax Computation solution and project. Visual Basic .NET creates an initial form and displays it in the main work area on the Form1.vb[Design] tab. The Visual Basic .NET window is maximized. The Solution Explorer window displays information about the State Tax Computation solution and project (Figure 3-11).

FIGURE 3-11

After Visual Basic .NET creates the new project, the solution and project name, State Tax Computation, displays in the Solution Explorer window (Figure 3-11 on the previous page). Form1.vb is selected in the Solution Explorer window to indicate that Form1.vb currently is active in the main work area. The Properties window displays information about Form1.vb.

Clicking the Create directory for Solutions check box in the New Project dialog box (Figure 3-8 on page VB 3.10) tells Visual Basic .NET to create a sub-directory with the same name as the project, in the project location. All of the files associated with the State Tax Computation project will be saved in this sub-directory, to separate them from other projects created in the Chapter3 folder.

The Large Icons button and Small Icons button (Figure 3-10 on the previous page) toggle how the Template area of the New Project dialog box displays. When the **Large Icons button** is selected, the template names display as large icons, as shown in Figure 3-10. When the **Small Icons button** is selected, the template names display in a list with smaller icons to their left.

Working with Form Properties for a Windows Application

A project can contain many forms. Visual Basic .NET always adds an initial form to a new Windows Application project. At run time, the form becomes the window in which the application displays. When you start a new project using the Windows Application template, Visual Basic .NET creates an initial form and displays it in the main work area on the Form1.vb[Design] tab, as shown in Figure 3-11 on the previous page. A **form** is an instance of the System.Windows.Forms.Form class in the .NET framework.

The first step in developing the user interface for the State Tax Computation application is to change several form properties, such as the size of and location where the application window displays on the desktop during run time. The hand drawing of the user interface created during interface design (Figure 3-4 on page VB 3.06) serves as a guide for setting the form properties and helps you develop a user interface that supports the inputs, processing, and outputs of data required by the application.

Changing the Size of a Form

During design time, you set the size of a form to define the size of the application window on the desktop during run time. When Visual Basic .NET creates the initial form, it sets the form to a default size.

Tip

Form Sizing

As you start developing the user interface, you should adjust the form size to accommodate the input area, output area, and other user interface elements.

The following steps set the size of the State Tax Computation form, which currently has the file name, Form1.vb.

To Change the Size of a Form

1. Click the Form1 form in the main work area. Point to the center sizing handle on the form's right border.

The Form1 form is active, as indicated by the change in the color of the Form1 form title bar. The Properties window displays the form name in the Object box. The mouse pointer changes to a double two-headed arrow, indicating the form can be sized (Figure 3-12).

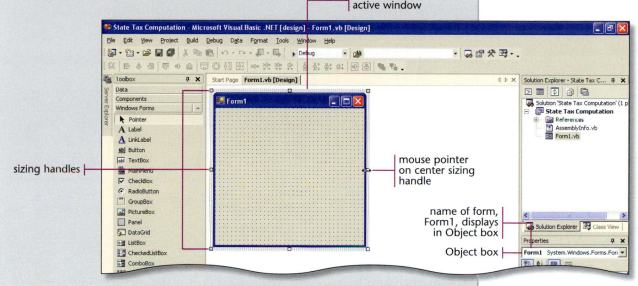

Form1 form is active window

sizing handles

mouse pointer on center sizing handle

name of form, Form1, displays in Object box

Object box

FIGURE 3-12

2. Drag the form's right border to the left to decrease the form width by approximately one-half inch.

The form's right border is moved approximately one-half inch to the left (Figure 3-13).

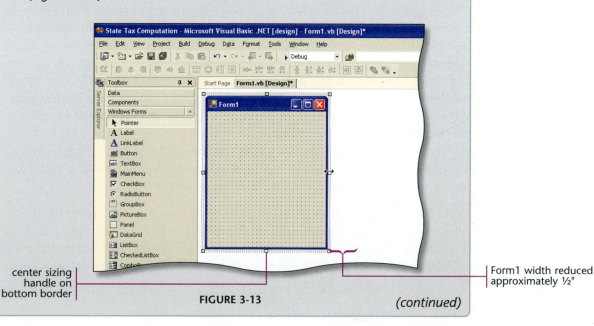

center sizing handle on bottom border

Form1 width reduced approximately ½"

FIGURE 3-13

(continued)

3. Point to the center sizing handle on the form's bottom border and then drag the form's bottom border up to decrease the form height approximately one-half inch.

The form's bottom border is moved up approximately one-half inch (Figure 3-14).

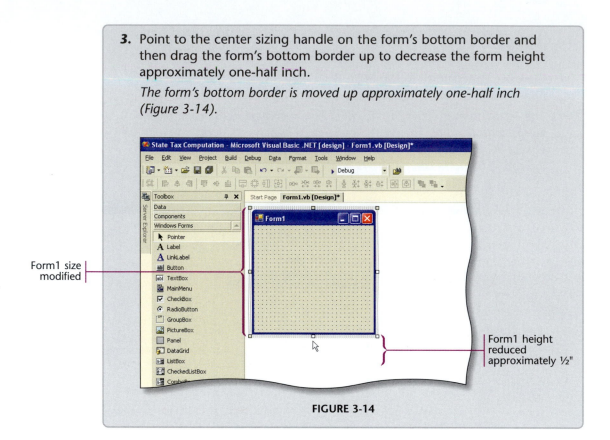

FIGURE 3-14

You can adjust a form's size at any point during design time. In the preceding steps, you modified the width and height of the form by dragging the form's right and bottom borders. You also can drag the lower-right corner of the form to change its width and height at the same time.

Using the Property Window

As you learned in Chapter 2, a property is an attribute of an object or control, such as its background color or the text that displays with it. Width and Height are properties of a form. The form's **Width property** defines the width of the form in pixels; the **Height property** defines the height of the form in pixels. A **pixel** is a single point on a display monitor. A typical PC monitor contains approximately 96 pixels per inch. As you resize the form by dragging its borders, Visual Basic .NET automatically updates the Width and Height properties in the Properties window

As you have learned, the Properties window contains a list of attributes for the object currently selected in the main work area. As shown in Figure 3-15, the Properties window consists of the following elements.

OBJECT BOX The **Object box** displays the name of the currently selected object or control. An object can be a control or form in the main work area or any item selected in the Solution Explorer window, including a solution, project, or other file. Clicking the Object box arrow displays a list of objects associated with the current form in the main work area, including the form itself. You can select a different object by selecting an object in the list or by clicking the object in the main work area.

PROPERTIES LIST   The **Properties list** displays the set of properties for the object named in the Object box and the current value of those properties.

TOOLBAR   The **toolbar** in the Properties window includes buttons that allow you to change the display of the Properties list. The **Categorized button** displays properties grouped by category, such as Appearance or Behavior, in the Properties list. The Properties list displays in categorized view by default. The **Alphabetic button** displays properties alphabetically in the Properties list. As shown in Figure 3-15, the **Properties button** is selected, indicating that a list of properties currently displays in the Properties list. The **Property Pages button** is activated when a project or solution is selected in the Solution Explorer window. Clicking the Property Pages button opens a dialog box with options you can set for a solution or project. Depending on the tasks you are completing in the Visual Basic .NET IDE, the buttons on the Properties window toolbar sometimes may change.

DESCRIPTION PANE   The **description pane** at the bottom of the Properties window displays information about the property currently selected in the Properties list.

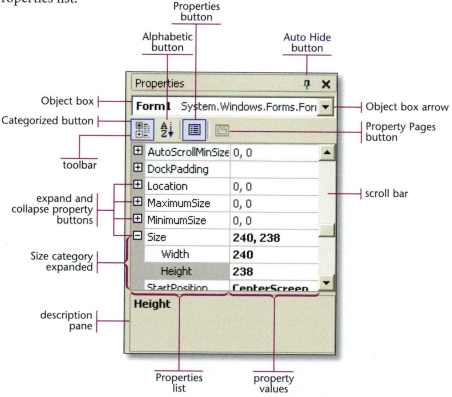

FIGURE 3-15

Because the Properties list for an object can include numerous properties, the Properties window includes a scroll bar that allows you to navigate the list. In categorized view, groups of properties are collapsed together for easier navigation through the Properties list. When a group of properties is collapsed, a plus (+) sign displays next to the group category name in the Properties list (Figure 3-15 on the previous page). Clicking the plus sign expands the group to display all of the properties in that group.

It is not necessary to set every property for each object you add to an interface because Visual Basic .NET assigns an initial value, called the **default value**, for each of the properties. Property values can be numbers, text, or a selection from a list. A property that determines a size of a control, for example, will have a property value that is a number. A property that displays a message on the screen will have a property value that is text. A property, such as a color with a few discrete values, will have a list of options for the property value. Clicking the property value arrow value displays the list of options from which you can select. For some properties, the property value has a button that opens a dialog box in which you can set property values. Clicking the button for the Font property value opens the Font dialog box, which allows you to set font face, style, color, and so on.

Tip

Setting Properties

As you develop the user interface for an application, you need to change only the property values for which you do not want to use the default values.

The commonly used properties of objects will be discussed as they are used in this book. When adding a new control to a form, you should navigate the Properties list to understand better the unique properties and property values for that control.

Changing StartPosition, Title, and FormBorderStyle Property Values

To develop the user interface of the State Tax Computation form, as shown in Figure 3-1 on page VB 3.02, you must modify several of the default form property values. The first form property to change is the StartPosition property. The **StartPosition property** of a form specifies the position where the application window displays on the Windows desktop when the application is run. The default value for the StartPosition property is **WindowsDefault**, which tells the .NET CLR to position the application window wherever Windows sees fit to display it on the screen. Changing the StartPosition property value from WindowsDefault to the value of **CenterScreen** sets the application window to display in the center of the user's screen.

Next, the title on the application window should convey the purpose or use of the application. The **Text property** of the form allows you to set the title that displays on the application window title bar at run time. The default value for the Text property is a generic name (Form1) that Visual Basic .NET assigns when creating the form. As specified by the project design, the Text property value must be changed to display State Tax Calculation on the application window title bar.

The third form property value to change is the FormBorderStyle property. The **FormBorderStyle property** controls the appearance of the border of a form. The FormBorderStyle property determines if a user can resize an application window at run time and how other objects on the form, such as the Minimize button, Maximize button, Control menu box, title bar, and Help button, behave or display. The FormBorderStyle property can take one of seven property values, as listed in Table 3-2.

Table 3-2 FormBorderStyle Property Values

CONTROL OR CHARACTERISTIC	FORMBORDERSTYLE PROPERTY VALUE						
	None	FixedSingle	Fixed3D	FixedDialog	Sizable	FixedToolWindow	SizableToolWindow
Minimize button	No	Available	Available	Available	Available	No	No
Maximize button	No	Available	Available	Available	Available	No	No
Control menu box	No	Yes	Yes	Yes	Yes	No	No
Title bar	No	Yes	Yes	Yes	Yes	Yes	Yes
Help button	No	Available	Available	Available	Available	No	No
Sizable	No	No	No	No	Yes	No	Yes

The default value for the FormBorderStyle property is Sizable. Using the **Sizable property value** displays the application window with borders the user can drag to resize the application window at run time. The State Tax Computation application window, like many Windows Application windows, should not be sizable. Allowing the user to resize the State Tax Computation application window would distort the display of the input and output areas and buttons, making the user interface difficult to use. To prevent a user from resizing the application window, set the FormBorderStyle property value to FixedDialog. Using the **FixedDialog property value** displays the application window in one size, with the appearance of a standard Windows dialog box.

The following steps change the StartPosition, Text, and FormBorderStyle property values of the State Tax Computation application window from the default values to the values discussed above.

To Change the StartPosition, Title, and FormBorderStyle Property Values of a Form

1. Click the title bar of the Form1 form to select the form. Scroll the Properties list until the FormBorderStyle property displays.

   The Form1 form is selected and the form name displays in the Object box in the Properties window (Figure 3-16).

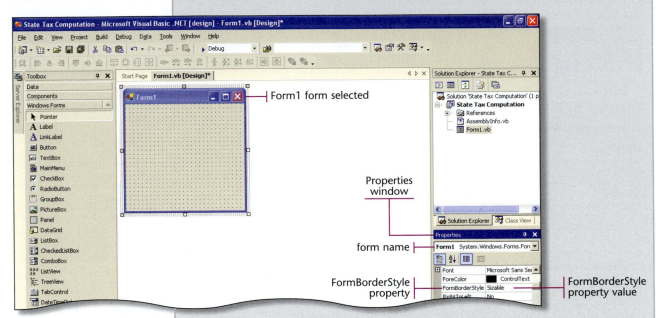

FIGURE 3-16

2. Click the Sizable value next to the FormBorderStyle property. Click the FormBorderStyle box arrow next to the value, Sizable.

   Clicking the FormBorderStyle box arrow displays a list of seven possible values for the FormBorderStyle property (Figure 3-17).

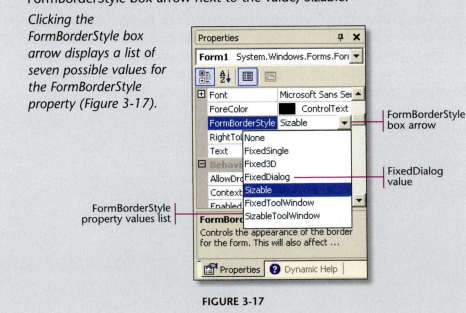

FIGURE 3-17

3. Click FixedDialog in the FormBorderStyle property values list.

The FormBorderStyle property value is set to FixedDialog. The Form1 form border changes to a slightly thinner border. The Form1 icon changes to indicate that the FormBorderStyle property value is FixedDialog (Figure 3-18).

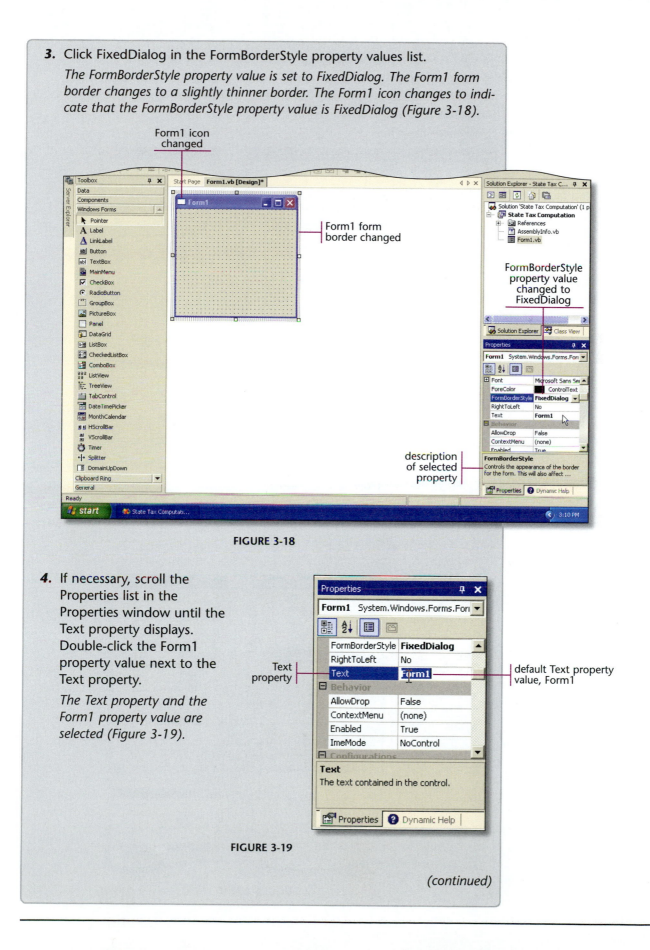

FIGURE 3-18

4. If necessary, scroll the Properties list in the Properties window until the Text property displays. Double-click the Form1 property value next to the Text property.

The Text property and the Form1 property value are selected (Figure 3-19).

FIGURE 3-19

(continued)

5. Type State Tax Computation as the Text property.

The Text property value is set to State Tax Computation although only a portion displays (Figure 3-20). The form title bar still displays the default property value, Form1.

form title bar displays
default property
value, Form1

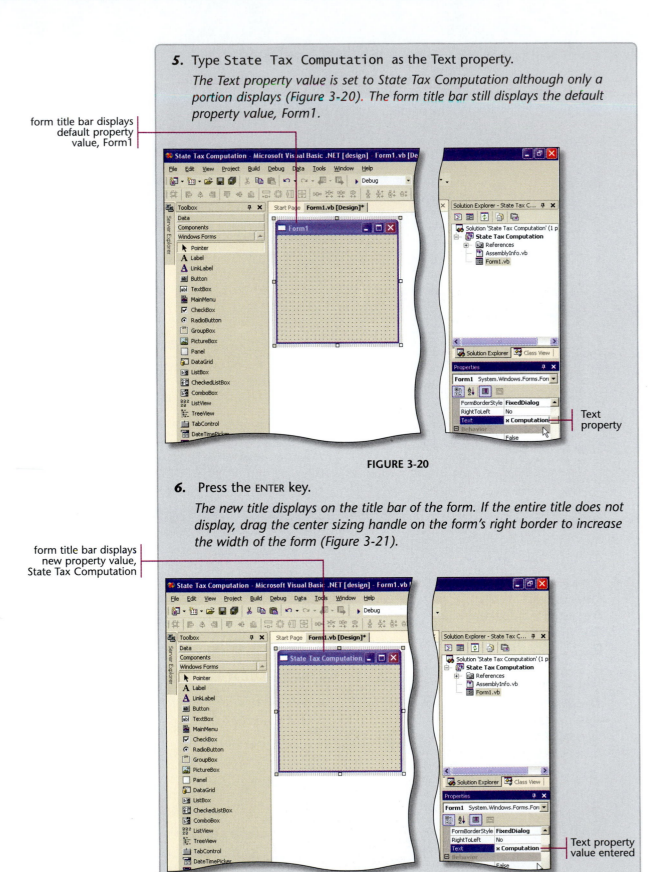

FIGURE 3-20

6. Press the ENTER key.

The new title displays on the title bar of the form. If the entire title does not display, drag the center sizing handle on the form's right border to increase the width of the form (Figure 3-21).

form title bar displays
new property value,
State Tax Computation

FIGURE 3-21

7. Scroll the Properties list in the Properties window until the StartPosition property displays. Click the WindowsDefaultLocation value next to the StartPosition property. Click the StartPosition box arrow next to the value, WindowsDefaultLocation.

Clicking the StartPosition box arrow displays a list of five possible values for the StartPosition property (Figure 3-22).

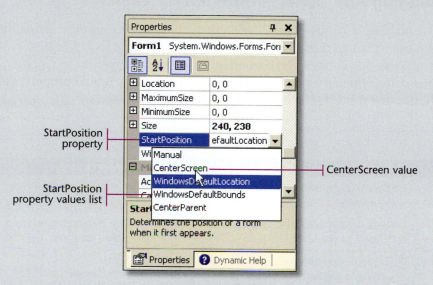

StartPosition property

StartPosition property values list

CenterScreen value

FIGURE 3-22

8. Click CenterScreen in the StartPosition property values list.

The StartPosition property value is set to CenterScreen (Figure 3-23). The CenterScreen property value indicates that the application window will display in the center of the screen during run time. During design time, no changes are visible on the form.

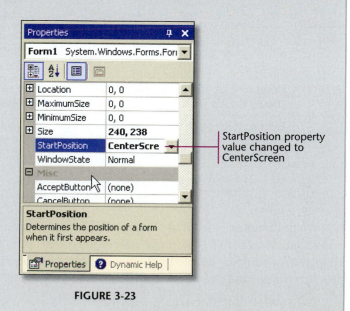

StartPosition property value changed to CenterScreen

FIGURE 3-23

During design time, the form remains sizable and displays in the upper-left corner of the main work area, regardless of the property values set for the FormBorderStyle and StartPosition properties. At run time, however, the property values will ensure that the form displays in the center of the screen and cannot be resized by the user.

Changing Additional Form Property Values

A form for a Windows Application project has numerous other properties and property values that allow you to customize the form to fit program requirements. Table 3-3 shows several commonly used form properties by category, with a brief description and a list of available property values. A bold property value indicates that this value is the default value for the property.

Table 3-3 **Form Properties**

CATEGORY	PROPERTY	DESCRIPTION	PROPERTY VALUES
Appearance	BackColor	Sets background color of application window	Any color selected from dialog box
	ForeColor	Sets default color for controls that are added to the form	Any color selected from dialog box
	FormBorderStyle	Dictates appearance of form border; whether the form is sizable; and how the Minimize and Maximize buttons, Control menu box, and Help button behave	None FixedSingle Fixed3D FixedDialog **Sizable** FixedToolWindow SizableToolWindow
	Text	Sets title to display on title bar of application window	Any value
Behavior	Enabled	Sets form to be usable during run time	**True** False
Layout	WindowState	Dictates how a window should display initially during run time	**Normal** Minimized Maximized
Window Style	ControlBox	Determines if a Windows control box should display on the form	**True** False
	Icon	Defines the icon that displays on the top-left corner of the window title bar and on the taskbar at run time	Any icon selected from a file via a dialog box

When designing a form, it is important to understand all of the form properties that are available so you can select the best options. The Visual Basic .NET Help system contains detailed information about all the form properties and property values and provides example uses for properties.

Working with Controls for a Windows Application

As you have learned, a form is an object in Visual Basic .NET. The State Tax Computation form includes four different types of controls, as shown in Figure 3-24. These controls and their functions include the following.

LABEL   A **Label control** is used to display text, such as Taxpayer's income, on a form. During run time, the person using the application cannot change the text displayed in a label.

TEXTBOX   A **TextBox control** is used to display text or allow users to enter text on a form. During run time, the contents of a TextBox control can be changed by the person using the application. A TextBox control frequently is used to allow a user to input values for processing by the application.

NUMERICUPDOWN   A **NumericUpDown control** is used to display or allow users to enter numbers on a form. During run time, the contents of a NumericUpDown control can be changed by the person using the application. Up and down arrows in the control allow the user to change the value displayed in the control; the user also can type a value in the control. The up and down arrows increment and decrement the displayed value within a predefined range. If the user enters a number outside of the range, the control changes the entered number to the closest allowable value within the predefined range.

BUTTON   A **Button control** is used during run time to initiate actions called events. A Button control usually is placed on the user interface to allow a user to indicate that the application should execute an action such as calculating a value, resetting values, or closing a window.

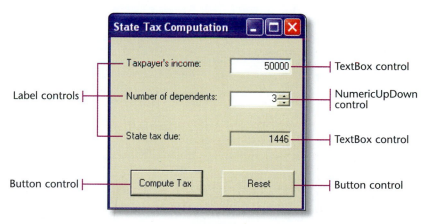

FIGURE 3-24

Adding Controls to a Form

You can add controls to a form using the Toolbox window, which displays on the left side of the Visual Basic .NET IDE (Figure 3-25 on the next page). The Toolbox window usually displays six tabs such as Windows Forms, Data, Components, and so on. The **Windows Forms tab**, which is selected by default, includes buttons that represent common controls used on a Windows form. By default, the Windows Forms sheet in the Toolbox window contains forty intrinsic controls. An **intrinsic control** is a control that is included on the Windows Forms sheet by default and cannot be removed. You can add additional controls to the Windows Forms sheet, by selecting from the thousands of additional controls available from Microsoft and third-party vendors. The remaining five tabs in the Toolbox window and specific controls and their functions are discussed as they are used in this book.

Adding Label Controls to a Form

The next step in developing the State Tax Computation application is to add the labels such as Taxpayer's income that are used to identify the input and output areas of the State Tax Computation window. You can add a control to a form using one of three methods: drawing, dragging, or double-clicking. The following steps show how to use the Toolbox window to add Label controls to the form by drawing.

To Add Label Controls to a Form by Drawing

1. If necessary, click the Windows Forms tab in the Toolbox window. Point to the Label button in the Toolbox window.

The Windows Forms sheet displays in the Toolbox window (Figure 3-25). The Label button adds a Label control to the form.

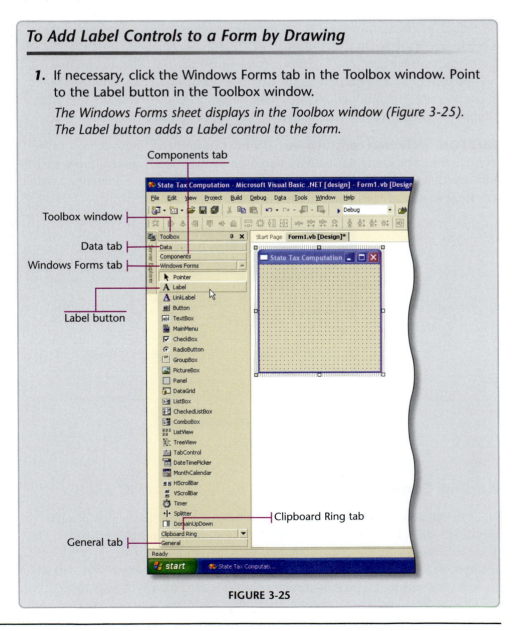

FIGURE 3-25

2. Click the Label button. Point to the upper-left corner of the form.

The Label button on the Windows Forms sheet is selected. When the mouse pointer is positioned over the form, the mouse pointer changes to cross hairs with a Label control indicator (Figure 3-26).

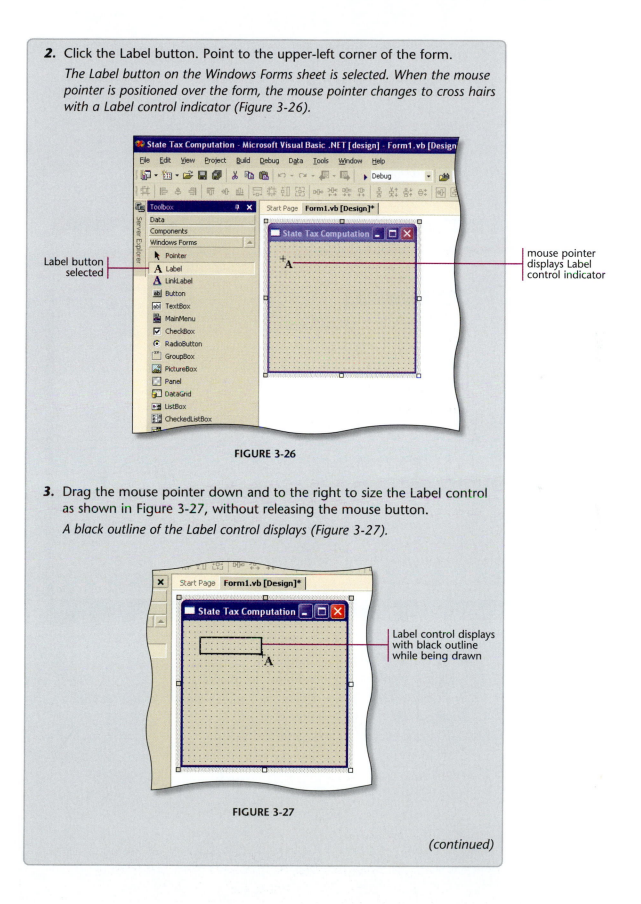

Label button selected

mouse pointer displays Label control indicator

FIGURE 3-26

3. Drag the mouse pointer down and to the right to size the Label control as shown in Figure 3-27, without releasing the mouse button.

A black outline of the Label control displays (Figure 3-27).

Label control displays with black outline while being drawn

FIGURE 3-27

(continued)

4. When the Label control outline is the desired size, release the mouse button.

The black outline of the Label control changes to a dotted gray border with sizing handles. The default Text property value of the Label control (Label1) displays in the control. The properties for the Label control display in the Properties window. The Pointer button is selected on the Windows Forms sheet, indicating that no controls are selected (Figure 3-28).

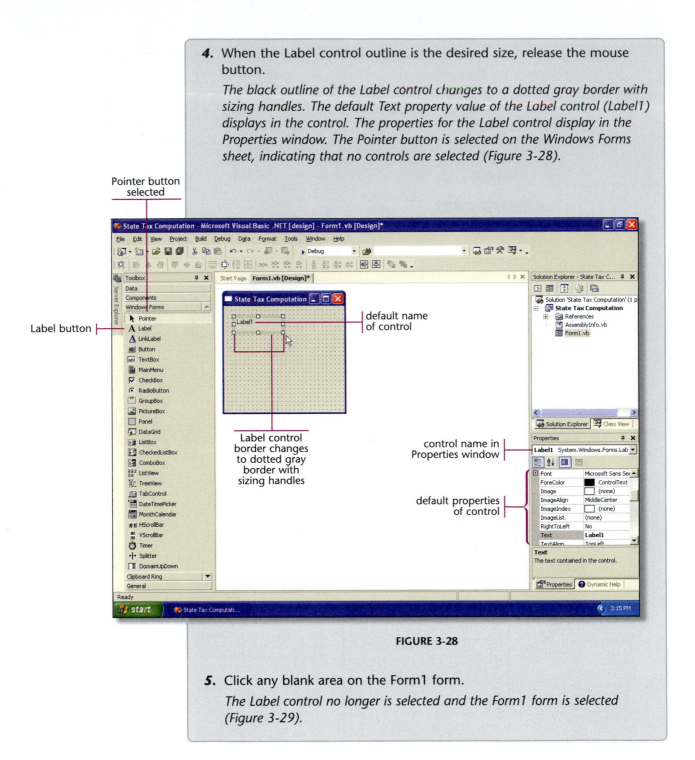

Pointer button selected

Label button

default name of control

Label control border changes to dotted gray border with sizing handles

control name in Properties window

default properties of control

FIGURE 3-28

5. Click any blank area on the Form1 form.

The Label control no longer is selected and the Form1 form is selected (Figure 3-29).

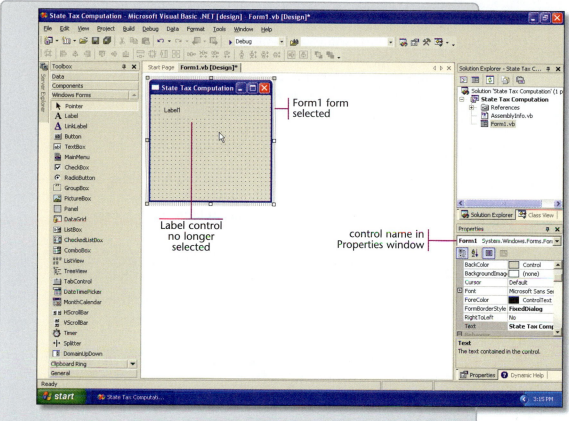

FIGURE 3-29

6. Repeat Step 2 through Step 5 two times to add two more Label controls to the form in the size and position shown in Figure 3-30.

Three Label controls display on the form. You do not need to position and size the controls precisely as shown because the control properties will be set later in the chapter.

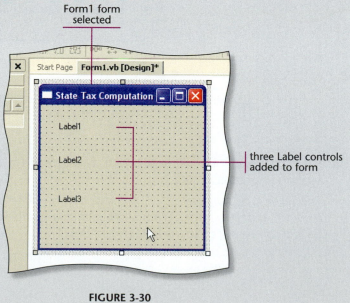

FIGURE 3-30

Three Label controls that will provide text descriptions of the input and output areas of the application window are added to the form. When you are adding controls to a form, the dots on the background of the form, called the **positioning grid**, serve as anchors for aligning the controls. As you position or size a control on a form, the top, bottom, left, and right borders of the controls always align themselves, or **snap**, to the dots that display on a form. This functionality helps you align controls with greater precision.

Adding TextBox Controls to a Form

As you have learned, you can add a control to a form using one of three methods: drawing, dragging, or double-clicking. The following steps use the dragging method to add two TextBox controls to the Form1 form.

To Add TextBox Controls to a Form by Dragging

1. Point to the TextBox button in the Toolbox window (Figure 3-31).

The TextBox button adds a TextBox control to the form.

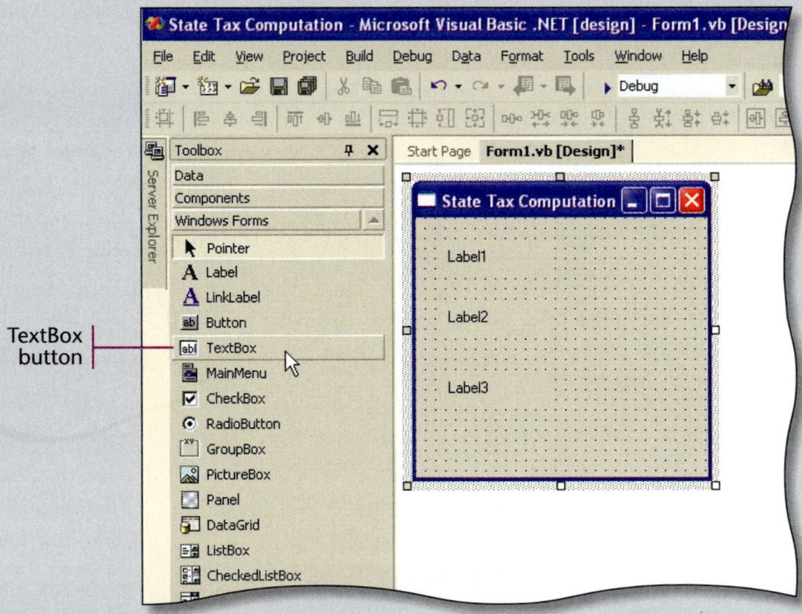

FIGURE 3-31

2. Drag the TextBox button to the right as shown in Figure 3-32, without releasing the mouse button.

The TextBox button is selected. When the mouse pointer is positioned over the form, the mouse pointer displays a plus sign to indicate that the selected control can be added to the form (Figure 3-32).

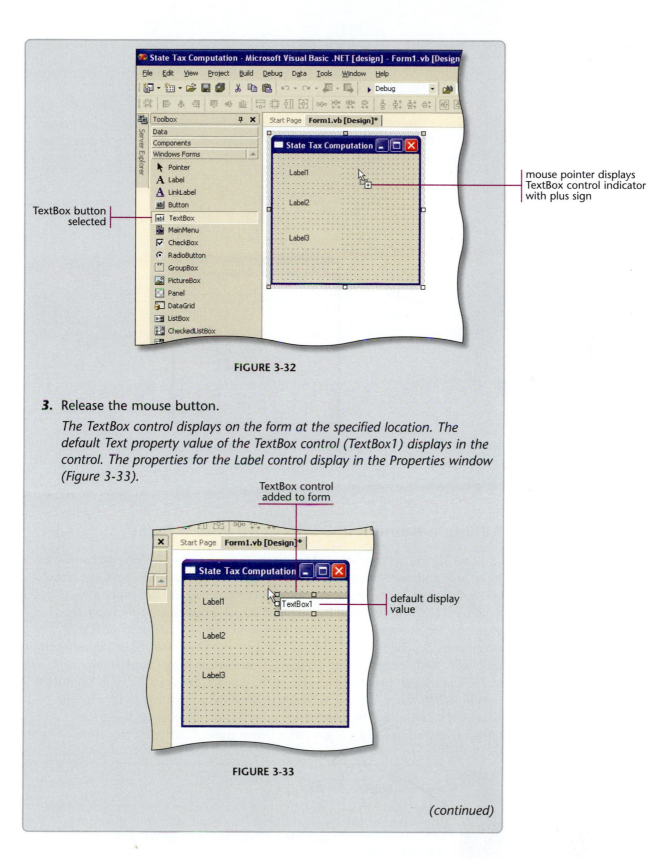

TextBox button selected

mouse pointer displays TextBox control indicator with plus sign

FIGURE 3-32

3. Release the mouse button.

The TextBox control displays on the form at the specified location. The default Text property value of the TextBox control (TextBox1) displays in the control. The properties for the Label control display in the Properties window (Figure 3-33).

TextBox control added to form

default display value

FIGURE 3-33

(continued)

4. Repeat Step1 through Step 3 to add a second TextBox control to the form in the size and position shown in Figure 3-34. Click any blank area on the Form1 form.

Two TextBox controls display on the form (Figure 3-34). You do not need to position and size the controls precisely as shown because the control proper-ties will be set later in the chapter. The TextBox control no longer is selected and the Form1 form is selected.

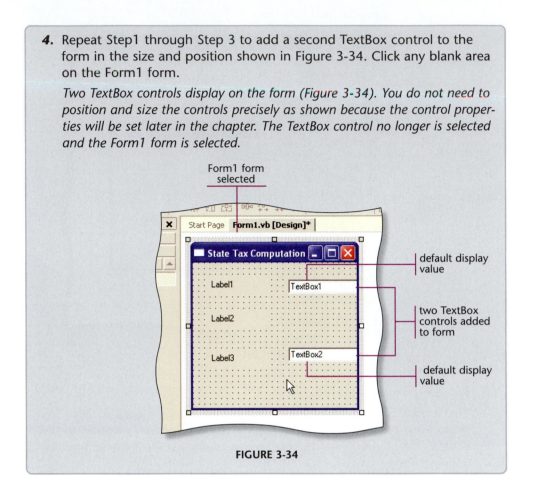

FIGURE 3-34

Adding a NumericUpDown Control to a Form

Two TextBox controls are added to the form, one for the Taxpayer's income input area and one to display State tax due in the output area. Next, you should add a NumericUpDown control. During run time, a user can input a value into a NumericUpDown control. In the State Tax Computation application, for example, the NumericUpDown control allows users to enter a value for Number of dependents. Up and down arrows in the control allow the user to increment and decrement the displayed value within a predefined range of 0 to 10. The user also can type a value in the control. If the user enters a number outside of the range, the control changes the entered number to the closest allowable value within the predefined range. The following steps use the dragging method to add a NumericUpDown control to the Form1 form.

NumericUpDown Ranges

If the user enters a number in a NumericUpDown control outside the range of the minimum and maximum allowed, the control automatically changes the entered number to the closest allowable value.

To Add a NumericUpDown Control to a Form by Dragging

1. Click the down scroll arrow in the Toolbox window until the NumericUpDown button displays on the Windows Forms sheet (Figure 3-35).

The NumericUpDown button adds a NumericUpDown control to a form.

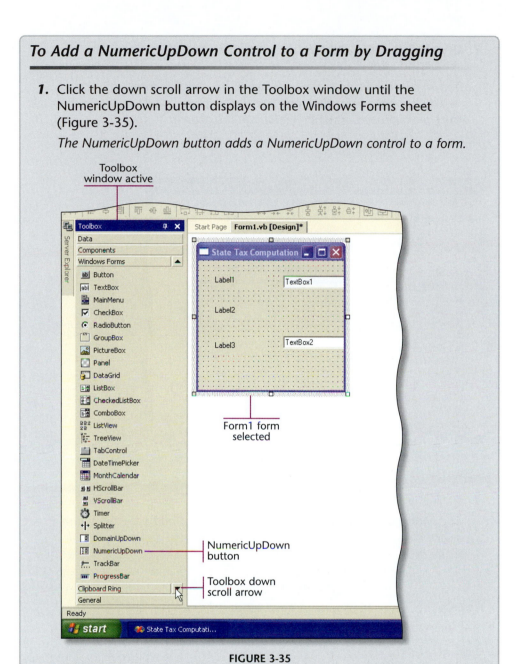

FIGURE 3-35

2. Drag the NumericUpDown button to the right of the Form1 form, as shown in Figure 3-36.

The NumericUpDown control displays at the specified location (Figure 3-36). You do not need to position and size the control precisely as shown, because the control properties will be set later in the chapter.

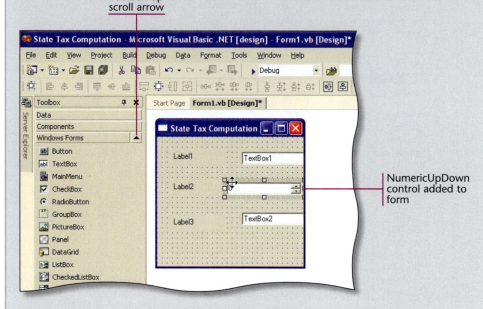

FIGURE 3-36

3. Click any blank area on the Form1 form.

The NumericUpDown control no longer is selected and the Form1 form is selected (Figure 3-37). The NumericUpDown control displays a default value of 0.

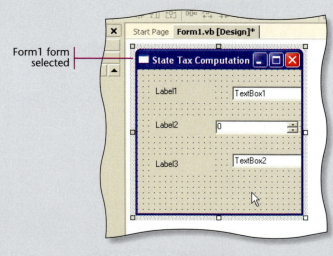

FIGURE 3-37

Adding Button Controls to a Form

The final two controls to add to the form are the two buttons used for the Compute Tax and Reset buttons on the application window. As you have learned, you can add a control to a form by double-clicking the control button on the Windows Forms sheet in the Toolbox window. The following steps use the double-clicking method to add two Button controls to the Form1 form.

To Add Button Controls to a Form by Double-Clicking

1. If necessary, click the up scroll arrow in the Toolbox window to display the Button button on the Windows Forms sheet. Point to the Button button.

The Button button adds a Button control to a form.

2. Double-click the Button button.

Visual Basic .NET adds a Button control to the top-left corner of the form (Figure 3-38).

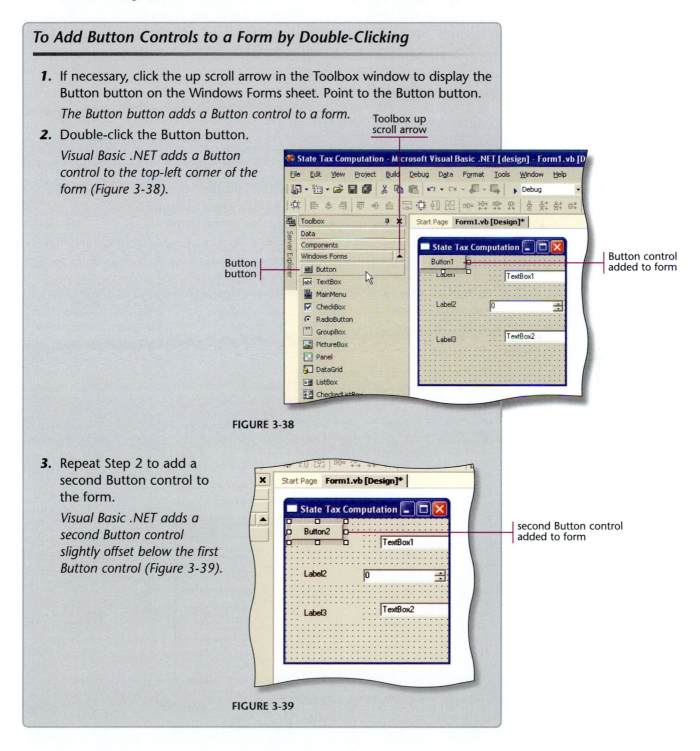

Toolbox up scroll arrow

Button button

Button control added to form

FIGURE 3-38

3. Repeat Step 2 to add a second Button control to the form.

Visual Basic .NET adds a second Button control slightly offset below the first Button control (Figure 3-39).

second Button control added to form

FIGURE 3-39

Whether you use the drawing, dragging, or double-clicking method to add a control to a form depends on your preference and the type of control you are adding to the form. As shown in the preceding steps, double-clicking a control button on the Windows Forms sheet adds a default-sized control to the upper-left corner of the form. If another control already is located at the upper-left corner of the form, double-clicking a control button adds the new control above and slightly offset from the previous control. If you add a control by double-clicking a control button on the Windows Forms sheet, you will need to move the control from the upper-left corner of the form, and frequently, you will want to change the control's size from the default.

Moving Controls on a Form

With all of the controls added to the form, you can move the controls to position them as they should display on the user interface in the application window. When working with forms, you may find it is faster to add all of the required controls to the form and then position them correctly on the form. If you position individual controls before adding all of the controls, you may have to reposition those controls to accommodate any additional controls.

The user interface design created earlier in the chapter (Figure 3-4 on page VB 3.06) serves as a guide for positioning controls on the form. To develop the user interface specified in the design of the project, the Button controls must be moved from the upper-left corner of the form.

You can move a control on a form by dragging the control to a new location or by setting properties in the Properties window. The following steps move the two Button controls on the form by dragging.

To Move Controls on a Form

1. Point to the center of the Button2 control, being sure not to point to a sizing handle.

The mouse pointer changes to a double two-headed arrow (Figure 3-40).

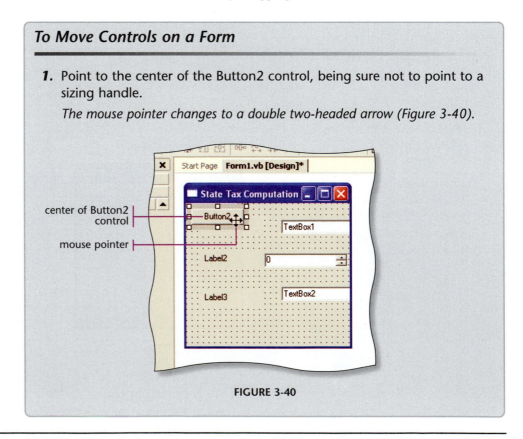

FIGURE 3-40

2. Drag the Button2 control to the bottom right of the form, as shown in Figure 3-41.

The Button2 control displays in the specified location. The outline of the Button2 control changes to a solid gray border with sizing handles (Figure 3-41).

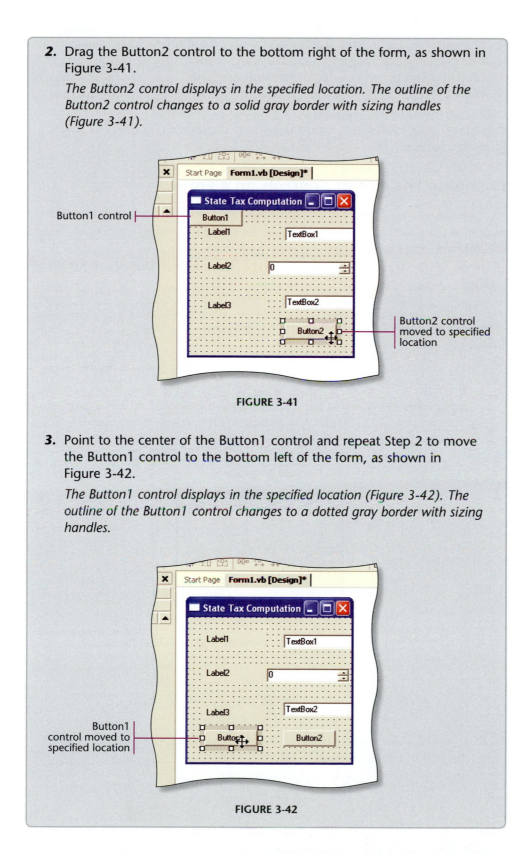

FIGURE 3-41

3. Point to the center of the Button1 control and repeat Step 2 to move the Button1 control to the bottom left of the form, as shown in Figure 3-42.

The Button1 control displays in the specified location (Figure 3-42). The outline of the Button1 control changes to a dotted gray border with sizing handles.

FIGURE 3-42

The location of a control on the form in design time determines where the control displays in the application window at the beginning of run time. The **Top property** and **Left property** are two properties that determine the location of the control at design time and the beginning of run time. Dragging a control on a form changes the property values of the control's Top and Left properties. The Top and Left property values determine, or set, the number of pixels that the control displays from the top and left sides of the form at design time and the beginning of run time. A control does not have to remain in its original location during run time. Changing a control's location during run time will be covered in a later chapter.

Changing the Size of Controls on a Form

You can change the size of a control by dragging the sizing handles on the border of the control or by setting properties in the Properties window. Perform the following steps to change the size of the Button controls to a size that will allow the button text to display as specified in the user interface design for the project.

To Change the Size of Controls on a Form

1. If necessary, click the Button1 control. Point to the bottom-right corner sizing handle on the border of the Button1 control.

Sizing handles display on the border around the Button1 button control. The mouse pointer changes to a diagonal two-headed arrow (Figure 3-43).

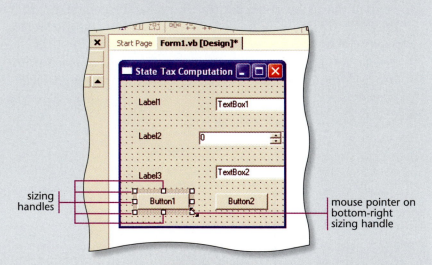

FIGURE 3-43

2. Drag the sizing handle down and to the right until the Button1 control displays in the size shown in Figure 3-44.

The Button1 control is resized (Figure 3-44).

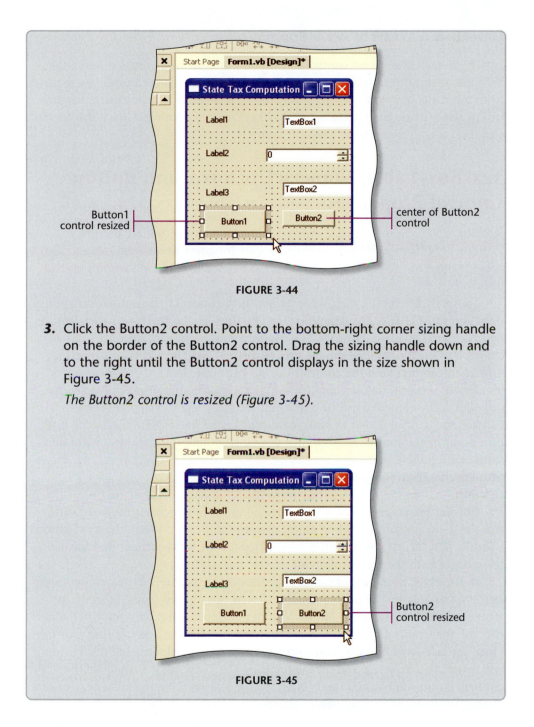

FIGURE 3-44

3. Click the Button2 control. Point to the bottom-right corner sizing handle on the border of the Button2 control. Drag the sizing handle down and to the right until the Button2 control displays in the size shown in Figure 3-45.

The Button2 control is resized (Figure 3-45).

FIGURE 3-45

The steps to set the location and size of a form and the locations and sizes of Button controls on a form are similar. This similarity is due to the fact that a Visual Basic .NET form is a type of control, just as Button, TextBox, and Label, are controls.

Deleting a Control on a Form

If you click the wrong control button on the Windows Forms sheet in the Toolbox or want to modify the controls used on a form, you can delete a control from a form at any point during design time. To delete a control, click the control to select it and then press the DELETE key. You also can right-click the control and then click Delete on the shortcut menu.

TextBox, Label, NumericUpDown, and Button Control Properties

TextBox, Label, NumericUpDown, and Button controls often are used in a Windows application. These controls are easy for users to understand, and they provide most of the input and output areas needed for an application's user interface.

To finish developing the user interface of the State Tax Computation application, you must change the default property values of the TextBox, Label, Button, and NumericUpDown controls. The property values for each control will be changed to position and size the controls correctly on the form and to define how users interact with the controls during run time. During run time, for instance, if a user wants to change a value in a specific input area, the user typically clicks the control used for that input area to select it. When a user selects a control, the control is said to have **focus** and Visual Basic .NET places the insertion point in the control or displays a dotted rectangle around the control on the form. A user also can use the TAB key on the keyboard to select, or set, the focus on a specific control. Using the TAB key to set the focus on a control is called **tabbing**.

The **TabIndex property** determines the order in which Visual Basic .NET sets the focus on controls when a user presses the TAB key. When the application window first displays at run time, Visual Basic .NET will set the initial focus on the control with the lowest value for the TabIndex property.

In the State Tax Computation application window, the TextBox control used as the input area for Taxpayer's income should have initial focus. Subsequent tabbing should set the focus on the Number of dependents NumericUpDown control, the Compute Tax Button control, and, finally, the Reset Button control. Once the last control in the TabIndex sequence is reached, pressing the TAB key will restart the sequence and set the focus on the Taxpayer's income TextBox control. If you want Visual Basic .NET to skip a control during tabbing, you can change the value of its **TabStop property** from True to False.

Common Properties of Controls

Many of the controls used in developing a Windows application share common properties. The Form, TextBox, and Label controls, for example, all have Text, Size, and Location properties. TextBox, Label, and NumericUpDown controls use the TabStop and TabIndex properties. Table 3-4 lists some of the more common properties for controls. Entries listed in bold in the table are the default property values. Appendix C contains a complete summary of the properties, events, and methods for controls introduced in this book.

Table 3-4 *Common Properties of Controls*

CATEGORY	PROPERTY	DESCRIPTION	PROPERTY VALUES
Appearance	BackColor	Sets the background color of the control	Select a color from a pop-up dialog box.
	Cursor	Defines which mouse pointer (cursor) displays when user moves the mouse over the control	Select a mouse pointer from a list of more than 20 mouse pointers.
	Font	Defines the text font to use if text displays in the control	Select a font style from a pop-up dialog box.
	ForeColor	Changes the foreground color, usually of the text that displays on the control	Select a color from a pop-up dialog box.
Behavior	Enabled	If True, control is usable at run time; if False, a user cannot change control value and control may display grayed out	**True** False
	TabStop	Determines whether the TAB key sets focus on the control during run time	**True** False
	TabIndex	Determines the order in which the TAB key navigates to the control	Any positive whole number
	Visible	If True, control displays at run time; if False, control does not display	**True** False
Data	Tag	Defines data to be stored with the control (data does not display to user)	Any text
Design	Locked	Ensures that a control cannot be moved during design time; prevents inadvertently moving the control once it is positioned	True **False**
	Name	Provides a descriptive, unique identifier for the control	Any text
	Size	Indicates height and width of the control in pixels	Two positive whole numbers, separated by a comma
	Location	Indicates distance from the top and left border of the form in pixels	Two positive whole numbers, separated by a comma

Although the properties in Table 3-4 are common among many different controls, the properties can cause different effects. Properties such as Size and Location, for example, have the same effect for each control. Other properties, such as Enabled and Font, cause different effects for different controls.

TextBox Control Properties

A TextBox control has many properties used to define how the control displays on the form and how the user interacts with the control during run time. The Height property, Width property, and **Location property** define the position and size of the TextBox control in the application window. The **ReadOnly property** determines whether or not the user can input data into the TextBox control at run time. The ReadOnly property value can be either True or False. The default value is False, meaning that users can input data into the TextBox control. Table 3-5 lists several of the properties associated with the TextBox control, with a brief description and a list of available property values. Entries listed in bold in the table are the default property values.

Table 3-5 *TextBox Control Properties*

CATEGORY	PROPERTY	DESCRIPTION	PROPERTY VALUES
Appearance	BorderStyle	Determines how the border of the TextBox control displays	None FixedSingle **Fixed3D**
	Text	Sets the text that displays inside the control	Any text with a character length up to the value specified in the MaxLength property
	TextAlign	Determines if text in the control displays left-aligned, right-aligned, or centered	**Left** Right Center
Behavior	AutoSize	Indicates whether the height of the control automatically changes when the font size in the control is changed	**True** False
	MaxLength	Sets the maximum number of characters a user can input into the text control	Any positive whole number from 0 through **32767**
	Multiline	Determines if text in the control displays on more than one line	True **False**
	ReadOnly	If True, a user cannot type or edit text in control during run time; if False, user can type and edit text in control	True **False**
	WordWrap	If MultiLine is True, text in control wraps to the next line when the text is longer than the width of the control	**True** False

Several of the properties of the two TextBox controls added to the form must be changed from the default values, according to the design of the application. Table 3-6 lists the properties and values for the two TextBox controls that require changes.

Table 3-6 TextBox Control Property Values for the State Tax Computation Application

CONTROL	PROPERTY	PROPERTY VALUE	EFFECT
TextBox1	Text	0	Sets 0 to display as the initial value in the control at run time
	Location: X	144	Indicates distance from left border of the form in pixels
	Location: Y	24	Indicates distance from top border of the form in pixels
	Size: Width	76	Sets the width of the control in pixels
	Size: Height	20	Sets the height of the control in pixels
	TextAlign	Right	Sets text to display right-aligned on the control
TextBox2	Text	0	Sets 0 to display as initial value in the control at run time
	TabStop	False	Indicates that TAB key should not set focus on the control when user navigates the window by tabbing during run time
	Location: X	144	Indicates distance from left border of the form in pixels
	Location: Y	112	Indicates distance from top border of the form in pixels
	Size: Width	76	Sets the width of the control
	Size: Height	20	Sets the height of the control
	ReadOnly	True	Prohibits user from entering data in control; sets background color to display as gray
	TextAlign	Right	Sets text to display right-aligned in the control

As defined in the user interface design for the State Tax Computation application, the first TextBox control, TextBox1, should allow a user to input a value for Taxpayer's income. The second TextBox control, TextBox2, should display the output value for State tax due. As shown in Figure 3-45 on page VB 3.37, the two TextBox controls currently display the default Text property values of TextBox1 and TextBox2. As listed in Table 3-6, the Text property values are changed to display zero (0) as the initial value at run time. Because it displays an output value, the TabStop property is set to False to indicate that TAB key should not set focus on the control when a user navigates the window by tabbing during run time.

The steps on the next page set the property values for the two TextBox controls, as listed in Table 3-6.

To Change Properties of TextBox Controls

1. Click the TextBox1 control. If necessary, scroll the Properties list until the Text property displays. Double-click the Text property value.

Sizing handles display around the TextBox1 control. The control name (TextBox1) displays in the Object box of the Properties window. The Text property displays in the Appearance property category in the Properties list, and the current Text property value, TextBox1, is selected (Figure 3-46).

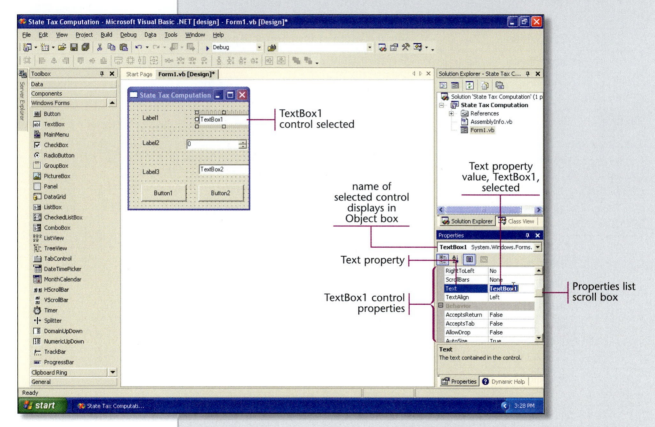

FIGURE 3-46

2. Type 0 as the new value, as indicated in Table 3-6, and then press the ENTER key.

The new Text property value, 0, displays in the Properties window and in the TextBox control on the form (Figure 3-47). You can use the BACKSPACE key or the LEFT ARROW and DELETE keys to correct mistakes made while typing.

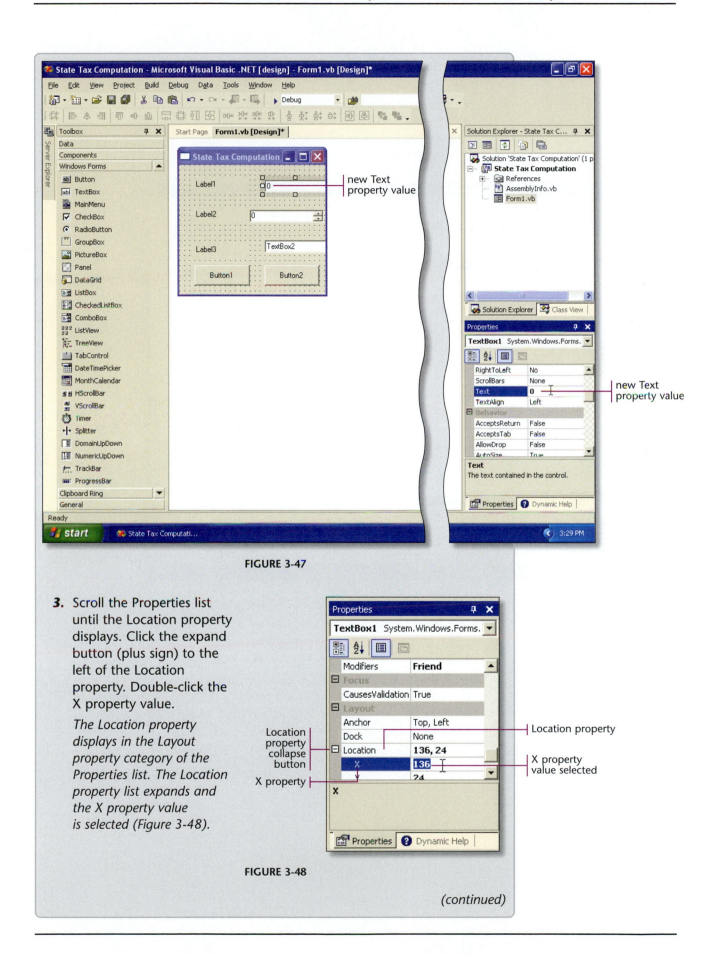

FIGURE 3-47

3. Scroll the Properties list until the Location property displays. Click the expand button (plus sign) to the left of the Location property. Double-click the X property value.

The Location property displays in the Layout property category of the Properties list. The Location property list expands and the X property value is selected (Figure 3-48).

FIGURE 3-48

(continued)

4. Type 144 as the X property value, as indicated in Table 3-6, and then press the ENTER key.

The TextBox control displays in the location indicated by the new X property value (Figure 3-49). The value updates in both the Location property and the X property, so that the X property value displays when the Location property is collapsed.

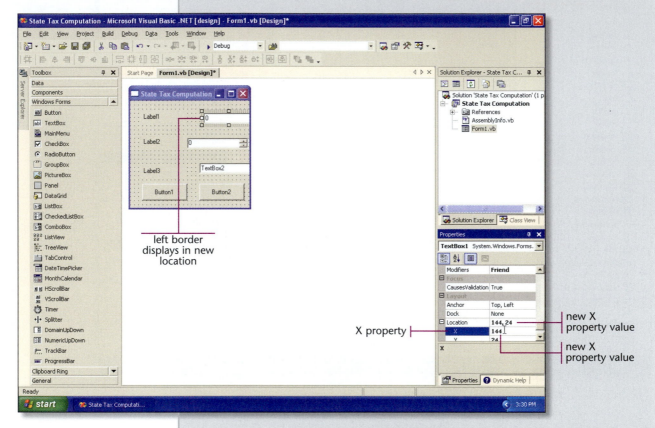

FIGURE 3-49

5. Repeat Steps 3 and 4 to change the Location: Y, Size: Width, and Size: Height, and TextAlign property values for the TextBox1 control, as shown in Table 3-6.

The TextBox1 control displays in the correct location with the size, value, and alignment as defined in the user interface design (Figure 3-50).

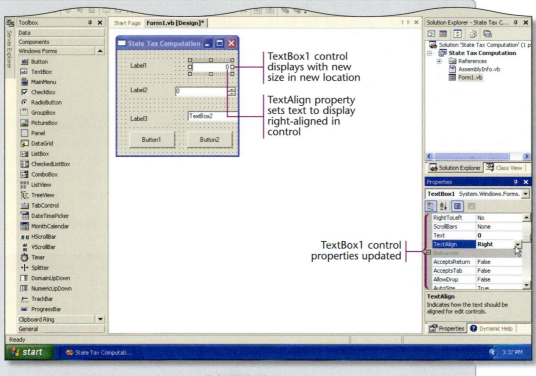

FIGURE 3-50

6. Repeat Steps 1 through 5 to change the Text, TabStop, Location: X, Location: Y, Size: Width, Size: Height, ReadOnly, and TextAlign property values for the TextBox2 control.

7. Select the Form1 form by clicking an empty area of the form that does not contain any other controls.

   The Form1 form is selected (Figure 3-51). The TextBox2 control displays in the correct location with the size, value, and alignment as defined in the user interface design.

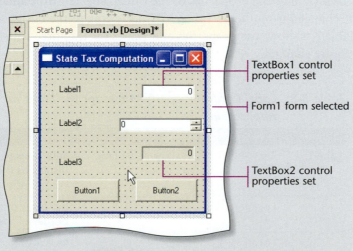

FIGURE 3-51

As shown in the preceding steps, the Properties window allows you to change the appearance of the TextBox controls by changing property values. By following the same basic steps, you can use the Properties window to change property values for most controls during design time.

Label Control Properties

As you have learned, a Label control such as Label1 is used to display text on a form. During run time, the person using the application cannot change the text in a label. The important properties for a Label control include the Location, Size, Font, and Text properties. Table 3-7 lists several of the properties associated with the Label control, with a brief description and a list of available property values.

Table 3-7   Label Control Properties

CATEGORY	PROPERTY	DESCRIPTION	PROPERTY VALUES
Appearance	FlatStyle	Determines the 3D appearance of the control	Flat Popup **Standard** System
	Image	Sets an image to display on the visible portion of the Label control, along with the Text	Select a picture from the hard drive using a dialog box.
	ImageAlign	If the Image property is set, determines where the image displays	Select a location from a pop-up graphical display map.
	Text	Defines the visible text that displays on the control	Any text with any character length

Several of the properties of the three Label controls added to the form must be changed from the default values, according to the design of the application. Table 3-8 shows the properties and values for the three Label controls that require changes.

Table 3-8   Label Control Property Values for the State Tax Computation Application

CONTROL	PROPERTY	VALUE	EFFECT
Label1	Text	Taxpayer's income:	Sets Taxpayer's income: to display as the initial value in the control at run time
	Location: X	16	Indicates distance from left border of the form in pixels
	Location: Y	24	Indicates distance from top border of the form in pixels

Table 3-8 *Label Control Property Values for the State Tax Computation Application (continued)*

CONTROL	PROPERTY	VALUE	EFFECT
	Size: Width	104	Sets the width of the control in pixels
	Size: Height	16	Sets the height of the control in pixels
Label2	Text	Number of dependents:	Sets Number of dependents: to display as the initial value in the control at run time
	Location: X	16	Indicates distance from left border of the form in pixels
	Location: Y	64	Indicates distance from top border of the form in pixels
	Size: Width	128	Sets the width of the control in pixels
	Size: Height	16	Sets the height of the control in pixels
Label3	Text	State tax due:	Sets State tax due: to display as the initial value in the control at run time
	Location: X	16	Indicates distance from left border of the form in pixels
	Location: Y	112	Indicates distance from top border of the form in pixels
	Size: Width	88	Sets the width of the control in pixels
	Size: Height	16	Sets the height of the control in pixels

The user interface design for the State Tax Computation application specifies that the Label controls should display to the left of the NumericUpDown and TextBox controls to provide descriptions of the controls. As shown in Figure 3-51 on page VB 3.45, the three Label controls currently display the default Text property values of Label1, Label2, and Label3. Table 3-8 lists the new Text property values that must be entered so the controls display descriptions of the NumericUpDown and TextBox controls. The property values also must be changed to set the location and size of each Label control.

The steps on the next page set the property values for the three Label controls, as listed in Table 3-8.

To Change Properties of Label Controls

1. Click the Label1 control. Scroll the Properties list until the Text property displays and then double-click the Text property.

   Sizing handles display around the Label1 control. The control name (Label1) displays in the Object box of the Properties window. The Text property is highlighted in the Properties list. The current Text property value, Label1, is selected.

2. Type Taxpayer's income: as the new Text property, as indicated in Table 3-8 on the previous page and then press the ENTER key.

   The new Text property value, Taxpayer's income:, displays in the Properties window and in the Label control on the form (Figure 3-52). You can use the BACKSPACE key or the LEFT ARROW and DELETE keys to correct mistakes made while typing.

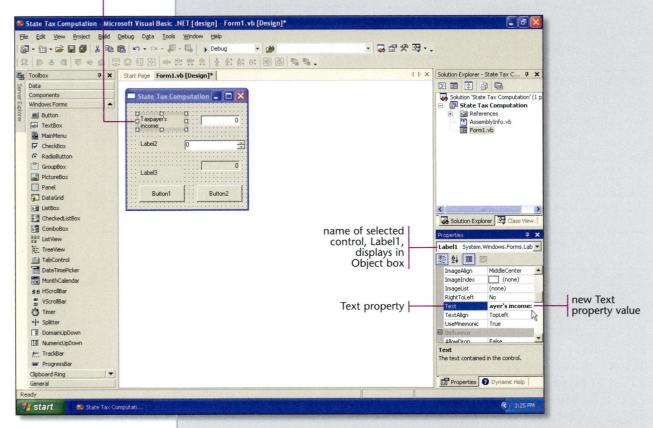

FIGURE 3-52

3. Scroll the Properties list until the Location property displays. Click the expand button (plus sign) to the left of the Location property and then double-click the X property value.

   The Location property displays in the Layout property category of the Properties list. The Location property expands and the X property value is selected (Figure 3-53).

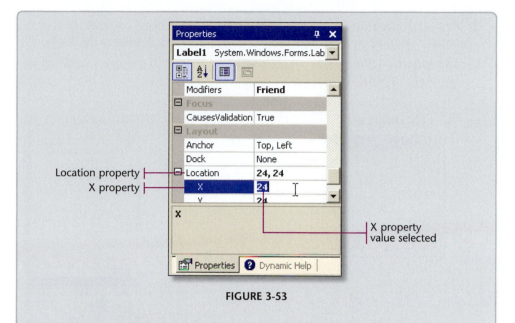

FIGURE 3-53

4. Type 16 as the X property value, as indicated in Table 3-8 on pages VB 3.46 and VB 3.47 and then press the ENTER key.

The Label control displays in the location indicated by the new X property value (Figure 3-54). The value updates in both the Location property and the X property so the X property value displays when the Location property is collapsed.

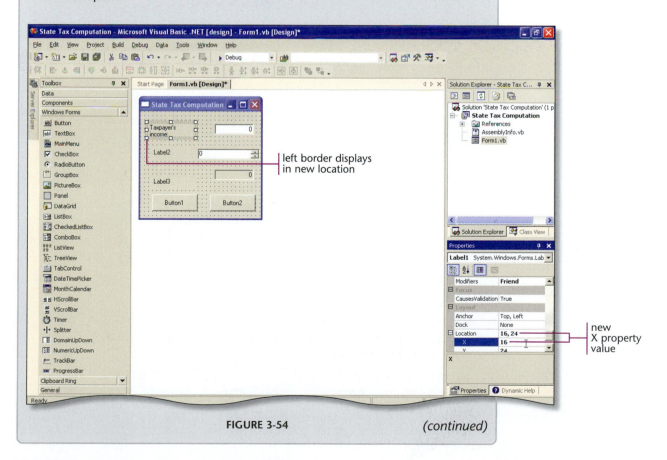

FIGURE 3-54   *(continued)*

5. Repeat Steps 3 and 4 to change the remaining property values for the Label1 control, as shown in Table 3-8 on pages VB 3.46 and VB 3.47.

The Label1 control displays in the correct location with the size as defined in the user interface design (Figure 3-55).

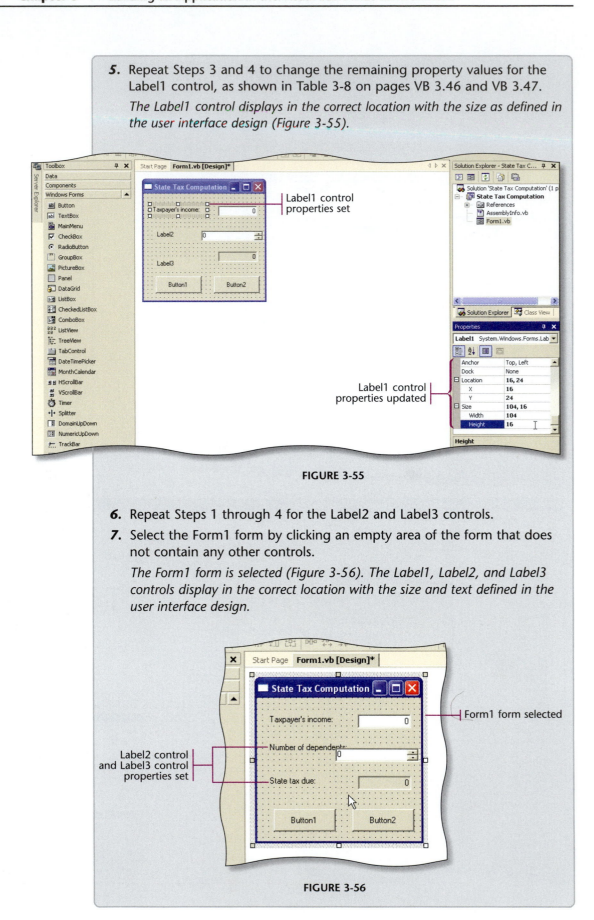

FIGURE 3-55

6. Repeat Steps 1 through 4 for the Label2 and Label3 controls.

7. Select the Form1 form by clicking an empty area of the form that does not contain any other controls.

The Form1 form is selected (Figure 3-56). The Label1, Label2, and Label3 controls display in the correct location with the size and text defined in the user interface design.

FIGURE 3-56

As shown in Figure 3-56, the Label controls now display on the form as they should display to a user using the State Tax Computation application.

NumericUpDown Control Properties

A NumericUpDown control allows the user to change an input value by typing it on the keyboard, using the UP ARROW or DOWN ARROW keys on the keyboard, or using the mouse to click the up and down arrows. The **Value property** defines the current value displayed in the control. The **Minimum property** and **Maximum property** determine the range of allowable values. If the user enters a number outside of the range set by the Minimum and Maximum property values, the control automatically changes the entered number to the closest allowable value. The property values for the Value, Minimum, and Maximum properties can be integer or decimal values, depending on the value of the **DecimalPlaces property**. The DecimalPlaces property defaults to 0, to indicate that only integer values are accepted as input. Table 3-9 lists several of the properties associated with the NumericUpDown control, with a brief description and a list of available property values.

Table 3-9 NumericUpDown Control Properties

CATEGORY	PROPERTY	DESCRIPTION	PROPERTY VALUES
Appearance	BorderStyle	Determines how the border of the control displays	None FixedSingle **Fixed3D**
	TextAlign	Defines if text in the control displays left-aligned, right-aligned, or centered	**Left** Right Center
	UpDownAlign	Determines if the up and down arrows on the control display on left or right side of the control	Left **Right**
	Value	Sets the value that displays in the control	Any value within the range set by the Minimum and Maximum property values
Behavior	InterceptArrowKeys	If True, a user can use the UP ARROW and DOWN ARROW keys to change the value in control; if False, the user cannot	**True** False
Data	DecimalPlaces	Defines numbers of decimal places that display in the value in the control	Any whole number from **0** to 99
	Increment	Defines amount to add or subtract from the displayed value each time user clicks the up or down arrow on control	Any positive number
	Maximum	Determines the highest allowable value in the control; if user enters a higher value, the value is set automatically to the Maximum value	Any number

(continued)

Table 3-9   NumericUpDown Control Properties (continued)

CATEGORY	PROPERTY	DESCRIPTION	PROPERTY VALUES
Data	Minimum	Determines the lowest allowable value in the control; if user enters a lower value, the value is set automatically to the Minimum value	Any number
	ThousandsSeparator	Determines if a Thousands separator character is used in the value, when appropriate; if True, the value displays with a Thousands separator character set on user's system; if False, no Thousands separator character displays	True **False**

Several of the properties of the NumericUpDown control must be changed from the default values, according to the application requirements. Table 3-10 shows the properties and values of the NumericUpDown control that require changes.

Table 3-10   NumericUpDown Control Property Values for the State Tax Computation Application

CONTROL	PROPERTY	VALUE	EFFECT
NumericUpDown1	Value	0	Sets 0 to display as the initial value in the control at run time
	Location: X	144	Indicates distance from left border of the form in pixels
	Location: Y	64	Indicates distance from top border of the form in pixels
	Size: Width	76	Sets the width of the control in pixels
	Size: Height	20	Sets the height of the control in pixels
	Minimum	0	Defines the lowest value allowed in the control
	Maximum	10	Defines the highest value allowed in the control
	TextAlign	Right	Sets text to display right-aligned in the control

As defined in the user interface design for the State Tax Computation application, the NumericUpDown control should accept only values for Number of dependents from 0 through 10 and the value should display right-aligned in the control. The property values also must be changed to set the location and size of the NumericUpDown control. The following steps set the property values of the NumericUpDown1 control, as listed in Table 3-10.

To Change Properties of a NumericUpDown Control

1. Click the NumericUpDown1 control.
2. Scroll the Properties list until the Location property displays.
3. Click the expand button (plus sign) to the left of the Location property.
4. Double-click the X property value.
5. Type 144 as the X property value, as indicated in Table 3-10, and then press the ENTER key.
6. Repeat Steps 1 through 5 to change the remaining property values for the NumericUpDown1 control, as shown in Table 3-10.
7. Click any blank area of the Form1 form.

   The Form1 form is selected (Figure 3-57). The NumericUpDown1 control displays in the correct location with size, value, minimum, maximum, and alignment as defined in the user interface design.

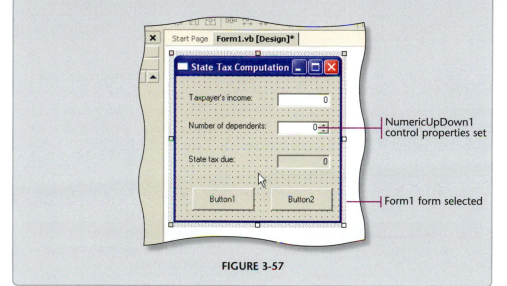

FIGURE 3-57

Button Control Properties

Adding one or more buttons to a user interface allows a user to initiate an action by clicking the button, which causes the code associated with the button to be executed. A Button control, for example, can instruct the application to calculate or process an output, based on inputs that have been provided. In the case of the State Tax Computation application, Button controls allow a user to tell the application to perform the computation or to reset the data on the form. Table 3-11 on the next page lists several of the properties associated with the Button control, with a brief description and a list of available property values.

Table 3-11   *Button Control Properties*

CATEGORY	PROPERTY	DESCRIPTION	PROPERTY VALUES
Appearance	FlatStyle	Determines the 3D appearance of the control	Flat Popup **Standard** System
	Image	Sets an image to display on the visible portion of the Label control, along with the Text	Select a picture from the hard drive using a dialog box.
	ImageAlign	If Image property is set, determines where the image displays	Select a location from a pop-up graphical display map.
	TextAlign	Determines where the Text should display on the button	Select one of nine locations from a pop-up graphical display map.

The Location and Size properties of the two Button controls already have been changed to position and size the buttons correctly on the form. The only other property change required is to change the Text property value to define the text that displays on the button face. Table 3-12 shows the properties and values of the Button1 and Button2 controls that require changes.

Table 3-12   *Button Control Property Values for the State Tax Computation Application*

CONTROL	PROPERTY	VALUE	EFFECT
Button1	Text	Compute Tax	Sets the text that displays on the button face to Compute Tax
Button2	Text	Reset	Sets the text that displays on the button face to Reset

The following steps set the property values of the Button1 and Button2 controls, as listed in Table 3-12.

To Change Properties of Button Controls

1. Click the Button1 control.
2. Scroll the Properties list until the Text property displays.
3. Double-click the Text property value.
4. Type Compute Tax as the Text property value, as indicated in Table 3-12, and then press the ENTER key.

5. Repeat Steps 1 through 4 to change the Text property value for the Button2 control, as shown in Table 3-12.

6. Click any blank area of the Form1 form.

The Form1 form is selected (Figure 3-58). The Button1 and Button2 controls display with the Text property values defined in the user interface design.

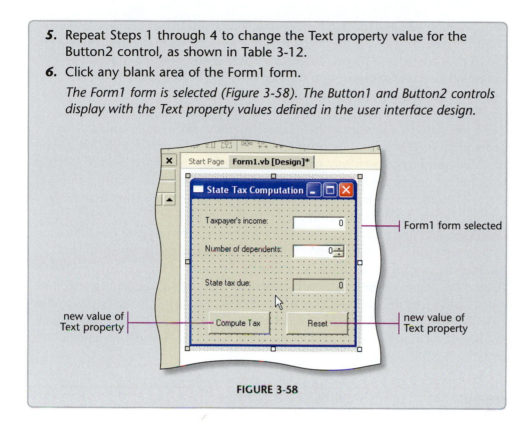

FIGURE 3-58

All of the controls have been added to the form and changed to reflect the desired user interface design. The user interface for the State Tax Computation application is complete. The TextBox, Label, NumericUpDown, and Button controls now display on the form as they should display in the application window at run time.

Changing the Name Property of Controls

As you have learned, Visual Basic .NET assigns unique default names to controls, such as Form1, Label1, Label2, TextBox1, and Button1. The **Name property** of a control reflects its name. Each control has its own unique default name to distinguish it from another instance of the same class of objects; Visual Basic .NET also adds a number to each default control name to ensure that the control name is unique. For example, because the form in the State Tax Computation application includes more than one TextBox control, Visual Basic .NET names the first TextBox control, TextBox1, and the second TextBox control, TextBox2.

It is useful to change the default name of a control to provide a more descriptive name. In general, you should rename controls that will have one or more properties changed at run time, such as controls used for input and output. You also should rename forms, which are a type of control. This is particularly true for Visual Basic .NET projects that include multiple forms. Because the State Tax Computation program includes only one form, it is not necessary to rename the form. You also do not need to rename controls that are used for static display, such as the Label controls in the State Tax Computation application.

Although Visual Basic .NET may initially set the text that displays in the control to match the name of the control, the text in a control and the name of the control are defined by two different properties and property values. For example, the text that displays on the Compute Tax button is set by the Text property; the name of the Button control, Button1, is set by the Name property.

Renaming controls is not a requirement of programming in Visual Basic .NET, but rather a convention that makes programs more understandable by programmers. When naming forms and controls, it is beneficial to follow a standardized **naming convention**, which is an agreed upon method for naming controls so the control can be identified easily in code. Companies or programming teams often maintain standards for the names of controls to ensure that everyone on the programming team understands the purpose of the controls.

When defining standards for naming forms and controls, you can follow some simple rules. First, the control name should indicate the type of control. Second, the control name should describe the purpose of the control. Following these rules, you can create naming conventions that use a three-letter prefix and a descriptive identifier as the name of the control. All forms, for example, would have the prefix of frm followed by a descriptive identifier. Using this convention, the Form1 form in the State Tax Computation application would be named frmStateTaxComputation.

Tip

Naming Forms

In a project with multiple forms, all forms in an application should be assigned an appropriate name other than the default name. When naming a form, use a prefix of frm followed by a descriptive identifier.

When creating naming standards for other controls, such as a TextBox, Label, NumericUpDown, or Button control, again you can use a three-letter prefix and a descriptive identifier as the name of the control. Each type of control would have a unique prefix, such as txt for a TextBox control and lbl for a Label control.

Tip

Naming Controls

A descriptive name should be used when naming a control used for input or output. A control that will not be changed during run time, such as a Label control, does not necessarily need a name. When naming a control, use a unique three-character prefix together with a descriptive identifier. The following three-character prefixes can be used for TextBox, Label, NumericUpDown, and Button controls:

txt – TextBox controls

lbl – Label controls

nud – NumericUpDown controls

btn – Button controls

Table 3-13 shows how these naming conventions apply to the input and output controls on the form in the State Tax Computation application.

Table 3-13 Control Names for the State Tax Computation Application

CURRENT CONTROL NAME PROPERTY VALUE	NEW NAME PROPERTY VALUE
TextBox1	txtIncome
TextBox2	txtTaxDue
NumericUpDown1	nudDependents
Button1	btnCompute
Button2	btnReset

The following steps change the Name property values of these controls to set the Name property values to the names listed in Table 3-13.

To Change the Name Property of Controls

1. Click the TextBox1 control.
2. Scroll the Properties list until the Name property displays in the Properties window.
3. Double click the Name property value.
4. Type txtIncome as the new Name property value for the TextBox1 control, as indicated in Table 3-13.
5. Repeat Steps 1 through 4 to set the Name property values for the TextBox2, NumericUpDown1, Button1, and Button2 controls.
6. Click any blank area on the Form1 form to select it.

   The Name property value of each control is set to the values indicated in Table 3-13. The form and controls show no visible change.

The steps followed to change the Name property value of a control are the same as those followed to change any other property value for a control. It is important to name controls correctly while creating the interface and before writing any code. Otherwise, if you refer to any of the control names in code and then change the name of a control, the name change may not be reflected automatically in your code and will cause unintended results.

Tip

Setting Control Names
Be certain to name your controls while designing the interface and before writing any code.

With the control names set, the required changes to the control properties for the State Tax Computation application are complete. The next step in developing the application is to write the code that executes when the user clicks the Compute and Reset buttons.

TextBox and NumericUpDown Control Methods

You began the development of the State Tax Computation application by developing the user interface, which consisted of a form and controls. You then set the properties of the controls. The final step in developing the State Tax Computation application is to write the code, or *actions,* that will occur in the application in response to specific events. Visual Basic .NET has its own language, which are the words and symbols used to write the code.

Events are messages sent to an object such as a control when the application runs. As you have learned, Visual Basic .NET controls are objects; just as a method is a message sent to an object, an event procedure is a message sent to a control. Events can be initiated when a user completes a task, such as clicking or dragging a control. Events also can be initiated by the application itself. Events trigger **event procedures**, which are groups of code statements, sometimes simply called code. **Code statements** are instructions to the computer written at design time for the computer to execute at run time.

In Visual Basic .NET, certain controls are capable of recognizing events. For example, most types of Visual Basic .NET controls that display in the application window recognize the **Click event**, which is an event initiated when the user clicks the left mouse button. Button controls are one type of control that can recognize the Click event. A control's name is used to associate an event with a specific control on a form, in order to tell Visual Basic .NET that an event initiated by that control should trigger the event procedure or code statements. For example, when the user clicks the left mouse button with the mouse pointer positioned on a specific Button control, such as btnCompute, the code in the btnCompute_Click event procedure executes.

A program that behaves as just described is called **event driven**. Code in event-driven programs executes only when a certain event, such as clicking a button, triggers the code to execute. Windows applications built using Visual Basic .NET are event driven.

Assignment Statements

Many times, the actions that you want to occur in the application in response to events can be expressed as changes in property values of controls on the form. The generalized code statement used to change the value of a control property is

controlname.propertyname = propertyvalue

where controlname is the name of the control, propertyname is the name of the property to change, and propertyvalue is the new value to which the property value should be changed. This type of code statement is known as an **assignment statement**, which is a code statement that changes the value of a variable or property of an object or control. Variables will be discussed in

Chapter 4. The assignment statement tells the application to set the control property on the left side of the statement to the property value on the right side of the statement. In the State Tax Computation application, for example, you can use an assignment statement to change the Text property of a TextBox control at run time so it displays the State tax due in the output area. Table 3-15 shows the general form of the assignment statement. Appendix D summarizes all of the general forms of statements introduced in this book.

Table 3-14 *Assignment Statement*

General form:	1. Object = newvalue 2. Object.Property = newvalue
Purpose:	To change the value of the object or object property on the left side of the equal sign to the value on the right side of the equal sign.
Examples:	1. `Button1.Text = "Compute Tax"` 2. `txtTaxDue.Text = 0.03 * (txtIncome.Text - 600 * nudDependents.Value)` 3. `i = 0`

Comment Statements

Programmers often add comments within their code statements as a form of **internal documentation**. A **comment** is text added within an event procedure that explains how the code in the event procedure works or why it was written. Comments are not executed in event procedures and are ignored by the .NET CLR. Comments are included only for informational purposes for you or for other programmers. Each comment line must begin with an apostrophe (') or the letters **REM**. The following general rules apply to the placement of comments in code statements.

Tip

Comment Placement

Use comments to remind yourself and other programmers of the purpose of code. Use comments in the following three ways:

1. Place a comment that identifies the file and its purpose at the top of every class or file that contains code. This type of comment typically is called a **comment header**.

2. Place a comment at the top of every event procedure or function.

3. Place comments near portions of code that need clarification or serve an important purpose.

The general form of a comment statement is shown in Table 3-15.

Table 3-15   *Comment Statement*

General form:	1. ' comment 2. REM comment
Purpose:	To insert explanatory comments in a program as internal documentation.
Examples:	1. ' Payroll: Overtime hour calculation ' Programmer: J. Quasney ' Date: September 23, 2003 ' Purpose: This project calculates total overtime pay for ' each department for a given time period. 2. REM Compute the overtime hours

---

In the code used for the State Tax Computation application, a comment header identifies the application, programmer, date, and purpose for the State Tax Computation application. Figure 3-59 shows the comment header. Visual Basic .NET automatically generates the line numbers shown in Figure 3-59 when the code is entered in the code window.

```
136    ' Chapter 3:     State Tax Computation
137    ' Programmer:    J. Quasney
138    ' Date:          September 2, 2003
139    ' Purpose:       This project calculates state income tax due based
140    '                on income level and number of dependents.
```

FIGURE 3-59

The code shown in Figure 3-59 includes **tab characters**, which are used to indent items on each line and are produced by pressing the TAB key. For example, in line 136, the tab character exists after the 3: and before the words, State Tax Computation.

Writing Code in the Code Window

During program design, you used pseudocode to design the program code to execute two tasks in the State Tax Computation application: computing state tax due when a user clicks the Compute Tax button and setting all values to 0 when a user clicks the Reset button (Figure 3-5 on page VB 3.08). The event procedure that is triggered when the user clicks the Compute Tax button, which is named btnComputeTax, is the btnCompute_Click event procedure. The btnCompute_Click event procedure calculates the State tax due based on a Taxpayer's income and Number of dependents entered by the user and then displays the result in the State tax due text box. The btnCompute_Click event procedure also includes a single comment statement to provide an explanation of the code. Figure 3-60 shows the code that needs to be entered to add the btnComputeTax_Click event procedure. The code is the Visual Basic .NET language for the pseudocode in Figure 3-5 on page VB 3.08.

```
142            ' Calculate tax and display the result in the txtTaxDue text box
143            txtTaxDue.Text = 0.03 * (txtIncome.Text - 600 * nudDependents.Value)
```

FIGURE 3-60

As shown in Line 143 of Figure 3-60, the code uses an assignment statement to assign the value of the calculation by changing the Text property of the txtTaxDue TextBox control. The right side of the assignment statement contains the equation used to calculate the state tax payment due by a taxpayer. The Taxpayer's income is referenced in the statement by using the Text property of the txtIncome TextBox control. The Number of dependents is referenced by using the Value property of the nudDependents NumericUpDown control. Both of these values are entered by the user at run time via the controls in the State Tax Computation application window. For example, the Text property of the txtIncome TextBox control is referenced by the code, txtIncome.Text.

Tip

Referencing Control Properties

In code, a reference to control properties is made by typing the name of the control followed by a period, and then the property name.

The code in Figure 3-59 and Figure 3-60 contains **line numbers** on the left side of each line. Visual Basic .NET automatically numbers all lines of code, regardless of whether you entered the lines or Visual Basic .NET generated the lines automatically. Visual Basic .NET includes an option to display line numbers in the code window. The default setting for this option is not to display line numbers. Programmers often display and print line numbers with code to facilitate communication when discussing the code. The remainder of this book will utilize line numbers when discussing, displaying, and printing code.

In Visual Basic .NET, the code window includes a built-in technology called Intellisense to help you write code. **Intellisense™** anticipates your needs during coding and displays prompts to assist you in coding. As you type in the code window, Intellisense assists you by helping to complete words as you type, displaying appropriate list boxes from which you can select events, properties, or methods, and highlighting typographical or syntax errors in your code. A **syntax error** is an error caused by code statements that violate one of the structure or syntax rules of the Visual Basic .NET language. For example, the assignment statement requires an object or property on the left of the equal sign and a valid object or property value on the right side of the equal sign. If you do not include one of the required elements on either side of the equal sign, then you have created code with a syntax error.

As you write code in the code window, using proper spacing and indenting code will make the code more readable. The TAB key often is used to align code properly. Using blank spaces is also acceptable, but more cumbersome to enter. Companies or programming teams usually maintain their own set of coding standards that instruct programmers how code should be indented or aligned in the code window. In this book, the TAB key is used to indent code.

The following steps turn on the display of line numbers and insert the comment header and the code for the btnCompute_Click event procedure.

To Show Line Numbers and Write Code for a Comment Header and the btnCompute_Click Event Procedure

1. Click Tools on the menu bar and then click Options. When the Options dialog box displays, click the Text Editor folder in the Options list.

2. If necessary, click the Basic folder below the Text Editor folder in the Options list. When the Basic options display, click Line numbers in the Display area.

The Options dialog box displays. The Text Editor folder and Basic subfolder are open in the Options list, and the Line numbers check box is selected in the Display area (Figure 3-61). The Options list consists of categories of options for working in the Visual Basic .NET IDE. The Basic options on the right side of the dialog box include the Line numbers check box that turns on line numbers.

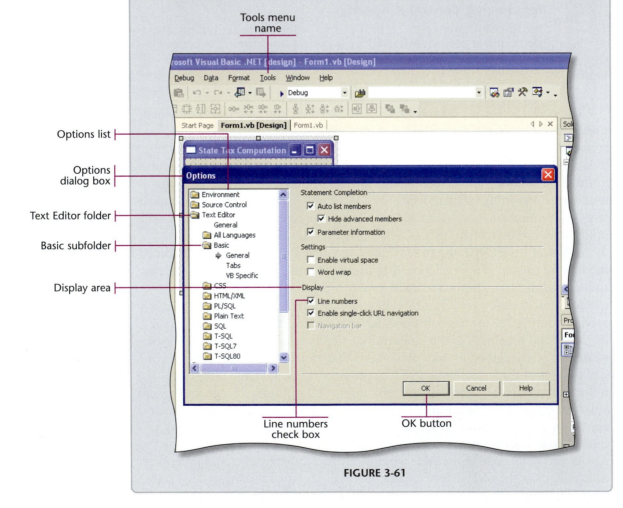

FIGURE 3-61

3. Click the OK button.

4. Double-click the Compute Tax button on the Form1 form in the main work area.

The code window opens in the main work area (Figure 3-62). The name of the current form, Form1, displays in the Object box in the Code window. The Click event is the default event for Button controls, so Visual Basic .NET automatically creates a Click event procedure when you double-click the button on the form. The event procedure name displays in the Procedure box. Visual Basic .NET inserts two lines of code for the Click event procedure, lines 137 and 139, as well as other code that is collapsed in the code region at line 4. The insertion point is placed inside the btnCompute_Click event procedure. Line numbers display on the left side of the code window.

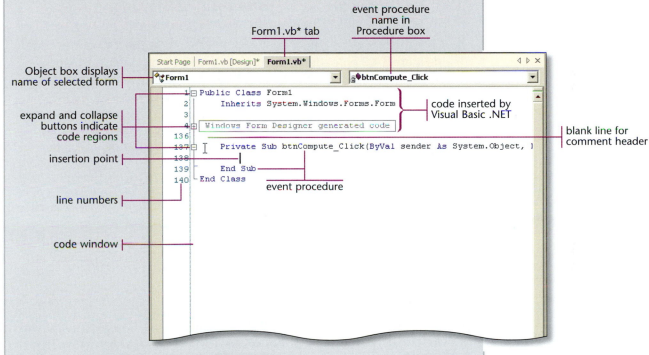

event procedure
name in
Procedure box

Form1.vb* tab

Object box displays
name of selected form

expand and collapse
buttons indicate
code regions

insertion point

line numbers

code window

code inserted by
Visual Basic .NET

blank line for
comment header

event procedure

FIGURE 3-62

5. Click the left side of the blank line above the word, Private, on line 137. Type the five comment header lines exactly as illustrated in Figure 3-59 on page VB 3.60. Do not type the line numbers. You can insert your own name as the programmer. Press the TAB key at the start of each line to indent each line of code properly as shown in the table. Press the TAB key after typing each colon to indent the text as illustrated in Figure 3-59. You may need to press the TAB key more than once after typing each colon to create the correct indentation. Press the ENTER key after each of the first four lines. Do not press the ENTER key after the last line.

When you click above the word, Private, the Procedure box changes to display Declarations. The code window displays the comment header for the State Tax Computation application (Figure 3-63 on the next page).

(continued)

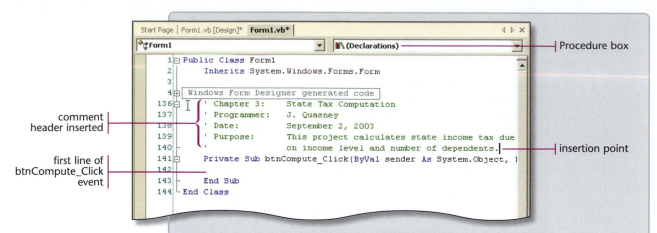

FIGURE 3-63

6. Click the blank line below the word, Private. Type line 142 of the code in Figure 3-60 on page VB 3.61. Type the first word in line 143 in Figure 3-60, including the period. Make sure you type the code using the correct case, because Visual Basic .NET is case-sensitive.

The first line of code, a comment that explains the first section of the code, displays in the code window. When you type the period after the control name in the second line, Intellisense displays a list box of the txtTaxDue control's properties and methods (Figure 3-64).

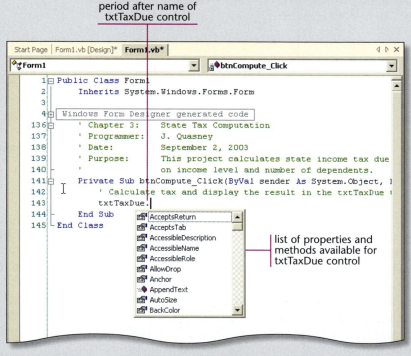

FIGURE 3-64

7. Type the letters te to select Text from the list.

As you type the letters, the list scrolls to display the Text property (Figure 3-65).

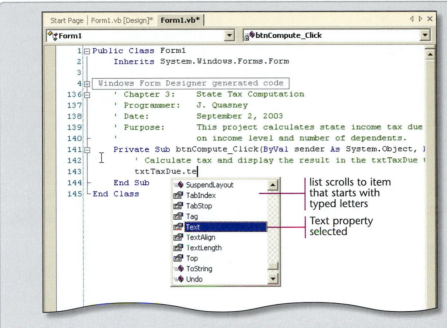

FIGURE 3-65

8. Press the TAB key.

Intellisense inserts the word, Text, in the code after the period (Figure 3-66). When working in the code window, the TAB key is used to enter a selection from the list.

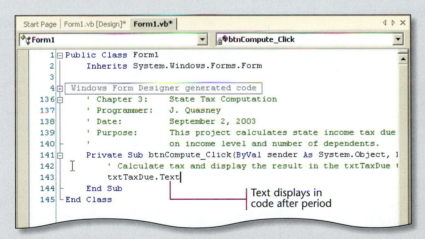

FIGURE 3-66

9. Type the remaining code in Line 143 in Figure 3-60 on page VB 3.61.

The code window scrolls horizontally as you type text that extends past the right edge of the window. The code will calculate the state income tax and then use the assignment statement to assign the result of the calculation to the Text property of the txtTaxDue TextBox control. The complete btnCompute_Click event procedure displays in the code window (Figure 3-67 on the next page).

(continued)

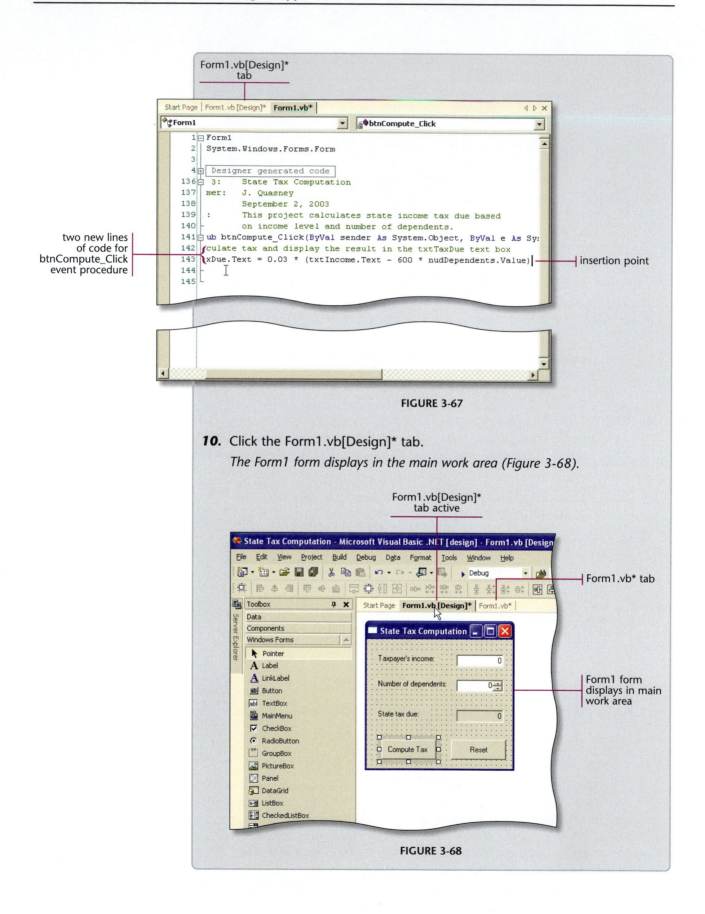

FIGURE 3-67

10. Click the Form1.vb[Design]* tab.

The Form1 form displays in the main work area (Figure 3-68).

FIGURE 3-68

The preceding steps showed how to write code for the btnCompute_Click event procedure for the btnComputeTax button. The code executes when the user clicks the Compute Tax button during run time. Steps 6 through 8 demonstrate the capabilities of the Intellisense system built into the Visual Basic .NET IDE. As shown in these steps, Intellisense assists coding by anticipating and displaying a list of properties, objects, and methods that are spelled similarly to the text you are typing.

As shown in Figure 3-62 on page VB 3.63, when the code window first opens, Visual Basic .NET places the insertion point inside the btnCompute_Click event procedure. The Click event is the default event for Button controls, so Visual Basic .NET automatically creates that event procedure when you double-click the button on the form.

Line numbers display in Figure 3-62, after the Line numbers option is set in the Options dialog box. Line numbers will continue to display and print in the code until the option is turned off. The option will remain set even after quitting and restarting Visual Basic .NET. If you are working in a computer lab, you may have to turn on the Line numbers option if it is not turned on.

As shown in the code window, an event procedure begins with the line that contains the text, Private Sub, and ends with the line that contains the text, End Sub. The line that starts with Private Sub is called the **event procedure declaration**. Because event procedures are methods for controls, the word, **Private**, indicates that this is a private method for the object. The word, **Sub**, which is short for Subroutine, indicates the beginning of a method. The next part of the event procedure declaration, btnCompute_Click, is the name of the event procedure. Finally, parameters to the event procedure are listed at the end of the event procedure declaration. Parameters are covered in more detail in Chapter 5. The line that includes the text, **End Sub**, indicates the end of the event procedure.

As indicated in the design of the application, the btnReset button must assign a value of 0 to the input and output controls in the application when clicked by a user. The btnReset_Click event procedure is assigned to the btnReset button so that it executes when the btnReset button is clicked.

As shown in Figure 3-69, the three assignment statements in lines 148 through 150 set the property values of the controls when the event procedure executes.

```
147          ' Set all input and output display values to 0
148          txtIncome.Text = "0"
149          nudDependents.Value = 0
150          txtTaxDue.Text = "0"
```

FIGURE 3-69

Line 148 sets the Text property value of the txtIncome TextBox control to the value of "0" (zero). Because Text boxes display alphanumeric characters, not numeric values, double quotation marks are used around the value to tell Visual Basic .NET to treat the 0 as a character, rather than a numeric value. Line 149 sets the Value property value of the nudDependents NumericUpDown control to 0, its minimum value. Because the Value property is a numeric property, it does not require the double quotation marks around the 0. Line 150 sets the Text property value of the txtTaxDue output TextBox control to a value of 0. Again, the 0 is in double quotation marks, meaning that Visual Basic .NET should treat the value as a character, not a numeric value.

The following steps insert the code for the btnReset_Click event procedure.

To Write Code for the btnReset_Click Event Procedure

1. Double-click the Reset button on the Form1 form in the main work area.

The code window opens in the main work area (Figure 3-70). Visual Basic .NET creates the btnReset_Click event procedure and places the insertion point inside the btnReset_Click event procedure. The event procedure name displays in the Procedure box.

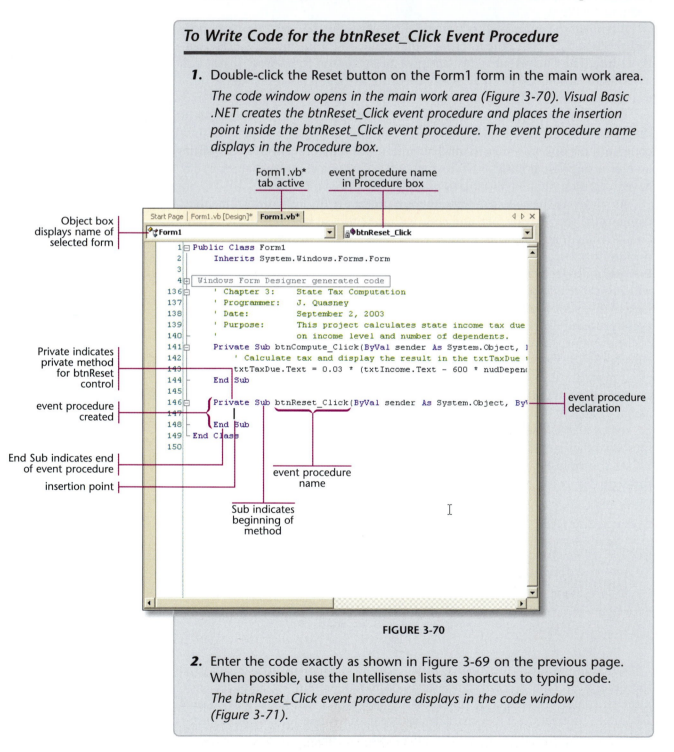

FIGURE 3-70

2. Enter the code exactly as shown in Figure 3-69 on the previous page. When possible, use the Intellisense lists as shortcuts to typing code.

The btnReset_Click event procedure displays in the code window (Figure 3-71).

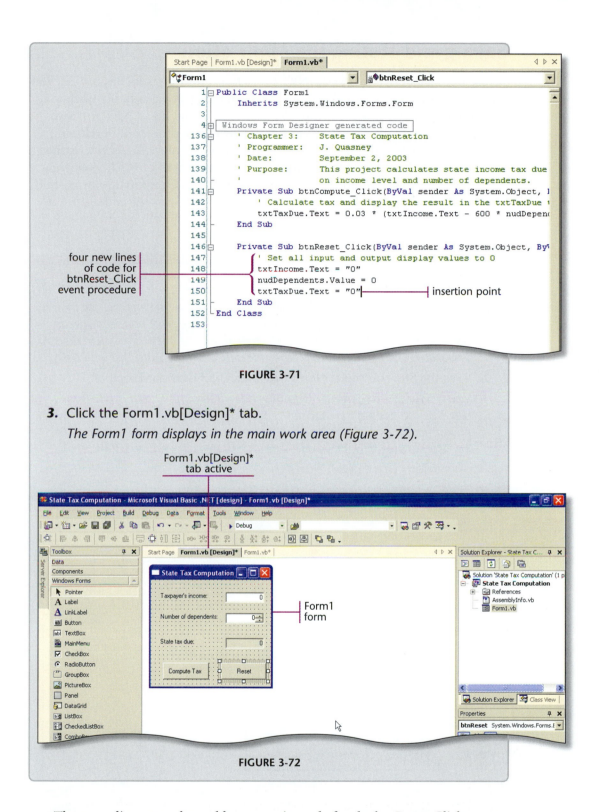

four new lines
of code for
btnReset_Click
event procedure

insertion point

FIGURE 3-71

3. Click the Form1.vb[Design]* tab.

The Form1 form displays in the main work area (Figure 3-72).

Form1.vb[Design]*
tab active

Form1
form

FIGURE 3-72

The preceding steps showed how to write code for the btnReset_Click event procedure for the btnReset button. The code for the State Tax Computation application is now complete, with code written to include comments that clarify the purpose of the project and the meaning of the code and two Click event procedures that are triggered when a user clicks either the Compute Tax or Reset button in the State Tax Computation application.

Saving and Testing the Application

Before testing a new Visual Basic .NET project or quitting Visual Basic .NET, you should save your work. You also should save your project periodically while you work on it and before you run it for the first time. Visual Basic .NET will save your project automatically when you run it. During the process of developing a project, however, you should save your work at regular intervals. As you learned in Chapter 2, a Visual Basic .NET project is saved as a set of files. The following steps to save the form and project files for the State Tax Computation project on the Data Disk in drive A and then run the application to test the code.

To Save and Test a Project

1. Click the Save All button on the Standard toolbar.

The asterisk next to Form1.vb [Design] on the window title bar and the main work area tab no longer display, indicating that the project has been saved. Because the project was created and saved initially on the Data Disk in drive A, Visual Basic .NET automatically saves the project on the Data Disk in drive A.

2. Click the Start button on the Visual Basic .NET Standard toolbar.

Visual Basic .NET opens the Output window temporarily and displays messages as the application starts. The State Tax Computation application window displays, and Visual Basic .NET sets the focus to the first text box. The application button displays on the Windows taskbar (Figure 3-73).

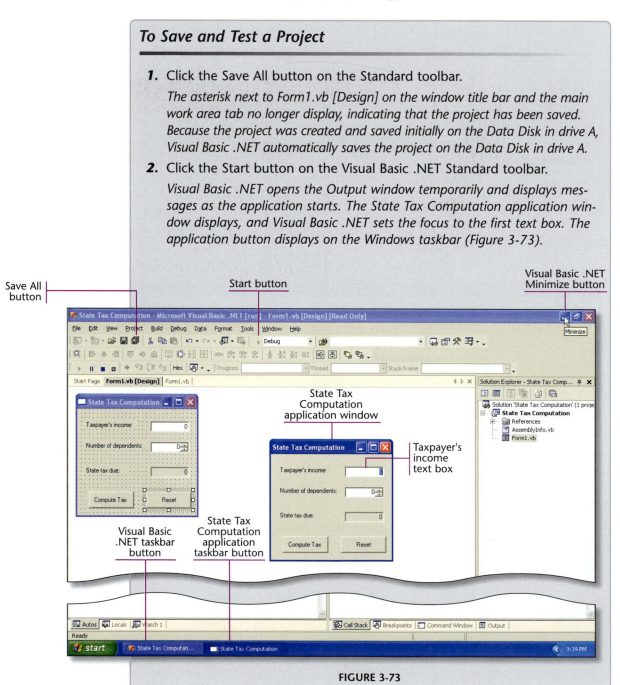

FIGURE 3-73

3. Click the Minimize button on the Visual Basic .NET title bar. Type 50000 in the Taxpayer's income text box and then point to the Number of dependents NumericUpDown box up arrow.

The Visual Basic .NET IDE is minimized. The State Tax Computation application runs in a window separate from the Visual Basic .NET application. The State Tax Computation application window displays as shown in Figure 3-74. The value, 50000, will be used as the input value for Taxpayer's income.

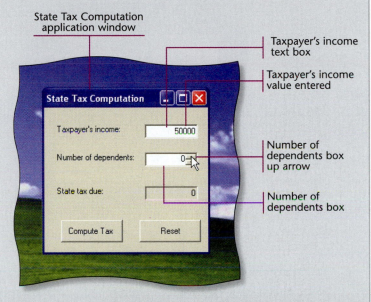

State Tax Computation
application window

Taxpayer's income
text box

Taxpayer's income
value entered

Number of
dependents box
up arrow

Number of
dependents box

FIGURE 3-74

4. Click the Number of dependents box up arrow until the number 3 displays.

The State Tax Computation application window displays as shown in Figure 3-75. The value, 3, will be used as the input value for Number of dependents.

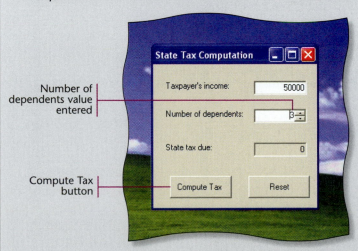

Number of
dependents value
entered

Compute Tax
button

FIGURE 3-75

(continued)

5. Click the Compute Tax button.

The State Tax Computation application calculates the State tax due based on the values input to the application. The resulting output value, 1446, displays in the State tax due text box (Figure 3-76). The result indicates that a taxpayer with a yearly income of $50,000 and 3 dependents owes a state tax of $1,446.

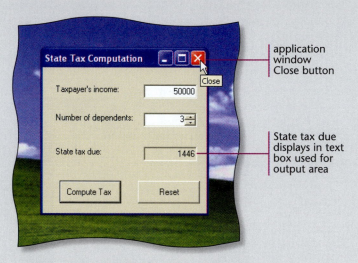

application window Close button

State tax due displays in text box used for output area

FIGURE 3-76

6. Click the Close button on the State Tax Computation application window title bar. Click the Visual Basic .NET taskbar button to display the Visual Basic .NET window.

The maximized Visual Basic .NET window displays and Visual Basic .NET returns to design time (Figure 3-77).

Visual Basic .NET returns to design time

Visual Basic .NET Close button

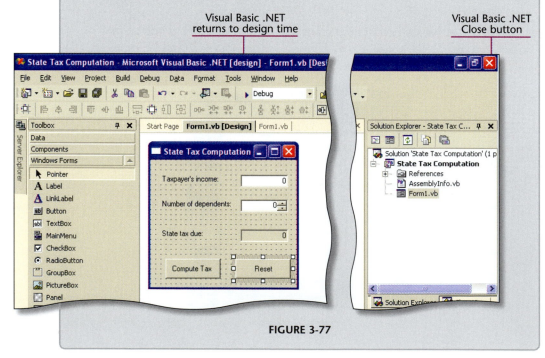

FIGURE 3-77

To test the State Tax Computation application fully, you should run the application again, trying different values for the Taxpayer's income and Number of dependents. As you enter the values and run the application, perform the calculation at the top of page VB 3.03 by hand and compare the results with the results of the program. You also should test the application by entering more than 10 dependents or a negative number for the number of dependents. If you enter more than 10 dependents or a negative number for the number of dependents, the NumericUpDown control should automatically change the value to the closest allowed value, either 0 or 10.

To test the Reset button, you should click it to test that the Reset button sets the three values in the application window to 0. Finally, you should test that you do not need to restart the application each time you want to perform another tax calculation. Instead, you should be able to click the Reset button each time you want to try another set of input values.

If your application does not run as expected, check your code and the property values set for the controls to make sure they match the specifications in this chapter. Other things to test include:

- Checking for incorrect spelling in text on Label controls
- Checking alignment and size of Label, TextBox, NumericUpDown, and Button controls
- Ensuring that the application window displays centered in the Windows environment
- Checking the application window to be sure it is not sizable
- Ensuring that tabbing using the TAB key on the keyboard properly moves the insertion point to the next control

Continue debugging the application by updating the property values and code to match the steps in this chapter until the application operates as designed.

Documenting the Application and Quitting Visual Basic .NET

The development process for the State Tax Computation application is complete. After finishing the development tasks on a project, the final step of the development cycle is to document the application. When you have completed working with Visual Basic .NET, you should quit the Visual Basic .NET system. The steps on the next page document the application and quit Visual Basic .NET. Line numbers are printed on the code listing.

To Document the Application and Quit Visual Basic .NET

1. If necessary, close the Output window. Click the Form1.vb[Design] tab, and then follow the steps on page VB 2.34 in Chapter 2 using the PRINT SCREEN key to print a record of the user interface design of the State Tax Computation form.

The State Tax Computation form is printed (Figure 3-78).

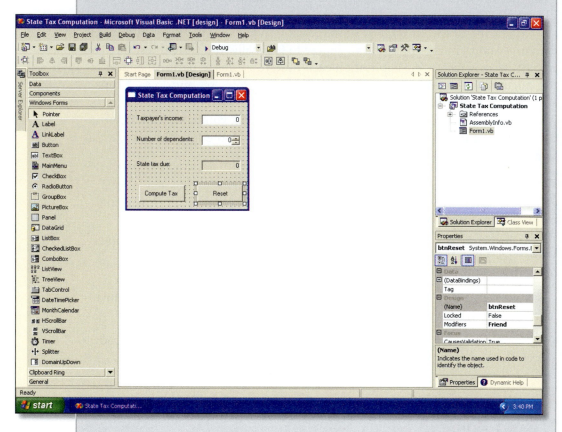

FIGURE 3-78

2. Click the Form1.vb tab. Click File on the menu bar and then click Page Setup.

3. When the Page Setup dialog box displays, click Line numbers and then click the OK button.

4. Follow the steps on page VB 2.40 in Chapter 2 using the Print command on the File menu to print a record of the code of the State Tax Computation form.

The State Tax Computation code is printed (Figure 3-79).

```
A:\Chapter3\State Tax Computation\State Tax Computation\Form1.vb                    1
 1 Public Class Form1
 2     Inherits System.Windows.Forms.Form
 3
 4  Windows Form Designer generated code
 5     ' Chapter 3:      State Tax Computation
 6     ' Programmer:     J. Quasney
 7     ' Date:           September 2, 2003
 8     ' Purpose:        This project calculates state income tax due based
 9     '                 on income level and number of dependents.
10     Private Sub btnCompute_Click(ByVal sender As System.Object, ByVal e As System.  ↵
       EventArgs) Handles btnCompute.Click
11         ' Calculate tax and display the result in the txtTaxDue text box
12         txtTaxDue.Text = 0.03 * (txtIncome.Text - 600 * nudDependents.Value)
13     End Sub
14
15     Private Sub btnReset_Click(ByVal sender As System.Object, ByVal e As System.  ↵
       EventArgs) Handles btnReset.Click
16         ' Set all input and output display values to 0
17         txtIncome.Text = "0"
18         nudDependents.Value = 0
19         txtTaxDue.Text = "0"
20     End Sub
21 End Class
```

FIGURE 3-79

5. Click the Visual Basic .NET Close button.

If you made changes to the project since the last time it was saved, Visual Basic .NET displays the Microsoft Visual Basic .NET dialog box. If you click the Yes button, you can resave your project and quit. If you click the No button, you will quit without saving changes. Clicking the Cancel button will close the dialog box.

Chapter Summary

In this chapter, you learned how to develop a Visual Basic .NET application, from the initial analysis and design of the user interface and program through development, testing, and documentation. In the process, you learned how to start a new project in Visual Basic .NET, develop a user interface on a form, and add Label, TextBox, NumericUpDown, and Button controls to a form. You learned common properties for forms and controls and learned how to change the appearance and behavior of forms and controls by setting property values for properties such as StartPosition, Text, Location, Size, TextAlign, Maximum, and Minimum. You also learned how to properly name forms and controls. You then learned how to write code for two Click event procedures and include comments to document the purpose of the code. You learned how line numbers assist programmers and how to display them in the code window. Finally, you saved and tested the application to ensure that it met the program requirements defined during the design phase.

What You Should Know

Having completed this chapter, you now should be able to perform the tasks shown in Table 3-16.

Table 3-16   Chapter 3 What You Should Know

TASK NUMBER	TASK	PAGE
1	Start a New Visual Basic .NET Project	VB 3.09
2	Change the Size of a Form	VB 3.13
3	Change the StartPosition, Title, and FormBorderStyle Property Values of a Form	VB 3.18
4	Add Label Controls to a Form by Drawing	VB 3.24
5	Add TextBox Controls to a Form by Dragging	VB 3.28
6	Add a NumericUpDown Control to a Form by Dragging	VB 3.31
7	Add Button Controls to a Form by Double-Clicking	VB 3.33
8	Move Controls on a Form	VB 3.34
9	Change the Size of Controls on a Form	VB 3.36
10	Change Properties of TextBox Controls	VB 3.42
11	Change Properties of Label Controls	VB 3.48
12	Change Properties of a NumericUpDown Control	VB 3.53
13	Change Properties of Button Controls	VB 3.54
14	Change the Name Property of Controls	VB 3.57
15	Show Line Numbers and Write Code for a Comment Header and the btnCompute_Click Event Procedure	VB 3.62
16	Write Code for the btnReset_Click Event Procedure	VB 3.68
17	Save and Test a Project	VB 3.70
18	Document the Application and Quit Visual Basic .NET	VB 3.74

Key Terms

Alphabetic button *(VB 3.15)*
assignment statement *(VB 3.58)*
Button control *(VB 3.23)*
Categorized button *(VB 3.15)*
CenterScreen *(VB 3.16)*
Click event *(VB 3.58)*
code statements *(VB 3.58)*
comment *(VB 3.59)*
comment header *(VB 3.59)*
DecimalPlaces property *(VB 3.51)*
default value *(VB 3.16)*
description pane *(VB 3.15)*
End Sub *(VB 3.67)*
events *(VB 3.58)*
event driven *(VB 3.58)*
event procedure declaration *(VB 3.62)*
event procedures *(VB 3.58)*
FixedDialog property value *(VB 3.17)*
focus *(VB 3.38)*
form *(VB 3.12)*
FormBorderStyle property *(VB 3.17)*
graphical user interface (GUI)
    (VB 3.06)
Height property *(VB 3.14)*
icon *(VB 3.06)*
Intellisense *(VB 3.61)*
internal documentation *(VB 3.59)*
intrinsic control *(VB 3.24)*
Label control *(VB 3.23)*
Large Icons button *(VB 3.12)*
Left property *(VB 3.35)*
line numbers *(VB 3.61)*
Location property *(VB 3.40)*

Maximum property *(VB 3.51)*
Minimum property *(VB 3.51)*
Name property *(VB 3.55)*
naming convention *(VB 3.56)*
NumericUpDown control *(VB 3.23)*
Object box *(VB 3.14)*
pixel *(VB 3.14)*
positioning grid *(VB 3.28)*
Private *(VB 3.67)*
Properties button *(VB 3.15)*
Properties list *(VB 3.15)*
Property Pages button *(VB 3.15)*
ReadOnly property *(VB 3.40)*
REM *(VB 3.59)*
Sizable property valve *(VB 3.17)*
Small Icons button *(VB 3.12)*
snap *(VB 3.28)*
StartPosition property *(VB 3.16)*
Sub *(VB 3.67)*
syntax error *(VB 3.61)*
tab characters *(VB 3.60)*
tabbing *(VB 3.38)*
TabIndex property *(VB 3.38)*
TabStop property *(VB 3.38)*
Text property *(VB 3.16)*
TextBox control *(VB 3.23)*
toolbar *(VB 3.15)*
Top property *(VB 3.35)*
user interface (UI) *(VB 3.06)*
Value property *(VB 3.51)*
Width property *(VB 3.14)*
WindowsDefault *(VB 3.16)*
Windows Forms tab *(VB 3.23)*

Homework Assignments

Label the Figure

Identify the elements shown in Figure 3-80.

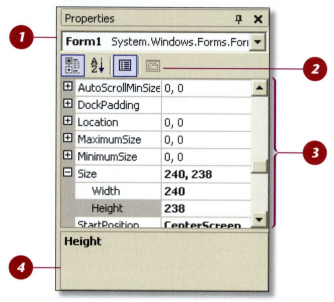

FIGURE 3-80

1. _____ 2. _____ 3. _____ 4. _____

Short Answer

1. When you create a new project, Visual Basic .NET always creates _____ form(s).

2. Briefly describe the following form properties: Text, FormBorderStyle, and Fixed Dialog.

3. A _____ control is used to display text on a form. A _____ control is frequently used as a way for the user to input information into the application. A _____ control is used during run time to initiate actions called events. By default, the _____ in the Toolbox window contains 40 intrinsic controls.

4. List the steps to delete a control from a form.

5. If you add three Label controls, three TextBox controls, and two Button controls to an empty form, what will be their default names? It is good programming practice to change the names of the controls you plan to reference in your code. Identify the property you use to change the name of a control, the window you use to change it, and the recommended prefixes for naming the following controls: TextBox; Label; NumericUpDown; and Button.

6. Assume you have a TextBox control on a form named txtVolume and you want to assign it the product of three other text boxes on the form named txtLength, txtWidth, and txtHeight. Write the assignment code statement.

7. Each comment line must begin with a(n) _____ or the letters
   _____.

8. If you want to assign the value zero (0) to a TextBox control, then write
   the zero as _____. If you want to assign the value zero (0) to a
   NumericUpDown control, then write the zero as _____.

9. Write assignment code statements for the following:
   a. Assign txtAnswer1 the value 3
   b. Assign txtAnswer2 the value of txtAnswer1 less 2
   c. Assign txtAnswer3 the product of txtAnswer1 and txtAnswer2
   d. Triple the value of txtAnswer3
   e. Assign txtAnswer4 the quotient of txtAnswer3 divided by txtAnswer2
   f. Increment txtAnswer5 by 1
   g. Decrement txtAnswer6 by 3
   h. Cube the value of txtAnswer7

Learn It Online

Start your browser and visit scsite.com/vbnet/exs. Follow the instructions in the
exercises below.

1. **Chapter Reinforcement TF, MC, and SA**   Click the True/False, Multiple
   Choice, and Short Answer link below Chapter 3. Print and then answer the
   questions.

2. **Practice Test**   Click the Practice Test link below Chapter 3. Answer each
   question, enter your first and last name at the bottom of the page, and then
   click the Grade Test button. When the graded practice test displays on your
   screen, click Print on the File menu to print a hard copy. Continue to take
   practice tests until you score 80% or better. Hand in a printout of the final
   practice test.

3. **Crossword Puzzle Challenge**   Click the Crossword Puzzle Challenge link
   below Chapter 3. Read the instructions, and then enter your first and last
   name. Click the Play button. Work the crossword puzzle. When you are finished, click the Submit button. When the crossword puzzle redisplays, click
   the Print button.

4. **Tips and Tricks**   Click the Tips and Tricks link below Chapter 3. Click a
   topic that pertains to Chapter 3. Right-click the information and then click
   Print on the shortcut menu. Construct a brief example of what the information relates to in Visual Basic .NET to confirm you understand how to use
   the tip or trick. Hand in the example and printed information.

5. **Newsgroups**   Click the Newsgroups link below Chapter 3. Click a topic that
   pertains to Chapter 3. Print three comments.

6. **Expanding Your Horizons**   Click the Articles for Visual Basic .NET below
   Chapter 3. Click a topic that pertains to Chapter 3. Print the information.
   Construct a brief example of what the information relates to in Visual Basic
   .NET to confirm you understand the contents of the article. Hand in the
   example and printed information.

7. **Search Sleuth**   Select three key terms from the Key Terms section of this
   chapter and then use the Google search engine at google.com (or any major
   search engine) to display and print two Web pages for each key term.

Debugging Assignment

Start Visual Basic .NET and open the project, Athas Construction, from the Chapter3/Athas Construction folder on the Data Disk. See the preface of this book for instructions for downloading the Data Disk or see your instructor for information about accessing the files required in this book. The Athas Construction application consists of several controls, including a TextBox control used to input Board Length, a NumericUpDown control used to input Number of boards, a second TextBox control used to display the output value for Total square feet, and three Label controls that provide descriptive labels for the TextBox and NumericUpDown controls. The application also includes two Button controls. Clicking the first Button control (Calculate) should compute the Total square feet based on the input for Board Length and Number of boards. The Total square feet is equal to the input length times the number of boards, which are one foot-wide pieces of flooring. Clicking the second Button control (Reset) should reset the values of the input and output controls to 0.

1. Fix any typographical or display problems on the form and the controls on the form. Make sure the controls line up in a visually appealing manner. Check that the TabIndex properties for the TextBox, NumericUpDown, and Button controls are logical. Check the StartPosition property value to ensure that the application will display in the center of the screen when the application starts.

2. Run the project and enter 10 for the Board Length and 5 for the Number of boards. Click the Calculate button on the lower left to check the resulting output. Note any errors in the processing and close the running application.

3. Double-click the Calculate Button control on the lower left of the form and fix any errors you found with the code. Run the project again and test the changes you just made.

4. With the application still running, click the Reset button on the lower right of the window and check its functionality. Note any errors in the processing and exit the running application.

5. Double-click the Reset Button control on the lower right of the form and fix any errors you found with this button. Insert a new line in the comment header indicating that you fixed bugs in the code.

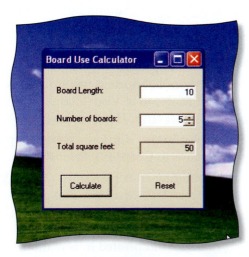

6. Run the project and enter 10 for the length and 5 for the number of boards. Click the Calculate button. The window should display as shown in Figure 3-81.

7. Print the form and all of the code for the project.

FIGURE 3-81

Programming Assignments

1 Designing a Visual Basic .NET Application

At Pacific Realty, real estate agents receive a commission rate that ranges from 1% (.01) to 7% (.07) on home sales in increments of .1% (.001), depending on the home sale price. Design an application that accepts the home sale price and a commission rate as inputs. The application should calculate and display the resulting commission and allow the user to reset the input and output values. The formula for calculating the commission is:

Commission = SalesPrice × CommissionRate

Perform the following tasks to design two solutions to the problem.

1. On paper, design a suitable user interface for the application. Be as specific as possible in naming controls and specifying their functions.

2. List all properties and property values for the form and any controls that the application requires. You need only to list those properties that must be changed from their default values.

3. On paper, write pseudocode for any events that need to be coded, based on your design in step 1.

4. Desk-check your design by testing your application on paper. Draw a three-column table with the two input values in columns 1 and 2, and the output value in column 3. Create three rows that contain various input values for the home sale price and commission rate. Test your program design by substituting the values in columns 1 and 2 into your pseudocode. Write the results in column 3. Double-check the values against the formula in the instructions to make certain the pseudocode properly solves the problem.

5. Create an alternate design to the solution, using at least one different control in the interface design. Repeat steps 1 through 4 for this alternate design.

2 Employee Payroll Calculation

You want to develop an application that computes an employee's weekly pay based on a standard salary plus overtime pay. Overtime pay is computed as 5% of weekly pay multiplied by the number of overtime hours worked.

Build an application with a user interface that resembles the one shown in Figure 3-82.

1. Design the application on paper based on the methods you learned in this chapter.

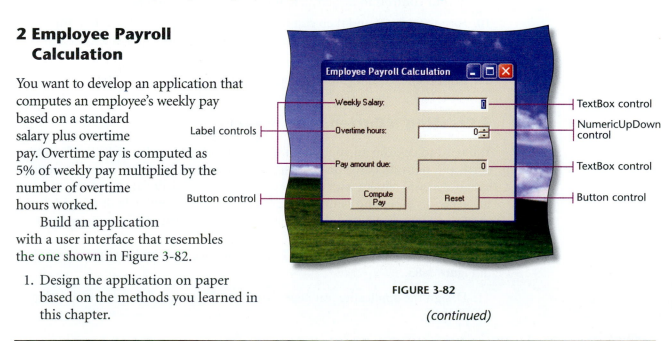

FIGURE 3-82

(continued)

2 Employee Payroll Calculation (*continued*)

2. Start a new project in Visual Basic .NET using the Windows Application template. Create the application in the Chapter3 folder of the Data Disk and name the project, Employee Payroll Calculation.

3. Add three Label controls, two TextBox controls, a NumericUpDown control, and two Button controls to the form.

4. Position, align, and size the controls appropriately, as shown in Figure 3-82 on the previous page.

5. Change the form's Text property value to Employee Payroll Calculation, the FormBorderStyle property value to FixedDialog, and the StartPosition property value to CenterScreen.

6. Change the Text property value of the Label and Button controls as follows:

Label1 control	Weekly Salary:
Label2 control	Overtime hours:
Label3 control	Pay amount due:
Button1 control	Compute Pay
Button2 control	Reset

7. Change the property values of the TextBox and NumericUpDown controls to set the initial display value to 0. Change the Name properties of the input and output controls to assign appropriate control names. Modify the TabStop, TabIndex, and ReadOnly properties, as necessary. The NumericUpDown control should have a Maximum value of 100, a Minimum value of 0, and an Increment value of 1.

8. Open the code window for the Compute Pay Button control and enter the code to make the computation. Insert appropriate comments for the project and the event procedure. The appropriate formula is PayAmount = Weekly Salary + .05 × Weekly Salary × Overtime Hours.

9. Return to the Form1.vb form and then open the code window for the Reset button control. Enter code in the event procedure that resets the input and output controls to display 0. Return to the Form1.vb form.

10. Save the project and then run the application to make certain no errors exist. If any errors are encountered, correct them, and save the form and the project again.

11. Print the form and all of the code for the project.

3 Creating a Currency Converter

You need to develop an application that can display the value of U.S. dollars in euros and pounds, based on changing currency exchange rates. Create an application that will allow a user to enter an amount in U.S. dollars and then calculate the values in euros and pounds. The exchange rates should default to the values shown in Figure 3-83, and the user should be able to vary the rates from .5 to 3 in increments of .01.

Perform the following tasks to build an application similar to the one shown in Figure 3-83.

1. Design the application on paper based on the methods you learned in this chapter.

2. Start a new Windows Application project in Visual Basic .NET. Create the application in the Chapter3 folder of the Data Disk and name the project, Currency Converter.

3. Set the title to display on the title bar of the form to Currency Converter.

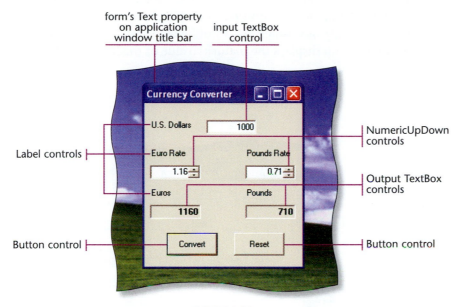

FIGURE 3-83

4. Place Label controls on the form to display the words U.S. Dollars, Euro Rate, Pounds Rate, Euros, and Pounds.

5. Set the form to be centered on the desktop when the application runs and do not allow the user to size the window during run time. (*Hint*: Use the StartPosition and FormBorderStyle properties.)

6. Add one TextBox control for input, two TextBox controls for output, and two NumericUpDown controls for input. Add two Button controls.

7. Set the Name property for all input, output, and Button controls. Set a Minimum, Maximum, and Increment for the NumericUpDown control. Set the DecimalPlaces property on the NumericUpDown controls to 2. Set defaults of 0 for the TextBox controls, 1.16 for the euro NumericUpDown control exchange rate, and .71 for the pounds NumericUpDown control exchange rate. Set the Text property of each Button control, as indicated in Figure 3-83. If necessary, set the text in the TextBox and NumericUpDown controls to display right-aligned. Modify the TabStop, TabIndex, and ReadOnly properties as necessary.

8. Write the code to display the result of calculations in the output TextBox controls. The calculation for each result is the amount in U.S. dollars multiplied by the exchange rate. Make sure the Reset button sets the exchange rates to the default, rather than 0. Be sure to add a comment header and appropriate comments to your code.

9. Save the project and then run the application to make certain no errors exist. If any errors are encountered, correct them, and save the form and the project again.

10. Print the form and all of the code for the project.

4 Maturity Calculator

You are planning to invest money and would like to know what your investment will be worth within a specified period. You have decided to develop an application similar to the one shown in Figure 3-84 that will allow entry of different amounts, different annual interest rates, and different number of years. This will aid you in determining how much you would like to invest. When a button is clicked, the application displays the maturity value of the investment based on quarterly compounding.

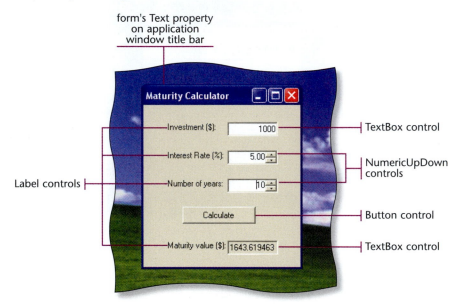

FIGURE 3-84

Perform the following tasks to build the application.

1. Design the application on paper based on the methods you learned in this chapter.

2. Open a new Windows Application project in Visual Basic .NET. Create the application in the Chapter3 folder of the Data Disk and name the project, Maturity Calculator.

3. Change the form title to Maturity Calculator. Set the form to be centered in the application window during run time and do not allow the user to size the form at run time.

4. Add four Label controls, two TextBox controls, two NumericUpDown controls, and one Button control to the form.

5. Position and size the controls as shown in Figure 3-84. Set the Text property of all the Label controls as shown in Figure 3-84.

6. Set the Text properties of the input and output TextBox controls to 0. Make the numbers appear right-justified in the boxes.

7. For the Interest Rate (%) NumericUpDown control, set the DecimalPlaces property to 2, set the range of allowed values from 3 to 8, set the increment to allow the user to increment the value by .01, and right-justify the value in the control.

8. For the Number of years NumericUpDown control, set the range of allowed values from 2 to 30, set the increment to allow the user to increment the value by 1, and right-justify the value in the control.

9. Make the Maturity value ($) output TextBox control read-only by setting its ReadOnly property to True.

10. Set TabStop and TabIndex properties appropriately for input controls and the Button control.

11. Rename the input and output controls using the following names: txtInvestment, nudInterestRate, nudYears, btnCalculate, and txtValue.

12. Write the Click event for the Button control. *Hint:* For the btnCalculate button Click event, type the following code statement:

```
txtValue.Text = txtInvestment.Text * (1 + nudInterestRate.Value / 400) ^ (4 * nudYears.Value)
```

13. Save the project and then run the application to make certain no errors exist. If any errors are encountered, correct them, and save the form and the project again.

14. Print the form and all of the code for the project.

5 Miles per Gallon Computation

The supervisor of Maria's Limousine maintenance department has asked you to develop an application to help prevent maintenance problems. At the end of each shift, drivers submit mileage and the amount of gas used for the day's trips. The supervisor would like you to develop an application that will take this information and compute the miles per gallon for the limousine for the shift. She can then take the information and compare it with historical values to see if the data is within an acceptable range.

6 Sales Tax Computation

Stan's Subs would like an application that calculates the sales tax for the front counter employees. The application should let the employee enter the amount of the customer's order and then calculate a 4% sales tax. When the employee clicks the Calculate button, the application should display the amount of the customer's order, the tax, and the total of the customer's order and tax added together.

7 Metric Conversion

As a part-time worker at McIntyre's Hardware store, you have been asked to use your Visual Basic .NET skills to assist with some routine calculations. Your first project is to develop an application for the Paint department to convert liters to pints and gallons. Use the knowledge gained in this chapter to develop an application to perform this calculation.

8 Calories Computation

Union Cafeteria has asked you to develop an application for determining the calorie count in an entrée. Based on the ingredients, the chef knows total number of grams of protein, fat, and carbohydrates for a recipe. There are four calories in a gram of protein, four calories in a gram of carbohydrates, and nine calories in a gram of fat. Create an application that will take the number of grams of each and then display the total calories when the user clicks a Compute Calories button.

9 Computing an Average

An instructor has asked you to develop a Visual Basic .NET application that takes four test scores and computes an average. The scores can range from 50 to 100. Use NumericUpDown controls to input the scores, and a ReadOnly TextBox control to display the result. As the value changes in the NumericUpDown control, change the average using the OnChange event of the NumericUpDown control. Use Visual Basic .NET Help for more information about the OnChange event. Include only one button for allowing scores to be reset to their default value of 100.

10 Rule-of-Thumb Calculation

Your friend is a tailor and performs rule-of-thumb calculations of various types to compute measurements of male customers. These rules are: Neck Size = 3 × (Weight / Waistline), Hat Size = (3 × Weight) / (2.125 × Waistline), and Shoe Size = 50 × (Waistline / Weight). He has asked you to create an application that will accept the required inputs, perform the various calculations, and output the results. Use the / (forward slash) to indicate arithmetic division in the code.

11 Computing Financial Ratios

As an intern at a financial services company, you have been asked to develop an application that computes several fundamental financial ratios based on readily available financial data. Ratios are the result of one financial value divided by another financial value. The equations for the required ratios are: Price earnings ratio = Market price per share / Earnings per share, Dividend payout ratio = Dividends per share / Earnings per share, and Dividend yield ratio = Dividends per share / Market price per share. The three inputs required are Market price per share, Earnings per share, and Dividends per share. Develop an application that accepts the necessary inputs, and then displays the ratios. Use the / (forward slash) to indicate arithmetic division in the code. Include a Reset button to set the values back to 0 in the window. Use at least one TextBox and at least one NumericUpDown control in the application.

4

Working with Variables, Constants, Data Types, and Expressions

Objectives

You will have
mastered the material in
this chapter when you can:

- Use the RadioButton and GroupBox
  controls
- Use the Layout toolbar to size and align controls
- Set a default button on a form
- Lock controls on a form
- Declare variables and constants
- Use variables and constants within code
- Describe Visual Basic .NET data types
- Convert between data types
- Code a form Load event procedure
- Use the Option Strict statement
- Use arithmetic expressions
- Describe the order of operator precedence in code
- Use the Pmt function
- Use the Format$ function

Introduction

Visual Basic .NET provides a variety of tools and constructs, such as controls, data types, and code structures, to help Visual Basic .NET programmers build Windows-based applications quickly and easily. This chapter concentrates on using these tools and constructs to develop the Windows application shown in Figure 4-1. The application uses two new controls: the GroupBox and the RadioButton. You will learn about the different types of variables and constants in Visual Basic .NET. You also will learn how to write code that performs mathematical operations. Finally, you will use some of the built-in functions that are supplied by Visual Basic .NET.

Chapter Four — Calculating Automobile Loan Payments

The Windows application developed in this chapter is the Automobile Loan Calculator, which calculates a customer's monthly automobile loan payment based on a loan amount, interest rate, and the term, or length, of the loan (Figure 4-1). To calculate a monthly payment, the user first enters the customer's desired loan amount in the Loan amount box. Next, the user selects an interest rate using the Current interest rate (%) box and then clicks an option button in the Years in loan area to select the term for the loan.

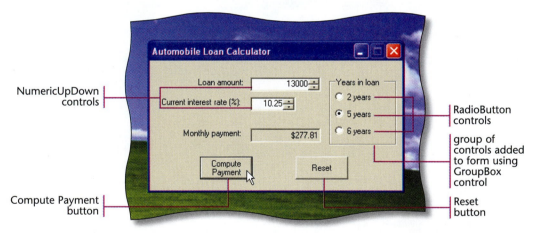

FIGURE 4-1

When the user clicks the Compute Payment button, the application first converts the user input data into values it can use in an equation. The application then computes and displays the monthly loan payment in the Monthly payment text box. The dealership currently extends loan amounts between $0 and $25,000, inclusive.

The calculation used to compute the monthly payment is represented by the following formula:

$$\text{MonthlyPayment} = (\text{InterestRate} \times (1 + \text{InterestRate}) \wedge \text{NumberofPayments}) / ((1 + \text{InterestRate}) \wedge \text{NumberofPayments} - 1) \times \text{LoanAmount}$$

where NumberofPayments is the number of months that the customer will have the loan, or 12 times the number selected in the Years in loan area. InterestRate is a monthly rate, which is determined by dividing the yearly Current interest rate by 12. The $\wedge$ symbol indicates that a number should be raised to a power using an exponent. For example, x^2 means x^2 and (1 + InterestRate) $\wedge$ NumberofPayments means $(1 + InterestRate)^{NumberofPayments}$. When the user clicks the Reset button, the Loan amount is set to 0, the Current interest rate (%) is set to 5.00, the Years in loan is set to 5 years, and the Monthly payment is set to $0.00.

Program Development

The development cycle for the Automobile Loan Calculator application consists of tasks that correspond to the six development cycle phases, as shown in Table 4-1.

Table 4-1 Automobile Loan Calculator Application Development Tasks

DEVELOPMENT PHASE	TASK NUMBER	TASK NAME	TASK
Analyze requirements	1	Analyze problem	Analyze the automobile loan calculator problem.
Design solution	2	Design interface	Design the user interface for the application, including input areas, output areas, and form controls.
	3	Design program	Design the logic for the code and write pseudocode.
Validate design	4	Validate design	Prove that the solution produces correct results for the automobile loan calculator program.
Implement design	5	Develop interface	Add user interface elements, such as input areas, output areas, and Button controls on a form.
	6	Write code	Write code to add event procedures for the buttons; add comment statements in code.
Test solution	7	Test	Test the application.
	8	Debug	Fix any problems with the application.
Document solution	9	Document	Print the program.

Analysis and Design

Figure 4-2 on the next page shows the requirements document that initiates the development cycle for the Automobile Loan Calculator application. The document shows the algorithm used to compute a monthly payment based on a loan amount, monthly interest rate, and the number of monthly payments to pay back the loan.

REQUEST FOR NEW APPLICATION

Date submitted:	September 15, 2004
Submitted by:	Steven Wang
Purpose:	Sales representatives often are asked to make quick estimates of monthly payments for customers who may take out a loan for an automobile purchase. Sales representatives would like an easy-to-use application that calculates monthly payments based on the loan amount, interest rate, and length of loan.
Application title:	Automobile Loan Calculator
Algorithms:	A monthly payment is calculated as follows: *MonthlyPayment = (InterestRate x (1 + InterestRate) ^ NumberofPayments) / ((1 + InterestRate) ^ NumberofPayments – 1) x LoanAmount* The *InterestRate* is a monthly interest rate (annual rate / 12). The *NumberofPayments* is the number of years for the loan x 12.
Notes:	1) Sales representatives are accustomed to the following terminology: ***Loan amount***, ***Current interest rate***, and ***Monthly payment.*** 2) The application should allow the user to enter values for the loan amount, current interest rate, and length of loan in years so the monthly payment can be computed. Loan amounts typically are incremented by amounts of $1000. Interest rates typically are incremented by values of .05%. 3) The general loan program only allows loans to be 2 years, 5 years, or 6 years. 4) At this time, users can obtain loans for a minimum amount of $0 and a maximum of $25,000, inclusive. This may change every few months, however. 5) The application also should allow the user to reset values for Loan amount and Monthly payment to zero (0) so that another calculation can be performed. Years in loan should be set to 5, which is the most common length of a loan. The interest rate should be reset to 5.0% because interest rates do not go below this in our general loan program. 6) The computation should be designated by the term, Compute Payment. The reset of the values should be designated by the term, Reset.

Approvals

Approval Status:	X	Approved
		Rejected
Approved by:	Lillian Bukiet	
Date:	September 17, 2004	
Assigned to:	J. Quasney, Programmer	

FIGURE 4-2

PROBLEM ANALYSIS The problem that the Automobile Loan Calculator application should solve is the calculation of a monthly payment for a customer based on the loan amount requested by the customer, the current interest rate, and the length of the loan. To complete the calculation and generate results, or output, for the user, the Automobile Loan Calculator application requires the user to input three values: Loan amount, Current interest rate, and Years in loan.

As stated in the formula of the requirements document in Figure 4-2, the application uses the following formula:

$$MonthlyPayment = (InterestRate \times (1 + InterestRate) \wedge NumberofPayments) /$$
$$((1 + InterestRate) \wedge NumberofPayments - 1) \times LoanAmount$$

to calculate the customer's monthly loan payment. The formula requires three inputs to complete one calculation and generate one output. The first input, loan amount, is represented by LoanAmount in the formula. The second input, Current interest rate, is a yearly interest rate. This input is divided by 12 to determine the monthly interest rate. The monthly interest rate is represented by InterestRate in the formula. The third input, Years in loan, is multiplied by 12 and represented by NumberofPayments in the formula. The application uses these inputs to calculate the output, monthly payment, which is represented by MonthlyPayment in the formula.

As indicated in the requirements document, the application also must provide a way to reset input and output values back to initial values, so that a user can calculate the monthly payment for another loan scenario. To reset these values, the application uses the formulas

LoanAmount = 0
Rate = 5
NumberofYears = 5
MonthlyPayment = $0.00

to tell the application to set the inputs — Loan amount (LoanAmount), Current interest rate (Rate), and Number of years (NumberofYears) and the output — Monthly payment (MonthlyPayment), back to the original values. Each element of the formula corresponds to an element in the requirements document.

INTERFACE DESIGN   The requirements for the application specify several input and output controls that should fit easily on a small form. The loan amount and interest rate inputs meet the criteria for a NumericUpDown control. As you learned in Chapter 3, a NumericUpDown control is used to display or allow users to enter numbers on a form. The up and down arrows increment and decrement the displayed value within a predefined range. If the user enters a number outside of the range, the control changes the number to the closest allowable value within the predefined range. As defined in the requirements document (Figure 4-2), the NumericUpDown control used to enter Loan amount should be set to increment or decrement by $1,000. The maximum value allowed in the NumericUpDown control — in this case, $25,000 — will be set by an event procedure that assigns a maximum value to the Maximum property of the Loan amount NumericUpDown control (Figure 4-3 on the next page). The NumericUpDown control used to enter Current interest rate will be set to increment or decrement by .05 with a minimum value of 5.00% and a maximum value of 15.00%. The output value meets the requirements for a read-only TextBox control. The output value in the TextBox control should be formatted as currency.

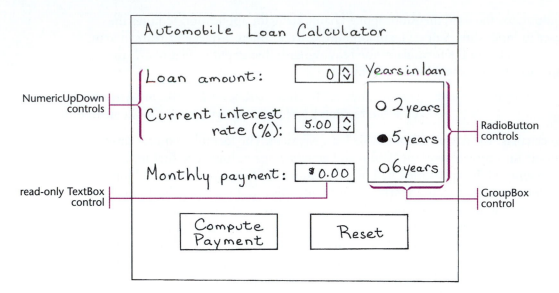

FIGURE 4-3

The application also must give users a way to select one of three options for the number of years for a loan. RadioButton controls, which are commonly called option buttons, allow a user to select one of several mutually exclusive, predefined values. The option buttons on the form are drawn with a box around them to indicate that they are grouped together. In the Automobile Loan Calculator application, three option buttons are grouped together as choices for Years in loan. To meet the specifications in the requirements document, the user can select 2 years, 5 years, or 6 years — the three types of loans allowed in the general loan program. The two actions listed in the requirements document — compute and reset — are designated by two Button controls at the bottom of the form.

PROGRAM DESIGN   The two program tasks include (1) calculating the monthly loan payment using the formula

$$\text{MonthlyPayment} = (\text{InterestRate} \times (1 + \text{InterestRate}) \wedge \text{NumberofPayments}) /$$
$$((1 + \text{InterestRate}) \wedge \text{NumberofPayments} - 1) \times \text{LoanAmount}$$

and (2) resetting the input and output values back to their original values, so the user can perform the calculation again using different input values. The user can execute these tasks by clicking the Compute Payment button or the Reset button on the user interface.

Figure 4-4 shows the pseudocode that represents the logic of the requirements. Table 4-2 outlines the event procedures defined in the pseudocode, along with the events that trigger the procedures and the actions performed by each.

Visual Basic .NET includes several built-in coding shortcuts, called functions. Some of these functions perform common financial calculations without the need to code a formula. The Visual Basic .NET Pmt function performs the same calculation shown in the pseudocode for the Compute Payment Click Event. The built-in functions remove some of the complexity of the code. They also reduce the probability of making a mistake when coding a complex formula. When the Compute Payment Click Event is coded, the Pmt function will be used to perform the calculation shown in the pseudocode.

```
Form Load Event
        LoanAmount.Maximum = MaximumLoanAllowed
End

Reset Button Click
        LoanAmount = 0
        InterestRate = 5%
        YearsInLoan = 5
        MonthlyPayment = 0
End

2-Years Click Event
        NumberOfPayments = 24
End

5-Years Click Event
        NumberOfPayments = 60
End

6-Years Click Event
        NumberOfPayments = 72
End

Compute Payment Click Event
        MonthlyPayment = (InterestRate X (1 + InterestRate) ^ NumberOfPayments) / ((1
+ InterestRate) ^ NumberOfPayments – 1) X LoanAmount
        Display MonthlyPayment
End
```

FIGURE 4-4

Table 4-2 **Automobile Loan Calculator Event Procedures**

EVENT PROCEDURE	EVENT	ACTION PERFORMED
Form Load	Form load event executes when user starts the application	Sets the maximum value allowed in the Loan amount NumericUpDown control
Reset Button Click	Click event executes when user clicks the Reset button	Resets the input and output values to original states
2-Years Click	Click event executes when user clicks the corresponding 2 years option button	Sets the NumberofPayments to 24 months (2 years, 12 months per year)
5-Years Click	Click event executes when user clicks the corresponding 5 years option button	Sets the NumberofPayments to 60 months (5 years, 12 months per year)
6-Years Click	Click event executes when user clicks the corresponding 6 years option button	Sets the NumberofPayments to 72 months (6 years, 12 months per year)
Compute Payment Click	Click event executes when user clicks the Compute Payment button	Performs the calculation in the requirements document to calculate and then display the monthly payment

VALIDATE DESIGN You can validate the program design by stepping through the requirements and making sure that the design addresses each requirement. The formula in the Algorithms section of the requirements document is handled in the design by the Computer Payment Click event (Figure 4-4 on the previous page). The items in the first note in the Notes section are shown as requested on the storyboard (Figure 4-3 on page VB 4.06). The requirements in the second and third notes also are handled on the storyboard by appropriate controls. The requirement in the fourth note is handled in the Form Load Event in the pseudocode by assigning a maximum value to the Maximum property of the Loan amount NumericUpDown control. The requirements of the fifth and sixth notes are met by the two buttons and the associated pseudocode.

As shown in Table 4-1 on page VB 4.03, after validating the program design, the next phase in the development cycle is to develop the user interface of the application using Visual Basic .NET.

Starting the Project and Creating the User Interface

The Automobile Loan Calculator application is a Windows application with a graphical user interface for user input and output display. The application is based on the Windows Application template provided by Visual Basic .NET. The following steps start Visual Basic .NET and start a new project using the Windows Application template.

To Start Visual Basic .NET and Start a New Project

1. Start Visual Basic .NET. When the Start Page displays, click the New Project button on the Start Page.

2. When the New Project dialog box displays, if necessary, click Create directory for Solution. Double-click the text, WindowsApplication1, in the Name box. Type Automobile Loan Calculator in the Name box.

   The new project name displays in the Name box, and the solution name displays in the New Solution Name box. Because the Create directory for Solution check box is selected, Visual Basic .NET will create a subdirectory with the same name as the project when it creates the project.

3. Click the Browse button. If necessary, click 3½ Floppy (A:) in the Look in box. Click Chapter4 and then click the Open button.

4. Click the OK button. After the new Automobile Loan Calculator project is created, if necessary, click the Maximize button on the Visual Basic .NET window title bar to maximize the Visual Basic .NET window. If necessary, close the Output window.

   Visual Basic .NET creates the new Automobile Loan Calculator solution and project. Visual Basic .NET creates an initial form and displays it in the main work area.

After Visual Basic .NET creates the new project, the solution and project name, Automobile Loan Calculator, display in the Solution Explorer window. Form1.vb is selected in the Solution Explorer window to indicate that the Form1.vb tab is selected in the main work area. The Properties window displays information about Form1.vb.

Setting Form Properties and Adding Controls

The next step is to set the properties of the Form1 form and add controls to the form to create the user interface. Several of the property values of the Form1 form must be changed. Table 4-3 lists the Form1 form property value changes that need to be made.

Table 4-3   Form1 Form Property Values for the Automobile Loan Calculator Application

PROPERTY	VALUE	EFFECT
Size: Width	360	Sets the width of the form in pixels
Size: Height	216	Sets the height of the form in pixels
FormBorderStyle	FixedDialog	Disallows resizing of the window at run time
StartPosition	CenterScreen	Causes the form to display in the center of the user's screen at the start of run time
MaximizeBox	False	Disables the Maximize button on the window's title bar at run time
Text	Automobile Loan Calculator	Sets the value of the window on the title bar

The user interface design also specifies that the Form1 form should include the following controls: three Label controls, two NumericUpDown controls, one TextBox control, two Button controls, a GroupBox control, and three RadioButton controls. Perform the steps on the next page to add the Label, NumericUpDown, TextBox, and Button controls by drawing them on the form.

To Set Form Properties and Add Controls

1. Select Form1 in the main work area. Set the properties of Form1 as specified in Table 4-3 on the previous page.

The form displays as shown in Figure 4-5. The Maximize button on the form title bar is inactive. The form is properly sized and the form title is set.

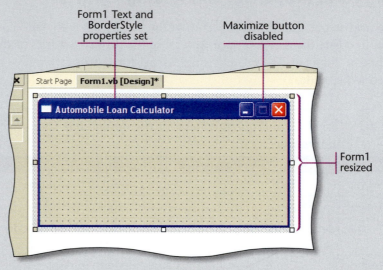

FIGURE 4-5

2. Add three Label controls, two NumericUpDown controls, one TextBox control, and two Button controls by selecting the appropriate control in the Toolbox window and drawing the control on Form1, as shown in Figure 4-6. These controls will be positioned precisely later in this chapter.

Three Label controls, two NumericUpDown controls, one TextBox control, and two Button controls display on the form (Figure 4-6).

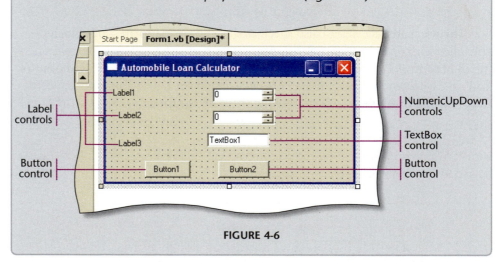

FIGURE 4-6

Adding a GroupBox Control to a Form

A **GroupBox control** is used as a container for other controls, as shown in Figure 4-1 on page VB 4.02. A **container control** serves as a holding area for other controls, indicating that the controls within the container are somehow related. In this application, the GroupBox control will serve as a container control for the three RadioButton controls.

When you draw the GroupBox control, the center of the GroupBox control displays with a positioning grid inside of it on the form so you can draw and position other controls inside the GroupBox control.

To Add a GroupBox Control to a Form

1. Add the GroupBox control by clicking the GroupBox button in the Toolbox window and drawing the GroupBox1 control on Form1, as shown in Figure 4-7.

The GroupBox1 control contains a positioning grid and has a thin border to indicate its size and location. The control name, GroupBox1, displays on top of the control (Figure 4-7).

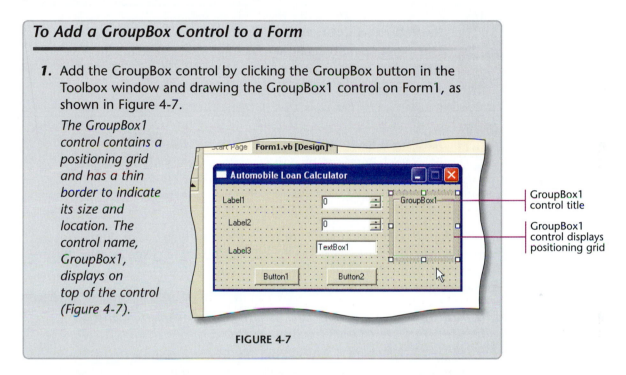

FIGURE 4-7

As shown in Figure 4-7, the default GroupBox control name, GroupBox1, displays on top of the control. You can change the control name by changing the value of the Text property to indicate the function of the controls it contains. The center of the GroupBox control contains a positioning grid so other controls can be drawn and positioned inside the GroupBox control. In the case of the GroupBox1 control, the RadioButton controls that indicate the length of the loan in years will be drawn and positioned inside the control (Figure 4-1 on page VB 4.02). When you add controls by drawing them inside a GroupBox control, dragging the GroupBox control to a new position also repositions the controls contained inside the GroupBox control.

> **Tip**
>
> **Using Container Controls**
> Container controls are used to serve as a holding area for other controls, indicating that the controls within the container are related.

Adding RadioButton Controls to Create a Group of Controls

The **RadioButton control** presents a set of choices, such as the number of years in a loan (Figure 4-1 on page VB 4.02). RadioButton controls are placed in **groups** that permit the user to make only one selection from a group of RadioButton controls, such as the number of years. For a RadioButton to be part of a group, it must be added directly inside the GroupBox control that serves as a container.

RadioButton Control

Use the RadioButton control to present a set of choices from which a user is permitted to make only one selection.

Adding a RadioButton Control to a Group

For a RadioButton to be part of a group, you must add it directly inside the GroupBox control that serves as a container.

The Automobile Loan Calculator offers three options for the number of years in a loan (2, 5, or 6). Perform the following steps to create a group of three RadioButton controls within the GroupBox1 control.

To Add RadioButton Controls to Create a Group of Controls

1. Drag the RadioButton button from the Toolbox window to the top of the GroupBox1 control. Be sure to release the mouse button while the mouse pointer is positioned within the borders of the GroupBox1 control.

A RadioButton control is added inside the GroupBox1 control (Figure 4-8).

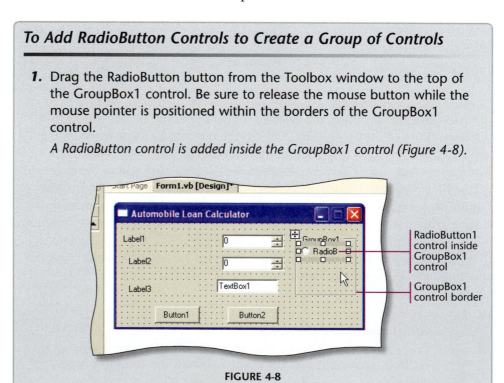

FIGURE 4-8

2. Repeat Step 1 two more times to place two more RadioButton controls inside the GroupBox1 control. Position the controls as shown in Figure 4-9.

The three RadioButton controls form a group of controls inside the GroupBox1 control (Figure 4-9).

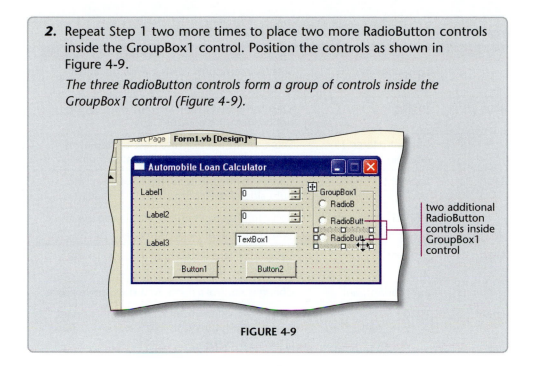

two additional RadioButton controls inside GroupBox1 control

FIGURE 4-9

The RadioButton controls were added to the form inside the GroupBox control in order to form a RadioButton group. When several RadioButton controls display in a group, only one of the RadioButton controls can be checked at any time. You do not need to write code to enforce this rule. The controls automatically enforce this rule. You can create multiple groups of RadioButton controls by adding additional container controls to the form for each RadioButton group. If the RadioButton controls on a form are not placed inside one or more container controls, all of the RadioButton controls function as one group and only one can be selected at a time.

Changing Control Properties

Several of the items listed in the requirements document for the Automobile Loan Calculator application (Figure 4-2 on page VB 4.04) require you to change the default property values for the controls. Table 4-4 on the next page lists property values for the Label, NumericUpDown, TextBox, and Button controls that must be set to meet these requirements.

Table 4-4 Control Property Values for the Automobile Loan Calculator Application

CONTROL	PROPERTY	VALUE	EFFECT
Label1	Text	Loan amount:	Sets Loan amount: to display as the initial value in the control at run time
	TextAlign	TopRight	Causes the text in the label to align to the right side of the control
Label2	Text	Current interest rate (%):	Sets Current interest rate (%): to display as the initial value in the control at run time
	TextAlign	TopRight	Causes the text in the label to align to the right side of the control
Label3	Text	Monthly payment:	Sets Monthly payment: to display as the initial value in the control at run time
	TextAlign	TopRight	Causes the text in the label to align to the right side of the control
NumericUpDown1	Name	nudLoanAmount	Changes control's name to a descriptive name
	Increment	1000	Causes the value in the control to increment or decrement by 1,000 when the up or down arrows are clicked
	TabIndex	0	Causes this control to be the first control on the form to receive focus
	TextAlign	Right	Sets text to display right-aligned in the control
NumericUpDown2	Name	nudRate	Changes control's name to a descriptive name
	DecimalPlaces	2	Sets the number of decimal places of the value to display in the control
	Increment	.05	Causes the value in the control to increment or decrement by .05 when the up or down arrows are clicked
	Maximum	15	Defines the highest value allowed in the control
	Minimum	5	Defines the lowest value allowed in the control
	TabIndex	1	Causes this control to be the second control on the form to receive focus
	TextAlign	Right	Sets text to display right-aligned in the control
	Value	5	Sets 5 to display as the initial value in the control at run time
TextBox1	Name	txtMonthlyPayment	Changes control's name to a descriptive name
	ReadOnly	True	Disallows the user from entering a value in the control at run time
	Text	$0.00	Sets $0.00 to display as the initial value in the control at run time
	TextAlign	Right	Sets text to display right-aligned in the control
Button1	Text	Compute Payment	Sets the text that displays on the button face to Compute Payment
	TabIndex	3	Causes this control to be the fourth control on the form to receive focus

Table 4-4 Control Property Values for the Automobile Loan Calculator Application *(continued)*

CONTROL	PROPERTY	VALUE	EFFECT
	Name	btnComputePayment	Changes control's name to a descriptive name
Button2	Text	Reset	Sets the text that displays on the button face to Reset
	TabIndex	4	Causes this control to be the fifth control on the form to receive focus
	Name	btnReset	Changes control's name to a descriptive name

The following step sets the property values of the Label controls, NumericUpDown controls, TextBox control, and Button controls on the Form1 form. Size and Position properties will be set later in this chapter.

To Change Properties of Controls

1. Change the property values of the three Label controls, two NumericUpDown controls, one TextBox control, and two Button controls, as listed in Table 4-4.

The controls display on Form1 as shown in Figure 4-10.

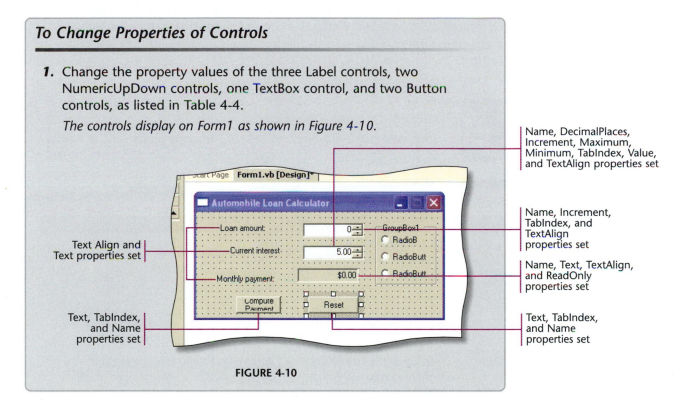

Name, DecimalPlaces, Increment, Maximum, Minimum, TabIndex, Value, and TextAlign properties set

Name, Increment, TabIndex, and TextAlign properties set

Name, Text, TextAlign, and ReadOnly properties set

Text Align and Text properties set

Text, TabIndex, and Name properties set

Text, TabIndex, and Name properties set

FIGURE 4-10

Recall that the NumericUpDown control allows the user to change the value displayed in the control by clicking the arrows or typing a value in the control. With the Increment property value for the nudLoanAmount control to 1000, the application will only allow a user to enter a Loan amount in increments of $1,000 dollars, by clicking the up and down arrows or typing a value. The DecimalPlaces and Value property values set for the nudRate control ensure that the Current interest rate (%) displays to the user with two decimal places and an initial value of 5.00. The values set for the Increment, Maximum, and Minimum properties only allow a user to input a Current interest rate (%) in increments of .05%, with a minimum value of 5.00% and a maximum value of 15.00%.

NumericUpDown Control
Use the NumericUpDown control to allow the user to enter numbers on a form by clicking the up and down arrows or by typing.

GroupBox Control Properties

The GroupBox control is used as a container for other controls. The GroupBox control has several properties that relate to its appearance.

- A GroupBox control can have only a rectangular shape.
- A GroupBox control can have a label, indicated by its Text property value.
- When RadioButton controls are added inside a GroupBox control, only one can be selected during run time.

In general, you do not name GroupBox controls because they seldom are referenced in code. If you do name a GroupBox control, however, use the grp prefix in the name. Table 4-5 lists the common properties of the GroupBox control.

Naming GroupBox Controls
When naming GroupBox controls, use the grp prefix for the name.

Table 4-5   GroupBox Control Properties

CATEGORY	PROPERTY	DESCRIPTION	PROPERTY VALUES
Appearance	FlatStyle	Determines the 3D appearance of the control	Flat Popup **Standard** System
	Text	Indicates the label to display on the upper-left edge of the control	Any value, or set blank if no label is desired.
Design	GridSize: Width and Gridsize: Height	Determines the size of the positioning grid within the control	Width and Height properties can be any positive whole number (**8, 8**).

Table 4-6 lists the two GroupBox control property values — Text and TabIndex — that must be changed for the Automobile Loan Calculator application.

Table 4-6 GroupBox Control Property Values for the Automobile Loan Calculator Application

CONTROL	PROPERTY	VALUE	EFFECT
GroupBox1	Text	Years in loan	Sets the caption of the control on the top-left side of the control
	TabIndex	2	Causes the first RadioButton in the GroupBox to be the third control on the form to receive focus

The following steps set the property values for the GroupBox control, as listed in Table 4-6.

To Change the Properties of a GroupBox Control

1. Click inside the GroupBox1 control, but not on one of the RadioButton controls in the GroupBox1 control. If the RadioButton controls obscure the inside of the GroupBox1 control, click the border of the GroupBox1 control to select it.

The GroupBox1 control is selected (Figure 4-11).

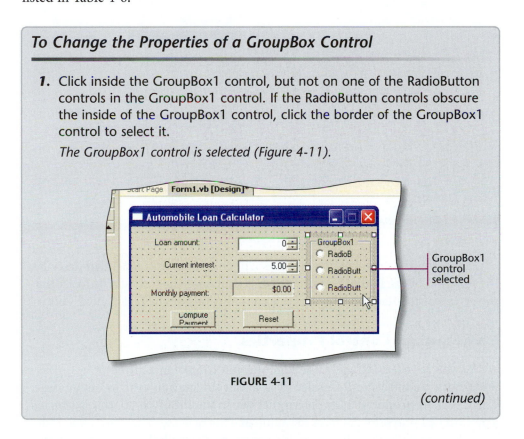

FIGURE 4-11

(continued)

2. Change the property values for the GroupBox1 control, as listed in Table 4-6.

The Text property of the GroupBox1 controls displays on top of the GroupBox1 control (Figure 4-12).

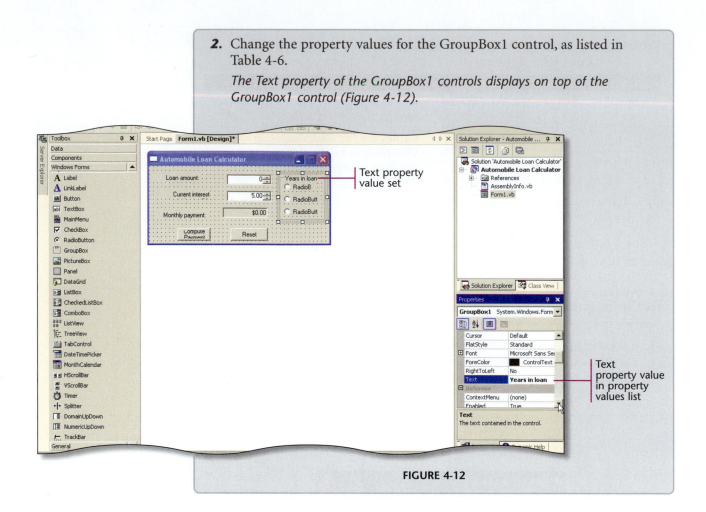

Text property value set

Text property value in property values list

FIGURE 4-12

The GroupBox control now displays with a Years in loan label that describes the function of the RadioButton controls it contains. The next step is to set the properties of the RadioButton controls contained inside the GroupBox1 control.

RadioButton Control Properties

As you have learned, only one RadioButton control in a group of RadioButton controls may be selected at a time during run time or design time. The **Checked property** value determines which RadioButton control is selected. The Checked property can have the value of True or False. The True value indicates that the RadioButton control is selected, or checked; the False value indicates that the RadioButton control is not selected. The RadioButton control also has a property, CheckAlign, whose value defines on which side of the control the option button displays. When naming a RadioButton control using the Name property value, use the rad prefix in the name to indicate a RadioButton control. Table 4-7 lists the common RadioButton control properties.

Naming RadioButton Controls
When naming RadioButton controls, use the rad prefix for the name.

Table 4-7 RadioButton Control Properties

CATEGORY	PROPERTY	DESCRIPTION	PROPERTY VALUES
Appearance	CheckAlign	Determines the location of the check box inside the control	Select a location from a pop-up graphical display map. **(MiddleLeft)**
	Checked	Determines whether the RadioButton is selected (checked) or not	True **False**
	FlatStyle	Determines the 3D appearance of the control	Flat Popup **Standard** System
	Image	Sets an image to display on the visible portion of the Label control, along with the Text	Select a picture from the hard disk using a dialog box.
	ImageAlign	If the Image property is set, determines where the image displays	Select a location from a pop-up graphical display map. **(MiddleCenter)**
	Text	Defines the visible text that displays on the control	Any text with any character length.
Behavior	AutoCheck	Causes the RadioButton to change state automatically (value of Checked property) when clicked	**True** False

The requirements for the Automobile Loan Calculator application require that the Text property values for the three RadioButton controls are 2 years, 5 years, and 6 years, respectively (Table 4-8). The requirements document also specifies that 5 years is the default number of years for a loan, which means the RadioButton2 control (5 years) should be set to display initially as checked during run time.

Table 4-8 RadioButton Control Property Values for the Automobile Loan Calculator Application

CONTROL	PROPERTY	VALUE	EFFECT
RadioButton1	Name	radTwoYears	Changes control's name to a descriptive name
	TabIndex	0	Causes focus on this control first when the GroupBox1 control receives focus
	Text	2 years	Sets the value of the label next to the check box
RadioButton2	Name	radFiveYears	Changes control's name to a descriptive name
	TabIndex	1	Second control to receive focus after the TAB key is pressed in the GroupBox1 control
	Text	5 years	Sets the value of the label next to the check box
RadioButton3	Name	radSixYears	Changes control's name to a descriptive name
	TabIndex	2	Third control to receive focus after the TAB key is pressed in the GroupBox1 control
	Text	6 years	Sets the value of the label next to the check box

The following steps set the property values for the three RadioButton controls, as listed in Table 4-8 on the previous page.

To Change the Properties of RadioButton Controls

1. Select the RadioButton1 control. Change the property values for the RadioButton1 control, as listed in Table 4-8.

The Name, TabIndex, and Text property values of the control are set. The Text property, 2 years, displays in the control. The new name of the control is radTwoYears (Figure 4-13).

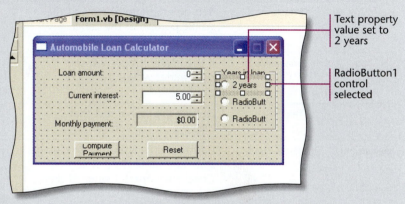

FIGURE 4-13

2. Select the RadioButton2 control. Change the property values for the RadioButton2 control, as listed in Table 4-8. Select the Checked property in the Properties window and then click the Checked property down arrow in the property values list.

The Name, TabIndex, and Text property values of the control are set. The Text property, 5 years, displays in the control. The new name of the control is radFiveYears. The Checked property is selected in the Properties window and the two possible Checked property values, True and False, display in the property values list (Figure 4-14).

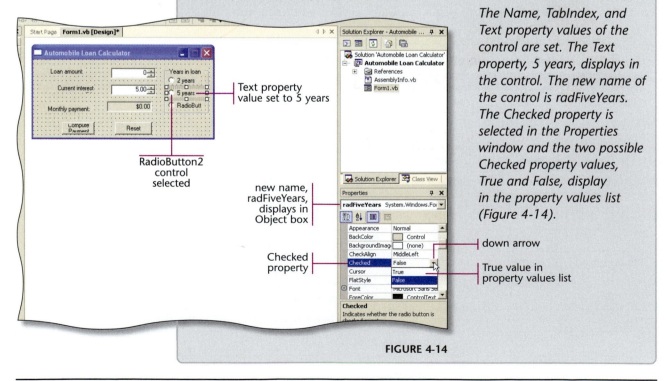

FIGURE 4-14

3. Click True in the Checked property values list.

The Checked property value is set to True, which sets the radFiveYears control to display as selected at run time (Figure 4-15). The filled circle in the radFiveYears control indicates that the control is selected.

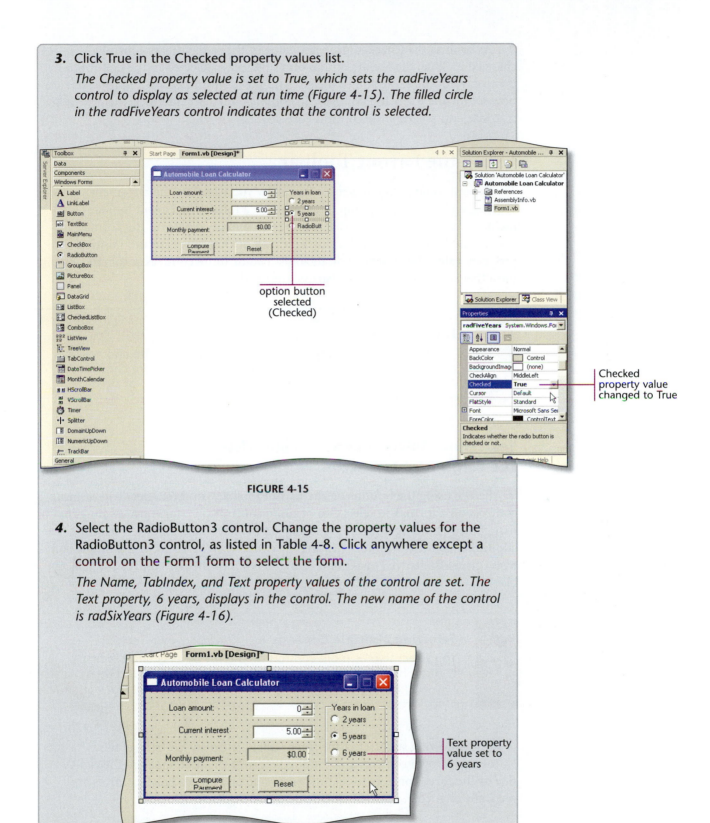

FIGURE 4-15

4. Select the RadioButton3 control. Change the property values for the RadioButton3 control, as listed in Table 4-8. Click anywhere except a control on the Form1 form to select the form.

The Name, TabIndex, and Text property values of the control are set. The Text property, 6 years, displays in the control. The new name of the control is radSixYears (Figure 4-16).

FIGURE 4-16

As soon as the Checked property value of the radFiveYears control is changed to True, the 5 years option button displays selected in the GroupBox1 control. With the exception of the size and position properties, all properties are now set for the form and controls. To complete the user interface, the next step is to size and position the controls correctly.

Using the Layout Toolbar

The Layout toolbar contains tools that allow you to adjust the alignment, spacing, and size of any group of controls on a form. The Layout toolbar includes buttons that map to all of the commands available on the Format menu. The Layout toolbar simplifies the task of changing Size and Position property values by allowing you to adjust two or more controls automatically until they are properly aligned, spaced, or sized.

Layout Toolbar

The Layout toolbar simplifies the task of changing Size and Position property values by allowing you to adjust two or more controls automatically until they are properly aligned, spaced, or sized.

Selecting Multiple Controls and Using the Align Rights Button

Before using the buttons on the Layout toolbar, you first select two or more controls on a form. You select two or more controls on a form by selecting the first control, holding down the CTRL key on the keyboard, and then selecting additional controls without releasing the CTRL key. When selecting multiple controls, Visual Basic .NET makes the sizing handles of the last control you select black.

Selecting Multiple Controls

You select two or more controls on a form by selecting the first control, holding down the CTRL key on the keyboard, and then selecting additional controls without releasing the CTRL key.

The following steps select the three Label controls used to label the NumericUpDown controls and the TextBox control and then align the right side of the three controls so that the right side of all three Label controls are vertically aligned.

To Select Multiple Controls and Use the Align Rights Button

1. Select the Label2 control, which has the Text property value of Current interest rate (%):.

The Label2 control is selected (Figure 4-17).

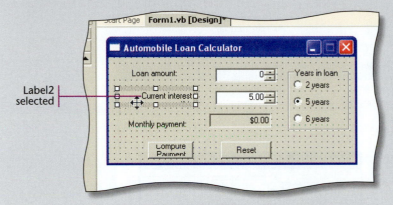

Label2 selected

FIGURE 4-17

2. Use the middle sizing handle on the left or right side of the Label2 control to size the control so that the text within the control displays on a single line. With the Label2 control selected, press and hold down the CTRL key, and then click the Label1 (Loan amount:) and Label3 (Monthly payment:) controls.

As the Label1 and Label3 controls are selected, sizing handles display around the selected controls (Figure 4-18).

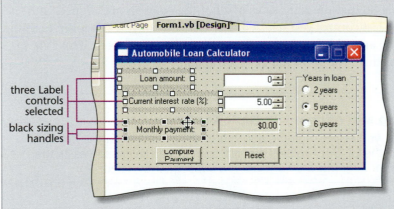

three Label controls selected

black sizing handles

FIGURE 4-18

(continued)

3. Click the Align Rights button on the Layout toolbar and then click the Make Vertical Spacing Equal button on the Layout toolbar. If necessary, click one of the controls and move all of the controls together to align them as shown in Figure 4-19.

The right borders of the three Label controls are aligned (Figure 4-19). The controls are set to have equal vertical spacing.

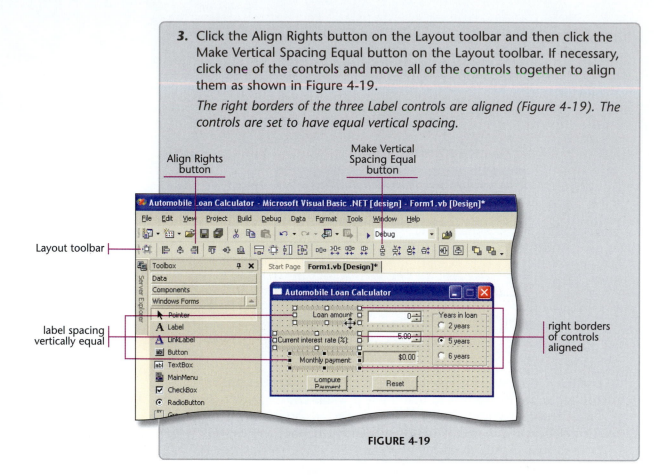

FIGURE 4-19

Clicking the Align Rights button changes the Position: Left property of the selected controls, so that the right sides of all of the controls are aligned with the right side of the last control you selected. The last control you select serves as the basis for aligning any additional controls you had already selected. This rule applies for all of the buttons on the Layout toolbar.

Sizing and Aligning Multiple Controls

When you select multiple controls and size and align the controls using the Layout toolbar, the last control you select serves as the basis for aligning the controls you subsequently select.

Sizing and Aligning Controls

When multiple controls used for input or output display in a column, it is good practice to size and align the controls together. You can use the Make Same Size button and Align Lefts button in conjunction to perform this task quickly. The following step sizes and aligns the input and output controls in the center of the form.

To Size and Align Input and Output Controls

1. Select the nudLoanAmount, nudRate, and txtMonthlyPayment controls by selecting one of the controls, holding down the CTRL key, and then selecting the other controls one at a time. Select the control which is best sized and positioned last, so that the other controls are sized and positioned based on that control. Click the Make Same Size button on the Layout toolbar and then click the Align Lefts button on the Layout toolbar. If the controls do not display as shown in Figure 4-20, then change the Height and Width property values in the property values list to 20 and 100, respectively, while the three controls are still selected.

The input and output controls are properly sized and aligned (Figure 4-20).

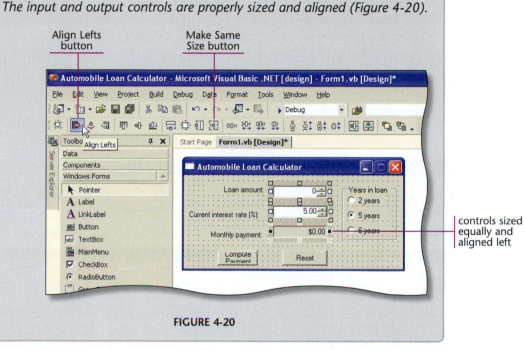

FIGURE 4-20

As you have learned, the last control you select serves as the basis for sizing and aligning all of the other controls. If none of the controls is the size or alignment you want to have for all of the controls, use the sizing handles to size a control properly and then move the control to the proper alignment. Once the control has the proper size and alignment, you can select the other controls and then select the properly sized one last. You then can use the Make Same Size button to size the controls and the Align Lefts or Align Rights button to align the controls.

Sizing and Aligning Button Controls

A good user interface design often requires that Button controls are centered on a form. The step on the next page sizes and aligns the Button controls at the bottom of the Form1 form and centers both buttons together horizontally.

To Size and Align Button Controls

1. Click anywhere on the Form1 form. Select the btnComputePayment and btnReset controls by selecting one of the controls, holding down the CTRL key, and then selecting the other control. If necessary, size and position one control first, and then make certain to select this control last. Click the Make Same Size button on the Layout toolbar and then click the Align Tops button on the Layout toolbar. If the controls do not display as shown in Figure 4-21, then change the Height and Width property values in the property values list to 32 and 75, respectively, while the two controls are still selected. Click the Increase Horizontal Spacing button on the Layout toolbar several times until the buttons are separated as shown in Figure 4-21. Click the Center Horizontally button on the Layout toolbar.

The Button controls are properly sized and aligned and are centered horizontally on the form (Figure 4-21).

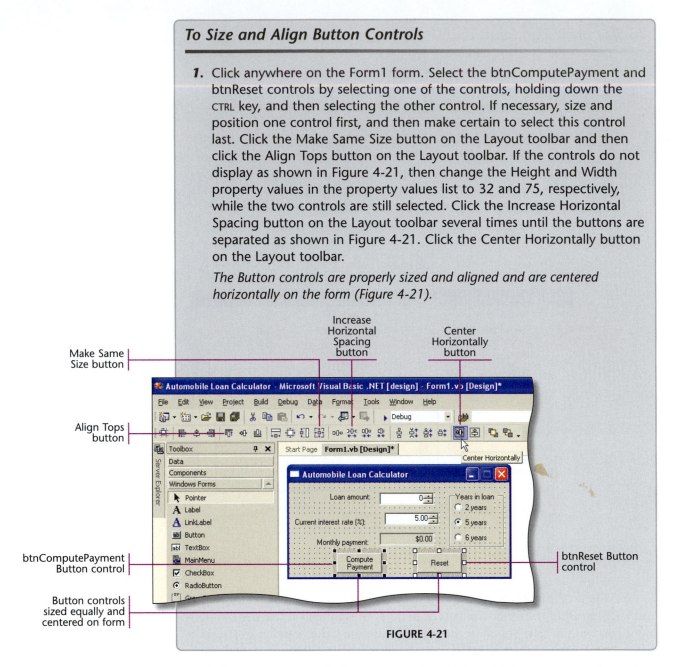

FIGURE 4-21

Each time you click the Increase Horizontal Spacing button on the Layout toolbar, Visual Basic .NET increases the horizontal spacing between the buttons. To undo this operation or decrease the spacing between the controls, click the Decrease Horizontal Spacing button. You can center a control on a form vertically or horizontally using the Center Vertically or Center Horizontally button on the Layout toolbar.

Sizing and Aligning Controls in a Group

Controls in a group, such as the RadioButton controls contained inside a GroupBox control, must be sized and aligned as a group. If you select a control that is in a group and then another control not in the same group, the buttons on the Layout toolbar have no effect on the alignment of the controls. The RadioButton controls in the GroupBox control should have their left sides aligned and should be equally spaced vertically. The following steps size and align the RadioButton controls in a group.

To Size and Align Controls in a Group

1. Select the radTwoYears, radFiveYears, and radSixYears controls by selecting one of the controls, holding down the CTRL key, and then selecting the other controls. Click the Make Same Size button on the Layout toolbar. Click the Make Vertical Spacing Equal button on the Layout toolbar. Make certain that the last control you select has been properly aligned and sized.

The RadioButton controls are sized properly and equally spaced vertically (Figure 4-22).

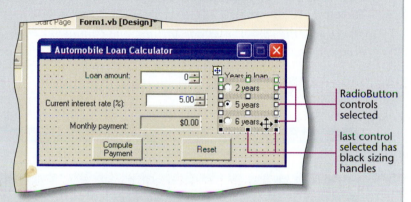

FIGURE 4-22

2. Click the Align Lefts button on the Layout toolbar. If the controls do not display as shown in Figure 4-23, then change the Height and Width property values in the property values list to 24 and 80, respectively, while all the controls are still selected.

The RadioButton controls are properly sized and aligned as shown in Figure 4-23.

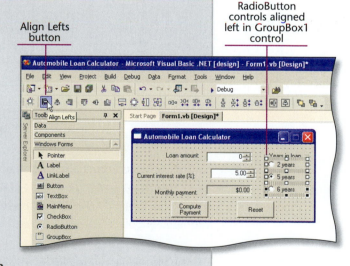

FIGURE 4-23

The Make Vertical Spacing Equal button allows you to make the space between the tops and bottoms of two or more controls the same. The Make Horizontal Spacing Equal button does the same for the left and right sides of two or more controls.

Aligning the Tops of Controls

The final step in sizing and aligning the controls is to align the tops of the controls. The following steps use the Align Tops button to align the tops of the controls, using the top of the nudLoanAmount control as the basis for alignment.

To Align the Tops of Controls

1. Select the nudLoanAmount control. With the nudLoanAmount control selected, hold down the CTRL key and then select the Label1 control and the GroupBox1 control. Click the Align Tops button on the Layout Toolbar.

The tops of the Label1, nudLoanAmount, and GroupBox1 controls are properly sized and aligned (Figure 4-24).

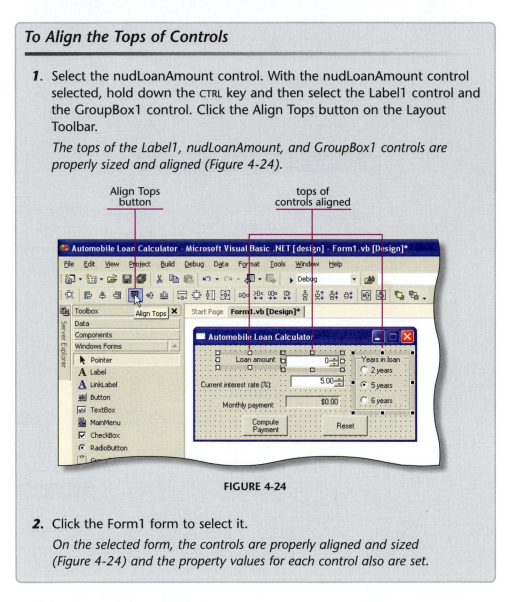

FIGURE 4-24

2. Click the Form1 form to select it.

On the selected form, the controls are properly aligned and sized (Figure 4-24) and the property values for each control also are set.

By choosing groups of controls selectively and using the functionality of the buttons on the Layout toolbar, you can size and align the controls on a form to achieve a polished and symmetrical appearance. Depending on how controls are initially added to a form, the steps to align and size the controls using the Layout toolbar can differ.

Now that the controls on the form are aligned properly, they should have the Size and Position property values shown in Table 4-9. The step below uses the Properties window to confirm that the controls use the size and position as shown in Table 4-9 to match the controls shown in Figure 4-25. The width of the nudRate control should not be the same as the other input and output controls, so you must set its width using the Properties window.

Table 4-9   Size and Position Property Values for Controls in the Automobile Loan Calculator Application

CONTROL	LOCATION: X (LEFT)	LOCATION: Y (TOP)	WIDTH	HEIGHT
Label1	40	24	100	23
Label2	8	52	136	23
Label3	40	96	100	23
nudLoanAmount	144	24	100	20
nudRate	144	52	64	20
txtMonthlyPayment	144	96	100	20
btnComputePayment	72	136	75	32
btnReset	208	136	75	32
GroupBox1	256	24	96	96
radTwoYears	8	16	80	24
radFiveYears	8	40	80	24
radSixYears	8	64	80	24

To Verify the Size and Position of Controls

1. Select each control and use the Properties window to verify that the Location: X, Location: Y, Height, and Width property values are set to the values listed in Table 4-9. Make certain to change the Width property of the nudRate control by setting the Width property in the property list.

The input and output controls are properly sized and aligned (Figure 4-25).

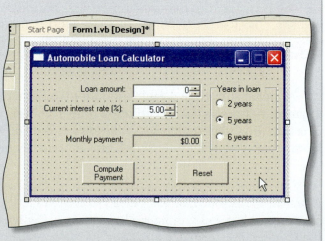

FIGURE 4-25

As shown in the previous steps, the order in which you perform some tasks when laying out a form impacts decisions you make about setting property values. For example, you should set the Text property value of a Label control before setting its Size property value, because the Size property value may need to be increased to accommodate more text.

Setting a Default Button on a Form and Locking Controls

At least two other properties and user interface design changes are best left until the bulk of the work on the form is complete and most controls are added and their properties are set. Such changes include setting the default button on a form so it is selected when a user presses the ENTER key and locking the controls on a form to ensure that controls cannot be moved accidentally during design time.

Setting the Default Button on a Form

Often, the user interface design of a form specifies one particular button on the form that executes the central task that the form was designed to accomplish. The Compute Payment button in the Automobile Loan Calculator application, for example, executes the central task of computing a monthly loan payment. In such instances, you should set that button to be the default button for a form. A **default button** on a form is specified by the **AcceptButton property**, which tells the application that pressing the ENTER key on the form is equivalent to clicking the button specified in the AcceptButton property. When the user presses the ENTER key or clicks the default button on a form that has the AcceptButton property set, the Click event procedure of the button specified by the AcceptButton executes.

> **Tip**
>
> **AcceptButton Property**
> One button on a form can be set to be the default button. The AcceptButton property of a form specifies this button. When the user presses the ENTER key or clicks the default button on a form that has the AcceptButton property set, the Click event procedure of the button specified by the AcceptButton property executes.

As noted above, the default button for the Form1 form is the Compute Payment button, so the AcceptButton property must be set to this button's name. The following steps set the AcceptButton property of Form1 to the name of the Compute Payment Button control, btnComputePayment.

To Set the Default Button on a Form

1. With the Form1 form selected, select the AcceptButton property in the Properties window. Click the AcceptButton down arrow in the property values list.

The three possible values of the AcceptButton property display in the property values list. The last two values are names of the two Button controls on Form1 (Figure 4-26).

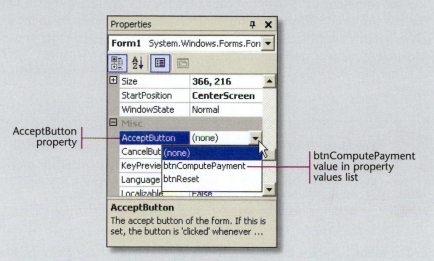

FIGURE 4-26

2. Click btnComputePayment in the AcceptButton property values list.

The AcceptButton property value is set to btnComputePayment (Figure 4-27). The AcceptButton property value indicates which button's Click event procedure executes when the user presses the ENTER key while using the application during run time. A black border displays around the btnComputePayment control on Form1.

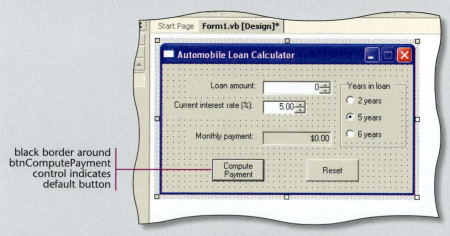

FIGURE 4-27

The Compute Payment button is now set as the default button based on the AcceptButton property. When the user presses the ENTER key while the window or any control on the window has focus during run time, the btnComputePayment_Click event procedure executes. The modifications to the controls on the Form1 form — including the size, alignment, position, tab order, and other properties — are now complete.

Locking Controls on a Form

After completing the layout of controls a form, Visual Basic .NET allows you to lock controls on a form. **Locking controls** disallows the ability to move controls or modify control sizes on a form during design time. Locking prevents the accidental moving or resizing of controls on a form. With Visual Basic .NET, you can either lock individual controls or all the controls on a form, including the form itself.

Locking Controls

Locking controls disallows the ability to move controls or modify control sizes on a form during design time. Locking prevents the accidental moving or resizing of controls on a form.

The following steps lock the Form1 control and all of the controls on the Form1 form.

To Lock Controls on a Form

1. If necessary, select Form1. Click Format on the menu bar.
The Format menu displays (Figure 4-28).

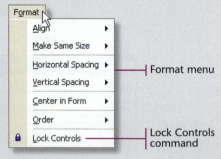

FIGURE 4-28

2. Click Lock Controls on the Format menu.
The sizing handles on Form1 no longer display and a black border appears around the form, indicating that the form and the controls on the form are locked (Figure 4-29). While the form and controls are locked, they cannot be resized or moved.

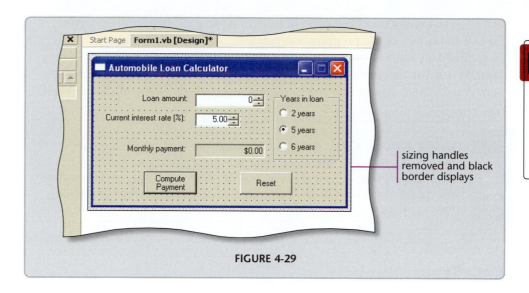

FIGURE 4-29

OTHER WAYS

1. Right-click anywhere on form, click Lock Controls on shortcut menu
2. Press ALT+O, L

After the form and controls are locked, sizing handles no longer display when you select the form, because the form cannot be resized. Similarly, if you select a control on the form, sizing handles will not display.

To lock an individual control, select the control and then click the Lock Controls command on the Format menu. To lock two or more controls, use the CTRL key to select additional controls, and then click the Lock Controls command on the Format menu.

To unlock a form or controls, you select the form or individual control and then click Lock Controls again on the Format menu. A lock icon next to the Lock Controls command on the Format menu indicates the current status of the selected form or control. With the form and controls locked, the user interface for the Automobile Loan Calculator application is now complete.

Declaring Constants and Variables

With the user interface complete, the next step is to write the code, or actions, that will occur within the application in response to specific events in the Automobile Loan Calculator application. As indicated in the program design, the code for the Automobile Loan Calculator requires six event procedures. One event procedure is needed for each of the two Button controls on the form, and one event procedure is needed for each of the three RadioButton controls. A sixth event procedure is needed to execute when the application starts, to set the maximum value allowed for the loan amount in the nudLoanAmount control. The maximum value allowed for the loan amount is stored in the code, so that the value can be changed in the code easily as the program requirements change over time.

A **value**, such as 150, 0.03, 8.14, "yes", "no", or the value allowed for the loan amount for the nudLoanAmount control, is a number or string that programmers use in the code. Variable and constants are used in code statements to store temporary values used by other code statements. A **variable** represents a location in computer memory that can change values as the code executes. Similarly, a **constant** represents a location in computer memory, but its value cannot change during execution of the code. Constants often are used to define values that are used many times in an application and were defined in the program requirements before the program was created.

When you want to use a constant in code, you first must declare the constant. When you **declare** a constant, you tell Visual Basic .NET the name and data type of the constant you want to use, along with the value of the constant.

Using Values, Constants, and Variables in Code

Use a value when it shows up only once in code. Use constants to store values that do not change and may be used more than once in the code. Use variables to store values that can change as the code executes.

Data Types

The **data type** of a variable or constant determines what kind of data the variable or constant can store, such as numeric or character. For example, the maximum value allowed for a loan amount is a numeric value. As shown in Table 4-10, Visual Basic .NET supports several data types for text (character) values, such as character and string, and several types for numeric values, such as decimal and integer.

Table 4-10   Visual Basic .NET Data Types

CATEGORY	DATA TYPE	DESCRIPTION	RANGE
Character	**Char**	16-bit (2 bytes) character	1 16-bit character
	String	Sequence of 0 or more 16-bit characters	0 to 2,000,000,000 16-bit characters
Integral	**Short**	16-bit integer value	-32,768 to 32,767
	Integer	32-bit (4 bytes) integer value	-2147483648 to 2147483647
	Long	64-bit (8 bytes) integer value	-9,223,372,036,854,775,808 to 9,223,372,036,854,775,807
	Byte	8-bit (1 byte) unsigned integer value	0 to 255
Nonintegral	**Decimal**	128-bit (16 bytes) fixed point	1.0e-28 to 7.9e28
	Single	32-bit floating point	+-1.5e-45 to +-3.4e38
	Double	64-bit floating point	+-5.0e-324 to +-1.7e308
Miscellaneous	**Boolean**	32-bit value	True or **False**
	Date	64-bit signed integer – each increment represents 100 nanoseconds elapsed since the beginning of January 1 in the year 1	January 1, 0001:00:00:00 to December 31, 9999:23:59:59
	Object	32-bit number that represents the location of the object in memory	Any object

Recall from Chapter 1 that an intermediate .NET system, known as the Common Language Runtime (CLR), takes control of the application and runs the application under the operating system. The CLR is the environment that executes Visual Basic .NET programs. The CLR also determines the data types that are allowed in Visual Basic .NET. Each data type corresponds to a data type in the CLR.

As shown in Table 4-10, each data type takes up a certain number of bytes in memory when the variable or constant is used. As you write the code for an application, you choose the data type for variables and constants in code. In general, you should try to use the data type that takes up the smallest amount of memory. In addition, where possible, you should try to use integral data types that represent whole numbers, such as 1, 5, and 1000, because arithmetic operations are fastest with whole numbers. If a variable or constant will not contain a decimal amount, use an integral data type. If a variable or constant might contain a decimal, use a nonintegral data type.

Choosing Data Types

Try to use the data type that takes up the smallest amount of memory.

Declaring Constants

As previously discussed, when you want to use a constant in code, you first must declare the constant by telling Visual Basic .NET the name, data type, and value of the constant. Using a constant in code ensures that, if the value stated in the requirements changes in the future, you only have to change the value in one place in the code. Using a constant also makes the value's purpose more clear because the value is given a meaningful name.

The following rules apply when choosing names for constants.

1. The name must begin with a letter, although the name can begin with an underscore as long as another valid character also is used in the name.
2. The name can be up to 16,383 characters in length.
3. The name cannot contain punctuation or blank spaces.

When naming constants, this book uses a naming convention that gives the constant a descriptive name but does not indicate the data type of the constant.

To declare a constant, you use the **Const keyword**. Table 4-11 on the next page shows the general form of a constant declaration statement. When declaring a constant, the general form of the constant declaration statement indicates that a data type is not needed. Good coding practice, however, dictates that a constant or variable always be declared with a data type. Declaring a data type (1) makes the code more readable to others and (2) eliminates the time-consuming process of having Visual Basic .NET determine the data type during run time. Code is more efficient and foolproof if all constants and variables are defined explicitly with a data type.

Table 4-11 Constant Declaration Statement

General forms:	1. Const name As type = value 2. Const name = value
Purpose:	The **constant declaration statement** declares a constant that cannot change during the execution of code. The name of the constant can be used in code to represent the value assigned to the constant. The use of a constant allows you to change the value in only one place in the code in the future if the value stated in the requirements changes.
Examples:	1. Const MaxVolume as Integer = 11 2. Const CurrencyString as String = "Dollars" 3. Const DrumCapacity = 1500.13

Declaring Constants and Variables 1

Although it is not generally required, good coding practice dictates that a constant or variable always be declared with a data type.

Declaring Constants and Variables 2

Code is more efficient and foolproof if all constants and variables are defined explicitly with a data type.

Figure 4-30 shows the code necessary to declare the constant needed in the Automobile Loan Calculator application. The constant, MaximumLoanAllowed, reflects the current maximum amount that the dealership will loan a customer. The code also contains the comment header for the form.

```
189    ' Chapter 4:     Automobile Loan Calculator
190    ' Programmer:    Jeff Quasney
191    ' Date:          September 22, 2004
192    ' Purpose:       This project calculates the monthly payment for
193    '                a loan based on loan amount, interest rate, and
194    '                length of the loan.
195    Const MaximumLoanAllowed As Integer = 25000
```

FIGURE 4-30

The following steps add the comment header and constant declaration statement to the Form1.vb form. The constant is not declared in any event procedure. By declaring the constant outside of any event procedure, the constant can be used in any event procedure within the form.

To Declare a Constant

1. Double-click the Form1 form in an area that does not contain a control. When the code window displays, click line 189.

The code window opens in the main work area (Figure 4-31). Visual Basic .NET creates the Form1_Load event procedure. The insertion point is on line 189.

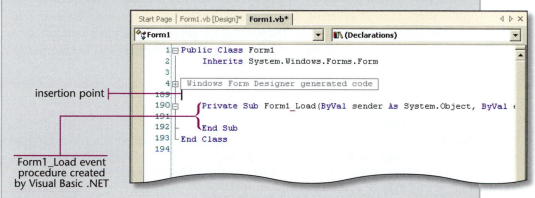

insertion point

Form1_Load event procedure created by Visual Basic .NET

FIGURE 4-31

2. Enter the seven lines of code from Figure 4-30. Press the ENTER key after entering the last line. When entering code, use the Intellisense feature whenever possible.

The comment header and a constant declaration statement display in the code window (Figure 4-32).

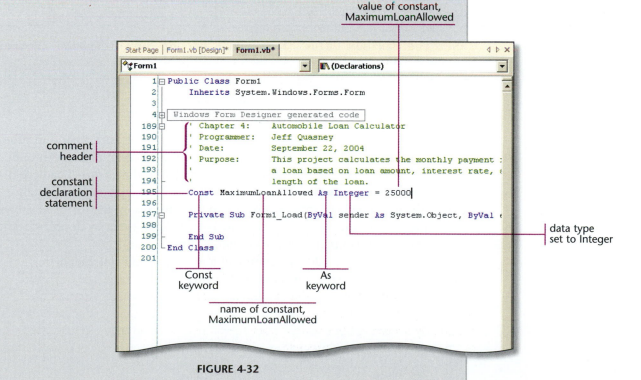

value of constant, MaximumLoanAllowed

comment header

constant declaration statement

data type set to Integer

Const keyword

As keyword

name of constant, MaximumLoanAllowed

FIGURE 4-32

Coding a Form Load Event Procedure

Like any other control, forms include event procedures. As previously noted, the Automobile Loan Calculator application includes an event procedure that executes when the application starts and the form loads. This event procedure sets the maximum value allowed for the loan amount in the nudLoanAmount control. The form event procedure that executes whenever the form initially displays to the user is a **form Load event**. The code you write for the Load event is code that you want to execute before the CLR allows the user to take any action on the form, such as entering data. You can see the list of Form events available for a form by selecting the item, (Base Class Events), in the Object box in the code window and then displaying the list of event procedures by clicking the Procedure box arrow.

> **Tip**
>
> **Form Load Event**
> The form Load event executes for a form whenever the form initially displays to the user. The code you write for the Load event is code that you want to execute before the CLR allows the user to take any action on the form, such as entering data.

The Automobile Loan Calculator application calls for assigning the nudLoanAmount.Maximum property the value of the constant, MaximumLoanAllowed, when the form first loads. A constant may be used in an assignment statement, but it can only be on the right side of an assignment statement. Figure 4-33 shows the assignment statement needed to set the property value nudLoanAmount.Maximum to the constant, MaximumLoanAmount.

```
198         ' Set the maximum value of the Loan amount NumericUpDown control
199         nudLoanAmount.Maximum = MaximumLoanAllowed
```

FIGURE 4-33

The line of code after the comment in Figure 4-33 sets the Maximum property of the nudLoanAmount to equal the value of the MaximumLoanAmount constant, 25000. The assignment statement is added to the Form1_Load event procedure, so that the property is set when the user starts the application and before the user is able to enter any data into the controls on the form. As shown in the previous steps, you start coding the Form1_Load event by double-clicking any area on the form that does not contain a control.

The following step adds the comment and assignment statements in Figure 4-33 to the Form1_Load event of Form1.

To Code a Form Load Event Procedure

1. Click line 198 in the Form1_Load event procedure and then enter the two lines of code from Figure 4-33.

The comment line and assignment statement display in the code window as lines 198 and 199 (Figure 4-34). Because the statement is part of the Form1_Load event procedure, the assignment statement will execute when the user starts the application.

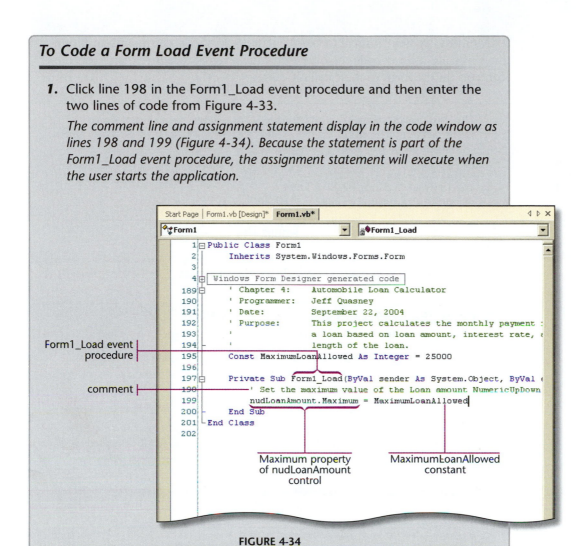

FIGURE 4-34

The Form1_Load event procedure can be used to set any or all of the properties of the Form1 form or controls. The reason that the nudLoanAmount.Maximum property is set in the procedure is that the requirements document for the application (Figure 4-2 on page VB 4.04) states that the value is likely to change in the future. By explicitly assigning this value in the code, the code only needs to be changed in one place if the value changes.

Setting the Reset Button Properties

As outlined in the program requirements, when the user clicks the Reset button during run time, four controls must be reset to their default property values. In the Automobile Loan Calculator application, the btnReset_Click event procedure is assigned to the btnReset control so that it executes when the btnReset button is clicked. The btnReset_Click event procedure is used to set the Value property value of the nudLoanAmount control to 0, the Value property value of the nudRate control to 5, the Checked property value of the radFiveYears control to True, and the Text property value of the txtMonthlyPayment control to $0.00. Figure 4-35 shows comments and four lines of code used to code the btnReset_Click event procedure that resets the controls on the form to their default values.

```
203          ' Reset Loan Amount and Monthly payment to zero. Reset
204          ' the interest rate to 5%, and select five years for the
205          ' length of the loan
206          nudLoanAmount.Value = 0
207          nudRate.Value = 5
208          radFiveYears.Checked = True
209          txtMonthlyPayment.Text = "$0.00"
```

FIGURE 4-35

The following step inserts the code for the btnReset_Click event procedure.

To Code the btnReset_Click Event Procedure

1. Click the Form1.vb[Design] tab and then double-click the btnReset control. When the code window displays, enter the seven lines of code from Figure 4-35.

The code window opens in the main work area (Figure 4-36). Visual Basic .NET creates the btnReset_Click event procedure, and the insertion point is positioned on line 203 in the procedure. The comment lines and assignment statements display in the code window as lines 203 through 209. The assignment statement will execute when the user clicks the Reset button during run time.

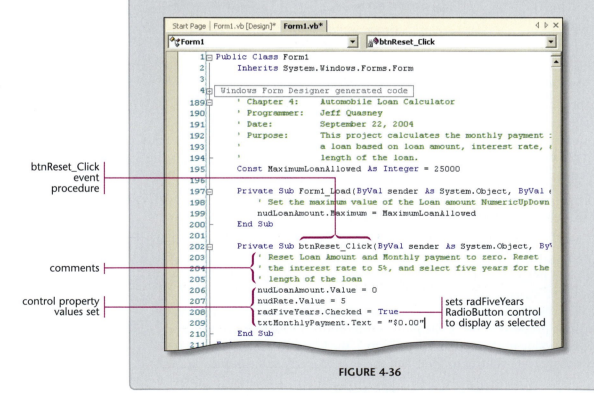

FIGURE 4-36

The code for the btnReset_Click event procedure is now complete. When a user clicks the Reset button during run time, the code will set the control property values as indicated in lines 206 through 209. The code in line 208, which sets the Checked property value of the radFiveYears RadioButton control to True, performs the same action as if the user clicked the 5 years option button in the Years in loan area of the form.

Using the Option Strict Statement

When you use an assignment statement, Visual Basic .NET does not require you to use the same data type on both sides of the assignment. Visual Basic .NET converts the variables or constants to the proper data type so it can make a valid assignment. This conversion process, however, can cause problems with code and makes code more unreadable for others. For example, if you leave the data conversions to Visual Basic .NET, you may try assigning an Integer variable with a value of 50,000 to a variable declared as a Short. In this case, the Integer value exceeds the maximum value that can fit in a Short variable. This condition causes a run time error to occur and the CLR halts the program.

The **Option Strict statement** can be used to instruct Visual Basic .NET to force you to ensure that all assignment statements use the same data type on both sides of the assignment. Option Strict also forces you to declare a data type for all variables and constants explicitly. Table 4-12 shows the general form of an Option Strict statement.

Table 4-12 Option Strict Statement	
General forms:	1. Option Strict On 2. Option Strict Off
Purpose:	When set to On, the Option Strict statement requires all constants and variable to be declared with a data type and requires assignment statements to have the same data type on each side of the assignment.
Examples:	1. `Option Strict On` 2. `Option Strict Off`

By default, Option Strict is set to Off, which means that Visual Basic .NET does not require a data type to be the same on each side of an assignment and that you do not need to declare a data type for each variable. For the remainder of this book, Option Strict will be set to On, meaning that you must declare a data type for all constants and variables and you must use the same data type on each side of an assignment statement.

If you use an Option Strict statement, the statement must be the first line of code entered in the code window. Figure 4-37 shows the Option Strict statement included in the code window.

```
1 Option Strict On
```

FIGURE 4-37

The following step inserts the code for an Option Strict statement that sets Option Strict setting to On.

To Code an Option Strict Statement

1. Click to the left of the keyword, Public, and to the right of the collapse button on line 1. Press the ENTER key, position the insertion point at the beginning of line 1, and then type the code Option Strict On as shown in Figure 4-37 on the previous page.

The Option Strict On statement displays as the first line of code (Figure 4-38). All lines of code are moved down and renumbered.

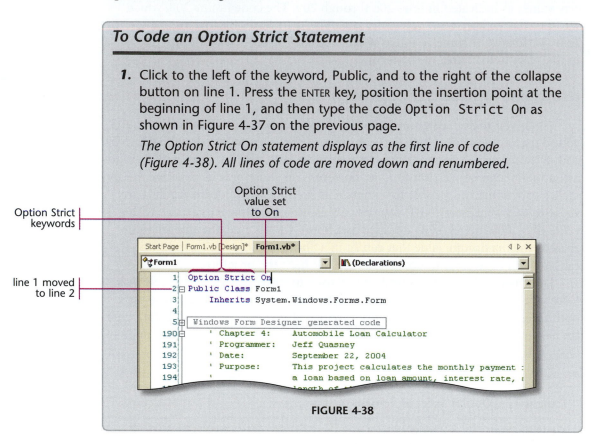

FIGURE 4-38

When the Option Strict statement is entered on the first line, all other lines of code are moved down and renumbered. The Option Strict On statement causes Visual Basic .NET to require that all assignment statements use the same data type on both sides of the equal sign and that a data type is declared for all constants and variables.

Declaring Global Variables

As with constants, variables also are used in code statements to store temporary values used by other code statements. Unlike a constant, which does not change as the code executes, a variable represents a location in computer memory that can change values as the code executes. If you want to use a variable in code, you first must declare the variable by telling Visual Basic .NET the name, data type, and value of the variable.

The rules for naming variables are the same as the rules for naming constants: the name must begin with a letter, although the name can begin with an underscore as long as another valid character also is used in the name, the name can be up to 16,383 characters in length, and cannot contain punctuation or blank spaces. Table 4-13 shows the prefixes used for naming variables in this book, based on the data type of the variable.

Table 4-13 Naming Convention for Variables

DATA TYPE	PREFIX
Short	shr
Integer	int
Long	lng
Byte	byt
Decimal	dec
Single	sng
Double	dbl
Char	chr
String	str
Boolean	bln
Date	dtm
Object	obj

To declare a variable, you use the **Dim statement**. Table 4-14 shows the general form of a Dim statement.

Table 4-14 Dim Statement (simple)

General form:	1. Dim variablename As datatype = initialvalue 2. Dim variablename As datatype 3. Dim variablename
Purpose:	The Dim statement declares a variable.
Examples:	1. `Dim intScore As integer = 0` 2. `Dim strName As String` 3. `Dim lngInStock`

Visual Basic .NET allows you to declare a variable either in a procedure or in the area of code outside of a procedure, in the general area of a class. Variables and constants have an attribute called scope. **Scope** refers to a variable or constant's accessibility and is defined by the placement of the variable declaration in the code. Depending on where a variable is declared, the scope of the variable can be limited so it is not usable everywhere in a project's code. The MaximumLoanAmount constant declared earlier in this chapter was declared in the general area of the form and has scope that is global to the form. The MaximumLoanAmount is a global constant. Variables typically are declared at the start of an event procedure, using the general forms in Table 4-14. A variable declared within an event procedure only has scope within that procedure and is considered a **local variable**. A declaration made outside of a specific event procedure and in the general area of the code, such as the constant declaration statement on line 195 in Figure 4-30 on page VB 4.36, has scope for all of the procedures in the form and is considered a **form level**, or **global, variable**.

When the user clicks a RadioButton control in the Automobile Loan Calculator application to specify the number of years in the loan, the CheckChanged event procedure of the RadioButton control executes. By placing an assignment to a global variable in the CheckChanged event procedure of each RadioButton control, you can tell Visual Basic .NET to update the global variable with the correct number of months in the loan whenever the user clicks a RadioButton control. Even after the event procedure has finished executing, the variable retains the newly assigned value. The name of this variable will be gdblMonths. The variable is named with a preceding character, g, to indicate that it is a global variable using the short data type.

Naming Global Variables

Append the letter g in front of the properly formed variable name when naming global variables. After the g, use a prefix to indicate data type and then add a descriptive word or words.

Figure 4-39 shows the declaration of the global variable, gdblMonths. The global variable is assigned an initial value of 60, which is the number of months in the 5 years loan, which serves as a default length of a loan. Just as with the global constant, MaximumLoanAllowed, the global variable, gdblMonths, is declared in the general section of the code. The coding standard used in this book requires that global variables be declared after the comment header for the code file and before any constant declarations.

```
196        Dim gdblMonths As Double = 60.0
```

FIGURE 4-39

Global Variable Placement

Place global variables after the comment header in the code, but before any constant declarations.

The following step inserts the code to declare a global variable for the Automobile Loan Calculator application.

To Declare a Global Variable

1. Click the end of line 195 and then press the ENTER key. Enter the line of code from Figure 4-39.

The declaration for the global variable, gdblMonths, displays in the code window as line 196 (Figure 4-40). The declaration for the global variable is entered below the comment header and above the constant declaration statement.

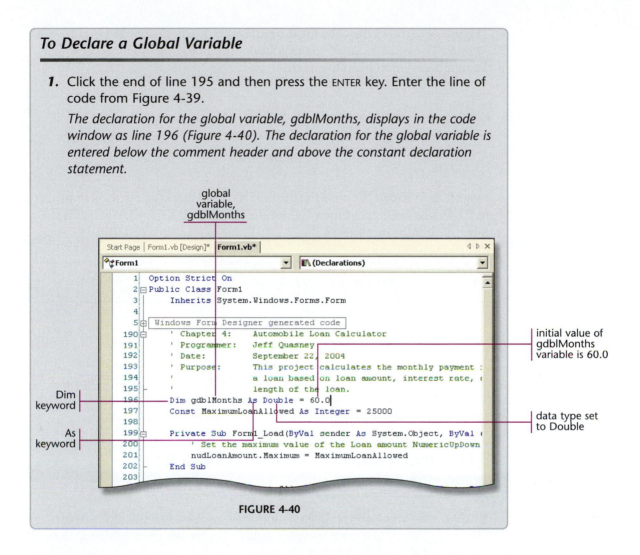

FIGURE 4-40

The gdblMonths variable now contains the number of months that corresponds to the default number of years in a loan.

Coding the Event Procedures for the RadioButton Controls

The next step in developing the Automobile Loan Calculator application is to code the event procedures for the RadioButton controls, so that the gdblMonths variable is set to the correct number of months, 24 (2 years), 60 (5 years), or 72 (6 years) depending on which RadioButton the user clicks.

The event procedure that executes when the user clicks a RadioButton is the CheckChanged event procedure. Figure 4-41 shows the code for the radTwoYears_CheckChanged event procedure. The value assigned to the gdblMonths global variable is 24.0, which is the number of months in two years.

```
215        gdblMonths = 24.0
```

FIGURE 4-41

Figure 4-42 shows the code for the radFiveYears_CheckChanged event procedure. The value assigned to the gdblMonths global variable is 60.0, which is the number of months in five years.

```
219              gdblMonths = 60.0
```

FIGURE 4-42

Figure 4-43 shows the code for the radSixYears_CheckChanged event procedure. The value assigned to the gdblMonths global variable is 72.0, which is the number of months in six years.

```
223              gdblMonths = 72.0
```

FIGURE 4-43

The following steps insert the code for the three event procedures that execute when the corresponding RadioButton control is clicked. The code in each event procedure sets the gdblMonths global variable to the correct number of months whenever the user clicks one of the RadioButton controls.

To Code the CheckChanged Event Procedures for RadioButton Controls

1. Click the Form1.vb[Design] tab and then double-click the radTwoYears control. When the code window displays, enter the code on line 215 of Figure 4-41 on the previous page.

    The assignment statement displays in the code window on line 215 (Figure 4-44). The value assigned to the gdblMonths global variable is 24.0, the number of months in two years.

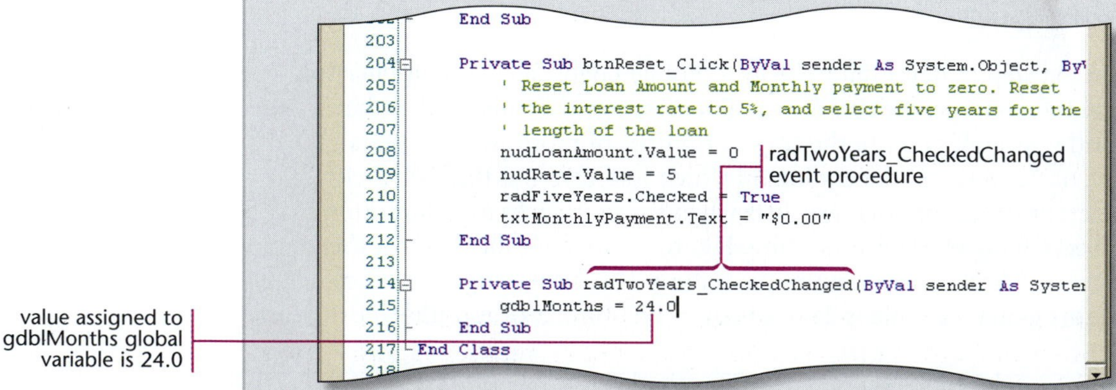

```
              End Sub
203
204    Private Sub btnReset_Click(ByVal sender As System.Object, ByV
205        ' Reset Loan Amount and Monthly payment to zero. Reset
206        ' the interest rate to 5%, and select five years for the
207        ' length of the loan
208        nudLoanAmount.Value = 0        radTwoYears_CheckedChanged
209        nudRate.Value = 5              event procedure
210        radFiveYears.Checked = True
211        txtMonthlyPayment.Text = "$0.00"
212    End Sub
213
214    Private Sub radTwoYears_CheckedChanged(ByVal sender As Syster
215        gdblMonths = 24.0
216    End Sub
217  End Class
218
```

value assigned to gdblMonths global variable is 24.0

FIGURE 4-44

2. Click the Form1.vb[Design] tab and then double-click the radFiveYears control. When the code window displays, enter the code on line 219 from Figure 4-42.

The assignment statement displays in the code window on line 219 (Figure 4-45). The value assigned to the gdblMonths global variable is 60.0, the number of months in five years.

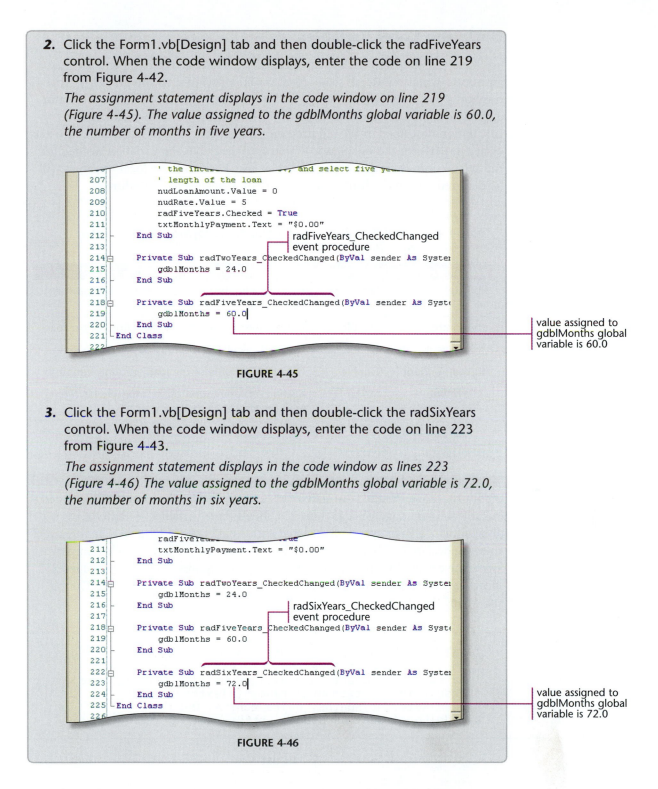

```
' the interest ..., and select five ye...
207       ' length of the loan
208       nudLoanAmount.Value = 0
209       nudRate.Value = 5
210       radFiveYears.Checked = True
211       txtMonthlyPayment.Text = "$0.00"
212   End Sub
213
214   Private Sub radTwoYears_CheckedChanged(ByVal sender As System
215       gdblMonths = 24.0
216   End Sub
217
218   Private Sub radFiveYears_CheckedChanged(ByVal sender As Syste
219       gdblMonths = 60.0|
220   End Sub
221   End Class
222
```

radFiveYears_CheckedChanged event procedure

value assigned to gdblMonths global variable is 60.0

FIGURE 4-45

3. Click the Form1.vb[Design] tab and then double-click the radSixYears control. When the code window displays, enter the code on line 223 from Figure 4-43.

The assignment statement displays in the code window as lines 223 (Figure 4-46) The value assigned to the gdblMonths global variable is 72.0, the number of months in six years.

```
      radFive...
211       txtMonthlyPayment.Text = "$0.00"
212   End Sub
213
214   Private Sub radTwoYears_CheckedChanged(ByVal sender As System
215       gdblMonths = 24.0
216   End Sub
217
218   Private Sub radFiveYears_CheckedChanged(ByVal sender As Syste
219       gdblMonths = 60.0
220   End Sub
221
222   Private Sub radSixYears_CheckedChanged(ByVal sender As Syste
223       gdblMonths = 72.0|
224   End Sub
225   End Class
226
```

radSixYears_CheckedChanged event procedure

value assigned to gdblMonths global variable is 72.0

FIGURE 4-46

The code in the previous steps declared, initialized, and modified the gdblMonths variable, which is used as the number of months for the calculation of the monthly loan payment.

Declaring Local Variables

The next step is to declare the local variables needed to complete the loan amount calculation. Recall that a local variable declared within an event procedure only has scope within that procedure. In the Automobile Loan Calculator application, the btnComputePayment_Click event procedure performs the calculation described in the requirements document. Five local variables are necessary to perform the calculation. Table 4-15 describes the variables needed for the calculation, their data types, and their use. Each of these local variables will be declared within the btnComputePayment_Click event procedure

Table 4-15   Local Variables in the btnComputePayment_Click Event Procedure

NAME	DATA TYPE	PURPOSE
dblRate	Double	The actual interest rate used in the final payment calculation
dblMonths	Double	The number of months for the length of the loan
dblPayment	Double	The final calculated monthly payment amount
dblLoanAmount	Double	The numeric value of the loan amount requested
strPayment	String	A string representation of the monthly payment used for display to the user

Figure 4-47 shows the comments used to describe the btnComputeLoan_Click event procedure and the Dim statements used to declare the local variables listed in Table 4-14 on page VB 4.43. Line 231 shows three variables — dblRate, dblMonths, dblPayment — all declared with a data type of Double. The three variables are declared with a data type of Double because the line of code that performs the calculation shown later in the chapter requires Double values. Line 232 shows two variables — dblLoanAmount and strPayment — declared as Double and String data types, respectively.

```
227         ' Validate inputs and compute the monthly payment using
228         ' the inputs. Determine the interest rate to be used
229         ' based on the input rate divided by 12.0. Display the
230         ' result in the txtMonthlyPayment Textbox.
231         Dim dblRate, dblMonths, dblPayment As Double
232         Dim dblLoanAmount As Double, strPayment As String
```

FIGURE 4-47

The following step inserts the comments and code to start the btnComputePayment_Click event procedure and declares the local variables within the event procedure.

To Declare Local Variables

1. Click the Form1.vb[Design] tab and then double-click the btnComputePayment control. When the code window displays, enter the six lines of code from Figure 4-47.

The comment lines and local variable declarations display in the code window as lines 227 through 232 (Figure 4-48).

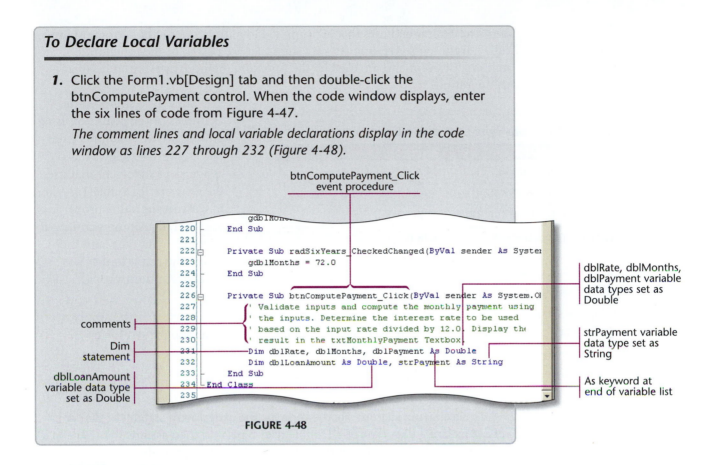

FIGURE 4-48

The code declares the variables within the btnComputePayment_Click event procedure. Therefore, these local variables may be used only within this event procedure. If you tried to refer to the variables in another event procedure, Visual Basic .NET would indicate a syntax error.

Converting Data Types

Because Option Strict is On, the btnComputePayment_Click event procedure must ensure that all data being used in the calculation has the same data type before making the calculation. One of the values used in the calculation, however, nudLoanAmount, uses a different data type. The Value property of the nudLoanAmount control has a Decimal data type.

To set the value to the correct data type, the Value property of the nudLoanAmount control must be converted from a Decimal data type to a Double data type. This is accomplished by converting the Value property of the nudLoanAmount to a Double data type, and then assigning the result to the dblLoanAmount variable, which is declared with a Double data type.

Visual Basic .NET includes several methods that allow you to convert the value of a variable or constant to another data type, and then use the result in a statement. For example, the **Convert.ToDouble() method** converts the value of a variable to a Double data type. The Visual Basic .NET online Help documentation includes additional explanations of the various methods available for data conversions. You place the item you want to convert inside the parentheses. The items within parentheses that are supplied to a function, method, or event are called arguments. **Arguments** are values that are passed to the function, method, or event and are used by the function, method, or event to perform its operation.

Table 4-16 shows some examples of the results of using data type conversion methods.

Figure 4-49 shows the assignment statement that uses the Convert.ToDouble() method to convert the Value property of the nudLoanAmount control to a Double data type, and then assign the result to the dblLoanAmount variable.

Table 4-16   Data Type Conversion Examples

STATEMENT	RESULT
Convert.ToString(498.72)	"498.72"
Convert.ToInt16(498.72)	499
Convert.ToBoolean(498.72)	True
Convert.ToDouble(498)	498.0

```
234          dblLoanAmount = Convert.ToDouble(nudLoanAmount.Value)
```

FIGURE 4-49

The following step inserts the code for the assignment statement that converts a Decimal data type to a Double data type, and then assigns the result to a local variable in the btnComputePayment_Click event procedure.

To Code an Assignment Statement to Convert a Data Type

1. Press the ENTER key twice. Enter the line of code from Figure 4-49.

Line 234 displays in the code window (Figure 4-50). This assignment statement uses the Convert.ToDouble() method to convert the nudLoanAmount.Value property to a Double data type and assign the result to the dblLoanAmount variable.

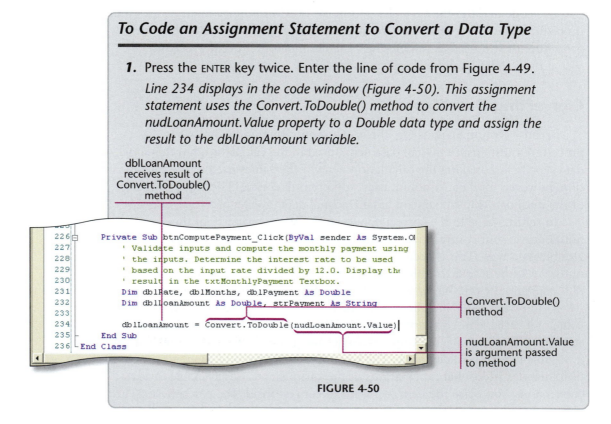

FIGURE 4-50

The assignment statement converts the value of the nudLoanAmount.Value property to a Double data type, and then assigns this value to the dblLoanAmount variable. Once converted and stored in the local variable, dblLoanAmount, this value can be used in other code statements in the btnComputePayment_Click event procedure that require the Double data type.

Numeric Expressions and Operator Precedence

An **expression** can perform a calculation, manipulate characters, call a function, or test data. A **numeric expression** is any expression that can be evaluated as a number. A numeric expression can include values, variables, and constants, as well as certain control properties. The data type of any value in an arithmetic expression must be one of the numeric data types from Table 4-10 on page VB 4.34. A numeric expression cannot contain string variables, string constants, or objects.

The values, variables, constants, and control properties in a numeric expression often are separated from each other by parentheses and arithmetic operators. An **arithmetic operator** is used to manipulate two or more numeric values. Commonly used arithmetic operators are the plus sign (+) used to sum two numbers and the asterisk (*) used to multiply two numbers. Table 4-17 shows seven arithmetic operators listed in the order of operator precedence. **Order of operator precedence** is a predetermined order that defines the sequence in which operators are evaluated and resolved when several operations occur in an expression.

Table 4-17 Arithmetic Operators

ARITHMETIC OPERATOR	MEANING
^	Used to raise a number to the power of an exponent
*	Used to multiply two numbers
/	Used to divide two numbers and return a decimal result
\	Used to divide two numbers and return an integer result
Mod	Used to divide two numbers and return only the remainder
+	Used to sum two numbers
–	Used to find the difference between two numbers or to indicate the negative value of a numeric expression

The process of raising a number to the power of an exponent is called exponentiation. For example, 4 ^ 2 is the same as 4^2 and is equal to 16, and 3 ^ 4 is the same as 3^4 and is equal to 81. In programming, the asterisk (*) is used to indicate multiplication and the forward slash (/) indicates division. Therefore, 8 * 4 is equal to 32, and 8 / 4 is equal to 2. For addition and subtraction, the traditional + and – signs are used.

Two arithmetic operators that may be unfamiliar to you are the backslash (\) and Mod, both of which are used to indicate a division operation. The backslash operator instructs Visual Basic .NET first to round the dividend and the divisor to integers (whole numbers) and then truncate any decimal portion of the quotient. For example, 5 \ 3 is equal to 1, and 6.8 \ 3.2 is equal to 2.

The **Mod operator** (also called the **modulo operator**) is used to divide two numbers and then return the remainder of the division operation as an integer. For example, 34 Mod 6 is equal to 4 because 34 divided by 6 is 5 with a remainder of 4. Also, 23 Mod 12 is equal to 11 because 23 divided by 12 is 1 with a remainder of 11.

A programmer must be concerned with both the form and evaluation of an expression. It is necessary to consider the purpose of the expression, as well as the rules for forming a valid expression, before you start to write expressions in Visual Basic .NET statements with confidence.

Forming Valid Numeric Expressions

The definition of a numeric expression dictates the manner in which a numeric expression can be validly formed. For example, the following statement formed to assign A twice the value of B is invalid:

A = 2B ' Invalid statement

Visual Basic .NET will reject the statement because a constant and a variable within the same expression must be separated by an arithmetic operator. The statement can be written validly as follows:

A = 2 * B

It also is invalid to use a string variable or string constant in a numeric expression. The following are invalid numeric expressions:

6 + "DEBIT" / C
"25" / B + "X" − 19

Evaluation of Numeric Expressions

As you form complex numeric expressions involving several arithmetic operations, it is important to consider the order in which Visual Basic .NET will evaluate the expression. For example, if you entered the statement:

A = 8 / 4 / 2

would the expression assign a value of 1 or 4 to A? The answer depends on how Visual Basic .NET evaluates the expression. If Visual Basic .NET completes the operation, 8 / 4, first and only then 2 / 2, the expression yields the value 1. If Visual Basic .NET completes the second operation, 4 / 2, first and only then 8 / 2, it yields 4.

Visual Basic .NET follows the normal algebraic rules to evaluate an expression. The normal algebraic rules that define the order in which the operations are evaluated are as follows: Unless parentheses dictate otherwise, reading from left to right in a numeric expression, all exponentiations are performed first, then all multiplications and/or divisions, then all integer divisions, then all modulo arithmetic, and finally, all additions and/or subtractions. Following these algebraic rules, Visual Basic .NET would evaluate the expression 8 / 4 / 2 to yield a value of 1.

Tip

Order of Operator Precedence

Unless parentheses dictate otherwise, reading from left to right in a numeric expression, all exponentiations are performed first, then all multiplications and/or divisions, then all integer divisions, then all modulo arithmetic, and finally, all additions and/or subtractions.

This order of operator precedence, which defines the order in which operators are evaluated, is sometimes called the rules of precedence, or the hierarchy of operations. The meaning of these rules can be made clear with some examples.

For example, the expression 18 / 3 ^ 2 + 4 * 2 is evaluated as follows:

$$18 / 3 \wedge 2 + 4 * 2 = 18 / 9 + 4 * 2$$
$$= 2 + 4 * 2$$
$$= 2 + 8$$
$$= 10$$

If you have trouble following the logic behind this evaluation, use the following technique. Whenever a numeric expression is to be evaluated, read, or scan, the expression from left to right five different times and apply the order of operator precedence rules outlined above each time you read the expression. On the first scan, every time you encounter an ^ operator, you perform exponentiation. In this example, 3 is raised to the power of 2, yielding 9.

On the second scan, moving from left to right again, every time you encounter the operators, * and /, perform multiplication and division. Hence, 18 is divided by 9, yielding 2, and 4 and 2 are multiplied, yielding 8.

On the third scan, from left to right, perform all integer division. On the fourth scan, from left to right, perform all modulo arithmetic. This example includes no integer division or modulo arithmetic so no operations are performed.

On the fifth scan, moving again from left to right, every time you encounter the operators, + and −, perform addition and subtraction. In this example, 2 and 8 are added to form 10.

The following expression includes all seven arithmetic operators and yields a value of 2. This particular expression assumes that Option Strict is set to Off, because a value, 4.8, with the Double data type, a Nonintegral data type, is used in an arithmetic expression that uses only integers.

$$3 * 9 \text{ Mod } 2 \wedge 2 + 5 \setminus 4.8 / 2 - 3 = 3 * 9 \text{ Mod } 4 + 5 \setminus 4.8 / 2 - 3 \quad \text{<-end of first scan}$$
$$= 27 \text{ Mod } 4 + 5 \setminus 2.4 - 3 \quad \text{<-end of second scan}$$
$$= 27 \text{ Mod } 4 + 2 - 3 \quad \text{<-end of third scan}$$
$$= 3 + 2 - 3 \quad \text{<-end of fourth scan}$$
$$= 2 \quad \text{<-end of fifth scan}$$

The expression below yields the value of −2.73, as follows:

$$2 - 3 * 4 / 5 \wedge 2 + 5 / 4 * 3 - 2 \wedge 3 = 2 - 3 * 4 / 25 + 5 / 4 * 3 - 8 \quad \text{<-end of first scan}$$
$$= 2 - 0.48 + 3.75 - 8 \qquad \text{<-end of second scan}$$
$$= -2.73 \qquad \text{<-end of third scan}$$

When operations of the same precedence are encountered, the normal rules of precedence apply. For example,

A − B − C is interpreted as (A − B) − C
A / B / C is interpreted as (A / B) / C
A ^ B ^ C is interpreted as (A ^ B) ^ C
A \ B \ C is interpreted as (A \ B) \ C
A Mod B Mod C is interpreted as (A Mod B) Mod C

Using Parentheses in Numeric Expressions

Parentheses may be used to change the order of operations. In Visual Basic .NET, parentheses normally are used to avoid ambiguity and to group terms in a numeric expression. The order in which the operations in an expression containing parentheses are evaluated can be stated as follows: when parentheses are inserted into an expression, the part of the expression within the parentheses is evaluated first, and then the remaining expression is evaluated according to the normal rules of operator precedence.

Use of Parentheses in a Numeric Expression
When parentheses are inserted into an expression, the part of the expression within the parentheses is evaluated first, and then the remaining expression is evaluated according to the normal rules of operator precedence.

If the first example was rewritten with parentheses, as (18 / 3) ^ 2 + 4 * 2, then it would be evaluated in the following manner:

$$(18 / 3) \wedge 2 + 4 * 2 = 6 \wedge 2 + 4 * 2$$
$$= 36 + 4 * 2$$
$$= 36 + 8$$
$$= 44$$

Evaluating expressions with parentheses should be done as follows: Make five scans from left to right within each pair of parentheses, and only after doing this, make the standard five passes over the entire numeric expression.

Evaluating Expressions with Parentheses
Make five scans from left to right within each pair of parentheses, and only after doing this, make the standard five passes over the entire numeric expression.

The expression below yields the value of 1.41, as follows:

$$(2 - 3 * 4 / 5) \wedge 2 + 5 / (4 * 3 - 2 \wedge 3) = (2 - 3 * 4 / 5) \wedge 2 + 5 / (4 * 3 - 8)$$
$$= (2 - 2.4) \wedge 2 + 5 / (12 - 8)$$
$$= (-0.4) \wedge 2 + 5 / 4$$
$$= 0.16 + 5 / 4$$
$$= 0.16 + 1.25$$
$$= 1.41$$

When coding a numeric expression, use parentheses freely when in doubt as to the valid form and evaluation of a numeric expression. For example, if you want Visual Basic .NET to divide 8 * D by 3 ^ P, the expression may correctly be written as 8 * D / 3 ^ P, but you also may write it as follows:

$$(8 * D) / (3 \wedge P)$$

> **Tip**
>
> **Use of Parentheses when Coding Expressions**
> When coding a numeric expression, use parentheses freely when in doubt as to the valid form and evaluation of a numeric expression. Adding parentheses helps to provide clarity when you are evaluating an expression.

For more complex expressions, Visual Basic .NET allows parentheses to be contained within other parentheses. When this occurs, the parentheses are said to be **nested**. In this case, Visual Basic .NET evaluates the innermost parenthetical expression first, and then goes on to the outermost parenthetical expression. Thus, 18 / 3 ^ 2 + (3 * (2 + 5)) is broken down in the following manner:

$$18 / 3 \wedge 2 + (3 * (2 + 5)) = 18 / 3 \wedge 2 + (3 * 7)$$
$$= 18 / 3 \wedge 2 + 21$$
$$= 18 / 9 + 21$$
$$= 2 + 21$$
$$= 23$$

Table 4-18 gives examples of the Visual Basic .NET equivalent of some algebraic statements and the equivalent Visual Basic .NET assignment statements.

Table 4-18   Algebraic Statements and Equivalent Assignment Statements

ALGEBRAIC STATEMENTS	EQUIVALENT VISUAL BASIC .NET ASSIGNMENT STATEMENTS
$H = \sqrt{X^2 + Y^2}$	H = (X ^ 2 + Y ^ 2) ^ 0.5
$S = AL^P K^{1-P}$	S = A * L ^ P * K ^ (1 - P)
$Q = \dfrac{-b + \sqrt{b^2 - 4ac}}{2a}$	Q = (-B + (B ^ 2 - 4 * A * C) ^ 0.5) / (2 * A)
$A = F \left[\dfrac{r}{(1 + r)^n - 1} \right]$	A = F * (R / (((1 + R) ^ N) - 1))
$P = \sqrt[3]{(x - p)^2 + y^2}$	P = ((X - P) ^ 2 + Y ^ 2) ^ (1 / 3)
$Z = \dfrac{ab}{x + \sqrt{x^2 - a^2}}$	Z = A * B / (X + (X ^ 2 - A ^ 2) ^ 0.5)

When coding expressions, be sure to avoid two common errors. First, check that you have surrounded the correct part of an expression with parentheses. Second, check that you have balanced the parentheses, by checking that the expression has as many close parentheses as open parentheses.

Construction of Error-Free Numeric Expressions

If you have written a numeric expression observing the order of operator precedence, Visual Basic .NET can translate the expression without generating any error messages. This is no guarantee, however, that Visual Basic .NET actually will be able to evaluate it. In other words, although a numeric expression may be formed in a valid fashion, Visual Basic .NET may not be able to evaluate it because of the numbers involved. In situations where error conditions arise during execution, Visual Basic .NET will halt the program and display a dialog box informing you of the error.

Applying the following rules when coding expressions should help you avoid such hazards:

1. Do not attempt to divide by 0.
2. Do not attempt to determine the square root of a negative value.
3. Do not attempt to raise a negative value to a nonintegral value.
4. Do not attempt to compute a value that is greater than the largest permissible value or less than the smallest permissible nonzero value for the data type.

Table 4-19 illustrates some examples of the combinations to be avoided in numeric expressions written in a Visual Basic .NET program.

Table 4-19 Invalid Numeric Expressions

ERROR	EXAMPLES

Division by 0	1. `Z = 2 * 8`
	    `A = 16`
	    `B = A - Z`
	    `C = A / B`
	2. `W = X / 0`

Negative number raised to Nonintegral value	`Value = -25` `Result = Value ^ (1 / 2)`
Number too large	`Dim Value As Single` `Value = 999999 ^ 500`

Coding an Expression to Calculate a Monthly Interest Rate

The formula used to compute the monthly payment requires that a monthly interest rate be used. In the Automobile Loan Calculator application, the user enters the current annual interest rate, which is expressed as a percentage. Therefore, the rate entered by the user must be divided by 100, and then divided by 12 in order to calculate the monthly rate to use in the final calculation. Figure 4-51 shows the numeric expression needed to calculate the monthly rate.

```
236              ' Set the true interest rate based on the input rate
237              ' divided by 12.0.
238              dblRate = (Convert.ToDouble(nudRate.Value) / 100.0) / 12.0
```

FIGURE 4-51

Line 238 first converts the Value property, which has the Decimal data type, of the nudRate control to the data type of Double. The result then is divided by 100.0. The result of that calculation then is divided by 12.0. Because Option Strict is On, all values in the expression must be of the same data type. The decimal place (.0) thus is added to the values 100 and 12 to make them 100.0 and 12.0, values of the Double data type. If the values 100 and 12 are used, Visual Basic .NET interprets the values as integers of the Short data type and will display an error message at run time. The following step inserts the code for an expression to calculate the monthly rate for use in the btnComputePayment_Click event procedure.

To Code an Expression to Calculate a Monthly Interest Rate

1. Enter the lines of code from Figure 4-51.

Lines 236 through 238 display in the code window (Figure 4-52). The assignment statement in line 238 calculates a monthly interest rate and then assigns the value to the dblRate variable.

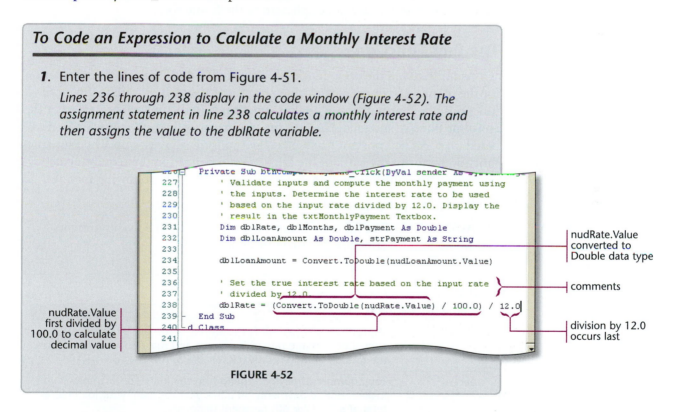

FIGURE 4-52

After line 238 executes, the dblRate variable contains a monthly interest rate expressed as a decimal value.

The next step is to use the variables, dblRate, gdblMonths, and dblLoanAmount to calculate the monthly payment.

Intrinsic Functions

Visual Basic .NET includes built-in functions, or **intrinsic functions,** that you can use in your code. For a complete list and descriptions of all these Visual Basic .NET functions, search online Help using the phrase, run-time library members. The Visual Basic .NET **run-time library** is divided into several categories, such as financial and date and time functions. These functions are not part of the .NET Framework class library discussed in Chapter 1, and are available only when coding Visual Basic .NET programs. Appendix E contains an overview of common .NET Framework class library classes. The fact that these intrinsic functions are not part of the .NET Framework class library is what makes them different from methods, such as Convert.ToDouble(), used earlier in this chapter. Intrinsic functions are accessible to Visual Basic .NET only. They are not available in other .NET languages. Visual Basic .NET includes intrinsic functions largely for backward compatibility with older versions of Visual Basic. In Visual Basic .NET, classes in the .NET Framework class library duplicate most functionality of intrinsic functions. The intrinsic financial functions, however, which are very useful, are not duplicated in the framework.

The Pmt Function

As indicated in the program design on page VB 4.06, the actual computation for the monthly payment is performed by one of Visual Basic .NET's financial functions, the Pmt function. The **Pmt function** is in the financial category of the run-time library functions. The Pmt function returns the payment for a loan based on periodic, constant payments and a constant interest rate. The Pmt function performs the work of the calculation described in the requirements document. The function is used in a code statement in the following manner:

Pmt(rate, nper, pv, fv, due)

As shown, the Pmt function accepts five arguments. The five arguments within the Pmt function are described in Table 4-20.

Table 4-20   Arguments Passed to the Pmt Function

ARGUMENT	DESCRIPTION
rate	Interest rate per period. For example, if you get a car loan at an annual percentage rate of 9 percent and make monthly payments, the rate per period is 0.09/12, or .0075.
nper	Total number of payment periods in the loan. For example, if you make monthly payments on a five year car loan, your loan has a total of 5 * 12 (or 60) payment periods.
pv	Present value that a series of payments to be made in the future is worth now (to the lender). For example, if you borrow $10,000 to buy a car, its pv is –10,000.
fv (optional)	Future value or cash balance you want after you have made the final payment. The future value of a loan is 0.
due (optional)	Number indicating when payments are due. Use 0 if payments are due at the end of the period, and use 1 if the payments are due at the beginning of the period.

Table 4-21 lists the other Visual Basic .NET intrinsic financial functions, their arguments, and their purpose.

Table 4-21 Intrinsic Financial Functions

FUNCTION	ARGUMENTS	PURPOSE
Ddb()	cost salvage life period factor (optional)	Calculates the depreciation of an asset for a specific period using the double-declining balance method or some other method you specify by changing the factor argument.
Fv()	rate nper pmt pv (optional) due (optional)	Calculates the future value of an annuity based on periodic, fixed payments and a fixed interest rate.
Ipmt()	rate per nper pv fv (optional) due (optional)	Calculates the interest payment for a given period of an annuity based on periodic, fixed payments and a fixed interest rate.
Irr()	valuearray() guess (optional)	Calculates the internal rate of return for a series of periodic cash flows. The series of cash flows is placed in the valuearray() argument.
Mirr()	valuearray() financerate reinvestrate	Calculates the modified internal rate of return for a series of periodic cash flows. The series of cash flows is placed in the valuearray() argument.
Nper()	rate pmt pv fv (optional) due (optional)	Calculates the number of periods for an annuity based on periodic, fixed payments and a fixed interest rate.
Npv()	rate valuearray()	Calculates the net present value of an investment based on a series of periodic cash flows and a discount rate. The series of cash flows is placed in the valuearray() argument.
Ppmt()	rate per nper pv fv (optional) due (optional)	Calculates the principal payment for a given period of an annuity based on periodic, fixed payments and a fixed interest rate.
Pv()	rate nper pmt fv (optional) due (optional)	Calculates the present value of an annuity based on periodic, fixed payments to be paid in the future and a fixed interest rate.

(continued)

Table 4-21 *Intrinsic Financial Functions (continued)*

FUNCTION	ARGUMENTS	PURPOSE
Rate()	nper pmt pv fv (optional) due (optional) guess (optional)	Calculates the interest rate per period for an annuity.
Sln()	cost salvage life	Calculates the straight-line depreciation of an asset for a single period.
Syd()	cost salvage life period	Calculates the sum-of-years digits representation of an asset for a specified period.

In the btnComputePayment_Click event procedure, the dblRate variable contains the monthly interest rate (rate), the dblMonths variable contains the number of months (nper), and the dblLoanAmount variable contains the value of the loan (pv). As indicated in Table 4-20 on page VB 4.58, for a loan, the Pmt function requires a negative value for the present value (pv) argument, because a payment is considered a debit (negative value) and the specifications call for displaying the payment as a positive number. The negative value of a variable is indicated by placing a minus sign (–) before the variable name.

Using a Negative Value

The negative value of a variable is indicated by placing a minus sign (–) before the variable name.

Figure 4-53 shows the code required to call the Pmt function and assign the result of the function to the dblPayment variable. Functions return a value and the value returned has a data type, just as any value does in code. Therefore, because Option Strict is set to On, the data type of the resulting value of the Pmt function, which is a Double, must match the data type of the variable it is assigned to, dblPayment.

```
240        ' Calculate the monthly payment using the .NET PMT
241        ' function. Format the result as currency and then
242        ' display the result in the txtMonthlyPayment Textbox.
243        dblPayment = Pmt(dblRate, gdblMonths, -dblLoanAmount)
```

FIGURE 4-53

The following step illustrates using the Pmt function.

To Use the Pmt Function

1. Enter the lines of code from Figure 4-53.

Lines 240 through 243 display in the code window (Figure 4-54). The assignment statement calls the Pmt function to calculate the monthly payment and assigns the result to the dblPayment variable.

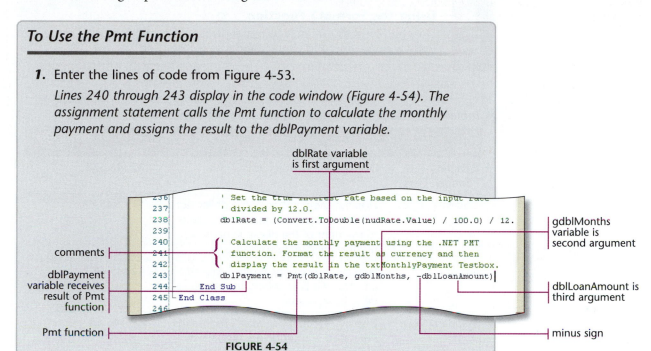

FIGURE 4-54

Figure 4-54 shows the Pmt function and the three arguments passed to it. The minus sign before the dblLoanAmount variable tells the Pmt function to calculate a payment on a loan. The result of the Pmt function is assigned to the dblPayment variable.

The Format$ Function

The statements in Figure 4-55 format the result of the Pmt function as dollars and cents and place the value in the txtMonthlyPayment TextBox control.

```
244         strPayment = Format$(dblPayment, "Currency")
245         txtMonthlyPayment.Text = strPayment
```

FIGURE 4-55

strPayment is a string variable declared at the top of the event procedure. The **Format$ function** is an intrinsic function that takes the first item in parentheses, dblPayment, and formats it as specified by the second item in the parentheses, "Currency". Currency is a predefined format name, which means Visual Basic .NET will display the value dblPayment in a more readable fashion in the Monthly payment text box. The Format$ function returns a value with a String data type. Table 4-22 on the next page summarizes the more frequently used predefined formats for the Format$ function in Visual Basic .NET. The last column in the table shows the result of formatting the value, 12345.678.

Tip

Using the Format$ Function
Use the Format$ function to make displayed numeric results more visually appealing and understandable to the user.

Table 4-22   Common Formats for the Format$ Function

FORMAT	DESCRIPTION	RESULT OF FORMATTING 12345.678
General Number, G, g	Displays the number as is	12345.678
Currency, C, c	Displays the number with a dollar sign, a thousands separator, and two digits to the right of the decimal; negative numbers display in parentheses	$12,345.68
Fixed, F, f	Displays at least one digit to the left and two digits to the right of the decimal separator	12345.68
Standard, N, n	Displays the number with a thousands separator; if appropriate, displays two digits to the right of the decimal	12,345.68
Percent, P, p	Displays the number multiplied by 100 with a % sign	1,234,567.80%
Scientific, E, e	Uses standard scientific notation	1.234568e+004
True/False	Displays False if the number is 0; otherwise, displays True	True
On/Off	Displays Off if the number is 0; otherwise, displays On	On
Yes/No	Displays No if the number is 0; otherwise, displays Yes	Yes

The following step enters the code shown in Figure 4-55 on the previous page in the btnComputePayment_Click event procedure.

To Use the Format$ Function

1. Press the ENTER key. Enter the lines of code from Figure 4-55 and do not press the ENTER key.

Lines 244 and 245 display in the code window (Figure 4-56). The first statement formats the dblPayment variable as currency and assigns the resulting string to the strPayment variable. Line 245 assigns the strPayment string variable to the Text property of the txtMonthlyPayment TextBox control.

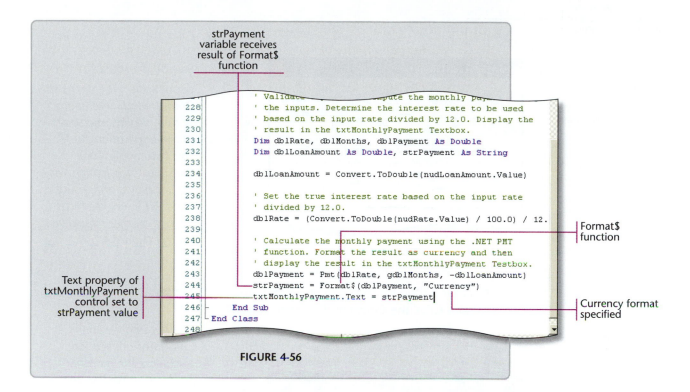

FIGURE 4-56

The preceding steps showed how to use the Format$ function to change the appearance of the output value, dblPayment. The Format$ function converts the value of the dblPayment variable to a string and then applies the Currency format to the result. The formatted string is assigned to the Text property of the txtMonthlyPayment control, meaning that the result is displayed to the user.

The coding phase for the Automobile Loan Calculator application is now complete and the application can be tested.

Saving, Testing, and Documenting the Project

The following steps save the form and project files for the Automobile Loan Calculator project on the Data Disk in drive A and then run the application to test the code.

To Save and Test the Project

1. Click the Save All button on the Standard toolbar.

The asterisk next to Form1.vb [Design] on the window title bar and the main work area tab no longer display, indicating that the project has been saved. Because the project was created and saved initially on the Data Disk in drive A, Visual Basic .NET automatically saves the project on the Data Disk in drive A.

(continued)

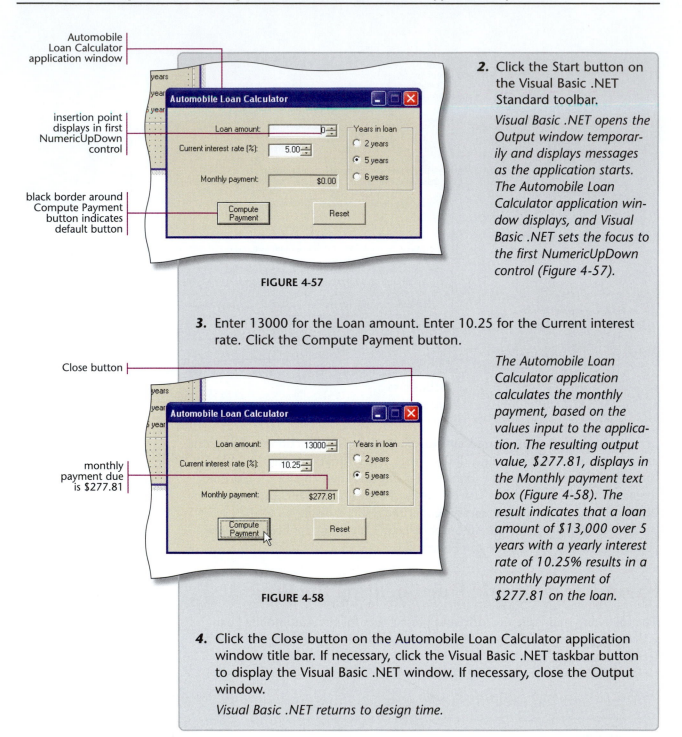

Automobile
Loan Calculator
application window

insertion point
displays in first
NumericUpDown
control

black border around
Compute Payment
button indicates
default button

FIGURE 4-57

Close button

monthly
payment due
is $277.81

FIGURE 4-58

2. Click the Start button on the Visual Basic .NET Standard toolbar.

Visual Basic .NET opens the Output window temporarily and displays messages as the application starts. The Automobile Loan Calculator application window displays, and Visual Basic .NET sets the focus to the first NumericUpDown control (Figure 4-57).

3. Enter 13000 for the Loan amount. Enter 10.25 for the Current interest rate. Click the Compute Payment button.

The Automobile Loan Calculator application calculates the monthly payment, based on the values input to the application. The resulting output value, $277.81, displays in the Monthly payment text box (Figure 4-58). The result indicates that a loan amount of $13,000 over 5 years with a yearly interest rate of 10.25% results in a monthly payment of $277.81 on the loan.

4. Click the Close button on the Automobile Loan Calculator application window title bar. If necessary, click the Visual Basic .NET taskbar button to display the Visual Basic .NET window. If necessary, close the Output window.

Visual Basic .NET returns to design time.

When testing the application, it is important to test the boundary conditions stated in the requirements. In the Automobile Loan Calculator application, the requirements state the boundary condition for the maximum loan amount to be $25,000. Therefore, you should test the value of 25000 for the Loan amount and some value higher than 25000 to make certain that the program behaves correctly.

Testing an Application

When testing an application, make certain that all rules are tested for their minimum and maximum values. Also, test any special cases that are specified in the requirements document.

Once you have tested the data validation rules for minimum and maximum values, the testing process for the Automobile Loan Calculator application is complete. The final step of the development cycle is to document the application. The following steps document the application and quit Visual Basic .NET. Line numbers are printed on the code listing.

To Document the Application and Quit Visual Basic .NET

1. If necessary, close the Output window. Click the Form1.vb [Design] tab, and then follow the steps on page VB 2.34 of Chapter 2 using the PRINT SCREEN key to print a record of the user interface design of the Automobile Loan Calculator form.

A record of the user interface design of the Automobile Loan Calculator application is printed (Figure 4-59).

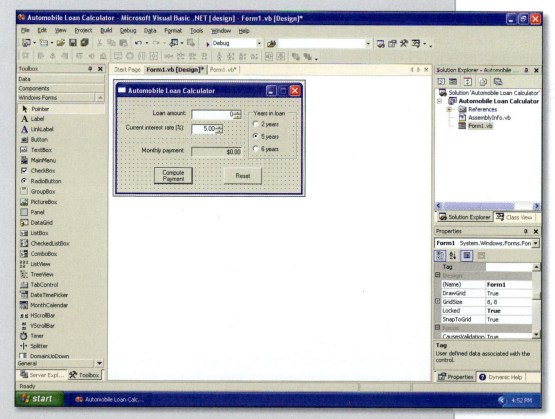

FIGURE 4-59

(continued)

2. Click the Form1.vb tab. Click File on the menu bar and then click Page Setup.

3. When the Page Setup dialog box displays, if necessary, click Line numbers and then click the OK button.

4. Follow the steps on page VB 2.40 of Chapter 2 using the Print command on the File menu to print a record of the code for the Automobile Loan Calculator application.

A record of the Automobile Loan Calculator application code is printed (Figure 4-60).

```
A:\Chapter4\Automobile Loan Calculator\Automobile Loan Calculator\Form1.vb                    1
 1 Option Strict On
 2 Public Class Form1
 3     Inherits System.Windows.Forms.Form
 4
 5 Windows Form Designer generated code
 6     ' Chapter 4:       Automobile Loan Calculator
 7     ' Programmer:      Jeff Quasney
 8     ' Date:            September 22, 2004
 9     ' Purpose:         This project calculates the monthly payment for
10     '                  a loan based on loan amount, interest rate, and
11     '                  length of the loan.
12     Dim gdblMonths As Double = 60.0
13     Const MaximumLoanAllowed As Integer = 25000
14
15     Private Sub Form1_Load(ByVal sender As System.Object, ByVal e As System.EventArgs) ↵
       Handles MyBase.Load
16         ' Set the maximum value of the Loan amount NumericUpDown control
17         nudLoanAmount.Maximum = MaximumLoanAllowed
18     End Sub
19
20     Private Sub btnReset_Click(ByVal sender As System.Object, ByVal e As System.        ↵
       EventArgs) Handles btnReset.Click
21         ' Reset Loan Amount and Monthly payment to zero. Reset
22         ' the interest rate to 5%, and select five years for the
23         ' length of the loan
24         nudLoanAmount.Value = 0
25         nudRate.Value = 5
26         radFiveYears.Checked = True
27         txtMonthlyPayment.Text = "$0.00"
28     End Sub
29
30     Private Sub radTwoYears_CheckedChanged(ByVal sender As System.Object, ByVal e As  ↵
       System.EventArgs) Handles radTwoYears.CheckedChanged
31         gdblMonths = 24.0
32     End Sub
33
34     Private Sub radFiveYears_CheckedChanged(ByVal sender As System.Object, ByVal e As ↵
       System.EventArgs) Handles radFiveYears.CheckedChanged
35         gdblMonths = 60.0
36     End Sub
37
38     Private Sub radSixYears_CheckedChanged(ByVal sender As System.Object, ByVal e As  ↵
       System.EventArgs) Handles radSixYears.CheckedChanged
39         gdblMonths = 72.0
40     End Sub
41
42     Private Sub btnComputePayment_Click(ByVal sender As System.Object, ByVal e As     ↵
       System.EventArgs) Handles btnComputePayment.Click
43         ' Validate inputs and compute the monthly payment using
44         ' the inputs. Determine the interest rate to be used
45         ' based on the input rate divided by 12.0. Display the
46         ' result in the txtMonthlyPayment Textbox.
47         Dim dblRate, dblMonths, dblPayment As Double
48         Dim dblLoanAmount As Double, strPayment As String
49
50         dblLoanAmount = Convert.ToDouble(nudLoanAmount.Value)
51
52         ' Set the true interest rate based on the input rate
53         ' divided by 12.0.
54         dblRate = (Convert.ToDouble(nudRate.Value) / 100.0) / 12.0
55
56         ' Calculate the monthly payment using the .NET PMT
57         ' function. Format the result as currency and then
58         ' display the result in the txtMonthlyPayment Textbox.
59         dblPayment = Pmt(dblRate, gdblMonths, -dblLoanAmount)
60         strPayment = Format$(dblPayment, "Currency")
61         txtMonthlyPayment.Text = strPayment
62     End Sub
63 End Class
64
```

FIGURE 4-60

5. Click the Visual Basic .NET Close button.

If you made changes to the project since the last time it was saved, Visual Basic .NET displays the Microsoft Visual Basic .NET dialog box. If you click the Yes button, you can save your project and quit. If you click the No button, you will quit without saving changes. Clicking the Cancel button will close the dialog box.

Chapter Summary

In this chapter, you learned how to use two new controls: the GroupBox control and the RadioButton control. You learned how to use the Layout toolbar to align and size controls quickly. You then learned how to set a default button on a form and lock a form and its controls, so that they could not be moved or resized accidently. You learned how to declare variables and constants and how data types are used. You also learned how to code mathematical expressions and the order of operator precedence. Finally, you learned how to use instrinsic functions, such as Pmt and Format$, and pass parameters to functions.

What You Should Know

Having completed this chapter, you now should be able to perform the tasks shown in Table 4-23.

Table 4-23   *Chapter 4 What You Should Know*

TASK NUMBER	TASK	PAGE
1	Start Visual Basic .NET and Start a New Project	VB 4.08
2	Set Form Properties and Add Controls	VB 4.10
3	Add a GroupBox Control to a Form	VB 4.11
4	Add RadioButton Controls to Create a Group of Controls	VB 4.12
5	Change the Properties of Controls	VB 4.15
6	Change the Properties of a GroupBox Control	VB 4.17
7	Change the Properties of RadioButton Controls	VB 4.20
8	Select Multiple Controls and Use the Align Rights Button	VB 4.23
9	Size and Align Input and Output Controls	VB 4.25
10	Size and Align Button Controls	VB 4.26
11	Size and Align Controls in a Group	VB 4.27
12	Align the Tops of Controls	VB 4.28
13	Verify the Size and Position of Controls	VB 4.29
14	Set the Default Button on a Form	VB 4.31
15	Lock Controls on a Form	VB 4.32
16	Declare a Constant	VB 4.37
17	Code a Form Load Event Procedure	VB 4.39
18	Code the btnReset_Click Event Procedure	VB 4.40
19	Code an Option Strict Statement	VB 4.42
20	Declare a Global Variable	VB 4.45
21	Code the CheckChanged Event Procedures for RadioButton Controls	VB 4.46
22	Declare Local Variables	VB 4.49
23	Code an Assignment Statement to Convert a Data Type	VB 4.50
24	Code an Expression to Calculate a Monthly Interest Rate	VB 4.57
25	Use the Pmt Function	VB 4.61
26	Use the Format$ Function	VB 4.62
27	Save and Test the Project	VB 4.63
28	Document the Application and Quit Visual Basic .NET	VB 4.65

Key Terms

AcceptButton property *(VB 4.30)*
argument *(VB 4.50)*
arithmetic operator *(VB 4.51)*
Boolean *(VB 4.34)*
Byte *(VB 4.34)*
Char *(VB 4.34)*
Checked property *(VB 4.18)*
Const keyword *(VB 4.35)*
constant *(VB 4.33)*
constant declaration statement
   (VB 4.36)
container control *(VB 4.11)*
Convert.ToDouble() method
   (VB 4.49)
data type *(VB 4.34)*
Date *(VB 4.34)*
Decimal *(VB 4.34)*
declare *(VB 4.34)*
default button *(VB 4.30)*
Dim statement *(VB 4.43)*
Double *(VB 4.34)*
expression *(VB 4.51)*
form level variable *(VB 4.44)*
form Load event *(VB 4.38)*
Format$ function *(VB 4.61)*

global variable *(VB 4.44)*
groups *(VB 4.12)*
GroupBox control *(VB 4.11)*
Integer *(VB 4.34)*
intrinsic function *(VB 4.58)*
local variable *(VB 4.44)*
locking controls *(VB 4.32)*
Long *(VB 4.34)*
Mod operator *(VB 4.52)*
modulo operator *(VB 4.52)*
nested *(VB 4.55)*
numeric expression *(VB 4.51)*
Object *(VB 4.34)*
Option Strict statement *(VB 4.41)*
order of operator precedence
   (VB 4.51)
Pmt function *(VB 4.58)*
RadioButton control *(VB 4.12)*
run-time library *(VB 4.58)*
scope *(VB 4.43)*
Short *(VB 4.34)*
Single *(VB 4.34)*
String *(VB 4.34)*
value *(VB 4.33)*
variable *(VB 4.33)*

Homework Assignments

Short Answer

1. Which arithmetic operation is performed first in the following numeric expressions?
   a. 8 / 6 * 4
   b. intCount + intCount1 – intX
   c. 8 * (intInventoryAmount + 3)
   d. (X * (3 / Y)) ^ 6 + Z ^ (2 ^ 2) + 8 Mod 5
   e. dblPrice / dblInventory + dblTax
   f. (B ^ 2 – 4 * A * C) / (2 * A)
2. Evaluate each of the following:
   a. 4 * 5 * 3 / 6 – 6 ^ 2 / 12
   b. (3 ^ 4) + 7 * 4
   c. 7 * 5 / 2 + 9 Mod 3 + 3

3. Calculate the numeric value for each of the following valid numeric expressions if A = 3.0, C = 5.0, W = 3.0, T = 3.0, X = 1.0, and Y = 2.0.
   a. (C − A * 3) + 8.1
   b. (A / (C + 1) * 4 − 5) / 2 + (4 Mod 3 \ 3)
   c. 50.0 / (X * Y) ^ W
   d. X + 7.0 * Y * W / 3.0 − 7.0 / (T − X / Y) + W ^ T

4. Repeat the above assignment for the case of A = 2.0, C = 3.0, W = 4.0, T = 4.0, X = 2.0, and Y = 2.0.

5. Which of the following are invalid variable names in Visual Basic .NET? Why?
   a. X
   b. PriCe
   c. Const
   d. R.3
   e. 531
   f. Dim
   g. _Sng
   h. A-Z
   i . Q9
   j. _Integer

6. Write a valid statement for each of the following algebraic statements. Use appropriate variable names.
   a. $q = (d + e)^{1/3}$
   b. $d = (A^2)^{3.2}$
   c. $Y = a_1x + a_2x^2 + a_3x^3 + a_4x^4$
   d. $v = 100 − (2/3)^{100 − B}$

7. If necessary, insert parentheses so that each numeric expression results in the value indicated on the right side of the arrow.
   a. 8 / 2 + 2 + 12 —> 14
   b. 8 ^ 2 − 1 —> 8
   c. 3.0 / 2.0 + 0.5 + 3.0 ^ 1.0 —> 5.0
   d. 12.0 Mod 5.0 \ 2.0 + 1.0 ^ 2.0 + 1.0 * 2.0 * 3.0 / 4.0 − 3.0 / 2.0 —> 0.5
   e. 12 − 2 − 3 − 1 − 4 —> 10
   f. 7 * 3 + 4 ^ 2 − 3 / 13 —> 22
   g. 3 * 2 − 3 * 4 * 2 + 3 —> − 60
   h. 3 * 6 − 3 + 2 + 6 * 4 − 4 / 2 ^ 1 —> 33

8. Consider the valid code below. What is displayed in the txtResult TextBox control when the code is executed?
   a. Dim A As Double = 2.0
      Dim B as Double = 3.0
      Dim D as Double
      D = (A ^ 4.0 / A * B) − (8 .0* B / 4.0)
      D = D + 1.0
      txtResult.Text = D

   b. Dim A As Double = 2.0
      Dim B As Double = 3.0
      Dim E1, E2, E3 As Double
      B = 4.0

```
El = A * B
E3 = 4.0 + 1.0
E2 = E2 / E3
A  = El + E2
txtResult.Text = A
```

9. What does the following code display in the Value1 and Value2 TextBox controls?

   dblAverage1 = 4.0 + 5.0 + 6.0 + 7.0 + 8.0 / 5.0

   dblAverage2 = (4.0 + 5.0 + 6.0 + 7.0 + 8.0) / 5.0

   txtValue1.Text = dblAverage1

   txtValue2.Text = dblAverage2

10. The _____ control is used as a container for other controls.

11. List the defaults for the following RadioButton controls.
    a. CheckAlign _____   b. Checked _____   c. FlatStyle _____
    d. ImageAlign _____   e. AutoCheck _____

12. The _____ toolbar contains tools that allow you to adjust the alignment spacing and size of any group of controls on a form.

13. Use the _____ key to select two or more controls at the same time.

14. When the user presses the ENTER key during run time and the form has the name of a Button control assigned as the _____ property, the Click event procedure assigned to the button executes.

15. _____ disallows the ability to modify controls on a form during design time.

16. _____ are numbers or strings that programmers will never change in the code. _____ represent a location in memory which can change values as the code executes. _____ represents a location in memory, but its value cannot change during execution of the code.

17. The _____ determines what kind of data the variables or constants can store.

18. A variable or constant name must begin with a(n) _____ and can be up to _____ characters in length.

19. The _____ statement is used to instruct Visual Basic .NET to force the programmer to make certain all assignments occur with the same type on both sides of the assignment and that all variables are explicitly declared.

20. The _____ function converts the value of a numeric argument to a Double data type.

21. To display a positive payment, append a _____ to the front of the present value argument in the Pmt function.

22. The _____ function is used to format a value so that it displays in a meaningful form.

Learn It Online

Start your browser and visit scsite.com/vbnet/exs. Follow the instructions in the exercises below.

1. **Chapter Reinforcement TF, MC, and SA** Click the True/False, Multiple Choice, and Short Answer link below Chapter 4. Print and then answer the questions.

2. **Practice Test** Click the Practice Test link below Chapter 4. Answer each question, enter your first and last name at the bottom of the page, and then click the Grade Test button. When the graded practice test displays on your screen, click Print on the File menu to print a hard copy. Continue to take practice tests until you score 80% or better. Hand in a printout of the final practice test.

3. **Crossword Puzzle Challenge** Click the Crossword Puzzle Challenge link below Chapter 4. Read the instructions, and then enter your first and last name. Click the Play button. Complete the crossword puzzle. When you are finished, click the Submit button. When the crossword puzzle redisplays, click the Print button.

4. **Tips and Tricks** Click the Tips and Tricks link below Chapter 4. Click a topic that pertains to Chapter 4. Right-click the information and then click Print on the shortcut menu. Construct a brief example of what the information relates to in Visual Basic .NET to confirm you understand how to use the tip or trick. Hand in the example and printed information.

5. **Newsgroups** Click the Newsgroups link below Chapter 4. Click a topic that pertains to Chapter 4. Print three comments.

6. **Expanding Your Horizons** Click the Articles for Visual Basic .NET below Chapter 4. Click a topic that pertains to Chapter 4. Print the information. Construct a brief example of what the information relates to in Visual Basic .NET to confirm you understand the contents of the article. Hand in the example and printed information.

7. **Search Sleuth** Select three key terms from the Key Terms section of this chapter and then use the Google search engine at google.com (or any major search engine) to display and print two Web pages for each key term.

Debugging Assignment

Start Visual Basic .NET and open the project, Kona's Coffee Supply, from the Chapter4\Konas Coffee Supply folder on the Data Disk. The project consists of a form that calculates the price of an order based on a quantity ordered, item price, and customer type. The calculate button calculates the total price for the order and then displays the result in a text box. Preferred customers and New customers receive a 4% discount. Delinquent customers pay an additional 5% on any order.

The Kona's Coffee Supply project contains bugs in the user interface and in the program code. Follow the steps below to debug the project.

1. Use the Layout toolbar to size and align controls that are not sized or aligned correctly. The Label controls should be right-aligned. The NumericUpDown controls and TextBox control should be left-aligned and sized the same. The Button controls should be centered on the form together and should be the same size.

2. The uppermost RadioButton control is not inside the GroupBox control container. Delete the control and add a new RadioButton control with correct properties in the appropriate location. Be sure not to lose the code associated with the control's event procedure.

3. The Compute Total button is not the default button. Make the Compute Total button the default button for the form.

4. Format the total as Currency in the code using the Format$ function.

5. A bug in the computation causes Delinquent customers to receive a 5% discount instead of a 5% penalty. Fix this bug.

6. Save the project and then run the project to test for any additional bugs. Enter 2500 for the quantity, 15.75 as the price, and select a Customer type of New. The application should display as shown in Figure 4-61 with a total of $37,800.00.

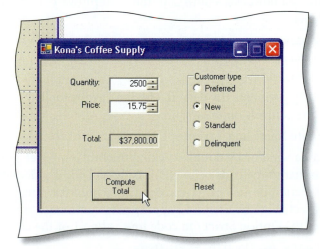

FIGURE 4-61

7. Document the form code for the Form1.vb form. Circle the lines of code you modified on the code printout.

Programming Assignments

1 Understanding Code Statements

Carefully read each of the following descriptions. Write code statements to accomplish specific tasks. Record your answers on a separate sheet of paper. Number your answers to correspond to the code descriptions.

1. Write a code statement that will display the characters, Salutations, in a Label control with a name of lblGreeting.

2. Write a code statement that will clear a TextBox control with the name of txtBlank.

3. Write a code statement that will create a variable called total. The variable should have a data type of Short.

4. When a RadioButton control with a name of radGreeting is checked, write a code statement that displays, Salutations, in a Label control with a name of lblGreeting; otherwise, when a second RadioButton control is checked the code statement should display, Farewell, in the same Label control.

2 Present Value Function

Start Visual Basic .NET. Open the project, Lottery Projection from the Chapter 4/Lottery Projection folder on the Data Disk. This application calculates the present value of payments received over a given number of years assuming a certain interest rate can be achieved in an investment in the same time frame. The calculation can be used to compare receiving a lump-sum lottery payment for a lottery winner versus receiving a certain number of payments over several years.

Perform the following tasks to complete the application.

1. Unlock the controls on the form.

2. Add the three RadioButton controls to the GroupBox1 control with the following labels:

```
10 yearly payments
20 yearly payments
25 yearly payments
```

Make 20 yearly payments the default. Use the Layout toolbar to size and align all of the controls on the form.

3. Set appropriate Name and Text properties for each of the new controls.

4. Open the code window by double-clicking the btnComputePV button and add code similar to the code below. This code will add a global variable in the general section of the Form1.vb code file to hold the number of years of payments selected by the user. Add appropriate comments to your code. Be sure to enter the Option Strict On code line as line 1 of the code.

```
Dim gdblYears As Double = 20.0
```

In the btnComputePV_Click event procedure, add code to declare variables that you will use in the event procedure as follows:

```
Dim dblAmount, dblPV As Double, strPV As String
```

5. After the code added in step 4, insert the following code to convert the Yearly payment amounts value to the data type Double and assign the result to the dblAmount variable.

```
dblAmount = Convert.ToDouble(txtAmount.Text)
```

6. Add the code to perform the calculation of the present value of the payments. The present value function, PV, accepts three inputs: the interest rate, the number of payments, and the amount of the payments. The interest rate is calculated from the Value property of the nudRate control. The number of payments is based on the item selected in the RadioButton group. Insert the following code after the code entered in step 5:

```
dblRate = Convert.ToDouble(nudRate.Value)/100
dblPV = PV(dblRate, gdblYears, -dblAmount)
```

7. To format the output value and display it on the form, insert code similar to the following code after the code inserted in step 6:

```
strPV = Format$(dblPV, "Currency")
txtPV.Text = strPV
```

8. Return to the Form1.vb[design] tab. Double-click the 10 yearly payments RadioButton and enter a line of code to set the gdblYears variable to the value 10.0. Repeat the process for the other two RadioButton controls using the appropriate value for the variable.

9. Lock the controls on the form and then save the project.

10. Run the project and correct any errors. If changes have been made, save the project again. The application window should display as shown in Figure 4-62 at run time.

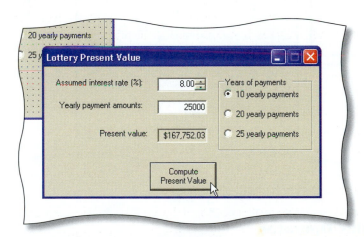

FIGURE 4-62

3 Production Lot Size Calculation

When a company manufactures several products, the management must decide how many units of one product should be produced before switching the manufacturing system over to produce another product. The number of units of a certain product to produce before switching to another product is called the lot size. Costs are associated both with having a number of units in inventory (CarryingCost) and with switching manufacturing to another product (SetupCost). If a company must produce a certain quantity of a product in a given year (UnitsPerYear), it must determine how many to produce at each production run in order to meet that quantity, keep inventory costs low, and keep the cost of switching the manufacturing system low. The production lot size tells the company how many units of a product to produce before changing the manufacturing over to another product.

The production lot size (ProductionLotSize) is calculated as follows:

$$\text{ProductionLotSize} = ((\,2 \times \text{UnitsPerYear} \times \text{SetupCost}) / \text{CarryingCost}\,)\,{\wedge}\,.5$$

Design and write a program that calculates the production lot size based on a number of units to produce each year, a setup cost, and an inventory cost to carry a unit in inventory for a year. Use NumericUpDown controls for the three input values. Limit the UnitsPerYear between 500 and 15,000, the SetupCost between $150 and $500, and the CarryingCost between $1 and $5. The completed application should display as shown in Figure 4-63.

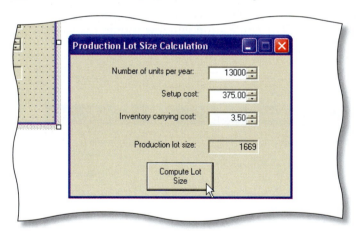

FIGURE 4-63

4 Modulus Operator

Write a program that will display the number of dollars and cents in two output TextBox controls based on user numeric input. For instance, if the user inputs 543, the program will display 5 in the Dollars output TextBox control and 43 in the Cents output TextBox control. For this program, use integer arithmetic and avoid using decimal variables and values. If necessary, review the integer remainder modular operator, Mod, introduced in this chapter. The completed application should display as shown in Figure 4-64.

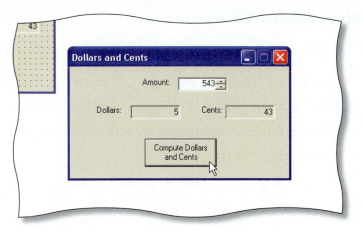

FIGURE 4-64

5 Using RadioButton Controls and Global Variables

Design and develop a project to assign a letter grade to a student's assignment based on a test score and other criteria. Use a NumericUpDown control to allow the instructor's assistant to enter a test score between 0 and 100. Use a group of RadioButton controls to determine the grade on Extra Credit Problem #1 – None, Average (3 point bonus), or Above average (5 point bonus). Use a second group of RadioButton controls to select whether a student handed in the assignment on time, with the default being On time. The other choices are 1 to 2 days late (5 point penalty) and more than 2 days late (automatic score of 0). Display the final total grade in a read-only TextBox control. Use global variables to keep track of which RadioButton control is checked before determining the final grade. The completed application should display as shown in Figure 4-65.

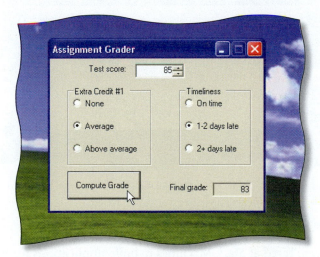

FIGURE 4-65

6 English to Metric Conversion

Design and develop a project to convert an English measurement in miles, yards, feet, and inches to a metric measurement in kilometers, meters, and centimeters. Use the following formula to change the English measurement to inches:

Total Inches = 63,360 × Miles + 36 × Yards + 12 × Feet + Inches

Use the following formula to determine the equivalent meters:

Meters = Total Inches / 39.37

Declare constants for all numeric values in the two formulas above. The variable used to represent the number of meters and the numeric constant 39.37 must be declared as the data type Double. The constants and data types in the first formula should be declared as integers. Convert the Total Inches in the second formula to a Double data type before using it in the calculation. Set Option Strict to On in your code.

(*Hint:* After the number of meters has been determined, the maximum number of kilometers can be computed from: Kilometers = Meters\ 1,000. Next, the remaining meters can be determined from: Remaining Meters = Meters – 1,000 * Kilometers. The number of integer meters in Remaining Meters then can be determined from: Integer Meters = Convert.ToInt32(Remaining Meters). Continue with the same technique to compute the number of centimeters.)

Use the following test data to test your program: 2 miles, 5 yards, 2 feet, and 7 inches. The result should be 3 kilometers, 224 meters, and 5.38 centimeters. The completed application should display as shown in Figure 4-66.

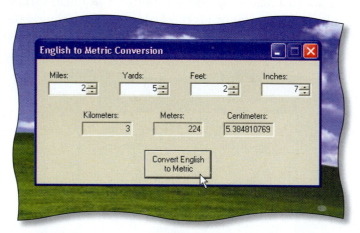

FIGURE 4-66

7 Multiple Groups of RadioButton Controls

You recently were hired at Stark Machines to build applications for its accounting department. One of your first assignments is to design and develop a Windows application to calculate employee yearly raises. You have decided that the yearly salary must be entered in a NumericUpDown control with a range of 10000 to 75000 for the salary. Use RadioButton controls to select the raise percentage rates of 8% for sales, 10% for labor, or 5% for management. Use a second RadioButton control group to designate whether an employee has worked more than 15 years, in which case the employee is entitled to an additional 2% raise.

8 Slope and Intercept Calculation

Using the concepts presented in this chapter, design and write a program that accepts two sets of (X, Y) coordinates, (X1, Y1) and (X2, Y2), and then calculates and displays the slope and Y intercept of the line that intersects the two coordinates. Use NumericUpDown controls to limit the coordinates to integer values between 0 and 20.

9 Using Events and Expressions

Write a Windows application for a self-service printing center that sells self-service copies at 4 cents per page, computer time at $3.00 per ten minutes, and computer laser printing at 9 cents per page. Use NumericUpDown controls to input quantities of each item. Next to each quantity, include a read-only TextBox control that displays the price of the quantity multiplied by the price per unit listed above. Update each TextBox control when the ValueChanged event of each NumericUpDown control executes. Also, include code that calculates the total in all three TextBox controls and then updates a fourth TextBox control at the bottom of the form with the total. Be sure to initialize all of the controls on the form correctly. The form should not contain any Button controls, only the controls mentioned above.

10 Writing an Expression for a Monthly Payment

Write a valid Visual Basic .NET expression for the Automobile Loan Payment formula in the project developed in this chapter. If you developed the Automobile Loan Payment application in this chapter, place the expression in your code as a substitute for the use of the Pmt function. Be sure to use any data type conversions necessary to conform to the restrictions of the Option Strict On statement. Test the change to be sure that you obtain the same results as the Pmt function.

5

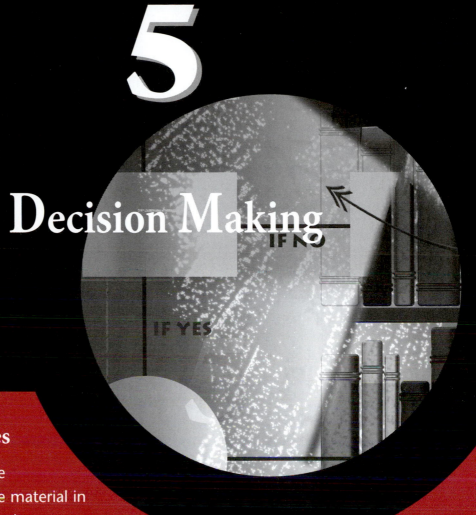

Decision Making

Objectives

You will have
mastered the material in
this chapter when you can:

- Use the ComboBox control
- Code an If...Then...Else statement
- Code a nested If...Then...Else statement
- Code a Select Case statement
- Validate user input
- Use the MessageBox class
- Use string concatenation in code
- Use relational operators in code
- Use logical operators in code

Introduction

This chapter concentrates on modifying the Windows application developed in Chapter 4 (Figure 5-1a) to add functionality as shown in Figure 5-1b. The modified application uses one new control: the ComboBox. In this chapter, you will learn how to add and set properties for the ComboBox control, so it functions as a drop-down list. You will learn how to write code that uses If...Then...Else and Select Case statements. You also will learn how to write code to display messages to the user. Finally, you will learn how to write code that uses relational operators, such as greater than (>), less than (<), and equal to (=), and logical operators, such as Not, And, and Or.

Chapter Five — Modifying the Automobile Loan Calculator Application

The Windows application developed in this chapter is an enhanced version of the Automobile Loan Calculator application developed in Chapter 4. In addition to the functionality included in the application in Chapter 4, the modified application allows the user to select a credit rating for the customer from a list of credit ratings. The five credit ratings in the credit rating list are: A – Excellent, B – Good, C – Average, D – Poor, and E – Low. The interest rate on the loan is determined by the customer's credit rating. A customer with an A – Excellent rating receives the lowest current interest rate available; this current interest rate is entered by the user. The interest rate for a customer with a B – Good rating is 10% higher than the current interest rate entered by the user; for a C – Average rating, it is 15% higher; for a D – Poor rating, it is 17% higher; and for an E – Low rating, it is 25% higher. If the user enters an E – Low credit rating for a customer, the application also sets the maximum loan amount to $5,000. If the user has not selected a credit rating, the application displays an error message. In the case of Figure 5-1(b), the credit rating of B – Good raises the interest rate by 10%, or from 10.25% to 11.275%.

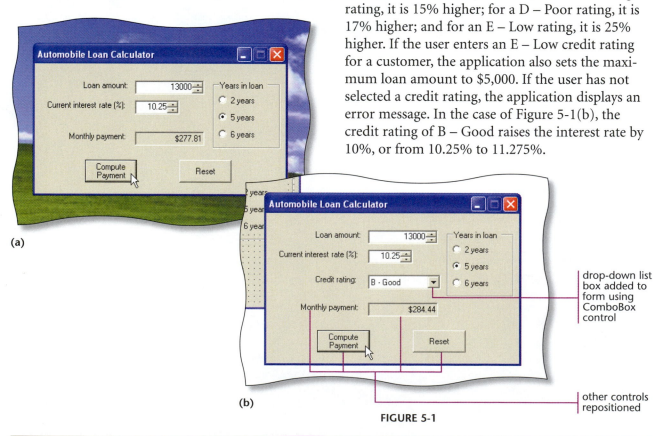

(a)

(b)

drop-down list box added to form using ComboBox control

other controls repositioned

FIGURE 5-1

When the user clicks the Compute Payment button, the application first checks the data input by the user to determine if it is valid. If the user has not selected a credit rating, the application displays an error message. If the user enters an E – Low credit rating for a customer, the application sets the maximum loan amount to $5,000. If the user enters more than $5,000 as the loan amount for a customer with an E – Low credit rating, the application displays an error message. After the input data is validated, the application computes and displays the monthly loan payment in the Monthly payment text box.

Program Development

The development cycle for the modified Automobile Loan Calculator application consists of tasks that correspond to the six development cycle phases, as shown in Table 5-1.

Table 5-1 Automobile Loan Calculator Application Modification Tasks

DEVELOPMENT PHASE	TASK NUMBER	TASK NAME	TASK
Analyze requirements	1	Analyze problem	Analyze the automobile loan calculator problem.
Design solution	2	Design interface	Update the design of the user interface for the application. Include new controls and specify changes to the layout of existing controls.
	3	Design program	Design the logic for the code and write pseudocode. Determine where to insert new code and which existing code to rewrite or delete.
Validate design	4	Validate design	Prove that the solution produces correct results for the automobile loan calculator program.
Implement design	5	Develop interface	Add and move user interface elements, such as input areas, output areas, and Button controls on the form.
	6	Write code	Write code to update event procedures for the buttons; revise comment statements in code. Add constants.
Test solution	7	Test	Test the application.
	8	Debug	Fix any problems with the application.
Document solution	9	Document	Print the program.

Analysis and Design

Figure 5-2 on the next page shows the requirements document that initiates the development cycle to modify the Automobile Loan Calculator application. The Notes area of the document includes rules that explain how the interest rate for a loan will be adjusted automatically by the program based on a customer's credit rating. These rules, such as notes 2 and 3, are called **business logic** or **business rules**, because they relate to the manner in which a business or organization operates. Knowledge of the business rules can help programmers develop more efficient algorithms to solve programming problems. Business rules, for instance, define formats, ranges, and other characteristics of input or output data. Business rules vary between different organizations and can change over time.

REQUEST FOR CHANGE TO APPLICATION

Date submitted:	October 1, 2004
Submitted by:	Steven Wang
Purpose:	The Automobile Loan Calculator requires an update based on new requirements from the Finance Manager. The interest rate given to a customer must now vary based on the customer's credit rating. We score customer's credit on a scale from A - Excellent through E - Low. We also place a ceiling on the maximum loan allowed to customers with low credit.
Application title:	Automobile Loan Calculator
Algorithms:	N/A
Notes:	1) Sales representatives are accustomed to the following terminology: *Credit rating* 2) The user should be forced to enter a credit rating for the customer. Depending on the credit rating, the interest rate is adjusted for the loan. The following credit ratings are used to classify the credit rating of customers. A – Excellent B – Good – Interest rate should be Current interest rate × 1.1 C – Average – Interest rate should be Current interest rate × 1.15 D – Poor – Interest rate should be Current interest rate × 1.17 E – Low – Interest rate should be Current interest rate × 1.25 3) The maximum amount that we can loan to a customer with a Low credit rating is $5,000. This amount may change every few months. 4) The application should also allow the user to reset all values on the screen to zero (0) or blank so that another calculation can be performed.

Approvals

Approval Status:	**X**	Approved
		Rejected
Approved by:	Lillian Bukiet	
Date:	October 4, 2004	
Assigned to:	J. Quasney, Programmer	

FIGURE 5-2

PROBLEM ANALYSIS   The primary problem that the modified Automobile Loan Calculator application should solve is the adjustment of the interest rate based on the customer's credit rating. The business logic outlined in note 2 of the requirements document can be expressed using the following formulas:

If the CreditRating is A – Excellent then

AdjustedInterestRate = InterestRate

If the CreditRating is B – Good then

AdjustedInterestRate = InterestRate × 1.1

If the CreditRating is C – Average then

AdjustedInterestRate = InterestRate × 1.15

If the CreditRating is D – Poor then

AdjustedInterestRate = InterestRate × 1.17

If the CreditRating is E – Low then

AdjustedInterestRate = InterestRate × 1.25

In the above formulas, InterestRate is the interest rate that the user enters in the Current interest rate (%) NumericUpDown control in the application. AdjustedInterestRate is the interest rate that the customer will be charged, based on his or her credit rating.

As indicated in note 4 of the requirements document in Figure 5-2, the application also must provide the user with the ability to reset input and output values back to initial values, so that a user can calculate the monthly payment for another loan. Because code already performs this task for the existing controls used in the application, you only need to add new code to reset values for the new Credit rating ComboBox control. To reset this value, the application uses the equation

CreditRating = ""

to tell the application to set the Credit rating input back to the original value. The "" represents an empty string, which is a value that is intentionally left blank.

INTERFACE DESIGN   As noted in the requirements document, the interface of the application must allow a user to select one credit rating from a list of five choices. A **ComboBox control** is used in Windows applications to present lists of choices. In this application, the properties of the ComboBox control are set so that it displays and functions as a drop-down list box. A **drop-down list box** is a user interface element used to present several discrete text choices to a user. With a drop-down list box, a user can select one of the five credit ratings from a list. To accommodate the ComboBox control and its associated label, the existing controls — the Monthly payment label, Monthly payment text box, Compute Payment button, and Reset button — should be moved down on the form (Figure 5-3 on the next page).

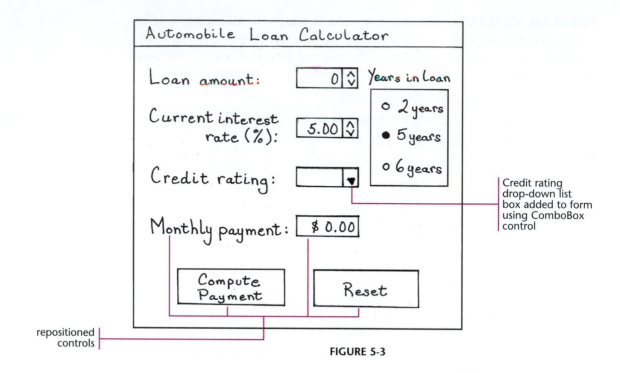

Credit rating drop-down list box added to form using ComboBox control

repositioned controls

FIGURE 5-3

Additionally, the program requires two messages that must display to users to inform them of errors in the input data. The first message displays when the user clicks the Compute Payment button, but has neglected to select a credit rating in the Credit rating list. The second dialog box displays when the user has selected the E – Low credit rating and has entered a loan amount greater than $5,000, the maximum allowed for those with the E – Low credit rating.

PROGRAM DESIGN   Figure 5-4 shows a flowchart that represents the logic for the Compute Payment Click event that executes when the user clicks the Compute Payment button. The flowchart includes several control structures that were introduced in Chapter 1 and are covered in detail in Appendix A and later in this chapter. The structures in Figure 5-4 include two If…Then…Else structures, a Select Case structure, and a nested If…Then…Else structure. The first If…Then…Else structure determines if the user selected a credit rating. If the user did not select a credit rating, then an error message displays to the user and the Compute Payment Click event procedure exits without performing any calculations. The second If…Then…Else structure is a **nested structure**, meaning that an If…Then…Else structure contains a second If…Then…Else structure within it. This structure determines which option button the user has selected for the number of years in the loan. This logic is a replacement for the logic coded in Chapter 4, where a global variable was set each time the user selected an option button. The third If…Then…Else structure first checks if the credit rating is E – Low. If the credit rating selected is E – Low, then a second test is performed to check if the loan amount input is greater than the maximum loan amount allowed for customers with a Low credit rating. If it is, then an error message displays to the user, the focus is set to the Credit rating ComboBox control, and the event procedure exits without performing any calculations. The fourth structure in the flowchart is a Select Case structure. This structure determines the correct formula to calculate the adjusted interest rate that a customer will be charged based on his or her credit rating.

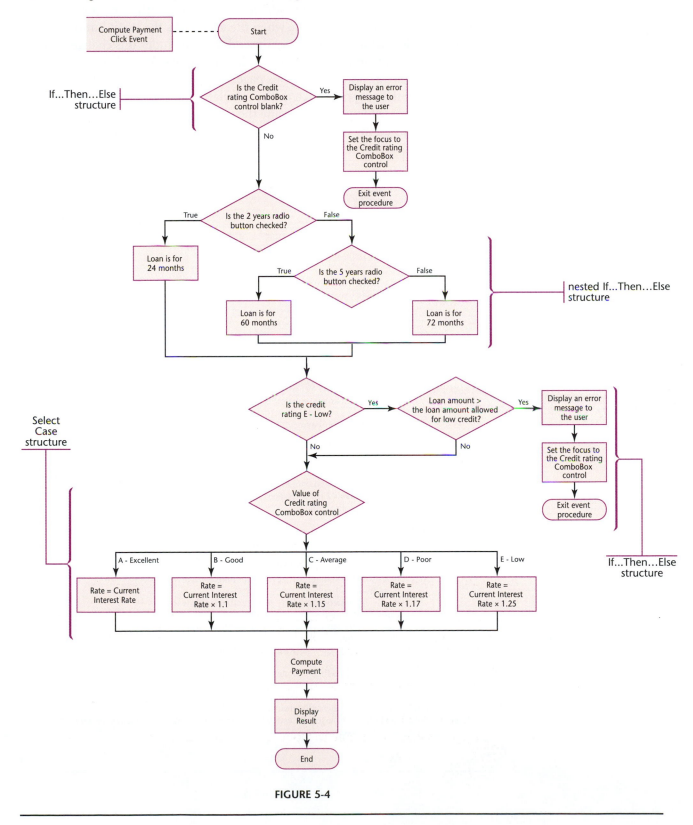

FIGURE 5-4

Figure 5-5 shows the pseudocode used to design the procedures needed to execute the two program tasks: (1) resetting the input and output values back to their original values, so the user can perform the calculation again using different input values, and (2) calculating the monthly loan payment. The code for the Reset Button Click event must be modified so it also resets the Credit rating drop-down list box to a blank value when the user clicks the Reset button. The last line of the Reset Button Click event pseudocode includes this change. The pseudocode for the Compute Payment Click event derives directly from the flowchart in Figure 5-4 on the previous page. The pseudocode includes logic that already exists in the program, such as the calculation of the payment amount. It also includes updated logic to determine the number of years in the loan and to establish an adjusted interest rate based on the customer's credit rating.

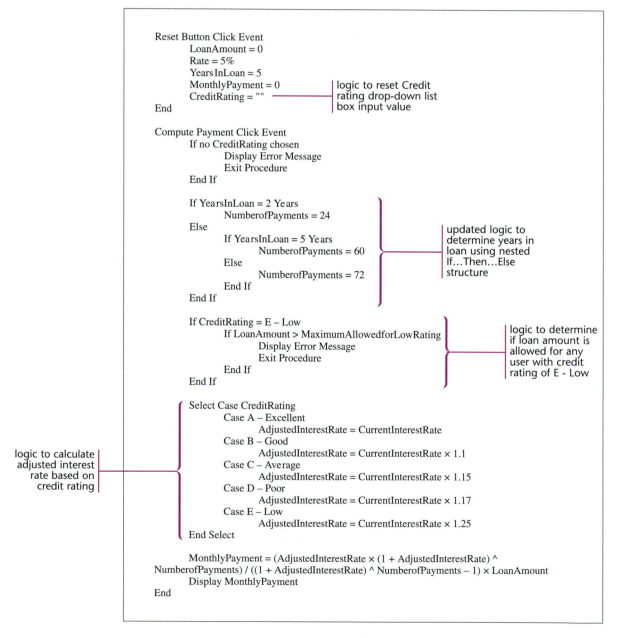

FIGURE 5-5

VALIDATE DESIGN   As explained in Chapter 4, you can validate the program design by stepping through the requirements and making certain that the design addresses each requirement. Even though the algorithm is being modified, not written from scratch, you should follow the steps outlined in Chapter 4 to validate the entire solution. The items in note 1 in the Notes section of the requirements document are shown as requested on the storyboard (Figure 5-3 on page VB 5.06). The program design addresses the credit rating adjustment formulas specified in note 2 of the requirements document, by including the Select Case block of pseudocode in the Compute Payment Button Click Event (Figure 5-5). The requirements in note 3 are handled by the third If block in the pseudocode (Figure 5-5), where the code tests to determine if the selected credit rating is E – Low. If the credit rating is E – Low and the loan amount requested is greater than the maximum loan amount allowed for customers with a Low credit rating, the application displays an error message and exits the procedure before any calculations are made. The requirement in note 4 is handled by updating the Reset Button Click Event pseudocode to assign a blank value to the Credit rating drop-down list box.

Having analyzed the problem, designed the interface, designed the program, and validated the design, the analysis and design of the application are complete. As shown in Table 5-1 on page VB 5.03, the next task in the development cycle is to develop the user interface of the application using Visual Basic .NET.

Opening the Project and Modifying the User Interface

The first step to implement the design of the revised Automobile Loan Calculator application is to update the user interface. The Form1 form must be resized and controls moved to allow for new controls to be added. Finally, controls must be added and properties of those controls must be set. Before you can begin developing the user interface, you first must start Visual Basic .NET and open the Automobile Loan Calculator project created in Chapter 4.

Starting Visual Basic .NET and Opening an Existing Project

The following steps start Visual Basic .NET and open the Automobile Loan Calculator project.

To Start Visual Basic .NET and Open an Existing Project

1. Insert the Data Disk in drive A. See page xvi in the preface of this book for instructions for downloading the Data Disk or see your instructor for information about accessing the files required in this book.
2. Start Visual Basic .NET. When the Start Page displays, click the Open Project button on the Start Page.

(continued)

3. If necessary, click the Look in box arrow and then click 3½ Floppy (A:). Double-click the Chapter5 folder.

Visual Basic .NET displays the Open Project dialog box. The Chapter5 folder displays in the Look in box.

4. Double-click the Automobile Loan Calculator folder. If necessary, click the Automobile Loan Calculator solution file (Automobile Loan Calculator.sln).

The Automobile Loan Calculator folder displays as the current folder in the Look in box. The Automobile Loan Calculator solution file displays as selected in the dialog box.

5. Click the Open button. If the Form1 form does not display in the main work area, double-click Form1.vb in the Solution Explorer window.

The Automobile Loan Calculator project opens in the Visual Basic .NET IDE. The Form1 form displays in the main work area. The gray border around the form indicates that the form is locked.

Unlocking a Form and Modifying the User Interface

As you learned in Chapter 4, while a form and controls are locked, they cannot be resized or moved. Before the new controls can be added to a locked form, the form must be unlocked. The next step is to increase the form height and then reposition existing output controls and button controls to create space for the ComboBox control and its associated Label control. Once the existing controls are repositioned, the new Label control and ComboBox control can be added.

The following steps increase the height of the Form1 form and reposition the Label3 (Monthly payment:) control, txtMonthlyPayment TextBox control, and the btnComputePayment and btnReset Button controls. Finally, the new Label and ComboBox controls are added to the form.

To Unlock a Form and Modify the Interface

1. Select the Form1 form in the main work area. Right-click the form and then click Lock Controls on the shortcut menu to unlock the form. Use the lower-middle sizing handle on the form to increase the form height to 248 pixels. View the Size property in the Properties window to verify that the Height property is set properly.

The form displays as shown in Figure 5-6. The Height property value is set to 248.

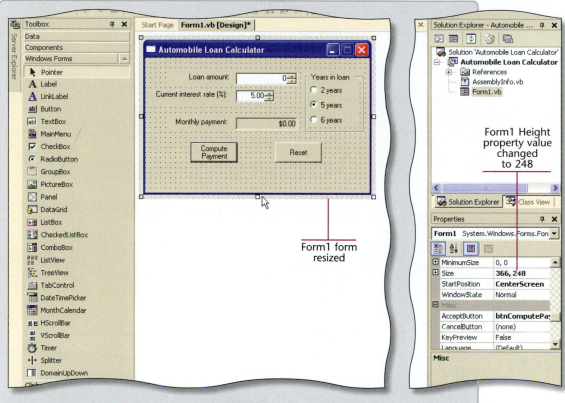

FIGURE 5-6

2. Select the Label3 control. With the Label3 control selected, hold down the CTRL key and then click the txtMonthlyPayment, btnComputePayment, and btnReset controls.

The four controls are selected (Figure 5-7). Sizing handles display around the selected controls, and the mouse pointer changes to a double two-headed arrow over the selected controls.

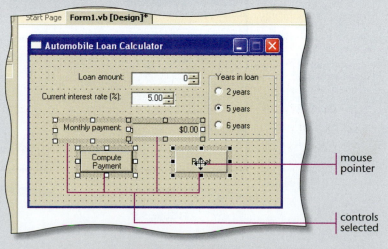

FIGURE 5-7

(continued)

3. Drag the four controls down four marks on the positioning grid. While moving the controls, be careful not to move the controls to the left or right.

The four controls are properly repositioned (Figure 5-8). The space above the Label3 and txtMonthlyPayment controls will be used to add the Label and ComboBox controls.

space for Label and ComboBox controls

controls moved down 4 marks on positioning grid

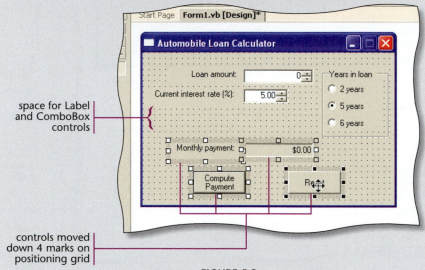

FIGURE 5-8

4. Add a Label control from the Toolbox window to the Form1 form. Position and size the Label control approximately as shown in Figure 5-9.

The Label4 control displays on the form (Figure 5-9).

Label4 control added below Label2 (Current interest rate (%):) control

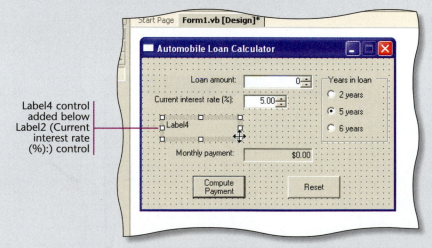

FIGURE 5-9

5. Add a ComboBox control from the Toolbox window to the Form1 form, and left-align the control with the nudRate control, as shown in Figure 5-10.

The ComboBox1 control displays on the form (Figure 5-10).

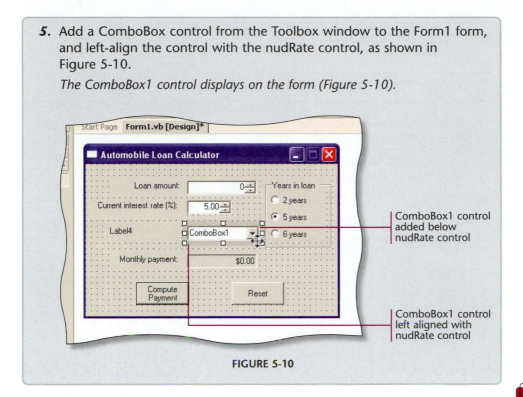

FIGURE 5-10

After unlocking a form or controls on a form, remember that the reason the controls were locked was that the original programmer did not want them repositioned. If you must reposition or resize existing controls, be sure to consult the original requirements document and any other documentation that exists for the previous version of the application. Often, programmers are asked to place controls at a certain location in a specific size in order to match an existing paper form. Also, users of the existing application may be surprised to see controls moved to a new location in a new version of the application.

Label Control Properties

The next step is to size and position the Label4 control to align with the Label controls already on the form. The Alignment and Text properties of the Label4 control also must be set to define the text value that displays in the control. Table 5-2 indicates the properties that must be changed for the Label4 controls.

Table 5-2 Label4 Control Property Values for the Modified Automobile Loan Calculator Application

PROPERTY	VALUE	EFFECT
Size: Width	104	Sets the width of the control in pixels
Size: Height	24	Sets the height of the control in pixels
Location: X (left)	32	Indicates distance from left border of the form in pixels
Location: Y (top)	88	Indicates distance from top border of the form in pixels
TextAlign	TopRight	Sets text to display top- and right-aligned in the control
Text	Credit rating:	Sets Credit rating: to display as the initial value in the control

The following step sets the properties of the Label4 control to the values listed in Table 5-2 on the previous page.

To Change Properties of a Label Control

1. Select the Label4 control. Set the properties of the control as indicated in Table 5-2.

The properties of the Label4 control are set. The control displays on the Form 1 form, as shown in Figure 5-11.

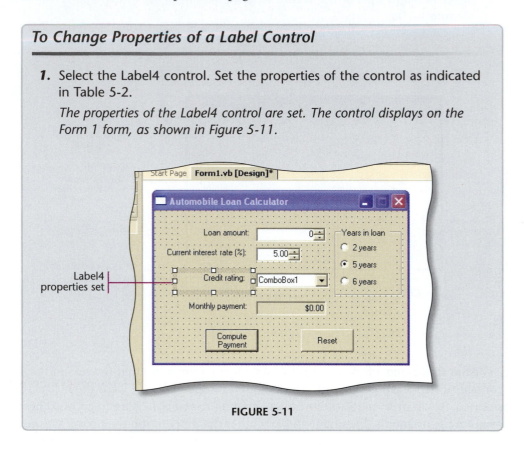

FIGURE 5-11

When modifying an application, you should make every effort to set control properties so that the modified application follows the same general style as the original application. For example, when adding new Label controls to a form, you should verify that the new controls use the same font and alignment as any existing Label controls.

ComboBox Control Properties

The next step is to change the properties of the ComboBox control to display the list of possible credit ratings for a customer. As previously noted, the ComboBox control is used in Windows applications to present lists of choices. In a list box, either part of the list or the entire list of choices can display. When the list of choices is too long to display in the list box, a scroll bar automatically is added so the user can scroll up and down through the list. When the user clicks an item to select it, the selected item displays in a highlighted color.

ComboBox Control
Use the ComboBox control to present a list of choices from which the user can select one.

With a ComboBox control, the appearance of the list and the method used to select an item are defined by the value of its **DropDownStyle property**. Table 5-3 summarizes how different DropDownStyle property values impact the appearance of the list and the methods of selecting an item from a ComboBox control at run time. Table 5-4 describes the DropDownStyle and other commonly used properties of a ComboBox control. Default property values appear in bold font.

Table 5-3   ComboBox DropDownStyle Property Values

DROPDOWNSTYLE	APPEARANCE OF LIST	ITEM SELECTION METHOD
Simple	List always displays; scroll bar added if list is longer than ComboBox height	Click item in list; scroll to view items, if list is longer than ComboBox height
DropDown	Drop-down list	Click item in list or type item directly in ComboBox text box
DropDownList	Drop-down list	Click item in list; typing directly in text box is disallowed

Table 5-4   ComboBox Control Properties

CATEGORY	PROPERTY	DESCRIPTION	PROPERTY VALUES
Appearance	DropDownStyle	Controls the list appearance and item selection method used (see Table 5-3)	Simple **DropDown** DropDownList
	Text	Sets the text that displays in the control's text box	Any text (defaults to the control name for controls with DropDown Style value of DropDown or DropDownList)
Behavior	DropDownWidth	Sets the width in pixels of the drop-down list box	A positive integer value (defaults to the width of the control)
	IntegralHeight	Indicates whether the visible list portion should display only complete items	**True** False
	ItemHeight	Sets the height in pixels of an item in the ComboBox	A positive integer value (**13**)
	MaxDropDownItems	Sets the maximum number of items in the drop-down list	An integer value between 1 and 100 (**8**)
	MaxLength	Sets the maximum number of characters the user can enter	A positive integer value
	Sorted	Controls whether items in the list portion are sorted automatically	True **False**

In the modified Automobile Loan Calculator application, the properties of the ComboBox1 control must be set so it displays and functions as a drop-down list box (Figure 5-1 on page VB 5.02). With a drop-down list box, the drop-down list of choices displays only when a user clicks the list box arrow. The user can select only one item from a discrete list of choices. When a user selects an item from the list by clicking it, the drop-down list closes and only the selected item displays in the control's text box.

To set a ComboBox control to display and function as a drop-down list, the DropDownStyle property value must be set to DropDownList. With the DropDownStyle property set to DropDownList (see Table 5-3 on the previous page), when the user clicks the ComboBox control's list box arrow a drop-down list of choices displays, from which the user can make one selection. Setting the DropDownStyle property value to DropDownList also means the user only can select an item in the list and cannot type a value in the text box portion of the control.

The Name property value of the ComboBox1 control also should be changed, to assign a unique, descriptive name. When naming ComboBox controls, use the cmb prefix for the name. Table 5-5 lists the property value changes needed for the ComboBox1 control on the Form1 form, including the changes to the DropDownStyle and Name property values.

Tip

Naming ComboBox Controls
When naming ComboBox controls, use the cmb prefix for the name.

Table 5-5   ComboBox1 Control Property Values for the Modified Automobile Loan Calculator Application

PROPERTY	VALUE	EFFECT
Name	cmbCreditRating	Changes control's name to a descriptive name
Size: Width	104	Sets the width of the control in pixels
Size: Height	21	Sets the height of the control in pixels
Location: X (left)	144	Indicates distance from left border of the form in pixels
Location: Y (top)	88	Indicates distance from top border of the form in pixels
TabIndex	3	Sets this control to be the fourth control to receive focus when the TAB key is pressed
DropDownStyle	DropDownList	Sets the ComboBox to display as a drop-down list of discrete choices from which the user can make one selection

The following steps modify the properties of the ComboBox1 control on the Form1 form.

To Change Properties of a ComboBox Control

1. Select the ComboBox1 control on the Form1 form. Enter the properties from Table 5-5 for the control, except for the DropDownStyle property.

2. Select the DropDownStyle property in the Properties window and then click the DropDownStyle down arrow in the property values list.

Clicking the drop-down arrow displays a list of three possible property values for the DropDownStyle property (Figure 5-12).

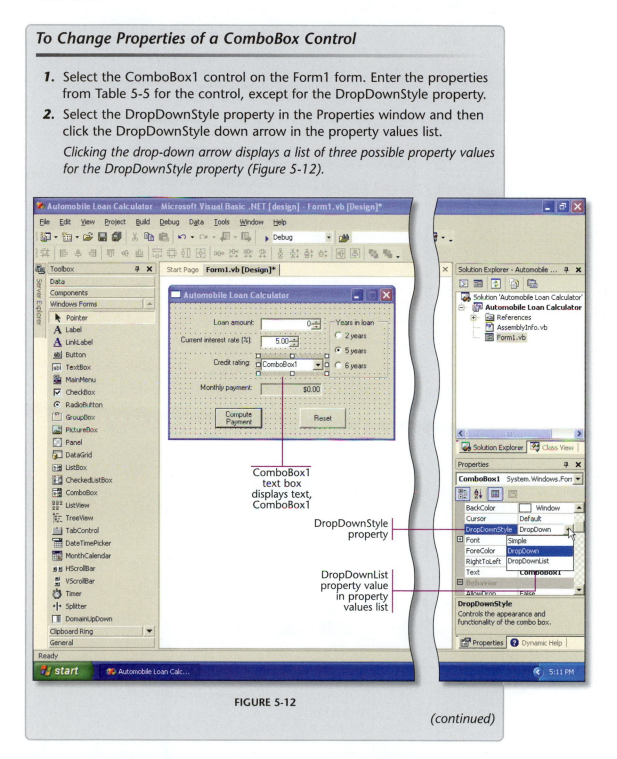

FIGURE 5-12

(continued)

3. Click DropDownList in the DropDownStyle property values list.

The DropDownStyle property value is set to DropDownList (Figure 5-13). The DropDownList property value indicates that the ComboBox control only will allow the user to select a value from the drop-down list; the user may not type a value into the ComboBox control's text box. On the Form 1 form, text no longer displays in the text box of the ComboBox1 control. The ComboBox1 control is renamed to cmbCreditRating.

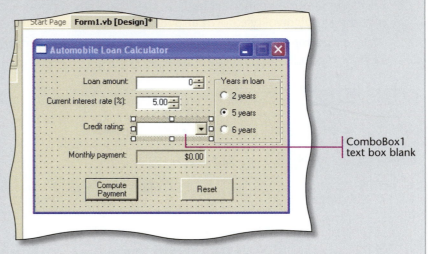

FIGURE 5-13

4. Select the Items property in the Properties window.

The word, (Collection), displays as the property value and a build button displays to the right of the property value (Figure 5-14).

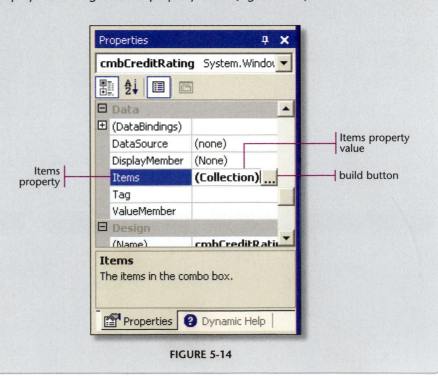

FIGURE 5-14

5. Click the Collection build button.

The String Collection Editor window displays and the insertion point displays in the String Collection text area (Figure 5-15).

String Collection
Editor window

insertion
point

String
Collection
text area

items in
ComboBox list
entered here

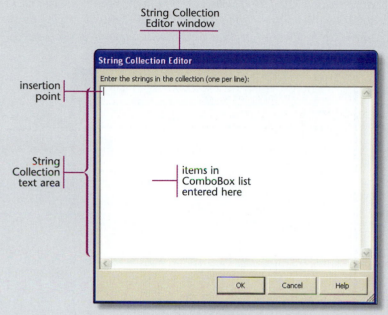

FIGURE 5-15

6. Type A - Excellent on line 1 in the String Collection text area.

A - Excellent displays on the first line in the String Collection text area (Figure 5-16).

first item in
ComboBox
list

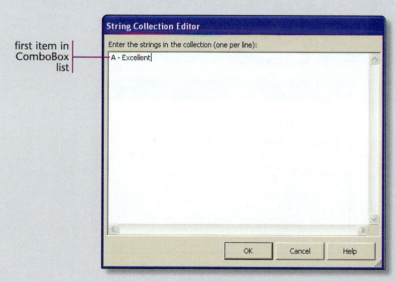

FIGURE 5-16

(continued)

7. Press the ENTER key. Type B – Good and then press the ENTER key. Type C – Average and then press the ENTER key. Type D – Poor and then press the ENTER key. Type E – Low and do not press the ENTER key.

Five items display in the String Collection text area. When the user clicks the down arrow on the control during run time, each item will display as a choice in the drop-down list of the cmbCreditRating control (Figure 5-17).

OK button

five items in ComboBox1 list

FIGURE 5-17

8. Click the OK button. If necessary, select the Form1 form. Click Lock Controls on the Format menu.

The Form1 form and its controls are locked. The user interface now is complete (Figure 5-18).

form and controls locked

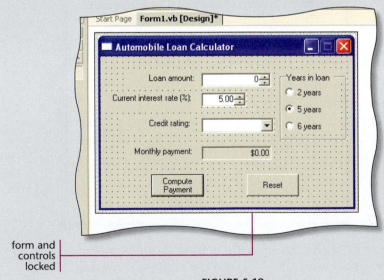

FIGURE 5-18

The String Collection Editor window allows you to enter and set the initial values or items for a ComboBox list. During design time, the values are not visible on the form. During run time, the values or items set in the String Collection Editor window display in the ComboBox list. The list also can be modified during run time by one or more methods that change the Items property of the control. The methods you can use in code to modify the list include methods such as Add, AddRange, Insert, and Remove.

The previous steps also set the TabIndex property to a value of 3. In Chapter 4, the TabIndex property of the GroupBox1 control was set to the value of 3. When the ComboBox1 TabIndex property is set to 3, Visual Basic .NET automatically updates all subsequent TabIndex properties by adding 1 to all of the values that were previously set to 3 or greater. Therefore, the GroupBox1 control's TabIndex property changes from 3 to 4, the btnComputePayment control's TabIndex property changes from 4 to 5, and the btnReset control's TabIndex property changes from 5 to 6.

> **Tip**
>
> **Setting TabIndex Properties**
> When you change the TabIndex property of a control to the same value of another control, Visual Basic .NET attempts to renumber subsequent TabIndex property values to maintain the same tabbing order.

Modifying Existing Code

Before you can add code to support the business logic outlined in the requirements document, several minor modifications must be made to the code that already exists in the Automobile Loan Calculator application. These modifications include:

- Updating the comment header to reflect the new functionality of the program
- Adding a new global constant for the maximum amount that a customer with a low credit rating can borrow
- Setting the ComboBox control's value to blank after the user clicks the Reset button
- Declaring two variables in the Compute Payment Click event procedure
- Updating the logic behind the RadioButton controls to be more efficient and intuitive

Modifying the Comment Header and Adding a Constant

When modifying an application with the goal of adding new functionality or fixing bugs, you should update the comment header to reflect the changes made. The updated or additional comments should clarify the reasons for the modifications and when the updates were made.

> **Tip**
>
> **Comments for Revisions**
> When modifying an application with the goal of adding new functionality or fixing bugs, you should update the comment header to reflect the changes made. The updated or additional comments should clarify the reasons for the modifications and when the updates were made.

Figure 5-19 shows a section of the general area of the Form1 form code after the modifications are made to the comment header and the constant declaration for MaximumLowCreditAllowed is updated. The MaximumLowCreditAllowed constant (line 222) is set to $5,000, the maximum amount that a customer with an E – Low credit rating is allowed to borrow.

```
212   ' Chapter 5:     Automobile Loan Calculator
213   ' Programmer:    Jeff Quasney
214   ' Date:          September 22, 2004
215   ' Purpose:       This project calculates the monthly payment for
216   '                a loan based on loan amount, interest rate, and
217   '                length of the loan.
218   ' Updated October 6, 2004 by Jeff Quasney
219   '                Base interest rate on the customer's credit rating
220   Dim gdblMonths As Double = 60.0
221   Const MaximumLoanAllowed As Integer = 25000
222   Const MaximumLowCreditAllowed As Double = 5000
```

FIGURE 5-19

The following step modifies the comment header and adds a new global constant, MaximumLowCreditAllowed, to the code.

To Modify the Comment Header and Add a Constant

1. Double-click the Form1 form to view code. Double-click the number 4 in line 212. Type 5 to replace the number 4. Enter lines 218, 219, and 222 as shown in Figure 5-19.

The comment header is modified to reflect the updates to the program. The constant, MaximumLowCreditAllowed is declared as data type Double and its value is set to 5000 (Figure 5-20).

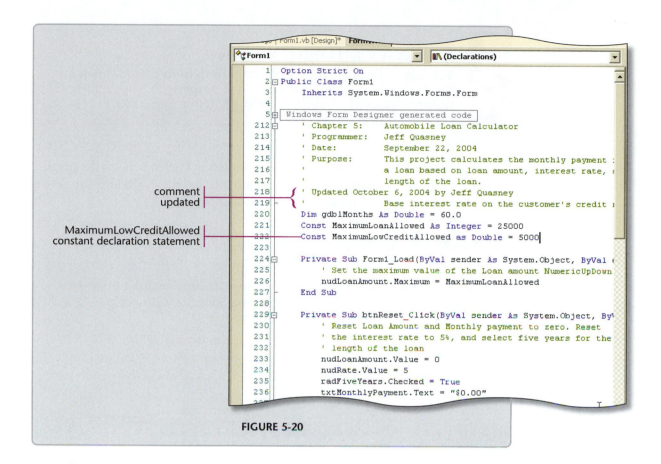

comment updated

MaximumLowCreditAllowed constant declaration statement

FIGURE 5-20

Resetting the ComboBox Value

When you add items to a ComboBox using the String Collection Editor, Visual Basic .NET assigns each item a consecutive number called an **index**. The first item is assigned an index of 0; the second item is assigned an index of 1; and so on. If no item is selected, the index is set to −1.

When a user selects an item from a ComboBox list during run time, the **SelectedIndex property** of the ComboBox control is assigned the value of that item's index. You also can use a code statement to change the control's SelectedIndex property. Adding code that sets the SelectedIndex property value to −1 indicates that no item is selected and thus resets the ComboBox control to its default value. Figure 5-21 shows the line of code needed to reset the cmbCreditRating control on the Form1 form to its default value, where no item is selected.

```
237        cmbCreditRating.SelectedIndex = -1
```

FIGURE 5-21

Tip

ComboBox SelectedIndex Property

You can write code to select an item from from a drop-down list by setting the control's SelectedIndex property. A SelectedIndex property value of –1 indicates that no item is selected.

The following step adds the line of code shown in Figure 5-21 on the previous page to the btnReset_Click event procedure, so that the procedure also resets the cmbCreditRating control to its original value.

To Modify the btnReset_Click Event Procedure

1. Click the Form1.vb[Design] tab and then double-click the btnReset button. Type line 237 of the code from Figure 5-21. Do not press the ENTER key after entering the code.

The assignment statement displays in the code window on line 237 (Figure 5-22). The assignment statement will execute when the user clicks the Reset button during run time.

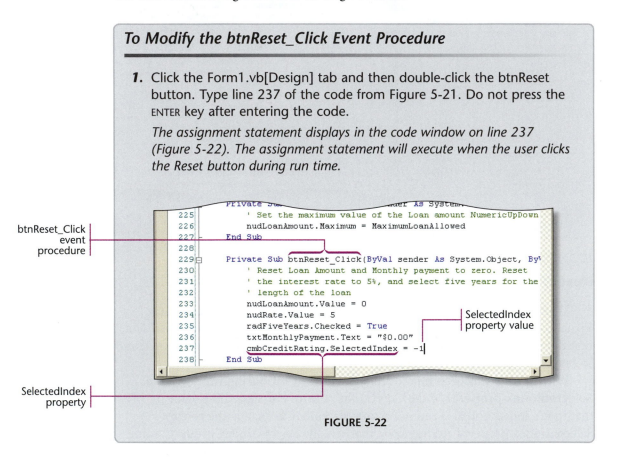

FIGURE 5-22

When the user clicks the Reset button, the code shown in Figure 5-22 executes. The values of the input and output controls are reset to values specified in the requirement documents on pages VB 4.04 and VB 5.04. You can change the SelectedIndex property value in line 237 of the code shown in Figure 5-22 to reset the cmbCreditRating control to a valid index for any of the items in the ComboBox control's drop-down list box. For example, if the requirements document had specified that the default credit rating should be B – Good, then you would change the code to set the SelectedIndex property to the value of 1.

Declaring Additional Variables

Two additional variables are needed in the btnComputePayment_Click event procedure that executes when the user clicks the Compute Payment button during run time. The two variable declarations are shown in Figure 5-23.

```
259          Dim dblAdjustedRate As Double, strErrorMessage As String
```

FIGURE 5-23

The first, dblAdjustedRate, holds the value of the interest rate after the customer's credit rating is used to adjust the interest rate entered by the user. Recall from Chapter 4 that the dblRate variable holds the interest rate entered by the user and is passed to the Pmt function as the interest rate parameter. In the modified program, the dblRate variable will hold the interest rate entered by the user. The dblAdjusted value will be passed to the Pmt function as the interest rate parameter. Therefore, the value must be of data type Double because the Pmt function expects a Double data type as the interest rate parameter.

The second variable, strErrorMessage, is used to hold the error message string that displays when a customer with an E – Low credit rating tries to borrow more than allowed for that credit rating. A variable is used because the error message must be put together from several strings before it is displayed to the user in a dialog box.

The following step adds the two variable declarations shown in Figure 5-23 to the btnComputePayment_Click event procedure.

To Declare Variables

1. Scroll the code window until line 258 displays. Enter line 259 as shown in Figure 5-23.

The variable declarations display in the code window on line 259 (Figure 5-24).

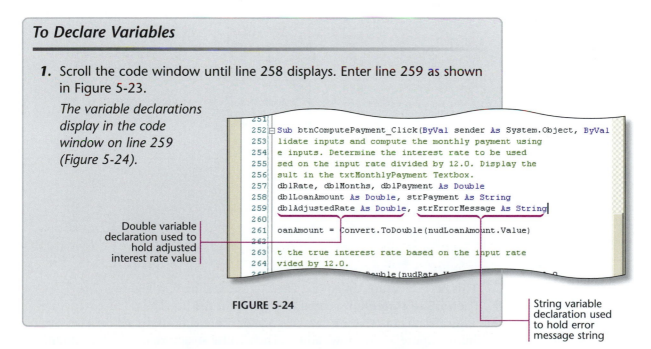

Double variable declaration used to hold adjusted interest rate value

String variable declaration used to hold error message string

FIGURE 5-24

The previous steps updated the comment header; declared a new constant, MaximumLowCreditAllowed; updated the btnReset_Click event procedure to reset the cmbCreditRating control; and declared two new variables, dblAdjustedRate and strErrorMessage. With these tasks complete, the next step is to write code to support the business logic described in the requirements document.

Decision-Making Control Structures

In previous chapters, the programs were designed to perform precisely the same computations for every set of data items that were processed. In some instances, however, you may not want a program to process each set of data items in exactly the same way. For example, a program designed to compute gross pay would have to use one formula to compute gross pay for employees who are paid on commission and another to compute gross pay for employees who are not. Therefore, the program must be coded to make a decision concerning which of two gross pay formulas to use.

In a program, **decision making** is the process of determining which of one or more paths to take. The sequential flow of control within procedures used in previous programs and illustrated by the flowchart in Figure 5-25 is not sufficient to solve problems that involve decision making. To develop an algorithm that requires deviation from a sequential flow of control, the code must include another control structure.

FIGURE 5-25

This new structure, called If…Then…Else, is shown in Figure 5-26a. The **If…Then…Else statement** is used to implement the If…Then…Else structure that indicates that a program can take one or more actions, based on a certain condition. Figure 5-26a shows an If…Then…Else structure in which a condition is evaluated and its result either is true or false — only these two choices are allowed. If the result of the condition is true, then one action is performed;

if the result is false, then a different action is performed. The action performed can be a single instruction or it can be another series of instructions. The If…Then…Else structure also is described in detail in Appendix A on page VB A.08.

The flowchart representation of a decision is the diamond-shaped symbol. One flowline will always be shown entering the symbol, and two flowlines always will be shown leaving the symbol. A condition that must be either true or false is written within the decision symbol. For example, a condition might ask whether two variables are equal or whether an expression is within a certain range. If the condition is true, one path is taken; if not, the other path is taken.

The **Select Case statement** is used to implement an extension of the If…Then…Else structure, in which there are more than two alternatives. This extended version of the If…Then…Else structure is called the **Select Case structure**. An example of the Select Case structure is illustrated in Figure 5-26b and described in Appendix A on page VB A.08.

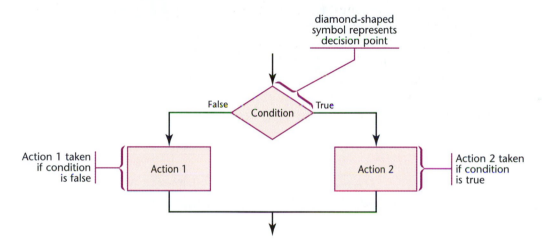

FIGURE 5-26a

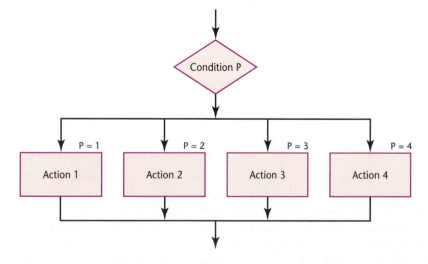

FIGURE 5-26b

The type of controls used to input the Loan amount, Current interest rate, and Years in loan ensure that any data input is valid. The only control used in this project that does not ensure that input data is valid is the cmbCreditRating control. With this control, a user might forget to select a credit rating from the list, which would leave the entry blank and be an invalid input. Thus, the code must test to ensure that a credit rating has been selected and is not blank. The logic for this code, which will be added to the btnComputeLoan_Click event procedure, requires the use of an If…Then…Else structure, as shown in Figure 5-27. In this flowchart, if the Credit rating is blank, then an error message displays and the focus is set to the cmbCreditRating control. If the Credit rating is not blank, then the input is valid and the procedure continues to execute.

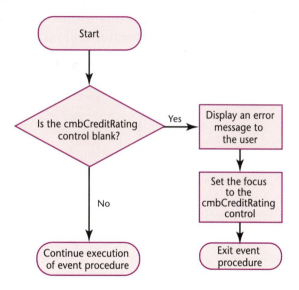

FIGURE 5-27

To implement the logic shown in the flowchart in Figure 5-27, the code requires the use of the MessageBox class, Focus method, and the If…Then…Else statement.

The MessageBox Class and the Show() Method

The **MessageBox class** is part of the .NET Framework class library and provides the ability to display a message to the user in a pop-up window, called a **message box**. In order to display a message box with a title on the title bar, you use the **Show() method** of the MessageBox class and pass the Show() method at least two parameters: the message to display and a title to display on the message box title bar. For example, the following statement displays the message box shown in Figure 5-28 with the title, No Credit Rating, and the message, Please enter the customer's credit rating in the Credit rating list box.

MessageBox.Show("Please enter the customer's credit rating in the Credit rating list box.", "No Credit Rating")

No Credit
Rating
message box

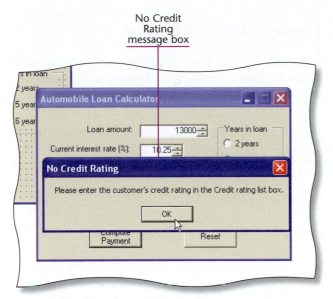

FIGURE 5-28

MessageBox Class

In order to display a message box with a title on the title bar, use the Show method of the MessageBox class and pass the Show method at least two parameters; the message to display and the title to display on the title bar.

The modified Automobile Loan Calculator application uses the MessageBox.Show method to display a message box if the user does not select a credit rating from the Credit rating list box.

The Focus() Method

As you learned in Chapter 3, when a user selects a control on a form, the control is said to have focus. Often, you must set the focus to a control during run time. For example, if the user does not select a credit rating, then a message box will display an error message and the focus should be set to the cmbCreditRating control, so that the user can locate the control quickly and select a credit rating. You can set the focus to a control during run time by using the Focus() method of the control. For example, when the following statement executes

cmbCreditRating.Focus()

the cmbCreditRating control receives focus.

The Focus() Method

Use the Focus() method to set the focus to controls during run time.

The If...Then...Else Statement

The function of the If...Then...Else statement is to perform selection — that is, to allow a program to choose whether to execute one or more lines of code. The general form of the If...Then...Else statement is shown in Table 5-6.

Table 5-6   If...Then...Else Statement

General form:	1. If condition Then clause Else clause
	2. If condition Then
	    clause 1
	    clause 2
	Else
	    clause 3
	End If
	3. If condition Then
	    clause
	End If
	
	Where condition is a relation that is either true or false and clause is a statement or series of statements; the Else keyword and subsequent clause are optional, as show in in General form 3 above.

Purpose:	If the condition is false and an Else clause is included, Visual Basic .NET executes the Else clause. After either clause is executed, control passes to the statement following the If in the first form, known as a single-line If...Then...Else statement, and to the statement following the corresponding End If in the second form, known as a block If...Then...Else statement.

Example:	1. `If lngAge > 65 Then  intCount = intCount + 1 Else strSwitch = "Y"`
	2. `If lngTax >= 0 Then`
	        `strSwitch1 = "Y"`
	        `txtOutput.Text = "Gross Pay"`
	    `Else`
	        `strSwitch1 = "N"`
	    `End If`
	3. `If strMarStatus = "M" Then`
	        `txtMarStatus.Text = "Married"`
	    `End If`

As indicated in Table 5-6, the If...Then...Else statement is used to indicate that a decision must be made, based on the evaluation of a condition. The condition appears between the keywords, If and Then. A condition is made up of two expressions and a relational operator. A condition is sometimes called a **relational expression**, because the condition specifies a relationship between expressions that is either true or false. In determining whether the condition is true or false, Visual Basic .NET first determines the single value of each expression in the condition. Visual Basic .NET then makes a comparison between the two expressions based on a relational operator. An expression also can consist of a single variable, constant, or value of the Boolean data type. Table 5-7 lists the valid relational operators.

Table 5-7   Relational Operators

RELATIONAL OPERATOR	MEANING
=	Is equal to
<	Is less than
>	Is greater than
<=	Is less than or equal to
>=	Is greater than or equal to
<>	Is not equal to

If the condition in an If...Then...Else statement is true, Visual Basic .NET acts upon the Then clause. A **single-line If...Then...Else statement**, as shown as General form 1 in Table 5-6, is used to perform a single task when the condition in the statement is true. A **block If...Then...Else statement**, as shown as General form 2 in Table 5-6, is used to execute more than one statement in response to a condition. If the condition in the statement is true, all of the statements in the Then clause are executed.

If the condition is false, Visual Basic .NET acts upon the Else clause. In either case, after executing the statements making up the clause, control passes to the statement following the If in the single-line If...Then...Else statement, and to the statement following the corresponding End If in the block If...Then...Else statement. If no Else clause is present and the condition is false, then control passes immediately to the statement following the If or corresponding End If.

As you have learned, you may declare variables anywhere in code. If you declare a variable in a block statement, however, such as the block If...Then...Else statement, the variable is valid only inside that block statement. This is known as **block-level scoping**.

In the modified Automobile Loan Calculator application, the user must enter a credit rating for the customer before the calculation can take place. If the user does not select a credit rating from the cmbCreditRating control, then an error message should display, informing the user to make a selection and no further processing should occur. To ensure that no further processing occurs, the **Exit Sub statement** (Table 5-8 on the next page) is used to tell Visual Basic .NET to exit the event procedure and return control to the user interface.

Tip

The Exit Sub Statement
In order to assure that no further processing occurs, the Exit Sub statement is used to tell Visual Basic .NET to leave the current procedure without executing any more code in the procedure.

Table 5-8 Exit Sub Statement

General form:	1. Exit Sub
Purpose:	The Exit Sub statement causes a procedure to terminate execution immediately.

Examples:	1. If blnDoneThen
	      Exit Sub
	   End If

The flowchart in Figure 5-27 represents the logic needed to check that the user has made a valid item selection in the cmbCreditRating control. The code that corresponds to the flowchart in Figure 5-27 is shown in Figure 5-29.

```
262
263         ' If the user has not selected a credit rating, inform
264         ' the user that a credit rating must be entered and then
265         ' exit the procedure
266         If cmbCreditRating.Text = "" Then
267             MessageBox.Show("Please enter the customer's credit rating in the Credit   ↙
        rating list box.", "No Credit Rating")
268             cmbCreditRating.Focus()
269             Exit Sub
270         End If
```

FIGURE 5-29

Line 266 contains the If statement that compares the Text property of the cmbCreditRating control with a blank string. If the Text property is blank — meaning that the user has not selected a credit rating value — then lines 267 through 269 execute. Line 267 displays an error message to the user in a message box. Line 268 uses the Focus() method of the cmbCreditRating control to place the insertion point in the cmbCreditRating control. Line 269 tells Visual Basic .NET to exit the event procedure, meaning that any code below this statement will not execute.

The following steps add the code shown in Figure 5-29 to the btnComputePayment_Click event procedure.

To Code an If...Then...Else Statement Using the Show() and Focus() Methods

---

1. Enter the first four lines of code shown in Figure 5-29.

After typing the fourth line, Intellisense™ finishes coding the block If statement by inserting the End If statement on line 268 (Figure 5-30).

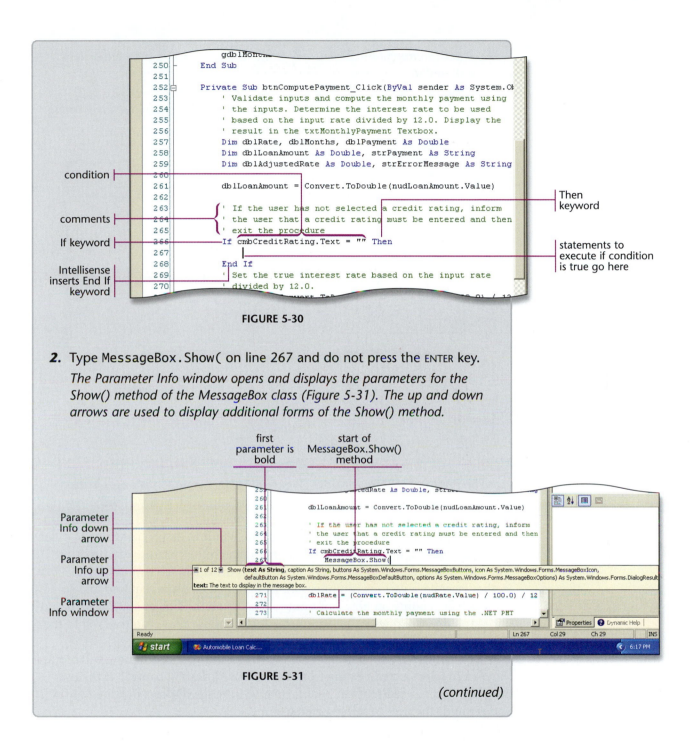

FIGURE 5-30

2. Type `MessageBox.Show(` on line 267 and do not press the ENTER key.

The Parameter Info window opens and displays the parameters for the Show() method of the MessageBox class (Figure 5-31). The up and down arrows are used to display additional forms of the Show() method.

FIGURE 5-31

(continued)

3. Enter the remainder of line 267 from Figure 5-29 and then enter lines 268 and 269.

Lines 263 through 271 display in the code window (Figure 5-32). The If...Then...Else statement validates that the user has selected a credit rating from the cmbCreditRating ComboBox.

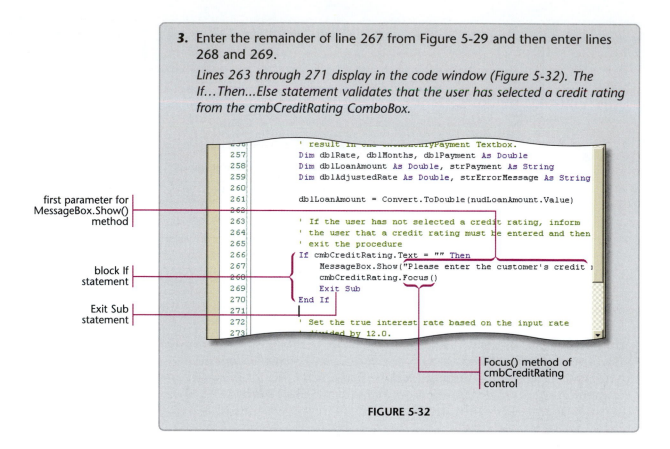

FIGURE 5-32

The **Parameter Info window** (Figure 5-31 on the previous page) is displayed by Intellisense™ whenever you begin coding a call to a method or event. The current parameter that you are coding displays as bold, and the description of the parameter displays at the bottom of the window. As you continue to enter more parameters, the description changes to match the current parameter. Methods and events may have several manners in which you can call them. That is, they may have various combinations of parameters, some required and some optional, depending on how you want to use the method or event. The scroll up and scroll down arrows in the Parameter Info window allow you to scroll to the various forms of the method or event.

With the If...Then...Else statement entered, the application now will require the user to select a credit rating from the cmbCreditRating control. If the user does not select a credit rating, an informative message displays in a message box and reminds the user to select a credit rating.

Implementing Selection Structures

Consider the If...Then...Else structure shown in Figure 5-33 and the corresponding methods of implementing the logic in Visual Basic .NET. Assume that strReg is a variable with the String data type representing a person's voter registration status. If strReg is equal to the value Y, the person is registered to vote. If strReg does not equal Y, the person is not registered to vote. intRegCnt and intNotRegCnt are counters that are incremented as specified in the flowchart, to keep a count of voter registration status for later reporting.

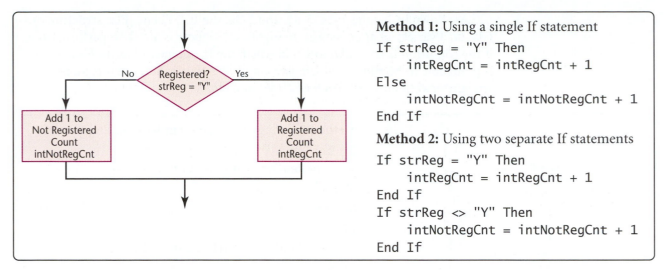

Method 1: Using a single If statement

```
If strReg = "Y" Then
    intRegCnt = intRegCnt + 1
Else
    intNotRegCnt = intNotRegCnt + 1
End If
```

Method 2: Using two separate If statements

```
If strReg = "Y" Then
    intRegCnt = intRegCnt + 1
End If
If strReg <> "Y" Then
    intNotRegCnt = intNotRegCnt + 1
End If
```

FIGURE 5-33

In the solution shown as Method 1 in Figure 5-33, an If...Then...Else statement resolves the logic indicated in the partial flowchart. The first line compares strReg to the value Y. If strReg is equal to Y, then intRegCnt is incremented by 1 in the Then clause. If strReg does not equal Y, intNotRegCnt is incremented by 1 in the Else clause. Regardless of the counter incremented, control passes to the statement following the End If.

Note that the first method could have been written as a single-line If...Then...Else statement without the End If. For readability purposes, however, it is recommended that you do not use the single-line If...Then...Else statement.

Single-line If...Then...Else Statement

For readability purposes, it is recommended that you do not use the single-line If...Then...Else statement.

In Method 2, strReg is compared to the value Y twice. In the first If...Then...Else statement, the counter intRegCnt is incremented by 1 if strReg is equal to Y. In the second If...Then...Else statement, the counter intNotRegCnt is incremented by 1 if strReg does not equal Y.

Although both methods are valid and both satisfy the If...Then...Else structure, the first method is more efficient, as it involves fewer lines of code and less execution time. Therefore, Method 1 is recommended as a solution over Method 2.

Else Clause

When using either form is possible, always use the Else clause with an If...Then...Else statement, rather than coding two separate If statements.

As shown in Figures 5-34, 5-35, and 5-36, the If…Then…Else structure can take on a variety of appearances. In Figure 5-34, there is a task to perform only if the condition is true. Method 1, in which the If statement has no Else clause, is preferable to Method 2, which uses a null Else clause, because it is more straightforward and involves fewer lines of code.

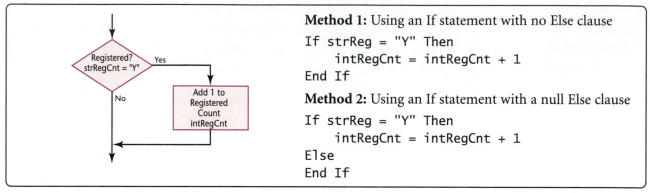

Method 1: Using an If statement with no Else clause

```
If strReg = "Y" Then
    intRegCnt = intRegCnt + 1
End If
```

Method 2: Using an If statement with a null Else clause

```
If strReg = "Y" Then
    intRegCnt = intRegCnt + 1
Else
End If
```

FIGURE 5-34

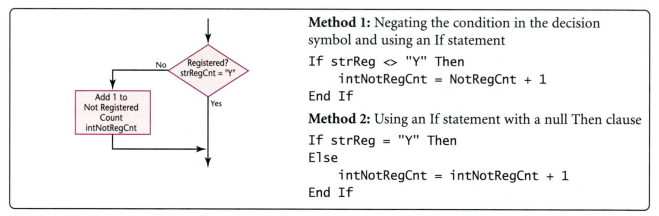

Method 1: Negating the condition in the decision symbol and using an If statement

```
If strReg <> "Y" Then
    intNotRegCnt = NotRegCnt + 1
End If
```

Method 2: Using an If statement with a null Then clause

```
If strReg = "Y" Then
Else
    intNotRegCnt = intNotRegCnt + 1
End If
```

FIGURE 5-35

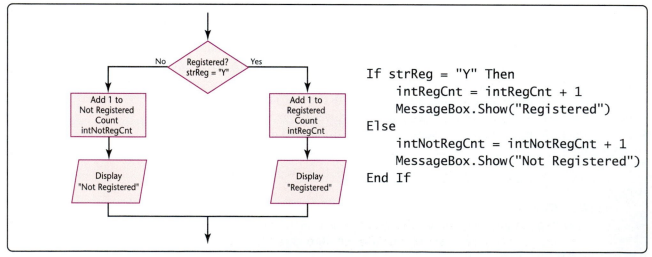

```
If strReg = "Y" Then
    intRegCnt = intRegCnt + 1
    MessageBox.Show("Registered")
Else
    intNotRegCnt = intNotRegCnt + 1
    MessageBox.Show("Not Registered")
End If
```

FIGURE 5-36

The If...Then...Else structure in Figure 5-35 illustrates how to increment the counter intNotRegCnt when the condition is false. In Method 1, the relation in the condition strReg = "Y" has been modified to read strReg <> "Y". Negating the relation is usually preferred when the program must execute additional tasks as a result of the condition being false.

In Method 2, when the condition strReg = "Y" is true, the null Then clause simply passes control to the statement following the End If. Either method is acceptable. Some programmers prefer always to include both a Then and an Else clause, even when one of them is null. Others prefer to negate the condition rather than include a null Then or Else clause.

In Figure 5-36, each task in the If...Then...Else structure is made up of multiple statements. If the condition strReg = "Y" is true, the two statements in the Then clause are executed. If the condition is false, the two statements in the Else clause are executed. Although there are alternative methods for implementing the If...Then...Else structure, the method presented in Figure 5-36 is fairly straightforward and involves fewer lines of code.

The Nested If...Then...Else Structure

As previously explained, a nested **If...Then...Else structure** is one in which the action to be taken for the true or false case includes yet another If...Then...Else structure. The second If...Then...Else structure is considered to be nested, or layered, within the first.

Study the partial program that corresponds to the nested If...Then...Else structure shown in Figure 5-37. In the partial program, if the condition intAge >= 18 is true, control passes to the If clause that starts on line 2. If the condition is false, the Else clause on line 9 is executed. If control does pass to line 2, then a second If tests to determine if strReg equals the value Y. If the condition on line 2 is true, lines 3 and 4 are executed. If the condition is false, then Visual Basic .NET executes lines 6 and 7.

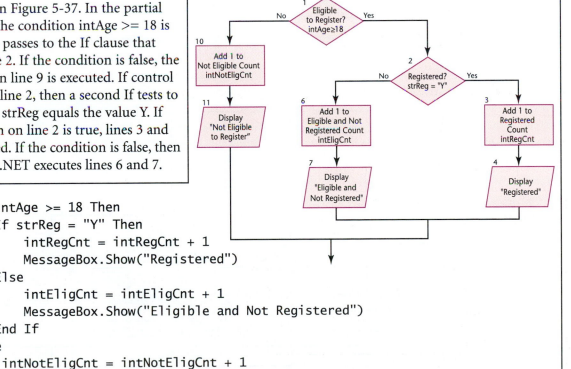

```
1    If intAge >= 18 Then
2        If strReg = "Y" Then
3            intRegCnt = intRegCnt + 1
4            MessageBox.Show("Registered")
5        Else
6            intEligCnt = intEligCnt + 1
7            MessageBox.Show("Eligible and Not Registered")
8        End If
9    Else
10       intNotEligCnt = intNotEligCnt + 1
11       MessageBox.Show("Not Eligible to Register")
12   End If
```

FIGURE 5-37

Visual Basic .NET requires that you end each If statement with a corresponding End If. Hence, the If on line 1 has a corresponding End If on line 12, and the If on line 2 has a corresponding End If on line 8.

Tip

End If Placement
Each If statement must have a corresponding End If.

```
1    If intAge >= 18 Then
2        If strReg = "Y" Then
3            If strVote = "Y" Then
4                intVote = intVote + 1
5            Else
6                intNVote = intNVote + 1
7            End If
8        Else
9            If strGender = "F" Then
10               intNRFem = intNRFem + 1
11           Else
12               intNRMale = intNRMale + 1
13           End If
14       End If
15   Else
16       If strGender = "F" Then
17           intNEFem = intNEFem + 1
18       Else
19           intNEMale = intNEMale + 1
20       End If
21   End If
```

In the partial program shown in Figure 5-37 on the previous page, note that only one of the three alternative tasks is executed for each record processed. Regardless of the path taken, control eventually passes to the statement immediately following the last End If on line 12.

If…Then…Else structures can be nested to any depth, but readability decreases as nesting increases. Consider the nested structure in Figure 5-38 and the corresponding implementation in Visual Basic .NET.

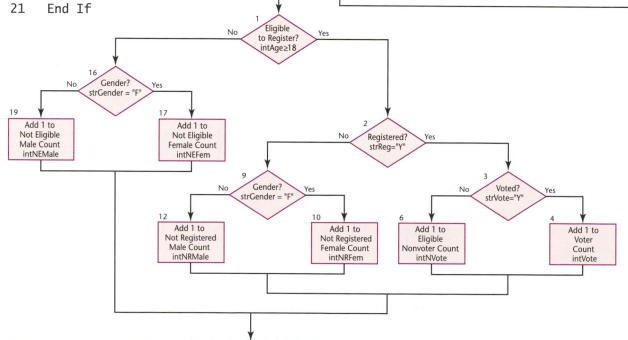

FIGURE 5-38

Figure 5-38 contains four nested If...Then...Else structures and six counters. The counters can be described in the following manner:

intNEMale: totals the number of males not eligible to register
intNEFem: totals the number of females not eligible to register
intNRMale: totals the number of males who are old enough to vote but have not registered
intNRFem: totals the number of females who are old enough to vote but have not registered
intNVote: totals the number of individuals who are eligible to vote but did not vote
intVote: totals the number of individuals who voted

In the partial program in Figure 5-38, line 1 corresponds to the decision at the very top of the flowchart. Lines 2 through 14 handle the true case to the right in the flowchart. Lines 16 through 20 fulfill the false case to the left in the flowchart.

Coding a Nested If...Then...Else Structure

The flowchart in Figure 5-39 shows the nested If...Then...Else structure for determining the number of months to use in the monthly payment calculation for the Automobile Loan Calculator application. The condition is evaluated based on the value of the Checked property of the three RadioButton controls in the GroupBox1 control. As shown in Figure 5-39, after the number of months is determined, the code continues to execute the rest of the btnComputePayment_Click event procedure.

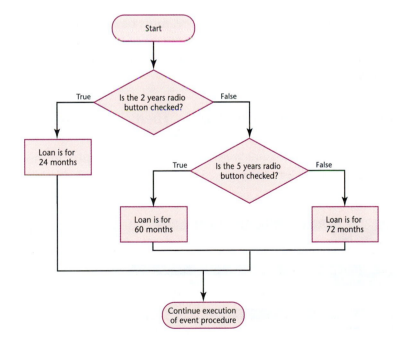

FIGURE 5-39

Figure 5-40 shows the code that corresponds to the flowchart. Each of the If...Then...Else statements has a corresponding End If statement. As the code was entered, the TAB key was pressed to indent the second If...Then...Else statement and help improve the readability of the code. Note that in lines 263 and 266, no Boolean operator is coded because the value being tested is of type Boolean. By its nature, a value which has the Boolean data type evaluates either to True or False. For example, if the value of radTwoYears.Checked is True in line 263, then the condition evaluates to True and the next line executed is line 264.

```
259
260         ' Set gdblMonths to the number of months that the loan
261         ' is for based on which radio button the user selected
262         ' for the number of years for the loan
263         If radTwoYears.Checked Then
264             gdblMonths = 24.0
265         Else
266             If radFiveYears.Checked Then
267                 gdblMonths = 60.0
268             Else
269                 gdblMonths = 72.0
270             End If
271         End If
```

FIGURE 5-40

In the modified Automobile Loan Calculator, this nested If...Then...Else statement will replace the three event procedures that executed when the corresponding RadioButton controls were clicked (radTwoYears_CheckChanged, radFiveYears_CheckChanged, and radSixYears_CheckChanged). The event procedures for the RadioButton controls, therefore, must be deleted before the new code can be added. The following steps delete the three RadioButton event procedures and add the nested If...Then...Else statement in Figure 5-40 into the btnComputePayment_Click event procedure.

To Delete Code and Code a Nested If...Then...Else Statement

1. Scroll the code window until lines 240 through 251 display in the code window. Select lines 240 through 251.

Lines 240 through 251 are highlighted (Figure 5-41).

lines 240 through 251 selected

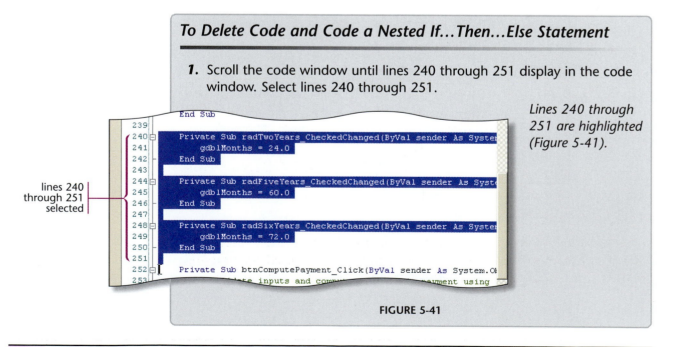

FIGURE 5-41

2. Press the DELETE key.

Lines 240 through 251 are deleted. All lines of code below line 239 are renumbered (Figure 5-42).

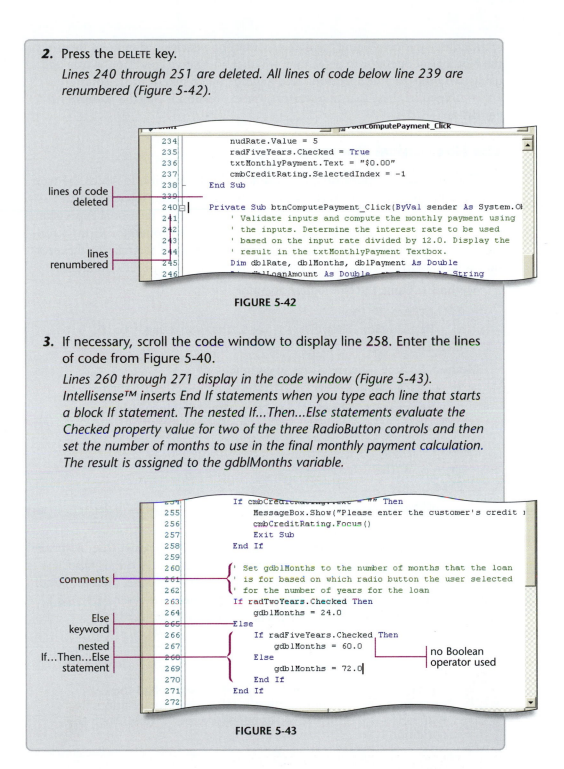

FIGURE 5-42

3. If necessary, scroll the code window to display line 258. Enter the lines of code from Figure 5-40.

Lines 260 through 271 display in the code window (Figure 5-43). Intellisense™ inserts End If statements when you type each line that starts a block If statement. The nested If...Then...Else statements evaluate the Checked property value for two of the three RadioButton controls and then set the number of months to use in the final monthly payment calculation. The result is assigned to the gdblMonths variable.

FIGURE 5-43

Logical Operators

In many instances, a decision to execute one alternative or another is based upon two or more conditions. In previous examples that involved two or more conditions, each condition was tested in a separate decision statement. This section discusses combining conditions within one decision statement by using the Not logical operator to determine whether a negative condition is true and using two other logical operators, And and Or. When two or more conditions are combined by these logical operators, the expression is called a **compound condition**.

The Not Logical Operator

The **Not logical operator** allows you to write a condition in which the true value is **complemented**, or reversed. Recall that a condition made up of two expressions and a relational operator is sometimes called a relational expression. A relational expression that is preceded by the Not logical operator forms a condition that is false when the relational expression is true. If the relational expression is false, then the condition is true. Consider the following If statements:

Method 1: Using the Not logical operator

```
If Not A > B Then
    MessageBox.Show("A is less than or equal to B.")
End If
```

Method 2: Using other relations to complement

```
If A <= B Then
    MessageBox.Show("A is less than or equal to B.")
End If
```

Method 3: Using a null Then

```
If A > B Then
Else
    MessageBox.Show("A is less than or equal to B.")
End If
```

In all three of these If...Then...Else statements, if A is greater than B, meaning the relational expression is true, then the condition, Not A > B, is false. If A is less than or equal to B, meaning the relational expression is false, then the condition, Not A > B, is true. All three methods are equivalent; however, Methods 1 and 2 are preferred over using a null Then, as shown in Method 3.

> **Tip**
>
> **Not Logical Operator**
>
> A relational expression that is preceded by the Not logical operator forms a condition that is false when the relational expression is true. If the relational expression is false, then the condition is true.

Because the Not logical operator can increase the complexity of a decision statement significantly, you should use it sparingly. As illustrated in Table 5-9, with Visual Basic .NET you may write the complement, or reverse, of a condition by using other relations.

Tip

Use of the Not Logical Operator

Because the Not logical operator can increase the complexity of the decision statement significantly, use it sparingly.

Table 5-9   Use of Other Relations to Complement a Condition

CONDITION	COMPLEMENT OF CONDITION	
	METHOD 1	METHOD 2
A = B	A <> B	Not A = B
A < B	A >= B	Not A < B
A > B	A <= B	Not A > B
A <= B	A > B	Not A <= B
A >= B	A < B	Not A >= B
A <> B	A = B	Not A <> B

To summarize, the Not logical operator requires the relational expression to be false for the condition to be true. If the relational expression is true, then the condition is false.

The And Logical Operator

The **And logical operator** is used to combine two or more conditions in an expression. When two or more conditions are combined by the And logical operator, the expression is called a compound condition. The And logical operator requires both conditions to be true for the compound condition to be true.

Tip

The And Logical Operator

The And logical operator requires both conditions to be true for the compound condition to be true.

Consider the following If statements:

Method 1: Using the And logical operator

```
If strGender = "M" And intAge > 20 Then
    MessageBox.Show(strEmpName)
End If
```

Method 2: Using nested If statements

```
If strGender = "M" Then
    If intAge > 20 Then
        MessageBox.Show(strEmpName)
    End If
End If
```

In both If…Then…Else statements on the previous page, if strGender is equal to the value M and intAge is greater than 20, then strEmpName is displayed before control passes to the line following the End If. If one of the conditions is false, then the compound condition is false, and control passes to the line following the End If without strEmpName being displayed. Although both methods are equivalent, Method 1 is more efficient, more compact, and more straightforward than Method 2.

Like a single condition, a compound condition can be only true or false. To determine the truth value of the compound condition, Visual Basic .NET must evaluate and assign a truth value to each individual condition. The truth value then is determined for the compound condition.

> **Tip**
>
> **Compound Conditions**
> A compound condition can be only true or false. To determine the truth value of the compound condition, Visual Basic .NET must evaluate and assign a truth value to each individual condition. The truth value then is determined for the compound condition.

For example, if intCount equals 4 and strCode equals "A", Visual Basic .NET evaluates the following compound condition in the manner shown:

If <u>intCount = 3</u> And <u>strCode = "A"</u> Then MessageBox.Show(strEmpSocSec)

      1. false   2. true

            3. false

Visual Basic .NET first determines the truth value for each condition, then concludes that the compound condition is false, because one of the conditions is false and the And logical operator requires that both conditions be true for the compound condition to be true.

A compound condition can be made up of several conditions separated by And operators. The flowchart shown in Figure 5-44 indicates that all three variables (T1, T2, and T3) must equal 0 to increment intCount by 1. The If…Then…Else statement in Figure 5-44 illustrates the use of a compound condition to implement the logic. The And operator requires all three conditions to be true for intCount to be incremented by 1. If any one of the three conditions is false, control is transferred to the line following the End If, and intCount is not incremented by 1. To summarize, the And logical operator requires all conditions to be true for the compound condition to be true.

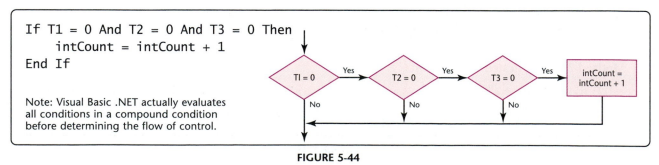

```
If T1 = 0 And T2 = 0 And T3 = 0 Then
    intCount = intCount + 1
End If
```

Note: Visual Basic .NET actually evaluates all conditions in a compound condition before determining the flow of control.

FIGURE 5-44

The Or Logical Operator

Like the And logical operator, the Or logical operator can combine two expressions to create a compound condition. The **Or logical operator** requires only one of two or more conditions to be true for the compound condition to be true. If all conditions are true, the compound condition also is true. Likewise, if all conditions are false, the compound condition is false.

> **Tip**
>
> **The Or Logical Operator**
>
> The Or logical operator requires only one of two or more conditions to be true for the compound condition to be true. If all conditions are true, the compound condition also is true. Likewise, if all conditions are false, the compound condition is false.

The use of the Or operator is illustrated below:

Method 1: Using the Or logical operator

```
If intDiv = 0 Or Expo > 1E30 Then
    MessageBox.Show("Warning")
End If
```

Method 2: Using two If...Then...Else statements

```
If intDiv = 0 Then
    MessageBox.Show("Warning")
End If
If Expo > 1E30 Then
    MessageBox.Show("Warning")
End If
```

In Method 1, if either intDiv equals 0 or Expo is greater than 1E30 (or 1 to the power of 30), the Then clause is executed. If both conditions are true, the Then clause also is executed. If both conditions are false, the Then clause is bypassed and control passes to the line following the End If.

Method 2 uses two If...Then...Else statements to resolve the same problem. Both methods are basically equivalent. Method 1, however, is more straightforward than Method 2. You also can write a single nested If...Then...Else statement without a logical operator that results in the same logic described in Methods 1 and 2.

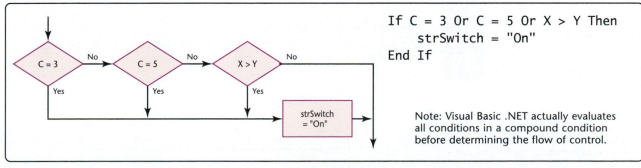

```
If C = 3 Or C = 5 Or X > Y Then
    strSwitch = "On"
End If
```

Note: Visual Basic .NET actually evaluates all conditions in a compound condition before determining the flow of control.

FIGURE 5-45

Figure 5-45 on the previous page illustrates a partial flowchart and the use of two Or operators to implement it. As with the And logical operator, the truth values of the individual conditions in the If statement in Figure 5-45 are first determined, and then the truth values for the conditions containing the Or logical operator are evaluated. For example, if C equals 4, X equals 4.9, and Y equals 4.8, the following condition is true:

```
If  C = 3  Or  C = 5  Or  X > Y  Then strSwitch = "On"
    1. false   2. false      3. true
       4. false
              5. true
```

In this If statement, Visual Basic .NET first evaluates the individual conditions. The first and second conditions are false, and the third condition is true. Next, Visual Basic .NET evaluates the leftmost Or, C = 3 Or C = 5. Because the truth values of these first two conditions are false, the truth value of C = 3 Or C = 5 also is false.

Finally, Visual Basic .NET evaluates the truth value of the condition resulting from the leftmost Or and the remaining rightmost Or, X > Y. Because the rightmost condition is true, the entire condition is determined to be true.

To summarize, the Or logical operator requires only one of the conditions to be true for the compound condition to be true. If both conditions are true, the compound condition also is true.

The Xor Logical Operator

Also used to create a compound condition, the **Xor logical operator** requires one of the two conditions to be true for the compound condition to be true. This Xor logical operator rarely is used. If both conditions are true, the compound condition is false. Likewise, if both conditions are false, the compound condition also is false. For example, if C = 3 and D = 4, then the following compound condition is false:

```
If  C = 3  Xor  D > 3  Then strSwitch = "On"
    1. true      2. true
         3. false
```

The Xor Logical Operator

The Xor logical operator requires one of the two conditions to be true for the compound condition to be true.

Other Logical Operators

An important characteristic of the And and Or logical operators is that if the left side is sufficient to decide the condition, the right side always is evaluated. For example, if the left side of the And operator evaluates to False, the right side still is evaluated, even though the left side sufficiently decides the condition. Two additional logical operators, the **AndAlso logical operator** and the **OrElse logical operator**, perform the And and Or operations, but include a feature called short-circuiting. If the left side of the AndAlso operator evaluates to False then the right side is not evaluated. If the left side of the OrElse operator evaluates to True, then the right side is not evaluated.

Combining Logical Operators

As you have learned, logical operators such as And, Or, Xor, AndAlso, and OrElse, can be combined in a decision statement to form a compound condition. The formation of compound conditions that involve more than one type of logical operator can create problems unless you fully understand the order in which Visual Basic .NET evaluates the entire condition. Consider the following decision statement:

```
If X > Y Or T = D And H < 3 Or Not Y = R Then
    intCount = intCount + 1
End If
```

To understand how Visual Basic .NET evaluates this statement, you must know if it evaluates operators from left to right, right to left, or one type of operator before another.

The order of evaluation of a series of logical operators is a part of what are called the **rules of precedence**. Just as Visual Basic .NET has rules of precedence for arithmetic operations (as discussed in Chapter 4), Visual Basic .NET also has rules of precedence for logical operators. Unless parentheses dictate otherwise, Visual Basic .NET reads from left to right and evaluates conditions using logical operators in this order:

1. Conditions containing arithmetic operators are evaluated first.
2. Conditions containing relational operators are evaluated second.
3. Conditions containing Not operators are evaluated third.
4. Conditions containing And/AndAlso operators are evaluated fourth.
5. Conditions containing Or/OrElse or Xor operators are evaluated fifth.

Tip

Logical Operator Rules of Precedence
Reading from left to right, unless parentheses dictate otherwise, Visual Basic .NET evaluates conditions containing arithmetic operators first; then those containing relational operators; then those containing Not operators; then those containing And/AndAlso operators; then those containing Or/OrElse or Xor operators.

Based on those rules of precedence, the compound condition in the previous If statement is evaluated as follows. Assume that D = 3, H = 3, R = 2, T = 5, X = 3, and Y = 2:

```
X > Y   Or   T = D   And   H < 3   Or   Not Y = R
1. true      2. false       3. false       4. true
                      6. false              5. false
          7. true
                         8. true
```

If you have trouble following the logic behind this evaluation, use this technique: Applying the rules of precedence, look or scan from *left to right* four different times. On the first scan, determine the truth value of each condition that contains a relational operator (X > Y, T = D, H < 3, Y = R). On the second scan, moving from left to right again, evaluate all conditions that contain Not operators. Because Y = R is true, Not Y = R is false. On the third scan, moving again from left to right, evaluate all conditions that contain And operators. Both T = D and H < 3 are false, therefore, T = D And H < 3 is false. On the fourth scan, moving from left to right, evaluate all conditions that contain Or operators. The first Or yields a truth value of true. The second Or yields, for the entire condition, a final truth value of true.

The Effect of Parentheses in the Evaluation of Compound Conditions

Parentheses can be used to change the order of precedence. In Visual Basic .NET, parentheses normally are used to avoid ambiguity and to group conditions with a desired logical operator. When parentheses are used in a compound condition, Visual Basic .NET evaluates that part of the compound condition within the parentheses first and then continues to evaluate the remaining compound condition according to the rules of precedence. For example, assuming C = 6 and D = 3, consider the following compound condition:

```
C = 7   And   D < 4   Or   D <> 0
1. false       2. true       3. true
        4. false
              5. true
```

Following the order of precedence for logical operators, the compound condition yields a truth value of true. If parentheses surround the last two conditions in the compound condition (D < 4 Or D <> 0), then Visual Basic .NET evaluates the Or operator before the And condition, and the compound condition yields a truth value of false, as shown at the top of the next page.

C = 7   And (D < 4   Or D <> 0)
‾‾‾‾   ‾‾‾‾   ‾‾‾‾‾
4. false   1. true   2. true

3. true

5. false

Parentheses can be used freely to reduce ambiguity in the evaluation of a compound condition. For example, if you want Visual Basic.NET to evaluate the compound condition

C > D And S = 4 Or X < Y And T = 5

you can incorporate it into a decision statement as it stands and it will be evaluated properly according to the rules of precedence. You also can write it as

(C > D And S = 4) Or (X < Y And T = 5)

to reduce the ambiguity and feel more certain of the outcome of the decision statement.

Parentheses and Logical Operators

Parentheses may be used to change the order of precedence. Parentheses can be used freely to reduce ambiguity in the evaluation of a compound condition.

Coding with a Logical Operator and String Expressions

Recall that the requirements document (Figure 5-2 on Page VB 5.04) includes a data validation requirement for customers with an E – Low credit rating. The condition states that if a customer has a low credit rating and wants to borrow more than the maximum loan amount allowed, an error message should display to the user and the loan amount must be reduced to an allowable value. Figure 5-46 illustrates this business logic in a flowchart.

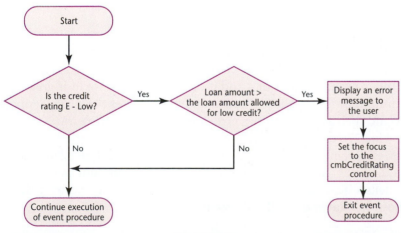

FIGURE 5-46

The first decision in Figure 5-46 on the previous page determines if the credit rating is E – Low. If it is not E – Low, then execution of the event procedure continues. If the credit rating is E – Low, then a second decision determines if the requested loan amount is greater than the maximum loan amount allowed for a customer with an E – Low credit rating. If it is not greater, then execution of the event procedure continues, which indicates that even though the credit rating is E – Low, the loan amount is acceptable. If the loan amount is greater than the maximum loan amount allowed for a customer with an E – Low credit rating, then an error message displays in a message box, focus is set to the cmbCreditRating control, and execution of the event procedure terminates.

The error message that displays includes a statement and the maximum amount a customer with the E – Low credit rating can borrow. To create this type of error message, string expressions and the concatenation operator are used.

In Visual Basic .NET, string expressions include string constants, string variables, character constants, character variables, string function references, and a combination of any number of these separated by the concatenation operator. The **concatenation (&) operator** joins two strings into one. For example, assume the variable strMoney is equal to the string, "5000", and the following code executes:

```
strErrorMessage = "Customers with this credit rating may only borrow " & strMoney
```

Then, the variable strErrorMessage will be equal to

Customers with this credit rating may only borrow 5000

A plus sign (+) can be used in the same manner as the & operator. To keep code unambiguous and avoid confusion with the plus sign used for addition, however, you should use the & operator whenever you want to concatenate strings.

Tip

String Concatenation
You should use the & operator whenever you want to concatenate strings.

The logic represented by the flowchart in Figure 5-46 translates into code in Figure 5-47. Line 273 uses the logical operator And to check the two conditions; that is, if E – Low is selected in the cmbCreditRating control as indicated by the SelectedIndex property value of 4 and if the loan amount input is greater than the MaximumLowCreditAllowed constant. Line 274 uses the string & operator, to create and then assign a custom error message to the strErrorMessage variable. Line 275 displays the error message defined as the variable, strErrorMessage, in line 274 to the user in a dialog box and line 276 sets the focus on the nudLoanAmount control where the loan amount was input. Line 277 tells Visual Basic .NET to exit the event procedure, meaning that any code below this statement will not execute.

```
272
273          If cmbCreditRating.SelectedIndex = 4 And dblLoanAmount >
         MaximumLowCreditAllowed Then
274              strErrorMessage = "Customers with this credit rating may only borrow " &
         MaximumLowCreditAllowed & "."
275              MessageBox.Show(strErrorMessage, "Check Loan Amount")
276              nudLoanAmount.Focus()
277              Exit Sub
278          End If
```

FIGURE 5-47

The following step inserts the code shown in Figure 5-47 into the btnComputeLoan_Click event procedure to evaluate the loan amount entered based on customer credit rating.

To Use a Logical Operator, Concatenation Operator, and the Focus() Method

1. Enter the lines of code from Figure 5-47.

Lines 272 through 278 display in the code window (Figure 5-48). The If...Then...Else statement validates that a customer with an E – Low credit rating cannot borrow more than the limit set by the MaximumLowCreditAllowed constant.

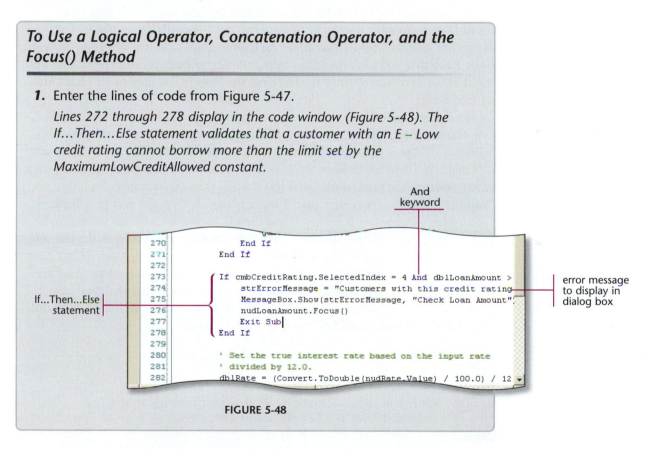

FIGURE 5-48

The two If...Then...Else statements coded thus far perform the data validation as specified in the requirements document; that is, that the monthly payment cannot be calculated unless the user has entered valid data and that a customer with an E – Low credit rating cannot borrow more than $5,000.00. The program enforces these limitations.

The Select Case Statement

The next step is to determine any adjustments to the interest rate based on the customer's credit rating. When the user clicks the Compute Payment button, the interest rate must be adjusted based on one of five possible values in the cmbCreditRating control. Rather than using a series of nested If...Then...Else statements to implement the logic, a Select Case statement (see page VB A.08 of Appendix A) provides a clearer and more maintainable structure for taking two or more different actions based on the value of a variable.

As previously discussed, the Select Case statement is used to implement an extension of the If...Then...Else structure in which there are more than two alternatives. This extended version of the If...Then...Else structure is a control structure called the Select Case structure. Table 5-10 shows the general form of a Select Case statement.

As indicated in Table 5-10, with a Select Case statement, you place the variable or expression you want to test after the keywords Select Case. Next, you assign the group of values that make each alternative case true after the keyword, Case. Each case contains the range of statements to execute, and you can add as many cases as required. After the last case, the Select Case statement ends with an End Select.

Example 1 in Table 5-10 tests the variable intAge against the expressionlist, beginning with the first Case clause and continuing downward until a match is found. If intAge is equal to 0, then a match occurs on the first case and the text box displays "Baby". The keyword Is is required when a relational operator, such as < (less than), is used. If intAge is less than 4, then the text box displays "Toddler". If intAge is greater than 4 but less than 8, then the text box displays "Youngster", and so on. If intAge is less than 0, then the Case Else is executed, and the text "Invalid Age" displays. Note that the Case Else clause is the last one in the list of cases. If a Case Else clause is included, then it must be the last case

Note that in Example 1, if intAge is equal to a value of 0, then all cases are true. Only the range of statements that correspond to the first matched case in a Select Case are executed, however. In Example 1 that means an intAge > 18 only executes the statement, txtAgeCategory.Text = "Adult".

Select Case Matching

Only the range of statements that corresponds to the first matched case in a Select Case is executed.

Table 5-10 Select Case Statement

General form:	Select Case testexpression
	    Case expressionlist
	        [statements]
	        .
	        .
	        .
	    Case Else
	        [statements]
	End Select
	
	where testexpression is a string or numeric variable or expression that is matched with the expressionlist in the corresponding Case clauses; and expressionlist is a numeric or string expression or a range of numeric or string expressions of the following form:
	1. expression, expression, . . . , expression
	2. expression To expression
	3. a relational expression where relation is <, >, >=, <=, =, or <>

Purpose:	The Select Case statement causes execution of the range of statements that follow the Case clause whose expressionlist matches the testexpression. If there is no match, then the range of statements in the Case Else clause is executed. Following the execution of a range of statements, control passes to the statement following the End Select.
| **Examples:** | 1. <br>```
Select Case intAge
    Case 0
        txtAgeCategory.Text = "Baby"
    Case Is < 4
        txtAgeCategory.Text = "Toddler"
    Case Is < 8
        txtAgeCategory.Text = "Youngster"
    Case Is < 12
        txtAgeCategory.Text = "PreTeen"
    Case Is < 18
        txtAgeCategory.Text = "Young Adult"
    Case Is >= 18
        txtAgeCategory.Text = "Adult"
    Case Else
        txtAgeCategory.Text = "Invalid Age"
End Select
```<br>2. <br>```
Select Case strCode
    Case "A", "B", "D"
        dblInterest = .015
        intTime = 24
    Case "C", "G" To "K"
        dblInterest = .014
        intTime = 36
    Case "L" To "Z"
        dblInterest = .013
        intTime = 48
    Case "E", "F"
        dblInterest = .012
        intTime = 60
End Select
``` |
| Notes: | If the Case Else clause is not included in a Select Case statement, as in Example 2, then it is the programmer's responsibility to ensure the testexpression falls within the range of at least one expressionlist found in the accompanying Case clauses. |

In Example 2 of Table 5-10 on the previous page, the variable strCode is matched against several different categories of letters. The first case is executed if strCode is equal to the value A, B, or D. The commas in a list of expressions following the keyword Case are mandatory. If strCode is equal to the value C or the letters G through K, then the second case is executed. The keyword To is required when specifying a range, such as "G" To "K". If strCode is equal to the values L through Z, the third case is executed. Finally, if strCode is equal to the value E or F, then the last case is executed.

Note in this example that there is no Case Else. The assumption here is that strCode contains no lowercase letters between A to Z, strCode is validated prior to the execution of the Select Case, and that strCode always is equal to an uppercase letter between A and Z. Hence, the Case Else is not required. If the rest of the code does not validate the expression, however, then you always should include a Case Else in the Select Case statement.

When specifying a range in a Case clause, make sure the smaller value is listed first. For example, the range, Case 3 To –1, is invalid; the range should be stated, Case –1 To 3. The same applies to string values. Whereas, Case "Eric" To "Ryan" is valid, Case "Ryan" To "Eric" is not, because Eric comes before Ryan in an alphabetical list ascending from A to Z.

Using Ranges in a Case Clause

When specifying a range in a Case clause, make sure the smaller value is listed first.

As indicated in Table 5-11, several ways to construct valid match expressions exist. In Example 1 in Table 5-11, the match expression is a list made up of the letters F to H, the letter S, and the value of the variable strEmpCode. In Example 2, the match expression includes the variable, dblEmpSalary, and the expression, dblMaxSalary – 2000.0. As indicated earlier, if a relational operator is used, then the keyword Is is required. The second value in the list of Example 2 shows that expressions with arithmetic operators are allowed. The third example includes a list of values with the keywords, Is and To.

Table 5-11   Valid Match Expressions

EXAMPLE	MATCH EXPRESSION
1	Case "F" To "H", "S", strEmpCode
2	Case Is = dblEmpSalary, Is = dblMaxSalary – 2000.0
3	Case Is < 12, 20 To 30, 48.6, Is > 100

Coding a Select Case Statement

In the modified Automobile Loan Calculator, the interest rate varies based on the credit rating selected by the user, as described in the requirements document. Figure 5-49 shows the flowchart for the logic for the Case structure used to determine the interest rate based on a customer's credit rating. Figure 5-50 shows the translation of the flowchart to the Select Case statement.

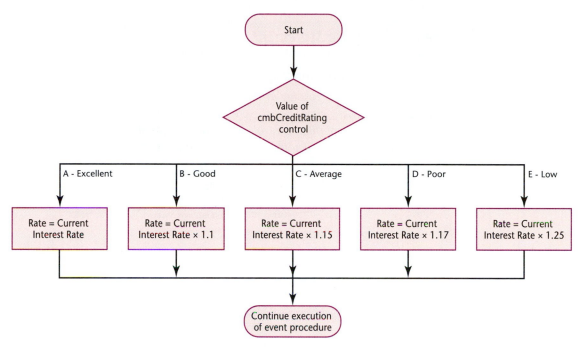

FIGURE 5-49

```
283
284         Select Case cmbCreditRating.SelectedIndex
285             Case 0 ' credit rating of A
286                 dblAdjustedRate = dblRate
287             Case 1 ' credit rating of B
288                 dblAdjustedRate = dblRate * 1.1
289             Case 2 ' credit rating of C
290                 dblAdjustedRate = dblRate * 1.15
291             Case 3 ' credit rating of D
292                 dblAdjustedRate = dblRate * 1.17
293             Case 4 ' credit rating of E
294                 dblAdjustedRate = dblRate * 1.25
295         End Select
```

FIGURE 5-50

As shown in Figure 5-50, Line 284 indicates that the expression tested by the Select Case statement is the value of the SelectedIndex property of the cmbCreditRating control. The in-line comments in the statements on lines 285, 287, 289, 291, and 293 indicate the credit rating that coincides with the SelectedIndex value. A Case Else is not necessary, because the data is validated for the SelectedIndex value earlier in the code and all possible values are accounted for in the Case clauses. Each of the five cases contains an assignment statement that calculates the adjusted interest rate based on the credit rating. For example, the requirements state that the credit rating of B – Good should cause the interest rate to be adjusted upwards by 10%. Therefore, the interest rate that the user inputs is multiplied by 1.1 to determine the adjusted interest rate to use in the final calculation.

The following step enters the Select Case statement shown in Figure 5-50 on the previous page.

To Code a Select Case Statement

1. Enter the lines of code from Figure 5-50.

Lines 283 through 295 display in the code window (Figure 5-51). The Select Case statement evaluates the credit rating the user selected in the cmbCreditRating ComboBox control. Based on the credit rating selected, assignment statements calculate the adjusted interest rate for the customer.

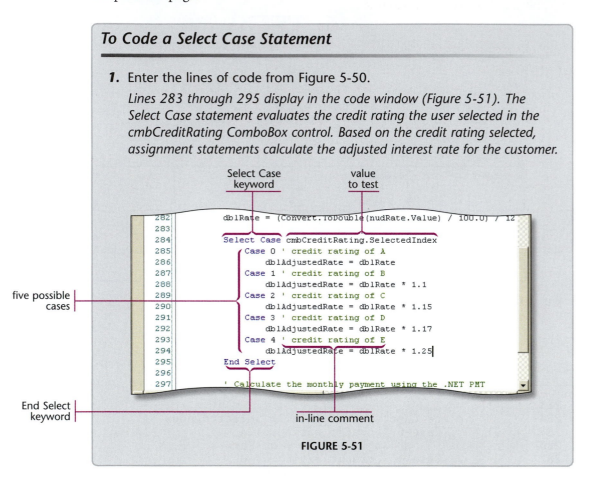

FIGURE 5-51

After the Select Case statement executes, the variable, dblAdjustedRate, contains the monthly interest rate to use in the final calculation. All of the values for the calculation shown on page VB 5.05 are now determined and the calculation can be performed.

Modifying a Parameter in a Function Call

The function call to the Pmt function currently accepts the dblRate variable as the interest rate parameter. The dblRate variable contains the interest rate entered by the user and does not take the customer's credit rating into account. The dblAdjustedRate variable contains the adjusted interest rate based on the customer's credit rating. The Select Case statement determines the correct value for the dblAdjustedRate. Therefore, the first parameter in the Pmt function call must be modified to accept the dblAdjustedRate variable instead of the dblRate variable. Figure 5-52 shows the modified call to the Pmt function.

```
300                    dblPayment = Pmt(dblAdjustedRate, gdblMonths, -dblLoanAmount)
```

FIGURE 5-52

The following step modifies the call to the Pmt function so that it accepts the dblAdjustedRate as the interest rate.

To Modify a Parameter in a Function Call

1. In line 300, click between the letters l and R in the dblRate parameter in the Pmt function call. Enter Adjusted to change the parameter name.

The parameter name is changed from the variable, dblRate, to the variable, dblAdjustedRate (Figure 5-53).

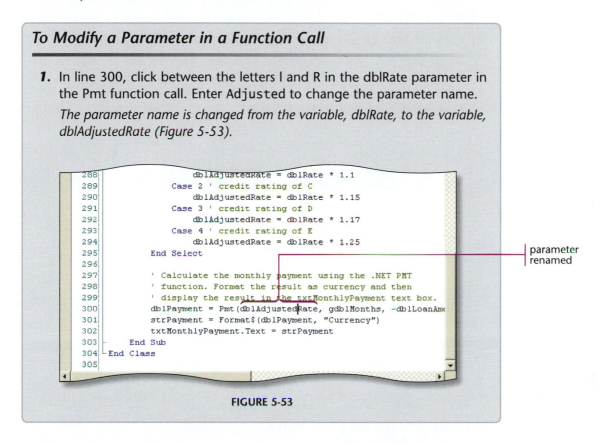

FIGURE 5-53

The preceding step modifies the first parameter sent to the Pmt function. The function now accepts the adjusted interest rate based on the customer's credit rating. The coding phase for the modified Automobile Loan Calculator application now is complete and the application can be tested.

Saving, Testing, and Documenting the Project

The steps on the next page save the form and project files for the modified Automobile Loan Calculator project on the Data Disk in drive A and then run the application to test the project.

To Save and Test the Project

1. Click the Save All button on the Standard toolbar.

The asterisk next to Form1.vb [Design] on the window title bar and the main work area tab no longer display, indicating that the project has been saved. Because the project was initially created and saved on the Data Disk in drive A, Visual Basic .NET automatically saves the project on the Data Disk in drive A.

2. Click the Start button on the Visual Basic .NET Standard toolbar.

Visual Basic .NET opens the Output window temporarily and displays messages as the application starts. The Automobile Loan Calculator application window displays, and Visual Basic .NET sets the focus to the first NumericUpDown control (Figure 5-54).

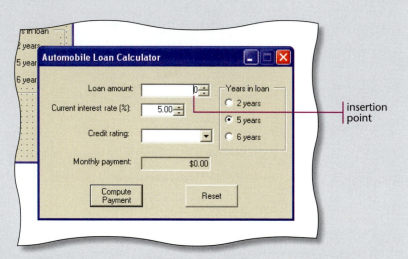

FIGURE 5-54

3. Enter 13000 for the Loan amount. Enter 10.25 for the Current interest rate in the second NumericUpDown control. Click the Compute Payment button.

The No Credit Rating message box displays, indicating that you must select a credit rating (Figure 5-55).

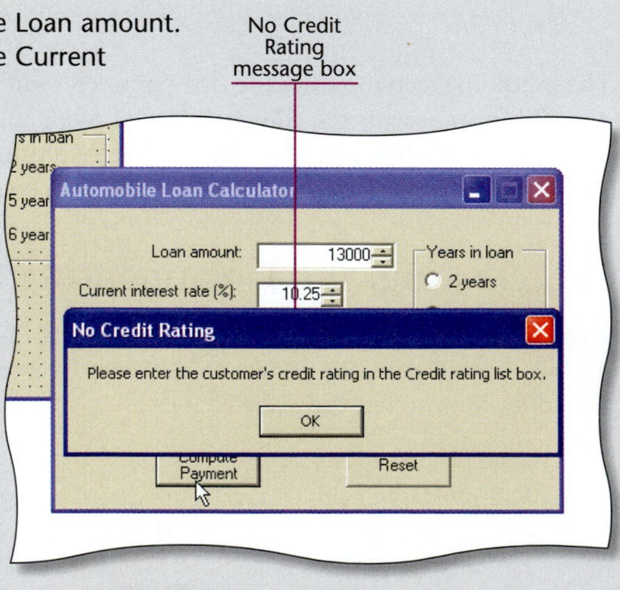

FIGURE 5-55

4. Click the OK button. Click the Credit rating box arrow and then select B – Good in the Credit rating drop-down list. Click the Compute Payment button.

The Automobile Loan Calculator application calculates the monthly payment, based on the values input to the application. The resulting output value, $284.44, displays in the Monthly payment text box (Figure 5-56). The result indicates that a loan amount of $13,000 over 5 years with a yearly interest rate of 10.25% for a customer with a B - Good credit rating will have a monthly payment of $284.44 on the loan.

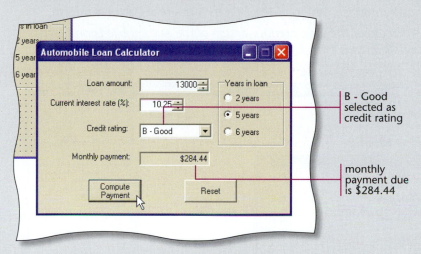

FIGURE 5-56

5. Click the Close button on the Automobile Loan Calculator application window title bar. If necessary, click the Visual Basic .NET taskbar button to display the Visual Basic .NET window. If necessary, close the Output window.

Visual Basic .NET returns to design time.

One important step when testing an application is to make certain that every line of code gets executed in your tests. When there are selection control structures, such as the If…Then…Else or Select Case structures, in the logic for your code, you should formulate test data that causes all of the conditions in the structures to execute. Such testing typically requires that you use multiple sets of test data. When choosing test data, using the flowchart shown in Figure 5-4 on page VB 5.07 may assist you in selecting data that will cause all of the code to execute.

Tip

Testing an Application
When testing an application, make certain that every line of code gets executed in your tests. Use carefully crafted sets of test data to ensure that all code executes.

The testing process for the modified Automobile Loan Calculator application is complete. The final step of the development cycle is to document the application. The following steps document the application and quit Visual Basic .NET. Line numbers are printed on the code listing.

To Document the Application and Quit Visual Basic .NET

1. Click the Form1.vb [Design] tab, and then follow the steps on page VB 2.34 of Chapter 2 using the PRINT SCREEN key to print a record of the user interface design of the Automobile Loan Calculator form.

A record of the user interface design of the Automobile Loan Calculator application is printed (Figure 5-57).

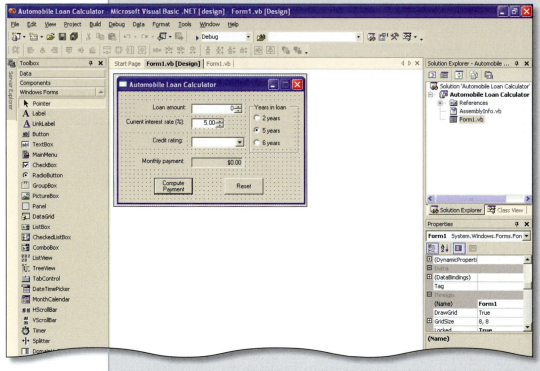

FIGURE 5-57

2. Click the Form1.vb tab. Click File on the menu bar and then click Page Setup.

3. When the Page Setup dialog box displays, if necessary, click Line numbers and then click the OK button.

4. Follow the steps on page VB 2.40 of Chapter 2 using the Print command on the File menu to print a record of the code for the Automobile Loan Calculator application.

A record of the Automobile Loan Calculator application code is printed (Figure 5-58).

A:\Chapter5\Automobile Loan Calculator\Automobile Loan Calculator\Form1.vb   2

```vb
64              End If
65          End If
66
67          If cmbCreditRating.SelectedIndex = 4 And dblLoanAmount >              ↙
    MaximumLowCreditAllowed Then
68              strErrorMessage = "Customers with this credit rating may only borrow " &   ↙
    MaximumLowCreditAllowed & "."
69              MessageBox.Show(strErrorMessage, "Check Loan Amount")
70              nudLoanAmount.Focus()
71              Exit Sub
72          End If
73
74          ' Set the true interest rate based on the input rate
75          ' divided by 12.0.
76          dblRate = (Convert.ToDouble(nudRate.Value) / 100.0) / 12.0
77
78          Select Case cmbCreditRating.SelectedIndex
79              Case 0 ' credit rating of A
80                  dblAdjustedRate = dblRate
81              Case 1 ' credit rating of B
82                  dblAdjustedRate = dblRate * 1.1
83              Case 2 ' credit rating of C
84                  dblAdjustedRate = dblRate * 1.15
85              Case 3 ' credit rating of D
86                  dblAdjustedRate = dblRate * 1.17
87              Case 4 ' credit rating of E
88                  dblAdjustedRate = dblRate * 1.25
89          End Select
90
91          ' Calculate the monthly payment using the .NET PMT
92          ' function. Format the result as currency and then
93          ' display the result in the txtMonthlyPayment text box.
94          dblPayment = Pmt(dblAdjustedRate, gdblMonths, -dblLoanAmount)
95          strPayment = Format$(dblPayment, "Currency")
96          txtMonthlyPayment.Text = strPayment
97      End Sub
98  End Class
99
```

A:\Chapter5\Automobile Loan Calculator\Automobile Loan Calculator\Form1.vb   1

```vb
1  Option Strict On
2  Public Class Form1
3      Inherits System.Windows.Forms.Form
4
5  Windows Form Designer generated code
6      ' Chapter 5:      Automobile Loan Calculator
7      ' Programmer:     Jeff Quasney
8      ' Date:           September 22, 2004
9      ' Purpose:        This project calculates the monthly payment for
10     '                 a loan based on loan amount, interest rate, and
11     '                 length of the loan.
12     ' Updated October 6, 2004 by Jeff Quasney
13     '                 Base interest rate on the customer's credit rating
14     Dim gdblMonths As Double = 60.0
15     Const MaximumLoanAllowed As Integer = 25000
16     Const MaximumLowCreditAllowed As Double = 5000
17
18     Private Sub Form1_Load(ByVal sender As System.Object, ByVal e As System.EventArgs) ↙
    Handles MyBase.Load
19         ' Set the maximum value of the Loan amount NumericUpDown control
20         nudLoanAmount.Maximum = MaximumLoanAllowed
21     End Sub
22
23     Private Sub btnReset_Click(ByVal sender As System.Object, ByVal e As System.   ↙
    EventArgs) Handles btnReset.Click
24         ' Reset Loan Amount and Monthly payment to zero. Reset
25         ' the interest rate to 5%, and select five years for the
26         ' length of the loan
27         nudLoanAmount.Value = 0
28         nudRate.Value = 5
29         radFiveYears.Checked = True
30         txtMonthlyPayment.Text = "$0.00"
31         cmbCreditRating.SelectedIndex = -1
32     End Sub
33
34     Private Sub btnComputePayment_Click(ByVal sender As System.Object, ByVal e As   ↙
    System.EventArgs) Handles btnComputePayment.Click
35         ' Validate inputs and compute the monthly payment using
36         ' the inputs. Determine the interest rate to be used
37         ' based on the input rate divided by 12.0. Display the
38         ' result in the txtMonthlyPayment Textbox.
39         Dim dblRate, dblMonths, dblPayment As Double
40         Dim dblLoanAmount As Double, strPayment As String
41         Dim dblAdjustedRate As Double, strErrorMessage As String
42
43         dblLoanAmount = Convert.ToDouble(nudLoanAmount.Value)
44
45         ' If the user has not selected a credit rating, inform
46         ' the user that a credit rating must be entered and then
47         ' exit the procedure
48         If cmbCreditRating.Text = "" Then
49             MessageBox.Show("Please enter the customer's credit rating in the Credit ↙
    rating list box.", "No Credit Rating")
50             cmbCreditRating.Focus()
51             Exit Sub
52         End If
53
54         ' Set gdblMonths to the number of months that the loan
55         ' is for based on which radio button the user selected
56         ' for the number of years for the loan
57         If radTwoYears.Checked Then
58             gdblMonths = 24.0
59         Else
60             If radFiveYears.Checked Then
61                 gdblMonths = 60.0
62             Else
63                 gdblMonths = 72.0
```

FIGURE 5-58

(continued)

5. Click the Visual Basic .NET Close button.

If you made changes to the project since the last time you saved it, Visual Basic .NET displays the Microsoft Visual Basic .NET dialog box. If you click the Yes button, you can resave your project and quit. If you click the No button, you will quit without saving changes. Clicking the Cancel button will close the dialog box.

Chapter Summary

In this chapter, you learned how to use a new control, the ComboBox control. You learned how to make significant modifications to an existing application. You learned how to use various forms of the If…Then…Else structure, including nesting If…Then…Else structures. You learned how to use logical and relational operators to perform a test and how to use the Select Case structure as an alternative to the If…Then…Else structure. You learned how to use the MessageBox class and the Focus() method to provide feedback to a user. Finally, you learned how to use the Exit Sub statement to halt execution of an event procedure.

What You Should Know

Having completed this chapter, you now should be able to perform the tasks shown in Table 5-12.

Table 5-12   Chapter 5 What You Should Know

TASK NUMBER	TASK	PAGE
1	Start Visual Basic .NET and Open an Existing Project	VB 5.09
2	Unlock a Form and Modify the Interface	VB 5.10
3	Change Properties of a Label Control	VB 5.14
4	Change Properties of a ComboBox Control	VB 5.17
5	Modify the Comment Header and Add a Constant	VB 5.22
6	Modify the btnReset_Click Event Procedure	VB 5.24
7	Declare Variables	VB 5.25
8	Code an If…Then…Else Statement Using the Show() and Focus() Methods	VB 5.32
9	Delete Code and Code a Nested If…Then…Else Statement	VB 5.40
10	Use a Logical Operator, a Concatenation Operator, and the Focus() Method	VB 5.51
11	Code a Select Case Statement	VB 5.56
12	Modify a Parameter in a Function Call	VB 5.57
13	Save and Test the Project	VB 5.58
14	Document the Application and Quit Visual Basic .NET	VB 5.60

Key Terms

And logical operator *(VB 5.43)*
AndAlso logical operator *(VB 5.47)*
block If…Then…Else statement
  (VB 5.31)
block-level scoping *(VB 5.31)*
business logic *(VB 5.03)*
business rules *(VB 5.03)*
ComboBox control *(VB 5.05)*
complemented *(VB 5.42)*
compound condition *(VB 5.42)*
concatenation (&) operator *(VB 5.50)*
decision making *(VB 5.26)*
DeMorgan's Laws *(VB 5.66)*
drop-down list box *(VB 5.05)*
DropDownStyle property *(VB 5.15)*
Exit Sub statement *(VB 5.31)*
If…Then…Else statement *(VB 5.26)*
index *(VB 5.23)*
message box *(VB 5.28)*

MessageBox class *(VB 5.28)*
nested If…Then…Else structure
  (VB 5.37)
nested structure *(VB 5.06)*
Not logical operator *(VB 5.42)*
Or logical operator *(VB 5.45)*
OrElse logical operator *(VB 5.47)*
Parameter Info window *(VB 5.34)*
relational expression *(VB 5.30)*
rules of precedence (logical operators)
  (VB 5.47)
Select Case statement *(VB 5.27)*
Select Case structure *(VB 5.27)*
SelectedIndex property *(VB 5.23)*
Show() method *(VB 5.28)*
single-line If…Then…Else statement
  (VB 5.31)
Xor logical operator *(VB 5.46)*

Homework Assignments

Short Answer

1. Given the following:

    $E = 500$

    $S = 700$

    $J = 1$

    $T = 60$

    $I = 40$

    Determine the truth value of the following compound conditions:

    a. $E < 400$ Or $J = 1$

    b. $S = 700$ And $T = 500$

    c. $S - T = 640$ And Not $(J = 1)$

    d. $T + I = S - 500$ Or $J = 0$

    e. $S < 300$ And $I < 50$ Or $J = 1$

    f. $S < 300$ And Not $(I < 50$ Or $J = 1)$

2. Determine a value of Q that will cause the condition below in the
   If…Then…Else statements to be true:

    a. `If Q > 8 Or Q = 3 Then`

        `    Z = Z / 10`

        `End If`

b. If Q + 10 >= 7 And Q > 0 Then
     strMessage = "Employee count exceeded."
  End If
c. If Q / 3 < 9 Then
     intCount = intCount + 1
  End If
d. If Q > 3 And Not (Q = 3) Then
     dblSum = dblSum + dblAmt
  End If

3. Write a series of code statements to perform the logic shown in Figure 5-59. Declare any variables you use and name the variables following the conventions used in this chapter.

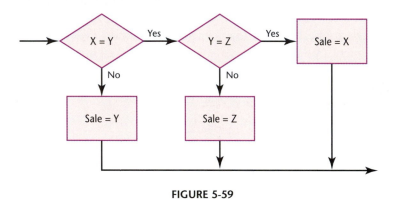

FIGURE 5-59

4. Construct code statements for each of the structures shown in Figure 5-60. Declare any variables you use and name the variables following the conventions used in this chapter.

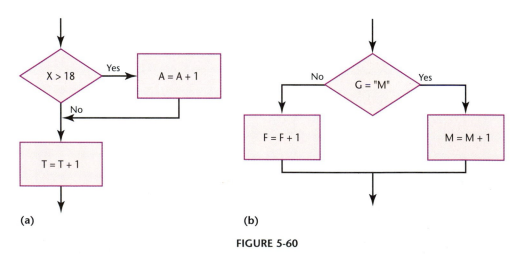

(a)   (b)

FIGURE 5-60

5. Construct code statements for each of the logic structures shown in Figure 5-61. Declare any variables you use and name the variables following the conventions used in this chapter.

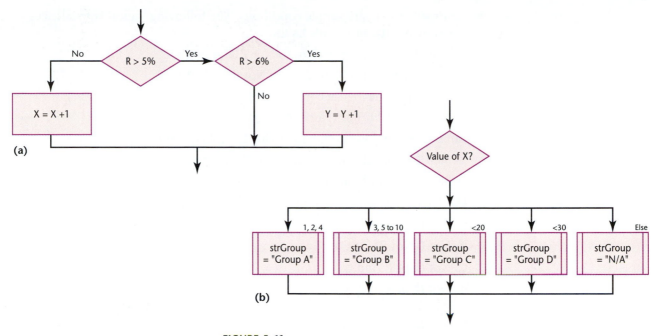

FIGURE 5-61

6. Given the conditions, S = 0, Y = 4, B = 7, T = 8, and X = 3, determine whether the message box displays for each of the following:

a. ```
If S > 0 Then
     MessageBox.Show ("Computation complete.")
End If
```

b. ```
If B = 4 Or T > 7 Then
     If X > 1 Then
          MessageBox.Show ("Computation complete.")
     End If
End If
```

c. ```
If X = 3 Or T > 2 Then
     If Y > 7 Then
          MessageBox.Show ("Computation complete.")
     End If
End If
```

d. ```
If X + 2 < 5 Then
     If B < Y + X Then
          MessageBox.Show ("Computation complete.")
     End If
End If
```

7. Given five variables, intA, intB, intC, intD, and intE, with previously defined values, write an If statement to increment the variable, intTotal, by 1 if all five variables have the exact value of 10.

8. Assume P and Q are simple conditions. The following logical equivalences are known as **DeMorgan's Laws:**

   Not (P Or Q) is equivalent to Not P And Not Q

   Not (P And Q) is equivalent to Not P Or Not Q

   For example, the logical equivalence

   Not ((P And Q) or (Not P And Q))

   can be broken down to the following logical equivalent in two steps:

   Step 1 = Not (P And Q) And Not (Not P and Q)

   Step 2 = (Not P or Not Q) And (P or Not Q)

   Use DeMorgan's Laws to write a logical equivalent for each of the following:

   a. Not P Or Not Q

   b. Not ((Not P) Or Q)

   c. Not (Not P And Q)

   d. Not (Not P And Not Q)

9. Given two positive-valued integer variables, intA and intB, write a sequence of statements to assign the variable with the larger value to intBig and the variable with the smaller value to intSmall. If intA and intB are equal, assign either to intSame. Be sure to show variable declarations.

10. The values of three variables, intU, intV, and intW, are positive and not equal to each other. Using If…Then…Else statements, determine which has the smallest value and assign this value to intLittle. Be sure to show variable declarations.

11. Write a partial program to set A = −1 if C and D are both 0, set A = −2 if neither C nor D is 0, and set A = −3 if either, but not both, C or D is 0.

12. In each of the following compound conditions, indicate the order of evaluation by Visual Basic .NET.

    a. S > 0 Or A > 0 Or T > 0

    b. S > 0 And A > 0 And Not T > 0

    c. Not S > 0 And T > 0 Xor P > 0

13. Given the following strings, write a partial program to (1) construct the concatenation, Format$ function, and (2) use the MessageBox.Show method to construct a statement that writes a message box to display a message box that reads, "Hayley Quintero, you are the winner of $10,000.00!". The message box should have the title, Hayley Quintero, Lucky Winner. Properly declare any necessary variables. Use the corresponding variables listed below for the first name, last name, and winnings amount, but do not code those values directly into the statements.

    strFirstName = "Hayley"

    strLastName = "Quintero"

    dblWinings = 10000.00

14. The _____ property of the ComboBox control can be used to indicate which list item is currently selected.

15. Use the _____ method of a TextBox control to position the insertion point in the TextBox control.

16. If the left side of the _____ operator evaluates to False, then the right side is not evaluated. If the left side of the _____ operator evalutes to True, then the right side is not evaluated.

17. The MessageBox class is part of the _____. Its sole method is the _____ method.

18. When the DropDownStyle property of a ComboBox control is set to the value, _____, a user is allowed to type a value into the ComboBox text box.

19. The _____ statement causes a procedure to halt execution immediately.

Learn It Online

Start your browser and visit scsite.com/vbnet/exs. Follow the instructions in the exercises below.

1. **Chapter Reinforcement TF, MC, and SA** Click the True/False, Multiple Choice, and Short Answer link below Chapter 5. Print and then answer the questions.

2. **Practice Test** Click the Practice Test link below Chapter 5. Answer each question, enter your first and last name at the bottom of the page, and then click the Grade Test button. When the graded practice test displays on your screen, click Print on the File menu to print a hard copy. Continue to take practice tests until you score 80% or better. Hand in a printout of the final practice test.

3. **Crossword Puzzle Challenge** Click the Crossword Puzzle Challenge link below Chapter 5. Read the instructions, and then enter your first and last name. Click the Play button. Complete the crossword puzzle. When you are finished, click the Submit button. When the crossword puzzle redisplays, click the Print button.

4. **Tips and Tricks** Click the Tips and Tricks link below Chapter 5. Click a topic that pertains to Chapter 5. Right-click the information and then click Print on the shortcut menu. Construct a brief example of what the information relates to in Visual Basic .NET to confirm you understand how to use the tip or trick. Hand in the example and printed information.

5. **Newsgroups** Click the Newsgroups link below Chapter 5. Click a topic that pertains to Chapter 5. Print three comments.

6. **Expanding Your Horizons** Click the Articles for Visual Basic .NET below Chapter 5. Click a topic that pertains to Chapter 5. Print the information. Construct a brief example of what the information relates to in Visual Basic .NET to confirm you understand the contents of the article. Hand in the example and printed information.

7. **Search Sleuth** Select three key terms from the Key Terms section of this chapter and then use the Google search engine at google.com (or any major search engine) to display and print two Web pages for each key term.

Debugging Assignment

Start Visual Basic .NET and open the project, Raintree Play, from the Chapter5\Raintree Play folder on the Data Disk. See page xvi in the preface of this book for instructions for downloading the Data Disk or see your instructor for information about accessing the files required in this book. The project consists of a form that helps a salesperson assist customers in configuring and pricing custom-built playground equipment. Certain rules exist to which each configuration must adhere:

- The user must select a Base model, but does not need to select any options.
- The Treetopper model cannot be configured with a sandbox.
- A playground cannot be configured with 2 swings.

The Raintree Play project contains bugs in the user interface and in the program code. Follow the steps below to debug the project.

1. All three ComboBox controls have a DropDownStyle property value of DropDown. The DropDownStyle property value for all three must be changed to the DropDownList, so that the user cannot type in the text boxes.

2. Spelling mistakes are in the Collection of the Item property of the Base model ComboBox control.

3. A flaw exists in the logic where the code determines if the Treetopper model is configured with a sandbox. Fix this logical error.

4. If a playground set is configured with 2 swings, focus should be set to the Option 1 ComboBox control after the error message displays.

5. The Case clause that determines which Option 1 item is selected is checking a range rather than a single value. Fix this error.

6. A Case clause in the Select Case statement is missing that determines the Base model price. Fix this error by adding `Case  1` as a Case clause.

7. The message box that displays if the user has not selected an item in the Base model ComboBox control should have the title, Error, on the title bar.

8. Lock the controls, save the project, and then run the project to test for any additional bugs. Select the SuperKids Regular base model with these options: a telescope, steering wheel, and sandbox. The application should display a Price of $1,020.00, as shown in Figure 5-62.

9. Document the form code for the Form1.vb form. Circle the lines of code you modified on the code printout.

FIGURE 5-62

Programming Assignments

1 The ComboBox Control and Decision Making

Start Visual Basic .NET. Open the project, Kim's Candies, from the Data Disk. This project contains a form and several controls with their properties already set. In this exercise, you will add additional controls and modify the code in the project.

The application computes the price of shipping and handling for a shipment of Kim's Candies. Kim's Candies ships five types of chocolates in boxes, usually in large quantities for special occassions and parties. The company has a minimum shipment of 10 boxes and a maximum shipment of 1,000 boxes. The prices per box are set in constants in the code. If the shipments are individually gift wrapped or customized, additional shipping and handling charges apply. The application should look similar to the one shown in Figure 5-63 on the next page.

Perform the following tasks to complete the application.

1. Unlock the controls on the form. Add a Label control and a ComboBox control and position the controls below the existing Label and NumericUpDown controls, as shown in Figure 5-63.

2. Change the DropDownStyle property value of the ComboBox control to DropDownList and change its name to cmbCandy. Add the following items to the list that displays in cmbCandy ComboBox control: Mint Chocolate, White Chocolate, Dark Chocolate, Swiss Chocolate, and Cherry Chocolate.

3. Open the code window by double-clicking the btnCompute button. Add the code, Option Strict On, as line 1 of the code. Add code similar to the code below to validate that the user has selected an item in the cmbCandy control. Add appropriate comments to your code.

```
If cmbCandy.Text = "" Then
    MessageBox.Show ("You must select the type of candy for this order.",  ↙
"Input Error")
    cmbCandy.Focus()
    Exit Sub
End If
```

4. At the top of the btnCompute_Click event procedure, declare the variables shown below. Be sure to add appropriate comments to your code.

```
    Dim dblOrderTotal as Double, dblOrderSize as Double
```
Directly below the code added in step 3, insert the following code with Select Case statement and Case clause to determine the type of candy ordered.

```
    dblOderSize = Convert.ToDouble(nudOrderSize.Value)
    Select Case cmbCandy.SelectedIndex
        Case 0
            dblOrderTotal = MintChocolatePerBox
    End Select
```

(continued)

1 The ComboBox Control and Decision Making *(continued)*

5. Complete the Select Case statement started in step 4 by adding four additional Case clauses for the other types of candy.

6. Add the code to adjust the order total for the type of packaging selected. Use code similar to the following nested If…Then…Else structure.

```
If radBasic.Checked Then
    dblOrderTotal = dblOrderTotal + BasicPackagingPerBox
Else
    If radGiftWrapped.Checked Then
        dblOrderTotal = dblOrderTotal + GiftWrappedPerBox
    Else
        dblOrderTotal = dblOrderTotal + SpecialWrapPerBox
    End If
End If
```

7. To format the output value and display it on the form, add the following line of code:

```
txtTotal.Text = Format$(dblOrderTotal * dblOrderSize, "Currency")
```

8. Lock the controls on the form and then save the project.

9. Run the project and correct any errors. If changes have been made, save the project again. In run time, the application window should display as shown in Figure 5-63.

10. Document the user interface and the code for the project.

FIGURE 5-63

2 Select Case and Nested If...Then...Else Structures

The Select Case statement can be written as a series of If...Then...Else statements. The following exercise demonstrates the differences in code between the Select Case and If...Then...Else statements. The application shown in Figure 5-64 on the next page is a quiz which contains five questions in the Question ComboBox control, and seven Answers in the Answer ComboBox control. After the user selects both a question and answer, the user can click either the Check with Select Case or Check with If...Then...Else buttons to determine if the question has been answered correctly. The first button uses the Select Case statement to determine if the answer is correct and the second button uses a nested If...Then...Else structure to determine if the answer is correct.

Perform the following tasks to build the application as shown in Figure 5-64.

1. Insert the Data Disk and start a new project in Visual Basic .NET. Create the project on the Data Disk in the Chapter5 folder in its own subfolder. Name the project, Visual Basic .NET Quiz.

2. Add two ComboBox controls, two label controls, and two Button controls to the form.

3. Name each of the controls appropriately and set appropriate properties on the form and controls using good practices introduced in this book. Be sure to set the ComboBox control's properties so it functions as a drop-down list box.

4. Populate the first ComboBox control with the following questions by clicking the Collections button of the Items property:

    1) Used to diagram structured code?

    2) Used to diagram obect-oriented design?

    3) Determines if TAB key causes focus?

    4) Controls program execution at run time?

    5) Shows a system in action?

5. Populate the second ComboBox control with the following answers:

    A) .NET Library

    B) TabStop

    C) Event diagram

    D) TabIndex

    E) The UML

    F) The CLR

    G) Flowchart

6. Write code in the first button's Click event procedure, using the Select Case statement to determine which question was asked. Use If...Then...Else statements within the Case clauses to determine if the questions were answered correctly. Indicate whether the answer is correct or incorrect in a message box. The correct answers are: 1 – G, 2 – E, 3 – B, 4 – F, 5 – C. Shown on the next page is an example of what a Case clause might look like, depending on the control names and variables used.

(continued)

2 Select Case and Nested If...Then...Else Structures *(continued)*

Case 3

```
If cmbAnswer.SelectedIndex = 5 Then
    MessageBox.Show ("Correct!", "Quiz")
Else
    MessageBox.Show ("Incorrect", "Quiz")
End If
```

The Case clause checks to see if the SelectedIndex property value of the first ComboBox is 3, meaning the fourth question is selected (Controls program execution at run time?), and then checks to see if the answer selected in the cmbAnswer control is the sixth item (The CLR). Before writing the code, create a flowchart that shows the program logic.

7. Repeat step 6 for the second button. Instead of using a Select Case statement, however, use nested If...Then...Else statements to construct the logic. Again, create a flowchart before writing the code.

8. Lock the controls on the form and then save the project.

9. Run the project and correct any errors. Make certain that both buttons always return the same answer. If changes have been made, save the project again. At run time, the application window should display as shown in Figure 5-64.

10. Document the user interface and the code for the project.

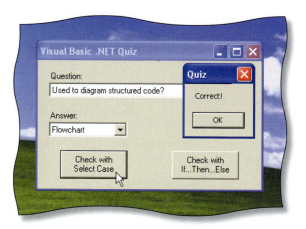

FIGURE 5-64

3 Stockbroker's Commission

Draw a flowchart and then develop an application that allows a user to enter a stock transaction and determine the stockbroker's commission. Each transaction includes the following data: the stock name, price per share, number of shares involved, and the stockbroker's name. Assume price per share = P. The stockbroker's commission is computed in the following manner: If the P (price per share) is less than or equal to $50.00, the commission rate is $0.19 per share; if P is greater than $50.00, the commission rate is $0.26 per share. If the number of shares sold is less than 150, the commission is 1.5 times the rate per share. Display the results in a message box, including the total commission earned.

Each message box result displayed should include the stock transaction data set and the commission paid the stockbroker in a grammatically correct set of sentences. After the message box displays, reset the input values to their original state.

4 ComboBox Controls and Selection Structures

Review the flowchart in Figure 1-25 on page VB 1.30. The flowchart is a representation of part of a cardiovascular disease risk assessment. Develop a program which performs the logic of the flowchart. Use four ComboBox controls for the following selections:

Age < 20, Age < 30, Age >= 30
Smoker, Nonsmoker
High Blood Pressure, Normal Blood Pressure
High Fat Diet, Normal Diet

Use If…Then…Else statements or Select Case statements in your code. Use proper data validation to ensure that the user has selected an item in each of the ComboBox controls, and display appropriate error messages and properly set focus if they have not. Display the final result in a message box.

5 Nested Select Case Statements

Design and build an application that works as a paper, scissors, and rock game. Draw a flowchart and write pseudocode before coding the application. Use two ComboBox controls to input the selections of the two players and label the ComboBox controls as Player 1 and Player 2. When the user clicks the Play Game button, a message box displays the winner. After the message box displays, both ComboBox controls are reset to a blank value and focus should be set to the first ComboBox control. Use a Select Case statement based on the value of the first ComboBox control. Within each Case, use a nested Select Case statement based on the value of the second ComboBox control to determine the winner.

6 Using ComboBox Control Properties

Max and Fritz's Pet Clinic has hired you for a small project. The veterinary assistants would like an application that calculates and displays total charges for veterinary services. The application should be designed with ComboBox controls to select the various services as follows:

- 3 levels of office visits (Routine - $15, Checkup - $25, and Extended - $35)
- 2 types of vaccinations (rabbies - $35, heartworm preventive - $25)
- Other services (grooming - $20, boarding - $15, dentistry - $22, x-rays - $65)
- Number of days of hospitalization (0 – 4 - $55/day)

As each service is selected the charge for the service should display in a TextBox control next to the ComboBox control. After all selections have been made, the charges should be added together to arrive at a total amount due and displayed

(continued)

6 Using ComboBox Control Properties (continued)

when a Button control is clicked. In case the patient's owner thinks the total is too high, the application should provide a way to reset the ComboBox controls, the corresponding service charges, and the total amount, so that the user can again select services. Use the concepts and techniques presented in this chapter to create the application.

7 Data Validation and Message Boxes

As a part-time employee of the PetsNow pet store, you have been asked to develop a small application for the salespeople. They require an application that allows them to enter the cost price of an item and select the margin (markup) using a NumericUpDown control. The markup should be a percentage that the item is marked up to determine the selling price. The application then should compute both the selling price of the item and the gross profit of the item. The gross profit is the difference between the cost price of the item to the store and the selling price to a customer. The selling price and gross profit should display for the salesperson. The salesperson should be notified if any errors occur when entering the cost price. Use the knowledge gained in this chapter to develop an appropriate application to perform these calculations.

8 Volume Computations

Use good design and programming techniques to develop a program to compute the volume of a box, cylinder, cone, and sphere. The selection of which calculation to make should be made from a ComboBox control. The application should include four input fields that allows a user to enter numbers with two decimal places; each input field also should indicate that the input value is measured in feet. Label the four input fields as: Length, Width, Height, and Radius. When the user clicks a button to perform the calculation, the button's event procedure should first determine that a selection for the calculation type was made. Next, the event procedure should ensure that non-zero, positive values have been entered only for the measurements needed for the particular formula being used. Finally, the calculation should be performed and a message box displayed to indicate the inputs and output in the following format:

The volume of a box with a length of 1.00 feet, a width of 2.00 feet, and a height of 3.00 feet has a volume of 6.00 cubic feet.

Use the following formulas to determine the volumes of the various shapes:

1. Volume of a box: $V = L \times W \times H$ where L is the length, W is the width, and H is the height of the box
2. Volume of a cylinder: $V = pi \times R \times R \times H$, where R is the radius, and H is the height of the cylinder
3. Volume of a cone: $V = (pi \times R \times R \times H)/3$, where R is the radius of the base, and H is the height of the cone
4. Volume of a sphere: $V = 4 \times pi \times R * R \times R/3$, where R is the radius of the sphere

In all of the above formulas, use the .NET Framework class library constant, Math.PI, for the value of pi.

6

Repetition and Multiple Forms

Objectives

You will have
mastered the material in
this chapter when you can:

- Add additional forms to a project
- Change the default icon on the title bar of a form
- Use ListView controls to display a list of items on a form
- Use CheckBox controls in an application
- Use the Anchor property of controls
- Work with Collections in code
- Code a Do Until loop
- Code a Do While loop
- Code a For...Next and a For Each...Next loop
- Code a concatenation operator
- Code a keyboard event
- Code a form Resize event procedure
- Work with multiple code windows
- Specify a Startup object for a project

Introduction

This chapter concentrates on developing the Windows application shown in Figure 6-1. The application contains two windows, one to display data and one to allow data entry. The application also uses a message box to provide output to the user. The application uses a new control in each window: the ListView control and the CheckBox control. In this chapter, you will learn how to add and set properties for these two controls. You also will learn to set the Anchor property for controls, so that the controls maintain their proper positions relative to the sides of the window when the user resizes the window. You will learn how to work with Collections in code to manage related data in an orderly manner. You will learn how to write code that includes loops using the Do Until, Do While, For…Next, and For Each…Next statements and how to code a concatenation operator, a keyboard event, and a form Resize event procedure. Finally, you will learn how to work with multiple code windows and specify a Startup object for a project to define which window displays when the application starts.

Chapter Six — Checking Daily Sales Totals

The Windows application developed in this chapter is the Today's Sales Check application, which calculates daily total sales for products entered by the user and two daily subtotals — one for items sold at a sale price and items sold at the regular price (Figure 6-1d). When the user starts the application, the Today's Sales Check window opens and displays an empty list (Figure 6-1a). The user clicks the Enter Today's Sales button to open the Today's Sales Entry window and begin entering the items sold that day (Figure 6-1c). After completing each entry, the user clicks the OK button or presses the ENTER key, which adds the data to the list in the Today's Sales Check window (Figure 6-1b) and then prompts the user to enter more data. The user continues to enter data in the Today's Sales Entry window until he or she has no more data to enter. Once finished, the user leaves the Item description text box blank and then clicks the OK button to return to the Today's Sales Check window (Figure 6-1b). Next, the user resizes the window to view all of the data entered (compare the size of Figure 6-1a with Figure 6-1b). Finally, the user clicks the Total Today's Sales button to calculate the total sales for the day, the total sales for items that were on sale, and the total sales for items that were not on sale (Figure 6-1d). The user can click the Clear Today's Sales List button to clear the list and begin again (Figure 6-1e).

When the user clicks the Total Today's Sales button to calculate daily total sales, the program first determines the number of items, or lines, in the list. Next, the program reads each line in the list and adds the amount in the Total Sales column to appropriate variables. Each amount in the Total Sales column is added to the total daily sales. If the item contains the value, Yes, in the On Sale column, the amount in the Total Sales column also is added to the total daily sales for items on sale. If the item contains the value, No, in the On Sale column, the amount in the Total Sales column also is added to the total daily sales for items not on sale. After reading each line in the list, the program displays the results in a message box.

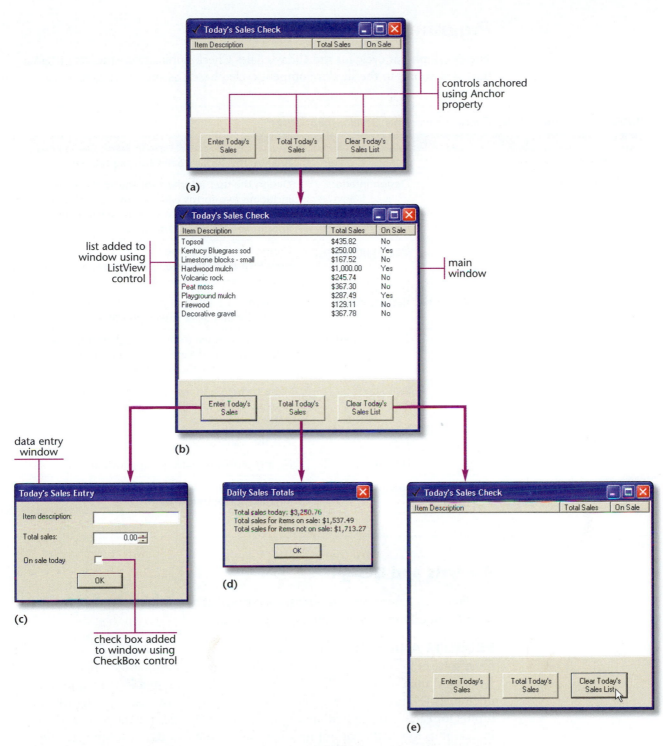

FIGURE 6-1

To fix any data entry errors for a specific item, the user can select a single item in the list in the Today's Sales Check window and press the DELETE key. The user then can re-enter the correct data using the Today's Sales Entry window. Finally, if the user wants to start over, he or she can click the Clear Today's Sales List button to clear all of the items in the list.

Program Development

The development cycle for the Today's Sales Check application consists of tasks that correspond to the six development cycle phases, as shown in Table 6-1.

Table 6-1   Today's Sales Check Application Development Tasks

DEVELOPMENT PHASE	TASK NUMBER	TASK NAME	TASK
Analyze requirements	1	Analyze problem	Analyze the Today's Sales Check problem.
Design solution	2	Design interface	Design the user interface for the application, including two forms with several controls and a message box. Set control properties to define appropriate layout and actions.
	3	Design program	Design the logic for the code and write pseudocode for the event procedures associated with the forms and controls.
Validate design	4	Validate design	Prove that the solution produces correct results for the Today's Sales Check problem.
Implement design	5	Develop interface	Add user interface elements, such as input areas, output areas, and Button controls on the forms. Set properties for the forms and controls.
	6	Write code	Write code to add event procedures for the buttons, form, and list box. Add comment statements in code.
Test solution	7	Test	Test the application.
	8	Debug	Fix any problems with the application.
Document solution	9	Document	Print the program, including the code and user interface for both forms.

Analysis and Design

Figure 6-2 shows the requirements document that initiates the development cycle to modify the Today's Sales Check application.

PROBLEM ANALYSIS   The problem that the Today's Sales Check application must solve is to allow data entry of an undetermined number of items, list the items, and then total the dollar amounts in the list. As stated in the requirements document (Figure 6-2), the application should require the user to enter three inputs for each item: an item description, total daily sales for the item, and an indicator as to whether or not the item was on sale that day. After the user finishes inputting all of the data for the items, the application must display a list of the items for the user to review for accuracy. If the user has entered an item incorrectly, the application should allow the user to delete the item and then add additional or corrected items.

REQUEST FOR NEW APPLICATION

Date submitted:	November 4, 2004
Submitted by:	Geetha Singh
Purpose:	As store manager, I need a quick way to do a daily comparison of total sales for items on sale versus items not on sale to help me analyze sales trends for our various landscaping products. Each day, I receive a hand-written list of total sales for each item; any sale items are marked as On Sale.
Application title:	Today's Sales Check
Algorithms:	Total daily sales should be summed in three different ways: • total daily sales • total sales for items on sale • total sales for items not on sale Calculations should be based on sales data entered by the user.
Notes:	1) The company uses the following terminology: *Item description, Total sales, On sale today.* 2) For each item, the application should require the user to: • enter an item description (1 to 50 characters) • enter total daily sales for each item ($0.00 to $1000.00) • check an indicator if the item was on sale that day The application should allow the user to enter as many items as necessary. The data entry area or screen should be designated by the term, Enter Today's Sales. 3) The application should display a list of the items entered by the user, so that he or she can check the data entry. It is important that the application allows the user to view as much of the list as possible, so that the user can check the data entered into the application against the hand-written list. If an item was entered incorrectly, the user should be able to delete the item from the list and then re-enter the item. 4) The application should also allow the user to clear the list of items, so that he or she can begin again. 5) The calculations should be designated by the term, Total Today's Sales. The clearing of the list of the items should be designated by the term, Clear Today's Sales List.

Approvals

Approval Status:	X	Approved
		Rejected
Approved by:	Ted Riedy	
Date:	November 8, 2004	
Assigned to:	J. Quasney, Programmer	

FIGURE 6-2

Once the list is complete and validated, the user should be able to tell the application to calculate three totals based on the data entered — the total daily sales in dollars, the total daily sales for sale items in dollars, and the total daily sales for non-sale items in dollars. Finally, the application should provide a way for the user to clear the list of items and begin the process again.

INTERFACE DESIGN   According to the requirements for the Today's Sales Check application, the application interface must handle two distinctly different requirements. First, the interface must provide an input area where a user can enter data for the items. Second, the interface must provide an output area to display the item list. Because the two requirements are distinctly different, they are best implemented using two separate forms to create two separate application windows: one to allow data entry and one to display the item list.

Tip

Using Multiple Forms
Use multiple forms in a project to separate distinct functionality into separate windows within the user interface.

When a project contains multiple forms, you must specify a Startup object in order to let Visual Basic .NET know which form to display first when run time begins. A **Startup object** can be any form or class that you want to have control when the application begins. Figure 6-3a shows a storyboard that meets the requirements for the first form, which will serve as the Startup object for the project.

As shown in Figure 6-3a, the first form is used to display the list of items entered by the user. Initially, the startup form is empty. Four functions are specified in the requirements document for this form. The user must be able to add items, calculate totals, clear the list, and delete items. The first three functions can be handled by adding Button controls to the form. When the user clicks the first button, the second form displays. When the user clicks the second button, the program reads the items in the list, totals the items in three ways, and then displays a message box with the results. When the user clicks the third button, the program clears the list. The user can complete the fourth function — deleting an item from the list — by selecting an item in the list and then pressing the DELETE key. The delete functionality is best handled this way, because this method is a common and familiar way to delete items in a list.

The list on the first form (Figure 6-3a) must contain three columns, each of which is associated with the three data elements required for each item — item description, total daily sales for the item, and an indication whether the item was on sale for the day. A **ListView control** is used to arrange and display a list of items into single or multiple columns, with or without column headings. The ListView control also allows you to display accompanying icons and additional text, called subitems, for each list item. As indicated in note 3 in the requirements document (Figure 6-2 on the previous page), the entire form should be resizable so that the user can view more or less data, if he or she chooses. This requirement also implies that the list should resize as the form resizes.

As shown in the storyboard in Figure 6-3b, the second form must be able to accept the data entered by the user for each of the list items. The form requires three inputs — the item description, the total daily sales for the item, and an indicator whether the item was on sale for the day. The first input, item description, is a text value with a maximum length of 50 characters and can be designed with a TextBox control. A NumericUpDown control is best used for input of total daily sales amount, which is a numeric amount with two decimal places and a range from $0 to $1,000. The indicator for whether or not an item is on sale can be added to the second form using a CheckBox control A **CheckBox control** is used to add check boxes to a form and provides a way for users to select one of two states: checked and unchecked. Finally, the form requires a Button control to function as an OK button that allows the user to enter the data in the form so it displays in the Today's Sales Check list.

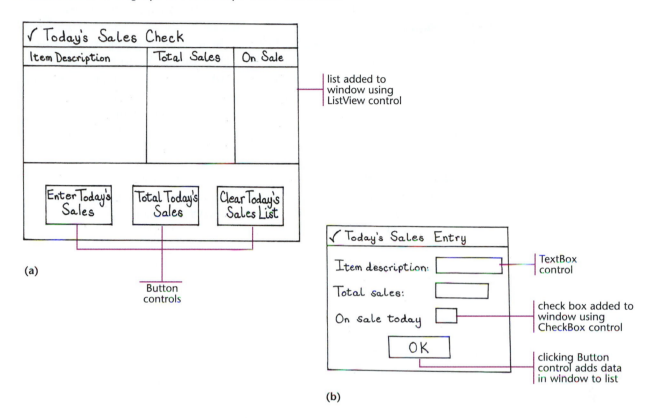

FIGURE 6-3

After the user enters data for the first item in the list, the application should allow the user either to click the OK button or press the ENTER key to add the data to the list in the Today's Sales Check window. To support this functionality, the OK button should be made the default button on the Today's Sales Entry form, so that pressing the ENTER key selects the OK button. Making the OK button the default button means the user does not need to use the mouse to perform data entry.

Tip

Data Entry Form Design

When designing a form for data entry, make sure that the user can perform all data entry without use of the mouse. Most users are accustomed to typing the data for one item and then pressing the ENTER key to move to the next item.

The final consideration for the interface design is how the two forms will interact. The Enter Today's Sales button on the first form (Figure 6-1a on page VB 6.03) opens the Today's Sales Entry form (Figure 6-1c on page VB 6.03). To make data entry more efficient, the application should continue to display the Today's Sales Entry form until data entry is complete, rather than requiring the user to click the Enter Today's Sales button after each item is entered to reopen the Today's Sales Entry form and continue data entry. To accomplish this, a **terminating condition** is used to let the program know when data entry is complete. In the Today's Sales Check application, the terminating condition is met when the user enters no data for the item description on the Today's Sales Entry form. By leaving the item description field blank and then clicking the OK button, the user indicates that he or she has finished entering data. Until the user completes these steps, which meet the requirements of the terminating condition, the application continues to display the Today's Sales Entry form and accept data entered by the user.

PROGRAM DESIGN   Figure 6-4 shows two flowcharts that represent the key logic in the application. The first flowchart (Figure 6-4a) represents the logic for the Enter Sales Click Event, which executes when the user clicks the Enter Today's Sales button. The logic includes a Do While structure, which causes the loop to repeat until the condition in the decision symbol — Is Item description blank? — is true. The Do While structure is covered in detail in Appendix A on page VB A.08.

The first task of the Enter Sales Click Event is to display the Today's Sales Entry form and request user input. In the Today's Sales Check application, the terminating condition is met when the user enters no data for the item description on the Today's Sales Entry form. As shown in the flowchart, if the user enters no text for the Item description, then the item description is blank and the looping process terminates. If the user enters a complete item description, then the looping process continues and the item is added to the list on the Today's Sales Check form. An If...Then...Else structure within the loop determines if the user has checked the check box to indicate that the item is on sale. If the item is on sale, then the value, Yes, is placed in the list with Item description and Total sales. If not, the value, No, is placed in the list with Item description and Total sales.

The second flowchart (Figure 6-4b) represents the logic for the Total Today's Sales Click Event, which totals the sales and displays the results. The flowchart contains a Do While structure, which causes the loop to repeat as long as the condition is true. Logic within the Do While structure executes once for each item in the list, determines the sales for each item, and adds it to the appropriate total. An If...Then...Else structure within the loop determines if the item was on sale or not. Based on the On Sale status of the item for the day, the structure then adds the sales for the item to the appropriate total. After the loop has terminated, the results are displayed.

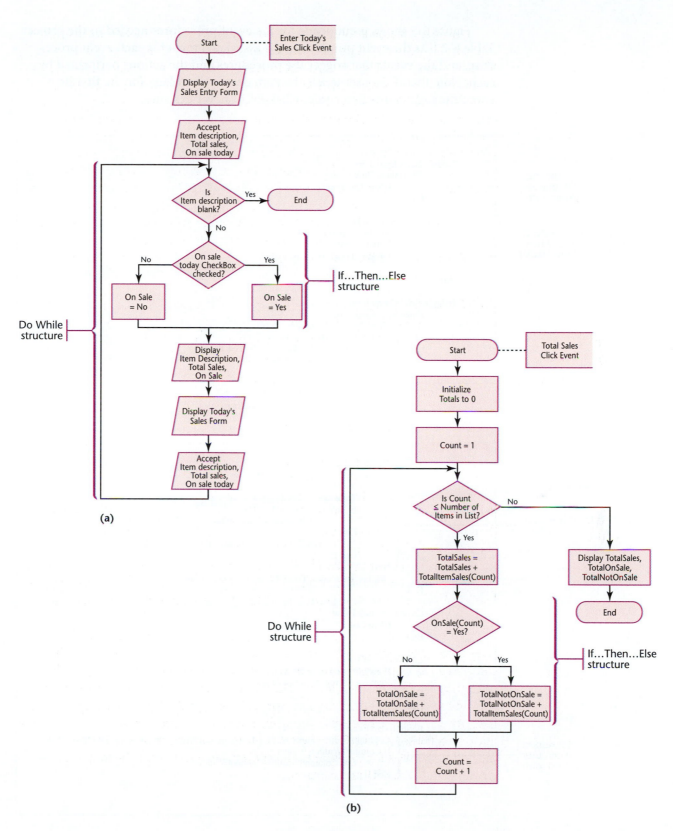

(a)

(b)

FIGURE 6-4

Figure 6-5 shows pseudocode for the event procedures needed in the project. Table 6-2 lists the event procedures, the associated form for each event procedure, and the events that trigger the procedures and the actions performed by each. Note that if the user leaves the item description blank for the first item entry, the logic in the Enter Sales Click Event never executes.

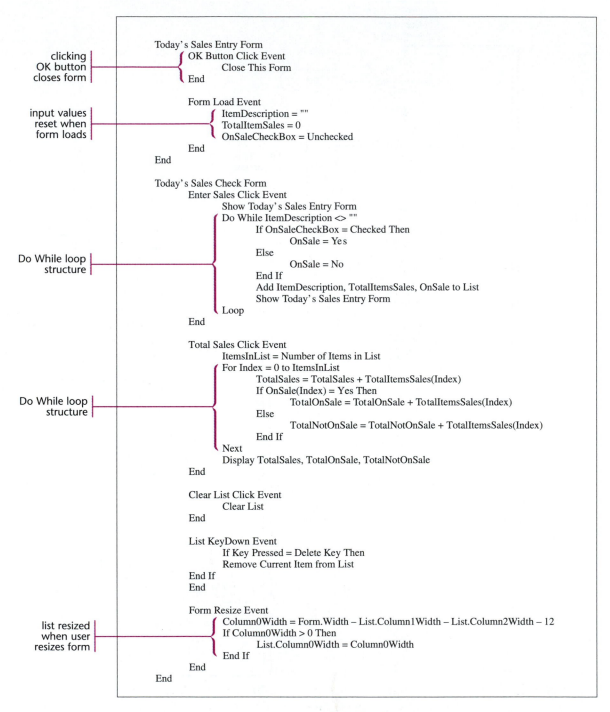

FIGURE 6-5

Table 6-2   Today's Sales Check Event Procedures

FORM	EVENT PROCEDURE	EVENT	ACTION PERFORMED
Today's Sales Entry	OK Button Click Event	Executes when the user clicks the OK button	Closes the form
	Form Load Event	Executes when the form displays for each item that is entered	Resets the input and output values to original states
Today's Sales Check	Total Sales Click Event	Executes when the user clicks the Total Today's Sales button	Reads each item in the ListView control and sums the total sales, total sales for items on sale, and total sales for items not on sale (After each item is summed, the results are displayed in a message box.)
	Enter Sales Click Event	Executes when the user clicks the Enter Today's Sales button	Adds an item to the list when the user clicks the OK button on the Today's Sales Entry form and then reopens the Today's Sales Entry form (The event procedure continues performing this operation (loops) until the user leaves the Item description blank.)
	Clear List Click Event	Executes when the user clicks the Clear Today's Sales List button	Removes all items from the ListView control
	List KeyDown Event	Executes when the user presses a key while the ListView control has focus	Removes the item currently selected in the ListView control from the ListView control
	Form Resize Event	Executes immediately after the user has resized the Today's Sales Entry form	Makes sure that the Item description column in the list displays as much information as possible when user resizes the form

VALIDATE DESIGN   The validation of the design is accomplished by stepping through the requirements document to ensure that all of the requirements are met in a sound manner and that the program logic is sound. The requirements in notes 1 and 2 are met with the design of the Today's Sales Entry form. The user quickly can enter the three data elements for each item; the controls and control properties used on the form place appropriate restrictions on the inputs. Note 3 is handled by the design of the Today's Sales Check form, which allows the user to resize the form to view as little or as much of the information as possible. The Clear Today's Sales List button on the Today's Sales Check form addresses the requirement in note 4. The Total Today's Sales button addresses the requirements in note 5 and the algorithm. When the user clicks the button, the event procedure reads each item in the list and adds the Total Sales for the item to appropriate totals. Two or more test data sets should be used to validate that program logic in the flowcharts and pseudocode will calculate the appropriate total and then display the total, as required.

As shown in Table 6-1 on page VB 6.04, after validating the program design, the next phase in the development cycle is to develop the user interface of the application using Visual Basic .NET.

Creating the User Interface

The Today's Sales Check application is a Windows application with a graphical user interface for user input and output display. The user interface consists of two forms, each of which contains several controls. The application is based on the Windows Application template provided by Visual Basic .NET. The following steps start Visual Basic .NET and then start a new project using the Windows Application template.

To Start Visual Basic .NET and Start a New Project

1. Insert the Data Disk in drive A. See page xvi in the preface of this book for instructions for downloading the Data Disk or see your instructor for information about accessing the files required in this book.

2. Start Visual Basic .NET. When the Start Page displays, click the New Project button on the Start Page.

3. When the New Project dialog box displays, if necessary, click Create directory for Solution. Double-click the text, WindowsApplication1, in the Name box. Type Today's Sales Check in the Name box.

The new project name displays in the Name box, and the solution name displays in the New Solution Name box. Because the Create directory for Solution check box is selected, Visual Basic .NET will create a subdirectory with the same name as the project when it creates the project.

4. Click the Browse button. If necessary, click 3½ Floppy (A:) in the Look in box. Click Chapter6 and then click the Open button.

5. Click the OK button. After the new Today's Sales Check project is created, if necessary, click the Maximize button on the Visual Basic .NET window title bar to maximize the Visual Basic .NET window. If necessary, close the Output window.

Visual Basic .NET creates the new Today's Sales Check solution and project. Visual Basic .NET creates an initial form and displays it in the main work area.

After Visual Basic .NET creates the new project, the solution and project name, Today's Sales Check, display in the Solution Explorer window. Form1.vb is selected in the Solution Explorer window to indicate that the Form1.vb[Design] tab is selected in the main work area. The Properties window displays information about Form1.vb. Later in this chapter, when the second form is added to the project, the Solution Explorer window also will display information about the second form.

Setting Form Properties and Adding Controls

The next step is to set the properties of the first form, the Form1 form, and add controls to the form. Several of the property values of the Form1 form must be changed. For example, the Form1 form should include a check mark icon on the title bar to distinguish the form from other applications running in Windows. Changing the property value for the **Icon property** allows you to set the form icon. The Name property also should be changed to assign the first form a name that distinguishes it from the second form. Table 6-3 lists the Form1 form property value changes that need to be made.

Naming Forms

If a project contains multiple forms, each form should be properly named so that the forms can be distinguished.

Table 6-3   Form1 Form Property Values for the Today's Sales Check Application

PROPERTY	VALUE	EFFECT
Size: Width	344	Sets the width of the form in pixels
Size: Height	240	Sets the height of the form in pixels
StartPosition	CenterScreen	Causes the form to display in the center of the user's screen at the start of run time
Text	Today's Sales Check	Sets the value of the title bar on the window
Name	frmTodaysSalesCheck	Changes the form's name to a descriptive name
Icon	CHECKMRK.ICO	Sets the icon that displays to the left of the title on the title bar

The user interface design also specifies that the Form1 form should include one ListView control and three Button controls. The ListView control allows you to display a list of items with several columns. The steps on the next page add the ListView and Button controls by drawing them on the form and then set the Form1 form properties shown in Table 6-3.

The steps use a new method to add the second and third Button controls. After the first Button control is added, the control is copied and then pasted twice. To copy the control, you select the control and then press CTRL+C. Once you have copied the control, you press CTRL+V to paste a new copy of the control on the form.

To Set Form Properties and Add Controls

1. Add a ListView control and a Button control by selecting the appropriate control in the Toolbox window and then drawing the controls on Form1, as shown in Figure 6-6. Select the Button1 control on Form1 and then press CTRL+C. Press CTRL+V two times.

   A ListView control and three Button controls are added to the form (Figure 6-6). The Button2 control is hidden below the Button3 control, so only two Button controls are visible on the form.

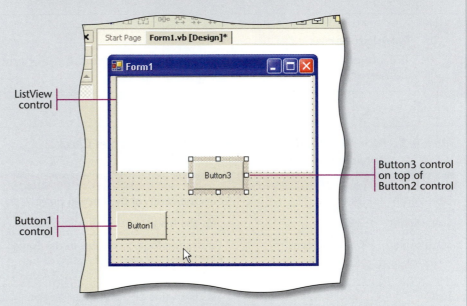

FIGURE 6-6

2. Drag the Button2 and Button3 controls so they are aligned horizontally with the Button1 control. Be sure to place Button2 in the center of the form and Button3 on the right of the form. Select Form1 in the main work area. Set the properties of Form1 as specified in Table 6-3 on the previous page, except for the Icon property. Select the Icon property value in the Properties window.

   The form properties are set and the form is sized properly, the name is changed to frmTodaysSalesCheck, and the form title is set. The Button controls partially display because they were not moved when the form was resized. When the Icon property is selected, the current form icon displays on the left side of the Icon property value and the Icon property ellipsis button displays (Figure 6-7).

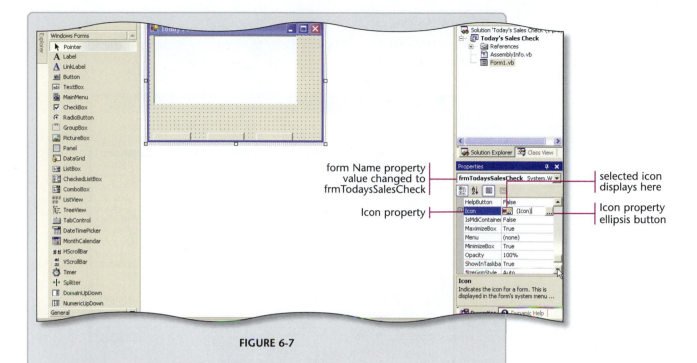

FIGURE 6-7

3. Click the Icon property ellipsis button. When the Open dialog box displays, use the Look in box to navigate to the C:\Program Files\ Microsoft Visual Studio .NET\Common7\Graphics\icons\Misc folder. Depending on how Visual Studio .NET or Visual Basic .NET was installed on your computer, the path to the Misc folder may vary.

The Open dialog box displays in which you can select an icon file. The icon files, which have the file extension, .ico, display in the file box (Figure 6-8).

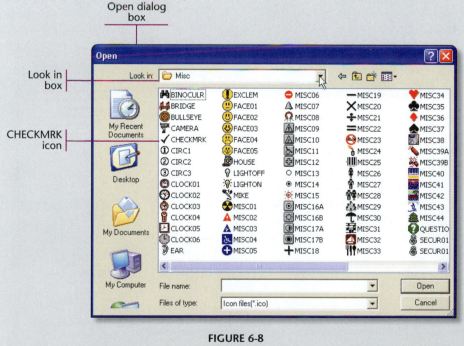

FIGURE 6-8

(continued)

4. Click the CHECKMRK icon.

The CHECKMRK icon is selected and the file name displays in the File name box (Figure 6-9).

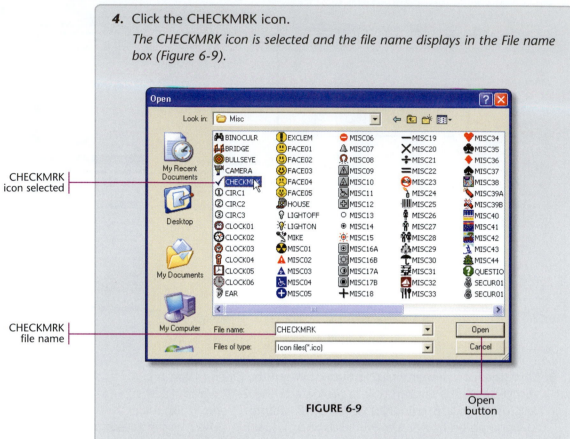

CHECKMRK icon selected

CHECKMRK file name

Open button

FIGURE 6-9

5. Click the Open button.

The icon on the left side of the Icon property value changes to a check mark. The title bar of the frmTodaysSalesCheck form now displays a check mark icon (Figure 6-10).

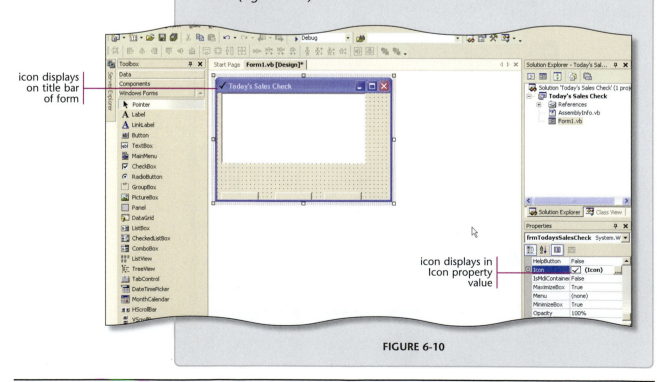

icon displays on title bar of form

icon displays in Icon property value

FIGURE 6-10

As indicated in the requirements document (Figure 6-2 on page VB 6.05), the frmTodaysSalesCheck form should remain sizable at run time, so that the user can resize the form to view all of the data in the item list. The default value for the FormBorderStyle property of the form is Sizable, so this property was not changed. The form is initially set at 344 pixels by 240 pixels to allow several items to display, without taking up too much space on the user's screen.

Changing Button Control Properties

The next step is to set the properties for the three Button controls, which must be named, sized, positioned, and labeled as described in the interface design on page VB 6.07. Table 6-4 lists the property values that must be set for the Button controls.

Table 6-4 Button Control Property Values for the frmTodaysSalesCheck Form

CONTROL	PROPERTY	VALUE	EFFECT
Button1	Text	Enter Today's Sales	Sets the text that displays on the button face to Enter Today's Sales
	TabIndex	1	Causes this control to be the second control on the form to receive focus
	Name	btnEnterSales	Changes the control's name to a descriptive name
	Size: Width	88	Sets the width of the control in pixels
	Size: Height	40	Sets the height of the control in pixels
	Location: X (left)	16	Indicates the distance from the left border of the form in pixels
	Location: Y (top)	152	Indicates the distance from the top border of the form in pixels
Button2	Text	Total Today's Sales	Sets the text that displays on the button face to Total Today's Sales
	TabIndex	2	Causes this control to be the third control on the form to receive focus
	Name	btnTotalSales	Changes the control's name to a descriptive name
	Size: Width	88	Sets the width of the control in pixels
	Size: Height	40	Sets the height of the control in pixels
	Location: X (left)	124	Indicates the distance from the left border of the form in pixels
	Location: Y (top)	152	Indicates the distance from the top border of the form in pixels
Button3	Text	Clear Today's Sales List	Sets the text that displays on the button face to Clear Today's Sales List
	TabIndex	3	Causes this control to be the fourth control on the form to receive focus
	Name	btnClearList	Changes the control's name to a descriptive name
	Size: Width	88	Sets the width of the control in pixels
	Size: Height	40	Sets the height of the control in pixels
	Location: X (left)	232	Indicates the distance from the left border of the form in pixels
	Location: Y (top)	152	Indicates the distance from the top border of the form in pixels

The following step sets the property values of the three Button controls on the frmTodaysSalesCheck form.

To Change the Properties of Button Controls

1. Change the property values of the three Button controls, as listed in Table 6-4 on the previous page.

The controls display on the frmTodaysSalesCheck form as shown in Figure 6-11.

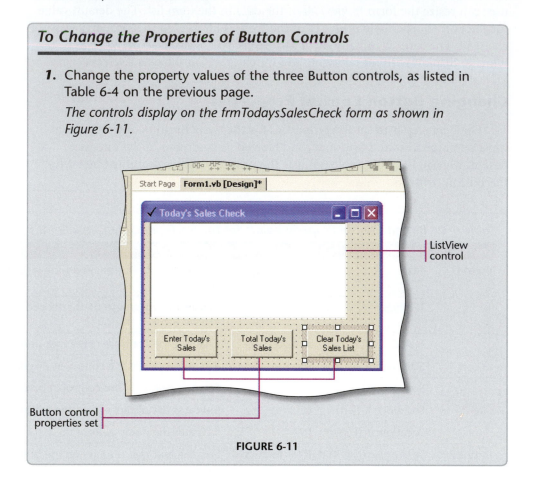

FIGURE 6-11

One additional property, the Anchor property, must be set for the Button controls on the frmTodaysSalesCheck form. The Anchor property, which defines the behavior of the Button controls when the frmTodaysSalesCheck form is resized, will be set later in this chapter.

ListView Control Properties

The next step is to set the properties for the ListView control (Figure 6-11). The properties of the ListView control define how the control displays a list of items and how the user interacts with the list.

The options for how the ListView control displays are similar to those available with Windows Explorer. Items can be viewed with large icons, small icons, list view, or detail view. The **View property** is used to set the display option for the ListView control. When the View property value is set to **LargeIcon view**, each list item displays as a full-sized icon with a label below it. When the View property value is set to **SmallIcon view**, each list item displays as a small icon with a label to its right. When the View property value is set to **List view**, each list item displays as a small icon with a label to its right and the list is arranged in columns with no column headers. In **Details view**, each list item displays on a separate line with additional information about each item arranged in columns. The leftmost column contains a label and optionally a small icon, and subsequent columns contain subitems. Each column has a header, which can display a caption for the column. The user can resize each column at run time.

Other properties control how the user interacts with the list. For example, the **MultiSelect property** specifies whether the user can select multiple items in the list. The **CheckBoxes property** determines if a check box appears with each item in the list, so the user can select multiple items.

Table 6-5 lists the commonly used properties of the ListView control.

Table 6-5 **ListView Control Properties**

CATEGORY	PROPERTY	DESCRIPTION	PROPERTY VALUES
Appearance	CheckBoxes	Determines whether a check box appears next to each item	True **False**
	FullRowSelect	Determines whether clicking an item selects all its subitems	True **False**
	GridLines	Determines whether grid lines appear between the rows and columns containing the items and subitems	True **False**
	View	Determines how items display in the control	**LargeIcon** Details SmallIcon List
Behavior	Activation	Determines the type of action the user must take to select (activate) an item	**Standard** OneClick TwoClick
	Alignment	Determines the alignment of list items	**Default** Left Top SnapToGrid
	AllowColumnReorder	Determines whether the user can drag column headers to reorder columns	True **False**
	AutoArrange	Determines whether icons are arranged automatically	**True** False
	Columns	Indicates the collection of all column headers used in the control	Collection of headers; default is an empty collection
	HeaderStyle	Determines the column header style when column headers are defined	None Nonclickable **Clickable**
	Items	Indicates a collection containing all list items	Collection of items; default is an empty collection
	MultiSelect	Determines whether multiple items can be selected	**True** False
	Scrollable	Determines whether a scroll bar is added to the control if not enough room is available to display all items	**True** False

The requirements for the Today's Sales Check application are that the user can view three columns in the ListView control — Item Description, Total Sales, and On Sale. The requirements also state that the user should be able to select one item at a time to delete the item from the list. In addition, you should assign a descriptive name to the ListView control using the Name property value. When naming a ListView control, use the lst prefix to indicate a ListView control. Table 6-6 lists the changes that must be made to the default properties of the ListView control on the frmTodaysSalesCheck form.

Naming ListView Controls
When naming Listview controls, use the lst prefix for the name.

Table 6-6   ListView Control Properties for the frmTodaysSalesCheck Form

CONTROL	PROPERTY	VALUE	EFFECT
ListView1	Name	lstTodaysSales	Changes the control's name to a descriptive name
	TabIndex	0	Causes this control to be the first control on the form to receive focus
	FullRowSelect	True	Causes all columns to be highlighted when the user selects an item in a row
	MultiSelect	False	Disallows selection of more than one row of items at a time
	View	Details	Shows the items in the list in a multicolumn view with column headers
	Size: Width	336	Sets the width of the control in pixels
	Size: Height	128	Sets the height of the control in pixels
	Location: X (left)	0	Indicates the distance from the left border of the form in pixels
	Location: Y (top)	0	Indicates the distance from the top border of the form in pixels

In addition to these properties, the **Columns property** must be set to define the number of columns that display in the list. As indicated by the user interface design, the ListView control should have three columns with column headers, labeled as Item Description, Total Sales, and On Sale. In order for the columns to be sized properly, the widths of the first two columns should be set to 190 and 79, respectively. The last column width does not need to be set, because it will take up the remaining width of the ListView control automatically. The following steps set the property values for the ListView control, as listed in Table 6-6, and set the Columns property to display the list with three columns.

To Change the Properties of a ListView Control

1. Click inside the ListView control to select it. Change the property values for the ListView control, as listed in Table 6-6. Select the Columns property of the lstTodaysSales control in the Properties window.

The property values are changed for the ListView control, which is renamed lstTodaysSales control. An area for the column headers displays at the top of the control (Figure 6-12).

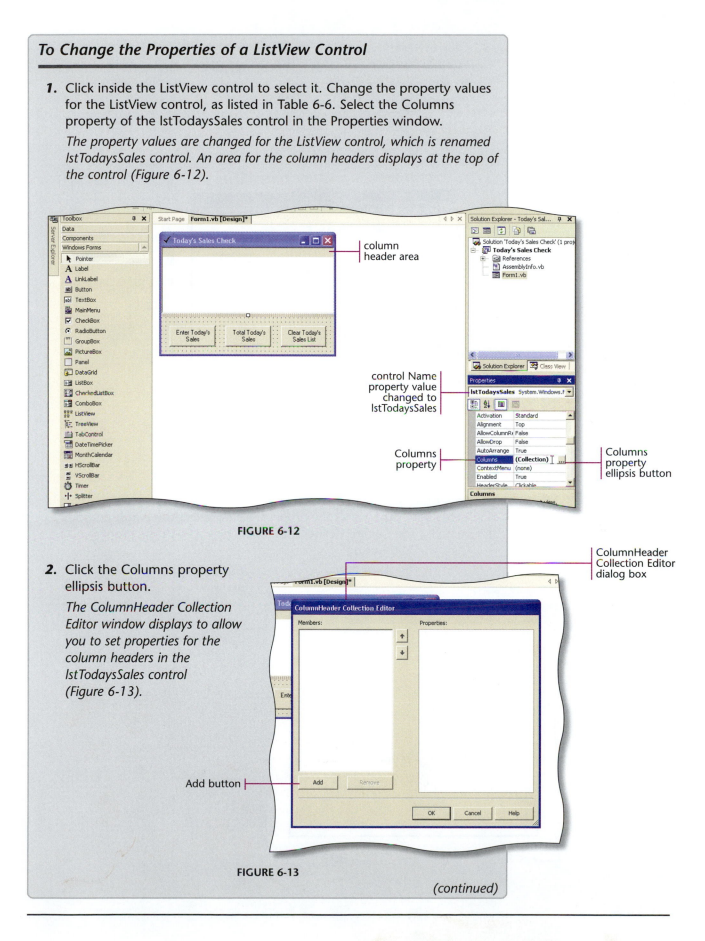

FIGURE 6-12

2. Click the Columns property ellipsis button.

The ColumnHeader Collection Editor window displays to allow you to set properties for the column headers in the lstTodaysSales control (Figure 6-13).

FIGURE 6-13

(continued)

3. Click the Add button.

The member, ColumnHeader1, is added to the Members list. A properties list for ColumnHeader1 displays in the ColumnHeader1 Properties list (Figure 6-14).

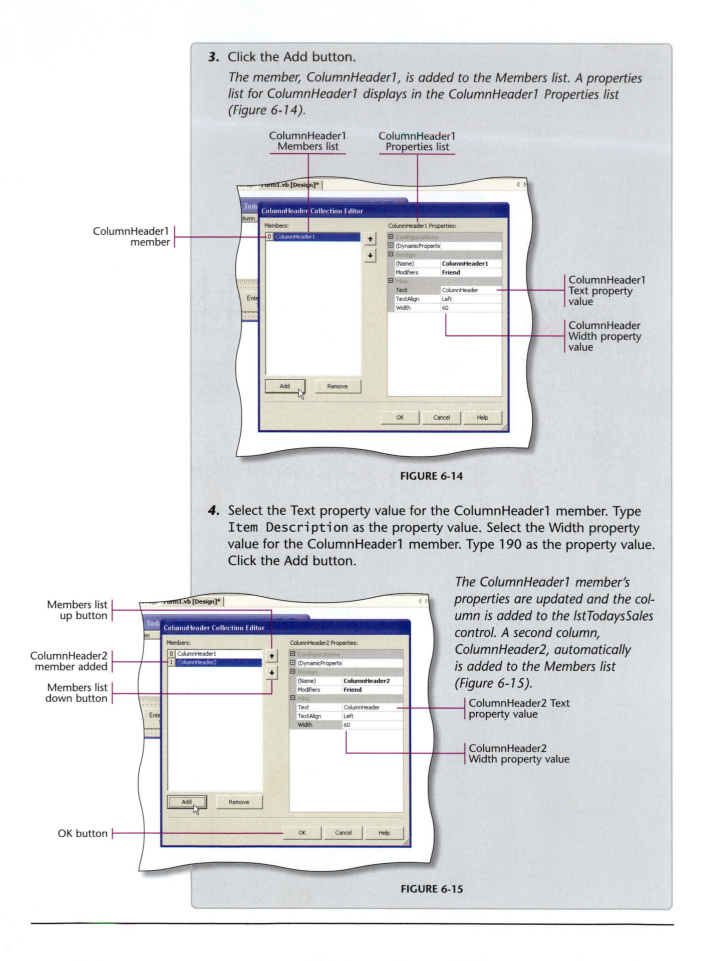

FIGURE 6-14

4. Select the Text property value for the ColumnHeader1 member. Type `Item Description` as the property value. Select the Width property value for the ColumnHeader1 member. Type 190 as the property value. Click the Add button.

The ColumnHeader1 member's properties are updated and the column is added to the lstTodaysSales control. A second column, ColumnHeader2, automatically is added to the Members list (Figure 6-15).

FIGURE 6-15

5. Select the Text property value for the ColumnHeader2 member. Type
Total Sales as the property value. Select the Width property value for
the ColumnHeader1 member. Type 79 as the property value. Click the
Add button. When the ColumnHeader3 member is added, select the
Text property value for the ColumnHeader3 member. Type On Sale as
the property value. Click the OK button.

*The column properties are set for the lstTodaysSales control. Three columns
with column headers display in the lstTodaysSales control, as shown in
Figure 6-16.*

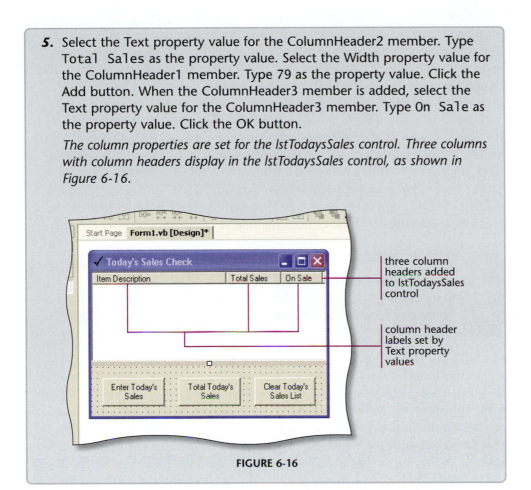

three column
headers added
to lstTodaysSales
control

column header
labels set by
Text property
values

FIGURE 6-16

As shown in Figure 6-12 on page VB 6.21, as soon as the View property
value is set to Detail, a column header displays at the top of the control. The
Columns property is a group, or collection, of headers. A **collection** is a group
of one or more objects that can be accessed and operated on as a single entity.
Collections manage an ordered set of items, which usually are other objects, such
as these column headers.

As shown in Figure 6-15, the **ColumnHeader Collection Editor window**
presents several options for each column header. You can name the column, add
a text label, adjust the alignment of the text label in the column header, and set
the initial width of the column. The Members list up and down arrow buttons,
located between the Members area and the ColumnHeader2 Properties area
(Figure 6-15), allow you to change the order of the column headers by selecting
a column header and then clicking one of the buttons to move the column
header up or down in the order of columns.

Anchoring Controls

In the previous applications developed in this book, the windows used in
application were not resizable during run time. In some applications, however,
you want to allow the user to resize a form in order to customize the view of that
application to his or her liking. When a form is resized, controls on the form

must be moved or resized as well in order to maintain a usable and balanced user interface. This requires adjusting the Size:Width, Size:Height, Position:X, and Position:Y property values for each of the controls. Rather than coding the changes in these values, Visual Basic .NET provides the ability to set a fixed location, or **anchor**, for controls to specified sides of a form.

The controls on a form include a property called the **Anchor property** that specifies the sides of the form to which the control is anchored. A control can anchor to the top, bottom, left, or right side of a form, or any combination of sides, such as top-left. If a control is anchored to a side, then Visual Basic .NET keeps the control the same distance from that side of the form when the form is resized. If necessary, Visual Basic .NET resizes the control in order to keep the control the appropriate distance from the side of the form.

Anchoring Controls

Use the anchor property to force controls to maintain a specific relationship with or distance from one or more sides of a form.

In the Today's Sales Check form, the four controls should be anchored so that the lstTodaysSales control takes up as much space as possible on the form, while still allowing the Button controls to be used on the bottom of the form. Anchoring the Button controls to the bottom of the form causes the buttons to remain spaced as they are and remain at the bottom of the form when it is resized. Anchoring the lstTodaysSales control to all four sides of the form causes the lstTodaysSales control always to touch the top, left, and right sides of the form as the form is resized. Anchoring to all four sides also ensures that there will be enough space for the Button controls at the bottom of the form, because the bottom of the lstTodaysSales control will always be the same distance from the bottom of the form.

The following steps anchor the Button controls to the bottom of the frmTodaysSalesCheck form and anchor the lstTodaysSales control to the four sides of the frmTodaysSalesCheck form. The steps use a new method to change property values, which allows you to change the same property on several controls at the same time. To use this method, you select multiple controls and then change the property value in the Properties window.

To Anchor Controls

1. Select the three Button controls on the frmTodaysSalesCheck form by selecting the btnEnterSales control, holding down the CTRL key, and then selecting the other two Button controls. Scroll to the Anchor property in the Layout category in the Properties window. Click the Anchor down arrow in the property values list.

   The graphical anchor map displays below the current Anchor property values for the controls (Top, Left). The graphical anchor map indicates that the Button controls are anchored to the top and left of the frmTodaysSalesCheck form (Figure 6-17).

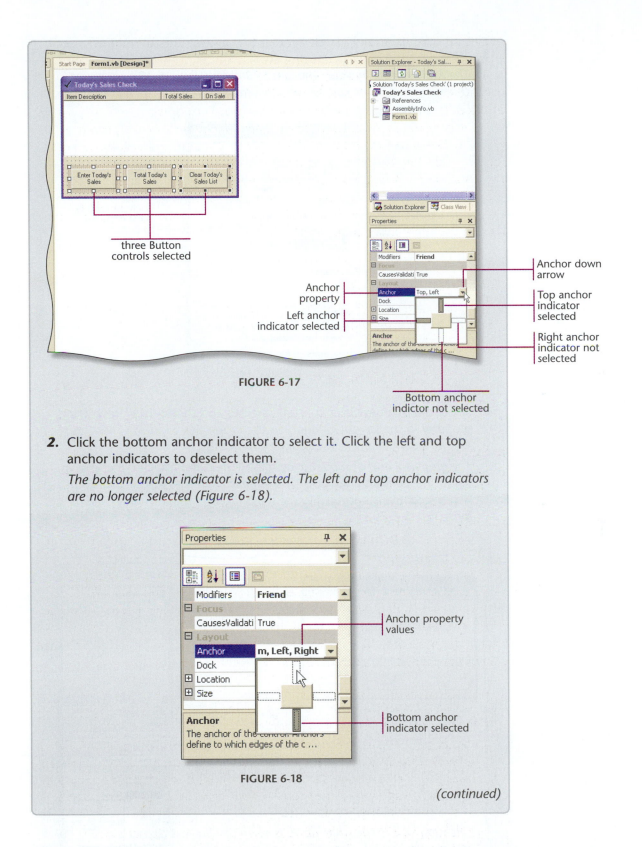

FIGURE 6-17

2. Click the bottom anchor indicator to select it. Click the left and top anchor indicators to deselect them.

The bottom anchor indicator is selected. The left and top anchor indicators are no longer selected (Figure 6-18).

FIGURE 6-18

(continued)

3. Press the ENTER key.

The Anchor property value changes to Bottom (Figure 6-19). No visible change occurs to the controls on the form.

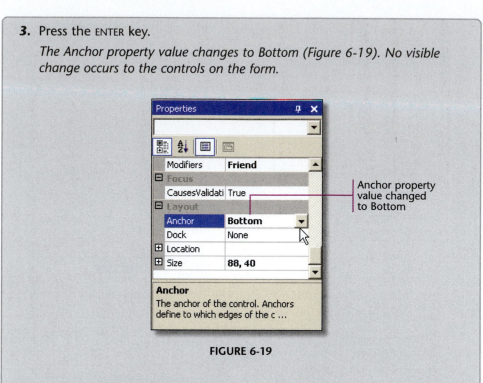

FIGURE 6-19

4. Select the lstTodaysSales control. Scroll to and then select the Anchor property in the Layout category in the Properties window. Click the Anchor down arrow in the property values list.

The graphical anchor map displays below the current Anchor property values for the controls (Top, Left). The graphical anchor map indicates that the ListView control is anchored to the top and left of the frmTodaysSalesCheck form (Figure 6-20).

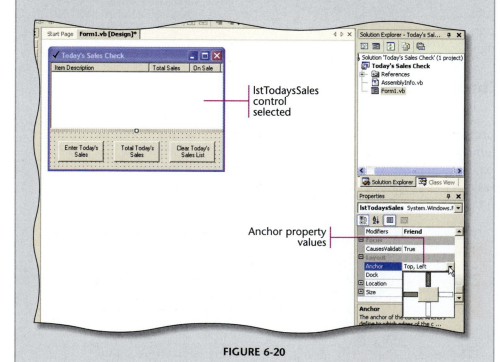

FIGURE 6-20

5. Click the bottom and right anchor indicators to select them.

All four anchor indicators are highlighted (Figure 6-21).

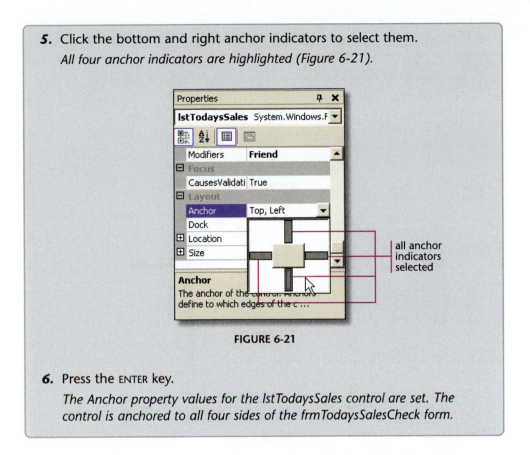

all anchor
indicators
selected

FIGURE 6-21

6. Press the ENTER key.

The Anchor property values for the lstTodaysSales control are set. The control is anchored to all four sides of the frmTodaysSalesCheck form.

As shown in Figure 6-17 on page VB 6.25, the Anchor property defaults to Top, Left. The graphical map that displays below the Anchor property value when the box arrow is clicked shows a representation of the control in the center of the map. As you click the anchor indicators, the indicator is highlighted gray, to indicate that the control is anchored to that side. If the anchor indicator is not highlighted gray, the control is not anchored to that side.

Changing the File Name of a Form

Because the Today's Sales Check application contains two forms, the first form should be given a new file name, before you add the second form. The file name of the first form currently is Form1.vb, as displayed in the Solution Explorer window. Changing a form's file name renames the file in which Visual Basic .NET saves the form. When renaming a form, include the word, Form, in the name to indicate that the file contains a form.

Changing a Form's File Name
When changing a form's file name, give the form a name that indicates that the file contains a form.

The steps on the next page change the Form1.vb form file name.

To Change the File Name of a Form

1. Right-click the Form1.vb form in the Solution Explorer window.
The form shortcut menu displays (Figure 6-22).

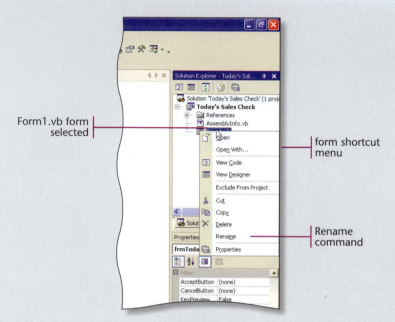

Form1.vb form
selected

form shortcut
menu

Rename
command

FIGURE 6-22

2. Click the Rename command on the shortcut menu. Type Todays Sales Form.vb as the new file name for the form and then press the ENTER key.
The form's file name is changed from Form1.vb to Todays Sales Form.vb. The new file name displays in the Solution Explorer window, on the main work area tab, and the Visual Basic .NET window title bar (Figure 6-23). The file name is shortened on the main work area tab, with an ellipsis.

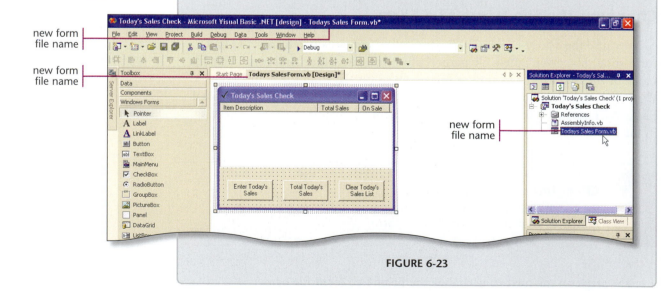

new form
file name

new form
file name

new form
file name

FIGURE 6-23

The **Form shortcut menu**, shown in Figure 6-22, contains many useful commands for working with form files. The **Open command** opens the form in the design mode in the main work area. The **View Code command** and **View Designer command** also bring up the form in the main work area in a code window or in design mode, respectively. The **Exclude From Project command** leaves the form in the project, but does not include the form when the project is run. This command may be useful for debugging a project. The **Cut command**, **Copy command**, and **Delete command** on the Form shortcut menu allow you to cut, copy, or delete the form file as you would any other file.

Adding a Form to a Project and Creating the Interface

The second form in the Today's Sales Check project is the Add Item Form (Figure 6-1 on page VB 6.03). Because Visual Basic .NET creates only one initial form when it creates a project, you must add a new form for the second form.

The new form is added in the Solution Explorer window using a template. A **template** is a Visual Basic .NET application component, such as a Windows form, an icon, or a Web page, that you easily can add to a project.

The following steps add a new form to the project.

To Add a Form to a Project

1. Right-click the Today's Sales Check project in the Solution Explorer window and then point to the Add command on the shortcut menu.

The project shortcut menu displays. When you point to the Add command, the Add submenu displays, to allow you to add various components to the project (Figure 6-24).

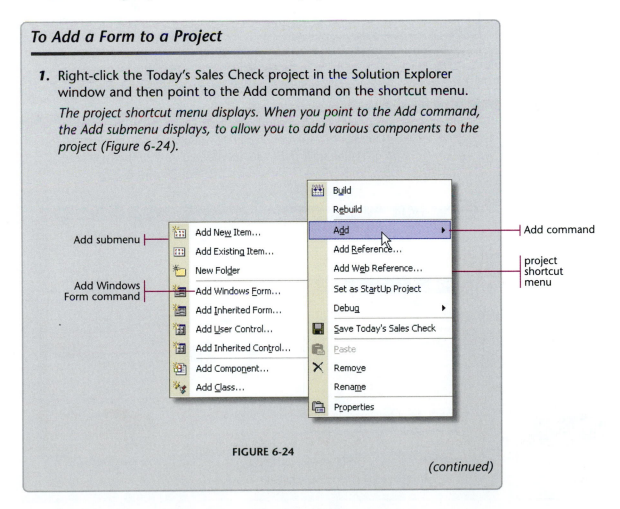

FIGURE 6-24

(continued)

2. Click the Add Windows Form command on the Add submenu. Select Form1 in the Name text box and then type Add Item Form to set, Add Item Form.vb, as the new file name for the form.

The Add New Item dialog box displays. The Windows Form template is the default selection in the Templates area (Figure 6-25). Add Item Form.vb is set as the new file name for the form.

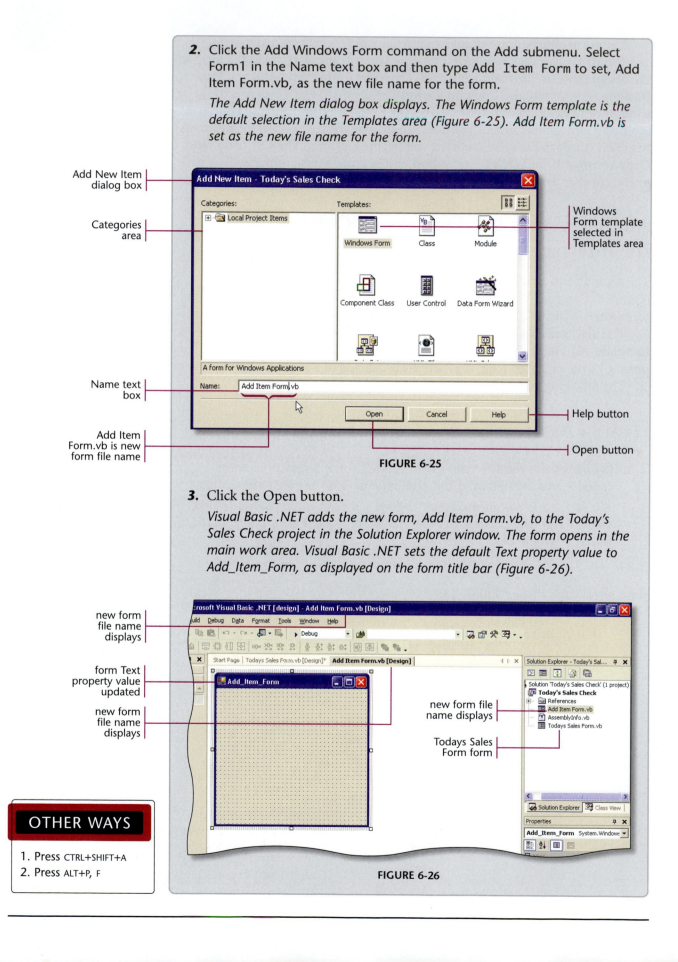

Add New Item dialog box

Categories area

Name text box

Add Item Form.vb is new form file name

Windows Form template selected in Templates area

Help button

Open button

FIGURE 6-25

3. Click the Open button.

Visual Basic .NET adds the new form, Add Item Form.vb, to the Today's Sales Check project in the Solution Explorer window. The form opens in the main work area. Visual Basic .NET sets the default Text property value to Add_Item_Form, as displayed on the form title bar (Figure 6-26).

new form file name displays

form Text property value updated

new form file name displays

new form file name displays

Todays Sales Form form

OTHER WAYS

1. Press CTRL+SHIFT+A
2. Press ALT+P, F

FIGURE 6-26

A Windows Form is just one of the 24 types of components that you can add to a project using a template. Figure 6-25 shows a partial list of templates that are available to add to a project using Visual Basic .NET. You also can use third-party templates or create your own templates, so that you can reuse custom components in multiple applications. For more information on the components you can add to a project using templates, click the Help button in the Add New Item dialog box (Figure 6-25).

Creating an Interface on a Newly Added Form

Just as with the initial form created when you start a new project, you must update the form properties of the newly added form to match the requirements for the project. The design for the Add Item Form form specifies that the form should include the following controls: two Label controls, one TextBox control, one NumericUpDown control, one CheckBox control, and one Button control. Table 6-7 lists the changes that need to be made to the Add Item Form form and control property values to complete the user interface. The StartPosition property value of the form is set to **CenterParent**, meaning that the form will display centered on top of the parent form. A **parent form** is the form that initiates the display of, or opens, the second form. In this case, the parent form is the frmTodaysSalesCheck form.

Table 6-7 Form and Control Properties for the Add Item Form Form

CONTROL	PROPERTY	VALUE	EFFECT
Add_Item_Form	Size: Width	272	Sets the width of the form in pixels
	Size: Height	186	Sets the height of the form in pixels
	StartPosition	CenterParent	Causes the form to display in the center of the frmTodaysSalesCheck form
	Text	Today's Sales Entry	Sets the value of the title bar on the window
	Name	frmAddItem	Changes the form's name to a descriptive name
	FormBorderStyle	FixedDialog	Disallows resizing of the window at run time
	AcceptButton	btnOK	Causes the btnOK Click event to execute when the user presses the ENTER key while the window is open
	MinimizeBox	False	Causes the form's Minimize button not to display
	MaximizeBox	False	Causes the form's Maximize button not to display
	ControlBox	False	Causes the form's control box not to display
Label1	Size: Width	96	Sets the width of the control in pixels
	Size: Height	16	Sets the height of the control in pixels
	Location: X (left)	8	Indicates the distance from the left border of the form in pixels

(continued)

Table 6-7 **Form and Control Properties for the Add Item Form Form** *(continued)*

CONTROL	PROPERTY	VALUE	EFFECT
Label1 (continued)	Location: Y (top)	16	Indicates the distance from the top border of the form in pixels
	Text	Item description:	Sets Item description: to display as the initial value in the control at run time
Label2	Size: Width	120	Sets the width of the control in pixels
	Size: Height	16	Sets the height of the control in pixels
	Location: X (left)	8	Indicates the distance from the left border of the form in pixels
	Location: Y (top)	48	Indicates the distance from the top border of the form in pixels
	Text	Total sales:	Sets Total sales: to display as the initial value in the control at run time
TextBox1	Size: Width	136	Sets the width of the control in pixels
	Size: Height	20	Sets the height of the control in pixels
	Location: X (left)	120	Indicates the distance from the left border of the form in pixels
	Location: Y (top)	16	Indicates the distance from the top border of the form in pixels
	Name	txtItemDescription	Changes control's name to a descriptive name
	MaxLength	50	Sets the maximum number of characters a user can enter in the control to 50
	TabIndex	0	Causes this control to be the first control on the form to receive focus
NumericUpDown1	Size: Width	88	Sets the width of the control in pixels
	Size: Height	20	Sets the height of the control in pixels
	Location: X (left)	120	Indicates the distance from the left border of the form in pixels
	Location: Y (top)	48	Indicates the distance from the top border of the form in pixels
	Name	nudTotalItemSales	Changes control's name to a descriptive name
	DecimalPlaces	2	Sets the number of decimal places of the value to display in the control
	Maximum	1000	Defines the highest value allowed in the control
	TabIndex	1	Causes this control to be the second control on the form to receive focus
	TextAlign	Right	Sets the text to be right-aligned in the control
Button1	Size: Width	72	Sets the width of the control in pixels
	Size: Height	24	Sets the height of the control in pixels
	Location: X (left)	95	Indicates the distance from the left border of the form in pixels
	Location: Y (top)	112	Indicates the distance from the top border of the form in pixels

Table 6-7 **Form and Control Properties for the Add Item Form Form** (continued)

CONTROL	PROPERTY	VALUE	EFFECT
Button1 (continued)	Name	btnOK	Changes control's name to a descriptive name
	Text	OK	Sets the text that displays on the button face to OK
	TabIndex	3	Causes this control to be the fourth control on the form to receive focus

The following step creates the interface of the new Add Item Form form by adding all of the controls to the Add Item Form form, and setting properties of the controls and the Add Item Form form, except the CheckBox control.

To Create the Interface on a Newly Added Form

1. Add two Label controls, one TextBox control, one NumericUpDown control, a CheckBox control, and a Button control to the form. Set the properties for the form and controls as indicated in Table 6-7. Set the AcceptButton property of the form last.

The form and controls display as shown in Figure 6-27.

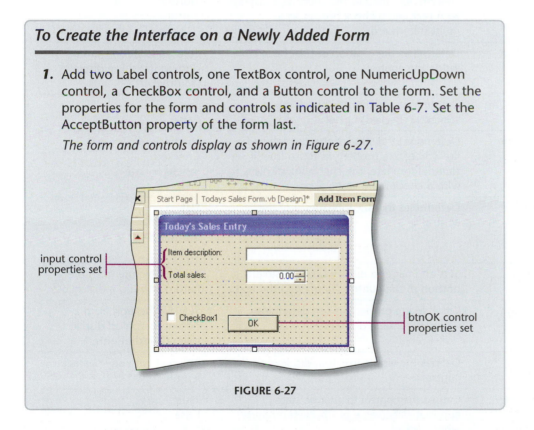

FIGURE 6-27

With the exception of the CheckBox control, the user interface for the frmAddItem form is complete. The AcceptButton property of the form is set last because the btnOK button control must have its Name property set first. The three input controls limit the user's input to acceptable values, as specified in the requirements document. The txtItemDescription control allows the user to enter only an item description of up to 50 characters in the control. The nudTotalItemSales control limits the Total sales to an amount from 0 to $1,000 dollars. The scroll buttons on the nudTotalItemSales control increment and decrement the value in the control by 1, because that is the default value for the Increment property of the control and the property value was not changed.

CheckBox Control Properties

The CheckBox control is used in applications to allow a user to specify one of two conditions, such as on or off, yes or no, or true or false. In the Today's Sales Check application, the CheckBox control on the frmAddItem form allows a user to indicate whether an item is or is not on sale today. Clicking the empty check box places a check mark in the check box to indicate the option is selected. Clicking a selected check box removes the check mark to indicate the option is not selected. Table 6-8 on the next page lists the common properties of the CheckBox control.

Table 6-8 **CheckBox Control Properties**

CATEGORY	PROPERTY	DESCRIPTION	PROPERTY VALUES
Appearance	Appearance	Determines whether the check box displays with text and a check box, or as a multi-state button	**Normal** Button
	CheckAlign	Determines the location of the check box inside the control	Select a location from a pop-up graphical display. **(MiddleLeft)**
	Checked	Determines whether the check box is selected (checked) or not	True **False**
	CheckState	Determines the state of the check box if the ThreeState property is set to true; if set to Indeterminate, the check box displays with a check mark and is shaded	**Unchecked** Checked Indeterminate
	FlatStyle	Determines the 3D appearance of the control	Flat Popup **Standard** System
	Image	Sets an image to display on the visible portion of the control, along with the text	Select a picture from the hard disk using a dialog box.
	ImageAlign	If the Image property is set, determines where the image displays	Select a location from a pop-up graphical display map. **(MiddleCenter)**
	Text	Defines the visible text that displays on the control	Any text with any character length
Behavior	AutoCheck	Causes the control to change state automatically (value of Checked property) when clicked	**True** False
	ThreeState	Determines whether the user can select the Indeterminate state of the check box	True **False**

Table 6-9 lists the control property values that must be changed for the CheckBox1 control used in the Today's Sales Check application. The check box in the control is aligned on the right side of the control.

Table 6-9   CheckBox Control Properties for the frmAddItem Form

CONTROL	PROPERTY	VALUE	EFFECT
CheckBox1	Name	chkOnSale	Changes control's name to a descriptive name
	Size: Width	128	Sets the width of the control in pixels
	Size: Height	24	Sets the height of the control in pixels
	Location: X (left)	8	Indicates the distance from the left border of the form in pixels
	Location: Y (top)	80	Indicates the distance from the top border of the form in pixels
	Text	On sale today	Sets the value of the label next to the check box
	TabIndex	2	Sets this control to be the third control to receive focus when the TAB key is pressed
	CheckAlign	MiddleRight	Causes the check box in the control to display on the right side of the control and to the right of the label in the control

The following steps set the property values for the CheckBox control, as listed in Table 6-9.

To Change the Properties of a CheckBox Control

1. Click the CheckBox1 control to select it. Change the property values for the CheckBox1 control, as listed in Table 6-9, except the CheckAlign property.

The chkOnSale control displays as shown in Figure 6-28. The Text property value, On sale today, displays on the control and the control is sized and positioned properly.

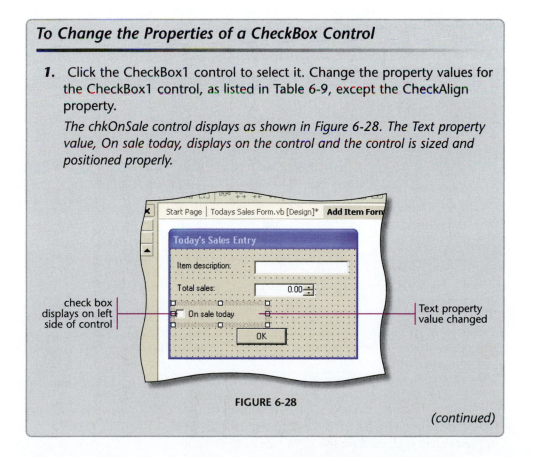

check box displays on left side of control

Text property value changed

FIGURE 6-28

(continued)

2. Scroll the Properties window until the CheckAlign property is visible and then select the CheckAlign property.

The CheckAlign property is selected (Figure 6-29).

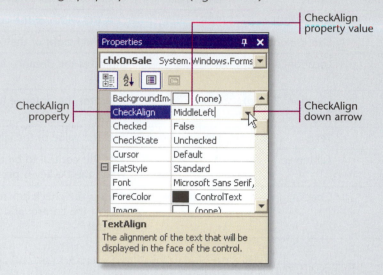

FIGURE 6-29

3. Click the CheckAlign down arrow in the property values list.

A graphical map displays, indicating that the current value of the CheckAlign property is MiddleLeft (Figure 6-30).

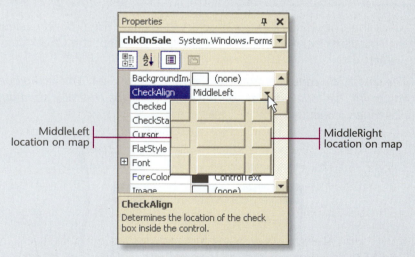

FIGURE 6-30

4. Select the MiddleRight indicator in the CheckAlign property value graphical map.

The text in the chkOnSale control moves to the left side of the control and the check box moves to the right side of the control (Figure 6-31).

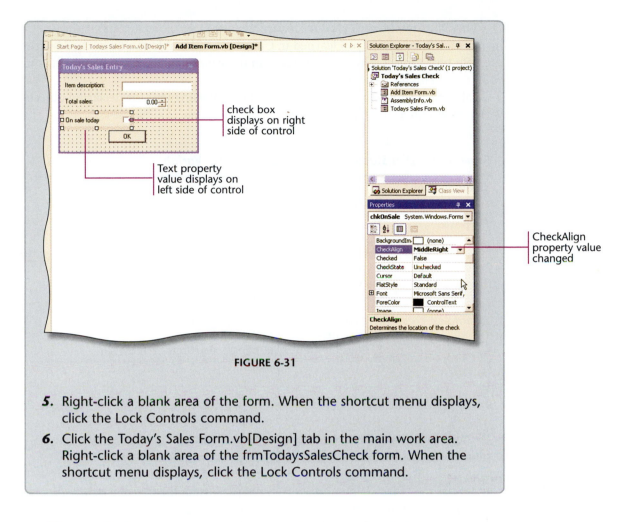

check box
displays on right
side of control

Text property
value displays on
left side of control

CheckAlign
property value
changed

FIGURE 6-31

5. Right-click a blank area of the form. When the shortcut menu displays, click the Lock Controls command.

6. Click the Today's Sales Form.vb[Design] tab in the main work area. Right-click a blank area of the frmTodaysSalesCheck form. When the shortcut menu displays, click the Lock Controls command.

The graphical map shown in Figure 6-30 shows that the check box can be placed in one of nine positions. When the CheckAlign property is set to MiddleRight, the check box displays on the right side of the control (Figure 6-31). The TextAlign property is set by default to align properly with the text in the Label controls above it. The user interface for the Today's Sales Check application now is complete.

Declaring Objects

As is the case with all forms, the Today's Sales Entry form is a class, which means an instance of the class must be created, or declared, before it can be used. An instance of a class, such as the Today's Sales Entry form, can be declared by using an object variable to hold the instance of the class.

Declaring an Object Using an Object Variable

In addition to storing values, a variable can refer to an object. Like other variables, an object variable is used to store temporary values used by other code statements as the code executes. In the case of an object variable, however, the value that the variable contains is the location of an object or an instance of a class, such as the Today's Sales Entry form, in memory.

The Dim statement is used to declare the object variable and create the instance of the class. As you learned in Chapter 4, a variable can be declared with the data type Object. Alternatively, you can indicate a specific class for which you want to declare the variable.

Table 6-10 shows the general form of the Dim statement for declaring object variables as either of type Object or of a specific class.

Table 6-10   *Dim Statement for Declaring Object Variables*

General form:	1. Dim variablename As [class or Object] 2. Dim variablename As New [class or Object]
Purpose:	The Dim statement declares a variable as either the general type Object or a specific class. If the New keyword is used, an instance of the class is created, allowing access to the properties and methods of the class. If the New keyword is omitted, then the variable is left unpopulated, but can be assigned the specified class in subsequent code.
Examples:	1. `Dim objMyButton As Button` 2. `Dim objList As New Collection` 3. `Dim objGenericObject As Object`

The **New keyword** determines whether the variable contains a complete instance of the object. If the New keyword is not used, then the variable is declared for future use in the code, but no memory is set aside for the contents of the object. When the New keyword is used, the object is said to be **instantiated** and memory is set aside for a complete copy of the object. When declaring object variables, use the obj prefix for the variable name.

Tip

Naming Object Variables
When declaring object variables, use the obj prefix for the variable name.

Showing a Form

As you have learned, a form is a class that includes properties, event procedures, and methods. When you create, design, and code a form, you are creating a class, which is only the description of what the form looks like and how it should behave during run time. The form does not become a window until an instance of the form's class is instantiated in code and the method that displays the form, such as the Show() or ShowDialog() method, is called. In the

Today's Sales Check application, Visual Basic .NET takes care of instantiating the frmTodaysSalesCheck form as an object, because it is set as the first object to display at run time (those steps appear later in this chapter). That means you do not need to write code to instantiate an object for the frmTodaysSalesCheck form. You do need to write code, however, to instantiate an object for the frmAddItem form.

After a form is instantiated in code, the Show() or ShowDialog()methods can be used to open the form and give focus to the opened form. If the **Show() method** is used in a form's code to open another form, then both forms still can receive focus and be accessed by the user. The newly opened form is **modeless**, meaning that the form displays and is available for use at any time, but permits the user to complete other actions in the application. Several modeless forms may be opened at the same time in an application and the user can switch between them.

The **ShowDialog() method** opens a form that is modal. Using a **modal** form means that the user must complete an action in that form, before completing other actions in the program. Using the ShowDialog() method to open a second modal form means that only the second form can have focus until it is closed, at which time focus returns to the original form. When the Show() method is used in code, the next line of code immediately executes after the form is opened. When the ShowDialog() method is used to open a form in code, the next line of code does not execute until the newly opened form is closed.

> **Tip**
>
> **Form.Show() versus Form.ShowDialog() Methods**
>
> The Show() method is used in a form's code to open another form and allow both forms to be accessed by the user and receive focus. The ShowDialog() method opens a form that is modal, meaning that only the second form can have focus until it is closed, at which time focus returns to the original form.

Figure 6-32 on the next page shows the comment header for the Today's Sales Check form. Figure 6-33 on the next page shows the comment header and two lines of code for the btnEnterSales_Click event procedure. Line 133 declares an object variable, objAddItemForm, and uses the New keyword to create an instance of the frmAddItem form. This means that a full copy of the form resides in the memory set aside for the objAddItemForm variable. Recall that this statement is necessary because the design and coding of the form only creates a class, which is a description of the form. By creating an instance of the form and assigning the instance to a variable, a usable copy of the form exists in memory at run time for you to use in the code. You access the form's properties and methods through use of the objAddItemForm variable. Line 135 uses the ShowDialog() method of the frmAddItem form to open the frmAddItem form so that the user can enter data for an item.

```
119        ' Chapter 6:    Today's Sales Check
120        ' Programmer:    J. Quasney
121        ' Date:          October 7, 2003
122        ' Purpose:       This form is the startup form for the Today's
123        '                Sales Check application. The application
124        '                accepts input of daily sales information totaled
125        '                by item. The application then calculates the
126        '                total sales for the day, the total sales for
127        '                the day for items on sale, and the total sales
128        '                for items not on sale.
```

FIGURE 6-32

```
130        ' Display a dialog box for data entry of each item's sales
131        ' totals for today. Display the dialog box until the user
132        ' enters an empty description for the item.
133        Dim objAddItemForm As New frmAddItem()
134
135        objAddItemForm.ShowDialog()
```

FIGURE 6-33

The following steps create the btnEnterSales_Click event procedure, enter the comment header shown in Figure 6-32, and enter the code shown in Figure 6-33.

> ### To Declare an Object and Show a Form
>
> **1.** If necessary, click the Todays Sales Form.vb[Design] tab in the main work area. Double-click the btnEnterSales button. When the code window displays, enter `Option Strict On` as the first line of code in the form.
>
> *The Option Strict On statement forces all variables in the form to be declared and all assignment statements to have the same data type on both sides of the assignment.*
>
> **2.** Click line 119 and enter the comment header as shown in Figure 6-32.
>
> **3.** Click line 130 and type the six lines of code shown in Figure 6-33.
>
> *Visual Basic .NET creates the btnEnterSales_Click event procedure. The comment header for the frmTodaysSalesCheck form displays as lines 119 through 128. Lines 130 through 135 display in the btnEnterSales_Click event procedure (Figure 6-34). Line 133 declares a new instance of the frmAddItem form. Line 135 uses the ShowDialog() method to cause the instance of the frmAddItem form to display.*

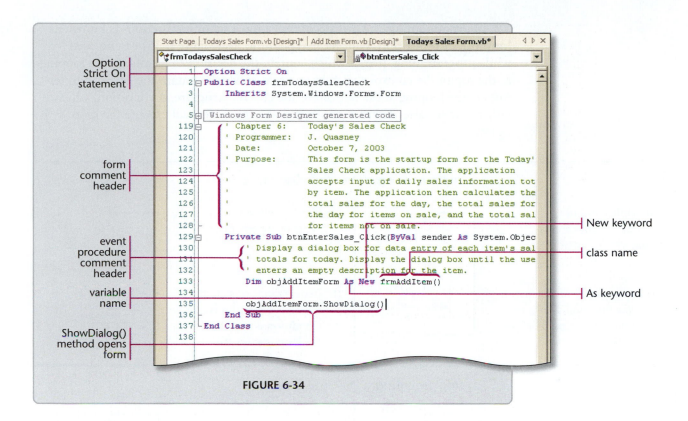

FIGURE 6-34

You assign an object to a variable, such as objAddItemForm, for the same reasons you assign any value to a variable. Using an object variable also is more efficient than repeatedly accessing the object itself through the necessary properties, just as you have accessed the properties of controls in code in previous chapters.

An object variable, however, does behave somewhat differently than the other variables used in expressions in this book. In addition to accessing properties of the object, you also can perform operations on an object variable by using the methods for the class to which the variable belongs. For example, if you assign a form object to a variable, you can use form methods such as Show(), ShowDialog(), Focus(), and others to perform operations on the object variable.

Repetition and the Do Statement

The next step is to write code for the loop that displays the frmAddItem form until the user has completed data entry. In previous chapters, the programs were designed to operate in a linear manner, with the exception of decision-making structures that allowed the code to perform one set of operations or another depending on conditions. One of the more powerful aspects of computer programming is the capability of performing a set of operations repeatedly based on certain conditions. For example, a program designed to read database records and total amounts in the records must be programmed to read the database repeatedly until no records remain.

In programming, the process of repeating a set of instructions is known as **looping**, or **repetition**. Four basic types of loops (Figure 6-35) can be used while programming, two of which contain the decision to terminate the looping at the top of the control structure and two of which contain the decision to terminate the looping at the bottom of the control structure. A condition, which is either true or false, determines whether the computer will execute the loop again.

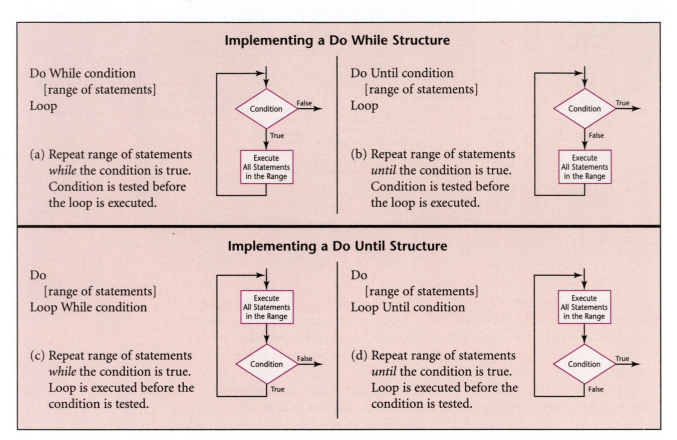

FIGURE 6-35

As shown at the top of each of the four flowcharts in Figure 6-35, alternative forms of the **Do statement** can be used to implement the four types of control structures.

The Do While and Do Until Statements

A common form of the Do statement, called the **Do While statement** (Figure 6-35a) repeatedly executes the series of statements in the loop as long as the condition is true. Another common form of the Do statement is the **Do Until statement** (Figure 6-35b), which repeatedly executes a series of instructions until the condition is true. Both the Do While and Do Until statements have forms that can be used to implement a loop when the decision to terminate is at the bottom of the loop (Figures 6-35c and 6-35d).

The general forms for the Do While and Do Until statements are shown in Tables 6-11 and 6-12.

Table 6-11   Do Until Statement

General form:	1. Do Until condition
	       statements
	   Loop
	2. Do
	      statements
	   Loop Until condition

Purpose:	This loop causes the statements between the Do and Loop statements to be executed repeatedly. The loop is executed until the condition becomes true. The first form tests the condition before looping and the second form tests the condition after executing the statements once.

Examples:	1. `Do Until intCount > 20`
	     `intCount = intCount + 1`
	  `Loop`
	2. `Do`
	     `intCount = intCount + 1`
	  `Loop Until intCount > 20`

Table 6-12   Do While Statement

General form:	1. Do While condition
	       statements
	   Loop
	2. Do
	      statements
	   Loop While condition

Purpose:	This loop causes the statements between the Do and Loop statements to be executed repeatedly. The loop is executed while the condition is still true. The first form tests the condition before looping and the second form tests the condition after executing the statements once.

Examples:	1. `Do While intCount <= 20`
	     `intCount = intCount + 1`
	  `Loop`
	2. `Do`
	     `intCount = intCount + 1`
	  `Loop While intCount <= 20`

Selecting the Proper Do Statement for a Program

Your program flowchart should indicate the type of Do loop to use in your program. The type you choose depends on the following two points:

1. If the decision to terminate is at the top of the loop, use Do While or Do Until (see Figures 6-35a and 6-35b). If the decision to terminate is at the bottom of the loop, use Loop While or Loop Until (see Figures 6-35c and 6-35d).

2. Use the keyword While if you want to continue execution of the loop while the condition is true. Use the keyword Until if you want to continue execution of the loop until the condition is true.

3. A Do While structure can be implemented using either a Do Until statement or a Do While statement. For example, to implement the Do While structure in Figure 6-36, you can write the following pseudocode:

Do Until ItemDescription = ""

> or

Do While ItemDescription <> ""

It is recommended that you select the Do statement that does not include a negation, because it is easier to read.

Do While Statement versus Do Until Statement

When implementing a Do While structure, always use the statement that does not require a negation, because it is easier to read.

Choosing a Proper Do Loop

If the decision to terminate is at the top of the loop, use Do While or Do Until. If the decision to terminate is at the bottom of the loop, use Loop While or Loop Until. Use the keyword While if you want to continue execution of the loop while the condition is true. Use the keyword Until if you want to continue execution of the loop until the condition is true.

The While...End While Statement

Visual Basic .NET also includes the **While...End While statement** for the purpose of implementing a Do While loop in a program. This statement works exactly the same as the Do...While statement. The **While keyword** initiates a Do While loop, and the **End While keywords** terminate it. Hence, the code below can be written as a Do While statement by replacing the While statement with the Do While keyword and replacing the End While keyword with the Loop statement. Table 6-13 shows the general form for the While...End While statement.

Table 6-13   While...End While Statement

General form:	1. While condition
	         statements
	     End While

Purpose:	This loop causes the statements between the While and End While statements to be executed repeatedly. The loop is executed while the condition is still true. The statement serves the same purpose as the first format of the Do While statement.

Examples:	1. While intCount <= 20
	         intCount = intCount + 1
	     End While

In this chapter, the Do...Until statement is used to implement the Do While structure. Because of their popularity in earlier versions of Visual Basic, however, you should be aware that the While...End While statement exists in many Visual Basic programs.

Implementing a Loop Using a Do Until Statement

The Today's Sales Check application requires that the frmAddItemForm form continue to accept data until the user has entered a blank for the Item description. Figure 6-36 shows the flowchart for the btnEnterSales_Click event procedure. A Do Until statement is the best choice to implement this type of loop, because the requirement is to loop until a condition is met. That condition is that the txtItemDescription control on the frmAddItemForm is blank when the user clicks the OK button.

The Do Until statement is used rather than the Do While statement because the Do While statement would require use of negation (<>) to implement the loop. The use of the Do Until statement in this situation allows for use of an equals sign (=) in the condition and makes the code more readable.

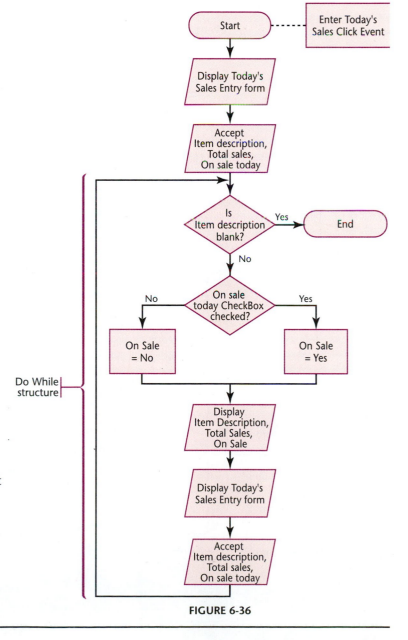

FIGURE 6-36

Figure 6-37 shows the Do Until statement that corresponds to the flowchart in Figure 6-36 and the pseudocode in Figure 6-5 on page VB 6.10.

```
136         Do Until objAddItemForm.txtItemDescription.Text = ""
137
138         Loop
```

FIGURE 6-37

The condition clause of the Do Until statement tests the value of the Text property of the txtItemDescription control on the objAddItemForm instance of the frmAddItemForm form. If the value is blank, then looping terminates and control passes to the statement following the Loop statement on line 138. The statements that execute within the loop will be added shortly.

The following step adds the code in Figure 6-37 to the btnEnterSales_Click event procedure.

To Code a Do Until Statement

1. Enter line 136 as shown in Figure 6-37.

Visual Basic .NET's Intellisense™ technology, which tries to understand what you are doing and helps you do it, completes the Do Until statement by adding a blank line and the Loop keyword (Figure 6-38).

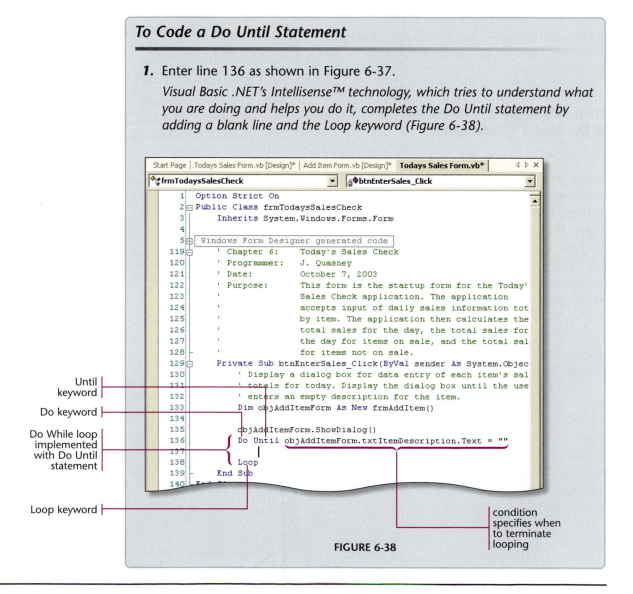

FIGURE 6-38

The Do Until statement loops until the Text property of the txtItemDescription control on the frmAddItemForm form is left blank by the user. Recall that the line of code above the Do Until statement (line 135) opens the frmAddItemForm using the ShowDialog() method. Therefore, the Do Until statement does not execute until the user closes the form by clicking the OK button or pressing the ENTER key. Later in this chapter, code will be written for the OK button on the frmAddItemForm to close the form when the user clicks the button. When the form closes, line 136 executes.

The next step is to write the statements that execute within the loop. The code within the loop involves the use of a collection, or ordered set of items.

Working with Collections in ListView Controls

As you have learned, a collection is a group of one or more objects that can be accessed and operated on as a single entity. Collections manage an ordered set of items, which usually are other objects. Most collections are based on the Collections class, which is part of the .NET Framework class library.

In this book, you have worked with collections on two previous occasions. First, in Chapter 5 on pages VB 5.19 and 5.20, you used the String Collection Editor window to enter a list, or collection, of items to display the ComboBox list. In that case, the entire collection serves as the property value for the Items property of the ComboBox control. A collection also was used on page VB 6.21, as the property value for the Column property of the ListView control.

In addition to Visual Basic .NET's Collection class, Visual Basic .NET includes several types of collections that are subclasses of the .NET Framework class library's Collections class. As shown in Table 6-14, Visual Basic .NET includes four methods in which you commonly use collections.

Table 6-14 Visual Basic .NET Collections

COLLECTION USED AS	EXAMPLE
A property of a control	Collection used as the property value for the Items property of the ListView control
An object in code by declaring a variable of type Collection	`Dim colStudents As New Collection()` Declares colStudents as a collection
An object in code by declaring a variable of type of one of the included subclasses of Collections	`Dim slsMyStock As New SortedList()` Declares slsMyStock as a sorted list collection
As a custom Collection type you create	You first determine the type of object that your collection will contain, such as InventoryItems. You create a class for InventoryItems. Next, create a collection to hold InventoryItems. The collection can only contain InventoryItems.

Notice that a generic type of collection simply is called, Collection. A collection of the type, Collection, is different from other types of collections that may have different properties and methods.

As you learned on page VB 5.32 of Chapter 5, Visual Basic .NET assigns a unique integer value, called an **index**, to each item in a collection. You can use the index to access items in the collection. The Items property for a ListView control contains a collection of objects of the **ListViewItem class**. That is, each item in a ListView control is an instance of the ListViewItem class. Recall that a class is like a data type, but describes objects rather than a single piece of data. An instance of the ListViewItem class must be created for each item you want to add to the ListView control.

Adding Items to a ListView Control

Before adding items to the lstTodaysSales control, an object must be created to hold the item and the object must be populated with the data entered by the user. Each item contains three pieces of information: the item description, the total sales for the item, and an indicator as to whether or not the item was on sale for the day. After the object is populated, the object containing the information is added to the lstTodaysSales control. Finally, the frmAddItem form is displayed again for the user to enter data.

Recall that the Details view of the ListView control also allows you to display additional text, called subitems, for each list item. Each item in a collection of type ListViewItem, such as the Items collection of the lstTodaysSales control, thus contains yet another collection called the SubItems collection. The **SubItems collection** is a property of a ListViewItem object. A ListViewItem can have many subitems in the SubItems collection. The Text property of each SubItem displays in a column in the ListView control when the View property of the ListView control is set to Details.

Figure 6-39 illustrates an example of the Items collection that makes up the Items property of the lstTodaysSales control. The example shows two items in the collection, which means that two rows of items will display in the lstTodaysSales control on the frmTodaysSalesCheck form. Each item in the collection can be referred to by the Index column.

As shown in Figure 6-39, each item has two properties that are used in this application: the Text property and the SubItems property. The Text property value is the text that the user enters in the Item description text box on the Today's Sales Entry form. The Text property of a ListViewItem always displays as the first column in the ListView control. For example, the Text property value, Topsoil, in the first item can be referenced by the following code:

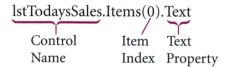

lstTodaysSales.Items(0).Text

Control Name Item Index Text Property

The **SubItems property** is yet another collection. That is, rather than the property value being a numeric or text value, the property value is a collection object. Each item in the SubItems collection has a unique index value, as do all collection items. The SubItems collection has several properties and methods,

Items Collection of Items Property

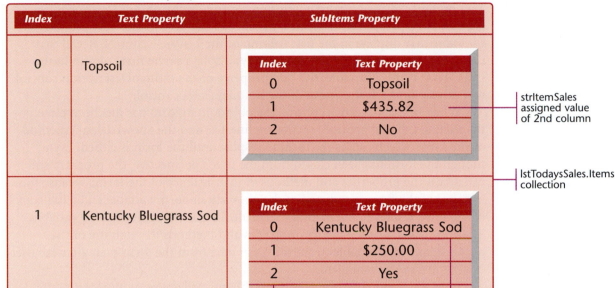

FIGURE 6-39

but the one of importance here is the Text property. The Text property value of each SubItem displays in a column in the ListView control. The Text property of the Items collection also can be obtained by referring to the Text property of the first subitem. Therefore, the SubItem with an index of 0 displays as the first column in the control. The SubItem with an index of 1 displays as the second column in the control. In the example shown in Figure 6-39, the value, $435.82, would display in the second column of the first row of the lstTodaysSales control. The value, $435.82, can be accessed with the following code:

lstTodaysSales.Items(0).SubItems(1).Text

Control	Item	SubItem	Text
Name	Index	Index	Property

Figure 6-40 shows the code that performs the operations described above.

```
137          Dim lviTodaysSales As New ListViewItem(objAddItemForm.txtItemDescription.  ↵
        Text)
138              lviTodaysSales.SubItems.Add(Format$(objAddItemForm.nudTotalItemSales.Value, ↵
        "Currency"))
139          If objAddItemForm.chkOnSale.Checked Then
140              lviTodaysSales.SubItems.Add("Yes")
141          Else
142              lviTodaysSales.SubItems.Add("No")
143          End If
144          lstTodaysSales.Items.Add(lviTodaysSales)
145          objAddItemForm.ShowDialog()
```

FIGURE 6-40

Line 137 declares a new ListViewItem object, named lviTodaysSales. The Text property of the txtItemDescription control on the objAddItemForm form is passed as a parameter to the new instance of the object. The Text property is the value that displays in the first column of the ListView control. Recall that the Text property of a ListViewItem always displays as the first column in the ListView control. Therefore, the Text property of the txtItemDescription control will display in the first column of the lstTodaysSales control.

When line 137 receives control, the objAddItemForm has just been closed by the user. Recall that control remains on line 135 and the ShowDialog() method of the form, which causes the form to display until the form is closed. Even though the form has been closed from the user's perspective, the program still can access the properties and methods of that instance of the form, because the instance of the form is assigned to the objAddItemForm variable and a full copy of the form resides in the memory set aside for the objAddItemForm variable. The code can access the form's properties and methods through use of the objAddItemForm variable to get the input data from the form even after the user closes the frmAddItem form.

Both the Items collection and the SubItems collection support the Add() method. Line 138 uses the Add() method of the SubItems collection to add the value in the NumericUpDown control (nudTotalItemSales.Value), on the objAddItemForm as a new subitem. The first subitem is the item description and has an index of 0. The second subitem contains the value from nudTotalItemSales.Value property and has an index of 1. Therefore, to refer to this data later in code, you use lviTodaysSales.SubItems(1).Text.

Lines 139 through 143 test the value of the chkOnSale control and add a new subitem to the lviTodaysSales object based on the value. Because either Yes or No is added as the second subitem, Visual Basic .NET automatically assigns this new subitem an index of 2. Therefore, to access this item later in code, you can use lviTodaysSales.SubItems(2) to access either the Yes or No value.

After the new ListViewItem object, lviTodaysSales, has been populated with the data from the objAddItemForm form, the item can be added to the lstTodaysSales Items collection, so it displays in the lstTodaysSales control in the frmTodaysSalesCheck form. This is accomplished in line 144 by using the Add() method of the Items collection. The lviTodaysSales object, which was populated with the data, is passed as a parameter. As soon as this line executes, the item is added to the collection and the item displays in the lstTodaysSales control in the frmTodaysSalesCheck form.

Finally, line 145 shows the objAddItemForm to the user again. Recall that this line of code only displays the form and gives the form focus. The form itself is an object that was created on line 133 with the New keyword when the objAddItemForm variable was declared.

Naming ListViewItem Objects
Use the lvi prefix when naming ListViewItem objects.

The following step adds the code shown in Figure 6-40 on the previous page to the btnEnterSales_Click event procedure.

To Write Code to Add Items to a ListView Control

1. Click line 137 and then type the code shown in Figure 6-40 on page VB 6.49.

The code within the Do Until loop displays as shown in Figure 6-41.

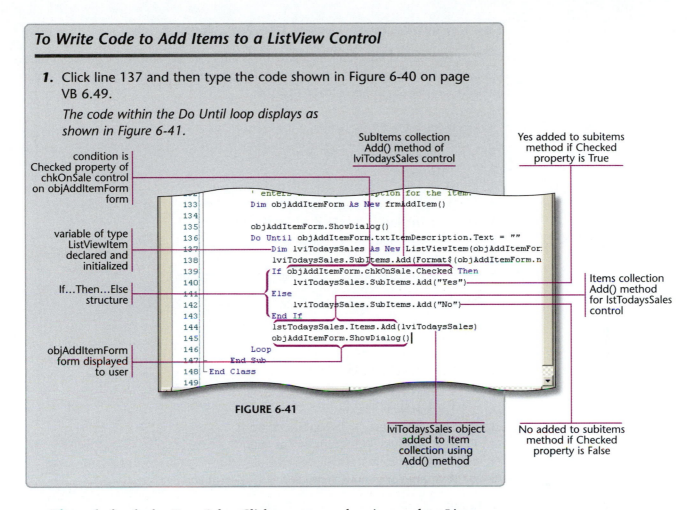

condition is Checked property of chkOnSale control on objAddItemForm form

SubItems collection Add() method of lviTodaysSales control

Yes added to subitems method if Checked property is True

variable of type ListViewItem declared and initialized

If...Then...Else structure

Items collection Add() method for lstTodaysSales control

objAddItemForm form displayed to user

```
 133    Dim objAddItemForm As New frmAddItem()
 134
 135    objAddItemForm.ShowDialog()
 136    Do Until objAddItemForm.txtItemDescription.Text = ""
 137        Dim lviTodaysSales As New ListViewItem(objAddItemFor:
 138        lviTodaysSales.SubItems.Add(Format$(objAddItemForm.n
 139        If objAddItemForm.chkOnSale.Checked Then
 140            lviTodaysSales.SubItems.Add("Yes")
 141        Else
 142            lviTodaysSales.SubItems.Add("No")
 143        End If
 144        lstTodaysSales.Items.Add(lviTodaysSales)
 145        objAddItemForm.ShowDialog()
 146    Loop
 147    End Sub
 148 End Class
 149
```

FIGURE 6-41

lviTodaysSales object added to Item collection using Add() method

No added to subitems method if Checked property is False

The code for the btnEnterSales_Click event procedure is complete. Lines 137 through 145 display within the Do Until statement (Figure 6-41). The lviTodaysSales object has block level scope within the Do Until statement. Line 138 adds an item to the lviTodaysSales ListViewItem object based on the value of the txtItemDescription control on the frmAddItemForm form. The If...Then...Else statement adds a SubItem to the lviTodaysSales object based on the checked property of the chkOnSale control. Line 144 adds the lviTodaysSales ListViewItem to the lstTodaysSales control. Finally, line 145 displays the instance of the frmAddItemForm so that the user can continue to enter data.

The For...Next Statement

The next step is to write the code for the btnTotalSales_Click event procedure, which totals the items in the lstTodaysSales control. To write this code, you will use the For...Next statement.

The **For...Next statement** statement is different from the Do statements in that it has an automatic counter and condition built in. For this reason, the For...Next statement is ideal for counter-controlled loops. A **counter-controlled loop** requires that you initialize a variable prior to the loop, increment the variable within the loop, and then test the variable prior to looping again to see if the condition has been met. When you use a For...Next statement to establish a loop, it is called a **For...Next loop**.

The Do While Loop versus the For...Next Loop

The two partial programs in Figure 6-42 illustrate the similarity between the Do While statements and the For...Next statements. Both partial programs compute the sum of the integers from 1 to 100.

(a) Using a Do While Loop

```
1      ' Looping Using Do While
2      intSum = 0
3      intCount = 1
4      Do While intCount <= 100
5          intSum = intSum + intCount
6          intCount = intCount + 1
7      Loop
8      MessageBox.Show("The sum is " & intSum)
```

Result

The sum is 5050

(b) Using a For...Next Loop

```
1      ' Looping Using For…Next
2      intSum = 0
3      For intCount = 1 To 100 Step 1
4          intSum = intSum + intCount
5      Next intCount
6      MessageBox.Show("The sum is" & intSum)
```

Result

The sum is 5050

FIGURE 6-42

The partial program in Figure 6-42a uses a Do While statement. Lines 2 and 3 initialize the running total, intSum, to 0 and the counter, intCount, to 1. Line 4 tests to determine whether the value of intCount is less than or equal to 100. If the condition is true, intSum is incremented by the value of intCount, and intCount is incremented by 1 before control transfers back to line 4. When the condition in the Do While statement is false, Visual Basic .NET terminates the loop, and line 8 displays the value of intSum.

The partial program in Figure 6-42b incorporates the For...Next statement to define the For...Next loop (lines 3 through 5). Read through this partial program carefully and see how it is much more efficient than the partial program in Figure 6-42a. Using a single For...Next statement, as in line 3 of Figure 6-42b, the functions of lines 3, 4, and 6 of the partial program in

Figure 6-42a are consolidated. Not only does the partial program in Figure 6-42b use less memory, it also is easier to read than the partial program in Figure 6-42a. As well, the For...Next statement executes faster than the Do statement.

For...Next versus Do While Statement

When possible, use the For...Next statement as opposed to a Do While statement because it is easier to read, uses less memory, is more efficient, and executes faster.

The Execution of a For...Next Loop

The execution of the For...Next loop shown in Figure 6-42b involves the following steps:

1. When the For statement is executed for the first time, the For...Next loop becomes active, and intCount is set equal to 1.
2. intCount is compared with 100. Because it is less than or equal to 100, the statements in the For loop, in this case line 4, are executed.
3. Control returns to the For statement, where the value of intCount is incremented by 1, the value that follows the keyword Step.
4. If the value of intCount is less than or equal to 100, execution of the For...Next loop continues.
5. When the value of intCount is greater than 100, control transfers to the statement (line 6) following the corresponding Next statement.

Table 6-15 shows the general form of the For...Next statement.

Table 6-15 For...Next Statement	

General form:	1. For k = initial value To limit value Step increment value
	          statements within For...Next loop
	     Next k
	or
	2. For k = initial value To limit value
	          statements within For...Next loop
	     Next k
	
	where k is a simple numeric variable called the loop variable, and the initial value, limit value, and increment value are numeric expressions

Purpose:	The For...Next statement causes the statements between the For and Next statements to be executed repeatedly in a loop until the value of k exceeds the limit value. When k exceeds the limit value, control transfers to the line immediately following the corresponding Next statement. If the increment value is negative, the test is reversed. The value of k is decremented each time through the loop, and the loop is executed until k is less than the limit value.
	(continued)

Table 6-15   For...Next Statement (continued)

Examples:	1. `For intItem = 1 To 20`
	`Next intItem`
	
	2. `For intAmount = -5 To 15 Step 2`
	`Next`
	
	3. `For intCount = 10 To -5 Step -3`
	`Next`
	
	4. `For intTax = 0 To 10 Step 0.1`
	`Next intTax`
	
	5. `For intTotal = intStart To intFinish Step intIncrement`
	`Next`
	
	6. `For S = A + 5 To C / D Step F * B`
	`Next`
	
	7. `For I = 20 To 20`
	`Next I`
	
	8. `For J = 20 To 1 Step -1`
	`Next J`

Note:	If the keyword Step is not used, then the increment value defaults to 1.

As shown in Figure 6-43, the **range** of a For...Next loop is the set of statements beginning with the For statement and continuing up to and including the Next statement that has the same loop variable.

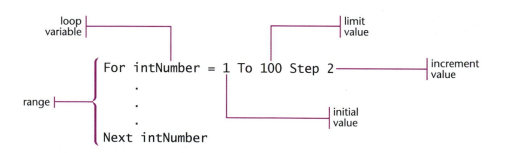

FIGURE 6-43

Table 6-16 summarizes several program tasks that can be completed using the For...Next loop.

Table 6-16   Using the For...Next Statement

TASK	REMARKS

Stepping by 1	Many applications call for incrementing, or **stepping**, the loop variable by 1 each time the For loop is executed. You may write such a For statement as follows:
	`For Rate = 1 To 12 Step 1`
	or
	`For Rate = 1 To 12`

Stepping by a value other than 1	Some applications call for the loop variable to be incremented by a value other than 1. You may write such a For statement as follows: `For Rate = 1 To 12 Step 3` The loop terminates when the loop variable Rate becomes 13 because this is greater than the value of the limit, which is 12.

Initializing the loop variable to a value other than 1	You may write such a For statement as follows:
	`For Rate = 8 To 16 Step 2`
	to intialize the loop variable to a value other than 1. Some applications call for initializing the loop variable to zero or some negative value. For example, the statements
	`For Temp = 0 To 10`
	or
	`For Temp = -6 To 12`
	are both valid. It is not necessary to initialize the loop variable to 1.

Decimal fraction values in a For statement	The values in a For statement can be decimal fraction numbers. You may write such a For statement as follows: `For Rate = 11.5 To 12.5 Step .1` This For statement loops between the values,11.5 and 12.5, inclusive, in increments of .1.
Negative values in a For statement	The values in a For statement can be negative. You may write such a For statement as follows: `For Rate = 8 To 0 Step -1` This statement loops and the Rate variable is decremented from 8 to 0. The negative step value in the For statement causes the test to be reversed, and the loop variable is decremented until it is less than the limit value.
Variables in a For statement	The values in a For statement can be variables as well as numeric constants. You may write such a For statement as follows: `For Rate = Rate1 To Rate2 Step Increment`
Using expressions as values in a For statement	The values in a For statement can be complex numeric expressions. You may write such a For statement as follows: `For Y = X / Z To A * B Step V ^ 2`
Redefining For...Next loop values	After the For statement is executed, the initial, limit, and increment values are set and cannot be altered while the For loop is active. Visual Basic .NET simply disregards any attempt to redefine them.
Iterations in a For loop	The number of **iterations**, or repetitions, specified by a For statement can be computed using the following formula: $$\text{Number of Iterations} = \frac{\text{LimitValue} - \text{InitialValue}}{\text{IncrementValue}} + 1$$ where the ratio is performed in integer arithmetic so that the quotient is truncated to the next lowest integer. For example, `For intTemp = -2 To 30 Step 2` Using the formula, the number of iterations is $\dfrac{30 - (-2)}{2} + 1 = 16 + 1 = 17$

Exiting a Loop Prematurely — The Exit Statement

Certain looping situations require a premature exit from the any loop. Visual Basic .NET includes the **Exit statement** for terminating any loop early. In Chapter 5, the Exit Sub form of the Exit statement was used to exit an event procedure if the user entered invalid input data. Although the Exit statement can be used to exit any loop, the Exit statement typically is reserved for use when an error condition or unusual circumstances occur in the statements in the loop.

> ### Tip
>
> **Using the Exit Statement**
> Use the Exit statement sparingly in order to keep the logic of code more readable. Typically, the use of the Exit statement is reserved for use when an error condition or unusual circumstance(s) occurs within a loop.

The general form of the Exit statement is given in Table 6-17.

Table 6-17   Exit Statement

General form:	1. Exit statement where statement is For, Do, Loop
Purpose:	The Exit statement allows for the premature exit of a For...Next or Do loop.
Examples:	1. `Exit For` 2. `Exit Do`

Nested For...Next Loops

Just as Visual Basic .NET allows you to write nested expressions and nested subroutines, you also can write nested For...Next loops. When the statements of one For...Next loop lie within the range of another For...Next loop, the loops are said to be **nested**, or **embedded**. Furthermore, the outer For...Next loop can be nested in the range of still another For...Next loop, and so on.

The program in Figure 6-44 utilizes two For...Next loops. The inner For...Next loop, formed by lines 4 through 6, is written so that all the statements in its range also lie within the range of the outer For...Next loop, lines 2 through 7.

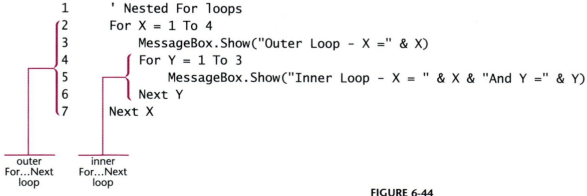

```
1    ' Nested For loops
2    For X = 1 To 4
3        MessageBox.Show("Outer Loop - X =" & X)
4        For Y = 1 To 3
5            MessageBox.Show("Inner Loop - X = " & X & "And Y =" & Y)
6        Next Y
7    Next X
```

outer For...Next loop   inner For...Next loop

FIGURE 6-44

When line 3 is executed in the partial program in Figure 6-44, the outer For...Next loop becomes active. The loop variable X is set to 1, and line 3 displays that value. When line 4 is executed, the inner For...Next loop becomes active. The loop variable Y is set to 1, and line 5 displays the values of both X and Y. With X equal to 1, control remains within the inner loop, which is executed three times, until Y exceeds 3. At this point, the inner loop is satisfied, and control passes to the outer For...Next loop, which executes line 7.

Control then passes back to line 2, where the loop variable X is incremented by 1 to become 2. After line 3 displays the new value of X, line 4 is executed, and the inner For...Next loop becomes active again. The loop variable Y is initialized to 1, and the process repeats itself.

When the outer loop is satisfied, control passes to the line after line 7. In Figure 6-44, the outer For...Next loop executes a total of four times, and the inner For...Next loop executes a total of 3 times 4, or 12.

When nesting occurs, all statements in the range of the inner For...Next loop also must be in the range of the outer For...Next loop. Visual Basic .NET does not allow the range of an inner For...Next loop to extend past the end of the range of an outer For...Next loop.

Implementing a Loop Using a For...Next Statement

As indicated in the program design, the code for the Today's Sales Check application requires a Total Sales Click event procedure to sum the total sales of all items, total sales for items on sale, and total sales for items not on sale when the user clicks the Total Today's Sales button.

Figure 6-45 shows the logic needed for this event procedure, the btnTotalSales_Click event procedure. The logic calls for a loop that executes for each row, or item, in the lstTodaysSales control. A For...Next statement can be used to code this loop because the loop is counter-controlled. The loop executes once for each item in the list, and the number of items can be determined before the loop begins execution.

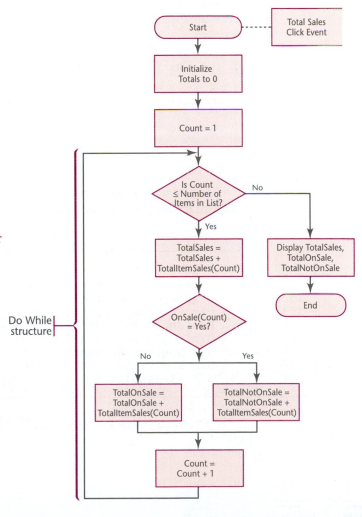

FIGURE 6-45

The btnTotalSales_Click event procedure requires several variables to do its work. Table 6-18 lists the variables needed by the btnTotalSales_Click event procedure.

Table 6-18   Variables in the btnTotalSales_Click Event Procedure

VARIABLE	DATA TYPE	INITIAL VALUE	PURPOSE
intIndex	Integer	Not set	Loop variable for For...Next loop
intListCount	Integer	Not set	Holds the number of items in the lstTodaysSales control
sngTotalSales	Single	0	Accumulates the total sales in the lstTodaysSales control
sngTotalOnSale	Single	0	Accumulates the total sales for items on sale in the lstTodaysSales control
sngTotalRegularPrice	Single	0	Accumulates the total sales for items not on sale in the lstTodaysSales control
sngItemSales	Single	Not set	Holds the value of the current item's sales total in the lstTodaysSales control
strResults	String	Not set	Message that contains totals displayed to the user
strItemSales	String	Not set	Holds a string representation of the sngItemSales variable

Figure 6-46 shows the comment header and variable declarations for the btnTotalSales_Click event procedure.

```
150        ' Read each item in the lstTodaysSales list box, determine
151        ' the amount in the second column, add the amount to the
152        ' appropriate totals, and then display the totals.
153        Dim intIndex, intListCount As Integer
154        Dim sngTotalSales As Single = 0
155        Dim sngTotalOnSale As Single = 0
156        Dim sngTotalRegularPrice As Single = 0
157        Dim sngItemSales As Single
158        Dim strResults As String, strItemSales As String
```

FIGURE 6-46

The code in Figure 6-47 shows the For...Next statement used to read each item in the lstTodaysSales control. The statements within the For...Next loop will be added shortly.

```
160         intListCount = Convert.ToInt32(lstTodaysSales.Items.Count)
161         For intIndex = 0 To intListCount - 1
162
163         Next
```

FIGURE 6-47

Line 160 determines the number of times that the For...Next loop should execute. The value is based on the Count property value of the Items collection of the lstTodaysSales control. The **Count property** of a collection is used to represent the total number of items in a collection. The Convert.ToInt32() method ensures that the value used in the loop is an Integer value. The value is assigned to the intListCount variable. The For...Next statement begins its iteration, or looping process, at 0 because the first item in the Items collection for the lstTodaysSales control has an index of 0. The loop's limit value is intListCount − 1. The reason that 1 is subtracted from intListCount is because the loop begins at 0, rather than 1. Because a Step clause is not included in the For statement, the increment value for the loop defaults to 1.

The following steps create the btnTotalSales_Click event procedure, add the comment header for the event procedure, declare variables for the btnTotalSales_Click event procedure, and then code the For...Next statement. The For...Next statement will do an iteration of the loop for each row in the lstTodaysSales control.

To Code a For...Next Statement

1. Click the Today's Sales Check.vb[Design] tab at the top of the main work area. Double-click the btnTotalSales button. When the code window displays, click line 150 and then enter the comments and variable declarations shown in Figure 6-46.

2. Enter the first two lines of code shown in Figure 6-47. Be sure to leave a blank line before the code statements starting in line 160.

   The comments for the btnEnterSales_Click event and the variable declarations display. After you press the ENTER key at the end of line 161, Intellisense™ inserts a blank line and the Next keyword as lines 162 and 163 (Figure 6-48 on the next page).

   (continued)

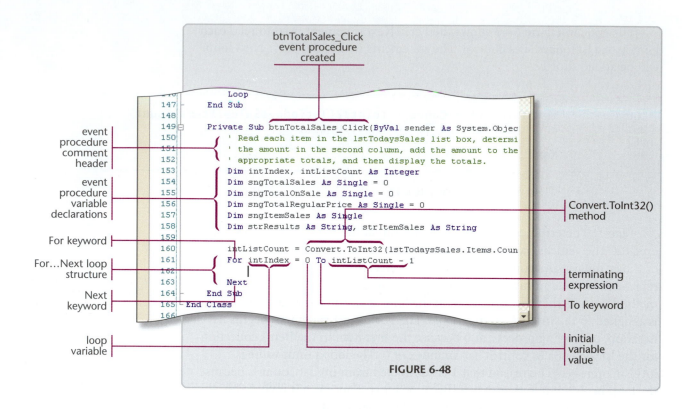

FIGURE 6-48

Accessing Items in a ListView Control

With the parameters of the loop defined, the next step is to begin to code the statements within the For…Next loop that read the items in the total sales of the lstTodaysSales control. To complete the computations required to display the totals shown in the message box in Figure 6-1d on page VB 6.03, each iteration of the For…Next loop needs to read the Total Sales column in the lstTodaysSales control. Recall that Total Sales is in the second column of the control and that the amount was added to the control using the SubItems collection of each added item. The Items property of the control contains one entry for each row that displays in the control. The SubItems(0) subitem contains information about the first column in the control. The SubItems(1) subitem contains information about the second column in the control. The Text property of each subitem contains the text that displays in the second and third column of the current row.

Figure 6-49 shows the code for assigning the Text property of the second column of the lstTodaysSales control to the variable, strItemSales. The current row in the table that is being read is designated by the Items(intIndex) portion of the code. The intIndex variable varies with each iteration of the For…Next loop. On the first iteration, intIndex is equal to 0, which indicates the first row in the lstTodaysSales control.

```
162    strItemSales = lstTodaysSales.Items(intIndex).SubItems(1).Text
```

FIGURE 6-49

The following step adds the line of code in Figure 6-49 to the btnTotalSales_Click event procedure.

To Write Code to Access an Item in a ListView Control

1. If necessary, click line 162. Enter the line of code from Figure 6-49.

Line 162 displays within the For...Next statement (Figure 6-50). The statement executes for each item in the lstTodaysSales control. The string in the second column of the current list row is assigned to the strItemSales variable.

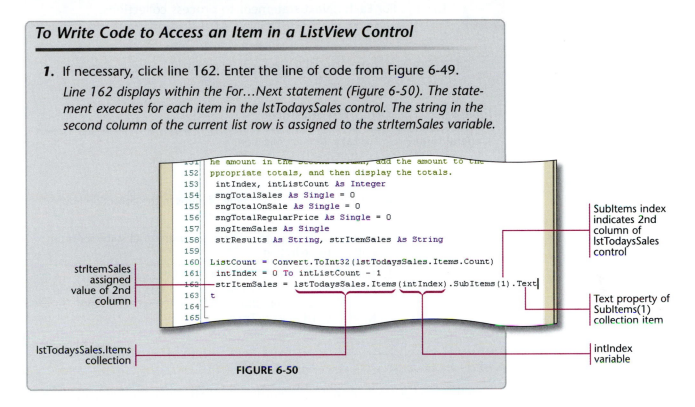

strItemSales assigned value of 2nd column

lstTodaysSales.Items collection

SubItems index indicates 2nd column of lstTodaysSales control

Text property of SubItems(1) collection item

intIndex variable

FIGURE 6-50

After line 162 executes, the strItemSales variable contains the value that displays in the row of the lstTodaysSales control indicated by the value of the intIndex variable. For example, if the first row contains a value of $133.50 for the Total Sales, then during the first iteration of the For...Next loop, line 162 assigns the value, 133.50, to the strItemSales variable.

The For Each...Next Statement

When working with a collection, Visual Basic .NET provides the For Each...Next statement, which is an alternative to the For...Next statement used to create the project in this chapter. The **For Each...Next statement**, which loops through a group of statements for each element in a collection, does not require a counter, because the statement automatically knows how to find the first item in the collection and when it has reached the last item in the collection.

The statements in the For Each...Next loop execute if at least one item exists in the collection. The statements execute for the first item in the collection; if the collection contains more than one item, the statements in the loop continue to execute for each item. When no more items exist, the loop terminates and program execution continues with the statement following the Next statement. Just as with the For...Next statement, you can nest For Each...Next statements.

The For Each...Next Statement
Use the For Each...Next statement to process collections.

Table 6-19 shows the general form for the For Each...Next statement.

Table 6-19	For Each...Next Statement

General form:	1. For Each item In collection
	         statements
	    Next item
	
	where item is of the object type of items in the collection and collection is the name of the collection

Purpose:	The For Each...Next statement repeats a group of statements for each item in a collection.

Example:	1. Dim lviListViewItem As ListViewItem
	   For Each lviListViewItem In ListView1.Items
	       MessageBox.Show(lviListViewItem.Text())
	   Next lviListViewItem

In the example in Table 6-19, the For Each...Next statement loops through the Items collection in a ListView control and displays the Text property of each item in a message box. The code in Figure 6-51 shows how the For...Next statement in the Today's Sales Check application can be rewritten as a For Each...Next statement.

```
160    Dim lviTodaysSales As ListViewItem
161    For Each lviTodaysSales In lstTodaysSales.Items
162        strItemSales = lviTodaysSales.SubItems(1).Text
              .
              .
              .
172    Next
```

FIGURE 6-51

As shown in Figure 6-51, line 160 declares the new loop variable, lviTodaysSales, for the For Each...Next loop. This declaration eliminates the need for the intIndex and intListCount variables, because the loop automatically cycles through the collection without a need to reference the index of each item. The lviTodaysSales variable is declared as a ListViewItem, because that is the class of the objects in the Items collection of the ListView control. Line 161 uses the For Each statement to set the looping variable to lviTodaysSales and the collection to loop through to the Items collection in lstTodaysSales. Compare line 162 in Figure 6-51 with line 162 in Figure 6-49 on page VB 6.60 to understand how the For Each…Next statement simplifies coding of references to items in the collection. The variable, lviTodaysSales, replaces the reference to lstTodaysSales.Items(intIndex). This is the case for all references to lstTodaysSales.Items(intIndex) in the code.

In this chapter, the For…Next statement is used to process the collection because it is the more common statement, one with which beginning Visual Basic .NET programmers should be familiar.

String Manipulation

All variables of the String data type are part of the String class. The String class includes many methods for the manipulation of String variables. For example, the **SubString() method** allows you to retrieve part of a string, called a **substring**, from a string, based on a start position and the number of characters to retrieve. Each character in a string has an index. The index of the first character in a string is 0. The index of the second character in a string is 1, and so on. Many of the common String class methods use indexes to perform operations on strings.

Table 6-20 lists the common methods used to manipulate strings.

Table 6-20 Common String Class Methods

METHOD	DESCRIPTION	EXAMPLE	RESULT
Chars()	Gets a character at the specified position in a string	strExample = "McKenna" strResult = strExample.Chars(3)	strResult = "e"
EndsWith()	Determines whether the end of a string matches a pass-in target	strExample = "McKenna" blnResult = strExample.EndsWith("na")	blnResult = True
Insert()	Inserts a passed-in string into the string at the index position specified	strExample = "Mcna" strResult = strExample.Insert(2, "Ken")	strResult = "McKenna"
Length()	Gets the number of characters in a string	strExample = "McKenna" intResult = strExample.Length()	intResult = 7
PadLeft()	Right-aligns the characters in this instance, padding on the left with spaces or a specified character for a specified total length	strExample = "Warning" strResult = strExample.PadLeft(12, "!")	strResult = "!!!!!Warning"
PadRight()	Left-aligns the characters in this instance, padding on the right with spaces or a specifiedcharacter for a specified total length	strExample = "Warning" strResult = strExample.PadRight(12, "!")	strResult = "Warning!!!!!"
Remove()	Deletes a specified number of characters from this instance beginning at a specified position	strExample = "McKenna" strResult = strExample.Remove(2, 3)	strResult = "Mcna"

(continued)

Table 6-20 *Common String Class Methods* (continued)

METHOD	DESCRIPTION	EXAMPLE	RESULT
Replace()	Replaces all occurrences of a specified character or string in this instance, with another specified character or string	strExample = "McKenna" strResult = strExample.Replace("nn", "l")	strResult = "McKela"
StartsWith()	Determines whether the start of a string matches a pass-in target	strExample = "McKenna" blnResult = strExample.StartsWith("na")	blnResult = False
SubString()	Retrieves a substring from the string	strExample = "McKenna" strResult = strExample.SubString(3, 2)	strResult = "en"
ToLower()	Returns a copy of the string in lowercase	strExample = "McKenna" strResult = strExample.ToLower()	strResult ="mckenna"
ToUpper()	Returns a copy of the string in uppercase	strExample = "McKenna" strResult = strExample.ToUpper ()	strResult = "MCKENNA"
Trim()	Removes all occurrences of a set of specified characters from the beginning and end of the string; default character to remove is the space character	strExample = " McKenna " strResult = strExample.Trim()	strResult = "McKenna"

The result of a String method does not change the original string itself. Instead, the result of the operation is returned in a copy of the string in memory. Therefore, you must assign the result to a variable to use the result in further program operations.

Tip

String Class Methods

The result of a String method does not change the original string itself. The result of the operation is returned in a copy of the string in memory. Therefore, you must assign the result to a variable to use the result in further program operations.

Manipulating Strings

After line 162 in Figure 6-51 on page VB 6.62 executes, the strItemSales variable contains a dollar amount for the total sales for the item expressed in Currency format. That is, the amount includes a dollar sign in front of it. Before the program can use the amount in a calculation, the dollar sign must be removed and the value converted from a String data type to a Numeric data type. The dollar sign can be removed by replacing the dollar sign with a zero (0). The **Replace() method** of the String class, as described in Table 6-19 on page VB 6.62, can be used to make this substitution and then assign the resulting string back to the original variable.

Figure 6-52 shows the code necessary to replace the dollar sign in the strItemSales variable with a 0 and assign the resulting string back to the strItemSales variable.

```
163                    strItemSales = strItemSales.Replace("$", "0")
```

FIGURE 6-52

The following step enters the line of code in Figure 6-52 into the btnTotalSales_Click event procedure.

To Code the String Replace() Method

1. If necessary, click line 163. Enter the line of code from Figure 6-52.

Line 163 displays in the code window (Figure 6-53). The Replace() method of the String class replaces the dollar sign, $, in the strItemSales variable with a zero, 0, so that the string can be converted to a number and used in an expression.

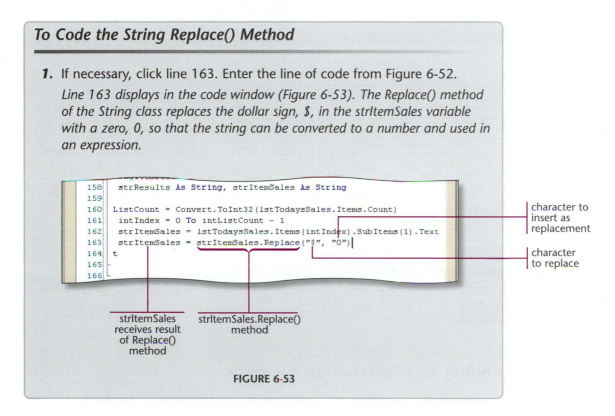

FIGURE 6-53

The total sales for an item now is stored in the strItemSales string. The next step is to convert the string to a numeric value and use the value in calculations.

Concatenation Operators

Chapter 4 introduced the string concatenation operator, &. Additional concatenation operators also can be used as shortcuts to simplify assignment statements where a variable is being modified by an expression. For example, the assignment statement

  intCount = intCount + 1

can be written as

  intCount += 1

using the **addition concatenation operator,** +=. The intCount variable is assigned the original value of intCount plus the expression, 1. All of the standard arithmetic operators and the string concatenation operators have a concatenation operator that provides a shortcut when writing assignment statements. Table 6-21 lists the concatenation operators and their meaning.

Table 6-21 *Concatenation Operators for Assignment Statements*

OPERATOR	EXAMPLE	MEANING
&= (string concatenation)	strAns &= " is my final answer."	strAns = strAns & " is my final answer."
*=	dblX *= 5.0	dblX = dblX * 5.0
+=	dblX += 5.0	dblX = dblX + 5.0
/=	dblX /= 5.0	dblX = dblX / 5.0
-=	dblX -= 5.0	dblX = dblX – 5.0
\=	intX \= 5	intX = intX \ 5
^=	dblX ^= 5.0	dblX = dblX ^ 5.0

The use of concatenation operators makes code more readable, so you should use them whenever possible in assignment statements.

Tip

Use of Concatenation Operators
Use the concatenation operators whenever possible in assignment statements to make code more readable.

Coding a Concatenation Operator

Concatenation operators can be used to simplify the code for the btnTotalSales_Click event procedure. As the For...Next loop in the btnTotalSales_Click event procedure executes, the total sales are accumulated in three variables that were declared earlier: sngTotalSales, sntTotalOnSale, and sngTotalRegularPrice (Table 6-19 on page VB 6.62). The statements that add the current item's total sales to these variables can use the addition concatenation operator, +=, to accumulate the totals. When creating the output string for the message box, the statements use the **string concatenation shortcut,** &=, to build the string one line at a time. The **ControlChars.NewLine constant** is used to start a new line at the end of each of the three output lines. The **ControlChars class** of constants includes many useful characters, such as the NewLine character, for building strings.

Figure 6-54 shows the statements for incrementing the three totals that must be calculated, which correspond to the pseudocode in Figure 6-5 on page VB 6.10. Before the current item's total sales can be used in an expression, the string that holds the value, strItemSales, must be converted to a single value, as shown in line 164.

```
164            sngItemSales = Convert.ToSingle(strItemSales)
165
166            sngTotalSales += sngItemSales
167            If lstTodaysSales.Items(intIndex).SubItems(2).Text = "Yes" Then
168                sngTotalOnSale += sngItemSales
169            Else
170                sngTotalRegularPrice += sngItemSales
171            End If
172        Next
173
174        strResults = "Total sales today: " & Format$(sngTotalSales, "Currency") &    ↙
        ControlChars.NewLine
175        strResults &= "Total sales for items on sale: " & Format$(sngTotalOnSale,    ↙
        "Currency") & ControlChars.NewLine
176        strResults &= "Total sales for items not on sale: " & Format$             ↙
        (sngTotalRegularPrice, "Currency")
177        MessageBox.Show(strResults, "Daily Sales Totals")
```

FIGURE 6-54

Line 166 increments the sngTotalSales variable by the value of the sngItemSales variable. The If…Then…Else statement in lines 167 through 171 increments either the sngTotalOnSale variable or the sngTotalRegularPrice variable based on the string in the third column of the lstTodaysSales control. The string is the Text property of the third SubItems member of the current item in the Items collection of the lstTodaysSales control:

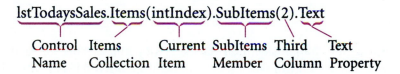

lstTodaysSales.Items(intIndex).SubItems(2).Text

| Control Name | Items Collection | Current Item | SubItems Member | Third Column | Text Property |

Finally, lines 174 through 176 use the string concatenation operator or the string concatenation shortcut to build the strResults string. The variables used to accumulate the totals are formatted as Currency for display. Line 177 uses the Show() method of the MessageBox class to display the results in a message box.

The steps on the next page add the code in Figure 6-54 to the btnTotalSales_Click event.

To Code Concatenation Operators

1. If necessary, click line 164. Enter the first nine lines of code shown in Figure 6-54.

2. Enter lines 174 through 177 as shown in figure 6-54. Be sure to leave a blank line before line 174.

   Lines 164 through 177 display in the code window. The code within the For...Next loop in lines 161 through 172 sums the sales for each item. The code after the For...Next loop creates an output message with the totals and then displays the message to the user (Figure 6-55).

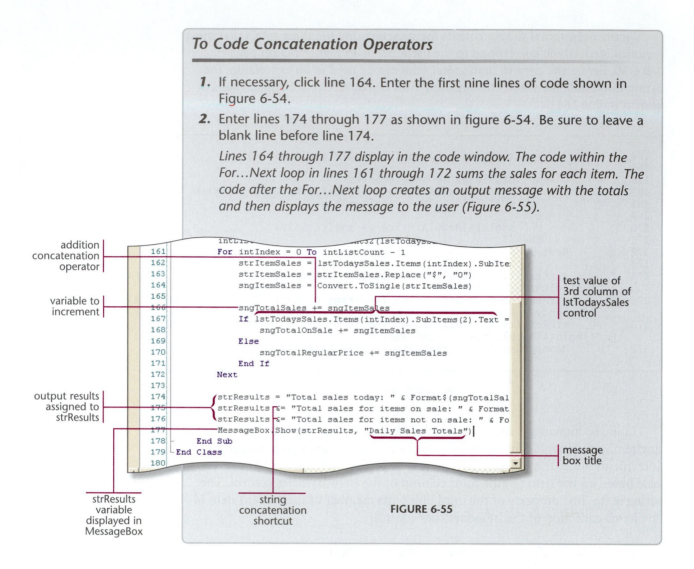

FIGURE 6-55

Lines 164 through 171 are inside the For...Next loop and execute for each item in the lstTodaysSales control when the user clicks the btnTotalSales control. Lines 174 through 177 execute after the loop has accumulated the proper totals. Finally, after the message box displays, the event procedure exits.

Removing Items from a ListView Control

The Clear(), Remove(), and RemoveAt() methods of the Items property of the ListView control are used to delete items from the Items property. The **Clear() method** removes all items. The **Remove() method** accepts one parameter of type ListViewItem and deletes one item in the list based on that parameter. The **RemoveAt() method** accepts a numeric index of type Integer and deletes the item at the index indicated by the parameter.

The Today's Sales Check application requires that the user be able to delete items in two ways. First, the user can click the Clear Today's Sales button to delete all items in the list. Second, the user can press the DELETE key to remove a single item, after selecting an item in the list.

Figure 6-56 shows the line of code needed to clear the lstTodaysSales control when the user clicks the btnClearList control. The Clear() method of the Items collection is used to clear the control.

```
181          lstTodaysSales.Items.Clear()
```

FIGURE 6-56

The following step creates the btnClearList_Click event procedure and enters the line of code shown in Figure 6-56.

To Write Code to Clear All Items in a ListView Control

1. Click the Todays Sales Form.vb[Design] tab in the main work area. Double-click the btnClearList button. When the code window displays, if necessary, click line 181 and then enter the line of code shown in Figure 6-56.

Visual Basic .NET creates the btnClearList_Click event procedure. Line 181 displays in the code window (Figure 6-57). Line 181 uses the Clear() method of the Items collection of the lstTodaysSales control to remove all of the items from the lstTodaysSales control.

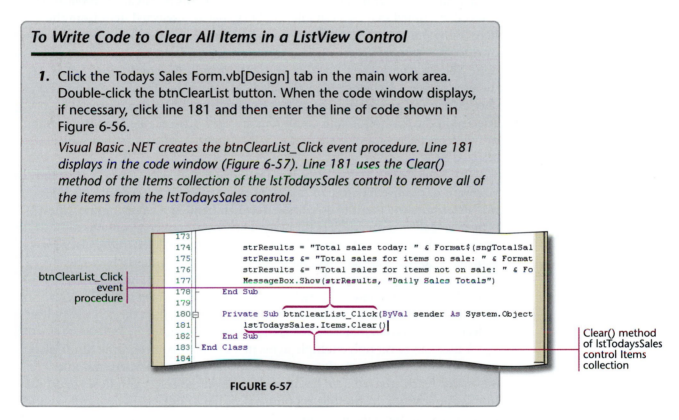

btnClearList_Click event procedure

Clear() method of lstTodaysSales control Items collection

FIGURE 6-57

The first method of deleting items — where the user can click the Clear Today's Sales button to delete all items in the list — is coded. Coding the second method requires coding a keyboard event procedure to determine when the user has pressed the DELETE key.

Keyboard Events

Most controls include three event procedures for handling user input from the keyboard. The **KeyDown event**, **KeyPress event**, and **KeyUp event** for a control occur when the user presses a key when the control has focus. All three events occur when the user presses a single key, in the order, KeyDown, KeyPress, and

KeyUp. The KeyUp event allows you to capture the moment when the user releases a key. The keyboard events often are used to validate user data. As a user enters data in a TextBox control, for example, the KeyDown event can be used to determine if the user has entered an invalid character for the particular input.

Because keyboard events are not the default events for controls, you cannot double-click the control on a form to create the event procedure for the keyboard event. Instead, you must use the Object and Procedure boxes at the top of the code window to create the event procedures.

Coding Keyboard Events

During the program design process for the Today's Sales Check application, it was determined that users should be able to delete a selected item from the item list by pressing the DELETE key. To implement this, a KeyDown event procedure for the lstTodaysSales control must be coded to delete the currently selected item. The logic in the KeyDown event procedure tells the application that, if the user presses a key when the lstTodaysSales control has focus, it should first check if the key pressed was the DELETE key and then determine if an item is selected in the control. If both conditions are True, then the RemoveAt() method of the Items collection of the lstTodaysSales control is called to remove the selected item.

The RemoveAt() method requires a parameter that is the index of the item you want to remove. Because of this, the KeyDown event procedure thus must first determine whether the user has selected an item by referencing the Count property of the SelectedIndices property. The Count property contains a numeric value which is a sum of the number of items selected in the ListView control. If no items are selected, the value of the Count property is 0. The **SelectedIndices property**, which is a collection property of the ListView control, contains the index for each item the user has selected in the ListView control. The first item selected is indicated by the index, 0, in the SelectedIndices collection; the second item selected is indicated by the index, 1, and so on.

A user can select only multiple items in a ListView control if the MultiSelect property value of the control is set to True. If the user has selected multiple items, then each selected item has its own index in the SelectedIndices collection. In this application, the MultiSelect property of the lstTodaysSales control is set to False, which means only one item can be selected at any time and the index for the selected item will always be set to 0 in the SelectedIndices collection. The RemoveAt() method thus can reference 0 as the index of the item you want to remove.

Figure 6-58 shows the code that corresponds to the pseudocode for the lstTodaysSales_KeyDown event procedure in Figure 6-5 on page VB 6.10.

```
185    If e.KeyCode = Keys.Delete And lstTodaysSales.SelectedIndices.Count > 0 Then
186        lstTodaysSales.Items.RemoveAt(lstTodaysSales.SelectedIndices(0))
187    End If
```

FIGURE 6-58

The following steps use the Object and Procedure boxes in the code window to create the lstTodaysSales_KeyDown event procedure and then add the code in Figure 6-58 to the new event procedure.

To Code a KeyDown Event to Remove Items from a ListView Control

1. Click the Object box arrow in the code window.

The list of objects for the frmTodaysSalesCheck form displays in the Object list (Figure 6-59).

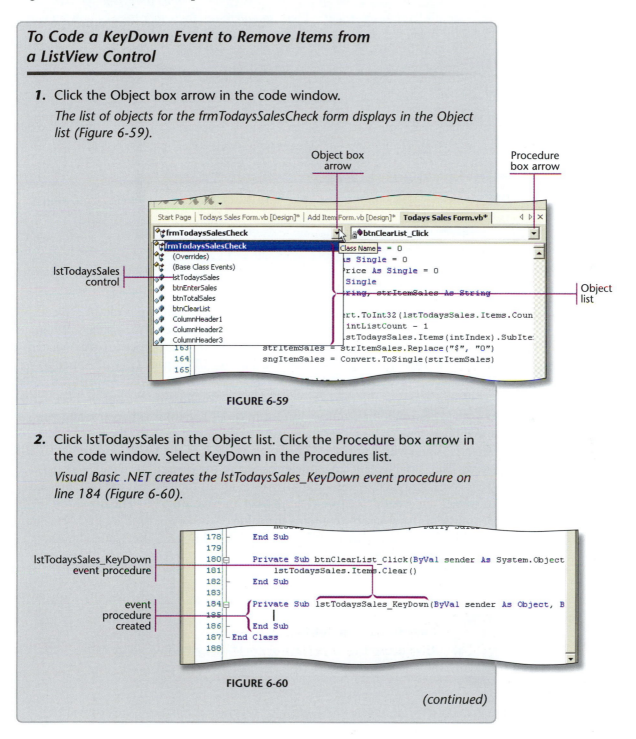

FIGURE 6-59

2. Click lstTodaysSales in the Object list. Click the Procedure box arrow in the code window. Select KeyDown in the Procedures list.

Visual Basic .NET creates the lstTodaysSales_KeyDown event procedure on line 184 (Figure 6-60).

FIGURE 6-60

(continued)

3. Enter the lines of code as shown in Figure 6-58 on page VB 6.70.

Lines 185 through 187 display in the code window (Figure 6-61). The event procedure executes when the user presses a key while the lstTodaysSales control has focus. The If...Then statement tests whether the key pressed was the DELETE key. If the user pressed the DELETE key, then Line 187 uses the RemoveAt() method of the Items collection of the lstTodaysSales control to delete the selected item from the lstTodaysSales control.

Keys.Delete constant

RemoveAt() method of lstTodaysSales control Items collection

Count property of SelectedIndices collection tested

index of first selected item in lstTodaysSales control

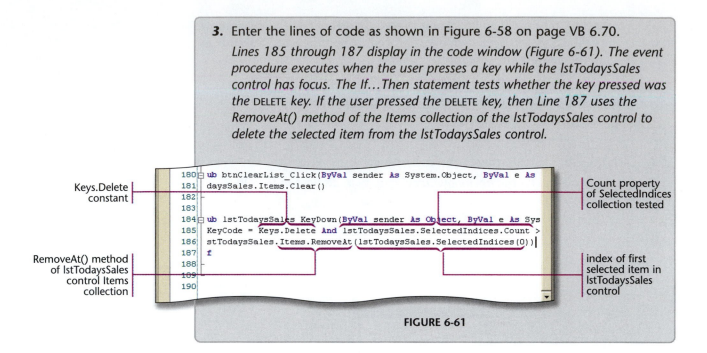

```
180 ⊟ ub btnClearList_Click(ByVal sender As System.Object, ByVal e As
181     daysSales.Items.Clear()
182 -
183
184 ⊟ ub lstTodaysSales_KeyDown(ByVal sender As Object, ByVal e As Sys
185     KeyCode = Keys.Delete And lstTodaysSales.SelectedIndices.Count >
186     stTodaysSales.Items.RemoveAt(lstTodaysSales.SelectedIndices(0))|
187     f
188 -
189
190
```

FIGURE 6-61

As shown in Figure 6-59 on the previous page, when you click the Object box arrow, a list of objects, including the controls on the form, displays. When you click the Procedure box arrow, the entire list of event procedures associated with the lstTodaysSales control displays. Table C-18 on page C.11 of Appendix C lists the event procedures and methods associated with the ListView control.

When you type the Keys keyword in Step 3, Intellisense™ displays a list of all possible keystrokes that you can test for in code. The list is exhaustive and you should use these codes rather than using strings, such as C for the letter C key, when working with keystrokes. The codes are part of the **Keys class** and are constants. The variable, e, is a parameter passed to the event procedure by Visual Basic .NET and includes useful information about the key that the user pressed to trigger the event procedure (Figure 6-58 on page VB 6.70) The **KeyCode property** of the e variable contains the value of the key pressed by the user. The variable, e, includes other useful properties. In addition to KeyCode, the Alt, Control, and Shift properties determine if the ALT, CONTROL, or SHIFT keys were pressed on the keyboard.

Tip

Keys Class Constants
Always use the Keys class of constants when working with keyboard input.

The Form Resize Event and Coding Additional Forms

The final coding steps for the Today's Sales Check application involve coding a Form Resize event for the frmTodaysSalesCheck form and writing the code for the frmSalesEntry form. The frmTodaysSalesCheck form requires coding to ensure the form is usable when the user resizes the form during run time. In particular, the list of items should resize properly to display the maximum amount of information when the user resizes the form.

The second task is to write code for the frmSalesEntry form. As indicated in the pseudocode in Figure 6-5 on page VB 6.10, the Form Load event should reset the input controls to their default values. Also, when the user clicks the OK button on the form, the form should close and return control to the frmTodaysSalesCheck form.

Coding a Form Resize Event

The **Resize() event** occurs when a form or control first displays or when the size changes because the user resizes the form. Code in the Resize event often is used to ensure that the user interface remains polished and usable during run time, even after the user resizes the form. The Resize event is not a default event and must be added to code using the Object and Procedure boxes in the code window.

When the user resizes the frmTodaysSalesCheck form, the Anchor property values set for the form controls ensure that the buttons and the lstTodaysSales control maintain their positions relative to the sides of the form. Anchoring does not cause the columns in the lstTodaysSales control to resize. The columns will remain the same size when the form is resized, unless code is written to modify the column sizes. The second and third columns, Total Sales and On Sale, contain data that does not vary greatly in its width. The size of those two columns should remain constant. The first column, however, contains item descriptions that range from 1 to 50 characters in length. As the width of the form changes when it is resized, the width of the first column also should change, in order to display as much information as possible.

The size of the first column can be adjusted by setting the Column's Width property. The value of the Width property should be the number of pixels remaining on the form, after accounting for the constant Width property values of the other two columns, and the width of the form border. The standard width of a form border on a FixedDialog style form is 12 pixels. The width of the first column thus can be calculated as

ItemColumnWidth = FormWidth – TotalSalesColumnWidth – OnSaleColumnWidth – 12

Figure 6-62 on the next page shows the code for the Resize event of the frmTodaysSalesCheck form, based on this formula.

```
191          ' When the form is resized, this event procedure makes
192          ' sure that the first column in the list box still displays
193          ' for the user.
194          Dim intColumn0Width As Integer
195
196          intColumn0Width = Me.Width - lstTodaysSales.Columns(1).Width - lstTodaysSales.↙
       Columns(2).Width - 12
197          If intColumn0Width > 0 Then
198              lstTodaysSales.Columns(0).Width = intColumn0Width
199          End If
```

FIGURE 6-62

As shown in the code, the intColumn0Width variable is assigned the number of pixels the first column can take up after taking into account the size of the Total Sales column, On Sale column, and the form border. The columns in the lstTodaysSales control are referred to by the Columns collection of the control. The first column is numbered, 0, and so on. The width of each column is referred to by the Column's Width property. The first column's width, therefore, is represented as lstTodaysSales.Column(0).Width in the code.

The following steps use the Object and Procedure boxes in the code window to create the frmTodaysSaleCheck_Resize event procedure and then enter the code shown in Figure 6-62.

To Code a Form Resize Event

1. Click the Object box arrow in the code window.

The list of objects for the frmTodaysSalesCheck form displays in the Object list (Figure 6-63).

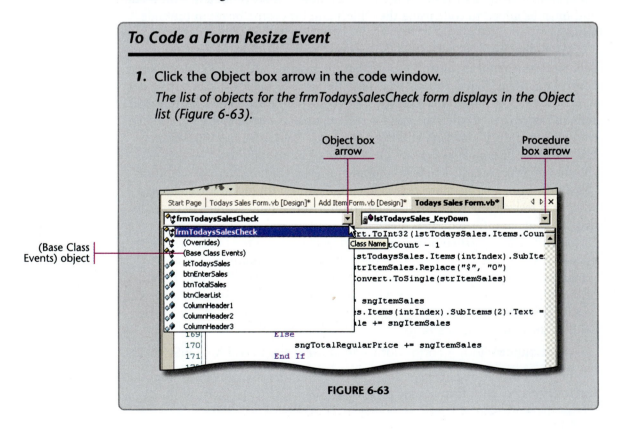

FIGURE 6-63

2. Click (Base Class Events) in the Object list. Click the Procedures box arrow in the Procedures box in the code window. Select Resize in the Procedures list.

Visual Basic .NET creates the frmTodaysSalesCheck_Resize event procedure on line 190 (Figure 6-64).

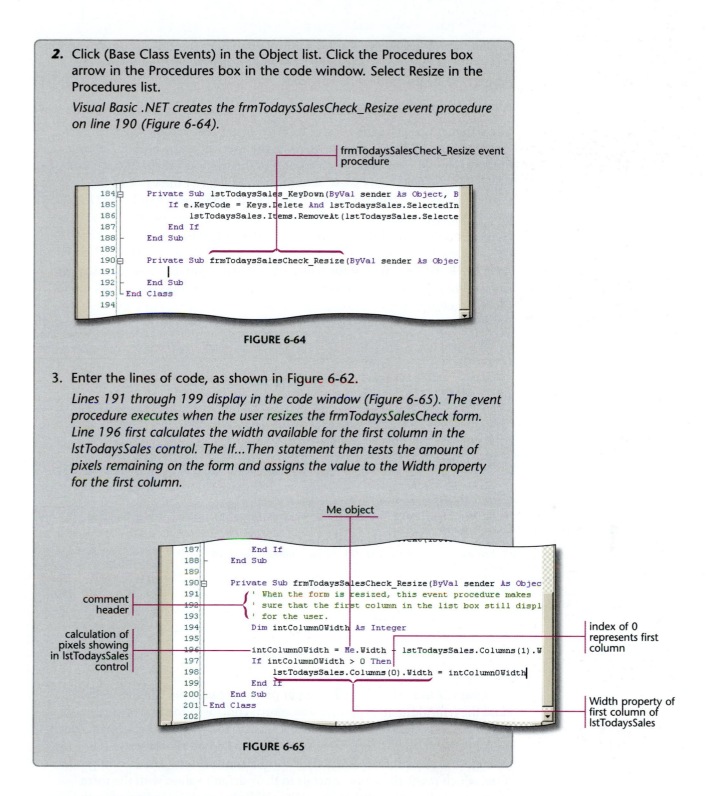

frmTodaysSalesCheck_Resize event procedure

```
184   Private Sub lstTodaysSales_KeyDown(ByVal sender As Object, B
185       If e.KeyCode = Keys.Delete And lstTodaysSales.SelectedIn
186           lstTodaysSales.Items.RemoveAt(lstTodaysSales.Selecte
187       End If
188   End Sub
189
190   Private Sub frmTodaysSalesCheck_Resize(ByVal sender As Objec
191
192   End Sub
193 End Class
194
```

FIGURE 6-64

3. Enter the lines of code, as shown in Figure 6-62.

Lines 191 through 199 display in the code window (Figure 6-65). The event procedure executes when the user resizes the frmTodaysSalesCheck form. Line 196 first calculates the width available for the first column in the lstTodaysSales control. The If...Then statement then tests the amount of pixels remaining on the form and assigns the value to the Width property for the first column.

Me object

comment header

calculation of pixels showing in lstTodaysSales control

```
187           End If
188       End Sub
189
190       Private Sub frmTodaysSalesCheck_Resize(ByVal sender As Objec
191           ' When the form is resized, this event procedure makes
192           ' sure that the first column in the list box still displ
193           ' for the user.
194           Dim intColumn0Width As Integer
195
196           intColumn0Width = Me.Width - lstTodaysSales.Columns(1).W
197           If intColumn0Width > 0 Then
198               lstTodaysSales.Columns(0).Width = intColumn0Width
199           End If
200       End Sub
201   End Class
202
```

index of 0 represents first column

Width property of first column of lstTodaysSales

FIGURE 6-65

The Me Keyword and Coding a Second Form

When coding a form, you often will find the need to refer to the current form's properties or methods. The **Me keyword** allows you to reference the current instance of a form or any other class within the form or class. The Me keyword also is useful for sending information about the current class to another procedure or method. For example, you can display the current form's Text property value using the following code

```
MessageBox.Show(Me.Text)
```

The statement displays the current form's title bar text in a message box.

In the frmAddItemForm form, when the user clicks the btnOK button, the form should close and return control to the frmTodaysSalesCheck form. Recall that the frmTodaysSalesCheck form will then test the value of the txtItemDescription control for a blank value. If the value is blank, the Do…Until loop in the frmTodaysSalesCheck form terminates. Otherwise, the values of the controls on the frmAddItemForm are added to the lstTodaysSales ListView control. You use the **Close() method** to close a form. Because the frmAddItemForm must be closed from within the frmAddItemForm form, the code uses the Me keyword to reference the current instance of the frmAddItemForm and use its Close() method.

Figure 6-66 shows the code for the frmAddItemForm form.

```
120    ' Chapter 6:      Today's Sales Check
121    ' Programmer:     J. Quasney
122    ' Date:           October 7, 2003
123    ' Purpose:        This form is the data entry form for the
124    '                 Today's Sales Check application. The form's
125    '                 parent is the Todays Sales Form form.
126    Private Sub btnOK_Click(ByVal sender As System.Object, ByVal e As System.  ↙
       EventArgs) Handles btnOK.Click
127        Me.Close()
128    End Sub
129
130    Private Sub frmAddItem_Load(ByVal sender As System.Object, ByVal e As System.  ↙
       EventArgs) Handles MyBase.Load
131        ' Initialize the Item description to blank, the Total
132        ' item sales today to 0, and the On sale today checkbox
133        ' to unchecked.
134        txtItemDescription.Text = ""
135        nudTotalItemSales.Value = 0
136        chkOnSale.Checked = False
137    End Sub
```

FIGURE 6-66

Line 127 in the btnOK_Click event procedure uses the Close() method to close the frmAddItemForm form and return control to the line of code in the btnEnterSales_Click event procedure of the frmTodaysSalesCheck form, which uses the ShowDialog() method to open the frmAddItemForm form. Lines 131 through 136 show the necessary code for the frmAddItem_Load event procedure, which resets the input controls to their default values with the form opens. Lines 134 through 136 specify the default values, as indicated in the requirements document.

The following steps add the code for the frmAddItemForm, as shown in Figure 6-66.

To Code a Close() Method Using the Me Keyword

1. Click the Add Item Form.vb[Design]* tab in the main work area. Double-click the btnOK button. Enter Option Strict On as the first line of code in the form.

2. Click line 120. Enter the comment header in lines 120 through 125, as shown in Figure 6-66.

3. Click line 127 and enter line 127, as shown in Figure 6-66.

   The Option Strict On statement and form comment header display in the general area of the form. The Me.Close() statement on line 127 in the btnOK_Click event procedure causes the frmAddItem form to close when the user clicks the OK button (Figure 6-67).

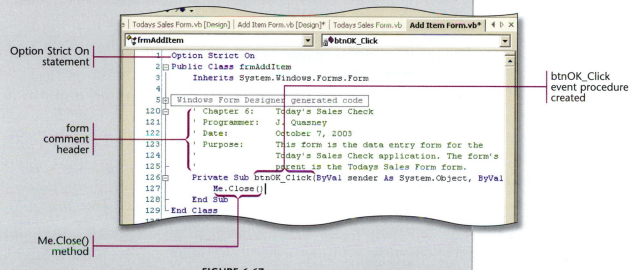

FIGURE 6-67

4. Click the Add Item Form.vb[Design]* tab in the main work area. Double-click any blank area on the form. When Visual Basic .NET creates the frmAddItem_Load event procedure, type lines 131 through 136, as shown in Figure 6-66.

   Lines 131 through 136 display in the frmAddItem_Load event procedure (Figure 6-68). Lines 134 through 136 reset the input controls to their default values.

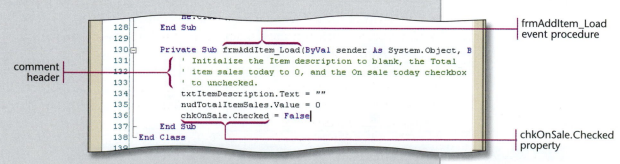

FIGURE 6-68

Setting the Startup Object for a Project

As you have learned, when Visual Basic .NET creates a new Windows Application project, it creates a form named Form1. By default, this form displays when run time begins. When working with multiple forms, or when renaming a form in a project with only one form, you must tell Visual Basic .NET which form to display first when run time begins. The form or class that initially executes during run time is called the Startup object. You set the Startup object in the project's **Property Pages**.

If the Startup object is not set after changing the default form's Name property, at run time, Visual Basic .NET indicates in an error message that it cannot find the Sub Main procedure. If you receive such an error, you most likely have not set the Startup object for the project.

The following steps open the Today's Sales Check Property Pages and set the Startup object to the frmTodaysSalesCheck form.

To Set the Startup Object for a Project

1. Click the Today's Sales Check project in the Solution Explorer window and then click the Property Pages button in the Properties window.

The Today's Sales Check Property Pages window displays. Form1 is selected as the current Startup object.

2. Click the Startup object box arrow. Select frmTodaysSalesCheck in the list.

The Startup object is set to frmTodaysSalesCheck, meaning that this form will display first when run time begins (Figure 6-69).

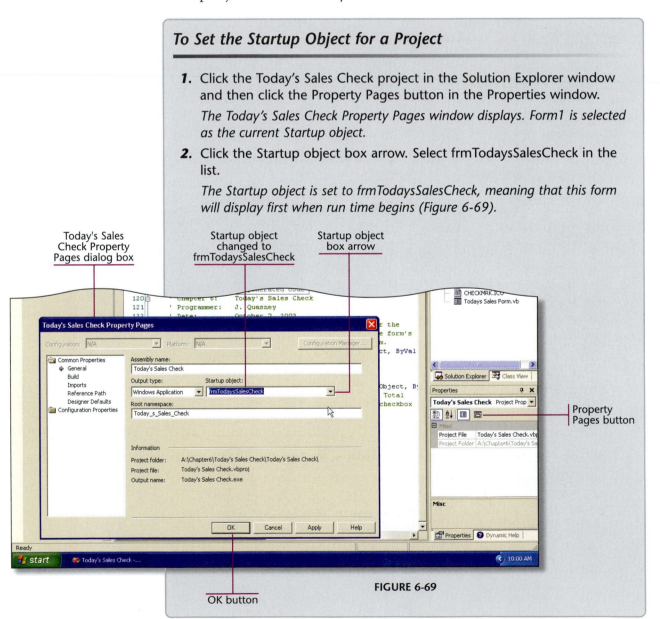

FIGURE 6-69

3. Click the OK button.

Once the Startup object is set, the value is saved with the project. The coding phase for the modified Today's Sales Check application now is complete and the application can be saved and tested.

Saving, Testing, and Documenting the Project

The following steps save the forms and project files for the Today's Sales Check project on the Data Disk in drive A and then run the application to test the project. The data in Table 6-22 is used to test the project.

Table 6-22   Test Data for the Today's Sales Check Project

Item description	Total sales	On sale today
Topsoil	435.82	No
Kentucky Bluegrass sod	250.00	Yes
Limestone blocks – small	167.52	No
Hardwood mulch	1000.00	Yes
Volcanic rock	245.74	No
Peat moss	367.30	No
Playground mulch	287.49	Yes
Firewood	129.11	No
Decorative gravel	367.78	No

To Save and Test the Project

1. Click the Save All button on the Standard toolbar.

The asterisks next to the tab names in the main work area tab no longer display, indicating that the project has been saved. Because the project was initially created and saved on the Data Disk in drive A, Visual Basic .NET automatically saves the project on the Data Disk in drive A.

2. Click the Start button on the Visual Basic .NET Standard toolbar. When the application starts, minimize the Visual Basic .NET window.

Visual Basic .NET opens the Output window temporarily and displays messages as the application starts. The Today's Sales Check application window displays, and Visual Basic .NET sets the focus to the lstTodaysSales control. The application button displays on the Windows taskbar.

(continued)

3. Click the Enter Today's Sales button. When the Today's Sales Entry window displays, enter the test data from Table 6-22 on the previous page. After each entry, click the OK button.

Each time the user clicks the OK button, the item is added to the Today's Sales Check window (Figure 6-70).

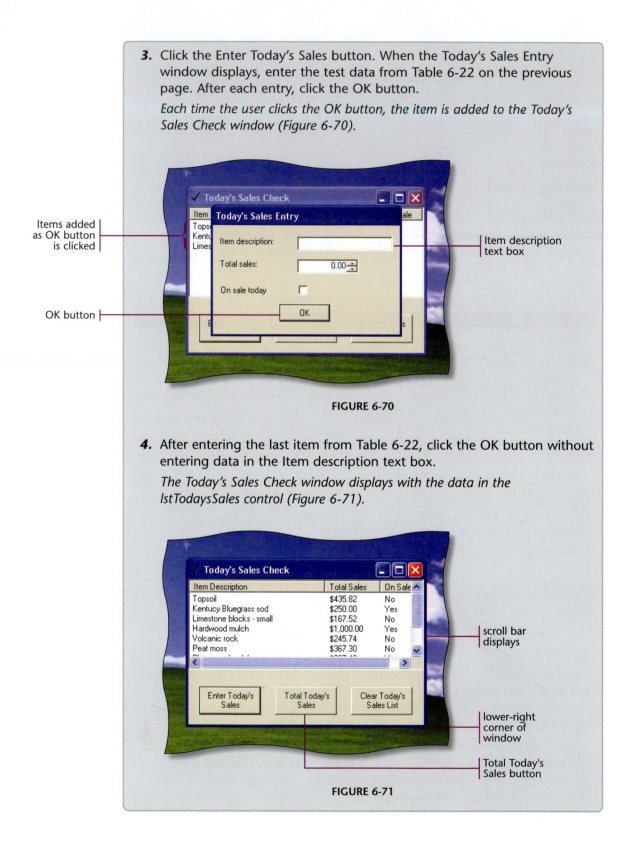

Items added as OK button is clicked

OK button

Item description text box

FIGURE 6-70

4. After entering the last item from Table 6-22, click the OK button without entering data in the Item description text box.

The Today's Sales Check window displays with the data in the lstTodaysSales control (Figure 6-71).

scroll bar displays

lower-right corner of window

Total Today's Sales button

FIGURE 6-71

5. Drag the lower-right corner of the Today's Sales Check window to expand the window as shown in Figure 6-72. Click the Total Today's Sales button.

   As the window is resized, the controls remain anchored on the form, and the width of the Item description column increases. The Daily Sales Totals message box displays with the sales totals (Figure 6-72).

Daily Sales
Totals
message box

FIGURE 6-72

6. Click the OK button to close the Daily Sales Totals message box. Click the Clear Today's Sales List button to clear the list. Click the Close button on the Today's Sales Check application window title bar. Click the Visual Basic .NET taskbar button to display the Visual Basic .NET window. If necessary, close the Output window.

   The Visual Basic .NET window maximizes and Visual Basic .NET returns to design time.

The testing process for the Today's Sales Check application is complete. The final step of the development cycle is to document the application. The steps on the next page document the application and quit Visual Basic .NET. Line numbers are printed on the code listing.

To Document the Application and Quit Visual Basic .NET

1. Click the Todays Sales Form.vb [Design] tab, and then follow the steps on page VB 2.34 of Chapter 2 using the PRINT SCREEN key to print a record of the user interface design of the Todays Sales Form form.

A record of the user interface design of the Todays Sales Form form is printed (Figure 6-73).

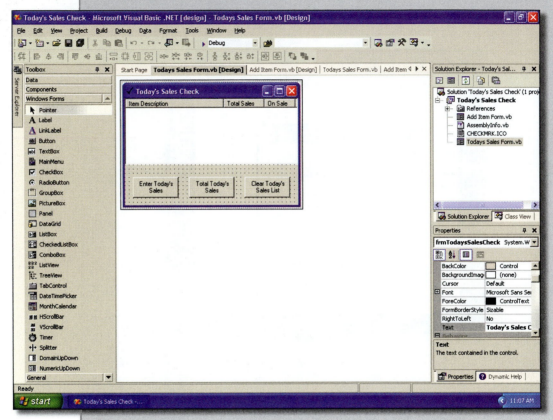

FIGURE 6-73

2. Click the Add Item Form.vb [Design] tab, and then follow the steps on page VB 2.34 of Chapter 2 using the PRINT SCREEN key to print a record of the user interface design of the Add Item Form form.

A record of the user interface design of the Add Item Form form is printed (Figure 6-74).

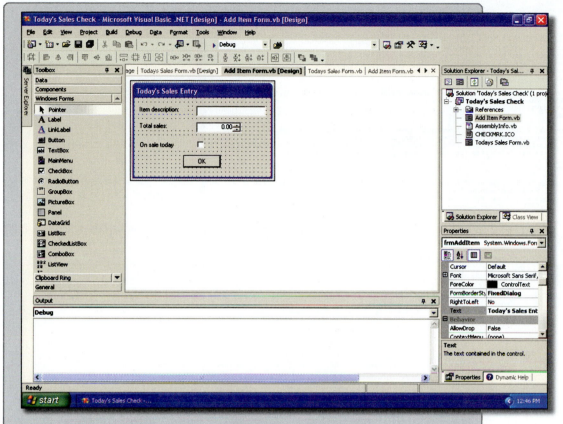

FIGURE 6-74

3. **Click the Todays Sales Form.vb tab. Click File on the menu bar and then click Page Setup.**

4. **When the Page Setup dialog box displays, if necessary, click Line numbers and then click the OK button.**

5. **Follow the steps on page VB 2.40 of Chapter 2 using the Print command on the File menu to print a record of the code of the Todays Sales Form form.**

   A record of the Todays Sales Form form code is printed (Figure 6-75 on the next page).

6. **Click the Add Item Form.vb tab. Click File on the menu bar and then click Page Setup.**

7. **When the Page Setup dialog box displays, if necessary click Line numbers and then click the OK button.**

8. **Follow the steps on page VB 2.40 of Chapter 2 using the Print command on the File menu to print a record of the code of the Add Item Form form.**

   A record of the Add Item Form form code is printed (Figure 6-76 on page VB 6.85).

(continued)

A:\Chapter6\Today's Sales Check\Today's Sales Check\Todays Sales Form.vb   2

```vb
        "Currency") & ControlChars.NewLine
63      strResults &= "Total sales for items not on sale: " & Format$    ↵
        (sngTotalRegularPrice, "Currency")
64      MessageBox.Show(strResults, "Daily Sales Totals")
65  End Sub
66
67  Private Sub btnClearList_Click(ByVal sender As System.Object, ByVal e As System.  ↵
    EventArgs) Handles btnClearList.Click
68      lstTodaysSales.Items.Clear()
69  End Sub
70
71  Private Sub lstTodaysSales_KeyDown(ByVal sender As Object, ByVal e As System.  ↵
    Windows.Forms.KeyEventArgs) Handles lstTodaysSales.KeyDown
72      If e.KeyCode = Keys.Delete And lstTodaysSales.SelectedIndices.Count > 0 Then
73          lstTodaysSales.Items.RemoveAt(lstTodaysSales.SelectedIndices(0))
74      End If
75  End Sub
76
77  Private Sub frmTodaysSalesCheck_Resize(ByVal sender As Object, ByVal e As System.  ↵
    EventArgs) Handles MyBase.Resize
78      ' When the form is resized, this event procedure makes
79      ' sure that the first column in the list box still displays
80      ' for the user.
81      Dim intColumn0Width As Integer
82
83      intColumn0Width = Me.Width - lstTodaysSales.Columns(1).Width - lstTodaysSales.  ↵
    Columns(2).Width - 12
84      If intColumn0Width > 0 Then
85          lstTodaysSales.Columns(0).Width = intColumn0Width
86      End If
87  End Sub
88 End Class
89
```

A:\Chapter6\Today's Sales Check\Today's Sales Check\Todays Sales Form.vb   1

```vb
1  Option Strict On
2  Public Class frmTodaysSalesCheck
3      Inherits System.Windows.Forms.Form
4
5  Windows Form Designer generated code
6      ' Chapter 6:      Today's Sales Check
7      ' Programmer:     J. Quasney
8      ' Date:           October 7, 2003
9      ' Purpose:        This form is the startup form for the Today's
10     '                 Sales Check application. The application
11     '                 accepts input of daily sales information totaled
12     '                 by item. The application then calculates the
13     '                 total sales for the day, the total sales for
14     '                 the day for items on sale, and the total sales
15     '                 for items not on sale.
16  Private Sub btnEnterSales_Click(ByVal sender As System.Object, ByVal e As System.  ↵
    EventArgs) Handles btnEnterSales.Click
17      ' Display a dialog box for data entry of each item's sales
18      ' totals for today. Display the dialog box until the user
19      ' enters an empty description for the item.
20      Dim objAddItemForm As New frmAddItem()
21
22      objAddItemForm.ShowDialog()
23      Do Until objAddItemForm.txtItemDescription.Text = ""
24          Dim lviTodaysSales As New ListViewItem(objAddItemForm.txtItemDescription.  ↵
    Text)
25          lviTodaysSales.SubItems.Add(Format$(objAddItemForm.nudTotalItemSales.Value, ↵
    "Currency"))
26          If objAddItemForm.chkOnSale.Checked Then
27              lviTodaysSales.SubItems.Add("Yes")
28          Else
29              lviTodaysSales.SubItems.Add("No")
30          End If
31          lstTodaysSales.Items.Add(lviTodaysSales)
32          objAddItemForm.ShowDialog()
33      Loop
34  End Sub
35
36  Private Sub btnTotalSales_Click(ByVal sender As System.Object, ByVal e As System.  ↵
    EventArgs) Handles btnTotalSales.Click
37      ' Read each item in the lstTodaysSales list box, determine
38      ' the amount in the second column, add the amount to the
39      ' appropriate totals, and then display the totals.
40      Dim intIndex, intListCount As Integer
41      Dim sngTotalSales As Single = 0
42      Dim sngTotalOnSale As Single = 0
43      Dim sngTotalRegularPrice As Single = 0
44      Dim sngItemSales As Single
45      Dim strResults As String, strItemSales As String
46
47      intListCount = Convert.ToInt32(lstTodaysSales.Items.Count)
48      For intIndex = 0 To intListCount - 1
49          strItemSales = lstTodaysSales.Items(intIndex).SubItems(1).Text
50          strItemSales = strItemSales.Replace("$", "0")
51          sngItemSales = Convert.ToSingle(strItemSales)
52
53          sngTotalSales += sngItemSales
54          If lstTodaysSales.Items(intIndex).SubItems(2).Text = "Yes" Then
55              sngTotalOnSale += sngItemSales
56          Else
57              sngTotalRegularPrice += sngItemSales
58          End If
59      Next
60
61      strResults = "Total sales today: " & Format$(sngTotalSales, "Currency") &
    ControlChars.NewLine
62      strResults &= "Total sales for items on sale: " & Format$(sngTotalOnSale,
```

FIGURE 6-75

```
A:\Chapter6\Today's Sales Check\Today's Sales Check\Add Item Form.vb                     1
 1  Option Strict On
 2  Public Class frmAddItem
 3      Inherits System.Windows.Forms.Form
 4
 5  Windows Form Designer generated code
 6      ' Chapter 6:      Today's Sales Check
 7      ' Programmer:     J. Quasney
 8      ' Date:           October 7, 2003
 9      ' Purpose:        This form is the data entry form for the
10      '                 Today's Sales Check application. The form's
11      '                 parent is the Todays Sales Form form.
12      Private Sub btnOK_Click(ByVal sender As System.Object, ByVal e As System.EventArgs) ↙
        Handles btnOK.Click
13          Me.Close()
14      End Sub
15
16      Private Sub frmAddItem_Load(ByVal sender As System.Object, ByVal e As System.      ↙
        EventArgs) Handles MyBase.Load
17          ' Initialize the Item description to blank, the Total
18          ' item sales today to 0, and the On sale today checkbox
19          ' to unchecked.
20          txtItemDescription.Text = ""
21          nudTotalItemSales.Value = 0
22          chkOnSale.Checked = False
23      End Sub
24  End Class
25
```

FIGURE 6-76

9. Click the Visual Basic .NET Close button.

If you made changes to the project since the last time it was saved, Visual Basic .NET displays the Microsoft Visual Basic .NET dialog box. If you click the Yes button, you can resave your project and quit. If you click the No button, you will quit without saving changes. Clicking the Cancel button will close the dialog box.

Chapter Summary

In this chapter, you learned how to use two new controls: the ListView control and the CheckBox control. You learned how to change the name and icon of forms and add additional forms to a project. You then learned how to write code for collections. You learned how to code looping structures, including the For…Next statement, the For Each…Next statement, the Do Until statement, and the Do While statement. You learned how to declare object variables and how to manipulate strings. You also learned how to work with keyboard events and how to code a form Resize event. Finally, you learned how to write code to open and close windows and set the Startup object for a project.

What You Should Know

Having completed this chapter, you now should be able to perform the tasks shown in Table 6-23.

Table 6-23 **Chapter 6 What You Should Know**

TASK NUMBER	TASK	PAGE
1	Start Visual Basic .NET and Start a New Project	VB 6.12
2	Set Form Properties and Add Controls	VB 6.14
3	Change the Properties of Button Controls	VB 6.18
4	Change the Properties of a ListView Control	VB 6.21
5	Anchor Controls	VB 6.24
6	Change the File Name of a Form	VB 6.28
7	Add a Form to a Project	VB 6.29
8	Create the Interface on a Newly Added Form	VB 6.33
9	Change the Properties of a CheckBox Control	VB 6.35
10	Declare an Object and Show a Form	VB 6.40
11	Code a Do Until Statement	VB 6.46
12	Write Code to Add Items to a ListView Control	VB 6.51
13	Code a For...Next Statement	VB 6.59
14	Write Code to Access an Item in a ListView Control	VB 6.61
15	Code the String Replace() Method	VB 6.65
16	Code Concatenation Operators	VB 6.68
17	Write Code to Clear All Items in a ListView Control	VB 6.69
18	Code a KeyDown Event to Remove Items from a ListView Control	VB 6.71
19	Code a Form Resize Event	VB 6.74
20	Code a Close() Method Using the Me Keyword	VB 6.77
21	Set the Startup Object for a Project	VB 6.78
22	Save and Test the Project	VB 6.79
23	Document the Application and Quit Visual Basic .NET	VB 6.82

Key Terms

addition concatenation operator *(VB 6.66)*

anchor *(VB 6.24)*

Anchor property *(VB 6.24)*

CenterParent *(VB 6.31)*

CheckBox control *(VB 6.07)*

CheckBoxes property *(VB 6.19)*

Clear() method *(VB 6.68)*

Close() method *(VB 6.76)*

collection *(VB 6.23)*

ColumnHeader Collection Editor window *(VB 6.23)*

Columns property *(VB 6.20)*

ControlChars class *(VB 6.66)*

ControlChars.NewLine constant *(VB 6.66)*

Copy command *(VB 6.29)*

Count property *(VB 6.59)*

counter-controlled loop *(VB 6.51)*

Cut command *(VB 6.29)*

Delete command *(VB 6.29)*

Details view *(VB 6.19)*

Do statement *(VB 6.42)*

Do Until statement *(VB 6.42)*

Do While statement *(VB 6.42)*

embedded *(VB 6.56)*

End While keywords *(VB 6.44)*

Exclude From Project command *(VB 6.29)*

Exit statement *(VB 6.56)*

For Each…Next statement *(VB 6.61)*

For…Next loop *(VB 6.51)*

For…Next statement *(VB 6.51)*

Form shortcut menu *(VB 6.29)*

Icon property *(VB 6.13)*

index *(VB 6.48)*

instantiated *(VB 6.38)*

iterations *(VB 6.55)*

KeyCode property *(VB 6.72)*

KeyDown event *(VB 6.69)*

KeyPress event *(VB 6.69)*

KeyUp event *(VB 6.69)*

Keys class *(VB 6.72)*

LargeIcon view *(VB 6.18)*

List view *(VB 6.18)*

ListView control *(VB 6.06)*

ListViewItem class *(VB 6.48)*

looping *(VB 6.41)*

Me keyword *(VB 6.75)*

modal *(VB 6.39)*

modeless *(VB 6.39)*

MultiSelect property *(VB 6.19)*

New keyword *(VB 6.38)*

nested *(VB 6.56)*

Open command *(VB 6.29)*

parent form *(VB 6.31)*

Property Pages *(VB 6.78)*

range *(VB 6.54)*

Remove() method *(VB 6.68)*

RemoveAt() method *(VB 6.68)*

repetition *(VB 6.41)*

Replace() method *(VB 6.64)*

Resize() event *(VB 6.73)*

SelectedIndices property *(VB 6.70)*

Show() method *(VB 6.39)*

ShowDialog() method *(VB 6.39)*

SmallIcon view *(VB 6.18)*

Startup object *(VB 6.06)*

stepping *(VB 6.55)*

string concatenation shortcut *(VB 6.66)*

SubItems collection *(VB 6.48)*

SubItems property *(VB 6.48)*

substring *(VB 6.63)*

SubString() method *(VB 6.63)*

template *(VB 6.29)*

terminating condition *(VB 6.08)*

View Code command *(VB 6.29)*

View Designer command *(VB 6.29)*

View property *(VB 6.18)*

While keyword *(VB 6.44)*

While…End While statement *(VB 6.44)*

Homework Assignments

Short Answer

1. Given the following partial program, what displays in the lstOutput control when the code is executed?

```
intF = 0
For I = 1 To 4
    intG = 0
    intF += 1
    For J = 1 To 3
        intG += intF
        Dim lviOutputItem As New ListViewItem(intF & " " & intG)
        lstOutput.Items.Add(lviOutputItem)
    Next J
Next I
```

2. Given the following partial program, how many times do the statements in the loop execute?

```
intCount = 11
intCount *= 2
Do While (intCount > 20 And intCount < 100)
    intCount +=2
Loop
```

3. Identify the syntax and logic error(s), if any, in each of the following For statements:

a. For intAmount = –1 To 10 Step –1

b. For intVar = 1 To –6

c. Dim intCount as String

   For intCount = 0 To 7

d. For intValue = 10 To 1

e. For intStart = A To B Step –B

4. How many items will be added to the lstOutput ListView control in the following code segment?

```
For intCount = 1 To 15
    For intCount2 = 1 To 20
        For intCount3 = 1 to 9
            Dim lviMyItem As New ListViewItem("A new item")
            lstOutput.Items.Add(lviMyItem)
        Next intCount3
    Next intCount2
Next intCount
```

5. Consider the following types of Do and For…Next statements.

a. Do While…Loop   b. Do Until…Loop

c. Do…Loop While   d. Do…Loop Until

e. For…Next   f. For Each…Next

Answer the following questions for each type of looping statement.
(1) Is the test made before or after the range of statements is executed?
(2) What is the minimum number of times the range of statements is executed?
(3) Does the loop terminate when the condition is true or false?

6. For each set below, write a Do statement and then a For statement. With the Do statement include the statements required to initialize and increment Initial.

Set	Initial	Limit	Increment	Set	Initial	Limit	Increment
1	1	25	2	4	5	1	-1
2	25	75	5	5	-3	10	0
3	5	5	1	6	4	10	0.1

7. Given the two valid programs below, how many times does the statement intDiff = intDiff – 10 execute before the loop terminates?

a.
```
intDiff = 1
For intCount = 1 to 100
    intDiff = intDiff +intCount
    If intDiff > 25 Then
        Exit For
    End If
    intDiff = intDiff - 10
Next
```

b.
```
intDiff = 50
intCount = -5
Do While intCount <= 3
    intCount = intCount + 2
    If intDiff = 0 Then
        Exit Do
    End If
    intDiff = intDiff - 10
Loop
```

8. Given a collection called colValues consisting of at most 50 items, write a partial program that counts the number of items in the collection that have a value in the Text property between 0 and 18, inclusive, between 26 and 29, inclusive, and between 42 and 47, inclusive. Use the following counters:

intLow: count of items with a value between 0 and 18 inclusive
intMiddle: count of items with a value between 26 and 29 inclusive
intHigh: count of items with a value between 42 and 47 inclusive

9. Given a collection called colF consisting of 10 items, write a partial program to shift all the items up one in the collection. The last of the ten items should replace the first item. Do not use any collection other than collection colF. Be sure not to destroy an item before it is shifted.

10. Evaluate each of the following. Assume strExample is equal to the following string for each:
If I have run farther it is because I have been carried in the arms of giants
   a. strExample.Length()
   b. strExample.ToUpper()
   c. strExample.Chars(5)
   d. strExample.EndWith("st")
   e. strExample.PadLeft(80, "*")
   f. strExample.ToLower()
   g. strExample.SubString(11, 3)
   h. strExample.StartsWith("If")
   i. strExample.Replace("run", "walked")
   j. strExample.Remove(6, 5)
   k. strExample.Replace("giants", "midgets")
   l. strExample.SubString(15, 6)

11. Rewrite the following as valid assignment statements without using concatenation operators.

    a. dblVal +=1

    b. dblVal /=15

    c. dblVal *=22

    d. dblVal ^=3

    e. dblVal −=35

    f. dblVal \=13

    g. strAns &="is not correct"

12. The _____ property determines whether a CheckBox control has two states or three states.

13. The _____ statement and the _____ statement can both be used in place of a For…Next statement for counter-controlled looping.

14. You open a new modal window using the _____ method of a form. You can open a new modeless window using the _____ method of a form.

15. Whenever a user presses a key while a control has focus during run time, the _____ event is invoked, followed by the _____ event, and finally the _____ event.

16. Use the statement _____ to prematurely terminate the execution of a For…Next statement. Use the statement _____ to prematurely terminate the execution of a Do Until statement.

17. When declaring a variable as an object, the _____ keyword creates an object in addition to declaring a variable.

18. The _____ collection, which is a property of the ListView control, contains one entry for each item the user sees in the control. The _____ collection of each item within the ListView control contains information about additional columns that display when the control's View property is set to Details. The _____ collection of a ListView control contains information about each column that displays when the control's View property is set to Details.

19. Write the code to display a message box that contains information about the current form's Height, Width, X, and Y properties.

20. What will happen if you use a value of zero for the increment in a For…Next loop?

Learn It Online

Start your browser and visit scsite.com/vbnet/exs. Follow the instructions in the exercises below.

1. **Chapter Reinforcement TF, MC, and SA** Click the True/False, Multiple Choice, and Short Answer link below Chapter 6. Print and then answer the questions.

2. **Practice Test** Click the Practice Test link below Chapter 6. Answer each question, enter your first and last name at the bottom of the page, and then click the Grade Test button. When the graded practice test displays on your screen, click Print on the File menu to print a hard copy. Continue to take practice tests until you score 80% or better. Hand in a printout of the final practice test.

3. **Crossword Puzzle Challenge** Click the Crossword Puzzle Challenge link below Chapter 6. Read the instructions, and then enter your first and last name. Click the Play button. Complete the crossword puzzle. When you are finished, click the Submit button. When the crossword puzzle redisplays, click the Print button.

4. **Tips and Tricks** Click the Tips and Tricks link below Chapter 6. Click a topic that pertains to Chapter 6. Right-click the information and then click Print on the shortcut menu. Construct a brief example of what the information relates to in Visual Basic .NET to confirm you understand how to use the tip or trick. Hand in the example and printed information.

5. **Newsgroups** Click the Newsgroups link below Chapter 6. Click a topic that pertains to Chapter 6. Print three comments.

6. **Expanding Your Horizons** Click the Articles for Visual Basic .NET below Chapter 6. Click a topic that pertains to Chapter 6. Print the information. Construct a brief example of what the information relates to in Visual Basic .NET to confirm you understand the contents of the article. Hand in the example and printed information.

7. **Search Sleuth** Select three key terms from the Key Terms section of this chapter and then use the Google search engine at google.com (or any major search engine) to display and print two Web pages for each key term.

Debugging Assignment

Start Visual Basic .NET and open the project, Software Consulting Experts, from the Chapter6\Software Consulting Experts folder on the Data Disk. See page xvi in the preface of this book for instructions for downloading the Data Disk or see your instructor for information about accessing the files required in this book. The project consists of two forms. The first form lists employees, hours worked, and hourly rate that are input by the user using the second form. The second form allows the user to enter the three data fields. After the user enters the data, the user clicks the Calculate Weekly Revenue button to generate total revenue for the week.

The Software Consulting Experts project contains bugs in the user interface and in the program code. Run the project to experience some of the problems listed in the steps below. Follow the steps below to debug the project.

1. The lstWeeklyHours control must be anchored so that it maintains its relative size and position with respect to the frmWeeklyReport form, as the form is resized. The control currently is not anchored correctly. The Button controls should maintain their positions relative to the right side of the form.

2. The lstWeeklyHours control requires three column headers: Employee Name, Hours, and Rate. The columns should have the following default widths: 190, 60, 60.

3. The Startup object for the project is not set correctly. Ensure that the Startup object is set to the frmWeeklyReport form. Also, the frmWeeklyReport form has the wrong icon set for its Icon property value. Change the Icon property value to the PC02 icon in the Computer folder where the icons that are installed with Visual Basic .NET are stored.

(continued)

(continued)

4. The Do Until loop tests for a blank value for the Employee name, only after the first record has been entered. This loop causes a blank value to be added to the list, if the user enters a blank value for Employee name as the first record. Correct this error by using the correct form of the Do Until loop for this problem.

5. The For…Next statement used to total the revenue does not properly count the items in the lstWeeklyHours control. The initial value for the loop begins the loop at the wrong index and the limit value ends at the wrong value. Correct this error by using the correct form of the For…Next statement for this problem.

6. The calculation to determine the new width for the first column of the lstWeeklyHours control has a flaw, which results in a poor user interface when the form is resized. Fix this error.

7. When the user presses the DELETE key to delete an item from the lstWeeklyHours control, the program does not ensure that the user first selected an item. Correct this omission by adding an additional condition to the If statement in the lstEmployeeHours click event.

8. Document the form code for both of the forms in the project. Circle the lines of code you modified on the code printout. Run the application. The application should function as shown in Figure 6-77.

FIGURE 6-77

Programming Assignments

1 Averaging Test Scores

Design and write a program that computes an average score for a class's scores on a test. The application should contain two forms. The first includes a two-column list and two buttons. The application should allow the instructor to continue to enter scores until a blank student name is entered.

1. Insert the Data Disk and start a new Windows Application project in Visual Basic .NET. Create the project on the Data Disk in the Chapter6 folder in its own subfolder. Name the project, Test Score Average.

2. Add a ListView control to the upper portion of the form and two Button controls to the lower portion of the form. Set the View property value of the ListView control to Details and the MultiSelect property value to False. Add two column headers to the form: Student Name and Test Score. Use appropriate widths for the columns. Label the buttons Enter Test Scores and Compute Average. Anchor the ListView control to all sides of the form. Anchor the Button controls to the bottom of the form. Give the controls appropriate names. Set the form's Icon property to the GRAPH01.ICO icon file in the Office icon folder.

3. Name the first form, frmAverage, and change the file name of the form to an appropriate name. Add a second form, which the instructor can use to enter the student names and test scores, to the project. Name the form, frmEnterScores, and change the file name of the form to an appropriate name. Add two Label controls, a TextBox control, a NumericUpDown control, and a Button control to the form. Set the Text properties of the Label controls to Student name: and Test score:. Limit input for the Student name to 30 characters. Set the limits on the NumericUpDown control between 0 and 100. Set the Name property of the controls to appropriate values. Set the OK button as the default button on the form.

4. Write a Form Load event procedure to reset the input values to blank for the Student name and 0 for the Test score. Write a Click event procedure for the Button control, which closes the form when the user clicks the button.

5. Return to the first form. Write a Resize event procedure for the form so that the first column in the ListView control shows as much information as possible and the second column maintains a consistent width.

6. Write an event procedure for the ListView control's KeyDown event, which tells the application to delete the currently selected item, if an item is selected and the user presses the key for the letter, d.

7. Write an event procedure for first Button control, so that the application continues to display and accept input from the second form, until the user enters no data for the Student name. Use a Do Until statement to display the form continuously. When the user clicks the OK button on the second form and the Student name is a nonblank value, the input data should be added to the ListView control in the appropriate columns.

8. Write an event procedure for the second button, which computes an average of all scores in the ListView control. The result should be displayed in a message box along with the number of scores included in the calculation. Use a For…Next loop to loop through each item in the ListView control. To compute the average, add up all of the scores and then divide the sum by the total number of items in the ListView control. Separate the output values in the message box with at least one linefeed.

9. Lock the controls on the forms. Set the frmAverage as the Startup object of the project and then save the project.

(continued)

1 Averaging Test Scores (continued)

10. Run the project and correct any errors. If changes have been made, save the project again. The application windows should display during run time, as shown in Figure 6-78.

FIGURE 6-78

2 Checking Daily Sales Totals Using the For Each...Next Statement

Create a version of the Today's Sales Check project completed in this chapter, except use the For Each...Next statement rather than the For...Next statement. Use the code in Figure 6-51 on page VB 6.62 as a starting point for replacing the For...Next statement. If you completed the Today's Sales Check application, use Windows Explorer to create a copy of the Today's Sales Check application in the Chapter6 folder on the Data Disk and name the new project, Today's Sales Check2. If not, develop the application as indicated in the chapter and use the For Each...Next statement as an alternative to the For...Next loop.

3 Computing a Factorial

The symbol N! represents the product of the first N positive integers. Thus 5! = 5 * 4 * 3 * 2 * 1. This is called 5 factorial. The general equation is:

N! = N * (N - 1) * (N - 2) * ... * 1

When a result is defined in terms of itself, it is called a recursive definition. Construct a program that will accept a positive integer from a NumericUpDown control and then compute its factorial when a Button control is clicked. The recursive definition used in the program is as follows:

If N = 1, then N! = 1, otherwise N! = N * (N - 1)!

4 Computing a Fibonacci Sequence

A sequence of Fibonacci numbers begins with integers 1 and 1, and continues endlessly, with each number being the sum of the preceding two numbers:

1, 1, 2, 3, 5, 8, 13, 21, 34, …

Design and develop a program to compute the first X integer numbers of the sequence. where the value of X is entered in a NumericUpDown control. Only accept values for X that are greater than 3 and less than or equal to 150. Display the results in a ListView control that has one column.

5 Money Changer

Design and develop a program that will make change for a one-dollar bill on a sale of less than or equal to one dollar. The program interface should include a NumericUpDown control with a range from 1 cent to 100 cents, in which the user can enter the amount of the sale. The program should determine the number of half dollars, quarters, dimes, nickels, and pennies to be returned to the customer. Develop the program logic to return as many half dollars as possible, then as many quarters as possible, and so on. For example, the output for a sale of $0.64 should be 0 Half Dollar, 1 Quarter, 1 Dime, 0 Nickels, and 1 Penny. After the change has been determined, the program should display the values in a message box. Use the string increment operator to build the output string. Choose an appropriate icon for the form in the application.

6 Reversing a String

Design and develop a program that reverses the text that a user enters into a TextBox control. The text can be from 1 to 50 characters in length. The program should display the reversed text in a message box when the user clicks a button. For example, if the user enters I want a new car in the TextBox control, a message box should display the message, rac wen a tnaw I.

7 Validating Telephone Numbers Using Substrings

Design and develop a program that validates the value a user enters into a TextBox control, to ensure that the entry is a valid telephone number. The application should accept a maximum of 12 characters. When the user clicks a button, the program should determine if the entry is of the form 999-999-9999, where the character, 9, represents any number. If the entry is a telephone number, display an appropriate message, along with the separate substrings that compose the telephone number without the dashes. If the entry is not a telephone number, then display a message as to the reason why the entry is not a valid telephone number, clear the TextBox control, and set focus to the TextBox control. Use the String class methods presented in this chapter to solve the problem. A few hints to help you code the String methods:

First, check that the user has entered two dashes in the appropriate spaces. Next, break the string into 3 substrings, represented as 999, 999, and 9999.

Use the Visual Basic .NET IsNumeric() function to determine whether each substring is a valid number. The function accepts one parameter and returns a True or False value.

8 Creating a Multiplication Table Using Nested For...Next Loops

Design and develop a program that creates a complete set of multiplication tables where both the multiplicand and the multiplier vary from 1 through 12. The table should display as 144 rows in a ListView control. The controls should have five columns: multiplicand, X, multiplier, =, and product. Use a For...Next loop nested in another For...Next loop to vary the multiplicand and multiplier.

9 MultiSelect and Edit ListView Contents

Follow the instructions for modifying the project developed in Programming Assignment 1 on page VB 6.93. Change the MultiSelect property on the ListView control so that the user can select multiple items. Change the ListView control's KeyPress event procedure to delete all selected records when the user presses the D key. Change the ListView control's event procedure to allow the user to edit the item that is the first item selected. If the user presses the E key while an item is selected, the frmEnterScores form should display, with the item's contents populating the input controls in the frmEnterScores form. When the user presses the OK button, the item's contents should update in the ListView control.

10 Using Strings to Create Pig Latin

In pig latin, a word such as television is converted to elevisiontay. For this problem, the translation from English to pig latin calls for taking the first consonant of the word and moving it to the end of the word, followed by an appended "ay." If a word begins with a vowel, then the vowel remains in its beginning position, and the string "way" is appended to the end of the word. For example, always becomes alwaysway.

First design and then write a Visual Basic .NET program that displays the pig latin translation for a string of English words (uppercase). Use the CharacterCasing property of a TextBox control to ensure that the input string is uppercase. Limit the string to 50 characters. Use the MultiLine property of the TextBox control to make the interface more appealing to the user. Also display the number of words that begin with a vowel, the total number of words in the string, and the percentage of words that begin with a vowel. Do not include punctuation in the converted string. Display the converted string and each count separated by NewLine characters in a message box. Use an icon of your choice as the icon for the form.

11 Palindromes

A palindrome is a word or phrase that is the same when read either backward or forward. For example, NOON is a palindrome, but MOON is not. First design and then write a Visual Basic .NET program that displays a message box indicating whether the text entered in a TextBox is a palindrome. Use the CharacterCasing property of a TextBox control to ensure that the input string is uppercase. Limit the string to 25 characters.

7

Using Menus, Common Dialogs, Procedures, Functions, and Arrays

Objectives

You will have
mastered the material in
this chapter when you can:

- Add a menu bar and menus to an application using the MainMenu control
- Add a shortcut menu to an application using the ContextMenu control
- Use the StatusBar control in an application
- Use the PictureBox control in an application
- Use common dialog boxes in an application to interact with the user
- Use one-dimensional and multidimensional arrays in code
- Write a function procedure to return a value
- Write a sub procedure
- Write code to pass arguments to function and sub procedures
- Describe the two methods for passing arguments to function and sub procedures
- Create an enhanced message box with the MessageBox.Show() method
- Use a collection of controls to access properties and methods in code

Introduction

This chapter concentrates on developing the Windows application shown in Figure 7-1. The application consists of one window with a menu bar at the top and a status bar at the bottom (Figure 7-1a). The application also includes a shortcut menu that allows users to select various commands (Figure 7-1i). The application uses message boxes to provide feedback to users, including an enhanced message box that provides options to users when they finish entering data (Figure 7-1d through Figure 7-1f). The application also uses a Font dialog box to allow users to change the font size used to display answer choices (Figure 7-1h).

In this chapter, you will learn how to add a menu bar, a shortcut menu, and a status bar to a form. You also will learn how to use enhanced message boxes and common dialog boxes, such as the Font dialog box, to interact with users. This chapter presents the concept of arrays and shows you how they work much like collections to allow you to manage related data in memory. You will also learn how to use a collection of controls to process a group of controls in code. Finally, you will learn how to write function procedures and sub procedures and how to pass arguments and return values from the function procedures and sub procedures.

Chapter Seven — Creating the Know Your Dogs Quiz

The Windows application developed in this chapter is the Know Your Dogs Quiz application (Figure 7-1a), which is used by a veterinarian to quiz potential part-time summer interns about their knowledge of dog breeds. The application displays a picture of a specific dog breed, which the user must identify by clicking one RadioButton control in a group of RadioButton controls. The current quiz question number displays on the status bar at the bottom of the window. The user can quit the application by using the Exit command on the File menu (Figure 7-1b). To navigate to the first, last, previous, or next question in the quiz, the user either chooses the commands on the Questions menu or presses the corresponding access keys (Figure 7-1c). The user also can navigate to the previous or next question in the quiz by clicking the Previous or Next button. If the user attempts to navigate to a previous question while viewing the first question, a message box displays and informs the user that he or she is at the beginning of the quiz (Figure 7-1d). If the user attempts to navigate to the next question while viewing the last question, a message box displays and provides the user with two options: to display the final quiz result and exit the application or continue checking his or her answers (Figure 7-1e).

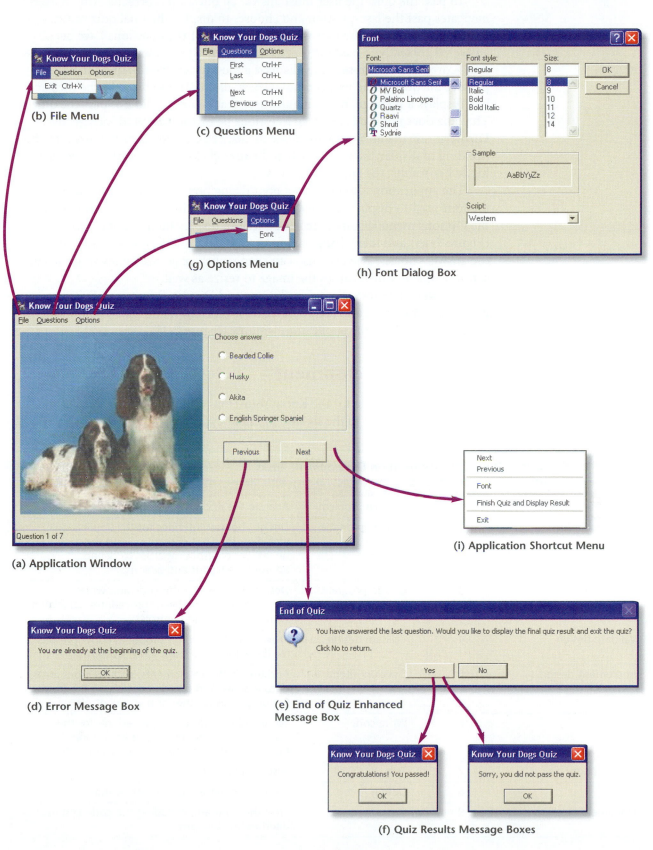

(b) File Menu

(c) Questions Menu

(g) Options Menu

(h) Font Dialog Box

(a) Application Window

(i) Application Shortcut Menu

(d) Error Message Box

(e) End of Quiz Enhanced Message Box

(f) Quiz Results Message Boxes

FIGURE 7-1

To pass the quiz, the user must answer all questions correctly. After a user navigates past the last question and chooses to display the final quiz result, a message box informs the user whether or not all of the questions have been answered correctly to pass the quiz (Figure 7-1f). If the user answered all questions correctly, the message box displays a message congratulating the user on passing the quiz. If the user did not answer all questions correctly, the message box displays a message informing the user that he or she did not pass the quiz. The quiz does not indicate which questions he or she answered incorrectly. Furthermore, the quiz does not allow the user to change his or her answers after deciding to display the results. When the user clicks the OK button after viewing his or her results, the application exits.

The application also includes a Font dialog box, so the user can change the font used to display the answer choices. By clicking the Font command on the Options menu (Figure 7-1g), the user can display the Font dialog box (Figure 7-1h) and then change the font, font style, and font size used to display the answer choices. The user also can change the image size by resizing the application window, which causes the image to resize as well.

The Next, Previous, Font, Finish Quiz and Display Result, and Exit commands just discussed also are available on a shortcut menu that displays when the user right-clicks the application window (Figure 7-1i).

Program Development

The development cycle for the Know Your Dogs Quiz application consists of tasks that correspond to the six development cycle phases, as shown in Table 7-1.

Table 7-1   Know Your Dogs Quiz Application Development Tasks

DEVELOPMENT PHASE	TASK NUMBER	TASK NAME	TASK
Analyze requirements	1	Analyze problem	Analyze the Know Your Dogs Quiz problem.
Design solution	2	Design interface	Design the user interface for the application, including the Font dialog box and the message boxes. Set control properties to define appropriate layout and actions.
	3	Design program	Design the logic for the code and write pseudocode for the event procedures associated with the forms and controls.
Validate design	4	Validate design	Prove that the solution produces correct results for the Know Your Dogs Quiz problem.
Implement design	5	Develop interface	Add user interface elements, such as input areas, output areas, and Button controls on the form. Set properties for the form and controls.
	6	Write code	Write code to add event procedures for the buttons, form, menus, and radio (option) buttons. Add comment statements in code.
Test solution	7	Test	Test the application.
	8	Debug	Fix any problems with the application.
Document solution	9	Document	Print the program, including the code and user interface for the form.

Analysis and Design

Figure 7-2 shows the requirements document that initiates the development cycle for the Know Your Dogs Quiz application.

REQUEST FOR NEW APPLICATION

Date submitted:	November 11, 2004
Submitted by:	Patricia Wolinsky
Purpose:	Each spring, I interview numerous high school candidates for summer internship positions at my veterinarian clinic. In order to help me select the candidates who will give the animals the best care, I screen them with quizzes regarding animals. I'd like a quiz that quickly tests a candidate's familiarity with several dog breeds. I will start the application for the user and proctor the quiz.
Application title:	Know Your Dogs Quiz
Algorithms:	If all questions are answered correctly, a message displays indicating that the candidate has passed the quiz. If any question is answered incorrectly, a message displays indicating that the candidate did not pass the quiz.
Notes:	1) The quiz consists of seven questions. Each question consists of an image and four possible answers. I have included an attached list and files for image file names, images, an icon for the application, answer choices, and the solutions.
	2) When the application begins, the first image and four answer choices for that image should display. The answer choices should be labeled, Choose answer.
	3) The application window should be resizable. When the user resizes the window, the image also should resize so that the user can get a better look. Similarly, the user should be able to increase the font of the answers.
	4) The user should be able to exit the application at any time and view the quiz result.
	5) The user should be able to navigate to the next and previous questions through use of the keyboard, buttons, a menu, and a shortcut menu. The user also should be able to navigate directly to the first or last question, using a menu.
	6) If the user attempts to navigate to a question before the first question, an error message box should display. If the user attempts to navigate past the last question, a message box should display and ask the user whether he or she wants to display the quiz results and exit the application or return to the quiz to continue checking answers.
	7) The application should include a status bar that tells the user which question of the seven questions currently is displayed.

Approvals

Approval Status:	X	Approved
		Rejected
Approved by:	Leslie Broda	
Date:	November 18, 2004	
Assigned to:	J. Quasney, Programmer	

FIGURE 7-2

PROBLEM ANALYSIS   The problem that the Know Your Dogs Quiz application must solve is to present seven quiz questions to a user, track the user's answers, and then display the quiz results to the user. As stated in the requirements document (Figure 7-2), the application begins by displaying the first question, which consists of an image and four possible answer choices. The user selects one of the four option buttons to indicate the answer he or she thinks matches the image. The user then navigates to another question using buttons, a menu, or the keyboard. After completing all seven of the questions, the user can review the chosen answers to determine if he or she correctly identified all of the images.

The requirements document also states that the application should include navigation elements that allow the user to move to the previous or next question in the question order. The user also must be able to navigate to the first or last question. The application also should allow the user to resize the application window to enlarge the image to get a better view and to change the font used to display the answer choices. Finally, the application should inform the user which question of the seven currently is displayed.

INTERFACE DESIGN   The interface for the Know Your Dogs Quiz application requires two forms and several message boxes. The first form displays the image, the choices for the answer, and navigational interface elements, such as menus and buttons. The second form is used as the Font dialog box that allows the user to modify the font used to display the answer choices.

Figure 7-3 shows a storyboard that outlines the interface requirements for the two forms and the message boxes. As shown in Figure 7-3, the main form includes a menu bar, a shortcut menu, an image, a GroupBox control that contains four RadioButton controls, two Button controls, and a status bar. The menu bar includes three menus with commands that allow the user to navigate the quiz, exit the application, or display the Font dialog box. Menus allow you to group commands logically in a concise manner that is familiar to users. Making commands accessible via menus instead of buttons helps ensure that the user interface does not become too cluttered. You can, however, duplicate important commands in Button controls or other controls for convenience. In this application, a **MainMenu control** is used to add the menu bar to the form.

Using Menus in an Application
Use menus to group commands logically in a concise manner. Duplicate important commands in Button controls or other controls for convenience.

The main form also includes a shortcut menu, in addition to the main menu. In Windows applications, a **shortcut menu** is used to provide users with an easily accessible menu of commands that are useful for the user given the context of the application. A user accesses a shortcut menu by right-clicking an area on the screen, desktop, or form, in this case. In this application, the shortcut menu duplicates often-used functions, such as navigating to the previous or next question. A **ContextMenu control** is used to add the shortcut menu to the form.

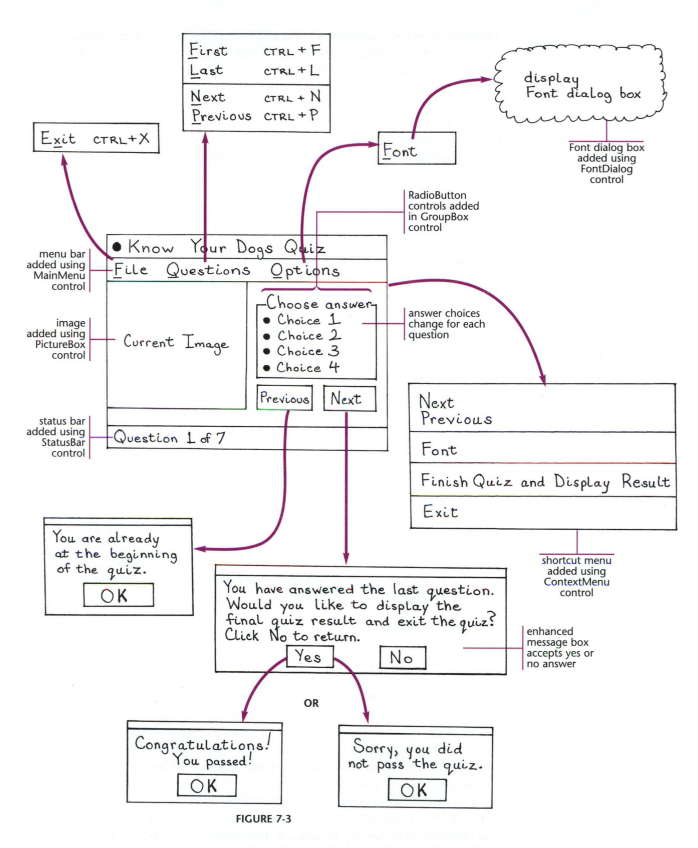

FIGURE 7-3

A PictureBox control is used to display the image on the form. A **PictureBox control** allows you to display a variety of image formats and perform some basic operations on the images, such as resizing. Finally, the form displays the current question number on a status bar. A **StatusBar control** allows you to place several panels containing status information in a window. Typically, a StatusBar control anchors to the bottom of a form.

The requirements document (Figure 7-2 on page VB 7.05) also states that the form should be resizable and that the image should resize along with the control. The PictureBox control, GroupBox control, and Button controls, therefore, must anchor to the proper sides of the form.

The second form, the Font dialog box, should display the Font dialog box that users are accustomed to using in Windows applications. The Font dialog box, along with other commonly used dialog boxes such as those used to open, save, or print files, is known as a **common dialog box**. Visual Basic .NET provides several controls, called **common dialog controls,** which are used to create and modify common dialog boxes in Visual Basic .NET. In the Know Your Dogs Quiz application, a common dialog control called the **FontDialog control** will be used to provide the interface for the Font dialog box that allows the user to modify the font used in the application.

Using Common Dialog Controls

Use common dialog controls whenever possible as a shortcut to creating and managing common dialog boxes, such as those used for font, save file, open file, and print.

Figure 7-3 on page VB 7.07 shows four message boxes that display when certain events occur. When the user attempts to navigate to a question before the first question, a message box displays an error message. When the user attempts to navigate beyond the last question, an enhanced message box containing an icon and two buttons displays. If the user clicks the Yes button to display the final quiz result, one of two message boxes displays to indicate the result. If the user clicks the No button, the message box closes and the main form displays. This enhanced message box is implemented by passing several optional parameters to the MessageBox.Show() method.

PROGRAM DESIGN   Figure 7-4 on page VB 7.10 shows two flowcharts that represent the key logic in the application. The first flowchart (Figure 7-4a) represents the logic for the procedure that changes the question that displays in the window at run time. The procedure accepts an argument that represents the question number the procedure should attempt to display in the window. This procedure is not an event procedure, but rather a sub procedure, which is a unit of code you name and can call from other procedures. A sub procedure only executes when called from code you write in other procedures. A sub procedure is used for this functionality because the logic is required many times in the program.

The logic in the flowcharts in Figure 7-4 uses a special type of variable, called an **array**, that can hold many values rather than just one value. An array provides a way to give several variables a common name and use an index to access each item. When writing pseudocode or code for an array, the array is written with the array name followed by the index in parentheses. The design consists of several arrays. The first array, Answers, consists of a list of answers entered by the user. The second array, Solution, consists of a list of correct answers and contains one entry for each question. The third array, QuestionChoice, contains the four answer choices for each question. This type of array has two indexes. The first index refers to the question number (1 to 7), and the second index refers to the question choice (1 to 4). When referring to an item in such an array, the indexes are in parentheses to the right of the variable name, and separated by commas. The last array, PictureFile, contains a list of file names for the image that displays with each question.

As outlined in the flowchart in Figure 7-4, the first task of the Display Question procedure is to determine whether the user is attempting to access a question before the first question. If so, the procedure next displays an error message and exits. If not, the procedure determines which RadioButton control was selected and then saves the answer in the correct location in the Answers array. The procedure then unchecks the checked RadioButton control so that no RadioButton control is selected when the next question displays. The next task for the procedure is to check whether the user is trying to navigate beyond the seventh question. If so, the procedure displays a message box that asks the user if he or she wants to display the final quiz result or continue with the quiz. If the user wants to continue with the quiz, the procedure sets the question number back to the last question and the procedure exits. If the user wants to see the result, the procedure scores the quiz, displays the result, and then exits.

If the user is navigating to a valid question number, beginning with the process symbol Count = 1, the procedure loops through each RadioButton control and updates the caption on the RadioButton control to the answer choices for the proper question. The procedure then sets the image on the form to the image in the PictureFile array that corresponds to the question number being displayed. The procedure updates the status bar with the current question number, sets a global variable to hold the value of the current question number, and exits.

The second flowchart (Figure 7-4b) represents the logic for a procedure that determines whether the user has passed the quiz. This special type of procedure, called a function procedure, returns a value to the function name in the procedure that called it. A function procedure is called by other code in much the same manner that methods or intrinsic functions are called. In this case, the decision statement that will correspond to the decision symbol containing the question Quiz Result = True in Figure 7-4a calls the function procedure. This function procedure, Quiz Result, loops once for each question and compares each item in the Answers array with the corresponding item in the Solution array. If any Answer item does not match the corresponding Solution item, the function procedure exits and returns a False value back to the function name in the line of code that called it. If all Answer items match the corresponding Solution items, the Do While structure exits and the function returns a True value back to the function name in the line of code that called it.

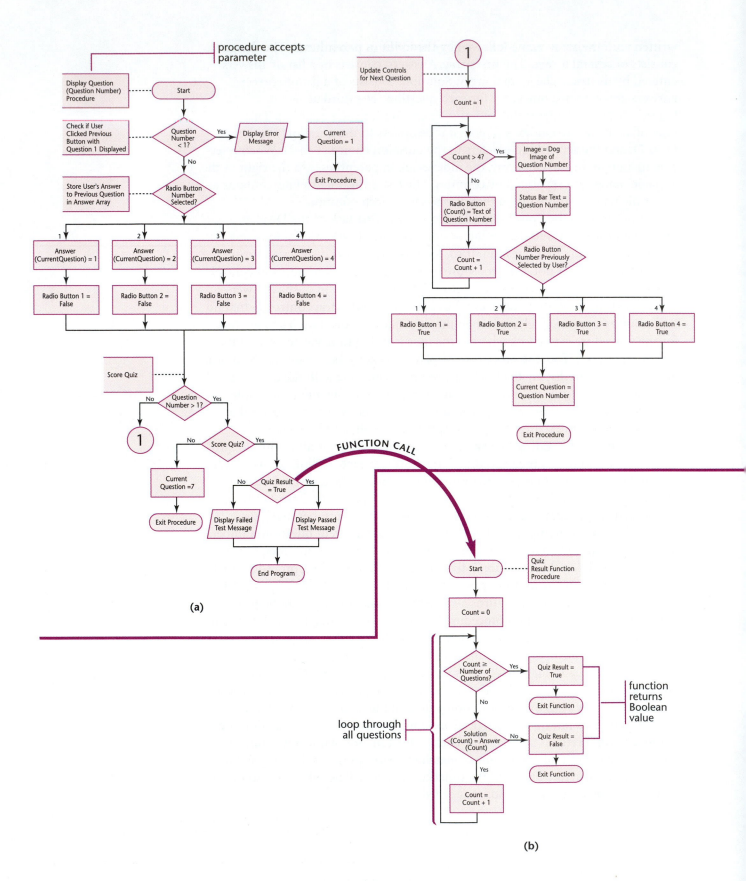

FIGURE 7-4

Figure 7-5 shows pseudocode for the procedures needed in the project, based on the flowcharts in Figure 7-4.

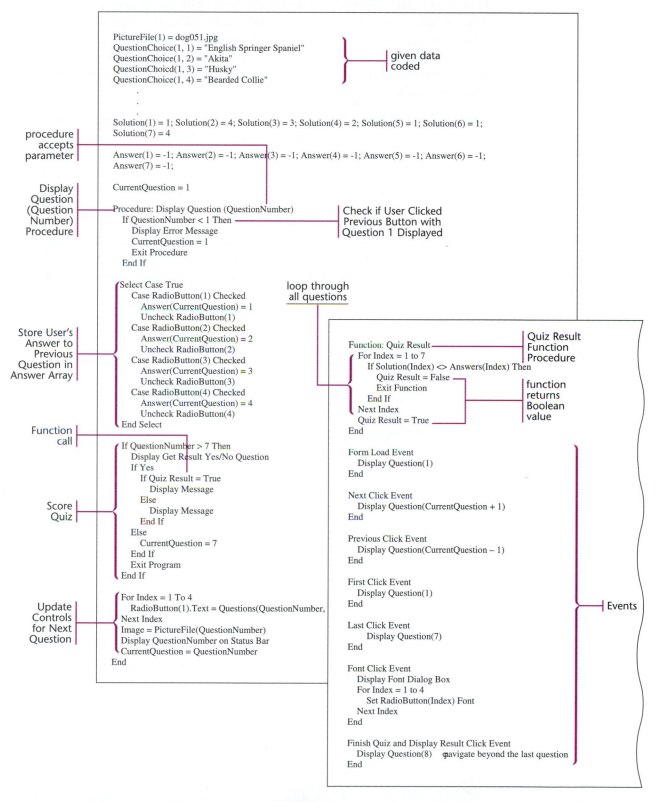

PictureFile(1) = dog051.jpg
QuestionChoice(1, 1) = "English Springer Spaniel"
QuestionChoice(1, 2) = "Akita"
QuestionChoicd(1, 3) = "Husky"
QuestionChoice(1, 4) = "Bearded Collie"
 .
 .
 .
Solution(1) = 1; Solution(2) = 4; Solution(3) = 3; Solution(4) = 2; Solution(5) = 1; Solution(6) = 1;
Solution(7) = 4

Answer(1) = -1; Answer(2) = -1; Answer(3) = -1; Answer(4) = -1; Answer(5) = -1; Answer(6) = -1;
Answer(7) = -1;

CurrentQuestion = 1

Procedure: Display Question (QuestionNumber)
    If QuestionNumber < 1 Then
        Display Error Message
        CurrentQuestion = 1
        Exit Procedure
    End If

    Select Case True
        Case RadioButton(1) Checked
            Answer(CurrentQuestion) = 1
            Uncheck RadioButton(1)
        Case RadioButton(2) Checked
            Answer(CurrentQuestion) = 2
            Uncheck RadioButton(2)
        Case RadioButton(3) Checked
            Answer(CurrentQuestion) = 3
            Uncheck RadioButton(3)
        Case RadioButton(4) Checked
            Answer(CurrentQuestion) = 4
            Uncheck RadioButton(4)
    End Select

    If QuestionNumber > 7 Then
        Display Get Result Yes/No Question
        If Yes
            If Quiz Result = True
                Display Message
            Else
                Display Message
            End If
        Else
            CurrentQuestion = 7
        End If
        Exit Program
    End If

    For Index = 1 To 4
        RadioButton(1).Text = Questions(QuestionNumber,
    Next Index
    Image = PictureFile(QuestionNumber)
    Display QuestionNumber on Status Bar
    CurrentQuestion = QuestionNumber
End

given data coded

procedure accepts parameter

Display Question (Question Number) Procedure

Check if User Clicked Previous Button with Question 1 Displayed

Store User's Answer to Previous Question in Answer Array

loop through all questions

Function: Quiz Result
    For Index = 1 to 7
        If Solution(Index) <> Answers(Index) Then
            Quiz Result = False
            Exit Function
        End If
    Next Index
    Quiz Result = True
End

Quiz Result Function Procedure

function returns Boolean value

Function call

Score Quiz

Update Controls for Next Question

Form Load Event
    Display Question(1)
End

Next Click Event
    Display Question(CurrentQuestion + 1)
End

Previous Click Event
    Display Question(CurrentQuestion – 1)
End

First Click Event
    Display Question(1)
End

Last Click Event
    Display Question(7)
End

Font Click Event
    Display Font Dialog Box
    For Index = 1 to 4
        Set RadioButton(Index) Font
    Next Index
End

Finish Quiz and Display Result Click Event
    Display Question(8)   navigate beyond the last question
End

Events

FIGURE 7-5

Pseudocode is only shown once for the navigation-related event procedures, such as Next Click Event, even though they are used in several event procedures. For example, the Next Button control, the Next main menu item, and the Next shortcut menu item all use the Next Click Event. When coding the navigation-related event procedures, however, you do not have to duplicate the code and, therefore, the pseudocode is not duplicated. Table 7-2 on page VB 7.13 lists the procedures, the events that trigger the event procedures, and the actions performed by each.

VALIDATE DESIGN   The validation of the design is accomplished by stepping through the requirements document to ensure that all of the requirements are met in a sound manner and that the program logic is sound. The requirements listed in note 1 are met with the arrays discussed in the Program Design, where the questions, solution, and file names for the images are stored in an array. The image files reside on the hard disk. The requirement in note 2 is met in the Form Load Event, which passes the value of 1 to the Display Question procedure, thus initiating the quiz. Note 3 will be addressed by setting properties of the image and form to ensure that they are sizable. The menu bar, shortcut menu, and buttons handle the requirements in notes 4 and 5 by providing navigation through the questions and the ability to exit the application at any time. The boundary conditions listed in note 6 occur when the user attempts to navigate beyond the first or seventh question. The Display Question procedure handles these conditions and displays appropriate messages. The status bar requirement listed in note 7 is addressed by the status bar that displays at the bottom of the application window. Finally, the requirements listed in the Algorithms section of the requirements document are handled by the Quiz Result function procedure, which validates the user's answers and returns a True or False value that indicates the result.

Table 7-2 Know Your Dogs Quiz Procedures

PROCEDURE	EVENT	ACTION PERFORMED
Display Question	N/A	Displays a question based on a question number passed to the procedure; does not allow user to navigate to a question beyond the first or last question; if user attempts to navigate beyond the last question, the procedure asks if user wants to see the quiz results; if user clicks the Yes button, the quiz results are displayed
Quiz Result	N/A	Determines whether user answered all questions correctly; returns a True or False value based on the result
Form Load Event	Executes when the form displays	Displays the first image and answer choices on the form
Next Button Click Event	Executes when the user clicks the Next button on the form	Calls the Display Question procedure and passes it the next question number
Next Main Menu Click Event	Executes when the user clicks the Next command on the Questions menu	Calls the Display Question procedure and passes it the next question number
Next Shortcut Menu Click Event	Executes when the user clicks the Next command on the shortcut menu	Calls the Display Question procedure and passes it the next question number
Previous Button Click Event	Executes when the user clicks the Previous button on the form	Calls the Display Question procedure and passes it the previous question number
Previous Main Menu Click Event	Executes when the user clicks the Previous command on the Questions menu	Calls the Display Question procedure and passes it the previous question number
Previous Shortcut Menu Click Event	Executes when the user clicks the Previous command on the shortcut menu	Calls the Display Question procedure and passes it the previous question number
First Main Menu Click Event	Executes when the user clicks the First command on the Questions menu	Calls the Display Question procedure and passes it the first question number
First Shortcut Menu Click Event	Executes when the user clicks the First command on the shortcut menu	Calls the Display Question procedure and passes it the first question number
Last Main Menu Click Event	Executes when the user clicks the Last command on the Questions menu	Calls the Display Question procedure and passes it the last question number
Last Shortcut Menu Click Event	Executes when the user clicks the Last command on the shortcut menu	Calls the Display Question procedure and passes it the last question number
Exit Menu Click Event	Executes when the user clicks the Exit command on the File menu	Exits the application
Exit Shortcut Menu Click Event	Executes when the user clicks the Exit command on the shortcut menu	Exits the application
Font Menu Click Event	Executes when the user clicks the Font command on the Options menu	Displays the Font dialog box, then sets the font of the RadioButton controls
Font Shortcut Menu Click Event	Executes when the user clicks the Font command on the shortcut menu	Displays the Font dialog box, then sets the font of the RadioButton controls
Finish Quiz and Display Result Shortcut Menu Click Event	Executes when the user clicks the Finish Quiz and Display Result command on the shortcut menu	Displays the quiz result and exits the application

Creating the User Interface

The Know Your Dogs Quiz application is a Windows application with a graphical user interface for user input and output display (Figure 7-1a on page VB 7.03). The user interface consists of a form that contains a menu bar, a shortcut menu, and several controls. The application is based on the Windows Application template provided by Visual Basic .NET. The following steps start Visual Basic .NET and then start a new project using the Windows Application template.

To Start Visual Basic .NET and Start a New Project

1. Insert the Data Disk in drive A.

2. Start Visual Basic .NET. When the Start Page displays, click the New Project button on the Start Page.

3. When the New Project dialog box displays, if necessary, click Create directory for Solution. Double-click the text, WindowsApplication1, in the Name box. Type Know Your Dogs Quiz in the Name box.

The new project name displays in the Name box, and the solution name displays in the New Solution Name box. Because the Create directory for Solution check box is selected, Visual Basic .NET will create a subdirectory with the same name as the project when it creates the project.

4. Click the Browse button. If necessary, click 3½ Floppy (A:) in the Look in box. Click Chapter7 and then click the Open button.

5. Click the OK button. After the new Know Your Dogs Quiz project is created, if necessary, click the Maximize button on the Visual Basic .NET window title bar to maximize the Visual Basic .NET window. If necessary, close the Output window.

Visual Basic .NET creates the Know Your Dogs Quiz solution and project. Visual Basic .NET creates an initial form and displays it in the main work area.

After Visual Basic .NET creates the new project, the solution and project name, Know Your Dogs Quiz, displays in the Solution Explorer window. Form1.vb is selected in the Solution Explorer window to indicate that the Form1.vb[Design] tab is selected in the main work area. The Properties window displays information about Form1.vb.

Setting Form Properties and Adding Controls

The next step is to set the properties of the Form1 form and add controls to the form. Several of the property values of the Form1 form must be changed. For example, the Form1 form should include a dog icon on the title bar to distinguish the form from other applications running in Windows. Table 7-3 lists the Form1 form property value changes that need to be made.

Table 7-3   Form1 Form Property Values for the Know Your Dogs Quiz Application

PROPERTY	PROPERTY VALUE	EFFECT
Size: Width	598	Sets the width of the form in pixels
Size: Height	392	Sets the height of the form in pixels
StartPosition	CenterScreen	Causes the form to display in the center of the user's screen at the start of run time
Text	Know Your Dogs Quiz	Sets the value of the title bar on the window
Icon	doggy.ico	Sets the icon that displays to the left of the title on the title bar

The user interface design (Figure 7-3 on page VB 7.07) also specifies that the Form1 form should include one PictureBox control, a GroupBox control that includes four RadioButton controls, a MainMenu control, a ContextMenu control, a StatusBar control, a FontDialog control, and two Button controls. The PictureBox control allows you to display an image to the user. The MainMenu and ContextMenu controls group related sets of commands. The StatusBar control anchors to the bottom of the form and allows you to display messages to the user. The FontDialog control includes methods that allow you to display a Font dialog box, so the user can select font options.

Some controls do not have typical visual interfaces that easily can be drawn on a form at design time. For example, a MainMenu control initially does not contain any commands on the menu and, thus, nothing displays for the menu on the form. Similarly, ContextMenu and FontDialog controls do not include interfaces that display during design time. When you add such controls to a form, Visual Basic .NET places an icon for the control in the Component Tray. The **Component Tray**, which is an area below the form that represents controls that do not have a visual interface on the form at design time, provides a way for users to access and set the properties of those controls, or components. When a MainMenu or ContextMenu control is selected in the Component Tray, Visual Basic .NET also displays the **Menu Designer**, which allows you to create the commands that display on the menus at run time. The Menu Designer will be used later in this chapter.

The steps on the following pages set the Form1 form properties, as shown in Table 7-3, and then add the controls by drawing them on the form.

To Set Form Properties and Add Controls

1. With Form1 selected, set the properties of the Form1 form as specified in Table 7-3 on page VB 7.15. To set the Icon property value, use the icon, doggy.ico, which is located in the Chapter7 folder on the Data Disk. Add a MainMenu control to the form by dragging the MainMenu button from the Toolbox window to the form.

The form properties are set and the form is sized properly, the icon displays on the title bar, and the form title is set. The MainMenu1 control displays in the Component Tray below the form (Figure 7-6). Because the MainMenu1 control is selected in the Component Tray, the Menu Designer displays at the top of the form, below the form's title bar.

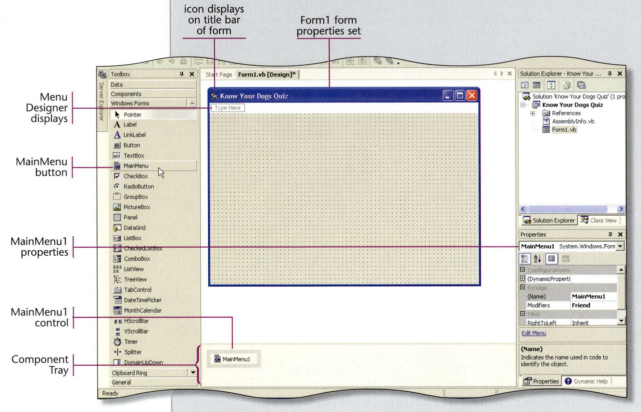

FIGURE 7-6

2. Add a StatusBar control by dragging the StatusBar button from the Toolbox window to the bottom of the Form1 form, as shown in Figure 7-7.

The StatusBar1 control anchors to the bottom, left, and right sides of the form (Figure 7-7). Visual Basic .NET automatically sets the height of the StatusBar1 control to a default height of 22 pixels. Because the MainMenu1 control no longer is selected in the Component Tray, Visual Basic .NET no longer displays the Menu Designer.

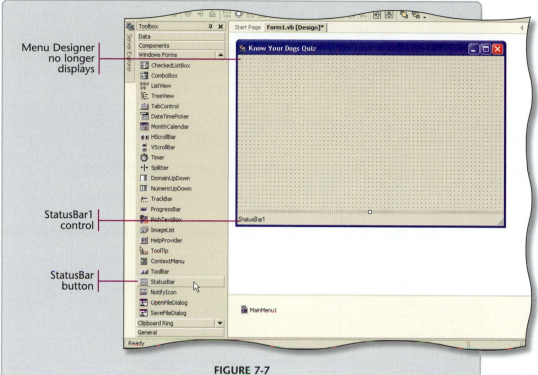

FIGURE 7-7

3. Add one PictureBox control, one GroupBox control, four RadioButton controls inside the GroupBox control, and two Button controls by dragging the appropriate buttons from the Toolbox window to Form1, as shown in Figure 7-8.

The controls are added to the form (Figure 7-8). The PictureBox control displays as a gray box.

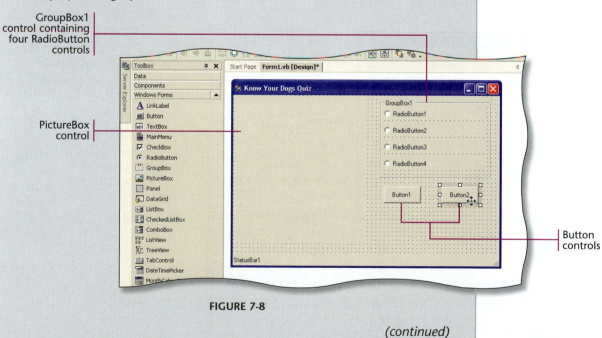

FIGURE 7-8

(continued)

4. Add a ContextMenu control to the form by dragging the ContextMenu button from the Toolbox window to the form.

Visual Basic .NET adds the ContextMenu1 control to the Component Tray (Figure 7-9). Because the ContextMenu1 control is selected in the Component Tray, Visual Basic .NET displays the Menu Designer at the top of the form.

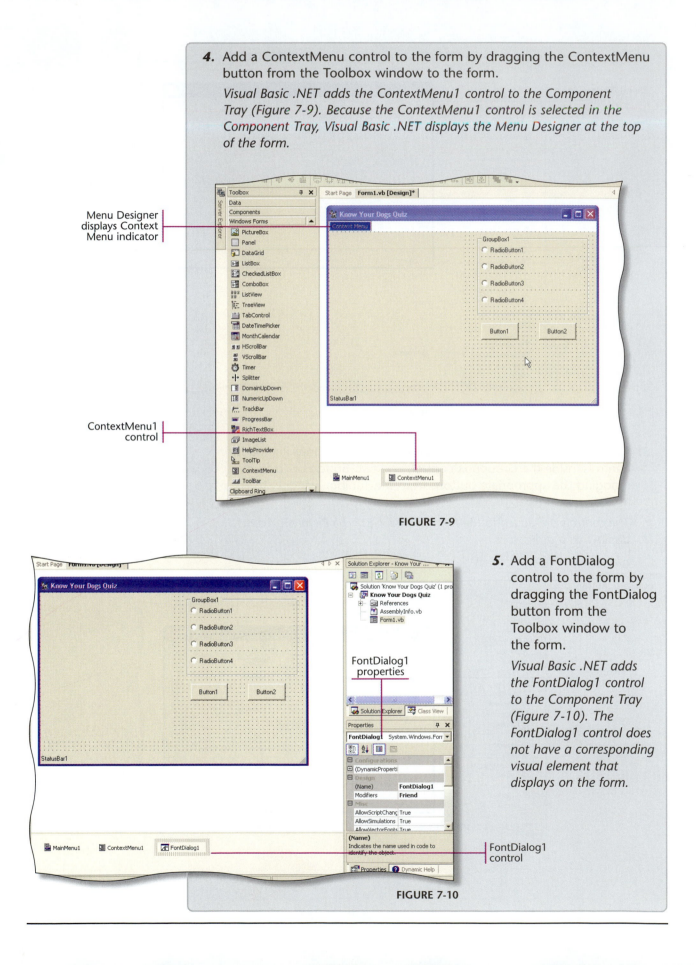

FIGURE 7-9

FIGURE 7-10

5. Add a FontDialog control to the form by dragging the FontDialog button from the Toolbox window to the form.

Visual Basic .NET adds the FontDialog1 control to the Component Tray (Figure 7-10). The FontDialog1 control does not have a corresponding visual element that displays on the form.

As indicated in the requirements document (Figure 7-2 on page VB 7.05), the Form1 form remains sizable at run time. When the user resizes the form, the PictureBox1 control also resizes to give the user a better view of the image displayed in the control.

As shown in Figure 7-10, when a control is selected in the Component Tray, Visual Basic .NET displays its properties in the Properties window so that you can modify its properties just as you modify control properties of controls that display on the form.

Changing GroupBox, RadioButton, and Button Control Properties

The next step is to set the properties for the GroupBox, RadioButton, and Button controls, which must be named, sized, positioned, and labeled as described in the interface design on page VB 7.06. Table 7-4 lists the property values that must be set for these controls.

Table 7-4   *GroupBox, RadioButton, and Button Control Property Values for the Know Your Dogs Quiz Application*

CONTROL	PROPERTY	PROPERTY VALUE	EFFECT
GroupBox1	Name	grpAnswer	Changes the control's name to a descriptive name
	Text	Choose answer	Sets the text that displays on the top of the control to Choose answer
	TabIndex	0	Causes this control to be the first control on the form to receive focus
	Size: Width	216	Sets the width of the control in pixels
	Size: Height	152	Sets the height of the control in pixels
	Location: X (left)	296	Indicates the distance from the left border of the form in pixels
	Location: Y (top)	8	Indicates the distance from the top border of the form in pixels
	Anchor	Top, Right	Anchors the control to the top and right of the form when the user resizes the form
RadioButton1	Name	radAnswer1	Changes the control's name to a descriptive name
	TabIndex	0	Causes this control to be the first control in the GroupBox to receive focus
	Size: Width	192	Sets the width of the control in pixels
	Size: Height	24	Sets the height of the control in pixels
	Location: X (left)	16	Indicates the distance from the left border of the GroupBox in pixels
	Location: Y (top)	24	Indicates the distance from the top border of the GroupBox in pixels

(continued)

Table 7-4 **GroupBox, RadioButton, and Button Control Property Values for the Know Your Dogs Quiz Application** *(continued)*

CONTROL	PROPERTY	PROPERTY VALUE	EFFECT
RadioButton2	Name	radAnswer2	Changes the control's name to a descriptive name
	TabIndex	1	Causes this control to be the second control in the GroupBox to receive focus
	Size: Width	192	Sets the width of the control in pixels
	Size: Height	24	Sets the height of the control in pixels
	Location: X (left)	16	Indicates the distance from the left border of the GroupBox in pixels
	Location: Y (top)	56	Indicates the distance from the top border of the GroupBox in pixels
RadioButton3	Name	radAnswer3	Changes the control's name to a descriptive name
	TabIndex	2	Causes this control to be the third control in the GroupBox to receive focus
	Size: Width	192	Sets the width of the control in pixels
	Size: Height	24	Sets the height of the control in pixels
	Location: X (left)	16	Indicates the distance from the left border of the GroupBox in pixels
	Location: Y (top)	88	Indicates the distance from the top border of the GroupBox in pixels
RadioButton4	Name	radAnswer4	Changes the control's name to a descriptive name
	TabIndex	3	Causes this control to be the fourth control in the GroupBox to receive focus
	Size: Width	192	Sets the width of the control in pixels
	Size: Height	24	Sets the height of the control in pixels
	Location: X (left)	16	Indicates the distance from the left border of the GroupBox in pixels
	Location: Y (top)	120	Indicates the distance from the top border of the GroupBox in pixels
Button1	Text	Previous	Sets the text that displays on the button face to Previous
	TabIndex	1	Causes this control to be the second control on the form to receive focus
	Name	btnPrevious	Changes the control's name to a descriptive name
	Size: Width	72	Sets the width of the control in pixels
	Size: Height	32	Sets the height of the control in pixels
	Location: X (left)	320	Indicates the distance from the left border of the form in pixels
	Location: Y (top)	176	Indicates the distance from the top border of the form in pixels
	Anchor	Top, Right	Anchors the control to the top and right of the form when the user resizes the form

Table 7-4 **GroupBox, RadioButton, and Button Control Property Values for the Know Your Dogs Quiz Application** *(continued)*

CONTROL	PROPERTY	PROPERTY VALUE	EFFECT
Button2	Text	Next	Sets the text that displays on the button face to Next
	TabIndex	2	Causes this control to be the third control on the form to receive focus
	Name	btnNext	Changes the control's name to a descriptive name
	Size: Width	72	Sets the width of the control in pixels
	Size: Height	32	Sets the height of the control in pixels
	Location: X (left)	408	Indicates the distance from the left border of the form in pixels
	Location: Y (top)	176	Indicates the distance from the top border of the form in pixels
	Anchor	Top, Right	Anchors the control to the top and right of the form when the user resizes the form

The following steps set the property values of the GroupBox, RadioButton, and Button controls on the Form1 form.

To Change Properties of the GroupBox, RadioButton, and Button Controls

1. Change the property values of the GroupBox, RadioButton, and Button controls, as listed in Table 7-4.

   The controls display on the Form1 form, as shown in Figure 7-11.

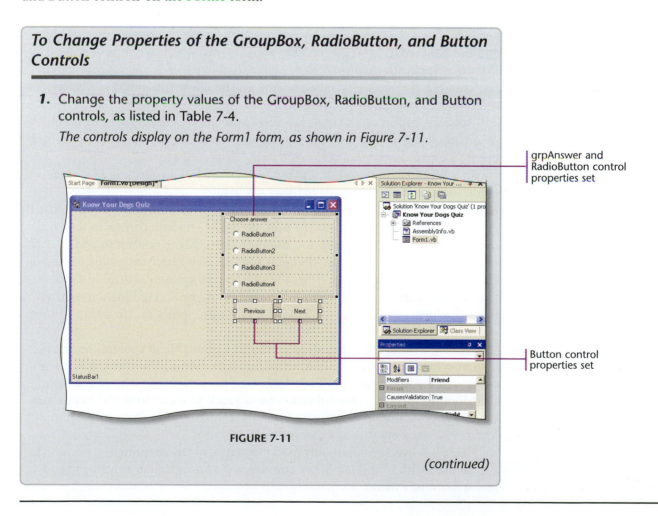

grpAnswer and RadioButton control properties set

Button control properties set

FIGURE 7-11

(continued)

2. Select the radAnswer2 control and then click the Send to Back button on the Layout toolbar. Select the radAnswer3 control and then click the Send to Back button on the Layout toolbar. Select the radAnswer4 control and then click the Send to Back button on the Layout toolbar.

The last step in the previous set of steps ensures that the controls are in the proper order within the GroupBox control. That is, the first RadioButton control is the top control within the GroupBox. Later in this chapter, the order of the controls will be important when writing code that places the answer choices in the RadioButton controls.

The properties of the GroupBox, RadioButton, and Button controls are set. The next task is to set properties for the new controls presented in this chapter, including the MainMenu, ContextMenu, StatusBar, PictureBox, and FontDialog controls. The first step is to set the properties for the MainMenu control to create a menu bar and menus on the form.

Creating Menus on a Menu Bar

The menu bar of the Know Your Dogs Quiz application consists of three menus: File, Questions, and Options (Figure 7-1a on page VB 7.03). A user selects one of these menus during run time either by clicking the menu name on the menu bar or by pressing an access key. An **access key** is an assigned letter key that allows the user to display a menu at run time by pressing the ALT key and the assigned letter key. Access key assignments, which are common in Windows applications, display as an underlined letter in the menu command. For example, the letter F is the access key for the File menu and thus displays underlined on the menu bar (Figure 7-1a).

Access keys also can be used to select menu commands. To select a menu command using an access key, you press only the access key of a command (not the ALT key) to choose that command in the displayed menu.

In a Windows application, a menu is composed of a collection of several menu items, including commands, menu separators, and submenus. The MainMenu and ContextMenu controls are the two menu controls used in Visual Basic .NET to add menus to forms. You use the MainMenu control to add a menu bar at the top of a form. You use the ContextMenu control to add shortcut menus to forms and controls. After you add one or both of these types of controls to a form during design time, you can select the menu control in the Component Tray and then use the Properties window and the Menu Designer to set the menu name, add menu items, and set properties for the menu commands, such as the caption and access key.

In Visual Basic .NET, the MainMenu and ContextMenu controls serve as containers for one or more MenuItems, much like GroupBox controls serve as containers for other controls. Each command on a menu is a MenuItem from the **MenuItem class**. A **MenuItem** behaves much like a control and has properties and events. You set the properties of a MenuItem in the Properties window, just as you set properties of other controls.

Table 7-5 lists the commonly used properties of the MenuItem class, which can be used with both MainMenu controls and ContextMenu controls to add menu items to a menu.

Table 7-5   *MenuItem Class Properties*

CATEGORY	PROPERTY	DESCRIPTION	PROPERTY VALUES
Misc	Checked	Indicates whether a check mark appears next to the text of the menu item	True **False**
	DefaultItem	Indicates whether the menu item is the default menu item	True **False**
	Enabled	Indicates whether the menu item is enabled	**True** False
	RadioCheck	Indicates whether the MenuItem is enabled, if checked, displays an option button instead of a check mark	True **False**
	Shortcut	Indicates the shortcut key associated with the menu item	Select from a list of keys (default is **None**)
	Text	Sets the text (caption) that displays on the menu for the menu item	Any text

The requirements for the Know Your Dogs Quiz application indicate three menu items on the menu bar: File, Questions, and Options. Each MenuItem object has a Name property that allows you to change the default MenuItem name to a descriptive name. When naming a MenuItem, you should use the mnu prefix to indicate a member of the MenuItem class.

Each menu item also requires an access key. To define an access key, type an ampersand (&) before the letter you want to assign as the access key when you enter the Text property value for the MenuItem object.

Several of the menu items also require shortcut keys. A shortcut key is one or more assigned keys that cause the event procedure for a menu item's Click event to execute. A **shortcut key** differs from an access key. While an access key is used to select a menu or menu command, a shortcut key is used to execute the command when a user presses the key or keys while the menu displays during run time. For example, as shown in Figure 7-3 on page VB 7.07, the shortcut key, CTRL+N, is assigned to the Next command on the Questions menu. If the user presses the keys, CTRL+N, when the Questions menu displays, the Next Main Menu Click Event procedure executes.

Table 7-6 on the next page lists the MenuItems that must be added to the MainMenu1 control to define the three menus and the associated menu commands, along with the properties that must be set for each MenuItem.

Tip

Naming a MenuItem
When naming a MenuItem, use the mnu prefix to indicate a member of the MenuItem class.

Table 7-6 MenuItem Properties for the MainMenu1 Control in the Know Your Dogs Quiz Application

MENU	COMMAND	PROPERTY VALUE	VALUE
File	File	Name	mnuFile
		Text	&File
	Exit	Name	mnuExit
		Text	E&xit
Questions	Questions	Name	mnuQuestions
		Text	&Questions
	First	Name	mnuFirst
		Text	&First
		Shortcut	CtrlF
	Last	Name	mnuLast
		Text	&Last
		Shortcut	CtrlL
	Next	Name	mnuNext
		Text	&Next
		Shortcut	CtrlN
	Previous	Name	mnuPrevious
		Text	&Previous
		Shortcut	CtrlP
Options	Options	Name	mnuOptions
		Text	&Options
	Font	Name	mnuFont
		Text	&Font

The following steps create the three menus in the Know Your Dogs Quiz application one at a time, using the MenuItem properties listed in Table 7-6.

To Create Menus on a Menu Bar for a Form

1. Click the MainMenu1 control in the Component Tray.

Visual Basic .NET displays a gray border around the MainMenu1 control in the Component Tray to indicate it is selected. The Menu Designer displays at the top of the Form1 form (Figure 7-12).

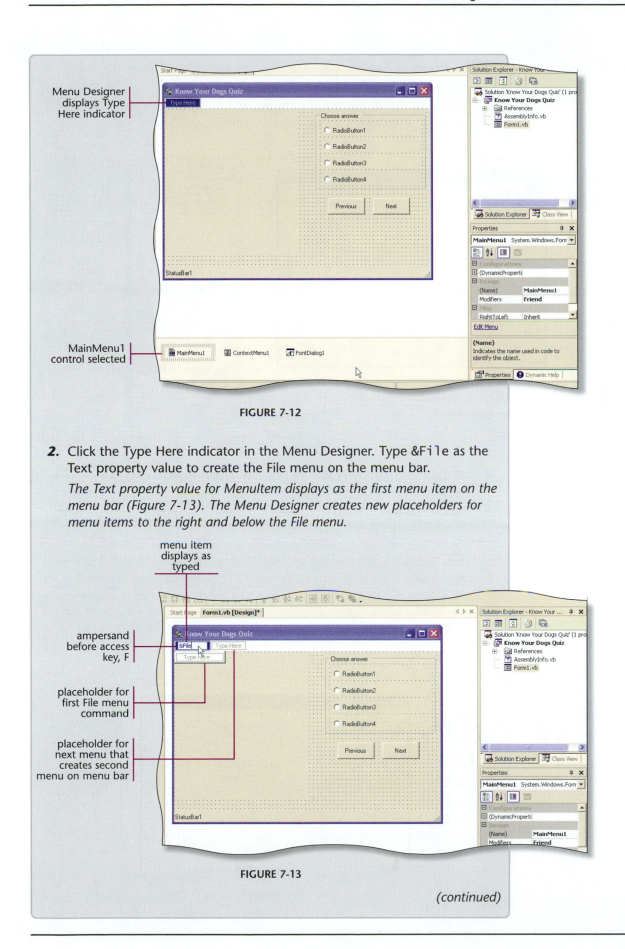

FIGURE 7-12

2. Click the Type Here indicator in the Menu Designer. Type &File as the Text property value to create the File menu on the menu bar.

The Text property value for MenuItem displays as the first menu item on the menu bar (Figure 7-13). The Menu Designer creates new placeholders for menu items to the right and below the File menu.

FIGURE 7-13

(continued)

3. Press the ENTER key.

The Menu Designer adds the File menu item to the menu bar. The letter F is underlined to indicate that it is the access key. The properties for the new menu item display in the Properties window (Figure 7-14).

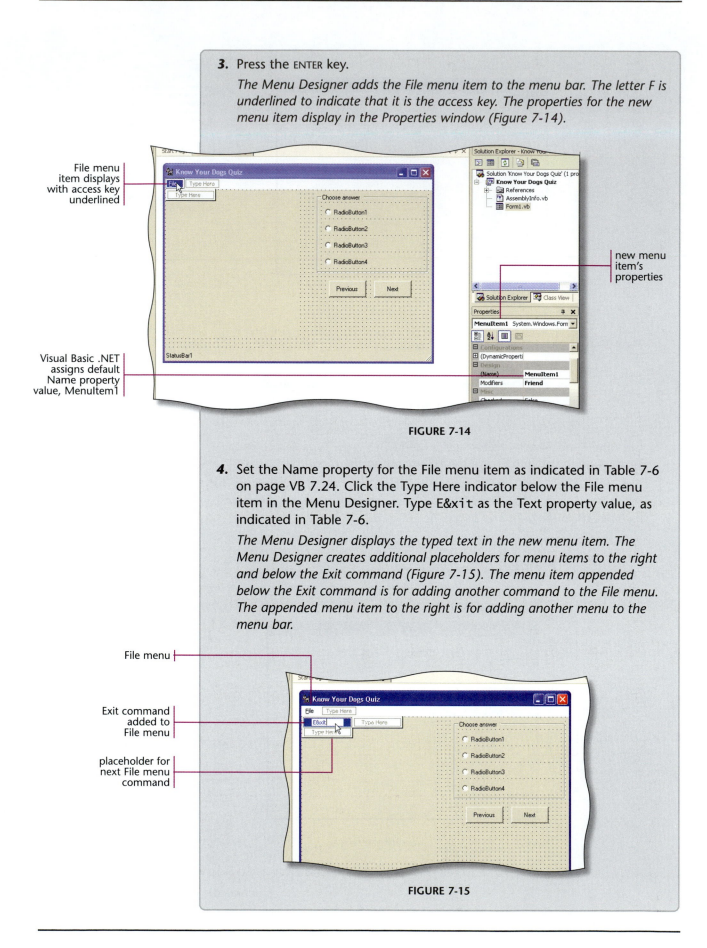

File menu item displays with access key underlined

new menu item's properties

Visual Basic .NET assigns default Name property value, MenuItem1

FIGURE 7-14

4. Set the Name property for the File menu item as indicated in Table 7-6 on page VB 7.24. Click the Type Here indicator below the File menu item in the Menu Designer. Type E&xit as the Text property value, as indicated in Table 7-6.

The Menu Designer displays the typed text in the new menu item. The Menu Designer creates additional placeholders for menu items to the right and below the Exit command (Figure 7-15). The menu item appended below the Exit command is for adding another command to the File menu. The appended menu item to the right is for adding another menu to the menu bar.

File menu

Exit command added to File menu

placeholder for next File menu command

FIGURE 7-15

5. Set the Name property for the Exit command as indicated in Table 7-6.

The Menu Designer adds the Exit command to the File menu. The Name property value is set to mnuExit in the Properties window (Figure 7-16).

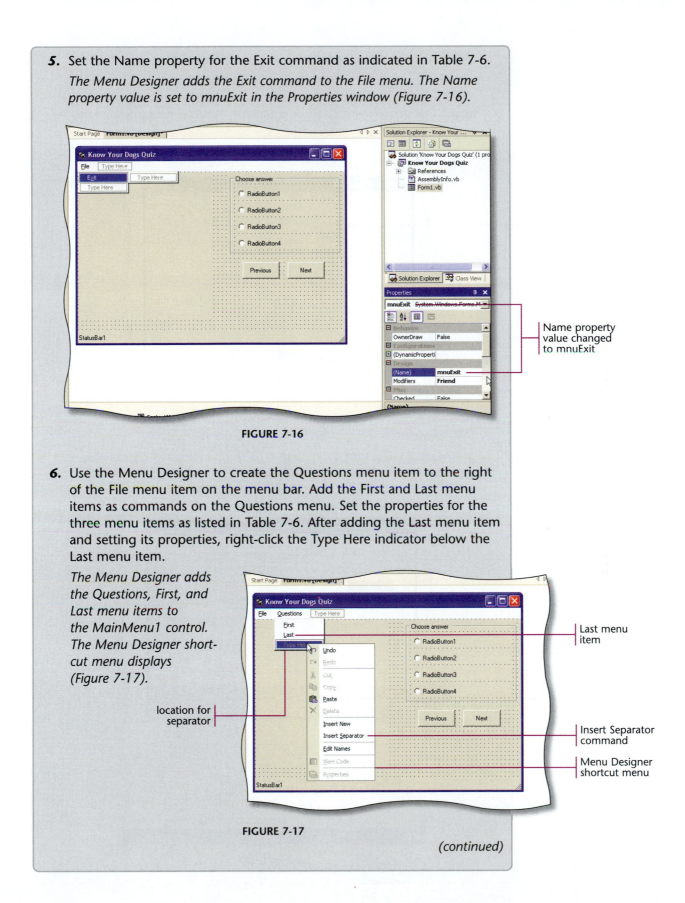

FIGURE 7-16

6. Use the Menu Designer to create the Questions menu item to the right of the File menu item on the menu bar. Add the First and Last menu items as commands on the Questions menu. Set the properties for the three menu items as listed in Table 7-6. After adding the Last menu item and setting its properties, right-click the Type Here indicator below the Last menu item.

The Menu Designer adds the Questions, First, and Last menu items to the MainMenu1 control. The Menu Designer short-cut menu displays (Figure 7-17).

FIGURE 7-17

(continued)

7. Click the Insert Separator command on the Menu Designer shortcut menu.

*The Menu Designer adds a separator to the Questions menu after the Last menu item (Figure 7-18). A **separator** is used to group related menu commands logically.*

separator added to menu

placeholder for next Questions menu command

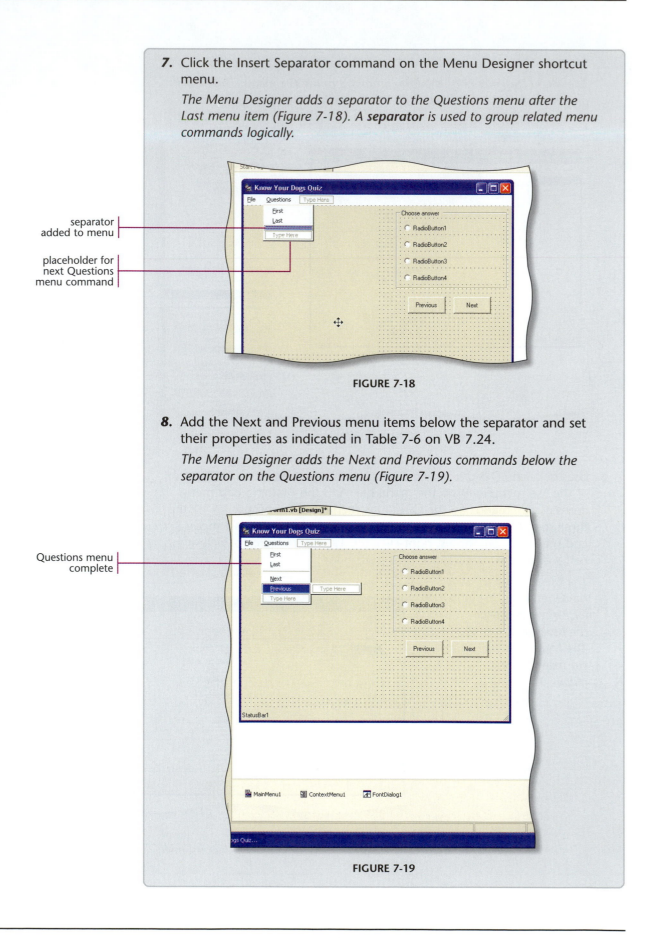

FIGURE 7-18

8. Add the Next and Previous menu items below the separator and set their properties as indicated in Table 7-6 on VB 7.24.

The Menu Designer adds the Next and Previous commands below the separator on the Questions menu (Figure 7-19).

Questions menu complete

FIGURE 7-19

9. Add the Options menu item to the right of the Questions menu item and set its properties as indicated in Table 7-6. Add the Font menu item below the Options menu item and set its properties as indicated in Table 7-6. Select the MainMenu1 control in the Component Tray and set the control's Name property to the value, mnuMain.

The menu bar displays at the top of the form with three menus: File, Questions, and Options. The name of the MainMenu control is changed to mnuMain in the Component Tray and the Properties window (Figure 7-20).

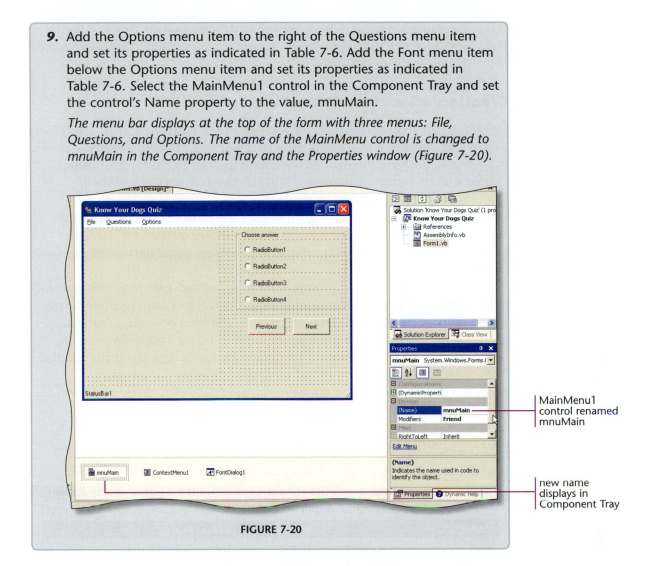

FIGURE 7-20

The previous steps illustrate how the Menu Designer allows you quickly to create complex menu structures. In addition to typing in the Type Here indicator, you also can drag a menu item to a new location within the same menu control using the Menu Designer. The steps showed you how to use the Menu Designer shortcut menu to add a menu separator between the Last and Next menu commands on the Questions menu. **Separators** are especially useful on large menus, where grouped menu items help the user find commands more quickly.

When you select the mnuMain control in the Component Tray, the Type Here indicators no longer display, but the menu items continue to display in the menu bar at the top of the form.

Creating a Shortcut Menu for a Form

Recall that a ContextMenu control allows you to create a shortcut menu for a form and controls. A shortcut menu also can be referred to as a **context menu**. In this book, the term, shortcut menu, is used to describe the types of menus created with a ContextMenu control. You can add as many ContextMenu controls to a form as required by the program and interface design. Each ContextMenu control can be assigned to the form or to one or more controls. When a ContextMenu control is assigned to a form or control, the user can right-click the form or control to display the shortcut menu next to the mouse pointer.

In the Know Your Dogs Quiz application, a ContextMenu control is assigned to the Form1 form. To assign a ContextMenu control to a form or control, you set the value of the **ContextMenu property** of the form or control to the name of the ContextMenu control. Because the controls on the Form1 form in the Know Your Dogs Quiz application are not assigned a ContextMenu control, the ContextMenu assigned to the Form1 form displays when the user right-clicks either the form or any control on the form.

Table 7-7 lists the MenuItem property values that must be set for the ContextMenu1 control to define the shortcut menu specified in the design of the Know Your Dogs Quiz application.

Table 7-7   MenuItem Properties for the ContextMenu1 Control in the Know Your Dogs Quiz Application

COMMAND	PROPERTY	PROPERTY VALUE
Next	Name	cmuNext
	Text	Next
Previous	Name	cmuPrevious
	Text	Previous
Font	Name	cmuFont
	Text	Font
Finish Quiz and Display Result	Name	cmuFinish
	Text	Finish Quiz and Display Result
Exit	Name	cmuExit
	Text	Exit

The following steps add the menu items in Table 7-7 to the ContextMenu1 control to create the shortcut menu. The control then is renamed to cmuShortcut and assigned to the Form1 form using the form's ContextMenu property.

To Create a Shortcut Menu for a Form

1. Click the ContextMenu1 control in the Component Tray.

The Menu Designer displays the Context Menu indicator at the top of the Form1 form (Figure 7-21). While the ContextMenu1 control is selected, the menu bar does not display. Although the ContextMenu1 control displays at the top of the form during design time, it will not display during run time until the user right-clicks the form or a control on the form.

Menu Designer displays Context Menu indicator

ContextMenu1 control selected

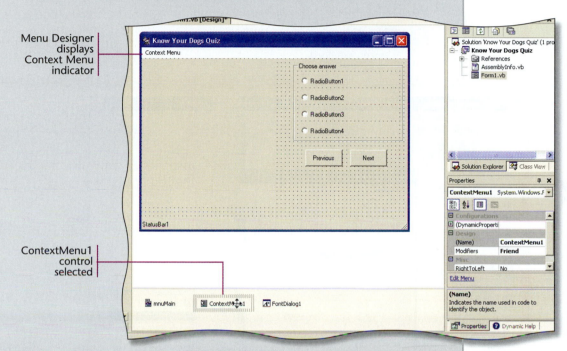

FIGURE 7-21

2. Click the Context Menu indicator. When the Type Here indicator displays, add the Next and Previous menu items below the Context Menu indicator and set the properties for the menu items as listed in Table 7-7. For the third menu item, type a dash (–) to indicate that a separator should display below the Previous command. Do not press the ENTER key.

The Next and Previous menu items display (Figure 7-22). Entering a single dash as a menu item is an alternate way of indicating to the Menu Designer to insert a separator at this location.

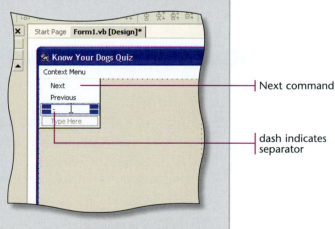

Next command

dash indicates separator

FIGURE 7-22

(continued)

3. Press the ENTER key. Add the Font command to the ContextMenu1 control and set its properties, as listed in Table 7-7 on page VB 7.30. Below the Font command, insert a separator. After the separator, add the Finish Quiz and Display Result command and set its properties, as listed in Table 7-7. Insert another separator. Finally, add the Exit command to the ContextMenu1 control and set its properties, as listed in Table 7-7.

The Menu Designer displays the completed shortcut menu (Figure 7-23). When the Finish Quiz and Display Result command is added, the Menu Designer automatically adjusts the width of the menu to accommodate the characters in the command name.

menu extended
to fit largest item

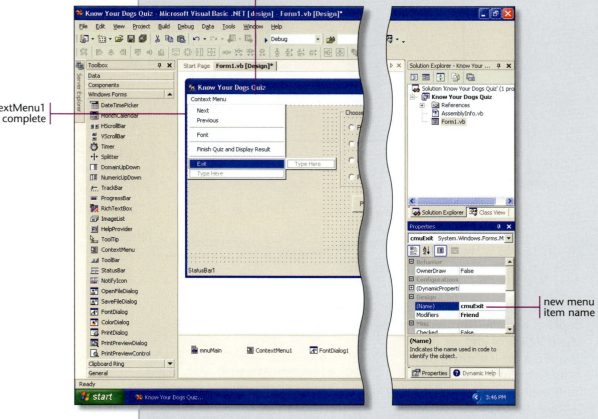

ContextMenu1
complete

new menu
item name

FIGURE 7-23

4. Select the ContextMenu1 control in the Component Tray and set the control's Name property value to cmuShortcut.

The new Name property value of the ContextMenu control is set to cmuShortcut in the Component Tray and in the Properties window (Figure 7-24).

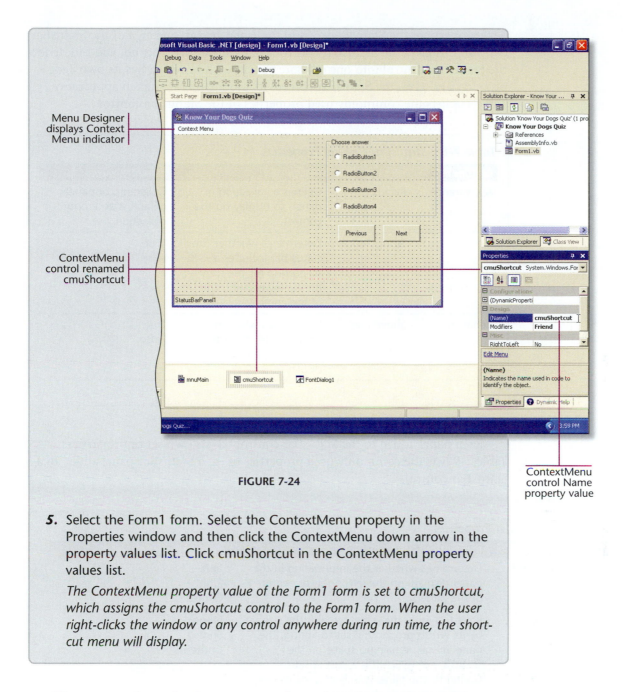

Menu Designer displays Context Menu indicator

ContextMenu control renamed cmuShortcut

ContextMenu control Name property value

FIGURE 7-24

5. Select the Form1 form. Select the ContextMenu property in the Properties window and then click the ContextMenu down arrow in the property values list. Click cmuShortcut in the ContextMenu property values list.

The ContextMenu property value of the Form1 form is set to cmuShortcut, which assigns the cmuShortcut control to the Form1 form. When the user right-clicks the window or any control anywhere during run time, the shortcut menu will display.

The commands on the shortcut menu do not have shortcut keys or access keys assigned to them. The user must right-click the window or any control during run time to display the control and then click the desired command to execute the associated event procedure. The Click event procedures for each menu item will be written later in the chapter.

StatusBar Control Properties

The StatusBar control at the bottom of the Form1 form is used to display the current question number and the total number of questions in the quiz. A StatusBar control can display text in two different ways. First, you can use the

Text property of the StatusBar control to display text in one area of the StatusBar control; this gives the StatusBar control a flat appearance. Second, you can divide the StatusBar control into one or more panels, each of which has its own Text property and gives the StatusBar control its more familiar sunken appearance. Table 7-8 lists the commonly used properties of the StatusBar control.

Table 7-8   **StatusBar Control Properties**

CATEGORY	PROPERTY	DESCRIPTION	PROPERTY VALUES
Appearance	Panels	Defines a collection of panels to display on the control	Collection of panels; default is an empty collection
	SizingGrip	Determines whether the status bar includes a sizing grip for the form on the lower-right side of the control	**True** False
Behavior	ShowPanels	Determines whether panels defined in the Panels property value display	True **False**

Each panel added to the StatusBar control has its own set of properties. Table 7-9 lists the commonly used properties of each StatusBar panel added to a StatusBar control.

Table 7-9   **StatusBar Panel Properties**

CATEGORY	PROPERTY	DESCRIPTION	PROPERTY VALUES
Appearance	Alignment	Determines whether the information in the panel displays on the left, right, or center of the panel	**Left** Right Center
	AutoSize	If set to None, the panel remains the size set by its Width property; if set to Spring, the panel fills all remaining space on the StatusBar of which it is a part; if set to Contents, the panel is only as large as the information inside the panel	**None** Spring Contents
	BorderStyle	Determines the appearance of the panel border	None Raised **Sunken**
	Icon	Sets an icon to display in the panel	File name of any icon
Behavior	MinWidth	Sets the minimum width in pixels to which the panel can be resized	Any positive whole number (default is **10**)

As shown in Figure 7-1a on page VB 7.03, the StatusBar control has a sunken appearance to help separate the information displayed in the panel from the rest of the form above it. To create the desired sunken appearance, you must add one panel to the StatusBar1 control. By default, the panel's BorderStyle property value is set to Sunken. The AutoSize property value should be set to Spring, so the panel takes up the entire status bar even after the user resizes the form. In addition, you should assign a descriptive name to the StatusBar control using the Name property value. When naming StatusBar controls that you refer to in code, use the stb prefix to indicate a StatusBar control. Table 7-10 lists the changes that must be made to the default properties of the StatusBar1 control in the Know Your Dogs Quiz Application.

Naming StatusBar Controls

When naming a StatusBar control, use the stb prefix to indicate a StatusBar control.

Table 7-10   StatusBar Control Properties for the Know Your Dogs Quiz Application

PROPERTY	PROPERTY VALUE	EFFECT
Name	stbQuestion	Changes the control's name to a descriptive name
Panels	(Collection)	Adds one panel to the Panels collection
ShowPanels	True	Sets the panels defined in the Panels property value to display

The steps on the following pages set the properties of the StatusBar1 control, as listed in Table 7-10, and add a panel to the Panels collection defined as the Panels property value.

Adding Panels to StatusBar Controls

Add panels to StatusBar controls when you want to give the StatusBar a sunken appearance or you want to display multiple pieces of information in the StatusBar control.

To Change the Properties of a StatusBar Control

1. Click the StatusBar1 control on the Form1 form. Change the Name property of the control to stbQuestion, as listed in Table 7-10. Select the Panels property in the Properties window and then click the Panels property ellipsis button.

The name of the StatusBar control is changed to stbQuestion. The StatusBarPanel Collection Editor displays to allow you to set properties for one or more panels in the stbQuestion control (Figure 7-25).

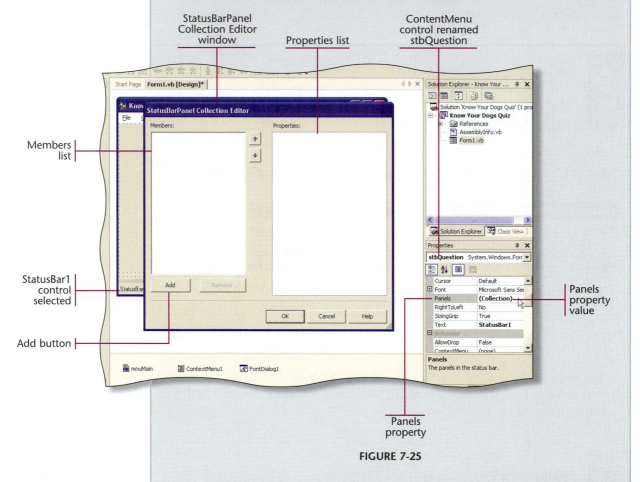

FIGURE 7-25

2. Click the Add button. When the StatusBarPanel1 panel is added, select the AutoSize property and then click the AutoSize box arrow.

The panel, StatusBarPanel1, is added to the Members list. Panels display on the left side of the window and the panels' properties display on the right side of the window. A list of properties for StatusBarPanel1 displays in the StatusBarPanel1 Properties list. The three possible values for the AutoSize property display in the property values list (Figure 7-26).

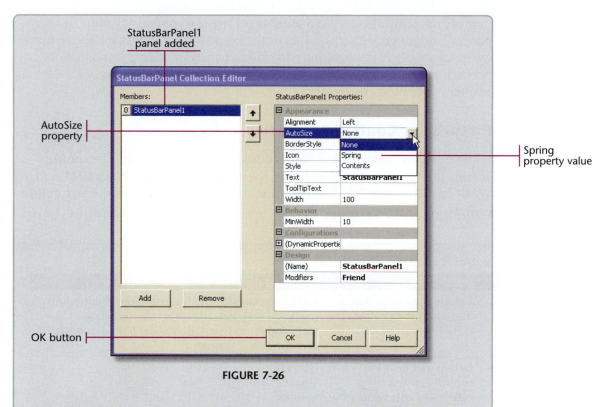

StatusBarPanel1
panel added

AutoSize
property

Spring
property value

OK button

FIGURE 7-26

3. Click the Spring property value and then click the OK button. When the StatusBarPanel Collection Editor window closes, select the ShowPanels property in the Properties window and change the ShowPanels property value to True.

The StatusBarPanel1 panel displays in the stbQuestion control. The panel displays with a sunken border style. The sizing grip for the form displays on the bottom right corner of the stbQuestion control (Figure 7-27).

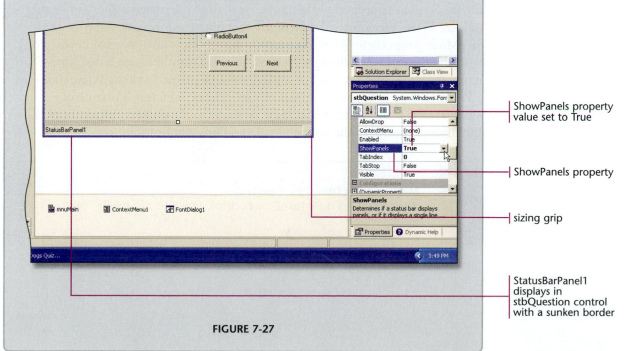

ShowPanels property
value set to True

ShowPanels property

sizing grip

StatusBarPanel1
displays in
stbQuestion control
with a sunken border

FIGURE 7-27

As previously discussed, a StatusBar control can contain any number of panels. You can use different values of the BorderStyle property for each panel to create effects, such as separating two sunken panels by adding a raised panel between them. You also can use icons in a panel to show the status of an element of your application graphically.

PictureBox Control Properties

PictureBox controls allow you to display images to the user. The control accepts several image types, including the popular JPEG, GIF, PNG, BMP, and WMF formats. Table 7-11 lists the commonly used properties of the PictureBox control.

Table 7-11   PictureBox Control Properties

CATEGORY	PROPERTY	DESCRIPTION	PROPERTY VALUES
Appearance	Image	Defines the image that displays in the control	Any image file with the file extensions of bmp, gif, jpg, jpeg, png, ico, emf, or wmf; any image matching those types also can be pasted into the control; default is **none**
Behavior	SizeMode	Determines how the control handles image placement and sizing	**Normal** StretchImage AutoSize CenterImage

The requirements document for the Know Your Dogs Quiz application (Figure 7-2 on page VB 7.05) specifies that the dog image should resize as the form resizes, so the user can view a larger image if desired. If the property value for the SizeMode property is left as Normal, then the image will retain its original size as the user resizes the form. By changing the property value for the SizeMode property to StretchImage, you ensure that the image will resize along with the control when the form resizes. You also should assign a descriptive name to the PictureBox control using the Name property value. When naming a PictureBox control, use the pic prefix to indicate a PictureBox control. Table 7-12 lists the changes that must be made to the default properties of the PictureBox control in the Know Your Dogs Quiz Application.

Naming PictureBox Controls
When naming a PictureBox control, use the pic prefix for the name.

Table 7-12 **PictureBox Control Properties for the Know Your Dogs Quiz Application**

PROPERTY	PROPERTY VALUE	EFFECT
Name	picQuestion	Changes the control's name to a descriptive name
SizeMode	StretchImage	Causes the image in the control to resize along with the control when the form resizes
Anchor	Top, Bottom, Left, Right	Anchors the control to all sides of the form, so the relative size of the image changes in conjunction with the form

The following steps set the properties of the PictureBox control, as listed in Table 7-12.

To Change the Properties of a PictureBox Control

1. Click the PictureBox1 control. Change the Name property value for the PictureBox1 control to picQuestion, as indicated in Table 7-12. Select the SizeMode property and click the SizeMode property down arrow.

The PictureBox1 control is renamed as picQuestion. The four possible values for the SizeMode property display in the property values list (Figure 7-28).

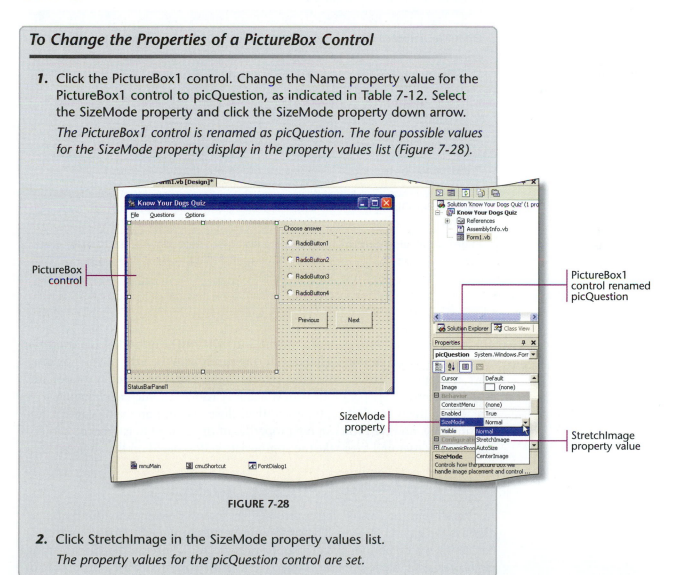

FIGURE 7-28

2. Click StretchImage in the SizeMode property values list.

The property values for the picQuestion control are set.

During design time, the picQuestion control displays as a gray box on the form. During run time, the Image property value of the control will be updated as the user navigates through the questions. Thus, it is not necessary to change the Image property during design time.

Common Dialog Controls

Windows applications often share requirements for certain types of input and therefore often use common dialog boxes to gather user input. For example, many Windows applications use similar dialog boxes, so users can open, print, preview, or save a file. As previously discussed, Visual Basic .NET includes several controls, called common dialog controls, that allow you to include common dialog boxes in a Windows application. Table 7-13 lists the types of common dialog controls available in Visual Basic .NET and their purpose.

Table 7-13 **Common Dialog Controls**

CONTROL	PURPOSE
OpenFileDialog control	Displays a dialog box that allows users to navigate to and select a file to open
SaveFileDialog control	Displays a dialog box that allows users to save a file
FontDialog control	Displays a dialog box that allows users to set a font and its attributes
ColorDialog control	Displays the color picker dialog box that allows users to set the color of an interface element
PrintDialog control	Displays a dialog box that allows users to select a printer and set its attributes
PrintPreviewDialog control	Displays a dialog box that displays how a PrintDocument object will appear when printed
PageSetupDialog control	Displays a dialog box that allows users to manipulate page settings, including margins and paper orientation

In Visual Basic .NET, you can use the **ShowDialog() method** of the control in code to display a common dialog box during run time. When the dialog box displays, it simply presents the available choices to the user. The dialog box does not actually perform the operations with which it is associated, such as changing a font. When the user selects options and then closes a common dialog control during run time, however, you can use properties of the control to gather the choices input by the user and then take the appropriate action based on the choices.

FontDialog Control Properties

Recall that the FontDialog control will let the user change the font that displays the answer choices. The various properties of the FontDialog control determine which options the dialog box presents to the user and define the range of choices available to the user. Table 7-14 lists the commonly used properties of the FontDialog control.

Table 7-14 *FontDialog Control Properties*

CATEGORY	PROPERTY	DESCRIPTION	PROPERTY VALUES
Misc	AllowScriptChange	Determines whether the user can change the character set of the font	**True** False
	AllowVectorFonts	Determines whether vector fonts can be selected	**True** False
	AllowVerticalFonts	Determines whether vertical fonts can be selected	**True** False
	FixedPitchOnly	Determines whether only fixed pitched fonts can be selected	**True** False
	Font	Defines the default font and font properties that are selected when the dialog box first displays	Select default font from a font dialog box (default is the default system font)
	FontMustExist	Determines whether to report an error if the selected font does not exist	True **False**
	MaxSize	Indicates the maximum point size that a user can select (0 to disable)	Any positive whole number (**0** to disable)
	MinSize	Indicates the minimum point size that a user can select (0 to disable)	Any positive whole number (**0** to disable)
	ScriptsOnly	Determines whether to exclude nonstandard fonts, such as Symbol character fonts	True **False**
	ShowApply	Determines whether to display the Apply button in the dialog box	True **False**
	ShowColor	Determines whether to display a color choice in the dialog box	True **False**
	ShowEffects	Determines whether to display the underline, strikethrough, and font color selections in the dialog box	**True** False
	ShowHelp	Determines whether to display the Help button in the dialog box	True **False**

The requirements document for the application states that the user should be able to change the font size used to display the answer choices on the RadioButton controls for better viewing of the possible answers. The application thus includes a FontDialog control to allow the user to change the font size. The default properties for a FontDialog control, however, allow the user to change several font options that might give the application a strange or confusing appearance. For example, using a standard FontDialog control, a user can select a font composed of mathematical symbols, which would make the answer choices unreadable.

For this application, the FontDialog box should limit the font sizes the user can select, so the text remains within the boundaries of the controls. You also should assign a descriptive name to the FontDialog control using the Name property value. When naming a FontDialog control, use the fod prefix to indicate a FontDialog control.

Tip

Naming FontDialog Controls

When naming a FontDialog control, use the fod prefix for the name.

Table 7-15 lists the changes that must be made to the default properties of the FontDialog control in the Know Your Dogs Quiz application.

Table 7-15 FontDialog Control Properties for the Know Your Dogs Quiz Application

PROPERTY	PROPERTY VALUE	EFFECT
Name	fodQuestion	Changes the control's name to a descriptive name
MaxSize	14	Sets the maximum font size the user can select to 14 points
MinSize	8	Sets the minimum font size the user can select to 8 points
ScriptsOnly	True	Excludes certain nonstandard fonts from the font list, such as symbols
ShowEffects	False	Removes options that allow the user to change the underline, strikethrough, and font color

The following step sets the property values for the FontDialog control, as indicated in Table 7-15.

To Change the Properties of a FontDialog Control

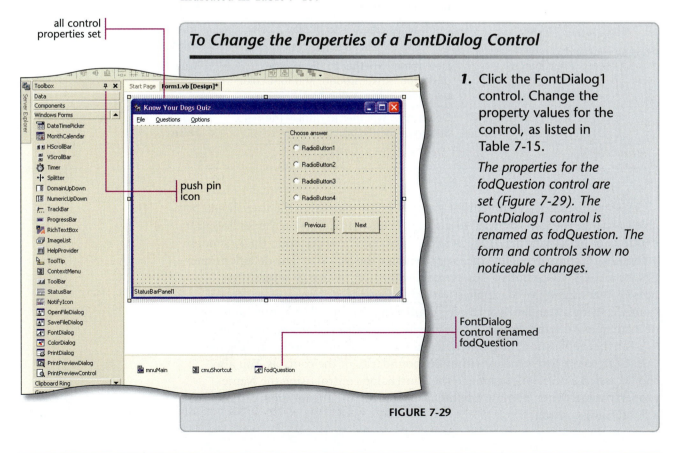

1. Click the FontDialog1 control. Change the property values for the control, as listed in Table 7-15.

    The properties for the fodQuestion control are set (Figure 7-29). The FontDialog1 control is renamed as fodQuestion. The form and controls show no noticeable changes.

FIGURE 7-29

Although the fodQuestion dialog box does not display during design time, the properties set will affect the display and options available on the control during run time. The other common dialog controls have different properties that relate to the control's particular function. For example, the OpenDialog control has a FileName property that contains the name of the file the user selected in the Open dialog box.

The user interface for the Know Your Dogs Quiz application now is complete. As indicated in Table 7-1 on page VB 7.04, the next task is to write the code for the project.

Arrays

As previously discussed, an array allows a programmer to represent many values with one variable name. The variable name assigned to represent an array is called the **array name**. The elements in the array are distinguished from one another by an index or **subscript**. Array indexes work just as the indexes worked with the collections discussed in previous chapters. In the array, the index is written inside a set of parentheses and is placed immediately to the right of the array name. A **array variable** is used to store and reference values that have been grouped into an array.

Consider the problem of writing a program to manipulate the monthly sales and generate a year-end report for a company. Figure 7-30 illustrates the difference between using an array and using simple variables to store the monthly sales.

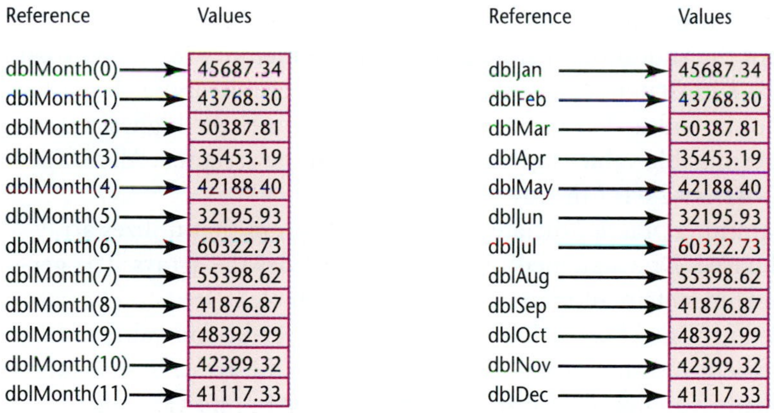

Reference	Values		Reference	Values
dblMonth(0) →	45687.34		dblJan →	45687.34
dblMonth(1) →	43768.30		dblFeb →	43768.30
dblMonth(2) →	50387.81		dblMar →	50387.81
dblMonth(3) →	35453.19		dblApr →	35453.19
dblMonth(4) →	42188.40		dblMay →	42188.40
dblMonth(5) →	32195.93		dblJun →	32195.93
dblMonth(6) →	60322.73		dblJul →	60322.73
dblMonth(7) →	55398.62		dblAug →	55398.62
dblMonth(8) →	41876.87		dblSep →	41876.87
dblMonth(9) →	48392.99		dblOct →	48392.99
dblMonth(10) →	42399.32		dblNov →	42399.32
dblMonth(11) →	41117.33		dblDec →	41117.33

(a) Using an Array   **(b)** Using Simple Variables

FIGURE 7-30

The monthly sales stored in an array require the same storage allocation as the sales represented using simple variables. The difference lies in the programming techniques that can access the different values grouped into an array. For example, using simple variables, you could use the following code to total the monthly sales results:

```
dblTotal = dblJan + dblFeb + dblMar + dblApr + dblMay +
           dblJun + dblJul + dblAug + dblSep + dblOct + dblNov
```

Each simple variable must explicitly appear in a statement, if the monthly sales are to be summed or displayed. Not only will the programming consume time, but also the variables must be placed properly in the program. The same functionality can be accomplished by entering all twelve values into the array dblMonth:

```
For intNumber = 0 To 11
    dblTotal += dblMonth(intNumber)
Next intNumber
```

In the For statement, the variable, intNumber, is initialized to 0. The expression in the second line gets the value for dblMonth(0), which is 45687.34. Then intNumber is incremented to 1, and the next value is assigned to dblMonth(1). This continues until dblMonth(11) is added as the twelfth value. Arrays created in Visual Basic .NET begin with an index of 0, meaning that is where you start counting the elements in the array.

The dblMonth2 and dblMonth(2) variables are different from each other. dblMonth2 is a simple variable, like the simple variables intSale, intIncrement, intDigit, or dblCost. dblMonth(2), by contrast, is the second element in the array dblMonth. Unlike the simple variable dblMonth2, the array element dblMonth(2) does not have to appear precisely in a statement in the code to be called upon in a program.

The Dim Statement for Arrays

Before arrays can be used, the amount of memory to be reserved must be declared in the program using the Dim statement for arrays. The main function of the **Dim statement for arrays** is to declare to Visual Basic .NET the necessary information about the allocation of storage locations in memory for arrays used in a program. The Dim statement for arrays also can declare the upper-bound value allowable for an index. The **upper-bound value** defines the highest value in the range of permissible values to which an index can be assigned. All arrays in Visual Basic .NET have 0 for the **lower-bound value**.

Good programming practice dictates that every program that utilizes array elements should have a Dim statement that properly defines the arrays. The general forms of the Dim statement for arrays are given in Table 7-16.

Arrays created in Visual Basic .NET always have a lower-bound value of 0, meaning that is where you start counting the elements in the array. If an array is to have five elements, you declare the array with an upper-bound value of 4. Such an array has indexes of 0, 1, 2, 3, and 4.

As shown in Table 7-16, an array can have one or more dimensions. The number of dimensions corresponds to the number of indexes used to identify an individual element. An array with only one dimension is considered to be a **one-dimensional array**. An array with more than one dimension is a **multidimensional array**, such as a two-dimensional or three-dimensional array. You can specify up to 32 dimensions, although more than three is extremely rare.

Table 7-16   The Dim Statement for Arrays

General Form:	1. Dim arrayname(upperlimit) As datatype = {initialvalue1, initialvalue2,...} 2. Dim arrayname(upperlimit) As datatype 3. Dim arrayname() As datatype = {initialvalue1, initialvalue2...} 4. Dim arrayname() As datatype where arrayname represents the array name and upperlimit represents the upper-bound value of the array. The upperlimit parameter can be repeated and separated by commas to define multidimensional arrays. Similarly, commas can be placed in the parentheses in forms 3 and 4 to define additional dimensions. For all arrays, the number of elements in the array is equal to upperlimit + 1, because the first element of all arrays has an index of 0.
Purpose:	The Dim statement for arrays declares array variables.
Examples:	1. `Dim intBalance(4) As Integer` 2. `Dim dblMoney() As Double = {2.0, 3.0, 4.0, 5.0}` 3. `Dim shrTable(9, 9) As Short` 4. `Dim strGrades( , ) As String = {{"A", "B"}, {"C", "D"}}` 5. `Dim intCounts() As Integer` 6. `Dim intValues (intUpperBound) As Integer`
Notes:	1. The lower-bound value of each dimension is 0. 2. In Visual Basic .NET, the maximum number of dimensions is 32. 3. If no upper-bound value is specified, as in the example of the General Form 2, 4, and 5, then the upper-bound value is set to the number of items to which you initialize the array (General Form 3) or is set as you assign values to array elements.

Array Dimensions

An array can have between 1 and 32 dimensions. The number of dimensions corresponds to the number of indexes used to identify an individual element.

In Table 7-16, the Dim statement in Example 1 reserves storage for five Integer elements in the one-dimensional numeric array, intBalance. A one-dimensional array requires only one index per element. These elements — intBalance(0), intBalance(1), intBalance(2), intBalance(3), and intBalance(4) — can be used in a program in much the same way as a simple variable can be used. For this Dim statement, elements intBalance(5), intBalance(6), and intBalance(-4) are not valid, because the upper-bound value for indexes is set to 4 and the lower-bound value is set to 0.

Indexes

Indexes must be within the lower-bound value and upper-bound value of an array.

In Table 7-16 on the previous page, the Dim statement in Example 2 declares a one-dimensional array of Double values. No upper-bound value is specified, meaning that the array size is based on the number of elements assigned to the array in code. The elements are initialized in brackets after an equals (=) sign. In the example, four elements are added to the array, meaning that the array's size is 4 and its upper-bound value is 3, because the first element has an index of 0. dblMoney(3), for instance, is equal to the value of 5.0. The Answers and Solution arrays used to store the user's answers and the solutions in the Know Your Dogs Quiz application, for example, both are one-dimensional arrays in which the elements are initialized.

The Dim statement in Example 3 declares a two-dimensional array. A two-dimensional array requires two indices per element. In this example, the Dim statement reserves storage locations for 100 elements for the array shrTable.

Example 4 in Table 7-16 declares a two-dimensional array and initializes four elements. Multidimensional arrays, such as the ones shown in examples 3 and 4, are discussed later in this chapter when you code the two-dimensional QuestionChoice array used to store the answer choices and image file names in the Know Your Dogs Quiz application.

Example 5 declares an array of integers of unknown size and does not initialize any elements.

Just as with simple variable declarations, if you need to declare several different arrays, you can list all of the arrays in the same Dim statement as follows:

```
Dim intX(20) As Integer, intCode(28) As Integer,
dblTemp(intRow, intColumn, intPlane) As Double
```

This Dim statement declares three different arrays, with the names intX, intCode, and dblTemp. Of the three arrays, intX and intCode are one-dimensional arrays and dblTemp is a three-dimensional array.

Example 6 in Table 7-16 declares an array of integers of UpperBound size, where UpperBound is assigned a value prior to the Dim statement. This type of declaration is discussed in the next section.

Dynamic Dimensioning of Arrays

Some applications call for dynamically dimensioned arrays. A **dynamically dimensioned array** is one that has a variable or expression, rather than a constant, as the upper-bound value. For example, a program may manipulate 60 elements of a one-dimensional array during one execution of the program, 100 elements the next time, and so on. Rather than modify the upper-bound value of the Dim statement each time the number of elements changes, Visual Basic .NET permits the size of an array in a Dim statement to be written as a simple variable, as in

```
Dim intCode(gintSize) As Integer
```

This Dim statement reserves a variable number of elements for the one-dimensional array intCode. After gintSize is assigned a value, the Dim statement sets that value of the upper-bound value and allocates the actual number of elements to the array intCode. Any For statements involved in the manipulation of the array must contain the same upper-bound value as the simple variable, gintSize, for their upper-bound value.

Declaring Arrays

Two aspects of the Know Your Dogs Quiz application design provide opportunities to use one-dimensional arrays, rather than simple variables. First, the application must track the user's answers to the questions in some manner. Second, the application must store the solutions to the quiz questions, to compare them with the user's answers and determine the quiz results. In both situations, using arrays instead of simple variables simplifies design and coding.

As shown in Figure 7-31, the user's answers can be stored in a one-dimensional array, named the gshrAnswers array. The gshrAnswers array includes seven elements, one for each question. The index value indicates the question number, with 0 indicating the first question, 1 indicating the second question, and so on. All values in the gshrAnswers array are initialized to -1, which indicates that the question has not been answered (Figure 7-31a). As the user navigates through the quiz, if he or she clicks the first RadioButton for the control, the corresponding element for the question receives a value of 0. If the user clicks the second RadioButton for the control, the corresponding element for the question receives a value of 1, and so on (Figure 7-31b). The question number currently displayed to the user will be tracked with a form-level variable, gshrQuestionNumber. As the user navigates through the quiz, the gshrQuestionNumber variable is updated in code to correspond to the index of the question number currently displayed.

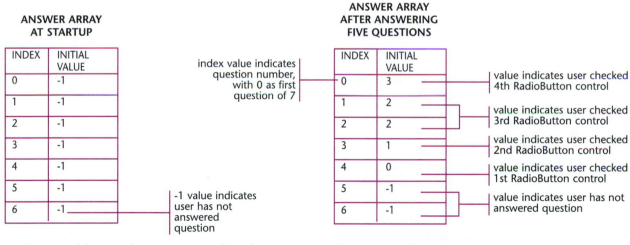

(a) Elements of the array shrAnswers assigned initial value of -1 when the application starts to indicate that questions are not answered.

(b) The status of the elements of the array shrAnswers is the initial value after the user answers the first five questions. The values of the first five elements are the user's answers.

FIGURE 7-31

The solutions to the quiz questions also can be stored in a one-dimensional array, named the gshrSolution array. As shown in Figure 7-32 on the next page, the gshrSolution array contains values corresponding to each of the seven questions. For example, an element with a value of 0 indicates that the correct answer for the corresponding question is the answer displayed on the first RadioButton control.

SOLUTION ARRAY

INDEX	INITIAL VALUE
0	0
1	3
2	2
3	1
4	0
5	0
6	3

value indicates which RadioButton control displays the correct answer

shrSolution array

FIGURE 7-32

Recall that the flowcharts shown in Figure 7-4 on page VB 7.10 are designed around an array. In the flowchart, the arrays start at 1. During the design phase, the design often begins counting at 1 to maintain clarity of the design. When the time comes to implement the design in code, however, you should recall that the index used in a Visual Basic .NET's array starts at 0, and write your code accordingly.

Designing and Coding Array Indexes
When working with arrays at design time, begin counting at 1 to maintain clarity of design. When implementing arrays in code, begin counting at zero (0), because zero refers to the initial element in the array.

Figure 7-33 shows the comment header, the Dim statements declaring the two one-dimensional arrays, and the declaration for the form level variable, gshrCurrentQuestion, which contains the current question number displayed to the user on the Form1 form. The arrays are initialized based on the information included in the requirements document and the list of answer choices and solutions.

```
320    ' Chapter 7:      Know Your Dogs Quiz
321    ' Programmer:     J. Quasney
322    ' Date:           November 24, 2004
323    ' Purpose:        This program generates a seven-question quiz. Each question
324    '                 includes an image and four choices in RadioButton controls.
325    '                 The user must answer all questions correctly to pass the quiz.
326    '                 The solution is stored in the gshrSolution array. The user answers
327    '                 are stored in the gshrAnswers array. Questions choices and image
328    '                 file names are stored in the gstrQuestions array.
329    Dim gshrSolution As Short() = {0, 3, 2, 1, 0, 0, 3}
330    Dim gshrAnswers As Short() = {-1, -1, -1, -1, -1, -1, -1}
331    Dim gshrCurrentQuestion As Short = 0
```

FIGURE 7-33

The following steps open the code window and enter the code shown in Figure 7-33 to declare two one-dimensional arrays.

To Declare Arrays

1. Right-click the Form1 form in the Solution Explorer. Click the View Code command on the shortcut menu. Click the push pin icon (shown in Figure 7-29 on page VB 7.42) on the Toolbox window to hide the window.

   Visual Basic .NET opens the code window.

2. Enter Option Strict On as the first line of code in the code window. Click line 320 and then type the code shown in Figure 7-33.

   The Toolbox window is hidden. The comment header for the form displays as lines 320 through 328, followed by declarations for the gshrSolution and gshrAnswers arrays and the form level variable, gshrCurrentQuestion, in the code window (Figure 7-34).

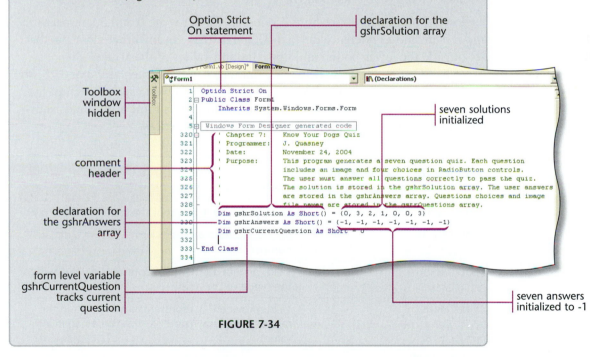

FIGURE 7-34

As shown in Figure 7-34, the code window displays much more code when the Toolbox window is hidden. When you are finished coding and are testing or debugging code, you should click the push pin icon to open the Toolbox window and make it available to make modifications to the user interface.

Lines 329 and 330 declare the two one-dimensional arrays that contain the solutions for the quiz (gshrSolution) and the answers given by the user (gshrAnwers). The arrays have the same data type and number of elements. Arrays that share these characteristics are called **parallel arrays**. The gshrCurrentQuestion variable contains the value of the current question that is displayed on the status bar. As the user navigates the quiz, this value will be updated in code to reflect the current question.

Indexes

As previously discussed, the elements in an array are distinguished from one another and referenced in code by an index. The index is written within parentheses and is placed immediately to the right of the array name. The index can be any valid number, variable, or numeric expression within the range of the array.

Using Indexes with Arrays

The index or subscript used to access an array element may be any valid number, variable, or numeric expression within the range of the array.

For example, if the array dblTax is declared as

```
Dim dblTax(50) As Double
```

the lower-bound and upper-bound values of the array are 0 and 50, respectively, and it is invalid to reference dblTax(-3), dblTax(51), or any other elements that are outside the lower-bound and upper-bound values of the array.

When Option Strict is set to On, noninteger indexes, such as 9.8 or 3.75, are disallowed. Otherwise, Visual Basic .NET uses the Convert class to attempt to convert the number to an Integer. Table 7-17 illustrates some additional examples of valid and invalid indexes used with array references.

Table 7-17 *Examples of Indexes*

ARRAY REFERENCE	COMMENT
dblTax(1)	Valid, provided 1 is within the range of the array
dblTax(-3)	Invalid, because an index never can be a negative number
dblTax(intI + intJ)	Valid, provided intI + intJ represents a value within the range of the array
dblTax(-X)	Valid, provided -X represents a value within the range of the array (note: X must be a negative value)
dblTax(9.8)	Valid, provided Option Strict is set to Off and the array has an upper bound of at least 10
dblTax(dblSSN(3))	Valid, provided dblSSN(3) represents a value within the range of the array
dblTax(intI + intJ / 4 + 3^intI)	Valid, provided intI + intJ / 4 + 3^intI represents a value within the range of the array

When coding a program, you must decide which variables will be indexed in the program and then use them consistently throughout the program. For example, if the array element is dblMonth(intNumber), you cannot use the variable dblMonth by itself without an index, nor can you use the variable with two subscripts. When you make these errors, Intellisense™ displays an error message in the code window.

Function Procedures

In Chapter 4, you learned about Visual Basic .NET's intrinsic functions, which you can use in code to perform common tasks. In Chapter 4, for example, you used the Pmt function to calculate loan payments. You can code your own **function procedures** to perform tasks and return a value back to the code that called it. Just as with the Pmt function, any function procedure you create can accept values as arguments and use those arguments to perform calculations. These function procedures always are declared with a data type, which represents the data type of the value that it returns.

You should use function procedures in your code when your design calls for a specific calculation or operations that will be used several times in your code and whose end result is a single value, such as an Integer or Boolean result.

Using Function Procedures

Use function procedures in your code when your design calls for a specific calculation or operations that will be used more than once in your code and whose end result is a single value.

Declaring a Function Procedure

As with variables and event procedures, it is good coding practice to declare function procedures in your code. A function declaration looks much like an event procedure declaration. The function declaration, however, also is similar to a variable declaration in that a function declaration includes a data type.

Table 7-18 on the next page shows the general form of a simple **Function statement** used to declare a function procedure.

Table 7-18   Function Statement (Simple)

General Form:	1. Function name(argument 1, ..., argument n) As datatype
	        statements
	End Function
	2. Private Function name(argument 1, ..., argument n) As datatype
	        statements
	End Function
	
	where the Function name is a valid name following the conventions of variable naming.

Purpose:	The Function statement declares a function procedure with arguments and a data type.

Example:	1. `Function CalculatePayment() As Double`
	      .
	      .
	      .
	   `End Function`
	2. `Private Function CalculatePayment() As Double`
	      .
	      .
	      .
	   `End Function`

Notes:	1. The **Private keyword** used in Example 2 specifies that the function procedure is only for use by the code within the form. The Private keyword is optional, but it is good coding practice to specify it to make the code more understandable.
	2. Arguments are optional. If used, arguments behave as local variables within the function procedure and are passed to the function procedure when it is called.
	3. Arguments use the general form:
	
	    Optional ByVal argumentname As datatype
	    ByVal argumentname As datatype
	    Optional ByRef argumentname As datatype
	    ByRef argumentname As datatype
	
	The keyword Optional indicates that the arguments are not required when the procedure is called. The keywords, ByVal and ByRef, are explained in detail later in the chapter.

You declare a function as an array data type in much the same way that you declare variables arrays. For example, the function declaration

```
Private Function InventoryCounts() As Integer()
```

declares a function procedure that returns an array of integers.

Although not listed in Table 7-18, Visual Basic .NET also supports several options for function declarations, which are useful when coding classes. For more information about alternative function declarations, see Visual Basic .NET Help.

Returning a Value and Exiting a Function Procedure

As you have learned, a function returns a value to the function name in the line of code that called it.

A function procedure exits due to one of four conditions occurring during execution:

1. A statement in the function procedure executes and sets the function name to a valid value based on its data type.
2. A Return statement executes in the function.
3. An Exit Function statement executes.
4. An End Function statement is reached.

In the first condition, a statement in the function executes and sets the function name to a valid value. The function then returns a value to the function name in the line of code that called it.

Alternatively, you can use the Return statement to return a value to the function name in the line of code that called it and exit a function. The **Return statement** consists of the keyword Return followed by the value you want to return to the function name in the line of code that called it. The value returned to the function name must use the same data type as the function.

> **Tip**
>
> **Returning a Value from a Function Procedure**
> You return a value from a function procedure to the line of code that called it by (1) setting the function name to a value within the function procedure before exiting it or (2) using the Return statement.

The **Exit Function statement** can be used at any point in the function procedure to return a value to the function name in the line of code that called it. If the value of the function name has not been set, then the default value of the function data type is returned. For example, Visual Basic .NET returns 0 as the value of the function name for a function declared as an Integer, if the function name has not been set to a value prior to execution of the Exit Function statement.

The **End Function statement**, as shown in the Function statement in Table 7-18, marks the end of the function. When the End Function statement executes, a value is returned to the function name in the line of code that called it.

Coding a Function Procedure

The Know Your Dogs Quiz application will use a function procedure named QuizResult() to determine whether the user answered all the questions correctly. In this case, the QuizResult() function should return a value of True if the user answers all of the questions correctly and a value of False if the user does not answer all of the questions correctly. Figure 7-35 shows a flowchart that outlines the logic used to determine whether the user answered all of the questions correctly. The logic exits in two places, each after the value of the function procedure is set. A counter-controlled Do While structure processes each item in the Solution and Answers arrays until the count exceeds the number of questions.

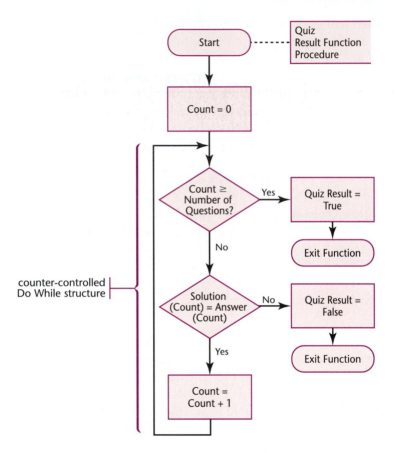

FIGURE 7-35

Figure 7-36 shows the function declaration for the QuizResult() function procedure and the Dim statement used to declare the shrIndex variable. The code following the declaration also is shown. Line 333 declares the QuizResult() function as a Boolean data type. The QuizResult() function loops through each question using the shrIndex variable as the looping variable. The shrIndex variable has a range of 0 to 6, which accounts for all seven answers and solutions in the arrays. Line 337 compares each element in the gshrSolution array with the corresponding element of the gshrAnswers array. As soon as an element in the gshrSolution array does not match the corresponding element in the gshrAnswers array, the QuizResult() function returns the value, False, using the Return statement, and it exits on line 338. If the loop executes successfully for all seven items and then exits, then line 341 sets the QuizResult value to True, which causes the value, True, to be returned to the function name in the line of code that called it. The QuizResult() function then exits, as shown in line 342.

```
333        Private Function QuizResult() As Boolean
334            Dim shrIndex As Short
335
336            For shrIndex = 0 To 6
337                If gshrSolution(shrIndex) <> gshrAnswers(shrIndex) Then
338                    Return False
339                End If
340            Next
341            QuizResult = True
342        End Function
```

FIGURE 7-36

The following steps add the declaration for the QuizResult() function and code it.

To Declare a Function Procedure and Use Arrays in Code

1. Enter line 333 as shown in Figure 7-36.

The Function statement displays in the code window. Visual Basic .NET completes the function procedure by adding the End Function keyword on line 335 (Figure 7-37).

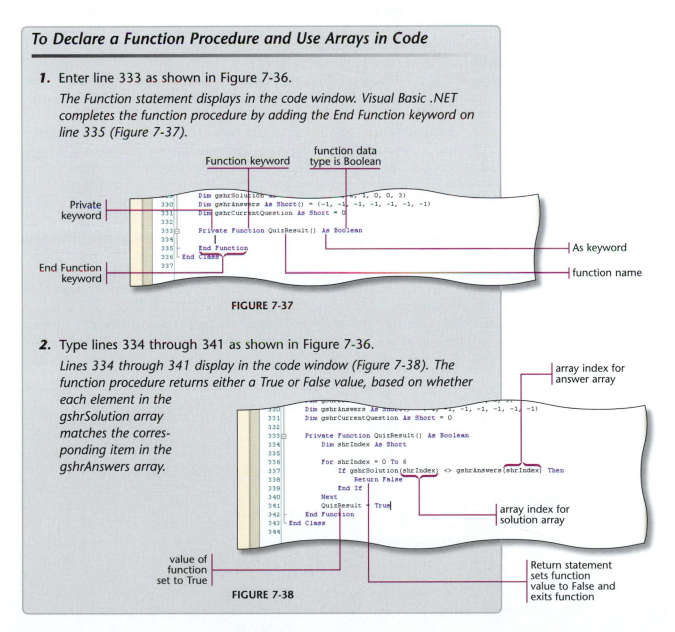

FIGURE 7-37

2. Type lines 334 through 341 as shown in Figure 7-36.

Lines 334 through 341 display in the code window (Figure 7-38). The function procedure returns either a True or False value, based on whether each element in the gshrSolution array matches the corresponding item in the gshrAnswers array.

FIGURE 7-38

Once coded, the QuizResult() function can be called from any other procedure or function in the Form1 form. The function exits in two places, each after the value of the function is set. If the Return statement in line 338 is reached within the function, the function exits and the value of False is returned to the function name in the line of code that called it. If the loop exits successfully, line 341 sets the value of the function to True. When the function exits on line 342, the value of True is returned to the function name in the line of code that called it.

Coding a Menu Command and Using a FontDialog Control

For each menu command in the three main menus on the menu bar and the shortcut menu, you must write code to define the action that occurs when the user clicks the menu command. Of all of the menu commands, two of the menu commands do not manipulate or rely on data in the quiz: the Exit command on the File menu and the Font command on the Options menu. The Click event procedures for these commands will be coded first. The Exit command's Click event procedure needs to close the form, thereby exiting the application. The Click event procedure for the Font command needs to display the Font dialog box. The code that uses the QuizResult() function will be discussed later in this chapter.

As previously discussed, you can use the ShowDialog() method of a control to display a common dialog box during run time. All common dialog boxes include a ShowDialog() method that opens the dialog box modally. When the ShowDialog() method executes, the current line of code waits until the dialog box closes. When the dialog box closes, the ShowDialog() method returns a value that the program uses to determine what actions were taken by the user while the dialog box displayed.

Figure 7-39 shows the code for two Click event procedures. The first is the Click event procedure for the Exit command on the File menu (lines 344 through 346). The second is the Click event procedure for the Font command on the Options menu (lines 348 through 356). Line 350 of the Font command's Click event procedure uses the ShowDialog() method to open a Font dialog box. When the Font dialog box closes, it returns a result that is compared against a constant, DialogResult.OK. The DialogResult.OK constant is a value that reflects

```
344    Private Sub mnuExit_Click(ByVal sender As System.Object, ByVal e As System.    ↙
       EventArgs) Handles mnuExit.Click
345        Me.Close() ' Exit application
346    End Sub
347
348    Private Sub mnuFont_Click(ByVal sender As System.Object, ByVal e As System.    ↙
       EventArgs) Handles mnuFont.Click
349        fodQuestion.Font = radAnswer1.Font
350        If fodQuestion.ShowDialog() = DialogResult.OK Then
351            radAnswer1.Font = fodQuestion.Font
352            radAnswer2.Font = fodQuestion.Font
353            radAnswer3.Font = fodQuestion.Font
354            radAnswer4.Font = fodQuestion.Font
355        End If
356    End Sub
```

FIGURE 7-39

the fact that the user clicked the OK button in the Font dialog box to close it. If the user clicked the OK button, the Font property value for the four RadioButton controls is updated to the values selected by the user in the dialog box.

The following steps create and code the mnuExit_Click (Exit command) and mnuFont_Click (Font command) event procedures.

To Code a Menu Command and Use a FontDialog Control in Code

1. Click the Form1.vb[Design] tab in the main work area. Double-click the Exit command on the File menu of the Form1 form.

   Visual Basic .NET creates the mnuExit_Click event procedure.

2. Type line 345 as shown in Figure 7-39.

3. Click the Form1.vb[Design] tab in the main work area. Double-click the Font command on the Options menu of the Form1 form.

   Visual Basic .NET creates the mnuFont_Click event procedure.

4. Type lines 349 through 355 as shown in Figure 7-39.

   Lines 349 through 355 display in the code window, as shown in Figure 7-40. When a user clicks the Exit command on the application's File menu, the mnuExit_Click event procedure closes the application window. When the user clicks the Font command on the Options menu, the mnuFont_Click event procedure opens a Font dialog box. Line 350 determines whether the user clicked the OK button to close the Font dialog box. If so, the mnuExit_Click procedure sets the font of the four RadioButton controls to the selected font.

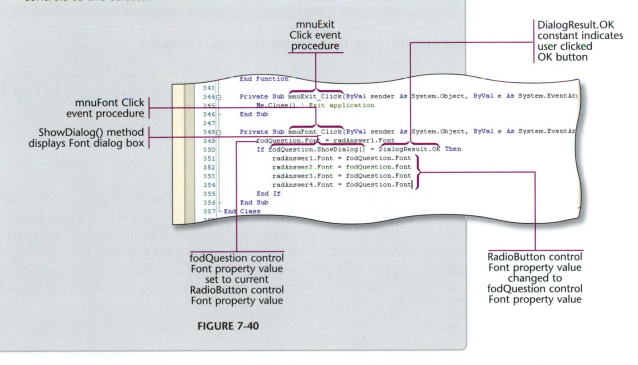

```
      End Function
343
344   Private Sub mnuExit_Click(ByVal sender As System.Object, ByVal e As System.EventAr(
345       Me.Close() ' Exit application
346   End Sub
347
348   Private Sub mnuFont_Click(ByVal sender As System.Object, ByVal e As System.EventAr
349       fodQuestion.Font = radAnswer1.Font
350       If fodQuestion.ShowDialog() = DialogResult.OK Then
351           radAnswer1.Font = fodQuestion.Font
352           radAnswer2.Font = fodQuestion.Font
353           radAnswer3.Font = fodQuestion.Font
354           radAnswer4.Font = fodQuestion.Font
355       End If
356   End Sub
357 End Class
```

mnuExit Click event procedure

DialogResult.OK constant indicates user clicked OK button

mnuFont Click event procedure

ShowDialog() method displays Font dialog box

fodQuestion control Font property value set to current RadioButton control Font property value

RadioButton control Font property value changed to fodQuestion control Font property value

FIGURE 7-40

The ShowDialog() method of the fodQuestion control returns a value that indicates how the dialog box closed. If the value is equal to the constant, DialogResult.OK, that indicates that the user closed the dialog box by clicking the OK button. Other possible values that can be returned by the ShowDialog() method include DialogResult.Cancel, which indicates that the user clicked the Cancel button in the dialog box to close it. In that instance, the font of the controls would not change.

Lines 351 through 354 update the font of the RadioButton controls by using the Font property of the fodQuestion control and the individual RadioButton controls. These lines of code actually set several font properties, such as font name and font size. You can set all font properties at once by using the Font property, or set individual font properties, such as the Font.Name and FontSize property, by referring to them separately.

Multidimensional Arrays

As previously discussed, the dimension of an array is defined by the number of indexes required to reference an individual element in an array. Thus far, the arrays used in the Know Your Dogs Quiz application have been one-dimensional, and each individual element in the array was referenced by an integer, a variable, or a single expression in the parentheses following the array name.

Visual Basic .NET allows arrays to have up to 32 dimensions. One- and two-dimensional arrays are the more commonly used arrays. Three-dimensional arrays are used less frequently in business applications, and arrays with more than three dimensions are rarely used in business. Arrays of more than three dimensions, however, are used often in scientific and engineering applications.

Manipulating Two-Dimensional Arrays

As illustrated in Table 7-16 on page VB 7.45, the number of dimensions in an array is declared in the Dim statement for the array. For example, the Dim statements

```
Dim dblCost(2, 4) As Double
```

or

```
Dim dblCost(,) As Double
```

both declare a two-dimensional array. A two-dimensional array usually is illustrated in the form of a table. The first index defines the number of rows in the table, and the second index defines the number of columns. Figure 7-41 shows the dblCost array as a 3 × 5 array as a table with three rows and five columns. As with all arrays created in Visual Basic .NET, the index begins with 0. The element located in the second row and second column is referenced as dblCost(1, 1) and is read as dblCost sub one one.

element referenced
as dblCost(1, 1)

	Columns 0	1	2	3	4
Rows 0	dblCost(0,0)	dblCost(0,1)	dblCost(0,2)	dblCost(0,3)	dblCost(0,4)
1	dblCost(1,0)	dblCost(1,1)	dblCost(1,2)	dblCost(1,3)	dblCost(1,4)
2	dblCost(2,0)	dblCost(2,1)	dblCost(2,2)	dblCost(2,3)	dblCost(2,4)

FIGURE 7-41

In Figure 7-42, the element found in the third row and fourth column is referenced as dblCost(2, 3) and is read as dblCost sub two three.

	Columns 0	1	2	3	4
Rows 0	4.0	3.2	−4.6	53.2	45.0
1	33.8	1.0	0.0	65.6	239.3
2	2.3	389.3	854.3	33.8	32.3

element referenced
as dblCost(2, 3)

FIGURE 7-42

Assuming that the elements of the array dblCost are assigned the values shown in Figure 7-42, the following statements are true:

dblCost(0, 2) is equal to -4.6.
dblCost(2, 4) is equal to 32.3.
dblCost(2, 2) is equal to 854.3.
dblCost(1, 0) is equal to dblCost(2, 3).
dblCost(3, 5) is outside the range of the array; it does not exist.
dblCost(2, 6) is outside the range of the array; it does not exist.
dblCost(−2, −5) is outside the range of the array; it does not exist.

Initializing Multidimensional Arrays

As shown in General Form 3 in Table 7-16, you can declare an array using the Dim statement and initialize the values for the array. The following code, for example, initializes all of the elements in the 4 × 3 shrArea array to 0, row by row:

```
Dim shrArea(3, 2) As Short
For intRow = 0 TO 3
    For intColumn = 0 TO 2
        shrArea(intRow, intColumn) = 0
    Next intColumn
Next intRow
```

Similarily, you can write the code as follows:

```
Dim shrArea() As Short = {{0, 0, 0}, {0, 0, 0}, {0, 0, 0}, {0, 0, 0}}
```

To initialize all elements to 1 on the main diagonal of a 4 × 4 array called shrTable, you can write the following code:

```
Dim shrTable(3, 3) As Short
For intRow = 0 TO 3
    shrTable(intRow, intRow) = 1
Next intRow
```

As a result, elements shrTable(0, 0), shrTable(1, 1), shrTable(2, 2), and shrTable(3, 3) are assigned the value of 1.

Two-dimensional arrays often are used to classify data. For example, if a company makes five models of a particular product and the production of each model involves a certain amount of processing time in minutes on any one of six different machines, the processing time can be summarized in a table of five rows and six columns, as illustrated in Figure 7-43.

PRODUCT PROCESSING MINUTES		Machine					
	Indexes	0	1	2	3	4	5
Model	0	13	30	5	17	12	45
	1	34	26	16	26	23	35
	2	32	16	25	33	29	34
	3	34	15	19	50	34	43
	4	15	22	25	17	24	45

FIGURE 7-43

The following statement reserves storage in memory for a two-dimensional array that will accommodate the data in the table shown in Figure 7-43.

```
Dim intTime(4, 5) As Integer
```

If intModel represents the model number (row of the table) and intMachine represents the machine (column of the table), then the index array variable intTime(intModel, intMachine) gives the time it takes for a model to be processed on a particular machine. The value of intModel can range from 0 to 4, and the value of intMachine can range from 0 to 5. If intModel is equal to 4 and intMachine is equal to 5, the table tells you the product processing time is 45 minutes. That is, model number 4 involves 45 minutes of processing on machine 5.

To sum all the elements in column 2 of the table in Figure 7-43 into a running total, intSum2, and to sum all the elements in row 4 into a running total, intSum4, you can write the following:

```
Dim intTime(5, 6)
intSum2 = 0
intSum4 = 0
For intModel = 0 TO 4
    intSum2 += intTime(intModel, 1)
Next intModel
For intMachine = 0 TO 5
    intSum4 += intTime(3, intMachine)
Next intMachine
```

These last three partial programs provide examples of how you can handle elements that appear in various rows and columns of two-dimensional arrays.

Arrays with More than Two Dimensions

The table in Figure 7-43 organizes information for one product with five different models. You also can create comparable tables for two different products, both of which have five different models that are processed on the six machines. To construct such a table, you can declare the array dblTime as a three-dimensional array, using the following Dim statement:

```
Dim dblTime(4, 5, 1)
```

In this Dim statement, the indexed variable dblTime(intModel, intMachine, intProduct) refers to the time it takes to process a given model number (intModel) on a particular machine (intMachine) for a specific product (intProduct). Figure 7-44 represents a conceptual view of some of the storage locations for a 5 × 6 × 2 array called dblTime. This three-dimensional array contains five rows, six columns, and two planes, for a total of 60 elements.

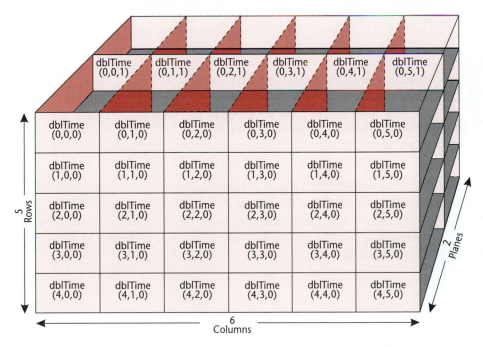

FIGURE 7-44

If elements other than product, model, and machine are required, you can add even more dimensions to the array.

Declaring a Two-Dimensional Array

The list of question answers and image file names used in the Know Your Dogs Quiz application can be represented in a two-dimensional array. Each question is represented by a row in a two-dimensional array. Each answer choice is represented by a column in the array. The image file name also is represented in another column in the array. Recall that the quiz has seven questions, each of which has four answer choices and one image file. A 7 × 5 array thus allows for all of the data to be contained in a two-dimensional array.

As you code the array, you should use line-continuation characters to make your code easier to read. A **line-continuation character** allows you to write long lines of code over several lines in the code window. In Visual Basic .NET, you can enter a line-continuation character by entering a space followed by the underscore character, _, followed by pressing the ENTER key. You then can continue typing the line of code on a new line in the code window.

Visual Basic .NET places the following limitations on use of the line-continuation character:

- You cannot follow a line-continuation character with a comment on the same line.
- You cannot place a line-continuation in the middle of an argument or keyword.

Visual Basic .NET also allows you to place several statements on one line in the code window, by separating the statements with a colon (:). Good coding practice, however, dictates that you avoid using this method, because it makes code more unreadable.

Using Line-Continuation Characters
Use line-continuation characters to break long lines of code over several lines in the code window, in order to make your code more readable.

Figure 7-45 shows the Dim statement that declares the two-dimensional array, gstrQuestions, and shows the data used to initialize the array. Although Figure 7-45 shows one statement, line-continuation characters are used to make the long statement display in a neat and orderly manner on lines 331 through 338 in the code window.

```
331  Dim gstrQuestions As String(,) = { _
332      {"English Springer Spaniel", "Akita", "Husky", "Bearded Collie", "dog051.jpg"}, _
333      {"Pug", "Whippet", "Fox Terrier", "English Setter", "dog50.jpg"}, _
334      {"Chow Chow", "Beagle", "Labrador Retriever", "Foxhound", "dog068.jpg"}, _
335      {"Great Dane", "Dachshund", "Samoyed", "Newfoundland", "dog044.jpg"}, _
336      {"Samoyed", "Pekingese", "English Setter", "Pomeranian", "dog088.jpg"}, _
337      {"Old English Sheepdog", "Saluki", "Rottweiler", "Poodle", "dog074.jpg"}, _
338      {"Collie", "Boston Terrier", "Bichon Frise", "Akita", "dog007.jpg"}}
339
```

FIGURE 7-45

The following step enters the code shown in Figure 7-45 to declare the two-dimensional array, gstrQuestions, and initialize the array.

To Declare a Two-Dimensional Array

1. Insert a new line after line 330 and then, enter lines 331 through 339 as shown in Figure 7-45.

The gstrQuestions array declaration displays. Visual Basic .NET initializes the two-dimensional array to the values shown on lines 332 through 338. Line-continuation characters make the code more readable (Figure 7-46).

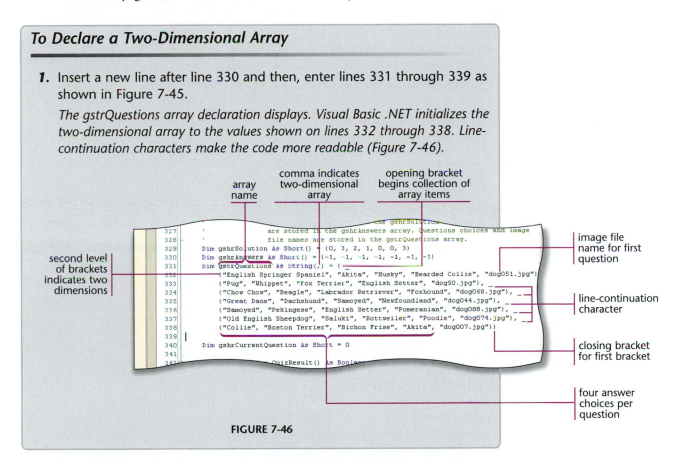

FIGURE 7-46

The two-dimensional array, gstrQuestions, contains all of the information supplied with the requirements document for the questions included in the quiz. Line-continuation characters neatly separate each row of the array, and tab characters vertically align the start of each row.

Array Methods

Visual Basic .NET includes several methods that you can use with array variables. For example, the GetUpperBound(N) method returns the upper-bound value for the index in a specific dimension of the array. N specifies the Nth dimension. If N is omitted, Visual Basic .NET uses 0. Table 7-19 lists the common methods available for array variables. See Help for more information about the arguments and return values for the methods.

Table 7-19   Array Methods

METHOD	DESCRIPTION	EXAMPLE
BinarySearch()	Searches a one-dimensional sorted array for a value	Array.BinarySearch(intMyArray, 5)
Clear()	Sets a range of elements in the array to 0, false, or null depending on the data type of the element	Array.Clear(intMyArray, 0, 4)
Copy()	Copies a section of one array to another array	Array.Copy(intMyArray,0, inDestinationArray, 0, 1)
CopyTo()	Copies all elements of a one-dimensional array to the specified one-dimensional array, starting at a specified starting point	myArrayZero.CopyTo(myArrayTwo, 3)
GetLength()	Gets the number of elements in the specified dimension of an array	intMyArray.GetLength(0)
GetUpperBound()	Gets the upper-bound value of the specified dimension of an array	intMyArray.GetUpperBound(0)
Reverse()	Reverses the order of the elements in a one-dimensional array or a portion of an array	Array.Reverse(intMyArray)
Sort()	Sorts the elements in a one-dimensional array	Array.Sort(intMyArray)

Sub Procedures

A **sub procedure** is a unit of code that executes when called from code in other procedures and event procedures. In Visual Basic .NET, a sub procedure is delimited in code by the Sub Procedure and End Procedure statements and called by using the sub procedure name. When the sub procedure is finished executing, control transfers back to the calling line of code.

Just like a function procedure, a sub procedure is a unit of code that you define when coding a task that will be repeated in the logic of a program's design. Unlike function procedures, sub procedures do not return values. In this book, you already have used one type of sub procedure, when you coded various event procedures.

Declaring Sub Procedures

A **Sub statement** is used to declare the name, arguments, and code that define a sub procedure. Table 7-20 shows the general form of a sub procedure Sub statement.

Table 7-20	*Sub Statement (Simple)*

General Form:	1. Sub name(argument 1, …, argument n)
	    statements
	End Sub
	2. Private Sub name(argument 1, …, argument n)
	    statements
	End Sub
	
	where the name is a valid sub procedure name following the conventions of variable naming.

Purpose:	The Sub statement declares a sub procedure with arguments.

Example:	1. `Sub CalculatePayment()`
	   `End Sub`
	2. `Private Sub CalculatePayment()`
	   `End Sub`

Notes:	1. The Private keyword specifies that the sub procedure is only for use by the code within the form. The Private keyword is optional, but it is good coding practice to specify it to make the code more understandable.
	2. Arguments are optional. If used, arguments behave as local variables within the sub procedure and are passed to the sub procedure when it is called.
	3. Arguments use the general form
	
	    Optional ByVal argumentname As datatype
	    ByVal argumentname As datatype
	    Optional ByRef argumentname As datatype
	    ByRef argumentname As datatype
	
	The keyword, Optional, indicates that the arguments are not required when the sub procedure is called. The keywords, ByVal and ByRef, are explained in detail later in the chapter.
	4. Other keywords that relate to object-oriented concepts can be used with the Sub statement. These statements, however, are beyond the scope of this chapter.

Like functions, sub procedures accept variables, constants, and expressions as arguments. A sub procedure, for instance, can accept a variable that represents an array. The data type of the argument in the call to the sub procedure or function must agree with the corresponding argument in the Sub or Function statement.

Tip

Argument Data Types
The data type of the argument in the call to the sub procedure or function must agree with the corresponding argument in the Sub or Function statement.

Passing Arguments Between Procedures

Sub procedures and function procedures use one of two methods to accept arguments: passing by value and passing by reference. When you use the **passing by value method** to pass an argument by a value, only the value of the variable, constant, or expression that you pass is sent to the sub procedure or function procedure. The **ByVal keyword** is used before the parameter name in the Sub statement to denote that the value is passed by value. ByVal is the default method for passing arguments.

When you use the **passing by reference method** to pass an argument by reference, you are passing the variable's location in the computer's memory to the sub procedure or function procedure. Therefore, any modification made to the argument within the sub procedure or function procedure is reflected in the variable after the function or sub procedure exits. The **ByRef keyword** is used before the argument name in the declaration to denote that the value is passed by reference. Passing variables by reference allows you to modify several arguments in the sub procedure or function procedure and send new values back to the calling line of code.

Exercise caution when using the passing by reference method, because passing variables by reference is slower than passing them by value. Passing variables by reference also can make code less readable.

> **Tip**
>
> **Passing By Reference**
> Exercise caution when using the passing by reference method, because passing variables by reference is slower than passing them by value. Passing variables by reference also can make code less readable.

In some situations, you may want to ensure that a variable that you pass to a sub procedure or function procedure is not modified. Even if the argument is passed by reference and is subject to modification in the sub procedure or function procedure, you can force the argument to be passed by value by enclosing the argument in parentheses. For example, the following line of code forces the dblIncome variable to be passed by value rather than by reference, even though the CalculateTax() sub procedure declares the argument to be passed by reference:

```
CalculateTax((dblIncome), intTaxBracket)
Private Sub CalculateTax(ByRef dblValue As Double)
```

Some situations require that you pass no arguments to a sub procedure or function procedure. For example, your program requirements might call for the display of the same message box in many places in the program logic. In this case, you can create a sub procedure that displays a message box, but requires no arguments and does not return a value.

The Optional keyword indicates that the program does not need to pass an argument to the sub procedure or function procedure. If you use an optional argument when declaring a sub procedure or function procedure, all subsequent arguments also must be optional. When calling a sub procedure or function procedure, the number of arguments in the call to the procedure must agree exactly with the number of arguments in the Sub or Function statement.

Tip	**Optional Arguments**
	If you use an optional argument when declaring a sub procedure or function procedure, all subsequent arguments also must be optional.

Tip	**Calling Sub Procedures and Functions**
	When calling a sub procedure or function procedure, the number of arguments in the call to the sub procedure or function procedure must agree exactly with the number of arguments in the Sub or Function statement.

Coding a Sub Procedure

In the Know Your Dogs Quiz application, the display of a question to the user is a recurring operation for several commands and buttons on the user interface. This operation thus is ideal for a sub procedure. The sub procedure that handles the display of a question to the user will be named DisplayQuestion(). Figure 7-47 shows a flowchart that outlines the logic required at the beginning of the DisplayQuestion() sub procedure.

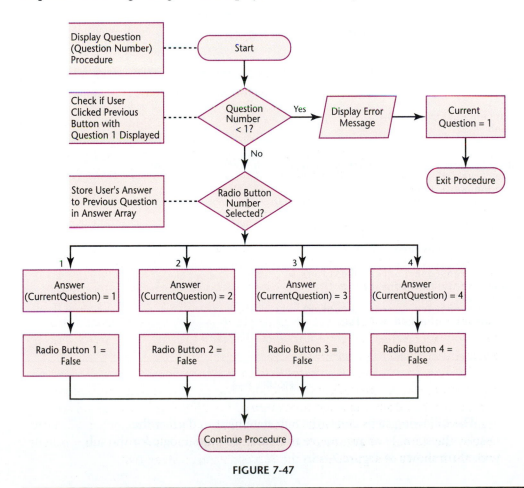

FIGURE 7-47

As outlined in the flowchart in Figure 7-47 on the previous page, the DisplayQuestion() sub procedure first determines whether the user is attempting to navigate to a question before the first question. If so, an error message displays and the sub procedure exits. A selection structure in the logic then determines which RadioButton control, if any, the user selected. The logic updates the gshrAnswers array with an appropriate value, based on the RadioButton control selected for the answer.

Figure 7-48 shows the beginning of the DisplayQuestion() sub procedure, which includes the code for the logic shown in Figure 7-47. Line 353 uses the Boolean constant, True, as the expression in a Select Case statement. Using the Boolean constant, True, means that the expressions in the Case clauses are compared with the value, True. For example, in line 354, Visual Basic .NET compares the value of the radAnswer1.Checked property with True. If the user has selected the first RadioButton control in the grpAnswer control as the answer to the question, then the radAnswer1.Checked property value is True.

The Select Case statement updates the question number element of the gshrAnswers array with a 0, 1, 2, or 3, based on which one of the four RadioButton controls has a Checked property value of True. In the RadioButton controls, 0 represents the first RadioButton control, 1 represents the second RadioButton control, and so on. This value is assigned to the array element, gshrAnswers(gshrCurrentQuestion). The index, gshrCurrentQuestion, is the question number that currently is displayed in the application.

```
342    Private Sub DisplayQuestion(ByVal shrQuestion As Short)
343        Dim shrIndex As Short
344
345        ' Check if user clicked Previous button with question 1 displayed
346        If shrQuestion < 0 Then
347            MessageBox.Show("You are already at the beginning of the quiz.", "Know    ↙
    Your Dogs Quiz")
348            gshrCurrentQuestion = 0
349            Exit Sub
350        End If
351
352        ' Store user's answer to previous question in gshrAnswers array
353        Select Case True
354            Case radAnswer1.Checked
355                gshrAnswers(gshrCurrentQuestion) = 0
356                radAnswer1.Checked = False
357            Case radAnswer2.Checked
358                gshrAnswers(gshrCurrentQuestion) = 1
359                radAnswer2.Checked = False
360            Case radAnswer3.Checked
361                gshrAnswers(gshrCurrentQuestion) = 2
362                radAnswer3.Checked = False
363            Case radAnswer4.Checked
364                gshrAnswers(gshrCurrentQuestion) = 3
365                radAnswer4.Checked = False
366        End Select
367    End Sub
```

FIGURE 7-48

The following steps create the Sub statement to declare the DisplayQuestion() sub procedure and enter the initial logic for the sub procedure shown in Figure 7-48.

To Code a Sub Procedure

1. Enter line 342 as shown in Figure 7-48.

The procedure declaration for the DisplayQuestion() sub procedure displays in the code window. Intellisense™ inserts the End Sub keyword on line 344 (Figure 7-49).

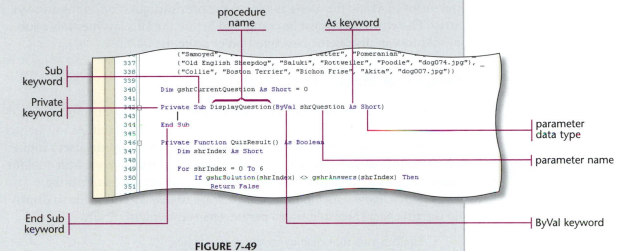

FIGURE 7-49

2. Enter lines 343 through 366 as shown in Figure 7-48.

The code displays in the code window, as shown in Figure 7-50. The Select Case statement sets a value in the gshrAnswers array and then sets all RadioButton controls to be unchecked when the next question displays in the application window. Lines 346 through 350 determine if the user is attempting to navigate to a question before the first question. If so, an error message displays and the sub procedure exits.

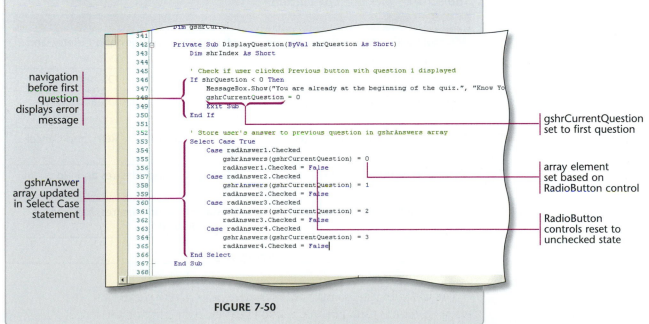

FIGURE 7-50

The DisplayQuestion() sub procedure executes only when called by other procedures. In the Know Your Dogs Quiz application, the DisplayQuestion() sub procedure will be used by event procedures, such as the btnNext_Click and btnPrevious_Click event procedures, to navigate the user through the quiz. The code for the DisplayQuestion() sub procedure includes familiar statements from previous chapters, such as the If…Then…Else statement to test whether the user attempts to navigate to a question before the first question and the Select Case statement to assign the user's answer to the previous question to the answers array. These two tasks must be completed before the DisplayQuestion() sub procedure can display the next question or score the quiz.

Enhanced MessageBox Features

The next section of code in the sub procedure requires the user to indicate to the program whether to score the quiz and display the result. As in Chapter 5, a message box will be used to display the options and accept the user's input. The MessageBox class includes several options that make it a versatile tool for interacting with the user. Previously, you used two parameters with the MessageBox.Show() method: the text message to display and a title to display on the title bar. Three additional parameters allow you to specify:

- The buttons that display in the message box
- An icon to display in the message box
- The default button to display in the message box

You add the additional parameters separated by commas after the first two parameters, the text and title.

Table 7-21 shows the values you use in the third MessageBox.Show() parameter that indicate the buttons that display in the message box.

Table 7-21   Message Box Buttons

PARAMETER	DESCRIPTION
MessageBoxButtons.AbortRetryIgnore	Message box includes Abort, Retry, and Ignore buttons
MessageBoxButtons.OK	Message box includes OK button
MessageBoxButtons.OKCancel	Message box includes OK and Cancel buttons
MessageBoxButtons.RetryCancel	Message box includes Retry and Cancel buttons
MessageBoxButtons.YesNo	Message box includes Yes and No buttons
MessageBoxButtons.YesNoCancel	Message box includes Yes, No, and Cancel buttons

Table 7-22 shows the values you can use in the fourth MessageBox.Show() parameter, to define which icon displays in the message box.

Table 7-22   Message Box Icons

PARAMETER	DESCRIPTION
MessageBoxIcon.Asterisk	Message box includes a symbol of a lowercase letter I in a circle
MessageBoxIcon.Error	Message box includes a symbol of a white X in a circle with a red background
MessageBoxIcon.Exclamation	Message box includes a symbol of an exclamation point in a triangle with a yellow background
MessageBoxIcon.Hand	Message box includes a symbol of a white X in a circle with a red background
MessageBoxIcon.Information	Message box includes a symbol of a lowercase letter I in a circle
MessageBoxIcon.None	Message box does not include an icon
MessageBoxIcon.Question	Message box includes a symbol of a question mark in a circle
MessageBoxIcon.Stop	Message box includes a symbol of a white X in a circle with a red background
MessageBoxIcon.Warning	Message box includes a symbol of an exclamation point in a triangle with a yellow background

The fifth parameter specifies the default button in the message box. The parameter can be a value such as MessageBoxDefaultButton.Button1, MessageBoxDefaultButton.Button2, or MessageBoxDefaultButton.Button3, to indicate which button should serve as the default button in the message box. The following code displays a message box with the message, "The selected font was not found on your computer. Would you like to search again?", the title, Font Error, the Yes and No buttons, and the Exclamation icon. The No button is selected as the default button.

```
MessageBox.Show("The selected font was not found on your
computer. Would you like to search again?", "Font Error",
MessageBoxButtons.YesNo, MessageBoxIcon.Exclamation,
MessageBoxDefaultButton.Button2)
```

After the user completes an action in a dialog box that contains a choice, such as clicking a Yes or No button, the MessageBox.Show() returns a result that indicates which button the user clicked. Table 7-23 shows the possible return values of the MessageBox.Show() method for which you can test in your code.

Table 7-23   MessageBox.Show() Method Return Values

VALUE	DESCRIPTION
DialogResult.Abort	User clicked the Abort button
DialogResult.Cancel	User clicked the Cancel button
DialogResult.Ignore	User clicked the Ignore button
DialogResult.No	User clicked the No button
DialogResult.None	No value was returned from the message box
DialogResult.OK	User clicked the OK button
DialogResult.Retry	User clicked the Retry button
DialogResult.Yes	User clicked the Yes button

Using an Array Method and an Enhanced Message Box

Figure 7-51 shows a flowchart that outlines the continued logic of the DisplayQuestion() sub procedure started in Figure 7-47. This portion of the logic tests to determine whether the user is attempting to navigate beyond the last question in the quiz. If so, an enhanced message box displays and gives the user the option to display the final quiz result and exit the application or to return to the quiz.

If the user chooses to display the final quiz result, then the QuizResult() function is used to grade the quiz. If the user answered all seven questions correctly, the message box displays a message congratulating the user on passing the quiz. If the user did not answer all questions correctly, the message box displays a message informing the user that he or she did not pass the quiz. If the user chooses not to display the final quiz result, the question number is set to 7 before the sub procedure exits.

As shown in the first decision point in Figure 7-51, if the question number was not greater than 7, then execution continues and the next question displays. The program logic used to display the next question is discussed later in the chapter.

Figure 7-52 shows additional code for the DisplayQuestion() sub procedure, based on the logic in Figure 7-51 and the pseudocode in Figure 7-5 on page VB 7.11. Line 369 uses an array method, GetUpperBound(), to determine whether the user is attempting to navigate beyond the upper-bound value of the gstrQuestions array. The GetUpperBound() method is called with an index of 0, indicating that the method should return the upper-bound value of the first dimension of the gstrQuestions array. For the gstrQuestions array, the upper-bound value for the first dimension is a value of 6, which represents the seventh question.

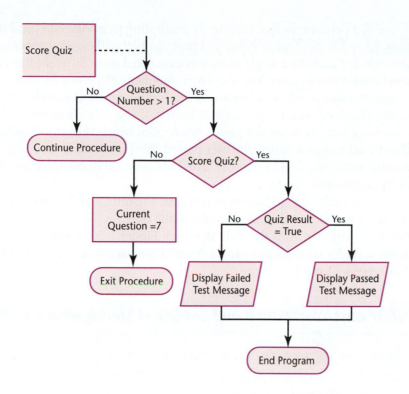

FIGURE 7-51

```
367
368        ' Score quiz
369        If shrQuestion > gstrQuestions.GetUpperBound(0) Then
370            If MessageBox.Show("You have answered the last question. Would you like to ↵
       display the final quiz result and exit the quiz?" _
371                              & ControlChars.NewLine & ControlChars.NewLine _
372                              & "Click No to return.", "End of Quiz", _
373                              MessageBoxButtons.YesNo, MessageBoxIcon.Question, _
374                              MessageBoxDefaultButton.Button2) = DialogResult.Yes Then
375                If QuizResult() Then
376                    MessageBox.Show("Congratulations! You passed!", "Know Your Dogs Quiz")
377                Else
378                    MessageBox.Show("Sorry, you did not pass the quiz.", "Know Your Dogs Quiz")
379                End If
380                Me.Close()
381            Else
382                gshrCurrentQuestion = Convert.ToInt16(gstrQuestions.GetUpperBound(0))
383            End If
384            Exit Sub
385        End If
```

FIGURE 7-52

If line 369 determines that the user is attempting to navigate beyond the last question, lines 370 displays an enhanced message box with several options. Lines 370 through 374 include a single statement organized onto different lines using line-continuation characters. The If…Then statement displays a message box with a test message, a title, a Yes button, a No button, and a Question icon. The No button (Button2) is set as the default button. If the user clicks the Yes button in the message box, then control passes to line 375, which calls the QuizResult() function to determine whether the user passed the quiz. A message box indicating the quiz result displays to the user. The Me.Close() statement on line 380 causes the application to exit.

If the user clicks the No button to continue the quiz, line 382 sets the current question number to the last question in the quiz.

The following step adds the code shown in Figure 7-52, which adds the GetUpperBound() array method and advanced message box features to the DisplayQuestion() sub procedure.

To Code an Array Method and Enhanced MessageBox

1. Enter lines 367 through 385 as shown in Figure 7-52.

Lines 367 through 385 display in the DisplayQuestion() sub procedure in the code window (Figure 7-53).

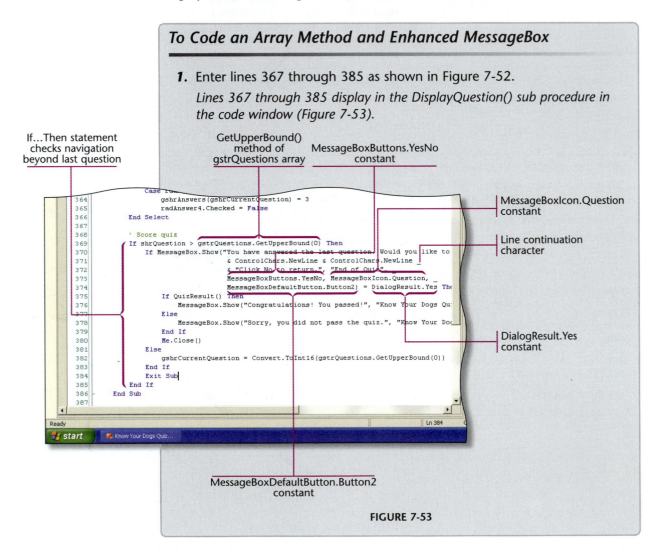

FIGURE 7-53

Line 369 uses the GetUpperBound() method of the gstrQuestions array to determine whether the user is attempting to navigate beyond the last question. Line 370 displays an advanced message box that gives the user the option to display the final quiz result and exit the application. If the user opts to display the final quiz result, line 375 calls the QuizResult() function procedure and tests the value returned by the function procedure. Because the function procedure returns a Boolean value or True or False, the result of the function procedure can be evaluated immediately in the If…Then…Else statement. Recall that when the function procedure is called, line execution resumes on line 375 only after the function procedure exits. The line-continuation characters used beginning in line 370 show how the code is easier to read when the arguments passed to a method or function are separated on different lines.

The next task is to add code to the DisplayQuestion() sub procedure, so it changes the question displayed to the user when the value of gshrQuestion is determined to be valid. You can do this using a control collection of the RadioButton controls.

Using a Control Collection

A **control collection** allows you to treat two or more controls as members of a collection, thereby allowing you to operate on the controls using indexes. This method of accessing controls in code, as opposed to using the control name, is useful when you need to loop through several related controls to perform a common operation on the controls.

A control collection is defined using the **Controls property** of the container control. For example, the four RadioButton controls contained in the grpAnswer control make up the control collection of the grpAnswer control. Generally, a control collection indexes the controls in the opposite order in which you add them to the form or other container control. The z-order of a control on a form determines the order in which the control exists in the form's control collection. In the steps beginning on page VB 7.21, the first RadioButton control was moved to the top of the z-order by clicking the Bring to Front button on the Layout toolbar. Thus, the first RadioButton control can be addressed in code either as radAnswer1 or grpAnswer.Controls(0). Both of these references to the control can be used interchangeably. The benefit of using the control name, radAnswer1, is that the reference is a unique and meaningful name. The benefit of using the indexed control array, grpAnswer.Controls(0), is that you can use a loop structure, such as a For…Next loop, to loop through several controls and perform the same operation on each very efficiently.

Tip

Using Control Collections
Use control collections when you need to perform the same operation on several controls with something in common, such as being grouped in a GroupBox control or form.

Figure 7-54 shows a flowchart that outlines the logic needed to change the display from one question to another on the form. A counter-controlled Do While structure loops through the RadioButton controls and updates the text on the controls, the image file name, and the status bar text for the next question. Finally, the logic sets a global variable that contains the index of the question current displaying on the form.

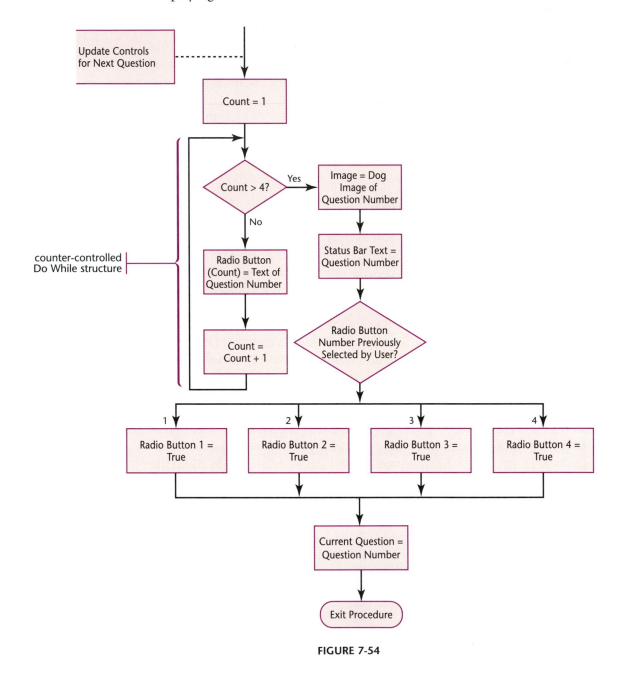

FIGURE 7-54

Figure 7-55 shows the last section of code for the DisplayQuestion() sub procedure. This code corresponds to the logic shown in Figure 7-54. The For…Next loop starting in line 388 sets the Text property value of the

RadioButton controls. Once the For…Next loop loops for all four RadioButton controls, the code changes the image of the dog, updates the text on the status bar, and updates the current question number before exiting the sub procedure.

```
386
387              ' Update controls for next question
388              For shrIndex = 0 To 3
389                  grpAnswer.Controls(shrIndex).Text = gstrQuestions(shrQuestion, shrIndex)
390              Next
391              picQuestion.Image = Image.FromFile(gstrQuestions(shrQuestion, 4))
392              stbQuestion.Panels(0).Text = "Question " & shrQuestion + 1 & " of " &
         gstrQuestions.GetUpperBound(0) + 1
393              Select Case gshrAnswers(shrQuestion)
394                  Case 0
395                      radAnswer1.Checked = True
396                  Case 1
397                      radAnswer2.Checked = True
398                  Case 2
399                      radAnswer3.Checked = True
400                  Case 3
401                      radAnswer4.Checked = True
402              End Select
403              gshrCurrentQuestion = shrQuestion
```

FIGURE 7-55

The following step adds the code shown in Figure 7-55 to the DisplayQuestion() sub procedure.

To Use a Control Collection

1. Enter lines 386 through 403 as shown in Figure 7-55.

Lines 386 through 403 display in the DisplayQuestion() sub procedure in the code window (Figure 7-56).

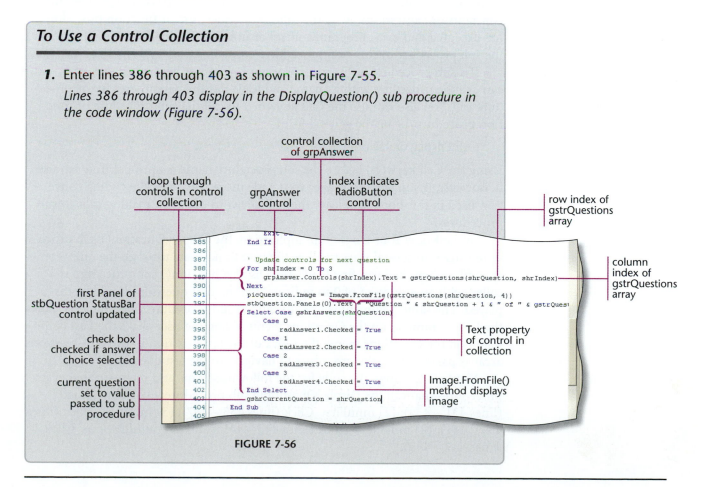

FIGURE 7-56

The For…Next loop starting in line 388 finds each control in the grpAnswer control collection and then sets the control's Text property value to the value corresponding to an element in the gstrQuestions two-dimensional array. Line 391 uses the Image.FromFile() method to update the Image property value of the picQuestion control with the proper image file name. Line 392 updates the Text property value of the panel in the stbQuestion StatusBar control to the current question number. Lines 393 through 402 ensure that the RadioButton controls reflect the answer choice selected by the user, if the user navigates to a previously answered question. Line 403 sets the global variable, gshrCurrentQuestion, to the value passed to the DisplayQuestion() sub procedure. This line of code executes only after the argument has been validated by the previous code, as shown in line 369 of Figure 7-52 on page VB 7.73.

The next step is to write the event procedures that call the DisplayQuestion() sub procedure.

Calling a Sub Procedure

You call a sub procedure in code in much the same manner that you call a function. A sub procedure, however, does not return a value. A sub procedure call in code generally is written on a line by itself. When passing arguments to a sub procedure or function procedure, you should check the sub procedure or function procedure declaration to determine which argument data types are used and whether the arguments are passed ByRef or ByVal. When passing arguments ByRef, you should ensure that the arguments you pass are variables, not constants or expressions. After the called sub procedure or function procedure has executed and exits, program control resumes at the line following the call to the sub procedure or function procedure.

If a sub procedure or function procedure does not have any arguments, you can call the procedure with its name and leave out the parentheses in the procedure call. You also can use the **Call keyword** to call the sub procedure or function procedure, using the general form

Call DisplayQuestion()

Using the Call keyword before the sub procedure name is optional. You can use it, however, if you feel this makes your code more readable. The coding convention used in this book is to leave the Call keyword off when making calls to sub procedures.

In the Know Your Dogs Quiz application, the DisplayQuestion() sub procedure is used in several ways to allow the user to navigate through the quiz. For example, when the form first loads, the DisplayQuestion() sub procedure is called with an argument of 0 to indicate that the first question should be displayed. The same argument is used to call the sub procedure when the user clicks the First command on the Questions menu. When the user clicks the Last command on the Questions menu, the index of the last question in the gstrQuestions array is passed to tell the procedure to navigate to the last question.

Figure 7-57 shows the code for the following form- and menu-related event procedures that call the DisplayQuestion() sub procedure: (1) Form1_Load (lines 431 – 433); (2) mnuFirst_Click (lines 435 – 437); (3) mnuLast_Click (lines 439 – 441); (4) mnuNext_Click (lines 443 – 445); and (5) mnuPrevious_Click (lines 447 – 449).

```
431      Private Sub Form1_Load(ByVal sender As System.Object, ByVal e As System.EventArgs) ↙
             Handles MyBase.Load
432          DisplayQuestion(0) ' Display the first question
433      End Sub
434
435      Private Sub mnuFirst_Click(ByVal sender As System.Object, ByVal e As System.          ↙
             EventArgs) Handles mnuFirst.Click
436          DisplayQuestion(0) ' Display the first question
437      End Sub
438
439      Private Sub mnuLast_Click(ByVal sender As System.Object, ByVal e As System.           ↙
             EventArgs) Handles mnuLast.Click
440          DisplayQuestion(Convert.ToInt16(gstrQuestions.GetUpperBound(0))) ' Display the ↙
             last question
441      End Sub
442
443      Private Sub mnuNext_Click(ByVal sender As System.Object, ByVal e As System.           ↙
             EventArgs) Handles mnuNext.Click
444          DisplayQuestion(gshrCurrentQuestion + Convert.ToInt16(1)) ' Display the next     ↙
             question
445      End Sub
446
447      Private Sub mnuPrevious_Click(ByVal sender As System.Object, ByVal e As System.       ↙
             EventArgs) Handles mnuPrevious.Click
448          DisplayQuestion(gshrCurrentQuestion - Convert.ToInt16(1)) ' Display the          ↙
             previous question
449      End Sub
```

FIGURE 7-57

The following steps add the code shown in Figure 7-57 to the Form1 form, so that the event procedures can call the DisplayQuestion() sub procedure.

To Call a Sub Procedure

1. Click the Form1.vb[Design] tab in the main work area. Double-click anywhere on the Form1 form. When Visual Basic .NET creates the Form1_Load event procedure, enter line 432 as shown in Figure 7-57.

2. Click the Form1.vb[Design] tab in the main work area. Double-click the First command on the Questions menu on the Form1 form. When Visual Basic .NET creates the mnuFirst_Click event procedure, enter line 436 as shown in Figure 7-57.

3. Click the Form1.vb[Design] tab in the main work area. Double-click the Last command on the Questions menu on the Form1 form. When Visual Basic .NET creates the mnuLast_Click event procedure, enter line 440 as shown in Figure 7-57.

4. Click the Form1.vb[Design] tab in the main work area. Double-click the Next command on the Questions menu on the Form1 form. When Visual Basic .NET creates the mnuNext_Click event procedure, enter line 444 as shown in Figure 7-57.

(continued)

5. Click the Form1.vb[Design] tab in the main work area. Double-click the Previous command on the Questions menu on the Form1 form. When Visual Basic .NET creates the mnuPrevious_Click event procedure, enter line 448 as shown in Figure 7-57 on the previous page.

The five event procedures display in the code window as shown in Figure 7-58. Each event procedure calls the DisplayQuestion() sub procedure and passes an appropriate argument.

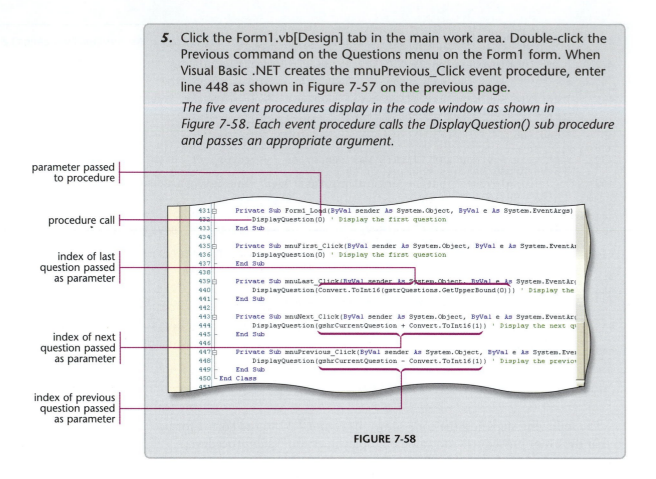

parameter passed to procedure

procedure call

index of last question passed as parameter

index of next question passed as parameter

index of previous question passed as parameter

```
431    Private Sub Form1_Load(ByVal sender As System.Object, ByVal e As System.EventArgs)
432        DisplayQuestion(0) ' Display the first question
433    End Sub
434
435    Private Sub mnuFirst_Click(ByVal sender As System.Object, ByVal e As System.EventAr
436        DisplayQuestion(0) ' Display the first question
437    End Sub
438
439    Private Sub mnuLast_Click(ByVal sender As System.Object, ByVal e As System.EventAr
440        DisplayQuestion(Convert.ToInt16(gstrQuestions.GetUpperBound(0))) ' Display the
441    End Sub
442
443    Private Sub mnuNext_Click(ByVal sender As System.Object, ByVal e As System.EventAr
444        DisplayQuestion(gshrCurrentQuestion + Convert.ToInt16(1)) ' Display the next q
445    End Sub
446
447    Private Sub mnuPrevious_Click(ByVal sender As System.Object, ByVal e As System.Eve
448        DisplayQuestion(gshrCurrentQuestion - Convert.ToInt16(1)) ' Display the previo
449    End Sub
450  End Class
451
```

FIGURE 7-58

The event procedures in Figure 7-58 illustrate the power of using sub procedures and functions to code logic commonly used in a program. Each of the five event procedures calls the DisplayQuestion() sub procedure for a different reason, based on the user's action. Only one line of code is needed for these procedures, because they perform the similar task of allowing the user to navigate the quiz in some manner. You can code additional event procedures in much the same manner.

Using the PerformClick() Method

When coding a program, you may find it practical to write code that performs a user action, such as clicking a button, within code, rather than relying on the user to complete the action. Almost all actions a user performs on controls can be performed from within code. The **PerformClick() method** is a method common to most controls that you call when you want to execute the Click event procedure for the control. Using the PerformClick() method to call the Click event procedure is not always the same as simply calling the Click event procedure directly based on a user action. For example, if you call the Click event procedure of a RadioButton control, the code in the Click event procedure will execute, but the state of the option button on the control does not change. Using the PerformClick() method ensures that any visual effects are handled, in addition to calling the Click event procedure.

In the Know Your Dogs Quiz application, several event procedures perform duplicate actions. For example, the action of moving to the next question occurs when the user clicks the Next command on the Questions menu, when the user clicks the Next button on the form, when the user clicks the Next command on the shortcut menu, and when the user presses the shortcut key, CTRL+N. The Click event procedure for the Next command on the Questions menu and the CTRL+N shortcut key — the mnuNext_Click event procedure — was coded earlier in this chapter. Therefore, the Click event procedures for the Next command on the shortcut menu and the Next button both can use event procedures to call the PerformClick() method to call the existing mnuNext_Click event procedure and cause the next question to display to the user.

Figure 7-59 shows how the PerformClick() method is used in seven Click event procedures to call other existing event procedures from within the code. The event procedures include those associated with the Previous and Next buttons on the form and the commands on the shortcut menu. As shown in Figure 7-59, these event procedures include the following: (1) btnPrevious_Click (lines 451 – 453); (2) btnNext_Click (lines 455 – 457); (3) cmuNext_Click (lines 459 – 461); (4) cmuPrevious_Click (lines 463 – 465); (5) cmuFont_Click (lines 467 – 469); (6) cmuFinish_Click (lines 471 – 473); and (7) cmuExit_Click (lines 475 – 477).

```
451    Private Sub btnPrevious_Click(ByVal sender As System.Object, ByVal e As System.    ↵
       EventArgs) Handles btnPrevious.Click
452        mnuPrevious.PerformClick() ' Click the Previous command on the Questions menu
453    End Sub
454
455    Private Sub btnNext_Click(ByVal sender As System.Object, ByVal e As System.    ↵
       EventArgs) Handles btnNext.Click
456        mnuNext.PerformClick() ' Click the Next command on the Questions menu
457    End Sub
458
459    Private Sub cmuNext_Click(ByVal sender As System.Object, ByVal e As System.    ↵
       EventArgs) Handles cmuNext.Click
460        mnuNext.PerformClick() ' Click the Next command on the Questions menu
461    End Sub
462
463    Private Sub cmuPrevious_Click(ByVal sender As System.Object, ByVal e As System.    ↵
       EventArgs) Handles cmuPrevious.Click
464        mnuPrevious.PerformClick() ' Click the Previous command on the Questions menu
465    End Sub
466
467    Private Sub cmuFont_Click(ByVal sender As System.Object, ByVal e As System.    ↵
       EventArgs) Handles cmuFont.Click
468        mnuFont.PerformClick() ' Click the Font command on the Options menu
469    End Sub
470
471    Private Sub cmuFinish_Click(ByVal sender As System.Object, ByVal e As System.    ↵
       EventArgs) Handles cmuFinish.Click
472        DisplayQuestion(Convert.ToInt16(gstrQuestions.GetUpperBound(0) + 1)) '    ↵
       Navigate past the last question
473    End Sub
474
475    Private Sub cmuExit_Click(ByVal sender As System.Object, ByVal e As System.    ↵
       EventArgs) Handles cmuExit.Click
476        mnuExit.PerformClick() ' Click the Exit command on the File menu
477    End Sub
```

FIGURE 7-59

The following steps add the code shown in Figure 7-59 on the previous page to the Form1 form.

To Use the PerformClick() Method

1. Click the Form1.vb[Design] tab in the main work area. Double-click the btnPrevious control on the Form1 form. When Visual Basic .NET creates the btnPrevious_Click event procedure, enter line 452 as shown in Figure 7-59.

2. Click the Form1.vb[Design] tab in the main work area. Double-click the btnNext control on the Form1 form. When Visual Basic .NET creates the btnNext_Click event procedure, enter line 456 as shown in Figure 7-59.

   The btnPrevious_Click and btnNext_Click event procedures display in the code window (Figure 7-60). The PerformClick() method simulates the user clicking the mnuPrevious and mnuNext buttons on the Questions menu.

btnPrevious_Click event procedure

PerformClick() method

btnNext_Click event procedure

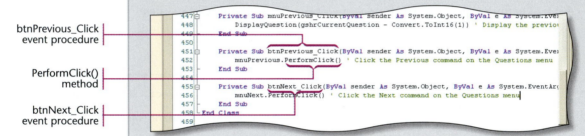

```
447   Private Sub mnuPrevious_Click(ByVal sender As System.Object, ByVal e As System.Eve)
448       DisplayQuestion(gshrCurrentQuestion - Convert.ToInt16(1)) ' Display the previou
449   End Sub
450
451   Private Sub btnPrevious_Click(ByVal sender As System.Object, ByVal e As System.Eve)
452       mnuPrevious.PerformClick() ' Click the Previous command on the Questions menu
453   End Sub
454
455   Private Sub btnNext_Click(ByVal sender As System.Object, ByVal e As System.EventAr(
456       mnuNext.PerformClick() ' Click the Next command on the Questions menu
457   End Sub
458 End Class
459
```

FIGURE 7-60

3. Click the Form1.vb[Design] tab in the main work area. Click the cmuShortcut control in the Component Tray. Double-click the Next command in the Menu Designer on the Form1 form. When Visual Basic .NET creates the cmuNext_Click event procedure, enter line 460 as shown in Figure 7-59.

4. Click the Form1.vb[Design] tab in the main work area. Double-click the Previous command in the Menu Designer on the Form1 form. When Visual Basic .NET creates the cmuPrevious_Click event procedure, enter line 464 as shown in Figure 7-59.

5. Click the Form1.vb[Design] tab in the main work area. Double-click the Font command in the Menu Designer on the Form1 form. When Visual Basic .NET creates the cmuFont_Click event procedure, enter line 468 as shown in Figure 7-59.

6. Click the Form1.vb[Design] tab in the main work area. Double-click the Finish Quiz and Display Result command in the Menu Designer on the Form1 form. When Visual Basic .NET creates the cmuFinish_Click event procedure, enter line 472 as shown in Figure 7-59.

7. Click the Form1.vb[Design] tab in the main work area. Double-click the Exit command in the Menu Designer on the Form1 form. When Visual Basic .NET creates the cmuExit_Click event procedure, enter line 476 as shown in Figure 7-59.

The event procedures for the shortcut menu display in the code window as shown in Figure 7-61. Each calls the other Click event procedures or the DisplayQuestion() sub procedure to perform an action.

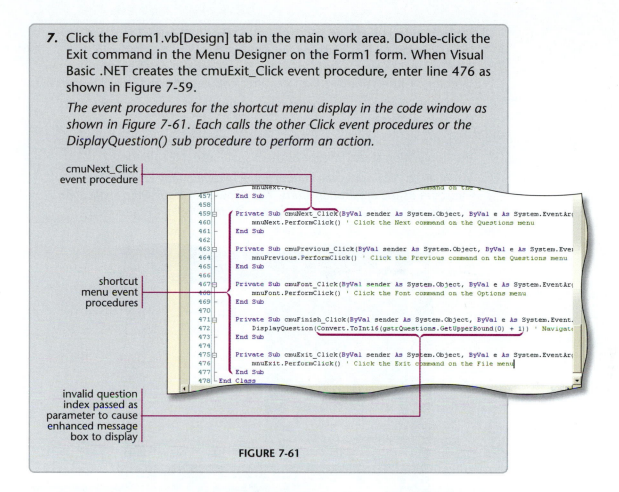

cmuNext_Click event procedure

shortcut menu event procedures

invalid question index passed as parameter to cause enhanced message box to display

FIGURE 7-61

The coding phase for the Know Your Dogs application now is complete and the application can be tested.

Saving, Testing, and Documenting the Project

The following steps save the form and project files for the Know Your Dogs Quiz project on the Data Disk in drive A and then run the application to test the project. Before running the project, the image files used in the quiz must be copied to the folder from which Visual Basic .NET runs the project.

To Save and Test the Project

1. Click the Save All button on the Visual Basic .NET Standard toolbar.

The asterisk next to the tab names on the window title bar and the main work area tab no longer display, indicating that the project has been saved. Because the project initially was created and saved on the Data Disk in drive A, Visual Basic .NET automatically saves the project on the Data Disk in drive A.

(continued)

2. Open Windows Explorer and browse to the A:\Chapter7 folder. Copy the seven image files with the file extension .jpg in the folder in the A:\Chapter7\Know Your Dogs Quiz\Know Your Dogs Quiz\bin directory. Close Windows Explorer after copying the files.

The seven image files just copied must be pasted in the same directory as the executable file.

3. Click the Start button on the Visual Basic .NET Standard toolbar. When the application starts, minimize the Visual Basic .NET window.

Visual Basic .NET opens the Output window temporarily and displays messages as the application starts. The Know Your Dogs Quiz application window and the first image and answer choices display (Figure 7-62).

FIGURE 7-62

4. Attempt to navigate to a question before the first question. Close the message box that displays the warning message.

5. Answer the questions in the quiz. While answering the questions, use all four methods to navigate to the next question: the Next button, the Next command on the Questions menu, the CTRL+N shortcut key, and the Next command on the shortcut menu. The correct answers are English Springer Spaniel, English Setter, Labador Retriever, Dachshund, Samoyed, Old English Sheepdog, and Akita. Navigate past the last question.

The enhanced message box displays, informing the user that he or she has answered the last question. The message box presents two buttons, Yes and No, and displays a question icon (Figure 7-63).

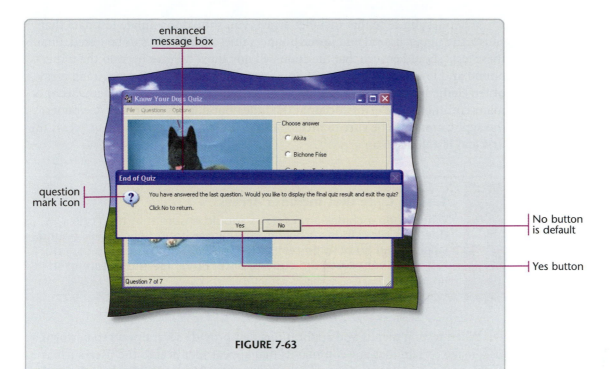

enhanced message box

question mark icon

No button is default

Yes button

FIGURE 7-63

6. Click the Yes button to view the quiz result.

The quiz result indicates that the user passed the quiz (Figure 7-64).

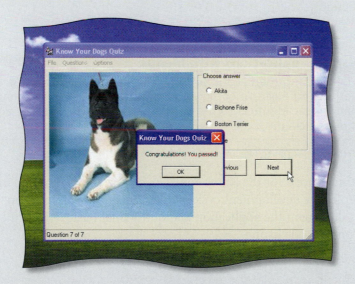

FIGURE 7-64

7. Click the Close button on the Know Your Dogs Quiz application window title bar. Click the Visual Basic .NET taskbar button to display the Visual Basic .NET window. If necessary, close the Output window.

The Visual Basic .NET window maximizes and Visual Basic .NET returns to design time.

When testing code that includes arrays, you should formulate test data that causes the upper-bound and lower-bound values of the arrays to be tested. First, these tests should ensure that the code will not allow indexes beyond the upper-bound and lower-bound values of an array to be referenced. That is, in an array of ten elements, the code should never allow access to the eleventh item. Second, many common logic errors occur at the index boundaries of arrays. As you test the application, also be sure to include test data that causes the code to access the first and last items in an array.

Testing Code that Includes Arrays

When code includes arrays, tests should ensure that the code does not allow indexes beyond the upper-bound and lower-bound values of an array to be referenced. Second, make sure to include test data that causes the code to access the first and last items in an array.

When testing menus and applications that provide several ways to perform a task, make certain that any commands that appear identical to the user, such as the Next command on the Question menu and the Next command on the short-cut menu, perform the exact same actions under all circumstances. Common errors occur when similar commands are coded separately, rather than in procedures or functions.

Testing Applications with Menus

When testing menus and applications that include several methods to perform commands, make certain that commands that appear identical to the user perform the exact same actions under all circumstances.

The testing process for the Know Your Dogs Quiz application is complete. The final step of the development cycle is to document the application. The following steps document the application and quit Visual Basic .NET. Line numbers are printed on the code listing.

To Document the Application and Quit Visual Basic .NET

1. Click the Form1.vb [Design] tab, and then follow the steps on page VB 2.34 of Chapter 2 using the PRINT SCREEN key to print a record of the user interface design of the Form1 form.

A record of the user interface design of the Know Your Dogs Quiz application is printed (Figure 7-65).

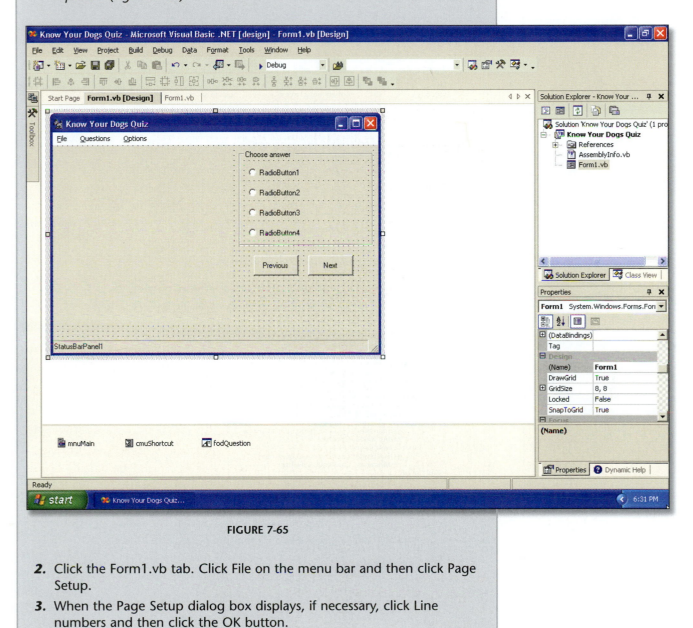

FIGURE 7-65

2. Click the Form1.vb tab. Click File on the menu bar and then click Page Setup.

3. When the Page Setup dialog box displays, if necessary, click Line numbers and then click the OK button.

(continued)

4. Follow the steps on page VB 2.40 of Chapter 2 using the Print command on the File menu to print a record of the code for the Know Your Dogs Quiz application.

A record of the Know Your Dogs Quiz application code is printed (Figure 7-66).

```
A:\Chapter7\Know Your Dogs Quiz\Know Your Dogs Quiz\Form1.vb                    1
 1 Option Strict On
 2 Public Class Form1
 3     Inherits System.Windows.Forms.Form
 4
 5  Windows Form Designer generated code
 6     ' Chapter 7:     Know Your Dogs Quiz
 7     ' Programmer:    J. Quasney
 8     ' Date:          November 24, 2004
 9     ' Purpose:       This program generates a seven question quiz. Each question
10     '                includes an image and four choices in RadioButton controls.
11     '                The user must answer all questions correctly to pass the quiz.
12     '                The solution is stored in the gshrSolution array. The user answers
13     '                are stored in the gshrAnswers array. Questions choices and image
14     '                file names are stored in the gstrQuestions array.
15     Dim gshrSolution As Short() = {0, 3, 2, 1, 0, 0, 3}
16     Dim gshrAnswers As Short() = {-1, -1, -1, -1, -1, -1, -1}
17     Dim gstrQuestions As String(,) = { _
18         {"English Springer Spaniel", "Akita", "Husky", "Bearded Collie", "dog051.jpg"}↵
        ' _
19         {"Pug", "Whippet", "Fox Terrier", "English Setter", "dog50.jpg"}, _
20         {"Chow Chow", "Beagle", "Labrador Retriever", "Foxhound", "dog068.jpg"}, _
21         {"Great Dane", "Dachshund", "Samoyed", "Newfoundland", "dog044.jpg"}, _
22         {"Samoyed", "Pekingese", "English Setter", "Pomeranian", "dog088.jpg"}, _
23         {"Old English Sheepdog", "Saluki", "Rottweiler", "Poodle", "dog074.jpg"}, _
24         {"Collie", "Boston Terrier", "Bichon Frise", "Akita", "dog007.jpg"}}
25
26     Dim gshrCurrentQuestion As Short = 0
27
28     Private Sub DisplayQuestion(ByVal shrQuestion As Short)
29         Dim shrIndex As Short
30
31         ' Check if user clicked Previous button with question 1 displayed
32         If shrQuestion < 0 Then
33             MessageBox.Show("You are already at the beginning of the quiz.", "Know  ↵
    Your Dogs Quiz")
34             gshrCurrentQuestion = 0
35             Exit Sub
36         End If
37
38         ' Store user's answer to previous question in gshrAnswers array
39         Select Case True
40             Case radAnswer1.Checked
41                 gshrAnswers(gshrCurrentQuestion) = 0
42                 radAnswer1.Checked = False
43             Case radAnswer2.Checked
44                 gshrAnswers(gshrCurrentQuestion) = 1
45                 radAnswer2.Checked = False
46             Case radAnswer3.Checked
47                 gshrAnswers(gshrCurrentQuestion) = 2
48                 radAnswer3.Checked = False
49             Case radAnswer4.Checked
50                 gshrAnswers(gshrCurrentQuestion) = 3
51                 radAnswer4.Checked = False
52         End Select
53
54         ' Score quiz
55         If shrQuestion > gstrQuestions.GetUpperBound(0) Then
56             If MessageBox.Show("You have answered the last question. Would you like to↵
    display the final quiz result and exit the quiz?" _
57                 & ControlChars.NewLine & ControlChars.NewLine _
58                 & "Click No to return.", "End of Quiz", _
59                 MessageBoxButtons.YesNo, MessageBoxIcon.Question, _
60                 MessageBoxDefaultButton.Button2) = DialogResult.Yes  ↵
    Then
61                 If QuizResult() Then
62                     MessageBox.Show("Congratulations! You passed!", "Know Your Dogs  ↵
    Quiz")
```

FIGURE 7-66a

A:\Chapter7\Know Your Dogs Quiz\Know Your Dogs Quiz\Form1.vb   2

```
63              Else
64                  MessageBox.Show("Sorry, you did not pass the quiz.", "Know Your    ↙
        Dogs Quiz")
65              End If
66              Me.Close()
67          Else
68              gshrCurrentQuestion = Convert.ToInt16(gstrQuestions.GetUpperBound(0))
69          End If
70          Exit Sub
71      End If
72
73      ' Update controls for next question
74      For shrIndex = 0 To 3
75          grpAnswer.Controls(shrIndex).Text = gstrQuestions(shrQuestion, shrIndex)
76      Next
77      picQuestion.Image = Image.FromFile(gstrQuestions(shrQuestion, 4))
78      stbQuestion.Panels(0).Text = "Question " & shrQuestion + 1 & " of " &        ↙
        gstrQuestions.GetUpperBound(0) + 1
79      Select Case gshrAnswers(shrQuestion)
80          Case 0
81              radAnswer1.Checked = True
82          Case 1
83              radAnswer2.Checked = True
84          Case 2
85              radAnswer3.Checked = True
86          Case 3
87              radAnswer4.Checked = True
88      End Select
89      gshrCurrentQuestion = shrQuestion
90  End Sub
91
92  Private Function QuizResult() As Boolean
93      Dim shrIndex As Short
94
95      For shrIndex = 0 To 6
96          If gshrSolution(shrIndex) <> gshrAnswers(shrIndex) Then
97              Return False
98          End If
99      Next
100     QuizResult = True
101 End Function
102
103 Private Sub mnuExit_Click(ByVal sender As System.Object, ByVal e As System.    ↙
    EventArgs) Handles mnuExit.Click
104     Me.Close() ' Exit application
105 End Sub
106
107 Private Sub mnuFont_Click(ByVal sender As System.Object, ByVal e As System.    ↙
    EventArgs) Handles mnuFont.Click
108     fodQuestion.Font = radAnswer1.Font
109     If fodQuestion.ShowDialog() = DialogResult.OK Then
110         radAnswer1.Font = fodQuestion.Font
111         radAnswer2.Font = fodQuestion.Font
112         radAnswer3.Font = fodQuestion.Font
113         radAnswer4.Font = fodQuestion.Font
114     End If
115 End Sub
116
117 Private Sub Form1_Load(ByVal sender As System.Object, ByVal e As System.EventArgs) ↙
     Handles MyBase.Load
118     DisplayQuestion(0) ' Display the first question
119 End Sub
120
121 Private Sub mnuFirst_Click(ByVal sender As System.Object, ByVal e As System.    ↙
    EventArgs) Handles mnuFirst.Click
122     DisplayQuestion(0) ' Display the first question
123 End Sub
```

FIGURE 7-66b

(continued)

```
        A:\Chapter7\Know Your Dogs Quiz\Know Your Dogs Quiz\Form1.vb                    3
124
125     Private Sub mnuLast_Click(ByVal sender As System.Object, ByVal e As System.      ↵
        EventArgs) Handles mnuLast.Click
126         DisplayQuestion(Convert.ToInt16(gstrQuestions.GetUpperBound(0))) ' Display the↵
        last question
127     End Sub
128
129     Private Sub mnuNext_Click(ByVal sender As System.Object, ByVal e As System.      ↵
        EventArgs) Handles mnuNext.Click
130         DisplayQuestion(gshrCurrentQuestion + Convert.ToInt16(1)) ' Display the next  ↵
        question
131     End Sub
132
133     Private Sub mnuPrevious_Click(ByVal sender As System.Object, ByVal e As System.   ↵
        EventArgs) Handles mnuPrevious.Click
134         DisplayQuestion(gshrCurrentQuestion - Convert.ToInt16(1)) ' Display the       ↵
        previous question
135     End Sub
136
137     Private Sub btnPrevious_Click(ByVal sender As System.Object, ByVal e As System.   ↵
        EventArgs) Handles btnPrevious.Click
138         mnuPrevious.PerformClick() ' Click the Previous command on the Questions menu
139     End Sub
140
141     Private Sub btnNext_Click(ByVal sender As System.Object, ByVal e As System.       ↵
        EventArgs) Handles btnNext.Click
142         mnuNext.PerformClick() ' Click the Next command on the Questions menu
143     End Sub
144
145     Private Sub cmuNext_Click(ByVal sender As System.Object, ByVal e As System.       ↵
        EventArgs) Handles cmuNext.Click
146         mnuNext.PerformClick() ' Click the Next command on the Questions menu
147     End Sub
148
149     Private Sub cmuPrevious_Click(ByVal sender As System.Object, ByVal e As System.   ↵
        EventArgs) Handles cmuPrevious.Click
150         mnuPrevious.PerformClick() ' Click the Previous command on the Questions menu
151     End Sub
152
153     Private Sub cmuFont_Click(ByVal sender As System.Object, ByVal e As System.       ↵
        EventArgs) Handles cmuFont.Click
154         mnuFont.PerformClick() ' Click the Font command on the Options menu
155     End Sub
156
157     Private Sub cmuFinish_Click(ByVal sender As System.Object, ByVal e As System.     ↵
        EventArgs) Handles cmuFinish.Click
158         DisplayQuestion(Convert.ToInt16(gstrQuestions.GetUpperBound(0) + 1)) '        ↵
        Navigate past the last question
159     End Sub
160
161     Private Sub cmuExit_Click(ByVal sender As System.Object, ByVal e As System.       ↵
        EventArgs) Handles cmuExit.Click
162         mnuExit.PerformClick() ' Click the Exit command on the Fil emenu
163     End Sub
164 End Class
165
```

FIGURE 7-66c

5. Click the Visual Basic .NET Close button.

If you made changes to the project since the last time it was saved, Visual Basic .NET displays the Microsoft Visual Basic .NET dialog box. If you click the Yes button, you can resave your project and quit. If you click the No button, you will quit without saving changes. Clicking the Cancel button will close the dialog box.

Chapter Summary

In this chapter, you learned how to use five new controls: the MainMenu control, the ContextMenu control, the StatusBar control, the PictureBox control, and the FontDialog control. You learned how to create menus for an application and how to write code for events that perform the same task, such as displaying the next question in a quiz. You then learned how to declare and initialize one- and two-dimensional arrays. You learned how to write code to manipulate and utilize elements of an array. You also learned how to write function procedures to perform common tasks that return a value and how to write sub procedures. You learned how to pass arguments to function procedures and sub procedures. You learned how to write code for common dialog boxes in order to interact with the user in a standard manner. Finally, you learned how to utilize enhanced message boxes to interact with the user.

What You Should Know

Having completed this chapter, you now should be able to perform the tasks shown in Table 7-24.

Table 7-24   Chapter 7 What You Should Know

TASK NUMBER	TASK	PAGE
1	Start Visual Basic .NET and Start a New Project	VB 7.14
2	Set Form Properties and Add Controls	VB 7.16
3	Change Properties of the GroupBox, RadioButton, and Button Controls	VB 7.21
4	Create Menus on a Menu Bar for a Form	VB 7.24
5	Create a Shortcut Menu for a Form	VB 7.31
6	Change the Properties of a StatusBar Control	VB 7.36
7	Change the Properties of a PictureBox Control	VB 7.39
8	Change the Properties of a FontDialog Control	VB 7.42
9	Declare Arrays	VB 7.49
10	Declare a Function Procedure and Use Arrays in Code	VB 7.55
11	Code a Menu Command and Use a FontDialog Control in Code	VB 7.57
12	Declare a Two-Dimensional Array	VB 7.63
13	Code a Sub Procedure	VB 7.69
14	Code an Array Method and Enhanced MessageBox	VB 7.74
15	Use a Control Collection	VB 7.77
16	Call a Sub Procedure	VB 7.79
17	Use the PerformClick() Method	VB 7.82
18	Save and Test the Project	VB 7.83
19	Document the Application and Quit Visual Basic .NET	VB 7.87

Key Terms

access key *(VB 7.22)*
array *(VB 7.08)*
array name *(VB 7.43)*
array variable *(VB 7.43)*
ByRef keyword *(VB 7.66)*
ByVal keyword *(VB 7.66)*
Call keyword *(VB 7.78)*
ColorDialog control *(VB 7.40)*
common dialog box *(VB 7.08)*
common dialog controls *(VB 7.08)*
Component Tray *(VB 7.15)*
context menu *(VB 7.30)*
ContextMenu control *(VB 7.06)*
ContextMenu property *(VB 7.30)*
control collection *(VB 7.75)*
Controls property *(VB 7.75)*
Dim statement for arrays *(VB 7.44)*
dynamically dimensioned array
    (VB 7.46)
End Function statement *(VB 7.53)*
Exit Function statement *(VB 7.53)*
FontDialog control *(VB 7.08)*
function procedure *(VB 7.51)*
Function statement *(VB 7.51)*
line-continuation character *(VB 7.62)*
lower-bound value *(VB 7.44)*
MainMenu control *(VB 7.06)*
Menu Designer *(VB 7.15)*

MenuItem *(VB 7.22)*
MenuItem class *(VB 7.22)*
multidimensional array *(VB 7.44)*
one-dimensional array *(VB 7.44)*
OpenFileDialog control *(VB 7.40)*
PageSetupDialog control *(VB 7.40)*
parallel arrays *(VB 7.49)*
passing by reference method
    (VB 7.66)
passing by value method *(VB 7.66)*
PageSetupDialog control *(VB 7.40)*
PerformClick() method *(VB 7.80)*
PictureBox control *(VB 7.07)*
PrintDialog control *(VB 7.40)*
PrintPreviewDialog control *(VB 7.40)*
Private keyword *(VB 7.52)*
Return statement *(VB 7.53)*
SaveFileDialog control *(VB 7.40)*
separator *(VB 7.29)*
shortcut menu *(7.06)*
ShowDialog() method *(VB 7.40)*
StatusBar control *(VB 7.08)*
sub procedure *(VB 7.64)*
Sub statement *(VB 7.65)*
subscript *(VB 7.43)*
upper-bound value *(VB 7.44)*

Homework Assignments

Short Answer

1. Use a _____ control to create a menu that appears at the top of a form at run time. Use a _____ control to create a shortcut menu that can be linked to a right-click event for any visible control on a form.

2. A _____ is a procedure that returns a value and has a data type. A _____ is a procedure that performs an action but does not have a value. You can return values in a procedure either by declaring the procedure as a _____ or by passing arguments by _____ and modifying the passed arguments in the procedure.

3. Write the Function statement for a private function that accepts two integer values, one double value, and two Decimal values and then returns a Boolean value.

4. Using a method of an array, write the one line of code that copies all elements after the fifth element in the array intI(20) to the array intJ(20).

5. Given the one-dimensional array intNumber that consists of 1,000 elements, write a partial program that will count the number of elements in the array intNumber that have a value less than 0; between 0 and 100, inclusive; and greater than 100. Use the following counters:

   shrLow: count of elements with a value less than 0

   shrMid: count of elements with a value between 0 and 100, inclusive

   shrHigh: count of elements with a value greater than 100

   Use the index intI to help reference the elements.

6. Given an array dblShift that has been declared to have 10 elements, assume that each element of the array dblShift has been assigned a value. Write a partial program to shift all the values up one location. That is, assign the value of dblShift(9) to dblShift(8), dblShift(8) to dblShift(7), and dblShift(1) to dblShift(9). Do not use any array other than the array dblShift. Be sure not to destroy a value before it is shifted.

7. Given the three arrays shrOriginal, shrModified, and shrResult, each declared to have 75 elements, assume that the elements of the arrays shrOriginal and shrModified have been assigned values. Write a partial program that compares each element of the array shrOriginal with its corresponding element in the array shrModified. Assign 1, 0, or −1 to the corresponding element in the array shrResult, as follows:

   1 if shrOriginal is greater than shrModified

   0 if shrOriginal is equal to shrModified

   −1 if shrOriginal is less than shrModified

(continued)

Short Answer (continued)

8. Identify the error(s), if any, in each of the following partial programs:

   a.
   ```
   Dim intX(500) As Integer, IntI as Integer
   Dim strOutput As String
   For intI = -50 To 450
       strOutput &= Convert.ToStrint(intX(intI)) & ", "
   Next intI
   ```

   b.
   ```
   Dim intX(400) As Integer, IntI as Integer
   Dim strOutput As String
   For intK = 400 To 1 Step -1
       strOutput &= Convert.ToString(intX(intK)) & ", "
   Next intK
   ```

9. Given the two two-dimensional arrays intR and intS, each of which has 20 rows and 20 columns and is of the Integer data type, write a partial program using a For loop to efficiently compute the sum (intSum) of the elements of the two arrays that have equal subscript values. That is, find the following:

   $intSum = intR(0, 0) + intR(1, 1) + \ldots + intR(20, 20) + intS(0, 0) + intS(1, 1) + \ldots intS(19, 19)$

10. Given the one-dimensional array intA, consisting of 43 elements, write the Dim statement and the For…Next loop to count the number of elements with negative, positive, and 0 values in the array.

11. Write a partial program to find the salesperson who has the least total sales for a given period. Assume that the total sales are in the array dblSales, that the corresponding salespersons' names are in the array strPerson, and that each array has an upper-bound value of 30.

12. Using the same arrays as in assignment 11, write a partial program to find the salesperson who has the greatest total sales for a given period.

13. Consider the valid code segment below. What displays in the message box when the code segment executes?

   ```
   Dim intFib(10)
   strResult = "N" & ControlChars.Tab & "Nth Fibonacci Nunber" _
   & ControlChars.NewLine
   intFib(1) = 1
   intFib(2) = 1
   strResult &= 1 & ControlChars.Tab & intFib(1)
   strResult &= 2 & ControlChars.Tab & intFib(2)
   For intNum = 3 To 10
       intFib(intNum) = intFib(intNum - 2) + intFib(intNum - 1)
       strResult &= intNum & ControlChars.Tab & intFib(intNum)
   Next intNum
   MessageBox.Show(strResult)
   ```

14. Using an array method, write a line of code to search a one-dimensional array of positive integers for the value 5 and then assign the result to the integer variable, intResult. Write the pseudocode for a function that performs the same operation but does not use any array methods other than GetUpperBound() and GetLowerBound(). The function should return the value −1 if the value is not found.

15. Assume that the array intA has four rows and four columns and that the elements of the array intA are assigned the following values:

    Array intA   A(0, 0) = 1 and A (2, 1) = 10

1	2	3	4
5	6	7	8
9	10	11	12
13	14	15	16

    Which of the following arrays below accurately represent the final arrangement of the array intA after the following code executes?

    ```
    For intI = 0 To 3
        For intJ = 0 To 3
            intA(intI, intJ) = intA(intJ, intI)
        Next intJ
    Next intI
    ```

    a.

1	2	3	4
5	6	7	8
9	10	11	12
13	14	15	16

    b.

1	5	9	13
5	6	10	14
9	10	11	15
13	14	15	16

    c.

1	2	2	4
5	6	6	8
9	10	10	12
13	14	14	16

    d.

16	15	14	13
12	11	10	9
8	7	6	5
4	3	2	1

    e. None of the above

16. Refer to the initial array intA given in assignment 15 above. What will be the final arrangement of the array intA after each of the following partial programs executes? Select your answer from the choices given in assignment 15.

    a.
    ```
    For intI = 0 To 3
        intA(intI, 2) = intA(intI, 1)
    Next intI
    ```
    b.
    ```
    intJ = 2
    For intI = 0 To 3
        intA(intI, intJ + 1) = intA(intI, intJ)
    Next intI
    ```

                                                              (continued)

Short Answer *(continued)*

c.
```
For intI = 0 To 3
    intA(intI, intI) = intA(intI - 2, intI + 2)
Next intI
```
d.
```
For intI = 0 To 3
    For intJ = 0 To 3
        intA(intI, intJ) = intA(intI, intJ)
    Next intJ
Next intI
```

17. Consider the function procedure and sub procedure declarations below. What is wrong with the each of the declarations?

a. `Dim Function FindValue() As Object`

b. `Private Sub AverageValues(ByRef intI, ByRef intK) As Double`

c. `Public Sub PrintDisclaimer(ByVal intK, ByRef strJ, ByRef strK)`

d. `Function DisplayErrorMessage(strI, strJ, "Error") As String`

18. Consider the code segments below. What is displayed in a message box after each code segment executes?

a.
```
Dim dblB As Double = 20.0, dblC As Double
Compute(10.0, dblB, "Parameters", dblC)
MessageBox.Show("The value of dblC =" & dblC)
Sub Compute (ByVal dblX As Double, ByVal dblY As Double, _
    ByVal strTerm As String, ByRef dblZ As Double)
        dblZ = 3 * dblX ^ 2 + dblY / 2 +strTerm.Length
End Sub
```

b.
```
MessageBox.Show(Convert.ToString(Formula(5, 6)))
Function Formula(ByVal dblX As Double, ByVal dblY As Double) _
    As Double
    Dim dblNum As Double
    dblNum = dblX * dblY + dblNum
    Formula = dblNum
End Function
```

Learn It Online

Start your browser and visit scsite.com/vbnet/exs. Follow the instructions in the exercises below.

1. **Chapter Reinforcement TF, MC, and SA**   Click the True/False, Multiple Choice, and Short Answer link below Chapter 7. Print and then answer the questions.

2. **Practice Test**   Click the Practice Test link below Chapter 7. Answer each question, enter your first and last name at the bottom of the page, and then click the Grade Test button. When the graded practice test displays on your screen, click Print on the File menu to print a hard copy. Continue to take practice tests until you score 80% or better. Hand in a printout of the final practice test.

3. **Crossword Puzzle Challenge**   Click the Crossword Puzzle Challenge link below Chapter 7. Read the instructions, and then enter your first and last name. Click the Play button. Complete the crossword puzzle. When you are finished, click the Submit button. When the crossword puzzle redisplays, click the Print button.

4. **Tips and Tricks**   Click the Tips and Tricks link below Chapter 7. Click a topic that pertains to Chapter 7. Right-click the information and then click Print on the shortcut menu. Construct a brief example of what the information relates to in Visual Basic .NET to confirm you understand how to use the tip or trick. Hand in the example and printed information.

5. **Newsgroups**   Click the Newsgroups link below Chapter 7. Click a topic that pertains to Chapter 7. Print three comments.

6. **Expanding Your Horizons**   Click the Articles for Visual Basic .NET below Chapter 7. Click a topic that pertains to Chapter 7. Print the information. Construct a brief example of what the information relates to in Visual Basic .NET to confirm you understand the contents of the article. Hand in the example and printed information.

7. **Search Sleuth**   Select three key terms from the Key Terms section of this chapter and then use the Google search engine at google.com (or any major search engine) to display and print two Web pages for each key term.

Debugging Assignment

Start Visual Basic .NET and open the Ganden Real Estate project from the Chapter7\Ganden Real Estate folder on the Data Disk. The project consists of a form that contains a StatusBar control, a MainMenu control, a ContextMenu control, Label controls, and TextBox controls. The program displays home listings stored in parallel arrays in the code. The Record menu is used to navigate through the home listings.

The Ganden Real Estate project contains bugs in the user interface and in the program code. Run the project to experience some of the problems listed in the steps below. Follow the steps to debug the project.

1. The menu items on the ContextMenu control do not perform any actions. Link the click event procedures on the ContextMenu menu items to click events on the Record menu. Use the PerformClick() method.

2. The StatusBar panel does not update correctly. Fix this bug. The StatusBar control displays a sizing grip even though the form is not sizable at run time. Remove the sizing grip from the StatusBar control.

3. The Record menu requires intuitive shortcuts. A separator should also be added to the Record menu to separate the first two and last two items.

4. The parallel arrays do not match in size when they are initialized in the code. Add two additional home prices for the final two homes as $145,500.00 and $163,200.00.

5. The sub procedure that computes the average price contains errors in the logic. The errors involve the bounds of the array.

6. The code that navigates the user to the first, last, next, and previous records is incorrect. The bounds of the array are not checked correctly and the array indexes are used improperly.

7. Lock the controls, save the project, and then run the project to test for any additional bugs. The application should display as shown in Figure 7-67.

8. Document the form code for the Form1.vb form. Circle the lines of code you modified on the code printout.

FIGURE 7-67

Programming Assignments

1 Passing Parameters to Function and Sub Procedures

Using the following steps, develop a program that illustrates the concepts of function procedures, sub procedures, passing by reference, and passing by value. The program performs the calculation of multiplying price by quantity to determine the total (Figure 7-68). The user chooses to either perform the calculation using a function procedure or using a sub procedure. The user also chooses how to pass the price and quantity to the function procedure or sub procedure.

1. Create the interface similar to the interface shown in Figure 7-68. Use appropriate names for controls, center the window on startup at run time, and make sure the window is not resizable at run time.

2. Write a function procedure that multiplies the price and quantity and returns a Double value for the total. The function procedure should accept both parameters by reference. After performing the calculation, the function procedure should set the input arguments to 0.

3. Write a sub procedure that multiplies the price and quantity and returns a Double value for the total. The sub procedure should include three arguments accepted by reference (price, quantity, and total). After performing the calculation, both sub procedures should set the input arguments to 0.

4. Write code for the first two Button controls' click event procedures. Check the value of the RadioButton controls in your code to determine how to call the appropriate procedure and how to pass the arguments. (**Hint:** To force an argument to be passed by value, enclose the argument in parentheses.)

5. Write code for the Reset button's click event procedures that sets all values to 0 and resets the RadioButton controls to their initial state.

6. Run the project and correct any errors. If changes have been made, save the project again. In run time, the application window should display as shown in Figure 7-68. Use the data shown in Figure 7-68 to perform the calculation using every possible choice of passing parameters and calling either the function procedure or the sub procedure. Write down your results in a clearly labeled table of input choices and output values.

7. Document the user interface and the code for the project.

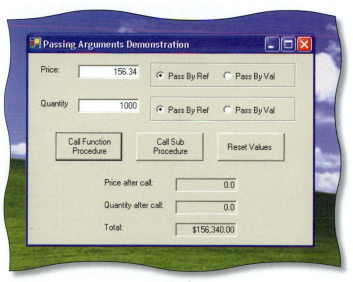

FIGURE 7-68

2 Enhanced MessageBox Features and StatusBar Panels

Develop a program that demonstrates the enhanced options for the MessageBox class. Use three GroupBox controls with RadioButton controls contained within each. The first GroupBox control should contain the various options for which buttons display in the message box. The second GroupBox control should contain the various options for which icon displays in the message box. The third GroupBox control should contain options for which button is the default button. Disable any RadioButton controls in the third GroupBox control that are not valid given other choices that the user has made. Use a sub procedure to handle the functionality of determining which buttons are valid in the third GroupBox control and properly handling which button is selected when one or more of these buttons become disabled. Use two TextBox controls to allow the user to type a message box title and a message. Add a Button control to the form to display the message box as designed by the user's selections in the GroupBox and TextBox controls. Use three panels on a StatusBar control to display the current selections made by the user.

3 Using a Two-Dimensional Array to Find Wind Chill Factors

Design and develop a program that accepts user input of a temperature between –20º F and 15º F and a wind velocity between 5 mph and 30 mph, both in multiples of five. Based on the user input, the program should look up the wind chill factor in a two-dimensional array and display it to the user. Use a function procedure to find the result and then return the result to the calling event procedure. Use the following table of wind chill factors to calculate the wind chill.

Table of Wind Chill Factors

Temperature in Fahrenheit	Wind Velocity in Miles per Hour					
	5	10	15	20	25	30
–20	–26	–46	–58	–67	–74	–79
–15	–21	–40	–51	–60	–66	–71
–10	–15	–34	–45	–53	–59	–64
–5	–10	–27	–38	–46	–51	–56
0	–5	–22	–31	–39	–44	–49
5	0	–15	–25	–31	–36	–41
10	7	–9	–18	–24	–29	–33
15	12	–3	–11	–17	–22	–25

In your program, initialize a two-dimensional array with the values above. Display the result in a message box. Use NumericUpDown controls to accept the input and do not allow selections of values not in the table.

Use the following sample data to test the program:

Temperature (°F)	Wind Velocity (mph)
−15	10
0	30
5	10

The output for the test data should be −40, −49, and −15.

4 Performing Calculations on Rows and Columns of an Array

Create an application that either sums or averages the rows or columns of a two-dimensional array depending on user choices. Use the following data for the array:

5	7	3	9	12
4	8	9	13	4
0	−1	−7	13	8
4	4	4	4	0

Create a menu bar with a File menu that includes a Perform Action command and an Exit command. The Perform Action command computes either the sum or the average of the rows or columns in the array and displays the result in a message box. The Exit command exits the application. Create a second menu on the menu bar called the Action menu. Add a Sum Rows command, Sum Columns command, Average Rows command, and Average Columns command to the Action menu. Use the RadioCheck and Check properties of each command to allow the user to select a command on the Action menu. The Perform Action command checks to see which command is selected on the Action menu to determine which operation to execute when the user clicks the Perform Action command. Note that the commands on the Action menu do not require any event procedures. Include appropriate shortcut keys for all commands. After the Perform Action command executes, the program should display the results in a message box. The message box should display results for each row or column separated by a ControlChars.NewLine character. The message box also should ask the user if he or she wants to continue or to exit the application.

5 Designing Menus to Change Control Properties

Develop a program that uses menus to modify and track the current properties of controls on a form. Add two PictureBox controls to a resizable form. Use the user interface design shown in Figure 7-69 as a guide to create a menu bar with four menus that change the property values of the two PictureBox controls. Use the Checked property of the commands on the Control menu to set whether one, both, or neither of the controls are affected by the commands selected in the other menus. Both PictureBox controls should start at the top-left corner of the form. Figure 7-69 shows the application after several commands have been executed and the control positions have been changed on the form. The Next Color command should set the BackColor property value of the control to Colors.Red, Colors.Green, or Colors.Orange. Loop through these colors using the next color whenever the Next Color command is used. The Previous Color command should set the BackColor property value of the control to Colors.Red, Colors.Green, or Colors.Orange. Loop through these colors using the previous color whenever the Previous Color command is used.

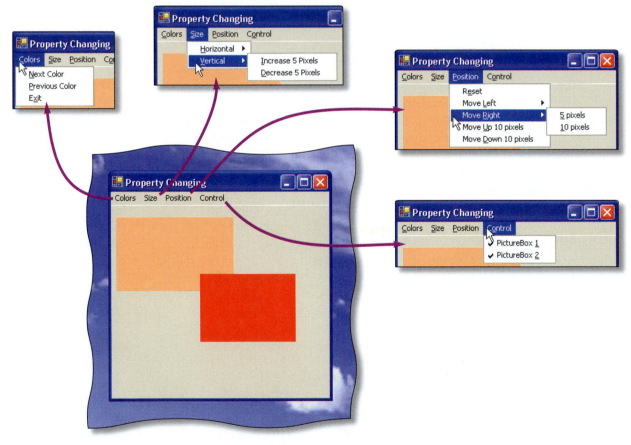

FIGURE 7-69

6 Merging Arrays

Merging is the process of combining two sorted lists into a single sorted list. In some cases, one list can be appended to the other, and the new list then can be sorted. Merging using this method, however, is not always the most efficient. Write a program that merges two arrays, intX and intY, into array intZ. Assume that the arrays intX and intY have been presorted and are in ascending sequence. Declare the array intX to have 15 elements, the array intY to have 13 elements, and the array intZ to have 28 elements. Display the contents of the array intZ in a TextBox control that has its MultiLine property set to True. Do not use any array methods in your code. (**Hint:** Be sure to take into consideration that the two arrays are not the same size. That is, when the shorter of the two arrays has been processed, assign the remaining elements of the longer array to the array intZ.)

Use the following sample data for the two initial arrays:

Array intX	15 elements	4, 9, 12, 15, 22, 33, 44, 66, 72, 84, 87, 92, 96, 98, 99
Array intY	13 elements	6, 8, 12, 16, 24, 31, 68, 71, 73, 74, 81, 93, 94

The resulting array should have the elements in the following order:

4, 6, 8, 9, 12, 12, 15, 16, 22, 24, 31, 33, 44, 66, 68, 71, 72, 73, 74, 81, 84, 87, 92, 93, 94, 96, 98, 99

7 Using Array Methods to Merge Arrays

Solve Programming Assignment 6 using array methods in a program that merges the two arrays, intX and intY, into the array intZ. (**Hint:** Copy the arrays to a larger array first, and then sort the array.)

8 Drawing a Histogram to Display Survey Results

Design and develop a program that displays a histogram using asterisks in a message box, as shown in Figure 7-70. Use the following data from survey results as the data for the histogram: 15, 8, 12, 3, 2, 0, 3, 9, 12, 8. Store the values in an array with the Integer data type. Display the results in two columns labeled Result and Histogram. Use the ControlChars.Tab constant to separate the columns. Build the entire output message in a string variable using nested For loops. The outer loop should loop from 0 to the upper-bound value of the array. The inner loop should loop from 1 to the value of the next survey result. The histogram should display as shown in Figure 7-70.

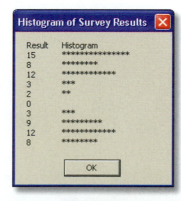

FIGURE 7-70

8

Debugging, Creating Executable Files, and Distributing a Windows Application

Objectives

You will have
mastered the material in
this chapter when you can:

- Describe the difference between syntax,
  logic, and run-time errors
- Find syntax errors during design time
- Find run-time errors and logic errors during run time
- Set breakpoints
- Execute one statement at a time by stepping
- Set the next statement to execute
- Evaluate variables using DataTips
- Evaluate variables and expressions using the QuickWatch and Watch windows
- Change values of variables using debug tools
- Use the Autos, Locals, and Me windows to examine variables and objects
- Use the Command window to execute commands
- Set the icon for an executable file
- Create an executable file
- Create a setup program to distribute a Windows application

Introduction

Chapter 8 concentrates on using the rich set of debugging tools available in Visual Basic .NET and creating an executable file and setup program to distribute an application to users.

Three general categories of errors that require debugging include syntax errors, logic errors, and run-time errors. This chapter discusses how you can find syntax errors during design time and logic errors and run-time errors during run time. You also will learn how to set breakpoints in code to pause the execution of a program temporarily. You will learn how to watch variables during execution and examine variables while a program is paused. The chapter also instructs you how to use stepping to execute a program, one code statement at a time. You will learn how to set an icon for a project's executable file and how to create an executable file for distribution to users. Finally, you will learn how to create a setup program used to distribute a Windows application to users.

Chapter Eight — Debugging the Modified Today's Sales Check Application

This chapter steps you through the process using Visual Basic .NET debugging techniques to debug a modified version of the Today's Sales Check application developed in Chapter 6. The modified version of the application in this chapter includes errors introduced using the hypothetical scenario in which another programmer tried to enhance the application without completely testing it during the implementation phase. Incomplete testing is a common cause of errors. The project thus requires debugging to find and fix the syntax, logic, and run-time errors before the application can move to the testing phase of the development cycle.

Visual Basic .NET provides several methods you can use to find the portion of the program that includes an error. These methods are called **debugging techniques**. The errors themselves are called **bugs**, and the process of detecting the bugs is called **debugging**.

The programming techniques introduced in the first seven chapters can help to minimize programming errors. These good design and development practices, combined with Visual Basic .NET's Intellisense™ technology, can help you avoid many errors, but they do not guarantee error-free programs. Carelessness or insufficient thought during a program's development can introduce problems that cause programs not to work as anticipated or produce erroneous results. When these types of problems occur, you can use debugging techniques to isolate the errors and correct the erroneous code.

As just mentioned, three general categories of errors that require debugging include syntax errors, logic errors, and run-time errors. A **syntax error** occurs when you violate a rule of the Visual Basic .NET language. A **logic error** occurs when a program does not behave as intended, due to poor design or incorrect implementation of the design. A **run-time error**, called an **exception**, is an error that occurs when conditions arise during run time that the CLR (Common Language Runtime, which executes the application) does not know how to handle.

Syntax errors generally are discovered during design time. As you write code statements, Visual Basic .NET can detect most syntax errors using Intellisense™ technology. Visual Basic .NET then highlights the error and reminds you to fix it by adding a task to the Task List window. No programming language, however, can detect all errors. Some syntax errors go undetected by Visual Basic .NET until an abnormal end occurs during run time or the program ends with the results in error. When you attempt to run a program with syntax errors, Visual Basic .NET then can detect the syntax errors and display appropriate diagnostic messages.

Logic errors and run-time errors generally are discovered in three ways:

1. During unit testing in the implementation phase of the development cycle
2. During integration and other testing during the test phase of the development cycle
3. When users run the program

To help you find and fix logic errors, Visual Basic .NET includes tools that allow you to set a breakpoint in a program to pause the program (Figure 8-1a on the next page) and to watch and modify variables during run time. For example, you can set a breakpoint on a code statement during design time. When the program is run in the IDE; the **breakpoint** causes the execution of code to pause at the statement. Figure 8-1a shows a breakpoint set in code at line 139 during design time, with the resulting breakpoint displaying in the Breakpoints window. The **Breakpoints window** contains a list of breakpoints currently set for code statements in the project. As shown in Figure 8-1b once a breakpoint is set at a line, Visual Basic .NET halts execution of the Today's Sales Check project at the breakpoint during run time. In this example, Visual Basic .NET halts execution at line 139, where the breakpoint is set. Once the program has paused at a breakpoint, you can instruct Visual Basic .NET to resume execution or execute the code line by line. Figure 8-1c shows that line 145 currently has control after stepping through the code in lines 139 through 144. While the program is paused, you can view and change the values of variables using the **Watch window** (Figure 8-1d).

Visual Basic .NET also includes tools that help you find and fix run-time errors. Recall that run-time errors, or exceptions, are errors that occur when conditions arise during run time that the CLR (Common Language Runtime, which executes the application) does not know how to handle. Chapter 4 discussed how to construct error-free numeric expressions to avoid exceptions on page VB 4.56. An example of such an exception is when the program code includes a numeric expression that attempts to divide by 0, an expression that is mathematically incorrect. Intellisense™ technology will not detect this as a syntax error during design time. The error also is not necessarily a logic error, because an attempt to divide by 0 could be due to invalid data input. When a program attempts to divide by 0 during run time, the CLR cannot continue with execution, so it displays an error to the user before terminating the program. Visual Basic .NET's debugging tools can help you find the cause of these exceptions or assist you in reproducing the conditions that caused the exception. Once you find the cause, either you can modify the program to avoid the exception or write code to handle the exception, rather than letting the CLR display an error and terminate the program.

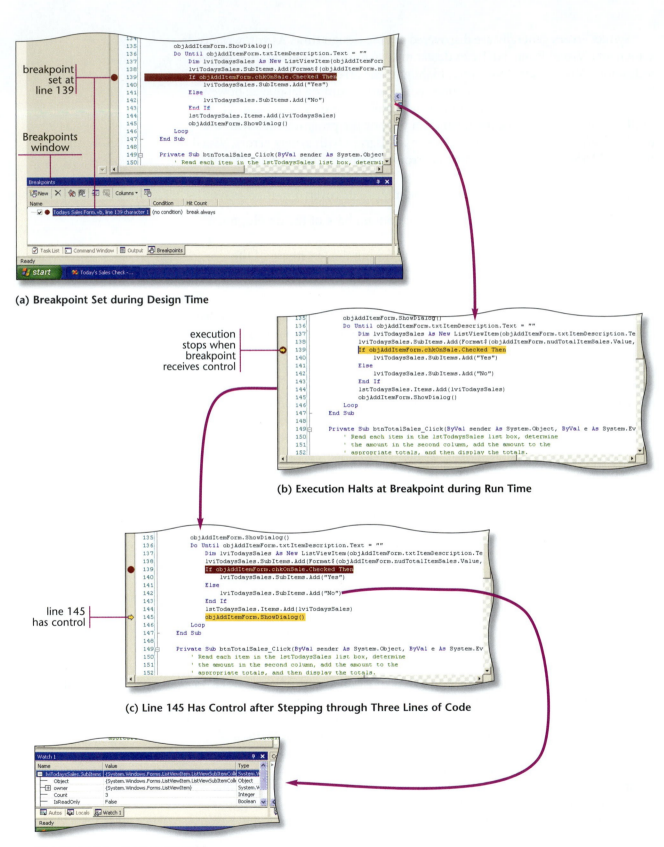

(a) Breakpoint Set during Design Time

(b) Execution Halts at Breakpoint during Run Time

(c) Line 145 Has Control after Stepping through Three Lines of Code

(d) lviTodaySales.SubItems Variable
Watched in Watch Window

FIGURE 8-1

The modified Today's Sales Check project in this chapter contains syntax errors, logic errors, and run-time errors. The following debugging process will be used to find and fix errors with the assistance of the Visual Basic .NET debugging tools:

- Determine the symptoms of an error
- Reproduce the error
- Determine which code statements are causing the error
- Fix the code statements
- Test the modified code to ensure that no unwanted side effects occur as a result of the modifications

The Debugging Process

To find and fix bugs, use the following steps: determine the symptoms of an error, reproduce the error, determine the errant code statements causing the error, fix the code statements, and then test the modified code to ensure that no unwanted side effects occur as a result of the modifications.

Starting Visual Basic .NET and Opening an Existing Project

The following steps start Visual Basic .NET and open the modified Today's Sales Check project.

To Start Visual Basic .NET and Open an Existing Project

1. Insert the Data Disk in drive A.

2. Start Visual Basic .NET. When the Start Page displays, click the Open Project button on the Start Page.

3. If necessary, click the Look in box arrow and then click 3½ Floppy (A:). Double-click the Chapter8 folder.

   Visual Basic .NET displays the Open Project dialog box. The Chapter8 folder displays in the Look in box.

4. Double-click the Today's Sales Check folder. If necessary, click the Today's Sales Check solution file (Today's Sales Check.sln).

   The Today's Sales Check folder displays as the current folder in the Look in box. The Today's Sales Check solution file displays as selected in the dialog box.

   (continued)

5. Click the Open button. If the Todays Sales Form form does not display in the main work area, double-click Todays Sales Form.vb in the Solution Explorer window.

The Today's Sales Check project opens in the Visual Basic .NET IDE. The Todays Sales Form form displays in the main work area. The gray border around the form indicates that the form is locked (Figure 8-2).

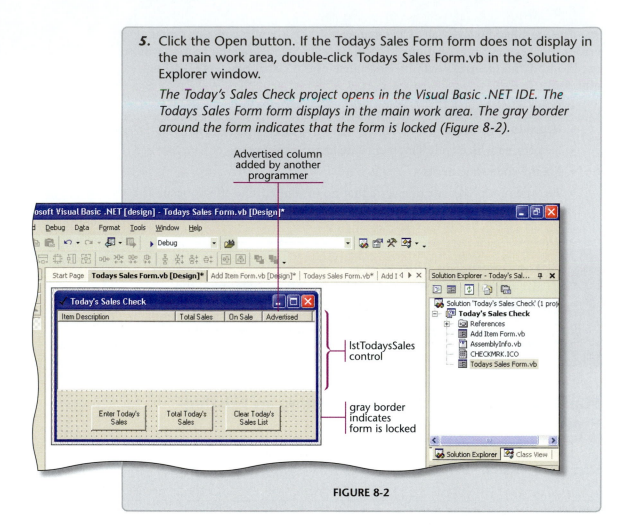

FIGURE 8-2

As shown in Figure 8-2, the lstTodaysSales control in the modified Today's Sales Check project includes a fourth column, the Advertised column. This column was added by another programmer attempting to enhance the Today's Sales Check project created in Chapter 6. The Advertised column should include a Yes or No value to indicate whether the item was recently advertised. The programmer also modified the Add Item Form form to include a CheckBox control where the user indicates the value to place in the Advertised column. When the user clicks the Total Today's Sales button, the program should total the sales for items that have the value, Yes, in the Advertised column, in addition to the other three totals.

Syntax Errors and the Task List Window

As you have learned, a syntax error occurs when the code violates a rule of the Visual Basic .NET language. Visual Basic .NET detects such errors as misspelled keywords, misspelled variable names, or missing keywords as syntax errors. For example, if you do not include the As keyword in a Dim statement when you declare a variable with a data type, Visual Basic .NET will detect a syntax error.

Finding and Fixing Syntax Errors

When Visual Basic .NET detects a syntax error, it takes two actions. First, Intellisense™ underlines the syntax error in the code window with a blue, wavy underline (Figure 8-3). When you move the mouse pointer over the syntax error, Intellisense™ displays a description of the syntax error. Second, an entry is added to the Task List window to remind you that you must fix the error. The entry includes a description of the error and a line number indicating where the error occurs in the code.

```
155            End If
156            lstTodaysSales.Items.Add(lviTodaysSales)
157            objAddItemForm.ShowDialog()
158        Loop
159    End Sub
160
161    Private Sub btnTotalSales_Click(ByVal sender As System.Object
162        ' Read each item in the lstTodaysSales list box, determin
163        ' the amount in the second column, add the amount to the
164        ' appropriate totals, and then display the totals.
165        Dim intIndex, intListCount As Intger
166        Dim sngTotalSales As Single = 0
167        Dim sngTotalOnSale As Single = 0
168        Dim sngTotalRegularPrice As Single = 0
169        Dim sngTotalAdvertised As Single
```

blue wavy underline indicates syntax error

FIGURE 8-3

If you attempt to run the project in the IDE while the code contains a syntax error, Visual Basic .NET displays a warning in a dialog box, indicating that errors exist in the code (Figure 8-4). The dialog box allows you to choose whether you want to continue execution despite the errors. If you choose to continue executing the code with syntax errors, the lines that contain the errors will not be accessible during run time. If the syntax error is severe enough, the entire procedure that contains the error may not be accessible during run time. For example, if the Click event procedure of a btnOK control contains a syntax error, Visual Basic .NET may not execute the Click event procedure when you click the btnOK button during run time.

dialog box indicates errors

Microsoft Development Environment

⚠ There were build errors. Continue?

Yes   No

FIGURE 8-4

Tip

Running Projects with Syntax Errors
If you choose to run a project and execute code while syntax errors exist in the code, the procedures that contain the errors may not be accessible during run time.

The following steps find and correct the syntax errors in the code of the Today's Sales Check project.

To Find and Fix Syntax Errors Using the Task List Window

1. With the Today's Sales Check project open, click View on the menu bar and then click Other Windows. When the Other Windows submenu displays, click Task List.

   The Task List window opens and displays at the bottom of the IDE (Figure 8-5). Five syntax errors display as tasks in the Task List window.

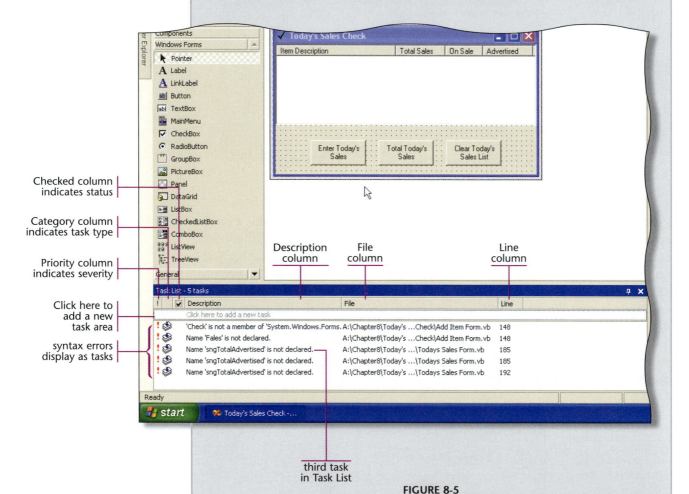

Checked column indicates status

Category column indicates task type

Priority column indicates severity

Click here to add a new task area

syntax errors display as tasks

Description column

File column

Line column

third task in Task List

FIGURE 8-5

2. Double-click the third task in the Task List.

   The Todays Sales Form.vb code window opens. Visual Basic .NET highlights the location of the third syntax error in the code, on line 185 of the Todays Sales Form form code (Figure 8-6). Another syntax error on the same line is underlined with a blue wavy underline. Visual Basic .NET highlights the third task in the Task List window. The task indicates that a syntax error is caused by a variable that is not declared as required by the Option Strict On statement.

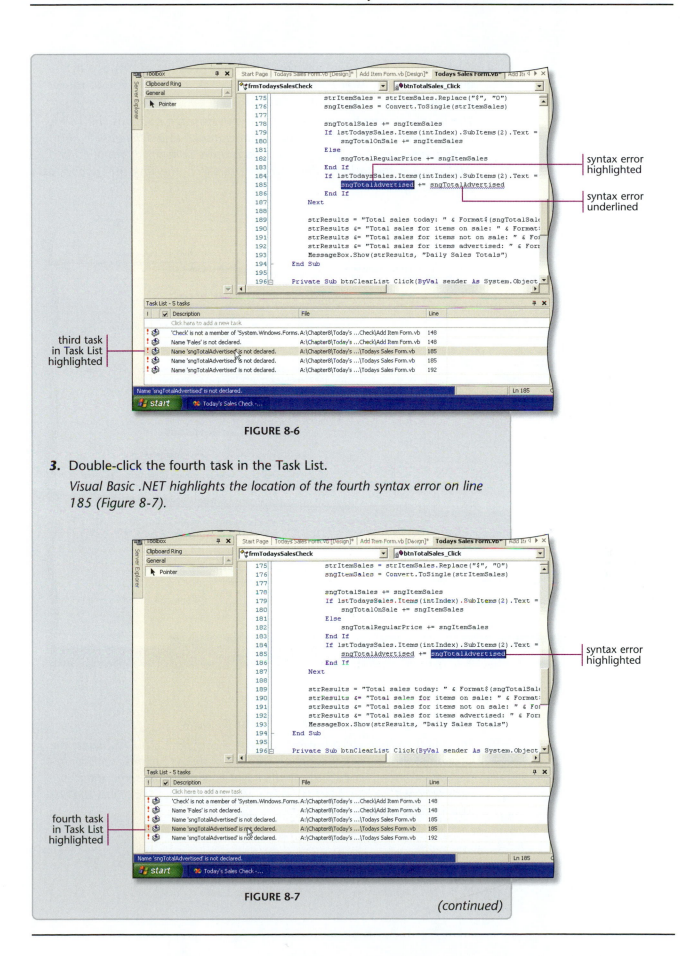

FIGURE 8-6

3. Double-click the fourth task in the Task List.

Visual Basic .NET highlights the location of the fourth syntax error on line 185 (Figure 8-7).

FIGURE 8-7

(continued)

4. Click line 169 and enter `Dim sngTotalAdvertised As Single` as the new line of code. After entering the code, click a different line to move the insertion point to another line of code.

The code to declare the variable, sngTotalAdvertised, displays as line 169 in the code window. After the insertion point is moved to a different line of code, the syntax errors on line 185 no longer are underlined. Visual Basic .NET removes the tasks for those syntax errors from the Task List window, as shown in Figure 8-8.

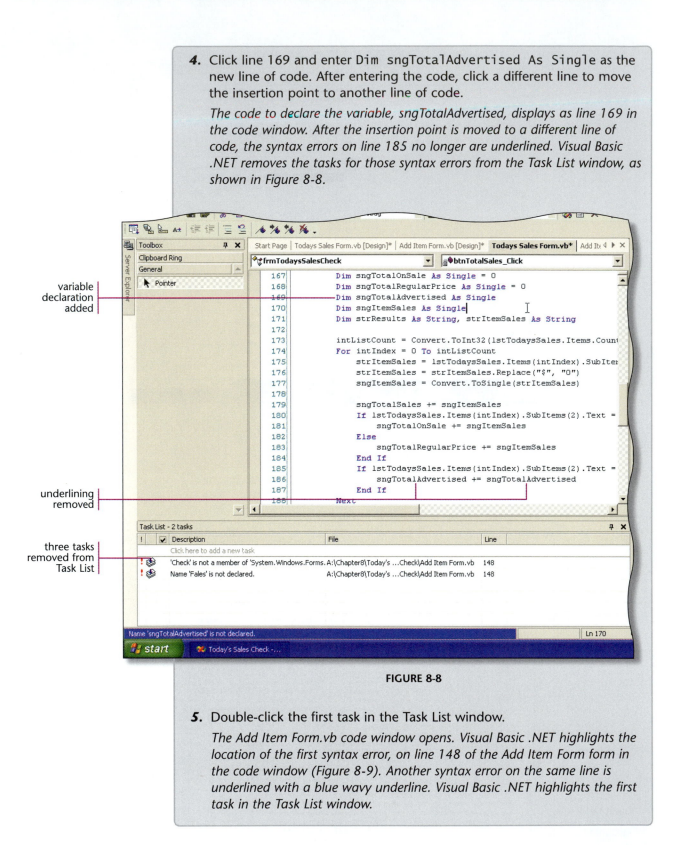

FIGURE 8-8

5. Double-click the first task in the Task List window.

The Add Item Form.vb code window opens. Visual Basic .NET highlights the location of the first syntax error, on line 148 of the Add Item Form form in the code window (Figure 8-9). Another syntax error on the same line is underlined with a blue wavy underline. Visual Basic .NET highlights the first task in the Task List window.

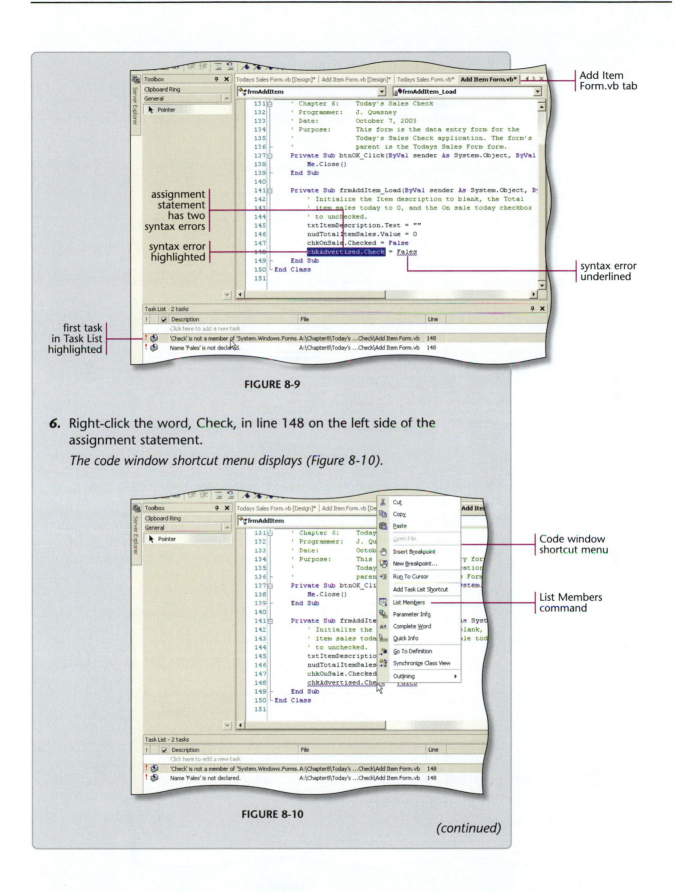

FIGURE 8-9

6. Right-click the word, Check, in line 148 on the left side of the assignment statement.

The code window shortcut menu displays (Figure 8-10).

FIGURE 8-10

(continued)

7. Click the List Members command.

*The properties and methods for the chkAdvertised control display in the Members list below line 148 (Figure 8-11). The **Members list** displays valid properties, variables, or methods for the class or structure to the left of the insertion point.*

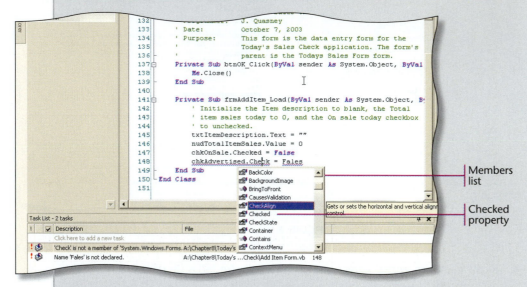

FIGURE 8-11

8. Double-click the property, Checked, in the Members list. Click another line in the code window.

Visual Basic .NET changes the text, Check, to Checked and then removes the blue wavy underline on the left side of the assignment statement. Visual Basic .NET also removes the tasks for that syntax error from the Task List window (Figure 8-12).

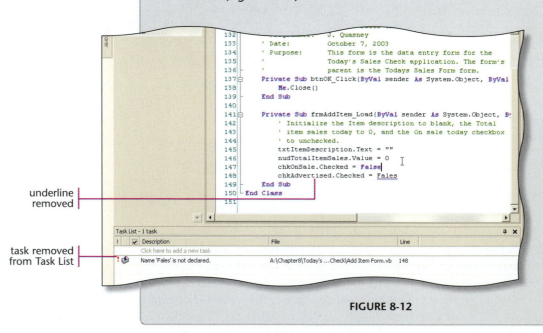

FIGURE 8-12

9. Double-click the value, Fales, on line 148. Type False to correct the spelling mistake. Click another line in the code window.

The underline indicating a syntax error no longer displays. The final syntax error is removed from the Task List window (Figure 8-13).

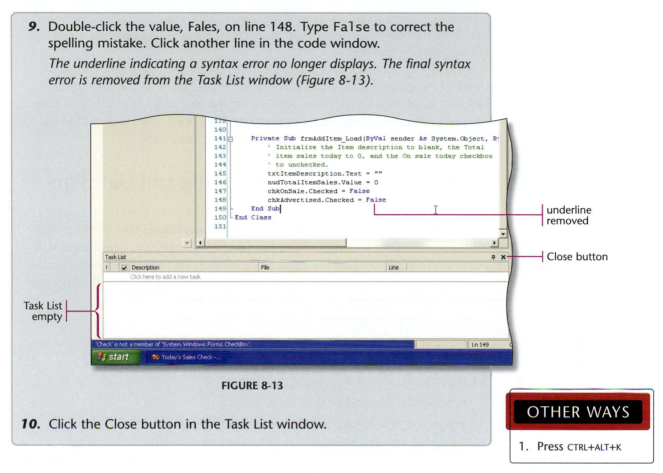

FIGURE 8-13

10. Click the Close button in the Task List window.

OTHER WAYS

1. Press CTRL+ALT+K

The Priority column in the Task List window (Figure 8-5 on page VB 8.08) includes an icon to indicate the severity of an error. The severity of an error can be high (red exclamation point), normal (no icon), or low (blue down arrow). Visual Basic .NET assigns all syntax errors a high severity, which displays as a red exclamation point in the Task List window. Table 8-1 shows the icons used in the Priority column to indicate the severity of errors in the Task List window.

Table 8-1 Priority Column Icons in the Task List Window

ERROR SEVERITY	ICON
Low	↓
Normal	None
High	!

The Category column in the Task List window indicates the type of task. The icon displayed in the Category column in Figure 8-5 represents a **Build Error**, meaning that Visual Basic .NET encountered the error when trying to build, or process, the code. The Category column can contain a number of icons depending on the type of task. The Checked column in the Task List window indicates whether the task is complete. Completed tasks display with a checked check box; uncompleted tasks display with a check box that is cleared or no check box.

When you correct a syntax error, Visual Basic .NET automatically deletes the task from the Task List, rather than marking the task as complete, in order to avoid cluttering the Task List.

You also can use the Task List window to create your own list of tasks for a project. To create a task, click the Click here to add a new task area in the Task List window and type a Description for the new task (Figure 8-5 on page VB 8.08). When tracking your own programming tasks, you may want to use the Checked column to track your progress toward completion.

Using Breakpoints with Stepping and DataTips

As you have learned, breakpoints help you find logic errors or run-time errors during design time. You can set a breakpoint for any line in the program where you want execution to pause, so you can review the code. The breakpoint tells Visual Basic .NET to pause (or break) execution at that point or when a certain condition occurs. To set a breakpoint, move the insertion point to the appropriate line and then use one of the following techniques:

- Click in the column to the left of the line number
- Right-click the line and then click the **Insert Breakpoint command** on the Code window shortcut menu
- Select the line and press the F9 key
- Select the line and press CTRL+B

When you set a breakpoint, the line is highlighted in red and a filled red circle icon appears to the left of the line. When you execute the program after setting one or more breakpoints, Visual Basic .NET halts execution each time a breakpoint receives control, opens the code window, and highlights the line where the breakpoint paused execution in yellow.

Tip

Using Breakpoints

Use a breakpoint to instruct Visual Basic .NET to halt execution at a specific line in the code, so you can inspect the program code when the line receives control.

To remove a breakpoint, move the insertion point to the line where the breakpoint is set and then press the F9 key. You also can right-click the line where the breakpoint is set and then click the **Remove Breakpoint command** on the code window shortcut menu. An alternative method for clearing breakpoints is to select the **Clear All Breakpoints command** on the Debug menu or press CTRL+SHIFT+F9. This technique can be useful if you have a number of breakpoints set and cannot remember where they are located in the program.

Setting a Breakpoint

While you can set as many breakpoints as you like in your code, you should select breakpoints carefully to save time in the debugging process. Commonly used code lines selected as breakpoints include lines immediately following input, calculations, and decision statements. The goal of setting breakpoints should be to examine variable values near the breakpoint or to follow the logic of the code near a breakpoint. Often, however, the process of setting breakpoints is one of trial and error.

> ### Setting Breakpoints
> The goal of setting breakpoints should be to examine variable values near the breakpoint or to follow the logic of the code near a breakpoint.

With the syntax errors corrected, the next step in the debugging process is to run the Today's Sales Check project to look for logic or run-time errors. When the system attempts to display the columns in the lstTodaysSales control, a logic error occurs. The following steps set a breakpoint to help debug the error.

To Run the Project and Set a Breakpoint

1. With the Today's Sales Check project open and the syntax errors in the previous set of steps corrected, click the Start button on the Visual Basic .NET Standard toolbar.

The Today's Sales Check application enters run time and the Today's Sales Check window displays (Figure 8-14). The Today's Sales Check window has two errors in the user interface: the Advertised column that should display on the far right (Figure 8-5 on page VB 8.08) is not visible and an unexpected scroll bar displays. This implies that the Advertised column is off to the right and the user must scroll to view it.

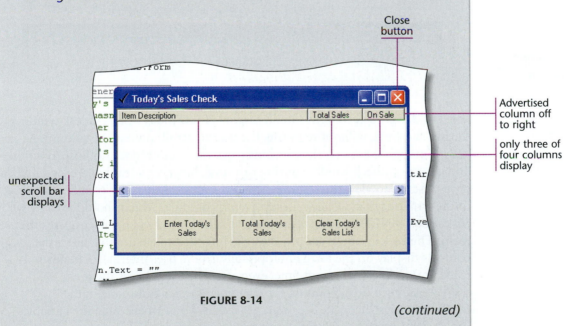

Close button

Advertised column off to right

only three of four columns display

unexpected scroll bar displays

FIGURE 8-14

(continued)

2. Click the Close button in the Today's Sales Check window to close the window. Click the Today's Sales Form.vb tab in the main work area.

Visual Basic .NET closes the Today's Sales Check window and returns to design time.

3. Scroll to the frmTodaysSalesCheck_Resize event procedure, which should have resized the Today's Sales Check window to display the Advertised column. Click the column at the left side of the code window, directly to the left of line 213.

Visual Basic .NET displays a filled red circle icon to the left of line 213 and the line becomes highlighted in red to indicate that the line is set as a breakpoint (Figure 8-15). With a breakpoint set at line 213, you can examine the variables in the procedure during run time to attempt to find the logic error.

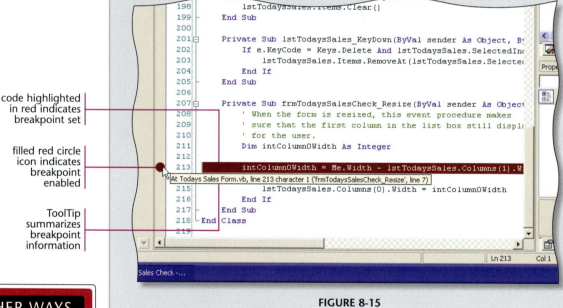

code highlighted in red indicates breakpoint set

filled red circle icon indicates breakpoint enabled

ToolTip summarizes breakpoint information

```
198         lstTodaysSales.Items.Clear()
199     End Sub
200
201     Private Sub lstTodaysSales_KeyDown(ByVal sender As Object, B:
202         If e.KeyCode = Keys.Delete And lstTodaysSales.SelectedInd
203             lstTodaysSales.Items.RemoveAt(lstTodaysSales.Selected
204         End If
205     End Sub
206
207     Private Sub frmTodaysSalesCheck_Resize(ByVal sender As Object
208         ' When the form is resized, this event procedure makes
209         ' sure that the first column in the list box still disple
210         ' for the user.
211         Dim intColumn0Width As Integer
212
213         intColumn0Width = Me.Width - lstTodaysSales.Columns(1).W:
    At Todays Sales Form.vb, line 213 character 1 ('frmTodaysSalesCheck_Resize', line 7)
215             lstTodaysSales.Columns(0).Width = intColumn0Width
216         End If
217     End Sub
218 End Class
219
```

Ln 213   Col 1

Sales Check -...

FIGURE 8-15

The Advertised column should display in the Today's Sales Check window during run time, without requiring the user to scroll to view the column. As shown in Figure 8-14 on the previous page, the column does not display in the Today's Sales Check window during run time, however, meaning a user would have to scroll to view the column. The error most likely is the result of an error in the frmTodaysSalesCheck_Resize event procedure, which should execute when Visual Basic .NET first draws the form at run time or when a user resizes the form. The code in the event procedure is intended to ensure that all of the controls display on the form appropriately, so the user interface remains polished and usable during run time, even after the user resizes the form.

By placing a breakpoint on the first line of executable code in the frmTodaysSalesCheck_Resize event procedure, you can examine the variables in the event procedure during run time to determine if a logic error exists. Execution pauses at the breakpoint when Visual Basic .NET first attempts to draw the window on the user's screen.

Using Stepping and DataTips

When Visual Basic .NET encounters a breakpoint during run time, it enters **break mode**. When the program is in break mode, you can do one of the following:

1. Press the F8 key (Step Into command on the Debug menu) to enter step mode and execute one statement at a time

2. Display the values of variables

3. Edit the program if the option to allow editing is turned on in the Options window

4. Delete or add new breakpoints

5. Click the Continue button (or press the F5 key) to continue execution of the program

As noted above, the **Step Into command** on the **Debug menu** is used to execute the program one statement at a time while the program is in break mode. When you click the Step Into command or press the F8 key, Visual Basic .NET enters step mode and then displays the first executable statement highlighted in yellow. Thereafter, each time you press the F8 key, Visual Basic .NET executes the highlighted statement and then displays the next executable statement with a yellow highlight. Using stepping with breakpoints allows you to pause execution at a certain point using a breakpoint and then continue execution using stepping, so you watch the logic of the code from the breakpoint forward.

Tip

Using the Step Into Command

If Visual Basic .NET is in design time, click the Step Into command or press the F8 key to change Visual Basic .NET from design time to break mode. If Visual Basic .NET is in break mode, click the Step Into command or press the F8 key to highlight the first executable statement. Press the F8 key to execute the next statement.

When Visual Basic .NET is in break mode, you cannot modify code. You can, however, determine the current value of variables. **DataTips** provide the quickest method of viewing the values of variables that are not objects. To view the value of a variable using a DataTip, you place the insertion point over the variable anywhere in the code window during break mode.

To modify code, you must return to design mode, modify the code, and then begin run time again to test your changes. To exit break mode, press the F5 key. Pressing the F5 key tells Visual Basic .NET to continue normal execution of the program, if no run-time errors have occurred. If you want to enter break mode again, press CTRL+BREAK. To return to normal execution of the program again, you can do one of the following:

1. Click the Continue button on the Debug toolbar (or press the F5 key) to continue normal execution.

2. Click Debug on the menu bar and then click the Step Into command (or press the F8 key) to activate step mode.

The following steps show Visual Basic .NET entering break mode when program execution reaches the breakpoint set at line 213. The steps also show the use of DataTips to view the value of variables and the use of the F8 key to step through the frmTodaysSalesCheck_Resize event procedure.

To Use Stepping and DataTips with Breakpoints

1. With a breakpoint set at line 213, click the Start button on the Visual Basic .NET Standard toolbar to enter run time. When execution halts at line 213, click the Breakpoints tab.

Visual Basic .NET begins run time and then enters break mode when the breakpoint at line 213 is reached (Figure 8-16). An arrow displays in the filled red circle breakpoint icon to the left of line 213. Visual Basic .NET highlights the code in line 213 in yellow. The Breakpoints window displays information about the breakpoint at line 213. The Debug and Debug Location toolbars display.

break mode
indicated on Visual
Basic .NET title bar

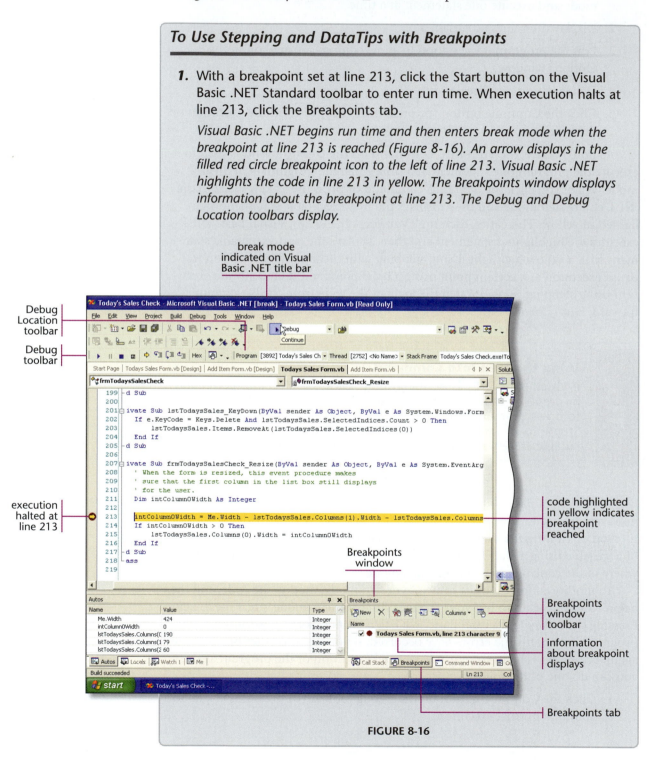

Debug
Location
toolbar

Debug
toolbar

execution
halted at
line 213

code highlighted
in yellow indicates
breakpoint
reached

Breakpoints
window

Breakpoints
window
toolbar

information
about breakpoint
displays

Breakpoints tab

FIGURE 8-16

2. Move the mouse pointer over the property, Me.Width, on the right side of the assignment statement in line 213. Move the mouse pointer over the variable, intColumn0Width, on the left side of the assignment statement in line 213.

A DataTip first displays with the current value of the Me.Width property as 424. Next, a DataTip displays with the current value of the intColumn0Width variable as 0, as shown in Figure 8-17.

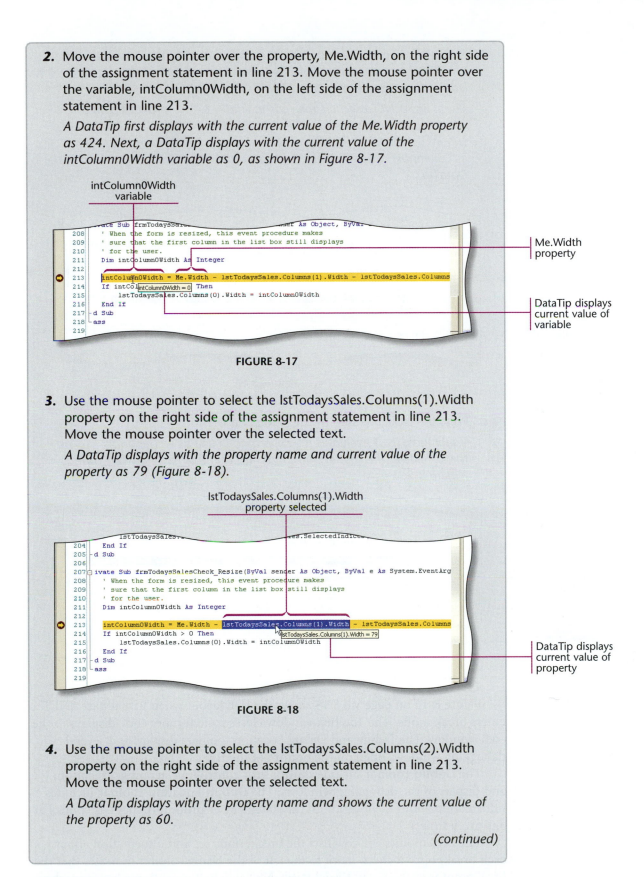

FIGURE 8-17

3. Use the mouse pointer to select the lstTodaysSales.Columns(1).Width property on the right side of the assignment statement in line 213. Move the mouse pointer over the selected text.

A DataTip displays with the property name and current value of the property as 79 (Figure 8-18).

FIGURE 8-18

4. Use the mouse pointer to select the lstTodaysSales.Columns(2).Width property on the right side of the assignment statement in line 213. Move the mouse pointer over the selected text.

A DataTip displays with the property name and shows the current value of the property as 60.

(continued)

5. Press the F8 key to execute line 214 and to step to the next statement. Move the mouse pointer over the variable, intColumn0Width, on the left side of the expression in line 214.

Visual Basic .NET executes the code in line 213. The arrow icon on the left side of the code window indicates that line 214 now has control (Figure 8-19). After the calculation executes in line 213, the variable, intColumn0Width in line 214 is assigned the value of 273, as shown in the DataTip.

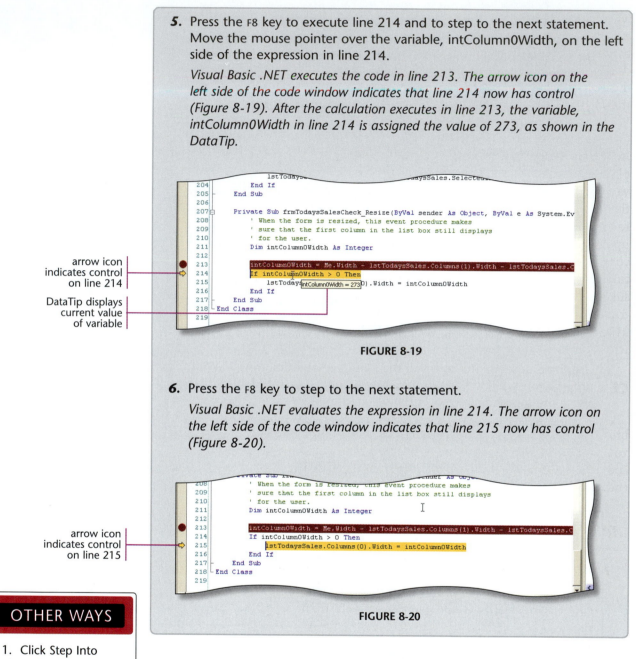

arrow icon indicates control on line 214

DataTip displays current value of variable

FIGURE 8-19

6. Press the F8 key to step to the next statement.

Visual Basic .NET evaluates the expression in line 214. The arrow icon on the left side of the code window indicates that line 215 now has control (Figure 8-20).

arrow icon indicates control on line 215

FIGURE 8-20

OTHER WAYS

1. Click Step Into button on Debug toolbar

Figure 8-16 on page VB 8.18 shows the IDE layout when Visual Basic .NET enters break mode. The Toolbox window closes so that more code displays in the code window. The Debug and Debug Location toolbars display, and several debugging windows open on the bottom of the IDE.

The **Debug toolbar** includes buttons for controlling stepping, execution, and display of the debugging windows. The **Debug Location toolbar** includes information about the location of the statement or procedure that has control at any given time.

The Breakpoints window lists the breakpoints set and information about each breakpoint. A check mark to the left of the Name column indicates that the breakpoint is enabled and Visual Basic .NET will halt execution when it reaches the breakpoint. The Condition column can include an expression to indicate whether the breakpoint should cause the program to halt execution only if the expression is true. For example, you can set a condition that halts execution at the breakpoint only if the value of the intColumn0Width is greater than 0. To set a condition for a breakpoint, right-click the breakpoint in the Breakpoints window and then click the Properties command on the Breakpoint shortcut menu. Several of the other debugging windows shown in Figure 8-16 on page VB 8.18, such as the Watch, Autos, Locals, and This (Me) windows, are discussed later in the chapter.

The value of the intColumn0Width variable in line 213 sets the width of the Item Description column in the lstTodaysSales control. The DataTips that displayed in the previous steps, however, indicate that the calculation used to set the value does not take the width of the Advertised column into account. As a result, the value of the intColumn0Width variable is being set too large to allow space for the Advertised column to display. The first column, Item Description, takes up 273 pixels, the second column, Total Sales, takes up 79 pixels, and the third column, On Sale, takes up 60 pixels. Twelve (12) pixels are used in the calculation on line 213 to account for the width of the form border. No value is subtracted for the width of the Advertised column. To fix this bug in the frmTodaysSalesCheck_Resize event procedure, you must modify the code in line 213 to subtract the width of the Advertised column from the form width, along with the other column widths.

Changing the Status of a Breakpoint

When you first set a breakpoint, Visual Basic .NET automatically enables the breakpoint. Once you use a breakpoint to find and determine the fix for a bug, you can disable the breakpoint, so you can test any changes you made to the code. The following steps disable the breakpoint on line 213 and implement the code change to fix the bug in the frmTodaysSalesCheck_Resize event procedure.

To Disable a Breakpoint and Correct a Logic Error

1. Right-click anywhere in line 213. When the code window shortcut menu displays, click the Disable Breakpoint command.

Visual Basic .NET disables the breakpoint. The icon to the left of line 213 changes to an empty red circle. Visual Basic .NET surrounds line 213 with a box, meaning that the breakpoint at that line is disabled (Figure 8-21).

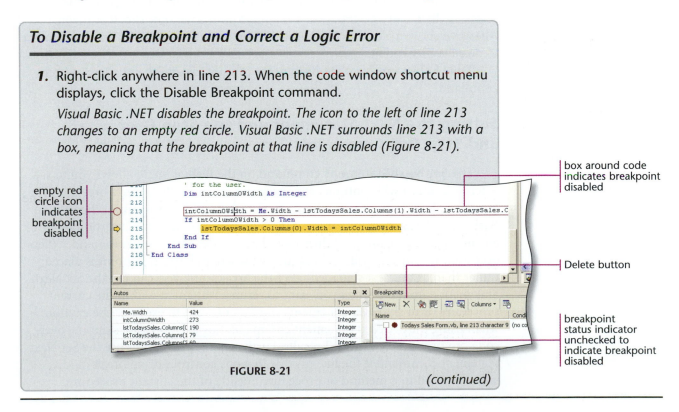

empty red circle icon indicates breakpoint disabled

box around code indicates breakpoint disabled

Delete button

breakpoint status indicator unchecked to indicate breakpoint disabled

FIGURE 8-21

(continued)

2. Click the Stop Debugging button on the Debug toolbar. Scroll the code window to the right, until the end of line 213 displays. Click after the text, 1stTodaysSales.Columns(2).Width. Enter – 1stTodaysSales .Columns(3).Width and then press the SPACEBAR.

The changes to line 213 display in the code window, as shown in Figure 8-22. The new line of code will subtract the width of the Advertised column from the form width, along with the Total Sales column, On Sale column, and form border widths, to determine the new width of the Item Description column when the user resizes the form.

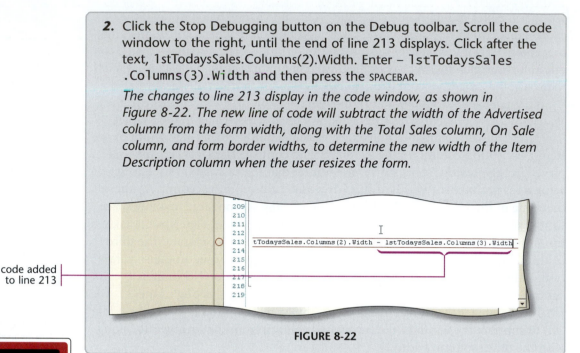

code added to line 213

FIGURE 8-22

When you save a project, Visual Basic .NET also saves any breakpoints with their current status. This allows you to keep disabled breakpoints set in troublesome code areas while you test recent modifications. If errors still occur, you can enable the breakpoints using the **Enable All Breakpoints command** on the Debug menu. Similarly, you can use the **Disable All Breakpoints command** to set the breakpoint status to disabled for all breakpoints. You also can remove breakpoints in the Breakpoints window by right-clicking a breakpoint and selecting the **Delete command** on the Breakpoints window shortcut menu. Alternatively, you can click the Delete button on the Breakpoints window toolbar to delete a breakpoint.

Table 8-2 summarizes the Breakpoint commands and the purpose of each command.

Setting the Next Statement and the Step Over and Step Out Commands

The **Set Next Statement command** on the Debug menu allows you to set where execution will continue, after program execution halts for a breakpoint. For example, assume that you have set a breakpoint in a program. When Visual Basic .NET halts execution at the statement, you can move the insertion point to any line in the program and then click the Set Next Statement command. When execution resumes, it will begin at the line where the insertion point is placed, rather than at the next statement after the breakpoint. You can use the Set Next Statement command when you want to rerun a statement within the current procedure or to skip over statements you do not want to execute. Use caution when using the Set Next Statement command, however, because skipping over code can produce unexpected results. Furthermore, you cannot use the Set Next Statement command if the line of code that has control during break mode includes a call to a method or procedure outside of the current procedure.

Table 8-2   Breakpoint Command Summary

BREAKPOINT COMMAND	STEPS TO EXECUTE	PURPOSE
Insert Breakpoint	1. Click column to the left of the code line 2. Right-click code line, click Insert Breakpoint command on shortcut menu	Sets a breakpoint at the current line and displays the new breakpoint in the Breakpoints window. Break mode will be initiated when the line receives control.
New Breakpoint	1. Press CTRL+B 2. Click New Breakpoint button on Breakpoints toolbar in Breakpoints window 3. Click New Breakpoint command on Debug menu	Opens the New Breakpoint window, which allows you to set a breakpoint. Unlike the Insert Breakpoint command, this command does not create a new breakpoint on the current line automatically.
Disable Breakpoint	1. Right-click breakpoint, click Disable Breakpoint on shortcut menu 2. Clear check box in Name column in Breakpoints window	Causes the breakpoint to be ignored by the debugger. The breakpoint remains for future use but does not affect execution until re-enabled.
Disable All Breakpoints	1. Click Disable All Breakpoints button on Breakpoints toolbar in Breakpoints window 2. Click Disable All Breakpoints command on Debug menu	Causes all breakpoints to be set to disabled status, meaning that all breakpoints will be ignored by the debugger.
Enable All Breakpoints	1. Click Enable All Breakpoints command on Debug menu	Causes all breakpoints to be set to enabled status, so that break mode will be initiated when a breakpoint receives control.
Remove Breakpoint	1. Click column to the left of code line set as breakpoint 2. Right-click code line, click Remove Breakpoint command on shortcut menu 3. Click Delete button on Breakpoints toolbar in Breakpoints window	Deletes the breakpoint from the Breakpoints window. Break mode will no longer be initiated when the line receives control.
Toggle Breakpoint	1. Position insertion point on code line and press the F9 key	If a breakpoint is not set on the line, a breakpoint is set on the line. If a breakpoint is set on the line, the breakpoint is removed.
Clear All Breakpoints	1. Press CTRL+SHIFT+F9 2. Click Clear All Breakpoints button on Breakpoints toolbar in Breakpoints window 3. Click Clear All Breakpoints command on Debug menu	Removes all breakpoints from the Breakpoints window.

> **Tip**
>
> **Using the Set Next Statement Command**
> Use caution when evaluating the program results following the use of the Set Next Statement command because skipping over code can produce unexpected results.

As you have learned, the Step Into command is used to execute the program one statement at a time while the program is in break mode. Visual Basic .NET includes two alternative forms of this command, which are used when stepping involves calls to other procedures. When using the Step Into command to step into a line that contains a procedure call, such as the execution of a method, Visual Basic .NET steps into the called procedure and steps to the first line in the called procedure as the next line to execute. When you use the **Step Over command,** Visual Basic .NET executes all of the code in the called procedure and then steps to the next statement in the current procedure. The Step Over command sets the next line after the call to the procedure as the next line to execute.

The **Step Out command** is used to execute all of the remaining code in a called procedure. When you use the Step Out command, Visual Basic .NET executes all of the remaining code in the current procedure and then steps to the line of code that called the procedure, if there was one. In the case of event procedures, no procedure initiates the call to the event procedure, so Visual Basic .NET resumes execution of the program without breaking.

When Visual Basic .NET is in design time, you can use the Step Into, Step Over, or Step Out command to begin execution of the project in break mode. Table 8-3 summarizes the stepping commands and the purpose of each command. Be aware that the keys for many of the operations differ if you do not have the Keyboard scheme set to Visual Basic 6 as set in Chapter 2. For example, the Step Into shortcut key is F11 by default, but changed to F8 when the Keyboard scheme is set to Visual Basic 6.

Table 8-3   Stepping Command Summary

STEPPING COMMAND	STEPS TO EXECUTE	PURPOSE
Set Next Statement	1. While in break mode, right-click code line, click Set Next Statement command on shortcut menu	Use this command to set the next statement to execute following a break.
Step Into	1. Press F8 2. Click Step Into button on Debug toolbar 3. Click Step Into command on Debug menu	Use this command to execute one statement at a time in break mode.
Step Out	1. Press CTRL+SHIFT+F8 2. Click Step Out button on Debug toolbar 3. Click Step Out command on Debug menu	Use this command to execute all remaining code in the current procedure or function and then halt in break mode when the procedure or function returns to the code line that called the procedure or function.

Table 8-3 Stepping Command Summary (continued)

STEPPING COMMAND	STEPS TO EXECUTE	PURPOSE
Step Over	1. Press SHIFT+F8 2. Click Step Over button on Debug toolbar 3. Click Step Over command on Debug menu	Use this command to execute one statement at a time in break mode, but execute all procedure and function calls without stepping through them.
Run to Cursor	1. While in break mode, right-click statement, click Run to Cursor command on shortcut menu	Use this command to execute all code up to the statement that contains the insertion point

Debugging Run-Time Errors by Watching Variables and Expressions

In addition to using break mode to help you debug logic errors, Visual Basic .NET allows you to enter break mode when a run-time error occurs. In break mode, you can isolate and view the values of particular variables and properties as a way of checking for errors. You specify which variables and properties you want to monitor by setting a **watch expression** for each variable or property before running the application. When the value of the variable or property changes, the watch expression then causes the application to halt execution and enter break mode. You also can check the value of any variable or property in break mode by using a QuickWatch.

Breaking on a Run-Time Error and Using a QuickWatch

As shown in Figure 8-23, when Visual Basic .NET encounters a run-time error during program execution, a Microsoft Development Environment dialog box displays. The dialog box gives you the option to break on the line of code that caused the error (Break button) or return to design time (Continue button).

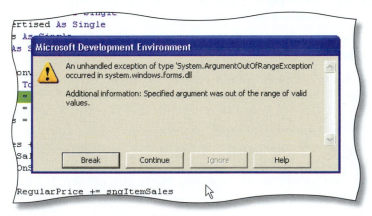

FIGURE 8-23

Recall that DataTips allow you to view the value of a variable during break mode. A **QuickWatch** not only allows you quickly to evaluate a variable or expression, but also to edit the value of a variable or expression during break mode. That is, with the program in a paused state, you can use the **QuickWatch window** to change the value currently used in the program at run time to any valid value for the variable. The QuickWatch window is modal, meaning that when the window is displaying, you must close the window before performing any other tasks in Visual Basic .NET.

> **Tip**
>
> **DataTip versus QuickWatch**
> A DataTip allows you to view the value of a variable during break mode. A QuickWatch not only allows you quickly to evaluate a variable or expression, but also to edit the value of a variable or expression during break mode.

The following steps enter two test data items in Table 8-4 into the Today's Sales Check application and then attempt to run the program to total the sales. After a run-time error is encountered, the QuickWatch window is used to evaluate the variable values. Because all breakpoints used thus far have been disabled, the breakpoints will be ignored by Visual Basic .NET.

Table 8-4   Test Data for Debugging the Today's Sales Check Project

ITEM DESCRIPTION	TOTAL ITEM SALES TODAY	ON SALE TODAY	ADVERTISED
Topsoil	435.82	No	Yes
Kentucky Bluegrass sod	250.00	Yes	Yes

To Break on a Run-Time Error and Use a QuickWatch

1. Click the Start button on the Visual Basic .NET Standard toolbar to run the Today's Sales Check project.

2. When the Today's Sales Check window displays, click the Enter Today's Sales button. Enter the test data as shown in Table 8-4. After entering the second item, click the OK button without entering a description in the Item Description text box.

   Visual Basic .NET begins executing the Today's Sales Check project. The test data values display in the lstTodaysSales control. The Advertised column displays, indicating that the logic error found earlier in line 213 has been corrected (Figure 8-24).

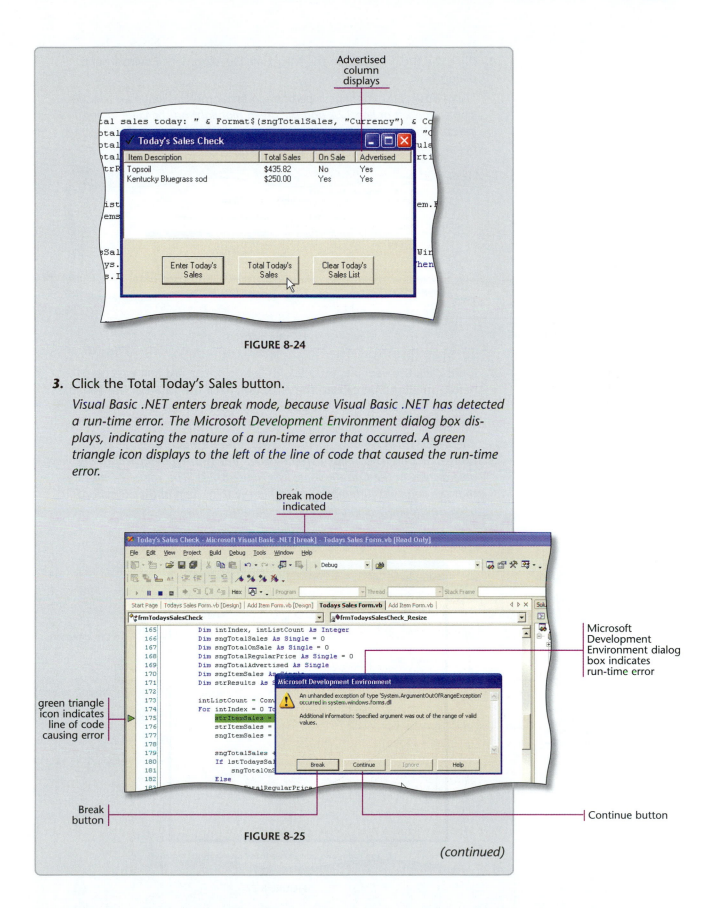

FIGURE 8-24

3. Click the Total Today's Sales button.

Visual Basic .NET enters break mode, because Visual Basic .NET has detected a run-time error. The Microsoft Development Environment dialog box displays, indicating the nature of a run-time error that occurred. A green triangle icon displays to the left of the line of code that caused the run-time error.

FIGURE 8-25

(continued)

4. Click the Break button in the Microsoft Development Environment dialog box.

Visual Basic .NET continues operating in break mode. The green triangle icon to the left of line 175 and the green highlight on the code in line 175 indicate the line of code that Visual Basic .NET last attempted to execute before entering break mode (Figure 8-26).

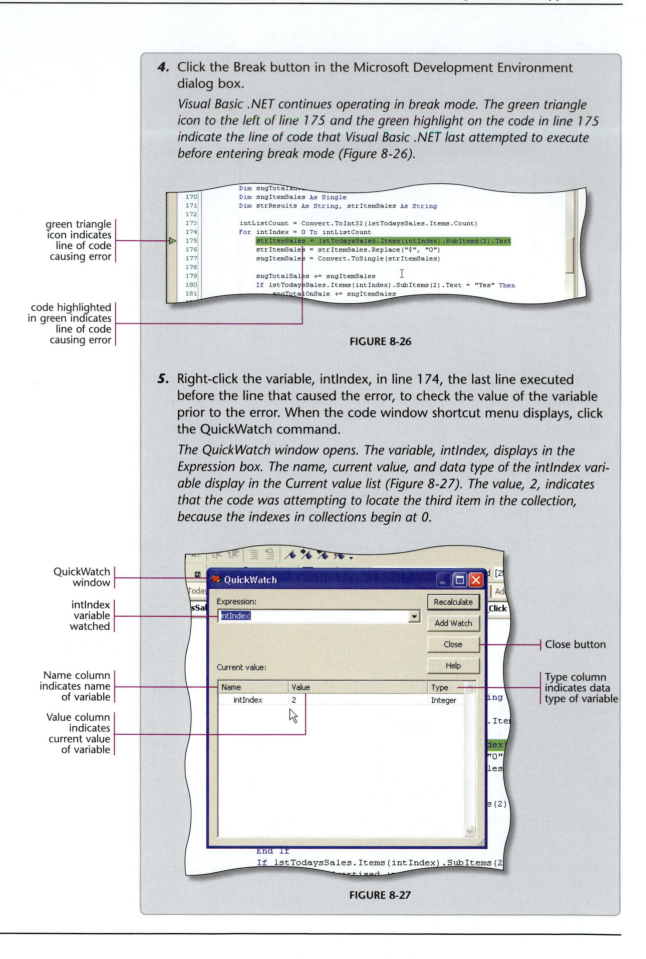

green triangle icon indicates line of code causing error

code highlighted in green indicates line of code causing error

FIGURE 8-26

5. Right-click the variable, intIndex, in line 174, the last line executed before the line that caused the error, to check the value of the variable prior to the error. When the code window shortcut menu displays, click the QuickWatch command.

The QuickWatch window opens. The variable, intIndex, displays in the Expression box. The name, current value, and data type of the intIndex variable display in the Current value list (Figure 8-27). The value, 2, indicates that the code was attempting to locate the third item in the collection, because the indexes in collections begin at 0.

QuickWatch window

intIndex variable watched

Name column indicates name of variable

Value column indicates current value of variable

Close button

Type column indicates data type of variable

FIGURE 8-27

6. Click the Close button in the QuickWatch window. Right-click the variable, intListCount, in line 174 to check the value of the variable prior to the error. When the code window shortcut menu displays, click the QuickWatch command.

The QuickWatch window opens. The variable, intListCount, displays in the Expression box. The name, current value, and data type of the intListCount variable display in the Current value list (Figure 8-28). The value, 2, indicates that the code correctly counted the number of items that were entered as test data.

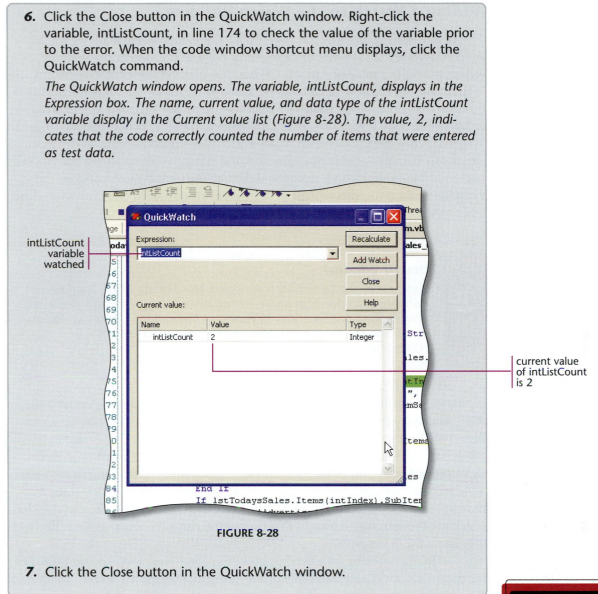

intListCount variable watched

current value of intListCount is 2

FIGURE 8-28

7. Click the Close button in the QuickWatch window.

The Expression box in the QuickWatch window can contain any expression you want to evaluate. For example, you can type, $intIndex - 2$, in the Expression box and the Name in the Current value list will change to the value, $intIndex - 2$. The Value in the Current value list will change to the value, 0, because the current value of intIndex is 2 and subtracting 2 yields a result of 0. By evaluating expressions in this manner, you can perform calculations involving any variables and values. You also can use other variables in the expression, as long as the variable is within the same scope as the variable chosen for the QuickWatch. Recall that scope refers to the sections of code for which the variable is valid.

As indicated by the dialog box shown in Figure 8-25 on page VB 8.27, the run-time error indicates that an index in the expression is invalid. Even after evaluating the values of the two variables shown in the QuickWatch window in Figure 8-27 and Figure 8-28, the reason for the run-time error is not obvious. Further investigation is needed to debug the run-time error.

Adding a Watch to the Watch Window

As shown in Figure 8-1d on page VB 8.04, a Watch window allows you to watch the values of variables or expressions during run time or break mode, as well as to edit the value of variables. When you edit the values of variables in any Watch window, the new value takes the place of the variable's value during break mode or run time. Visual Basic .NET allows you to add variables and expressions to up to four Watch windows, which are named Watch 1, Watch 2, Watch 3, and Watch 4. While the QuickWatch window provides a quick, simple way to evaluate or edit a single variable or expression, the Watch windows allows you to evaluate multiple variables and expressions. Unlike the QuickWatch window, the variables and expressions remain in the Watch window even after you save, close, and reopen the project.

Tip

Watch Window

Use one of the four Watch windows to evaluate more than one variable or expression and edit variables. When you add variables and expressions to a Watch window, the variables and expressions remain in the Watch window even after you save, close, and reopen the project.

In the Today's Sales Check project, a run-time error is causing Visual Basic .NET to display the Microsoft Development Environment dialog box shown in Figure 8-25 on page VB 8.27, when it tries to execute line 175. The code in line 175 is part of the For…Next loop of the btnTotalSales_Click event procedure. By setting a breakpoint in the loop and adding variables in the loop to a Watch window, you can watch values of the variables change as the loop executes. In the For…Next loop of the btnTotalSales_Click event procedure, the variables to watch are those in the statement that caused the run-time error, as most likely they are causing the error.

The following steps set a breakpoint in the For…Next loop and add watches for the intIndex variable, the value of the Text property for the second column in the lstTodaysSales control, and the intListCount variable. Recall from the previous set of steps that the application is in break mode and paused on line 175.

To Add a Watch to the Watch Window and Set a Breakpoint in a Loop

1. With the application in break mode and paused on line 175, right-click the intIndex variable on line 174. When the code window shortcut menu displays, click the Add Watch command.

Visual Basic .NET opens the Watch 1 window and adds the intIndex variable to the Watch list (Figure 8-29). The variable name, current value, and data type display in the list.

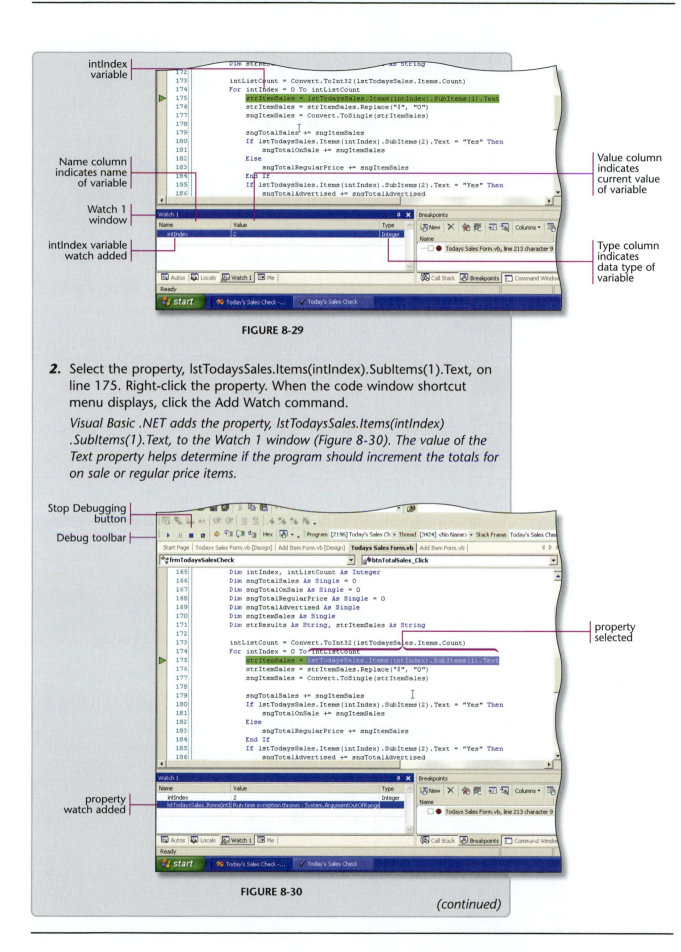

FIGURE 8-29

2. Select the property, lstTodaysSales.Items(intIndex).SubItems(1).Text, on
line 175. Right-click the property. When the code window shortcut
menu displays, click the Add Watch command.

*Visual Basic .NET adds the property, lstTodaysSales.Items(intIndex)
.SubItems(1).Text, to the Watch 1 window (Figure 8-30). The value of the
Text property helps determine if the program should increment the totals for
on sale or regular price items.*

FIGURE 8-30

(continued)

3. Right-click the intListCount variable on line 174. When the code window shortcut menu displays, click the Add Watch command.

Visual Basic .NET adds the intListCount variable to the Watch list.

4. Click the Stop Debugging button on the Debug toolbar.

Visual Basic .NET returns to design mode.

5. Click to the left of line 175 to set a breakpoint at line 175.

Line 175, the line that caused the run-time error, becomes a breakpoint. The breakpoint displays in the Breakpoints window.

The previous steps added three watches to the Watch window and set a breakpoint. You can remove a watch from the Watch window by (1) highlighting it in the Watch window and then pressing the DELETE key or (2) by right-clicking the watch in the Watch window and clicking the **Delete Watch command** on the Watch window shortcut menu.

Tip

Removing a Watch

You can remove a watch from the Watch window by (1) highlighting it in the Watch window and then pressing the DELETE key or (2) by right-clicking the watch in the Watch window and clicking the Delete Watch command on the Watch window shortcut menu.

The next steps run the program with the breakpoint set on line 175 and use the Watch window to evaluate the watched variables and property. The breakpoint set on line 175 pauses the program during each iteration of the For…Next loop in lines 174 through 188.

To Watch Variables and Use a Breakpoint in a Loop

1. Click the Start button on the Visual Basic .NET Standard toolbar to enter run time.

2. When the Today's Sales Check window displays, click the Enter Today's Sales button. Enter the test data as shown in Table 8-4 on page VB 8.26. After entering the second item, click the OK button without entering a description in the Item Description text box.

Visual Basic .NET begins executing the Today's Sales Check project. The test data values display in the lstTodaysSales control.

3. Click the Total Today's Sales button.

Visual Basic .NET enters break mode when the breakpoint on line 175 receives control. The current values of the three watched variables display in the Watch 1 window. The value of the variable, intIndex, displays in red to indicate that the code changed the value during execution. The Breakpoints window indicates that the breakpoint on line 175 is enabled and the bold font on the breakpoint indicates that this breakpoint caused break mode to begin (Figure 8-31).

break mode
indicated on
title bar

breakpoint halts
execution

current values
of watched
variables
display

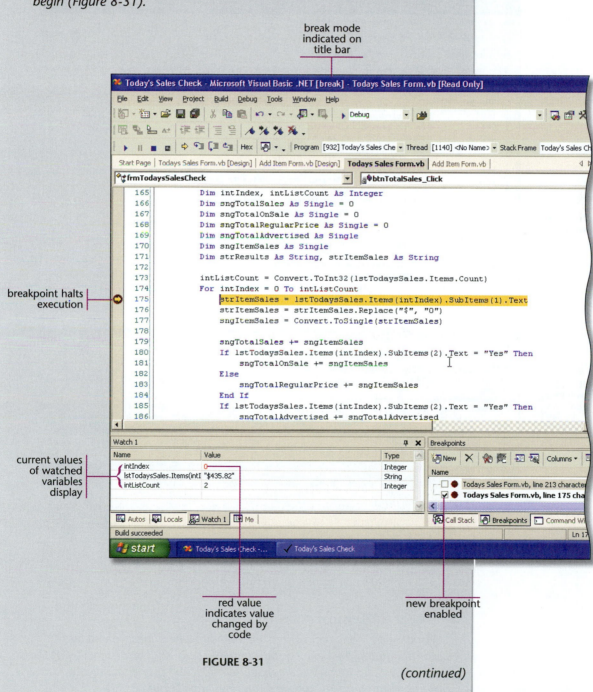

red value
indicates value
changed by
code

new breakpoint
enabled

FIGURE 8-31

(continued)

4. Press the F5 key to resume running the project.

Visual Basic .NET again enters break mode when line 175 receives control during the next iteration of the For...Next loop. The current values of the watched variables display in the Watch 1 window. Any values that changed since the first time the variables were added to the watch list are displayed in red (Figure 8-32).

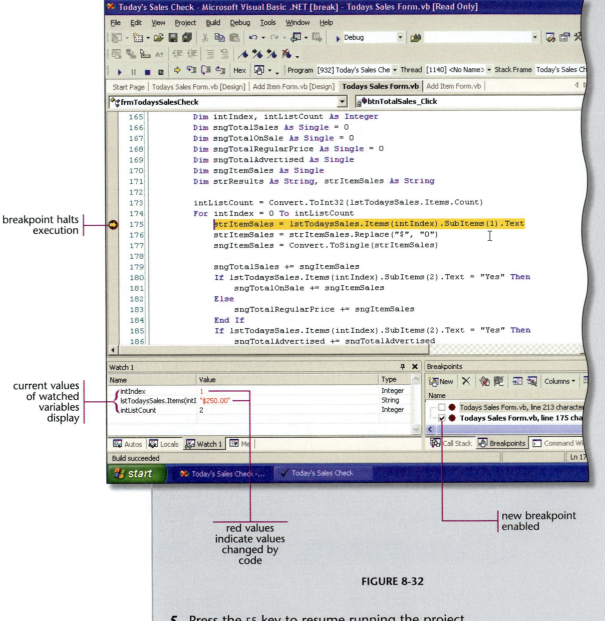

breakpoint halts execution

current values of watched variables display

red values indicate values changed by code

new breakpoint enabled

FIGURE 8-32

5. Press the F5 key to resume running the project.

Visual Basic .NET again enters break mode when line 175 receives control during the next iteration of the For...Next loop. The value of the lstTodaysSales.Items(intIndex).SubItems(1).Text property indicates that the value of the property causes a run-time error (Figure 8-33).

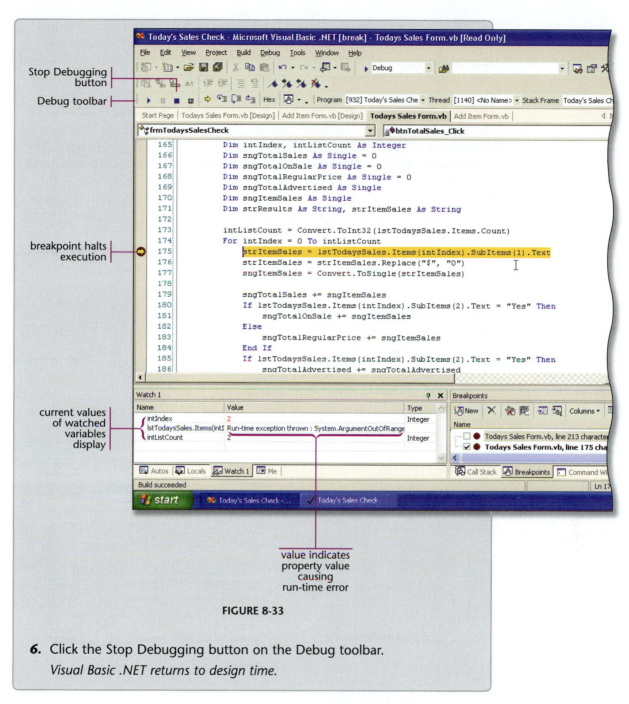

Stop Debugging button

Debug toolbar

breakpoint halts execution

current values of watched variables display

value indicates property value causing run-time error

FIGURE 8-33

6. Click the Stop Debugging button on the Debug toolbar.

Visual Basic .NET returns to design time.

As shown in the previous steps, when execution pauses during the first iteration of the For…Next loop (Figure 8-31 on page VB 8.33), the Watch window displays the value of the second watched variable as $435.82, or the Total Sales value that displays in the second column for the first item in the lstTodaysSales control. During the second iteration of the For…Next loop (Figure 8-32), the Watch window displays the value of the second watched variable as $250.00, or the Total Sales that displays in the second column of the second item in the lstTodaysSales control. At this point, the For…Next loop should terminate, because the loop has evaluated both test data values. As shown in Figure 8-33, however, the loop iterates yet again.

The unexpected iteration of the loop indicates that the run-time error is caused by an incorrect looping constraint. When the loop executes one more time than necessary, the program attempts to find a Total Sales value in the third row (Items(2)) of the lstTodaysSales control. Because no such value exists, a run-time error results. With this information, you can determine that the way to fix the bug is to subtract 1 from the intListCount variable that is the limit value of the For…Next loop. As you have learned, the For…Next statement begins its iteration at 0 because the index of a collection starts numbering at 0, not 1. The Count property of a collection is used to represent the total number of items in a collection. If the Count property stored in the variable, intListCount, is 3, then the loop should take into account three index values of 0, 1, and 2. In this example, the current code takes into account four index values of 0, 1, 2, and 3, which causes a run-time error when the index value of 3 is used.

The following steps fix the run-time error by modifying the limit value of the For…Next loop on line 175 and then disables the breakpoint on line 175.

To Fix a Run-Time Error in a For…Next Loop

1. Click the end of line 174. Type – 1 to fix the error.

2. Right-click line 175. When the code window shortcut menu displays, click the Disable Breakpoint command.

The updated code displays on line 174. Visual Basic .NET disables the breakpoint on line 175 (Figure 8-34).

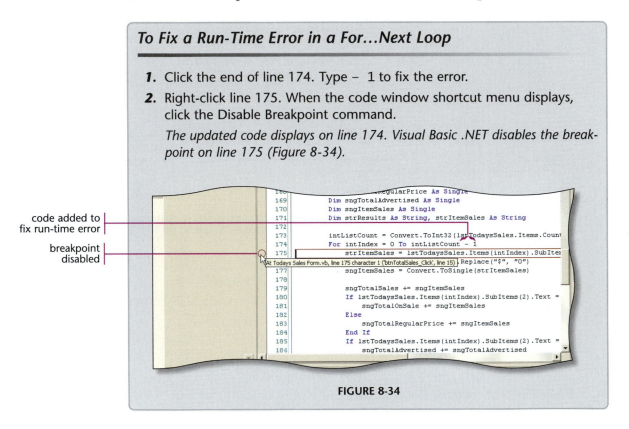

code added to fix run-time error

breakpoint disabled

FIGURE 8-34

With the loop's limit value changed to intListCount – 1, the run-time error is fixed. The next step is to retest the application to determine if the code contains additional logic or run-time errors.

The Autos, Locals, and Me Windows

Visual Basic .NET provides several other debugging tools for evaluating and modifying variable values during run time. These tools, which include the Autos, Locals, and Me windows, behave in a manner similar to the Watch window. Unlike the Watch window, however, these windows do not require you to add a watch to display variable or property values. Visual Basic .NET automatically populates the windows with variables, based on certain criteria for each window. The **Autos window**, for example, displays variables used in the current statement and the previous statement. The **Locals window** displays variables local to the current procedure. The **Me window** allows you to examine the data members of the object associated with the current method. Table 8-5 summarize the criteria that determine which variables display in the Autos, Locals, and This (Me) windows.

Table 8-5   Criteria for Debugging Windows

WINDOW NAME	CRITERIA	KEY COMBINATIONS TO OPEN WINDOW
Autos	Variables in the current statement and previous statement	Press CTRL+ALT+V, A
Locals	Local variables in the current procedure	Press CTRL+ALT+V, L
Me	Data members for the object associated with the current method. For example, the form when working in event procedures. The window is called the Me window in Visual Basic and the This window in C++ and C#.	Press CTRL+ALT+V, T

By default, these debugging windows display as tabs at the bottom of the IDE when the IDE is in break mode. You can click the Autos, Locals, or Me tab to open the corresponding window. If the tab for the window does not display in the IDE, you use the key combinations listed in Table 8-5 to open the corresponding window.

Using the Autos Window

The Autos window is useful because it displays the values of variables in the current statement and the previous statement. You use the Autos window when the IDE is in break mode and you want to view the values of the variables close to the statement that currently has control. The variables listed in the Autos window automatically change as you use stepping or breakpoints to move from one line of code to another. The Autos window thus saves you the effort of setting watches for the variables or opening the QuickWatch window individually for each variable.

Tip

The Autos Window
Use the Autos window in break mode to evaluate and modify variables in the current statement and previous statement.

The following steps use the test data in Table 8-4 on page VB 8.26 to locate another logic error in the program code and then use the Autos window to assist in debugging the error. The logic error results in an incorrect result when totaling the sales for the items that were advertised.

To Use the Autos Windows to Evaluate Variables

1. Click the Start button on the Visual Basic .NET Standard toolbar to enter run time.

2. When the Today's Sales Check window displays, click the Enter Today's Sales button. Enter the test data as shown in Table 8-4. After entering the second item, click the OK button without entering a description in the Item Description text box.

Visual Basic .NET begins executing the Today's Sales Check project. The test data values display in the lstTodaysSales control.

3. Click the Total Today's Sales button to determine if the application displays the expected results in the Daily Sales Totals message box.

The Daily Sales Totals message box displays correct values for all totals except Total sales for items advertised. The value, which should be $685.82, displays as $0.00 (Figure 8-35). This result indicates that a bug is causing the application to display an incorrect total.

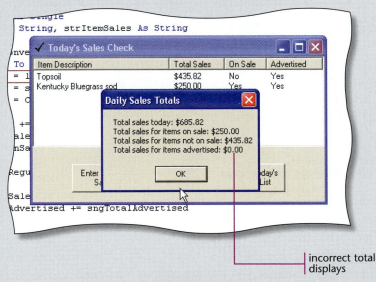

incorrect total
displays

FIGURE 8-35

4. Click the breakpoint status check box in the Breakpoints window to enable the breakpoint on line 175.

The breakpoint at line 175 becomes enabled. Visual Basic .NET remains in run time and the Today's Sales Check application continues to execute (Figure 8-36).

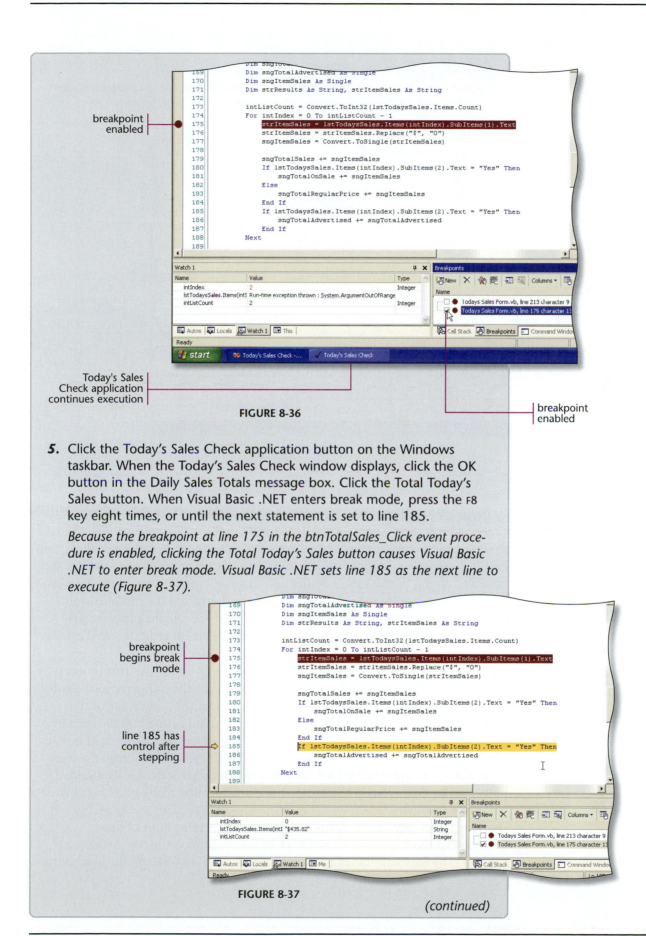

FIGURE 8-36

5. Click the Today's Sales Check application button on the Windows taskbar. When the Today's Sales Check window displays, click the OK button in the Daily Sales Totals message box. Click the Total Today's Sales button. When Visual Basic .NET enters break mode, press the F8 key eight times, or until the next statement is set to line 185.

Because the breakpoint at line 175 in the btnTotalSales_Click event procedure is enabled, clicking the Total Today's Sales button causes Visual Basic .NET to enter break mode. Visual Basic .NET sets line 185 as the next line to execute (Figure 8-37).

FIGURE 8-37

(continued)

6. Click the Autos tab at the bottom of the IDE.

The Autos window displays variables that are in the current statement, line 185, and the previous executable statement, line 183 (Figure 8-38).

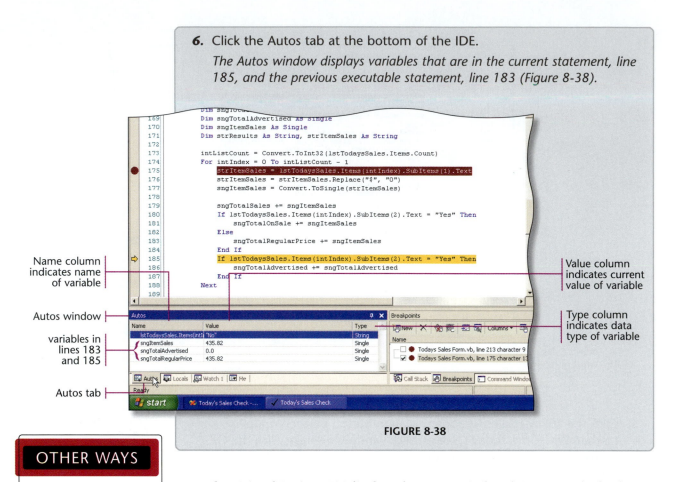

Name column indicates name of variable

Value column indicates current value of variable

Type column indicates data type of variable

Autos window

variables in lines 183 and 185

Autos tab

FIGURE 8-38

OTHER WAYS

1. Press CTRL+ALT+V, A

When Visual Basic .NET displays the Autos window (Figure 8-38), the four variables located on lines 183 and 185 display in the Name column. Visual Basic .NET does not consider line 184 an executable statement, because it includes the End If keyword, which does not execute. In the Autos window, the values of the variables display in the Value column and the data types display in the Type column. You can modify the values in the Value column, and the modified value will be reflected in the program if you continue to execute the program. Use caution when modifying variables during break mode, in order to avoid causing any unexpected program errors.

The first line of the Autos window in Figure 8-38 shows the Text property value of the SubItems(2) collection of the first row of the lstTodaysSales control. The value that the condition should check is the Text property value of the Advertised column to determine if the value is Yes, indicating that the item in the row is advertised. If so, the total for the items advertised is increased in line 186 by the amount in the Total Sales column for the row. Recall from the test data that both values entered for the Advertised column were Yes. The value however, displays as No in the Autos window, indicating that something is wrong with the value being tested by the condition in line 185. Further inspection shows that the SubItems index of 2, refers to the third column of the lstTodaysSales control, On Sale, instead of the fourth column, the Advertised column. The SubItems index must be changed from 2 to 3 to fix the logic error.

The following steps fix the logic error found using the Autos window.

To Fix a Logic Error

1. Click the Stop Debugging button on the Debug toolbar.

Visual Basic .NET returns to design time.

2. Change the index of the SubItems item in line 185 from the value, 2, to the value, 3.

The correction to line 185 displays in the code window (Figure 8-39).

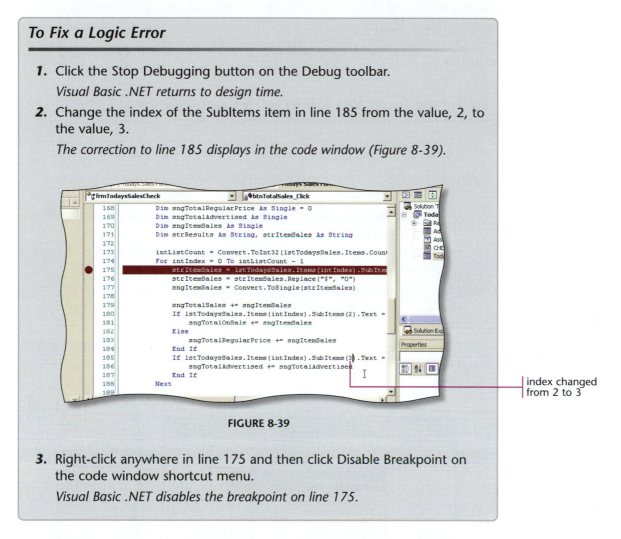

index changed
from 2 to 3

FIGURE 8-39

3. Right-click anywhere in line 175 and then click Disable Breakpoint on the code window shortcut menu.

Visual Basic .NET disables the breakpoint on line 175.

The steps above correct the logic error so that the condition in line 185 checks the value in the Advertised column (column 4) of the lstTodaysSales control to determine if the item was advertised and, if it was, then adds its Total Sales (column 2) to the total for items advertised. The next step is to retest the program to verify that the bug is fixed.

Using the Locals Window

The Locals window displays variables within the scope of the current procedure, as you use stepping or breakpoints to move from one procedure to another. The current procedure is the procedure that contains the code statement that has control.

The Locals Window

Use the Locals window in break mode to evaluate and modify variables in the current procedure.

The following steps use the test data in Table 8-4 on page VB 8.26 to locate another logic error in the program code and then use the Locals window to assist in debugging the error. The error indicates that another problem exists with the totaling of the sales for advertised items, because the result still displays as $0.00.

To Use the Locals Window to Evaluate Variables

1. Click the Start button on the Visual Basic .NET Standard toolbar to enter run time.

2. When the Today's Sales Check window displays, click the Enter Today's Sales button. Enter the test data as shown in Table 8-4. After entering the second item, click the OK button without entering a description in the Item Description text box.

Visual Basic .NET begins executing the Today's Sales Check project. The test data values display in the lstTodaysSales control.

3. Click the Total Today's Sales button to determine if the application displays the expected results in the Daily Sales Totals message box.

The Daily Sales Totals message box displays $0.00 for the Total sales for items advertised (Figure 8-40). This result indicates that yet another bug is causing an incorrect total to display.

incorrect total still displays

FIGURE 8-40

4. Click the breakpoint status check box in the Breakpoints window to enable the breakpoint on line 175.

The breakpoint on line 175 becomes enabled. Visual Basic .NET remains in run time and the Today's Sales Check application continues to execute.

5. Click the Today's Sales Check application button in the Windows taskbar. When the Today's Sales Check window displays, click the OK button in the Daily Sales Totals message box. Click the Total Today's Sales button. Click the Locals tab at the bottom of the IDE.

Because the breakpoint at line 175 in the btnTotalSales_Click event procedure is enabled, clicking the Total Today's Sales button causes Visual Basic .NET to enter break mode. The Locals window displays variables that are in scope in the btnTotalSales_Click event procedure (Figure 8-41).

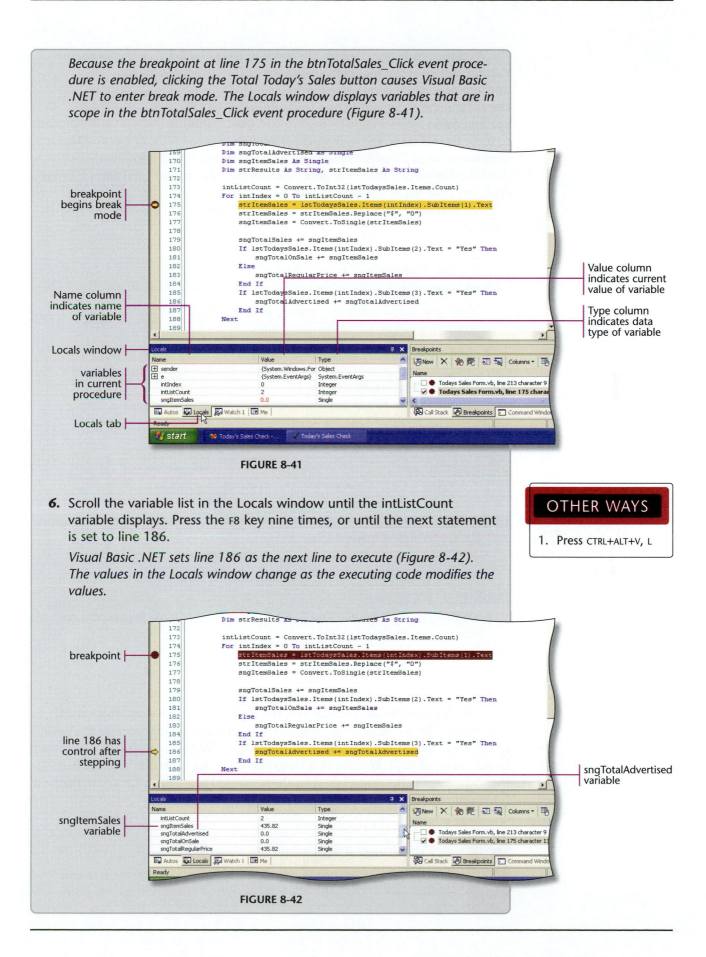

FIGURE 8-41

6. Scroll the variable list in the Locals window until the intListCount variable displays. Press the F8 key nine times, or until the next statement is set to line 186.

Visual Basic .NET sets line 186 as the next line to execute (Figure 8-42). The values in the Locals window change as the executing code modifies the values.

FIGURE 8-42

As shown in Figure 8-42 on the previous page, the Locals window shows that the values of the sngItemSales is correct, but that the value for SngTotalAdvertised is calculated as $0.00. Further inspection shows that the assignment statement in line 186 is incrementing the value of the sngTotalAdvertised variable by the value of itself, meaning it always will calculate to 0. To fix this error, the assignment statement in line 186 must be modified to increment the sngTotalAdvertised variable by the value of the sngItemSales variable. The sngItemSales variable contains the value of the Total Sales column (column 2) of the lstTodaysSales control.

The following steps correct the bug found with the assistance of the Autos window.

To Fix an Assignment Logic Error

1. Click the Stop Debugging button on the Debug toolbar.
   Visual Basic .NET returns to design time.

2. Select the variable, sngTotalAdvertised, on the right side of the assignment statement in line 186. Type `sngItemSales` to replace the variable, sngTotalAdvertised.
   The correction to line 186 displays in the code window (Figure 8-43).

```
178
179            sngTotalSales += sngItemSales
180            If lstTodaysSales.Items(intIndex).SubItems(2).Text =
181                sngTotalOnSale += sngItemSales
182            Else
183                sngTotalRegularPrice += sngItemSales
184            End If
185            If lstTodaysSales.Items(intIndex).SubItems(3).Text =
186                sngTotalAdvertised += sngItemSales
187            End If
188        Next
189
```

sngTotalAdvertised changed to sngItemSales

FIGURE 8-43

3. Right-click anywhere in line 175 and then click Disable Breakpoint on the code window shortcut menu.
   Visual Basic .NET disables the breakpoint on line 175.

With the modification of line 186, the sngTotalAdvertised variable now is incremented by the value of the sngItemSales variable, which contains the value of the Total Sales column (column 2) of the lstTodaysSales control. As indicated in the previous steps, an error in a program can result from one or more bugs in the code. After correcting a bug, you always should test your code to determine if it fixes the error appropriately.

Tip

Testing While Debugging
When fixing bugs, continue diligently to test your code to make certain that other bugs do not result in the same program error.

With the logic error corrected on line 186, the project can be tested once again and then saved.

Testing and Saving the Project

The following steps test the Today's Sales Check project with the test data supplied in Table 8-4 on page VB 8.26. Once the correctness of the project is verified, the project is saved.

To Test and Save the Project

1. Click the Start button on the Visual Basic .NET Standard toolbar to enter run time.

2. When the Today's Sales Check window displays, click the Enter Today's Sales button. When the Today's Sales Entry window displays, enter the test data as shown in Table 8-4. After entering the second item, click the OK button without entering a description in the Item Description text box.

Visual Basic .NET begins executing the Today's Sales Check project. The Today's Sales Check window displays with the data in the lstTodaysSales control.

3. Click the Total Today's Sales button.

The Daily Sales Totals message box displays the correct sales totals (Figure 8-44). This result indicates that the bugs have been fixed and the program is operating correctly.

total displays correct value

FIGURE 8-44

4. Click the Stop Debugging button on the Debug toolbar. Click the Save All button on the Visual Basic .NET Standard toolbar.

Because the project initially was created and saved on the Data Disk in drive A, Visual Basic .NET automatically saves the project on the Data Disk in drive A.

The modified Today's Sales Check project is now debugged and tested. Before preparing the application for distribution to users, the chapter will discuss two additional debugging features — viewing collection items and using the Command window.

Viewing Collection Items and Using the Command Window

The variables examined using the debugging tools up to this point in the chapter have been variables and properties of simple data types, such as Single and String. Visual Basic .NET debugging tools also allow you to view variables of type Object, such as collections, while in break mode. Visual Basic .NET also allows you to use the Command window to issue commands and view the results of Visual Basic .NET statements.

Viewing Collection Items

The debugging windows, such as the Watch, Locals, and Autos windows, display a plus (+) sign next to a variable name when the variable is an object that contains at least one property that you can view. The plus sign indicates that the list of additional properties is collapsed. Clicking the plus sign expands the list, so you can view the items in the collection. Some properties may be of type Object themselves, such as the SubItems collection of the ListView control. In this case, a plus sign will allow you to expand the SubItems list, so you can view that collection as well.

The process of debugging the Today's Sales Check application offers the opportunity to view the contents of a collection in order to understand better how Visual Basic .NET organizes the items in a collection. The following steps add the Items(intIndex) property of the lstTodaysSales control to the Watch 1 window, so you can view the text property value of the second SubItems property of the Items property. The lstTodaysSales.Items(intIndex) variable represents the Items collections of the lstTodaysSales control, and the intIndex variable refers to the current row being accessed in the For…Next loop in the code.

> ### To View Collection Items in a Watch Window
>
> **1.** Click the empty red circle icon to the left of line 175 to enable the breakpoint at line 175. Click the Start button on the Visual Basic .NET Standard toolbar to enter run time.
>
> **2.** When the Today's Sales Check window displays, click the Enter Today's Sales button. Enter the test data as shown in Table 8-4 on page VB 8.26. After entering the second item, click the OK button without entering a description in the Item Description text box.
>
> *Visual Basic .NET begins executing the Today's Sales Check project. The test data values display in the lstTodaysSales control.*

3. Click the Total Today's Sales button. Press the F8 key nine times to step to line 186. If necessary, click the Watch 1 tab at the bottom of the IDE.

4. Select lstTodaysSales.Items(intIndex) on line 185, as shown in Figure 8-45. Right-click the selection and then click the Add Watch command on the code window shortcut menu.

A watch for lstTodaysSales.Item(intIndex) is added to the Watch 1 window. A plus sign (+) displays to the left of the variable name in the Name column (Figure 8-45).

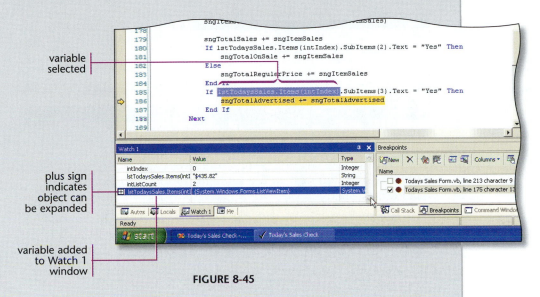

FIGURE 8-45

5. Click the plus sign in the Name column of the lstTodaysSales.Item(intIndex) watch in the Watch window.

A tree view of the members of the lstTodaysSales.Items(intIndex) object displays, as shown in Figure 8-46. If necessary, scroll the Watch 1 window to view as many of the members as possible.

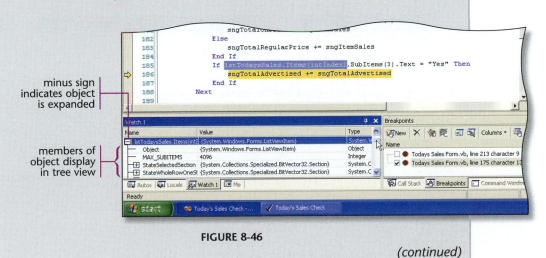

FIGURE 8-46

(continued)

6. Scroll the Watch 1 window until the subItems property displays in the Watch 1 window.

The subItems property displays in the Watch1 window. The Value column indicates that the number of subItems, or the Length of the subItems, is 4 (Figure 8-47). The number 4 corresponds to the four columns that display in the lstTodaysSales control.

subItems
property

plus sign
indicates property
can be expanded

Length=4
indicates four
subitems

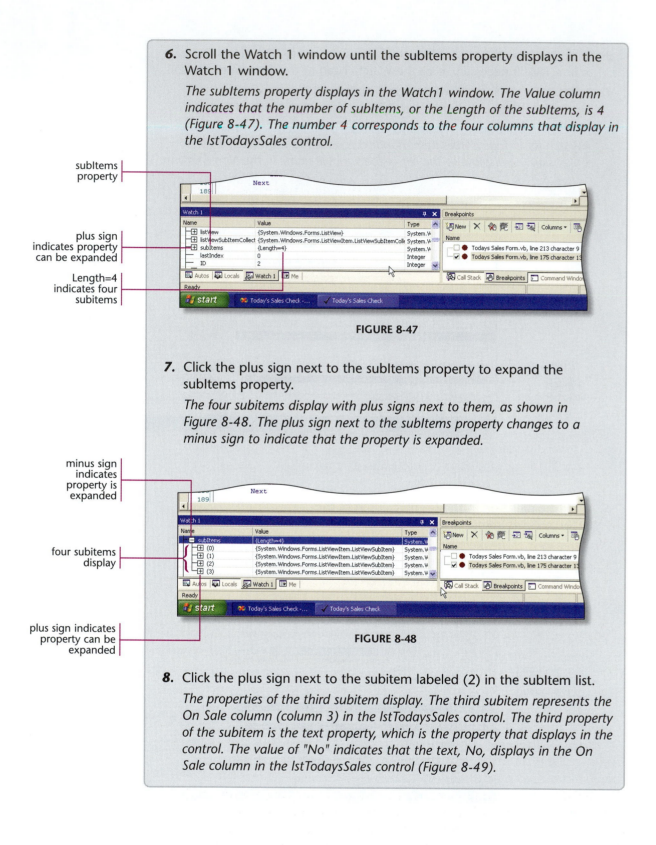

FIGURE 8-47

7. Click the plus sign next to the subItems property to expand the subItems property.

The four subitems display with plus signs next to them, as shown in Figure 8-48. The plus sign next to the subItems property changes to a minus sign to indicate that the property is expanded.

minus sign
indicates
property is
expanded

four subitems
display

plus sign indicates
property can be
expanded

FIGURE 8-48

8. Click the plus sign next to the subitem labeled (2) in the subItem list.

The properties of the third subitem display. The third subitem represents the On Sale column (column 3) in the lstTodaysSales control. The third property of the subitem is the text property, which is the property that displays in the control. The value of "No" indicates that the text, No, displays in the On Sale column in the lstTodaysSales control (Figure 8-49).

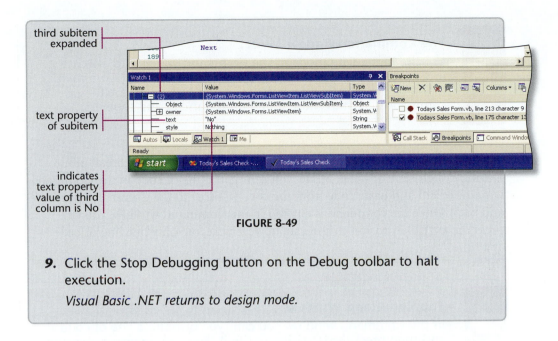

third subitem expanded

text property of subitem

indicates text property value of third column is No

FIGURE 8-49

9. Click the Stop Debugging button on the Debug toolbar to halt execution.

Visual Basic .NET returns to design mode.

The previous steps show how to navigate through a collection in a Watch window. In Figure 8-46 on page VB 8.47, the lstTodaysSales.Items(intIndex) variable is watched. This variable represents the Items collections of the lstTodaysSales control. The intIndex refers to the current row being accessed in the For…Next loop in the code. When you use the other debugging windows, such as the Locals and Autos windows, the process for viewing items and subitems in a collection is similar.

Using the Command Window

The **Command window** (Figure 8-50 on page VB 8.51) allows you to run commands and statements from a prompt. The Command window has two modes, one for running commands, the other for running statements. When in **Command mode**, you type commands in the IDE to complete tasks. For example, you can type the command, > saveall, to save all of the files in the open project. The effect is the same as clicking the Save All button on the Standard toolbar in the IDE. When in **Immediate mode**, the Command window allows you to execute and test Visual Basic .NET code statements without changing any of the actual program code.

While using the Command window, you switch from Immediate to Command mode by entering the **cmd command**. You switch from Command to Immediate mode by entering the **immed command**. When in Command mode, the title, Command Window, displays on the Command window title bar and the prompt, >, displays in the last line of the Command window. When in Immediate mode, the title, Command Window - Immediate displays on the Command window title bar and no prompt displays. You can issue commands while in Immediate mode, however, by typing the > prompt before the command you want to execute. For example, if you type > cmd, the Command window switches from Immediate mode to Command mode. Intellisense™ is available in both modes of the Command window.

The Command Window Modes

Use the Immediate mode of the Command window to execute individual Visual Basic .NET code statements. Use the Command mode of the Command window to enter Visual Basic .NET commands, such as those found on the menu and toolbars.

The Command window is available in both design time and break mode. During design time or break mode, you can type a line of code in the Command window or cut and paste code from the code window to the Command window and back. Once the command is entered in the Command window, you can press the ENTER key to run it. You can, however, execute only one line of code at a time.

The Command Window

In the Command window, you can type or paste a line of code and then press the ENTER key to run it. You can, however, execute only one line of code at a time.

When using the Immediate mode of the Command window during break mode, you can execute statements using variables that are active in the code. You can create expressions using these variables and evaluate the expressions. When in Immediate mode, you can determine the value of a variable or expression in code by typing a question mark (?) followed by the expression or variable name. You can only evaluate expressions in Immediate mode while the IDE is in break mode.

Using the Immediate Window

You can only evaluate expressions in Immediate mode while the IDE is in break mode.

You open the Command window in Command mode by clicking the Command Window command on the Other Windows submenu of the View menu. You also can press CTRL+G to open the Command window in Command mode. You open the Command window in Immediate mode by clicking the Immediate command on the Windows submenu of the Debug menu. You also can press CTRL+ALT+A to open the Command window in Immediate mode. Table 8-6 shows several uses for the Command window, along with an example of when that use would be beneficial.

Table 8-6 Uses of the Command Window

PURPOSE	MODE	EXAMPLE
Copy and paste a line of code that possibly is causing a bug	Immediate mode during break mode	`? intMyIndex` displays the value of the variable intMyIndex
Modify the value of a variable or property	Immediate mode during break mode	`intMyIndex = 0` changes the value of the variable intMyIndex to 0
Issue a command	Command during design time	`> Project.AddWindowsForm` performs the same action as clicking the Add Windows Form command on the Project menu
Issue a command	Command during break mode	`Project.AddWindowsForm` performs the same action as clicking the Add Windows Form command on the Project menu

The following steps enter break mode while running the Today's Sales Check project and then enter commands in the Command window.

To Enter Commands in the Command Window

1. Right-click the filled red circle icon to the left of line 175 and then click the Disable Breakpoint command on the shortcut menu to disable the breakpoint at line 175. Click the empty red circle icon to the left of line 213 to enable the breakpoint at line 213. Press the F5 key to enter run time.

   The breakpoint on line 175 is disabled and the breakpoint on line 213 is enabled. After run time begins, the program enters break mode when line 213 receives control, due to the breakpoint set on that line.

2. Click the Debug menu and point to the Windows command. Click the Immediate command on the Windows submenu.

   The Command window displays in Immediate mode as shown in Figure 8-50.

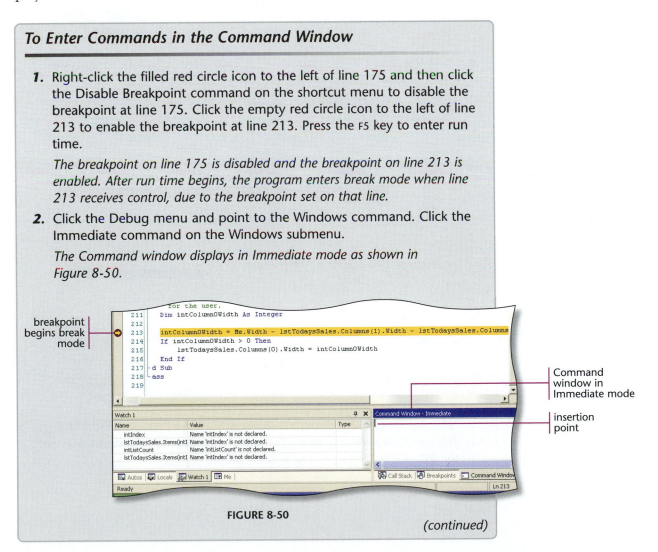

FIGURE 8-50

(continued)

3. At the insertion point in the Command window, type `?intColumn0Width` and then press the ENTER key.

The Command window returns and displays the current value of the intColumn0Width variable in line 213 (Figure 8-51).

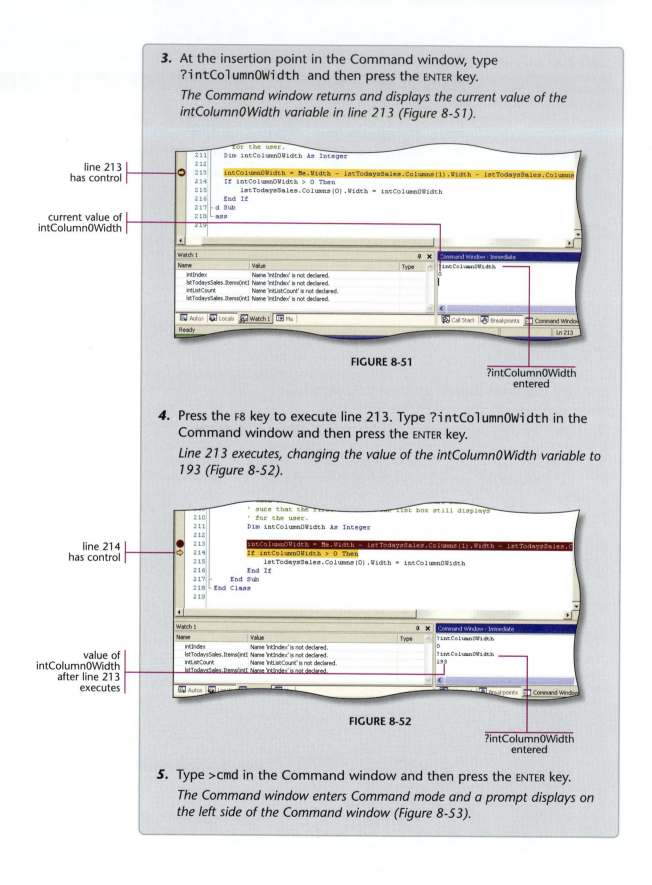

line 213 has control

current value of intColumn0Width

FIGURE 8-51

?intColumn0Width entered

4. Press the F8 key to execute line 213. Type `?intColumn0Width` in the Command window and then press the ENTER key.

Line 213 executes, changing the value of the intColumn0Width variable to 193 (Figure 8-52).

line 214 has control

value of intColumn0Width after line 213 executes

FIGURE 8-52

?intColumn0Width entered

5. Type `>cmd` in the Command window and then press the ENTER key.

The Command window enters Command mode and a prompt displays on the left side of the Command window (Figure 8-53).

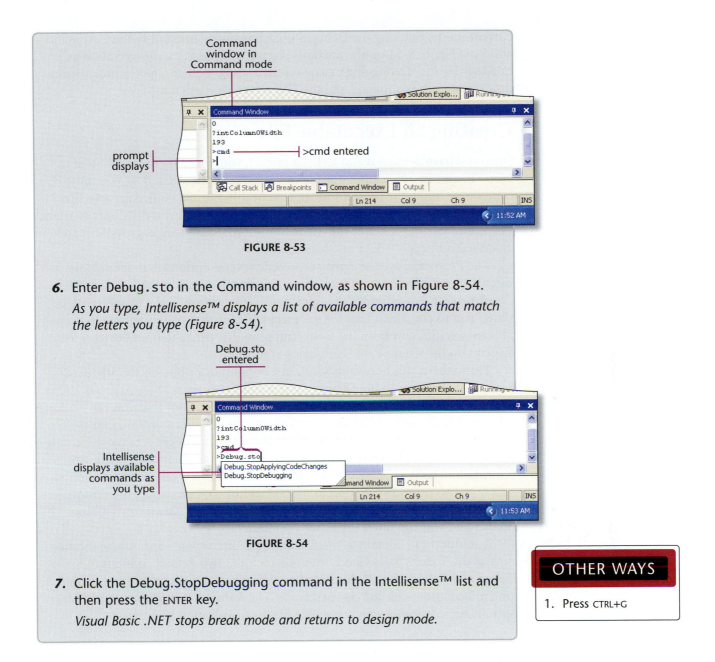

FIGURE 8-53

6. Enter Debug.sto in the Command window, as shown in Figure 8-54.

As you type, Intellisense™ displays a list of available commands that match the letters you type (Figure 8-54).

FIGURE 8-54

7. Click the Debug.StopDebugging command in the Intellisense™ list and then press the ENTER key.

Visual Basic .NET stops break mode and returns to design mode.

OTHER WAYS

1. Press CTRL+G

As shown in Figure 8-50 on page VB 8.51, the Command window only contains the insertion point when it initially launches in Immediate mode. Figures 8-51 and 8-52 show the results of using the ? command to request the value of a variable or expression. If the ? command is not used, then any statement can be executed. For example, if you entered

```
intColumn0Width = 0
```

in the Command window after line 214 executes, Visual Basic .NET would change the value of intColumn0Width from 193 back to 0 in the program. Figure 8-53 shows the >cmd command used to enter Command mode in the Command window. The Command window title bar changes to show the current mode. Entering the Debug.StopDebugging command in the Command window (Figure 8-54 on the previous page) performs the same operation as clicking the Stop Debugging button on the Debug toolbar. The Command window executes the command and the IDE returns to design mode.

Creating an Executable File

Once you have debugged and tested a project, you are ready to distribute it to users. To run an application outside of the Visual Basic .NET IDE, you must compile, or build, the project into an **executable file**, also called an **.exe file**. The resulting executable file includes the application that you distribute to users. The executable file contains the Microsoft Intermediate Language (MSIL) code described on page VB 1.24 of Chapter 1.

The Property Pages of a project provide several options that define how Visual Basic .NET builds and interacts with a project, such as the Today's Sales Check project. For example, the Application icon option in the Property Pages allows you to choose an icon for the executable file that you distribute to users. This icon is different from the form Icon property, which defines the icon that displays on the window title bar during run time.

Throughout this book, the Solution Configurations box on the Standard toolbar has been set to the Debug configuration (Figure 2-12 on page VB 2.12). A **configuration** is a stored set of values for certain options that you can set for a solution. Visual Basic .NET allows you to set options for a solution, save the settings as a configuration, and then change the settings and create a second configuration. For example, you can specify that one configuration stores debugging information, such as breakpoints, in the executable file, while a second configuration intended for distribution to users does not contain debugging information in the executable. The executable without the debugging information is smaller and will run faster on a user's computer.

A solution can contain as many configurations as you want. A new solution, such as the Today's Sales Check solution, includes two default configurations, Debug and Release. The **Debug configuration** has options set to store debugging information with the executable file. The **Release configuration** includes options set to optimize the executable file for distribution to users.

Selecting a Solution Configuration

After you debug and test a project, set the configuration to Release before creating the executable that you distribute to users.

The following steps set an application icon for the Today's Sales Check application, set the configuration for building the application, and create an executable file.

To Set Project Options and Create an Executable File

1. Click the Today's Sales Check project in the Solution Explorer window. Click the Property Pages icon on the Properties toolbar in the Properties window. When the Today's Sales Check Property Pages display, click the Build item in the Common Properties folder.

The Today's Sales Check Property Pages window opens and the Build options display (Figure 8-55).

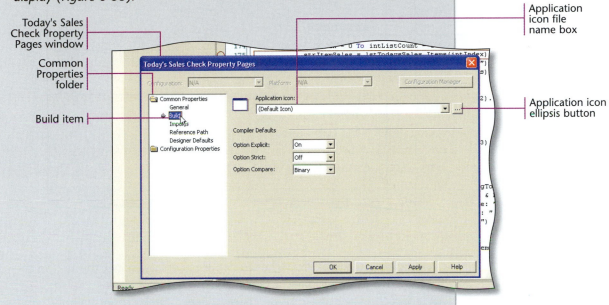

FIGURE 8-55

2. Click the Application icon ellipsis button. Select the CHECKMRK.ICO file located in the A:\Chapter8\Today's Sales Check\Today's Sales Check folder and then click the Open button.

Visual Basic .NET updates the file name in the Application icon box and displays the icon to the left of the Application icon box (Figure 8-56).

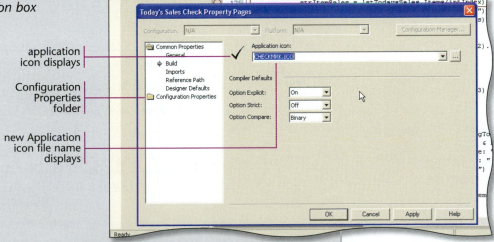

FIGURE 8-56

(continued)

3. Click the Configuration Properties folder and, if necessary, select the Debugging item in the Configuration Properties folder.

The Debugging options display in the Today's Sales Check Property Pages window. The configuration currently is set to Active(Debug), as shown in Figure 8-57.

Configuration box

Debugging item

OK button

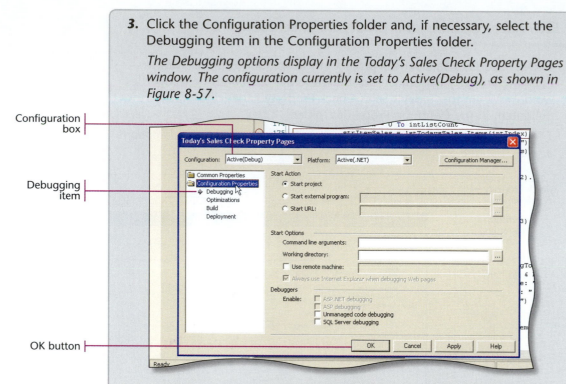

FIGURE 8-57

4. Click the General Properties folder. If necessary, select the text in the Assembly name box and type **Todays Sales Check**.

5. Click the OK button in the Today's Sales Check Property Pages window.

The configuration for the Today's Sales Check project remains set to Active(Debug).

6. Click the Solution Configurations box arrow on the Standard toolbar. Select Release in the Solution Configurations list. Click Build on the menu bar.

The configuration for the Today's Sales Check project is set to Release, meaning that the executable file can be built (compiled) and distributed to users. The Build menu displays (Figure 8-58).

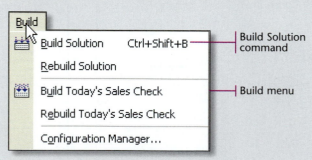

Build Solution command

Build menu

FIGURE 8-58

7. Click the Build Solution command on the Build menu.

Visual Basic .NET displays several messages that scroll as they display in the Output window. When the build is complete, the build results display in the Output window (Figure 8-59).

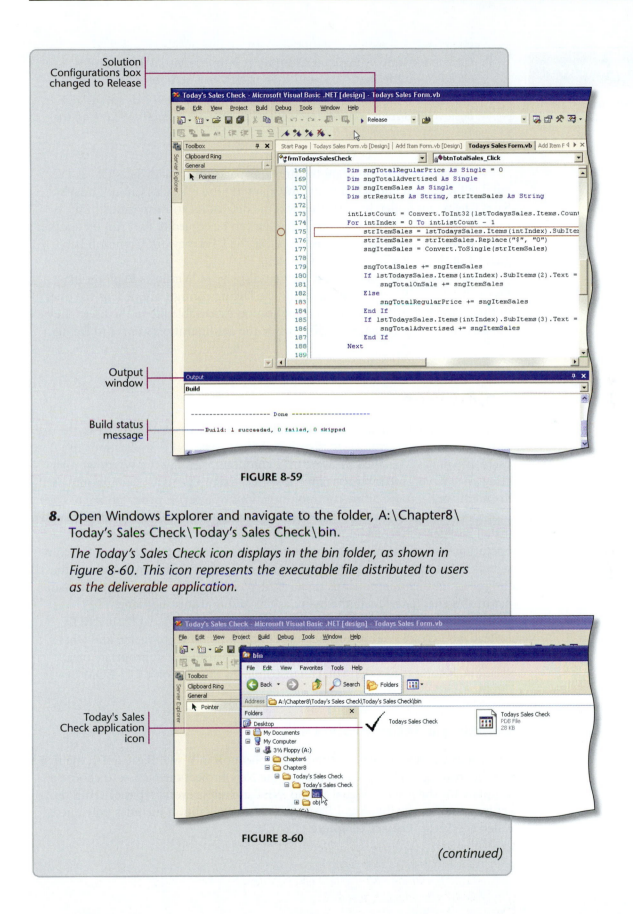

Solution
Configurations box
changed to Release

Output
window

Build status
message

FIGURE 8-59

8. Open Windows Explorer and navigate to the folder, A:\Chapter8\
Today's Sales Check\Today's Sales Check\bin.

*The Today's Sales Check icon displays in the bin folder, as shown in
Figure 8-60. This icon represents the executable file distributed to users
as the deliverable application.*

Today's Sales
Check application
icon

FIGURE 8-60

(continued)

9. Click the Windows Explorer Close button. In the Visual Basic .NET IDE, click File on the menu bar and then click Close Solution.

If changes were made to the project since the last time it was saved, Visual Basic .NET displays the Microsoft Visual Basic .NET dialog box. Clicking the Yes button resaves and then closes the project.

As shown in Figure 8-60 on the previous page, the Todays Sales Check executable file is built and saved to the A:\Chapter8\Today's Sales Check\Today's Sales Check\bin folder, because that was the default location specified in the project's Property Pages. The executable file can be copied to and run on another user's computer, as long as that user has the .NET Framework Common Language Runtime installed on the computer.

The Todays Sales Check .PDB file that displays in Windows Explorer in Figure 8-60 is a file created and used by the Debug configuration. This file does not need to be distributed with the application executable file to the user. The file was created by Visual Basic .NET while the configuration was set to Debug.

Creating a Setup Project for a Windows Application

Visual Basic .NET provides tools that allow you to create customized, easy-to-use setup programs that you use to distribute Visual Basic .NET applications to users. If you have installed software on a computer running the Windows operating system, you probably are familiar with the setup programs commonly used to install applications. Some common functions of a **setup program** are to copy program files to the Program Files folder, install icons on the user's desktop, and install a folder and icons on the All Programs submenu. In the Windows XP operating system, the All Programs submenu is the menu that contains the commands to start applications installed on the computer. This is equivalent to the Programs submenu in previous versions of Windows. For simplicity, the remainder of this chapter refers to the menu as the All Programs submenu.

Creating a setup program does not involve coding in Visual Basic .NET. Instead, you create a **setup project** and specify which files to install and where to install them. Visual Basic .NET takes care of creating the appropriate files, such as a Setup.exe file, that you can distribute to the user on a CD-ROM or via the Internet.

Creating a Setup Project

Just as when you create a Windows application in Visual Basic .NET, the first step in creating a setup project is to use the New Project dialog box to choose a template for the project. Visual Studio .NET includes several types of setup project templates, while the Visual Basic .NET standard edition includes only one, called the **Setup Project template**.

A setup project allows you to specify the files to install on the user's computer. These files include any files Visual Basic .NET created when you built the project, as well as databases, Help files, and any other required files. The setup project also allows you to specify shortcuts to be added to the user's desktop or the All Programs submenu, so the user can run the application that is installed on the computer.

The following steps create a new setup project and then add the executable file for the Today's Sales Check application to the setup project.

To Create a Setup Project and Add an Executable File

1. With the Today's Sales Check solution closed, click Project on the New submenu of the File menu. When the New Project dialog box displays, select Setup and Deployment Projects in the Project Types box. If necessary, select A:\Chapter8 in the Location text box. Enter Todays Sales Check Setup in the Name text box and then click the Setup Project icon in the Templates box.

The New Project dialog box displays. The project name displays in the Name text box, and the project location displays in the Location text box. Visual Basic .NET will create the Today's Sales Check setup project in the specified location (Figure 8-61). Depending on the version of Visual Basic .NET installed on your computer, the list of templates may differ from those shown in Figure 8-61.

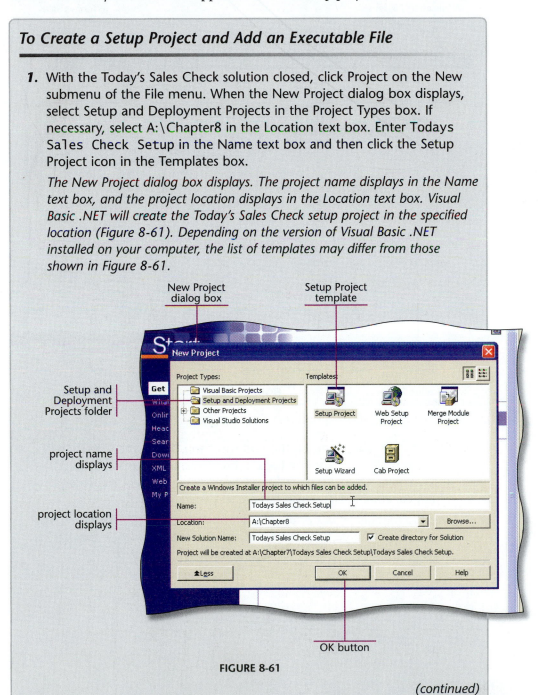

FIGURE 8-61

(continued)

2. Click the OK button. After Visual Basic .NET creates the new project, right-click the Application Folder folder in the File System window. When the shortcut menu displays, point to the Add command.

Visual Basic .NET creates a new setup project. The project and solution display in the Solution Explorer window. Two windows (Files and Folders) display in the main work area. The Add submenu displays when you point to the Add command on the shortcut menu (Figure 8-62).

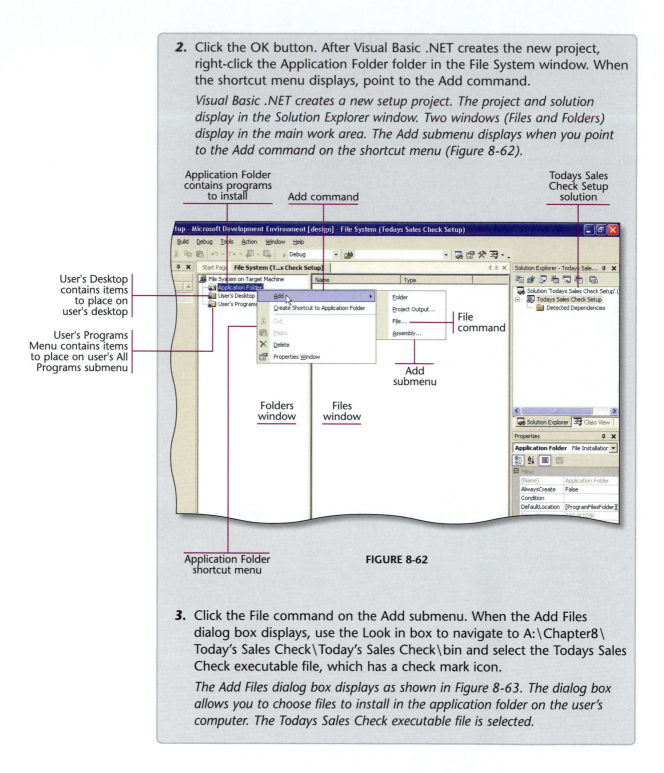

FIGURE 8-62

3. Click the File command on the Add submenu. When the Add Files dialog box displays, use the Look in box to navigate to A:\Chapter8\ Today's Sales Check\Today's Sales Check\bin and select the Todays Sales Check executable file, which has a check mark icon.

The Add Files dialog box displays as shown in Figure 8-63. The dialog box allows you to choose files to install in the application folder on the user's computer. The Todays Sales Check executable file is selected.

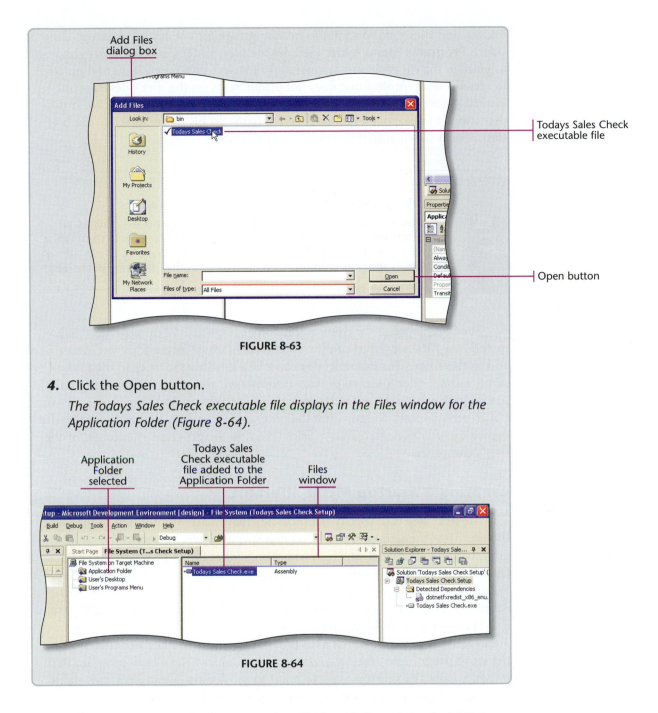

Add Files
dialog box

Todays Sales Check
executable file

Open button

FIGURE 8-63

4. Click the Open button.

The Todays Sales Check executable file displays in the Files window for the Application Folder (Figure 8-64).

Application
Folder
selected

Todays Sales
Check executable
file added to the
Application Folder

Files
window

FIGURE 8-64

As shown in Figure 8-62, a setup project displays differently in the IDE than a project created using the Windows Application template. See Figure 8-2 on page VB 8.06 to compare the IDE for a setup project with the IDE for a Windows Application project. With the setup project, the Solution Explorer displays the list of files within the solution. The **Folders window** on the left of the main work area displays folders that represent locations on the user's computer. You place files, folders, and shortcuts in these folders, depending on what and where you want to install these items on the user's computer. The **Application Folder folder** includes the files you want to install in the application's Program Files folder on the user's computer. The **User's Desktop folder** contains files, folders, and shortcuts you want to install on the user's Windows desktop. The **User's Programs Menu folder** includes the files, folders, and shortcuts you want to place in the All Programs submenu of the user's computer. It is good practice to create a setup project that does not install items on the user's desktop, but instead places the items in a folder on the user's All Programs submenu. If the user wants to place one of more program items on his or her desktop, the user can create a shortcut to the program on the desktop.

Tip

Installing Items on the All Programs Submenu

It is good practice to create a setup project that does not install items on the user's desktop. Instead, it should place the items in a folder on the user's All Programs submenu by putting these files in the User's Programs Menu folder while creating the setup project.

The files placed in the Application Folder (Figure 8-62 on page VB 8.60) include the files needed to run the application and any other files you want to add to this folder. For example, you can add a ReadMe file or Help file to the Application Folder folder to provide information about the application. Any files placed in the Application Folder of the setup project are not seen by the user on his or her Windows desktop after the program is installed. Rather, these files are copied to a folder named Todays Sales Check in the Program Files folder of the user's computer.

Creating a Startup Menu Shortcut

The next step is to specify the shortcuts that the setup program creates when the user runs the setup program. You first specify where you want the setup program to create the shortcut. Next, you specify what file or program the shortcut launches when the user opens the shortcut. The setup program for the Todays Sales Check Setup program should create a folder on the user's All Programs submenu. This folder will contain a shortcut to the Todays Sales Check program.

The following steps instruct the setup program to add a folder named Todays Sales Check to the user's All Programs submenu. The steps then instruct the setup program to create a shortcut to the Todays Sales Check program in this folder. Finally, the shortcut is set to point to the Todays Sales Check executable file installed in the Program Files\Todays Sales Check folder.

To Create a Startup Menu Shortcut

1. Right-click the User's Programs Menu folder in the Folders window. Click the Add command on the User's Programs Menu shortcut menu.

The User's Programs Menu shortcut menu displays. No files display in the Files window, indicating that no items have been added to the User's Programs Menu folder (Figure 8-65).

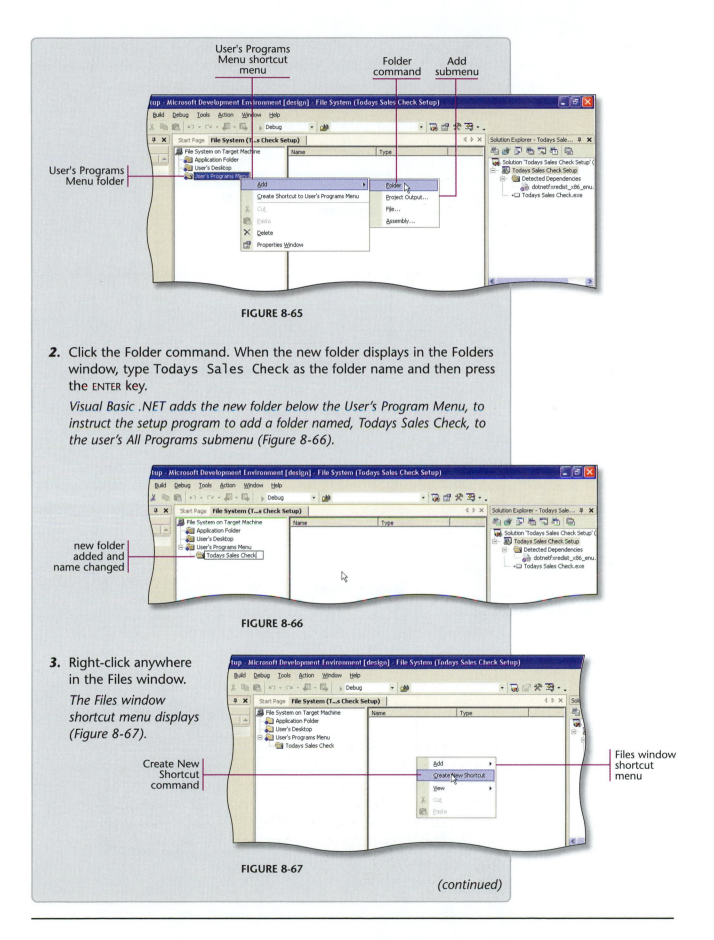

FIGURE 8-65

2. Click the Folder command. When the new folder displays in the Folders window, type Todays Sales Check as the folder name and then press the ENTER key.

Visual Basic .NET adds the new folder below the User's Program Menu, to instruct the setup program to add a folder named, Todays Sales Check, to the user's All Programs submenu (Figure 8-66).

FIGURE 8-66

3. Right-click anywhere in the Files window.

The Files window shortcut menu displays (Figure 8-67).

FIGURE 8-67

(continued)

4. Click the Create New Shortcut command. When the Select Item in Project dialog box displays, double-click the Application Folder folder.

The Select Item in Project dialog box displays as shown in Figure 8-68. The dialog box allows you to select an item for creating a shortcut. The Todays Sales Check.exe file in the Application Folder folder is selected.

Todays Sales
Check.exe
executable
program file

OK button

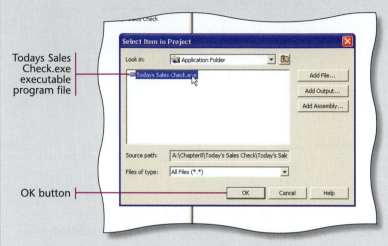

FIGURE 8-68

5. Click the OK button. In the Files window, type Todays Sales Check as the name for the shortcut.

Visual Basic .NET adds a shortcut to the executable to the Todays Sales Check subfolder. When the user runs the setup program, the setup program will add the shortcut to the Todays Sales Check folder on the user's All Programs submenu (Figure 8-69).

shortcut will be
placed in Todays
Sales Check folder on
All Programs submenu

shortcut to
Todays Sales
Check.exe

current Icon
property
is None

Icon property

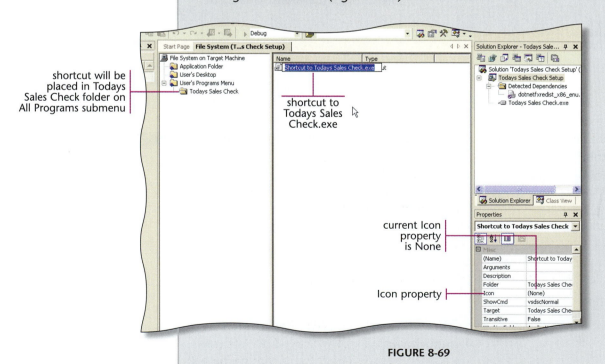

FIGURE 8-69

6. Click the Icon property value in the Properties window. Click the Icon property box arrow and then click Browse in the Icon property values list.

The default icon for a new shortcut is the Windows shortcut default icon. The Icon dialog box allows you to associate a new icon with the shortcut.

7. When the Icon dialog box displays, click the Browse button. When the Select Item in Project dialog box displays, double-click the Application Folder folder.

8. Select Executable Files (*.exe) in the Files of type list. Click the Todays Sales Check.exe file and then click the OK button.

9. Click the OK button in the Icon dialog box.

The icon for the shortcut is changed from the default Windows shortcut icon to the check mark icon associated with the Todays Sales Check.exe executable file in the Application Folder.

When the setup program runs, it creates a Todays Sales Check subfolder (Figure 8-66 on page VB 8.63) on the user's All Programs submenu. The setup program then adds a shortcut to the Todays Sales Check.exe executable file to the Todays Sales Check subfolder. If no subfolder is specified, then the program shortcut is added directly to the All Programs submenu. Unless the program being installed is a general-purpose program, such as a word processor, it is recommended that the setup program install shortcuts in a program subfolder, not in the All Programs submenu.

Installing Shortcuts on the All Programs Submenu

Unless the program being installed is a general-purpose program, such as a word processor, it is recommended that shortcuts not be installed on the All Programs submenu.

When you create a shortcut in the setup program, you specify the file to which the shortcut links. You can create a shortcut to any file already added to the setup program. In the previous steps, for example, you created a shortcut to the Todays Sales Check.exe file, which already was in the Application Folder folder. The shortcut name entered in the Files window — in this case, Todays Sales Check — is the shortcut name that displays in the Todays Sales Check folder on the user's All Programs submenu. Finally, the default icon for the new shortcut is changed from the default Windows shortcut icon by setting the Icon property of the shortcut to the icon associated with the Todays Sales Check.exe executable file in the Application Folder.

Setting Setup Project Options and Building the Setup Program

As with Windows application projects, Visual Basic .NET allows you to set the options for a setup project using the Property Pages window. The Property Pages window for a setup project differs from the Property Pages window for a Windows application, as shown in Figure 8-55 on page VB 8.55.

When you create a setup project, Visual Basic .NET creates a Windows installer file with the extension, msi. The **Windows installer file**, which is the file distributed to the user, contains the information about how Windows should perform the program installation, such as the location on the user's computer to place the program files and what shortcuts to create. Recent Windows operating systems, such as Windows XP, include an application called the **Windows Installer**, which understands how to read and interpret the Windows installer (.msi) file. The Windows Installer program is known as a **bootstrapper** and is responsible for starting and executing the setup instructions. When you create a setup project, you can change the **Bootstrapper option** on the Property Pages to set whether or not to include the Windows Installer along with your setup project. The Windows Installer adds between 1 and 2 megabytes of disk space to your setup project. If users must install the program on a Windows system with an operating system version prior to Windows XP, you should include the Windows Installer. If the size of the setup project is an issue for the distribution of your files, and you are certain that your users have the Windows Installer on their computers, you can choose not to include the Windows Installer. For example, if you want to distribute the setup program on a floppy disk, you would not want to include the Windows Installer.

Tip

Including the Windows Installer in a Setup Program
If users must install the program on a Windows system with an operating system version prior to Windows XP, you should include the Windows Installer.

Table 8-7 shows the commonly used options available on the Property Pages for a setup project.

Table 8-7   Common Setup Project Options

OPTION	VALUE	DESCRIPTION
Package files	As loose compressed files	Files to install placed in the same directory as the Windows installer (.msi) file
	In setup file	Files packaged inside of the Windows installer (.msi) file
	In cabinet file	Files packaged together in one or more .cab files, which are created in the same directory as the Windows installer (.msi) file
Bootstrapper	None	No bootstrapper is included
	Windows Installer Bootstrapper	Windows Installer version 1.5 application included with the setup program distributed to users
	Web Bootstrapper	Bootstrapper included allows for Web downloads of the setup program
Compression	Optimized for speed	Files compressed to install faster, but results in a larger setup program size
	Optimized for size	Files compressed to be smaller size, but may result in slower installation
	None	Files not compressed

The following steps set the Bootstrapper option for the project to the value, None, so that the Windows Installer is not included with the setup program. This ensures that the setup program fit on a floppy disk. The steps then build the setup program for distribution to the user.

To Set Options and Build a Setup Program

1. Click the Todays Sales Check Setup project in the Solution Explorer window. Then, click the Property Pages button in the Properties window.

2. When the Property Pages window displays, click the Bootstrapper box arrow.

The option values for the Bootstrapper option display in the Bootstrapper list. The Windows Installer Bootstrapper is the default option (Figure 8-70).

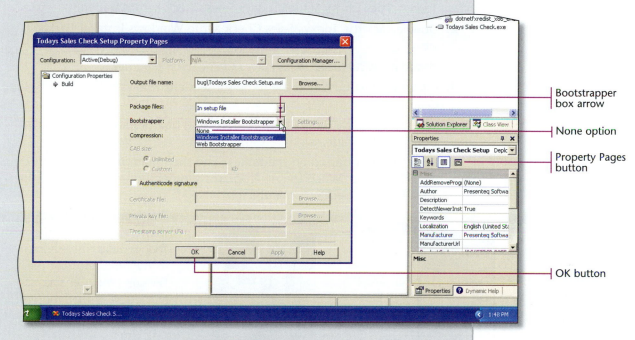

FIGURE 8-70

3. Click None in the Bootstrapper list. Click the OK button.

4. When the Property Pages window closes, click the Build Solution command on the Build menu.

Visual Basic .NET takes up to several minutes to build the setup project and displays status messages in the Output window.

5. When the Output window indicates that the build is complete, close Visual Basic .NET.

The Visual Basic .NET window closes. The Todays Sales Check setup program now is built and ready for distribution to users.

The setup program is created without a bootstrapper. The setup project contains a Windows installer (.msi) file that includes the information about where to place to Todays Sales Check.exe executable file and which folders and shortcuts to create on the user's All Programs submenu.

Testing a Setup Program

The next step is to run the setup program to verify that it operates as intended and installs the Today's Sales Check application correctly. The following steps test the setup program for the Today's Sales Check application.

To Test a Setup Program

1. Open Windows Explorer and navigate to the folder, A:\Chapter8\ Todays Sales Check Setup\Todays Sales Check Setup\Debug.

2. Double-click the Todays Sales Check Setup Windows Installer Package icon.

Windows executes the Todays Sales Check Setup program.

3. Click the Next button in the three subsequent Todays Sales Check Setup dialog boxes.

4. When the Todays Sales Check Setup dialog box displays the Installation Complete message, click the Close button.

5. Click the Start button on the taskbar and then point to All Programs on the Start menu. When the All Programs submenu displays, point to the Todays Sales Check command.

The Todays Sales Check shortcut displays on the Todays Sales Check submenu indicating that the Windows Installer successfully installed the program (Figure 8-71).

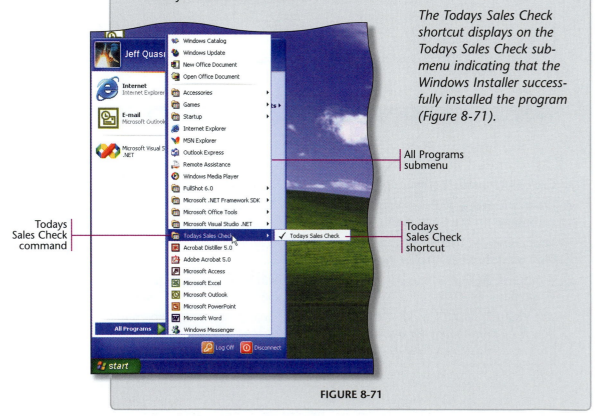

Todays Sales Check command

All Programs submenu

Todays Sales Check shortcut

FIGURE 8-71

Once the Today's Sales Check application is installed on the user's computer, the user can start the application using the same basic steps used to start any Windows application:

1. Click the Start button on the taskbar and then point to All Programs on the Start menu.
2. Point to Todays Sales Check on the All Programs submenu.
3. Point to Todays Sales Check on the Todays Sales Check submenu.
4. Click Todays Sales Check.

To uninstall the application, the user can use the Add or Remove Programs icon in the Control Panel. If you need to test the setup program again, you first must uninstall the Today's Sales Check application.

Chapter Summary

In this chapter, you learned how to use Visual Basic .NET's extensive set of debugging tools. You learned how to find and correct syntax errors in code using the Task List. You learned how to set breakpoints to pause execution during run time and use stepping to execute one line of code at a time. You learned several methods of evaluating variables and expressions, including DataTips, the QuickWatch window, the Watch windows, the Autos window, and the Locals window. You also learned how the Command window allows you to execute commands and Visual Basic .NET code statements. You learned how to set options to prepare an application for distribution to users and then how to create an executable file to distribute to users. Finally, you learned how to create a setup program for a Windows application to distribute an application to users.

What You Should Know

Having completed this chapter, you now should be able to perform the tasks shown in Table 8-8.

Table 8-8   Chapter 8 What You Should Know

TASK NUMBER	TASK	PAGE
1	Start Visual Basic .NET and Open an Existing Project	VB 8.05
2	Find and Fix Syntax Errors Using the Task List Window	VB 8.08
3	Run the Project and Set a Breakpoint	VB 8.15
4	Use Stepping and DataTips with Breakpoints	VB 8.18
5	Disable a Breakpoint and Correct a Logic Error	VB 8.21
6	Break on a Run-Time Error and Use a QuickWatch	VB 8.26
7	Add a Watch to the Watch Window and Set a Breakpoint in a Loop	VB 8.30
8	Watch Variables and Use a Breakpoint in a Loop	VB 8.32
9	Fix a Run-Time Error in a For...Next Loop	VB 8.36
10	Use the Autos Windows to Evaluate Variables	VB 8.38

(continued)

Table 8-8 Chapter 8 What You Should Know (continued)

TASK NUMBER	TASK	PAGE
11	Fix a Logic Error	VB 8.41
12	Use the Locals Window to Evaluate Variables	VB 8.42
13	Fix an Assignment Logic Error	VB 8.44
14	Test and Save the Project	VB 8.45
15	View Collection Items in a Watch Window	VB 8.46
16	Enter Commands in the Command Window	VB 8.51
17	Set Project Options and Create an Executable File	VB 8.55
18	Create a Setup Project and Add an Executable File	VB 8.59
19	Create a Startup Menu Shortcut	VB 8.62
20	Set Options and Build a Setup Program	VB 8.67
21	Test a Setup Program	VB 8.68

Key Terms

Application Folder folder (*VB 8.61*)
Autos window (*VB 8.37*)
bootstrapper (*VB 8.66*)
Bootstrapper option (*VB 8.66*)
break mode (*VB 8.17*)
breakpoint (*VB 8.03*)
Breakpoints window (*VB 8.03*)
bugs (*VB 8.02*)
Build Error (*VB 8.13*)
Clear All Breakpoints command (*VB 8.14*)
cmd command (*VB 8.49*)
Command mode (*VB 8.49*)
Command Window (*VB 8.49*)
configuration (*VB 8.54*)
DataTips (*VB 8.17*)
Debug configuration (*VB 8.54*)
Debug Location toolbar (*VB 8.20*)
Debug menu (*VB 8.17*)
Debug toolbar (*VB 8.20*)
debugging (*VB 8.02*)
debugging techniques (*VB 8.02*)
Delete command (*VB 8.22*)
Delete Watch command (*VB 8.32*)
Disable All Breakpoints command (*VB 8.22*)
Enable All Breakpoints command (*VB 8.22*)
exception (*VB 8.02*)
.exe file (*VB 8.54*)
executable file (*VB 8.54*)

Folders window (*VB 8.61*)
immed command (*VB 8.49*)
Immediate mode (*VB 8.49*)
infinity (*VB 8.78*)
Insert Breakpoint command (*VB 8.14*)
Locals window (*VB 8.37*)
logic error (*VB 8.02*)
Me window (*VB 8.37*)
Members list (*VB 8.12*)
nan (*VB 8.78*)
QuickWatch (*VB7.26*)
QuickWatch window (*VB 8.26*)
Release configuration (*VB 8.54*)
Remove Breakpoint command (*VB 8.14*)
run-time error (*VB 8.02*)
Set Next Statement command (*VB 8.22*)
setup program (*VB 8.58*)
setup project (*VB 8.58*)
Setup Project template (*VB 8.58*)
Step Into command (*VB 8.17*)
Step Out command (*VB 8.24*)
Step Over command (*VB 8.24*)
syntax error (*VB 8.02*)
User's Desktop folder (*VB 8.61*)
User's Programs Menu folder (*VB 8.62*)
watch expression (*VB 8.25*)
Watch window (*VB 8.03*)
Windows Installer (*VB 8.66*)
Windows installer file (*VB 8.66*)

Homework Assignments

Label the Figure

Identify the 16 components of the Visual Basic .NET debugging tools shown in Figure 8-72.

1. _____
2. _____
3. _____
4. _____
5. _____
6. _____
7. _____
8. _____

9. _____
10. _____
11. _____
12. _____
13. _____
14. _____
15. _____
16. _____

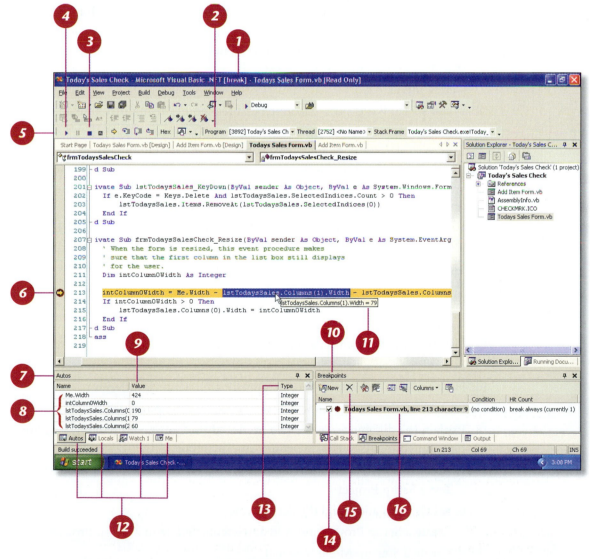

FIGURE 8-72

Short Answer

1. A(n) _____ occurs when you violate a rule of the Visual Basic .NET language.

2. Program errors are called _____, and the activity involved in their detection is called _____.

3. List three methods you can use to enter break mode.

   _____

   _____

   _____

4. You set _____ on code statements during _____ time, which cause the execution of code to pause at the statement during _____ time.

5. The _____ window shows variable values within one line of the current line that has control. The _____ window shows all variables within the same scope as the current line. The _____ window shows all variables associated with the current class or object being debugged.

6. _____, also called exceptions, are errors that occur when conditions arise during run time that the CLR does not know how to handle.

7. You clear all breakpoints by invoking the _____ command on the Debug menu.

8. When Visual Basic .NET encounters a breakpoint during run time, it enters _____ mode.

9. _____ provide the quickest method of viewing the values of variables that are not objects.

10. When you save a project, Visual Basic .NET _____ (does, does not) remember the breakpoints and the status of the breakpoints.

11. You can check the value of any variable or property in break mode by opening the _____ window.

12. Explain the difference between a syntax error, a logic error, and a run-time error.

13. What two actions does Visual Basic .NET take when it discovers a syntax error?

14. List five ways you can set a breakpoint in a procedure.

15. List at least five actions you can take when a program is in break mode.

16. How are Watch windows and the QuickWatch window different?

17. Identify all the debugging windows and explain the purpose of each.

18. Explain the differences in the two modes of the Command window and how their functionality varies, depending on the mode of the IDE.

19. Reorder these steps in the required sequence for creating a setup project.

    a. Test a Setup Project

    b. Set Options and Build the Setup Project

    c. Create a Setup Project and Add an Executable File to a Setup Project

    d. Create a Startup Menu Shortcut

20. For the following situations, indicate the best options to set for a setup program assuming that the users have the .NET Framework installed on their computers.

SITUATION	PACKAGE FILES	BOOTSTRAPPER	COMPRESSION
Windows XP on a CD-ROM			
Any Windows user over the Web			
Any Windows user on a CD-ROM			

Learn It Online

Start your browser and visit scsite.com/vbnet/exs. Follow the instructions in the exercises below.

1. **Chapter Reinforcement TF, MC, and SA** Click the True/False, Multiple Choice, and Short Answer link below Chapter 8. Print and then answer the questions.

2. **Practice Test** Click the Practice Test link below Chapter 8. Answer each question, enter your first and last name at the bottom of the page, and then click the Grade Test button. When the graded practice test displays on your screen, click Print on the File menu to print a hard copy. Continue to take practice tests until you score 80% or better. Hand in a printout of the final practice test.

3. **Crossword Puzzle Challenge** Click the Crossword Puzzle Challenge link below Chapter 8. Read the instructions, and then enter your first and last name. Click the Play button. Complete the crossword puzzle. When you are finished, click the Submit button. When the crossword puzzle redisplays, click the Print button.

4. **Tips and Tricks** Click the Tips and Tricks link below Chapter 8. Click a topic that pertains to Chapter 8. Right-click the information and then click Print on the shortcut menu. Construct a brief example of what the information relates to in Visual Basic .NET to confirm you understand how to use the tip or trick. Hand in the example and printed information.

5. **Newsgroups** Click the Newsgroups link below Chapter 8. Click a topic that pertains to Chapter 8. Print three comments.

6. **Expanding Your Horizons** Click the Articles for Visual Basic .NET below Chapter 8. Click a topic that pertains to Chapter 8. Print the information. Construct a brief example of what the information relates to in Visual Basic .NET to confirm you understand the contents of the article. Hand in the example and printed information.

7. **Search Sleuth** Select three key terms from the Key Terms section of this chapter and then use the Google search engine at google.com (or any major search engine) to display and print two Web pages for each key term.

HOMEWORK ASSIGNMENTS

Programming Assignments

1 Debugging a Windows Application Project Using the Task List

Start Visual Basic .NET and open the project, Graphics Sample, from the Chapter8\Graphics Sample folder on the Data Disk. The Graphics Sample application plots four points input by the user. Default values are supplied to begin. The points are connected with straight lines and then a special curve, known as a cardinal spline, is drawn based on the location of the points. The purpose of the application is to demonstrate some of the graphics capabilities of Visual Basic .NET.

The Graphics Sample application contains several syntax errors, which are listed in the Task List. Additionally, the Task List contains other entries with instructions that you should follow. Perform the following steps using the Task List as a guide.

1. Use the Task List to find and fix all of the syntax errors that have an icon representing a Build Error in the Category column. Eight syntax errors exist in the project.

2. Two tasks have blue arrow icons in the Category column. The blue arrow icons identify a task list shortcut that links a user-defined task to specific lines of code. Double-click the first user-defined task with a blue arrow icon and follow the instructions in the task to modify code.

3. Double-click the second user-defined task with a blue arrow icon and follow the instructions in the task to modify code.

4. When you complete the tasks in steps 2 and 3, click the check box in the task to indicate that the task is complete.

5. The final task contains instructions for a final code modification to fix a run-time error condition. Follow the instructions in the task.

6. Run the project. Correct any errors caused during the debugging process. Test the application using X and Y coordinate values at the upper and lower limits of the acceptable range. After making final changes to fix any bugs, save the project again. The application window should display as shown in Figure 8-73.

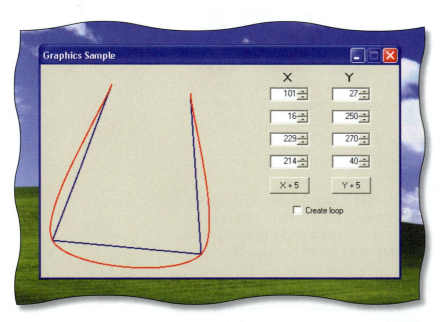

FIGURE 8-73

2 Debugging Logic and Run-Time Errors

Open the project, Weekly Revenue, from the Chapter8\Weekly Revenue folder on the Data Disk. The Weekly Revenue application accepts data items entered by the user when the user presses the INSERT key while the ListView control has focus. The user also can press the DELETE key to delete items from the list. As items are added and deleted, the application automatically updates totals on the lower-right side of the window (Figure 8-74 on the next page). The Weekly Revenue project currently contains several logic errors. Perform the following steps to debug the project.

1. Run the project. Press the INSERT key to add a new data item of your choice to the list. A run-time error occurs. The line of code that has control, line 167, should not execute until the user has opened and the closed the data entry form. Click the Continue button to exit break mode. Fix the statement or statements that caused this error.

2. Run the project. Press the INSERT key and add a new data item of your choice. A logic error occurs. Set a breakpoint on the line of code above the line causing the run-time error, exit break mode, and run the project again. When the breakpoint pauses execution, use the Autos window to help you determine the cause of the error in the For…Next loop. Fix the errors and disable the breakpoint.

3. Run the project. Press the INSERT key and add a new data item of your choice. Use a DataTip to determine the value of the strHours variable. Use a QuickWatch window to evaluate the value of lstWeeklyHours.Items(intIndex).SubItems(2).Text.
   Modify the QuickWatch by adding .Replace("$", "0") to the end of the expression and then clicking the Recalculate button. Write the values that display on a sheet of paper and label the items Programming Assignment 2, Step 3 Values. The QuickWatch window and DataTips show that line 171 assigns the wrong column's value to the strHours variable. Exit break mode and fix this error.

4. Run the project. Press the INSERT key and add a new data item of your choice. Check the totals on the lower-right side of the window. One of the totals is incorrect. Exit break mode, enable the breakpoint on line 166, run the application, and then press the INSERT key to add a new data item. When execution halts at the breakpoint, add the following variables to the Watch 1 window: strRate, sngRate, strHours, sngHours. Write the initial values of these variables as shown in the Watch 1 window on the same sheet of paper and label the items as Programming Assignment 2, Step 4 Initial Values. Use the F8 key to step through the code until the For…Next loop exits. Watch the variables in the Watch window. Write the final values of these variables as shown in the Watch 1 window after the For…Next loop exits on the same sheet of paper and label the items as Programming Assignment 2, Step 4 Initial Values. The Watch window indicates that the sngRate and strRate variables are being assigned the wrong value. Exit break mode and fix this error.

5. Run the project. Press the INSERT key and add three new data items of your choice. Attempt to delete the second item by pressing either the DELETE key or the D key. While in run time, set a breakpoint on line 150 and try the delete operation again. Use the F8 key to step twice. Exit break mode and fix the error that causes the line of code with the RemoveAt() method to execute improperly.

(continued)

2 Debugging Logic and Run-Time Errors *(continued)*

6. Run the project. Add the test data shown in Figure 8-74. The application should display the totals as shown at the bottom of Figure 8-74.

FIGURE 8-74

3 Debugging Run-Time Errors and Numeric Exceptions

Open the project, Variable Expenses, from the Chapter8\Variable Expenses folder on the Data Disk. The Variable Expenses application contains several run-time errors that occur when the test data meets certain conditions.

The Variable Expenses application (Figure 8-75) is used to calculate the net income that a product manager can expect for a particular product, based on projected sales, projected quantity of items sold, the variable cost for producing each unit, and the fixed costs associated with producing the product. After a user enters the information and clicks the Calculate button, the application determines the net income for the scenario and also calculates a useful ratio called the contribution margin ratio.

Use the test data shown in Table 8-9 to test the application, discover the various run-time errors, and fix the errors.

Table 8-9 Test Data for the Variable Expenses Application

QUANTITY	PRICE (SALES IN DOLLARS PER UNIT)	VARIABLE EXPENSES PER UNIT	FIXED EXPENSES
300	$300	$125	$34,000
300	$300	$125	$1,000
0	$200	$100	$40,000
500	$0	$20	$22,000
200	$150	$0	$20,000
500	$200	$175	$35,000

1. Run the project. Use the first and second rows of test data in Table 8-9 to test the application. The second set of test data results in a run-time error.

2. Return to design mode and open the code window for the Form1 form. Set Option Strict to On for the form. Several syntax errors result from setting Option Strict to On. Open the Task List to view the errors resulting from setting Option Strict to On.

3. Declare all necessary variables and perform the necessary data conversions in the code to perform the calculations properly without syntax errors.

4. Correct the run-time error that results from the data in row 2 of Table 8-9. Do not modify the range of the NumericUpDown controls to fix the error. Rather, use the proper data types in the code and perform the necessary data conversions to handle the numeric data properly.

5. Test the project. Use all of the test data in Table 8-9 and take note of the results in the Contribution margin ratio box. Results of Nan and Infinity are a result of exceptions handled by Visual Basic .NET when numeric values are invalid. Nan means the value is not a numeric value. **Infinity** means that an expression evaluated to infinity, which is not a valid numeric value. Change the code to place proper restrictions on the input data, display error messages to the user when they input data resulting in the invalid results, and prevent the program from performing the calculations when the user inputs data that will result in invalid results.

FIGURE 8-75

6. Format all output to TextBox controls to currency where currency values are used. Ratios are not currency values.

Figure 8-75 shows the application after the changes are made.

4 Creating a Setup Program for a Windows Application

Create a setup program for the Weekly Revenue Windows application debugged in Programming Assignment 2 on page VB 8.75, or any other completed Windows application from this chapter or a previous chapter. The installed application should execute from a folder named Weekly Revenue on the user's All Programs submenu. The user also should be able to click a shortcut to a ReadMe file associated with the application. Perform the following steps to create and test the setup program.

1. Create a new setup project using the Setup Project template. Name the project Weekly Revenue Setup.

2. Add the file, Weekly Revenue.exe, from the Weekly Revenue/Debug/bin folder on the Data Disk to the Application Folder folder of the setup project.

(continued)

4 Creating a Setup Program for a Windows Application *(continued)*

3. Add the file, ReadMe.doc, from the Chapter8/ProgAssn4 folder on the Data Disk to the Application Folder folder of the setup project.

4. Create a Weekly Revenue folder in the User's Program Menu folder of the setup project.

5. Add shortcuts for both the executable file and ReadMe file to the Weekly Report folder in the User's Program Menu folder.

6. Change the icons for both shortcuts created in step 5 to the icons of the files to which they link.

7. If you are building the setup project on a hard disk, set the options on the Property Pages of the project to include the Windows Installer program, set compression to optimize for speed, and package the files in the setup file. If you are building the setup project on a floppy disk, set the options on the Property Pages of the project not to include the Windows Installer program, set compression to optimize for size, and package the files in the setup file.

8. Click the Build Solution command on the Build menu to build the setup program.

9. Test the setup program by executing the setup program and ensuring that the application is installed correctly and that the Weekly Revenue application and ReadMe file both execute from the All Programs submenu. Finally, uninstall the application.

5 Exceptions and the Exceptions Window

The Exceptions window lists all of the exceptions, or types of run-time errors, of which Visual Basic .NET is aware. You can open the Exceptions window by clicking the Exceptions command on the Debug menu while a project is open. For example, the System.OverflowException exception can be found in the Exceptions window by clicking the System folder and then scrolling down to the System.OverflowException exception. When an exception is selected, you can modify what actions the IDE takes when an exception occurs at run time. Using the Visual Basic .NET Help system and the Exceptions window, develop an application that causes two types of exceptions, the System.OverflowException exception and the System.DivideByZeroException exception. Use short data types and multiplication to cause the System.OverflowException exception, and division by 0 to cause the System.DivideByZeroException. Create a user-friendly interface using TextBox controls for input and and output, using Button controls to cause a calculation to take place. In the Exceptions window, define how the IDE should handle these exceptions by changing the value of the When exception is thrown parameter to either Break into Debugger or Continue. Run the program and write down how the IDE handles each exception based on the value of the When exception is thrown parameter. Finally, use the debugging tools used in this chapter to examine the values of the variables when the errors arise and write them down.

9

Designing, Creating, and Using a Class

Objectives

You will have
mastered the material in
this chapter when you can:

- Understand when to create a class when designing a solution
- Design a class using the UML
- Create a new class in Visual Basic .NET
- Create a constructor for a class
- Create a property for a class
- Code a Get property procedure
- Code a Set property procedure
- Create a method for a class
- Create a class by using inheritance
- Draw a UML object diagram for an object
- Use a class in a Visual Basic .NET program

Introduction

As you have learned, the .NET Framework provides a programmer with a rich set of commonly used classes, known as the .NET Framework class library. In the previous chapters, these classes were utilized to develop a wide range of applications. In developing some programs, however, you will need to create a new class to provide functionality not provided by the classes in the .NET Framework class library.

This chapter concentrates on creating a new class using Visual Basic .NET. The projects developed in Chapters 10 through 12 extend and utilize this new class to develop an employee compensation review system that integrates several applications into a complete program solution (Figure 9-1).

In developing the employee compensation review system, you first will learn when to use a class in the design of a solution. You will learn how to use the UML to formalize the design of an application using class diagrams. You then will learn how to create a new class library. A class library is a collection of code that defines and provides functionality for one or more related classes. This chapter also shows you how to create a constructor for a class, so that objects created using the class can be initialized. You will learn how to add properties and methods to a class and how to write Get and Set procedures for properties, so that the user of a class can determine and set property values. This chapter also discusses how to use inheritance to create subclasses. Finally, you will learn how to implement the class by developing a Windows application to test the class and how to represent an instantiated object using the UML.

Chapter Nine — Creating the Employee Class

The remaining four chapters in this book focus on creating a complete solution to a problem in four stages. The problem involves compensation adjustments for employees, based on their review dates. Each of these four chapters extends the solution, until a complete solution — called the Compensation Review System — is developed.

The human resources department at Ekstrom Optics Corporation requires an application that allows managers to input employee compensation adjustments that are determined during each employee's annual performance and compensation review. The company classifies employees as either salaried or hourly. The company places limits on the minimum and maximum percentage that a manager can increase an employee's compensation, based on the employee's location. Any changes in employee compensation then must be sent to the company's payroll vendor, who is responsible for calculating, printing, and mailing payroll checks.

Figure 9-1 illustrates the use of the Compensation Review System from the point of view of the users involved in the process. When using the system, a user, such as a human resources manager, will run a report and then use the report to determine which employees are due for a compensation review. After completing the review, the manager then uses a Web page on the company intranet to update the employee compensation information. After the updates are complete, a manager or other designated employee then uses another application to generate a file listing compensation updates for the payroll processing vendor. The vendor then uses a Web service to retrieve this file over the Internet.

Step 1 — Manager uses report to determine which employees require a compensation review

Step 2 — Manager uses Web page to update compensation

Step 3 — File created for payroll processing vendor

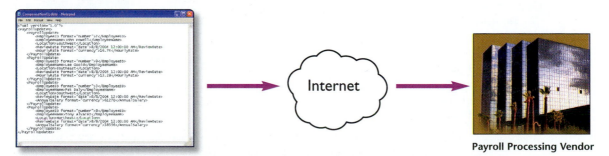

Payroll Processing Vendor

Step 4 — XML file available to Payroll Processing vendor via the Web

FIGURE 9-1

Figure 9-2 on the following pages show the complete view of the programs developed in the remaining chapters of this book, the chapters in which the components of the system are developed, and the underlying data and classes used by the programs.

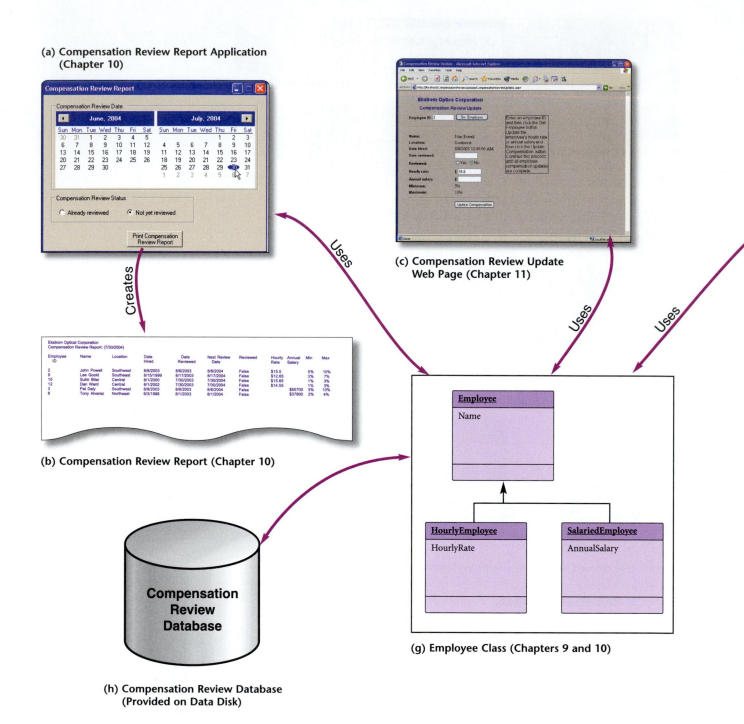

(a) Compensation Review Report Application (Chapter 10)

(b) Compensation Review Report (Chapter 10)

(c) Compensation Review Update Web Page (Chapter 11)

(g) Employee Class (Chapters 9 and 10)

(h) Compensation Review Database (Provided on Data Disk)

FIGURE 9-2

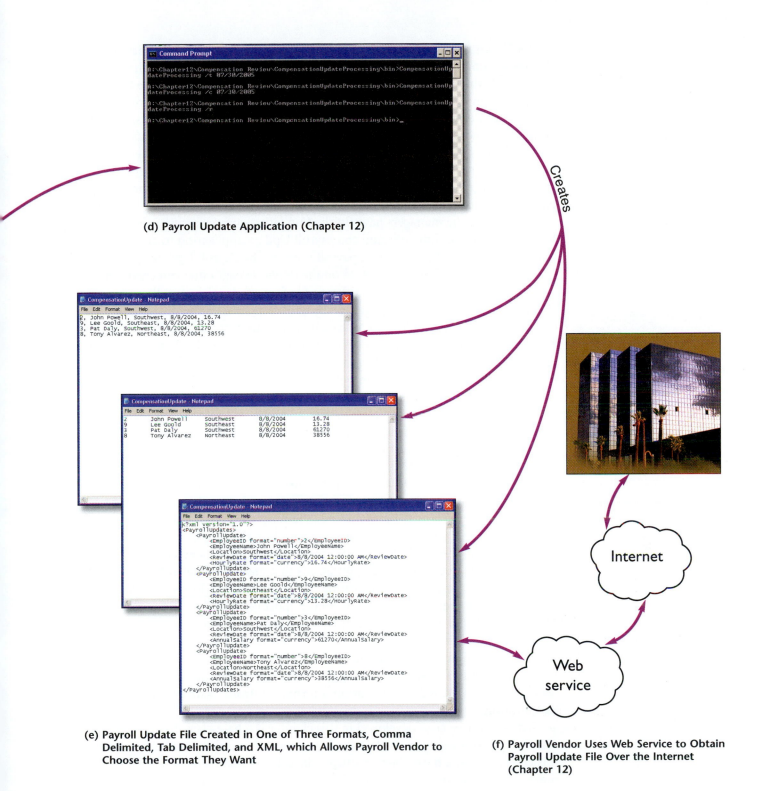

(d) Payroll Update Application (Chapter 12)

Creates

(e) Payroll Update File Created in One of Three Formats, Comma
Delimited, Tab Delimited, and XML, which Allows Payroll Vendor to
Choose the Format They Want

(f) Payroll Vendor Uses Web Service to Obtain
Payroll Update File Over the Internet
(Chapter 12)

FIGURE 9-2 *(continued)*

Each month, managers use the Compensation Review Report application (Figure 9-2a on the previous page) to create a report (Figure 9-2b on the previous page) listing the employees who report to the manager and are due for a compensation review in the following month. Along with basic employee information, the Compensation Review Report lists the employee's current salary or hourly rate and the minimum and maximum allowable pay increase based on the employee's location. The manager determines the adjustment to the employee's compensation and then inputs the new compensation information into the Compensation Review Update Web page (Figure 9-2c on the previous page) located on the company's intranet.

After all of the managers have finished updating compensation information for the month, the company runs the Payroll Update application to create a file that can be sent to the company's payroll vendor. The Payroll Update application is a console application (Figure 9-2d on the previous page) that can create the payroll update file in up to three different file formats for the payroll vendor (Figure 9-2e on the previous page). The payroll vendor uses the file to update its database, so that the vendor has up-to-date compensation information for each employee and can accurately calculate and print payroll checks. The payroll vendor obtains the new payroll information over the Internet, by using a Web service (Figure 9-2f on the previous page).

Chapter 9 focuses on developing the behind-the-scenes classes necessary to complete the system. An Employee class will be created to make management of the employee information easier when writing code (Figure 9-2g on the previous page). The class and applications created in Chapters 10 through 12 use the Employee class created in Chapter 9 in order to interact with the Compensation Review database (Figure 9-2h on the previous page). The Compensation Review database, which is supplied on the Data Disk, stores the employee compensation review information. For the programmer, the Employee class provides the benefit of reusability. Each application or class can reuse the Employee class when interacting with the database, thus eliminating the need for a great deal of redundant code in the class and applications that require access to the data.

Chapter 10 concentrates on creating the Compensation Review Report application and the Compensation Review Report generated by the application. An additional class is created in Chapter 10 to assist with this task. Chapter 11 focuses on developing the Compensation Review Update Web page, which each manager uses to input information on each employee's compensation adjustment. Chapter 12 focuses on creating the Web service that the payroll vendor uses to acquire updated compensation information from Ekstrom Optics Corporation.

The Employee class developed in this chapter is a base class. In object-oriented programming, each class can have one or more classes at higher levels; this class is called a **base class** or a **superclass**. Each base class can have one or more classes at lower levels; such a class is called a subclass. This chapter also develops two subclasses based on the Employee class – the HourlyEmployee subclass and the SalariedEmployee subclass. The relationship between base classes and subclasses often is represented using a high-level class diagram, which is a UML diagram used to show the hierarchical relationship among classes.

Figure 9-3a shows the high-level class diagram that represents the Employee class and its two subclasses, the HourlyEmployee subclass and the SalariedEmployee subclass. The Employee class encompasses common properties and methods of both hourly and salaried employees. The HourlyEmployee and SalariedEmployee subclasses are based on the Employee class and thus have all of the methods and properties it has; the subclasses also contain unique methods and properties specific to each type of employee. The three classes — Employee, HourlyEmployee, and SalariedEmployee — compose the Compensation Review class library. These three classes, which serve as a basis for the Ekstrom Optics Compensation Review System, contain information regarding each employee's personal and salary information.

In addition to designing and creating the Compensation Review class library used in the remaining chapters, Chapter 9 also addresses developing a Windows application to test the Employee class and the HourlyEmployee and SalariedEmployee subclasses (Figure 9-3b). The Employee Class Test application tests the classes by demonstrating the use of the Compensation Review class library. When the application starts, one instance of each of the three classes is instantiated as an object. When the user selects a RadioButton for a particular class or object, three properties of that object display in the Properties area of the Employee Class Test application window, as shown in Figure 9-3b. A user can update the properties of each object by selecting the RadioButton for that object, changing the property values in the Properties area, and then clicking the Set Properties button.

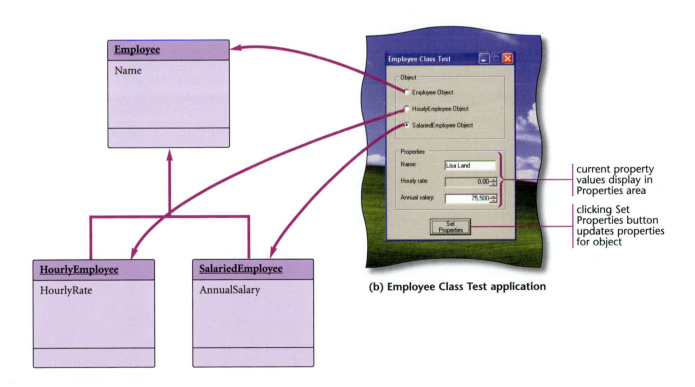

(a) Compensation Review class library

(b) Employee Class Test application

FIGURE 9-3

Program Development

The development cycle for the Compensation Review class library and the Employee Class Test application consists of tasks that correspond to the six development cycle phases, as shown in Table 9-1. The Employee Class Test application is a unit test program used to test the functionality of the Employee class and its subclasses — the HourlyEmployee and SalariedEmployee classes.

Table 9-1 Compensation Review Class Library and Employee Class Test Application Development Tasks

DEVELOPMENT PHASE	TASK NUMBER	TASK NAME	TASK
Analyze requirements	1	Analyze problem	Analyze the Ekstrom Optics Compensation Review System problem.
Design solution	2	Design classes	Design the classes used in the complete system.
	3	Design interface and program	Design the user interface for a unit test program to test the classes, including input areas, output areas, and form controls. Design the logic and write pseudocode for the unit test program.
Validate design	4	Validate design	Prove that the unit test program produces correct results for testing the classes.
Implement design	5	Write code for classes	Write code to implement the design of the three classes.
	6	Write code and develop interface for program	Write a unit test program called the Employee Class Test application that will be used to test the Employee class and its related classes. Add user interface elements, such as input areas, output areas, and controls on a form.
Test solution	7	Test program	Use the Employee Class Test application to test the classes.
	8	Debug classes and program	Fix any problems with the Employee Class Test application and the classes.
Document solution	9	Document classes and program	Print the code for the classes. Print the Employee Class Test application's form and code.

Analysis and Design

Figure 9-4 shows the requirements document that initiates the development cycle for the Ekstrom Optics Compensation Review System. The requirements document outlines the needs for the entire system and serves as a general basis for the programs developed in the remaining chapters in this book. The programs developed in the remaining chapter each require a more detailed requirements document; these are presented in the introduction of each subsequent chapter.

an hourly rate. The compensation for salaried employees is expressed as an annual salary.

5) After all managers have completed the compensation reviews, the human resources department needs to run an application that gathers the updated compensation information and saves the information in a file. The application should allow for creation of three different file formats: a comma-delimited text file, a tab-delimited text file, and an XML file. This XML file is sent to the company's payroll vendor, who uses the information in the file to update the payroll records used to calculate and print employee payroll checks.

6) The payroll vendor has requested that Ekstrom Optics make the XML file available to the vendor via a Web service. A Web service application thus is required to meet the payroll vendor's request.

Approvals

Approval Status:	X	Appr
		Rejec
Approved by:	Jonathan Ingra	
Date:	January 11, 20(	
Assigned to:	J. Quasney, Pr	

REQUEST FOR NEW APPLICATION

Date submitted:	January 4, 2005
Submitted by:	Samantha O'Conner
Purpose:	The human resources department would like to add more automation to the compensation review process. Each month, managers should receive a report listing the employees who need a compensation review in the next month. The manager should then use a Web page to update the employee's compensation. Finally, the updated compensation information should be made available to our payroll vendor, who is responsible for printing, calculating, and distributing payroll checks each month.
Application title:	Compensation Review System
Algorithms:	The company has an existing Compensation Review database that is available for use in the system. The Compensation Review database contains information for the minimum and maximum percentage increases for yearly compensation adjustment for each of the company's regions. The percentage increases vary based on regional location.
Notes:	1) The Compensation Review database is available for use in this project. The first table in the database includes a record for each employee, which includes an employee ID, name, date hired, date reviewed, employee location, and review status indicator of whether the employee has been reviewed. The second table in the database includes the minimum and maximum percentage increases in compensation for each location. 2) An application is required to compute if an employee is eligible for review and then print a report that managers can use to identify employees requiring a compensation review in the next 30 days. An employee is eligible for review if his or her last review date or hire date falls at least one year from the date that the report is run. The application should allow the user to select a date for which to run the report. 3) A Web page is required to allow a manager to update an employee's compensation. The Web page should allow the manager to enter an employee ID and then view the current employee information. The manager then should be able to update the compensation information for that employee. The Web page should display the minimum and maximum percentage increase in compensation based on the employee's location. After updating all of the employees' salaries, the manager should be able to view a Web page report that summarizes the compensation adjustments made by the manager. 4) The company employs two types of employees: Hourly and Salaried. The compensation for hourly employees is expressed as

FIGURE 9-4

PROBLEM ANALYSIS The problem that the Ekstrom Optics Compensation Review System must solve is to automate many of the manual tasks involved in the annual employee compensation review and update process. The requirements document indicates that the overall system includes four programs for various users. Table 9-2 lists the individual programs that make up the Compensation Review System. As you learned in Chapter 1, developers often break systems into smaller pieces to simplify development and reduce errors. The developer then follows the six phases in the development cycle to design, code, and test each individual component. The four programs in the Compensation Review System will be developed in Chapters 10 through 12. Each program will be completely designed, developed, and tested, following the six phases in the development cycle.

Table 9-2   Programs in the Compensation Review System

PROGRAM	REQUIREMENT FROM REQUIREMENTS DOCUMENT	CHAPTER IN WHICH PROGRAM IS DEVELOPED
Compensation Review Report Application	Note 2	Chapter 10
Compensation Review Update Web Page	Note 3	Chapter 11
Compensation Update Application	Note 5	Chapter 12
Compensation Update Web Service	Note 6	Chapter 12

As indicated in note 1 in the requirements document, most of the applications share a common requirement: most of the applications needs to access the employee compensation information that is stored in the Compensation Review database. When several programs require similar functionality, or if you anticipate that this may be the case in the future, an object-oriented approach to the solution should be considered in the design of the solution.

Tip

Considering Object-Oriented Design
When several programs require similar functionality, or if you anticipate that this may be the case in the future, an object-oriented approach to the solution should be considered in the design of the solution.

The common functionality needed in each program is the ability to retrieve employee information from the Compensation Review database provided by Ekstrom Optics. One way to address this requirement is to write the code to retrieve the employee data needed from the database and then copy the code to each program that needs this functionality. Many drawbacks exist in this approach. For example, if something about the data retrieval process changes, then the developer would need to incorporate the changes in each program, rebuild all of the programs, and then redistribute the programs to users.

Object-oriented design and programming offers a better solution. Using object-oriented design and programming, a developer can use a stand-alone object to encapsulate the functionality of retrieving and manipulating information from the database tables. Each program that requires the functionality makes use of the common class, which is built into a separate file and is reusable in many programs. In the case of the Compensation Review System, the concept of an employee lends itself to encapsulation in an object. The requirements document states that the company has two types of employees — hourly and salaried — and that each type has its pay represented differently. The methods and properties specific to the two types of employees are represented by the two subclasses, HourlyEmployee and SalariedEmployee.

This chapter focuses on the object-oriented design and development of the classes that represent the two types of employees. A unit test program also will be developed to test the classes. The classes developed in this chapter will be reused in Chapters 10 through 12. For a review of object-oriented terminology and the UML, see Chapter 1 and Appendix A.

CLASS AND INTERFACE DESIGN   The problem analysis suggests that the development should take an object-oriented approach to contain the concept of the two types of employees. The requirements document states that employees have several common attributes: employee ID, name, date hired, date last reviewed, location, review status, a maximum amount that a manager can raise the compensation, and a minimum amount that a manager can raise the compensation. The requirements document also indicates that the Compensation Review System must help a manager determine the next review date for the employee.

In object-oriented design, a class describes similar objects. Visual Basic .NET provides the syntax and tools necessary to create classes. When you write code, classes behave like data types. You declare object variables as classes, rather than data types. For example, in Chapter 6, variables were declared as collections based on the Collection class, which is a class in the .NET Framework class library. Each collection included properties and methods. Similarly, classes you develop can include properties and methods.

When deciding how to design classes and their properties and methods to solve a problem, consider the following rules of thumb as you review the program requirements:

- Look for nouns that denote people, places, things, or procedures. Often, these nouns correspond to the classes you need to build.
- Look for adjectives that describe things about those nouns. Often, these adjectives correspond to properties in the class.
- Look for verbs that express actions that the nouns can complete or express actions that can be taken on the nouns. These verbs often correspond to the methods in the class.

Tip

Designing Classes

When deciding how to design classes and their properties and methods to solve a problem, consider the following rules of thumb as you review the program requirements:

- Look over the requirements for nouns that denote people, places, things, or procedures. Often, these nouns correspond to the classes you need to build.
- Look for adjectives that describe things about those nouns. Often, these adjectives correspond to properties in the class.
- Look for verbs that express actions that the nouns can complete or express actions that can be taken on the nouns. These verbs often correspond to the methods in the class.

In the case of the Compensation Review System, the word, employee, is a noun that denotes a class of people. This suggests that a class of employees could be created and given a unique name, such as Employee. The word, employee, occurs more than once in the program requirements, which indicates that there is more than one type or class of employee to consider in the problem.

The adjectives used to describe the noun, employee, include employee ID, name, date hired, date last reviewed, location, review status, a maximum amount that a manager can raise the compensation, and a minimum amount that a manager can raise the compensation. These adjectives can be expressed as properties in the Employee class.

The verb, compute, expresses an action that can be taken regarding an employee — in this case, computing if an employee is eligible for review based on the next review date. This computation action can be expressed as a method of the Employee class.

Note 4 in the requirements document identifies two additional adjectives, or attributes, for employees: hourly rate and annual salary. Each employee has only one of these attributes, depending on whether he or she is hourly or salaried. One way to design these attributes in the Employee class is to include both attributes in the Employee class. This practice, however, is discouraged for a number of reasons. For one, including both attributes in the Employee class would allow each employee to have both an annual salary and an hourly rate. This would be confusing and could lead to erroneous results.

A better solution is to design two additional classes, one for each type of employee. These classes — named the HourlyEmployee and SalariedEmployee classes — both include all of the properties and the method of the Employee class. Each class also includes an additional property to indicate the employee's compensation, either an hourly rate or an annual salary. Figure 9-5 shows the high-level class diagram that describes the Employee, HourlyEmployee, and SalariedEmployee classes.

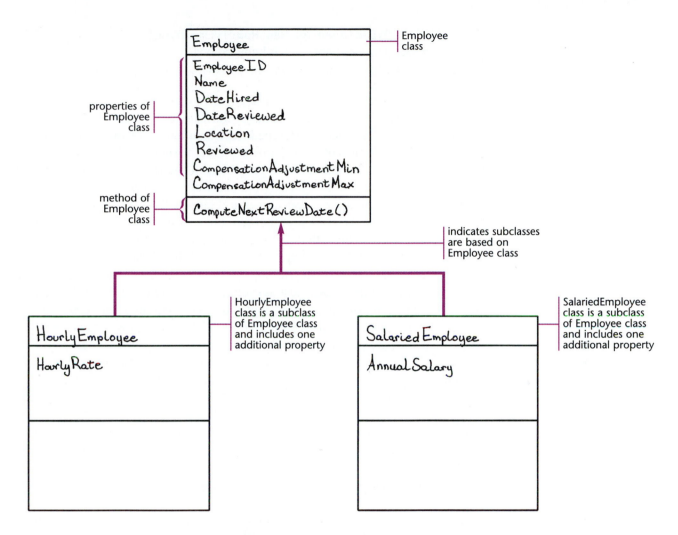

FIGURE 9-5

Tip

Designing Subclasses

When determining when to create a subclass for a class, look for mutually exclusive properties of the items in the class in question. Then, create subclasses based on the mutually exclusive properties.

The high-level class diagram in Figure 9-5 shows the eight properties and one method of the Employee class. The HourlyEmployee and SalariedEmployee subclasses share all of the properties and methods of the Employee class, but each includes one additional property that describes the compensation information for an employee. Once the classes are created in code, variables can be declared with the type of Employee, HourlyEmployee, or SalariedEmployee, as long as the classes are made available to the program in which the variables are declared. For example, the following code declares a variable of type HourlyEmployee and then sets the values for the name and hourly rate properties of the employee:

```
Dim objMyEmployee As New HourlyEmployee()
objMyEmployee.Name = "Johnny Sabol"
objMyEmployee.HourlyRate = 24.55
```

Variables declared as objects behave much like variables declared with standard data types, but can include many values and actions instead of one. For example, a variable declared of type Integer can have only one value at any time during the execution of a program. An object variable declared as an HourlyEmployee can include the nine properties of the HourlyEmployee class all at once, and the values can be updated and accessed, as shown in the code above.

In this chapter, the three classes shown in Figure 9-5 on the previous page will be coded. That is, the classes, properties, and method will be created. The coding required for the logic that gets the data from the Compensation Review database will be completed in Chapter 10 in an additional class.

Chapter 9 also focuses on developing the Employee Class Test application to provide a way to test the classes, just as every project developed in this book has been tested. The Employee Class Test application is a Windows application that will utilize the Employee, HourlyEmployee, and SalariedEmployee classes in order to unit test the classes. To test the classes, the Employee Class Test application should declare variables with a data type corresponding to each class. Then, the application should allow a user to view and modify the values assigned to properties of the classes.

Figure 9-6 shows the user interface for the Employee Class Test application. RadioButton controls in a GroupBox control allow the user to select an object to test. When the object is selected, the values of one or more of its properties display in the Properties GroupBox control. The property values that display depend on the object selected. For example, if the user selects the Employee Object RadioButton control, the Name property value displays in the Properties GroupBox control; if the user selects the HourlyEmployee Object RadioButton control, then the Name and HourlyRate property values display in the Properties GroupBox control. The user can modify the value for each of the object's property values in the Properties GroupBox control and then update the values by clicking the Set Properties button. If the user selects a different object and then reselects the modified object, then the updated property values display in the Properties GroupBox control.

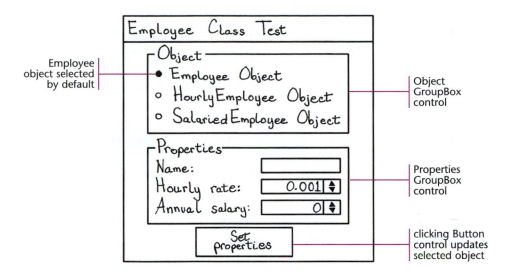

Employee object selected by default

Object GroupBox control

Properties GroupBox control

clicking Button control updates selected object

FIGURE 9-6

PROGRAM DESIGN As stated, the coding for the three classes will not include any code for accessing the data in the Compensation Review database. When using the classes, a programmer will be able to declare variables of the types Employee, HourlyEmployee, and SalariedEmployee. The programmer then can access and set the properties of the object. The logic to access the employee compensation information stored in the Compensation Review database will be programmed in another class in Chapter 10.

Figure 9-5 on page VB 9.13 lists the class names, properties, and method needed for the base class and two subclasses. For the coding in this chapter, the design in Figure 9-5 suffices for the program design because no additional logic is coded in this phase in the development of the Compensation Review System.

The Employee Class Test application requires coding to perform actions when the user clicks RadioButton controls or the Set Properties button. Figure 9-7 on the next page shows the pseudocode for the Employee Class Test application. The pseudocode first declares three global variables — one for each of the three classes. The RadioButton CheckedChanged event procedures and Set Properties Button Click event procedures behave as described in Table 9-3 on page VB 9.17.

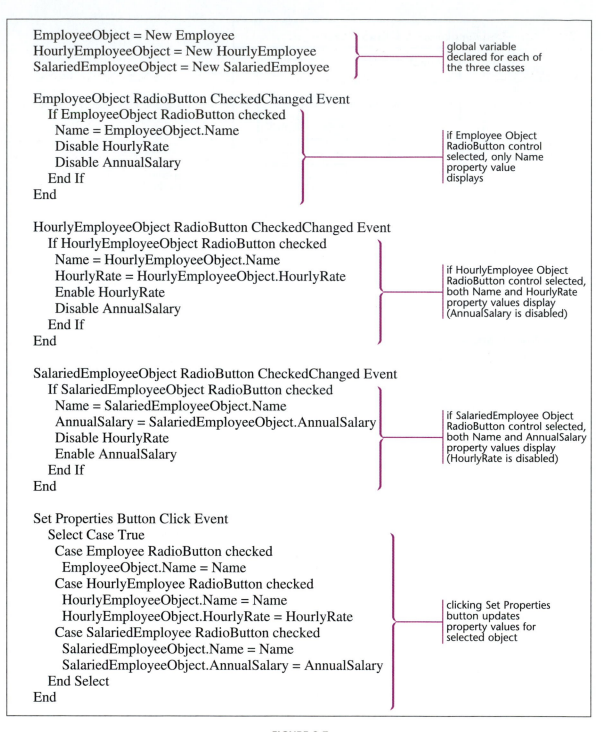

EmployeeObject = New Employee
HourlyEmployeeObject = New HourlyEmployee
SalariedEmployeeObject = New SalariedEmployee

> global variable declared for each of the three classes

EmployeeObject RadioButton CheckedChanged Event
  If EmployeeObject RadioButton checked
    Name = EmployeeObject.Name
    Disable HourlyRate
    Disable AnnualSalary
  End If
End

> if Employee Object RadioButton control selected, only Name property value displays

HourlyEmployeeObject RadioButton CheckedChanged Event
  If HourlyEmployeeObject RadioButton checked
    Name = HourlyEmployeeObject.Name
    HourlyRate = HourlyEmployeeObject.HourlyRate
    Enable HourlyRate
    Disable AnnualSalary
  End If
End

> if HourlyEmployee Object RadioButton control selected, both Name and HourlyRate property values display (AnnualSalary is disabled)

SalariedEmployeeObject RadioButton CheckedChanged Event
  If SalariedEmployeeObject RadioButton checked
    Name = SalariedEmployeeObject.Name
    AnnualSalary = SalariedEmployeeObject.AnnualSalary
    Disable HourlyRate
    Enable AnnualSalary
  End If
End

> if SalariedEmployee Object RadioButton control selected, both Name and AnnualSalary property values display (HourlyRate is disabled)

Set Properties Button Click Event
  Select Case True
    Case Employee RadioButton checked
      EmployeeObject.Name = Name
    Case HourlyEmployee RadioButton checked
      HourlyEmployeeObject.Name = Name
      HourlyEmployeeObject.HourlyRate = HourlyRate
    Case SalariedEmployee RadioButton checked
      SalariedEmployeeObject.Name = Name
      SalariedEmployeeObject.AnnualSalary = AnnualSalary
  End Select
End

> clicking Set Properties button updates property values for selected object

FIGURE 9-7

Table 9-3   Employee Class Test Event Procedures

EVENT PROCEDURE	EVENT	ACTION PERFORMED
EmployeeObject RadioButton CheckedChanged Event	Executes when the user clicks the EmployeeObject RadioButton control	Displays the Name property value of the Employee object in the Name text box and disables the Hourly rate and Annual salary NumericUpDown controls.
HourlyEmployeeObject RadioButton CheckedChanged Event	Executes when the user clicks the HourlyEmployeeObject RadioButton control	Displays the Name and HourlyRate property values of the HourlyEmployee object in the Name text box and Hourly rate NumericUpDown control. Disables the Annual salary NumericUpDown control.
SalariedEmployeeObject RadioButton CheckedChanged Event	Executes when the user clicks the SalariedEmployeeObject RadioButton control	Displays the Name and AnnualSalary property values of the SalariedEmployee object in the Name text box and Annual salary NumericUpDown control. Disables the Hourly rate NumericUpDown control.
Set Properties Button Click Event	Executes when the user clicks the Set Properties button	Sets properties of the active object based on the RadioButton control currently selected. The values in the Name text box and two NumericUpDown controls are used to update or set the property values.

VALIDATE DESIGN   The validation of the design can be accomplished for the design tasks considered in this chapter. The Employee, HourlyEmployee, and SalariedEmployee classes solve the problem of encapsulating information about the two types of employees. These classes can be reused by the four applications required for the Compensation Review System. The use of the Employee Class Test application serves as validation of the classes. The design of the Employee Class Test application allows for the declaration of objects of the three classes and retrieving and setting property values of those objects.

As shown in Table 9-1 on page VB 9.08, after validating the program design, the next phase in the development cycle is to develop the three classes using Visual Basic .NET.

Creating a Class Library

When you start a new project in Visual Basic .NET, in addition to choosing the Windows Application template for the new project, you can choose to create a **Class Library project**. A **class library** is a collection of code that contains one or more related classes, which are a type of reusable component in object-oriented programming. In Visual Basic .NET, developers can use pre-written classes from the .NET Framework class library or they can create a new class library with classes that address specific program requirements. Additionally, classes can be coded into any type of application developed using Visual Basic .NET. This chapter focuses on creating a new class library, the Compensation Review class library, which contains the three classes outlined in the program design shown in Figure 9-5 on page VB 9.13.

The following steps start Visual Basic .NET and then start a new Class Library project using the Class Library template.

To Start Visual Basic .NET and Start a Class Library Project

1. Insert the Data Disk in drive A. See the preface of this book for instructions for downloading the Data Disk or see your instructor for information about accessing the files required in this book.

2. Start Visual Basic .NET. When the Start Page displays, click the New Project button on the Start Page.

3. When the New Project dialog box displays, if necessary, click Create directory for Solution to select it. Click the Class Library icon in the Templates area. Double-click the text, ClassLibrary1, in the Name box. Type Compensation Review in the Name box.

The new project name displays in the Name box, and the solution name displays in the New Solution Name box. Because the Create directory for Solution check box is selected, Visual Basic .NET will create a subdirectory with the same name as the project when it creates the project.

4. Click the Browse button. If necessary, click 3½ Floppy (A:) in the Look in box. Click Chapter9 and then click the Open button.

5. Click the OK button. After the new Compensation Review project is created, if necessary, click the Maximize button on the Visual Basic .NET window title bar to maximize the Visual Basic .NET window. If necessary, close the Output window.

Visual Basic .NET creates the Compensation Review solution and project. Because classes do not contain forms by default, the Start Page is displayed in the main work area. Visual Basic .NET adds a Class1.vb file to the Compensation Review project in the Solution Explorer window (Figure 9-8).

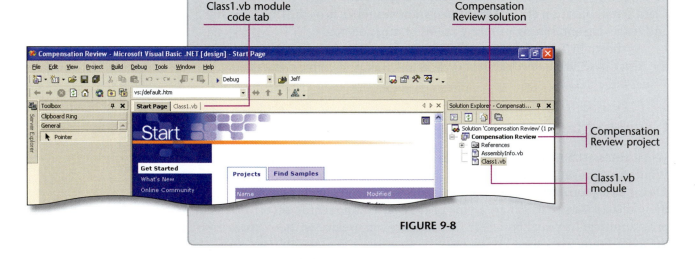

FIGURE 9-8

After Visual Basic .NET creates the new project, the solution and project name, Compensation Review, display in the Solution Explorer window. The new Class1.vb file created in the steps above is created as a starting point for the first class in the class library. Visual Basic .NET does not create an initial form for the project because classes in class libraries typically do not contain a user interface.

Creating a Class

A class library may contain one or more classes. Each class contains the code for the properties and methods of that class. The code that you write for a class is very similar to the code that you have written for forms.

Figure 9-9 shows the high-level class diagram for the Employee, HourlyEmployee, and SalariedEmployee classes. The Employee class serves as a base class for the HourlyEmployee and SalariedEmployee classes, which are known as subclasses of the Employee class. A subclass includes all of the properties and methods of its base class. Therefore, although not explicitly shown in Figure 9-9, the HourlyEmployee and SalariedEmployee classes include all eight properties and the method of the Employee class. The Employee class does not include any additional properties associated with the HourlyEmployee and SalariedEmployee classes.

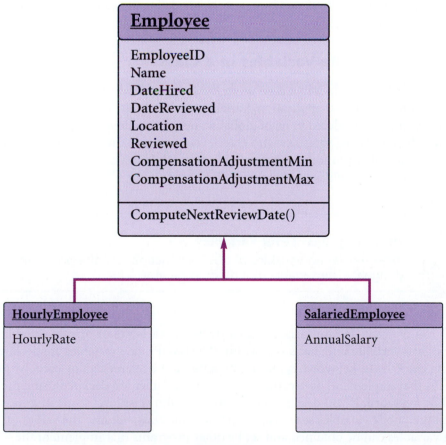

FIGURE 9-9

When coding classes, you always should write code for the base class or classes first. For more complex classes, you then should declare the properties and methods for the base class and all related subclasses before writing code that implements the business logic of the design. This practice is known as writing a **stub** for a class. Writing stubs allows you to code the outline of the classes in order to finalize the structure and correctness of the classes as designed in the high-level class diagram. A second advantage to writing stubs is that other developers gain access to the structure of the classes so that they can design and begin writing other programs that implement the classes.

Coding Classes

When coding classes, you always should write code for base classes first. Next, create stubs that only declare properties and methods for the base class and all related subclasses, without implementing the business logic of the design.

In this chapter, the code will be written for the Employee, HourlyEmployee, and SalariedEmployee classes. Because the logic in the classes is basic, the code for the classes resembles stubs that you would write for a more complex class. As mentioned above, the first step is to write the code for the base class, which is the Employee class.

Declaring Private Variables in a Class

You declare variables in a class using the same methods for declaring variables in a Windows application. Variables declared outside of functions or procedures are considered to be of global scope, or **class level scope**, to the class. When declaring variables with class level scope, use the prefix, m, to designate the variable as a module level variable. A **module** is a collection of code stored in one file, such as the Employee.vb class file.

Declaring Class Level Variables

When declaring variables of class level scope, use the prefix, m, to designate the variable as a module variable.

You typically declare variables as either public variables or private variables. A **private variable** only has scope within the class. Private variables are declared using the **Private keyword**. A **public variable** can be referenced, or used, by programs that implement, or use, the class. Public variables are declared using the **Public keyword**. If you declare public variables with class level scope in a class, then the public variables serve as properties of the class, because the values of the variables can be obtained and set by other programs that implement the class. For example, in a class named Employee with a public variable named

EmployeeID, code in another program can reference the value of the variable by using the code, Employee.EmployeeID, and thus change the value of the property. If the variable is private, then the code in the other program has no access to Employee.EmployeeID and thus cannot change the property value. In this case, the code results in a syntax error. In general, it is best to avoid use of public variables in a class, in order to limit the ability of other programs to control the values of the properties. Later in this chapter, you will learn how to code properties using a more acceptable approach.

Tip

Using Private Variables to Store Class Properties
Use private variables, not public variables, to store the values of a class's properties.

The Employee class requires eight properties: EmployeeID, Name, DateHired, DateReviewed, Location, Reviewed, CompensationAdjustmentMax, and CompensationAdjustmentMin. The values of these properties must be stored in variables within the class. Figure 9-10 shows the code necessary to declare the eight private variables that will store the values of the eight properties of the Employee class. The variables used to store these property values are themselves not the properties of the Employee class. This distinction will be discussed later in this chapter when the code for the properties is complete.

```
 1 Option Strict On
 2 Public Class Employee
 3      Private mintEmployeeID As Integer
 4      Private mstrName As String
 5      Private mdtmDateHired As Date
 6      Private mdtmDateReviewed As Date
 7      Private mstrLocation As String
 8      Private mblnReviewed As Boolean
 9      Private mdecCompensationAdjustmentMin As Decimal
10      Private mdecCompensationAdjustmentMax As Decimal
```

FIGURE 9-10

The following steps open the code window and enter the code shown in Figure 9-10 to set the name of the Employee class and declare private variables within the Employee class.

To Declare Private Variables in a Class

1. Right-click the Class1.vb class in the Solution Explorer window. Click the Rename command on the shortcut menu, type `Employee.vb` as the new module name, and then press the ENTER key.

(continued)

2. If necessary, right-click the Employee.vb class in the Solution Explorer window and then click the View Code command on the shortcut menu.

Visual Basic .NET opens the code window. The first line of code in the code window declares a class named Class1 (Figure 9-11).

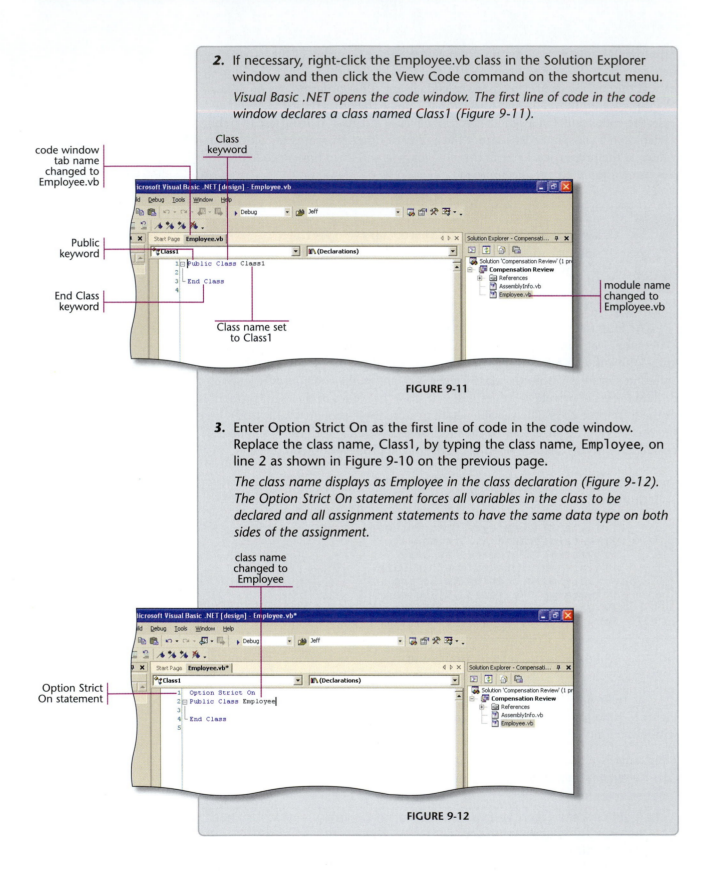

code window tab name changed to Employee.vb

Class keyword

Public keyword

End Class keyword

Class name set to Class1

module name changed to Employee.vb

FIGURE 9-11

3. Enter Option Strict On as the first line of code in the code window. Replace the class name, Class1, by typing the class name, Employee, on line 2 as shown in Figure 9-10 on the previous page.

The class name displays as Employee in the class declaration (Figure 9-12). The Option Strict On statement forces all variables in the class to be declared and all assignment statements to have the same data type on both sides of the assignment.

class name changed to Employee

Option Strict On statement

FIGURE 9-12

4. Type lines 3 through 10 as shown in Figure 9-10 on page VB 9.21.

The eight variable declarations display in the code window as shown in Figure 9-13.

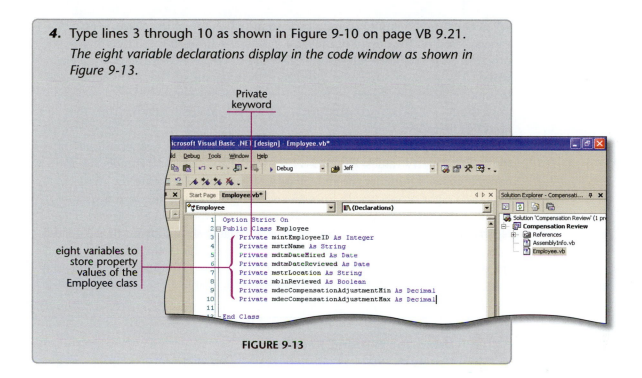

FIGURE 9-13

The code entered in the steps above properly names the Employee class. Line 2 includes the **Class statement** with the Public modifier that declares the Employee class in much the same way that you declare variables. The **End Class keyword** on line 12 denotes the end of the code for the class. The next step is to write the code that initializes the eight variables declared in the class.

Creating a Constructor for a Class

As you learned earlier in Chapter 6 (on page VB 6.38), when you instantiate an object in code, you use the New keyword to create a new instance of the object in memory. The New keyword tells Visual Basic .NET to set aside memory for the instance of the object, which includes memory for the object's properties. The New keyword is used to indicate a **constructor**, which is used to control the creation of an object. Every object in Visual Basic .NET includes a constructor. When you use the New keyword in conjunction with an object variable, such as a collection, you are calling the object's constructor to control the creation of the object in memory.

By default, Visual Basic .NET creates a hidden constructor for each class that you create. Good programming practice, however, dictates that you code a constructor for each class you create rather than allowing Visual Basic .NET to create a default constructor.

Tip

Creating Constructors
Good programming practice dictates that you code a constructor for each class you create rather than allowing Visual Basic .NET to create a default constructor.

A constructor should contain code to initialize any of the class's property values, based on the design of the class. A constructor also may contain calls to procedures or even creation of other objects. To create a constructor for a class, you declare a sub procedure in the class with the name of New. Whenever code in another program creates an instance of the class, the code in the New() sub procedure — the class's constructor — executes and creates (initializes) the object in memory.

In the Employee class, the constructor will perform the task of initializing the eight property values. Figure 9-14 shows the code necessary to declare the constructor and initialize the eight class level variables that store the values of the class's eight properties. In lines 15 and 16, the Nothing keyword is used to initialize the date variables of mdtmDateHired and mdtmDateReviewed. The **Nothing keyword** is used to indicate that a variable should be set to the default value of that variable's data type. In the case of variables of the Date data type, the default value is midnight on January 1 of the year 1. Rather than typing that value in code, the Nothing keyword serves as a shortcut.

Using the Nothing Keyword
Use the Nothing keyword to set a variable to the default value of the variable's data type.

```
12      Public Sub New()
13          mintEmployeeID = 0
14          mstrName = ""
15          mdtmDateHired = Nothing
16          mdtmDateReviewed = Nothing
17          mstrLocation = ""
18          mblnReviewed = False
19          mdecCompensationAdjustmentMin = 0
20          mdecCompensationAdjustmentMax = 0
21      End Sub
```

FIGURE 9-14

Note that the variable names shown in Figure 9-14 use the prefix, m, to designate each of the variables as a module variable, combined with a prefix to indicate the data type. The variable, mdtmDateHired, for example, uses the prefix of m combined with dtm to indicate that this variable is a module variable with a Date data type. For a review of naming conventions for variables based on data types, see Table 4-13 on page VB 4.43.

When another program instantiates an object of the Employee class, the code in the New() sub procedure is called automatically, resulting in the initialization of the eight variables in lines 13 through 20 of Figure 9-14. The following steps create and code the New() constructor for the Employee class.

To Create a Constructor for a Class

1. Enter line 12 as shown in Figure 9-14.

The Sub statement displays in the code window to declare the New() sub procedure. Visual Basic .NET completes the sub procedure by adding the End Sub keyword on line 14 (Figure 9-15).

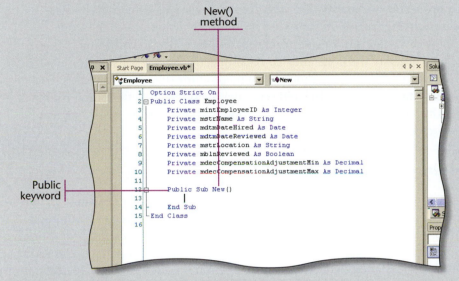

New()
method

Public
keyword

FIGURE 9-15

2. Type lines 13 through 20 as shown in Figure 9-14.

Lines 13 through 20 display in the code window (Figure 9-16). The New() sub procedure is the class constructor that executes whenever another program creates an instance of the class. The procedure initializes the eight private variables in the class.

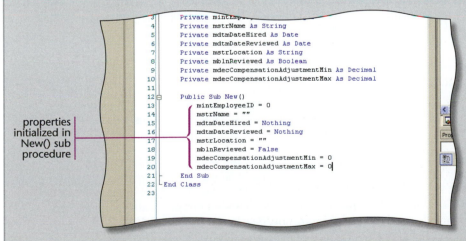

properties
initialized in
New() sub
procedure

FIGURE 9-16

The Employee class, the eight private variables in the Employee class, and the class constructor are coded. Another program now can create an Employee object and be sure that the variables within the class are initialized properly. The next step is to write the properties and methods for the Employee class.

Adding Properties and Methods to a Class

The properties and methods of the Employee class, as shown in the class diagram in Figure 9-9 on page VB 9.19, must be written as code in the Employee.vb file. You declare properties and methods in code, much as you declare variables and constants. For example, the New() constructor created earlier in this chapter acts much like a method for the Employee class. Each property and method is declared separately, and the code that **implements**, or does the work for, the property or method is coded within the property or method declaration.

Adding a Property to a Class

As previously discussed, when coding properties for classes, you could declare properties of a class as public variables within the class — but good coding practice dictates that you avoid this approach for creating properties for classes. Instead, Visual Basic .NET includes syntax for a property declaration specifically designed to declare properties within classes. A property declaration is similar to a variable declaration, but also allows you to write code to limit how the property's value is read or to set and define any rules or limits for the property's value.

Table 9-4 shows the general form of a simple **Property statement** used to code a property declaration that declares properties within a class declaration.

Table 9-4 Property Statement (Simple)	

General Form:	1. [Public | Private | Protected] Property Name(argument 1, ..., argument n) As datatype
	    Get and Set property procedures
	    End Property
	
	2. [Public | Private | Protected] [ReadOnly | WriteOnly] Property name() As datatype
	    Get and/or Set property procedures
	    End Property
	
	where at least one of the keywords, Public, Private, or Protected, is used and, in the second form, either the ReadOnly or WriteOnly keyword is used. The Property name is a valid name following the conventions of variable naming. All arguments must be passed by value (ByVal).

Purpose:	The Property statement declares a Get and/or a Set property procedure.

Table 9-4	*Property Statement (Simple) (continued)*

Examples:	1. `Public Property Name() As String`
	   `End Property`
	2. `Private Property Name() As Integer`
	   `End Property`
	3. `Public ReadOnly Property Name() As Date`
	   `End Property`
	4. `Public WriteOnly Property Name() As Object`
	   `End Property`

Notes:	1. If the ReadOnly keyword is used, then the Set property procedure is not required. 2. If the WriteOnly keyword is used, then the Get property procedure is not required. 3. If the Public keyword is used, no restrictions exist on the use of the property outside the class. 4. If the **Protected keyword** is used, then the property is accessible only within the class and any subclasses of the class in which the property is declared. 5. If neither the Public, Private, or Protected keywords are used, the property is Private by default.

Coding a Get Property Procedure

As indicated in Table 9-4, Visual Basic .NET has two types of property procedures: A **Get property procedure** is used to retrieve, or read, a property value; a **Set property procedure** is used to assign, or write, a value to a property. If a class requires that a property value can be written, or updated, but cannot be read, then the property is a **write-only property** and the Get property procedure can be eliminated from the Property statement.

Table 9-5 shows the general form of the **Get statement** used to implement the Get property procedure. The Set statement used to implement the Set property procedure will be discussed in the next section.

Table 9-5	*Get Statement*

General Form:	1. `Get`
	     `statements`
	  `End Get`
	
	where the Get statement occurs nested within a Property declaration.

Purpose:	The Get statement declares a Get property procedure.
Example:	1. `Get` `End Get`
Notes:	1. Use the Return statement to return the value to the calling expression. 2. The value returned in the Get property procedure must match the data type of the property to which it belongs. 3. The Get statement can appear only within a Property statement. 4. Only one Get statement is allowed in a property.

Figure 9-17 shows the code necessary to get the value of the mintEmployeeID private class variable, whenever another program needs to retrieve the value of the EmployeeID property of an Employee object. For example, a program using the Employee object uses the code

```
intMyValue = objEmployee.EmployeeID
```

to retrieve the value of the EmployeeID property of an Employee object and then assign the value to the intMyValue variable. When the line of code executes, the Get property procedure executes within the EmployeeID property.

```
23      Public Property EmployeeID() As Integer
24          Get
25              Return mintEmployeeID
26          End Get
27          Set(ByVal intEmployeeID As Integer)
28
29          End Set
30      End Property
```

FIGURE 9-17

As stated earlier, the code in Figure 9-17 can be avoided by declaring the mintEmployeeID as a Public variable. Although using a Public variable is not recommended, if this was the coding tactic used, then a program using the Employee object would use the following code to access the property:

```
intMyValue = objEmployeeID.mintEmployeeID
```

The following steps add the EmployeeID property to the Employee class and code the Get property procedure for the property.

To Add a Property to a Class and Code a Get Property Procedure

1. Enter line 23 as shown in Figure 9-17.

The Property statement displays in the code window. Visual Basic .NET completes the Property statement by adding the End Property keyword on line 30 and inserting Get and Set property procedures within the property (Figure 9-18).

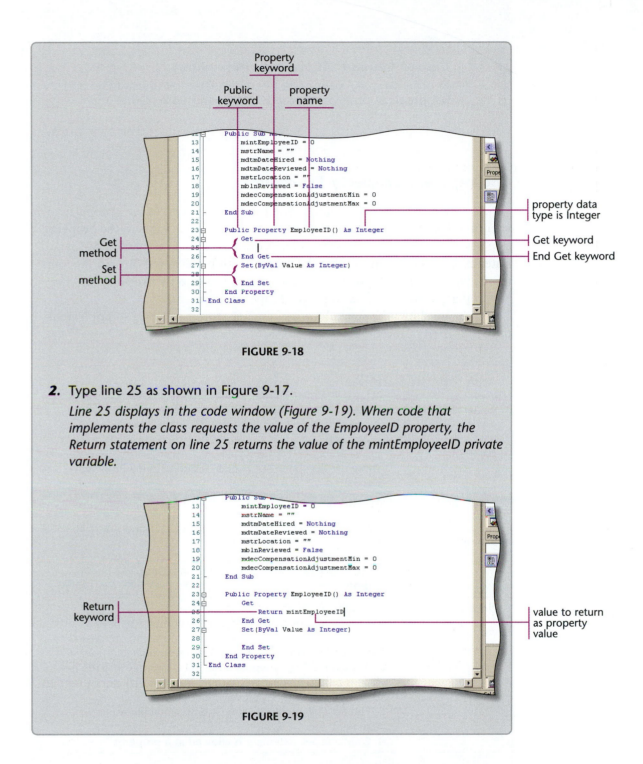

FIGURE 9-18

2. Type line 25 as shown in Figure 9-17.

Line 25 displays in the code window (Figure 9-19). When code that implements the class requests the value of the EmployeeID property, the Return statement on line 25 returns the value of the mintEmployeeID private variable.

FIGURE 9-19

As shown in Figure 9-19, after line 23 is entered, Intellisense automatically enters several lines of code in the Property statement for the EmployeeID property. First, Intellisense completes the Property statement by adding the End Property keyword on line 30 and then it inserts Get and Set statement blocks to define Get and Set property procedures. If the property does not require either a Get or a Set property procedure, then you should delete the Get or Set statement block rather than leaving it empty, in order to make the code clearer.

Unused Get and Set Property Procedures
In order to make your code clearer, delete any unused Get and Set property procedures inserted by Intellisense, rather than leaving them empty.

Coding a Set Property Procedure

As previously defined, a Set property procedure is used to set a property to a value and is called when a program needs to assign a new value to the property. The new property value is passed to the procedure as an argument of the Set statement. If a class requires that the property can be retrieved or read, but cannot be written, or updated, then the property is a **read-only property** and the Set property can be eliminated from a Property statement.

Table 9-6 shows the general form of the **Set statement** used to implement the Set property procedure.

Table 9-6 Set Statement	

General Form:	1. Set (argument 1, …, argument n)
	        statements
	    End Set
	
	where the Set statement occurs nested within a Property declaration.

Purpose:	The Set statement declares a Set property procedure with arguments.

Examples:	1. Set ()
	    End Set
	2. Set (ByVal dblEmployeeID As Double)
	    End Set

Notes:	1. Arguments must be passed using ByVal. 2. Arguments are optional. If used, arguments behave as local variables within the Set property procedure and are passed to the procedure when it is called. If no arguments are specified, as in Example 1, then Visual Basic .NET assumes that the new value is passed in a variable named Value, which can be used to set the value in the Set procedure code. 3. The Set statement can appear only within a Property statement. 4. Only one Set statement is allowed in a property.

Figure 9-20 shows the code necessary to set the value of the mintEmployeeID private class variable, whenever another program sets the EmployeeID property of an Employee object. For example, a program using the Employee object uses the code

```
objEmployee.EmployeeID = 0
```

to set the EmployeeID property of an Employee object named objEmployee to the value 0. The value 0 then is passed as the parameter, intEmployeeID, to the Set property procedure of the EmployeeID property.

```
28              mintEmployeeID = intEmployeeID
```

FIGURE 9-20

The following step enters the line of code shown in Figure 9-20 to code a Set property procedure to set the value of the EmployeeID property and then assign, or pass, the value to the Set method of the EmployeeID property.

To Code a Set Property Procedure

1. Change the variable name, Value, to intEmployeeID on line 27. Enter line 28 as shown in Figure 9-20.

Line 28 displays in the code window (Figure 9-21). The code sets the value of the EmployeeID property, which then is assigned to the mintEmployeeID private variable of the Employee class.

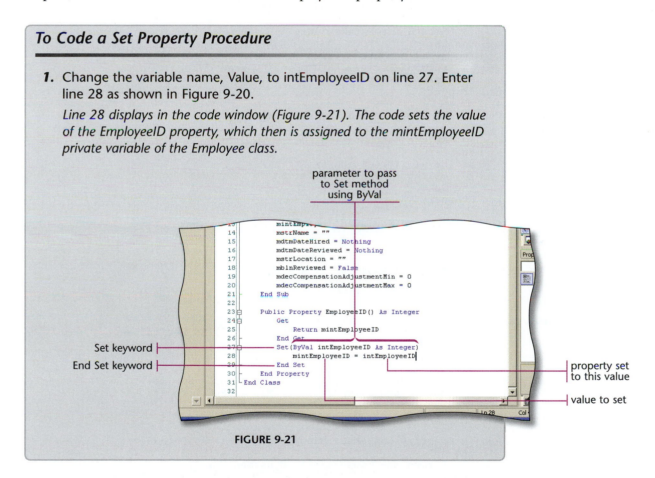

FIGURE 9-21

Coding the Remaining Properties

The coding of the seven remaining properties is similar to coding the EmployeeID property. The Employee class requires a property declaration and a Get and Set property procedure for each property. Figure 9-22 on the next page shows the code necessary for the seven remaining properties.

```
32      Public Property Name() As String
33          Get
34              Return mstrName
35          End Get
36          Set(ByVal strName As String)
37              mstrName = strName
38          End Set
39      End Property
40
41      Public Property DateHired() As Date
42          Get
43              Return mdtmDateHired
44          End Get
45          Set(ByVal dtmDateHired As Date)
46              mdtmDateHired = dtmDateHired
47          End Set
48      End Property
49
50      Public Property DateReviewed() As Date
51          Get
52              Return mdtmDateReviewed
53          End Get
54          Set(ByVal dtmDateReviewed As Date)
55              mdtmDateReviewed = dtmDateReviewed
56          End Set
57      End Property
58
59      Public Property Location() As String
60          Get
61              Return mstrLocation
62          End Get
63          Set(ByVal strLocation As String)
64              mstrLocation = strLocation
65          End Set
66      End Property
67
68      Public Property Reviewed() As Boolean
69          Get
70              Return mblnReviewed
71          End Get
72          Set(ByVal blnReviewed As Boolean)
73              mblnReviewed = blnReviewed
74          End Set
75      End Property
76
77      Public Property CompensationAdjustmentMin() As Decimal
78          Get
79              Return mdecCompensationAdjustmentMin
80          End Get
81          Set(ByVal decCompensationAdjustmentMin As Decimal)
82              mdecCompensationAdjustmentMin = decCompensationAdjustmentMin
83          End Set
84      End Property
85
86      Public Property CompensationAdjustmentMax() As Decimal
87          Get
88              Return mdecCompensationAdjustmentMax
89          End Get
90          Set(ByVal decCompensationAdjustmentMax As Decimal)
91              mdecCompensationAdjustmentMax = decCompensationAdjustmentMax
92          End Set
93      End Property
```

FIGURE 9-22

The following step enters the code to declare the seven remaining properties for the Employee class.

To Code the Remaining Properties

1. Unpin the Toolbox window from the main work area in order to display more code in the main work area. Enter lines 32 through 93 as shown in Figure 9-22.

The code for the Employee class properties displays (Figure 9-23). As the code was entered, the Intellisense feature of Visual Basic .NET completes the Property statement by adding the End Property keyword and inserting Get and Set property procedures within the property. Each property thus includes Get and Set property procedures that return or set the values of the properties of the Employee class, which are held in the private variables within the class.

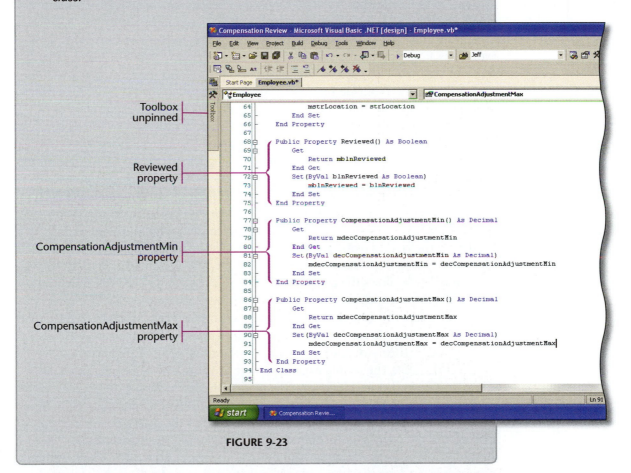

FIGURE 9-23

All eight of the properties of the Employee class now are coded. Get and Set property procedures often contain more code than is shown in the Employee class. For example, private functions and sub procedures can be used within a class and then provide functionality to code in the property procedures. As code is added, a class may become quite complex. However, because the class can be reused over and over by other programs without modification to the class, the programmer only has to maintain code for that class, instead of many programs.

Coding a Method for a Class

Function procedures and sub procedures are used to declare and code methods in classes. In Chapter 2 you learned that forms are one type of class and that, when you code a form, you are coding a class. A method that returns a value should be coded as a function procedure. A method that does not need to return a value should be coded as a sub procedure.

> **Tip**
>
> **Declaring Methods**
> A method that returns a value should be coded as a function procedure. A method that does not need to return a value should be coded as a sub procedure.

Just as with a Property statement used to declare a property, Visual Basic .NET provides additional options when declaring methods. For example, a developer can use the keyword, Public or Protected, in place of the Private keyword in a Function or Sub statement (see Table 7-18 on page VB 7.52 and Table 7-20 on page VB 7.65). If the Public keyword is used, no restrictions exist on the use of the method outside the class. If the Protected keyword is used, then the method is accessible only within the class and any subclasses of the class in which the method is declared. If neither the Public, Private, or Protected keywords are used, the method is Private by default.

Recall from the requirements document (Figure 9-4 on page VB 9.09) that one of the programs in the Compensation Review System must compute if an employee is eligible for review. As defined during program design and showed in the high-level class diagram (Figure 9-9 on page VB 9.19), this computation action is expressed as a method of the Employee class. The Employee class requires a method to compute the next review date for the Employee represented in an instance of the class.

Figure 9-24 shows the code for the function procedure used to create the ComputeNextReviewDate() method that computes an employee's next review date and return the next review date. The method uses two private variables. The first, dtmNextDateReviewed, stores the computed value of the next review date. The second, intReviewCycleYears, indicates the number of years in the review cycle (in this case, the number of years is set to 1, because reviews are annual). The value for intReviewCycleYears is added to the last review date in order to determine the next review date. Line 99 uses the AddYears() method of the Date data type to add the value of intReviewCycleYears to the mdtmDateReviewed private variable, which stores the value for the DateReviewed property of the Employee class. Date variables require methods, such as the AddYears() method, to perform mathematical operations on them because of the special nature of dates. The **AddYears() method** is used to add a number of years passed as a parameter to a date variable. Other methods for the Date data type include AddMonths(), AddDays(), and AddMinutes().

Manipulating Date Variables

Date variables require methods, such as the AddYears() method, to perform mathematical operations on them because of the special nature of dates.

```
95      Public Function ComputeNextReviewDate() As Date
96          Dim dtmNextDateReviewed As Date
97          Dim intReviewCycleYears As Integer = 1
98
99          dtmNextDateReviewed = mdtmDateReviewed.AddYears(intReviewCycleYears)
100         Return dtmNextDateReviewed
101     End Function
```

FIGURE 9-24

When another program uses the ComputeNextReviewDate() method of the Employee class, the program must place the result of the method in a variable. For example, the following line of code gets, or retrieves, the next review date for an instance of the Employee object named objFirstEmployee and then places the result in a Date variable named dtmCheckDate.

```
dtmCheckDate = objFirstEmployee.ComputeNextReviewDate()
```

The following steps enter the code shown in Figure 9-24 to create the ComputeNextReviewDate() method for the Employee class.

To Code a Method for a Class

1. Enter line 95 as shown in Figure 9-24.

The function declaration for the ComputeNextReviewDate() method displays in the code window (Figure 9-25). Intellisense inserts the End Function keyword on line 97.

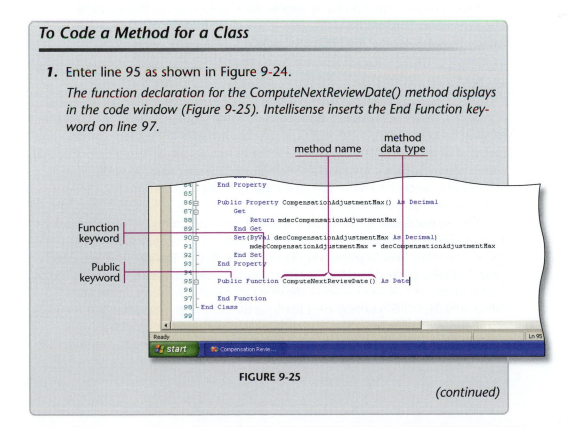

FIGURE 9-25

(continued)

2. Enter lines 96 through 100 as shown in Figure 9-24.

The code displays in the code window, as shown in Figure 9-26. The AddYears() method adds one year to the date stored in the mdtmDateReviewed private class variable that holds the value of the ReviewDate property of the Employee class. After the new date is computed, the value is returned by line 100 to the program that used the method.

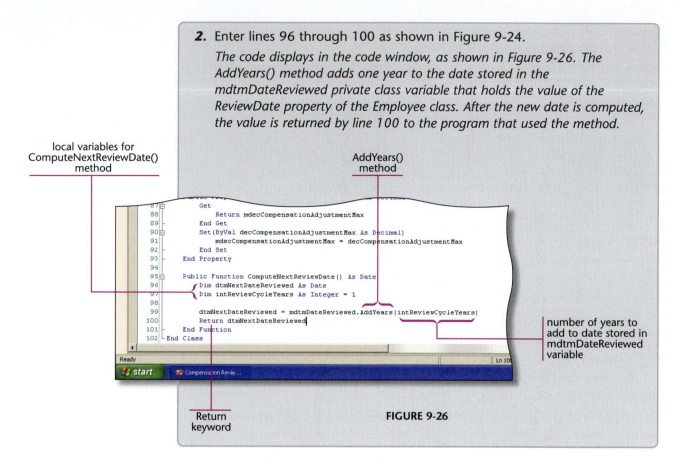

local variables for
ComputeNextReviewDate()
method

AddYears()
method

number of years to
add to date stored in
mdtmDateReviewed
variable

Return
keyword

FIGURE 9-26

The coding for the Employee class in the Compensation Review class library now is complete. The next step is to create the HourlyEmployee and SalariedEmployee subclasses that are based on the Employee class.

Subclasses

A subclass, sometimes called a **derived class** or **descendant class**, is a class that is based on another class. By default, a subclass includes all of the properties and methods of its base class. **Inheritance** is the object-oriented design principle that allows you to borrow functionality, including properties and methods, from other classes to create a new class. You **inherit** properties and methods from a base class to create a new subclass.

Inheritance is one of the most important concepts in object-oriented design and programming. Inheritance allows for reusability of code, which saves time and reduces mistakes in attempting to rewrite code that has already been developed and tested. For example, if a project requires classes for automobile objects, boat objects, and airplane objects, the developer first can create a base class called Vehicle, which encompasses many of the common properties and methods of the three vehicle types. The Vehicle base class would have properties and methods shared by all three vehicles, such as the properties for MaximumSpeed,

MilesPerGallon, Weight, MaximumNumberofPassengers and methods for Accelerate, Stop, Load, and Unload. Each of the three vehicle classes inherits from the Vehicle class, meaning that they all share those common properties and methods. Each subclass, however, also includes its own unique properties and methods that differentiate it from the other classes. The Boat class, for example, may have a NumberofSails property, while the Airplane class may have a WingType property.

In the Compensation Review class library, the HourlyEmployee and SalariedEmployee subclasses inherit all of the properties and methods of the Employee class. The code that has been written for the Employee class is reused for the HourlyEmployee and SalariedEmployee classes. The following sections describe the process of continuing to create the Compensation Review class library by creating the HourlyEmployee and SalariedEmployee classes, writing code to define them as subclasses that inherit the properties and methods from the Employee class, and declaring a new property for each of the subclasses.

Adding a Class to a Class Library

You add additional classes to a Class Library project in much the same way that you add additional forms to Windows application projects. Each of the .vb files in a class library, such as the Employee.vb file, can contain one or more classes. Alternatively, you can add additional .vb files, called modules, to a project to hold additional classes. In order to keep code more maintainable, each class should be coded in a separate module in a Class Library project.

Tip

Adding Classes to a Class Library Project
In order to keep code more maintainable, code each class in the class library in a separate module in the Class Library project.

Figure 9-27 on the next page shows the high-level class diagram that illustrates the relationship between the Employee class and the HourlyEmployee class. The HourlyEmployee class is a subclass of the Employee class and therefore should be coded in the same class library as the Employee class. The HourlyEmployee class includes nine properties and one method. Only one property, however, must be coded in the HourlyEmployee class; the HourlyEmployee class inherits the other eight properties and the method from the Employee class.

The high-level class diagram in Figure 9-27 also includes further details on the properties and methods of the classes. Each property and method includes a colon followed by a data type. While not all methods include data types, the ComputeNextReviewDate() method returns a date value. If a method accepts arguments, the arguments and their data types also should be indicated in the parentheses following the name of the method.

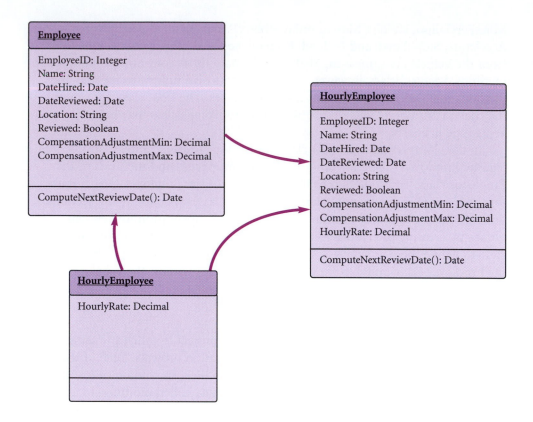

FIGURE 9-27

Adding Detail to High-Level Class Diagrams

To add detail to a high-level class diagram, indicate the data types for properties and methods after the property or method name by adding a colon followed by the data type of the property or method. If a method accepts arguments, indicate the arguments and their data types in the parentheses after the name of the method.

The first step in creating the HourlyEmployee class is to add a new class module to the Compensation Review Class Library project. The following steps add a new class module to the Class Library project; this class module will contain the HourlyEmployee subclass of the Employee class.

To Add a Class to a Class Library

1. Right-click the Compensation Review project in the Solution Explorer window. When the shortcut menu displays, point to the Add command.
The Add submenu displays (Figure 9-28).

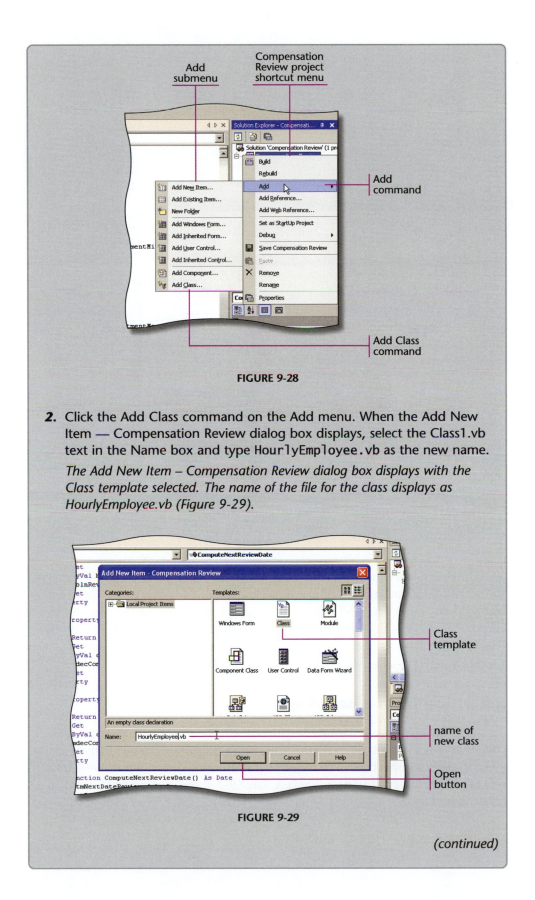

FIGURE 9-28

2. Click the Add Class command on the Add menu. When the Add New Item — Compensation Review dialog box displays, select the Class1.vb text in the Name box and type HourlyEmployee.vb as the new name.

The Add New Item – Compensation Review dialog box displays with the Class template selected. The name of the file for the class displays as HourlyEmployee.vb (Figure 9-29).

FIGURE 9-29

(continued)

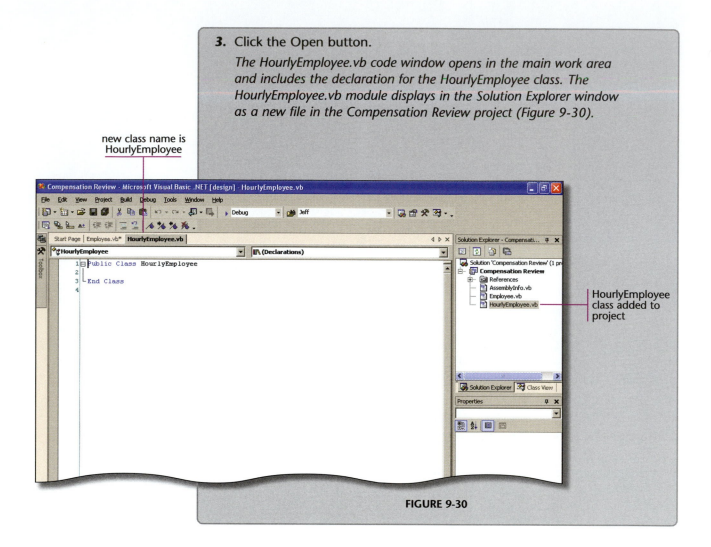

3. Click the Open button.

The HourlyEmployee.vb code window opens in the main work area and includes the declaration for the HourlyEmployee class. The HourlyEmployee.vb module displays in the Solution Explorer window as a new file in the Compensation Review project (Figure 9-30).

new class name is
HourlyEmployee

HourlyEmployee
class added to
project

FIGURE 9-30

The Add Class command works exactly like the Add Form command, except the default template selected on the Add New Item dialog box is the Class template. When Visual Basic .NET creates the new class, it uses the file name of the class file as the default class name. The new class thus is named HourlyEmployee (line 1 in Figure 9-30), because the default class name corresponds to the file name, HourlyEmployee.vb.

Inheriting from a Base Class

After declaring a new HourlyEmployee class, the next step is to write the code that tells Visual Basic .NET that the HourlyEmployee class actually is a subclass of the Employee class. The **Inherits statement** allows you to inherit from one other class to create a new subclass. Table 9-7 shows the general form of the Inherits statement.

Table 9-7   Inherits Statement

General Form:	Inherits classname
	where classname is another class in the current project or a class included in one of the references in the project.
Purpose:	The Inherits statement allows you to create a new subclass from a base class.
Example:	`Inherits Employee`
Notes:	1. Visual Basic .NET only allows one Inherits statement per class, which means that a subclass can inherit only from one base class. 2. The Inherits statement must be the first statement of the class.

As stated in the first note, a class in Visual Basic .NET may inherit from only one other class. Other object-oriented programming languages may allow you to inherit from multiple classes. While it is possible to use other features of Visual Basic .NET to accomplish this goal, it is beyond the scope of this book.

Figure 9-31 shows the Inherits statement necessary for the HourlyEmployee class to inherit from the Employee class. After this line of code is added, the HourlyEmployee class includes all of the properties and methods of the Employee class. The default constructor of the HourlyEmployee class is the constructor of the Employee class. If no more code was included in the HourlyEmployee class, you could instantiate an instance of the HourlyEmployee class and have access to all of the properties and methods already coded for the Employee class.

```
3       Inherits Employee
```

FIGURE 9-31

The step on the next page adds the code shown in Figure 9-31 to the HourlyEmployee class module, so that it inherits from the Employee base class.

Inheriting from Multiple Classes
When designing programs for Visual Basic .NET, avoid designing solutions that involve inheriting from multiple classes.

To Inherit from a Base Class

1. Enter Option Strict On as the first line of code in the code window. Click line 3 and then type the line of code shown in Figure 9-31 on the previous page.

The Inherits statement displays in the code window, meaning that the HourlyEmployee class inherits from the Employee class (Figure 9-32). All of the methods and properties of the Employee class are available to all instances of the HourlyEmployee class.

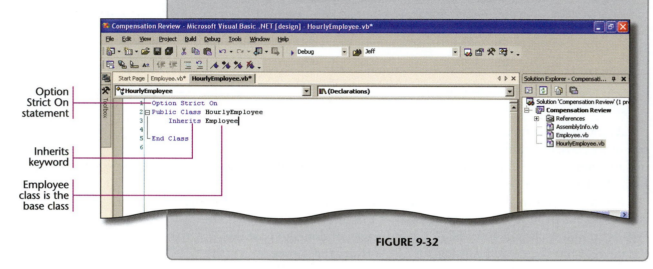

FIGURE 9-32

After you type the Inherits keyword, Intellisense displays a list of classes available for inheritance. The list includes the Employee class developed earlier in this chapter. Intellisense knows about the Employee class because the Employee class is in the same project as the HourlyEmployee class. Intellisense knows about the other classes in the list because those classes are available in the .NET Framework class library references in the References folder in the Solution Explorer window.

Creating a Private Variable for a Property in a Subclass

The HourlyEmployee class includes one property, the HourlyRate property, in addition to the eight properties inherited from the Employee class. The HourlyEmployee class thus requires a private variable to store the value of the HourlyRate property, which needs to be of the data type Decimal. Figure 9-33 shows the line of code necessary to declare the private variable for the property in the subclass.

```
5        Private mdecHourlyRate As Decimal
```

FIGURE 9-33

The following step adds the code shown in Figure 9-33 to create a private variable for the HourlyRate property in the HourlyEmployee class.

To Create a Private Variable for a Property in a Subclass

---

1. Enter line 5 as shown in Figure 9-33.

The mdecHourlyRate variable declaration displays in the code window (Figure 9-34). The variable holds the value of the HourlyRate property of the HourlyEmployee class.

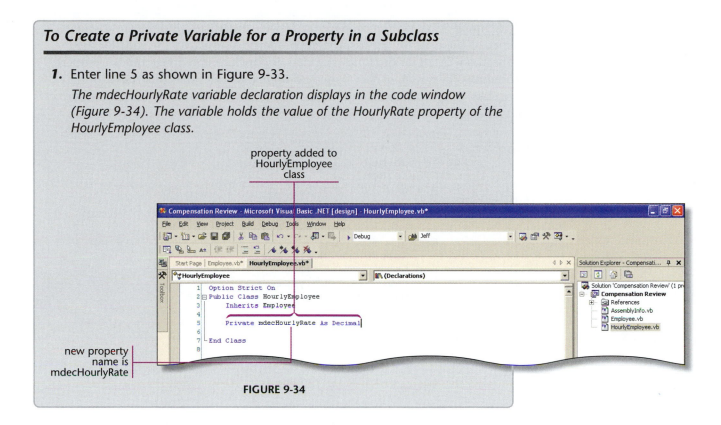

FIGURE 9-34

Creating a Constructor and a Property in a Subclass

The HourlyEmployee class requires a constructor to initialize the private variable and a property declaration for the HourlyRate property of the class. The New() constructor only needs to initialize the mdecHourlyRate variable. When another program instantiates an instance of the HourlyEmployee class, the New() constructor in the HourlyEmployee class executes to initialize the mdecHourlyRate variable. The properties defined in the Employee class also must be initialized.

Code will be added to the HourlyEmployee constructor to execute the Employee class constructor. By default, the constructor automatically is called, but the code is added in this project to reinforce the idea that the constructor of the Employee class is called. That is, if the call to the base class constructor is omitted in this case, the base class constructor is still called. This is not always the case, but the discussion of the special cases is out of the scope of this book. In previous chapters, the Me object was used to allow a form to refer to itself. With classes, a similar object, called the **MyBase object**, allows a class to refer to its base class without needing to use the base class name. To call the constructor in the Employee class from the HourlyEmployee class, the code, MyBase.New(), should appear as the first line of the HourlyEmployee constructor.

Tip

Constructors of Subclasses

In general, it is good practice to add the line of code, MyBase.New(), as the first line in the constructor of a subclass to ensure that the constructor of the base class is called first.

Figure 9-35 shows the code for the New() constructor and the HourlyRate property. The code for the HourlyRate property is similar to the code for the properties written for the Employee class and includes both Get and Set property procedures. The MyBase.New() method on line 8 forces the constructor of the base class, Employee, to execute whenever a new instance of the HourlyEmployee class is created.

```
7        Public Sub New()
8            MyBase.New()
9            mdecHourlyRate = 0
10       End Sub
11
12       Public Property HourlyRate() As Decimal
13           Get
14               Return mdecHourlyRate
15           End Get
16           Set(ByVal decHourlyRate As Decimal)
17               mdecHourlyRate = decHourlyRate
18           End Set
19       End Property
20 End Class
```

FIGURE 9-35

The following steps enter code to create the constructor for the HourlyEmployee subclass and the HourlyRate property.

To Create a Constructor and a Property in a Subclass

1. Type lines 7 through 10 as shown in Figure 9-35.

The Sub statement displays in the code window to declare the New() sub procedure for the HourlyEmployee class, which is the constructor for the class (Figure 9-36). The constructor initializes the value of the mdecHourlyRate private variable, which holds the value of the HourlyRate property of the class. Visual Basic .NET completes the sub procedure by adding the End Sub keyword on line 10.

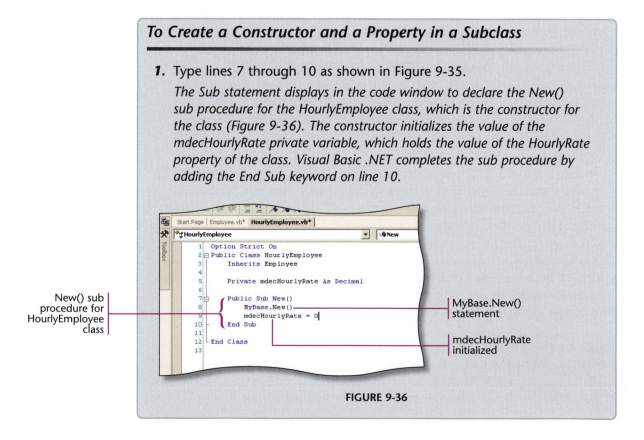

FIGURE 9-36

2. Type line 12 as shown in Figure 9-35.

The Property statement for the HourlyRate property displays in the code window. Visual Basic .NET completes the Property statement by adding the End Property keyword on line 19 and inserting Get and Set property procedures within the property (Figure 9-37).

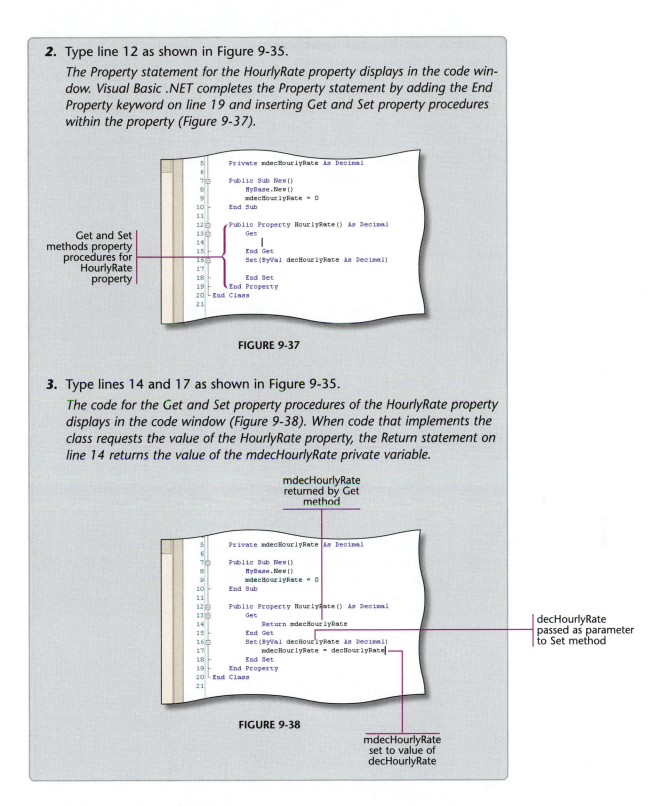

Get and Set methods property procedures for HourlyRate property

```
 5    Private mdecHourlyRate As Decimal
 6
 7    Public Sub New()
 8        MyBase.New()
 9        mdecHourlyRate = 0
10    End Sub
11
12    Public Property HourlyRate() As Decimal
13        Get
14
15        End Get
16        Set(ByVal decHourlyRate As Decimal)
17
18        End Set
19    End Property
20 End Class
21
```

FIGURE 9-37

3. Type lines 14 and 17 as shown in Figure 9-35.

The code for the Get and Set property procedures of the HourlyRate property displays in the code window (Figure 9-38). When code that implements the class requests the value of the HourlyRate property, the Return statement on line 14 returns the value of the mdecHourlyRate private variable.

mdecHourlyRate returned by Get method

```
 5    Private mdecHourlyRate As Decimal
 6
 7    Public Sub New()
 8        MyBase.New()
 9        mdecHourlyRate = 0
10    End Sub
11
12    Public Property HourlyRate() As Decimal
13        Get
14            Return mdecHourlyRate
15        End Get
16        Set(ByVal decHourlyRate As Decimal)
17            mdecHourlyRate = decHourlyRate
18        End Set
19    End Property
20 End Class
21
```

decHourlyRate passed as parameter to Set method

FIGURE 9-38

mdecHourlyRate set to value of decHourlyRate

The code for the HourlyEmployee subclass is complete. In addition to the HourlyRate property, the subclass includes all of the properties and methods of the Employee class. The next step is to create the third class in the Compensation Review Class Library project, the SalariedEmployee class.

Creating Additional Subclasses

You create and code the SalariedEmployee class using the same techniques used to create the HourlyEmployee class. The SalariedEmployee class is a subclass of the Employee class. Figure 9-39 illustrates the relationship between the Employee class and the SalariedEmployee class. The SalariedEmployee class includes one additional property — the AnnualSalary property. The resulting SalariedEmployee class includes nine properties and one method. Only one property, however, requires coding in the SalariedEmployee class, because the SalariedEmployee class inherits the other properties and method from the Employee class.

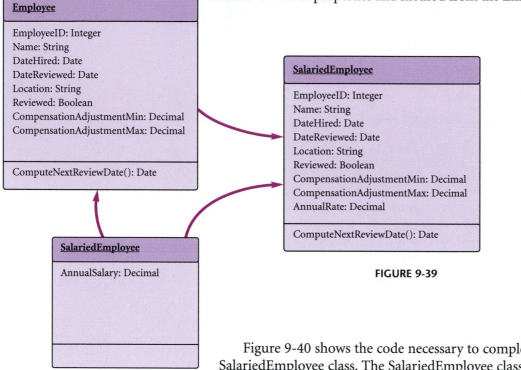

FIGURE 9-39

Figure 9-40 shows the code necessary to complete the SalariedEmployee class. The SalariedEmployee class inherits from the Employee class, as shown in line 3 of the code.

```
1 Option Strict On
2 Public Class SalariedEmployee
3     Inherits Employee
4
5     Private mdecAnnualSalary As Decimal
6
7     Public Sub New()
8         MyBase.New()
9         mdecAnnualSalary = 0
10    End Sub
11
12    Public Property AnnualSalary() As Decimal
13        Get
14            Return mdecAnnualSalary
15        End Get
16        Set(ByVal decAnnualSalary As Decimal)
17            mdecAnnualSalary = decAnnualSalary
18        End Set
19    End Property
20 End Class
```

FIGURE 9-40

The following steps add the SalariedEmployee class to the Compensation Review class library and then enter the code for the class as shown in Figure 9-40.

To Create an Additional Subclass

1. Right-click the Compensation Review project in the Solution Explorer window. When the shortcut menu displays, click the Add command.

2. Click the Add Class command on the Add menu. When the Add New Item – Compensation Review dialog box displays, select the Class1.vb text in the Name box and type SalariedEmployee.vb as the new name.

3. Click the Open button. When the SalariedEmployee.vb code window displays, enter the lines of code as shown in Figure 9-40.

The SalariedEmployee.vb code window opens in the main work area and includes the declaration for the SalariedEmployee class (Figure 9-41). The SalariedEmployee.vb module displays in the Solution Explorer window as a new file in the Compensation Review project. The code for the SalariedEmployee class displays in the code window, including the Inherits statement, the property declaration for the AnnualSalary property, and the Get and Set property procedures.

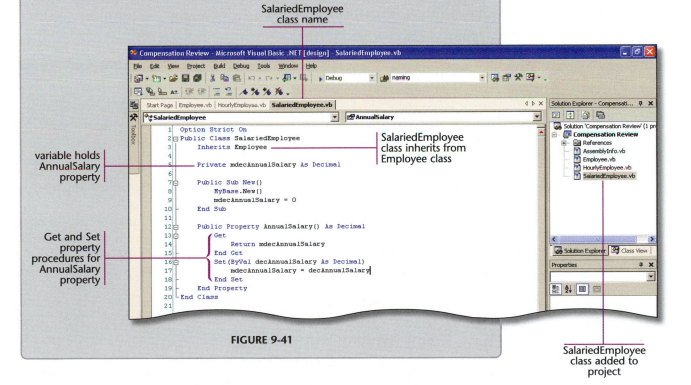

FIGURE 9-41

Aggregation

Aggregation is another key object-oriented concept, which often is contrasted with inheritance. **Aggregation**, or **composition**, is a special type of relationship among classes in which a class consists of one or more other classes. Inheritance is said to define an "is a" relationship between two classes; aggregation, however, is said to describe a "has a" relationship between classes.

Using the example of the Vehicle class, a car *is a* type of vehicle, just as a boat *is a* type of vehicle. The Vehicle class provides common properties and methods for all types of vehicles; the subclasses inherit these properties and methods. In this project, an hourly employee *is a* type of employee and a salaried employee *is a* type of employee. Inheritance thus is used to allow the HourlyEmployee and SalariedEmployee subclasses to inherit properties and methods from the base class, Employee.

With aggregation or composition, one class has, or is composed of, one or more other classes, rather than inheriting the properties and methods of another class. Using a Car class as an example, a car *has a* transmission, but it *is not a* type of transmission. The Car class thus aggregates the functionality of the Transmission class (along with other classes, such as the Engine class) to provide required functionality. A Car class might aggregate the functionality of the Transmission class by declaring a property in the Car class as the type Transmission in code and then calling its ShiftGear() method of the Transmission property, as if the method was its own. The following code shows some of the code required for such a situation.

```
Public Class Car
   Private mTransmission As New Transmission()
   Public Sub New()
     mTransmission.ShiftGear(1)
   End Sub
     .
     .
     .
End Class
```

As noted above, in this chapter, the HourlyEmployee and SalariedEmployee subclasses inherit from the Employee class. With the completion of the third class, the SalariedEmployee class, the coding for the Compensation Review class library is complete. The class library is ready to be built and saved, so that other programs can use it. The next step is to build and save the class library and then document the code.

Building, Saving, and Documenting the Class Library

In previous chapters, the development of a Windows application project resulted in an executable file with a .EXE file extension after Visual Basic .NET builds the project. The building of a class library results in a non-executable file with a .DLL file extension. The **.DLL file** is not executable because class libraries are designed for use by other applications and provide no functionality on their own. Building the Compensation Review class library results in a file named

Compensation Review.dll. This file contains all of the information and functionality for other programs to implement the Employee, HourlyEmployee, and SalariedEmployee classes. Later in this chapter, you will learn how to use the class library in other programs.

> **Building Class Libraries**
> The result of building a class library is a non-executable file with a .DLL file extension. The .DLL file is not executable because class libraries are designed for use by other applications and provide no functionality on their own.

The following steps build, save, and document the Compensation Review class library.

To Build, Save, and Document the Class Library

1. Right-click the Compensation Review project in the Solution Explorer window. When the shortcut menu displays, click the Build command.

Visual Basic .NET automatically saves the class files and then opens the Output window and displays several messages while building the project (Figure 9-42). The result of the build is the creation of the Compensation Review.dll file in the A:\Chapter9\Compensation Review\ Compensation Review\bin folder on the Data Disk.

2. Click the Employee.vb tab and then follow the steps on page VB 2.40 of Chapter 2 to use the Print command on the File menu to print a record of the code for the Employee class.

3. Click the HourlyEmployee.vb tab and then follow the steps on page VB 2.40 of Chapter 2 to use the Print command on the File menu to print a record of the code for the HourlyEmployee class.

4. Click the SalariedEmployee.vb tab and then follow the steps on page VB 2.40 of Chapter 2 to use the Print command on the File menu to print a record of the code for the SalariedEmployee class.

A record of the code for the three classes is printed (Figure 9-43 on pages VB 9.50 and VB 9.51).

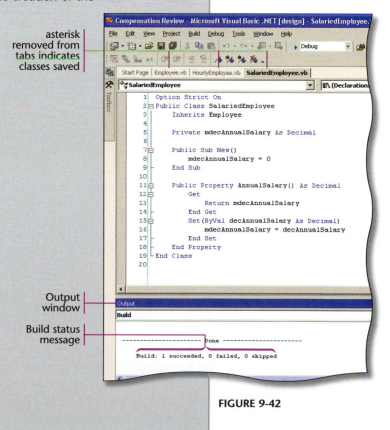

asterisk removed from tabs indicates classes saved

Output window

Build status message

FIGURE 9-42

(continued)

A:\Chapter9\Compensation Review\Compensation Review\Employee.vb   2

```
 68     Public Property Reviewed() As Boolean
 69         Get
 70             Return mblnReviewed
 71         End Get
 72         Set(ByVal blnReviewed As Boolean)
 73             mblnReviewed = blnReviewed
 74         End Set
 75     End Property
 76
 77     Public Property CompensationAdjustmentMin() As Decimal
 78         Get
 79             Return mdecCompensationAdjustmentMin
 80         End Get
 81         Set(ByVal decCompensationAdjustmentMin As Decimal)
 82             mdecCompensationAdjustmentMin = decCompensationAdjustmentMin
 83         End Set
 84     End Property
 85
 86     Public Property CompensationAdjustmentMax() As Decimal
 87         Get
 88             Return mdecCompensationAdjustmentMax
 89         End Get
 90         Set(ByVal decCompensationAdjustmentMax As Decimal)
 91             mdecCompensationAdjustmentMax = decCompensationAdjustmentMax
 92         End Set
 93     End Property
 94
 95     Public Function ComputeNextReviewDate() As Date
 96         Dim dtmNextDateReviewed As Date
 97         Dim intReviewCycleYears As Integer = 1
 98
 99         dtmNextDateReviewed = mdtmDateReviewed.AddYears(intReviewCycleYears)
100         Return dtmNextDateReviewed
101     End Function
102 End Class
103
```

(a)

A:\Chapter9\Compensation Review\Compensation Review\Employee.vb   1

```
 1 Option Strict On
 2 Public Class Employee
 3     Private mintEmployeeID As Integer
 4     Private mstrName As String
 5     Private mdtmDateHired As Date
 6     Private mdtmDateReviewed As Date
 7     Private mstrLocation As String
 8     Private mblnReviewed As Boolean
 9     Private mdecCompensationAdjustmentMin As Decimal
10     Private mdecCompensationAdjustmentMax As Decimal
11
12     Public Sub New()
13         mintEmployeeID = 0
14         mstrName = ""
15         mdtmDateHired = Nothing
16         mdtmDateReviewed = Nothing
17         mstrLocation = ""
18         mblnReviewed = False
19         mdecCompensationAdjustmentMin = 0
20         mdecCompensationAdjustmentMax = 0
21     End Sub
22
23     Public Property EmployeeID() As Integer
24         Get
25             Return mintEmployeeID
26         End Get
27         Set(ByVal intEmployeeID As Integer)
28             mintEmployeeID = intEmployeeID
29         End Set
30     End Property
31
32     Public Property Name() As String
33         Get
34             Return mstrName
35         End Get
36         Set(ByVal strName As String)
37             mstrName = strName
38         End Set
39     End Property
40
41     Public Property DateHired() As Date
42         Get
43             Return mdtmDateHired
44         End Get
45         Set(ByVal dtmDateHired As Date)
46             mdtmDateHired = dtmDateHired
47         End Set
48     End Property
49
50     Public Property DateReviewed() As Date
51         Get
52             Return mdtmDateReviewed
53         End Get
54         Set(ByVal dtmDateReviewed As Date)
55             mdtmDateReviewed = dtmDateReviewed
56         End Set
57     End Property
58
59     Public Property Location() As String
60         Get
61             Return mstrLocation
62         End Get
63         Set(ByVal strLocation As String)
64             mstrLocation = strLocation
65         End Set
66     End Property
67
```

FIGURE 9-43

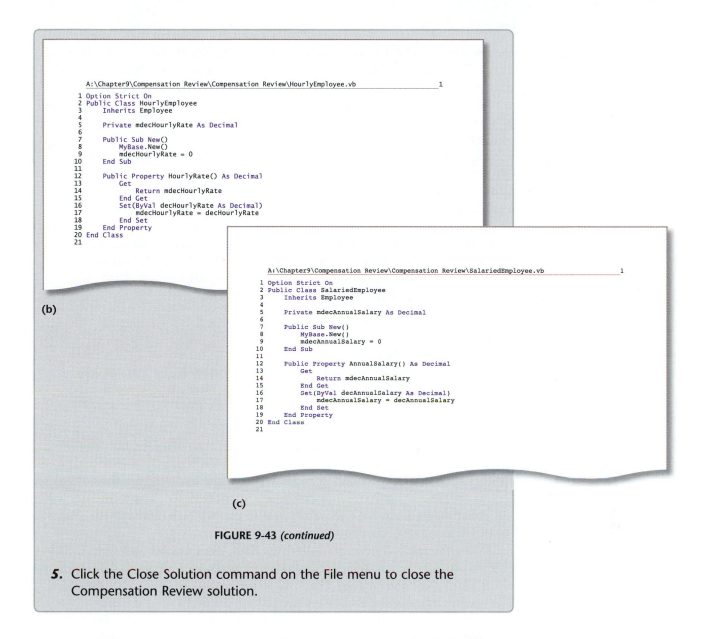

```
A:\Chapter9\Compensation Review\Compensation Review\HourlyEmployee.vb                1
 1 Option Strict On
 2 Public Class HourlyEmployee
 3     Inherits Employee
 4
 5     Private mdecHourlyRate As Decimal
 6
 7     Public Sub New()
 8         MyBase.New()
 9         mdecHourlyRate = 0
10     End Sub
11
12     Public Property HourlyRate() As Decimal
13         Get
14             Return mdecHourlyRate
15         End Get
16         Set(ByVal decHourlyRate As Decimal)
17             mdecHourlyRate = decHourlyRate
18         End Set
19     End Property
20 End Class
21
```

(b)

```
A:\Chapter9\Compensation Review\Compensation Review\SalariedEmployee.vb              1
 1 Option Strict On
 2 Public Class SalariedEmployee
 3     Inherits Employee
 4
 5     Private mdecAnnualSalary As Decimal
 6
 7     Public Sub New()
 8         MyBase.New()
 9         mdecAnnualSalary = 0
10     End Sub
11
12     Public Property AnnualSalary() As Decimal
13         Get
14             Return mdecAnnualSalary
15         End Get
16         Set(ByVal decAnnualSalary As Decimal)
17             mdecAnnualSalary = decAnnualSalary
18         End Set
19     End Property
20 End Class
21
```

(c)

FIGURE 9-43 *(continued)*

5. Click the Close Solution command on the File menu to close the Compensation Review solution.

The development phase for the Compensation Review class library now is complete and the class library can be tested by using a class in code.

Using a Class in Code

The remainder of this chapter concentrates on creating the EmployeeClassTest application that tests some of the functionality of the classes in the Compensation Review class library. This application will be created to instantiate objects in each of the three classes developed in the class library and allow the user to be able to get and set properties for each of the three objects.

The EmployeeClassTest application is a unit test program that is used to test the three classes in the Compensation Review class library. Developers often create applications, called unit test programs, to test the functionality of portions of a larger project. As discussed in Chapter 1, this practice is known as unit testing. Unit testing allows a programmer to validate the correctness of discrete portions of a project. End users do not see these unit test programs, as they are for the sole use of the developer.

Figure 9-44 shows the three objects created in the EmployeeClassTest application and how the objects interact with the user interface, using a type of UML diagram called an object diagram. An **object diagram** shows the status of a particular instance of a class at a point in time, including the values of properties. As indicated by the object diagram, when the EmployeeClassTest application starts, the code creates one object for each class in the Compensation Review class library. The three objects are represented as global variables named gobjEmployee, gobjHourlyEmployee, and gobjSalariedEmployee. Each object represents an individual employee stored in memory.

Object Diagrams

Use object diagrams to represent an instance of a class at a particular point in time, including the values of properties.

The object diagram looks much like a detailed class diagram, but with some important differences. The name of the object, which is the variable name, appears at the top of the diagram and is separated by a colon from the object's class name. The object name and class name are underlined. The properties in the object diagram appear with values next to them, which represent the state of the object at a particular point in time.

When the application starts and Visual Basic .NET creates each object, each object's property values, such as Name and AnnualSalary, are set to default values of blank, Nothing, or zero. These values are set by each object's constructor. The user interface of the EmployeeClassTest application allows the user to update the Name property value for the gobjEmployee object, the Name and HourlyRate property values for the gobjHourlyEmployee object, and the Name and AnnualSalary property values for the gobjSalariedEmployee object. The user selects which object's properties to view (get) or update (set) by selecting the object's associated RadioButton control in the Object GroupBox control. When the user selects one of the RadioButton controls, the code displays the corresponding object's property values in the controls in the Properties GroupBox control. Because each type of object includes different properties, the type of object selected determines which controls in the Properties GroupBox control are accessible. For example, the Hourly rate NumericUpDown control is not accessible when the SalariedEmployee Object RadioButton control is selected. Figure 9-44 shows the object diagram for the gobjSalariedEmployee object, after the user enters new property values in the Properties GroupBox control and then clicks the Set Properties button.

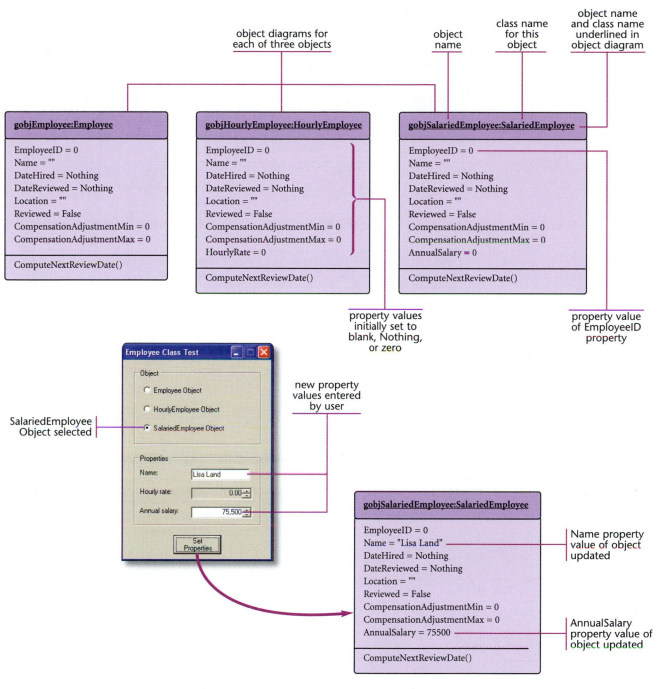

FIGURE 9-44

Starting a New Project and Creating a User Interface

The first steps in creating the EmployeeClassTest application are to start a new project and then add controls and set properties for the form and controls. Table 9-8 on the next page lists the Form1 form property value changes that need to be made.

Table 9-8 *Form1 Form Property Values for the EmployeeClassTest Application*

PROPERTY	PROPERTY VALUE	EFFECT
Size: Width	256	Sets the width of the form in pixels
Size: Height	368	Sets the height of the form in pixels
StartPosition	CenterScreen	Causes the form to display in the center of the user's screen at the start of run time
MaximumBox	False	Causes the form to not display a Maximize button on the title bar on the window
Text	Employee Class Test	Sets the value of the title bar on the window
FormBorderStyle	FixedDialog	Disallows resizing of the form during run time

The user interface design shown in Figure 9-6 on page VB 9.15 also specifies that the Form1 form requires two GroupBox controls, three RadioButton controls, one TextBox control, two NumericUpDown controls, and a Button control. Table 9-9 lists the property values that must be set for these controls.

Table 9-9 *GroupBox, RadioButton, TextBox, NumericUpDown, and Button Control Property Values for the EmployeeClassTest Application*

CONTROL	PROPERTY	PROPERTY VALUE	EFFECT
GroupBox1	Text	Object	Sets the text that displays on the top of the control to Object
	TabIndex	0	Causes this control to be the first control on the form to receive focus
	Size: Width	215	Sets the width of the control in pixels
	Size: Height	128	Sets the height of the control in pixels
	Location: X (left)	18	Indicates the distance from the left border of the form in pixels
	Location: Y (top)	16	Indicates the distance from the top border of the form in pixels
GroupBox2	Text	Properties	Sets the text that displays on the top of the control to Properties
	TabIndex	1	Causes this control to be the second control on the form to receive focus
	Size: Width	215	Sets the width of the control in pixels
	Size: Height	120	Sets the height of the control in pixels

Table 9-9 *GroupBox, RadioButton, TextBox, NumericUpDown, and Button Control Property Values for the EmployeeClassTest Application (continued)*

CONTROL	PROPERTY	PROPERTY VALUE	EFFECT
GroupBox2 (continued)	Location: X (left)	18	Indicates the distance from the left border of the form in pixels
	Location: Y (top)	160	Indicates the distance from the top border of the form in pixels
RadioButton1	Name	radEmployeeObject	Changes the control's name to a descriptive name
	TabIndex	0	Causes this control to be the first control in GroupBox1 to receive focus
	Size: Width	152	Sets the width of the control in pixels
	Size: Height	24	Sets the height of the control in pixels
	Location: X (left)	16	Indicates the distance from the left border of the GroupBox1 in pixels
	Location: Y (top)	24	Indicates the distance from the top border of the GroupBox1 in pixels
	Checked	True	Sets this control as the default button in the GroupBox1
RadioButton2	Name	radHourlyEmployeeObject	Changes the control's name to a descriptive name
	TabIndex	1	Causes this control to be the second control in the GroupBox1 to receive focus
	Size: Width	152	Sets the width of the control in pixels
	Size: Height	24	Sets the height of the control in pixels
	Location: X (left)	16	Indicates the distance from the left border of the GroupBox1 in pixels
	Location: Y (top)	56	Indicates the distance from the top border of the GroupBox1 in pixels
RadioButton3	Name	radSalariedEmployeeObject	Changes the control's name to a descriptive name
	TabIndex	2	Causes this control to be the third control in the GroupBox1 to receive focus
	Size: Width	152	Sets the width of the control in pixels
	Size: Height	24	Sets the height of the control in pixels
	Location: X (left)	16	Indicates the distance from the left border of the GroupBox1 in pixels
	Location: Y (top)	88	Indicates the distance from the top border of the GroupBox1 in pixels
Label1	Size: Width	80	Sets the width of the control in pixels
	Size: Height	16	Sets the height of the control in pixels

(continued)

Table 9-9 *GroupBox, RadioButton, TextBox, NumericUpDown, and Button Control Property Values for the EmployeeClassTest Application (continued)*

CONTROL	PROPERTY	PROPERTY VALUE	EFFECT
Label1 (continued)	Location: X (left)	8	Indicates the distance from the left border of the GroupBox2 in pixels
	Location: Y (top)	24	Indicates the distance from the top border of the GroupBox2 in pixels
	Text	Name:	Sets Name: to display as the initial value in the control at run time
Label2	Size: Width	80	Sets the width of the control in pixels
	Size: Height	16	Sets the height of the control in pixels
	Location: X (left)	8	Indicates the distance from the left border of the GroupBox2 in pixels
	Location: Y (top)	56	Indicates the distance from the top border of the GroupBox2 in pixels
	Text	Hourly rate:	Sets Hourly rate: to display as the initial value in the control at run time
Label3	Size: Width	80	Sets the width of the control in pixels
	Size: Height	16	Sets the height of the control in pixels
	Location: X (left)	8	Indicates the distance from the left border of the GroupBox2 in pixels
	Location: Y (top)	88	Indicates the distance from the top border of the GroupBox2 in pixels
	Text	Annual salary:	Sets Annual salary: to display as the initial value in the control at run time
TextBox1	Size: Width	100	Sets the width of the control in pixels
	Size: Height	20	Sets the height of the control in pixels
	Location: X (left)	96	Indicates the distance from the left border of the GroupBox2 in pixels
	Location: Y (top)	24	Indicates the distance from the top border of the GroupBox2 in pixels
	Name	txtName	Changes the control's name to a descriptive name
	Text	<blank>	Sets the text that displays in the text box to an empty string
	TabIndex	0	Causes this control to be the first control in the GroupBox2 to receive focus
	MaxLength	75	Sets the maximum number of characters that can be typed in the control
NumericUpDown1	Size: Width	104	Sets the width of the control in pixels
	Size: Height	20	Sets the height of the control in pixels
	Location: X (left)	96	Indicates the distance from the left border of the GroupBox2 in pixels

Table 9-9 ***GroupBox, RadioButton, TextBox, NumericUpDown, and Button Control Property Values for the EmployeeClassTest Application*** (continued)

CONTROL	PROPERTY	PROPERTY VALUE	EFFECT
NumericUpDown1 (continued)	Location: Y (top)	56	Indicates the distance from the top border of the GroupBox2 in pixels
	Increment	.5	Causes the value in the control to increment or decrement by .5 when the up or down arrows are clicked
	Maximum	75	Defines the highest value allowed in the control
	TabIndex	1	Causes this control to be the second control in the GroupBox2 to receive focus
	Name	nudHourlyRate	Changes the control's name to a descriptive name
	DecimalPlaces	2	Sets the number of decimal places of the value to display in the control
NumericUpDown2	Size: Width	104	Sets the width of the control in pixels
	Size: Height	20	Sets the height of the control in pixels
	Location: X (left)	96	Indicates the distance from the left border of the GroupBox2 in pixels
	Location: Y (top)	88	Indicates the distance from the top border of the GroupBox2 in pixels
	Increment	500	Causes the value in the control to increment or decrement by 500 when the up or down arrows are clicked
	Maximum	125000	Defines the highest value allowed in the control
	TabIndex	2	Causes this control to be the third control in the GroupBox2 to receive focus
	Name	nudAnnualSalary	Changes the control's name to a descriptive name
Button1	Text	Set Properties	Sets the text that displays on the button face to Set Properties
	TabIndex	2	Causes this control to be the third control on the form to receive focus
	Name	btnSetProperties	Changes the control's name to a descriptive name
	Size: Width	80	Sets the width of the control in pixels
	Size: Height	32	Sets the height of the control in pixels
	Location: X (left)	85	Indicates the distance from the left border of the form in pixels
	Location: Y (top)	296	Indicates the distance from the top border of the form in pixels

The following steps start a new Windows application project, called the EmployeeClassTest project, and then create the user interface for the Employee Class Test application. The form properties are set using the property values listed in Table 9-8 on page VB 9.54. The control properties are set using the property values listed in Table 9-9 on pages VB 9.54 through VB 9.57.

To Start a New Project and Create the User Interface

1. If necessary, click the Show Start Page command on the Help menu. When the Start Page displays, click the New Project button on the Start Page.

2. When the New Project dialog box displays, if necessary, click Create directory for Solution. Click the Windows Application icon in the Templates area. Double-click the text, WindowsApplication1, in the Name box. Type EmployeeClassTest in the Name box.

   The new project name displays in the Name box, and the solution name displays in the New Solution Name box. Because the Create directory for Solution check box is selected, Visual Basic .NET will create a subdirectory with the same name as the project when it creates the project.

3. Click the Browse button. If necessary, click 3½ Floppy (A:) in the Look in box. Click Chapter9 and then click the Open button.

4. Click the OK button. If necessary, close the Output window.

   Visual Basic .NET creates the EmployeeClassTest solution and project. Visual Basic .NET creates an initial form and displays it in the main work area.

5. With Form1 selected, set the properties of the Form1 form as specified in Table 9-8 on page VB 9.54. Add and then set the property values of the controls as listed in Table 9-9 on pages VB 9.54 through VB 9.57. Add the three RadioButton controls to the first GroupBox control. Add the TextBox control and two NumericUpDown controls to the second GroupBox control, as shown in Figure 9-45.

   The properties of the Form1 form and controls are set and the controls display on the Form1 form, as shown in Figure 9-45.

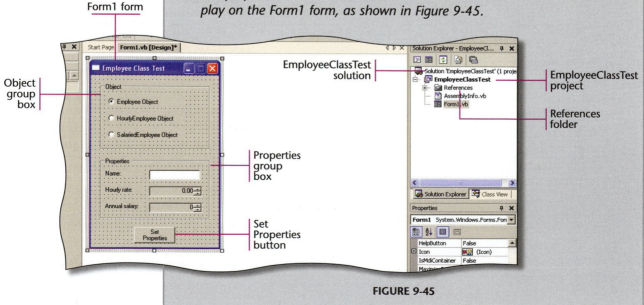

FIGURE 9-45

After Visual Basic .NET creates the new project, the solution and project name, EmployeeClassTest, display in the Solution Explorer window. The Form1 form shown in Figure 9-45 includes two GroupBox controls. The first, the Object GroupBox, allows the user to select an object for which properties display in the Properties GroupBox. Controls in the Properties GroupBox become enabled depending on which Object the user selects in the Object GroupBox. The Set Properties button allows the user to update the values of the properties of the Object from the values in the Properties GroupBox.

The user interface for the EmployeeClassTest application is now complete. The next step is to write the code for the EmployeeClassTest project.

Adding a Reference to a Class

Before you can use the classes in the Compensation Review class library in a project, the project must be aware of the Compensation Review class library. As shown in Figure 9-45, a References folder displays below the project in the Solution Explorer window. As discussed in Chapter 2, the References folder contains a list of the classes used by the project. By default, a Windows application project contains five references in the References folder. You also can add your own references to classes used by your project to the References folder.

The following steps create the radEmployeeObject_CheckedChanged event procedure and add a reference to the Compensation Review class library to the EmployeeClassTest project.

To Add a Reference to a Class

1. Double-click the Employee Object radio button on the Form1 form. When Visual Basic .NET creates the radEmployeeObject_ CheckedChanged event procedure, right-click the References folder in the Solution Explorer window.

Visual Basic .NET creates the radEmployeeObject_CheckedChanged event procedure. The References shortcut menu displays (Figure 9-46).

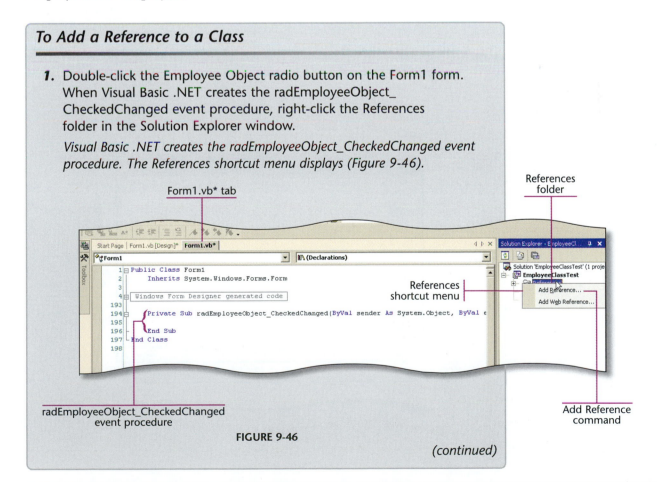

FIGURE 9-46

(continued)

2. Click the Add References command on the References shortcut menu.

The Add Reference dialog box displays (Figure 9-47). The dialog box displays a list of reusable components, including several class libraries.

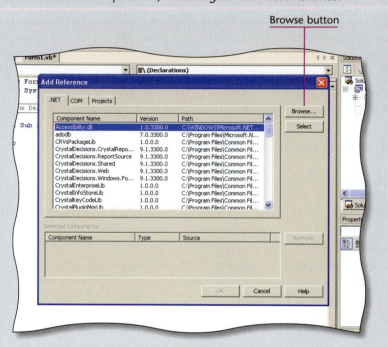

FIGURE 9-47

3. Click the Browse button.

The Select Component dialog box displays (Figure 9-48).

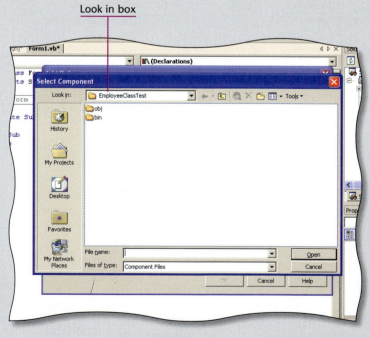

FIGURE 9-48

4. Use the Look in box to navigate to the A:\Chapter9\Compensation Review\Compensation Review\bin folder. If necessary, click the Compensation Review.dll component to select it.

The Select Component dialog box displays all files with the .dll extension. The CompensationReview.dll component that was created earlier in this chapter is selected (Figure 9-49).

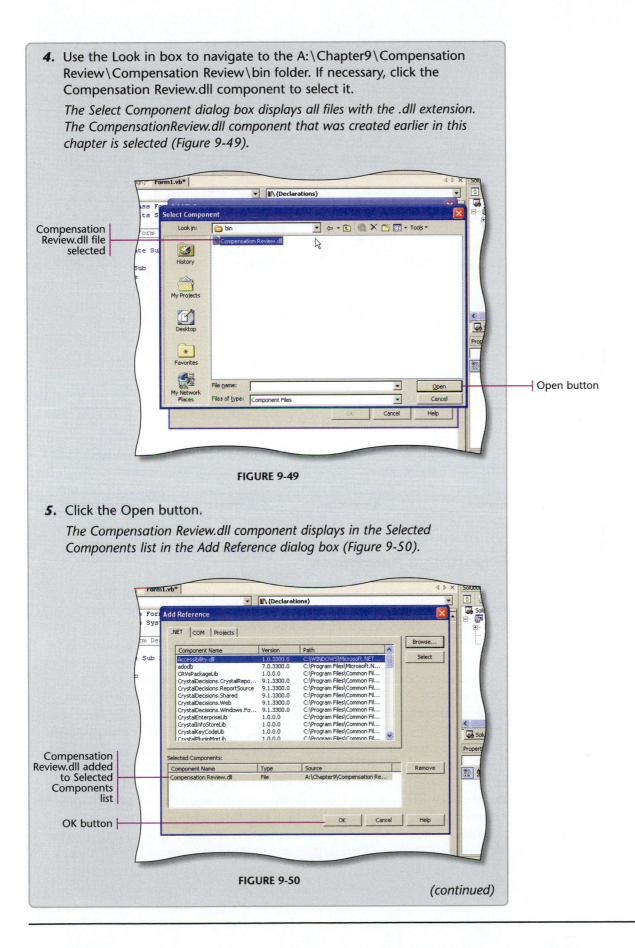

Compensation Review.dll file selected

Open button

FIGURE 9-49

5. Click the Open button.

The Compensation Review.dll component displays in the Selected Components list in the Add Reference dialog box (Figure 9-50).

Compensation Review.dll added to Selected Components list

OK button

FIGURE 9-50

(continued)

6. Click the OK button. If necessary, expand the References folder to view the references in the EmployeeClassTest project.

The Compensation Review class library displays in the References folder of the EmployeeClassTest project (Figure 9-51).

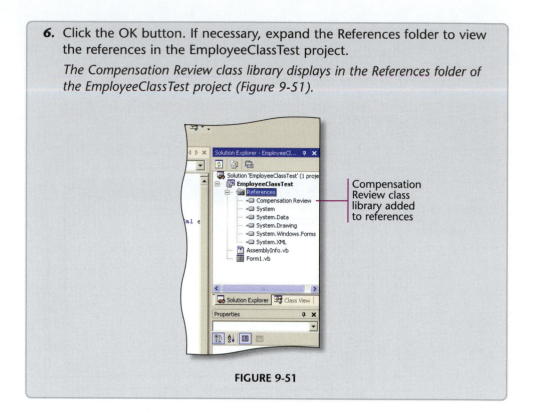

FIGURE 9-51

With the reference to the Compensation Review class library added, Visual Basic .NET allows the EmployeeClassTest application to access any of the classes within that class library. If the reference is not added, the EmployeeClassTest application has no way of knowing about the classes in the Compensation Review class library.

Importing a Namespace

For every project, Visual Basic .NET automatically sets a namespace. A **namespace**, also called a **root namespace**, provides a unique identifier for all entities in a project, such as classes. The namespace is used to qualify, or name, each entity. A project's namespace is displayed in the Property Pages for every Visual Basic .NET project (see Figure 6.69 on page VB 6.78 for an example).

The namespace set for the Compensation Review class library is Compensation_Review. If you want to use any classes in the Compensation Review class library in another project, you can reference any of the three classes using the Compensation_Review namespace. For example, the Employee class can be referenced in code as Compensation_Review.Employee.

Rather than using the namespace, Compensation_Review, before each reference to the Employee class and other classes, Visual Basic .NET provides a shortcut that allows you to eliminate the need for using the namespace when referencing those classes in code. The **Imports statement** provides this shortcut, allowing you to reference elements in a namespace without qualification. Any element in the imported namespace does not need the namespace identifier when it is referenced in code. For example, you can use the identifier Employee rather than Compensation_Review.Employee to reference the Employee class, if the namespace Compensation_Review is imported using the Imports statement.

Table 9-10 shows the general form of the Imports statement.

Table 9-10	Imports Statement
General Form:	1. Imports namespace 2. Imports alias = namespace 3. Imports namespace.element 4. Imports alias = namespace.element where the namespace is a valid namespace in the current project or in a reference in the current project and where element is a valid class or other entity in the namespace.
Purpose:	The Imports statement allows you to reference elements in a namespace without qualification. That is, elements, such as classes, in the imported namespace do not need the namespace identifier placed before the class name when referencing the class.
Example:	1. `Imports System` 2. `Imports mvbstr = System` 3. `Imports Microsoft.VisualBasic.Strings` 4. `Imports mvbstr = Microsoft.VisualBasic.Strings`
Notes:	1. Imports statements must appear after any Option statement. 2. Any number of Imports statements may be used. 3. Imports statements must be placed before any declarations, including class declarations, and before any references to variables or constants. 4. A reference to a class or class library used as the namespace in the Import statement must have been added to the project.

Figure 9-52 shows the Imports statement used to import the Compensation_Review namespace in the EmployeeClassTest application. By importing the Compensation_Review namespace, you can reference classes in the namespace, such as the Employee class, with only the class name.

```
1 Option Strict On
2 Imports Compensation_Review
```

FIGURE 9-52

The steps on the next page enter the code shown in Figure 9-52 to the Form1.vb form, in order to import the Compensation_Review namespace.

To Import a Namespace

1. Enter line 1 of the code as shown in Figure 9-52 on the previous page. Type the keyword, `Imports`, followed by a space.

The Option Strict On statement displays in line 1 in the code window. A list displays the available namespaces for the Imports statement, including the Compensation_Review namespace that represents the Compensation Review class library (Figure 9-53).

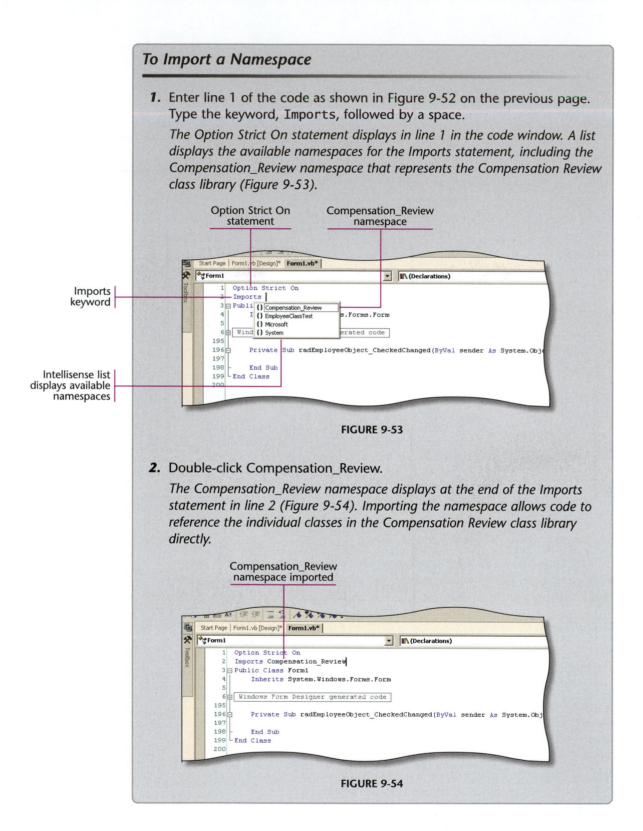

FIGURE 9-53

2. Double-click Compensation_Review.

The Compensation_Review namespace displays at the end of the Imports statement in line 2 (Figure 9-54). Importing the namespace allows code to reference the individual classes in the Compensation Review class library directly.

FIGURE 9-54

The three classes in the Compensation Review class library now are ready to be used in code in the same manner as you have used other classes in code throughout this book. The next step is to declare variables using the classes in the Compensation Review class library.

Creating an Object from a Class in Code

The EmployeeClassTest application includes three global variables, corresponding to the three classes in the Compensation Review class library. Each variable stores an instance of one of the classes. Figure 9-55 shows the code used to declare the three variables.

```
196        Private gobjEmployee As New Employee()
197        Private gobjHourlyEmployee As New HourlyEmployee()
198        Private gobjSalariedEmployee As New SalariedEmployee()
```

FIGURE 9-55

The following steps create three global object variables for the three classes in the Compensation Review class library.

To Create Objects from Classes

1. Type the first four words of line 196 as shown in Figure 9-55, followed by a space. If necessary, scroll the Intellisense list to the Employee keyword.

Intellisense displays a list of data types and classes. The Employee class is included in the list of available classes, because a reference was added to the Compensation Review class library and the Compensation_Review namespace was imported (Figure 9-56).

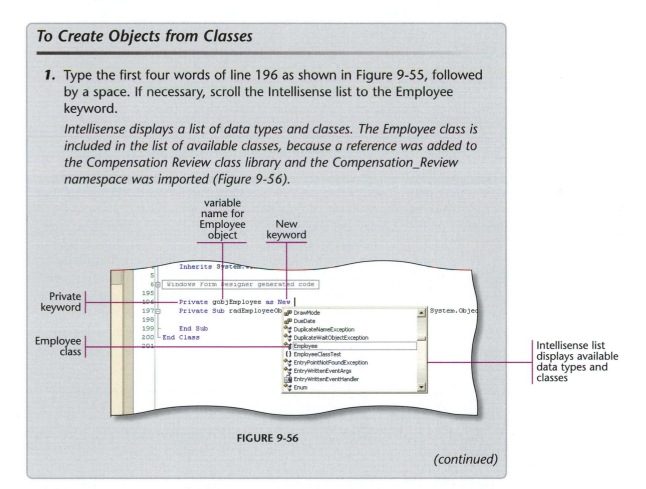

FIGURE 9-56

(continued)

2. Double-click Employee. Enter lines 197 and 198 as shown in Figure 9-55 on the previous page.

Lines 197 and 198 display in the general area of the Form1 form code in the code window (Figure 9-57).

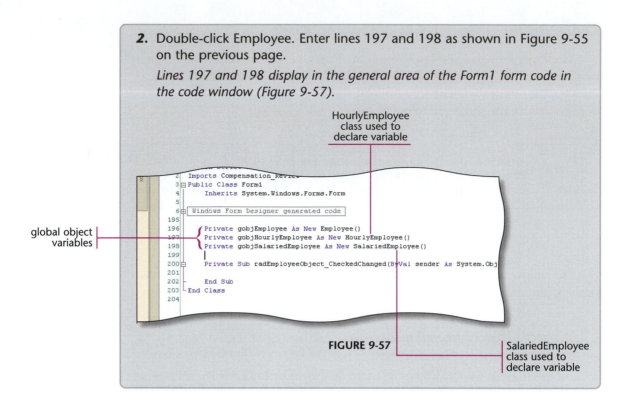

HourlyEmployee class used to declare variable

global object variables

```
 2   Imports Compensation_Rev
 3 ⊟ Public Class Form1
 4       Inherits System.Windows.Forms.Form
 5
 6 ⊞   Windows Form Designer generated code
195
196     Private gobjEmployee As New Employee()
197     Private gobjHourlyEmployee As New HourlyEmployee()
198     Private gobjSalariedEmployee As New SalariedEmployee()
199
200 ⊟   Private Sub radEmployeeObject_CheckedChanged(ByVal sender As System.Obj
201
202 ⊦     End Sub
203 └ End Class
204
```

FIGURE 9-57

SalariedEmployee class used to declare variable

As shown in Figure 9-56 on the previous page, the code used to declare a variable with a data type of a class is similar to the code used to declare any other variable. The Employee class displays in the Intellisense list in Figure 9-56 for two reasons. First, the Employee class is part of the Compensation Review class library that was added as a reference to the project. Adding the Compensation Review class library to the project allows the project to have access to the classes in the class library. Intellisense includes the capability to find the classes in the class library and display them in the list.

The second reason that the Employee class appears in the Intellisense list is that the Imports statement on line 2 allows the code in the Form1.vb file to reference the classes in the Compensation Review class library using only the class name, without the namespace. For example, if the Imports statement was eliminated from line 2, then the declaration of a variable of the type Employee would require the namespace of the class library to precede the class name. That is, the variable declaration would appear as follows:

```
Private gobjEmployee As New Compensation_Review.Employee()
```

if the Imports statement was omitted on line 2.

The three declared variables are of types that correspond to the three classes created in the Compensation Review class library developed earlier in this chapter. The methods and properties of these classes now may be accessed through these variables. The next step is to write the code that executes when the user selects one of three RadioButton controls.

Using Objects in Code to Get and Set Property Values

Throughout this book, the projects have used classes in the .NET Framework class library. Using the classes in the Compensation Review class library in code parallels the use of classes in the .NET Framework class library. Once a variable is declared as a type of class, the properties and methods of the class can be referenced in code by placing the name of the property or method after a period that follows the variable name. For example, you reference the Name property value of a variable declared as the Employee class with the code, gobjEmployee.Name.

Figure 9-58 shows the code for the CheckedChanged event procedure for each of the three RadioButton controls on the Form1 form. When the user clicks one of the RadioButton controls, the If statement in each event procedure determines if the RadioButton control is selected or checked. The code then updates the selected RadioButton control in the Properties group box with property values from the object corresponding to the RadioButton control that the user clicked. For example, in lines 212 and 213, the code updates the values displayed in the txtName and nudHourlyRate controls, if the user clicks the HourlyEmployee Object radio button on the form.

Finally, each CheckedChanged event procedure sets the ReadOnly property to True to disable the controls in the Properties group box, depending on which RadioButton control the user clicked. For example, lines 205 and 206 disable the nudHourlyRate and nudAnnualSalary controls when the user selects the Employee Object radio button, because the Employee object does not include either the HourlyRate or the AnnualSalary properties.

```
200     Private Sub radEmployeeObject_CheckedChanged(ByVal sender As System.Object, ByVal ⤶
        e As System.EventArgs) Handles radEmployeeObject.CheckedChanged
201         If radEmployeeObject.Checked Then
202             txtName.Text = gobjEmployee.Name
203             nudHourlyRate.Value = nudHourlyRate.Minimum
204             nudAnnualSalary.Value = nudAnnualSalary.Minimum
205             nudHourlyRate.ReadOnly = True
206             nudAnnualSalary.ReadOnly = True
207         End If
208     End Sub
209
210     Private Sub radHourlyEmployeeObject_CheckedChanged(ByVal sender As System.Object, ⤶
        ByVal e As System.EventArgs) Handles radHourlyEmployeeObject.CheckedChanged
211         If radHourlyEmployeeObject.Checked Then
212             txtName.Text = gobjHourlyEmployee.Name
213             nudHourlyRate.Value = gobjHourlyEmployee.HourlyRate
214             nudAnnualSalary.Value = nudAnnualSalary.Minimum
215             nudHourlyRate.ReadOnly = False
216             nudAnnualSalary.ReadOnly = True
217         End If
218     End Sub
219
220     Private Sub radSalariedEmployeeObject_CheckedChanged(ByVal sender As System.Object⤶
        , ByVal e As System.EventArgs) Handles radSalariedEmployeeObject.CheckedChanged
221         If radSalariedEmployeeObject.Checked Then
222             txtName.Text = gobjSalariedEmployee.Name
223             nudHourlyRate.Value = nudHourlyRate.Minimum
224             nudAnnualSalary.Value = gobjSalariedEmployee.AnnualSalary
225             nudHourlyRate.ReadOnly = True
226             nudAnnualSalary.ReadOnly = False
227         End If
228     End Sub
```

FIGURE 9-58

The following steps enter the code shown in Figure 9-58 on the previous page to the Form1 form.

To Get Property Values of an Object in Code

1. Enter lines 201 through 207 as shown in Figure 9-58.

2. Click the Form1.vb[Design]* tab in the main work area. Double-click the HourlyEmployee Object radio button on the Form1 form. When Visual Basic .NET creates the radHourlyEmployeeObject_CheckedChanged event procedure, enter lines 211 through 217 as shown in Figure 9-58.

3. Click the Form1.vb[Design]* tab in the main work area. Double-click the SalariedEmployee Object radio button on the Form1 form. When Visual Basic .NET creates the radSalariedEmployeeObject_CheckedChanged event procedure, enter lines 221 through 227 as shown in Figure 9-58.

The CheckedChanged event procedures for the RadioButton controls display in the code window as shown in Figure 9-59. Each event procedure gets property values for the corresponding object and then sets property values for the controls in the Properties GroupBox control.

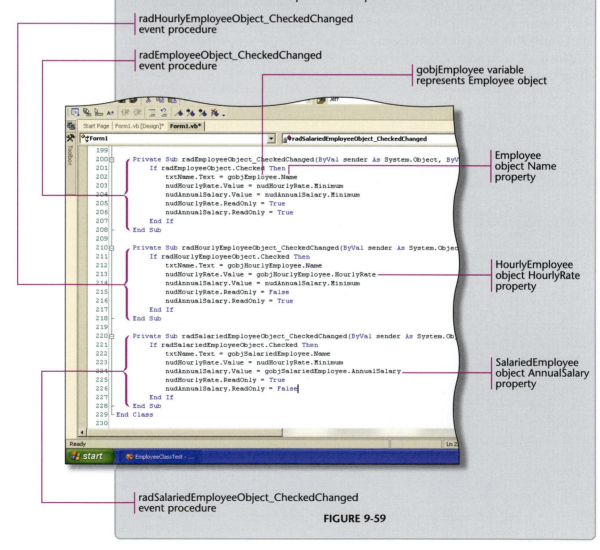

radHourlyEmployeeObject_CheckedChanged event procedure

radEmployeeObject_CheckedChanged event procedure

gobjEmployee variable represents Employee object

Employee object Name property

HourlyEmployee object HourlyRate property

SalariedEmployee object AnnualSalary property

radSalariedEmployeeObject_CheckedChanged event procedure

FIGURE 9-59

As shown in the previous steps, using classes created in Visual Basic .NET uses the same coding techniques as using any other class in the .NET Framework class library. The use of property values in lines 202, 212, and 222 in Figure 9-59 demonstrates the use of the Get() property methods coded earlier in this chapter. For example, when line 202 executes, Visual Basic .NET calls the Get() method of the Name property of the Employee class.

The next step is to code the btnSetProperties_Click event procedure so that the correct object's properties are updated when the user clicks the Set Properties button on the Form1 form.

In the EmployeeClassTest application, object properties must be updated depending on which object's RadioButton control is selected when the user clicks the Set Properties button. The properties of the three global variables always contain current property values while the program executes. Figure 9-60 shows the code necessary to accomplish this task. The code for the btnSetProperties_Click event procedure first uses a Select Case statement to determine which RadioButton control is selected by determining which Checked property value is set to True. Each of the three cases of the Select Case statement sets a value for one of the object's properties. For example, line 233 references the Name property of the gobjEmployeeObject with the code, gobjEmployeeObject.Name.

```
230     Private Sub btnSetProperties_Click(ByVal sender As System.Object, ByVal e As
        System.EventArgs) Handles btnSetProperties.Click
231         Select Case True
232             Case radEmployeeObject.Checked
233                 gobjEmployee.Name = txtName.Text
234             Case radHourlyEmployeeObject.Checked
235                 gobjHourlyEmployee.Name = txtName.Text
236                 gobjHourlyEmployee.HourlyRate = nudHourlyRate.Value
237             Case radSalariedEmployeeObject.Checked
238                 gobjSalariedEmployee.Name = txtName.Text
239                 gobjSalariedEmployee.AnnualSalary = nudAnnualSalary.Value
240         End Select
241     End Sub
```

FIGURE 9-60

The step on the next page enters the code shown in Figure 9-60 to create the btnSetProperties_Click event procedure that sets the property values of objects based on which RadioButton control is selected by the user when the Set Properties button is clicked.

To Set Property Values of an Object in Code

1. Click the Form1.vb[Design]* tab in the main work area. Double-click the Set Properties button on the Form1 form. When Visual Basic .NET creates the btnSetProperties_Click event procedure, enter lines 231 through 240 as shown in Figure 9-60 on the previous page.

The Select Case statement determines which RadioButton control that the user selected. Depending on which RadioButton control the user selected, the code sets a value for one of the corresponding object's properties, using values from the controls in the Properties GroupBox control (Figure 9-61).

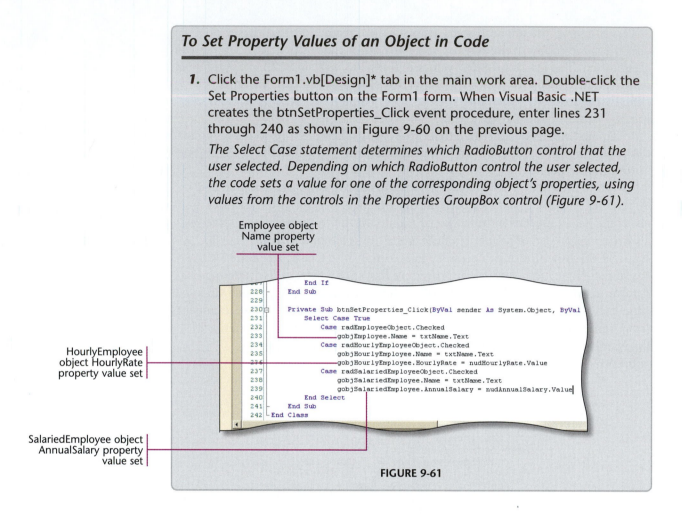

Employee object Name property value set

HourlyEmployee object HourlyRate property value set

SalariedEmployee object AnnualSalary property value set

```
                  End If
228   -    End Sub
229
230 □     Private Sub btnSetProperties_Click(ByVal sender As System.Object, ByVal
231            Select Case True
232                Case radEmployeeObject.Checked
233                    gobjEmployee.Name = txtName.Text
234                Case radHourlyEmployeeObject.Checked
235                    gobjHourlyEmployee.Name = txtName.Text
236                    gobjHourlyEmployee.HourlyRate = nudHourlyRate.Value
237                Case radSalariedEmployeeObject.Checked
238                    gobjSalariedEmployee.Name = txtName.Text
239                    gobjSalariedEmployee.AnnualSalary = nudAnnualSalary.Value
240            End Select
241   -    End Sub
242 └ End Class
```

FIGURE 9-61

As shown in Figure 9-61, the code in each case of the Select Case statement only sets the property values of the object corresponding to the currently selected RadioButton control. Each of the three objects has a Name property because the Employee class contains a Name property and the HourlyEmployee and SalariedEmployee classes inherit the Name property from the Employee class. The Employee class does not include a property for compensation, such as HourlyRate or AnnualSalary; therefore, none is set in the first case of the Select Case statement.

The coding phase for the EmployeeClassTest application now is complete and the application can be tested.

Saving, Testing, and Documenting the Project

The following steps save the form and project files for the EmployeeClassTest project on the Data Disk in drive A and then run the application to test the project.

To Save and Test the Project

1. Click the Save All button on the Standard toolbar.

The asterisks next to Form1.vb [Design] in the window title bar and the main work area tab no longer display, indicating that the project has been saved. Because the project initially was created and saved to the Data Disk in drive A, Visual Basic .NET automatically saves the project to the Data Disk in drive A.

2. Click the Start button on the Visual Basic .NET Standard toolbar. When the EmployeeClassTest application starts, minimize the Visual Basic .NET window. Type Sandy Grant in the Name text box in the EmployeeClassTest application window and then click the Set Properties button.

Visual Basic .NET opens the Output window temporarily and displays messages as the application starts. The EmployeeClassTest application window displays. The Employee Object radio button is selected and the name property for the Employee object is set to Sandy Grant (Figure 9-62).

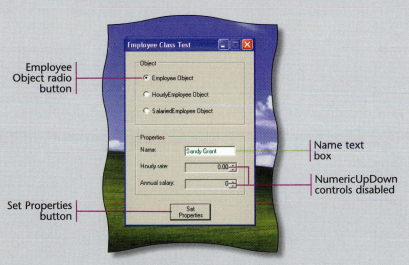

Employee Object radio button

Name text box

NumericUpDown controls disabled

Set Properties button

FIGURE 9-62

3. Click the HourlyEmployee Object radio button. Type Randolph Jefferson in the Name text box. Type 10.25 as the Hourly rate. Click the Set Properties button.

When the HourlyEmployee Object radio button is clicked, the controls in the Properties area are reset to their initial values of blank and zero, because no values have been set for the HourlyEmployee Object. The user then can type new values in the controls in the Properties area.

(continued)

4. Click the Employee Object radio button.

The value set for the Employee object's Name property in Step 2 again displays in the Properties area (Figure 9-63).

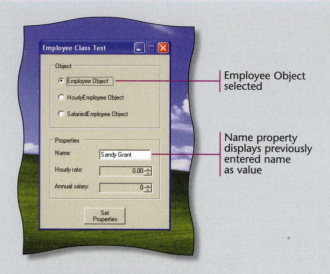

FIGURE 9-63

5. Type Emerson Grant in the Name box and click the Set Properties button.

The Name property of the Employee object is updated with the new value.

6. Click the SalariedEmployee Object radio button. Type Lisa Land as the Name and type 75,500 as the Annual salary. Click the Set Properties button.

The Annual salary NumericUpDown control is active. The new property values display in the controls in the Properties area (Figure 9-64).

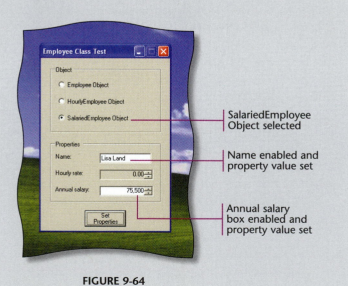

FIGURE 9-64

7. Continue changing the properties of the three objects and making certain that the proper values display as each radio button is selected, until you are satisfied that the application works as designed and you understand how the objects and properties relate to what is displayed on the screen. If necessary, use the debugging techniques introduced in Chapter 8 to examine the variables and objects in the code.

8. Click the Close button on the EmployeeClassTest application window title bar. If necessary, click the Visual Basic .NET taskbar button to display the Visual Basic .NET window. If necessary, close the Output window.

Visual Basic .NET returns to design time.

The tests demonstrate the instantiation of each of the three classes in the Compensation Review class library and the ability to set and get properties in all three classes. The EmployeeClassTest application functions as designed, allowing the user to retrieve and then modify property values for each of the three objects declared in the Form1.vb code. The values of the properties are retrieved each time the user clicks the corresponding radio button in the Object area.

The testing process for the EmployeeClassTest application and the Compensation Review class library is complete. The final step of the development cycle is to document the EmployeeClassTest application. The following steps document the EmployeeClassTest application and quit Visual Basic .NET. Line numbers are printed on the code listing.

To Document the Application and Quit Visual Basic .NET

1. If necessary, close the Output window. Click the Form1.vb [Design] tab, and then follow the steps on page VB 2.34 of Chapter 2 to use the PRINT SCREEN key to print a record of the user interface design of the Form1 form.

A record of the user interface design of the EmployeeClassTest application is printed.

2. Click the Form1.vb tab. Click File on the menu bar and then click Page Setup.

3. When the Page Setup dialog box displays, if necessary, click Line numbers and then click the OK button.

(continued)

4. Follow the steps on page VB 2.40 of Chapter 2 to use the Print command on the File menu to print a record of the code for the EmployeeClassTest application.

A record of the EmployeeClassTest application code is printed (Figure 9-65).

```
A:\Chapter9\EmployeeClassTest\EmployeeClassTest\Form1.vb                                          1

 1 Option Strict On
 2 Imports Compensation_Review
 3 Public Class Form1
 4     Inherits System.Windows.Forms.Form
 5
 6  Windows Form Designer generated code
 7
 8     Private gobjEmployee As New Employee()
 9     Private gobjHourlyEmployee As New HourlyEmployee()
10     Private gobjSalariedEmployee As New SalariedEmployee()
11
12     Private Sub radEmployeeObject_CheckedChanged(ByVal sender As System.Object, ByVal e↵
       As System.EventArgs) Handles radEmployeeObject.CheckedChanged
13         If radEmployeeObject.Checked Then
14             txtName.Text = gobjEmployee.Name
15             nudHourlyRate.Value = nudHourlyRate.Minimum
16             nudAnnualSalary.Value = nudAnnualSalary.Minimum
17             nudHourlyRate.ReadOnly = True
18             nudAnnualSalary.ReadOnly = True
19         End If
20     End Sub
21
22     Private Sub radHourlyEmployeeObject_CheckedChanged(ByVal sender As System.Object,  ↵
       ByVal e As System.EventArgs) Handles radHourlyEmployeeObject.CheckedChanged
23         If radHourlyEmployeeObject.Checked Then
24             txtName.Text = gobjHourlyEmployee.Name
25             nudHourlyRate.Value = gobjHourlyEmployee.HourlyRate
26             nudAnnualSalary.Value = nudAnnualSalary.Minimum
27             nudHourlyRate.ReadOnly = False
28             nudAnnualSalary.ReadOnly = True
29         End If
30     End Sub
31
32     Private Sub radSalariedEmployeeObject_CheckedChanged(ByVal sender As System.Object,↵
       ByVal e As System.EventArgs) Handles radSalariedEmployeeObject.CheckedChanged
33         If radSalariedEmployeeObject.Checked Then
34             txtName.Text = gobjSalariedEmployee.Name
35             nudHourlyRate.Value = nudHourlyRate.Minimum
36             nudAnnualSalary.Value = gobjSalariedEmployee.AnnualSalary
37             nudHourlyRate.ReadOnly = True
38             nudAnnualSalary.ReadOnly = False
39         End If
40     End Sub
41
42     Private Sub btnSetProperties_Click(ByVal sender As System.Object, ByVal e As System↵
       .EventArgs) Handles btnSetProperties.Click
43         Select Case True
44             Case radEmployeeObject.Checked
45                 gobjEmployee.Name = txtName.Text
46             Case radHourlyEmployeeObject.Checked
47                 gobjHourlyEmployee.Name = txtName.Text
48                 gobjHourlyEmployee.HourlyRate = nudHourlyRate.Value
49             Case radSalariedEmployeeObject.Checked
50                 gobjSalariedEmployee.Name = txtName.Text
51                 gobjSalariedEmployee.AnnualSalary = nudAnnualSalary.Value
52         End Select
53     End Sub
54 End Class
55
```

FIGURE 9-65

5. Click the Visual Basic .NET Close button.

If you made changes to the project since the last time it was saved, Visual Basic .NET displays the Microsoft Visual Basic .NET dialog box. If you click the Yes button, you can resave your project and quit. If you click the No button, you will quit without saving changes. Clicking the Cancel button will close the dialog box and not quit Visual Basic .NET.

Chapter Summary

In this chapter, you learned when to create classes to solve a problem and how to design classes using the UML. You learned how to create a new class library and then create a class and subclasses in the class library. You then learned how to create constructors, properties, and methods for classes, including creating a method to perform arithmetic operations on variables and properties of the Date data type. You learned how to inherit from base classes to create new subclasses. You also learned how to build a class to create a .DLL file. Finally, you learned how to use a class library in code and access the classes within the class library.

What You Should Know

Having completed this chapter, you should now be able to perform tasks shown in Table 9-11.

Table 9-11   Chapter 9 What You Should Know

TASK NUMBER	TASK	PAGE
1	Start Visual Basic .NET and Start a Class Library Project	VB 9.18
2	Declare Private Variables in a Class	VB 9.21
3	Create a Constructor for a Class	VB 9.25
4	Add a Property to a Class and Code a Get Property Procedure	VB 9.28
5	Code a Set Property Procedure	VB 9.31
6	Code the Remaining Properties	VB 9.33
7	Code a Method for a Class	VB 9.35
8	Add a Class to a Class Library	VB 9.39
9	Inherit from a Base Class	VB 9.42
10	Create a Private Variable for a Property in a Subclass	VB 9.43
11	Create a Constructor and a Property in a Subclass	VB 9.44
12	Create an Additional Subclass	VB 9.47
13	Build, Save, and Document the Class Library	VB 9.49
14	Start a New Project and Create the User Interface	VB 9.58
15	Add a Reference to a Class	VB 9.59
16	Import a Namespace	VB 9.64
17	Create Objects from Classes	VB 9.65
18	Get Property Values of an Object in Code	VB 9.68
19	Set Property Values of an Object in Code	VB 9.70
20	Save and Test the Project	VB 9.71
21	Document the Application and Quit Visual Basic .NET	VB 9.73

Key Terms

AddYears() method *(VB 9.34)*
aggregation *(VB 9.48)*
base class *(VB 9.06)*
class level scope *(VB 9.20)*
class library *(VB 9.17)*
Class Library project *(VB 9.17)*
Class statement *(VB 9.23)*
composition *(VB 9.48)*
constructor *(VB 9.23)*
derived class *(VB 9.36)*
descendant class *(VB 9.36)*
.DLL file *(VB 9.48)*
End Class keyword *(VB 9.23)*
Get statement *(VB 9.27)*
Get property procedure *(VB 9.27)*
implements *(VB 9.26)*
Imports statement *(VB 9.62)*
inherit *(VB 9.36)*
inheritance *(VB 9.36)*

Inherits statement *(VB 9.40)*
module *(VB 9.20)*
MyBase object *(VB 9.43)*
namespace *(VB 9.62)*
Nothing keyword *(VB 9.24)*
object diagram *(VB 9.52)*
Private keyword *(VB 9.20)*
private variable *(VB 9.20)*
Property statement *(VB 9.26)*
Protected keyword *(VB 9.27)*
Public keyword *(VB 9.20)*
public variable *(VB 9.20)*
read-only property *(VB 9.30)*
root namespace *(VB 9.62)*
Set statement *(VB 9.30)*
Set property procedure *(VB 9.27)*
stub *(VB 9.20)*
superclass *(VB 9.06)*
write-only property *(VB 9.27)*

Homework Assignments

Short Answer

1. Describe the situations in which the requirements of a program may lead you to design a class to help solve the problem.

2. Assume that the Employee class developed in this chapter is available to you. On paper, write the code for a class named Volunteer, which is a subclass of the Employee class, but does not include any additional properties or methods beyond those available in the Employee class.

3. Describe the purpose of a constructor and when constructors execute. Include a description of how constructors are called when subclasses are created, as they were in the code in this chapter.

4. Given the following class in Visual Basic .NET code, draw the associated high-level class diagram for the class.

```
Public Class DiseaseRisk
  Public Age As Integer
  Public Smoker as Boolean
  Public HighBloodPressure as Boolean
  Public Function Assessment() As String
    Return "Stub value"
  End Function
End Class
```

5. On paper, write the code for the property declarations and property procedures for each of the following situations:

   a. A property named LastVisit, which is a date. The property is available to any program implementing the class to which it belongs. The property only can be read and the property is stored in a private variable named dtmLastVisit.

   b. A property named HitCount, which is an integer. The property is available only to the class to which it belongs. The property can be read and updated. Updating the value adds 1 to the current property value, which is stored in a private variable named intHits.

   c. A property named Total, which is a decimal value. The property is available only to the class and any subclasses created from the class. The property only can be updated. Updating the value adds a passed value to the current value of the property, which is stored in a private variable named decTotal.

6. Assume that the classes developed in this chapter are available to you. A new class is needed for a StudentEmployee class. The StudentEmployee class is a subclass of the HourlyEmployee class and also includes two String properties for the student's school and instructor. On paper, write the code for the class declaration for the StudentEmployee class, variables to store the property values, and the constructor. Do not write the code for the properties.

7. Draw the high-level class diagram for the class library described in Homework Assignment 6. Include the Employee, HourlyEmployee, SalariedEmployee, and StudentEmployee classes.

8. Write the lines of code that would allow you to avoid coding all of the property procedures for the Employee class. Indicate which lines of code in this chapter could be eliminated or replaced by using these lines of code.

9. Write the code for a public, read-only property named Volume that accepts three arguments — Length, Width, and Height — as Integers and then returns an Integer value that is the result of multiplying all of the arguments together.

10. Describe the process of and reasoning for writing stubs for classes.

11. Explain how the Imports statement makes your code more readable and in what cases you can use the Imports statement.

12. Explain what happens when the MyBase.New() statement executes. Explain why the use of the MyBase.New() statement is optional in the program developed in this chapter.

13. Use the _____ keyword before the class name to declare a new class. If the class is based on another class, use the _____ keyword in the first statement of the class to indicate this. All classes end with the _____ keyword.

14. A property that should be available only to its class should be declared with the _____ keyword. A property that should be available only to both its class and any subclasses created from the class should be declared with the _____ keyword. A property that should be made generally available should be declared with the _____ keyword.

(continued)

Short Answer *(continued)*

15. A read-only class only requires a _____ property procedure. A write-only class only requires a _____ property procedure.

16. Building a class library results in a file with a _____ extension. The file should be added as a _____ to any other programs that wish to use classes in the class library. Any namespaces in the class library should be _____ in order to make access to its classes more readable in code.

Learn It Online

Start your browser and visit scsite.com/vbnet/exs. Follow the instructions in the exercises below.

1. **Chapter Reinforcement TF, MC, and SA** Click the True/False, Multiple Choice, and Short Answer link below Chapter 9. Print and then answer the questions.

2. **Practice Test** Click the Practice Test link below Chapter 9. Answer each question, enter your first and last name at the bottom of the page, and then click the Grade Test button. When the graded practice test displays on your screen, click Print on the File menu to print a hard copy. Continue to take practice tests until you score 80% or better. Hand in a printout of the final practice test.

3. **Crossword Puzzle Challenge** Click the Crossword Puzzle Challenge link below Chapter 9. Read the instructions, and then enter your first and last name. Click the Play button. Complete the crossword puzzle. When you are finished, click the Submit button. When the crossword puzzle redisplays, click the Print button.

4. **Tips and Tricks** Click the Tips and Tricks link below Chapter 9. Click a topic that pertains to Chapter 9. Right-click the information and then click Print on the shortcut menu. Construct a brief example of what the information relates to in Visual Basic .NET to confirm you understand how to use the tip or trick. Hand in the example and printed information.

5. **Newsgroups** Click the Newsgroups link below Chapter 9. Click a topic that pertains to Chapter 9. Print three comments.

6. **Expanding Your Horizons** Click the Articles for Visual Basic .NET below Chapter 9. Click a topic that pertains to Chapter 9. Print the information. Construct a brief example of what the information relates to in Visual Basic .NET to confirm you understand the contents of the article. Hand in the example and printed information.

7. **Search Sleuth** Select three key terms from the Key Terms section of this chapter and then use the Google search engine at google.com (or any major search engine) to display and print two Web pages for each key term.

Note: If you plan to complete the project and all the exercises in this chapter, it is recommended that you use a hard disk or Zip disk for your solutions, because they will not all fit on a floppy disk.

Debugging Assignment

Start Visual Basic .NET and open the Burgers solution from the Chapter9\
Burgers\Burgers folder on the Data Disk. The solution consists of two projects:
the Burger Class Library project and the BurgerBuilder Windows Application
project. The Burger class library includes three classes: a base class and two
subclasses. The BurgerBuilder Windows application is used as a unit test
program to test the classes in the Burger class library.

The classes in the Burger class library and the BurgerBuilder Windows application
(Figure 9-66) contain bugs in the code. Run the BurgerBuilder Windows
application to experience some of the problems listed in the steps below. Follow
the steps to debug the project.

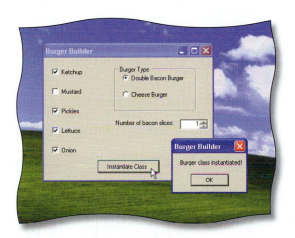

FIGURE 9-66

1. Review the code for the Burger class library. The GetCondimentList()
method of the Burger class is not accessible to programs that use the Burger
class and its subclasses. Fix this error by modifying the declaration of the
method.

2. The constructors of the subclasses do not initialize the properties inherited
from the base class correctly. Add a line of code to the beginning of each
subclass's constructor to fix this error.

3. The NumberofBaconSlices property of the DoubleBaconBurger class is read-
only. The users of this class also must be able to set this property. Add this
functionality to the class.

4. The CheeseBurger class inherits from the wrong class. The design of the class
indicates that this class should inherit from the Burger class. Fix this error in
the code.

(continued)

Debugging Assignment *(continued)*

5. Review the code for the BurgerBuilder Windows application, which is the second project in the solution. The BurgerBuilder Windows application, which should allow you to test the Burger class library, does not access the class library properly. The project requires a reference to the Burger class library. In order to shorten the names used in the code to access the classes in the class library, the program requires an Imports statement. Correct these two deficiencies in the BurgerBuilder application.

6. The BurgerBuilder Windows application does not access at least one of the properties and one of the methods in the classes correctly. Use Intellisense to correct these mistakes, which can be found in the Task List window.

7. Save the projects and then run the Windows application to test for any additional bugs. The BurgerBuilder Windows application should display as shown in Figure 9-66 on the previous page.

8. Document the three classes in the Burger class library and the form code for the BurgerBuilder Windows application. On the code printout, circle the lines of code you modified.

Programming Assignments

1 Creating a Base Class and Subclasses

Using the following steps, design and develop a program that illustrates the concepts of classes and subclasses.

1. Use the Class Library template to start a new project in Visual Basic .NET. Create the solution on the Data Disk in a new folder named A:\Chapter9\CheckingAccount.

2. Rename the Class1.vb module to CheckingAccount.vb. Open the module in the main work area and change the name of the class to CheckingAccount. Add the Option Strict On statement as line 1 in the module.

3. Declare four private variables to store the values of the properties in the class. The properties are as follows: FirstName as String, LastName as String, AccountNumber as Integer, and Balance as Decimal.

4. Create a constructor for the CheckingAccount class that initializes property values to set the FirstName and LastName to blank and the AccountNumber and Balance to zero.

5. Create Get and Set property procedures for the FirstName, LastName, and AccountNumber properties. Create only a Get property procedure for the Balance property.

6. Create two methods for the class. The first method, Deposit(), should accept a decimal value as the amount to deposit. The method should update the Balance property value. The second method, WriteCheck(), should accept a decimal value as the amount of a check. The WriteCheck() method should be of type Boolean and should update the Balance property value only if the amount of the check does not cause the Balance to go below zero. If the

amount of the check would cause the balance to go below zero, return False as the value of the method. Otherwise, update the Balance property value and return True as the value of the method.

7. Add a new module that will contain a second class, which is a subclass of the CheckingAccount class. Name the module BasicChecking.vb and name the class in the module BasicChecking. Inherit from the CheckingAccount class to create the subclass. Add a read-only property named MaxChecks as an Integer and initialize the value to 10.

8. Add a new module that will contain a third class, which is a subclass of the CheckingAccount class. Name the module TotalChecking.vb and name the class in the module TotalChecking. Inherit from the CheckingAccount class to create the subclass. Add a read-only property named MonthlyFee as a Decimal and initialize the value to 8.50. Add a second property named InternetEnabled as a Boolean data type. Allow the user of the class to both set and get the property value of the InternetEnabled property. Change the namespace of the class to CheckingAccount. Build the class library using the Build command.

9. In the same solution, start a new Visual Basic .NET project to create a Windows application to use as a unit test program. Name the project CheckingAccountClassTest. Create the user interface as shown in Figure 9-67 to provide controls that allow the user to update all values of three different global object variables stored in the form. The Account number ranges from 0 to 100. The deposit and check amounts range from 0 to 10000. The InternetEnabled CheckBox control is enabled only when the TotalChecking Object RadioButton is selected, or checked. Add a reference to the CheckingAccount class library. Import the namespace of the class library. Declare one global variable of each class in the class library. Create event procedures for the two RadioButton controls so that the corresponding object's properties display in the Properties GroupBox control when changed. Write event procedures for the Make Deposit and Write Check buttons so that they update appropriate object properties when clicked. Be sure to disable any controls that should not allow updates depending on the selection made in the Object GroupBox control. Write an event procedure for the Set Properties button that updates the properties of the object selected in the Object GroupBox control.

10. Run the CheckingAccountClassTest application and correct any errors. If changes have been made, save the projects again. During run time, the CheckingAccountClassTest application window should display as shown in Figure 9-67.

11. Document the code for both projects and the user interface for the unit test program.

FIGURE 9-67

2 Creating a Class

Create a class library named Chairs based on the class diagram shown in Figure 9-68.

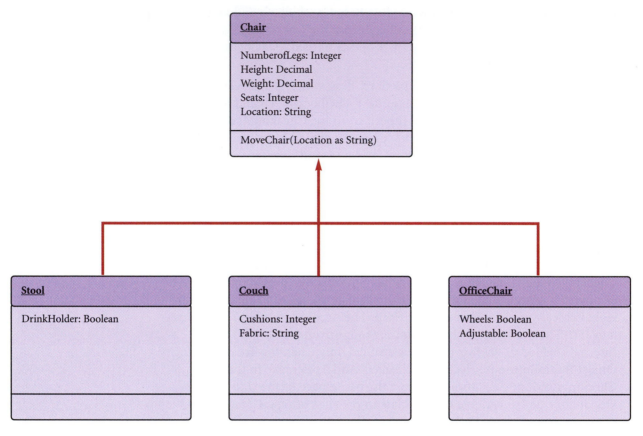

FIGURE 9-68

The constructor of the Couch subclass accepts a parameter for the number of people who can sit on the couch. The parameter should be used to initialize the Seats property value. When creating a Couch object in another program, the number of seats should be passed as a parameter as follows:

```
Dim MyCouch As New Couch(3)
```

The constructors of the Stool and OfficeChair classes should initialize the Seats property value to 1. The Chair constructor should initialize the Seats property value to 0.

The Location property is read-only. The MoveChair() method accepts a string as a new location for the chair and updates the Location property value.

Build the class library and then create a Windows application in the same solution to use as a unit test program for the class library. The user interface for the application should operate in much the same manner as the EmployeeClassTest application developed in this chapter and have an Object area and a Properties area on the form. The Properties area should include controls to display the property values for the selected object. (Use a GroupBox containing groups of RadioButton controls for properties that are of the Boolean data type.) If the property is not in use for the object selected, disable the appropriate control. Make sure that the user can update all of the properties of the objects, except for the read-only Location property. Add a Move Chair button and a TextBox control to the user interface that allow the user to input a location and then click the Move Chair button to execute the MoveChair() method of whichever object is selected.

3 Collections in a Class

Create a class library that contains one class named Scores, which is a class containing a collection of test scores. Properties of the class include a collection that stores the sum of all of the scores, the average score, the minimum score, the maximum score, and the number of scores. The class diagram of the Scores class is shown below. The – signs preceding the properties indicate that the properties are private. The + symbols preceding the properties and methods indicate that they are public.

<table>
<tr><td><u>Scores</u></td></tr>
<tr><td>–ScoreCollection: Collection
+Sum: Integer
+Average: Decimal
+Minimum: Integer
+Maximum: Integer
+NumberofScores: Integer</td></tr>
<tr><td>+AddScore(NewScore as Integer)</td></tr>
</table>

Declare the ScoreCollection variable as a private, class level variable in the class. The AddScore method accepts an integer value and then adds the value as a new item in the ScoreCollection collection. The Sum, Average, Minimum, Maximum, and NumberofScores properties are read-only properties of the class.

Build the class library and then develop a Windows application in the same solution to serve as a unit test program for the class. Allow the user to input scores using a NumericUpDown control. Include an Add Score button and buttons that cause a message box to display each of the public properties of the class.

4 Using Aggregation to Create a New Class

Create a new class library and add a class named Point that consists of two Integer properties: X and Y. Create appropriate Get and Set property procedures for the properties. The Set property procedure should allow only values from 0 through 100. If an attempt is made to set the value lower than 0, then the value should be set to 0. If an attempt is made to set the value higher than 100, then the value should be set to 100.

Create a second class named Line. The Line class should be composed of two properties named Point1 and Point2, both with the data type of Point. The Line class should include one method, named ComputeSlope(), which performs a

(continued)

4 Using Aggregation to Create a New Class *(continued)*

calculation that determines the slope of the line created by the two points in the class. Draw class diagrams for the two classes. Draw object diagrams for the classes, in which a Line named MyLine has an X1 value of 1, a Y1 value of 2, a X2 value of 12, and a Y2 value of 64. When drawing the object diagram, take into consideration that the MyLine object aggregates, or is composed of, two Point objects.

Build the class library and then create a Windows application in the same solution that acts as a unit test program for the classes. The program allows the user to use NumericUpDown controls to modify the X and Y values of each of the two points in the line. A Button control should call the ComputeSlope() method to find the slope and then allow the user to display the slope of the line. To set the properties of the points in code, use code such as the following:

```
MyLine.Point1.X = 1
MyLine.Point1.Y = 2
```

5 More Class Aggregation

Using the solution created in Programming Assignment 4, create a third class named Triangle. The Triangle class should consist of three properties of the data type Point. Create a ComputeArea() method that computes the area of the triangle described by the three points in the Triangle class. Given three points — (X1, Y1), (X2, Y2), and (X3, Y3) — the area of the triangle formed by the three points is computed using the formula:

$$\frac{1}{2}\left((X2 - X1)(Y3 - Y1) - (Y2 - Y1)(X3 - X1)\right)$$

Build the class library and then create a unit test program similar to that created in Programming Assignment 4, but allow the user to enter the values for three points. A button on the form should call the ComputeArea() method to compute the area of the triangle.

6 Volume Computations Class Library

Create a class library named VolumeComputations that contains four classes, each corresponding to one of the volume computations discussed in Programming Assignment 8 on page VB 5.74. Name each class appropriately, based on the type of object that the class describes. Use properties for the length, width, height, and radius of the objects. For each class, include a public method named Volume() that returns a decimal value for the volume of the object. Build the class into a .DLL file for use by other applications.

In the same solution, create a Windows application named Volume Computation to use as a unit test program to test the class library created above. The user interface should operate as described in Programming Assignment 8 on page VB 5.74. However, the calculations should be performed using the class library.

10

Accessing Databases with ADO.NET, Handling Exceptions, and Printing

Objectives

You will have
mastered the material in
this chapter when you can:

- Use the MonthCalendar control in an application
- Use the PrintDialog control in an application
- Use the PrintDocument control in an application
- Write code in a class
- Understand database connections
- Write code to connect to a database
- Understand how the CLR handles exceptions during run time
- Code a Try…Catch…Finally statement to handle exceptions
- Read records from a database
- Understand the role of SQL in interacting with a database
- Use simple SQL SELECT statements to query a database
- Understand the functionality and major components of Crystal Reports

Introduction

This chapter concentrates on developing the Windows application used to create the Compensation Review report, as shown in Figure 10-1. This Windows application allows users to choose the start date for the report on a calendar. After the user selects a date on the calendar, clicks the appropriate option button, and then clicks the Print Compensation Review Report button, a Print dialog box is displayed to allow the user to select printer options. Finally, the application reads records from the Compensation Review database, determines which records to print, and then prints the records on the report.

In this chapter, you will learn how to develop an application that connects to a database and reads records from a database. You will learn how to write code for a class and how to use a Visual Basic .NET class to access a database. You also will learn how to use controls that display a calendar in the application window and allow the user to print information. This chapter presents the concept of testing for exceptions that occur during run time and writing code to handle these exceptions, such as those that occur if a database is not accessible when an application needs to read records from it. Finally, this chapter presents an overview of the Crystal Reports software used to design, display, and print reports in Visual Basic .NET.

Chapter Ten — Creating the Compensation Review Report Application

The Windows application developed in this chapter is the Compensation Review Report application (Figure 10-1), which managers will use to print a Compensation Review report listing those employees who require a compensation review one month (30 days) from a given date. The Compensation Review Report application uses a new class, called the Employees class, in addition to .NET Framework classes that encapsulate the operations of connecting to and reading records from the Compensation Review database (Figure 10-1c). To generate a report (Figure 10-1e), the manager first uses a MonthCalendar control to select the start date for the report (Figure 10-1a). The manager then clicks the Not yet reviewed option button to indicate that the report should include the records for employees who have not yet been reviewed. The manager then clicks the Print Compensation Review Report button, which causes the PrintDialog common dialog control to display a standard Windows Print dialog box (Figure 10-1b). After the manager clicks the Print button in the dialog box, the Compensation Review report (Figure 10-1e) prints to the printer selected in the Print dialog box (Figure 10-1b). The control that prints the document is the PrintDocument control, which does not display on the form.

When the manager clicks the Print Compensation Review Report button, the Compensation Review Report application instantiates an instance of a new class, called the Employees class (Figure 10-1d), which includes collections of HourlyEmployee and SalariedEmployee objects. The Compensation Review Report application uses the Employees class (Figure 10-1d) to determine which employee records to print on the report. The date selected by the manager sets the start date for a one-month (30-day) window of time that the application

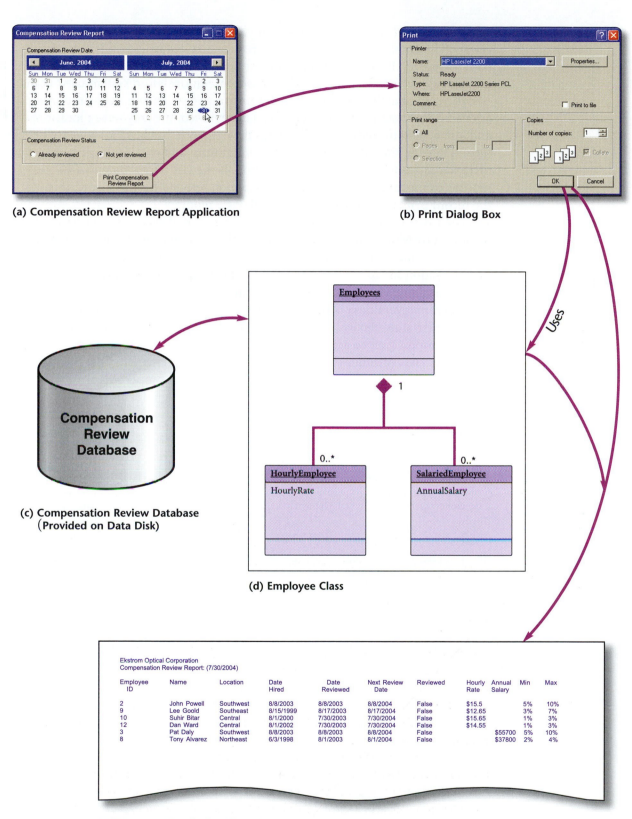

(a) Compensation Review Report Application

(b) Print Dialog Box

(c) Compensation Review Database
(Provided on Data Disk)

(d) Employee Class

(e) Compensation Review Report

FIGURE 10-1

uses to determine if employees have not yet been reviewed and thus are due for review. The employee information is stored in the Compensation Review database (Figure 10-1c) that is supplied on the Data Disk. The source of the information in the database is assumed to be another information system used in the company. The database includes one table with a record listing each employee's ID, name, location, date hired, and date last reviewed, the employee's location, and a review status indicator of whether the employee has been reviewed. The second table in the database includes the minimum and maximum percentage increases in compensation for each location. If the last review date was 12 months or more prior to the one-month period selected for the report, then the record prints on the Compensation Review report.

The Compensation Review report created in this chapter allows managers to determine which employees to review in the next 30 days. After reviewing the report and completing the employee review, the manager will use the Compensation Review Update Web page to be developed in Chapter 11 to update each employee's salary or hourly rate.

The Employees class developed in this chapter is added as the fourth class in the Compensation Review class library developed in Chapter 9. The Employees class is composed of, or aggregated from, other existing classes. In particular, the Employees class includes two properties that are collections. The first property is a collection of HourlyEmployee objects and the second property is a collection of SalariedEmployee objects. The collections include the information for those employees who are due for a review and thus should have their employee records printed on the Compensation Review report.

Program Development

The development cycle for the Employees class and the Compensation Review Report application consists of tasks that correspond to the six development cycle phases, as shown in Table 10-1. The Compensation Review Report application is the first end-user application developed for the Ekstrom Optics Compensation Review System.

Table 10-1 Employees Class and Compensation Review Report Application Development Tasks

DEVELOPMENT PHASE	TASK NUMBER	TASK NAME	TASK
Analyze requirements	1	Analyze problem	Analyze the Compensation Review Report problem.
Design solution	2	Design classes	Design the Employees class used in the Compensation Review Report application and other applications developed in subsequent chapters.
	3	Design interface and program	Design the user interface for the Compensation Review Report application, including input areas, report layout, and form controls. Design the logic and write pseudocode for the program.
Validate design	4	Validate design	Prove that the solution produces correct results for the Compensation Review report.
Implement design	5	Write code for classes	Write code to implement the design of the Employees class.
	6	Write code and develop interface for program	Write code for the Compensation Review Report application and add user interface elements, such as input areas, output areas, and controls on a form. Write the code to add event procedures and use the Employees class to create the Compensation Review report.
Test solution	7	Test program	Test the Compensation Review Report application and the Employees class.
	8	Debug classes and program	Fix any problems with the Compensation Review Report application and the Employees class.
Document solution	9	Document classes and program	Print the code for the Employees class. Print the Compensation Review Report application's form and code.

Analysis and Design

Figure 10-2 on the next page shows the requirements document that initiates the development cycle for the Compensation Review Report application.

REQUEST FOR NEW APPLICATION

Date submitted:	January 25, 2004
Submitted by:	Samantha O'Conner
Purpose:	The human resources department requires a Compensation Review Report application as part of the Compensation Review System. Managers will use the application to generate a Compensation Review report to decide which employees require a compensation review within a month of a given date.
Application title:	Compensation Review Report
Algorithms:	The company has an existing Compensation Review database that is available for use by the Compensation Review Report application. When the user chooses to print the report, employee records from the database should print on the report if their last review date plus one year is within the 30 days following the date selected by the user.
Notes:	1) The Compensation Review database provided is a sample database containing a partial list of Employees. The database is a Microsoft Access database on the enclosed Data Disk and is named Compensation Review.mdb.
	2) The user interface should allow the user to select a date for which to run the report. The selected date should be used as the start date for the one-month (30-day) window of time that is used to determine if employees have not yet been reviewed and thus are due for review. Employees needing review within that 30-day range should print on the Compensation Review report.
	3) The minimum date allowed should be January 1, 2004. The maximum date allowed should be December 31, 2010.
	4) By default, the report should print those employees in need of a review. The report also should allow the option of printing employees who already have been reviewed.
	5) A report header should include the name of the report and the date selected by the user. Column headers should print for each field in the Employees table of the database. Additionally, a column is needed to print the next review date for each employee.
	6) The report should list hourly employees first, followed by salaried employees.
	7) A sample report layout also is attached. Note that employee information for each record is included on one line.

Approvals

Approval Status:	X	Approved
		Rejected
Approved by:	Jonathan Ingram	
Date:	February 1, 2004	
Assigned to:	J. Quasney, Programmer	

FIGURE 10-2

PROBLEM ANALYSIS The problem that the Compensation Review Report application must solve is to print a report listing employees in need of a compensation review within one month of a given date. The application also must be capable of printing a report listing those employees who already have been reviewed within one month of a given date. The user interface of the application must provide a way for the user to (1) enter a date and (2) choose whether to print a report listing employees not yet reviewed or employees already reviewed.

The requirements document shown in Figure 10-2 states that the application must format the Compensation Review report in a certain manner. Although the sample report layout provided with the requirements document is not shown here, the requirements document notes that the report header should include the report name and the date selected by the user. For each employee record printed in the report, several items of information, including the next review date, should print on one line. The report also should include a column header for each item of information. Finally, the report should list all hourly employees first, followed by all salaried employees.

The process of requesting information from a database based on certain criteria is called a **query**. In the Compensation Review Report application, the query retrieves a list of employees needing review or a list of those who already have been reviewed. This same query also is used in the applications developed later in this chapter and in Chapter 11 to retrieve employee information from the Compensation Review database.

As you learned in Chapter 9, when several programs require similar functionality, an object-oriented approach to the solution should be considered in the design of the solution. The duplicate requirements for the functionality provided by the query suggest that creating a new class to encapsulate the functionality of retrieving information from the database could ease the programming requirements for the other applications. Each program that requires the functionality can make use of the class.

INTERFACE DESIGN   The interface for the Compensation Review report requires one form. The user interface needs an element to allow the user to select a date for which to run the report. The interface also must allow the user to choose which report type to print.

Figure 10-3 shows a storyboard that outlines the interface requirements for the Compensation Review Report application. The Compensation Review Report window, which is displayed when the application runs, includes a calendar that allows the user to navigate to and select a date. A **MonthCalendar control** is used to display the calendar and allow the user to select a date. Properties of the MonthCalendar control can be set to limit the values that the user can select, based on the limitations specified in note 3 in the requirements document. The MonthCalendar control is contained by a GroupBox control that is used to label and separate the calendar from other controls. A second GroupBox control includes two RadioButton controls that correspond to the two types of reports that the user can choose. A Button control initiates the printing of the report, which is based on the date selected in the MonthCalendar control and the report type selected in the RadioButton controls. If the user selects the Already reviewed RadioButton, then the report prints only those employees who have been reviewed by the manager for the selected period.

As shown in Figure 10-3 on the next page, when the user clicks the Print Compensation Review Report button, the Print dialog box is displayed. The Print dialog box displays using a common dialog control called the **PrintDialog control**. The Print dialog box allows the user to select a printer and configure options for the selected printer. After the user clicks the OK button on the Print dialog box, the report prints.

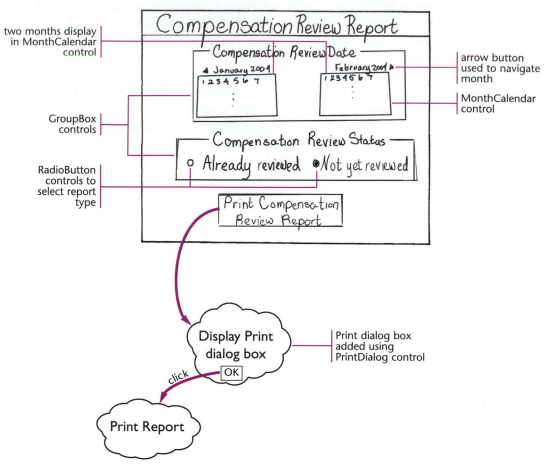

FIGURE 10-3

PROGRAM DESIGN The three classes designed and coded in Chapter 9 — the Employee class, the HourlyEmployee class, and the SalariedEmployee class — did not include any code for accessing the data in the Compensation Review database. A new class named Employees will perform the task of retrieving employee records from the Compensation Review database for the applications developed in this chapter and the next two chapters. As discussed in Chapter 9, you could code the database access logic directly in the Compensation Review Report application and then copy the code to each program that needs this functionality, but that approach has many drawbacks.

The first reason for creating the Employees class to encapsulate the database access logic is that other applications can reuse the logic if the logic is coded in a class. Using object-oriented design and programming, a developer can create the new Employees class to encapsulate the functionality of retrieving information from the database. The other applications then can use the Employees class to provide that functionality.

Second, a good design and coding practice is to separate all of the code that defines business logic, including database access, from the user interface code. This practice allows other programmers using different interface design tools to reuse the components of an application that encapsulate the business logic. For example, the database access code included in the Employees class can be used in both the Compensation Review Report Windows application developed in this chapter and the Compensation Review Update Web page developed in Chapter 11. The separation of the business logic from the user interface also allows project managers to divide tasks among different developers or groups of developers more easily.

Separating Business Logic and the User Interface
When designing applications in which business logic may be reused, separate the functionality of the business logic from the user interface code by placing the business logic in classes.

The Employees class will be added as the fourth class to the Compensation Review class library. The other three classes, developed in Chapter 9, are the Employee, HourlyEmployee, and SalariedEmployee classes. Figure 10-4 shows the high-level class diagram for the Employees class. The class **exposes**, or makes available, two public properties for use by other programs. The first property is a collection of HourlyEmployee objects and the second property is a collection of SalariedEmployee objects. The two boxes below the Employees class represent the collections. The filled diamond symbol indicates that the Employees class is composed of HourlyEmployee and SalariedEmployee objects. The 0..* implies that the collections in the Employees class must include zero or more HourlyEmployee and SalariedEmployee objects. The employees represented in the two collections in the Employees class are those who meet the criteria selected by the user in the Compensation Review Report application. For example, if the user sets the report date as 9/1/2004 and selects the Not yet reviewed RadioButton control, any hourly or salaried employees eligible for review during that month will be represented in the HourlyEmployee and SalariedEmployee objects that compose the Employees class.

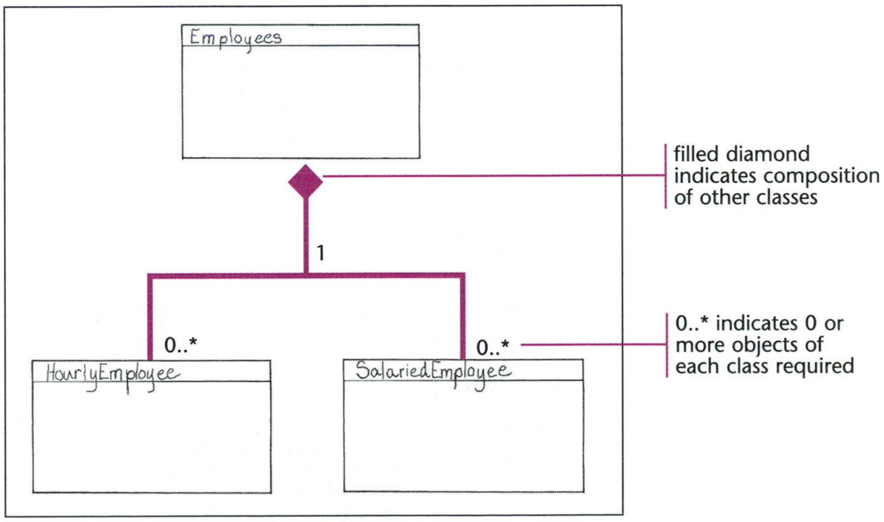

The constructor of the Employees class accepts two parameters. Recall that the constructor is a procedure named New() that executes when an object of the class type is instantiated. The first parameter, ReviewDate, is the date the user selects in the MonthCalendar control. The second, ReportType, is a Boolean variable that determines whether to select employees who have or have not been reviewed, based on the RadioButton control selected by the user.

FIGURE 10-4

filled diamond indicates composition of other classes

0..* indicates 0 or more objects of each class required

Figure 10-5 shows two flowcharts that represent the key logic in the Employees class and Compensation Review Report application. Figure 10-5a represents the logic for the constructor of the Employees class. In general, when accessing data in a database, a program first must locate and connect to the database. The program also must create a data reader object using a class in the .NET Framework class library that connects to the database and performs a query and returns information from the database. Next, the program performs operations, such as reading the data, on the data. Finally, the program closes the data reader object. The constructor of the Employees class opens the Compensation Review database and then sends a command to the database to read the records for hourly employees. The database returns a set of records that the constructor reads in a loop. The fields in each record correspond to a property of the HourlyEmployee class; the values in these fields are used to set the property

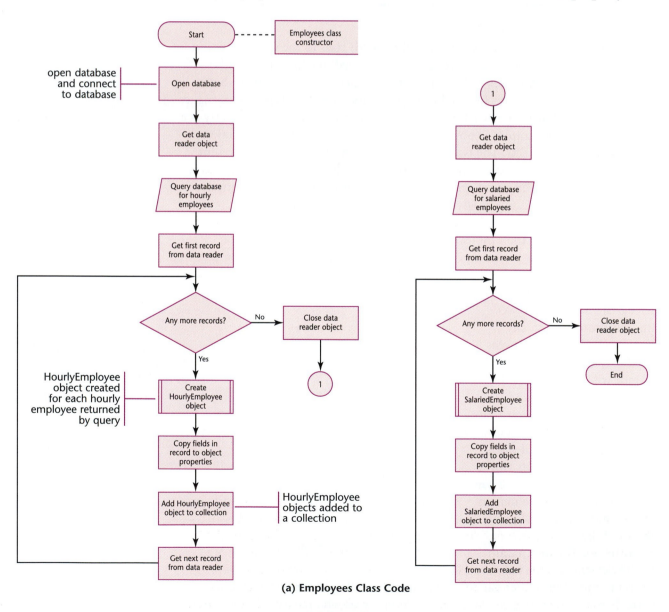

(a) Employees Class Code

FIGURE 10-5

values of a new HourlyEmployee object. Next, the same process is repeated for salaried employees. The result is that two properties are initialized for the Employees class and both properties are collections of employees that must print on the report.

Figure 10-5b represents the logic for the Compensation Review Report application. When the user clicks the Print Compensation Review Report button, the input values from the MonthCalendar control and RadioButton controls are passed to the constructor of the Employees class, resulting in a new Employees object. When the Employees object is created, the logic for the constructor of the Employees class shown in Figure 10-5a executes. The application then creates a report header, followed by the report body, which includes one line for each hourly employee, followed by one line for each salaried employee. Finally, the application prints the report.

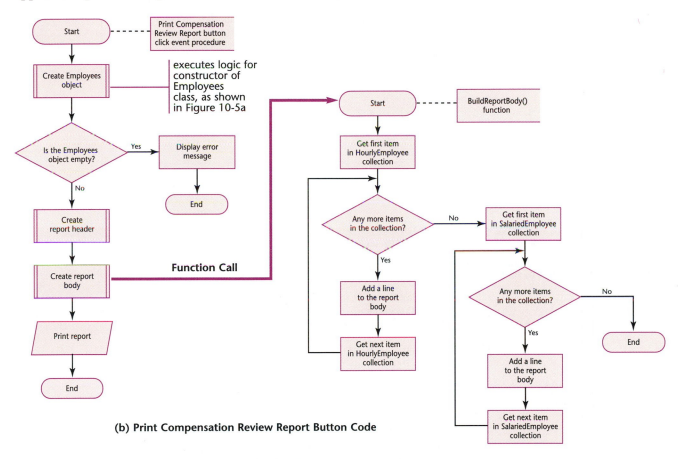

(b) Print Compensation Review Report Button Code

FIGURE 10-5 *(continued)*

Figure 10-6 on the next page shows the pseudocode for the procedures needed in the projects, based on the flowcharts in Figure 10-5. Figure 10-6a shows the procedure that handles opening the database and the logic for the Employees class constructor. After the first hourly employee record is read, a Do While statement causes the loop to repeat until all hourly employee records are read; a second Do While statement loops until all salaried employee records are read. The HourlyEmployee and SalariedEmployee objects are used in the loops. The pseudocode in Figure 10-6b shows the procedures that handle the creation and printing of the report header and the lines in the body of the report.

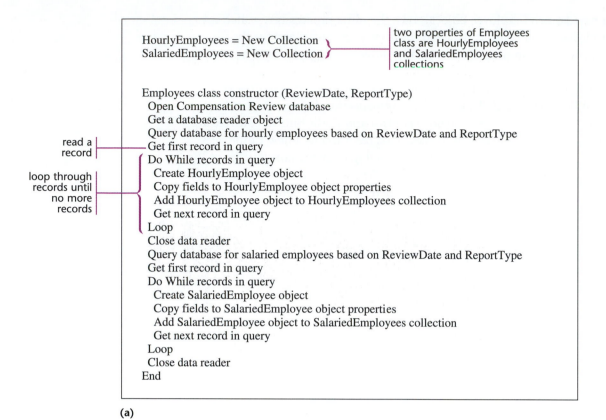

HourlyEmployees = New Collection
SalariedEmployees = New Collection

> two properties of Employees class are HourlyEmployees and SalariedEmployees collections

Employees class constructor (ReviewDate, ReportType)
  Open Compensation Review database
  Get a database reader object
  Query database for hourly employees based on ReviewDate and ReportType

read a record →   Get first record in query

loop through records until no more records →
  Do While records in query
    Create HourlyEmployee object
    Copy fields to HourlyEmployee object properties
    Add HourlyEmployee object to HourlyEmployees collection
    Get next record in query
  Loop

  Close data reader
  Query database for salaried employees based on ReviewDate and ReportType
  Get first record in query
  Do While records in query
    Create SalariedEmployee object
    Copy fields to SalariedEmployee object properties
    Add SalariedEmployee object to SalariedEmployees collection
    Get next record in query
  Loop
  Close data reader
End

(a)

instantiate an Employees object using values input by user →

Procedure: Print Compensation Review Report
  Create Employees object (ReviewDate, ReportType)
  If Employees.HourlyEmployees.Count = 0 and Employees.SalariedEmployees.Count = 0 Then
    Display Error Message
    Exit Procedure
  End If

  Create Report Header
  Create Report Body (Employees)
  Print Report
  End

Procedure: Create Report Body (Employees)
  NumberOfHourlyEmployees = Number of HourlyEmployee objects in Employees.HourlyEmployees collection

loop through hourly employees and add to report →
  For Index = 0 to NumberOfHourlyEmployees
    Concatenate Employee(Index) properties to report body
  Next

  NumberOfSalariedEmployees = Number of SalariedEmployee objects in Employees.SalariedEmployees collection

loop through salaried employees and add to report →
  For Index = 0 to NumberOfSalariedEmployees
    Concatenate Employee(Index) properties to report body
  Next
  End

(b)

FIGURE 10-6

VALIDATE DESIGN   The validation of the design is accomplished by stepping through the requirements document to ensure that all of the requirements are met in a sound manner and that the program logic is sound. The MonthCalendar control on the user interface provides the user with a way to enter a date within the allowable range. The RadioButton controls provide the user with a way to choose which type of report to run. A Print dialog box provides the user with a common interface for selecting print options before printing the report.

The new Employees class handles the functionality of retrieving records from a database and storing the values as objects until an application needs the information. The logic in the Compensation Review Report Windows application instantiates an Employees object, and then loops through the objects in the two collections in the properties. A properly formatted header prints on the report, followed by the records retrieved in the Employees class. The Employees class also can be reused by other applications, such as those developed in Chapters 11 and 12.

As shown in Table 10-1 on page VB 10.05, after validating the program design, the next phase in the development cycle is to develop the new Employees class in the Compensation Review class library using Visual Basic .NET.

Connecting to a Database Using ADO.NET

Almost all programs require some level of interaction with data that exists outside of the program. Often the data exists in a database. A **database** is a collection of data organized in a manner that allows access, retrieval, and use of that data. A database consists of one or more tables. A **table** is a group of related data that organizes the data in rows. Each of these rows represents a record. A **record** contains information about a particular item, product, event, or person, such as an employee. Records are made up of individual data elements, and each element, such as employee name, location, and review date, is called a **field**.

Before learning about reading data from a database, you should understand the Compensation Review database. Figure 10-7 on the next page shows the Compensation Review database. The database includes three tables — Employee, Location, and CompensationAdjustment. The Employee table, which includes information about each employee, contains 15 records, or rows. The fields in the Employee table are identified by the column names in the first row of the Employee table, such as Name, DateHired, HourlyRate, and AnnualSalary. Each employee record has a non-zero value in either the HourlyRate field or the AnnualSalary field. Examining this field allows you to make the determination as to whether an employee is an hourly employee or a salaried employee. The Location table includes a LocationID and name for the five employee locations. Each record in the Employee table includes a LocationID that corresponds to one of the five rows in the Location table. The CompensationAdjustment table includes minimum and maximum raise percentages for each location, as identified by LocationID.

Employee table

EmployeeID	Name	LocationID	DateHired	DateReviewed	Reviewed	HourlyRate	AnnualSalary
1	Dennis Kiest	1	12/8/2000	12/8/2003	☐	$0.00	$62,000.00
2	John Powell	2	8/8/2003	8/8/2003	☐	$15.50	$0.00
3	Pat Daly	2	8/8/2003	8/8/2003	☐	$0.00	$55,700.00
4	Joseph Ritram	1	7/4/2002	7/20/2003	☐	$12.40	$0.00
5	Jan Shapiro	4	7/15/1999	7/17/2004	☐	$17.55	$0.00
6	Sarah Knipfer	3	2/5/2000	2/15/2003	☐	$0.00	$46,700.00
7	Robert Frett	5	5/22/2001	5/25/2004	☐	$0.00	$53,560.00
8	Tony Alvarez	3	6/3/1998	8/1/2003	☐	$0.00	$37,800.00
9	Lee Goold	4	8/15/1999	8/17/2003	☐	$12.65	$0.00
10	Suhir Bitar	5	8/1/2000	7/30/2003	☐	$15.65	$0.00
11	Phyllis Li	2	9/14/1999	9/10/2003	☐	$0.00	$65,300.00
12	Dan Ward	5	8/1/2002	7/30/2003	☐	$14.55	$0.00
13	Mel Voogd	3	11/4/1999	11/15/2003	☐	$0.00	$53,050.00
14	Lucy Dunn	4	1/15/1998	1/30/2004	☐	$18.95	$0.00
15	Raj Dutt	1	2/3/2000	2/15/2004	☐	$0.00	$71,475.00

Compensation
Review
database

Location table

LocationID	Location
1	West
2	Southwest
3	Northeast
4	Southeast
5	Central

CompensationAdjustment table

LocationID	Min	Max
1	3	5
2	5	10
3	2	4
4	3	7
5	1	3

FIGURE 10-7

Figure 10-8 shows the table design for each of the three tables in the Compensation Review database. As shown in Figure 10-8, each field in a database is assigned a data type, much like variables in programs. The data type of a field may be text, integer, currency, date/time, or even object. Figure 10-8 also shows the indexes and primary keys of each table. An **index** is a group of one or more fields that can be used to sort fields and identify records in a table. Indexes work behind the scenes, much like the indexes in a book, to make the retrieval of data faster. A table can include no indexes or any number of indexes. A **primary key** is a type of index that provides a unique identifier for each record. As shown in Figure 10-8, each of the three tables in the Compensation Review database includes at least one index. Each index also serves as the primary key for the table and, therefore, is listed as both an index and a primary key in the Table Indexes area for each table. The EmployeeID field serves as the primary key for the Employee table; the LocationID field serves as the primary key for the CompensationAdjustment and Location tables.

When a database is created, relationships can be defined among tables. A **relationship** defines how different tables and the fields within those tables are related. Figure 10-9 shows the relationships among the tables in the Compensation Review database. As shown in Figure 10-9, the relationship between the Location table and the Employees table is a many-to-one relationship. The line between the tables is labeled with an infinity symbol (∞) and the number 1. The placement of these symbols indicates that many employees can be in one location. The relationship between the Location table and CompensationAdjustment table is a one-to-one relationship. The line between the tables is labeled with the number 1 on either side of the line, indicating that each record in the Location table has exactly one corresponding record in the CompensationAdjustment table.

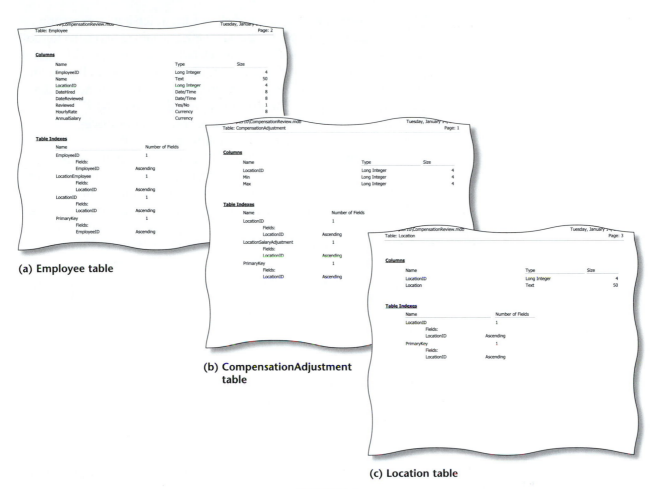

(a) Employee table

(b) CompensationAdjustment table

(c) Location table

FIGURE 10-8

Relationships for Compensation Review Database

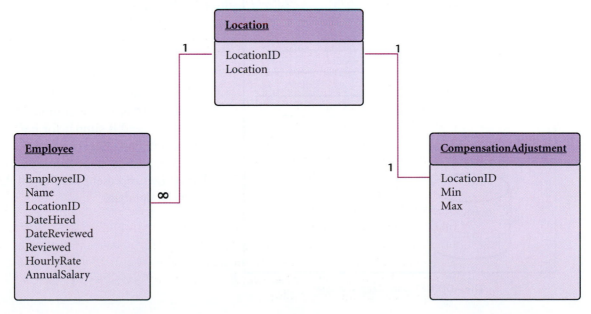

FIGURE 10-9

The .NET framework provides a set of classes for accessing information stored in databases, called **ADO.NET**. The ADO.NET database access technologies make available a wide range of database-related classes that provide access to a number of standard types of databases and data storage technologies. The Compensation Review database used in this project is a Microsoft Access database, which is one of the types of databases supported by ADO.NET.

The System.Data.OleDb namespace is one of several namespaces that compose ADO.NET functionality in Visual Basic .NET. The **System.Data.OleDb namespace**, which provides access to databases that use the standard OLE DB database access technology, such as Microsoft Access databases, describes a collection of classes used to provide outside programs with access to the database. For other database technologies, a different namespace might be used to provide access. For example, the **System.Data.SqlClient namespace** provides database access to Microsoft SQL Server 2000 databases.

As noted above, the System.Data.OleDb namespace describes a collection of classes used to communicate with the database, including classes that allow a program to connect to a database, read data from a database, and send commands to a database. The first step in giving a program access to data in a database is to create a connection to the database using the **OleDbConnection class**. The OleDbConnection class tells the program where to find the database and what kind of database with which the program must communicate. Next, the program must use the connection to read records from the database. The **OleDbDataReader class** provides functionality to read data from a database once an OleDbConnection object has been created for the connection to the database. Finally, commands must be sent to the database to request information from the database. The **OleDbCommand class** provides the mechanisms to build and send commands to the database using an OleDbDataReader object.

Figure 10-10 shows the ADO.NET data access model, which illustrates the relationship between a program, the three types of classes listed above, and a database. The model shown in Figure 10-10 is a general model for ADO.NET and is similar for both the System.Data.OleDb and the System.Data.SqlClient namespaces. The arrows represent the flow of data from the database.

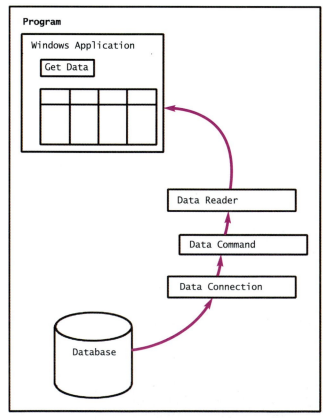

The ADO.NET Data Access Model

FIGURE 10-10

Starting Visual Basic .NET and Adding a New Class to a Project

In order to provide the database access functionality required for the Compensation Review System, the program design specifies that a new class, the Employees class, must be added to the Compensation Review class library. Figure 10-11 shows the detailed class diagram for the Employees class. The Employees class is composed of, or aggregated from, the HourlyEmployee and SalariedEmployee classes. The class diagram indicates that the Employees class can be composed of several HourlyEmployee objects and several SalariedEmployee objects.

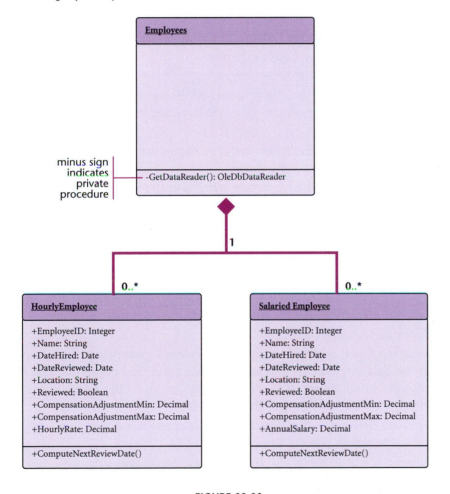

FIGURE 10-11

The first step for creating the Employees class is to add a new class to the Compensation Review class library.

> **Note 2**
>
> Database access is much faster from a hard drive rather than a floppy drive. If permitted by your instructor, you may want to copy the Chapter10 folder on the Data Disk to your hard drive to complete the project in this chapter.

The following steps start Visual Basic .NET and then add a new class to the Compensation Review class library using the Class template. The new class is the Employees class, which will perform the database access functions needed by the Compensation Review Report application.

To Start Visual Basic .NET and Add a New Class to the Compensation Review Class Library

---

1. Insert the Data Disk in drive A. Using Windows Explorer, copy the Compensation Review folder from the A:\Chapter9 folder to the A:\Chapter10 folder.

2. Start Visual Basic .NET. When the Start Page displays, click the Open Project button on the Start Page.

3. If necessary, click the Look in box arrow and then click 3½ Floppy (A:). Double-click the Chapter10 folder.

   Visual Basic .NET displays the Open Project dialog box. The Chapter10 folder becomes the current folder in the Look in box.

4. Double-click the Compensation Review folder. If necessary, click the Compensation Review solution file (Compensation Review.sln).

   The Compensation Review folder becomes the current folder in the Look in box. The Compensation Review solution file is displayed as selected in the dialog box.

5. Click the Open button. When the Compensation Review project displays in the Solution Explorer window, right-click the Compensation Review project. When the shortcut menu displays, point to the Add command and then click Add Class on the Add menu.

   The Add New Item - Compensation Review dialog box displays and the Class template is selected by default.

6. Select the text in the Name box and type Employees.vb as the new name. Click the Open button.

   Visual Basic .NET adds the Employees.vb module to the Compensation Review class library.

After Visual Basic .NET creates the new class module, the class module name, Employees.vb, displays in the Solution Explorer window.

Creating a Database Connection String

As you have learned, a program requires an OleDbConnection object to communicate with a database and OleDbDataReader and OleDbCommand objects to read records from tables in the database. The constructor of an OleDbConnection object requires a parameter that gives the OleDbConnection object information about the type of database and the location of the database to which the program will connect. These two pieces of information, provider and data source, are the minimum requirements for creating a connection to a database using the OleDbConnection namespace. Other optional information can include a user name and password for a password-protected database. The information is sent to the OleDbConnection object in a string called a **connection string**. In the case of the Compensation Review database, the database is a Microsoft Access database stored in the A:\Chapter10 folder and the connection string for the Compensation Review database is:

```
"Provider=Microsoft.Jet.OLEDB.4.0; Data Source=A:\Chapter10\CompensationReview.mdb"
```

Tip

Connection Strings

The constructor of an OleDbConnection object requires a parameter that gives the OleDbConnection object information about the type of database and the location of the database to which the program will connect. These two pieces of information, provider and data source, are the minimum requirements for creating a connection to a database using the OleDbConnection namespace. To determine the connection string for various database sources, use the Visual Basic .NET Help system or the documentation provided with the database software.

As shown in the connection string, the string consists of two portions: the Provider, or type of database, and the Data Source, or location of the database. Different types of databases may use slightly different formats and Provider and Data Source names in the connection string. To determine the connection string for other types of database sources, use the Visual Basic .NET Help system or the documentation provided with the database software.

Figure 10-12 on the next page shows the initial code for the Employees class. The private variables, mobjHourlyEmployees and mobjSalariedEmployees, store the values of the two properties of the Employees class. The variables are collections that will contain collections of HourlyEmployee and SalariedEmployee objects. Lines 6 and 7 declare OleDbCommand and OleDbDataReader variables for use in the class. The OleDbConnection variable will be declared later in this chapter. Line 9 declares a constant, g_strConnectionString, which contains the value of the connection string for the Compensation Review database.

```
 1 Option Strict On
 2 Imports System.Data.OleDb
 3 Public Class Employees
 4     Private mobjHourlyEmployees As New Collection()
 5     Private mobjSalariedEmployees As New Collection()
 6     Private objOleDbCommand As OleDbCommand
 7     Private objOleDbDataReader As OleDbDataReader
 8
 9     Private Const g_strConnectionString As String = "Provider=Microsoft.Jet.OLEDB.4.0;"↙
        & _
10                                                      "Data Source=A:\Chapter10\        ↙
        CompensationReview.mdb"
11
12 End Class
```

FIGURE 10-12

Figure 10-13 shows the property declarations for the HourlyEmployeeList and SalariedEmployeeList properties of the Employees class. The code declares the properties as read-only, with the data type of Collection. The values of the two properties are stored in the variables, mobjHourlyEmployee and mobjSalariedEmployee, respectively.

```
12     Public ReadOnly Property HourlyEmployeeList() As Collection
13         Get
14             Return mobjHourlyEmployees
15         End Get
16     End Property
17
18     Public ReadOnly Property SalariedEmployeeList() As Collection
19         Get
20             Return mobjSalariedEmployees
21         End Get
22     End Property
```

FIGURE 10-13

The following steps open the code window and enter the code shown in Figure 10-12 to set the name of the Employees class, declare private variables within the Employee class, and create a database connection string for the Compensation Review database.

To Declare Private Variables and Create a Database Connection String

---

1. If necessary, double-click the Employees.vb class module in the Solution Explorer window. When the Employees.vb code window opens, type the code as shown in Figure 10-12.

Visual Basic .NET opens the code window. The Option Strict On statement, Imports statement, private variable declarations, and constant to store the database connection string display in the code window.

2. Type the code as shown in Figure 10-13.

Two read-only property declarations display in the code window. The ReadOnly keyword in lines 12 and 18 ensure that the properties are read-only. The HourlyEmployeeList and SalariedEmployeeList properties are of the data type Collection (Figure 10-14).

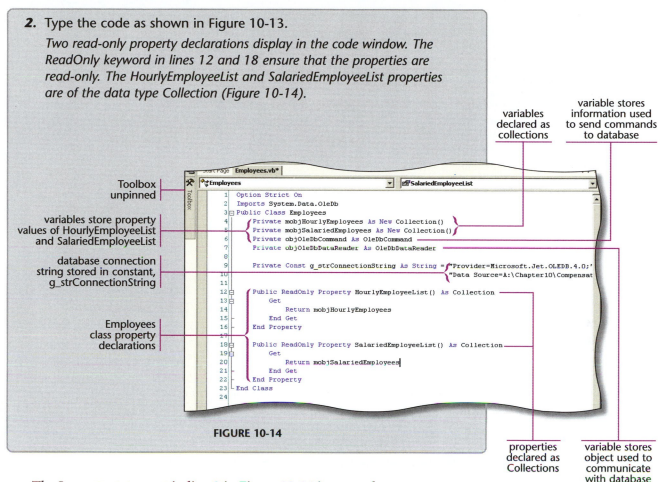

FIGURE 10-14

The Imports statement in line 2 in Figure 10-14 imports the System.Data.OleDb namespace to make the classes used to access the database available to the program. The code in lines 6 and 7 declares OleDbCommand and OleDbDataReader objects as variables to store information about how to access and read data from the database.

The next step is to write code that uses the OleDbDataReader object to read records from the database.

Try...Catch Exception Handling

Visual Basic .NET provides syntax for handling errors and exceptions that may occur during the execution of code. **Structured exception handling** is code that detects and responds to run-time errors in a logical and straightforward manner. The **Try...Catch...Finally statement** is used to implement structured exception handling. If you are concerned that some code may generate an exception during execution, you can place that code in the Try clause of the Try...Catch...Finally statement. If an exception occurs, the code in the Catch clause executes the code that can handle the error condition or alert the user to the error in an informative manner. As you learned in Chapter 8, if the exception occurs and the code is not in a Try clause, then the CLR displays an error message and halts the program. In the Employees class, a Try...Catch...Finally statement will be used to ensure that any errors caused during database processing are handled in a straightforward manner.

Table 10-2 shows the general form of the Try...Catch...Finally statement used to implement structured exception handling.

Table 10-2   Try...Catch...Finally Statement

General Form:	1. Try
	    statements
	Catch [exception as datatype]
	    statements
	End Try
	
	2. Try
	    statements
	Catch [exception as datatype]
	    statements
	Finally
	    statements
	End Try
	
	where the statements following the Try statement include the statements being tested for exceptions. Only one Try clause and one Finally clause are allowed. Multiple Catch clauses are allowed if an exception object follows the Catch keyword. An Exit Try statement may be placed in either the Try clause or the Catch clause to cause the Try...Catch...Finally statement to exit.

Purpose:	The Try...Catch...Finally statement provides syntax for structured exception handling.

Example:	1. Try
	        intX = intY / intZ
	    Catch System.DivideByZeroException
	        MessageBox.Show("You may not divide by zero.")
	    End Try
	
	2. Try
	        intX = intY / intZ
	    Catch Ex As System.DivideByZeroException
	        MessageBox.Show("You may not divide by zero.")
	    Finally
	        MessageBox.Show("This message always displays.")
	    End Try
	
	3. Try
	        intX = intY / intZ
	    Catch Ex As System.DivideByZeroException
	        MessageBox.Show("You may not divide by zero.")
	    Catch ex As New Exception
	        MessageBox.Show("Other exceptions skip the Finally clause.")
	        Exit Try
	    Finally
	        MessageBox.Show("Finally clause reached.")
	    End Try

Table 10-2 Try...Catch...Finally Statement (continued)

Notes:	1. The code in the Finally clause executes in all cases either after the code in the Try clause executes or after the code in the Catch clause executes. The exception is when an Exit Try statement is used to exit the Try...Catch...Finally statement, in which case the Finally clause does not execute.
	2. If an exception is not caught in a Try...Catch...Finally statement, Visual Basic .NET handles the exception through normal exception handling, such as displaying a run-time error and halting execution of the program.
	3. If a Catch clause is not included, a Finally clause must be included.
	4. The Finally clause is optional and does not have to be included if a Catch clause is included. In this book, the form of the statement without the Finally clause is referred to as the Try...Catch statement.

If an exception occurs in a particular class or procedure, instead of taking any action on the exception, you may want to halt execution of that class or procedure and then send the exception back to the code that called the class or procedure. This practice is known as **throwing exceptions**. The **Throw statement** is used to send, or throw, exceptions back to the line of code that called the module that caused the exception. Table 10-3 shows the general form of the Throw statement used to throw an exception.

Table 10-3 Throw Statement

General Form:	1. Throw exception
Purpose:	The Throw statement creates an exception that can be handled with structured exception handling code or left to the CLR to handle.
Examples:	1. Throw exMyException
Notes:	1. The Throw statement can be used anywhere in code and is not limited to use within the Try... Catch...Finally statement.

Figure 10-15 on the next page shows an illustration of the Try...Catch statement and Throw statement used in a series of three modules. All three modules use the Try...Catch form shown in example 1 of Table 10-2 and do not include the Finally clause. The code in the Try clause of Module 1 calls a procedure in Module 2. Module 2 calls a procedure in Module 3. The code in the Try clause of the Module 3 causes an exception. The exception is caught in the Catch clause; the Throw statement sends the exception back to Module 2. The same sequence of events occurs in Module 2. Module 1 finally catches and handles the exception by displaying an error message. If structured error handling was not used, then the code in Module 3 would cause a run-time error. Exceptions not handled in code automatically are thrown back to the CLR, which displays run-time errors. By preventing the CLR from displaying a run-time error and halting execution,

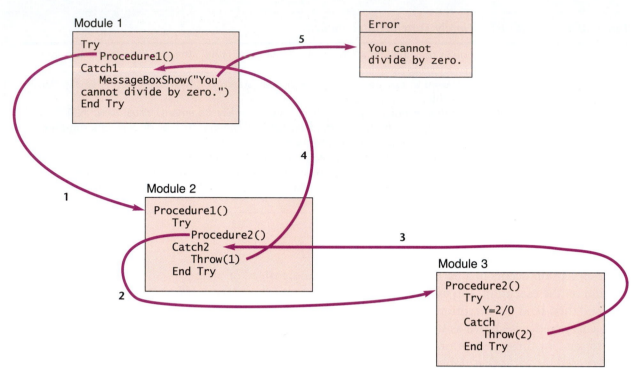

Example of Try...Catch Exception Handling

FIGURE 10-15

the error can be handled in code in a more graceful manner and the program does not necessarily need to halt. In the Employees class, any exceptions that occur in the database access code will be thrown back to the program that instantiated an Employees object.

Preparing a Data Command and a Data Reader

Because the two properties of the Employees class — HourlyEmployeeList and SalariedEmployeeList — both require data from the database, the database must be read twice. The code to query the database can be placed in a function, called the GetDataReader() function. As shown in Figure 10-16, the GetDataReader() function returns an OleDbDataReader object. The function accepts a command to execute against the database. The structure of the command is discussed later in this chapter.

```
24    Private Function GetDataReader(ByVal strSQL As String) As OleDbDataReader
25        Try
26            objOleDbCommand.CommandText = strSQL
27            objOleDbDataReader = objOleDbCommand.ExecuteReader
28        Catch objException As Exception
29            Throw objException
30        End Try
31        Return objOleDbDataReader
32    End Function
```

FIGURE 10-16

The code in the function is encapsulated in the Try clause of a Try…Catch statement. Line 26 sets the **CommandText property** of an OleDbCommand object to the command string passed to the function. Line 27 uses the **ExecuteReader() method** of the OleDbCommand class to execute the command against the database. The records returned by the command are stored in the objOleDbDataReader object and passed back to the calling line of code using the Return statement in line 31. If any of the database operations in lines 26 or 27 cause an exception, then the Catch statement in line 28 catches the exception in the variable named objException. The exception then is thrown back to the calling procedure using the Throw statement in line 29.

The following step adds the code shown in Figure 10-16 to the Employees class module.

To Prepare a Data Command and a Data Reader and Code a Try…Catch Statement

1. Enter lines 24 through 32 as shown in Figure 10-16.

The private GetDataReader() function displays in the code window (Figure 10-17). Because the function is private, it only is available to other procedures in the Employees class module. The Try…Catch statement allows the program to continue running even after a serious error is encountered. The Throw statement in line 29 throws any exceptions back to the line of code that called the GetDataReader() function. This allows any serious errors to be handled in a common location, and prevents the CLR from displaying a cryptic run-time error message to the user and halting execution of the class and of the calling program.

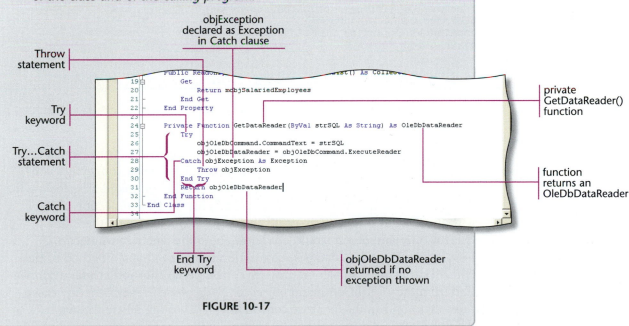

FIGURE 10-17

The GetDataReader() function reads the database by executing a command on the database that is passed to the function as a parameter. Structured exception handling ensures that any database errors that occur do not result in a run-time error, but rather that the errors are captured in an object and processed in code. The exceptions are thrown back to the line of code that called the function, and the exception can be handled in that code.

The next step is to create the constructor of the Employees class that will call the GetDataReader() function to query the database for hourly employee and salaried employee records.

Creating a Connection to a Database

The connection to the Compensation Review database is accomplished by passing the connection string to the OleDbConnection object's constructor. Figure 10-18 shows the code necessary to create the connection to the Compensation Review database. The code is written in the constructor of the Employees class and encapsulated in a Try…Catch statement, so that if any database operation fails — such as the database not being found because it does not exist — an exception is thrown to the line of code that called the Employees class constructor.

```
12    Public Sub New(ByVal ReviewedStatus As Boolean, ByVal ReviewDate As Date)
13        Dim strSQL, strHourlyEmployeeSQL, strSalariedEmployeeSQL As String
14        Dim objOleDbConnection As OleDbConnection
15
16        Try
17            objOleDbConnection = New OleDbConnection(g_strConnectionString)
18            objOleDbCommand = New OleDbCommand()
19            objOleDbCommand.Connection = objOleDbConnection
20            objOleDbCommand.Connection.Open()
21        Catch objException As Exception
22            Throw objException
23        End Try
24    End Sub
```

FIGURE 10-18

As shown in Figure 10-18, line 17 sends the connection string, which is stored in the g_strConnectionString constant, to the OleDbConnection constructor. Line 18 creates a new instance of the OleDbCommand class for use in the Employees constructor. Line 19 associates the OleDbConnection object with the OleDbCommand object. If this line was not executed, then the OleDbCommand object would not know about the database connection. Finally, line 20 opens a database connection using the Open() method of the OleDBCommand.Connection property. The **Open() method** creates a connection from the OleDbCommand object to the database in memory. Any exceptions that occur in the database code in lines 17 through 20 are thrown back to the line of code that called the constructor by the Throw statement in line 22.

The following step adds the code shown in Figure 10-18 to create the Employees class constructor and connect to the database.

To Connect to a Database

1. Type lines 12 through 24 as shown in Figure 10-18.

The New() constructor is created for the Employees class above the GetDataReader() function in the code. A Try...Catch statement contains the code that connects to the database using the connection string specified in the g_strConnectionString variable (Figure 10-19).

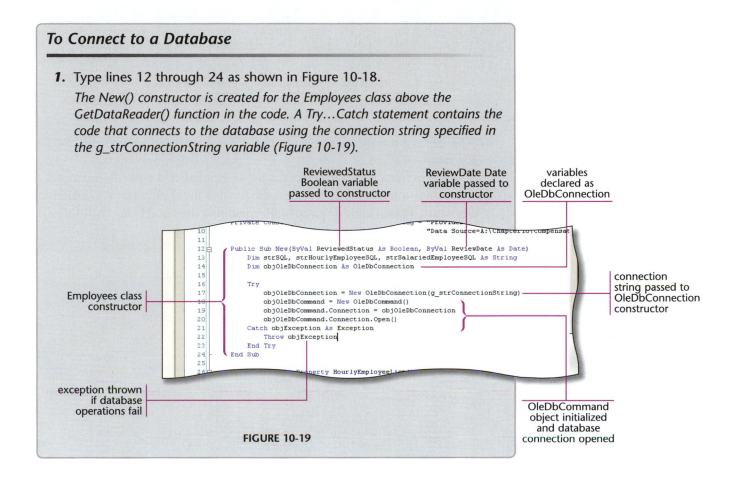

ReviewedStatus Boolean variable passed to constructor

ReviewDate Date variable passed to constructor

variables declared as OleDbConnection

Employees class constructor

connection string passed to OleDbConnection constructor

exception thrown if database operations fail

OleDbCommand object initialized and database connection opened

FIGURE 10-19

With the code added in the step above, the database is open and prepared for reading. The next step is to create and execute a command against the database.

Reading Records from a Database Using ADO.NET

Before reading records from the database, an OleDbDataReader object must be instantiated and initialized. Records are read from a database using a database query, and the results are stored as objects in the OleDbDataReader object. When using the values from a database in Visual Basic .NET, you process the records that are returned in the OleDbDataReader object, rather than processing the actual records that exist in the database.

Visual Basic .NET also does not include the syntax to query and manipulate databases. Instead, the code must include a query that is sent to the database in a string. The following sections describe the process of building a command for a database query and sending the command to the database.

Creating SQL Statements

SQL, which is an abbreviation for Structured Query Language, is a standard language used to create statements to send requests to and retrieve data from databases. SQL statements are English-like strings that are sent as commands to a database management system. SQL is used in almost all common database management systems, including Microsoft Access.

SQL includes four types of statements to manipulate and query data in a database: SELECT, INSERT, UPDATE, and DELETE. A **SELECT statement** is used to query records from a database. In this chapter, a simple SELECT statement is used to query the Compensation Review database.

Figure 10-20 shows an example of a simple SQL SELECT statement. This simple form of a SELECT statement includes three parameters:

1. The fields you want to retrieve from the database listed after the SELECT keyword.
2. The tables from which to select the fields listed after the FROM keyword.
3. The conditions for which to select the records listed after the WHERE keyword. These conditions are built much like the conditions built for If…Then…Else statements in the Visual Basic language.

Simple Example of SQL Select Statement

Simple format of the SELECT statement:

SELECT fields FROM tables WHERE conditions

Example:

SELECT Name, Address, City FROM Customers WHERE City = "Nashville"

Table: Customers

Name	Address	City	State	Zip	Phone
Bob Jones	3432 Broxton	Nashville	TN	53232	654-555-3423
Mary Jane	6842 Oak Ln.	Memphis	TN	54343	647-555-3922
Lane Stevens	3948 131st Street	Memphis	TN	54343	647-555-8398
Tonya Jackson	9873 State Street	Nashville	TN	53433	654-555-8473

Result of SELECT Statement

Name	Address	City
Bob Jones	3432 Broxton	Nashville
Tonya Jackson	9873 State Street	Nashville

FIGURE 10-20

Coding a SQL SELECT Statement to Read Hourly Employee Records

The process of creating and printing the Compensation Review report requires the Compensation Review Report application to retrieve specific information stored in the Compensation Review database. As discussed previously, the database uses three tables that store information. The relationships among the three tables are shown in Figure 10-9 on page VB 10.15. Figure 10-21 shows the SQL SELECT statement needed to query the Compensation Review database for the employee records to print on the Compensation Review report.

Figure 10-21 shows the SQL SELECT statement for retrieving all of the employee records that must print on the report. The SELECT clause includes three items. Each item includes a table name, a period, and then a field name to indicate which fields should be selected from each table. The first item uses an asterisk (*) as the field name. The asterisk indicates that all fields in the Employee table should be selected.

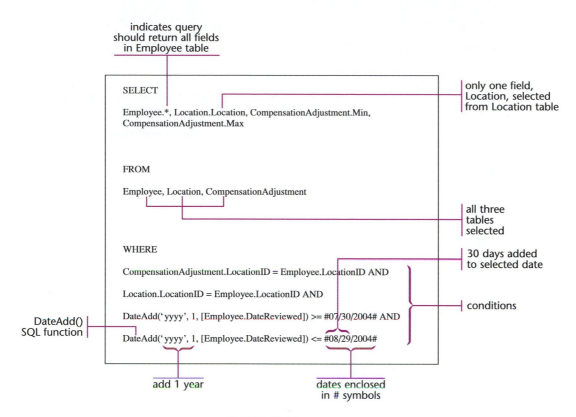

indicates query
should return all fields
in Employee table

SELECT

only one field,
Location, selected
from Location table

Employee.*, Location.Location, CompensationAdjustment.Min,
CompensationAdjustment.Max

FROM

Employee, Location, CompensationAdjustment

all three
tables
selected

WHERE

30 days added
to selected date

CompensationAdjustment.LocationID = Employee.LocationID AND

Location.LocationID = Employee.LocationID AND

conditions

DateAdd()
SQL function

DateAdd('yyyy', 1, [Employee.DateReviewed]) >= #07/30/2004# AND

DateAdd('yyyy', 1, [Employee.DateReviewed]) <= #08/29/2004#

add 1 year

dates enclosed
in # symbols

FIGURE 10-21

Because the SELECT statement must return data from all three tables, the
FROM clause lists the names of the three tables in the Compensation Review
database. The WHERE clause of the SELECT statement lists several conditions.
The first two conditions join the LocationID fields stored in each table. The conditions perform the task of making sure that the SELECT statement returns the
proper Location field and the corresponding minimum (Min) and maximum
(Max) compensation adjustment percentages for the location where the
employee works.

The last two conditions of the WHERE clause ensure selection of only those
employees who require a compensation review within 30 days of the date
selected by the user in the MonthCalendar control. In the case of the SELECT
statement shown in Figure 10-21, the selected review date is July 30, 2004. The
DateAdd() function is a SQL function, not a Visual Basic .NET function, which
is used here to add one year to each employee's last review date. The date resulting from the DateAdd() function call is compared against the selected date and
another date 30 days beyond the selected date.

Figure 10-22 on the next page shows the code that builds the SELECT statement to query the Compensation Review database. The SELECT statement is
stored in the strSQL variable, as shown in line 25. The SELECT statement is built
in a Try…Catch statement, because other database operations will be added that
may result in exceptions during run time.

```
24          Try
25              strSQL = "SELECT Employee.*, Location.Location, CompensationAdjustment.Min, ↵
    " & _
26                  "CompensationAdjustment.Max FROM Employee,Location,            ↵
    CompensationAdjustment " & _
27                  "WHERE CompensationAdjustment.LocationID = Employee.LocationID " & ↵
    _
28                  "AND Location.LocationID = Employee.LocationID " & _
29                  "AND Employee.Reviewed = " & Convert.ToString(ReviewedStatus) & " ↵
    AND " & _
30                  "DateAdd('yyyy', 1, [Employee.DateReviewed]) >= #" & ReviewDate. ↵
    ToShortDateString & "# AND " & _
31                  "DateAdd('yyyy', 1, [Employee.DateReviewed]) <= #" & ReviewDate. ↵
    AddDays(30).ToShortDateString & "#"
32          Catch objException As Exception
33              Throw objException
34          End Try
```

FIGURE 10-22

The following step adds the code shown in Figure 10-22 to the constructor of the Employees class.

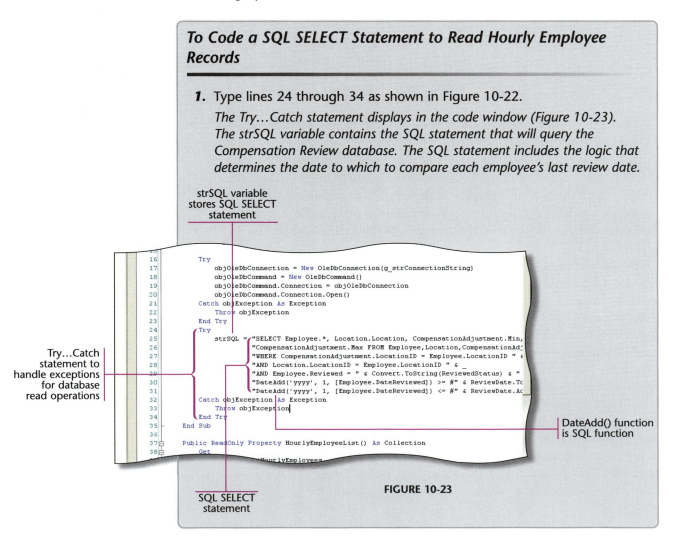

To Code a SQL SELECT Statement to Read Hourly Employee Records

1. Type lines 24 through 34 as shown in Figure 10-22.

The Try...Catch statement displays in the code window (Figure 10-23). The strSQL variable contains the SQL statement that will query the Compensation Review database. The SQL statement includes the logic that determines the date to which to compare each employee's last review date.

FIGURE 10-23

Later in this chapter, an additional condition is added to the query so that the SELECT statement returns only hourly employee or salaried employee records.

The flowchart in Figure 10-24 shows the logic necessary to query the database and read hourly employee records and then populate the HourlyEmployees property of the Employees class. The second task — populating the HourlyEmployees property of the Employees class — has been implemented for the constructor. The next step is to write the code to query the database for hourly employees.

A strSQL variable in line 25 stores the SELECT statement for querying all employees who match the criteria selected by the user on the user interface. An additional condition must be added to the SELECT statement so that the query returns only records for hourly employees. Figure 10-25 show the code to complete the SELECT statement for returning hourly employee records. Line 33 accomplishes this by restricting the returned records to only those employees who have a value of 0 in the AnnualSalary field, because any employee with an annual salary of 0 is an hourly employee. Line 34 of the code calls the GetDataReader() function coded earlier in this chapter to send the SELECT statement that returns only hourly employees from the database. The result of the GetDataReader() function call is that the objOleDbDataReader object contains objects representing hourly employee records that match the criteria selected by the user.

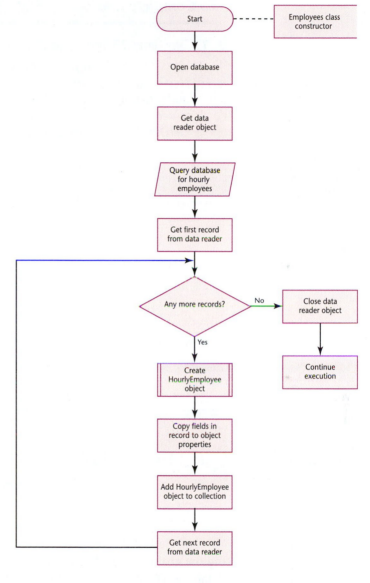

FIGURE 10-24

```
33          strHourlyEmployeeSQL = strSQL & " AND Employee.AnnualSalary = 0"
34          objOleDbDataReader = GetDataReader(strHourlyEmployeeSQL)
```

FIGURE 10-25

The following step adds the two lines of code shown in Figure 10-25 on the previous page to finish building the SQL SELECT statement for querying the hourly employees in the database.

To Complete Coding the SQL SELECT Statement

1. Type lines 33 and 34 as shown in Figure 10-25.

Lines 33 and 34 display in the code window. Line 33 concatenates the strSQL variable in line 25 with an additional condition that limits the query to only hourly employees. The resulting SELECT statement is stored in the strHourlyEmployeeSQL variable that is passed to the private GetDataReader() function (Figure 10-26).

strHourlyEmployeeSQL variable stores query for only hourly employee records

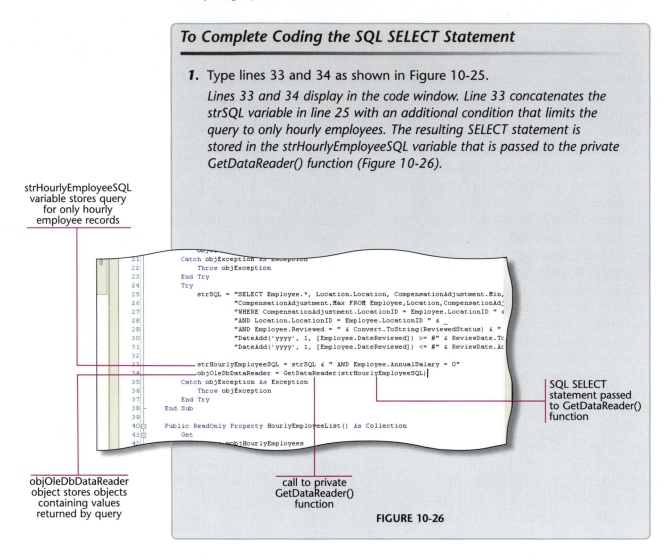

```
21        Catch objException As Exception
22            Throw objException
23        End Try
24        Try
25            strSQL = "SELECT Employee.*, Location.Location, CompensationAdjustment.Min,
26                "CompensationAdjustment.Max FROM Employee,Location,CompensationAdj;
27                "WHERE CompensationAdjustment.LocationID = Employee.LocationID " &
28                "AND Location.LocationID = Employee.LocationID " & _
29                "AND Employee.Reviewed = " & Convert.ToString(ReviewedStatus) & "
30                "DateAdd('yyyy', 1, [Employee.DateReviewed]) >= #" & ReviewDate.To
31                "DateAdd('yyyy', 1, [Employee.DateReviewed]) <= #" & ReviewDate.Ad
32
33            strHourlyEmployeeSQL = strSQL & " AND Employee.AnnualSalary = 0"
34            objOleDbDataReader = GetDataReader(strHourlyEmployeeSQL)
35        Catch objException As Exception
36            Throw objException
37        End Try
38    End Sub
39
40    Public ReadOnly Property HourlyEmployeeList() As Collection
41        Get
42                    objHourlyEmployees
```

SQL SELECT statement passed to GetDataReader() function

objOleDbDataReader object stores objects containing values returned by query

call to private GetDataReader() function

FIGURE 10-26

The GetDataReader() function returns a OleDbDataReader object containing the group of hourly employees requested from the Compensation Review database. The group of employee records in the object must be stored as either HourlyEmployee objects or SalariedEmployee objects in the collections that are the properties of the Employees class. The next step is to loop through the records in the OleDbDataReader object and store the values in the appropriate collection.

Using a Loop to Read Records

The process of reading records from the objOleDbDataReader object is similar to the process used to read through items in a collection. Figure 10-27 shows the code for the Do While loop that reads each record returned by the query for hourly employees. The code implements the loop shown in the flowchart in Figure 10-24 on page VB 10.31. For each record returned by the query and stored in the objOleDbDataReader object, the Do While loop creates a new HourlyEmployee object and then stores the fields from the query in the properties of the new HourlyEmployee object. After the properties are set for the new HourlyEmployee object, the object is added to the HourlyEmployees property collection of the Employees class.

```
35          Do While (objOleDbDataReader.Read())
36              Dim objEmployee As New HourlyEmployee()
37              objEmployee.HourlyRate = Convert.ToDecimal(objOleDbDataReader.Item("      ↙
        HourlyRate"))
38              objEmployee.EmployeeID = Convert.ToInt32(objOleDbDataReader.Item("      ↙
        EmployeeID"))
39              objEmployee.Name = Convert.ToString(objOleDbDataReader.Item("Name"))
40              objEmployee.Location = Convert.ToString(objOleDbDataReader.Item("      ↙
        Location"))
41              objEmployee.DateHired = Convert.ToDateTime(objOleDbDataReader.Item("      ↙
        DateHired"))
42              objEmployee.DateReviewed = Convert.ToDateTime(objOleDbDataReader.Item("↙
        DateReviewed"))
43              objEmployee.Reviewed = Convert.ToBoolean(objOleDbDataReader.Item("      ↙
        Reviewed"))
44              objEmployee.CompensationAdjustmentMin() = Convert.ToDecimal(      ↙
        objOleDbDataReader.Item("Min"))
45              objEmployee.CompensationAdjustmentMax() = Convert.ToDecimal(      ↙
        objOleDbDataReader.Item("Max"))
46              mobjHourlyEmployees.Add(objEmployee, Convert.ToString(objEmployee.      ↙
        EmployeeID))
47          Loop
48          objOleDbDataReader.Close()
```

FIGURE 10-27

The code in lines 37 through 45 demonstrates the necessity of performing data conversions using the Convert class when reading records from a database. When the Option Strict On statement is used, care must be taken to perform the necessary data conversions.

Line 48 closes the objOleDbDataReader object using its Close() method. Closing the objOleDbDataReader object allows the object to be reused for the query for salaried employees.

The step on the next page adds the code shown in Figure 10-27 to the Try…Catch statement in the Employees class constructor. The code creates a loop to read the records retrieved by the query for hourly employees.

To Use a Loop to Read Hourly Employee Records

1. Type lines 35 through 48 as shown in Figure 10-27 on the previous page.

Lines 35 through 48 display in the code window. The Do While loop executes once for each record in the objOleDbDataReader object. Line 36 declares a new HourlyEmployee object for each record. The objEmployee object's properties are set to the values read from the database (Figure 10-28).

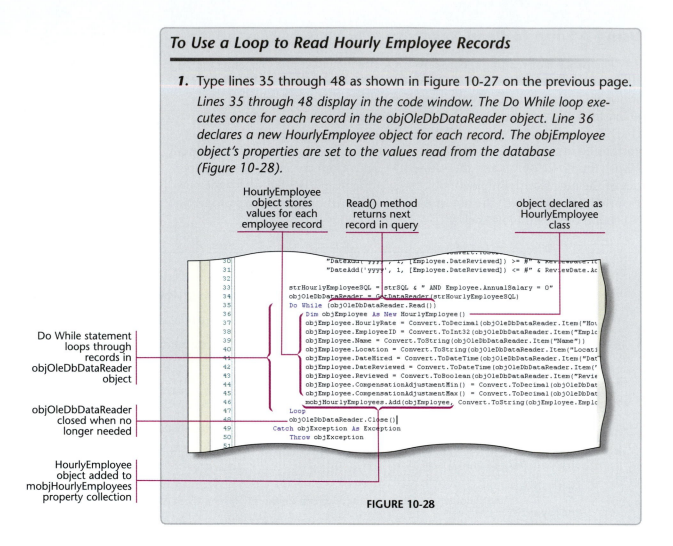

HourlyEmployee object stores values for each employee record

Read() method returns next record in query

object declared as HourlyEmployee class

Do While statement loops through records in objOleDbDataReader object

objOleDbDataReader closed when no longer needed

HourlyEmployee object added to mobjHourlyEmployees property collection

```
30        "DateAdd('yyyy', 1, [Employee.DateReviewed]) >= #" & ReviewDate.T
31        "DateAdd('yyyy', 1, [Employee.DateReviewed]) <= #" & ReviewDate.Ac
32
33    strHourlyEmployeeSQL = strSQL & " AND Employee.AnnualSalary = 0"
34    objOleDbDataReader = GetDataReader(strHourlyEmployeeSQL)
35    Do While (objOleDbDataReader.Read())
36        Dim objEmployee As New HourlyEmployee()
37        objEmployee.HourlyRate = Convert.ToDecimal(objOleDbDataReader.Item("Hou
38        objEmployee.EmployeeID = Convert.ToInt32(objOleDbDataReader.Item("Emplo
39        objEmployee.Name = Convert.ToString(objOleDbDataReader.Item("Name"))
40        objEmployee.Location = Convert.ToString(objOleDbDataReader.Item("Locati
41        objEmployee.DateHired = Convert.ToDateTime(objOleDbDataReader.Item("Dat
42        objEmployee.DateReviewed = Convert.ToDateTime(objOleDbDataReader.Item("
43        objEmployee.Reviewed = Convert.ToBoolean(objOleDbDataReader.Item("Revie
44        objEmployee.CompensationAdjustmentMin() = Convert.ToDecimal(objOleDbDat
45        objEmployee.CompensationAdjustmentMax() = Convert.ToDecimal(objOleDbDat
46        mobjHourlyEmployees.Add(objEmployee, Convert.ToString(objEmployee.Emplo
47    Loop
48    objOleDbDataReader.Close()
49    Catch objException As Exception
50        Throw objException
51
```

FIGURE 10-28

After the code entered in the previous steps executes, the HourlyEmployees property of the Employees class is initialized with values from the hourly employee records retrieved from the Compensation Review database. The code added to constructor of the Employees class populates the mobjHourlyEmployees variable that stores the value of the HourlyEmployeeList property of the Employees class. The next step is to write similar code for the salaried employee records.

The flowchart shown in Figure 10-29 shows the logic necessary to query the Compensation Review database for the salaried employee records to print on the Compensation Review report. Information for each employee then is read and stored in the SalariedEmployees property of the Employees class.

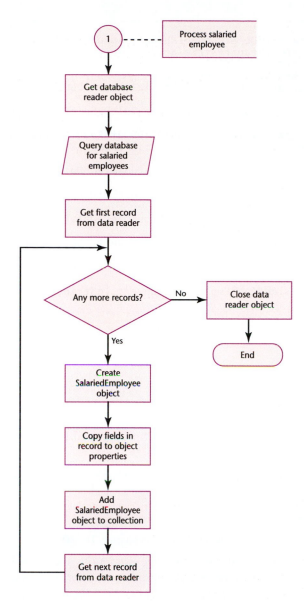

FIGURE 10-29

Figure 10-30 on the next page shows the code necessary to implement the logic shown in the flowchart in Figure 10-29. Line 50 completes the SELECT statement by adding an additional condition to the SELECT statement stored in the strSQL variable, so that it returns only salaried employee records. Lines 51 through 65 perform the same tasks for the salaried employees as were performed for the hourly employees, except that the code creates a SalariedEmployee object for each record in the objOleDbDataReader object and then adds the resulting object to the SalariedEmployees property of the Employees class.

```
50              strSalariedEmployeeSQL = strSQL & " AND Employee.AnnualSalary > 0"
51              objOleDbDataReader = GetDataReader(strSalariedEmployeeSQL)
52              Do While (objOleDbDataReader.Read())
53                  Dim objEmployee As New SalariedEmployee()
54                  objEmployee.AnnualSalary = Convert.ToDecimal(objOleDbDataReader.Item(" ↙
        AnnualSalary"))
55                  objEmployee.EmployeeID = Convert.ToInt32(objOleDbDataReader.Item("    ↙
        EmployeeID"))
56                  objEmployee.Name = Convert.ToString(objOleDbDataReader.Item("Name"))
57                  objEmployee.Location = Convert.ToString(objOleDbDataReader.Item("     ↙
        Location"))
58                  objEmployee.DateHired = Convert.ToDateTime(objOleDbDataReader.Item("   ↙
        DateHired"))
59                  objEmployee.DateReviewed = Convert.ToDateTime(objOleDbDataReader.Item("↙
        DateReviewed"))
60                  objEmployee.Reviewed = Convert.ToBoolean(objOleDbDataReader.Item("     ↙
        Reviewed"))
61                  objEmployee.CompensationAdjustmentMin() = Convert.ToDecimal(          ↙
        objOleDbDataReader.Item("Min"))
62                  objEmployee.CompensationAdjustmentMax() = Convert.ToDecimal(          ↙
        objOleDbDataReader.Item("Max"))
63                  mobjSalariedEmployees.Add(objEmployee, Convert.ToString(objEmployee.  ↙
        EmployeeID))
64              Loop
65              objOleDbDataReader.Close()
```

FIGURE 10-30

The following step adds the code shown in Figure 10-30 to the constructor of the Employees class to populate the mobjSalariedEmployees variable that stores the value of the SalariedEmployeeList property of the Employees class.

> ### To Code a SQL SELECT Statement and Loop to Read Salaried Employee Records
>
> ---
>
> **1.** Type lines 50 through 65 as shown in Figure 10-30.
>
> *Lines 50 through 65 display in the code window as shown in Figure 10-31. The code concatenates the strSQL variable with another condition for the SELECT statement to limit the retrieved records to only salaried employees. Line 51 calls the private GetDataReader() function to gather the requested salaried employee records. The Do While loop creates a SalariedEmployee object for each record returned by the database query and adds the object to the SalariedEmployeeList property.*

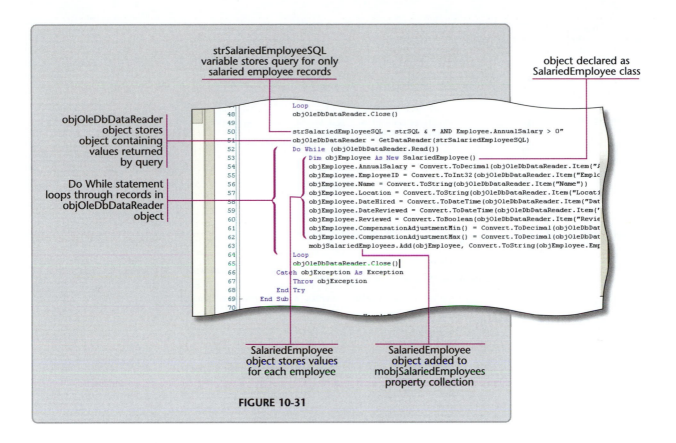

FIGURE 10-31

The code for the Employees class now is complete. When an object is instantiated using the Employees class, the two properties of the class are populated by reading the Compensation Review database. Another programmer using the class can access the data stored in the database through the properties, which are collections.

Figure 10-32 on the next page shows the code from the Employees class that performs the tasks for the database operations. The lines of code shown in Figure 10-32 are the important statements for OleDB database access. In general, the actions performed in Figure 10-32 are similar when reading through the records for any database. The code is shown in the order in which it executes when the Employees constructor executes. Lines 85 and 86 from the GetDataReader() function are shown in two places because the GetDataReader() function is called twice.

In general, the process for accessing data in a database first requires that a database connection object is declared and instantiated. Next, if records will be returned by the database query, then a data reader must be declared in addition to a data command used to send requests to the database. Before a data command can perform an action, an instantiated data connection must be associated with the data command object.

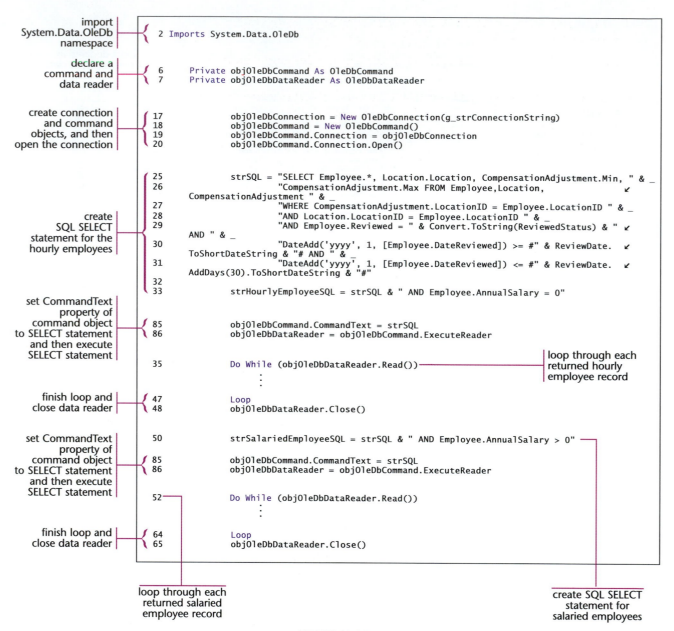

FIGURE 10-32

Building, Saving, and Documenting the Class Library

With the coding for the new Employees class complete, the next step is to build the Compensation Review class library so that the .DLL file includes the new class. The current version of the .DLL file in the \bin directory of the project includes only the three classes coded in Chapter 9.

The following steps build, save, and document the Compensation Review class library.

To Build, Save, and Document the Class Library

1. Right-click the Compensation Review project in the Solution Explorer window. When the shortcut menu displays, click the Build command.

   Visual Basic .NET automatically saves the class files and then opens the Output window and displays several messages while building the project. The result of the build is the creation of the Compensation Review.dll file in the A:\Chapter10\Compensation Review\Compensation Review folder on the Data Disk.

2. Follow the steps on page VB 2.40 of Chapter 2 to use the Print command on the File menu to print a record of the code for the Employees class.

   A record of the code for the Employees class is printed (Figure 10-33 on this and the next page).

```
A:\Chapter10\Compensation Review\Compensation Review\Employees.vb                           1
 1 Option Strict On
 2 Imports System.Data.OleDb
 3 Public Class Employees
 4     Private mobjHourlyEmployees As New Collection()
 5     Private mobjSalariedEmployees As New Collection()
 6     Private objOleDbCommand As OleDbCommand
 7     Private objOleDbDataReader As OleDbDataReader
 8
 9     Private Const g_strConnectionString As String = "Provider=Microsoft.Jet.OLEDB.4.0;" _
       & _
10                                                      "Data Source=A:\Chapter10\
       CompensationReview.mdb"
11
12     Public Sub New(ByVal ReviewedStatus As Boolean, ByVal ReviewDate As Date)
13         Dim strSQL, strHourlyEmployeeSQL, strSalariedEmployeeSQL As String
14         Dim objOleDbConnection As OleDbConnection
15
16         Try
17             objOleDbConnection = New OleDbConnection(g_strConnectionString)
18             objOleDbCommand = New OleDbCommand()
19             objOleDbCommand.Connection = objOleDbConnection
20             objOleDbCommand.Connection.Open()
21         Catch objException As Exception
22             Throw objException
23         End Try
24         Try
25             strSQL = "SELECT Employee.*, Location.Location, CompensationAdjustment.Min, _
       " & _
26                      "CompensationAdjustment.Max FROM Employee,Location,
       CompensationAdjustment " & _
27                      "WHERE CompensationAdjustment.LocationID = Employee.LocationID " &
       _
28                      "AND Location.LocationID = Employee.LocationID " & _
29                      "AND Employee.Reviewed = " & Convert.ToString(ReviewedStatus) & "
       AND " & _
30                      "DateAdd('yyyy', 1, [Employee.DateReviewed]) >= #" & ReviewDate.
       ToShortDateString & "# AND " & _
31                      "DateAdd('yyyy', 1, [Employee.DateReviewed]) <= #" & ReviewDate.
       AddDays(30).ToShortDateString & "#"
32
33             strHourlyEmployeeSQL = strSQL & " AND Employee.AnnualSalary = 0"
34             objOleDbDataReader = GetDataReader(strHourlyEmployeeSQL)
35             Do While (objOleDbDataReader.Read())
36                 Dim objEmployee As New HourlyEmployee()
37                 objEmployee.HourlyRate = Convert.ToDecimal(objOleDbDataReader.Item("
       HourlyRate"))
38                 objEmployee.EmployeeID = Convert.ToInt32(objOleDbDataReader.Item("
       EmployeeID"))
39                 objEmployee.Name = Convert.ToString(objOleDbDataReader.Item("Name"))
40                 objEmployee.Location = Convert.ToString(objOleDbDataReader.Item("
       Location"))
41                 objEmployee.DateHired = Convert.ToDateTime(objOleDbDataReader.Item("
       DateHired"))
42                 objEmployee.DateReviewed = Convert.ToDateTime(objOleDbDataReader.Item("
       DateReviewed"))
43                 objEmployee.Reviewed = Convert.ToBoolean(objOleDbDataReader.Item("
       Reviewed"))
44                 objEmployee.CompensationAdjustmentMin() = Convert.ToDecimal(
       objOleDbDataReader.Item("Min"))
45                 objEmployee.CompensationAdjustmentMax() = Convert.ToDecimal(
       objOleDbDataReader.Item("Max"))
46                 mobjHourlyEmployees.Add(objEmployee, Convert.ToString(objEmployee.
       EmployeeID))
47             Loop
48             objOleDbDataReader.Close()
49
```

FIGURE 10-33

(continued)

```
A:\Chapter10\Compensation Review\Compensation Review\Employees.vb                                    2
50              strSalariedEmployeeSQL = strSQL & " AND Employee.AnnualSalary > 0"
51              objOleDbDataReader = GetDataReader(strSalariedEmployeeSQL)
52              Do While (objOleDbDataReader.Read())
53                  Dim objEmployee As New SalariedEmployee()
54                  objEmployee.AnnualSalary = Convert.ToDecimal(objOleDbDataReader.Item("
AnnualSalary"))
55                  objEmployee.EmployeeID = Convert.ToInt32(objOleDbDataReader.Item("
EmployeeID"))
56                  objEmployee.Name = Convert.ToString(objOleDbDataReader.Item("Name"))
57                  objEmployee.Location = Convert.ToString(objOleDbDataReader.Item("
Location"))
58                  objEmployee.DateHired = Convert.ToDateTime(objOleDbDataReader.Item("
DateHired"))
59                  objEmployee.DateReviewed = Convert.ToDateTime(objOleDbDataReader.Item("
DateReviewed"))
60                  objEmployee.Reviewed = Convert.ToBoolean(objOleDbDataReader.Item("
Reviewed"))
61                  objEmployee.CompensationAdjustmentMin() = Convert.ToDecimal(
objOleDbDataReader.Item("Min"))
62                  objEmployee.CompensationAdjustmentMax() = Convert.ToDecimal(
objOleDbDataReader.Item("Max"))
63                  mobjSalariedEmployees.Add(objEmployee, Convert.ToString(objEmployee.
EmployeeID))
64              Loop
65              objOleDbDataReader.Close()
66          Catch objException As Exception
67              Throw objException
68          End Try
69      End Sub
70
71      Public ReadOnly Property HourlyEmployeeList() As Collection
72          Get
73              Return mobjHourlyEmployees
74          End Get
75      End Property
76
77      Public ReadOnly Property SalariedEmployeeList() As Collection
78          Get
79              Return mobjSalariedEmployees
80          End Get
81      End Property
82
83      Private Function GetDataReader(ByVal strSQL As String) As OleDbDataReader
84          Try
85              objOleDbCommand.CommandText = strSQL
86              objOleDbDataReader = objOleDbCommand.ExecuteReader
87          Catch objException As Exception
88              Throw objException
89          End Try
90          Return objOleDbDataReader
91      End Function
92 End Class
93
```

FIGURE 10-33 (continued)

The previous steps left the solution and project open in the IDE because additional programs for the Compensation Review System, such as the Compensation Review Report application, will be added to the Compensation Review solution.

The development phase for the Employees class now is complete, and other programs, such as those in the Compensation Review System, can use the Compensation Review class library. The first program in the Compensation Review System to utilize the Employees class is the Compensation Review Report application.

Creating the User Interface

The remainder of this chapter concentrates on creating the Compensation Review Report application that uses the classes in the Compensation Review class library. Code in the application will instantiate the Employees class and pass parameters to the constructor of the class. When an object with a type of the Employees class is instantiated, records are read from the tables in the Compensation Review database and are used to populate the values stored in the two collection properties of the Employees class. Those records then are printed on a report.

The first step is to create the Compensation Review Report project in the Compensation Review solution. All of the remaining projects created in this and subsequent chapters will be created in the Compensation Review solution. This practice allows for the entire solution to be built and maintained together.

To Add a New Project to a Solution

1. Right-click the Compensation Review solution in the Solution Explorer. When the shortcut menu displays, point to the Add command.

2. Click the New Project command.

3. When the Add New Project dialog box displays, if necessary, click the Windows Application template in the Templates area. Select the text in the Name box, type Compensation Review Report as the new project name, and then click the OK button.

4. Right-click the References folder for the Compensation Review Report and then click the Add Reference command on the References shortcut menu. When the Add Reference dialog box displays, click the Browse button and use the Select Component dialog box to add a reference to the Compensation Review.dll component located in the A:\Chapter10\ Compensation Review\Compensation Review\bin folder.

Visual Basic .NET adds the Compensation Review Report project to the Compensation Review solution.

After adding the reference to the project, the project can utilize the four classes — Employee, HourlyEmployee, SalariedEmployee, and Employees — in the Compensation Review class library.

Setting Form Properties and Adding Controls

The next steps in creating the Compensation Review Report application are to add controls to a form and set properties for the form and controls. Table 10-4 on the next page lists the changes that need to be made to the Form1 form property values.

Table 10-4   *Form1 Form Property Values for the Compensation Review Report Application*

PROPERTY	PROPERTY VALUE	EFFECT
Size: Width	454	Sets the width of the form in pixels
Size: Height	344	Sets the height of the form in pixels
StartPosition	CenterScreen	Causes the form to display in the center of the user's screen at the start of run time
MaximumBox	False	Causes the form to not display a Maximize button on the title bar on the window
Text	Compensation Review Report	Sets the value of the title bar on the window
FormBorderStyle	FixedDialog	Disallows resizing of the form during run time

The Form1 form requires two GroupBox controls, two RadioButton controls, a Button control, and a MonthCalendar control. Table 10-5 lists the property values that must be set for the GroupBox, RadioButton, and Button controls.

Table 10-5   *GroupBox, RadioButton, and Button Control Property Values for the Compensation Review Report Application*

CONTROL	PROPERTY	PROPERTY VALUE	EFFECT
GroupBox1	Text	Compensation Review Date	Sets the text that displays on the top of the control to Compensation Review Date
	TabIndex	0	Causes this control to be the first control on the form to receive focus
	Size: Width	416	Sets the width of the control in pixels
	Size: Height	176	Sets the height of the control in pixels
	Location: X (left)	16	Indicates the distance from the left border of the form in pixels
	Location: Y (top)	16	Indicates the distance from the top border of the form in pixels
GroupBox2	Text	Compensation Review Status	Sets the text that displays on the top of the control to Compensation Review Status
	TabIndex	1	Causes this control to be the second control on the form to receive focus
	Size: Width	288	Sets the width of the control in pixels
	Size: Height	56	Sets the height of the control in pixels
	Location: X (left)	16	Indicates the distance from the left border of the form in pixels
	Location: Y (top)	200	Indicates the distance from the top border of the form in pixels

Table 10-5 GroupBox, RadioButton, and Button Control Property Values for the Compensation Review Report Application (continued)

CONTROL	PROPERTY	PROPERTY VALUE	EFFECT
RadioButton1	Name	radAlreadyReviewed	Changes the control's name to a descriptive name
	TabIndex	0	Causes this control to be the first control in GroupBox2 to receive focus
	Size: Width	120	Sets the width of the control in pixels
	Size: Height	24	Sets the height of the control in pixels
	Location: X (left)	16	Indicates the distance from the left border of GroupBox2 in pixels
	Location: Y (top)	24	Indicates the distance from the top border of GroupBox2 in pixels
RadioButton2	Name	radNotYetReviewed	Changes the control's name to a descriptive name
	TabIndex	1	Causes this control to be the second control in GroupBox2 to receive focus
	Size: Width	120	Sets the width of the control in pixels
	Size: Height	24	Sets the height of the control in pixels
	Location: X (left)	152	Indicates the distance from the left border of GroupBox2 in pixels
	Location: Y (top)	24	Indicates the distance from the top border of GroupBox2 in pixels
	Checked	True	Sets this control as the default button in GroupBox2
Button1	Text	Print Compensation Review Report	Sets the text that displays on the button face to Print Compensation Review Report
	TabIndex	2	Causes this control to be the third control on the form to receive focus
	Name	btnPrint	Changes the control's name to a descriptive name
	Size: Width	112	Sets the width of the control in pixels
	Size: Height	32	Sets the height of the control in pixels
	Location: X (left)	168	Indicates the distance from the left border of the form in pixels
	Location: Y (top)	272	Indicates the distance from the top border of the form in pixels

The step on the next page creates the user interface for the Compensation Review Report application. The form properties are set using the property values listed in Table 10-4; the control properties are set using the property values listed in Table 10-5. The properties for the MonthCalendar control are set later in this chapter.

To Set Form Properties and Add Controls

1. With Form1 selected, set the properties of the Form1 form as specified in Table 10-4 on page VB 10.42. Add the controls to the form as shown in Figure 10-34 and set the property values of the controls as listed in Table 10-5 on pages VB 10.42 and VB 10.43. Add the MonthCalendar control to the GroupBox1 control. Add the two RadioButton controls to the GroupBox2 control.

The properties of the Form1 form and controls are set and the controls display on the Form1 form, as shown in Figure 10-34. The properties of the MonthCalendar control will be set later in this chapter.

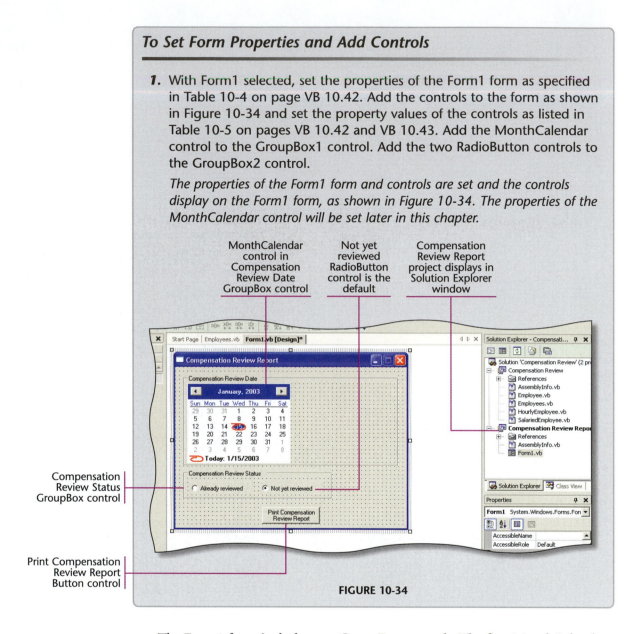

FIGURE 10-34

The Form1 form includes two GroupBox controls. The first MonthCalendar control in the first GroupBox control allows the user to select a date for which to check the review status of employees. The RadioButton controls in the second GroupBox control allow the user to choose whether to print the report for employees who have been reviewed or employees not yet reviewed. The Print Compensation Review Report button allows the user to print the report based on the criteria defined by the selections in the MonthCalendar and RadioButton controls.

MonthCalendar Control Properties

The MonthCalendar control allows the user to set and view dates and date ranges using a familiar calendar as an interface. The control can display as many months at one time as necessary; it also can be set to limit the date that the user can select to a specific date range. Table 10-6 lists the commonly used properties of the MonthCalendar control.

Table 10-6   MonthCalendar Control Properties

CATEGORY	PROPERTY	DESCRIPTION	PROPERTY VALUES
Appearance	CalendarDimensions: Height	The number of rows of months to display in the control	Any integer value from **1** to 12
	CalendarDimensions: Width	The number of columns of months to display in the control	Any integer value from **1** to 12
Behavior	FirstDayOfWeek	The first day of the week that displays in the left column of each month	**Default** Monday Tuesday Wednesday Thursday Friday Saturday Sunday
	MaxDate	The maximum date that the user can select	Choose a date from a drop-down calendar **(12/31/9998)**
	MaxSelectionCount	The maximum number of dates that the user can select at any time	Any integer value **(7)**
	MinDate	The minimum date that the user can select	Monday drop-down calendar (1/1/1753)
	ScrollChange	The scroll rate in number of months moved when the user clicks an arrow button on the control	Any positive integer value up to 20,000. The default is the number of months currently displayed.
	SelectionRange:Start	The date marking the beginning of the currently selected range	Any valid date in the control
	SelectionRange:End	The date marking the end of the currently selected range	Any valid date in the control
	ShowToday	Determines whether today's date displays at the bottom of control	**True** False
	ShowTodayCircle	Determines whether today's date is circled in the control	**True** False
	ShowWeekNumbers	Determines whether the week number (1 – 52) displays for each week in the calendar	True **False**
	TodaysDate	The current day	Choose a date from a drop-down calendar
Misc	AnnuallyBoldedDates	An array of recurring dates that the control bolds for every year	Select individual dates in a dialog box
	BoldedDates	An array of individual, non-recurring dates that the control bolds	Select individual dates in a dialog box
	MonthlyBoldedDates	An array of recurring dates that the control bolds for each month	Select individual dates in a dialog box

The user interface design for the Compensation Review Report application (Figure 10-3 on page VB 10.08) requires that the MonthCalendar control display two months at once and limit the user to selecting one date between 1/1/2004 and 12/31/2010. Table 10-7 lists the changes that must be made to the default property values of the MonthCalendar control on the Form1 form. When naming a MonthCalendar control, use the cal prefix to indicate a MonthCalendar control.

Tip

Naming MonthCalendar Controls
When naming a MonthCalendar control, use the cal prefix for the name.

Table 10-7 **MonthCalendar Control Properties for the Compensation Review Report Application**

CATEGORY	PROPERTY	VALUE	EFFECT
Appearance	CalendarDimensions: Width	2	Causes 2 months to display side by side in the control
	CalendarDimensions: Height	1	Causes 1 month to display vertically in the control
Behavior	MaxDate	12/31/2010	Sets the maximum date that the user can select in the control
	MaxSelectionCount	1	Sets the maximum number of dates the user can select at any time to 1
	MinDate	1/1/2004	Sets the minimum date that the user can select in the control
	Name	calReviewDate	Changes the control's name to a descriptive name
	ScrollChange	1	Causes the calendar to increment by 1 month when the user clicks an arrow button on the control
	ShowToday	False	Causes the control not to highlight the current date
	TabIndex	0	Causes the control to be the first in GroupBox1 to receive focus
Layout	Location: X	8	Indicates the distance from the left border of GroupBox1 in pixels
	Location: Y	16	Indicates the distance from the top border of GroupBox1 in pixels

The following step sets the properties of the MonthCalendar control to those shown in Table 10-7.

To Change the Properties of a MonthCalendar Control

1. Click the MonthCalendar control. Change the Name property value for the MonthCalendar control to calReviewDate as listed in Table 10-7. Set the remaining properties of the control as listed in Table 10-7.

The MonthCalendar control is renamed calReviewDate and displays two months as shown in Figure 10-35.

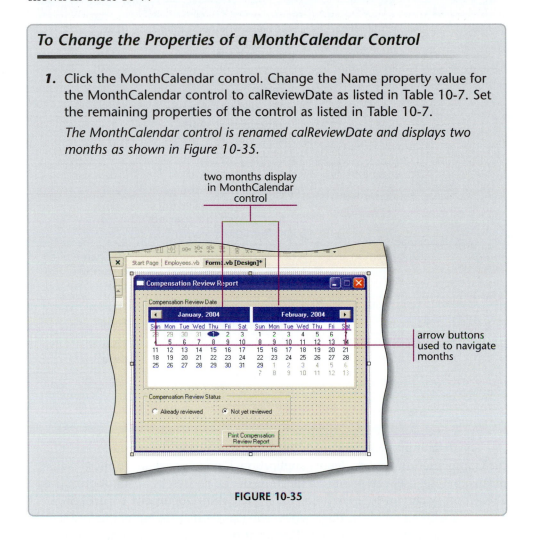

FIGURE 10-35

At run time, the calReviewDate MonthCalendar control will display the month of the current date. The user clicks the arrow buttons on the control to navigate to the date for which he or she wants to run the report.

Adding PrintDialog and PrintDocument Controls to a Form

You probably are familiar with the Print dialog box that offers you choices for setting print options when you print a document from a Windows application. The PrintDialog control provided by Visual Basic .NET allows use of a common Print Dialog box in a Windows application. Table 10-8 on the next page lists the commonly used properties of the PrintDialog control.

Table 10-8 PrintDialog Control Properties

CATEGORY	PROPERTY	DESCRIPTION	PROPERTY VALUES
Misc.	AllowPrintToFile	Determines whether a Print to file check box displays on the Print dialog box	**True** False
	AllowSelection	Determines whether the Selection radio button displays on the dialog box, allowing the user to print just a selection from the document	True **False**
	AllowSomePages	Determines whether the Pages radio button displays on the dialog box, allowing the user to print just selected pages from the document	True **False**
	Document	A document control associated with the dialog box	The name of a document control
	PrintToFile	Reflects the state of the Print to file check box	True **False**
	ShowNetwork	Determines whether the Network button displays on the dialog box	**True** False

The default property values for the PrintDialog meet the requirements of the Compensation Review Report application. Using the default property values means that the user can print to a file, if he or she desires, but cannot print only a selection or certain pages of a document. The **PrintDocument control** provides you with an object through which you can create a document before sending the document to the printer. Before printing, you set the properties that describe what to print using the **PrinterSettings** and **PageSettings** classes, and call the **Print()** method to actually print the document. After creating a document using the PrintDocument control and before printing, you also can use the **PrintPreview control** to allow you to preview the document.

Table 10-9 lists the changes that must be made to the default property values of the PrintDialog and PrintDocument controls. The only changes required are the Name properties. When naming a PrintDocument or PrintDialog control, use the obj or doc prefix for the name. Recall that the obj prefix is sufficient to name any control or variable that is an object.

Naming PrintDocument and PrintDialog Controls
When naming a PrintDocument or PrintDialog control, use the obj or doc prefix for the name.

Table 10-9 **PrintDialog and PrintDocument Control Properties for the Compensation Review Report Application**

CONTROL	PROPERTY	VALUE	EFFECT
PrintDialog1	Name	objPrintDialog	Changes the control's name to a descriptive name
PrintDocument	Name	objPrintDocument	Changes the control's name to a descriptive name

In the Compensation Review Report application, a header and the employee information are created and assigned to the objPrintDocument control. The Print() method then is called after all of the records are formatted and assigned to the objPrintDocument control.

The following steps set the properties of the PrintDialog and PrintDocument controls to those shown in Table 10-9.

To Change the Properties of PrintDialog and PrintDocument Controls

1. Click the PrintDialog control in the Component Tray. Change the Name property value of the PrintDialog control as shown in Table 10-9.

2. Click the PrintDocument control in the Component Tray. Change the Name property value of the Print-Document control as shown in Table 10-9.

   The names on the controls change in the Component Tray (Figure 10-36).

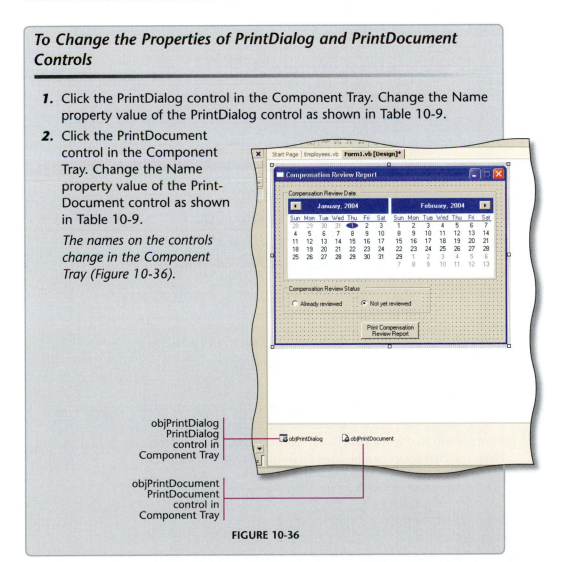

objPrintDialog PrintDialog control in Component Tray

objPrintDocument PrintDocument control in Component Tray

FIGURE 10-36

The user interface for the Compensation Review Report application now is complete. The next task is to write the code for the Compensation Review Report application.

Printing a Report

The .NET Framework class library provides a rich set of classes that support printing documents and graphics to a printer. Most of the classes relating to printing reside in the **System.Drawing.Printing namespace**. The PrintDocument control provides a visible representation of the **PrintDocument class**, which is part of the System.Drawing.Printing namespace.

Several methods exist for producing output using the PrintDocument class or object. One useful object contained in each PrintDocument object is the **Graphics object**. In this chapter, the **DrawString() method** of the Graphics object of a PrintDocument object will be used to print the string containing the report. Two common properties of the Graphics object are the Font property and the Brush property. The **Font property** and the **Brush property** allow you to specify font and color information about strings you place on a Graphics object using the DrawString() method. Figure 10-37 shows the relationship among these controls, classes, and objects.

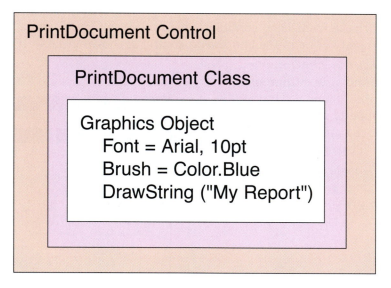

FIGURE 10-37

Before using the DrawString() method, the program must create a string to send as a parameter to the DrawString() method. The string includes all of the information that must print on the report. Space characters, Tab characters, and NewLine characters can be used to format the string properly.

Using PrintDialog and PrintDocument Controls in Code

In this chapter, the DrawString() method of the Graphics property of the PrintDocument class will be used to draw the Compensation Review report. A complete string containing the report will be created in code, and then the DrawString() method will be called to print the report to the printer selected by the user. The objPrintDocument control includes an instance of the PrintDocument class that can be used to print the report.

The first action the program performs is to display the Print dialog box so that the user can choose a printer. Just as with the FontDialog control used in Chapter 7, the ShowDialog() method displays the dialog box.

Figure 10-38 and Figure 10-39 show the initial code for the Form1 form. Figure 38 shows the code for the Option Strict On statement and the Imports statement necessary for the program. Recall that the Imports statement allows you to reference elements in a namespace without qualification, so elements in the imported namespace do not need the namespace identifier when they are referenced in code. For example, you can use the identifier Employee rather than Compensation_Review.Employee to reference the Employee class in the Compensation_Review class library, if the namespace Compensation_Review is imported using the Imports statement. Figure 10-39 shows the code for the btnPrint_Click event procedure that executes when the user clicks the Print Compensation Review Report button.

```
1 Option Strict On
2 Imports Compensation_Review
```

FIGURE 10-38

```
134      Private Sub btnPrint_Click(ByVal sender As System.Object, ByVal e As System.    ↙
         EventArgs) Handles btnPrint.Click
135          objPrintDialog.Document = objPrintDocument
136          If (objPrintDialog.ShowDialog() = DialogResult.OK) Then
137              objPrintDocument.DefaultPageSettings.Landscape = True
138              objPrintDocument.Print()
139          End If
140      End Sub
```

FIGURE 10-39

Line 135 in the btnPrint_Click event procedure associates the objPrintDocument control with the objPrintDialog control before the Print dialog box displays. This allows the Print dialog box to determine and take action on some properties of a PrintDocument control or object. For example, if the objPrintDocument control contained information to be printed, the objPrintDialog control could display information such as a page count on the Print dialog box. In this chapter, no properties have been set for the objPrintDocument control, so no additional action is taken by the objPrintDialog control.

Line 136 uses the ShowDialog() method to display the Print dialog box and determine if the user has clicked the OK button in the Print dialog box. If not, the procedure exits and the user interface regains control of the application. If the user clicks the OK button on the Print dialog box, then the **DefaultSettings.Landscape property** of the objPrintDocument control is set to True. This causes any information drawn on the control to be done so in landscape orientation. Line 138 calls the Print() method of the objPrintDocument control. The Print() method causes the **PrintPage event procedure** of the objPrintDocument control to execute. The objPrintDocument_PrintPage event procedure will be coded later in this chapter.

The following steps open the code window and add the code shown in Figures 10-38 and 10-39 on the previous page.

To Use a PrintDialog Control and a PrintDocument Control in Code

1. Double-click the btnPrint Button control on the Form1 form. When the code window displays, type the code as shown in Figure 10-38.

2. Enter lines 135 through 139 as shown in Figure 10-39. Visual Basic .NET automatically adds lines 134 and 140 to the code.

   The code window displays as shown in Figure 10-40. The Imports statement allows the code to reference elements in the Compensation_Review namespace without qualification, which makes the code more readable. Intellisense automatically creates the btnPrint_Click event procedure.

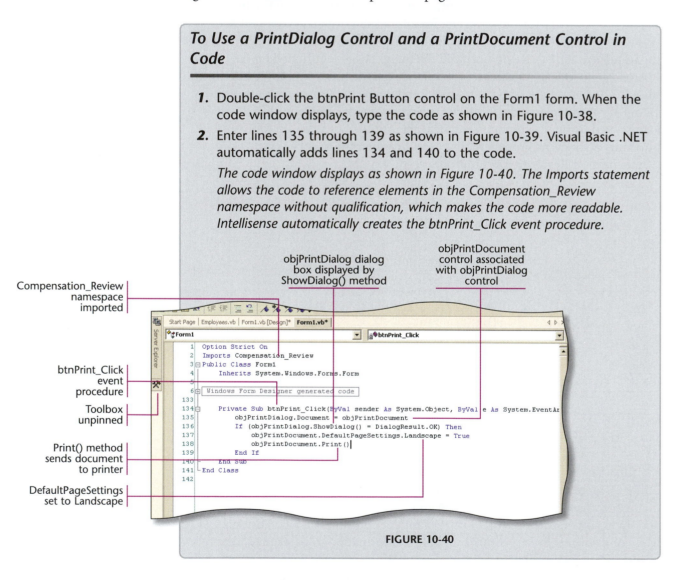

FIGURE 10-40

The coding for the btnPrint_Click event procedure is complete. The event procedure displays a Print dialog box, sets the document to landscape orientation, and then calls the Print() method of the objPrintDocument control. The next step is to code functions that build the report header and report body.

Building a Report Header

As you have learned, before sending the report to the printer, the program first builds a string containing the complete contents of the report. In the Compensation Review Report application, two functions handle the process of building the string. The first function builds the report header, and the second function builds the report body. Both functions return string variables containing the appropriate information.

The report header is a string that contains the company name, the report name, the date selected by the user, and column headers for each piece of information printed for each employee. Figure 10-41 shows the code necessary to build the report header string.

```
142     Private Function BuildReportHeader() As String
143         Dim strHeader As String
144
145         strHeader = "Ekstrom Optical Corporation" & ControlChars.NewLine & _
146                     "Compensation Review Report: (" & _
147                     calReviewDate.SelectionStart.ToShortDateString & _
148                     ")" & ControlChars.NewLine & ControlChars.NewLine & _
149                     "Employee" & ControlChars.Tab & _
150                     "Name" & ControlChars.Tab & ControlChars.Tab & _
151                     "Location" & ControlChars.Tab & ControlChars.Tab & _
152                     "Date" & ControlChars.Tab & ControlChars.Tab & _
153                     "    Date" & ControlChars.Tab & ControlChars.Tab & _
154                     "Next Review" & ControlChars.Tab & _
155                     "Reviewed" & ControlChars.Tab & _
156                     "Hourly" & ControlChars.Tab & _
157                     "Annual" & ControlChars.Tab & _
158                     "  Min" & ControlChars.Tab & _
159                     "  Max" & ControlChars.Tab & ControlChars.NewLine & _
160                     "    ID" & ControlChars.Tab & _
161                     ControlChars.Tab & ControlChars.Tab & ControlChars.Tab & _
162                     ControlChars.Tab & ControlChars.Tab & _
163                     "Hired" & ControlChars.Tab & ControlChars.Tab & _
164                     "  Reviewed" & ControlChars.Tab & _
165                     "    Date" & ControlChars.Tab & ControlChars.Tab & _
166                     ControlChars.Tab & ControlChars.Tab & _
167                     "Rate" & ControlChars.Tab & _
168                     "Salary" & ControlChars.NewLine & ControlChars.NewLine
169         Return strHeader
170     End Function
```

FIGURE 10-41

Line 142 declares the BuildReportHeader() function and indicates that the function returns the data type of String. Lines 145 through 168 build a long string that contains all of the necessary information for the report header. Space characters, Tab characters, and NewLine characters assist in formatting the header. Typically, before you enter the code to build the report, you should lay out a report on a report layout sheet to determine the proper spacing and necessary control characters needed.

Laying Out a Report
Use a report layout sheet to determine the proper spacing and necessary control characters needed to format a report properly.

Line 147 uses the **ToShortDateString() method** of a date variable to convert the date selected by the user — calReviewDate.SelectionStart — to a string formatted as MM/DD/YYYY. For example, if the user selected January 15, 2005 on the control, then the ToShortDateString() method returns 01/15/2005. Line 169 returns the strHeader variable to the calling line of code.

The following step adds the code shown in Figure 10-41 on the previous page to create a private function that returns a string containing a report header.

To Build a Report Header

1. Type lines 142 through 170 as shown in Figure 10-41.

Lines 142 through 170 display in the code window. The BuildReportHeader() function creates and returns a string containing a multi-line report header for the Compensation Review report. Control characters properly format the report header (Figure 10-42).

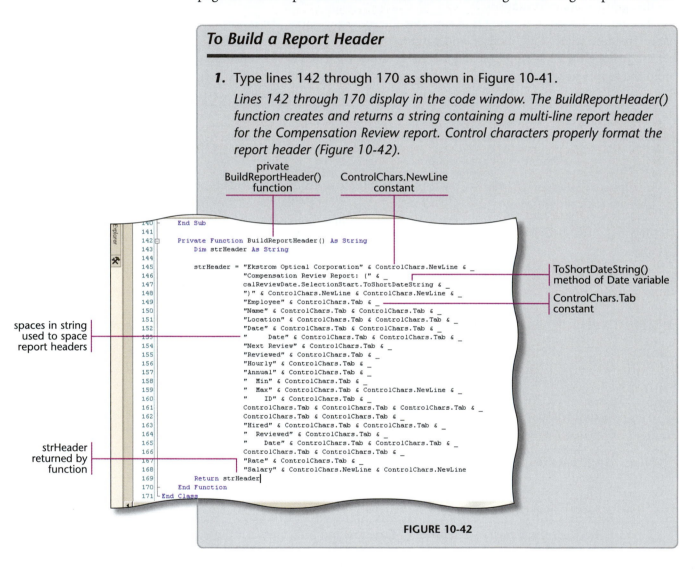

FIGURE 10-42

The code for the BuildReportHeader() function is complete. The function returns the strHeader variable to the calling line of code. The next step is to code a function to build the report body in a similar manner.

Building a Report Body

The Compensation Review report requires a line on the report for each employee who meets the criteria specified by the user and, if appropriate, is calculated to be eligible for review within 30 days of a given date. The BuildReportBody() function handles this requirement. When an instance of the Employees object is created, the object stores information for the selected employees in two properties. The properties are collections of either HourlyEmployee objects or SalariedEmployee objects. Later in this chapter, code will be written to instantiate an Employees object and then pass that object to the BuildReportBody() function.

Figure 10-43 shows a flowchart that outlines the logic used to get the HourlyEmployee and SalariedEmployee objects from the Employees object and then build a string from the properties and methods of the objects. Two Do While loops in the flowchart read the HourlyEmployee and SalariedEmployee objects. The loops exit when they have finished processing all of the items in the collections.

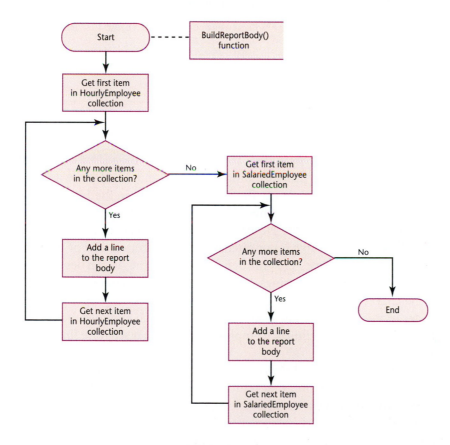

FIGURE 10-43

Figure 10-44 shows the function declaration for the BuildReportBody() function and the code that corresponds to the first loop in the flowchart in Figure 10-43 on the previous page. The function returns a String data type.

```
172    Private Function BuildReportBody(ByVal objEmployees As Employees) As String
173        Dim strBody As String
174        Dim objHourlyEmployee As HourlyEmployee
175        Dim objSalariedEmployee As SalariedEmployee
176
177        For Each objHourlyEmployee In objEmployees.HourlyEmployeeList
178            strBody = strBody & _
179                    objHourlyEmployee.EmployeeID & ControlChars.Tab & ControlChars. ↙
        Tab & _
180                    Convert.ToString(objHourlyEmployee.Name).PadRight(15, Convert. ↙
        ToChar(" ")) & ControlChars.Tab & _
181                    Convert.ToString(objHourlyEmployee.Location).PadRight(10,        ↙
        Convert.ToChar(" ")) & ControlChars.Tab & _
182                    objHourlyEmployee.DateHired & ControlChars.Tab & _
183                    objHourlyEmployee.DateReviewed & ControlChars.Tab & _
184                    objHourlyEmployee.ComputeNextReviewDate() & ControlChars.Tab & _
185                    objHourlyEmployee.Reviewed & ControlChars.Tab & _
186                    ControlChars.Tab & "$" & objHourlyEmployee.HourlyRate &          ↙
        ControlChars.Tab & ControlChars.Tab & _
187                    Convert.ToString(objHourlyEmployee.CompensationAdjustmentMin &   ↙
        "%").PadLeft(6, Convert.ToChar(" ")) & ControlChars.Tab & _
188                    Convert.ToString(objHourlyEmployee.CompensationAdjustmentMax &   ↙
        "%").PadLeft(6, Convert.ToChar(" ")) & ControlChars.NewLine
189        Next
190    End Function
```

FIGURE 10-44

The use of the HourlyEmployee and SalariedEmployee classes illustrates the power of object-oriented programming. Lines 174 and 175 declare an object for each of those classes and then use them as the variables in the For Each statements in the loop. The loop in lines 177 through 189 executes once for each HourlyEmployee object in the HourlyEmployees property of the Employees object. The strBody variable is concatenated with each iteration of the loop, as shown in line 178. Lines 179 through 188 convert the properties of the HourlyEmployee object to strings. Space characters, Tab characters, and NewLine characters help to format the line of information properly. A NewLine character in line 188 is the last character added to each employee's information, to instruct the code to print each employee record on a separate line of the report.

The following steps add the code shown in Figure 10-44 to create a private BuildReportBody() function that returns a string containing the report body for the Compensation Review report.

To Build the Report Body

1. Enter lines 172 through 175 as shown in Figure 10-44.

Lines 172 through 177 display in the code window. Intellisense automatically inserts the End Function statement on line 177. Two objects, objHourlyEmployee and objSalariedEmployee, are declared with types corresponding to each of the subclasses of the Employee class (Figure 10-45).

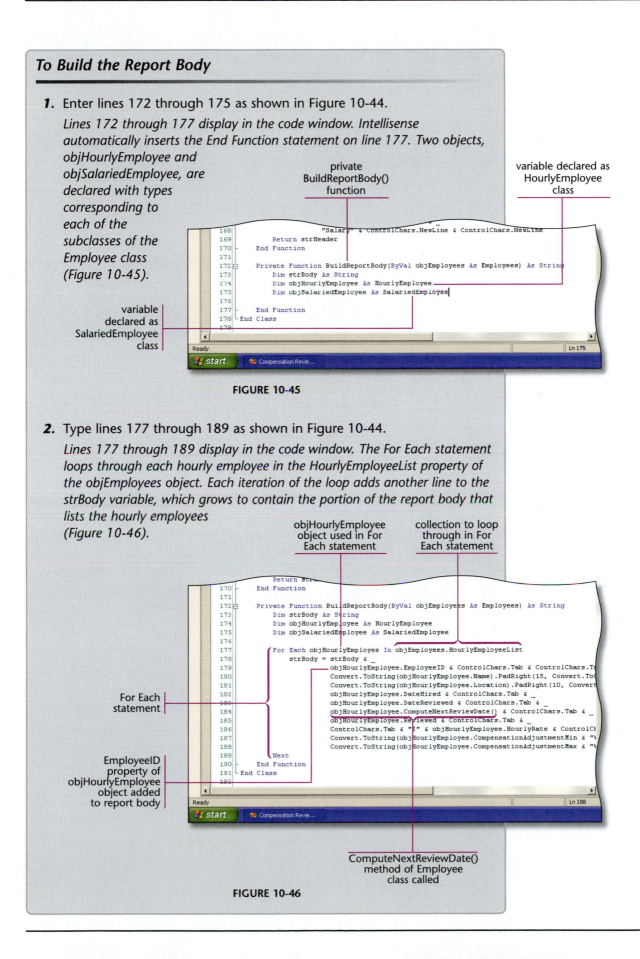

FIGURE 10-45

2. Type lines 177 through 189 as shown in Figure 10-44.

Lines 177 through 189 display in the code window. The For Each statement loops through each hourly employee in the HourlyEmployeeList property of the objEmployees object. Each iteration of the loop adds another line to the strBody variable, which grows to contain the portion of the report body that lists the hourly employees (Figure 10-46).

FIGURE 10-46

The code shown in Figure 10-46 on the previous page creates the lines of the report for hourly employees. The code carefully formats the information for each employee, using various ToString() methods and control characters. As indicated in the flowchart in Figure 10-43 on page VB 10.55, a second, similar loop is required to add salaried employee records to the report.

Figure 10-47 shows the code necessary to create a line on the report for each salaried employee record returned by the query.

```
190        For Each objSalariedEmployee In objEmployees.SalariedEmployeeList
191            strBody = strBody & _
192                    objSalariedEmployee.EmployeeID & ControlChars.Tab & ControlChars↙
       .Tab & _
193                    Convert.ToString(objSalariedEmployee.Name).PadRight(15, Convert.↙
       ToChar(" ")) & ControlChars.Tab & _
194                    Convert.ToString(objSalariedEmployee.Location).PadRight(10,        ↙
       Convert.ToChar(" ")) & ControlChars.Tab & _
195                    objSalariedEmployee.DateHired & ControlChars.Tab & _
196                    objSalariedEmployee.DateReviewed & ControlChars.Tab & _
197                    objSalariedEmployee.ComputeNextReviewDate() & ControlChars.Tab &↙
           _
198                    objSalariedEmployee.Reviewed & ControlChars.Tab & ControlChars.  ↙
       Tab & _
199                    ControlChars.Tab & ControlChars.Tab & "$" & objSalariedEmployee.↙
       AnnualSalary & _
200                    Convert.ToString(objSalariedEmployee.CompensationAdjustmentMin &↙
       "%").PadLeft(6, Convert.ToChar(" ")) & ControlChars.Tab & _
201                    Convert.ToString(objSalariedEmployee.CompensationAdjustmentMax &↙
       "%").PadLeft(6, Convert.ToChar(" ")) & ControlChars.NewLine
202        Next
203        Return strBody
```

FIGURE 10-47

The following step adds the code shown in Figure 10-47 to complete the BuildReportBody() function.

> ### To Finish Building the Report Body
>
> **1.** Type lines 190 through 203 as shown in Figure 10-47.
>
> *Lines 190 through 203 display in the code window. The For Each statement loops through each salaried employee in the SalariedEmployeeList property of the objEmployees object. Each iteration of the loop adds another line to the strBody variable, which grows to contain the portion of the report body that lists the salaried employees (Figure 10-48).*

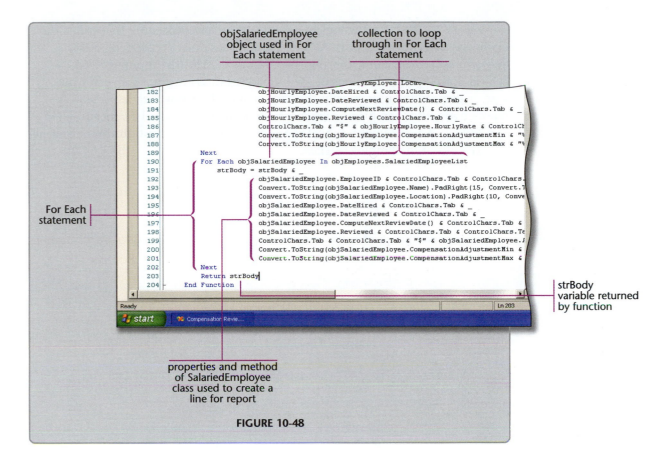

objSalariedEmployee object used in For Each statement

collection to loop through in For Each statement

```
182        objHourlyEmployee.DateHired & ControlChars.Tab & _
183        objHourlyEmployee.DateReviewed & ControlChars.Tab & _
184        objHourlyEmployee.ComputeNextReviewDate() & ControlChars.Tab & _
185        objHourlyEmployee.Reviewed & ControlChars.Tab & _
186        ControlChars.Tab & "$" & objHourlyEmployee.HourlyRate & ControlCh
187        Convert.ToString(objHourlyEmployee.CompensationAdjustmentMin & "%
188        Convert.ToString(objHourlyEmployee.CompensationAdjustmentMax & "%
189     Next
190     For Each objSalariedEmployee In objEmployees.SalariedEmployeeList
191        strBody = strBody & _
192        objSalariedEmployee.EmployeeID & ControlChars.Tab & ControlChars.
193        Convert.ToString(objSalariedEmployee.Name).PadRight(15, Convert.T
194        Convert.ToString(objSalariedEmployee.Location).PadRight(10, Conve
195        objSalariedEmployee.DateHired & ControlChars.Tab & _
196        objSalariedEmployee.DateReviewed & ControlChars.Tab & _
197        objSalariedEmployee.ComputeNextReviewDate() & ControlChars.Tab & _
198        objSalariedEmployee.Reviewed & ControlChars.Tab & ControlChars.Te
199        ControlChars.Tab & ControlChars.Tab & "$" & objSalariedEmployee.S
200        Convert.ToString(objSalariedEmployee.CompensationAdjustmentMin & _
201        Convert.ToString(objSalariedEmployee.CompensationAdjustmentMax & _
202     Next
203     Return strBody
204 End Function
```

Ready   Ln 203

start   Compensation Revie...

For Each statement

strBody variable returned by function

properties and method of SalariedEmployee class used to create a line for report

FIGURE 10-48

Line 203 returns the strBody variable to the line of code that called the BuildReportBody() function. The variable contains all of the employee information properly formatted and ready for printing.

The next step is to write the event procedure that creates an instance of the Employees object, calls the BuildReportHeader() and BuildReportBody() functions, and prints the report to the printer selected by the user.

Sending Output to a Printer

As indicated in the program design, the code for the Compensation Review Report application requires code that instantiates an Employees object, creates the report header, creates the report body, and then sends the report to the printer. Finally, if any exceptions occur during the creation of the Employees object, they must be caught in a Catch clause of a Try...Catch statement and handled by sending the error to the calling line of code or displaying a user-friendly error message.

Figure 10-49 shows the logic needed for the event procedure that prints the Compensation Review report. After the Employees object is created, a test determines if any records to print exist. If both the HourlyEmployees and SalariedEmployees collections of the Employees class are empty, an error message displays to the user. Finally, the code creates the report header, creates the report body, and then prints the report. All of the logic should be encapsulated in a Try...Catch statement, so that the code handles any exceptions that occur in the creation of the Employees class.

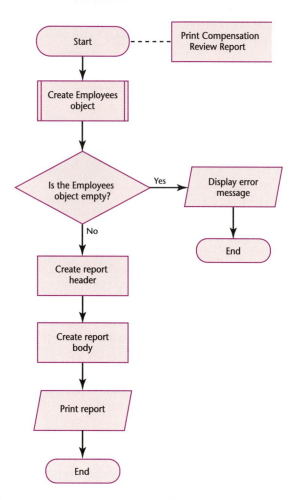

FIGURE 10-49

Figure 10-50 shows the Try clause of the Try...Catch statement, which implements the logic shown in Figure 10-49. Line 206 declares the PrintPage event procedure for the objPrintDocument control. The PrintPage event occurs when the Print() method is called for a PrintDocument object. In this application, the Print() method is called from the btnPrint_Click event procedure coded earlier in this chapter.

```
206     Private Sub objPrintDocument_PrintPage(ByVal sender As System.Object, ByVal e As ↙
        System.Drawing.Printing.PrintPageEventArgs) Handles objPrintDocument.PrintPage
207         Dim objFont As Font
208         Dim objBrush As Brush
209         Dim intHeight As Integer
210         Dim strCompensationReviewReport As String
211
212         Try
213             Dim objEmployees As New Employees(radAlreadyReviewed.Checked, ↙
        calReviewDate.SelectionRange.Start)
214             If objEmployees.HourlyEmployeeList.Count = 0 And objEmployees. ↙
        SalariedEmployeeList.Count = 0 Then
215                 MessageBox.Show("No employees to print for this date and status.", "No↙
        Employees to Print")
216                 Exit Try
217             Else
218                 objFont = New Font("Arial", 10)
219                 objBrush = New SolidBrush(Color.Blue)
220                 intHeight = objFont.Height
221                 strCompensationReviewReport = BuildReportHeader()
222                 strCompensationReviewReport &= BuildReportBody(objEmployees)
223                 e.Graphics.DrawString(strCompensationReviewReport, objFont, objBrush, ↙
        0, intHeight)
224             End If
225     End Sub
```

FIGURE 10-50

As you have learned, the DrawString() method requires that a Font object
and a Brush object be passed to the method. Lines 207 and 208 declare a Font
object, objFont, and a Brush object, objBrush, using the Font class and Brush
class. The **Font class** defines a particular format for text, including font name,
size, and style attributes. The **Brush class** serves as a container that holds other
objects that describe information about drawing to a graphics device, or an
object that supports graphics, such as a printer. Line 218 sets the objFont variable to an Arial font with a point size of 10. Line 219 creates a SolidBrush object
in the objBrush container and sets the brush color to Color.Blue. Setting the
brush color to Color.Blue causes output to the printer to be blue, if a color
printer is used. Both the objFont and objBrush objects are passed to the
DrawString() method on line 223.

Lines 213 instantiates an Employees object and passes two parameters to the
Employees class constructor — the state of the radAlreadyReviewed RadioButton
control and the date selected on the calReviewDate MonthCalendar control.
When line 213 executes, all of the code in the constructor, including the code
to connect to and read records from the database, executes and populates the
HourlyEmployees and SalariedEmployees properties of the objEmployees object.
Line 214 checks that at least one item exists in one of the two properties of the
Employees class. If no items exist, then an error message displays and the **Exit
Try statement** on line 216 exits the Try…Catch statement, which causes the
procedure to exit.

Lines 221 and 222 call the BuildReportHeader() and BuildReportBody functions. The code concatenates the strings returned by the two functions into the
strCompensationReviewReport variable. Finally, on line 223, the DrawString()
method of the e.Graphics object is called. The method accepts the report string,
the Font object, the Brush object, and the height of the font as parameters. The

printer object named e is a parameter passed to the objPrintDocument_PrintPage event procedure in line 206 and is an object in the PrintPageEventArgs class of the .NET Framework class library. The **PrintPageEventArgs class** is a robust class that allows for page formatting and fine-tuning the printing process.

Catching Exceptions

The Try…Catch statements coded thus far in this chapter used the Throw statement to handle the exceptions. Rather than having a run-time error occur when a run-time error condition is met, the code sends the exception back to the line of code that called the procedure or object in which the error occurred. When using Try…Catch…Finally exception handling, at some point, you must write code that does something with the exceptions that occur.

Figure 10-51 shows the Catch clause of the Try…Catch statement in the objPrintDocument_PrintPage event procedure. If any exceptions occur in the creation of the Employees object or in the printing of the report to the printer, a message box displays an error message and the program terminates, using the End statement. While the error message coded in line 227 may not be of much use to the user, other options exist for handling the error. The Catch statement in line 225 declares a new object of type Exception. When used in this manner, the Catch clause catches all exceptions, and information about the specific exception is stored in the objException variable next to the Catch keyword. This practice allows information about the exception to be displayed to the user or written to a log file to allow a developer to analyze when the error occurs.

> **Tip**
>
> **Handling Exceptions**
> When a variable of type Exception is placed next to the Catch keyword, the Catch clause catches all exceptions, and information about the specific exception is stored in the variable next to the Catch keyword. This practice allows information about the exception to be displayed to the user or written to a log file to allow a developer to analyze when the error occurs.

```
225         Catch objException As Exception
226            MessageBox.Show("The following Exception was encountered: " & objException↵
       .Message _
227                          & ControlChars.NewLine & "The program will now end. Please↵
       contact an administrator for help.")
228            End
229        End Try
```

FIGURE 10-51

The use of a message box to display the exception encountered is utilized here to illustrate the concept of exception handling using the Try…Catch statement. All exceptions do not need to result in the termination of the program. Other options for handling the exceptions may include attempting corrective measures for whichever error occurred. For example, the End statement in line

228 can be eliminated and control of the program could return to the user interface after the message box from line 226 displays. The Finally clause also can be used to take care of any clean-up work in the code, such as attempting to close a database before the program finally terminates.

The following steps create the objPrintDocument_PrintPage event procedure for the objPrintDocument control and then add the code shown in Figure 10-50 on page VB 10.61 and Figure 10-51 to the event procedure.

To Send Output to a Printer and Catch an Exception

1. Click the Form1.vb[Design]* tab at the top of the code window. When the Form1 form displays, double-click the objPrintDocument control in the Component Tray.

The Form1.vb* tab displays in the code window. Visual Basic .NET creates a new event procedure for the objPrintDocument_PrintPage event procedure.

2. Type lines 207 through 224 as shown in Figure 10-50 on page VB 10.61.

Lines 207 through 224 display in the code window.

3. Type lines 225 through 229 as shown in Figure 10-51.

Lines 225 through 229 display in the code window as shown in Figure 10-52. The objPrintDocument_PrintPage event procedure executes when the Print() method is called from the btnPrint_Click event procedure. An Employees object is instantiated within a Try...Catch statement, causing the code that reads records from the database to execute. If any database operations fail, the code in the Catch clause displays an error message box and exits the program.

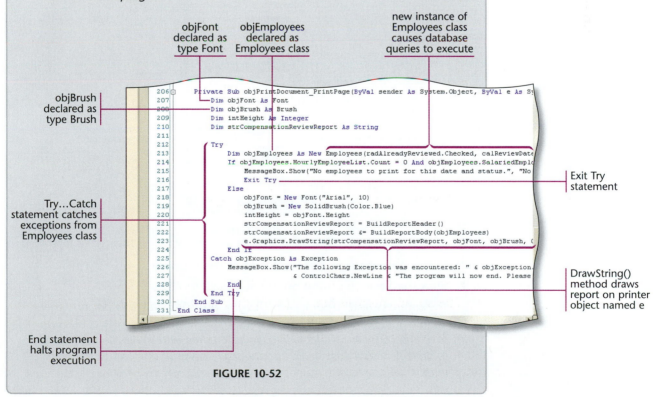

FIGURE 10-52

The coding phase for the Compensation Review Report application now is complete and the application can be tested.

Saving, Testing, and Documenting the Project

The following steps save the form and project files for the Compensation Review Report project on the Data Disk in drive A and then run the application to test the project.

To Set the Startup Project, Save the Project, and Test the Project

1. Click the Compensation Review solution in the Solution Explorer. Click the property value next to the Startup project property in the Properties window. Click the box arrow in the property value of the Startup project.

The two projects in the Compensation Review solution display in the list box. The Compensation Review class library currently is selected (Figure 10-53).

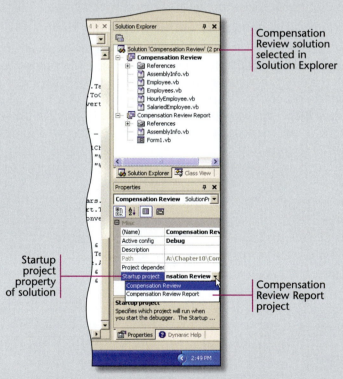

Compensation Review solution selected in Solution Explorer

Startup project property of solution

Compensation Review Report project

FIGURE 10-53

2. Click Compensation Review Report in the list box.

3. Click the Save All button on the Standard toolbar.

The asterisks next to Form1.vb [Design] in the window title bar and the main work area tab no longer display, indicating that the project has been saved. Because the project initially was created and saved to the Data Disk in drive A, Visual Basic .NET automatically saves the project to the Data Disk in drive A.

4. Click the Start button on the Visual Basic .NET Standard toolbar.

5. When the Compensation Review Report application window displays, use the arrow buttons at the top of the MonthCalendar control to navigate the months and then select July 30, 2004 using the MonthCalendar control.

Visual Basic .NET opens the Output window temporarily and displays messages as the application starts. The Compensation Review Report application window displays (Figure 10-54). The date, July 30, 2004, is selected in the MonthCalendar control.

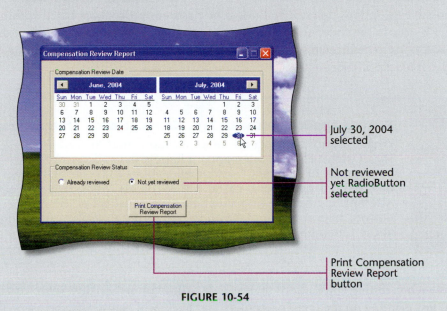

July 30, 2004 selected

Not reviewed yet RadioButton selected

Print Compensation Review Report button

FIGURE 10-54

6. Click the Print Compensation Review Report button. When the Print dialog box displays, select a printer and then click the OK button.

The Compensation Review report prints to the printer selected in the Print dialog box (Figure 10-55). Any employees who require review between July 30, 2004 and August 29, 2004 print on the report.

Report header

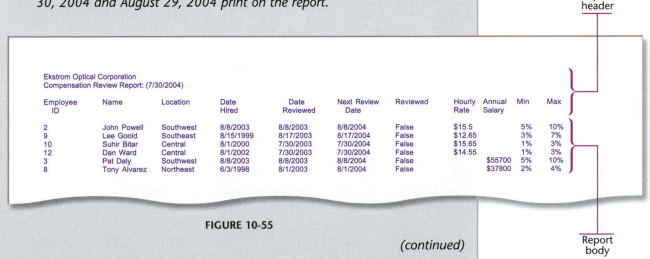

Ekstrom Optical Corporation
Compensation Review Report: (7/30/2004)

Employee ID	Name	Location	Date Hired	Date Reviewed	Next Review Date	Reviewed	Hourly Rate	Annual Salary	Min	Max
2	John Powell	Southwest	8/8/2003	8/8/2003	8/8/2004	False	$15.5		5%	10%
9	Lee Goold	Southeast	8/15/1999	8/17/2003	8/17/2004	False	$12.65		3%	7%
10	Suhir Bitar	Central	8/1/2000	7/30/2003	7/30/2004	False	$15.65		1%	3%
12	Dan Ward	Central	8/1/2002	7/30/2003	7/30/2004	False	$14.55		1%	3%
3	Pat Daly	Southwest	8/8/2003	8/8/2003	8/8/2004	False		$55700	5%	10%
8	Tony Alvarez	Northeast	6/3/1998	8/1/2003	8/1/2004	False		$37800	2%	4%

FIGURE 10-55

(continued)

Report body

> **7.** Click the Close button on the Compensation Review Report application window title bar. If necessary, click the Visual Basic .NET taskbar button to display the Visual Basic .NET window. If necessary, close the Output window.
>
> *Visual Basic .NET returns to design time.*

When testing the functions of applications that include Try…Catch…Finally statements to handle exceptions, you should create or obtain a list of all of the possible exceptions that can be thrown by classes or procedures called within the Try blocks in the code. Attempt to create testing situations that cause all of the exceptions to be thrown so that you test all of the exception handling in the Catch blocks of code.

Tip

Testing Applications with Try…Catch…Finally Statements

When testing the functions of applications that include Try…Catch…Finally statements to handle exceptions, create or obtain a list of all of the possible exceptions that can be thrown by classes or procedures called within the Try blocks in your code. Attempt to create testing situations that cause all of the exceptions to be thrown so that you test all of the exception handling in the Catch blocks of code.

When testing applications that include printing functionality, make certain to test printing on the types of printers that likely will be used by the users of the application. Ensure that all margins are appropriate and that all information prints on the page. If you use color printing or uncommon fonts in the application, make sure that these special features are available on the printers users of the application might use.

Tip

Testing Applications that Print

When testing applications that include print functionality, consider the following:

- Make certain to test printing on the types of printers that will be used by the users of the application

- Ensure that all margins are appropriate and that all information prints on the page

- If you use color printing or uncommon fonts in the application, make sure that these special features are available on the printers users of the application might use

When testing an application that connects to a database, test the application in situations in which the database is not available. In addition, use a test database, as in this chapter, during development of the application. Populate the database with data that tests the extreme values of each field in the database. If the application totals or performs calculations on information in the database, create test situations that may cause the total to overflow the data type of the variable. Make certain that the application handles all of these situations correctly.

Tip

Testing Database Applications

When testing applications that connect to databases, consider the following:

- Use a test database rather than a database that is in use

- Populate the database with data that tests the extreme values of each field in the database

- If the application totals or performs calculations on information in the database, create test situations that may cause the total to overflow

---

The testing process for the Compensation Review Report application is complete. The final step of the development cycle is to document the application. The following steps document the application and quit Visual Basic .NET. Line numbers are printed on the code listing.

To Document the Application and Quit Visual Basic .NET

1. Click the Form1.vb [Design] tab and then follow the steps on page VB 2.34 of Chapter 2 to use the PRINT SCREEN key to print a record of the user interface design of the Form1 form.

A record of the user interface design of the Compensation Review Report application is printed.

2. Click the Form1.vb tab. Click File on the menu bar and then click Page Setup.

3. When the Page Setup dialog box displays, if necessary, click Line numbers and then click the OK button.

(continued)

4. Follow the steps on page VB 2.40 of Chapter 2 to use the Print command on the File menu to print a record of the code for the Compensation Review Report application.

A record of the Compensation Review Report application code is printed (Figure 10-56).

```
A:\Chapter10\Compensation Review\Compensation Review Report\Form1.vb                              1
 1 Option Strict On
 2 Imports Compensation_Review
 3 Public Class Form1
 4     Inherits System.Windows.Forms.Form
 5
 6 Windows Form Designer generated code
 7
 8     Private Sub btnPrint_Click(ByVal sender As System.Object, ByVal e As System.      ↵
    EventArgs) Handles btnPrint.Click
 9         objPrintDialog.Document = objPrintDocument
10         If (objPrintDialog.ShowDialog() = DialogResult.OK) Then
11             objPrintDocument.DefaultPageSettings.Landscape = True
12             objPrintDocument.Print()
13         End If
14     End Sub
15
16     Private Function BuildReportHeader() As String
17         Dim strHeader As String
18
19         strHeader = "Ekstrom Optical Corporation" & ControlChars.NewLine & _
20                     "Compensation Review Report: (" & _
21                     calReviewDate.SelectionStart.ToShortDateString & _
22                     ")" & ControlChars.NewLine & ControlChars.NewLine & _
23                     "Employee" & ControlChars.Tab & _
24                     "Name" & ControlChars.Tab & ControlChars.Tab & _
25                     "Location" & ControlChars.Tab & ControlChars.Tab & _
26                     "Date" & ControlChars.Tab & ControlChars.Tab & _
27                     "    Date" & ControlChars.Tab & ControlChars.Tab & _
28                     "Next Review" & ControlChars.Tab & _
29                     "Reviewed" & ControlChars.Tab & _
30                     "Hourly" & ControlChars.Tab & _
31                     "Annual" & ControlChars.Tab & _
32                     "  Min" & ControlChars.Tab & _
33                     "  Max" & ControlChars.Tab & ControlChars.NewLine & _
34                     "    ID" & ControlChars.Tab & _
35                     ControlChars.Tab & ControlChars.Tab & ControlChars.Tab & _
36                     ControlChars.Tab & ControlChars.Tab & _
37                     "Hired" & ControlChars.Tab & ControlChars.Tab & _
38                     "  Reviewed" & ControlChars.Tab & _
39                     "    Date" & ControlChars.Tab & ControlChars.Tab & _
40                     ControlChars.Tab & ControlChars.Tab & _
41                     "Rate" & ControlChars.Tab & _
42                     "Salary" & ControlChars.NewLine & ControlChars.NewLine
43         Return strHeader
44     End Function
45
46     Private Function BuildReportBody(ByVal objEmployees As Employees) As String
47         Dim strBody As String
48         Dim objHourlyEmployee As HourlyEmployee
49         Dim objSalariedEmployee As SalariedEmployee
50
51         For Each objHourlyEmployee In objEmployees.HourlyEmployeeList
52             strBody = strBody & _
53                         objHourlyEmployee.EmployeeID & ControlChars.Tab & ControlChars. ↵
    Tab & _
54                         Convert.ToString(objHourlyEmployee.Name).PadRight(15, Convert. ↵
    ToChar(" ")) & ControlChars.Tab & _
55                         Convert.ToString(objHourlyEmployee.Location).PadRight(10, ↵
    Convert.ToChar(" ")) & ControlChars.Tab & _
56             objHourlyEmployee.DateHired & ControlChars.Tab & _
57             objHourlyEmployee.DateReviewed & ControlChars.Tab & _
58             objHourlyEmployee.ComputeNextReviewDate() & ControlChars.Tab & _
59             objHourlyEmployee.Reviewed & ControlChars.Tab & _
60             ControlChars.Tab & "$" & objHourlyEmployee.HourlyRate & ↵
    ControlChars.Tab & ControlChars.Tab & _
61                         Convert.ToString(objHourlyEmployee.CompensationAdjustmentMin & ↵
    "%").PadLeft(6, Convert.ToChar(" ")) & ControlChars.Tab & _
```

FIGURE 10-56

```
A:\Chapter10\Compensation Review\Compensation Review Report\Form1.vb                    2
62                     Convert.ToString(objHourlyEmployee.CompensationAdjustmentMax &  ↵
       "%").PadLeft(6, Convert.ToChar(" ")) & ControlChars.NewLine
63          Next
64       For Each objSalariedEmployee In objEmployees.SalariedEmployeeList
65          strBody = strBody & _
66                     objSalariedEmployee.EmployeeID & ControlChars.Tab & ControlChars↵
       .Tab & _
67                     Convert.ToString(objSalariedEmployee.Name).PadRight(15, Convert.↵
       ToChar(" ")) & ControlChars.Tab & _
68                     Convert.ToString(objSalariedEmployee.Location).PadRight(10,      ↵
       Convert.ToChar(" ")) & ControlChars.Tab & _
69                     objSalariedEmployee.DateHired & ControlChars.Tab & _
70                     objSalariedEmployee.DateReviewed & ControlChars.Tab & _
71                     objSalariedEmployee.ComputeNextReviewDate() & ControlChars.Tab &↵
       _
72                     objSalariedEmployee.Reviewed & ControlChars.Tab & ControlChars. ↵
       Tab & _
73                     ControlChars.Tab & ControlChars.Tab & "$" & objSalariedEmployee.↵
       AnnualSalary & _
74                     Convert.ToString(objSalariedEmployee.CompensationAdjustmentMin &↵
       "%").PadLeft(6, Convert.ToChar(" ")) & ControlChars.Tab & _
75                     Convert.ToString(objSalariedEmployee.CompensationAdjustmentMax &↵
       "%").PadLeft(6, Convert.ToChar(" ")) & ControlChars.NewLine
76          Next
77          Return strBody
78       End Function
79
80       Private Sub objPrintDocument_PrintPage(ByVal sender As System.Object, ByVal e As  ↵
       System.Drawing.Printing.PrintPageEventArgs) Handles objPrintDocument.PrintPage
81          Dim objFont As Font
82          Dim objBrush As Brush
83          Dim intHeight As Integer
84          Dim strCompensationReviewReport As String
85
86          Try
87             Dim objEmployees As New Employees(radAlreadyReviewed.Checked,          ↵
       calReviewDate.SelectionRange.Start)
88             If objEmployees.HourlyEmployeeList.Count = 0 And objEmployees.          ↵
       SalariedEmployeeList.Count = 0 Then
89                MessageBox.Show("No employees to print for this date and status.", "No↵
       Employees to Print")
90                Exit Try
91             Else
92                objFont = New Font("Arial", 10)
93                objBrush = New SolidBrush(Color.Blue)
94                intHeight = objFont.Height
95                strCompensationReviewReport = BuildReportHeader()
96                strCompensationReviewReport &= BuildReportBody(objEmployees)
97                e.Graphics.DrawString(strCompensationReviewReport, objFont, objBrush, ↵
       0, intHeight)
98             End If
99          Catch objException As Exception
100            MessageBox.Show("The following Exception was encountered: " & objException↵
       .Message _
101                          & ControlChars.NewLine & "The program will now end. Please↵
       contact an administrator for help.")
102            End
103         End Try
104      End Sub
105   End Class
106
```

FIGURE 10-56 *(continued)*

5. Click the Visual Basic .NET Close button.

If you made changes to the project since the last time it was saved, Visual Basic .NET displays the Microsoft Visual Basic .NET dialog box. If you click the Yes button, you can resave your project and quit. If you click the No button, you will quit without saving changes. Clicking the Cancel button will close the dialog box and not quit Visual Basic .NET.

Using Crystal Reports to Create a Report

Visual Basic .NET includes **Crystal Reports** software that assists in the design and printing of reports. The two general components of the Crystal Reports software are the Crystal Reports Designer and the Crystal Reports Viewers. The **Crystal Reports Designer** allows you to create a report layout using a database as a source of information. The **Crystal Reports Viewers** include controls for viewing reports designed in the Crystal Reports Designer. Visual Basic .NET includes controls for viewing reports in both Windows applications and Web applications. Using the **CrystalReportViewer control**, you can have your Visual Basic .NET application generate reports and send them to a window on the desktop, to a browser, or to a printer.

The Compensation Review report developed in this chapter did not use Crystal Reports to design and print the report. Crystal Reports requires that the code in the user interface interact directly with the database used as a source of information for the report. One design decision made for the Compensation Review report was that the code in the user interface should use a class to access the database so that the code used to interact with the database was in a central location — the Compensation Review class library. Crystal Reports, therefore, was not a tool that could meet this requirement.

This section provides an overview of the Crystal Reports software, including how to design and print a report similar to the Compensation Review report. The section discusses some of the features of Crystal Reports using the Compensation Review report as an example.

Adding a Crystal Report to a Project

Before you design a report for a Windows application, a Crystal Report module must be added to a Windows application project by right-clicking the appropriate project in the Solution Explorer (the Compensation Review project in this case), pointing to Add on the shortcut menu, clicking Add New Item on the Add menu, and adding a report entitled CrystalReport1.rpt. As shown in Figure 10-57, the Add New Item dialog box includes a **Crystal Report template**. Figure 10-57 shows the Add New Item dialog box after a new item is added to a Windows application project named CrystalReportsOverview. The report name displays as CrystalReport1.rpt. The .rpt file extension is used to designate a Crystal Reports module.

When to Use Crystal Reports

Use Crystal Reports for printing reports when your design allows for the user interface code to co-exist with the database access code.

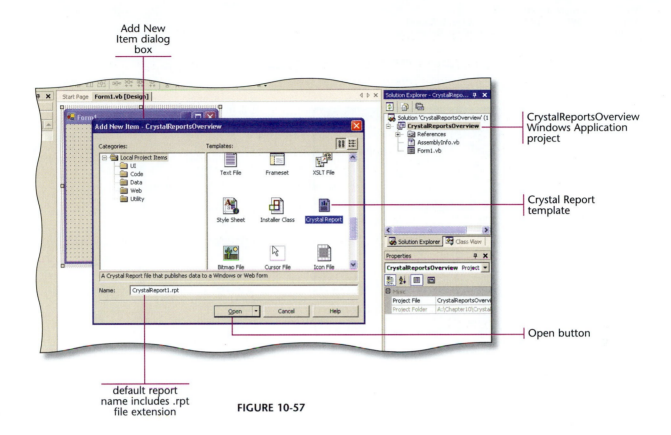

Add New
Item dialog
box

CrystalReportsOverview
Windows Application
project

Crystal Report
template

Open button

default report
name includes .rpt
file extension

FIGURE 10-57

Using a Report Expert to Create a Report

After you click the Open button on the Add New Item dialog box, Visual Basic .NET adds several references to the project, adds the .rpt module to the project, and opens the Crystal Report Gallery. In the example used here, the .rpt module is named creCompensationReviewReport.rpt and was named in the Add New Item dialog box. The cre prefix is used to name a new Crystal Report. Visual Basic .NET opens the .rpt file in the main work area and opens the **Document Outline window** on the left side of the IDE. The **Crystal Report Gallery** (Figure 10-58 on the next page) provides three choices for creating a new report and lists these choices in the Create a New Crystal Report Document area. When the Using the Report Expert RadioButton is selected, the Choose an Expert area is active and a report type can be chosen. The **Report Expert** provides a wizard to step through the creation of a new report layout by requesting information about the report.

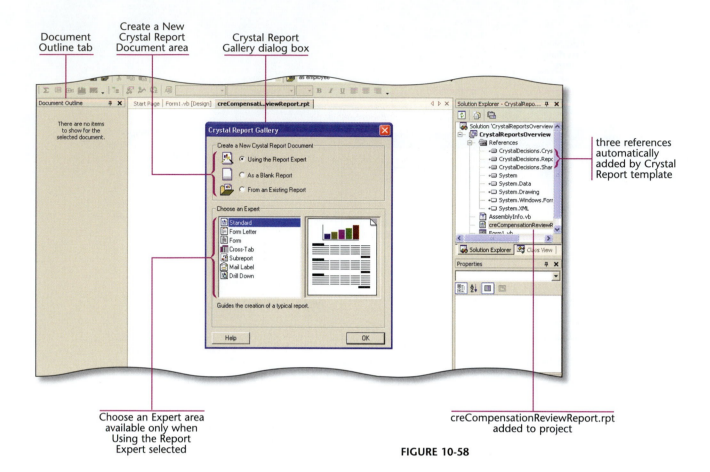

Document
Outline tab

Create a New
Crystal Report
Document area

Crystal Report
Gallery dialog box

three references
automatically
added by Crystal
Report template

Choose an Expert area
available only when
Using the Report
Expert selected

creCompensationReviewReport.rpt
added to project

FIGURE 10-58

When you are designing a report from a database, the Standard Report Expert provides most of the necessary functionality. The **Standard Report Expert** provides the features present in the Compensation Review report, such as a header and the ability to print one database record per report line.

After you choose the Standard Report Expert, Visual Basic .NET displays the Report Expert as shown in Figure 10-59. The Standard Report Expert includes several tabs across the top of the dialog box. The wizard steps through the options in each of the tabs. The Data tab includes a list of data sources. The data sources correspond to the Data Source parameter used in the connection string created earlier in this chapter, on page VB 10.20. The OLE DB (ADO) data source can be used to connect to the Compensation Review Microsoft Access database.

Tip

Using the Standard Report Expert
Use the Standard Report Expert to set database connection strings, queries, report fields, and a report layout. After using the Report Expert, you can fine tune the report in the IDE.

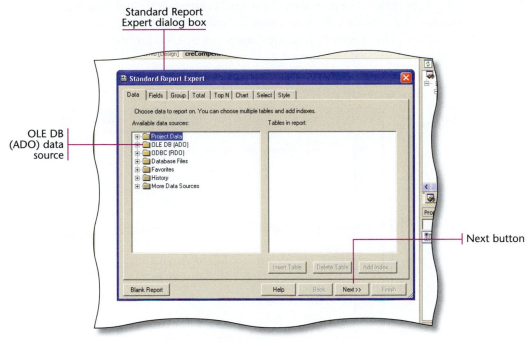

FIGURE 10-59

After you select the OLE DB (ADO) data source, the Standard Report Expert wizard displays a list of OLE DB (ADO) data providers. The second item in the list shown in Figure 10-60 is the Microsoft Jet 4.0 OLE DB Provider, which is the same provider used in the connection string created earlier in this chapter.

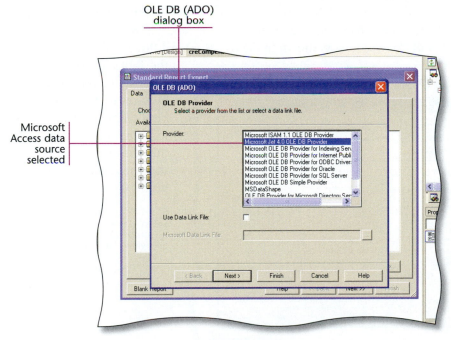

FIGURE 10-60

After you select the provider, the wizard requests optional database connection information, such as a user ID and password, as shown in Figure 10-61. The connection to the Compensation Review database does not require these optional parameters.

OLE DB (ADO) dialog box

Database Name set to CompensationReview.mdb file

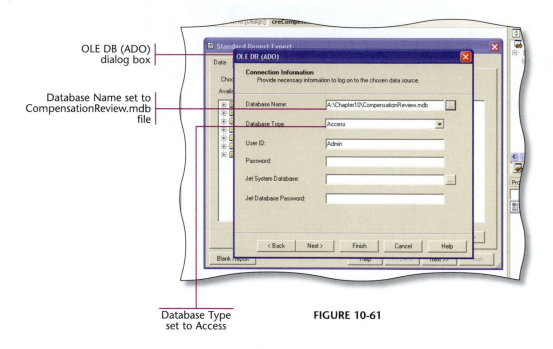

Database Type set to Access

FIGURE 10-61

After you click the Finish button on the OLE DB (ADO) dialog box, Visual Basic .NET displays the information in the Available data sources area. The data source includes the three table names from the Compensation Review database. You click each table name to add the table to the Tables in report area on the right side of the window, as shown in Figure 10-62. All three tables are added to the Tables in report area because the report wizard requires that a query be built from the three tables in much the same manner that the SQL SELECT statement was built earlier in this chapter.

Data tab

database and tables listed

tables from Compensation Review database added

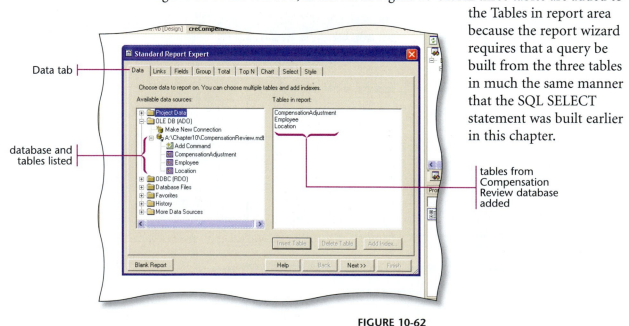

FIGURE 10-62

The information required on the Data tab is now complete. After you click the Next button, the wizard opens the Links tab. The Links tab automatically discovers and displays the relationships among the three tables in the database (Figure 10-63). If necessary, you can add additional links to the tables on the Links tab.

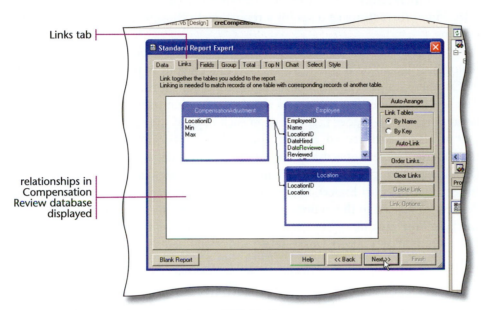

FIGURE 10-63

After you click the Next button on the Links tab, the wizard opens the Fields tab. The Fields tab allows you to specify which fields from the tables to print on the report. Figure 10-64 shows the Fields tab after the eight fields for the Compensation Review report have been added to the Fields to Display list. The Formula button allows you to create new fields by using calculations on fields in the Available Fields list. Such formulas may include concatenation of strings or mathematical formulas. The Column Heading text box on the Fields tab allows you to specify a user-friendly column heading for each field in the report.

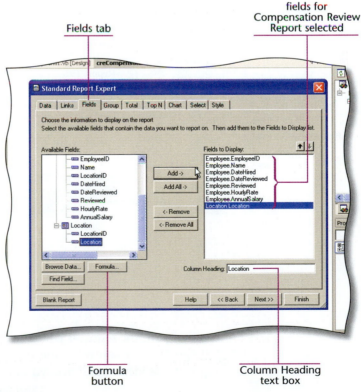

FIGURE 10-64

Additional tabs on the Standard Report Expert dialog box allow you to group records on the report or create totals and subtotals on the report. The Top N tab allows you to create summary lines in the report that include basic statistical information. The Chart tab allows you to place graphical charts, such as bar or pie charts, on a report. The Select tab allows you to create a SQL SELECT statement that selects the records to print on the report. The Style tab includes a selection of formatting options for a report, including colors and report layout options.

After you click the Finish button on the Standard Report Expert dialog box, Visual Basic .NET creates the report layout in the creCompensationReviewReport.rpt tab in the main work area (Figure 10-65). The layout includes five sections: a report header that prints at the beginning of the report, a page header that prints on each page of the report, a details section that prints for each record, a report footer that prints once at the end of the report, and a page footer that prints at the end of each page of the report. The Details section includes the fields and field names specified on the Fields tab of the Standard Report Expert dialog box. The items in each section can be moved, deleted, or resized in the main work area. Properties, such as font size and color, can be set for each item. The Field Explorer displays on the left side of the IDE. The Field Explorer allows you to select additional items to add to the report.

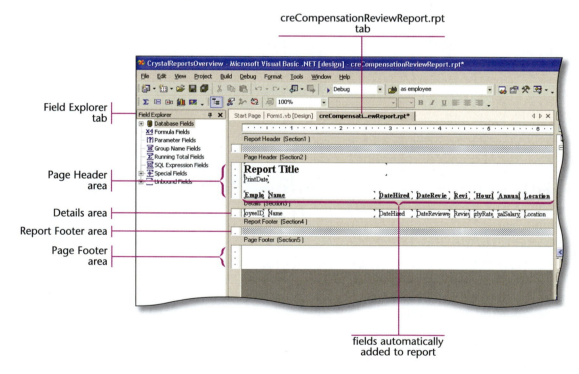

FIGURE 10-65

The design of the report is complete. The next step is to add a CrystalReportViewer control to the Windows application that allows the new report to be viewed and printed during run time.

Using the CrystalReportViewer Control

The CrystalReportViewer control displays in the Windows Forms tab of the Toolbox, just as the other Windows controls with which you are familiar. Figure 10-66 shows a CrystalReportViewer control on the Form1 form of the CrystalReportsOverview project. The control has been resized to display on most of the form. The control includes a toolbar at the top of the control, a Group Tree area on the left side of the control, the report display area on the right side of the control, and three status bar panels on the bottom of the form. You set properties of the control to disable or enable the display of any of the items on the control. Figure 10-66 shows that the name of the control has been changed to crvCompensationReviewReport. Use the crv prefix when naming CrystalReportViewer controls. The ReportSource of the control is set to the .rpt module file created using the Standard Report Expert. The ReportSource property is required in order to associate the viewer control with a Crystal Report.

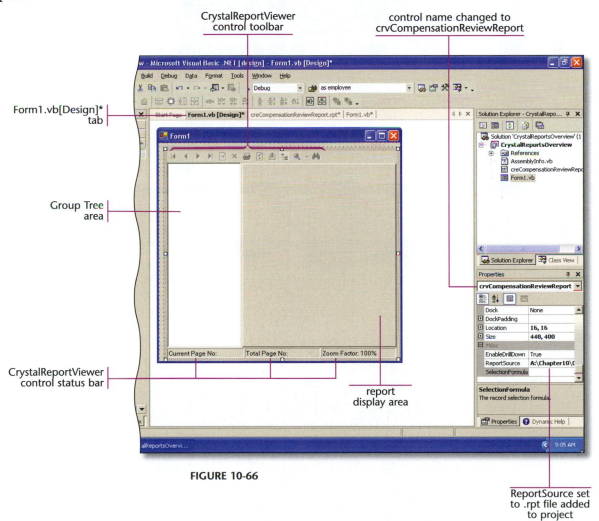

FIGURE 10-66

Running a Crystal Reports Report

Figure 10-67 shows the Form1 form during run time. When the application starts, the control automatically generates the report shown in the report display area. The report in Figure 10-67 is zoomed to a factor of 50%. Clicking the Print button on the toolbar causes a Print dialog box to display. A PrintDialog control is not necessary on the form in order for the Print dialog box to display for a Crystal Report. A SQL SELECT statement was not added to the Standard Report Expert, meaning that all records in the Employees table of the Compensation Review database will print on the report.

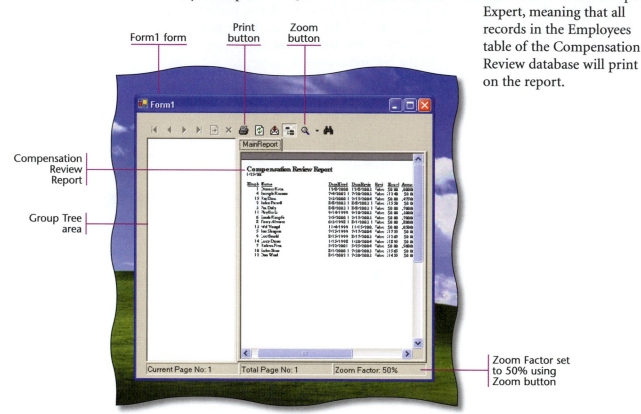

FIGURE 10-67

Crystal Reports is a large component of Visual Basic .NET, and its many features are beyond the scope of this book. To learn more about Crystal Reports, use the Visual Basic .NET Help system.

Chapter Summary

In this chapter, you learned how to design a class containing other classes and create a class containing a collection. You learned how to connect to a database and query records from a database. You learned how to handle exceptions in your code using the Try…Catch…Finally statement and how to report exceptions to a user. You then learned how to read records and data in the fields in records. You learned how to use three new controls: the MonthCalendar control, the PrintDialog control, and the PrintDocument control. You learned how to print from Visual Basic .NET by formatting a string and sending the string to a printer. Finally, you learned how Crystal Reports allows you to create, display, and print reports from a database.

What You Should Know

Having completed this chapter, you now should be able to perform the tasks shown in Table 10-10.

Table 10-10	Chapter 10 What You Should Know	
TASK NUMBER	**TASK**	**PAGE**
1	Start Visual Basic .NET and Add a New Class to the Compensation Review Class Library	VB 10.18
2	Declare Private Variables and Create a Database Connection String	VB 10.20
3	Prepare a Data Command and a Data Reader and Code a Try...Catch Statement	VB 10.25
4	Connect to a Database	VB 10.27
5	Code a SQL SELECT Statement to Read Hourly Employee Records	VB 10.30
6	Complete Coding the SQL SELECT Statement	VB 10.32
7	Use a Loop to Read Hourly Employee Records	VB 10.34
8	Code a SQL SELECT Statement and Loop to Read Salaried Employee Records	VB 10.36
9	Build, Save, and Document the Class Library	VB 10.39
10	Add a New Project to a Solution	VB 10.41
11	Set Form Properties and Add Controls	VB 10.44
12	Change the Properties of a MonthCalendar Control	VB 10.47
13	Change the Properties of PrintDialog and PrintDocument Controls	VB 10.49
14	Use a PrintDialog Control and a PrintDocument Control in Code	VB 10.52
15	Build a Report Header	VB 10.54
16	Build the Report Body	VB 10.57
17	Finish Building the Report Body	VB 10.58
18	Send Output to a Printer and Catch an Exception	VB 10.63
19	Set the Startup Project, Save the Project, and Test the Project	VB 10.64
20	Document the Application and Quit Visual Basic .NET	VB 10.67

Key Terms

ADO.NET *(VB 10.16)*
Brush class *(VB 10.61)*
Brush property *(VB 10.50)*
CommandText property *(VB 10.25)*
connection string *(VB 10.19)*
Crystal Report template *(VB 10.70)*
Crystal Report Gallery *(VB 10.71)*
Crystal Reports *(VB 10.70)*
Crystal Reports Designer *(VB 10.70)*
Crystal Reports Viewers *(VB 10.70)*
CrystalReportViewer control
   (VB 10.70)
database *(VB 10.13)*
DefaultSettings.Landscape property
   (VB 10.52)
Document Outline window
   (VB 10.71)
DrawString() method *(VB 10.50)*
ExecuteReader() method *(VB 10.25)*
Exit Try statement *(VB 10.61)*
exposes *(VB 10.09)*
field *(VB 10.13)*
Font class *(VB 10.61)*
Font property *(VB 10.50)*
Graphics object *(VB 10.50)*
index *(VB 10.14)*
MonthCalendar control *(VB 10.07)*
OleDbCommand class *(VB 10.16)*
OleDbConnection class *(VB 10.16)*
OleDbDataReader class *(VB 10.16)*
Open() method *(VB 10.26)*

PageSettings *(VB 10.48)*
primary key *(VB 10.14)*
Print () *(VB 10.48)*
PrintDialog control *(VB 10.07)*
PrintDocument class *(VB 10.50)*
PrintDocument control *(VB 10.48)*
PrinterSettings *(VB 10.48)*
PrintPage event procedure *(VB 10.52)*
PrintPageEventArgs class *(VB 10.62)*
PrintPreview control *(VB 10.48)*
query *(VB 10.07)*
record *(VB 10.13)*
relationship *(VB 10.14)*
Report Expert *(VB 10.71)*
SELECT statement *(VB 10.28)*
Standard Report Expert *(VB 10.72)*
SQL *(VB 10.27)*
structured exception handling
   (VB 10.21)
System.Drawing.Printing namespace
   (VB 10.50)
System.Data.OleDb namespace
   (VB 10.16)
System.Data.SqlClient namespace
   (VB 10.16)
table *(VB 10.13)*
Throw statement *(VB 10.23)*
throwing exceptions *(VB 10.23)*
ToShortDateString() method
   (VB 10.54)
Try…Catch…Finally statement
   (VB 10.21)

Homework Assignments

Short Answer

1. A database is composed of one or more _____, which are composed of _____, each represented by a row in the table. Columns, called _____, represent individual data elements that make up each record.

2. A _____ is used to begin communication with a database and describes the type and location of a database. To access a Microsoft Access database, you must provide at least the _____ and _____ parameters.

3. Explain the benefits of structured exception handling and when you should include structured exception handling in your code.

4. Given the following table, write a SQL SELECT statement that queries the table for all male students whose age is from 23 through 25. The query should return the student's name and age.

Table: Students

STUDENTID	NAME	ADVISOR	AGE	GENDER	MAJOR
791	Stephanie Brown	Jenkins	19	Female	Business
236	Shannon Shager	Liu	25	Female	Business
618	Geoff Berg	Smith	24	Male	Finance
256	Andrew Schilling	Jenkins	22	Male	History
902	Gary Sang	Abernathy	23	Male	Biology

5. For the table and SQL SELECT statement described in question 4, list the results of the query.

6. Given the following table and SQL SELECT statement, list the results of the query.

Table: Inventory

PRODUCTID	PRODUCTNAME	WEIGHT	COST	NUMBERINSTOCK
KJ3943	Spade shovel	30	45.00	45
UI3020	18" Lawn mower	100	384.49	42
TR4391	Dog house	250	59.00	67
UK8732	12" Wet saw	56	750.00	34
GV3900	36" Riding mower	234	3398.00	27
HU3093	40" Riding mower	834	5955.00	45

SQL SELECT Statement:

```
SELECT NumberInStock, ProductName FROM Inventory WHERE Weight > 100
```

(continued)

Short Answer *(continued)*

7. Given the following tables, write a SQL SELECT statement that queries the tables for all cities with populations greater than 30,000. The query should return the city name, square miles, and state name.

Table: Cities

CITY	POPULATION	SQUAREMILES	STATE
Morton	72938	32	TX
Springfield	89234	36	TX
Worth	14548	8	TX
Trenton	38493	25	OK
Elwood	3293	10	NV

Table: States

STATE	STATENAME
TX	Texas
OK	Oklahoma
NM	New Mexico
AZ	Arizona
NV	Nevada

8. For the tables and SQL SELECT statement described in question 7, list the results of the query.

9. Given the following tables and SQL SELECT statement, list the results of the query.

Table: Stocks

DATEPURCHASED	STOCKSYMBOL	SHARESOWNED	PURCHASEPRICE
5/17/2004	INTC	200	18.73
5/25/2004	MSFT	150	30.34
7/26/2004	CSCO	150	20.04
8/10/2004	RHAT	400	5.45
8/10/2004	SUNW	700	6.15
8/30/2004	COMS	200	5.50

Table: StockSymbols

STOCKSYMBOL	COMPANYNAME	COMPANYSTATE
INTC	Intel	California
MSFT	Microsoft	Washington
CSCO	Cisco	California
RHAT	Red Hat	North Carolina
SUNW	Sun Microsystems	California
COMS	3Com	California

SQL SELECT Statement:

```
SELECT StockSymbols.CompanyName, Stocks.DatePurchased,
StockSymbols.CompanyState FROM Stocks, StockSymbols WHERE
Stocks.StockSymbol = StockSymbols.StockSymbol AND CompanyState =
"California"
```

10. Given the following Try...Catch...Finally statement, indicate the output for each set of initial values listed in Table 10-11. All variables are declared as Integer variables.

```
Try
   intA = intB / intC
   intX = intY * intZ
Catch Ex As System.DivideByZeroException
   MessageBox.Show("A divide by zero exception occurred.")
Catch Ex as System.Exception
   MessageBox.Show("An unknown exception occurred!")
Finally
   MessageBox.Show("The program will now exit.")
   End
End Try
```

Table 10-11 Initial Values

a. intB = 45, intC = 5, intY = 99, intZ = 394
b. intB = 34, intC = 0, intY = 2000000000, intZ = 4
c. intB = 4354, intC = 0, intY = 439, intZ = 32
d. intB = 64, intC = 8, intY = 416, intZ = 2000000000

(continued)

Short Answer *(continued)*

11. Name the two .NET Framework class library ADO.NET namespaces that commonly are used to handle database access. Indicate in which cases each namespace is appropriate for use.

12. Describe the relationship between a data reader, a data command, and a data connection.

13. Explain the benefits of separating the business logic, including database access code, from the user interface portion of a program.

14. Before being sent to a printer, text can first be drawn on a _____ object, which is a class of the _____ .NET Framework class library, using the _____ method of the Graphics object.

15. List at least six considerations you should take into account when testing an application that includes database and printing functionality.

Learn It Online

Start your browser and visit scsite.com/vbnet/exs. Follow the instructions in the exercises below.

1. **Chapter Reinforcement TF, MC, and SA**   Click the True/False, Multiple Choice, and Short Answer link below Chapter 10. Print and then answer the questions.

2. **Practice Test**   Click the Practice Test link below Chapter 10. Answer each question, enter your first and last name at the bottom of the page, and then click the Grade Test button. When the graded practice test displays on your screen, click Print on the File menu to print a hard copy. Continue to take practice tests until you score 80% or better. Hand in a printout of the final practice test.

3. **Crossword Puzzle Challenge**   Click the Crossword Puzzle Challenge link below Chapter 10. Read the instructions, and then enter your first and last name. Click the Play button. Complete the crossword puzzle. When you are finished, click the Submit button. When the crossword puzzle redisplays, click the Print button.

4. **Tips and Tricks**   Click the Tips and Tricks link below Chapter 10. Click a topic that pertains to Chapter 10. Right-click the information and then click Print on the shortcut menu. Construct a brief example of what the information relates to in Visual Basic .NET to confirm you understand how to use the tip or trick. Hand in the example and printed information.

5. **Newsgroups**   Click the Newsgroups link below Chapter 10. Click a topic that pertains to Chapter 10. Print three comments.

6. **Expanding Your Horizons**   Click the Articles for Visual Basic .NET below Chapter 10. Click a topic that pertains to Chapter 10. Print the information. Construct a brief example of what the information relates to in Visual Basic .NET to confirm you understand the contents of the article. Hand in the example and printed information.

7. **Search Sleuth**   Select three key terms from the Key Terms section of this chapter and then use the Google search engine at google.com (or any major search engine) to display and print two Web pages for each key term.

Note: If you plan to complete the project and all the exercises in this chapter, it is recommended that you use a hard disk or Zip disk for your solutions, because they will not all fit on a floppy disk.

Debugging Assignment

Start Visual Basic .NET and open the Checking Accounts solution from the Chapter10\Checking Accounts folder on the Data Disk. The solution consists of a Windows application that reads records from an Accounts table in a Microsoft Access database stored in the A:\Chapter10\CheckingAccounts.mdb file on the Data Disk. When the program starts, the records are read into an array. A user interface allows the user to click arrow buttons to navigate the records. The user can print a record while viewing it.

The Checking Accounts Windows application contains bugs in the code. Run the application to experience some of the problems listed in the steps below. Follow the steps to debug the project.

1. Review the code for the Checking Accounts Windows application. The connection string for the database contains an error. This causes the program to throw an exception and a run-time error displays when the program executes. Fix the connection string.

2. To avoid other database related errors, place a Try…Catch statement around the code that accesses the database. Display a user-friendly error message if an exception is thrown. Test the Try…Catch statement by forcing an error in the database access by using an invalid connection string.

3. The SQL SELECT statement does not return all of the fields in the table in the database. Replace the field names in the SELECT clause of the SQL SELECT statement with an asterisk to indicate that all fields in the table should be selected.

4. The Do While statement does not read through all of the records correctly. Add logic to the code to ensure that a record is accessed before the loop begins. If the SQL SELECT statement does not return any records from the database, the code in the loop should not execute.

5. The code that sets the date in the MonthCalendar control sets the wrong date when a record is displayed. Correct the problem by using Visual Basic .NET debugging tools to analyze the values of the record's fields in debug mode.

6. When a record prints, the output is not aligned properly on the report. Modify the report format using Space, Tab, and NewLine characters to make the report more readable. Make sure the report prints using the Arial font and a font height of 5.

7. Save the project and then run the project to test for any additional bugs. The Checking Accounts Windows application should display as shown in Figure 10-68a on the next page. A page of the report should print as shown in Figure 10-68b.

8. Document the Checking Accounts Windows application form code. On the code printout, circle the lines of code you modified.

Debugging Assignment *(continued)*

(a)

(b)

FIGURE 10-68

Programming Assignments

1 Creating a Data Lookup Program

Using the following steps, design and develop a program that illustrates the concepts of using a database to look up information based on user input. The program should allow a user to enter two criteria for a product search. The program then should display each individual search result, or record that meet the search criteria, in a message box.

1. Use the Windows Application template in Visual Basic .NET to start a new project named Product List. Create the solution on the Data Disk in a new folder named A:\Chapter10\Product List.

2. Create a user interface similar to that shown in Figure 10-69 on page VB 10.88. Set form and control property values to center the window on startup at run time, and ensure that the window is not resizable at run time. For the Color ComboBox control, set property values to assign the name, cmbColor, and allow the user to select Black, White, Grey, or Beige. For the Manufacturer ComboBox control, set property values to assign the name, cmbManufacturer, and allow the user to select Sony, Aiwa, Panasonic, or Toshiba.

3. Create an event procedure for the Search Table button. The event procedure first should check that the user has selected a value in both ComboBox controls. If not, the code in the event procedure should display an appropriate error message box and then exit the event procedure.

4. In a Try...Catch statement, write code that opens the database. Use the connection string of "Provider=Microsoft.Jet.OLEDB.4.0; Data Source = A:\Chapter10\ProductList.mdb". Declare a new OleDbConnection object, a new OleDbCommand object, and a new OleDbDataReader object for use in the data access code.

5. In the same Try...Catch statement, write code that sets the

   ```
   OleDbCommand.CommandText property to the statement, "SELECT *
   From ProductList WHERE Color = '" & cmbColor.Text & "' AND
   Manufacturer = '" & cmbManufacturer.Text & "'"
   ```

6. Enter the following code to instruct the program to execute the OleDbCommand object on the OleDbDataReader object:
   `objOleDbDataReader= objOleDbDataCommand.ExecuteReader`

7. Code a Do While statement that loops through the OleDbDataReader object.

8. Within the Do While statement, build a string composed of the fields returned by the SELECT statement. The fields are as follows: ProductName, Price, InStock, Color, and Manufacturer. All fields in the table are of the String data type. For example, the following code concatenates the ProductName fields onto a string named strOutput:

   ```
   strOutput &= objOleDbDataReader.Item("ProductName")
   ```

9. Within the Do While statement, display the string for the record before looping to the next record. Display the record in a message box. After the user clicks the OK button in the message box, the next record should display in a new message box until all of the records returned by the query display.

10. In the Catch clause of the Try...Catch statement, enter code to display a user-friendly message that indicates that an error occurred while the program was accessing the database. Use the End statement to exit the program.

(continued)

1 Creating a Data Lookup Program *(continued)*

11. Run the Product List application and correct any errors. If you have made changes, save the project again. During run time, the Product List application window should display as shown in Figure 10-69.

12. Document the code and user interface for the project.

FIGURE 10-69

2 Using MonthCalendar Controls to Select Date Ranges

Develop a Windows application that allows the user to use two MonthCalendar controls to select two date ranges. Both MonthCalendar controls should limit input to dates between 1/1/2005 and 12/31/2006. The controls should allow the user to select up to seven days in a date range.

Add two buttons to the Form1 form. The first button, labeled Display Date Properties, should display the following values of the SelectionStart property of both MonthCalendar controls in a user-friendly format: Month, Day, Year, DayofWeek, DayofYear, DaysinMonth. The second button, labeled Compare Start Dates, should use the Compare() method of one of the SelectionStart properties to compare the SelectionStart dates of the two controls. The Compare() method returns a value indicating whether a date is greater than, equal to, or less than another date. Use Visual Basic .NET Help to determine how to evaluate the results of the Compare() method. Display the result of the Compare() method in a message box that indicates which MonthCalendar control has the earliest SelectionStart date.

3 Printing Using PrintDialog and PrintDocument Controls

Design and develop a Windows application named StudentID that accepts input for and prints a student identification card based on user input entered in several input controls on a form. Add appropriate controls to the Form1 form to accept the following inputs: Name (String of 50 characters), Date of Birth (any date from 1950 through 1988), Address (String of 30 characters), City (String of 15 characters), State (ComboBox control choice of Maine, Vermont, New Hampshire, or New York), and Major (String of 20 characters).

Use a MonthCalendar control to allow the user to input the Date of Birth. Add a GroupBox control with two RadioButton controls that are labeled Landscape and Portrait, with Landscape being the default print orientation. Add two Button controls to the form to create a New button and a Print button. The New button clears input controls; the Print button prints the information to the selected printer using the print orientation selected in the RadioButton controls. Use a PrintDialog box control to allow the user to select a printer. The information should print in a format similar to the following:

Name	Major
Address	Date of Birth
City, State	

Use the PadRight() function with a value of 55 to pad the Name and Address. Print using the Arial font with a font size of 12.

4 Printing a Report and Reading from a Database

Design and develop a Windows application named Inventory Report that reads from a database and prints a report of all the records in the database. The Microsoft Access database is named Inventory.mdb and is stored in the A:\Chapter10 folder on the Data Disk. The fields in the table named Inventory are named as follows: ProductID (Integer), ProductName (String), NumberInStock (Integer), Location (String), and DateOfLastReorder (Date). Print a header on the report that includes Inventory Report as the report name and the current date. The report header also should include column headers for each field in the records printed on the report. Print a line for each record in the database using appropriate spacing. Print using Portrait mode to the default printer, so that it is not necessary to use a PrintDialog control. The user interface for the Inventory Report application requires only a Button control to initiate the printing of the report. Use a Try…Catch…Finally statement for structured exception handling to catch any database errors that may occur.

5 Totaling and Subtotaling Data in a Database

Design and develop a Windows application named Inventory Totals that reads from a database and creates a total and subtotals for the records in the database. The Microsoft Access database is named Inventory.mdb and is stored in the A:\Chapter10 folder on the Data Disk. The table and fields in this database are described in Programming Assignment 4. Create a user interface that includes two ListView controls on the Form1 form. In the first ListView control, include a column for each field in the Inventory table. In the Form_Load event of the Form1 form, include code in a Try…Catch statement that reads the records in the Inventory table and adds an item to the ListView control for each record. Each field in the record should be added as a column in the ListView control. Add a new clause to the end of the SELECT statement created in Programming Assignment 4 that reads: "ORDER BY Location". The ORDER BY clause will sort the records in the data reader by Location.

(continued)

PROGRAMMING ASSIGNMENTS

Add a Label control and a read-only TextBox control to the Form1 form. Use Inventory total: as the label for the TextBox. As the code reads the Inventory table in the Form_Load event procedure, update the Inventory total: TextBox with a total of the values in the NumberInStock fields for all records. The second ListView control should have two columns: Location and NumberInStock. As the code reads the records, keep a running subtotal of the NumberInStock for each Location. In the loop that reads the records, whenever the Location changes, add the running subtotal and Location name to the second ListView control. The result should be that the second ListView control contains a row for each location in the Inventory table and a subtotal of the number of items in stock at each location.

6 Instantiating an Object Using a Database

Design and create a class named InventoryItem to read records from a database and set property values of the class using the values stored in a table in the database. The Microsoft Access database is named Inventory.mdb and is stored in the A:\Chapter10 folder on the Data Disk. The table and fields in this database are described in Programming Assignment 4. An instance of the InventoryItem class should represent one record in the database. The class constructor should accept a ProductID (Integer) as an parameter and then query the database for the product using a SELECT statement such as:

SELECT * FROM Inventory WHERE ProductID = intProductID

If the product is not found based on ProductID, use the Throw statement to throw an exception and exit the InventoryItem class constructor. Use the following syntax to throw a general exception:

```
Throw New System.Exception()
```

If the product is found, set the values of properties in the class to the value of each field in the Inventory table. Use read-only properties for each property in the class.

Create a Windows application in the same solution that uses the class. Recall that you should build the class and then add a reference to the .DLL file created for the class to the Windows application. The application should allow the user to input a Product ID number in a text box and then click a Button control to instantiate an instance of the InventoryItem class. In the code, instantiate an InventoryItem object by passing the Product ID entered by the user. Place the instantiation in a Try…Catch statement. Catch the System.Exception exception in a Catch statement as follows:

```
Catch objException As System.Exception
```

If the exception is thrown, display a user-friendly error message. If the exception is not thrown, display the properties of the new object in a message box. Display each property value on a separate line in the message box.

7 Learning About Crystal Reports

Use the Visual Basic .NET Help tools to learn how to specify a SQL SELECT statement when using the Crystal Reports Standard Report Expert. Determine the method used to pass parameters to the report so that the report prints records based on user input. Write a short description of your findings.

11

Creating Web Applications and Writing Data to a Database

Objectives

You will have
mastered the material in
this chapter when you can:

- Declare a public procedure in a module
- Use optional parameters in a procedure
- Use SQL SELECT statements to read individual records from a database
- Use SQL UPDATE statements to update individual records in a database
- Start a new ASP.NET Web application
- Understand Web applications and Web forms
- Explain when to use HTML controls and Web controls in a Web application
- Use Table and Horizontal Rule HTML controls on a Web form
- View HTML code for a Web form
- Use Label, TextBox, and Button Web controls on a Web form
- Test a Web application
- Understand how ASP.NET, the CLR, and Microsoft Internet Information
  Services interact to run a Web application

Introduction

This chapter concentrates on developing the Web application shown in Figure 11-1. A Web application is a program that a user interacts with through a Web browser. The Web application developed in this chapter allows a manager to indicate a compensation adjustment for an employee. The manager uses the report generated by the Compensation Review Report application developed in Chapter 10 to determine which employees require compensation reviews. After a review is complete, the manager can use the Web application to select an employee and then enter the review date and an hourly rate or annual salary adjustment.

In this chapter, you will learn how to write code that updates records in a database, as well as how to declare optional parameters for a procedure. You also will learn how to create a new type of application — a Web application. Finally, you will learn how to use controls in Web applications, just as you used controls in Windows applications.

Chapter Eleven — Creating the Compensation Review Update Web Application

The Web application developed in this chapter is the Compensation Review Update Web page, which is used to adjust an employee's annual salary or hourly rate during the employee's compensation review (Figure 11-1a). The user interface for the Web application displays in the user's Web browser. When a user uses his or her Web browser to navigate to the application, the application displays a Web page that accepts an employee number as input. When the user clicks the Get Employee button, the code in the Employees class (Figure 11-1b) accesses the appropriate employee record from the Compensation Review database (Figure 11-1d). If the record exists, the user enters the date reviewed and a new annual salary or hourly rate on the Web page. The user knows whether to enter a new annual salary or a new hourly rate based upon which of the two fields has a value. After entering the data, the user clicks the Update Compensation button, which calls the Update Compensation procedure (Figure 11-1c) to update the appropriate employee record in the Compensation Review database.

An application such as the Compensation Review Update application typically fills in the Date reviewed value on the Web page for the user automatically. The project developed in this chapter, however, is working with test data, and the actual dates when the tests will be performed are unknown. For the purposes of this chapter, therefore, the application will not fill in the review date automatically, but will request that the user enter a valid date for the Date reviewed in the format MM/DD/YY.

The user continues updating employee records until he or she has updated all the records indicated in the Compensation Review report created in Chapter 10. If the user attempts to update an employee's salary twice, the application displays an error message to the left of the Update Compensation button. When the user completes the updates, he or she can use the Compensation Review Report application developed in Chapter 10 to view a report that lists those employees reviewed by the user (Figure 11-1b).

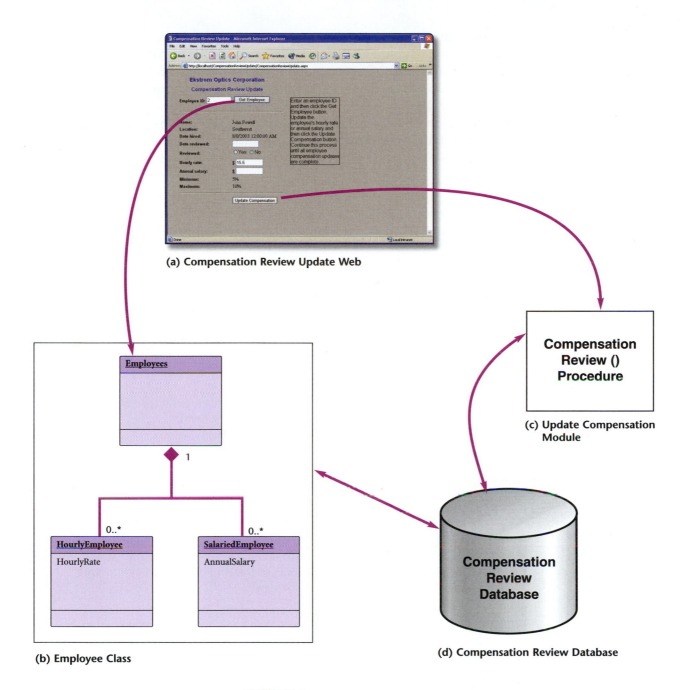

(a) Compensation Review Update Web

(b) Employee Class

(c) Update Compensation Module

(d) Compensation Review Database

FIGURE 11-1

When the user clicks the Get Employee button, the Compensation Review Update Web application uses a new option in the Employees class (Figure 11-1b) to query the Compensation Review database for one employee's compensation information. The new option in the constructor of the Employees class allows the user of the class to send an Employee ID as a parameter to the constructor and then queries the database for the employee record. After instantiating an Employees object with only one employee, the Web application then displays the employee's information on the Web page.

After entering new compensation information, the user clicks the Update Compensation button. The click event procedure of the Update Compensation button calls the Update Compensation procedure (Figure 11-1c) in the Compensation Review class library. The Update Compensation procedure is not part of a class, but is a separate code module containing a public procedure that updates the Employee table in the Compensation Review database with the new compensation information entered by the user.

Program Development

The development cycle for the Compensation Review Update Web application consists of tasks that correspond to the six development cycle phases, as shown in Table 11-1.

Table 11-1   Compensation Review Update Web Application Development Tasks

DEVELOPMENT PHASE	TASK NUMBER	TASK NAME	TASK
Analyze requirements	1	Analyze problem	Analyze the Compensation Review Update problem.
Design solution	2	Design class changes and module	Design the changes to the Employees class and the module that will update data in the database. Design the logic and write pseudocode for the module.
	3	Design program and interface	Design the user interface for the Compensation Review Update Web application, including input areas and Web page controls. Design the logic and write pseudocode for the program.
Validate design	4	Validate design	Prove that the solution produces correct results for the Compensation Review Update Web application.
Implement design	5	Write code for class and module	Write code to implement the design of the changes to the Employees class and the code for the new module.
	6	Write code	Write code for the Compensation Review Update Web application and add user interface elements, such as input areas, output areas, and controls on a Web page. Write the code to add event procedures and use the Employees class and new module to get and update employee information.
Test solution	7	Test	Test the Compensation Review Update Web application, the Employees class, and the new module.
	8	Debug	Fix any problems with the Compensation Review Report Web application, the Employees class, and the new module.
Document solution	9	Document	Print the code for the new module and the changes to the Employees class. Print the user interface and code for the Compensation Review Update Web application.

Analysis and Design

Figure 11-2 shows the requirements document that initiates the development cycle for the Compensation Review Update Web application.

REQUEST FOR NEW APPLICATION

Date submitted:	February 3, 2004
Submitted by:	Samantha O'Conner
Purpose:	The human resources department requires a Compensation Review Update application as part of the Compensation Review System. Managers use the report generated by the Compensation Review Report application to determine which employees require a compensation review; after completing these reviews, the managers will use the Web application to update each employee's date reviewed and hourly rate or annual salary adjustment. The application should be accessible through a Web browser on a Web page.
Application title:	Compensation Review Update
Algorithms:	When the user clicks the Update Compensation button, (1) the Employees table in the Compensation Review database should be updated with new compensation information and (2) the database field named Reviewed should be set to the value of True.
Notes:	1) The Compensation Review database provided is a sample database containing a partial list of employees. It is a Microsoft Access database on the enclosed Data Disk and is named Compensation Review.mdb.
	2) The user interface should allow the user to enter an employee ID and then click a button to retrieve employee information for a single employee.
	3) The employee information that must display includes: name, location, date hired, date reviewed, reviewed status, hourly rate or annual salary, the minimum amount the compensation can be increased, and the maximum amount the compensation can be increased.
	4) After entering new compensation information, the user should be able to click an Update Compensation button. This results in the compensation being updated in the Compensation Review database and the Reviewed field on the employee record being set to True.
	5) If an employee record is not found or if an error occurs while accessing the Compensation Review database, the Web page should display a user-friendly error message.

Approvals

Approval Status:	X	Approved
		Rejected
Approved by:	Jonathan Ingram	
Date:	February 10, 2004	
Assigned to:	J. Quasney, Programmer	

FIGURE 11-2

PROBLEM ANALYSIS   The problem that the Compensation Review Update Web application must solve is to allow a user to view a single employee's information and then update the employee's review date and compensation information. The user interface must provide a way for the user to (1) enter an Employee ID, (2) enter a review date, and (3) modify the employee's compensation information. The requirements document shown in Figure 11-2 states that the application must display all of the information in the Employee table of the

Compensation Review database. The application should allow the user only to update either the hourly rate or annual salary, depending on the type of employee displayed.

The Compensation Review Update Web application must run in the user's Web browser. As you learned in Chapter 1, Visual Basic .NET allows you to create Web applications that run in a Web browser. Web applications execute on a Web server, which serves Web pages to a browser. The Compensation Review Update Web application will be created on a Web server to meet this requirement.

The process of updating records in the Employee table of the Compensation Review database should be handled by a class or procedure that exists outside of the Compensation Review Update Web application. As you learned in Chapter 10, business logic, including database access, is best coded separately from the user interface.

INTERFACE DESIGN   The interface for the Compensation Review Update Web application requires one Web page. The user interface needs elements to allow the user to enter an Employee ID and display employee information for a single employee. The interface also must allow the user to modify compensation information and then update the Employee table in the Compensation Review database with the new compensation information.

Figure 11-3 shows a storyboard that outlines the interface requirements for the Web page used in the Compensation Review Update Web application. The Web page includes a title that is displayed on the title bar of the user's Web browser. The Web page also includes many interface elements similar to those used in Windows applications. Visual Basic .NET, however, uses two different sets of controls for Web applications — Web controls and HTML controls. Although many of the Web and HTML controls have the same names as their Windows application counterparts, the controls reside in separate namespaces — System.Web.UI.WebControls and System.Web.UI.HtmlControls. Web and HTML controls typically have functionality similar to their corresponding Windows controls, but often provide fewer properties, methods, and event procedures.

Tip

Designing with Web and HTML Controls
When designing a Web application, keep in mind that Web and HTML controls typically include similar functionality to their Windows controls counterparts, but often provide fewer properties, methods, and event procedures.

As shown in Figure 11-3, the Web page used in the Compensation Review Update Web application includes Label controls, TextBox controls, RadioButton controls, and Button controls. All of these controls display in an HTML table, which is used to format the Web page so that all controls remain in specific locations while the Web page displays.

All of the controls on the Web page are read-only, except for the Employee ID TextBox control and the TextBox control for either the Hourly rate or the Annual salary. To view employee information for a specific employee, the user enters the employee's Employee ID in a text box and then clicks the Get

Employee button. If the Employee ID is found in the database, then the employee's information displays in the controls. If the employee is not found or if a database error occurs, then an error message displays in the lower-left corner of the Web page. The error message displays on the Web page because Visual Basic .NET does not include a straightforward technique to allow Web applications to display pop-up message boxes like those displayed by several of the Windows applications developed in this book.

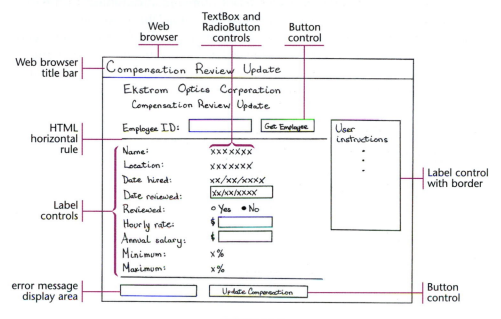

FIGURE 11-3

PROGRAM DESIGN   Figure 11-4 on the next page shows two flowcharts that represent the key logic necessary for the Compensation Review Update Web application. The first flowchart (Figure 11-4a) represents the logic for the tasks performed when the user clicks the Get Employee button on the Compensation Review Update Web application. The first task is to create an instance of the Employees class to retrieve an employee record that has the Employee ID entered by the user. The Employees class thus must include logic to locate an individual employee record in the Compensation Review database. To provide this logic, the Employees class constructor must be changed, so that the SQL SELECT statement created in the constructor in Chapter 10 can search for a single employee record. The SQL SELECT statement looks for a record with an Employee ID that matches the Employee ID entered by the user. If the SQL SELECT statement returns an employee record, then the data from that record is added to either the HourlyEmployees or the SalariedEmployees collection. The logic in the flowchart in Figure 11-4a then checks if either an HourlyEmployee object or a SalariedEmployee object exists in the new Employees object. If it does, the information from the object is displayed on the Web page. If neither object exists, because the SQL SELECT statement did not locate a record with a matching Employee ID, then an error message is displayed in the lower-left portion of the Web page.

The second flowchart (Figure 11-4b) represents the logic for the UpdateCompensation() procedure that is part of the Compensation Review class library. The UpdateCompensation() procedure is a procedure that exists outside of any class in the Compensation Review class library. The procedure is public and can be called by any program that includes a reference to the Compensation Review class library. As shown in Figure 11-4b, the UpdateCompensation() procedure first opens a connection to the database and creates a database command object, objOleDbCommand. A **database command object**, which is similar to the OleDbDataReader data reader object used in Chapter 10, allows a program to send SQL commands to a database, in situations in which the program does not require an SQL command to return any

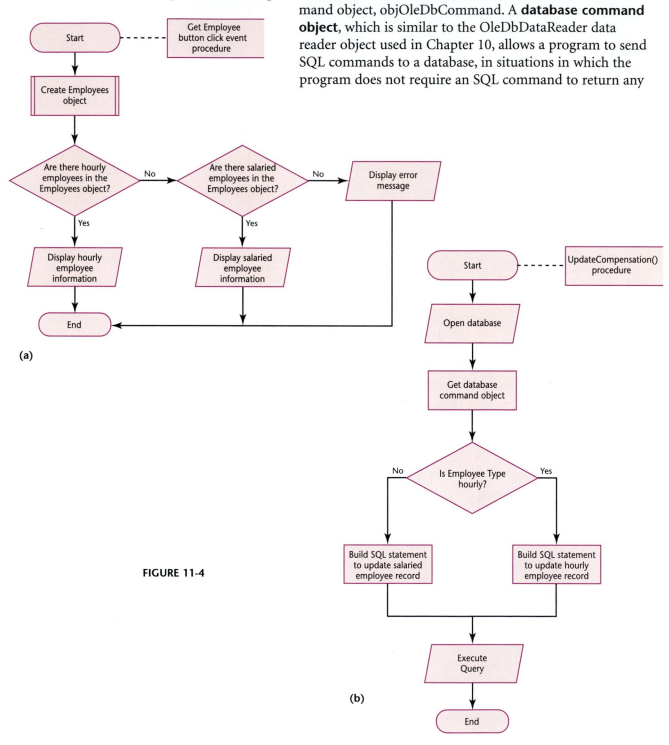

FIGURE 11-4

records. In the case of the UpdateCompensation() procedure, for example, an SQL UPDATE statement is built and sent to the database to update employee compensation information. An **UPDATE statement** is used to set values of fields for existing records in a database.

The database command object also can be used with INSERT and DELETE statements, because they do not require data to be returned. The database command object is not used with the SELECT statement, which is used to retrieve records from a database; instead, the data reader object is used.

Figure 11-5 shows pseudocode for the click event procedure and the UpdateCompensation() procedure needed in the project. The Get Employee Click Event shown in Figure 11-5a first instantiates a new Employees object. The Employees object constructor includes a new, optional parameter: EmployeeID. If a value for EmployeeID is sent to the constructor, then the object is built and stores information about the employee whose database record matches the EmployeeID parameter. The information for the selected employee is stored in one of two properties, which are collections of either HourlyEmployee objects or SalariedEmployee objects. The pseudocode then shows an If…Then…Else statement that determines if the employee record is found and then populates the fields on the Web page with the proper employee information.

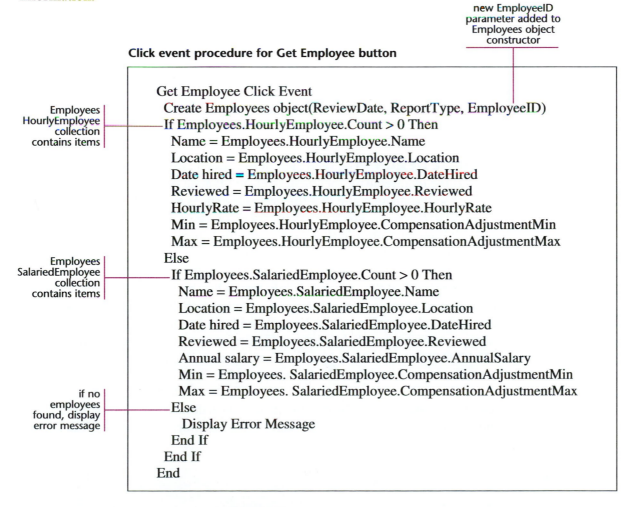

Click event procedure for Get Employee button

new EmployeeID parameter added to Employees object constructor

Get Employee Click Event
  Create Employees object(ReviewDate, ReportType, EmployeeID)

Employees HourlyEmployee collection contains items

  If Employees.HourlyEmployee.Count > 0 Then
    Name = Employees.HourlyEmployee.Name
    Location = Employees.HourlyEmployee.Location
    Date hired = Employees.HourlyEmployee.DateHired
    Reviewed = Employees.HourlyEmployee.Reviewed
    HourlyRate = Employees.HourlyEmployee.HourlyRate
    Min = Employees.HourlyEmployee.CompensationAdjustmentMin
    Max = Employees.HourlyEmployee.CompensationAdjustmentMax
  Else

Employees SalariedEmployee collection contains items

    If Employees.SalariedEmployee.Count > 0 Then
      Name = Employees.SalariedEmployee.Name
      Location = Employees.SalariedEmployee.Location
      Date hired = Employees.SalariedEmployee.DateHired
      Reviewed = Employees.SalariedEmployee.Reviewed
      Annual salary = Employees.SalariedEmployee.AnnualSalary
      Min = Employees. SalariedEmployee.CompensationAdjustmentMin
      Max = Employees. SalariedEmployee.CompensationAdjustmentMax

if no employees found, display error message

    Else
      Display Error Message
    End If
  End If
  End

FIGURE 11-5a

The UpdateCompensation() procedure shown in Figure 11-5b accepts four arguments: EmployeeID, EmployeeType, DateReviewed, and Compensation. The EmployeeID indicates which employee record to update. The EmployeeType argument is used to determine whether to update the HourlyRate field or the AnnualSalary field in the Employee table of the Compensation Review database. The Compensation argument is a value for either an hourly rate or an annual salary, which is used to update the database. The UpdateCompensation() procedure builds an SQL UPDATE statement to update the database and then uses a database command object to pass the SQL UPDATE statement to the database.

UpdateCompensation() procedure in Compensation Review class library

```
Procedure: UpdateCompensation (EmployeeID, EmployeeType, DateReviewed, Compensation)
  Open Compensation Review database
  Get a database command object
  If EmployeeType = Hourly Then
    Create SQL statement to update hourly employee record
  Else
    Create SQL statement to update salaried employee record
  End If
  Execute SQL statement using database command object
End
```

FIGURE 11-5b

VALIDATE DESIGN The validation of the design is achieved by stepping through the requirements document to ensure that all of the requirements are met in a sound manner and that the program logic is sound. The user interface is built as a Web page, which allows the user to access the Web application from any Web browser. Note 2 in the requirements document on page VB 11.05 is accomplished by two user interface components and their related code: a TextBox control that accepts an Employee ID as input and a Get Employee Button control that the user can click to search for that specific Employee ID in the database. After a successful search is completed, the Web page displays the required employee information. Notes 4 and 5 are handled by the Update Compensation button click event and UpdateCompensation() procedures. The SQL UPDATE statement updates the Compensation Review database with the new compensation and sets the Reviewed field to True.

As shown in Table 11-1 on page VB 11.04, after validating the program design, the next phase in the development cycle is developing a procedure to update employee records with new compensation information using Visual Basic .NET.

Creating a Public Procedure in a Class Library

The logic needed to update the Employee table in the Compensation Review database does not quite fit into the design of the classes in the Compensation Review class library that were created in Chapters 9 and 10. Typically, the design of a class that interacts with a database includes the ability both to read information from and to write information to the database. The classes created in Chapters 9 and 10, however, only had the ability to read data, because the programs did not require functionality to write information to the database.

The Employees class can be modified to include the ability to write updated compensation information to the Employee table of the Compensation Review database. To illustrate the concept of declaring and accessing public procedures in a class library, or .DLL files, the UpdateCompensation() procedure will be coded in a public procedure, rather than a class. The public procedure can be added to a class library, just as new classes were added to the Compensation Review class library in Chapters 9 and 10. Programs that add a reference to the Compensation Review class library also have access to the public procedure in the class library and can call the procedure in the same manner that they call other procedures. Figure 11-6 shows the structure of the Compensation Review class library (CompensationReview.dll) after the creation of the UpdateCompensation module and UpdateCompensation() procedure.

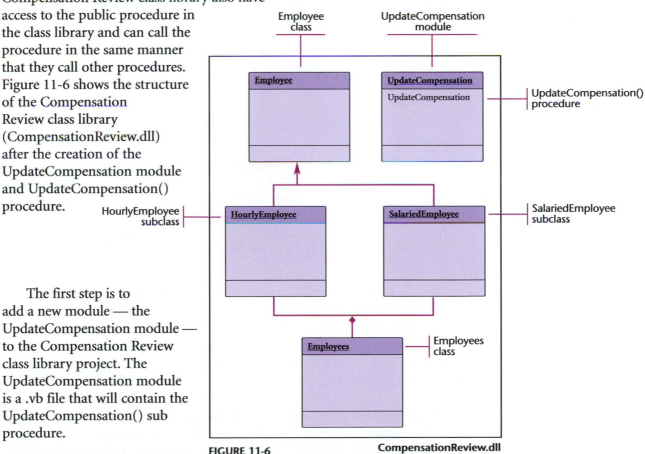

FIGURE 11-6   **CompensationReview.dll**

The first step is to add a new module — the UpdateCompensation module — to the Compensation Review class library project. The UpdateCompensation module is a .vb file that will contain the UpdateCompensation() sub procedure.

Note 2

Database access is much faster from a hard drive rather than a floppy drive. If permitted by your instructor, you may want to copy the Chapter11 folder on the Data Disk to your hard drive to complete the project in this chapter.

The following steps start Visual Basic .NET, open the Compensation Review solution, and then add a new module to the Compensation Review class library project.

To Start Visual Basic .NET and Add a New Module to a Project

1. Insert the Data Disk in drive A. Using Windows Explorer, if necessary copy the Compensation Review folder and Compensation Review.mdb database file from the A:\Chapter10 folder to the A:\Chapter11 folder.

2. Start Visual Basic .NET. When the Start Page displays, click the Open Project button on the Start Page.

3. If necessary, click the Look in box arrow and then click 3½ Floppy (A:). Double-click the Chapter11 folder.

   Visual Basic .NET displays the Open Project dialog box. The Chapter11 folder becomes the current folder in the Look in box.

4. Double-click the Compensation Review folder. If necessary, click the Compensation Review solution file (Compensation Review.sln).

   The Compensation Review folder becomes the current folder in the Look in box. The Compensation Review solution file is selected in the dialog box.

5. Click the Open button. When the Compensation Review project displays in the Solution Explorer window, right-click the Compensation Review project. When the shortcut menu displays, point to the Add command and then click Add New Item on the Add menu.

   The Add New Item - Compensation Review dialog box displays.

6. Click the Module template in the Templates area. Select the text in the Name box and type UpdateCompensation.vb as the new name. Click the Open button.

   Visual Basic .NET adds the UpdateCompensation.vb module to the Compensation Review class library.

After Visual Basic .NET creates the new module, the module name, UpdateCompensation.vb, displays in the Solution Explorer window below the Compensation Review project. The code written in the UpdateCompensation.vb module will be accessible to the code in the Compensation Review class library. Public procedures declared in the UpdateCompensation.vb module will be available to any program that adds a reference to the Compensation Review class library. You can create a class library project that includes only procedures and does not contain any classes. The typical use for class library projects, however, is to encapsulate classes.

Adding a Public Procedure to a Module

The UpdateCompensation.vb module added in the previous steps creates an empty module to which code — such as the UpdateCompensation() procedure — can be added. Figure 11-7 shows the initial lines of code for the UpdateCompensation module. The Option Strict On and Imports statements are placed before the module declaration in line 3. In order for a module and procedure to be available to programs that reference the .DLL file in which they are built, the module and procedure declarations must include the keyword, Public. The word Public thus must be added to the module declaration in line 3 and the procedure declaration in line 7. As shown in line 7, the UpdateCompensation() procedure accepts four parameters — an EmployeeID, an EmployeeType, the DateReviewed, and a new Compensation amount for the employee.

```
 1 Option Strict On
 2 Imports System.Data.OleDb
 3 Public Module UpdateCompensation
 4     Const g_strConnectionString As String = "Provider=Microsoft.Jet.OLEDB.4.0;" & _
 5                                   "Data Source = A:\Chapter11\
       CompensationReview.mdb"
 6
 7     Public Sub UpdateCompensation(ByVal EmployeeID As Integer, ByVal EmployeeType As
       String, ByVal DateReviewed As Date, ByVal Compensation As Decimal)
 8         Dim objOleDbConnection As OleDbConnection
 9         Dim objOleDbCommand As OleDbCommand
10         Dim strSQL As String
11
12         objOleDbConnection = New OleDbConnection(g_strConnectionString)
13         objOleDbCommand = New OleDbCommand()
14         objOleDbCommand.Connection = objOleDbConnection
15         objOleDbCommand.Connection.Open()
16
17     End Sub
18 End Module
```

FIGURE 11-7

Figure 11-7 also shows the database object declarations and code to create a connection to the Compensation Review database. Line 4 sets the database connection string in the constant, g_strConnectionString. Line 9 declares the database command object, OleDbCommand, which will be used to send commands to the Compensation Review database.

Line 12 sends the connection string, which is stored in the g_strConnectionString constant, to the OleDbConnection constructor. Line 13 creates a new instance of the OleDbCommand class; Line 14 then associates the OleDbConnection object with the OleDbCommand object. If this line was not executed, then the OleDbCommand object would not know about the database connection. Finally, line 15 opens a database connection using the Open() method of the OleDbCommand.Connection property.

The following step adds the code shown in Figure 11-7 on the previous page to declare the public procedure, UpdateCompensation(), and open a database connection.

To Declare a Public Procedure in a Module and Open a Database Connection

1. When the UpdateCompensation.vb code window opens, type lines 1 and 2 and add the word Public to line 3 as shown in Figure 11-7. Enter the remaining code as shown in Figure 11-7.

Visual Basic .NET opens the code window. The Option Strict On statement and Imports statement display at the top of the code window. Lines 4 through 6 of the module declare the database connection string. The objects used to connect to the database are declared and initialized in lines 8 through 15 (Figure 11-8).

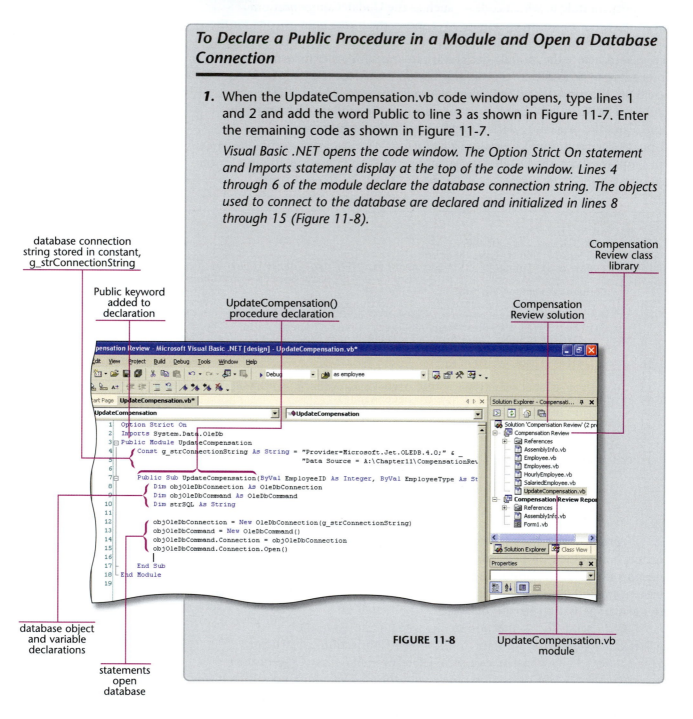

database connection string stored in constant, g_strConnectionString

Public keyword added to declaration

UpdateCompensation() procedure declaration

Compensation Review class library

Compensation Review solution

database object and variable declarations

statements open database

FIGURE 11-8

UpdateCompensation.vb module

Figure 11-8 shows the location of the UpdateCompensation.vb module in the Solution Explorer. The database objects are declared and initialized in the code shown in Figure 11-8, much as was done in the code entered in Chapter 10 to communicate with the Compensation Review database.

Writing Data to a Database Using ADO.NET

The next step is to write the code to create and execute the SQL command that updates the database with new employee compensation information. The process of writing to a database is similar to the process of reading a database. To write to a database, an SQL command is created in a string variable and sent to the database using the OleDbCommand object declared in line 9. As you learned on page VB 10.09 of Chapter 10, an SQL UPDATE statement updates records in a database. In the Compensation Review Update Web application, an SQL UPDATE statement will be used to update employee records with the new compensation information entered by the user.

Figure 11-9 shows the logic necessary to open the database and send an UPDATE statement to the database. The steps in the previous section provided the code for opening the database and getting a database command object. The next step is to code the remainder of the logic shown in Figure 11-9.

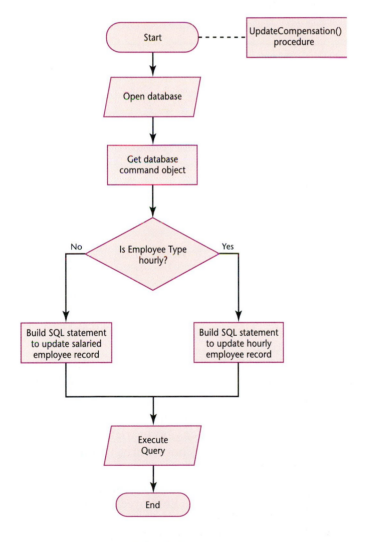

FIGURE 11-9

Creating an SQL UPDATE Statement to Update Employee Records

As you have learned, an UPDATE statement sets values of fields for existing records in a database. In this chapter, an UPDATE statement is used to update employee records in the Compensation Review database.

Figure 11-10 shows an example of an SQL UPDATE statement. The UPDATE statement includes three sections:

1. The name of the table you want to update in the database, listed after the UPDATE keyword.
2. The field names and new field values, listed after the SET keyword and separated by commas.
3. The conditions for which to update the records, listed after the WHERE keyword.

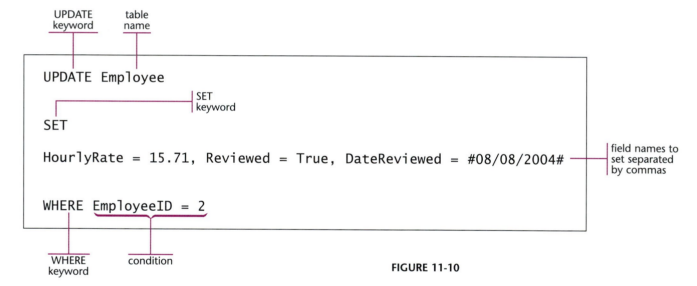

```
UPDATE Employee

SET

HourlyRate = 15.71, Reviewed = True, DateReviewed = #08/08/2004#

WHERE EmployeeID = 2
```

UPDATE keyword   table name   SET keyword   field names to set separated by commas   WHERE keyword   condition

FIGURE 11-10

The example shown in Figure 11-10 shows that, when the Employee field is equal to the EmployeeID value, the HourlyRate, Reviewed, and DateReviewed fields of the Employee table are updated to the values 15.71, True, and 08/08/2004, respectively.

Figure 11-11 shows the If…Then…Else statement that builds the SQL UPDATE statement based on the employee type. The EmployeeType is passed as a parameter to the UpdateCompensation() procedure. If the EmployeeType is Hourly, then the UPDATE statement updates the HourlyRate of the Employee table with the value of the Compensation variable, which also is passed to the procedure. If the EmployeeType is not Hourly, then the UPDATE statement updates the AnnualSalary field. The WHERE clause of the UPDATE statement indicates that the UPDATE statement should update only the record in which the EmployeeID matches the EmployeeID variable passed to the

UpdateCompensation() procedure. When the employee information is updated, the DateReviewed also is set to a date entered on the Web page. A program typically updates such a date with the computer system's date. Because the Compensation Review System is working with test data, however, the program developed in this chapter must allow the user to enter a review date rather than relying on the computer system's current date.

```
17          If EmployeeType = "Hourly" Then
18              strSQL = "UPDATE Employee SET HourlyRate = " & Convert.ToString(      ↙
            Compensation) & ", DateReviewed = #" & DateReviewed.ToShortDateString & "#"
19          Else
20              strSQL = "UPDATE Employee SET AnnualSalary = " & Convert.ToString(    ↙
            Compensation) & ", DateReviewed = #" & DateReviewed.ToShortDateString & "#"
21          End If
22          strSQL &= " , Reviewed = True" & _
23                  " WHERE EmployeeID = " & Convert.ToString(EmployeeID)
```

FIGURE 11-11

Figure 11-11 shows the code that builds the UPDATE statement to query the Compensation Review database. The UPDATE statement is stored in the strSQL variable, as shown in lines 18 and 20. The string can be passed to the OleDbCommand object for execution of the command.

The following step adds the code shown in Figure 11-11 to the UpdateCompensation() procedure to build an SQL UPDATE statement and assign the statement to the strSQL string variable.

To Code an SQL UPDATE Statement to Update Employee Records

1. Type lines 17 through 23 as shown in Figure 11-11.

Lines 17 through 23 display in the code window (Figure 11-12).

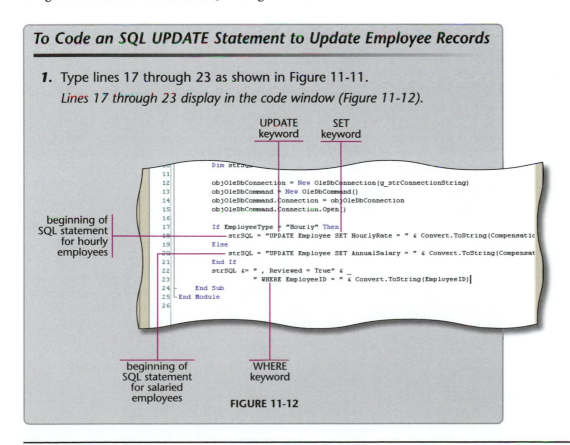

FIGURE 11-12

The code first determines the type of employee, based on the EmployeeType parameter passed to the procedure. The code then builds the beginning of the UPDATE statement based on the employee type and stores the beginning of the SQL UPDATE statement in the strSQL variable. Lines 22 and 23 complete the UPDATE command by setting the Reviewed field to True and the DateReviewed to the date entered by the user and then specifying a condition for the UPDATE command.

Executing an SQL UPDATE Statement

In Chapter 10, you learned that the ExecuteReader() method of the OleDbCommand class executes a SELECT statement on a database and returns a set of records. The OleDbCommand object includes a second method, which executes database commands that do not retrieve records, but rather add, update, or delete records in the database. The **ExecuteNonQuery() method** of the OleDbCommand object executes SQL statements that do not return records, such as the INSERT, UPDATE, and DELETE statements.

Figure 11-13 shows the two lines of code necessary to set the CommandText property of the objOleDbCommand object and then use the ExecuteNonQuery() method to execute the SQL UPDATE statement that updates the employee record with the new compensation amount, review data, and reviewed status.

```
24        objOleDbCommand.CommandText = strSQL
25        objOleDbCommand.ExecuteNonQuery()
```

FIGURE 11-13

The following step adds the code shown in Figure 11-13 to the UpdateCompensation() procedure to execute the SQL UPDATE statement on the Compensation Review database.

To Execute an SQL UPDATE Statement

1. Type lines 24 and 25 as shown in Figure 11-13.

Lines 24 and 25 display in the code window (Figure 11-14).

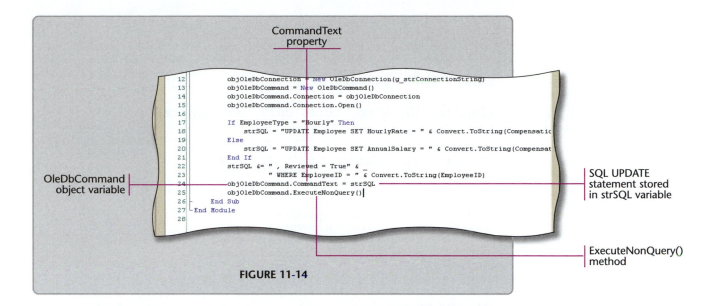

CommandText property

OleDbCommand object variable

SQL UPDATE statement stored in strSQL variable

ExecuteNonQuery() method

```
12        objOleDbConnection = New OleDbConnection(g_strConnectionString)
13        objOleDbCommand = New OleDbCommand()
14        objOleDbCommand.Connection = objOleDbConnection
15        objOleDbCommand.Connection.Open()
16
17        If EmployeeType = "Hourly" Then
18            strSQL = "UPDATE Employee SET HourlyRate = " & Convert.ToString(Compensatio
19        Else
20            strSQL = "UPDATE Employee SET AnnualSalary = " & Convert.ToString(Compensat
21        End If
22        strSQL &= " , Reviewed = True" & _
23              " WHERE EmployeeID = " & Convert.ToString(EmployeeID)
24        objOleDbCommand.CommandText = strSQL
25        objOleDbCommand.ExecuteNonQuery()
26    End Sub
27 End Module
28
```

FIGURE 11-14

Line 24 assigns the SQL UPDATE statement stored in the strSQL variable to the CommandText property of the objOleDbCommand object. Line 25 then executes the SQL UPDATE statement by calling the ExecuteNonQuery() method of the objOleDbCommand object.

The coding of the UpdateCompensation() procedure, which is responsible for performing the compensation updates on the Employees table in the Compensation Review database, is complete. Later in the chapter, the UpdateCompensation() procedure will be built in the same .DLL class library file as the four classes developed in Chapters 9 and 10.

Using the SQL Insert and Delete Statements

Two additional SQL statements not used in the Compensation Review solution are the SQL INSERT and DELETE statements.

The SQL **INSERT statement** adds records to a table or tables in a database. Figure 11-15 on the next page shows an example of an SQL INSERT statement. This simple form of an INSERT statement includes three parameters:

1. The name of the table you want to update in the database, listed after the INSERT keyword.
2. The field names you want to update, enclosed in parentheses and separated by commas, listed after the table name.
3. The values for the fields, listed in parentheses after the VALUES keyword. The values must match the number and data type of the field names listed after the table name.

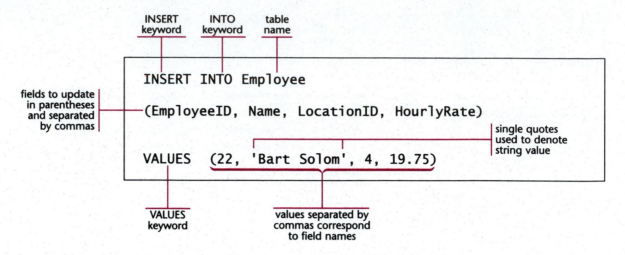

FIGURE 11-15

The SQL **DELETE statement** deletes records from a table in a database. Figure 11-16 shows an example of an SQL DELETE statement. This simple form of a DELETE statement includes two parameters:

1. The table name from which to delete a record or records. The table name is placed after the DELETE and FROM keywords.
2. The conditions for which to delete the records, listed after the WHERE keyword.

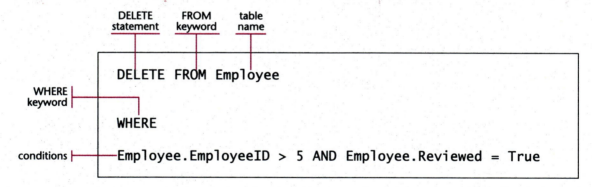

FIGURE 11-16

The combination of the SELECT, UPDATE, INSERT, and DELETE SQL statements provides you with the full functionality you need to perform most typical database operations. The SQL language is a universal database language used in almost all relational database management systems, including Microsoft Access.

Using Optional Parameters in a Procedure

In some situations, a procedure or method can perform a variety of operations. In addition to using conditional statements to control the actions performed by a procedure, Visual Basic .NET also can use optional parameters in a procedure declaration. An **optional parameter** is a parameter that may or may not be passed to a procedure, and does not have to be passed by the code that calls the procedure. If the parameter is not passed, then the procedure being called automatically detects this and sets the parameter to a specified default value.

Figure 11-17a shows the outline of a procedure declaration that includes an optional parameter. The **Optional keyword** is placed before the ByVal or ByRef keyword. The parameter name and parameter data type are followed by a default value. If the calling code does not include the parameter in the call to the procedure, then the procedure assumes the value of the parameter to be the default value specified in the procedure declaration. Figure 11-17b also shows two examples of calling the declared procedure. The first example shows a call to the procedure without the optional parameter. In this case, the procedure uses the default value, "None", to initialize the Dept parameter. The second example shows a call to the procedure with both parameters specified. The value, "Accounting", overrides the default value, "None", when the procedure executes.

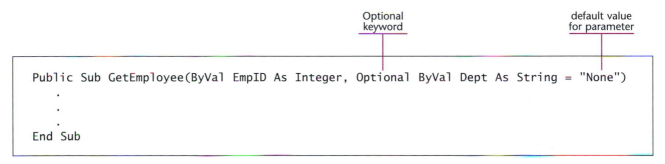

```
                                             Optional                              default value
                                             keyword                               for parameter

    Public Sub GetEmployee(ByVal EmpID As Integer, Optional ByVal Dept As String = "None")
        .
        .
        .
    End Sub
```

FIGURE 11-17a

```
    GetEmployee(5) ————————————| call to procedure without
                               | optional parameter

              example 1

    GetEmployee(6, "Accounting") ——————| call to procedure including
                                       | optional parameter

                                       | optional parameter

              example 2
```

FIGURE 11-17b

Adding an Optional Parameter to a Procedure

The Compensation Review Update Web application requires the ability to get and display an employee record from the Employee table in the Compensation Review database. The Employees class and SELECT statement developed in Chapter 10 includes much of the functionality needed to query the Compensation Review database. The Update Compensation Review Web application requires that a minor change be made to the SELECT statement to allow the Employees class to get information for one individual employee record, given an Employee ID.

The solution to this problem of finding just one employee is to send an optional parameter to the New() constructor of the Employees class. This optional parameter will be the Employee ID of the employee for which information is needed. If the optional parameter is passed to the constructor, then a different form of the SELECT statement that queries the database for only an individual employee record is built. The value of –1 will be used to initialize the EmployeeID. If the EmployeeID is –1 when the New() constructor executes, then the constructor executes as designed in Chapter 10. The value –1 is used because it is an invalid EmployeeID and serves as a flag within the code.

Figure 11-18 shows the code necessary to add the optional parameter to the New() constructor of the Employees class. The optional parameter, EmployeeID, is added in line 12, with the default value specified as –1. Line 10 of the code also modifies the connection string of the database so that the class looks for the database in the A:\Chapter11 folder, rather than the A:\Chapter10 folder.

```
9     Private Const g_strConnectionString As String = "Provider=Microsoft.Jet.OLEDB.4.0;" ↙
      & _
10                                                      "Data Source=A:\Chapter11\         ↙
      CompensationReview.mdb"
11
12    Public Sub New(ByVal ReviewedStatus As Boolean, ByVal ReviewDate As Date, Optional ↙
      ByVal EmployeeID As Integer = -1)
```

FIGURE 11-18

The following steps modify the connection string and add an optional parameter to the constructor declaration for the Employees class in the Compensation Review class library.

To Add an Optional Parameter to a Procedure

1. Double-click the Employees.vb module in the Solution Explorer window.
    The Employees.vb module opens in the main work area.
2. Modify lines 10 and 12 as shown in Figure 11-18 to change the folder name for the Data Source of the connection string and to add an optional parameter to the New() constructor declaration.
    The code displays as shown in Figure 11-19. The folder for the database is changed to A:\Chapter11. The optional parameter, EmployeeID, displays with an initial value of –1.

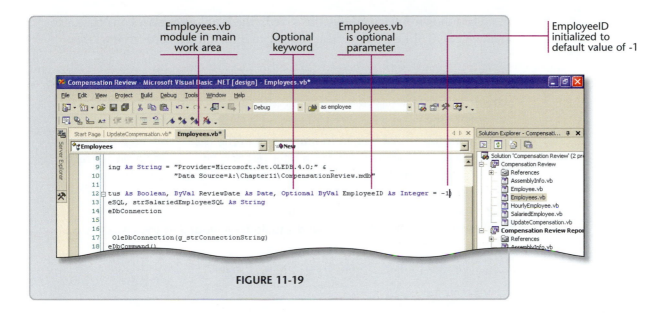

FIGURE 11-19

With the connection string and constructor declaration properly coded, the next step is to modify the string that stores the value of the SQL SELECT statement so that it queries a specific employee record if the optional parameter, EmployeeID, is passed to the constructor.

Selecting an Individual Record from a Table

The SELECT statement built in the Employees class constructor on page VB 10.28 of Chapter 10 must be modified so that if the optional parameter, EmployeeID, is passed to the constructor, the SELECT statement will select the employee record for the employee with the same EmployeeID as that passed in the parameter. Figure 11-20 shows the modifications to the Employees class constructor code and the new code required to build the SELECT statement if an EmployeeID is passed to the constructor. The string concatenation and line continuation characters on line 29 must be removed before adding the If…Then…Else statement beginning on line 30. Line 31 shows the new condition added to the SELECT statement; this condition requires that the employee record returned from the database have an EmployeeID that matches the EmployeeID passed as the optional parameter to the New() constructor. Lines 33 and 34 already are coded in the constructor. The End If statement in line 35 ends the If…Then…Else statement.

```
29                      "AND Employee.Reviewed = " & Convert.ToString(ReviewedStatus) & " ↙
         AND "
30              If EmployeeID <> -1 Then
31                  strSQL &= "EmployeeID = " & Convert.ToString(EmployeeID)
32              Else
33                  strSQL &= "DateAdd('yyyy', 1, [Employee.DateReviewed]) >= #" &       ↙
         ReviewDate.ToShortDateString & "# AND " & _
34                          "DateAdd('yyyy', 1, [Employee.DateReviewed]) <= #" &         ↙
         ReviewDate.AddDays(30).ToShortDateString & "#"
35              End If
```

FIGURE 11-20

The following steps modify the code in the Employees class constructor to create an SQL SELECT statement to read an individual record from a table.

To Code an SQL SELECT Statement to Read an Individual Record from a Table

1. With the Employees.vb module open in the main work area, remove the string concatenation character (&) and line continuation character (_) from line 29 of the Employees class constructor as shown in Figure 11-20 on the previous page.

2. Type lines 30 through 32 and line 35 as shown in Figure 11-20. Lines 33 and 34 are already coded and should be included in the Else clause of the If statement.

Lines 30 through 35 display as shown in Figure 11-21.

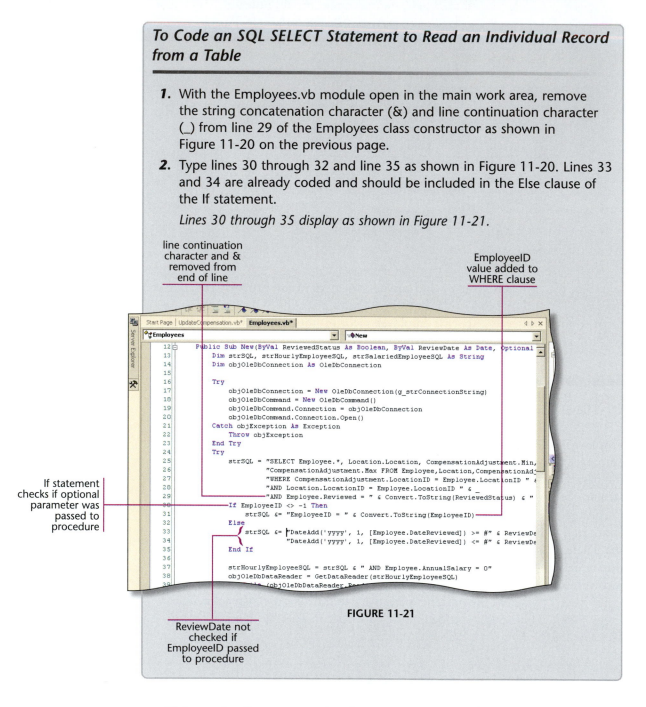

line continuation character and & removed from end of line

EmployeeID value added to WHERE clause

If statement checks if optional parameter was passed to procedure

ReviewDate not checked if EmployeeID passed to procedure

FIGURE 11-21

If the optional parameter, EmployeeID, is passed to the procedure, then the SQL SELECT command is built with a condition that includes the EmployeeID. If the optional parameter is not passed, then the SQL SELECT command is built in lines 33 and 34, as it was coded in Chapter 10.

The modifications to the Compensation Review class library are complete. A new module, UpdateCompensation, now is included in the class library and includes one public procedure, the UpdateCompensation() procedure. In addition to the functionality coded in Chapter 10, the Employees class now allows the ability to query the database for just one employee's record. The optional EmployeeID parameter is passed to the Employees class constructor to indicate that just one employee's record should be retrieved from the database.

Building, Saving, and Documenting the Class Library

Now the class library must be built and the code documented. With the coding for the new UpdateCompensation module and changes to the Employees class complete, the next step is to build the Compensation Review class library so that the .DLL file includes the new UpdateCompensation() procedure and changes to the Employees class. The current version of the .DLL file in the \bin directory of the project includes only the three classes (Employee, HourlyEmployee, SalariedEmployee) coded in Chapter 9 and the one class (Employees) coded in Chapter 10.

The following steps build, save, and document the Compensation Review class library with the UpdateCompensation module and changes to the Employees class.

To Build, Save, and Document the Class Library

1. Right-click the Compensation Review project in the Solution Explorer window. When the shortcut menu displays, click the Build command.

   Visual Basic .NET automatically saves the class files and then opens the Output window and displays several messages while building the project. The result of the build is the creation of the Compensation Review.dll file in the A:\Chapter11\Compensation Review\Compensation Review folder on the Data Disk.

2. Follow the steps on page VB 2.40 of Chapter 2 to use the Print command on the File menu to print a record of the code for the Employees class.

   A record of the code for the Employees class is printed. Figure 11-22 on the next page shows a record of the modified code.

   (continued)

```
A:\Chapter11\Compensation Review\Compensation Review\Employees.vb                    1
 1 Option Strict On
 2 Imports System.Data.OleDb
 3 Public Class Employees
 4     Private mobjHourlyEmployees As New Collection()
 5     Private mobjSalariedEmployees As New Collection()
 6     Private objOleDbCommand As OleDbCommand
 7     Private objOleDbDataReader As OleDbDataReader
 8
 9     Private Const g_strConnectionString As String = "Provider=Microsoft.Jet.OLEDB.4.0;"↙
       & _
10                                                      "Data Source=A:\Chapter11\       ↙
       CompensationReview.mdb"
11
12     Public Sub New(ByVal ReviewedStatus As Boolean, ByVal ReviewDate As Date, Optional ↙
       ByVal EmployeeID As Integer = -1)
13         Dim strSQL, strHourlyEmployeeSQL, strSalariedEmployeeSQL As String
14         Dim objOleDbConnection As OleDbConnection
15
16         Try
17             objOleDbConnection = New OleDbConnection(g_strConnectionString)
18             objOleDbCommand = New OleDbCommand()
19             objOleDbCommand.Connection = objOleDbConnection
20             objOleDbCommand.Connection.Open()
21         Catch objException As Exception
22             Throw objException
23         End Try
24         Try
25             strSQL = "SELECT Employee.*, Location.Location, CompensationAdjustment.Min,↙
       " & _
26                     "CompensationAdjustment.Max FROM Employee,Location,              ↙
       CompensationAdjustment " & _
27                     "WHERE CompensationAdjustment.LocationID = Employee.LocationID " &↙
       _
28                     "AND Location.LocationID = Employee.LocationID " & _
29                     "AND Employee.Reviewed = " & Convert.ToString(ReviewedStatus) & " ↙
       AND "
30             If EmployeeID <> -1 Then
31                 strSQL &= "EmployeeID = " & Convert.ToString(EmployeeID)
32             Else
33                 strSQL &= "DateAdd('yyyy', 1, [Employee.DateReviewed]) >= #" &        ↙
       ReviewDate.ToShortDateString & "# AND " & _
34                         "DateAdd('yyyy', 1, [Employee.DateReviewed]) <= #" &          ↙
       ReviewDate.AddDays(30).ToShortDateString & "#"
35             End If
36
37             strHourlyEmployeeSQL = strSQL & " AND Employee.AnnualSalary = 0"
38             objOleDbDataReader = GetDataReader(strHourlyEmployeeSQL)
```

FIGURE 11-22

3. Click the UpdateCompensation.vb tab in the main work area. Follow the steps on page VB 2.40 of Chapter 2 to use the Print command on the File menu to print a record of the code for the UpdateCompensation.vb module.

A record of the code for the UpdateCompensation.vb module is printed (Figure 11-23).

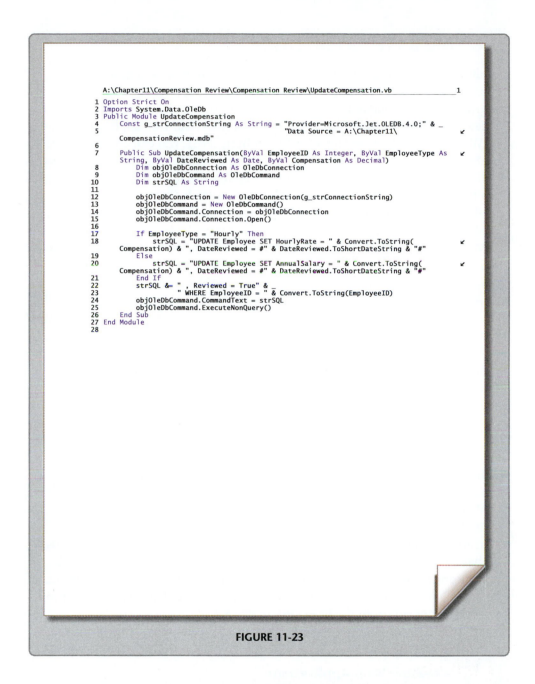

```
A:\Chapter11\Compensation Review\Compensation Review\UpdateCompensation.vb                1
1  Option Strict On
2  Imports System.Data.OleDb
3  Public Module UpdateCompensation
4      Const g_strConnectionString As String = "Provider=Microsoft.Jet.OLEDB.4.0;" & _
5                                     "Data Source = A:\Chapter11\        ↵
   CompensationReview.mdb"
6
7      Public Sub UpdateCompensation(ByVal EmployeeID As Integer, ByVal EmployeeType As  ↵
   String, ByVal DateReviewed As Date, ByVal Compensation As Decimal)
8          Dim objOleDbConnection As OleDbConnection
9          Dim objOleDbCommand As OleDbCommand
10         Dim strSQL As String
11
12         objOleDbConnection = New OleDbConnection(g_strConnectionString)
13         objOleDbCommand = New OleDbCommand()
14         objOleDbCommand.Connection = objOleDbConnection
15         objOleDbCommand.Connection.Open()
16
17         If EmployeeType = "Hourly" Then
18             strSQL = "UPDATE Employee SET HourlyRate = " & Convert.ToString(  ↵
   Compensation) & ", DateReviewed = #" & DateReviewed.ToShortDateString & "#"
19         Else
20             strSQL = "UPDATE Employee SET AnnualSalary = " & Convert.ToString(  ↵
   Compensation) & ", DateReviewed = #" & DateReviewed.ToShortDateString & "#"
21         End If
22         strSQL &= " , Reviewed = True" & _
23             " WHERE EmployeeID = " & Convert.ToString(EmployeeID)
24         objOleDbCommand.CommandText = strSQL
25         objOleDbCommand.ExecuteNonQuery()
26     End Sub
27 End Module
28
```

FIGURE 11-23

The previous steps left the solution and project open in the IDE because the Compensation Review Update Web application still must be added to the Compensation Review solution.

The development phase for the changes to the Compensation Review class library now is complete, and other programs, such as those in the Compensation Review System, can use the Compensation Review class library.

Creating a Web Application

Recall that the first program in the Compensation Review System to utilize the Employees class is the Compensation Review Report application. The second program in the Compensation Review System to utilize the Compensation Review class library is the Compensation Review Update Web application.

When you start a new project in Visual Basic .NET, you can choose to create an ASP.NET Web Application project instead of a Windows application project. As discussed on page VB 1.06 of Chapter 1, a Web application is a collection of Web forms and code that runs on a Web server. A **Web form** is similar to the Windows forms that you have developed, but is based on the Web controls and HTML controls in the .NET Framework class library. Web forms are stored as HTML (Hypertext Markup Language) by Visual Basic .NET. HTML is the standard language used to create and display Web pages in Web browsers. The user thus can interact with a Web form via his or her Web browser.

A **Web server** includes software that accepts and processes requests from a Web browser on a client, or user's computer. Based on the request that it receives from the Web browser, the Web server determines what to send back to the user's Web browser. Typically, the Web server sends HTML back to the Web browser, which the Web browser translates and displays for the user as a Web page. Microsoft's Web server software, called **Internet Information Services (IIS)**, can run Web applications built using Visual Basic .NET.

Visual Basic .NET requires that a special version of the CLR be running as a part of IIS in order to execute Web applications. **ASP.NET** is the technology that runs as an add-on to IIS to allow IIS to execute Web applications built using Visual Basic .NET. An **ASP.NET Web Application** is a Web application created in Visual Basic .NET that uses ASP.NET technology to provide functionality over the Web.

A Web page created using Visual Basic .NET is an **.aspx file**, with a file extension of .aspx. A Web page that is named Home in a Web application thus will have a page name of Home.aspx. Visual Basic .NET requires that all Web applications, including ASP.NET Web applications, be created on a Web server. Because a Web server can run only on a computer's hard drive, Web application projects cannot run from the Data Disk in drive A.

Creating Web Applications
Because a Web server can run only on a computer's hard drive, Web application projects cannot run from the Data Disk in drive A.

Figure 11-24 shows the components of the Web server and client required to request and view a Web application created using Visual Basic .NET. The IIS Web server accepts and processes the request from the Web browser on the client computer and sends it to the ASP.NET Web application. Based on the request that the ASP.NET Web application receives from the Web browser, the ASP.NET Web application and IIS determine what response to send back to the user's Web browser. Typically, the response is HTML that is sent to the client's Web browser to be displayed as a Web page.

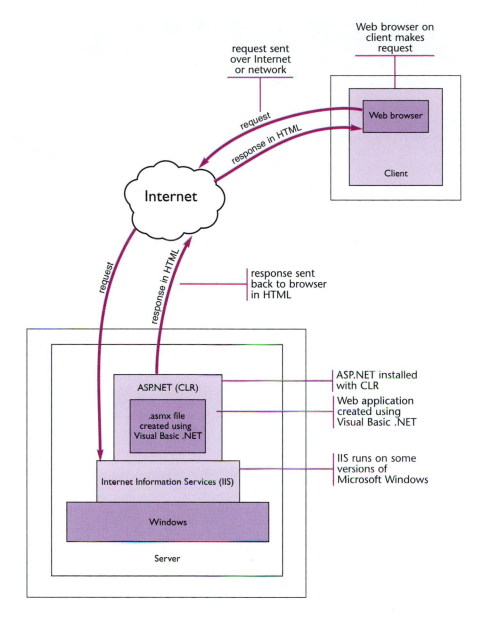

FIGURE 11-24

Starting a New ASP.NET Web Application Project

As shown in Figure 11-3 on page VB 11.07 and in Figure 11-25 on the next page, the user interface design of the Compensation Review Update Web application includes one Web page. When Visual Basic .NET creates a new ASP.NET Web Application, a default Web form is added to the project, just as a default Windows form is added to a Windows Application project. The Web form is used in design mode to create the user interface for the Web page.

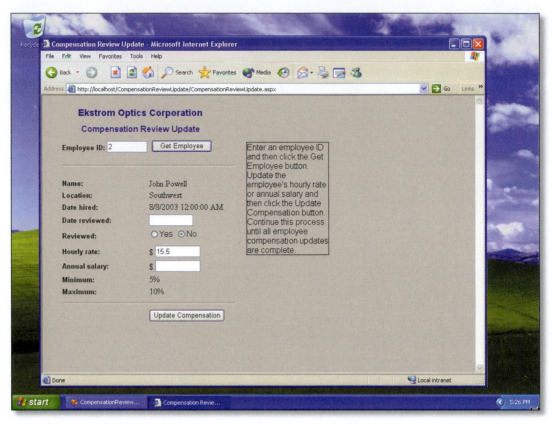

FIGURE 11-25

The following steps add a new ASP.NET Web Application project to the Compensation Review solution, using the **ASP.NET Web Application template**. The new project is named CompensationReviewUpdate and is created on the current computer's Web server. The default Web form is renamed to CompensationReviewUpdate.aspx.

Note: If you plan on completing the project in this chapter, you must have access to an Internet Information Services (IIS) Server that has been configured with ASP.NET. The steps in this chapter assume that IIS has been configured on the same computer on which Visual Basic .NET is installed and that the InetPub folder is located on C:\InetPub. If necessary, see your instructor for assistance in setting up IIS.

To Start a New ASP.NET Web Application Project

1. Right-click the Compensation Review solution in the Solution Explorer window. When the shortcut menu displays, click the Add command. When the Add shortcut menu displays, click the Add New Project command.

2. When the Add New Project dialog box displays, click the ASP.NET Web Application icon in the Templates area.

The ASP.NET Web Application template is selected in the Templates area. The project location changes to a Web page URL (Figure 11-26). The URL includes the server name of **localhost**, which indicates that the Web server is located on the current computer.

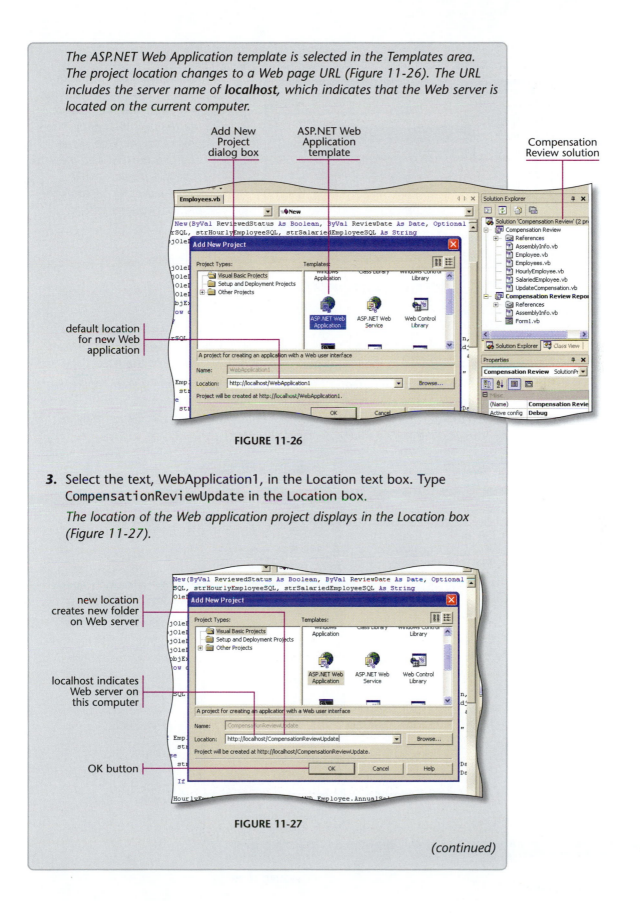

FIGURE 11-26

3. Select the text, WebApplication1, in the Location text box. Type CompensationReviewUpdate in the Location box.

The location of the Web application project displays in the Location box (Figure 11-27).

FIGURE 11-27

(continued)

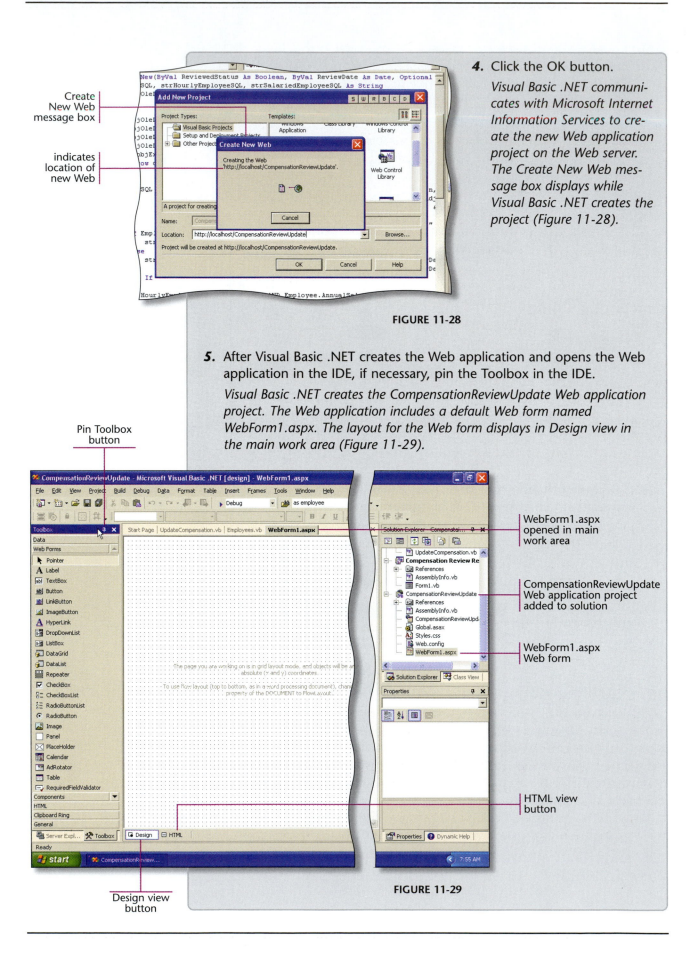

4. Click the OK button.

Visual Basic .NET communicates with Microsoft Internet Information Services to create the new Web application project on the Web server. The Create New Web message box displays while Visual Basic .NET creates the project (Figure 11-28).

FIGURE 11-28

5. After Visual Basic .NET creates the Web application and opens the Web application in the IDE, if necessary, pin the Toolbox in the IDE.

Visual Basic .NET creates the CompensationReviewUpdate Web application project. The Web application includes a default Web form named WebForm1.aspx. The layout for the Web form displays in Design view in the main work area (Figure 11-29).

FIGURE 11-29

6. Right-click the WebForm1.aspx Web form in the Solution Explorer window. When the shortcut menu displays, click the Rename command. Type CompensationReviewUpdate.aspx as the new Web form name.

The new Web form name, CompensationReviewUpdate.aspx, displays in the Visual Basic .NET title bar, on the tab in the main work area, and as the new Web form name in the Solution Explorer window (Figure 11-30).

CompensationReviewUpdate.aspx displays in toolbar

Web form name changed to CompensationReviewUpdate.aspx

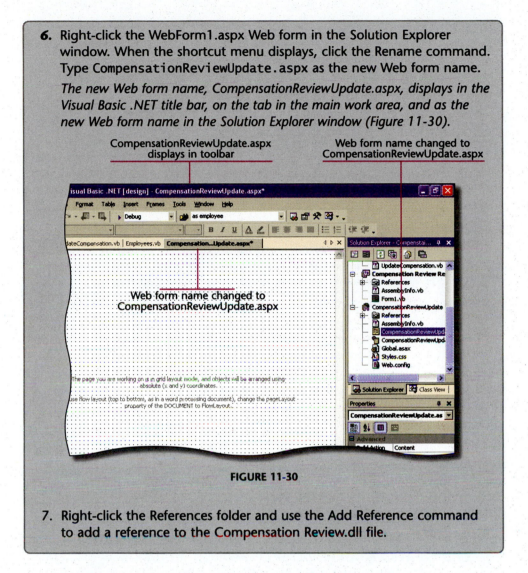

FIGURE 11-30

7. Right-click the References folder and use the Add Reference command to add a reference to the Compensation Review.dll file.

After Visual Basic .NET creates the new project, the solution and project name, CompensationReviewUpdate, displays in the Solution Explorer window. The Web form, WebForm1.aspx, is renamed to CompensationReviewUpdate.aspx. Figure 11-29 shows the Web form grid layout area in the main work area. Web forms do not have borders. The client's Web browser determines the size and borders for the Web page generated from the Web form. Therefore, the Web form layout consumes the entire main work area.

Figure 11-29 also shows the Web Forms controls in the Toolbox window. Many of these controls appear similar to the Windows controls used earlier in this book. As previously discussed, however, these controls are in a different part of the .NET Framework class library. They have different properties and methods than their Windows counterparts, but they can be used to solve many similar user interface design problems.

Web Form Properties

Web forms have properties just as Windows forms do. In the CompensationReviewUpdate Web form, the background color must be changed to gray. The background color for a Web form is set using the **bgColor property** of the form. The **title property** defines the title that displays in the Web browser title bar when the page is active in a Web browser. The title property of the Web page must be changed from WebForm1, the default name, to Compensation Review Update.

Table 11-2 shows the common form properties that are used on Web forms.

Table 11-2 Web Form Properties

PROPERTY	DESCRIPTION	PROPERTY VALUES
Background	A background image that displays on the form	Choose an image from a dialog box
bgColor	The background color of the form	Choose a color from a dialog box
Text	The text foreground color of text that is added to the form	Choose a color from a dialog box
Title	The title that displays in the Web browser title bar when the page is active in a Web browser	Any value

The following steps change the Web property values to set the background color of the CompensationReviewUpdate Web form to gray and to change the title to Compensation Review Update.

To Change Web Form Properties

1. Click anywhere on the grid in the main work area to select the CompensationReviewUpdate Web form. Click the bgColor property value in the Properties list.

2. When the Color Picker dialog box displays, click the System Colors tab. Click the ActiveBorder color in the Color list box.

   A list of system colors displays in the Color list box in the System Colors tab of the Color Picker dialog box. The selected color displays in the Color area below the list box (Figure 11-31).

3. Click the OK button.

   The background color of the CompensationReviewUpdate Web page changes to gray.

4. If necessary, scroll to the title property in the Properties list. Type Compensation Review Update as the new value of the title property.

   The Web form properties now are set.

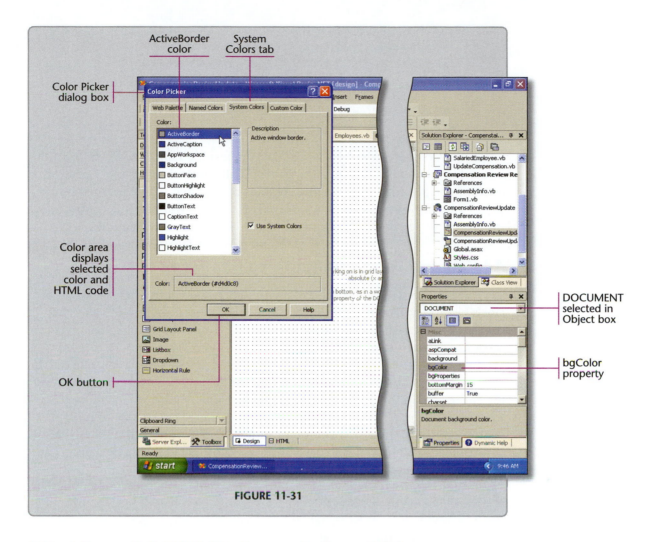

FIGURE 11-31

Working with HTML Controls for a Web Application

The next step is to begin adding controls to the Web form to create the user interface for the Compensation Review Update Web application. Web forms can include two types of controls: HTML controls and Web controls. **HTML controls** include standard HTML elements, such as text, tables, images, and checkboxes. HTML controls are used in a Web page when standard HTML is needed to format Web pages and display static information to users. HTML controls are not used if special ASP.NET processing or Visual Basic .NET code is needed for the controls. HTML controls are not processed by ASP.NET, which means they have limited functionality for interacting with the user. For example, you cannot change the Text property on an HTML Label control at run time as you can with a Label control in a Windows application.

Tip

Using HTML Controls
HTML controls are used when standard HTML is needed on a Web page to format Web pages and display static information to users. HTML controls are not used when special ASP.NET processing or Visual Basic .NET code is needed for the controls.

In the Compensation Review Update Web form, a Table HTML control will be used to align other controls. The **Table HTML control** allows other controls or text to be placed in the rows and columns of the table. As the user resizes his or her Web browser window, the Table HTML control will keep the controls in the user interface aligned and properly spaced in the browser window.

Adding and Formatting a Table HTML Control

The Compensation Review Update user interface requires that a column of labels be displayed on the left side of the page and that a column of values be displayed to the right of the labels. A Table HTML control with two columns can accommodate this layout.

Cells in a Table HTML control can be merged together to act like one cell. If all the cells in a row are merged together, then the resulting merged cell takes up the entire row. In this project, several of the cells in the table will be merged, so that two Horizontal Rule HTML controls can be added to separate some of the controls and assist the user in navigating the page. The **Horizontal Rule HTML control** places a line on a Web page that can be formatted to any thickness. The first row in the table also will be merged into one cell, to allow a Label, TextBox, and Button control to share the top row, as indicated in the user interface design in Figure 11-3 on page VB 11.07.

The following steps add a Table HTML control to the Web form and format the rows and columns of the table.

To Add and Format a Table HTML Control

1. If necessary, click the HTML tab in the Toolbox window. Drag a Table control from the Toolbox window to the Web form as shown in Figure 11-32.

The available HTML controls display in the Toolbox window. The CompensationReviewUpdate Web form displays a Table control. By default, the table includes three rows and three columns (Figure 11-32).

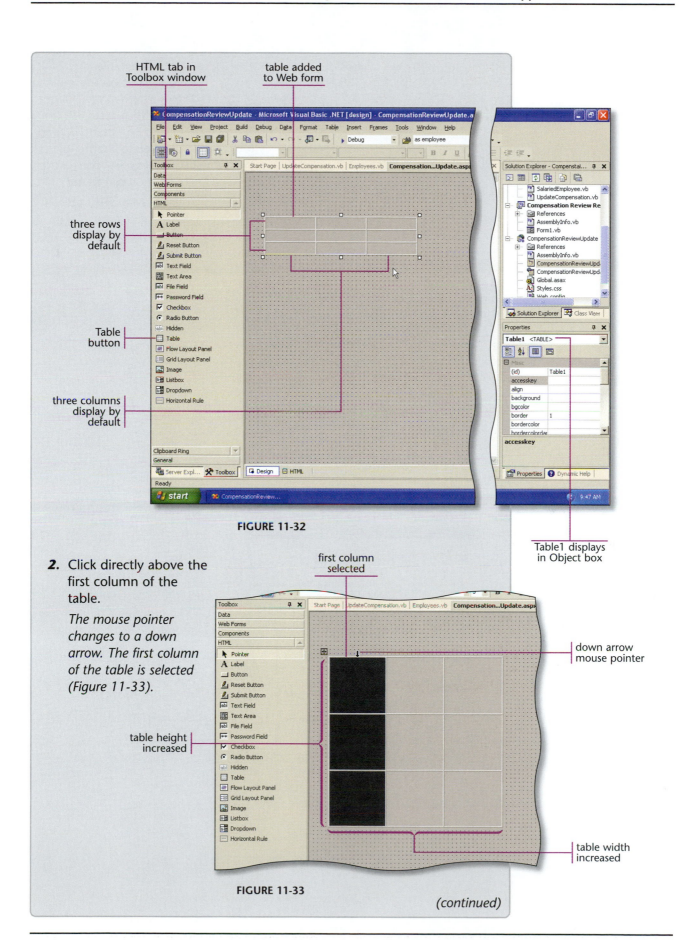

HTML tab in Toolbox window

table added to Web form

three rows display by default

Table button

three columns display by default

Table1 displays in Object box

FIGURE 11-32

2. Click directly above the first column of the table.

The mouse pointer changes to a down arrow. The first column of the table is selected (Figure 11-33).

first column selected

down arrow mouse pointer

table height increased

table width increased

FIGURE 11-33

(continued)

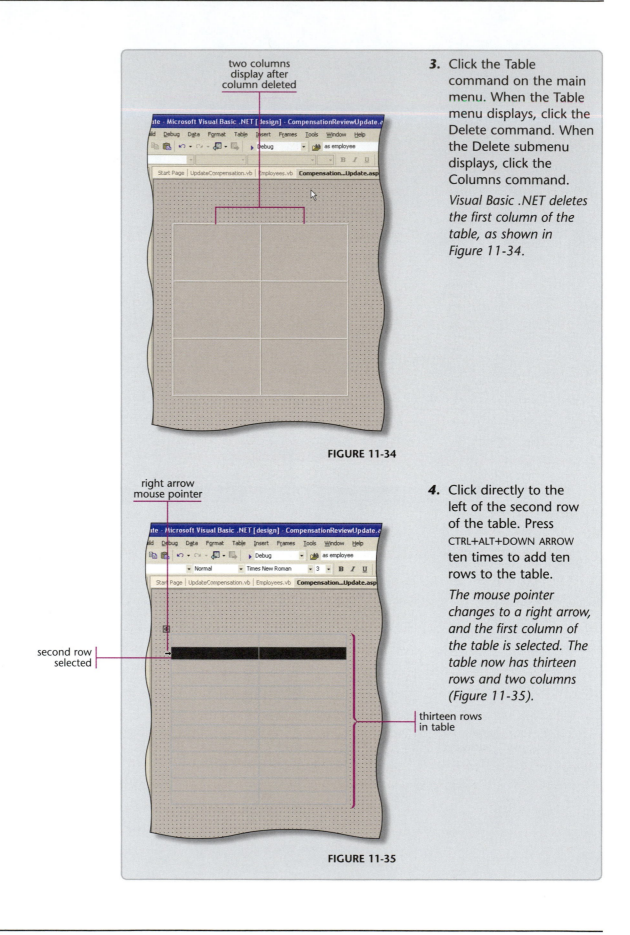

two columns
display after
column deleted

FIGURE 11-34

right arrow
mouse pointer

second row
selected

thirteen rows
in table

FIGURE 11-35

3. Click the Table command on the main menu. When the Table menu displays, click the Delete command. When the Delete submenu displays, click the Columns command.

Visual Basic .NET deletes the first column of the table, as shown in Figure 11-34.

4. Click directly to the left of the second row of the table. Press CTRL+ALT+DOWN ARROW ten times to add ten rows to the table.

The mouse pointer changes to a right arrow, and the first column of the table is selected. The table now has thirteen rows and two columns (Figure 11-35).

5. With the second row of the table still selected, click the Merge Cells command on the Table menu. Select the first row of the table and then click the Merge Cells command on the Table menu. Select the twelfth row of the table and then click the Merge Cells command on the Table menu.

Rows 1, 2, and 12 each are displayed in the table with one column (Figure 11-36).

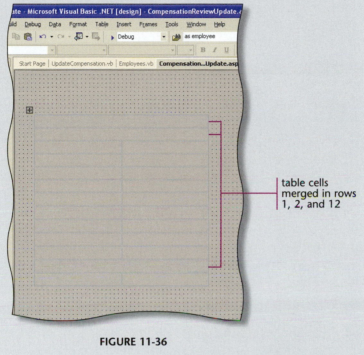

table cells merged in rows 1, 2, and 12

FIGURE 11-36

The Table HTML control serves as a guide for adding other controls. The border of the Table HTML control does not display to the user, but, as the user resizes his or her Web browser window, the Table HTML control keeps the controls aligned and properly spaced in the browser window.

Adding Text to a Table HTML Control

The next step is to enter the text labels in the first column of the Table HTML control. The text labels that are displayed on the left side of the Web page can be typed directly into the Table HTML control on the Web form. The text can be formatted after it is entered into the table cells.

The steps on the next page add text to the cells of the Table HTML control on the Web form.

To Add Text to a Table HTML Control

1. Click in the first row of the Table HTML control on the Web form. Type Employee ID: as the text label.

The text label, Employee ID:, is displayed in row 1, column 1 of the Table HTML control (Figure 11-37).

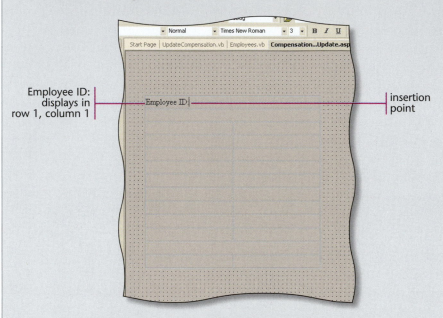

Employee ID:
displays in
row 1, column 1

insertion
point

FIGURE 11-37

2. Type the text in the table cells in column 1 as shown in Figure 11-38.

The text labels are displayed in the Table HTML control (Figure 11-38).

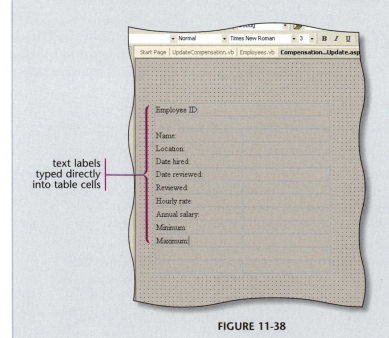

text labels
typed directly
into table cells

FIGURE 11-38

When a Web form is displayed in the main work area, the Design and Formatting toolbars display at the top of the Visual Basic .NET window. Figure 11-39 shows the buttons on the toolbars. The Show Borders button on the Design toolbar toggles the display of table borders on the Web form. The Show Grid button toggles the display of the grid layout used to position and align controls on the Web form.

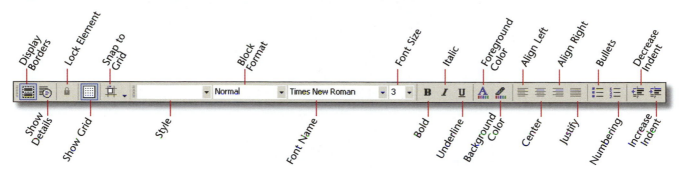

FIGURE 11-39

The buttons on the Formatting toolbar are used to perform formatting functions on text and other elements on the Web form. For example, the Formatting toolbar can be used to bold text or change the font name of text by using the Font Name list.

The following steps format the text that was added to the Table HTML control in the previous steps.

To Format Text on the Web Form

1. Click directly above column 1 of the Table HTML control to select the first column.

The cells in column 1 of the Table HTML control are selected (Figure 11-40).

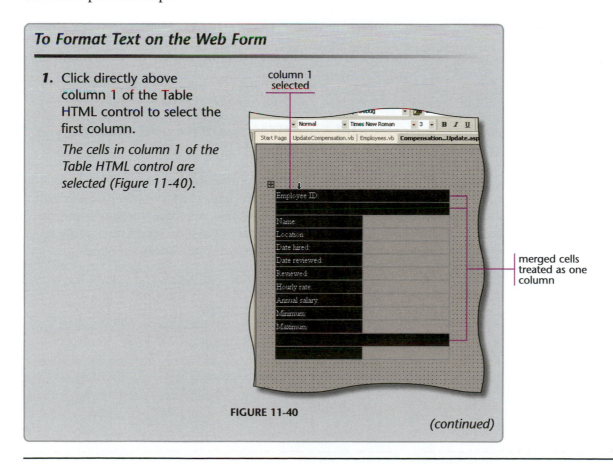

FIGURE 11-40

(continued)

2. Click the Font Name box arrow on the Formatting toolbar and then click Arial in the Font Name list. Click the Bold button on the Formatting toolbar.

The text in the first column of the Table HTML control displays in the Arial bold font (Figure 11-41).

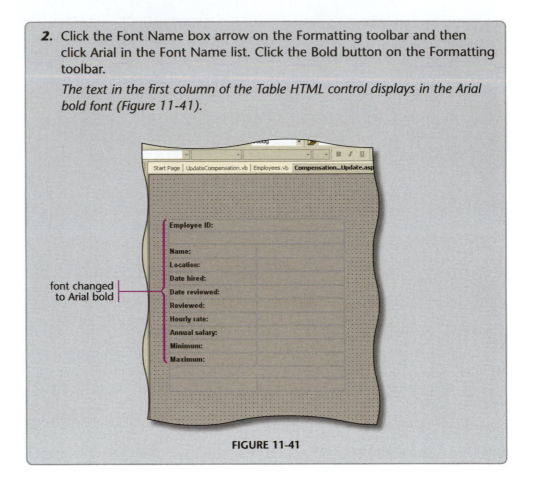

font changed to Arial bold

FIGURE 11-41

The labels now are placed and formatted as they should be in the final Update Compensation Review Web application. The font is changed to Arial bold to make the user interface easier to read.

Adding a Horizontal Rule HTML Control and Viewing HTML Code

The next step is to add two Horizontal Rule HTML controls to the table in order to separate some of the elements in the table. As previously discussed, the Horizontal Rule HTML control places a line on a Web page that can be formatted to any thickness. The Horizontal Rule HTML control serves little purpose other than to separate certain portions of a Web page visually.

Tip

Using Horizontal Rule HTML Controls
Use a Horizontal Rule HTML control to separate certain portions of a Web page visually for better readability.

The following steps add two Horizontal Rule HTML controls to the Web form and then format the controls. After the Horizontal Rule HTML controls are added, the HTML for the Web page is displayed by using the HTML view button. The HTML is viewed in order to confirm that as a Web form is built, Visual Basic .NET is building the HTML code behind the scenes.

To Add and Format a Horizontal Rule HTML Control and View HTML Code for a Web Form

1. Drag a Horizontal Rule HTML control from the Toolbox window to the second row of the Table HTML control on the Web form. Drag a second Horizontal Rule HTML control from the Toolbox window to the twelfth row of the Table HTML control on the Web form. Drag the bottom-center sizing handle of each Horizontal Rule HTML control approximately 1 pixel down to increase the width of the controls.

A Horizontal Rule HTML control displays across the length of rows 2 and 12 in the Table HTML control (Figure 11-42).

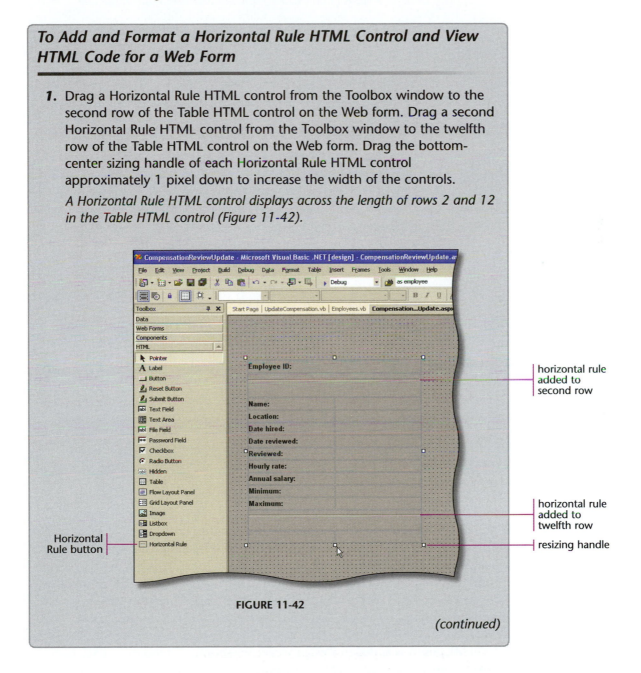

FIGURE 11-42

(continued)

2. Click the HTML view button below the main work area.

The HTML code for the Web form displays (Figure 11-43). As controls are added to the form, Visual Basic .NET automatically adds the HTML for the controls, as shown in the HTML view. The top portion of the HTML includes special code for ASP.NET that Visual Basic .NET inserted automatically.

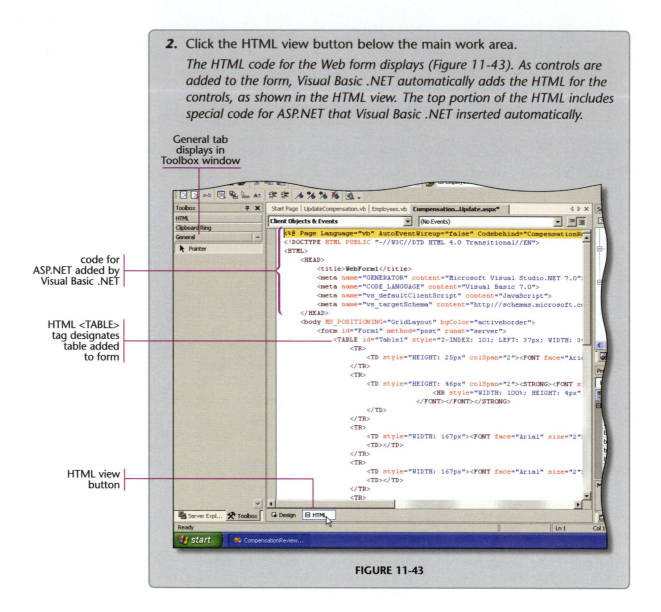

FIGURE 11-43

The first Horizontal Rule HTML control serves to separate the Employee ID input area from the area where employee information is displayed. The second Horizontal Rule HTML control separates the employee information from the Update Compensation button and the error message area.

As you design the Web form in design mode, Visual Basic .NET automatically generates the HTML code for the .aspx Web page (Figure 11-43). If you are proficient in programming HTML code, you can create or edit the HTML code in HTML view, in addition to using Design view to design the Web form. All of the HTML controls added in Design view correspond to standard HTML code that you can view and edit in HTML view.

Working with Web Controls for a Web Application

While HTML controls allow for a familiar and standard user interface for Web pages, the controls lack the robustness of the types of controls used to create Windows applications in Visual Basic .NET. The .NET Framework thus includes Web controls that fill the functionality gap between HTML controls and Windows controls. HTML controls correspond directly with specific HTML code, and the Web browser takes care of doing the behind-the-scenes work to display the HTML controls to the user. **Web controls**, by contrast, are handled on the Web server and are processed by ASP.NET. While they display on the client as HTML, the processing required for the events and methods of the Web controls is handled by ASP.NET on the Web server.

Visual Basic .NET includes many Web controls that correspond to the Windows controls used to create Windows applications. The behavior and appearance of the Web controls, however, often are different than what one would expect when using the corresponding Windows control. Visual Basic .NET also includes some Web controls that do not have equivalent Windows controls, and some Windows controls do not have corresponding Web controls. For example, the AdRotator Web control used to display banner ads on a Web page does not have a corresponding Windows control. Similarly, Visual Basic .NET does not include a ListView Web control.

Adding Web Controls to a Web Form

The Compensation Review Update Web application requires that the property values of several controls change during run time. For example, code must be able to change the employee information that is displayed on the Web page when the user wants to view an employee record. Label Web controls are needed to display this employee information on the Web page, along with a title and instructions. TextBox Web controls are required to accept an Employee ID, a review date, and compensation information. Button controls are needed to tell the Web application to search for an employee and to update the employee compensation information.

The Web Forms tab in the Toolbox window displays the available Web controls that you can place on a Web form. You can drag, double-click, or draw to add a Web control to a Web form, using the same techniques you use to add Windows controls to a Windows form.

The step on the next page adds Label, TextBox, and Button Web controls to the CompensationReviewUpdate Web form, as specified in the design of the user interface in Figure 11-3 on page VB 11.07.

To Add Web Controls to the Web Form

1. Click the Design view button and then click the Web Forms tab in the Toolbox window to display the available Web controls. Drag nine Label controls, four TextBox controls, and two Button controls from the Toolbox window to the Web form, as shown in Figure 11-44. Size the controls as shown in Figure 11-44. If necessary, drag the controls to place them in the appropriate cells on the Web form.

The Web controls display on the Web form as shown in Figure 11-44.

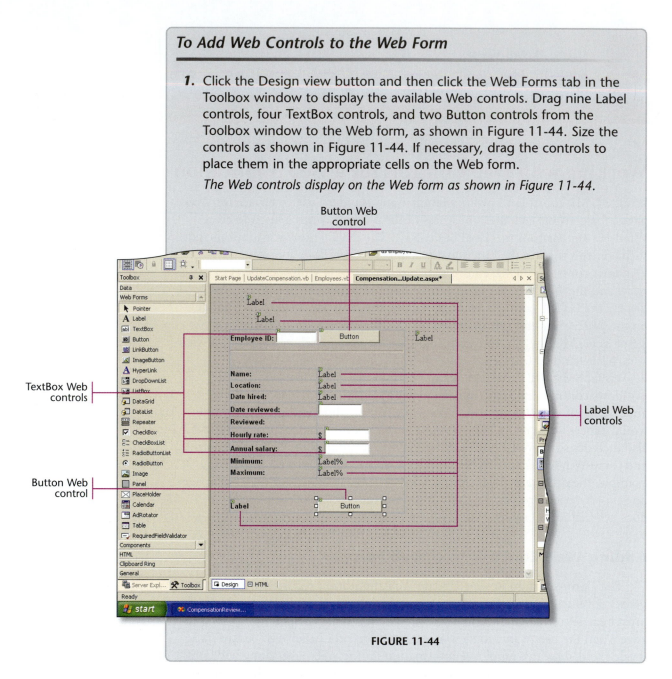

FIGURE 11-44

Label and TextBox Web Control Properties

Recall that HTML controls are used in a Web page to display static information to users. A **Label Web control** is used when you need to change a label's contents, or Text property value, during run time and display the contents as read-only text on a Web page.

The Compensation Review Update Web page uses Label Web controls in three different ways. First, they are used to label the top of the Web page with the company name and application name. Second, they are used to display output, including the employee name, location, date hired, minimum compensation adjustment, maximum compensation adjustment, and error messages, to the user. Finally, a Label Web control is used to provide instructions to the user on the right side of the Web page.

Working with Web Controls for a Web Application • **VB 11.47**

Table 11-3 shows the properties and values for the nine Label controls on the Web form.

Table 11-3   Label Web Control Property Values for the Compensation Review Update Web Application

CONTROL	PROPERTY	VALUE	EFFECT
Label1	Text	Ekstrom Optics Corporation	Sets the text that displays on the control at run time
	Width	248px	Sets the width of the control in pixels (px)
	Height	24px	Sets the height of the control in pixels (px)
	ForeColor	Blue	Sets the font foreground color
	Font:Bold	True	Sets the font of the text to bold
	Font:Name	Arial	Sets the font name for the text that displays on the control to Arial
	Font:Size	Larger	Causes the font to display in a larger font size in the Web browser
Label2	Text	Compensation Review Update	Sets the text that displays on the control at run time
	Width	237px	Sets the width of the control in pixels (px)
	Height	21px	Sets the height of the control in pixels (px)
	ForeColor	Blue	Sets the foreground color used for text
	Font:Bold	True	Sets the font of the text to bold
	Font:Name	Arial	Sets the font name for the text that displays on the control to Arial
Label3	Text	[lblName]	Sets the text that displays on the control at run time
	ID	lblName	Changes the control's name to a descriptive name
Label4	Text	[lblLocation]	Sets the text that displays on the control at run time
	ID	lblLocation	Changes the control's name to a descriptive name
Label5	Text	[lblDateHired]	Sets the text that displays on the control at run time
	ID	lblDateHired	Changes the control's name to a descriptive name
Label6	Text	[lblMin]	Sets the text that displays on the control at run time
	ID	lblMin	Changes the control's name to a descriptive name
Label7	Text	[lblMax]	Sets the text that displays on the control at run time
	ID	lblMax	Changes the control's name to a descriptive name
Label8	Text	[lblMessage]	Sets the text that displays on the control at run time
	ID	lblMessage	Changes the control's name to a descriptive name

(continued)

Table 11-3 *Label Web Control Property Values for the Compensation Review Update Web Application*
(continued)

CONTROL	PROPERTY	VALUE	EFFECT
Label9	Text	Enter an Employee ID and then click the Get Employee button. Update the employee's hourly rate or annual salary and then click the Update Compensation button. Continue this process until all employee compensation updates are complete.	Sets the text that displays on the control at run time
	BorderWidth	1px	Causes a 1-pixel border to display around the text in the control

A **TextBox Web control** is used to display output on a Web form when code requires access to read or write the value of the TextBox control. For example, in this Web application, a TextBox Web control is used to display the values for EmployeeID, DateReviewed, HourlyRate, and AnnualSalary, so that the user can view the current values and then enter new values to run a new query or to update the Compensation Review database.

Web controls use the ID property rather than the Name property to identify the controls. The naming conventions for Web controls, however, are the same as those used for Windows controls. The TextBox controls in the Compensation Review Update Web application require that the ID properties of the controls be

Tip

Naming Web Controls

Web controls use the ID property rather than the Name property to identify the controls. Use the same naming conventions for Web controls that you use for Windows controls.

changed to descriptive names: txtEmployeeID, txtDateReviewed, txtHourlyRate, and txtAnnualSalary.

The following steps set the properties of the Label Web controls on the CompensationReviewUpdate Web form to the values shown in Table 11-3 and change the names used for the TextBox Web controls.

To Change Properties of Label and TextBox Web Controls

1. Set the property values of the Label Web controls as shown in Table 11-3. If necessary, resize controls so that the text fits in each control. Resize the Label Web controls in the table so that each control fills the cell in which it is placed.

   The Label Web control properties are set and the controls display on the CompensationReviewUpdate form as shown in Figure 11-45.

2. Set the ID properties of the four TextBox Web controls to txtEmployeeID, txtDateReviewed, txtHourlyRate, and txtAnnualSalary.

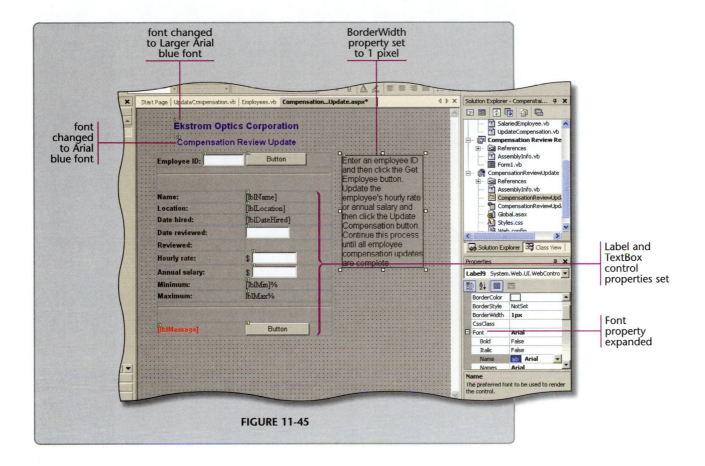

FIGURE 11-45

Button Web Control Properties

Button Web controls behave much as Button controls behave in Windows applications. When the user clicks a button, the Click event procedure executes. The Compensation Review Update Web application includes two Button controls: Get Employee and Update Compensation. Table 11-4 shows the properties and values of the Button controls that require changes.

Table 11-4 Button Control Property Values for the Compensation Review Update Web Application

CONTROL	PROPERTY	VALUE	EFFECT
Button1	ID	btnGetEmployee	Changes the control's name to a descriptive name
	Text	Get Employee	Sets the text that displays on the button face to Get Employee
Button2	ID	btnUpdateCompensation	Changes the control's name to a descriptive name
	Text	Update Compensation	Sets the text that displays on the button face to Update Compensation

The following step sets the property values of the Button controls to those listed in Table 11-4 on the previous page.

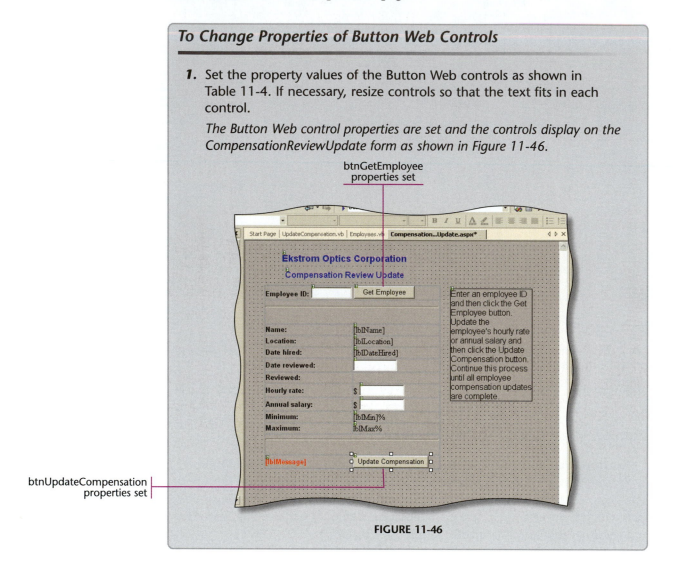

To Change Properties of Button Web Controls

1. Set the property values of the Button Web controls as shown in Table 11-4. If necessary, resize controls so that the text fits in each control.

The Button Web control properties are set and the controls display on the CompensationReviewUpdate form as shown in Figure 11-46.

FIGURE 11-46

RadioButton Web Control Properties

The RadioButton Web controls were not added to the form earlier in this chapter because a **RadioButton Web control** behaves differently than a RadioButton control in a Windows application. The RadioButton Web controls are more difficult to size if properties are not set at the time the controls are drawn on the form. With Web applications, the GroupName property of the RadioButtons that should be grouped together must be set to the same value. By setting the GroupName property of RadioButtons to the same value, only one of the RadioButton Web controls that share the GroupName can be selected at any time.

Table 11-5 shows the properties and values of the RadioButton Web controls that must be set.

Table 11-5 RadioButton Web Control Property Values for the Compensation Review Update Web Application

CONTROL	PROPERTY	VALUE	EFFECT
RadioButton1	Text	Yes	Sets the text that displays on the RadioButton face to Yes
	GroupName	Reviewed	Places the control in a RadioButton group with the radNotReviewed RadioButton
	ID	radReviewed	Changes the control's name to a descriptive name
RadioButton2	Text	No	Sets the text that displays on the RadioButton face to No
	GroupName	Reviewed	Places the control in a RadioButton group with the radReviewed RadioButton
	ID	radNotReviewed	Changes the control's name to a descriptive name

The following steps add the RadioButton Web controls and set the property values of the RadioButton Web controls to those listed in Table 11-5.

To Add and Change Properties of RadioButton Web Controls

1. Drag a RadioButton Web control to the table cell in the seventh row and second column of the HTML table.

The RadioButton1 Web control displays in the Table HTML control as shown in Figure 11-47.

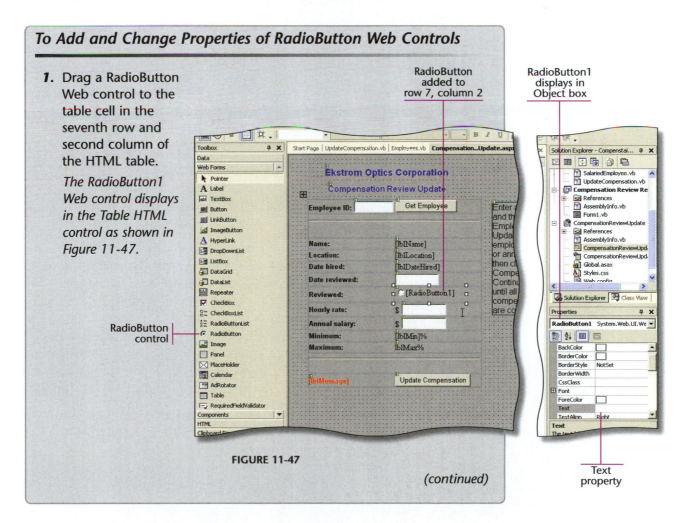

FIGURE 11-47

(continued)

2. Set the properties of the RadioButton1 control as shown in Table 11-5 on the previous page. Resize the control to the left side of the cell so that a second RadioButton Web control can be added next to it.

3. Add another RadioButton Web control to the right of the first RadioButton control. Set the properties for the second RadioButton Web control as shown in Table 11-5.

The two RadioButton Web controls display in the Table HTML control (Figure 11-48).

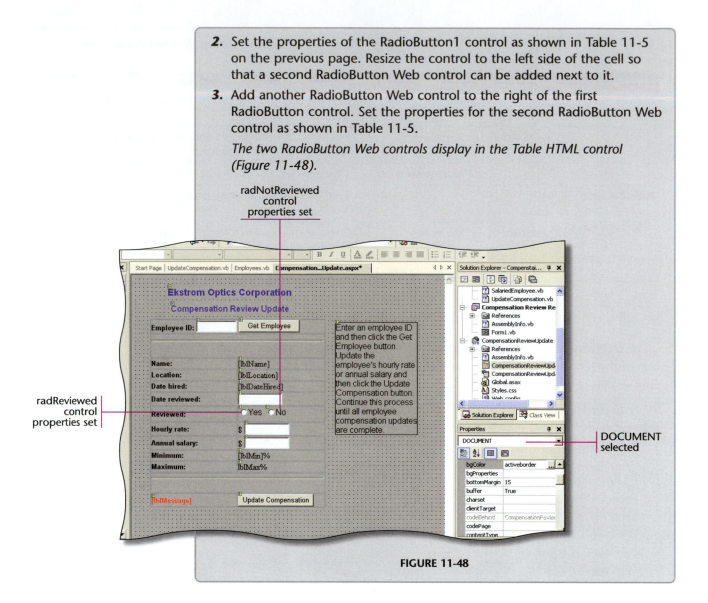

FIGURE 11-48

Using the same GroupName property value for both RadioButton Web controls ensures that the two controls behave as a RadioButton group. Only one of the RadioButton Web controls that share the same GroupName can be selected at any time. When the user clicks one of the radio buttons at run time, the other radio button automatically is deselected.

All of the controls have been added to the form and changed to reflect the desired user interface design. The user interface for the Compensation Review Update Web application is complete. The next step in developing the application is to write the code that executes when the user clicks the Button controls on the form.

Coding a Web Application

Coding a Web application involves the same process as coding a Windows application. When coding a Web application, however, remember that you can write event procedures only for Web controls; you cannot write event procedures for HTML controls. If you attempt to double-click an HTML control to write code for it, Visual Basic .NET displays an error message indicating that you should change the control to a Web control. Similarly, you cannot access the properties of HTML controls in the code of a Web form. If you need to set properties of controls during run time, use a Web control to implement your design.

> **Tip**
>
> **Using Web Controls versus HTML controls**
> You cannot write event procedures for HTML controls or access the properties of HTML controls in the code of a Web form. If you need to associate a control with an event procedure or set controls properties during run time, use a Web control to implement your design.

Figure 11-49 shows the flowchart for the btnGetEmployee_Click event procedure. An Employees object is instantiated using the optional EmployeeID parameter. When the Employees object is instantiated with the optional EmployeeID parameter, the object will contain either 0 or 1 employee object. If the passed EmployeeID is not found in the database, then the Employees object contains no HourlyEmployee or SalariedEmployee objects.

A nested If…Then…Else statement determines if the Employees object contains either HourlyEmployee or SalariedEmployee objects. If the Employees object contains HourlyEmployee or SalariedEmployee objects, then the employee information is displayed. Otherwise, an error message is displayed in the lblMessage TextBox Web control in the lower-left corner of the Web page.

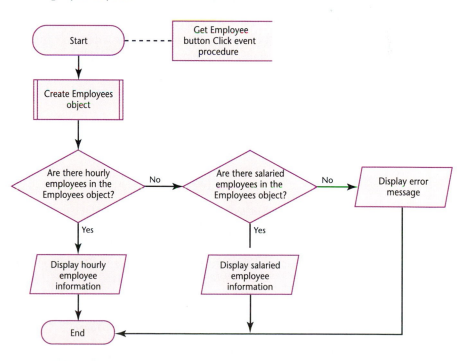

FIGURE 11-49

Writing Code for a Web Application

Figure 11-50 shows the code for the beginning of the btnGetEmployee_Click event procedure. The Option Strict On statement and an Imports statement are shown as the first two lines of code for the form. As previously discussed, the Option Strict On statement is used to ensure that all assignment statements use the same data type on both sides of the assignment; the Imports statement allows you to reference elements in a namespace without qualification, so elements in the imported namespace do not need the namespace identifier when they are referenced in code. For example, you can use the identifier Employee rather than Compensation_Review.Employee to reference the Employee class in the Compensation_Review class library, if the namespace Compensation_Review is imported using the Imports statement.

Visual Basic .NET generates lines 38 through 40 for the form automatically. The **Page_Load event procedure** executes whenever the user first accesses the Web page resulting from the Web form. Visual Basic automatically generates the Page_Load event with the comment line shown in line 26 for each Web form.

Lines 43 through 50 in Figure 11-50 show the initial code to declare variables, to begin a Try…Catch statement, and to declare object variables. Line 42 shows the declaration for the btnGetEmployee_Click event procedure that executes when the user clicks the Get Employee button on the Web page. Line 43 starts the Try…Catch statement. Line 44 shows the instantiation of an Employees object with the Text property of the txtEmployeeID control sent as the optional third parameter to the object's constructor. Recall that the first two parameters of the constructor are ignored by the constructor when the third parameter is passed. The value of False is used as the parameter for the reviewed status. A date of 1/1/1700 is used as the parameter for which to search for employees requiring a review. Any date can be used for this parameter's value because the value will not be used by the constructor when an Employee ID is passed as a parameter. Line 48 starts the Catch statement, and line 49 shows the code for displaying an error message in the lblMessage TextBox Web control if an exception is thrown during the instantiation of the Employees object.

```
 1  Option Strict On
 2  Imports Compensation_Review
        .
        .
        .
38      Private Sub Page_Load(ByVal sender As System.Object, ByVal e As System.EventArgs) ↵
        Handles MyBase.Load
39          'Put user code to initialize the page here
40      End Sub
41
42      Private Sub btnGetEmployee_Click(ByVal sender As System.Object, ByVal e As System. ↵
        EventArgs) Handles btnGetEmployee.Click
43          Try
44              Dim objQueryEmployees As New Employees(False, #1/1/1700#, Convert.ToInt16( ↵
        txtEmployeeID.Text))
45                  Dim objHourlyEmployee As HourlyEmployee
46                  Dim objSalariedEmployee As SalariedEmployee
47
48          Catch ex As Exception
49              lblMessage.Text = "Employee not found or database error."
50          End Try
51      End Sub
```

FIGURE 11-50

The following steps open the code window for the CompensationReviewUpdate Web form and add the code shown in Figure 11-50 to instantiate an Employee object.

To Write Code for a Web Application

1. Double-click the Get Employee button on the Web form. When the code window opens, type lines 1 and 2 as shown in Figure 11-50.

Visual Basic .NET creates the btnGetEmployee_Click event procedure and automatically generates several lines of code for the Web form. The Option Strict On and Imports statements are added to the code.

2. Enter lines 43 through 50 as shown in Figure 11-50.

Lines 43 through 50 display in the btnGetEmployee_Click event procedure in the code window as shown in Figure 11-51. The code declares several objects in a Try...Catch statement. An Employees object is instantiated with the optional EmployeeID parameter, meaning that the object should contain only one employee.

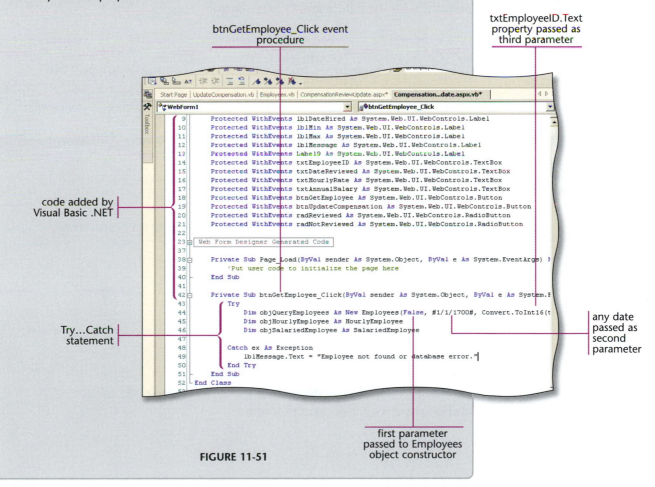

btnGetEmployee_Click event procedure

txtEmployeeID.Text property passed as third parameter

code added by Visual Basic .NET

Try...Catch statement

any date passed as second parameter

first parameter passed to Employees object constructor

FIGURE 11-51

As shown in Figure 11-51 on the previous page, writing code for a Web application is similar to writing code for a Windows application. Visual Basic .NET automatically inserts code in a Web form and hides some of the code in a code region, as shown in line 23.

Writing Code to Set Properties of Web Controls

The next step is to write the code to display the employee information for an hourly employee if an hourly employee is found in the instantiated Employees object. Figure 11-52 shows the code that determines if the Employees object contains an HourlyEmployee object. The If statement in Line 48 tests if an HourlyEmployee object exists in the objQueryEmployees object. If an HourlyEmployee object was found, then the HourlyEmployee object is assigned to the objHourlyEmployee object using the For Each statement in line 49. Lines 50 through 54 illustrate the concept that setting properties for Web controls is the same as setting properties for Windows controls in code. Line 55 sets the txtAnnualSalary control to a read-only state because the user should not be able to change the annual salary for an hourly employee. Lines 56 and 57 set the properties for the lblMin and lblMax controls.

```
48              If objQueryEmployees.HourlyEmployeeList.Count > 0 Then
49                  For Each objHourlyEmployee In objQueryEmployees.HourlyEmployeeList
50                      lblName.Text = objHourlyEmployee.Name
51                      lblLocation.Text = objHourlyEmployee.Location
52                      lblDateHired.Text = Convert.ToString(objHourlyEmployee.DateHired)
53                      txtHourlyRate.ReadOnly = False
54                      txtHourlyRate.Text = Convert.ToString(objHourlyEmployee.HourlyRate)
55                      txtAnnualSalary.ReadOnly = True
56                      lblMin.Text = Convert.ToString(objHourlyEmployee.              ↙
        CompensationAdjustmentMin)
57                      lblMax.Text = Convert.ToString(objHourlyEmployee.              ↙
        CompensationAdjustmentMax)
58                      If objHourlyEmployee.Reviewed Then
59                          radReviewed.Checked = True
60                          txtDateReviewed.Text = Convert.ToString(objHourlyEmployee. ↙
        DateReviewed)
61                      Else
62                          radNotReviewed.Checked = True
63                      End If
64                      lblMessage.Text = ""
65                  Next
66              End If
```

FIGURE 11-52

The following step adds the code shown in Figure 11-52 to the btnGetEmployee_Click event procedure.

To Write Code to Set Properties of Web Controls

1. Enter lines 48 through 66 as shown in Figure 11-52.

Lines 48 through 66 display in the code window. If an HourlyEmployee object exists in the Employees object, then the Web controls on the Web form are populated with the properties of the HourlyEmployee object (Figure 11-53).

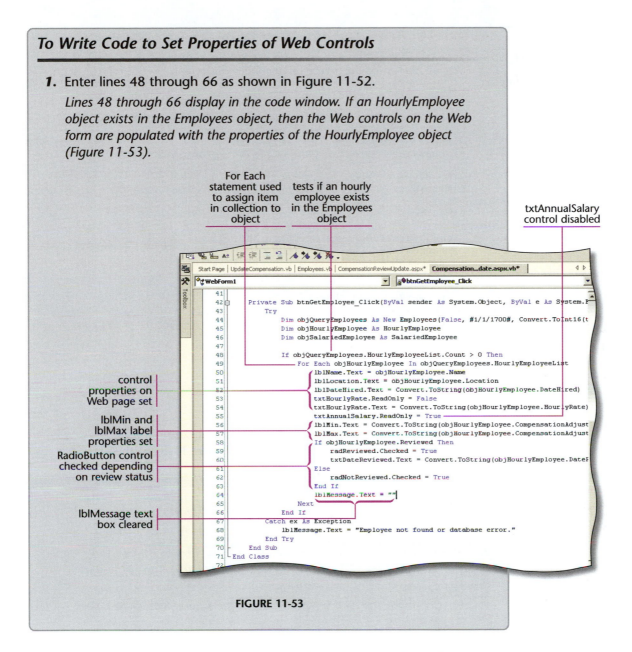

FIGURE 11-53

The If…Then…Else statement in lines 58 through 66 sets the radReviewed control to be selected or deselected, based on the review status of the employee, as defined by the Reviewed parameter. When the Reviewed status is set to True, then the btnReviewed RadioButton is checked in line 59. Line 60 updates the txtDateReviewed TextBox with the reviewed date if the employee has been reviewed already.

The next step is to write similar code for salaried employees. Figure 11-54 on the next page shows the code for setting control properties on the Web form if a SalariedEmployee object is found in the objQueryEmployees object. Line 67 checks if a SalariedEmployee was found during the database query. Lines 68 through 84 perform tasks similar to those completed for hourly employees in the last step.

```
66              Else
67                  If objQueryEmployees.SalariedEmployeeList.Count > 0 Then
68                      For Each objSalariedEmployee In objQueryEmployees.      ↙
        SalariedEmployeeList
69                          lblName.Text = objSalariedEmployee.Name
70                          lblLocation.Text = objSalariedEmployee.Location
71                          lblDateHired.Text = Convert.ToString(objSalariedEmployee.  ↙
        DateHired)
72                          txtAnnualSalary.ReadOnly = False
73                          txtAnnualSalary.Text = Convert.ToString(objSalariedEmployee.  ↙
        AnnualSalary)
74                          txtHourlyRate.ReadOnly = True
75                          lblMin.Text = Convert.ToString(objSalariedEmployee.  ↙
        CompensationAdjustmentMin)
76                          lblMax.Text = Convert.ToString(objSalariedEmployee.  ↙
        CompensationAdjustmentMax)
77                          If objSalariedEmployee.Reviewed Then
78                              radReviewed.Checked = True
79                              txtDateReviewed.Text = Convert.ToString(  ↙
        objSalariedEmployee.DateReviewed)
80                          Else
81                              radNotReviewed.Checked = True
82                          End If
83                          lblMessage.Text = ""
84                      Next
85                  Else
86                      lblMessage.Text = "Employee not found."
87                  End If
```

FIGURE 11-54

The following step adds the code shown in Figure 11-54 to the btnGetEmployee_Click event procedure.

To Complete the Code to Set Properties of Web Controls

1. Enter lines 66 through 87 as shown in Figure 11-54.

Lines 66 through 87 display in the code window. If a SalariedEmployee object exists in the Employees object, then the Web controls on the Web form are populated with the properties of the SalariedEmployee object (Figure 11-55).

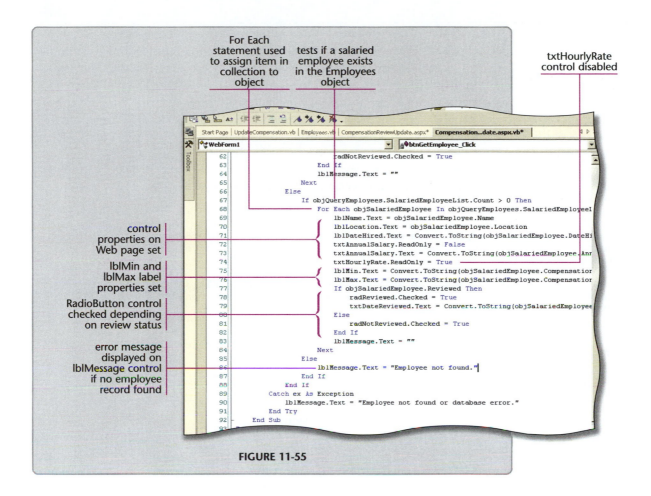

FIGURE 11-55

The code entered in the step above performs a similar task to the code entered for the HourlyEmployee object. The code for a salaried employee is almost duplicated from the code for an hourly employee. One key difference is whether the txtHourlyRate or txtAnnualSalary TextBox control is enabled. Lines 85 through 87 update the error message label control in the event that the Employees object does not contain either an HourlyEmployee object or a SalariedEmployee object.

Calling a Procedure in a Class Library

The code for the btnGetEmployee_Click event procedure is complete. The next step is to write the code for the btnUpdateCompensation_Click event procedure. When the user clicks the btnUpdateCompensation Button control, the Click event procedure of the control should call the UpdateCompensation() procedure in the UpdateCompensation module of the Compensation Review class library. The parameters required by the procedure are the EmployeeID, DateReviewed, EmployeeType — Hourly or Salaried — and the Compensation. Figure 11-56 on the next page shows the code necessary to call the UpdateCompensation() procedure in the UpdateCompensation module. An If…Then…Else statement determines the type of employee and makes the proper call to the procedure based on the employee type.

The UpdateCompensation() code in the procedure is contained in a Try…Catch statement in case the UpdateCompensation() procedure has trouble writing the new information to the database. If any errors occur, the Catch statement in lines 101 and 102 exception ensures that a user-friendly error message displays on the lblMessage control when an exception is thrown. If the exception is not caught when an exception is thrown, then Visual Basic .NET generates an error message that might be confusing to the user.

```
94      Private Sub btnUpdateCompensation_Click(ByVal sender As System.Object, ByVal e As ↵
        System.EventArgs) Handles btnUpdateCompensation.Click
95          Try
96              If txtAnnualSalary.ReadOnly Then
97                  UpdateCompensation.UpdateCompensation(Convert.ToInt32(txtEmployeeID. ↵
        Text), "Hourly", Convert.ToDateTime(txtDateReviewed.Text), Convert.ToDecimal( ↵
        txtHourlyRate.Text))
98              Else
99                  UpdateCompensation.UpdateCompensation(Convert.ToInt32(txtEmployeeID. ↵
        Text), "Salaried", Convert.ToDateTime(txtDateReviewed.Text), Convert.ToDecimal( ↵
        txtAnnualSalary.Text))
100             End If
101         Catch ex As Exception
102             lblMessage.Text = "Update not completed. Try again or see the database ↵
        administrator."
103         End Try
104     End Sub
```

FIGURE 11-56

The UpdateCompensation procedure is called using the code

`UpdateCompensation.UpdateCompensation()`

because both the module name and procedure name are identical. If the call was made as

`UpdateCompensation()`

then ASP.NET and the CLR would not know whether you meant the UpdateCompensation module or the UpdateCompensation() procedure. Using the procedure call as shown in lines 97 and 99 clears up this confusion by placing the procedure name after the module name.

The following step creates the btnUpdateCompensation_Click event procedure and then adds the code shown in Figure 11-56 to the btnUpdateCompensation _Click event procedure.

To Write Code to Call a Procedure in a Class Library

1. Click the CompensationReviewUpdate.aspx tab at the top of the main work area. Double-click the Update Compensation button. When the code window opens, enter lines 95 through 103 as shown in Figure 11-56.

Visual Basic .NET creates the btnUpdateCompensation_Click event procedure. Lines 95 through 103 display in the code window as shown in Figure 11-57.

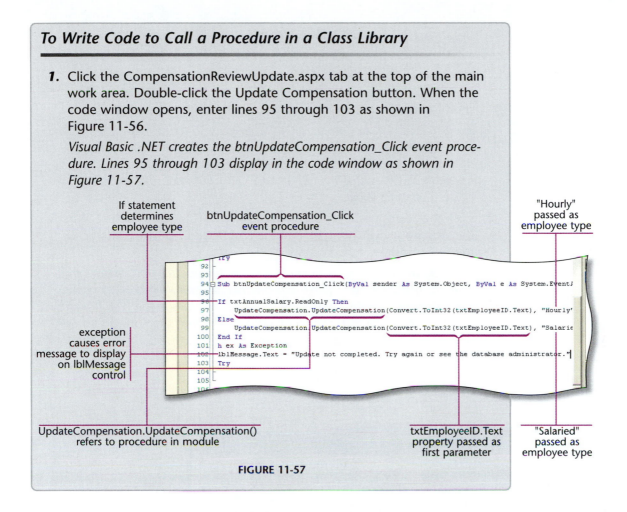

FIGURE 11-57

The code uses the ReadOnly state of the txtAnnualSalary control to determine the type of employee currently displayed. Based on the ReadOnly property, the procedure calls the UpdateCompensation() procedure in the UpdateCompensation module of the Compensation Review class library.

The coding phase for the Compensation Review Update Web application now is complete and the application can be tested.

Saving, Testing, and Documenting the Project

The steps on the next page save the form and project files for the Compensation Review Update project on the Web server and then run the Web application to test the project. When the application runs, the Internet Explorer Web browser automatically opens and the Compensation Review Update Web page displays in the browser. The first step to run the application is to make the Compensation Review Update application the startup project for the Compensation Review solution.

To Save and Test the Project

1. Click the Save All button on the Standard toolbar. Right-click the Compensation Review Update project in the Solution Explorer. When the shortcut menu displays, click the Set as Startup Project command.

   The asterisks next to CompensationReview.aspx in the window title bar and the main work area tab no longer display, indicating that the project has been saved. Because the project initially was created and saved to the C:\InetPub\wwwroot folder, Visual Basic .NET automatically saves the project to that same folder.

2. Click the Start button on the Visual Basic .NET Standard toolbar. When the Web page displays, type 2 in the Employee ID box and then click the Get Employee button.

   Visual Basic .NET opens the Output window temporarily and displays messages as the application starts. The Internet Explorer Web browser opens. The Compensation Review Update Web page displays in the Web browser, and the URL of the Web page displays in the Address drop-down list box. After the Get Employee button is clicked, the employee information displays (Figure 11-58).

URL of Web application

Microsoft Internet Explorer window

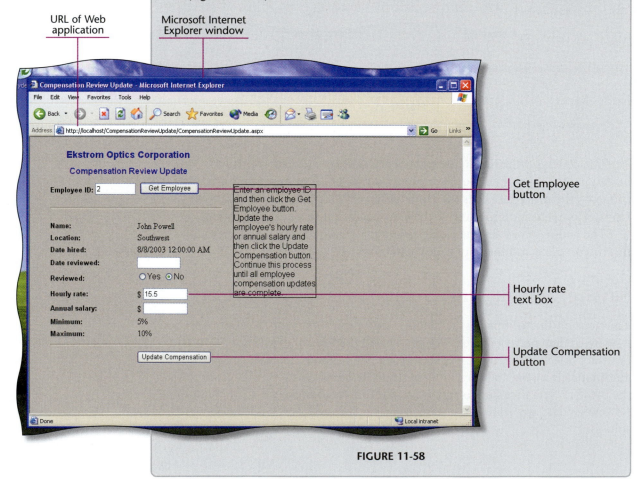

FIGURE 11-58

3. Type 08/08/2004 in the Date reviewed box. Change the Hourly rate to 15.75. Click the Update Compensation button.

The new reviewed date and hourly rate display in the text boxes (Figure 11-59).

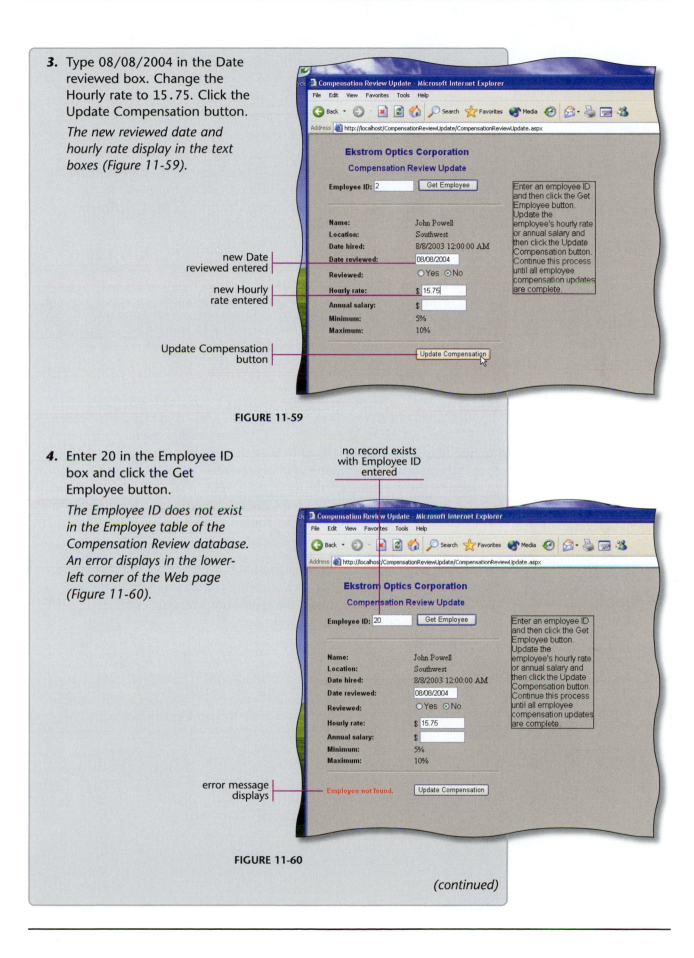

FIGURE 11-59

4. Enter 20 in the Employee ID box and click the Get Employee button.

The Employee ID does not exist in the Employee table of the Compensation Review database. An error displays in the lower-left corner of the Web page (Figure 11-60).

FIGURE 11-60

(continued)

> **5.** Click the Close button on the Microsoft Internet Explorer window. If necessary, click the Visual Basic .NET taskbar button to display the Visual Basic .NET window. If necessary, close the Output window.
>
> *Visual Basic .NET returns to design time.*

When testing Web applications, make certain that the page layout remains intact and usable as the user resizes the Web page. If multiple Web forms are used, make certain that the Back and Forward buttons of the Web browser behave correctly and do not result in undesirable effects.

Tip

Testing Web Applications

When testing Web applications, make certain that the page layout remains intact and usable as the user resizes the Web page. If multiple Web forms are used, make certain that the Back and Forward buttons of the Web browser behave correctly and do not result in undesirable effects.

Other users can access a Web application on your computer if they know the URL to access the IIS server on your computer. Each computer is assigned a unique address — called an IP address — that can be used to access the Web server if the network or computer administrator has allowed access to the server. For example, if you completed the project in this chapter and your computer's IP (Internet Protocol) number is 192.168.1.2, then the Web page developed in this chapter could be accessed from another computer, using the following URL:

http://192.168.1.2/CompensationReviewUpdate/CompensationReviewUpdate.aspx

The testing process for the Compensation Review Update Web application is complete. The final step of the development cycle is to document the application. The following steps document the application and quit Visual Basic .NET. Line numbers are printed on the code listing.

Tip

Printing Web Forms

Visual Basic .NET allows you to print the user interface for Web applications using the Print command on the File menu.

To Document the Application and Quit Visual Basic .NET

1. If necessary, close the Output window. Click the CompensationReviewUpdate.aspx tab, and then click the Print command on the File menu to print a record of the user interface design of the CompensationReviewUpdate Web form.

A record of the user interface design of the Compensation Review Update Web application is printed (Figure 11-61).

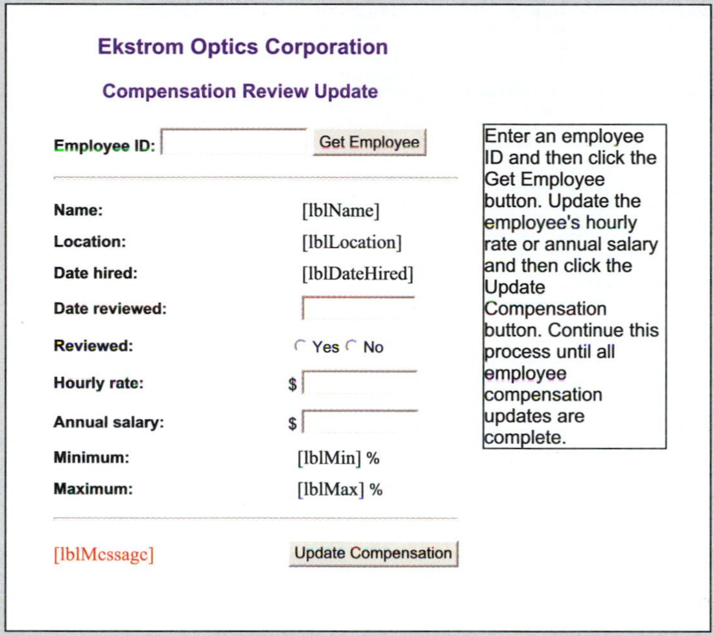

Ekstrom Optics Corporation

Compensation Review Update

Employee ID:		Get Employee

Enter an employee ID and then click the Get Employee button. Update the employee's hourly rate or annual salary and then click the Update Compensation button. Continue this process until all employee compensation updates are complete.

Name:	[lblName]
Location:	[lblLocation]
Date hired:	[lblDateHired]
Date reviewed:	
Reviewed:	○ Yes ○ No
Hourly rate:	$
Annual salary:	$
Minimum:	[lblMin] %
Maximum:	[lblMax] %

[lblMessage]   Update Compensation

FIGURE 11-61

2. Click the CompensationReviewUpdate.aspx.vb tab. Click File on the menu bar and then click Page Setup.

3. When the Page Setup dialog box displays, if necessary, click Line numbers and then click the OK button.

4. Follow the steps on page VB 2.40 of Chapter 2 to use the Print command on the File menu to print a record of the code for the Compensation Review Update Web application.

A record of the Compensation Review Update Web application code is printed (Figure 11-62 on the next page).

(continued)

```
       C:\Inetpub\wwwroot\CompensationReviewUpdate\CompensationUpdate.aspx.vb                    1

 1 Option Strict On
 2 Imports Compensation_Review
 3 Public Class WebForm1
 4     Inherits System.Web.UI.Page
 5     Protected WithEvents Label1 As System.Web.UI.WebControls.Label
 6     Protected WithEvents Label2 As System.Web.UI.WebControls.Label
 7     Protected WithEvents lblName As System.Web.UI.WebControls.Label
 8     Protected WithEvents lblLocation As System.Web.UI.WebControls.Label
 9     Protected WithEvents lblDateHired As System.Web.UI.WebControls.Label
10     Protected WithEvents lblMin As System.Web.UI.WebControls.Label
11     Protected WithEvents lblMax As System.Web.UI.WebControls.Label
12     Protected WithEvents lblMessage As System.Web.UI.WebControls.Label
13     Protected WithEvents Label9 As System.Web.UI.WebControls.Label
14     Protected WithEvents txtEmployeeID As System.Web.UI.WebControls.TextBox
15     Protected WithEvents txtDateReviewed As System.Web.UI.WebControls.TextBox
16     Protected WithEvents txtHourlyRate As System.Web.UI.WebControls.TextBox
17     Protected WithEvents txtAnnualSalary As System.Web.UI.WebControls.TextBox
18     Protected WithEvents btnGetEmployee As System.Web.UI.WebControls.Button
19     Protected WithEvents btnUpdateCompensation As System.Web.UI.WebControls.Button
20     Protected WithEvents radReviewed As System.Web.UI.WebControls.RadioButton
21     Protected WithEvents radNotReviewed As System.Web.UI.WebControls.RadioButton
22
23 Web Form Designer Generated Code
24
25     Private Sub Page_Load(ByVal sender As System.Object, ByVal e As System.EventArgs) ↵
       Handles MyBase.Load
26         'Put user code to initialize the page here
27     End Sub
28
29     Private Sub btnGetEmployee_Click(ByVal sender As System.Object, ByVal e As System. ↵
       EventArgs) Handles btnGetEmployee.Click
30         Try
31             Dim objQueryEmployees As New Employees(False, #1/1/1700#, Convert.ToInt16( ↵
       txtEmployeeID.Text))
32             Dim objHourlyEmployee As HourlyEmployee
33             Dim objSalariedEmployee As SalariedEmployee
34
35             If objQueryEmployees.HourlyEmployeeList.Count > 0 Then
36                 For Each objHourlyEmployee In objQueryEmployees.HourlyEmployeeList
37                     lblName.Text = objHourlyEmployee.Name
38                     lblLocation.Text = objHourlyEmployee.Location
39                     lblDateHired.Text = Convert.ToString(objHourlyEmployee.DateHired)
40                     txtHourlyRate.ReadOnly = False
41                     txtHourlyRate.Text = Convert.ToString(objHourlyEmployee.HourlyRate)
42                     txtAnnualSalary.ReadOnly = True
43                     lblMin.Text = Convert.ToString(objHourlyEmployee.                  ↵
       CompensationAdjustmentMin)
44                     lblMax.Text = Convert.ToString(objHourlyEmployee.                  ↵
       CompensationAdjustmentMax)
45                     If objHourlyEmployee.Reviewed Then
46                         radReviewed.Checked = True
47                         txtDateReviewed.Text = Convert.ToString(objHourlyEmployee.     ↵
       DateReviewed)
48                     Else
49                         radNotReviewed.Checked = True
50                     End If
51                     lblMessage.Text = ""
52                 Next
53             Else
54                 If objQueryEmployees.SalariedEmployeeList.Count > 0 Then
55                     For Each objSalariedEmployee In objQueryEmployees.               ↵
       SalariedEmployeeList
56                         lblName.Text = objSalariedEmployee.Name
57                         lblLocation.Text = objSalariedEmployee.Location
58                         lblDateHired.Text = Convert.ToString(objSalariedEmployee.     ↵
       DateHired)
59                         txtAnnualSalary.ReadOnly = False
```

FIGURE 11-62

```
C:\Inetpub\wwwroot\CompensationReviewUpdate\CompensationUpdate.aspx.vb                2
60                      txtAnnualSalary.Text = Convert.ToString(objSalariedEmployee.   ↵
        AnnualSalary)
61                      txtHourlyRate.ReadOnly = True
62                      lblMin.Text = Convert.ToString(objSalariedEmployee.            ↵
        CompensationAdjustmentMin)
63                      lblMax.Text = Convert.ToString(objSalariedEmployee.            ↵
        CompensationAdjustmentMax)
64                  If objSalariedEmployee.Reviewed Then
65                      radReviewed.Checked = True
66                      txtDateReviewed.Text = Convert.ToString(objSalariedEmployee↵
        .DateReviewed)
67                  Else
68                      radNotReviewed.Checked = True
69                  End If
70                  lblMessage.Text = ""
71              Next
72          Else
73              lblMessage.Text = "Employee not found."
74          End If
75      End If
76  Catch ex As Exception
77      lblMessage.Text = "Employee not found or database error."
78  End Try
79  End Sub
80
81  Private Sub btnUpdateCompensation_Click(ByVal sender As System.Object, ByVal e As  ↵
    System.EventArgs) Handles btnUpdateCompensation.Click
82      Try
83          If txtAnnualSalary.ReadOnly Then
84              UpdateCompensation.UpdateCompensation(Convert.ToInt32(txtEmployeeID.   ↵
    Text), "Hourly", Convert.ToDateTime(txtDateReviewed.Text), Convert.ToDecimal(      ↵
    txtHourlyRate.Text))
85          Else
86              UpdateCompensation.UpdateCompensation(Convert.ToInt32(txtEmployeeID.    ↵
    Text), "Salaried", Convert.ToDateTime(txtDateReviewed.Text), Convert.ToDecimal(    ↵
    txtAnnualSalary.Text))
87          End If
88      Catch ex As Exception
89          lblMessage.Text = "Update not completed. Try again or see the database     ↵
    administrator."
90      End Try
91  End Sub
92 End Class
93
```

FIGURE 11-62 (continued)

5. Click the Visual Basic .NET Close button.

If you made changes to the project since the last time you saved it, Visual Basic .NET displays the Microsoft Visual Basic .NET dialog box. If you click the Yes button, you can resave your project and quit. If you click the No button, you will quit without saving changes. Clicking the Cancel button will close the dialog box and not quit Visual Basic .NET.

Chapter Summary

In this chapter, you learned how to add optional parameters to a procedure. You learned how to update records in a database table using an SQL UPDATE statement. You learned how to add a module to a class library and write a public procedure in the module. You learned how to create a new Web application project and add HTML controls to a Web page. You then learned how to add Web controls, including Label, TextBox, RadioButton, and Button controls, to a Web page. You learned how to write code for a Web application. Finally, you learned how ASP.NET, the CLR, and Microsoft Internet Information Services interact to run a Web application.

What You Should Know

Having completed this chapter, you now should be able to perform tasks shown in Table 11-6.

Table 11-6 Chapter 11 What You Should Know

TASK NUMBER	TASK	PAGE
1	Start Visual Basic .NET and Add a New Module to a Project	VB 11.12
2	Declare a Public Procedure in a Module and Open a Database Connection	VB 11.14
3	Code an SQL UPDATE Statement to Update Employee Records	VB 11.17
4	Execute an SQL UPDATE Statement	VB 11.18
5	Add an Optional Parameter to a Procedure	VB 11.22
6	Code an SQL SELECT Statement to Read an Individual Record from a Table	VB 11.24
7	Build, Save, and Document the Class Library	VB 11.25
8	Start a New ASP.NET Web Application Project	VB 11.30
9	Change Web Form Properties	VB 11.34
10	Add and Format a Table HTML Control	VB 11.36
11	Add Text to a Table HTML Control	VB 11.40
12	Format Text on the Web Form	VB 11.41
13	Add and Format a Horizontal Rule HTML Control and View HTML Code for a Web Form	VB 11.43
14	Add Web Controls to the Web Form	VB 11.46
15	Change Properties of Label and TextBox Web Controls	VB 11.48
16	Change Properties of Button Web Controls	VB 11.50
17	Add and Change Properties of RadioButton Web Controls	VB 11.51
18	Write Code for a Web Application	VB 11.55

Table 11-6 *Chapter 11 What You Should Know* (continued)

TASK NUMBER	TASK	PAGE
19	Write Code to Set Properties of Web Controls	VB 11.57
20	Complete the Code to Set Properties of Web Controls	VB 11.58
21	Write Code to Call a Procedure in a Class Library	VB 11.61
22	Save and Test the Project	VB 11.62
23	Document the Application and Quit Visual Basic .NET	VB 11.65

Key Terms

ASP.NET *(VB 11.28)*
ASP.NET Web Application *(VB 11.28)*
ASP.NET Web Application template *(VB 11.30)*
.aspx file *(VB 11.28)*
bgColor property *(VB 11.34)*
Button Web control *(VB 11.49)*
database command object *(VB 11.08)*
DELETE statement *(VB 11.20)*
ExecuteNonQuery() method *(VB 11.18)*
Horizontal Rule HTML control *(VB 11.36)*
HTML controls *(VB 11.35)*
INSERT statement *(VB 11.19)*
Internet Information Services (IIS) *(VB 11.28)*
Label Web control *(VB 11.46)*
localhost *(VB 11.31)*
Optional keyword *(VB 11.21)*
optional parameter *(VB 11.21)*
Page_Load event procedure *(VB 11.54)*
RadioButton Web control *(VB 11.50)*
Table HTML control *(VB 11.36)*
TextBox Web control *(VB 11.48)*
title property *(VB 11.34)*
UPDATE statement *(VB 11.09)*
Web controls *(VB 11.45)*
Web form *(VB 11.28)*
Web server *(VB 11.28)*

Homework Assignments

Short Answer

1. When is the use of optional parameters beneficial in the development process?

2. Which of the following procedure declarations include incorrect syntax? Why?

   a. `Public Sub PrintValue(ByVal Optional strValue As String = "")`

   b. `Private Function PrintValue(Optional strValue As String =` `Your Name) As Boolean`

   c. `Public Sub PrintValue(Optional blnValue = True)`

   d. `Private Sub PrintValue(Optional strValue As String = "")`

3. Use the _____ property of a Web form to change the Web form's background color. Use the _____ property of a Web form to change the name of the Web page in the Web browser's title bar.

4. A _____ runs Microsoft's Web server software, which is called _____. _____ runs on top of the Web server and is responsible for executing Web applications.

5. When using OleDbCommand objects to perform operations on a database, use the _____ method if the operation returns records and the _____ method if the operation does not return records.

6. When naming a Web control, use the _____ property to identify the control.

7. Explain some of the key differences between Windows controls and Web controls. In your answer, explain how some of these differences influence the design of a user interface.

8. Explain the key differences between HTML controls and Web controls. Explain when to use each when designing a Web application and why one type might be better than the other in certain situations.

9. Use the _____ property to group RadioButton Web controls together so that only one control at a time can be selected — that is, only one control can have a True value for its _____ property.

10. The _____ event procedure is inserted automatically in the code for the initial Web form in a new ASP.NET Web Application project. This event procedure corresponds to the _____ event procedure commonly used in Windows applications.

11. When testing Web applications, pay particular attention to how the Web page behaves when the user clicks the _____ and _____ buttons of the Web browser.

12. Given the following table, write an SQL UPDATE statement that updates all male students whose age is from 23 through 25 with a new Advisor named Stevens. (See Figure 11-10 on page VB 11.16 and Figure 11-15 on page VB 11.20 for examples.)

Table: Students

STUDENTID	NAME	ADVISOR	AGE	GENDER	MAJOR
791	Stephanie Brown	Jenkins	19	Female	Business
236	Samir Sain	Liu	25	Female	Business
618	Geoff Berg	Smith	24	Male	Finance
256	Terrell Davis	Jenkins	22	Male	History
902	Minh Phan	Canowitz	23	Male	Biology

13. For the table shown in Exercise 12 above, write the SQL DELETE statement that deletes all students with a Major of Business and an age less than 22.

14. Given the table structure shown in Exercise 12 above, write the SQL INSERT statements that insert the following two records into the table. Do not include empty fields in the INSERT statement.

583	Allison Jones	Smith	18	Female	History
577	Jon Stern		21	Male	

Learn it Online

Start your browser and visit scsite.com/vbnet/exs. Follow the instructions in the exercises below.

1. **Chapter Reinforcement TF, MC, and SA**   Click the True/False, Multiple Choice, and Short Answer link below Chapter 11. Print and then answer the questions.

2. **Practice Test**   Click the Practice Test link below Chapter 11. Answer each question, enter your first and last name at the bottom of the page, and then click the Grade Test button. When the graded practice test displays on your screen, click Print on the File menu to print a hard copy. Continue to take practice tests until you score 80% or better. Hand in a printout of the final practice test.

3. **Crossword Puzzle Challenge**   Click the Crossword Puzzle Challenge link below Chapter 11. Read the instructions, and then enter your first and last name. Click the Play button. Complete the crossword puzzle. When you are finished, click the Submit button. When the crossword puzzle redisplays, click the Print button.

4. **Tips and Tricks**   Click the Tips and Tricks link below Chapter 11. Click a topic that pertains to Chapter 11. Right-click the information and then click Print on the shortcut menu. Construct a brief example of what the information relates to in Visual Basic .NET to confirm you understand how to use the tip or trick. Hand in the example and printed information.

(continued)

Learn it Online (continued)

5. **Newsgroups**   Click the Newsgroups link below Chapter 11. Click a topic that pertains to Chapter 11. Print three comments.

6. **Expanding Your Horizons**   Click the Articles for Visual Basic .NET below Chapter 11. Click a topic that pertains to Chapter 11. Print the information. Construct a brief example of what the information relates to in Visual Basic .NET to confirm you understand the contents of the article. Hand in the example and printed information.

7. **Search Sleuth**   Select three key terms from the Key Terms section of this chapter and then use the Google search engine at google.com (or any major search engine) to display and print two Web pages for each key term.

Note: If you plan to complete the project and all the exercises in this chapter, it is recommended that you use a hard disk or Zip disk for your solutions, because they will not all fit on a floppy disk.

Debugging Assignment

Start Visual Basic .NET and open the Furniture Pricing solution from the Chapter11\Furniture Pricing folder on the Data Disk. The solution consists of a Windows application that reads records from a Pricing table in a Microsoft Access database stored in the A:\Chapter11\FurniturePricing.mdb file on the Data Disk. When the program starts, the user can enter a Product ID to look up a product and product pricing information. Some of the fields on the interface are calculated by the application from values stored in the database table. The user is allowed to modify some information and update the database with the new information. Some of the processing for the application is done in a class library, which is a second project in the Furniture Pricing solution.

The Furniture Pricing Windows application contains bugs in the code. Run the application to experience some of the problems listed in the steps below. Follow the steps to debug the project.

1. Review the code for the Furniture Pricing Windows application. One of the calculations accepts an optional parameter to perform a calculation. The declaration of the parameter is incorrect. Fix the declaration so that the optional parameter is of type Decimal and initializes to −1.

2. The procedures in the module in the class library are not accessible to the code in the Furniture Pricing project. Fix the declarations of both the module and the procedure or procedures so that they are accessible to all programs that have a reference to the class library.

3. The code that builds the SQL UPDATE statement to update the table in the database is incorrect. Find and fix the errors in the code that builds the SQL UPDATE string.

4. If the user searches for a record and the record is not found, the application terminates with a run-time error. Add exception handling code so that the application displays user-friendly error messages and does not terminate if no record is found when the user searches for a record.

5. If the SQL UPDATE statement causes an exception, the application displays a run-time error and terminates. Add exception handling code so that the application displays user-friendly error messages and does not terminate in the event of an error with the table update.

6. Save the project and then run the project to test for any additional bugs. The Furniture Pricing Windows application should display as shown in Figure 11-63. Test with Product IDs ranging from 1 to 7.

7. Document the Furniture Pricing Windows application form code. On the code printout, circle the lines of code you modified.

FIGURE 11-63

Programming Assignments

1 Creating a Web Application

Using the following steps, design and develop a Web application that illustrates the concepts covered in this chapter. The program should allow a user to enter a sales price and commission rate to calculate a commission on a sale. You will need access to an Internet Information Services Web Server configured with ASP.NET in order to complete this exercise. Follow these steps to create the Web application:

1. Use the Web Application template in Visual Basic .NET to start a new project named SalesCommission. Create the solution on the Web in a new folder named SalesCommission.

2. Create a user interface similar to that shown in Figure 11-64 on the next page by first adding a Table HTML control that can be used to arrange controls on the Web form. Set the form title to Sales Commission Calculator and set the bgColor of the Web form to gray. Change the file name of the Web form to SalesCommission.aspx.

(continued)

1 Creating a Web Application *(continued)*

3. Change the Table HTML control so that it includes 2 columns and 5 rows. Type the three HTML labels in the Table HTML control as shown in Figure 11-64 in the first column.

4. Merge the cells in the fourth row of the Table HTML control. Add a Horizontal Rule HTML control to this row and increase the height of the control so that it displays as shown in Figure 11-64.

5. Add TextBox Web controls to the three cells in the second column as shown in Figure 11-64. Modify the TextBox controls so that they take up the width and height of the table cells in which they are placed. Change the third TextBox control to a read-only state. Name the controls appropriately. Set the Text property values of all of the TextBox controls to 0.

6. Add a Button Web control to each cell in the last row of the Table HTML control. Change the ID of the first Button control to btnComputePay and the second Button control to btnReset. Change the Text property values of the controls to read as shown in Figure 11-64.

7. Double-click the btnComputePay control. When the code window displays, write code to multiply the values in the two TextBox controls together, divide the result by 100, and display the result in the third read-only TextBox control.

8. Click the SalesCommission.aspx tab in the main work area. When the Web form displays, double-click the btnReset button. When the code window displays, write code for the btnReset_Click event procedure to reset the Text properties of the TextBox controls to 0.

9. Run the SalesCommission application and correct any errors. If you make any changes to fix errors, save the project again. During run time, the SalesCommission application window should display as shown in Figure 11-64.

10. Document the code and user interface for the project.

FIGURE 11-64

2 Reading and Updating Data in a Database

Design and develop a Windows application that finds product information stored in a database, displays the information, and allows the user to update the information. The database, named Products.mdb, is in the Chapter11 folder on the Data Disk and includes one table named Product. The Product table includes three fields: ProductID, ProductName, and InStock. The data types of the fields are Integer, String, and Integer. Figure 11-65 shows the contents of the Product table.

At the top of the Windows form, include a NumericUpDown control that ranges from 1 to 10000 and accepts a ProductID. A Button control next to the NumericUpDown control should select a product record from the Product table and display the product name and number of items in stock in controls on the lower portion of the form. The product name should display in a read-only control. The user should be able to modify the number in stock using a NumericUpDown control that also is used to display the number in stock. A second button control, labeled Update, should update the Product table with the new in stock amount entered by the user. Use message boxes to display any database errors that may occur.

Products

ProductID	ProductName	InStock
101	TV Tuner PCI card	17
871	Wireless Mouse	33
934	Mouse with Web Wheel	20
1660	Force Feedback Joystick	34
2245	High-resolution Webcamera	60
2896	10/100 Networking Card	17
3178	25 ft Cat5 Network Cable	65
4354	Notebook Security Lock	47
4540	15 inch Flat Panel Monitor	54
4912	4 ft USB 2.0 Cable	92
5685	17 inch Flat Panel Monitor	77

FIGURE 11-65

3 English to Metric Conversion Web Application

Design and develop a Web application to convert an English measurement in miles, yards, feet, and inches to a metric measurement in kilometers, meters, and centimeters. The algorithms and design considerations are listed in Programming Assignment 6 of Chapter 4, on page VB 4.78. Use a Table HTML control to align and size the input controls properly. Do not take into account invalid input data. Use Label Web controls to display the output.

4 Slope and Intercept Calculation Web Application

Using the concepts presented in this chapter, design and develop a Web application that accepts two sets of (X, Y) coordinates — (X1, Y1) and (X2, Y2) — and then calculates and displays the slope and Y intercepts of the line that intersects the two coordinates. Use TextBox controls to accept the user input. Place the calculations in a Try...Catch statement so that any invalid data used in a calculation can result in a user-friendly message being displayed on the Web page. Convert the text input to Int32 values. When converting the text input to integer values, try to catch situations in which the conversion is invalid. Use Visual Basic .NET Help to find the error type thrown when the Convert.ToInt32() method attempts to convert an invalid value to a number. Catch this exception in one Catch clause and display a unique error message for this type of error. Catch all other exceptions in a second Catch clause. For example, if a user enters XYZ for one of the values, then the Convert.ToInt32() method should throw an exception that is caught and displayed on the Web page.

5 Using a DropDownList Web Control in a Web Application

Design and develop a Web application that implements the logic of the cardiovascular disease risk assessment flowchart shown in Figure 1-25 of Chapter 1, on page VB 1.30. Use four DropDownList Web controls for the four selections represented by the flowchart. See Programming Assignment 5 in Chapter 5, on page VB 5.73, for hints on designing and developing the application. Display the final result in a TextBox Web control. Use appropriate labels for all of the controls and use a Table HTML control to assist in the positioning of the controls. Include two Button Web controls. The first should perform the calculation, and the second should reset all controls to their original states.

6 Reading, Writing, and Deleting Records from a Database

Design and develop a Windows application similar to the Today's Sales Check application developed in Chapter 6. Use the solution to the Today's Sales Check application as a starting point for developing a new version of the application that uses information from a database, rather than information entered by the user. If you developed the Today's Sales Check application in Chapter 6, copy the folder containing the solution to the Chapter11 folder on the Data Disk. If you did not develop the solution, see your instructor in order to obtain the files necessary to complete this problem, or use the steps in Chapter 6 to develop the Today's Sales Check application.

Make the following modifications to the Today's Sales Check application so that the application reads from a database to populate the ListView control on the frmTodaysSalesCheck form. Add code to the frmTodaysSalesCheck_Load event procedure and general area of the form code to read data from the TodaysSalesCheck.mdb Microsoft Access database supplied in the Chapter11 folder of the Data Disk. The table name to read is TodaysSales. The field names are ItemDescription, TotalSales, and OnSale. The data types of the fields are String, Decimal, and Boolean.

Modify the code in the frmAddItemForm to insert a record into the table using an SQL INSERT statement such as:

```
INSERT INTO TodaysSales (ItemDescription, TotalSales, OnSale)
VALUES ("Mulch", 354.54, True)
```

Use structured exception handling where appropriate. Add code to the lstTodaysSales_KeyDown event procedure to delete the record from the database as well as the ListView control. Remove the Clear Today's Sales List button from the form and remove the button's event procedures.

12

Creating Console Applications, Understanding XML, and Creating Web Services

Objectives

You will have mastered the material in this chapter when you can:

- Start a new Console application
- Use parameters in a Console application
- Write code to create a comma-delimited text file
- Write code to create a tab-delimited text file
- Write code to create an XML file
- Start a new ASP.NET Web service application
- Understand the structure of XML files
- Write code to read an XML file
- Use a Web service in code
- Debug Console applications and Web services

Introduction

This chapter concentrates on developing the Console application shown in Figure 12-1, along with a Web service that sends data to another program. The Console application developed in this chapter allows a user to extract data from a database and create a data file in one of three file formats. The file created using the Console application contains the records that were updated using the Web application developed in Chapter 11. The file then can be obtained by another user or program using a Web service. The Web service runs on a Web server, allowing a user or program to execute the Web service and obtain the file over the Internet.

In this chapter, you will learn how to create two new types of applications: a Console application and a Web service. You will learn how to write code to create comma-delimited and tab-delimited text files. You also will learn how to write code to create and read XML files. You will learn how to use a Web service in code and how to test the Web services that you create. Finally, you will learn how to debug Console applications and Web services.

Chapter Twelve — Creating the Payroll Update Console Application and Web Service

The Compensation Review System for Ekstrom Optics Corporation requires two additional components. First, an application must produce a file for the company's payroll vendor, who is responsible for printing and mailing payroll checks each month. The file, which is created once each month, informs the payroll vendor of any updated compensation information for the one-month (30-day) period since the last file was generated. The updated payroll information, which is updated using the Compensation Review Web application created in Chapter 11, must be sent to the payroll vendor on the last day of each month to ensure that the vendor uses updated information to print payroll checks during the following month.

The Compensation Review System requires that the user be able to create the file in one of three file formats: comma-delimited (Figure 12-1b), tab-delimited (Figure 12-1c), and XML (Figure 12-1d). The Compensation Update Processing application is the Console application used to create the desired file (Figure 12-1a). Users execute and interact with a Console application using the Command Prompt window in Windows. To execute the application, the user enters the name of the application at the command prompt in the Command Prompt window. The user then enters command-line parameters to indicate specific options to the application. In the Compensation Update Processing Console application, for example, the user enters parameters to indicate the type of file that the Console application should create and a review date.

After the user creates the payroll update file using the Compensation Update Processing Console application, the payroll vendor obtains the file via a Web service program. The Compensation Update Service Web service acts like a function procedure that the payroll vendor uses to obtain the file. The Web service runs on a Web server, allowing the payroll vendor to execute the Web service and obtain the file over the Internet (Figure 12-1e).

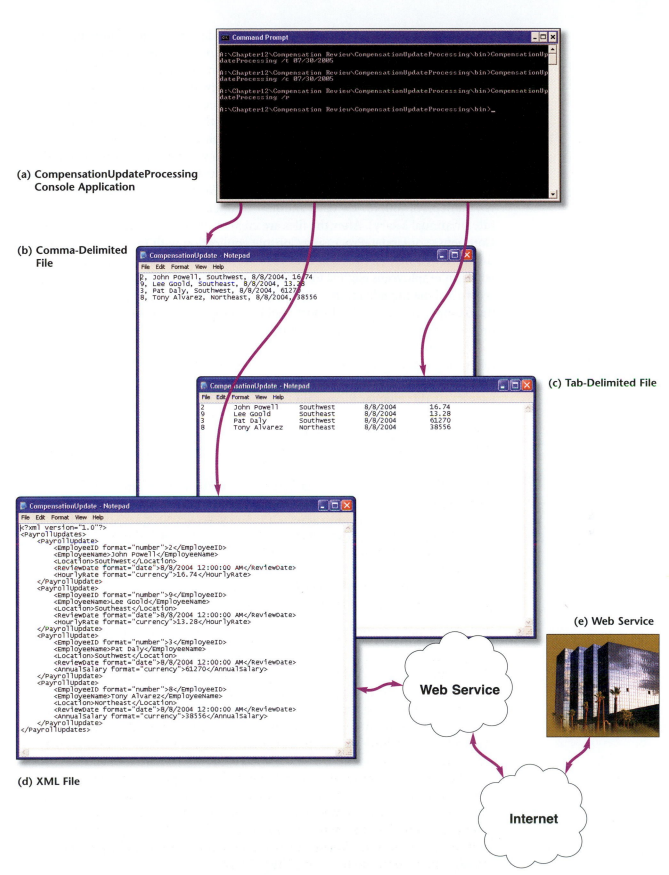

(a) CompensationUpdateProcessing Console Application

(b) Comma-Delimited File

(c) Tab-Delimited File

(d) XML File

(e) Web Service

FIGURE 12-1

When the user enters the CompensationUpdateProcessing command at the command prompt, along with either the /c, /t, or /x option and a date (Figure 12-1a on the previous page), the program queries the Compensation Review database for employees whose next review date is 30 days after the date entered. After the program retrieves the employee information, the program determines which type of file to write based on the option entered by the user. A /c instructs the program to write a comma-delimited text file (Figure 12-1b on the previous page), a /t instructs the program to write a tab-delimited text file (Figure 12-1c on the previous page), and an /x instructs the program to write an XML file (Figure 12-1d on the previous page). Each file includes the Employee ID, name, location, review date, and new compensation amount (either hourly rate or annual salary). After the files are created successfully, the user can run the CompensationUpdateProcessing Console application with the /r option to reset the Reviewed field in the Employee table from True to False. This is done so that when an employee is eligible for a review in the following year, the employee's record will be included in the Compensation Review report that is generated by the Compensation Review Report application (created in Chapter 10), which provides managers with a list of employees eligible for review.

A Console application that generates three different file formats will give Ekstrom Optics the option to work with any number of payroll vendors who support at least one of the three formats. Because the current payroll vendor uses XML, this chapter focuses on creating an XML file that can be obtained via a Web service.

Once the XML file is created, the payroll vendor then can obtain the XML file via a Web service and update the payroll records so that the employees' next paychecks reflect their new compensation amounts. The Compensation Update Service Web service provides this functionality. The vendor can use any programming language that supports using Web services, such as Visual Basic .NET, Java, or C#, to call the Compensation Update Service Web service over the Internet and obtain the XML file.

Program Development

The development cycle for the Compensation Update Processing Console application and Compensation Update Service Web service consists of tasks that correspond to the six development cycle phases, as shown in Table 12-1.

Table 12-1 **Compensation Update Processing Console Application and Compensation Update Service Web Service Development Tasks**

DEVELOPMENT PHASE	TASK NUMBER	TASK NAME	TASK
Analyze requirements	1	Analyze problem	Analyze the Compensation Update Processing and Compensation Update Service problem.
Design solution	2	Design interface	Design the options for the Compensation Update Processing Console application and the programmatic interface for the Compensation Update Service Web service.
	3	Design program	Design the logic for the code and write pseudocode for the Compensation Update Processing Console application and Compensation Update Service Web service.
Validate design	4	Validate design	Prove that the solution produces correct results for the Compensation Update Processing and Compensation Update Service problem.
Implement design	5	Write code for module	Write code to implement the design of the code for the new module needed in the Compensation Review class library.
	6	Write code for Console application	Write code for the Compensation Update Processing Console application.
	7	Write code for Web service	Write code for the Compensation Update Service Web service.
Test solution	8	Test Console application	Test the Compensation Update Processing Console application.
	9	Test Web service	Test the Compensation Update Service Web service.
	10	Debug	Fix any problems with the Compensation Update Processing Console application or Compensation Update Service Web service.
Document solution	11	Document	Print the code for the new procedure in the Compensation Review class library. Print the code for the Compensation Update Processing Console application and Compensation Update Service Web service.

Analysis and Design

Figure 12-2 shows the requirements document that initiates the development cycle for the Compensation Update Processing Console application and Compensation Update Service Web service.

REQUEST FOR NEW APPLICATION

Date submitted:	February 17, 2004
Submitted by:	Samantha O'Conner
Purpose:	The human resources department requires a Compensation Update Processing application as part of the Compensation Review System. A manager will run the application once per month after reviews have been completed. The application should generate a file that will be accessed by our payroll vendor using a Web service. The Web service should be named the CompensationUpdateService.
Application title:	Compensation Update Processing Console application and Compensation Update Service Web service
Algorithms:	The Compensation Update Processing application should create a file listing data for all employees with a reviewed status of True and whose next review date is within 30 days of a date that is given as an argument in the command for the application.
Notes:	1) The Compensation Review database provided is a sample database containing a partial list of employees. It is a Microsoft Access database on the enclosed Data Disk and is named Compensation Review.mdb. The database is basically the same as the database used in Chapter 11, only the sample database includes fewer records and has been updated to ensure the test data will return results. The database thus includes fourrecords for employees who have been reviewed between 07/30/2004 and 08/29/2004. 2) The Compensation Update Processing application should be a Console application that can generate files in one of three different file formats: comma-delimited, tab-delimited, or XML. Having an application that generates three different file formats gives us the option to use any different payroll vendor who supports one of the three formats. Our current payroll vendor needs the data in an XML format. 3) The Compensation Updage Processing Console application should allow four possible arguments: 　　/c MM/DD/YYYY – creates a comma-delimited file 　　/t MM/DD/YYYY – creates a tab-delimited file 　　/x MM/DD/YYYY – creates an XML file 　　/r – resets the Reviewed status in the Employee table to False 3) The employee information that must be included in the output files includes: Employee ID, name, location, date reviewed, and hourly rate or annual salary. 4) The Compensation Update Service should be a Web service that includes a function that returns a string containing the information in the XML version of the file created by the Compensation Update Processing Console application.

Approvals

Approval Status:	X	Approved
		Rejected
Approved by:	Jonathan Ingram	
Date:	February 24, 2004	
Assigned to:	J. Quasney, Programmer	

FIGURE 12-2

PROBLEM ANALYSIS   The problem that the Compensation Update Processing Console application must solve is to query the Employee table of the Compensation Review database for employee records that have a reviewed status of True and are eligible for a review within a month of a date entered by the user. After gathering the employee records that meet the requirements, the Console application must create and write a file that includes the gathered data in one of three possible formats. The application also must be capable of resetting the reviewed status of the records to False.

The resetting of the reviewed status for the employee records requires database access. Therefore, the code for this functionality should exist in a class library. As you learned in Chapter 10, business logic, including database access, is best coded separately from the user interface of the application.

The problem that the Compensation Update Service Web service must solve is to provide a means for an outside payroll vendor to request and retrieve the XML file created by the Compensation Update Processing Console application. As you learned in Chapter 1, a Web service is a program that provides information to another program over the Internet or an intranet, but does not have a user interface. Visual Basic .NET allows you to create Web services that are function procedures that are accessible over the Internet or an intranet. A Web service executes on a Web server, just as a Web application, such as the Compensation Review Update Web application created in Chapter 11, does. The Compensation Update Service Web service program will be created on a Web server rather than on the floppy drive to meet the requirement that Web services must be created on a Web server.

INTERFACE DESIGN   Although Console applications and Web services do not include graphical user interfaces, the methods that users must employ to access and interact with the applications should be specified in the design of the application. The Console application requires that the user execute the application by entering a command in the Command Prompt window and then specifying which action the program should take by entering command-line arguments. A **command-line argument** is any additional word or phrase that follows the command name to provide the program with more information about what actions to take. In the case of the Compensation Update Processing Console application, the command used to execute the application will be CompensationUpdateProcessing, and the two command-line arguments will specify the file format (/c, /t, /x, or /r) to create and a review date. Table 12-2 on the next page shows the arguments that the user can pass to the Console application.

Tip

Designing Console Applications and Web Services

Although Console applications and Web services do not include a graphical user interface, the methods that users must employ to access and interact with the applications should be specified in the design of the application.

Table 12-2   Command-Line Arguments for the Compensation Update Processing Console Application

ARGUMENTS	EXAMPLE	MEANING
/c or /C MM/DD/YYYY	CompensationUpdateProcessing /C 07/30/2005	Create a comma-delimited file for employees whose next review date is within the 30-day period after 07/30/2005
/t or /T MM/DD/YYYY	CompensationUpdateProcessing /t 07/30/2005	Create a tab-delimited file for employees whose next review date is within the 30-day period after 07/30/2005
/x or /X MM/DD/YYYY	CompensationUpdateProcessing /x 07/30/2005	Create an XML file for employees whose next review date is within the 30-day period after 07/30/2005
/r or /R	CompensationUpdateProcessing /r	Reset the reviewed status of all employee records to False

The Compensation Update Service Web service does not include a user interface, but the user, who is another programmer, must know the conventions that should be used to call the Web service. A Web service acts as a container for one or more functions and procedures that the consumer (the other programmer) of the Web service can call. The requirements document states that the Web service should include one function that returns a String value containing the information in the XML version of the file. This function will be named, GetCompensationUpdate(), to reflect the functionality provided by the function.

PROGRAM DESIGN   Figure 12-3 shows a flowchart that outlines the logic carried out when the Compensation Update Processing Console application begins execution. The first procedure to execute when the Console applications begins is called Main(). The application first determines if either two or three arguments have been passed to it. By default, one hidden argument always is passed to a Console application. The application, therefore, checks to see if the user has typed either one (/r) or two (/c, /t, or /x with a date) arguments on the command line (see Table 12-2 above for a list of possible arguments). If the user has not entered a valid number of arguments, then the application halts after displaying an error message in the Command Prompt window.

If the user has typed a valid number of arguments next to the command used to execute the application, CompensationUpdateProcessing, then the application takes an action depending on the value of the first argument. In the case of the /c or /t arguments, the application calls the CreateTextFile() procedure, which is described later in this section. In the case of the /x argument, the application calls the CreateXMLFile() procedure, which also is described later in this section. In the case of the /r argument, the application calls the UpdateReviewedStatus() public procedure, which is used to update all records in the Employee table, by changing the Reviewed field value of True to False. Because the UpdateReviewedStatus() procedure must access the Compensation Review database to perform these updates, the new procedure should be created in the Update Compensation module created in Chapter 11.

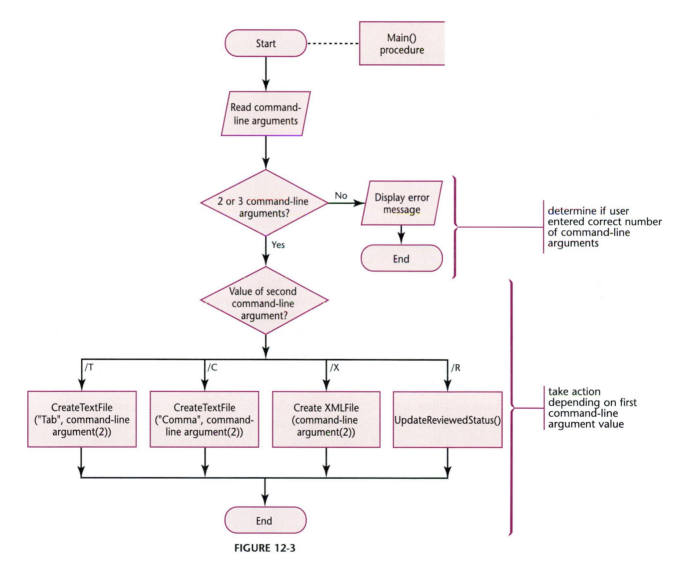

FIGURE 12-3

Figure 12-4 shows pseudocode that corresponds to the logic shown in the flowchart in Figure 12-3 on the previous page. The first command-line argument is converted to uppercase, so that the argument remains valid, regardless of whether the user types it as uppercase or lowercase.

```
Main()
  If Number of Command-line arguments <> 2 And Number of Command-line arguments <> 3 Then
    Write error message to Console
  End
  End If

  Select Case UpperCase(Command-line argument(1))
    Case "/T"
      CreateTextFile("Tab", Command-line argument(2))
    Case "/C"
      CreateXMLFile("Comma", Command-line argument(2))
    Case "/X"
      CreateXMLFile(Command-line argument(2))
    Case "/R"
      UpdateReviewedStatus()
  End Select
End
```

FIGURE 12-4

Figure 12-5 shows two flowcharts that represent the key logic in the CreateTextFile() and CreateXMLFile() procedures of the Console application. Figure 12-5a indicates that the CreateTextFile() procedure accepts an argument that determines the delimiter used in creating the text file. A **delimiter** is a character or string that sets fields apart in a text file. In the case of the CreateTextFile() procedure, the delimiter can be either a comma, which is indicated by using a /c command-line argument, or a tab, which is indicated by a /t command-line argument. The CreateTextFile() procedure first creates an Employees object that contains those employees whose review date is within 30 days of the date given by the user as the second command-line argument and whose records have the Reviewed field set to True. The logic shown in Figure 12-5a then loops through the hourly and salaried employees in the Employees object and writes the information for each employee to a text file. When writing the individual fields for each employee, the procedure will use the delimiter between each field written to the text file — either a comma or a tab character.

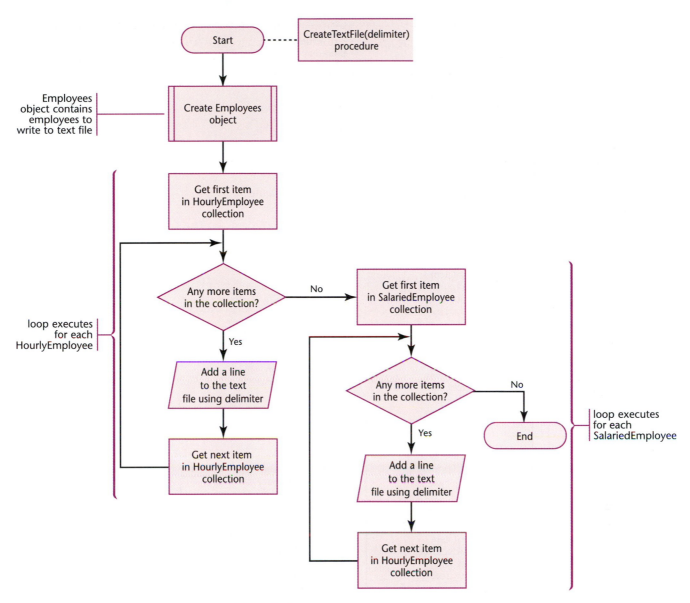

FIGURE 12-5a

Figure 12-5b on the next page shows the logic for the CreateXMLFile() procedure in the Console application. The procedure first creates an Employees object that contains those employees whose review date is within 30 days of the date given by the user as the second command-line argument and whose records have the Reviewed field set to True. Individual data elements and groups of data are arranged in a hierarchy in an XML file, and the flowchart indicates some of the elements that must be written to the XML file to create this hierarchy. For example, the entire set of employee elements is encapsulated in an XML element called PayrollUpdates. The logic shown in Figure 12-5b then loops through the hourly and salaried employees in the Employees object and writes the information for each employee to an XML file. The PayrollUpdates XML element that is started at the top of the flowchart must be closed when all employee information has been written to the file. The structure of XML files will be discussed in detail later in this chapter.

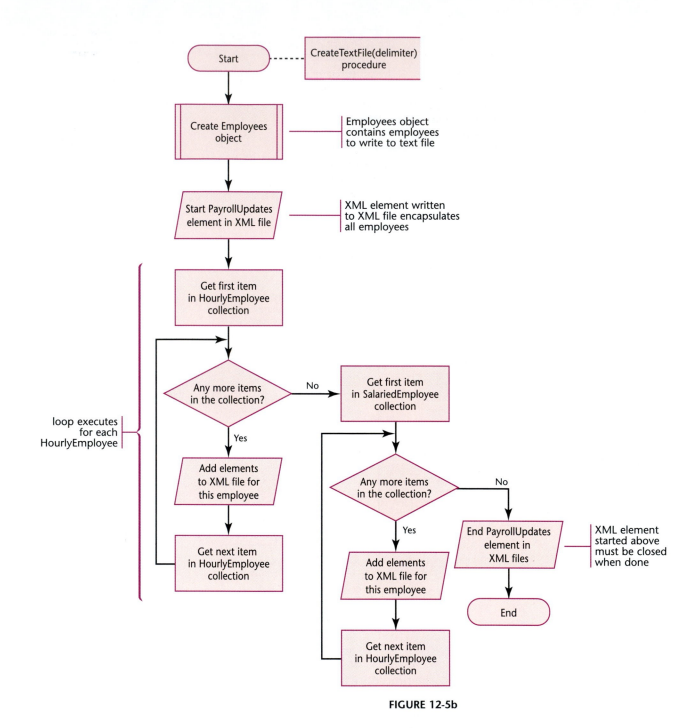

FIGURE 12-5b

Figure 12-6 shows pseudocode for both the CreateTextFile() and CreateXMLFile() procedures. The pseudocode corresponds to the logic shown in the flowcharts in Figure 12-5a on the previous page and Figure 12-5b. The pseudocode indicates where the text file or XML file must be created. Both text files and XML files first must be created and opened before the program can write any data to the files. The program must specify the location of the files on the floppy disk or hard disk. The pseudocode for the CreateXMLFile() procedure also indicates the XML elements that must be written for each employee record.

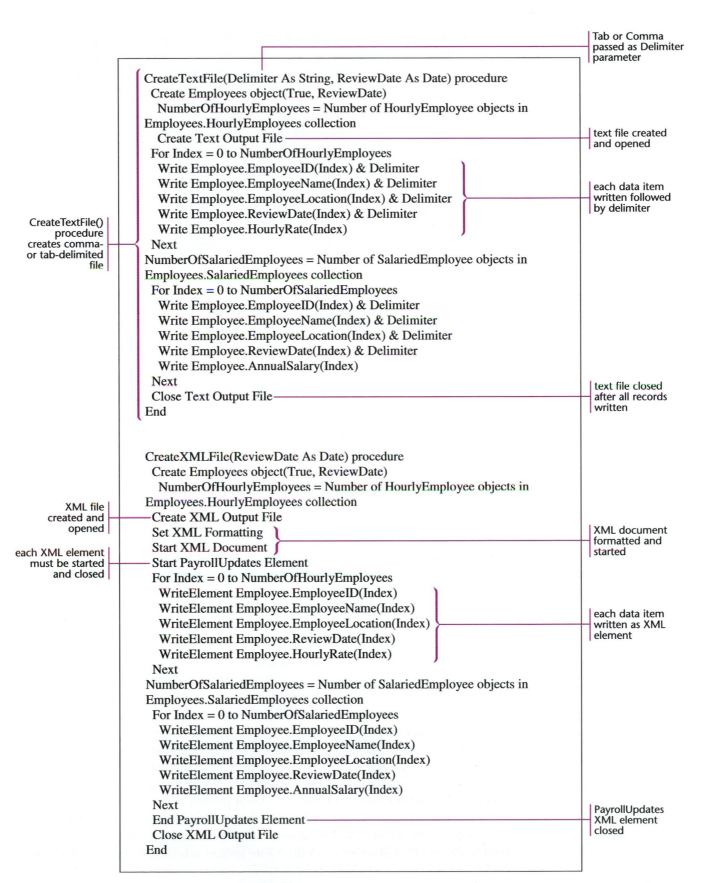

Tab or Comma passed as Delimiter parameter

```
CreateTextFile(Delimiter As String, ReviewDate As Date) procedure
  Create Employees object(True, ReviewDate)
    NumberOfHourlyEmployees = Number of HourlyEmployee objects in
Employees.HourlyEmployees collection
    Create Text Output File
  For Index = 0 to NumberOfHourlyEmployees
    Write Employee.EmployeeID(Index) & Delimiter
    Write Employee.EmployeeName(Index) & Delimiter
    Write Employee.EmployeeLocation(Index) & Delimiter
    Write Employee.ReviewDate(Index) & Delimiter
    Write Employee.HourlyRate(Index)
  Next
NumberOfSalariedEmployees = Number of SalariedEmployee objects in
Employees.SalariedEmployees collection
  For Index = 0 to NumberOfSalariedEmployees
    Write Employee.EmployeeID(Index) & Delimiter
    Write Employee.EmployeeName(Index) & Delimiter
    Write Employee.EmployeeLocation(Index) & Delimiter
    Write Employee.ReviewDate(Index) & Delimiter
    Write Employee.AnnualSalary(Index)
  Next
  Close Text Output File
End
```

text file created and opened

each data item written followed by delimiter

CreateTextFile() procedure creates comma- or tab-delimited file

text file closed after all records written

```
CreateXMLFile(ReviewDate As Date) procedure
  Create Employees object(True, ReviewDate)
    NumberOfHourlyEmployees = Number of HourlyEmployee objects in
Employees.HourlyEmployees collection
    Create XML Output File
  Set XML Formatting
  Start XML Document
  Start PayrollUpdates Element
  For Index = 0 to NumberOfHourlyEmployees
    WriteElement Employee.EmployeeID(Index)
    WriteElement Employee.EmployeeName(Index)
    WriteElement Employee.EmployeeLocation(Index)
    WriteElement Employee.ReviewDate(Index)
    WriteElement Employee.HourlyRate(Index)
  Next
NumberOfSalariedEmployees = Number of SalariedEmployee objects in
Employees.SalariedEmployees collection
  For Index = 0 to NumberOfSalariedEmployees
    WriteElement Employee.EmployeeID(Index)
    WriteElement Employee.EmployeeName(Index)
    WriteElement Employee.EmployeeLocation(Index)
    WriteElement Employee.ReviewDate(Index)
    WriteElement Employee.AnnualSalary(Index)
  Next
  End PayrollUpdates Element
  Close XML Output File
End
```

XML file created and opened

each XML element must be started and closed

XML document formatted and started

each data item written as XML element

PayrollUpdates XML element closed

FIGURE 12-6

The GetCompensationUpdate() function of the Compensation Update Service Web service reads the XML file created by the Compensation Update Processing application. The function then sends the relevant portion of the XML file to the user or program requesting the file as a String return value.

VALIDATE DESIGN   The validation of the design is achieved by stepping through the requirements document to ensure that all of the requirements are met in a reasonable manner and that the program logic is sound. The Compensation Update Processing Console application queries the Employee table in the Compensation Review database to find employees who recently have received a compensation review. The user specifies one command-line argument to request that the application create either a comma-delimited (/c), a tab-delimited (/t), or an XML file (/x). A second command-line argument allows the user to request that the application reset the Reviewed field of the employee records from True back to False. A new public procedure in the Compensation Review class library will handle the functionality of updating the database.

The Compensation Update Service Web service includes the GetCompensationUpdate() function that allows the payroll vendor to read the XML file created by the Compensation Update Processing Console application. The GetCompensationUpdate() function of the Web service then returns the relevant portion of the XML file as a String return value to the requesting program, such as a Web browser.

As shown in Table 12-1 on page VB 12.05, after validating the program design, the next phase in the development cycle is to use Visual Basic .NET to develop the public procedure that performs the database update operations and add it to the UpdateCompensation() module of the Compensation Review class library.

Adding a Public Procedure to a Module

The Console application requires functionality to reset the Reviewed field in the Employee table to False when the user executes the application with the /r option. Resetting this value requires database access. As you learned in Chapter 10, business logic, including the code to access a database, should be programmed outside of the user portion of the code. The UpdateCompensation() module of the Compensation Review class library provides the best place to place database access code that does not fit into one of the classes.

As outlined in the program design, the UpdateReviewedStatus() procedure updates records in the Employee table by setting the Reviewed field to True. Figure 12-7 shows the code for the UpdateReviewedStatus() procedure that accomplishes this task. Lines 33 through 35 include database access code that declares and initializes objects used to connect to the database; this code mirrors some of the code written for other procedures in the Compensation Review class library. Line 38 includes the significant functionality of the procedure, the SQL UPDATE statement that updates the Employee records in the database. The statement excludes a condition after the SET clause, which means that the statement will update the Reviewed field of all employee records in the Employee table to the value of True, whether they were reviewed or not. Line 40 assigns the

SQL UPDATE statement to the CommandText of the objOleDbCommand variable; in line 41, the ExecuteNonQuery() method of the objOleDbCommand variable executes the SQL UPDATE statement.

SQL UPDATE Statements

To update all records in a table, do not include a WHERE condition in the SQL UPDATE statement.

```
28     Public Sub UpdateReviewedStatus()
29         Dim objOleDbConnection As OleDbConnection
30         Dim objOleDbCommand As OleDbCommand
31         Dim strSQL As String
32
33         objOleDbConnection = New OleDbConnection(g_strConnectionString)
34         objOleDbCommand = New OleDbCommand()
35         objOleDbCommand.Connection = objOleDbConnection
36         objOleDbCommand.Connection.Open()
37
38         strSQL = "UPDATE Employee SET Reviewed = True"
39
40         objOleDbCommand.CommandText = strSQL
41         objOleDbCommand.ExecuteNonQuery()
42     End Sub
```

FIGURE 12-7

A new procedure — the UpdateReviewedStatus() procedure — must be added to the UpdateCompensation module of the Compensation Review class library project. The UpdateCompensation module is a .vb file that already contains the UpdateCompensation() procedure developed in Chapter 11.

- If you did not complete the code for the Compensation Review class library in Chapter 11 and you plan to complete the coding in this chapter, see your instructor to obtain the files necessary to complete the coding in this chapter or follow the steps in Chapter 11 to complete the Compensation Review class library.

- Database access is much faster from a hard drive rather than a floppy drive. If permitted by your instructor, you may want to copy the Chapter12 folder on the Data Disk to your hard drive to complete the project in this chapter.

The steps on the next page start Visual Basic .NET, open the Compensation Review solution, and then add a new procedure to the UpdateCompensation module of the Compensation Review class library project.

To Start Visual Basic .NET and Add a New Public Procedure to a Module

1. Insert the Data Disk in drive A. Start Visual Basic .NET. When the Start Page displays, click the Open Project button on the Start Page.

2. If necessary, click the Look in box arrow and then click 3½ Floppy (A:). Double-click the Chapter12 folder.

Visual Basic .NET displays the Open Project dialog box. The Chapter12 folder becomes the current folder in the Look in box.

3. Double-click the Compensation Review folder. If necessary, click the Compensation Review solution file (Compensation Review.sln).

The Compensation Review folder becomes the current folder in the Look in box. The Compensation Review solution file is selected in the dialog box.

4. Click the Open button. When the Compensation Review project displays in the Solution Explorer window, double-click the UpdateCompensation.vb module.

The UpdateCompensation.vb module opens in the code window.

5. Type lines 28 through 42 as shown in Figure 12-7 on the previous page.

Lines 28 through 42 display in the code window. The code includes the complete UpdateReviewedStatus() public procedure (Figure 12-8).

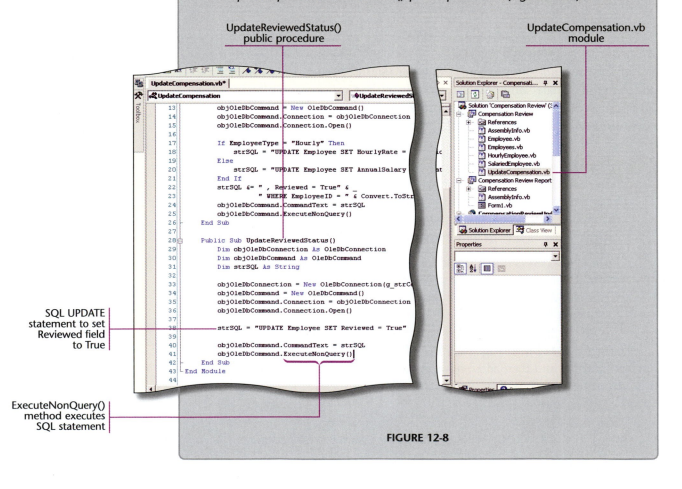

UpdateReviewedStatus() public procedure

UpdateCompensation.vb module

SQL UPDATE statement to set Reviewed field to True

ExecuteNonQuery() method executes SQL statement

FIGURE 12-8

Figure 12-8 shows the location of the UpdateCompensation.vb module in the Solution Explorer window. The objects used to connect to the database are declared and initialized in lines 33 through 35, much as was done in the code entered in Chapter 10 to communicate with the Compensation Review database. The SQL UPDATE statement sets the Reviewed field of all employee records in the Employees table to the value of True. The ExecuteNonQuery() method of the objOleDbCommand variable executes the SQL UPDATE statement.

Building, Saving, and Documenting the Class Library

With the coding for the new UpdateReviewedStatus() procedure complete, the next step is to rebuild the Compensation Review class library so that the .DLL file includes the new procedure.

The following steps build, save, and document the Compensation Review class library with the new UpdateReviewedStatus() procedure in the UpdateCompensation.vb module.

To Build, Save, and Document the Class Library

1. Right-click the Compensation Review project in the Solution Explorer window. When the shortcut menu displays, click the Build command.

Visual Basic .NET automatically saves the class files and then opens the Output window and displays several messages while building the project. The result of the build is the Compensation Review.dll file in the A:\Chapter12\ Compensation Review\Compensation Review\bin folder on the Data Disk.

2. Click the UpdateCompensation.vb tab in the main work area. Follow the steps on page VB 2.40 of Chapter 2 to use the Print command on the File menu to print a record of the code for the UpdateCompensation.vb module.

A record of the code for the UpdateCompensation.vb module is printed (Figure 12-9).

```
A:\Chapter12\Compensation Review\Compensation Review\UpdateCompensation.vb          1
 1 Option Strict On
 2 Imports System.Data.OleDb
 3 Public Module UpdateCompensation
 4     Const g_strConnectionString As String = "Provider=Microsoft.Jet.OLEDB.4.0;" & _
 5                                              "Data Source = A:\Chapter12\
   CompensationReview.mdb"
 6
```

```
27
28     Public Sub UpdateReviewedStatus()
29         Dim objOleDbConnection As OleDbConnection
30         Dim objOleDbCommand As OleDbCommand
31         Dim strSQL As String
32
33         objOleDbConnection = New OleDbConnection(g_strConnectionString)
34         objOleDbCommand = New OleDbCommand()
35         objOleDbCommand.Connection = objOleDbConnection
36         objOleDbCommand.Connection.Open()
37
38         strSQL = "UPDATE Employee SET Reviewed = True"
39
40         objOleDbCommand.CommandText = strSQL
41         objOleDbCommand.ExecuteNonQuery()
42     End Sub
43 End Module
44
```

FIGURE 12-9

The development phase for the changes to the Compensation Review class library now are complete, and other programs, such as those in the Compensation Review System, can use the Compensation Review class library.

The previous steps left the solution and project open in the IDE because the Console application and Web service still must be added to the Compensation Review solution.

Creating a Console Application

Recall that the first program in the Compensation Review System to utilize the Employees class is the Compensation Review Report application developed in Chapter 10. The second program in the Compensation Review System to utilize the Compensation Review class library is the Compensation Review Update Web application developed in Chapter 11. The third and final application to use the Employees class and Compensation Review class library is the Compensation Update Processing Console application developed in this chapter.

When you start a new project in Visual Basic .NET, you can choose to create a Console application project instead of a Windows application project. As discussed on page VB 1.07 of Chapter 1, a Console application is an application in which the user interface consists of a command prompt where users type instructions that execute in the Command Prompt window, also called the **Console window**. Before Microsoft introduced the Windows graphical interface, the user interface for a PC consisted solely of a **command-line interface**, in which users interacted with applications using text commands. The command-line interface lives on as the Command Prompt in Windows. You open the Command Prompt window by using the Command Prompt command on the Accessories menu of the Windows Start menu or All Programs submenu.

Once you open the Command Prompt window, you can execute any program simply by typing the program name. The Command Prompt supports special commands for use in the command-line environment. For example, the CD command is used to navigate to a different folder. By default, the Command Prompt window displays the current folder name as the command prompt.

A variety of circumstances dictate when you may want to create a Console application. Console applications can be executed by scripts that administrators run when they need to perform common administrative tasks. You also may want to use Console applications when writing unit test programs, because Console applications avoid the sometimes time-consuming task of creating a graphical user interface.

Tip

Developing Console Applications

Consider developing a Console application when the program performs administrative tasks that may be scripted by a computer or network administrator. You also may want to use Console applications when writing unit test programs, because Console applications avoid the sometimes time-consuming task of creating a graphical user interface.

The end result of a Console application is an executable file with an .EXE file extension, whose name can be typed by the user in the Command Prompt window.

Starting a New Console Application Project

The Compensation Update Processing Console application must be added to the Compensation Review solution. When Visual Basic .NET creates a new Console application, it adds only an empty code module to the project. You cannot add forms or controls to the Console application, because the Console application uses a command-line interface, not a graphical user interface.

The following steps add a new Console application project to Compensation Review solution, using the **Console Application template**. The new project is named CompensationUpdateProcessing, and the default module in the project is renamed CompensationUpdateProcessing.vb. A reference to the Compensation Review class library also is added to the new Console application project.

To Start a New Console Application Project

1. Right-click the Compensation Review solution in the Solution Explorer window. When the shortcut menu displays, click the Add command. When the Add submenu displays, click the New Project command.

2. When the Add New Project dialog box displays, click the Console Application icon in the Templates area. Select the text in the Name box. Type CompensationUpdateProcessing in the Name box.

The Console Application template is selected in the Templates area. The location of the Console application project displays in the Location box (Figure 12-10).

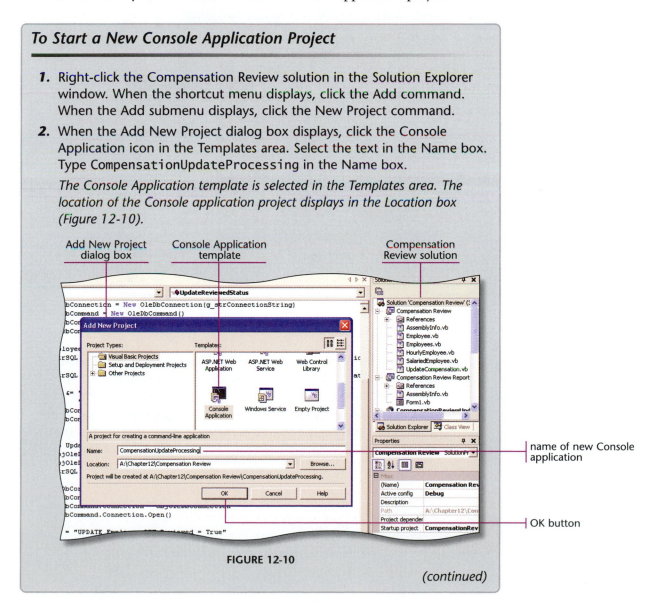

FIGURE 12-10

(continued)

3. Click the OK button.

Visual Basic .NET adds the new CompensationUpdateProcessing Console application to the Compensation Review solution.

4. Right-click the References folder in the CompensationUpdateProcessing project in the Solution Explorer window. When the shortcut menu displays, use the Add Reference command to add a reference to the Compensation Review.dll component located in the A:\Chapter12\ Compensation Review\Compensation Review\bin folder.

Visual Basic .NET adds a reference to the Compensation Review class library in the Reference folder. The default code module, Module1.vb, opens in the code window in the main work area. The code module includes a procedure declaration for a procedure named Main() (Figure 12-11).

Module1.vb
opened in main
work area

CompensationUpdateProcessing
Console application project
added to solution

Main()
procedure
created
automatically

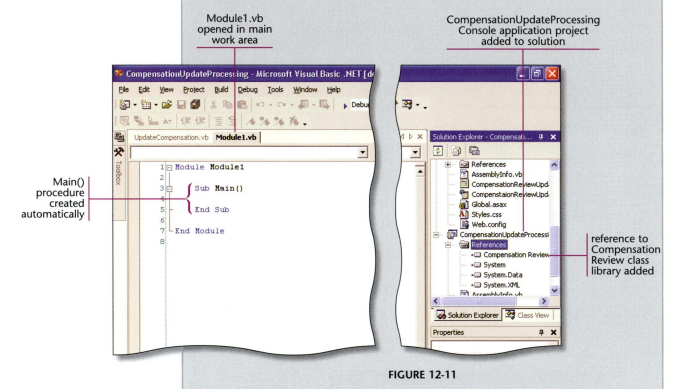

reference to
Compensation
Review class
library added

FIGURE 12-11

5. Right-click the Module1.vb module in the Solution Explorer window. When the shortcut menu displays, click the Rename command. Type CompensationUpdateProcessing.vb as the new module name.

The new module name, CompensationUpdateProcessing.vb, displays in the Visual Basic .NET title bar, on the tab in the main work area, and as the new module name in the Solution Explorer window (Figure 12-12).

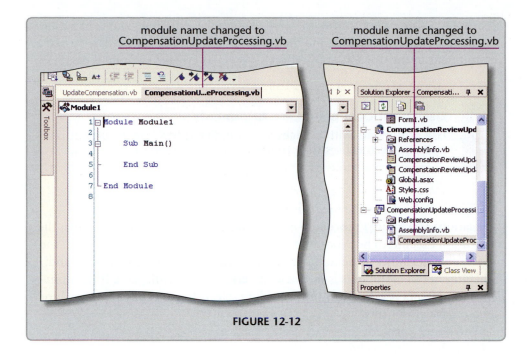

FIGURE 12-12

After Visual Basic .NET creates the new project, the solution and project names, CompensationUpdateProcessing, display in the Solution Explorer window. The default module, Module1.vb, is renamed CompensationUpdateProcessing.vb. Figure 12-11 shows the code for the new module. By default, all Console applications execute the **Main() procedure** first. Visual Basic .NET, therefore, automatically adds a Main() procedure to the module of the application. Console applications do not include forms or other user interface elements.

Working with Command-Line Arguments

When developing a Windows application or Web application, a programmer implements graphical user interface elements, such as buttons and text boxes, which allow the user to interact with the program and cause the program to perform a number of tasks. When developing a Console application, the programmer provides a similar level of functionality by allowing the user to enter command-line arguments next to the program command in the Command Prompt window. The programmer informs the user of the valid options for the command-line arguments. Often, if a user enters invalid command-line arguments, a command displays a text message to the user and indicates the valid options. Some commands also include a help option that causes the program to display a list of the valid command-line arguments for the program.

When deciding which options to give the user with command-line arguments, design the commands to give the user as much flexibility as possible and use arguments with intuitive syntax. For example, in the case of the Console application developed in this chapter, the arguments /c and /C tell the program to create a comma-delimited file, the arguments /t and /T tell the program to create a tab-delimited file, and the arguments /x and /X tell the program to create an XML file. Backslashes commonly are used to indicate that an argument serves as a switch.

A **command-line switch** causes the program to take a discrete course of action. Alternatively, data that is passed to the program, such as the review date passed as an argument in the Console application, typically is entered without a backslash.

Tip

Designing Command-Line Arguments
Use arguments with a backslash to indicate that the argument is a switch, which causes the program to take a discrete course of action.

Figure 12-13 shows the logic for the Main() procedure of the Console application. The Main() procedure is the procedure that executes first when the application executes. The procedure initially reads the command line. Then the procedure determines if the number of arguments entered by the user is valid. If the number of arguments is not valid, an error message displays. If the number of arguments is valid, then the procedure selects the appropriate procedure based on the arguments.

The Main() procedure typically checks for invalid arguments and invalid combinations of arguments. For brevity, the code in this chapter excludes many tests for invalid arguments that the user might enter. If the user enters an invalid switch, then the program simply exits.

```
             Start  - - - - - - -   Main()
                                     procedure

         Read command-
         line arguments

                                            No
      2 or 3 command-line    ----------->  Display error
         arguments?                          message

              Yes                              End

       Value of second
       command-line
       argument?

     /T              /C              /X              /R

 CreateTextFile   CreateTextFile   Create XMLFile   UpdateReviewedStatus()
 ("Tab", command-  ("Comma", command-  (command-line
  line             line argument(2))   argument(2))
  argument(2))

                        End
```

FIGURE 12-13

Figure 12-14 shows an example of the CompensationUpdateProcessing command in a Command Prompt window. The command prompt consists of the current directory, which is C:\> in Figure 12-14. The command includes two command-line arguments — the /t argument and a date. When the user presses the ENTER key after typing the command, the program executes and the two command-line arguments are passed as parameters to the program.

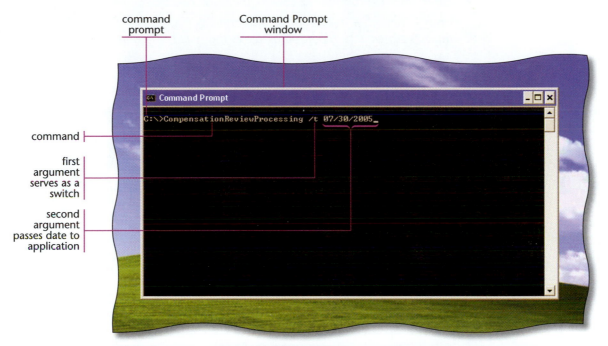

FIGURE 12-14

ENTERING INITIAL CONSOLE APPLICATION CODE   Figure 12-15 shows the code for the beginning of the CompensationUpdateProcessing.vb module. The Option Strict On statement and an Imports statement are shown as the first four lines of code for the module. As previously discussed, the Option Strict On statement is used to ensure that all assignment statements use the same data type on both sides of the assignment; the Imports statement allows you to reference elements in a namespace without qualification, so elements in the imported namespace do not need the namespace identifier when you reference them in code. For example, you can use the identifier Employee rather than Compensation_Review.Employee to reference the Employee class in the Compensation_Review class library, if the namespace Compensation_Review has been imported using the Imports statement.

```
1 Option Strict On
2 Imports Compensation_Review
3 Imports System.IO
4 Imports System.Xml
```

FIGURE 12-15

The following step adds the code shown in Figure 12-15 on the previous page to the CompensationUpdateProcessing.vb module already open in the code window.

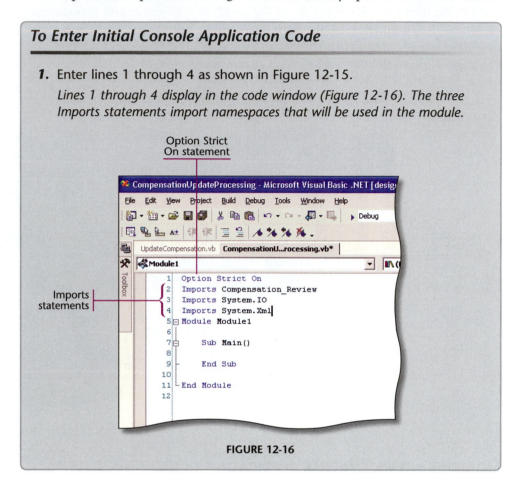

To Enter Initial Console Application Code

1. Enter lines 1 through 4 as shown in Figure 12-15.

Lines 1 through 4 display in the code window (Figure 12-16). The three Imports statements import namespaces that will be used in the module.

FIGURE 12-16

Lines 2 through 4 in Figure 12-16 import three namespaces: Compensation_Review, System.IO, and System.Xml. As previously noted, the Compensation_Review namespace allows you to reference classes in the Compensation_Review class library. The **System.IO namespace** provides classes to support basic input and output (IO) tasks required to manipulate data, such as loading data from a file or downloading data from a Web site. The **System.Xml namespace** provides standards-based support for processing XML.

VALIDATING THE NUMBER OF COMMAND-LINE ARGUMENTS

Figure 12-17 shows the code that corresponds to the first decision in the flow-chart shown in Figure 12-13 on page VB 12.22. The If…Then statement tests the Environment.GetCommandLineArgs.Length property to determine if the user typed one or two arguments on the command line. The **Environment object** contains a variety of information about the operating system and other properties of the user's working environment. The **GetCommandLineArgs property** of the Environment object contains information about the command-line arguments typed by the user. The **GetCommandLineArgs.Length property** of the Environment object contains the value of the number of arguments the user typed on the command line, plus 1. The extra argument is actually the name of the command typed by the user, such as CompensationUpdateProcessing, in the case of the CompensationUpdateProcessing Console application.

```
 7          If Environment.GetCommandLineArgs.Length <> 2 And Environment.
        GetCommandLineArgs.Length <> 3 Then
 8              Console.WriteLine("This command requires the /t, /c, /x, or /r switch. A
        date is required next to the /t, /c, or /x switch. Such as,
        CompensationUpdateProcessing /x 08/03/2004.")
 9              End
10          End If
```

FIGURE 12-17

Line 8 in Figure 12-17 uses the **Console.WriteLine() method** to write text to the Command Prompt window. The **Console object** represents the Command Prompt window in which the user typed the command.

The following step adds the code shown in Figure 12-17 to the CompensationUpdateProcessing.vb module already open in the code window.

To Enter Code to Validate Command-Line Arguments

1. Enter lines 7 through 10 as shown in Figure 12-17.

Lines 7 through 10 display in the code window (Figure 12-18). The code makes certain that the user entered either one or two command-line arguments along with the command name in the Command Prompt window.

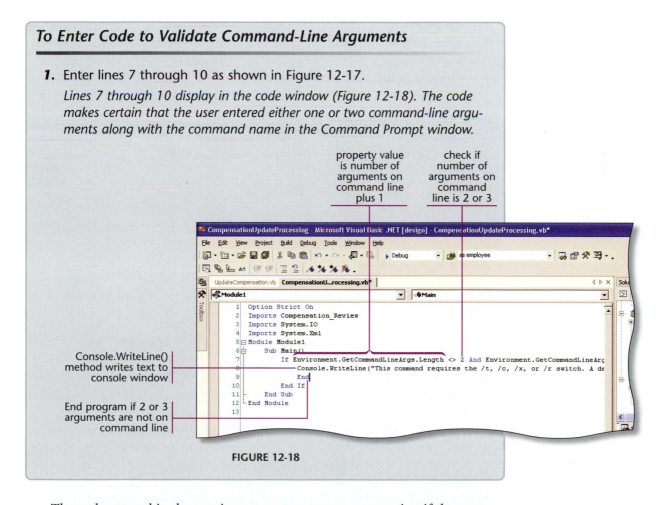

FIGURE 12-18

The code entered in the previous step stops program execution if the user entered too many arguments or no arguments.

DETERMINING THE TYPE OF FILE TO CREATE Figure 12-19 shows the code for the second decision point in the flowchart shown in Figure 12-13 on page VB 12.22. The GetCommandLineArgs() collection property of the Environment object contains an item for each argument. The GetCommandLineArgs(0) item includes the name of the command typed by the user — in this case, CompensationUpdateProcessing. The GetCommandLineArgs(1) item includes the name of the /t, /c, /x, or /r option entered by the user. The GetCommandLineArgs(2) item includes the date entered by the user.

As shown in Figure 12-19, lines 11 through 20 use a Select Case structure to determine what command-line switch the user entered and then execute the appropriate code in response to the user entry. The **UCase() function** in line 11 returns the uppercase version of the first command-line argument, Environment.GetCommandLineArgs(1). If the user entered the argument, /t or /T, the code instructs the program to execute the CreateTextFile() procedure using tabs as the delimiters when creating the text file. If the user entered the argument, /c or /C, the code instructs the program to execute the CreateTextFile() procedure using commas as the delimiters when creating the text file. If the user entered the argument, /x or /X, the code instructs the program to execute the CreateXMLFile() procedure to create an XML file. The CreateTextFile() and CreateXMLFile() procedures will be developed later in this chapter. Finally, the use of the /r or /R command-line argument causes the procedure to call the UpdateReviewedStatus() procedure in the Compensation Review library created earlier in this chapter.

```
11          Select Case UCase(Environment.GetCommandLineArgs(1))
12              Case "/T"
13                  CreateTextFile("Tab", Convert.ToDateTime(Environment.      ↙
        GetCommandLineArgs(2)))
14              Case "/C"
15                  CreateTextFile("Comma", Convert.ToDateTime(Environment.    ↙
        GetCommandLineArgs(2)))
16              Case "/X"
17                  CreateXMLFile(Convert.ToDateTime(Environment.GetCommandLineArgs(2)))
18              Case "/R"
19                  UpdateReviewedStatus()
20          End Select
```

FIGURE 12-19

The following step adds the code shown in Figure 12-19 to the Main() procedure to determine which of the four valid command-line switches the user entered in the Command Prompt window.

To Enter Code to Determine the Type of File to Create

1. Type lines 11 through 20 as shown in Figure 12-19.

Lines 11 through 20 display in the code window (Figure 12-20). The Select Case statement performs an action for each of the four possible command-line switches. Visual Basic .NET underlines the calls to the CreateTextFile() and CreateXMLFile() procedures with a blue wavy line, because these procedures have not been coded yet.

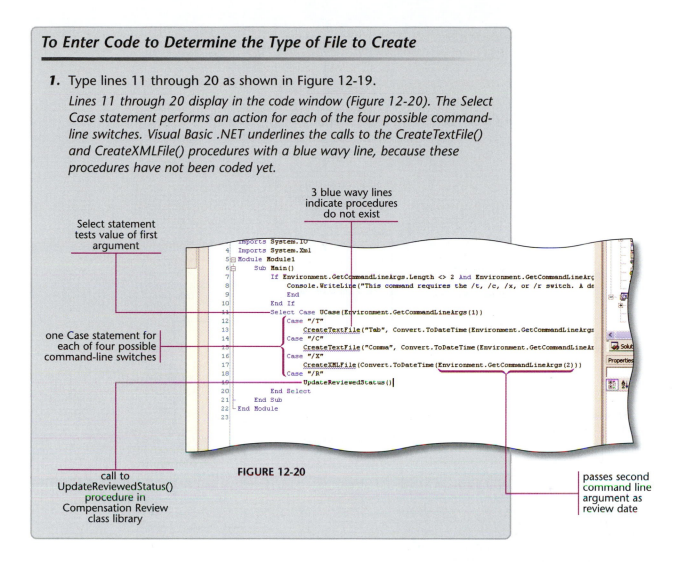

3 blue wavy lines indicate procedures do not exist

Select statement tests value of first argument

one Case statement for each of four possible command-line switches

call to UpdateReviewedStatus() procedure in Compensation Review class library

FIGURE 12-20

passes second command line argument as review date

The code entered in the previous step shows the structure of the typical Main() procedure. The code first validates arguments, and then a Select Case statement calls procedures or functions based on the arguments entered by the user. Main() procedures for Console applications usually do not include business logic.

Creating and Writing to Text Files

The flowcharts shown in Figure 12-21 on the next page represent the logic for both the CreateTextFile() and CreateXMLFile() procedures of the Console application. As shown in the flowcharts, both procedures require the program to create files and then write to those same files. The .NET Framework class library provides a special object for creating, reading from, and writing to text files and XML files, just as objects were used to write data to a printer in the project developed in Chapter 10 and objects were used to write to a database in Chapter 11. This section discusses the .NET Framework class library objects used to interact with text files.

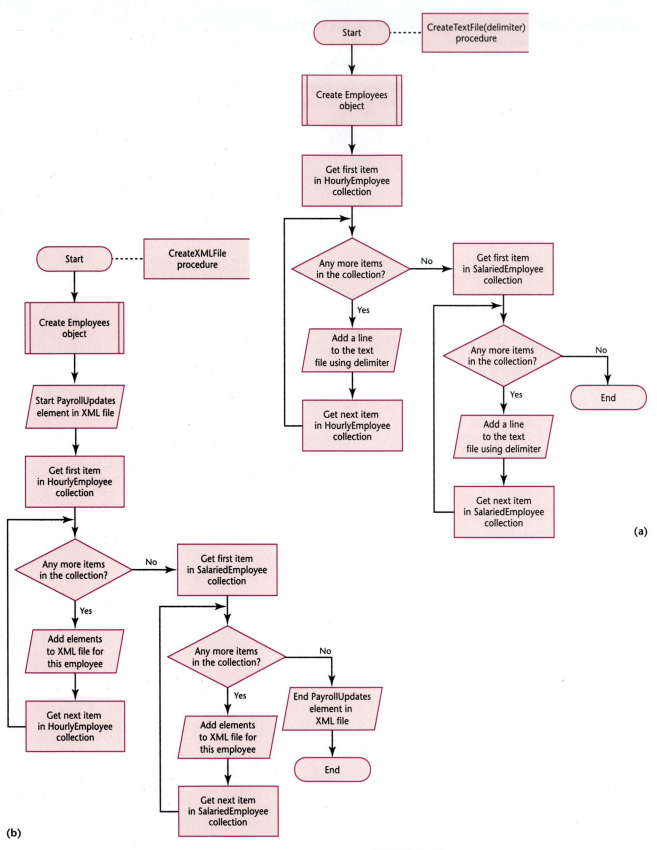

FIGURE 12-21

The **StreamWriter class** in the .NET Framework class library allows you to create and write to text files. The **StreamReader class** allow you to read from text files. You create a StreamWriter object by passing a file name to the class constructor, such as

```
Dim objFile As IO.StreamWriter = New IO.StreamWriter("A:\Chapter12\NewTextFile.txt")
```

When the code executes and the StreamWriter object is instantiated, the new file, NewTextFile.txt, is created in the A:\Chapter12 folder. Additionally, the file is open, meaning that additional code can write text data to the file.

When writing to a file, you can choose to write the text information in any manner you wish, including placing all the information on one line or writing one character per line. Typically, organized files contain discrete records, and each record is written on one line. Fields for each record are separated by placing a delimiter between the fields. In the case of the Compensation Update Processing application, the requirements state that employee information should be written to the text file with either a tab or a comma used as the delimiter between the fields within each record. A **tab-delimited file** is a text file in which one record exists per line and fields in the record are separated by a tab character. A **comma-delimited file** is a text file in which one record exists per line and fields in the record are separated by a comma.

Figure 12-22 shows an example of a tab-delimited file. Each column separated by a tab represents a field. Each line in the file represents a record. Such files often are known as sequential files, because records are written to and read from the files in a sequential order.

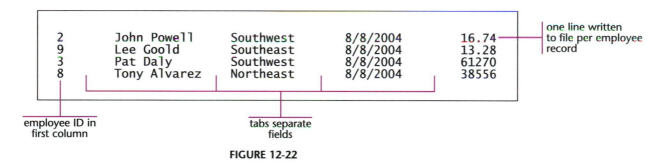

FIGURE 12-22

Figure 12-23 shows an example of a comma-delimited file. Fields do not show as columns, but instead are separated by commas followed by a space. Each line in the file represents a record.

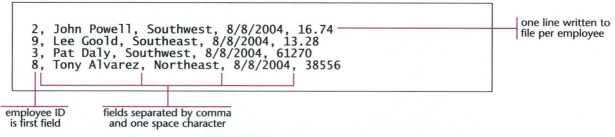

FIGURE 12-23

Text File Objects and Creating and Opening a Text File

The Compensation Update Processing application requires that either a tab-delimited or comma-delimited file be written to the Data Disk, depending on the command-line argument entered by the user. The CreateTextFile() procedure will handle both of these situations, by writing the same information to a text file, only using a different character as the field delimiter in the file, depending on the command-line argument entered by the user.

Figure 12-24 shows the code that begins the CreateTextFile() procedure in the Console application. The procedure accepts two parameters. The first indicates whether the procedure should create a comma-delimited file or a tab-delimited one. The second parameter is used as the next review date when creating the Employees object. Lines 25 through 27 instantiate an Employees object and declare the HourlyEmployee and SalariedEmployee objects needed to read the Employees object. Line 28 creates a new instance of the IO.StreamWriter class, passing the text file name to create as a parameter. When this line executes, the CompensationUpdate.txt file is created in the Chapter12 folder on the Data Disk, and the file is ready to be written to by the procedure.

```
23      Private Sub CreateTextFile(ByVal strFileType As String, ByVal dtmDateReviewed As    ↙
        Date)
24          Try
25              Dim objEmployees As New Employees(True, dtmDateReviewed)
26              Dim objHourlyEmployee As HourlyEmployee
27              Dim objSalariedEmployee As SalariedEmployee
28              Dim objTextFile As IO.StreamWriter = New IO.StreamWriter("A:\Chapter12\    ↙
        CompensationUpdate.txt")
29              Dim strFieldSeparator As String
30
31              If strFileType = "Tab" Then
32                  strFieldSeparator = ControlChars.Tab
33              Else
34                  strFieldSeparator = ", "
35              End If
36          Catch ex As Exception
37              Console.Write("An error occurred while getting employee records or creating↙
        the text file.")
38              End
39          End Try
40      End Sub
```

FIGURE 12-24

Lines 29 through 35 determine the first parameter passed to the procedure from the Select Case statement and then set the delimiter to be used when writing employee information to the text file. Finally, if any errors occur when creating the text file or Employees object, the Try…Catch statement writes an error message to the Command Prompt window with the Console.Write() method.

The following step adds the code shown in Figure 12-24 to create the CreateTextFile() procedure. Several objects are declared, including a StreamWriter object that will be used to write to a text file.

To Create and Open a Text File

1. Type lines 23 through 40 as shown in Figure 12-24.

Lines 23 through 40 display in the code window (Figure 12-25).

creates an Employees object and declares Employee objects

CreateTextFile() procedure

declares a new StreamWriter object to write to text file and creates text file

writes a message to console window if an error occurs

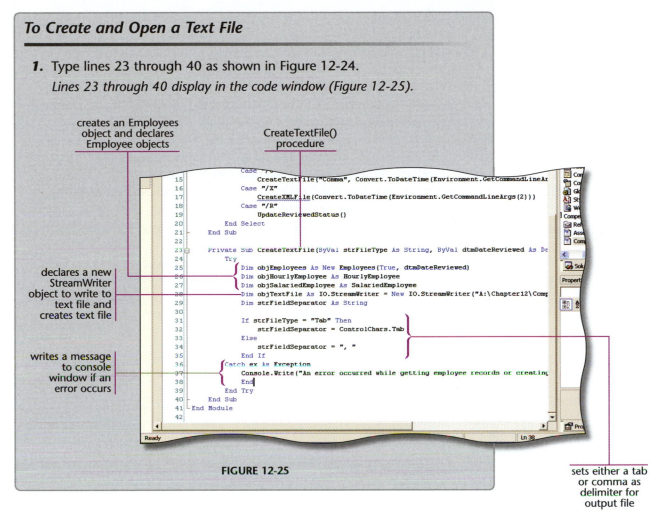

```
         Case "7u"
15           CreateTextFile("Comma", Convert.ToDateTime(Environment.GetCommandLineAr
16         Case "/X"
17           CreateXMLFile(Convert.ToDateTime(Environment.GetCommandLineArgs(2)))
18         Case "/R"
19           UpdateReviewedStatus()
20       End Select
21     End Sub
22
23     Private Sub CreateTextFile(ByVal strFileType As String, ByVal dtmDateReviewed As Da
24       Try
25         Dim objEmployees As New Employees(True, dtmDateReviewed)
26         Dim objHourlyEmployee As HourlyEmployee
27         Dim objSalariedEmployee As SalariedEmployee
28         Dim objTextFile As IO.StreamWriter = New IO.StreamWriter("A:\Chapter12\Comp
29         Dim strFieldSeparator As String
30
31         If strFileType = "Tab" Then
32           strFieldSeparator = ControlChars.Tab
33         Else
34           strFieldSeparator = ", "
35         End If
36       Catch ex As Exception
37         Console.Write("An error occurred while getting employee records or creating
38         End
39       End Try
40     End Sub
41   End Module
42
```

Ready   Ln 38

FIGURE 12-25

sets either a tab or comma as delimiter for output file

The code in the new CreateTextFile() procedure is placed in a Try…Catch statement. If any errors occur while creating the Employees object (line 25) or creating the text file (line 28), the Catch clause displays an error message to the user and then terminates execution of the program.

The code entered in the previous step results in the creation of an Employees object and the creation and opening of the CompensationUpdate.txt text file on the Data Disk. The field delimiter that will be written between each of the data fields in the text file is set to either a tab character — as indicated by the ControlChars.Tab in line 32 — or a comma followed by a space, as shown in line 34. All of the code is encapsulated in a Try…Catch statement so that if any operation causes a run-time error, the program exits and displays an error message to the user.

Writing to a Text File

The **Write() method** of the StreamWriter object writes a string value or the value of most Visual Basic .NET data types to a text output file. Here, the data is written as a string value to the text file. The **WriteLine() method** of the StreamWriter() object writes a value to a text output file and also appends a NewLine character to the end of the output, so that the next piece of data written to the object starts on a new line. If no arguments are passed to the

WriteLine() method, then a NewLine character is inserted into the file. As you have learned, information written to the StreamWriter object is written sequentially, so all output is appended to the last record written to the object.

Figure 12-26 shows the use of both the Write() and WriteLine() methods of the StreamWriter class. Two For Each loops loop through the HourlyEmployee and SalariedEmployee objects in the objEmployees object. Five fields from each employee's record are written to the text file: EmployeeID, Name, Location, DateReviewed, and HourlyRate or AnnualSalary. After each of the five fields is written, the WriteLine() method with no arguments on lines 43 and 51 inserts a NewLine character to ensure that the next employee's information begins on a new line in the text file. Finally, line 53 closes the text file so that no more information can be written to the file.

```
37          For Each objHourlyEmployee In objEmployees.HourlyEmployeeList
38              objTextFile.Write(objHourlyEmployee.EmployeeID & strFieldSeparator)
39              objTextFile.Write(objHourlyEmployee.Name & strFieldSeparator)
40              objTextFile.Write(objHourlyEmployee.Location & strFieldSeparator)
41              objTextFile.Write(objHourlyEmployee.DateReviewed & strFieldSeparator)
42              objTextFile.Write(objHourlyEmployee.HourlyRate)
43              objTextFile.WriteLine()
44          Next
45          For Each objSalariedEmployee In objEmployees.SalariedEmployeeList
46              objTextFile.Write(objSalariedEmployee.EmployeeID & strFieldSeparator)
47              objTextFile.Write(objSalariedEmployee.Name & strFieldSeparator)
48              objTextFile.Write(objSalariedEmployee.Location & strFieldSeparator)
49              objTextFile.Write(objSalariedEmployee.DateReviewed & strFieldSeparator)
50              objTextFile.Write(objSalariedEmployee.AnnualSalary)
51              objTextFile.WriteLine()
52          Next
53          objTextFile.Close()
```

FIGURE 12-26

The following step adds the code shown in Figure 12-26 to write information from the HourlyEmployee and SalariedEmployee objects to the text file.

To Write to a Text File

1. Type lines 37 through 53 as shown in Figure 12-26.

Lines 37 through 53 display in the code window (Figure 12-27). Two For Each loops in the code loop through the HourlyEmployee and SalariedEmployee objects in the Employees object. The Write() method of the StreamWriter class writes individual data elements to the file, separated by the string indicated in the strFieldSeparator variable. The WriteLine() method on line 43 and 51 writes a NewLine character to the text file to start a new line for each employee in the file.

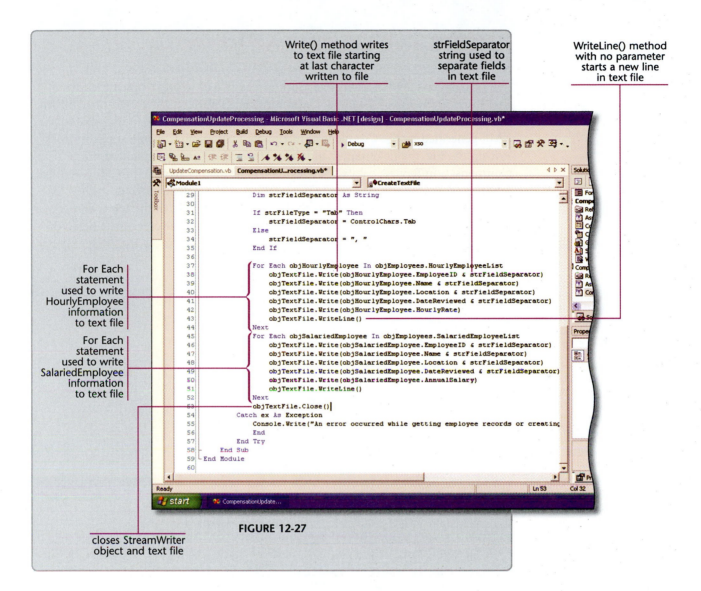

FIGURE 12-27

Callouts around the figure:

- Write() method writes to text file starting at last character written to file
- strFieldSeparator string used to separate fields in text file
- WriteLine() method with no parameter starts a new line in text file
- For Each statement used to write HourlyEmployee information to text file
- For Each statement used to write SalariedEmployee information to text file
- closes StreamWriter object and text file

Lines 37 through 52 write the employee information to the text file. The WriteLine() methods of the StreamWriter class is used to write a NewLine character after each employee's information. The **Close() method** of the StreamWriter class is used in line 53 to terminate the program's access to the text file.

The coding for the CreateTextFile() procedure is complete. The next step is to write the CreateXMLFile() procedure for the Compensation Update Processing application.

Creating and Writing to XML Files

In recent years, XML has gained in popularity as a format for storing and exchanging data. **XML** (Extensible Markup Language) is a text-based file format that stores elements of data in a hierarchical and self-describing method. An **XML file** stores information in the XML format. Figure 12-28 shows an example of the XML generated by the Compensation Update Processing Console application. Within the file, the field names and values from the Employee table of the Compensation Review database are evident. The data is arranged in a hierarchical manner, which is indicated by the indentation of the individual lines in the file. Some of the fields are described with data types. Each field in the file is named, and each field has a tag that indicates the beginning and the end of the field.

```xml
<?xml version="1.0"?>
<PayrollUpdates>
    <PayrollUpdate>
        <EmployeeID format="number">2</EmployeeID>
        <EmployeeName>John Powell</EmployeeName>
        <Location>Southwest</Location>
        <ReviewDate format="date">8/8/2004 12:00:00 AM</ReviewDate>
        <HourlyRate format="currency">16.74</HourlyRate>
    </PayrollUpdate>
    <PayrollUpdate>
        <EmployeeID format="number">9</EmployeeID>
        <EmployeeName>Lee Goold</EmployeeName>
        <Location>Southeast</Location>
        <ReviewDate format="date">8/8/2004 12:00:00 AM</ReviewDate>
        <HourlyRate format="currency">13.28</HourlyRate>
    </PayrollUpdate>
    <PayrollUpdate>
        <EmployeeID format="number">3</EmployeeID>
        <EmployeeName>Pat Daly</EmployeeName>
        <Location>Southwest</Location>
        <ReviewDate format="date">8/8/2004 12:00:00 AM</ReviewDate>
        <AnnualSalary format="currency">61270</AnnualSalary>
    </PayrollUpdate>
    <PayrollUpdate>
        <EmployeeID format="number">8</EmployeeID>
        <EmployeeName>Tony Alvarez</EmployeeName>
        <Location>Northeast</Location>
        <ReviewDate format="date">8/8/2004 12:00:00 AM</ReviewDate>
        <AnnualSalary format="currency">38556</AnnualSalary>
    </PayrollUpdate>
</PayrollUpdates>
```

FIGURE 12-28

Figure 12-29 takes a closer look at the XML shown in Figure 12-28. Figure 12-29 shows the XML file shown in Figure 12-28 as it appears when viewing the file using Microsoft Internet Explorer. Many modern browsers support viewing XML files by opening the file or navigating to the file.

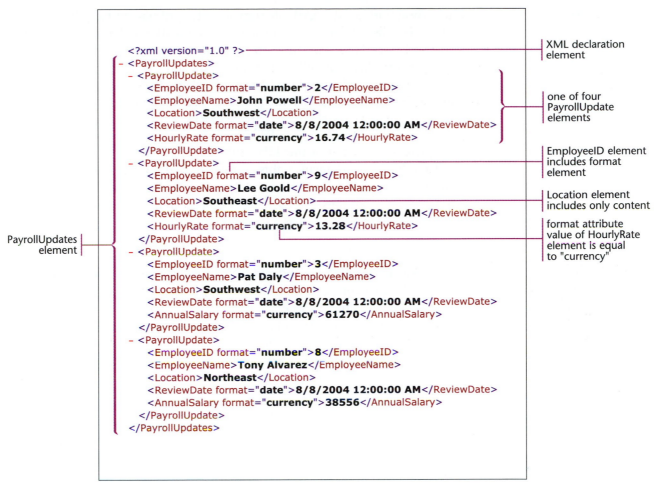

FIGURE 12-29

XML Declarations and Elements

The XML shown in Figure 12-29 includes an XML declaration and an XML element at the top of its hierarchy. The **XML declaration** in the first line of the XML file identifies the version of XML used in the document. As shown in Figure 12-29, a simple XML declaration takes the form

```
<?xml version="1.0"?>
```

to declare that the file is an XML file that uses version 1.0 of XML. A declaration in the first line is required for all XML files.

The second line 2 of the XML file starts the element named PayrollUpdates. An **element** is a discrete piece of information in an XML file that is delimited by a start tag and an end tag. The **start tag**, <PayrollUpdates>, is on the second line, and the **end tag**, </PayrollUpdates>, is on the last line. All XML elements must have a start tag and an end tag that use the element name to define the element that the tags enclose. Together, the start tag and end tag

```
<PayrollUpdates></PayrollUpdates>
```

are a complete XML element named PayrollUpdates.

The PayrollUpdates element in this example does not contain any content between the start and end tags. When an element does not contain content, an XML shortcut that combines the start and end tags can be used. The XML in the previous example can be written as a single tag

```
<PayrollUpdates/>
```

which encapsulates the start tag and end tag in one tag. Note that the slash appears after the element name in this tag, as opposed to the end tag, where it displays before the element name.

The PayrollUpdates element in Figure 12-29 on the previous page encompasses all other elements in the file and contains four PayrollUpdate elements. Each PayrollUpdate element starts with a <PayrollUpdate> start tag and ends with a </PayrollUpdate> end tag. Each PayrollUpdate element includes five additional elements to store one employee's compensation update information, as outlined in the requirements document for the Compensation Update Processing application. The five additional elements in each PayrollUpdate are EmployeeID, EmployeeName, Location, ReviewDate, and HourlyRate or AnnualSalary.

As shown in Figure 12-29, an XML element can consist of a start tag, an element name, an attribute name, an attribute value, content, and an end tag. The following line illustrates all of these pieces of an XML element:

```
<elementname attributename = attributevalue>content</elementname>
```

The EmployeeID element is an example of an element that includes a start tag, an element name, an attribute name, an attribute value, content, and an end tag. The **content**, which is the data that the XML file contains, is located between the start and end tags. For example, the line

```
<Location>Southeast</Location>
```

indicates that the content of the Location element is Southeast. An XML element can have only one content value, but the content can be in a variety of data formats, including numbers and strings.

The EmployeeID, ReviewDate, HourlyRate, and AnnualSalary elements also include additional information about the elements in the start tags. This additional information contained in a start tag is an attribute. An **attribute** is used to provide more information about an element; an element can contain any number of attributes. The following element contains an attribute that describes the format of the element:

```
<HourlyRate format="currency">10.98</HourlyRate>
```

Attributes exist as name/value pairs separated by an equals sign. In the above example, the attributename is format and the attributevalue is currency.

The previous discussion defines the important aspects of XML files. XML files are versatile and include a number of other options in their structure.

XML File Objects and Creating and Opening an XML File

Figure 12-30 shows the code necessary to declare the CreateXMLFile() procedure and declare several objects necessary for the procedure. The **XmlTextWriter class** is similar to the StreamWriter class used to write the text files, but also contains additional methods and properties that make working with XML files much easier. You use the **XmlTextReader class** to read XML files, just as the StreamReader object is used to read text files.

The constructor for the XmlTextWriter class accepts the file name as the first parameter. Line 67 instantiates an XmlTextWriter object and then creates an empty file named CompensationUpdate.xml in the Chapter12 folder on the Data Disk.

```
60      Private Sub CreateXMLFile(ByVal dtmDateReviewed As Date)
61          Try
62              Dim objEmployees As New Employees(True, dtmDateReviewed)
63              Dim objHourlyEmployee As HourlyEmployee
64              Dim objSalariedEmployee As SalariedEmployee
65              Dim objXMLFile As XmlTextWriter
66
67              objXMLFile = New XmlTextWriter("A:\Chapter12\CompensationUpdate.xml", ↙
        Nothing)
68          Catch ex As Exception
69              Console.Write("An error occurred while getting employee records or creating↙
        the XML file.")
70              End
71          End Try
72      End Sub
```

FIGURE 12-30

The step on the next page adds the code shown in Figure 12-30 to create the CreateXMLFile() procedure. Several objects are declared, including the XmlTextWriter object used to write to an XML file.

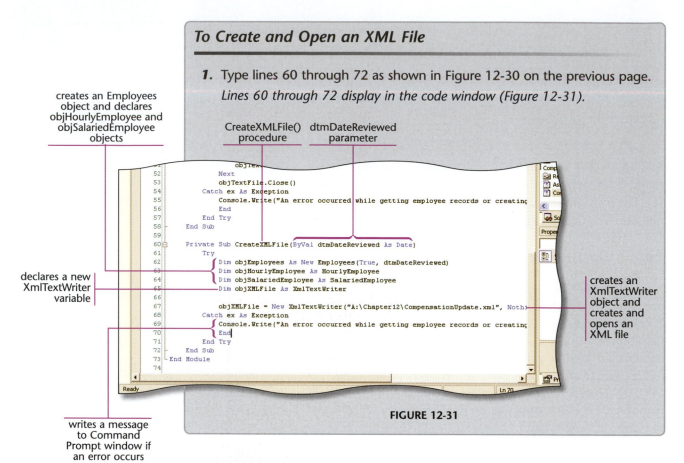

To Create and Open an XML File

1. Type lines 60 through 72 as shown in Figure 12-30 on the previous page. *Lines 60 through 72 display in the code window (Figure 12-31).*

creates an Employees object and declares objHourlyEmployee and objSalariedEmployee objects

CreateXMLFile() procedure

dtmDateReviewed parameter

declares a new XmlTextWriter variable

creates an XmlTextWriter object and creates and opens an XML file

writes a message to Command Prompt window if an error occurs

FIGURE 12-31

The code entered in the previous step declares the objects necessary for the procedure and creates and opens the CompensationUpdate.xml XML file. The code in the new CreateXMLFile() procedure is placed in a Try...Catch statement. If any errors occur while creating the Employees object (line 62) or creating the XML file (line 67), the Catch clause writes an error message to the Command Prompt window and then terminates execution of the program.

Formatting and Initializing an XML Object

Before writing XML elements to the XmlTextWriter object, the XmlTextWriter element should be initialized and the XML declaration, <?xml version="1.0"?>, should be added to the XML file. Figure 12-32 shows three formatting properties that are used to format the XML written by the XmlTextWriter object. Lines 68 through 70 set the Formatting, Indentation, and IndentChar properties of the XmlTextWriter object. The Formatting property is set to cause XML elements to be indented in the file. This property value makes the file easier to read because subsequent child elements are indented and the hierarchical nature of the XML file becomes apparent. The Indentation and IndentChar properties set the indentation to four space characters for each level of indentation.

```
68              objXMLFile.Formatting = Formatting.Indented
69              objXMLFile.Indentation = 4
70              objXMLFile.IndentChar = Convert.ToChar(" ")
71              objXMLFile.WriteStartDocument()
72              objXMLFile.WriteStartElement("PayrollUpdates")
```

FIGURE 12-32

The WriteStartDocument() method in line 71 writes the <?xml version="1.0"> line to the XML file to declare the XML file properly. Line 72 uses the **WriteStartElement() method** of the XmlTextWriter class to write the start tag of the PayrollUpdates element, which encapsulates all of the other data that will be written to the XML file. The WriteStartElement() method writes the string <PayrollUpdates> to the XML file on a new line after the XML declaration written by line 71. Later in this chapter, the code to write the end tag of the PayrollUpdates element will be written.

The following step adds the code shown in Figure 12-32 to the CreateXMLFile() procedure. The code sets properties for the XmlTextWriter object so that the object properly formats the XML in the XML file. The code then prepares the XML file for writing and creates the start tag for the first element of the XML file.

To Format and Initialize an XML Object

1. Type lines 68 through 72 as shown in Figure 12-32.

Lines 68 through 72 display in the code window (Figure 12-33). Lines 68 through 70 set properties of the XmlTextWriter object. Lines 71 and 72 use methods of the XmlTextWriter object to write the first two lines to the XML file.

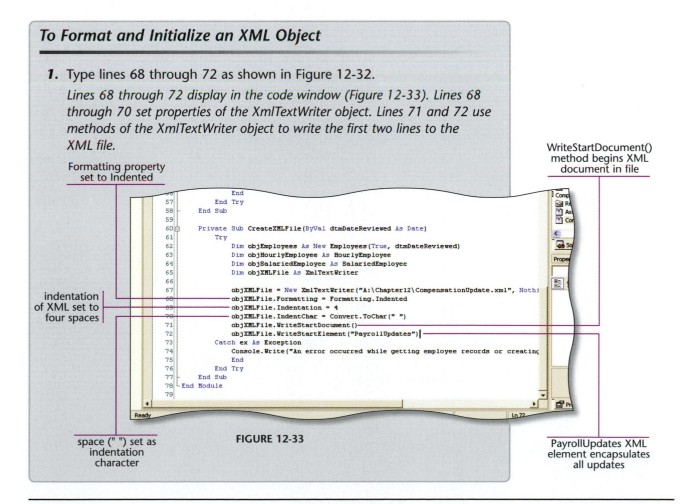

Formatting property set to Indented

WriteStartDocument() method begins XML document in file

indentation of XML set to four spaces

space (" ") set as indentation character

PayrollUpdates XML element encapsulates all updates

FIGURE 12-33

Figure 12-33 on the previous page shows the calls to the methods that format the XML. The calls to the methods used to format the XML should be made before any elements are written to the file.

XML Formatting Methods
The calls to the methods used to format the XML should be made before any elements are written to the file.

Writing an XML Element with an Attribute

As you have learned, an XML element can consist of a start tag, an element name, an attribute name, an attribute value, content, and an end tag, using the form

```
<elementname attributename = attributevalue>content</elementname>
```

Each part of an XML element can be written to the XML file separately, using methods of the XmlTextWriter class. The WriteStartElement() method writes the start tag and element name. The **WriteAttributeString() method** writes the attribute name and attribute value to the XML file. The **WriteString() method** writes the content for an element to an XML file. Finally, the **WriteEndElement() method** writes the end tag. The following code shows the method calls that write the XML shown above:

```
objXMLTextWriter.WriteStartElement("elementname")
objXMLTextWriter.WriteAttributeString("attributename", "attributevalue")
objXMLTextWriter.WriteString("content")
objXMLTextWriter.WriteEndElement()
```

The WriteEndElement() method does not require a parameter because the WriteEndElement() method always ends, or closes, the last unclosed element written to the file. That is, the method writes an end tag for the last element that has a start tag with no end tag.

Figure 12-34 shows the code necessary to start the For Each loop that reads through the HourlyEmployee objects in the objEmployees object. The code also starts writing the first PayrollUpdate element. Lines 75 through 78 use the methods described above to write the EmployeeID element to the XML file. The attribute named format, with a value of number, is written for the element.

```
73          For Each objHourlyEmployee In objEmployees.HourlyEmployeeList
74              objXMLFile.WriteStartElement("PayrollUpdate")
75              objXMLFile.WriteStartElement("EmployeeID")
76              objXMLFile.WriteAttributeString("format", "number")
77              objXMLFile.WriteString(Convert.ToString(objHourlyEmployee.EmployeeID))
78              objXMLFile.WriteEndElement()
79          Next
```

FIGURE 12-34

The following step adds the code shown in Figure 12-34 to the CreateXMLFile() procedure. The code begins a PayrollUpdate element in the XML file and then writes an EmployeeID start tag and value to the XML file, along with an attribute that designates the format or data type of the EmployeeID value as a number.

To Write an XML Element with an Attribute

1. Type lines 73 through 79 as shown in Figure 12-34.

Lines 73 through 79 display in the code window (Figure 12-35). The For Each loop executes once for each HourlyEmployee object in the objEmployees object.

starts a new XML element named PayrollUpdate for each HourlyEmployee

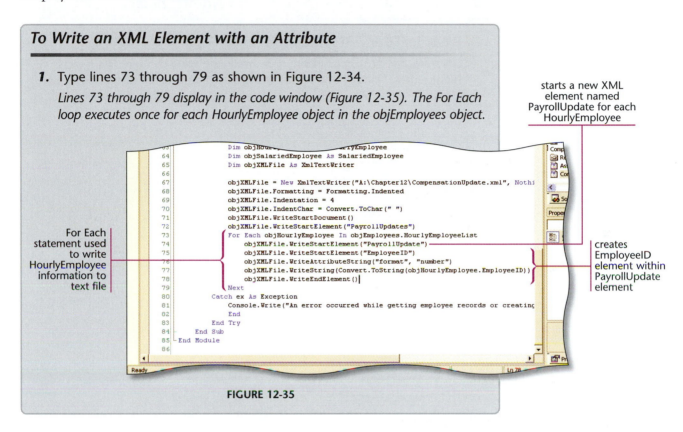

For Each statement used to write HourlyEmployee information to text file

creates EmployeeID element within PayrollUpdate element

FIGURE 12-35

The code entered in the previous step starts the PayrollUpdate element. After all five elements are written for an employee, the PayrollUpdate element will be closed. The code to close the PayrollUpdate element will be added later in this chapter.

Writing an XML Element with No Attributes

Often, an XML element contains only content, with no attributes. In this case, the **WriteElementString() method** can write the entire element and the content in one method call. The element name is sent as the first parameter to the WriteElementString() method, and the content is sent as the second parameter. Figure 12-36 shows two lines of code that use the WriteElementString() to write the EmployeeName and Location elements to the XML file.

```
80          objXMLFile.WriteElementString("EmployeeName", objHourlyEmployee.Name)
81          objXMLFile.WriteElementString("Location", objHourlyEmployee.Location)
```

FIGURE 12-36

The following step adds the code shown in Figure 12-36 on the previous page to the CreateXMLFile() procedure. The code writes the EmployeeName and Location elements and their values to the XML file.

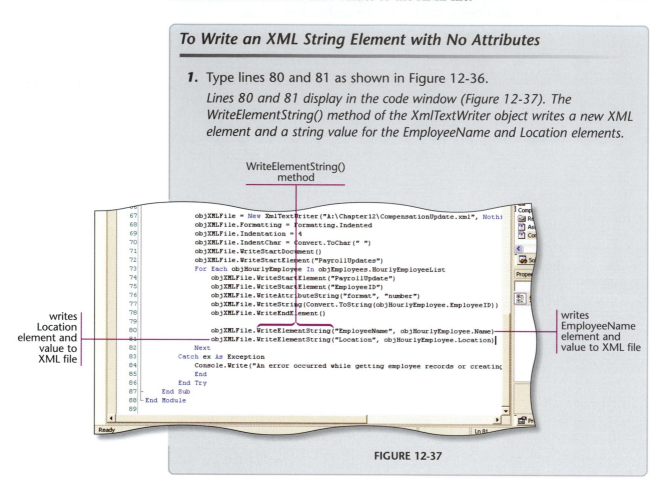

To Write an XML String Element with No Attributes

1. Type lines 80 and 81 as shown in Figure 12-36.

Lines 80 and 81 display in the code window (Figure 12-37). The WriteElementString() method of the XmlTextWriter object writes a new XML element and a string value for the EmployeeName and Location elements.

WriteElementString() method

```
67   objXMLFile = New XmlTextWriter("A:\Chapter12\CompensationUpdate.xml", Nothi
68   objXMLFile.Formatting = Formatting.Indented
69   objXMLFile.Indentation = 4
70   objXMLFile.IndentChar = Convert.ToChar(" ")
71   objXMLFile.WriteStartDocument()
72   objXMLFile.WriteStartElement("PayrollUpdates")
73   For Each objHourlyEmployee In objEmployees.HourlyEmployeeList
74       objXMLFile.WriteStartElement("PayrollUpdate")
75       objXMLFile.WriteStartElement("EmployeeID")
76       objXMLFile.WriteAttributeString("format", "number")
77       objXMLFile.WriteString(Convert.ToString(objHourlyEmployee.EmployeeID))
78       objXMLFile.WriteEndElement()
79
80       objXMLFile.WriteElementString("EmployeeName", objHourlyEmployee.Name)
81       objXMLFile.WriteElementString("Location", objHourlyEmployee.Location)
82   Next
83   Catch ex As Exception
84       Console.Write("An error occurred while getting employee records or creating
85   End
86   End Try
87   End Sub
88   End Module
89
```

writes Location element and value to XML file

writes EmployeeName element and value to XML file

Ready   Ln 81

FIGURE 12-37

The code in Figure 12-37 writes a start tag, content, and an end tag for both the EmployeeName and Location elements. For example, if an employee's location is South, then line 81 instructs the program to write the Location element in the file as

```
<Location>South</Location>
```

Writing the Final XML Elements for Hourly Employee Data

Figure 12-38 shows the code to write the last two XML elements for hourly employee records — ReviewDate and HourlyRate — to the XML file. The WriteStartElement() methods in lines 83 and 88 write the start tags for the elements. The WriteAttributeString() methods in lines 84 and 89 write the data types as attributes within the start tags of the elements. The WriteString() methods on lines 85 and 90 write the content of the elements, which are properties of the objHourlyEmployee object. The WriteEndElement() methods on lines 86 and 91 write the end tags for the ReviewDate and HourlyRate elements. Finally, line 92 writes the XML end tag for the PayrollUpdate element that was started on line 74.

```
83                    objXMLFile.WriteStartElement("ReviewDate")
84                    objXMLFile.WriteAttributeString("format", "date")
85                    objXMLFile.WriteString(Convert.ToString(objHourlyEmployee.DateReviewed↙
        ))
86                    objXMLFile.WriteEndElement()
87
88                    objXMLFile.WriteStartElement("HourlyRate")
89                    objXMLFile.WriteAttributeString("format", "currency")
90                    objXMLFile.WriteString(Convert.ToString(objHourlyEmployee.HourlyRate))
91                    objXMLFile.WriteEndElement()
92                    objXMLFile.WriteEndElement()
```

FIGURE 12-38

The following step adds the code shown in Figure 12-38 to the CreateXMLFile() procedure. The code writes the ReviewDate and HourlyRate elements and their values to the XML file. Finally, the code writes an end tag to close the PayrollUpdate element.

To Write the Final XML Elements for Hourly Employee Data

1. Type lines 83 through 92 as shown in Figure 12-38.

   Lines 83 through 92 display in the code window (Figure 12-39). The last two elements for an HourlyEmployee object are written to the XML file using the WriteStartElement(), WriteAttributeString(), WriteString(), and WriteEndElement() methods.

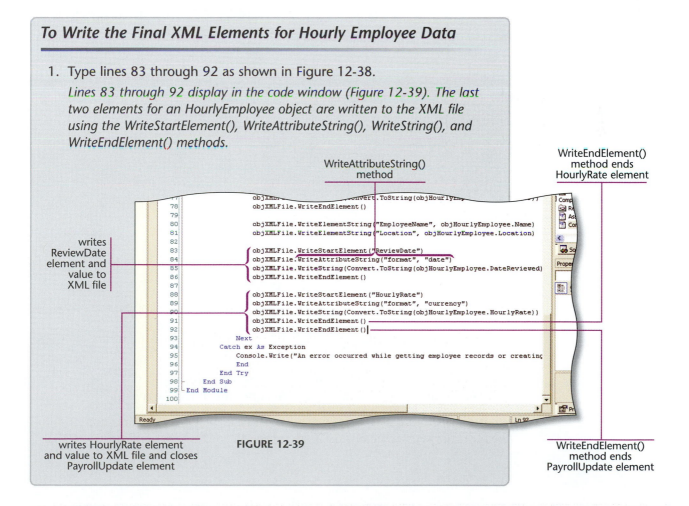

FIGURE 12-39

Code now has been written to write all five elements of information to the XML file for the HourlyEmployee objects in the objEmployees object. The next step is to write similar code for the SalariedEmployee objects.

Writing XML Elements for Salaried Employees Data and Closing the XmlTextWriter Object

Figure 12-40 shows the code that writes the SalariedEmployee information to the XML file. The code mirrors that written for the HourlyEmployee objects, with the exception of writing the AnnualSalary property to the XML file instead of the HourlyRate property. Finally, line 115 writes the end tag for the PayrollUpdates element, whose start tag was written before the first For Each statement. This closes the PayrollUpdates tag. Line 116 then closes the XmlTextWriter object so that no more data can be written to the XML file.

```
94              For Each objSalariedEmployee In objEmployees.SalariedEmployeeList
95                  objXMLFile.WriteStartElement("PayrollUpdate")
96                  objXMLFile.WriteStartElement("EmployeeID")
97                  objXMLFile.WriteAttributeString("format", "number")
98                  objXMLFile.WriteString(Convert.ToString(objSalariedEmployee.EmployeeID↙
    ))
99                  objXMLFile.WriteEndElement()
100
101                 objXMLFile.WriteElementString("EmployeeName", objSalariedEmployee.Name↙
    )
102                 objXMLFile.WriteElementString("Location", objSalariedEmployee.Location↙
    )
103
104                 objXMLFile.WriteStartElement("ReviewDate")
105                 objXMLFile.WriteAttributeString("format", "date")
106                 objXMLFile.WriteString(Convert.ToString(objSalariedEmployee.            ↙
    DateReviewed))
107                 objXMLFile.WriteEndElement()
108
109                 objXMLFile.WriteStartElement("AnnualSalary")
110                 objXMLFile.WriteAttributeString("format", "currency")
111                 objXMLFile.WriteString(Convert.ToString(objSalariedEmployee.            ↙
    AnnualSalary))
112                 objXMLFile.WriteEndElement()
113                 objXMLFile.WriteEndElement()
114             Next
115             objXMLFile.WriteEndElement()
116             objXMLFile.Close()
```

FIGURE 12-40

The following step adds the code shown in Figure 12-40 to the CreateXMLFile() procedure. The code writes SalariedEmployee object properties to the XML file in the same manner that HourlyEmployee object properties were written in the previous steps. After looping through the SalariedEmployee objects, the code then closes the initial PayrollUpdates element and then closes the XML file.

To Write Salaried Employee Data and Close the XmlTextWriter Object

1. Type lines 94 through 116 as shown in Figure 12-40.

Lines 94 through 116 display in the code window (Figure 12-41). The code writes SalariedEmployee properties, including the AnnualSalary property to the XML file. The Close() method of the XmlTextWriter object closes the file, so that no more data can be written to the file.

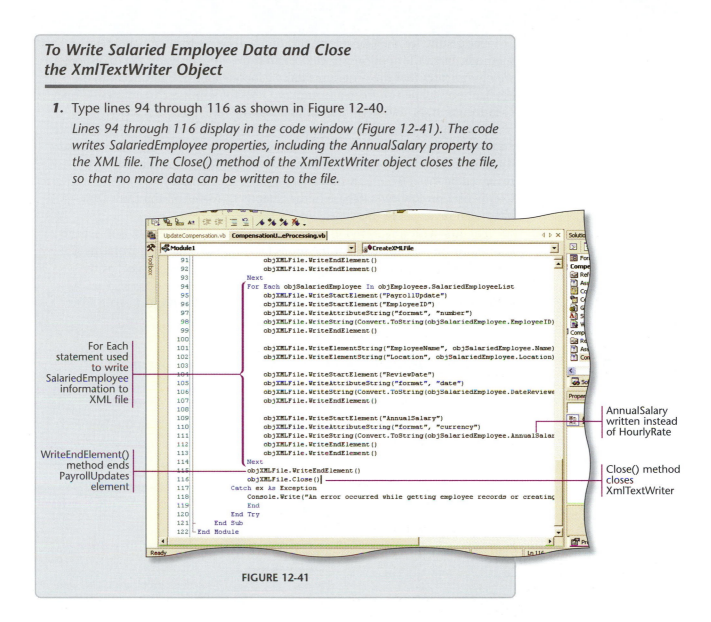

For Each statement used to write SalariedEmployee information to XML file

WriteEndElement() method ends PayrollUpdates element

AnnualSalary written instead of HourlyRate

Close() method closes XmlTextWriter

FIGURE 12-41

The coding phase for the Console application now is complete and the application can be tested.

Saving, Testing, and Documenting the Console Application

Because Console applications do not include a user interface, they require special considerations for testing the application. For example, if the application requires command-line arguments, the values of arguments must be known to the IDE when running the project from the IDE before the Start button is clicked. To do this, you must specify the command-line arguments in an option setting in the project's Property Pages.

The testing for the Console application will be performed using two methods. First, the application will be run from the IDE using the /x option, which indicates that the program should generate an XML file. Second, the application will be run from a Command Prompt window three times — once each for the /t, /c, and /r command-line arguments.

When testing the application, a date of 07/30/2005 will be used as the date argument that represents the employee's next review date. This date will ensure that the employees whose data is selected and written to the file have been reviewed between 07/30/2004 and 08/29/2004. Four employees in the Compensation Review database in the Chapter12 folder on the Data Disk have been reviewed in this timeframe.

The first action required to test the application from the IDE is to set the command-line arguments that the project should use when run from the IDE. The following steps set the CompensationUpdateProcessing project as the startup project for the Compensation Review solution. The steps also set command-line arguments that the project uses when the project is run from the IDE, rather than from a Command Prompt window.

To Set the Startup Project and Command-Line Arguments for Testing

1. Right-click the CompensationUpdateProcessing project in the Solution Explorer window.

The shortcut menu displays (Figure 12-42).

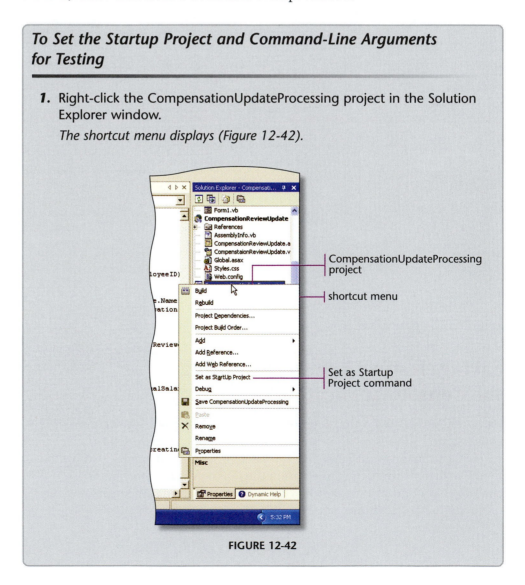

FIGURE 12-42

2. Click the Set as Startup Project command on the shortcut menu.

Visual Basic .NET sets the CompensationUpdateProcessing project as the startup project, and the project displays with a bold font in the Solution Explorer window.

3. Click the Property Pages button in the Properties window. When the CompensationUpdateProcessing Property Pages dialog box displays, click the Configuration Properties folder.

The CompensationUpdateProcessing Property Pages dialog box displays. When the Configuration Properties folder is selected, several Start Options, including command-line arguments, display in the dialog box (Figure 12-43).

CompensationUpdateProcessing
Property Pages dialog box

CompensationUpdateProcessing
project set as startup project

Configuration
Properties group

Command line
arguments box

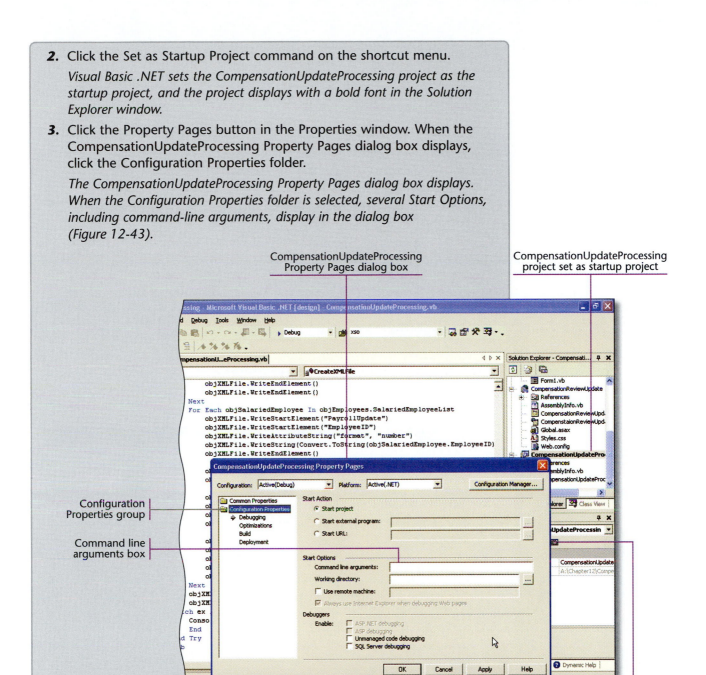

FIGURE 12-43

Property Pages
button

(continued)

4. Type /x 07/30/2005 in the Command line arguments box.

The command-line arguments display in the Command line arguments box (Figure 12-44). The command-line arguments specified here will be used for the Console application when the project is run from the IDE.

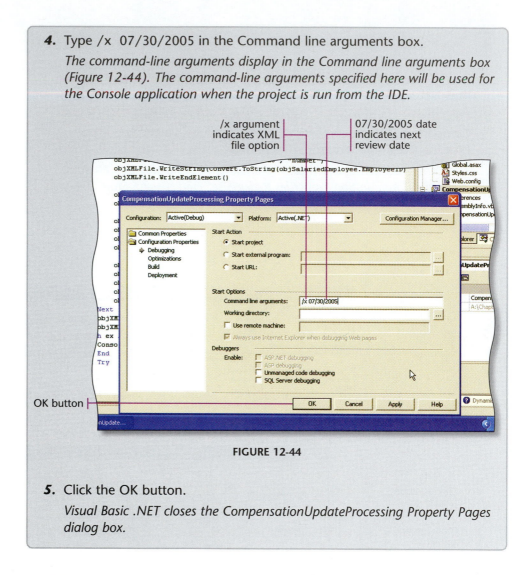

/x argument indicates XML file option

07/30/2005 date indicates next review date

OK button

FIGURE 12-44

5. Click the OK button.

Visual Basic .NET closes the CompensationUpdateProcessing Property Pages dialog box.

The previous steps prepare the project for testing within the IDE. When running a Console application from the IDE, you can use the debugging techniques described in Chapter 8.

Debugging Console Applications

When running a Console application from the IDE, you can use the debugging techniques described in Chapter 8. Before running the Console application, use the project's Property Pages to set command-line arguments, using the Command line arguments box in the Start Options area of the Configuration Properties folder.

The next step is to build and run the application. In order to test all of the command-line argument options for the program, the project first is tested in the IDE using the /x 07/30/2005 arguments. Next, a Command Prompt window is opened and the application is run from a command prompt three more times, using the following arguments:

```
/t 07/30/2005
/c 07/30/2005
/r
```

The /x 07/30/2005 arguments create an XML file in the Chapter12 folder of the Data Disk in drive A. The /t 07/30/2005 and /c 07/30/2005 arguments each create and write a text file (tab-delimited and comma-delimited, respectively) in the Chapter12 folder on the Data Disk. Finally, the /r option resets the Reviewed field in the Employee table to False, so that the employee can be reviewed again the following year.

The following steps build and save the project files for the CompensationUpdateProcessing project on the Data Disk in drive A and then run the application to test the project both from the IDE and from a Command Prompt window.

To Build, Save, and Test the Console Application

1. Right-click the CompensationUpdateProcessing project in the Solution Explorer. When the shortcut menu displays, click the Build command.

Visual Basic .NET automatically saves the class files, then opens the Output window and displays several messages while building the project (Figure 12-45). The result of the build is the CompensationUpdateProcessing.exe file in the A:\Chapter12\Compensation Review\CompensationUpdateProcessing folder on the Data Disk.

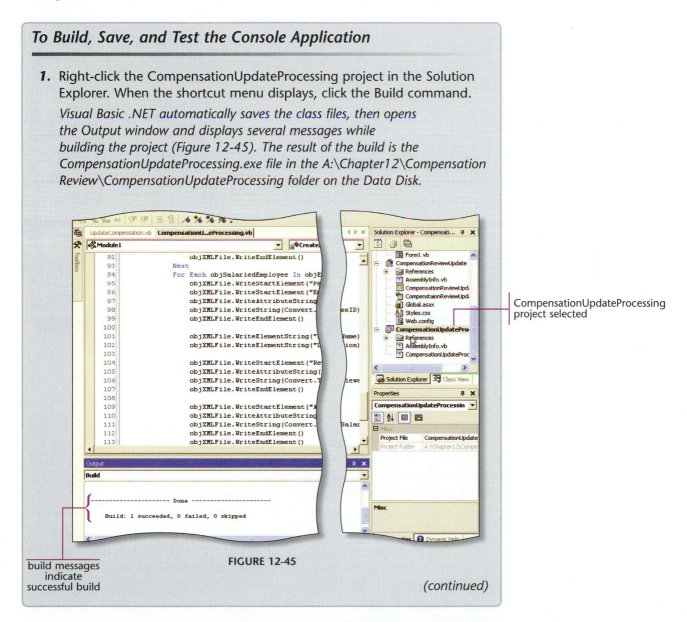

build messages indicate successful build

CompensationUpdateProcessing project selected

FIGURE 12-45

(continued)

2. Click the Start button on the Visual Basic .NET Standard toolbar.

Visual Basic .NET executes the CompensationUpdateProcessing Console application in a Command Prompt window, using the command-line arguments entered in the Property Pages. The window quickly displays and then disappears when the execution is complete. When the application finishes running, the last message in the Output window indicates the result of the application's execution. The result code of 0 indicates that the program did not generate a run-time error (Figure 12-46).

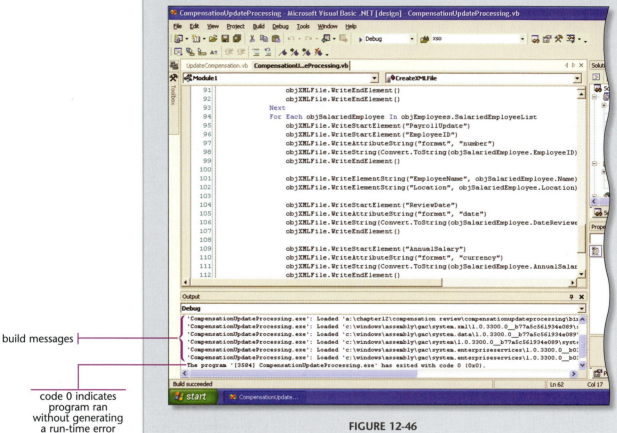

build messages

code 0 indicates program ran without generating a run-time error

FIGURE 12-46

3. Minimize the Visual Basic .NET window. Click the Command Prompt command on the Accessories menu of the Windows Start menu. When the Command Prompt window displays, type A: and press the ENTER key. Type cd\Chapter12\Compensation Review\ CompensationUpdateProcessing\bin to change the current folder to the location of the executable file for the CompensationUpdateProcessing application.

A Command Prompt window opens, and the command prompt indicates the current folder name.

4. Type CompensationUpdateProcessing /t 07/30/2005 and press the ENTER key. Using the Windows Notepad application, open the file, A:\Chapter12\CompensationUpdate.txt, on the Data Disk.

The application executes after the ENTER key is pressed. The resulting text file displays in the Notepad application (Figure 12-47).

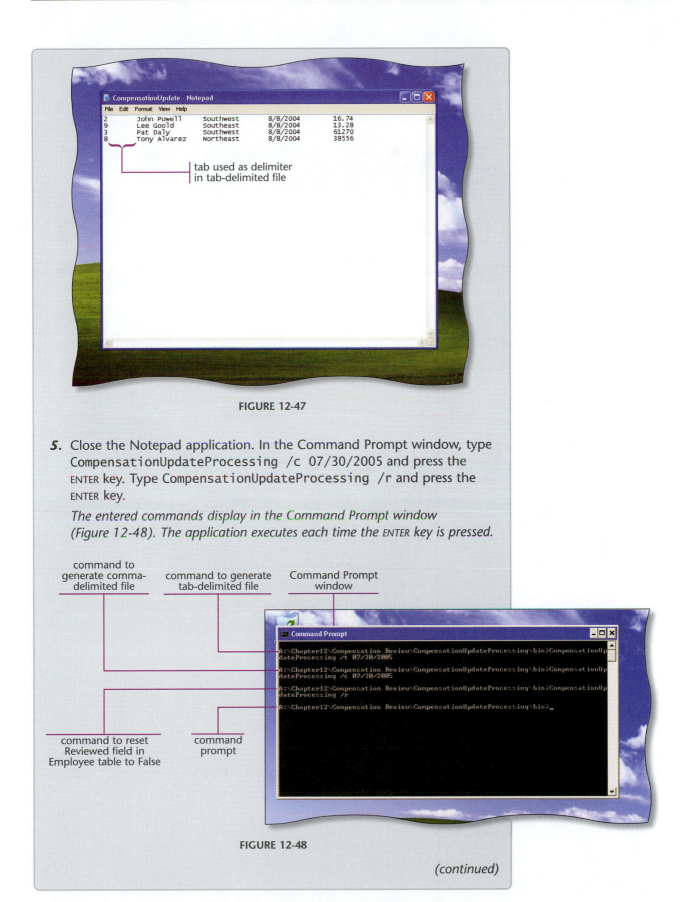

FIGURE 12-47

5. Close the Notepad application. In the Command Prompt window, type CompensationUpdateProcessing /c 07/30/2005 and press the ENTER key. Type CompensationUpdateProcessing /r and press the ENTER key.

The entered commands display in the Command Prompt window (Figure 12-48). The application executes each time the ENTER key is pressed.

command to generate comma-delimited file

command to generate tab-delimited file

Command Prompt window

command to reset Reviewed field in Employee table to False

command prompt

FIGURE 12-48

(continued)

6. Using the Windows Notepad application, open the file, A:\Chapter12\CompensationUpdate.txt, on the Data Disk.

The CompensationUpdate.txt file now includes the comma-delimited version of the output data (Figure 12-49).

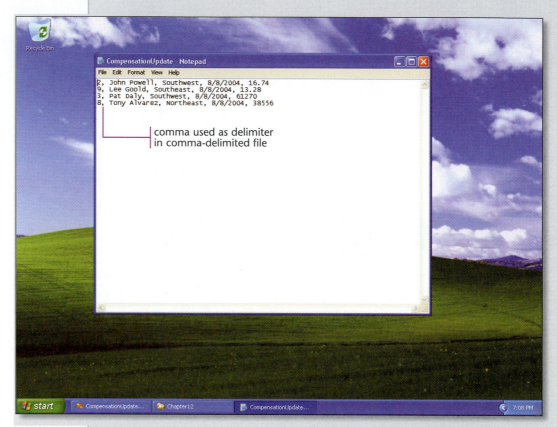

FIGURE 12-49

7. Close the Notepad application. In the Command Prompt window, type CompensationUpdateProcessing/x 07/30/2005 and press the ENTER key.

8. Using the Open command on the File menu of the Notepad application, open the file, A:\Chapter12\CompensationUpdate.xml, on the Data Disk.

The CompensationUpdate.xml file displays in the Notepad application (Figure 12-50).

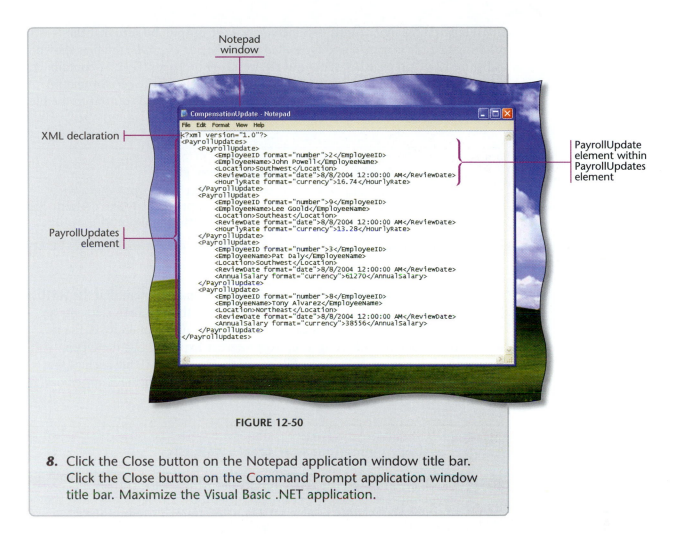

FIGURE 12-50

8. Click the Close button on the Notepad application window title bar. Click the Close button on the Command Prompt application window title bar. Maximize the Visual Basic .NET application.

The steps above test all four command-line switches for the Console application. When testing Console applications, test all possible combinations of command-line arguments.

Testing Console Applications

When testing Console applications, test all possible combinations of command-line arguments.

When testing applications that include text file output, be sure that the resulting text file is named and formatted properly. For example, the files shown in Figure 12-47 on page VB 12.51 and Figure 12-49 on page VB 12.52 contain identical data, but the files are formatted differently. Also make certain that no extraneous information is written to the files and that the fields output to the file are not truncated.

Testing Applications that Create Text Files

When testing applications that include text file output, be sure that the text file is named and formatted properly. Make certain that no extraneous information is written to the files and that the fields output to the file are not truncated.

When testing applications that create XML files, make certain that the XML is formatted properly and is valid XML. Make certain that all XML elements are closed properly. One method you can use to test the validity of an XML file is to attempt to open the file using Microsoft Internet Explorer. Use the Open command on the Internet Explorer File menu to open an XML file such as that created in the previous set of steps. Internet Explorer will indicate if any errors exist in the formatting of the XML file.

Testing Applications that Create XML Files

When testing applications that create XML, make certain that the XML is formatted properly and is valid XML. Make certain that elements are closed properly. One method you can use to test the format and validity of an XML file is to attempt to open the file using Microsoft Internet Explorer.

The testing process for the Console application is complete. The final step of the development cycle is to document the application. The following step documents the application. Line numbers are printed on the code listing.

To Document the Console Application

1. Follow the steps on page VB 2.40 of Chapter 2 to use the Print command on the File menu to print a record of the code for the Console application.

A record of the Console application code is printed (Figure 12-51).

```
C:\Shared\JeffWork\VB .NET\...\CompensationUpdateProcessing.vb                    1
1 Option Strict On
2 Imports Compensation_Review
3 Imports System.IO
4 Imports System.Xml
5 Module Module1
6     Sub Main()
7         If Environment.GetCommandLineArgs.Length <> 2 And Environment.       ↙
   GetCommandLineArgs.Length <> 3 Then
8             Console.WriteLine("This command requires the /t, /c, /x, or /r switch. A  ↙
   date is required next to the /t, /c, or /x switch. Such as,                ↙
   CompensationUpdateProcessing /x 08/03/2004.")
9             End
10        End If
11        Select Case UCase(Environment.GetCommandLineArgs(1))
12            Case "/T"
13                CreateTextFile("Tab", Convert.ToDateTime(Environment.        ↙
   GetCommandLineArgs(2)))
14            Case "/C"
15                CreateTextFile("Comma", Convert.ToDateTime(Environment.      ↙
   GetCommandLineArgs(2)))
16            Case "/X"
17                CreateXMLFile(Convert.ToDateTime(Environment.GetCommandLineArgs(2)))
18            Case "/R"
19                UpdateReviewedStatus()
20        End Select
21    End Sub
22
23    Private Sub CreateTextFile(ByVal strFileType As String, ByVal dtmDateReviewed As  ↙
   Date)
24        Try
25            Dim objEmployees As New Employees(True, dtmDateReviewed)
26            Dim objHourlyEmployee As HourlyEmployee
27            Dim objSalariedEmployee As SalariedEmployee
28            Dim objTextFile As IO.StreamWriter = New IO.StreamWriter("A:\Chapter12\  ↙
   CompensationUpdate.txt")
29            Dim strFieldSeparator As String
30
31            If strFileType = "Tab" Then
32                strFieldSeparator = ControlChars.Tab
33            Else
34                strFieldSeparator = ", "
35            End If
36
37            For Each objHourlyEmployee In objEmployees.HourlyEmployeeList
38                objTextFile.Write(objHourlyEmployee.EmployeeID & strFieldSeparator)
39                objTextFile.Write(objHourlyEmployee.Name & strFieldSeparator)
40                objTextFile.Write(objHourlyEmployee.Location & strFieldSeparator)
41                objTextFile.Write(objHourlyEmployee.DateReviewed & strFieldSeparator)
42                objTextFile.Write(objHourlyEmployee.HourlyRate)
43                objTextFile.WriteLine()
44            Next
45            For Each objSalariedEmployee In objEmployees.SalariedEmployeeList
46                objTextFile.Write(objSalariedEmployee.EmployeeID & strFieldSeparator)
47                objTextFile.Write(objSalariedEmployee.Name & strFieldSeparator)
48                objTextFile.Write(objSalariedEmployee.Location & strFieldSeparator)
49                objTextFile.Write(objSalariedEmployee.DateReviewed & strFieldSeparator↙
   )
50                objTextFile.Write(objSalariedEmployee.AnnualSalary)
51                objTextFile.WriteLine()
52            Next
53            objTextFile.Close()
54        Catch ex As Exception
55            Console.Write("An error occurred while getting employee records or        ↙
   creating the text file.")
56            End
57        End Try
58    End Sub
```

(a)

FIGURE 12-51

(continued)

C:\Shared\JeffWork\VB .NET\...\CompensationUpdateProcessing.vb   3

```
        creating the XML file.")
119            End
120        End Try
121    End Sub
122 End Module
123
```

C:\Shared\JeffWork\VB .NET\...\CompensationUpdateProcessing.vb   2

```
59
60    Private Sub CreateXMLFile(ByVal dtmDateReviewed As Date)
61      Try
62        Dim objEmployees As New Employees(True, dtmDateReviewed)
63        Dim objHourlyEmployee As HourlyEmployee
64        Dim objSalariedEmployee As SalariedEmployee
65        Dim objXMLFile As XmlTextWriter
66
67        objXMLFile = New XmlTextWriter("A:\Chapter12\CompensationUpdate.xml",  ↙
Nothing)
68        objXMLFile.Formatting = Formatting.Indented
69        objXMLFile.Indentation = 4
70        objXMLFile.IndentChar = Convert.ToChar(" ")
71        objXMLFile.WriteStartDocument()
72        objXMLFile.WriteStartElement("PayrollUpdates")
73        For Each objHourlyEmployee In objEmployees.HourlyEmployeeList
74            objXMLFile.WriteStartElement("PayrollUpdate")
75            objXMLFile.WriteStartElement("EmployeeID")
76            objXMLFile.WriteAttributeString("format", "number")
77            objXMLFile.WriteString(Convert.ToString(objHourlyEmployee.EmployeeID))
78            objXMLFile.WriteEndElement()
79
80            objXMLFile.WriteElementString("EmployeeName", objHourlyEmployee.Name)
81            objXMLFile.WriteElementString("Location", objHourlyEmployee.Location)
82
83            objXMLFile.WriteStartElement("ReviewDate")
84            objXMLFile.WriteAttributeString("format", "date")
85            objXMLFile.WriteString(Convert.ToString(objHourlyEmployee.DateReviewed↙
))
86            objXMLFile.WriteEndElement()
87
88            objXMLFile.WriteStartElement("HourlyRate")
89            objXMLFile.WriteAttributeString("format", "currency")
90            objXMLFile.WriteString(Convert.ToString(objHourlyEmployee.HourlyRate))
91            objXMLFile.WriteEndElement()
92            objXMLFile.WriteEndElement()
93        Next
94        For Each objSalariedEmployee In objEmployees.SalariedEmployeeList
95            objXMLFile.WriteStartElement("PayrollUpdate")
96            objXMLFile.WriteStartElement("EmployeeID")
97            objXMLFile.WriteAttributeString("format", "number")
98            objXMLFile.WriteString(Convert.ToString(objSalariedEmployee.EmployeeID↙
))
99            objXMLFile.WriteEndElement()
100
101            objXMLFile.WriteElementString("EmployeeName", objSalariedEmployee.Name↙
)
102            objXMLFile.WriteElementString("Location", objSalariedEmployee.Location↙
)
103
104            objXMLFile.WriteStartElement("ReviewDate")
105            objXMLFile.WriteAttributeString("format", "date")
106            objXMLFile.WriteString(Convert.ToString(objSalariedEmployee.          ↙
DateReviewed))
107            objXMLFile.WriteEndElement()
108
109            objXMLFile.WriteStartElement("AnnualSalary")
110            objXMLFile.WriteAttributeString("format", "currency")
111            objXMLFile.WriteString(Convert.ToString(objSalariedEmployee.          ↙
AnnualSalary))
112            objXMLFile.WriteEndElement()
113            objXMLFile.WriteEndElement()
114        Next
115        objXMLFile.WriteEndElement()
116        objXMLFile.Close()
117      Catch ex As Exception
118        Console.Write("An error occurred while getting employee records or
```

(c)

(b)

FIGURE 12-51 (continued)

The development phase for the Console application now is complete. The output files generated by the Console application and stored on the Data Disk can be used by the CompensationUpdateService Web service.

The previous steps left the solution and project open in the IDE because the CompensationUpdateService Web service still must be added to the Compensation Review solution.

Creating a Web Service

As you learned in Chapter 1, a Web service runs on a Web server and includes a collection of functions and procedures that are available for use by other programmers over the intranet or an intranet. Like classes, Web services do not include a user interface.

Visual Basic .NET requires the same environment to run Web services that it required to run the Web application developed in Chapter 11. That is, a special version of the CLR must be running as a part of IIS in order to execute Web services. ASP.NET is the technology that runs as an add-on to IIS to allow IIS to execute Web services that have been built using Visual Basic .NET. Web services can be developed in a multitude of programming languages, including Visual Basic .NET, Java, and C#, on almost any operating system that runs a Web server. For this reason, Web services have gained in popularity as a tool for allowing disparate systems to interact over the Internet. Rather than running or developing specific software functionality in-house, programmers and companies can take advantage of Web services already developed by others.

All Web services interact using XML. A client program sends a request to the Web service in XML, and then the Web service sends a response, sometimes including return values, in XML. If you are developing or using Web services in Visual Basic .NET, ASP.NET and Visual Basic .NET handle much of the work in processing the XML. Other languages often require that you translate a call to the Web service to XML, and then translate the return value from XML to data that your program can understand. Visual Basic .NET abstracts much of the XML work and presents an XML Web service function or procedure just like any other function or procedure you have worked with in this book. The XML processing is all done behind the scenes by the CLR.

> **Tip**
>
> **Developing Web Services**
> Develop a Web service as a solution to a problem when other programmers require interaction with a particular piece of functionality, such as a function or procedure, over the Internet or an intranet.

An **ASP.NET Web service** is a Web service created in Visual Basic .NET that uses ASP.NET technology to provide functions and procedures over the Web. A Web service created using Visual Basic .NET is saved as an **.asmx file**, with a file extension of .asmx. A Web service that is named GetEmployee thus will have a file name of GetEmployee.asmx. Visual Basic .NET requires that all Web services, including ASP.NET Web services, be created on a Web server. Because a Web server can run only on a computer's hard drive, Web service projects cannot run from the Data Disk in drive A.

Creating Web Services

Because a Web server can run only on a computer's hard drive, Web service projects cannot run from drive A.

Figure 12-52 shows the components of the Web server and client program required to make a request to a Web service that was created using Visual Basic .NET. The IIS Web server accepts and processes the request from the client program on the client computer and sends it to the ASP.NET Web service. Based on the request that the ASP.NET Web service receives from the client program, the ASP.NET Web service and IIS determine what response to send back to the client program. The response always is sent back in XML format, which the client program must interpret.

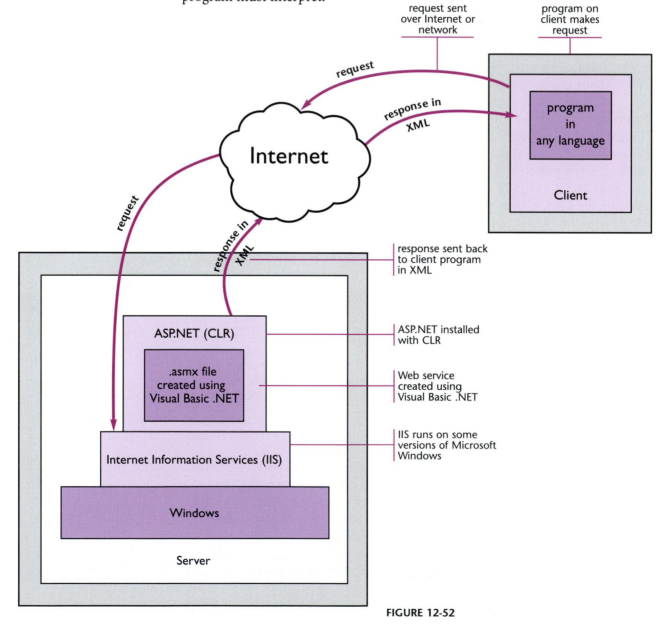

FIGURE 12-52

Starting a New ASP.NET Web Service Project

The Compensation Update Service Web service includes one function that returns a string value. As you have learned, a Web service does not include a user interface. When Visual Basic .NET creates a new Web service project, an empty code module thus is added to the project. ASP.NET Web service modules have the extension of .asmx.vb.

The following steps add a new ASP.NET Web service project to the Compensation Review solution, using the **ASP.NET Web Service template**. The new project is named CompensationUpdateService and is created on the current computer's Web server.

> **Note**
>
> If you plan on completing the project in this chapter, you must have access to an Internet Information Services (IIS) Server that has been configured with ASP.NET. The steps in this chapter assume that IIS has been configured on the same computer on which Visual Basic .NET is installed and that the InetPub folder is located at C:\InetPub. If necessary, see your instructor for assistance in setting up IIS.

To Start a New ASP.NET Web Service Project

1. Right-click the Compensation Review solution in the Solution Explorer window. When the shortcut menu displays, click the Add command. When the Add submenu displays, click the New Project command.

2. When the Add New Project dialog box displays, click the ASP.NET Web Service icon in the Templates area. Select the text, WebApplication1, in the Location text box. Type `CompensationUpdateService` in the Location box.

The ASP.NET Web Service template is selected in the Templates area. The project location changes to a Web page URL (Figure 12-53). The URL includes the server name of localhost, which indicates that the Web server is located on the current computer. The new name of the Web service project displays in the Location box.

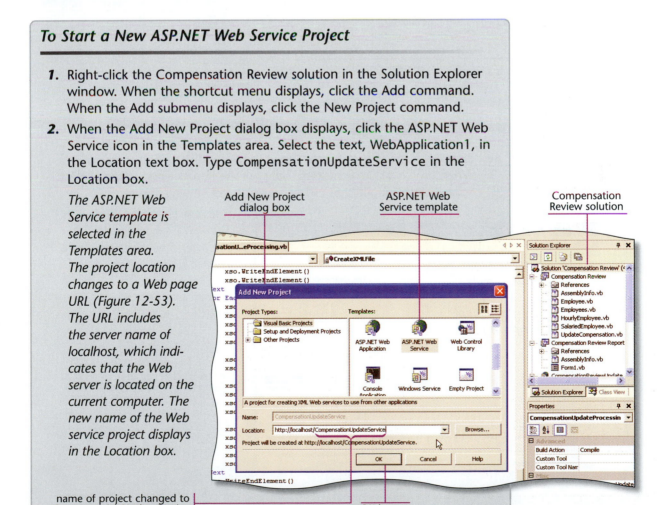

name of project changed to CompensationUpdateService

FIGURE 12-53

(continued)

3. Click the OK button.

Visual Basic .NET communicates with Microsoft Internet Information Services to create the new Web service project on the Web server. The Create New Web message box displays while Visual Basic .NET creates the project. After the project is created, Visual Basic .NET opens the Service1.asmx.vb module in the code window (Figure 12-54). Visual Basic .NET also adds several other files to the new project, as shown in the Solution Explorer window.

Service1.asmx.vb module opened in code window   CompensationUpdateService .vsdisco file   CompensationUpdateService project

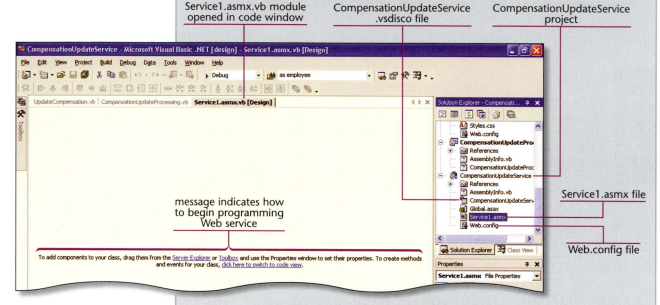

message indicates how to begin programming Web service

Service1.asmx file

Web.config file

FIGURE 12-54

4. Right-click the Service1.asmx file in the Solution Explorer window. When the shortcut menu displays, click the Rename command. Enter CompensationUpdateService.asmx as the new file name.

The new file name displays in the Solution Explorer window and in the tab in the main work area (Figure 12-55).

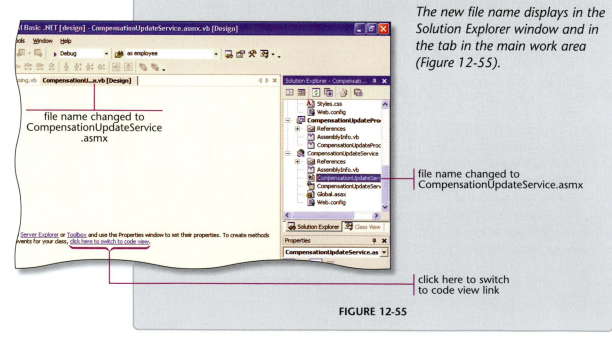

file name changed to CompensationUpdateService .asmx

file name changed to CompensationUpdateService.asmx

click here to switch to code view link

FIGURE 12-55

5. Click the click here to switch to code view link in the main work area.

Visual Basic .NET opens the code window for the CompensationUpdateService module (Figure 12-56). Several lines of code already exist in the module. Visual Basic .NET provides a function template for creating a function in the Web service that can be accessed by other programmers.

CompensationUpdateService.asmx.vb opened in code window

code automatically inserted by Visual Basic .NET

comments and function template automatically added by Visual Basic .NET

End Class keyword automatically added by Visual Basic .NET

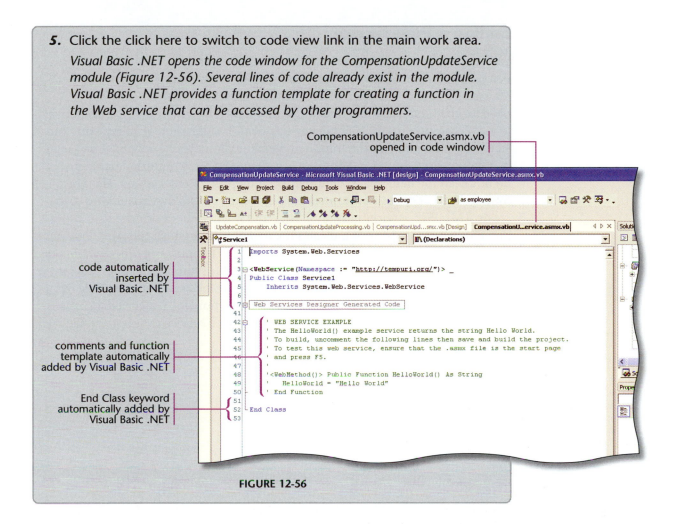

FIGURE 12-56

Each XML Web service needs a unique namespace in order for applications that are using the Web service to distinguish it from other services on the Web. By default, ASP.Net Web services use the namespace, http://tempuri.org/, for this purpose. Visual Basic .NET thus automatically adds this namespace in line 3 of the code shown in Figure 12-56. While the namespace, http://tempuri.org/, is appropriate to use during development, the final Web service should be identified by a namespace that you control. For example, you can use your school or company's Internet domain name as part of the namespace. Also note that although namespaces look like URLs, they do not have to point to actual Web sites or other resources.

After Visual Basic .NET creates the new project, the solution and project names, CompensationUpdateService, display in the Solution Explorer window. The module, Service1.asmx, is renamed CompensationUpdateService.asmx. Figure 12-54 shows the module in the main work area. While you can add components to the module, as shown in Figure 12-54, you cannot add user interface components, such as TextBox controls, because Web services do not include a user interface.

Coding a Web Service

Figure 12-57 shows the code for the beginning of the CompensationUpdateService.asmx.vb module. The Option Strict On statement and an Imports statement are shown as the first four lines of code for the module. As previously discussed, the Option Strict On statement is used to ensure that all assignment statements use the same data type on both sides of the assignment; the Imports statement allows you to reference elements in a namespace without qualification, so elements in the imported namespace do not need the namespace identifier when they are referenced in code. The **System.Web.Services namespace** consists of the classes that enable you to create XML Web services using ASP.NET and XML Web service clients. As previously discussed, line 4 indicates the namespace in which the Web service exists — in this case, the default namespace http://tempuri.org. The line of code is written as XML, which is denoted by the < and > symbols on either side of the statement. Line 5 of the code changes the name of the class in the module from Service1 to the more descriptive name, CompensationUpdateService. Using a descriptive name helps programmers using the Web service to recognize the purpose of the module more easily.

```
1 Option Strict On
2 Imports System.Web.Services
3 Imports System.Xml
4 <WebService(Namespace:="http://tempuri.org/")> _
5 Public Class CompensationUpdateService
```

FIGURE 12-57

Tip

Naming Classes in Web Services
When coding a Web service, change the names of classes in the modules from the default names to more descriptive names. Using a descriptive name helps programmers using the Web service to recognize the purpose of the module more easily.

The following step adds the first three lines of code shown in Figure 12-57 to the CompensationUpdateService.asmx.vb module and changes line 5 of the module.

To Start Coding a Web Service

1. Type lines 1 through 3 as shown in Figure 12-57. Modify line 5 as shown in Figure 12-57.

Lines 1 through 5 display as shown in Figure 12-58. The Imports statements import two namespaces for objects that will be used to code the module. The Compensation_Review namespace is not imported, because the classes in the class library are not needed in this Web service.

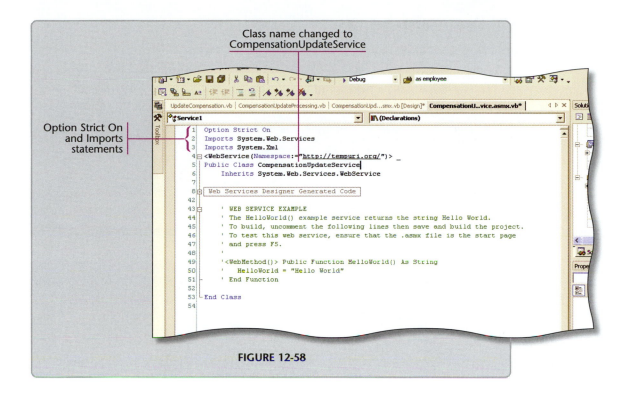

FIGURE 12-58

Declaring a Function in a Web Service

The next step is to declare a function in the Web service. As defined in the requirements document in Figure 12-2 on page VB 12.06, the Web service must read the XML file created by the Console application and then return the XML to the client program as a string value. Just as with any other function, this function must be declared within the Web service code module. Figure 12-59 shows the code necessary to declare the GetCompensationUpdate() function that returns a string value.

```
43    <WebMethod()> Public Function GetCompensationUpdate() As String
44
45    End Function
```

FIGURE 12-59

Line 43 shows a special XML element that must precede all function declarations that are to be made available as Web service functions or procedures. The **<WebMethod()> directive** tells Visual Basic .NET that the function is to be made available to outside users of the Web service.

The step on the next page replaces the comments in line 43 through 51 (which were generated automatically when the Web service was created initially) with the code shown in Figure 12-59. The code declares a function as a Web method with a data type of String.

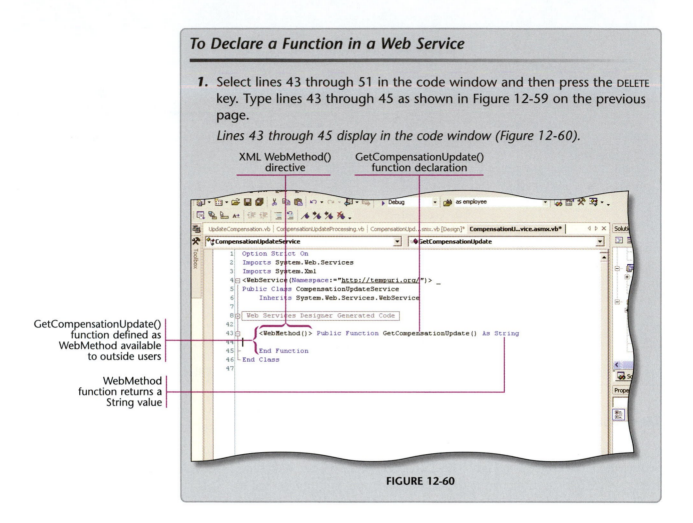

To Declare a Function in a Web Service

1. Select lines 43 through 51 in the code window and then press the DELETE key. Type lines 43 through 45 as shown in Figure 12-59 on the previous page.

Lines 43 through 45 display in the code window (Figure 12-60).

FIGURE 12-60

The commented code in the module is deleted and replaced by the declaration for the GetCompensationUpdate() function, as shown in Figure 12-60. The <WebMethod()> directive indicates to Visual Basic .NET that the function should be accessible as a Web service.

With the function declared, the next step is to write the code that reads the XML file and then returns the XML to the client program as a string value.

Working with an XML Document

The file that must be returned to the client program is an XML document. Visual Basic .NET provides a robust set of classes in the .NET Framework class library for working with XML files.

The **XmlDocument object** is a powerful object that can be used to process XML files and documents. The XmlDocument object provides a Load() method that reads an XML document from disk into memory. Figure 12-61 shows the code for the GetCompensationUpdate() function. Line 44 declares the objCompensationUpdateXML variable as an XmlDocument. The Load() method in line 48 reads the CompensationUpdate.xml file from disk into the objCompensationUpdateXML object. Once the document is loaded, operations can be performed on the XML document using a variety of methods and properties of the XmlDocument class.

```
44          Dim objCompensationUpdateXML As New XmlDocument()
45          Dim strResult As String
46
47          Try
48              objCompensationUpdateXML.Load("A:\Chapter12\CompensationUpdate.xml")
49              strResult = objCompensationUpdateXML.LastChild.InnerXml
50          Catch ex As Exception
51              strResult = "The following error occurred while processing your request"
52              strResult &= ex.InnerException.ToString()
53          End Try
54
55          Return strResult
```

FIGURE 12-61

Line 49 uses the InnerXml property of the LastChild property of the XmlDocument class to access the XML in the XML document that must be returned to the calling program. The **LastChild property** indicates the last XML element in the document. In the case of the CompensationUpdate.xml file, this indicates all XML in the <PayrollUpdates> element (Figure 12-62). In other words, the <?xml version ="1.0"?> element is excluded, because this element does not need to be returned to the user. The **InnerXML property** indicates all of the XML from the LastChild property should be returned. The XML extracted from the CompensationUpdate.xml file in the objCompensationUpdateXML object then is assigned to the strResult variable. This variable is returned as the result of the GetCompensationUpdate() function.

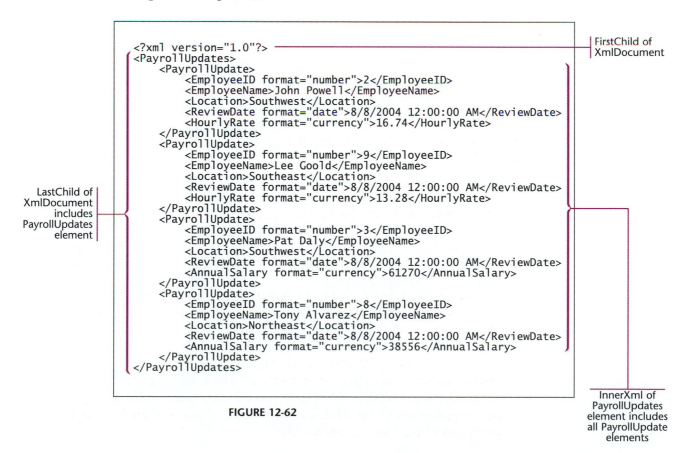

FIGURE 12-62

The following step adds the code shown in Figure 12-61 on the previous page to the GetCompensationUpdate() function. The code loads an XML document from the Data Disk and sends the XML as the return value of the function.

To Read and Process an XML Document

1. Type lines 44 through 55 as shown in Figure 12-61.

Lines 44 through 55 display in the code window (Figure 12-63).

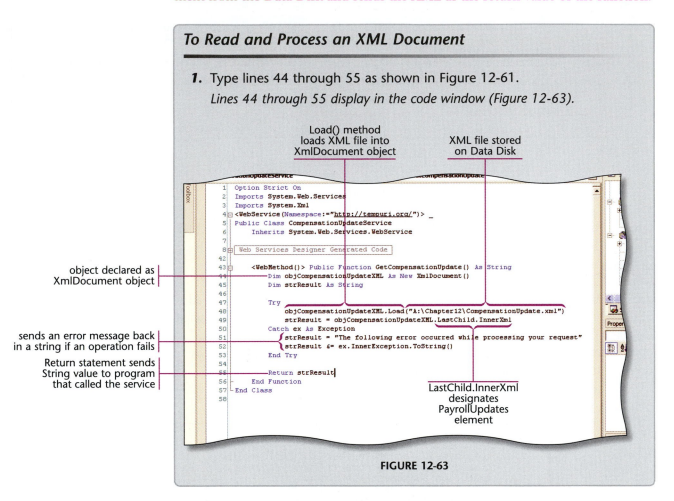

FIGURE 12-63

As shown in Figure 12-63, a Try…Catch statement encapsulates the major functionality of the code, from lines 44 to 53. The Load() method of the XmlDocument object loads the XML file created by the Console application. The LastChild.InnerXML property of the XmlDocument object then is returned by the function.

If the program encounters an error while reading the XML file, then the client program receives a string informing the user of the error. Errors may include the file not existing or an error in the formatting of the XML in the CompensationUpdate.xml file.

The coding phase for the Web service now is complete, and the application can be tested.

Saving, Testing, and Documenting the Web Service

You typically develop Web services for use by other programmers. When testing a Web service, you must use another program to initiate the call to the Web service, much in the same way that you used a unit test application to test the Compensation Review class library in Chapter 9. Visual Basic .NET provides a basic unit test program that you can use for testing Web services that you develop in Visual Basic .NET. The unit test program allows you to use the Visual Basic .NET debugging tools to debug Web service applications.

In order to use the Web services test program, you simply run the Web service in the IDE. Visual Basic .NET opens the Web service unit test program Web page in Microsoft Internet Explorer. The Web page allows you to execute Web services, and, if necessary, enter any parameters that the Web service requires. Finally, the unit test page displays the results of the Web service after the service executes.

The Web services test Web page also provides some valuable information about the Web service. For example, the Web page indicates how another programmer should formulate a call to the Web service, and provides information about the format of the data returned by the Web service.

The following steps save the code module and project files for the CompensationUpdateProcessing Web service on the Web server and then run and test the Web service.

To Save and Test the Web Service

1. Click the Save All button on the Standard toolbar. Right-click the CompensationUpdateProcessing project in the Solution Explorer window. When the shortcut menu displays, click the Set as Startup Project command.

The asterisks next to CompensationUpdateProcessing.asmx in the window title bar and the main work area tab no longer display, indicating that the project has been saved. Because the project initially was created and saved to the C:\InetPub\wwwroot folder, Visual Basic .NET automatically saves the project to that same folder.

(continued)

2. Click the Start button on the Visual Basic .NET Standard toolbar.

Visual Basic .NET opens the Output window temporarily and displays messages as the application starts. The Web service test Web page opens in Microsoft Internet Explorer. The test Web page displays the name of the application at the top of the page and includes a link that initiates execution of the GetCompensationUpdate() function in the Web service. The Web page also lists helpful informational instructions regarding the Web service (Figure 12-64).

Microsoft Internet Explorer window   URL of Web service

GetCompensationUpdate link for GetCompensationUpdate() function

instructions for changing the Web service namespace

example of new namespace in C# language

example of new namespace in Visual Basic language

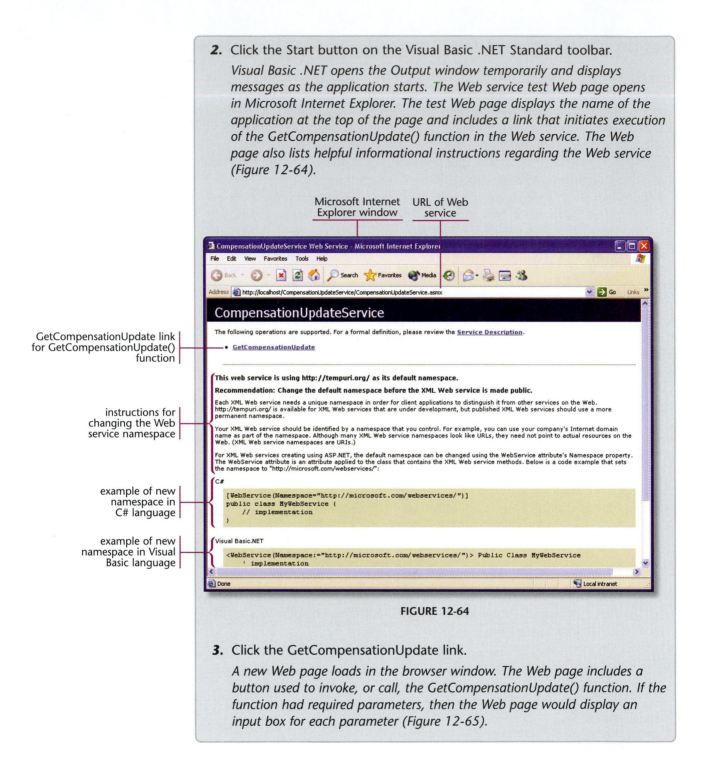

FIGURE 12-64

3. Click the GetCompensationUpdate link.

A new Web page loads in the browser window. The Web page includes a button used to invoke, or call, the GetCompensationUpdate() function. If the function had required parameters, then the Web page would display an input box for each parameter (Figure 12-65).

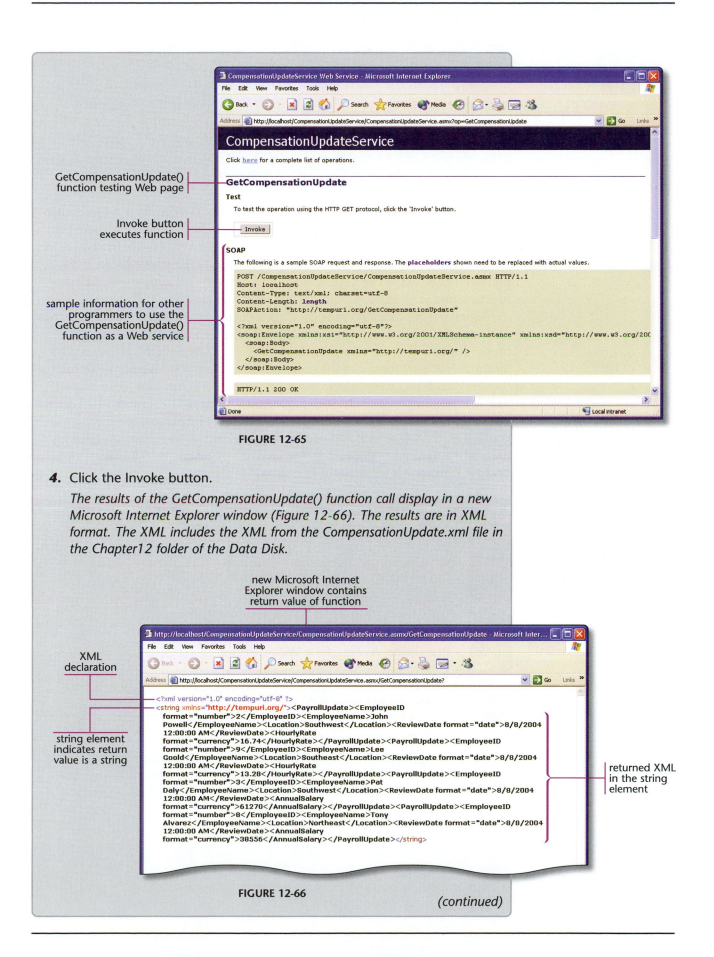

GetCompensationUpdate() function testing Web page

Invoke button executes function

sample information for other programmers to use the GetCompensationUpdate() function as a Web service

FIGURE 12-65

4. Click the Invoke button.

The results of the GetCompensationUpdate() function call display in a new Microsoft Internet Explorer window (Figure 12-66). The results are in XML format. The XML includes the XML from the CompensationUpdate.xml file in the Chapter12 folder of the Data Disk.

new Microsoft Internet Explorer window contains return value of function

XML declaration

string element indicates return value is a string

returned XML in the string element

FIGURE 12-66

(continued)

> **5.** Click the Close button on both the Microsoft Internet Explorer application window title bars. If necessary, click the Visual Basic .NET taskbar button to display the Visual Basic .NET window. If necessary, close the Output window.
>
> *Visual Basic .NET returns to design time when the browser windows are closed.*

The Web pages shown in the steps above are not how another programmer would call the Web service. The Web pages are only for testing and debugging purposes. If another programmer were to include the Web service in another program, he or she would not have access to the test Web pages shown in the previous set of steps. The programmer only calls the GetCompensationUpdate() function just as he or she would call any other function.

When testing code that includes Web services, make certain that the function and procedure calls operate as intended and return the expected results in the proper format. The test Web page shown in Figure 12-65 on the previous page indicates the exact format of the code another programmer would use to call the Web service. If you must inform other programmers about how to access your Web service, simply print the Web page shown in Figure 12-65 and distribute the information to the other programmers. When providing access for another programmer to a Web service that you have created, at the very least you must give the other programmer the URL of the Web service .asmx file. The use of an existing Web service is discussed later in this chapter.

Tip

Testing Code that Includes Web Services
When testing code that includes Web services, make certain that the function and procedure calls operate as intended and return the expected results in the proper format.

Tip

Providing Access to a Web Service
If you must inform other programmers about how to access your Web service, simply print the Web page shown in Figure 12-65 and distribute the information to the other programmers.

The testing process for the CompensationUpdateService application is complete. The final step of the development cycle is to document the application. The following steps document the application and quit Visual Basic .NET. Line numbers are printed on the code listing.

To Document the Web Service and Quit Visual Basic .NET

1. Follow the steps on page VB 2.40 of Chapter 2 to use the Print command on the File menu to print a record of the code for the CompensationUpdateService Web service.

A record of the CompensationUpdateService Web service code is printed (Figure 12-67).

```
c:\inetpub\wwwroot\CompensationUpdateService\CompensationUpdateService.asmx.vb                    1
 1 Option Strict On
 2 Imports System.Web.Services
 3 Imports System.Xml
 4 <WebService(Namespace:="http://tempuri.org/")> _
 5 Public Class CompensationUpdateService
 6     Inherits System.Web.Services.WebService
 7
 8  Web Services Designer Generated Code
 9
10     <WebMethod()> Public Function GetCompensationUpdate() As String
11         Dim objCompensationUpdateXML As New XmlDocument()
12         Dim strResult As String
13
14         Try
15             objCompensationUpdateXML.Load("A:\Chapter12\CompensationUpdate.xml")
16             strResult = objCompensationUpdateXML.LastChild.InnerXml
17         Catch ex As Exception
18             strResult = "The following error occurred while processing your request"
19             strResult &= ex.InnerException.ToString()
20         End Try
21
22         Return strResult
23     End Function
24 End Class
25
```

FIGURE 12-67

2. Click the Visual Basic .NET Close button.

If you made changes to the project since the last time it was saved, Visual Basic .NET displays the Microsoft Visual Basic .NET dialog box. If you click the Yes button, you can resave your project and quit. If you click the No button, you will quit without saving changes. Clicking the Cancel button will close the dialog box without quitting Visual Basic .NET.

Using a Web Service

Every programming language or programming platform that supports the use of Web services provides different methods for coding the calls to the Web service functions. As discussed in the previous section, the Visual Basic .NET Web services test Web page provides much of the information you should provide to another programmer who wants to use your Web service.

You can use a Web service in any type of Visual Basic .NET project, including a Web service project. To use a Web service you first must add a Web reference to the Web service. You add a Web service reference by right-clicking a project name in the Solution Explorer and then clicking the Add Web Reference command on the shortcut menu. You also can right-click the References folder of a project and click the Add Web Reference command on the shortcut menu. You then type the URL of the Web service in the Add Web Reference dialog box. For example, if you want to add a Web reference to the CompensationUpdateService Web service that is on the Web server located on your current computer, then the URL is as follows:

http://localhost/CompensationUpdateService/CompensationUpdateService.asmx

After entering the URL, you then click the Add Reference button on the dialog box.

After adding the reference, you then can change the name of the reference to a user-friendly name. Figure 12-68 shows a Windows application project in the Solution Explorer in which a Web reference to the CompensationUpdateService Web service has been added as described above.

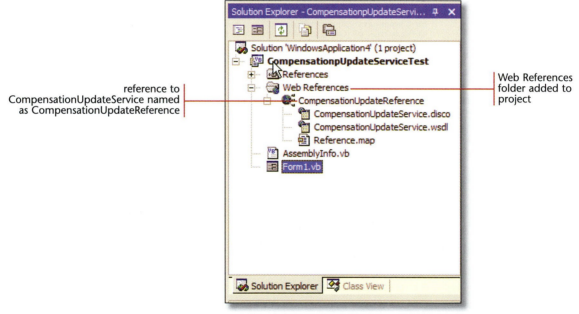

FIGURE 12-68

Once you have added the reference, you access the function and sub procedures in the Web service in much the same manner as you have accessed classes, functions, and procedure in class libraries. Figure 12-69 shows code that declares a Web service object of the CompensationUpdateService type and then calls the GetCompensationUpdate() function procedure in the Web service. The string containing the XML that results from the function call is assigned to a string variable and then is displayed in a message box. This technique demonstrates the power of Web services because the function procedure can exist on any Web server accessible by the computer running the program, including Web servers available on the Internet.

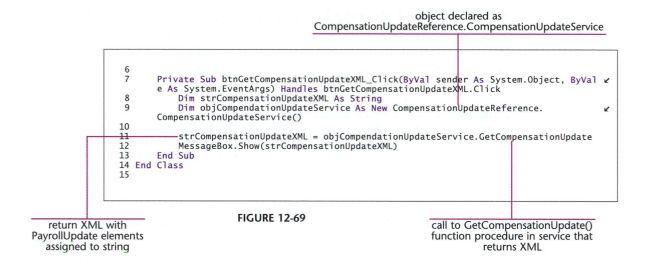

FIGURE 12-69

The XML Web Services link on the Visual Basic .NET Start Page provides the ability to find other users' public Web services, and provides the ability for you to publish a Web service for the world to see. You can add a reference to any of the public Web services you find on the XML Web Services page on the Start Page and add the provided functionality to any program you create in Visual Basic .NET. Available Web services include weather information, stock information, and calendaring services.

Chapter Summary

In this chapter, you learned how to create a new Console application and write code to process command-line arguments. You learned how to create text files and write data to a text file using tabs and commas as delimiters. You also learned how to create XML files and write XML elements to an XML file using several methods. You learned how to create a new Web service and write functions that are accessible to other programmers who want to use the Web service. You then learned how to read an XML file from a disk and send the XML as the return value of a function to a requesting client program. Finally, you learned how to debug and test Console applications and Web services.

What You Should Know

Having completed this chapter, you now should be able to perform tasks shown in Table 12-3.

Table 12-3   Chapter 12 What You Should Know

TASK NUMBER	TASK	PAGE
1	Start Visual Basic .NET and Add a New Public Procedure to a Module	VB 12.16
2	Build, Save, and Document the Class Library	VB 12.17
3	Start a New Console Application Project	VB 12.19
4	Enter Initial Console Application Code	VB 12.24
5	Enter Code to Validate Command-Line Arguments	VB 12.25
6	Enter Code to Determine the Type of File to Create	VB 12.27
7	Create and Open a Text File	VB 12.31
8	Write to a Text File	VB 12.32
9	Create and Open an XML File	VB 12.38
10	Format and Initialize an XML Object	VB 12.39
11	Write an XML Element with an Attribute	VB 12.41
12	Write an XML String Element with No Attributes	VB 12.42
13	Write the Final XML Elements for Hourly Employee Data	VB 12.43
14	Write Salaried Employee Data and Close the XmlTextWriter Object	VB 12.45
15	Set the Startup Project and Command-Line Arguments for Testing	VB 12.46
16	Build, Save, and Test the Console Application	VB 12.49
17	Document the Console Application	VB 12.55
18	Start a New ASP.NET Web Service Project	VB 12.59
19	Start Coding a Web Service	VB 12.62
20	Declare a Function in a Web Service	VB 12.64
21	Read and Process an XML Document	VB 12.66
22	Save and Test the Web Service	VB 12.67
23	Document the Web Service and Quit Visual Basic .NET	VB 12.71

Key Terms

.asmx file *(VB 12.57)*
ASP.NET Web service *(VB 12.57)*
ASP.NET Web Service template *(VB 12.59)*
attribute *(VB 12.37)*
Close() method *(VB 12.33)*
comma-delimited file *(VB 12.29)*
command-line argument *(VB 12.07)*
command-line interface *(VB 12.18)*
command-line switch *(VB 12.22)*
Console Application template *(VB 12.19)*
Console object *(VB 12.25)*
Console window *(VB 12.18)*
Console.WriteLine() method *(VB 12.25)*
content *(VB 12.36)*
delimiter *(VB 12.10)*
element *(VB 12.36)*
end tag *(VB 12.36)*
Environment object *(VB 12.24)*
GetCommandLineArgs.Length property *(VB 12.24)*
GetCommandLineArgs property *(VB 12.24)*
InnerXML property *(VB 12.65)*
LastChild property *(VB 12.65)*
Main() procedure *(VB 12.21)*
start tag *(VB 12.36)*
StreamReader class *(VB 12.29)*
StreamWriter class *(VB 12.29)*
System.IO namespace *(VB 12.24)*
System.Web.Services namespace *(VB 12.62)*
System.Xml namespace *(VB 12.24)*
tab-delimited file *(VB 12.29)*
UCase function *(VB 12.26)*
<WebMethod()> directive *(VB 12.63)*
Write() method *(VB 12.31)*
WriteAttributeString() method *(VB 12.40)*
WriteElementString() method *(VB 12.41)*
WriteEndElement() method *(VB 12.40)*
WriteLine() method *(VB 12.31)*
WriteStartElement() method *(VB 12.39)*
WriteString() method *(VB 12.40)*
XML *(VB 12.34)*
XML declaration *(VB 12.35)*
XmlDocument object *(VB 12.64)*
XML file *(VB 12.34)*
XmlTextReader class *(VB 12.37)*
XmlTextWriter class *(VB 12.37)*

KEY TERMS

Homework Assignments

Short Answer

1. Describe one or more situations in which you would develop a Console application. Describe one or more situations in which you would develop a Web service.

2. A command-line _____ often is referred to as a(n) _____ when it is used to cause the program to take a discrete course of action.

3. Information about a user's operating system can be gathered using the _____ class of the .NET Framework class library. The _____ returns the number of arguments in the command line used to start the program.

4. The _____ class is used to write to a text file, and the _____ class is used to read from a text file. The _____ class is used to write to an XML file, and the _____ class is used to read from an XML file.

5. Write the declaration for a StreamWriter object that creates and opens a file named, Products.txt, in the C:\Inventory folder. Write the statement that closes the file.

6. All XML elements must include a(n) _____ tag and a(n) _____ tag that enclose _____. In addition, an XML element optionally can include _____ or _____.

7. Identify the errors in the following XML documents.

   a.
   ```
   <PET>
      <DOG name="Fritz"></DOG>
      <CAT>Sugar<CAT>
      </PET>
   ```
   b.
   ```
   <?xml version="1.0"?>
   <TOOLS>
      <TOOL type="Phillips">Screwdriver
      <TOOL/>
      <TOOL type="regular>Screwdriver</TOOL>
   <TOOLS>
   ```
   c.
   ```
   <?xml version="1.0"?>
   <BOOKS>
      <BOOK>
         <TITLE>The Cat in the Hat</TITLE>
         <AUTHOR>Dr. Seuss</AUTHOR>
      </BOOK>
      <BOOK title="Green Eggs and Ham" author="Dr. Seuss"/>
   <BOOK>
   ```

8. Use the _____ method of the XmlTextWriter class to begin writing an element, but not to write content or attributes. Use the _____ method of the XmlTextWriter class to write an element and content, without attributes.

9. Write the calls to methods of the XmlTextWriter class that create the following XML.

   a.

   ```
   <?xml version="1.0"?>
   <CUSTOMER>
      <NAME>Sean McGill</NAME>
      <LASTPURCHASE date="07/15/2004">40 gallons fuel</LASTPURCHASE>
      <PAYMENTMETHOD>Credit Card</PAYMENTMETHOD>
   </CUSTOMER>
   ```

   b.

   ```
   <?xml version="1.0"?>
   <HOUSE>
      <ROOM>
         <WALL side="north"/>
         <WALL side="south"/>
         <WALL side="east"/>
         <WALL side="west"/>
         <DOOR side="west"/>
      </ROOM>
   </HOUSE>
   ```

10. When debugging Console applications that accept arguments in the IDE, the desired command-line arguments must be in the _____ box in the project's Property Pages, before running the program.

11. Calls to Web services are sent in _____ format. A Web service executes on a(n) _____; a Web service created using Visual Basic .NET is saved with the file extension, _____.

12. Describe the situation in which a function or procedure requires the <WebMethod()> directive before the function or procedure's declaration.

13. The _____ class in the .NET Framework class library can be used to read XML documents from XML files on disk.

(continued)

Learn It Online

Start your browser and visit scsite.com/vbnet/exs. Follow the instructions in the exercises below.

1. **Chapter Reinforcement TF, MC, and SA**   Click the True/False, Multiple Choice, and Short Answer link below Chapter 12. Print and then answer the questions.

2. **Practice Test**   Click the Practice Test link below Chapter 12. Answer each question, enter your first and last name at the bottom of the page, and then click the Grade Test button. When the graded practice test displays on your screen, click Print on the File menu to print a hard copy. Continue to take practice tests until you score 80% or better. Hand in a printout of the final practice test.

3. **Crossword Puzzle Challenge**   Click the Crossword Puzzle Challenge link below Chapter 12. Read the instructions, and then enter your first and last name. Click the Play button. Complete the crossword puzzle. When you are finished, click the Submit button. When the crossword puzzle redisplays, click the Print button.

4. **Tips and Tricks**   Click the Tips and Tricks link below Chapter 12. Click a topic that pertains to Chapter 12. Right-click the information and then click Print on the shortcut menu. Construct a brief example of what the information relates to in Visual Basic .NET to confirm you understand how to use the tip or trick. Hand in the example and printed information.

5. **Newsgroups**   Click the Newsgroups link below Chapter 12. Click a topic that pertains to Chapter 12. Print three comments.

6. **Expanding Your Horizons**   Click the Articles for Visual Basic .NET below Chapter 12. Click a topic that pertains to Chapter 12. Print the information. Construct a brief example of what the information relates to in Visual Basic .NET to confirm you understand the contents of the article. Hand in the example and printed information.

7. **Search Sleuth**   Select three key terms from the Key Terms section of this chapter and then use the Google search engine at google.com (or any major search engine) to display and print two Web pages for each key term.

> *Note:* If you plan to complete the project and all the exercises in this chapter, it is recommended that you use a hard disk or Zip disk for your solutions, because they will not all fit on a floppy disk.

Debugging Assignment

Start Visual Basic .NET and open the Mailing List solution from the Chapter12\Mailing List folder on the Data Disk. The solution consists of a Windows application that reads records from a database named MailingList.mdb, which is stored on the Data Disk in the Chapter12\Mailing List folder. When the program starts, the user can enter a range of postal codes for which to select mailing labels. The requested mailing list information then is stored in a text file named MailingList.txt in the Chapter12 folder on the Data Disk.

The Mailing List application contains bugs in the code. Run the application to experience some of the problems listed in the steps below. Follow the steps to debug the project.

1. Review the code for the Mailing List Windows application. The loop that reads the database records does not terminate properly. The code does not place the contents of the last record into the gstrMailingList array.

2. The code that declares the text file does not instantiate an instance of the object. Code must be added to instantiate the object by passing the text file name, MailingList.txt, to the constructor of the object.

3. The mailing list should be written to the text file so that the city, state, and postal code are formatted with a comma after the city name and a space after the state. All three values should be written on one line. Currently, the values are written on three separate lines.

4. The requirements for the text file format ask that each address be separated by two blank lines. Add the appropriate lines of code to write two blank lines to the text file after each entry.

5. The SQL SELECT statement that reads the records does not include the proper conditions. Make certain that the conditions find records with zip codes greater than or equal to the first zip code entered by the user and less than or equal to the second zip code entered by the user.

6. The MailingList.txt text file is not closed after the data is written to the file. Add the appropriate code to close the text file.

7. Document the Mailing List Windows application form code. On the code printout, circle the lines of code you modified.

```
Bobbie McSween
33 Benzing Way
Doriswood, TN 37212

Melanie Parker
238 Thruss Ave.
Manchester, TN 37205

Emerson Fonesca
219 Sewanee Rd.
Nashville, TN 37211

Angela Bonte
3948 Wimpole Dr.
Nashville, TN 37214

Jenita Brown
343 Cabot Rd.
Nashville, TN 37211
```

FIGURE 12-70

Programming Assignments

1 Creating a Console Application with Arguments

Using the following steps, design and develop a Console application that illustrates the concepts covered in this chapter. When running in the Command Prompt window, the program should allow a user to type the command for the application, followed by a number of options for arguments. Follow these steps to create the Console application:

1. Use the Console Application template in Visual Basic .NET to start a new project named ConsoleMath. Create the solution on the Web in a new folder named ConsoleMath.

2. Create a new sub procedure, DisplayError(), that will be used in the Main() procedure to display an error in the Command Prompt window if the user makes a mistake while entering arguments. The procedure writes a user-friendly error message to the Command Prompt.

3. The application should allow for four combinations of arguments. In the Main() procedure, use an If...Then statement to check if the user entered at least one command-line argument after the command name. If not, call the DisplayError() procedure and halt execution. Start a Select Case statement, such as

    ```
    Select Case (UCase(Environment.GetCommandLineArgs(1))
    ```

    to process the command-line options.

4. The first Case clause in the Select Case statement should check if the first argument is a /S. If the user entered /S as the first argument, check that the user also entered exactly two additional arguments after the /S. If not, call the DisplayError() procedure and exit the Select Case statement. If two arguments are entered, then assume the arguments are numeric, multiply the arguments together to obtain the area of a rectangle of the dimensions entered, and display the results in a user-friendly message in the Command Prompt window.

5. Write code similar to that written in Step 4 above for an additional situation:

    ```
    /C 9 9 9
    ```

    where the number 9 represents additional numeric arguments. For the /C switch, multiply the last three arguments together to compute the volume of a cube.

6. Write code similar to that written in Step 4 above for an additional situation:

    ```
    /A 9 9...9
    ```

    where the user enters an unlimited number of additional arguments after the /A parameter. If no additional arguments are entered after the /A switch, call the DisplayError() procedure. Use a loop to read the additional parameters. Determine the average of the values and display the average in a user-friendly message to the Command Prompt window.

7. Before the program exits, the program should write the operating system version to the Command Prompt window. Write the value of the Environment.OSVersion.ToString property to the command line as the last line of the Main() procedure.

8. Run the ConsoleMath application from a Command Prompt window and correct any errors you find while running the application. If you make any changes to fix errors, save the project again. After running the application from the Command Prompt window, the Command Prompt window should display as shown in Figure 12-71.

9. Document the code for the project.

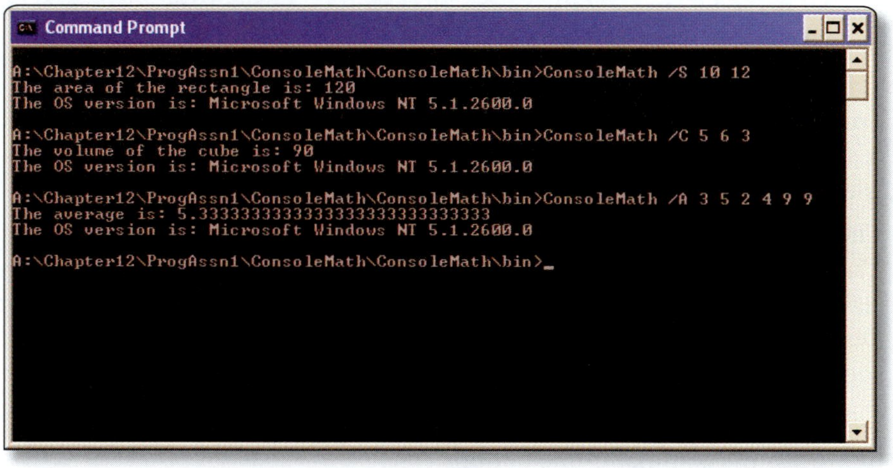

FIGURE 12-71

2 Creating a Web Service

Design and develop a new Web service that performs the loan computation as described in the requirements document on page VB 4.04. Use the code shown in Figure 4-53 on page VB 4.60 to perform the computation. The function in the Web service should be named ComputeMonthlyPayment(), and the function should accept three parameters: loan amount, interest rate, and number of months. Otherwise, the function should return the monthly payment. When testing the application, the unit test Web page will allow you to enter the three values as arguments to pass to the function. Enter the following arguments: loan amount of $13,000; interest rate of 10.25%; and number of months of 60 months. The Web service should return a value of a monthly payment of $277.81.

3 Writing to a Text File

Design and develop a Windows application that takes user input on a Windows form and then writes the information to a tab-delimited text file. The application should prompt for a music CD name, artist, number of songs, year released, and rating. The CD name and artist should be input using TextBox controls that accept no more than 25 characters. Allow input of the number of songs from 1 to 20 with a NumericUpDown control. Allow the year to be input in a TextBox control that accepts no more than 4 characters. Use four RadioButton controls in a GroupBox control to accept a rating, from 1 through 4. When the user clicks a Button control labeled, Write CD Information, the application should write the information as one record to a text file named CDInfo.txt in the Chapter12\ProgAssn3 folder of the Data Disk. Be sure to open the text file in the form's general area and close the file in the form's Closing() event procedure. When testing the application, enter at least five records. Use the Windows Notepad application to open the CDInfo.txt text file and print the output.

4 Reading a Text File and Writing an XML File

Design and develop a Console application that reads a text file from the Data Disk and creates an XML file from the records and fields in the text file. The text file named Inventory.txt is stored on the Data Disk in the Chapter12\ProgAssn4 folder. Create an XML file on the Data Disk in the Chapter12\ProgAssn4 folder named Inventory.xml. Use code similar to the following to open the file:

```
Dim objReader As IO.TextReader
objReader = IO.File.OpenText("A:\Chapter12\ProgAssn4\
Inventory.txt")
```

Use code such as the following to read from the file:

```
Do While objReader.Peek > -1
   strLine = objReader.ReadLine()
Loop
```

Use code such as the following to place the individual fields in a line of the file — such as the file read in the code above — into individual array elements:

```
Dim strFields(2) As String
strFields = strLine.Split(ControlChars.Tab)
```

The second line of code above places the three fields in a record into individual array elements in the strFields array. The first field is the item name, the second is the number in stock, and the third is the location. For each record in the text file, write an XML element. For example, the XML file should appear as follows:

```
<?xml version="1.0"?>
<INVENTORY>
   <ITEM amount="5" location="north">3/4 inch
plywood</ITEM>
   <ITEM amount="7" location="south">propane tanks</ITEM>
</INVENTORY>
```

5 Using Several Interfaces to Access a Class

Design and develop a class to be used by several types of applications. The class, ProductInformation, should accept a ProductID in its constructor. The constructor should read the ProductID, ProductName, ProductDescription, QuantityInStock, and ProductCost and set properties for the ProductInformationClass based on the values of these fields in a database. The database is stored on the Data Disk in the Chapter12\ProductInformation.mdb file. The table name is Products. The properties in the class all should be read-only properties. The class constructor should throw an exception if the ProductID is not found.

Create four projects that all perform similar tasks using the ProductInformation class. All four projects and the class should exist in the same solution named ProductInfo. Create one project type of each of the following types: Windows application, Web application, Web service, and Console application. All applications should accept a ProductID as input, and then instantiate an instance of the ProductInformation class by passing the input ProductID to the class constructor. Valid ProductID values include the numbers 1 through 12. After instantiating an instance of the class, each program should display all five properties of the ProductInformation object that was created. In the case of the Web service, the values should be concatenated in a string, separated by commas, and returned to the calling program. Each project should display or return a user-friendly error message if the constructor throws an exception.

APPENDIX

A

Flowcharting, Pseudocode, and the Unified Modeling Language (UML)

Appendix A explains how to prepare, use, and read program flowcharts, pseudocode, and basic Unified Modeling Language (UML) diagrams. Chapter 1 includes an introduction to flowcharting and flowchart symbols beginning on page VB 1.14. Pseudocode is introduced on page VB 1.16, and the UML is discussed briefly on page VB 1.20.

Guidelines for Preparation of Flowcharts

Before the flowchart can be drawn, a thorough analysis of the problem, the input data, and the desired output results must be performed. The program logic required to solve the problem also must be determined. On the basis of this analysis, a **general flowchart** illustrating the main path of the logic can be sketched. This flowchart can be refined until the overall program logic is fully determined. This general flowchart is used to make one or more **detailed flowcharts** of the various branches of and detours from the main path of the program logic. After each detailed flowchart has been freed of logical errors and other undesirable features, such as unnecessary steps, the actual coding of the program in a computer language can be undertaken.

Straight-Line Flowcharts

Figure A-1 illustrates a general, straight-line flowchart. A **straight-line flowchart** is one in which the symbols are arranged sequentially, without any deviations or looping, until the terminal symbol that represents the end of the flowchart is reached. Once the operation indicated in any one symbol has been performed, that operation is never repeated.

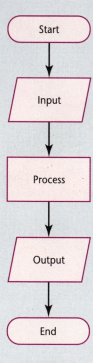

FIGURE A-1

Flowcharts with Looping

A general flowchart that illustrates an iterative, or repeating, process known as **looping** is shown in Figure A-2. The logic illustrated by this flowchart is in three major parts: initialization, process, and wrap-up. A flowline exits from the bottom symbol in Figure A-2 and enters above the diamond-shaped decision symbol that determines whether the loop is to be executed again. This flowline forms part of a loop inside which some operations are executed repeatedly until specified conditions are satisfied. This flowchart shows the input, process, and output pattern; it also uses a decision symbol that shows where the decision is made to continue or stop the looping process.

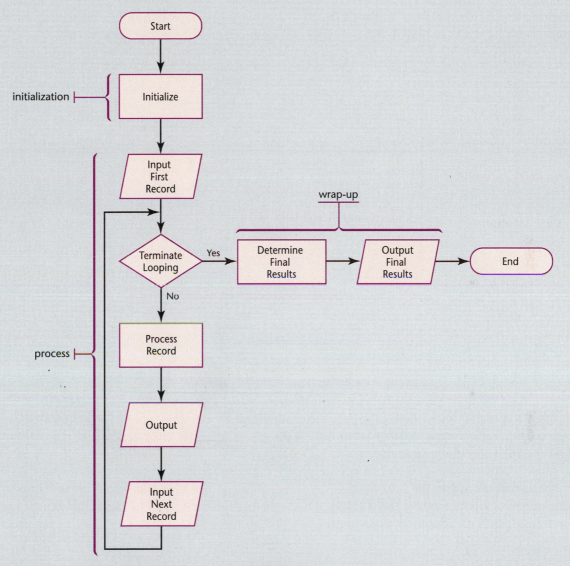

FIGURE A-2

Figure A-2 contains three braces that show the initialization, process, and wrap-up operations. For example, setting the program counters to 0 may represent an initialization operation and displaying the values of counters may represent a wrap-up operation.

Like the straight-line flowchart, a flowchart with looping need not have all the symbols shown in Figure A-2, or a flowchart can have many more symbols. For example, the process symbol within the loop in Figure A-2, when applied to a particular problem, may expand to include branching forward to bypass a process or backward to redo a process. It also is possible that through the use of decision symbols, the process symbol in Figure A-2 could be expanded to include several loops, some of which might be independent from each other and some of which might be within other loops.

A flowchart shows a process that is carried out. Flowcharts are flexible; they can show any logical process no matter how complex it may be, and they can show it in whatever detail is needed.

The two flowcharts illustrated in Figure A-3 represent the same program that accepts and then displays a record. Then the program loops back to the accepting operation and repeats the sequence, accepting and displaying any number of records. A connector symbol, represented by a circle with a letter or number in it (in this case, A), indicates the continuation of the looping process.

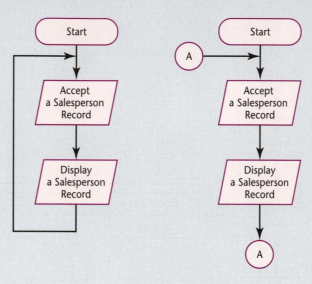

Endless Loops

FIGURE A-3

Although the flowcharts in Figure A-3 illustrate two ways a loop can be represented, the particular loop that is shown is an **endless loop**, also called an **infinite loop**. This type of loop should be avoided when constructing programs. In order to make a program finite, you must define it so it will terminate when specified conditions are satisfied.

Figure A-4 illustrates the use of a counter that terminates the looping process. Note that the counter is first set to 0 in the initialization step. After an account is read and a message is printed, the counter is incremented by 1 and tested to find whether it is now equal to 15. If the value of the counter is not 15, the looping process continues. If the value of the counter is 15, the looping process terminates.

For the flowchart used in Figure A-4, the exact number of accounts to be processed must be known beforehand. In practice, this will not always be the case because the number of accounts may vary from one run to the next.

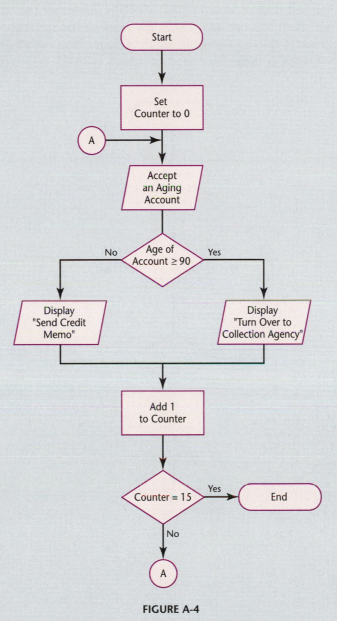

FIGURE A-4

A way to solve this type of problem is shown in Figure A-5, which illustrates the use of an end-of-file test to terminate the looping process. The value −999999 has been chosen to be the last account number. This kind of value sometimes is known as the **sentinel value** because it guards against continuing past the end-of-file. Also, the numeric item chosen for the last value cannot possibly be confused with a valid item because it is outside the range of the account numbers. Programs using an end-of-file test, such as the one shown in Figure A-5, are far more flexible and less limited than programs that do not, such as those illustrated in Figures A-3 and A-4 on pages VB A.04 and VB A.05.

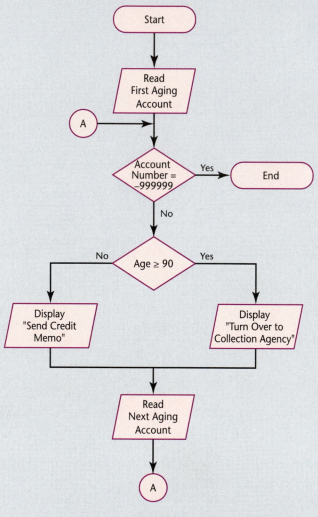

FIGURE A-5

Another flowchart with a loop is shown in Figure A-6. Figure A-6 illustrates the concept of counting. The flowchart incorporates the end-of-file test.

Simple computer programs do not require complex flowcharts and sometimes do not require flowcharts at all. As programs become more complex with many different paths of execution, however, a flowchart not only is useful but usually is a prerequisite for successful analysis and coding. Indeed, developing the problem solution by arranging and rearranging the flowchart symbols can lead to a more efficient solution.

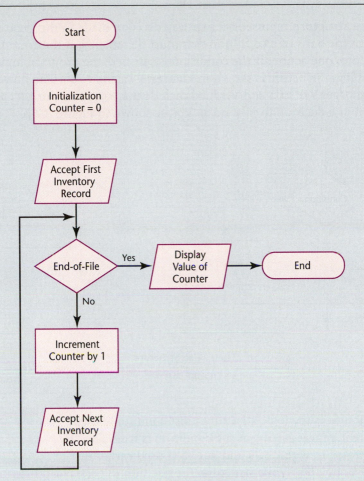

FIGURE A-6

Control Structures

The logic of almost any procedure or method can be constructed from the following three basic logic structures:

1. Sequence
2. If…Then…Else or Selection
3. Do While or Repetition

The following are two common extensions to these logic structures:

Do Until

Select Case (an extension of the If…Then…Else logic structure)

The **Sequence structure** is used to show one action or one action followed by another, as illustrated in Figures A-7a and A-7b. Every flowchart in this book includes this control structure.

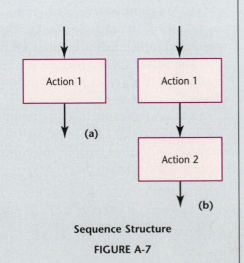

Sequence Structure

FIGURE A-7

The **If…Then…Else structure** represents a two-way decision made in the logic of the program. The decision is made on the basis of a condition that must be satisfied. If the condition is not satisfied, the program logic executes one action. If the condition is satisfied, the program logic executes a different action. This type of logic structure is shown in Figures A-8a and A-8b. The flowcharts presented in Figures A-4 and A-5 on pages VB A.05 and VB A.06 include this logic structure. The If…Then…Else structure also can result in a decision to take no action, as shown in Figure A-8b.

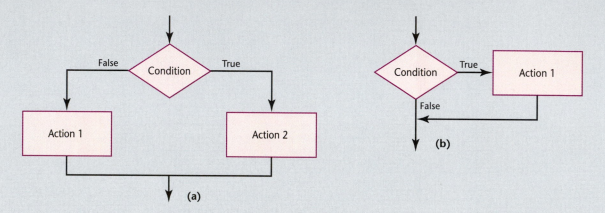

If…Then…Else Structure

FIGURE A-8

The **Do While structure** is the logic structure most commonly used to create a process that will repeat as long as the condition is true. The Do While structure is illustrated in Figure A-9 and has been used earlier in Figures A-2, A-5, and A-6. In a Do While structure, the decision to perform the action within the structure is at the top of the loop; as a result, the action will not occur if the condition is never satisfied.

The **Do Until structure** (Figure A-10) also is used for creating a process that will be repeated. The major differences between the Do Until and the Do While structures are that (1) the action within the structure of a Do Until always will be executed at least once, (2) the decision to perform the action within the structure is at the bottom of the Do Until loop, and (3) the Do Until loop exits when the condition is true.

Figure A-10 illustrates the Do Until structure, and the flowchart presented in Figure A-4 on page VB A.05 includes a Do Until structure.

The **Select Case structure** is similar to the If…Then…Else structure except that it provides more than two alternatives. Figure A-11 illustrates the Select Case structure.

A logical solution to a programming problem can be developed through the use of just these five logic structures. The program will be easy to read, easy to modify, and reliable; most important of all, the program will do what it is intended to do.

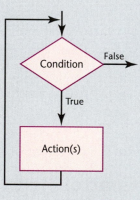

Do While Structure

FIGURE A-9

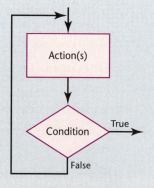

Do Until Structure

FIGURE A-10

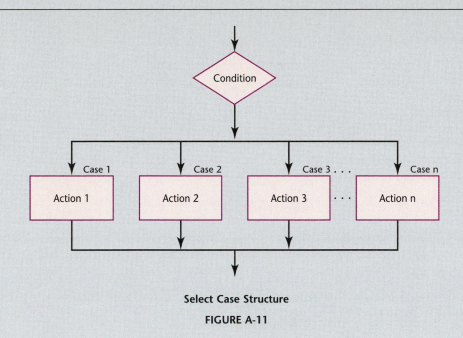

Select Case Structure

FIGURE A-11

Flowcharting Tips

The following recommendations can help make flowcharts more efficient and easier for others to understand. These suggestions assume that the input, processing, and output of the problem are defined properly in a requirements document.

1. Sketch a general flowchart and the necessary detail flowcharts before coding the problem. Repeat this step until you are satisfied with your flowcharts.

2. Use the control structures described on pages VB A.07 and VB A.08.

3. Put yourself in the position of the reader, keeping in mind that the purpose of the flowchart is to improve the reader's understanding of the solution to the problem.

4. Show the flow of processing from top to bottom and from left to right. When in doubt, use arrowheads as required to indicate the direction of flow.

5. Draw the flowchart so that it is neat and clear. Use the connector symbols to avoid excessively long flowlines.

6. Choose labels for each symbol that explain the function of the symbols in a clear and precise manner.

7. Avoid endless loops; construct loops so they will be terminated when specific conditions are satisfied.

The reason that flowcharts are so important is simple: the difficulties in programming lie mostly in the realm of logic, not in the syntax and semantics of the computer language. In other words, most computer errors are mistakes in logic, and a flowchart aids in detecting these types of mistakes.

Pseudocode

Pseudocode is a program design technique that uses natural English and resembles Visual Basic .NET code. It is an intermediate notation that allows the logic of a program to be formulated without diagrams or charts. Pseudocode resembles Visual Basic .NET in that specific operations can be expressed as commands that the program will execute. The following three examples illustrate pseudocode:

> Accept Employee Record
> MaleCounter = MaleCounter +1
> Display Employee Record

What makes pseudocode appealing to many programmers is that it has no formal syntax, which allows programmers to concentrate on the design of the program rather than on the peculiarities of the programming language's syntax.

Although pseudocode has no formal rules, the following guidelines are commonly accepted by most programmers:

1. Begin the pseudocode with a program, procedure, or method title statement.

> Monthly Sales Analysis Report Procedure

2. End the pseudocode with a terminal program statement.

> End

3. Begin each statement on a new line. Use simple and short imperative sentences that contain a single transitive verb and a single object.

> Accept EmployeeNumber
> Subtrate 10 From Quantity

4. Express assignments as a formula or as an English-like statement.

> $WithholdingTax = 0.20 \times (GrossPay - 38.46 \times Dependents)$

or

> Compute WithholdingTax

5. To avoid errors in the design, avoid using logic structures not available in the programming language being used.

6. For the If…Then…Else structure, use the following conventions:

   a. Indent the true and false tasks.

   b. Use End If as the structure terminator.

   c. Vertically align the If, Else, and End If statements.

These conventions for the If…Then…Else structure are illustrated in Figures A-12 and A-13.

```
If Balance < 500 then
        Display Credit OK
Else
        Display Credit not OK
End If
```

FIGURE A-12

```
If GenderCode = male Then
        MaleCount = MaleCount + 1
        If Age > 21 Then
                MaleAdultCount = MaleAdultCount + 1
        Else
                MaleMinorCount = MaleMinorCount + 1
        End If
Else
        FemaleCount = FemaleCount + 1
        If Age > 21 Then
                FemaleAdultCount = FemaleAdultCount + 1
        Else
                FemaleMinorCount = FemaleMinorCount + 1
        End If
End If
```

FIGURE A-13

7. For the Do While structure, use the following conventions:
   a. If the structure represents a counter-controlled loop, begin the structure with Do.
   b. If the structure does not represent a counter-controlled loop, begin the structure with Do While.
   c. Specify the condition on the Do While or Do line.
   d. Use End Do as the last statement of the structure.
   e. Align the Do While or Do and the End Do vertically.
   f. Indent the statements within the loop.

The conventions for the Do While structure are illustrated in Figures A-14 and A-15 on the next page.

8. For the Do Until structure, use the following conventions:
   a. Begin the structure with Do Until.
   b. Specify the condition on the Do Until line.
   c. Use End Do as the last statement of the structure.
   d. Align the Do Until and the End Do vertically.
   e. Indent the statements within the loop.

```
SumFirst100Integers Procedure
        Sum = 0
        Do Integer = 1 to 100
                Sum = Sum + Integer
        End Do
        Display sum
End
```

FIGURE A-14

```
EmployeeFileList Procedure
        Display report and column headings
        EmployeeCount = 0
        Accept first Employee record
        Do While Not End-of-File
                Add 1 to EmployeeCount
                Display Employee record
                Accept next Employee record
        End Do
        Display EmployeeCount
End
```

FIGURE A-15

The conventions for the Do Until structure are illustrated in Figure A-16.

```
SumFirst100Integers Procedure
        Sum = 0
        Integer = 1
        Do Until Integer >100
                Sum = Sum + Integer
                Integer = Integer + 1
        End Do
        Display Sum
End
```

FIGURE A-16

9. For the Select Case structure, use the following conventions:

   a. Begin the structure with Select Case, followed by the variable to be tested.

   b. Use End Case as the structure terminator.

   c. Align Select Case and End Case vertically.

   d. Indent each alternative.

   e. Begin each alternative with Case, followed by the value of the variable that equates to the alternative.

   f. Indent the action of each alternative.

These conventions are illustrated in Figure A-17.

```
Select Case CustomerCode
        Case 100
                High-RiskCustomerCount = High-RiskCustomerCount + 1
        Case 200
                LowRiskCustomerCount = LowRiskCustomerCount + 1
        Case 300
                RegularCustomerCount = RegularCustomerCount + 1
        Case 400
                SpecialCustomerCount = SpecialCustomerCount + 1
End Case
```

FIGURE A-17

For an additional example of pseudocode, see Figure 1-14 in Chapter 1 on page VB 1.16.

The Unified Modeling Language (UML)

Just as flowcharts describe algorithms, object-oriented design (OOD) has a standard method to depict, or diagram, concepts for design purposes. The Unified Modeling Language (UML) is a notation used to describe object behaviors and interaction. The UML is a graphical language used to represent how a system behaves or should behave. The UML is a relatively new language, having been developed in the 1990s from a number of competing object-oriented design tools.

In OOD, each class can have one or more lower levels, called **subclasses**, or one or more higher levels, called **base classes**, or **superclasses**. For example, a class for Secretaries is a subclass of the Employee class. Person is a base class or superclass of Employee. The relationship among the classes, subclasses, and base classes is called the **hierarchy**. A **high-level class diagram** is a UML diagram used to show the hierarchical relationships among classes (Figure A-18).

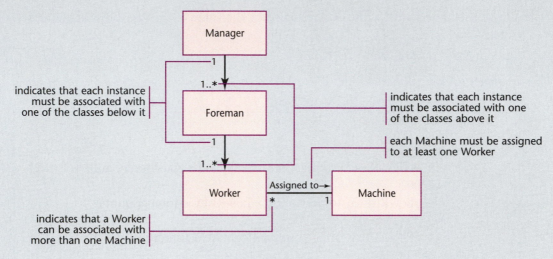

FIGURE A-18

Associations describe the manner in which instances of a class, or objects, are related. For example, two instances of a Worker class can have the association of being coworkers. This type of association is **bidirectional**, meaning each instance is associated with the other. Some associations are **unidirectional**, which means only one class is associated with the other. For example, a Worker instance can be assigned to operate an injection molder machine, which is an instance of the class Machines. The Worker is associated with the injection molder instance because a Worker must know how to operate the injection molder, but the injection molder does not have any information about or relationship to the Worker. In this way, the association between the Worker and Machine class is unidirectional.

The high-level class diagram shown in Figure A-18 depicts a hierarchy in which an instance of the Manager class can have several instances of the Foreman class associated with it; each instance of the Foreman class can have several workers associated with it; and each instance of the Worker class can be assigned to exactly one machine. Each class is represented by a box with the class name inside the box. Relationships are designated by lines between the classes.

The 1 below the Manager class indicates that each Manager class must have at least one Foreman class associated with it; the 1 below the Foreman class indicates that each Foreman class must have at least one Worker class associated with it. The 1..* above the Foreman class indicates that each Foreman class must be associated with at least one Manager class above it; the 1..* above the Worker class indicates that each Worker class must be associated with at least one Foreman class above it. The Assigned to label indicates that each Worker class is assigned to one Machine class. The 1 next to the Machine class indicates that each Machine class must be assigned at least one Worker class. The * next to the Worker class indicates that a worker can be associated with more than one Machine class.

Object-oriented programming (OOP) and OOD use many unique terms to describe program elements. In object-oriented terminology, the data stored about an object is called an attribute or property. An **attribute** or **property** is an identifying characteristic of individual objects, such as a name, weight, or color. An **operation** is an activity that reads or manipulates the data of an object. In OOD, an operation is a type of service. In OOP, the code that may be executed to perform a service is called a **method**.

A **detailed class diagram** is used to provide a visual representation of an object, its attributes, and its methods (Figure A-19 and Figure A-20). Figure A-19 shows the general form of a detailed class diagram. Figure A-20 shows a specific example of a detailed class diagram for the Foreman class. The Foreman class contains six attributes and five methods. The rules of the UML prescribe that each attribute and method begin with lowercase letters and that each method name is followed by parentheses. The parentheses indicate that the methods are procedures in the class. A detailed class diagram also can have additional notations.

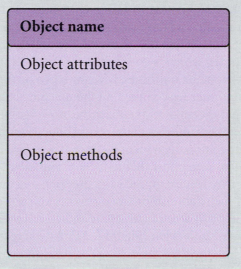

FIGURE A-19

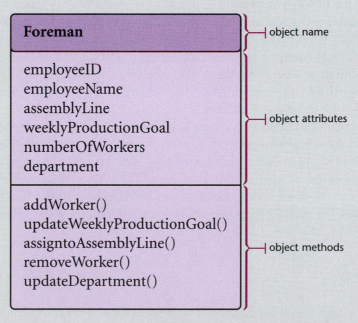

FIGURE A-20

Messages and Events

Message sending is a key component of object-oriented design because it describes how objects work together. For an object to do something, it must be sent a message. The **message** must have two parts: (1) the name of the object to which the message is being sent; and (2) the name of the operation that will be performed by the object. As you have learned, an operation is an activity that reads or manipulates the data of an object. An operation also can send additional messages while it performs its task.

Messages are sent through an interface to the object. Just as a user interface allows a program to accept data and instructions from the user, the **interface** is the way that an object receives messages.

As an example, suppose each time an assembly-line worker turns on a machine (an object), the machine tracks how many times it has been turned on by incrementing a counter. To turn on the machine, the worker presses a button on a panel to send a message to the machine. The button on the panel is the interface to the on method of the machine, and pressing the button is the event that sends a message to execute the on method. When the on method executes, part of its operation is to increment the numberTimesOn counter, which is an attribute of the machine. Suppose that the shop also uses an automated system to operate its machines. Machines can be turned on remotely using a computer. The interface that the computer uses to turn on the machine is different from the one the worker uses. The on method that executes on the machine, however, remains the same and the on method still increments the numberTimesOn counter attribute when it executes.

In OOD terminology, the operation, increment counter, is a service and the message, turn machine on, is called a **request for service**. Remember that in OOP terminology, the service is called a method and the message is what is sent when an event, such as a user pressing the on button, occurs. **Sequence diagrams** are used to represent the relationships among events and objects. In a sequence diagram, messages or events are shown as lines with arrows, classes are shown across the top in rectangles, and class names are underlined and prefaced by a colon (Figure A-21). As you read the sequence diagram, time progresses from top to bottom and the time the object is active is shown by vertical rectangles.

Figure A-21 illustrates a sequence diagram for a Foreman assigning a Worker to a Machine. The Foreman object in the first column interacts with other objects through the Foreman Interface. The Foreman sends a message through the Foreman Interface to find a Worker based on the worker's name. Next, the Foreman finds a Machine to assign the Worker based on the worker's skill. Finally, the assignment is made.

As shown in Figure A-21, nothing happens in a system unless a message is sent when an event occurs. At the conclusion of an operation, the system again will do nothing until another event occurs. This relationship of events causing operations is a key feature of OOP, and programs that are constructed in this way are said to be **event driven**.

The UML is a powerful tool because it can be used to describe any item, process, or concept in the real or imagined world. Its usefulness goes well beyond the programming world. People working in different disciplines or working in different industries can communicate concepts using the UML in a standard and well-understood manner. Another feature of the UML is that many types of diagrams provide different views of the same system, or object, in addition to the ones shown here. Different views of the same system are useful depending on a person's or object's role in the system.

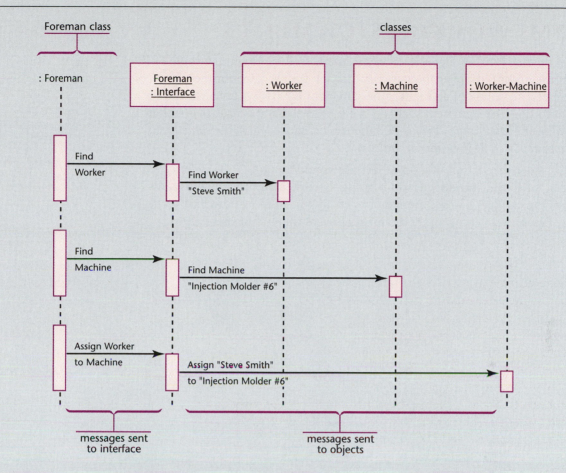

FIGURE A-21

HOMEWORK ASSIGNMENTS

1. In the flowchart in Figure A-22, what are the value of I and the value of J at the instant just after the statement J = J + 1 is executed for the fifth time? The value of I and J after the statement I = I + 2 is executed the tenth time? (A statement such as J = J + 1 is valid and is read as *the new value of J equals the old value of J plus one* or, equivalently, *the value of J is to be replaced by the value of J plus one.*)

2. Consider the section of a flowchart shown in Figure A-23. It assumes that an absent-minded person is going to work. This individual usually has the car keys but occasionally forgets them. Does the flowchart section in Figure A-23 incorporate the most efficient method of representing the actions to be taken? If not, redraw the flowchart portion given in Figure A-23.

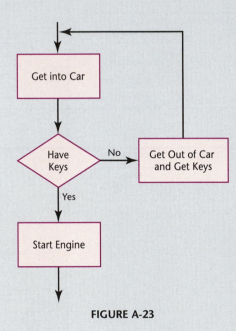

FIGURE A-23

3. In Figure A-24, the flowchart for a small program, what values of I and of J are printed when the output symbol is executed for the fiftieth time?

4. An opaque urn contains three diamonds, four rubies, and two pearls. Construct a flowchart that describes the following events: Take a gem from the urn. If it is a diamond, lay it aside. If it is not a diamond, return it to the urn. Continue in this fashion until all the diamonds have been removed. After all the diamonds have been removed, repeat the same procedure until all the rubies have been removed. After all the rubies have been removed, continue in the same fashion until all the pearls have been removed.

5. In the flowchart represented by Figure A-25, what is the value of I and the value of J at the instant the terminal symbol with the word End is reached?

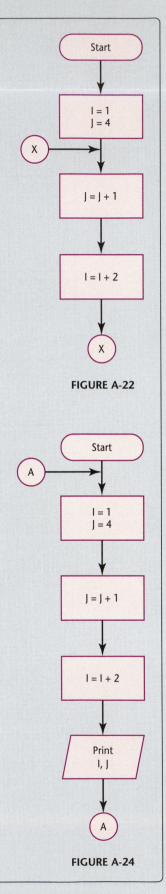

FIGURE A-22

FIGURE A-24

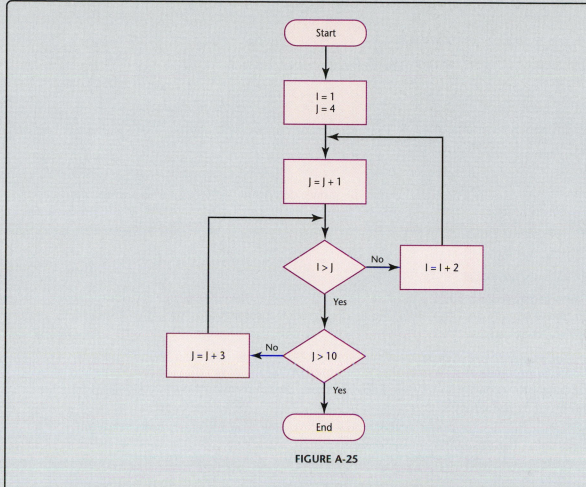

FIGURE A-25

6. Draw one flowchart, and only one, that will cause the mechanical mouse to go through any of the four mazes shown in Figure A-26. At the beginning, a user will place the mouse on the entry side of the maze, in front of the entry point, facing up toward the maze. The instruction Move to next cell will put the mouse inside the maze. Each maze has four cells. After that, the job is to move from cell to cell until the mouse emerges on the exit side. If the mouse is instructed to *Move to next cell* when a wall is in front of it, it will hit the wall and fall apart. Obviously, the mouse must be instructed to test whether it is *Facing a wall* before any *Move*. The physical movements and logical tests the mechanical mouse can complete are listed below Figure A-26.

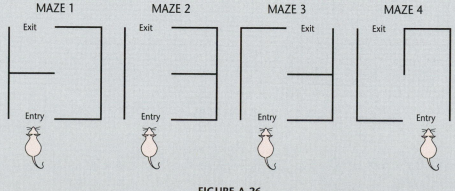

FIGURE A-26

(continued)

6. (continued)

a. Physical movement:

(1) Move to next cell. (The mouse will move in the direction it is facing.)

(2) Turn right.

(3) Turn left.

(4) Turn around 180 degrees. (All turns are made in place, without moving to another cell.)

(5) Halt.

b. Logic:

(1) Facing a wall? (Through this test, the mouse determines whether a wall is immediately in front of it, that is, on the border of the cell it is occupying and in the direction it is facing.)

(2) Outside the maze?

(3) On the entry side?

(4) On the exit side?

7. Develop a detailed class diagram for an electric dishwasher. List at least eight attributes, including number of racks, model, and color. List at least six methods, including addDishes() and addDetergent().

8. Develop a high-level class diagram that shows the relationships among a manufacturer's inventory of finished products in its warehouses. The company has many warehouses that are managed by the inventory control supervisor. Each warehouse contains many bins of products. Each bin contains one product type.

9. Develop a sequence diagram that shows how the inventory control supervisor in assignment 8 assigns a product to a bin in a warehouse.

B

Changing Screen Resolution and the IDE Layout

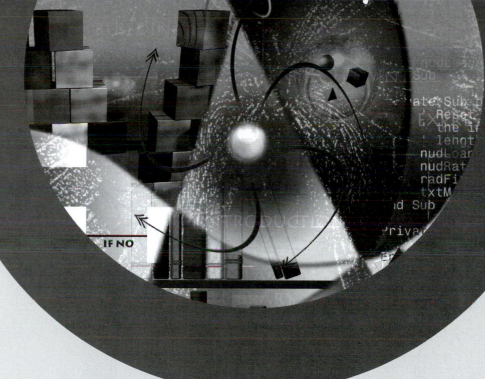

Appendix B explains how to change your screen resolution to the resolution used in this book. The appendix also explains how to rearrange windows and toolbars to change the layout of the Visual Basic .NET IDE, so that it is better suited to your preferred work habits.

Changing Screen Resolution

The following steps show how to change your screen's resolution from 800 by 600 pixels to 1024 by 768 pixels, which is the screen resolution used in this book.

To Change Screen Resolution

1. Click the Start button on the Windows taskbar, and then point to Control Panel on the Start menu.

The Start menu displays, and Control Panel is highlighted on the Start menu (Figure B-1).

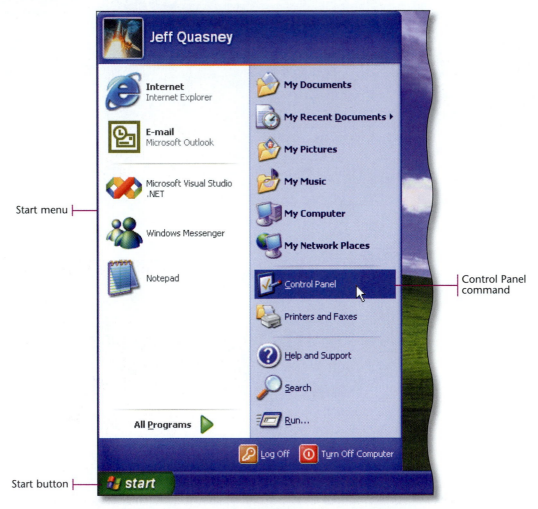

FIGURE B-1

2. Click Control Panel.

The Control Panel window opens (Figure B-2).

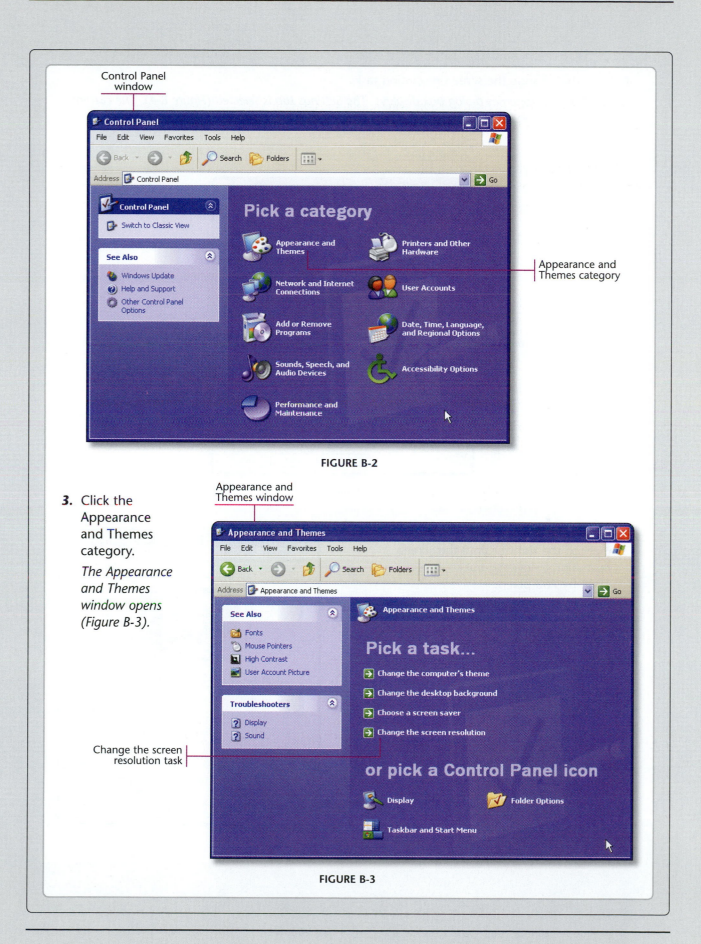

Control Panel window

Appearance and Themes category

FIGURE B-2

3. Click the Appearance and Themes category.

The Appearance and Themes window opens (Figure B-3).

Appearance and Themes window

Change the screen resolution task

FIGURE B-3

4. Click the Change the screen resolution task.

The Display Properties dialog box displays. The Settings tab is selected (Figure B-4). The current screen resolution displays in the screen resolution area.

Display Properties
dialog box

Screen resolution
area

Screen resolution
trackbar

current screen
resolution is
800 by 600 pixels

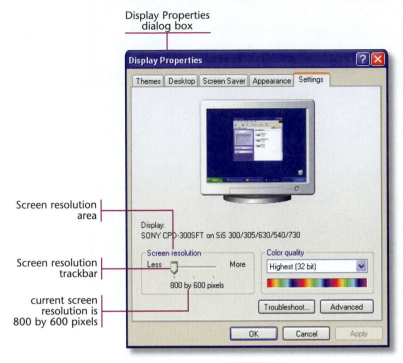

FIGURE B-4

5. Drag the Screen resolution trackbar one mark to the right or until the screen resolution below the trackbar reads, 1024 by 768 pixels.

As the trackbar is moved one mark to the right, the screen resolution displayed below the trackbar changes to 1024 by 768 pixels (Figure B-5).

trackbar moved one
tick mark to the right

screen resolution
now reads 1024
by 768 pixels

OK button

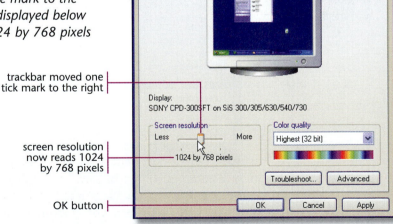

FIGURE B-5

6. Click the OK button.

The Display Properties dialog box closes. The Windows desktop displays at a screen resolution of 1024 by 768 pixels, as shown in Figure B-6. Compare Figure B-6 with Figure B-3 to see the difference in the display between the 800 by 600 screen resolution and the 1024 by 768 screen resolution. With a higher resolution, more items can fit on the screen but the items, such as windows, text, and icons, display at a smaller size.

screen resolution
changed to 1024 by 768

Close button

FIGURE B-6

7. Click the Close button on the Appearance and Themes window title bar.

The new screen resolution is set.

You can experiment with various screen resolutions. Depending on your monitor and the video adapter installed in your computer, the screen resolutions available on your computer will vary.

When designing a user interface in the IDE, remember to take into consideration the screen resolutions available to the majority of the users of the application. A good rule of thumb is to test your application in all of the screen resolutions in which the application likely is to be used.

Changing the IDE Layout

The Visual Basic .NET IDE is fully customizable and allows you to arrange the contents of the IDE in a manner suitable to your work habits. This section contains some examples of various layouts used to get the most out of the IDE. You should experiment with various layouts to find the one that works best for you. If you need to change the layout back to the Visual Studio .NET default, you can open the Options dialog box from the Tools menu and then click the Reset Window Layout button.

Sample IDE Layouts

Figure B-7 shows a common layout for programmers developing Windows applications using Visual Basic .NET. The Task List, Command Window, and Output tabs display at the bottom of the IDE. The Full Screen toolbar is docked to the right of the Standard toolbar. Clicking the Full Screen button on the Full Screen toolbar quickly changes the view of the main work area to a larger view. The larger view makes it easier to focus on that which you are working. The Debug toolbar is docked to the right of the Layout toolbar.

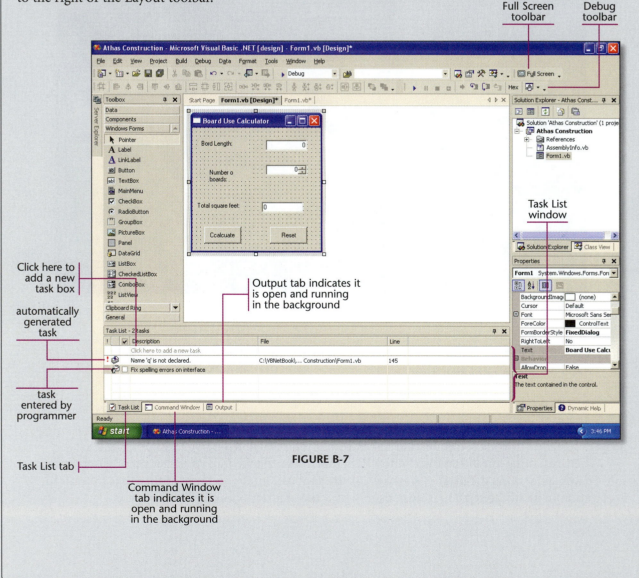

FIGURE B-7

As you are working, Visual Basic .NET automatically generates a new task in the **Task List** for any syntax errors in your code (Figure B-7). The tasks in the Task List serve as reminders of things that must be completed before you are done working on the code. You also can add tasks or reminders to the Task List by clicking the Click here to add a new task box directly above the Task List.

The **Command Window** allows you to test new code statements quickly without running the entire project (Figure B-7). The **Output window** displays the build results from the last time you ran the project. The contents of the Output window also serve as a reminder of bugs you must fix in the project. To view these windows, click the Command Window or Output tab at the bottom of the IDE.

Figure B-8 shows the result of undocking several of the windows from the IDE. This technique is useful if your computer only supports lower screen resolutions. By undocking the windows, you can move some windows out of the way, but still have quick access to the windows when necessary. To undock a window, drag the title bar of the window until you see a floating outline of the window, and then release the mouse button. To dock an undocked window, drag the window to the upper, lower, left, or right edge of the IDE. An outline of the window will snap to the edge as you move the mouse pointer towards the edge where you want to dock the window. When the window snaps to the desired position, release the mouse button to dock the window.

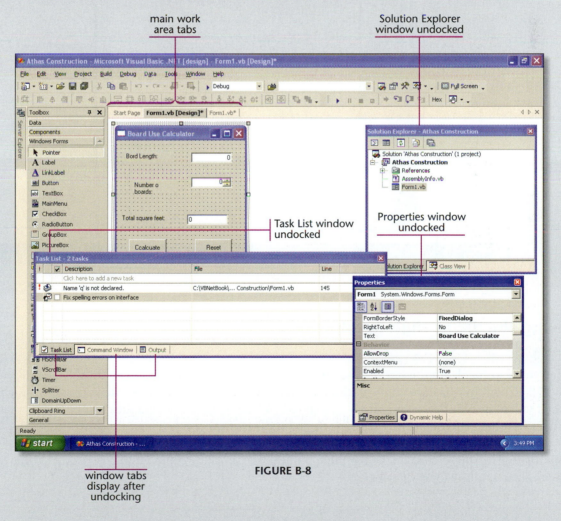

FIGURE B-8

Figure B-9 shows the main work area of the IDE in **Multiple Document Interface** (**MDI**) **mode**. In MDI mode, the IDE displays three separate windows in the main work area, instead of window tabs (Figure B-8 on the previous page). Using MDI mode is practical if you want to display a combination of form windows, code windows, and Help topics on the screen at one time. MDI mode also is useful for viewing multiple code windows, so that you can copy and paste code between the windows.

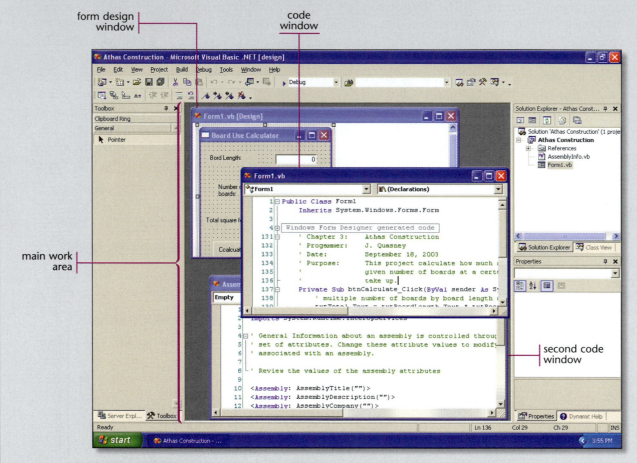

FIGURE B-9

Viewing the IDE at High Resolution

The higher the resolution you can tolerate while working in the IDE, the more information that you can make available on the screen at one time. Figure B-10 shows an example of the Visual Basic .NET IDE at 1280 by 1024 screen resolution. Much higher resolutions are possible with today's high-powered video cards and large monitors. In Figure B-10, the main work area illustrates a layout that displays a number of frequently used windows and toolbars in the IDE. The right side of the IDE is set up to display the Solution Explorer window, the Properties window, and the Dynamic Help window. Additional toolbars have been docked at the top of the IDE, including the Full Screen toolbar, the Debug toolbar, and the Query toolbar.

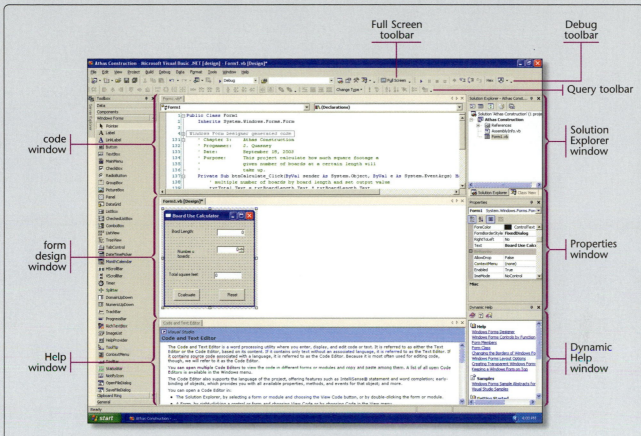

FIGURE B-10

APPENDIX

C

Visual Basic .NET Common Control Summary

Appendix C summarizes the commonly used properties,
events, and methods for controls introduced in this book
for developing applications in Visual Basic .NET.

Control Properties, Methods, and Events

The following tables summarize the properties, method, and events for the controls presented in this book. Default property values appear in bold font. The page number on which the control is first discussed in the book is shown next to the table title.

Common Properties of Controls

Table C-1 summarizes properties that are shared by a number of common Visual Basic .NET controls.

Table C-1 Common Properties of Controls (VB 3.39)

CATEGORY	PROPERTY	DESCRIPTION	PROPERTY VALUES
Appearance	BackColor	Sets the background color of the control	Select a color from a pop-up dialog box.
	Cursor	Defines which mouse pointer (cursor) displays when user moves the mouse over the control	Select a mouse pointer from a list of more than 20 mouse pointers.
	Font	Defines the text font to use if text displays in the control	Select a font style from a pop-up dialog box.
	ForeColor	Changes the foreground color, usually of the text that displays on the control	Select a color selected from a pop-up dialog box.
Behavior	Enabled	If True, control is usable at run time; if False, a user cannot change control value and control may display grayed out	**True** False
	TabStop	Determines whether the TAB key sets focus on the control during run time	**True** False
	TabIndex	Determines the order in which the TAB key navigates to the control	Any positive whole number
	Visible	If True, control displays at run time; if False, control does not display	**True** False
Data	Tag	Defines data to be stored with the control (data does not display to user)	Any text
Design	Locked	Ensures that a control cannot be moved during design time; prevents inadvertently moving the control once it is positioned	True **False**
	Name	Provides a descriptive, unique identifier for the control	Any text
	Size	Indicates height and width of the control in pixels	Two positive whole numbers, separated by a comma
	Location	Indicates distance from the top and left border of the form in pixels	Two positive whole numbers, separated by a comma

Common Control Methods and Events

Table C-2 summarizes the methods and events that are shared by a number of common Visual Basic .NET controls.

Table C-2   Common Methods and Events for Controls (N/A)

METHOD OR EVENT	DESCRIPTION
Enter event	Occurs when the control is entered
Focus method	Sets focus to the control
GotFocus event	Occurs when the control receives focus
Hide method	Conceals the control from the user
KeyPress event	Occurs when a key is pressed while the control has focus
LostFocus event	Occurs when the control loses focus; can be used to validate that the user has entered valid data
MouseMove event	Occurs when the mouse pointer is moved over the control
MouseWheel event	Occurs when the mouse wheel moves while the control has focus
Show method	Displays the control to the user

Form Properties

Table C-3 summarizes the more common properties of Form controls.

Table C-3   Form Properties (VB 3.22)

CATEGORY	PROPERTY	DESCRIPTION	PROPERTY VALUES
Appearance	BackColor	Sets background color of application window	Any color selected from dialog box
	ForeColor	Sets default color for controls that are added to the form	Any color selected from dialog box
	FormBorderStyle	Dictates appearance of form border; whether the form is sizable; and how the Minimize and Maximize buttons, Control menu box, and Help button behave	None FixedSingle Fixed3D FixedDialog **Sizable** FixedToolWindow SizableToolWindow
	Text	Sets title to display on title bar of application window	Any value
Behavior	Enabled	Sets form to be usable during run time	**True** False
Layout	WindowState	Dictates how a window should display initially during run time	**Normal** Minimized Maximized
Window Style	ControlBox	Determines if a Windows control box should display on the form	**True** False
	Icon	Defines the icon that displays on the top-left corner of the window title bar and on the taskbar at run time	Any icon selected from a file via a dialog box

Common Form Methods and Events

Table C-4 summarizes the more common methods and events of Form controls.

Table C-4   Common Form Methods and Events (VB 4.38)

METHOD OR EVENT	DESCRIPTION
Activate method	Activates the form and gives it focus
Activated event	Occurs when the form is activated in code or by the user
Click event	Occurs when the form is clicked
Close method	Closes the form
Closed event	Occurs when the form is closed in code or by the user
DragDrop event	Occurs when a drag-and-drop operation to the form is completed
Load event	Occurs before a form is displayed for the first time; if form subsequently is deactivated or hidden, and then reactivated or shown, event does not execute
Resize event	Event occurs when the Height or Width of the form is changed by the user or in code

TextBox Control Properties

Table C-5 summarizes the more common properties of the TextBox control.

Table C-5 TextBox Control Properties (VB 3.40)

CATEGORY	PROPERTY	DESCRIPTION	PROPERTY VALUES
Appearance	BorderStyle	Determines how the border of the TextBox control displays	None FixedSingle **Fixed3D**
	Text	Sets the text that displays inside the control	Any text with a character length up to the value specified in the MaxLength property
	TextAlign	Determines if text in the control displays left-aligned, right-aligned, or centered	**Left** Right Center
Behavior	AutoSize	Indicates whether the height of the control automatically changes when the font size in the control is changed	**True** False
	MaxLength	Sets the maximum number of characters a user can input into the text control	Any positive whole number from 0 through **32767**
	Multiline	Determines if text in the control displays on more than one line	True **False**
	ReadOnly	If True, a user cannot type or edit text in a control during run time; if False, user can type and edit text in control	True **False**

Table C-5 TextBox Control Properties (VB 3.40) *(continued)*

CATEGORY	PROPERTY	DESCRIPTION	PROPERTY VALUES
	WordWrap	If MultiLine is True, text in control wraps to next line when the text is longer than the width of the control	**True** False

Common TextBox Control Methods and Events

Table C-6 summarizes the more common methods and events of the TextBox control.

Table C-6   Common TextBox Control Methods and Events (VB 3.58)

METHOD OR EVENT	DESCRIPTION
AppendText method	Appends text to the current text of the control
Clear method	Clears all text from the control
Click event	Occurs when the control is clicked
Copy method	Copies the current selection in the control to the Clipboard
Cut method	Moves the current selection in the control to the Clipboard
DoubleClick event	Occurs when the control is double-clicked
Paste method	Replaces the current selection in the control with the contents of the Clipboard
SelectAll method	Selects all text in the text box
TextChanged	Occurs when the Text property value changes for any reason

Label Control Properties

Table C-7 summarizes the more common properties of the Label control.

Table C-7   Label Control Properties (VB 3.46)

CATEGORY	PROPERTY	DESCRIPTION	PROPERTY VALUES
Appearance	FlatStyle	Determines the 3D appearance of the control	Flat Popup **Standard** System
	Image	Sets an image to display on the visible portion of the Label control	Select a picture from the hard drive using a dialog box.
	ImageAlign	If the Image property is set, determines where the image displays	Select a location from a pop-up graphical display map. (**MiddleCenter**)
	Text	Defines the visible text that displays on the control	Any text with any character length

NumericUpDown Control Properties

Table C-8 summarizes the more common properties of the NumericUpDown control.

Table C-8 NumericUpDown Control Properties (VB 3.51)

CATEGORY	PROPERTY	DESCRIPTION	PROPERTY VALUES
Appearance	BorderStyle	Determines how the border of the control displays	None FixedSingle **Fixed3D**
	TextAlign	Defines if text in the control displays left-aligned, right-aligned, or centered	**Left** Right Center
	UpDownAlign	Determines if the up and down arrows on the control display on left or right side of the control	Left **Right**
	Value	Sets the value that displays in the control	Any value within the range set by the Minimum and Maximum property values
Behavior	InterceptArrowKeys	If True, user can use the UP ARROW and DOWN ARROW keys to change the value in the control; if False, the user cannot	**True** False
Data	DecimalPlaces	Defines numbers of decimal places that display in the value in the control	Any whole number from 0 to 99
	Increment	Defines amount to add or subtract from the displayed value each time user clicks the up or down arrow on control	Any positive number
	Maximum	Determines highest allowable value in the control; if user enters a higher value, the value is set automatically to the Maximum value	Any number
	Minimum	Determines lowest allowable value in the control; if a user enters a lower value, the value is set automatically to the Minimum value	Any number
	ThousandsSeparator	Determines if a Thousands separator character is used in the value, when appropriate; if True, value displays with a Thousands separator character set on user's system; if False, no Thousands separator character displays	True **False**

Common NumericUpDown Control Methods and Events

Table C-9 summarizes the more common methods and events of the NumericUpDown control.

Table C-9   Common NumericUpDown Control Methods and Events (VB 3.58)

METHOD OR EVENT	DESCRIPTION
DownButton method	Imitates the user clicking the down arrow on the control one time
UpButton method	Imitates the user clicking the up arrow on the control one time
ValueChanged event	Occurs when the Value property of the control has been changed in some way

Button Control Properties

Table C-10 summarizes the more common properties of the Button control.

Table C-10   Button Control Properties (VB 3.54)

CATEGORY	PROPERTY	DESCRIPTION	PROPERTY VALUES
Appearance	FlatStyle	Determines the 3D appearance of the control	Flat Popup **Standard** System
	Image	Sets an image to display on the visible portion of the Button control, along with the text	Select a picture from the hard drive using a dialog box.
	ImageAlign	Image property is set, determines where the image displays	Select a location from a pop-up graphical display map.
	TextAlign	Determines where text should display on the button	Select one of nine locations from a pop-up graphical display map.

Common Button Control Methods and Events

Table C-11 summarizes the more common methods and events of the Button control.

Table C-11   Common Button Control Methods and Events (VB 3.60)

METHOD OR EVENT	DESCRIPTION
Click event	Occurs when the user clicks the Button control
PerformClick method	Imitates a user clicking the Button control; causes the Click event to execute

GroupBox Control Properties

Table C-12 summarizes the more common properties of the GroupBox control.

Table C-12 GroupBox Control Properties (VB 4.16)

CATEGORY	PROPERTY	DESCRIPTION	PROPERTY VALUES
Appearance	FlatStyle	Determines the 3D appearance of the control	Flat Popup **Standard** System
	Text	Indicates the label to display on the upper-left edge of the control	Any value, or set blank if no label is desired
Design	GridSize: Width and Gridsize: Height	Determines the size of the positioning grid within the control	Width and Height properties can be any positive whole number (8, 8)

RadioButton Control Properties

Table C-13 summarizes the more common properties of the RadioButton control.

Table C-13 RadioButton Control Properties (VB 4.19)

CATEGORY	PROPERTY	DESCRIPTION	PROPERTY VALUES
Appearance	CheckAlign	Determines the location of the check box inside the control	Select a location from a pop-up graphical display map. (**MiddleLeft**)
	Checked	Determines whether the RadioButton is selected (checked) or not	True **False**
	FlatStyle	Determines the 3D appearance of the control	Flat Popup **Standard** System
	Image	Sets an image to display on the visible portion of the Label control along with the text	Select a picture from the hard drive using a dialog box.
	ImageAlign	If the Image property is set, determines where the image displays	Select a location from a pop-up graphical display map. (**MiddleCenter**)
	Text	Defines the visible text that displays on the control	Any text with any character length
Behavior	AutoCheck	Causes the RadioButton to change state (value of Checked property) automatically when clicked	**True** False

Common RadioButton Control Methods and Events

Table C-14 summarizes the more common methods and events of the RadioButton control.

Table C-14   Common RadioButton Control Methods and Events (VB 4.45)

METHOD OR EVENT	DESCRIPTION
CheckChanged event	Occurs when the value of the Checked property of the control changes

ComboBox Control Properties

Table C-15 summarizes the more common properties of the ComboBox control.

Table C-15   ComboBox Control Properties (VB 5.15)

CATEGORY	PROPERTY	DESCRIPTION	PROPERTY VALUES
Appearance	DropDownStyle	Controls the appearance and functionality of the ComboBox (see Table 5-3)	Simple **DropDown** DropDownList
	Text	Sets the text that displays in the control's text box	Any text (defaults to the control name for controls with DropDownStyle value of DropDown or DropDownList)
Behavior	DropDownWidth	Sets the width in pixels of the drop-down box	A positive integer value (defaults to the width of the control)
	IntegralHeight	Indicates whether the visible list portion should display only complete items	**True** False
	ItemHeight	Sets the height in pixels of an item in the ComboBox	A positive integer value (**13**)
	MaxDropDownItems	Sets the maximum number of items in the drop-down list	An integer value between 1 and 100 (**8**)
	MaxLength	Sets the maximum number of characters the user can enter	A positive integer value
	Sorted	Controls whether items in the list portion are sorted automatically	True **False**

Common ComboBox Control Methods and Events

Table C-16 summarizes the more common methods and events of the ComboBox control.

Table C-16   Common ComboBox Control Methods and Events (N/A)

METHOD OR EVENT	DESCRIPTION
FindString method	Finds the first item in the ComboBox that starts with the specified string
FindStringExact method	Finds the item that exactly matches the specified string
SelectionValueChanged event	Occurs when the SelectedValue property changes

ListView Control Properties

Table C-17 summarizes the more common properties of the ListView control.

Table C-17   ListView Control Properties (VB 6.19)

CATEGORY	PROPERTY	DESCRIPTION	PROPERTY VALUES
Appearance	CheckBoxes	Determines whether a check box appears next to each item	True **False**
	FullRowSelect	Determines whether clicking an item selects all its subitems	True **False**
	GridLines	Determines whether grid lines appear between the rows and columns containing the items and subitems	True **False**
	View	Determines how items display in the control	**LargeIcon** Details SmallIcon List
Behavior	Activation	Determines the type of action the user must take to select (activate) an item	**Standard** OneClick TwoClick
	Alignment	Determines the alignment of list items	**Default** Left Top SnapToGrid
	AllowColumnReorder	Determines whether the user can drag column headers to reorder columns	True **False**
	AutoArrange	Determines whether icons are arranged automatically	**True** False
	Columns	Indicates the collection of all column headers used in the control	Collection of headers; default is an empty collection

Table C-17   ListView Control Properties (VB 6.19) (continued)

CATEGORY	PROPERTY	DESCRIPTION	PROPERTY VALUES
	HeaderStyle	Determines the column header style when column headers are defined	None Nonclickable **Clickable**
	Items	Indicates a collection containing all list items	Collection of items; default is an empty collection
	MultiSelect	Determines whether multiple items can be selected	**True** False
	Scrollable	Determines whether a scroll bar is added to the control if not enough room is available to display all items	**True** False

Common ListView Control Methods and Events

Table C-18 summarizes the more common methods and events of the ListView control.

Table C-18   Common ListView Control Methods and Events (VB 6.47)

METHOD OR EVENT	DESCRIPTION
ArrangeIcons method	Arranges items in the control when they are displayed as icons
Clear method	Removes all items and columns from the control
EnsureVisible method	Ensures that the specified item is visible within the control, scrolling the contents of the control if necessary
GetItemAt method	Retrieves the item at the specified location
GetItemRect method	Retrieves the bounding rectangle for an item within the control
ItemActivate event	Occurs when an item is activated
ItemCheck event	Occurs when the check state of an item changes
SelectedIndexChanged event	Occurs when the index of the selected item in the control changes
Sort method	Sorts the items of the control
StyleChanged event	Occurs when the style of the control changes

CheckBox Control Properties

Table C-19 summarizes the more common properties of the CheckBox control.

Table C-19 *CheckBox Control Properties (VB 6.34)*

CATEGORY	PROPERTY	DESCRIPTION	PROPERTY VALUES
Appearance	Appearance	Determines whether the check box displays with text and a check box, or as a multi-state button	**Normal** Button
	CheckAlign	Determines the location of the check box inside the control	Select a location from a pop-up graphical display. (**MiddleLeft**)
	Checked	Determines whether the CheckBox is selected (checked) or not	True **False**
	CheckedState	Determines the state of the check box if the ThreeState property is set to true; if set to Indeterminate, the check box displays with a check mark and is shaded	**Unchecked** Checked Indeterminate
	FlatStyle	Determines the 3D appearance of the control	Flat Popup **Standard** System
	Image	Sets an image to display on the visible portion of the control, along with the text	Select a picture from the hard disk using a dialog box.
	ImageAlign	If the Image property is set, determines where the image displays	Select a location from a pop-up graphical display map. (**MiddleCenter**)
	Text	Defines the visible text that displays on the control	Any text with any character length
Behavior	AutoCheck	Causes the control to change state automatically (value of Checked property) when clicked	**True** False
	ThreeState	Determines whether the user can select the indeterminate state of the check box	True **False**

Common CheckBox Control Methods and Events

Table C-20 summarizes the more common methods and events of the CheckBox control.

Table C-20   Common CheckBox Control Methods and Events (N/A)

METHOD OR EVENT	DESCRIPTION
CheckedChanged event	Occurs when the value of the Checked property of the control changes

MenuItem Class Properties

Table C-21 summarizes the more common properties of the ComboBox control.

Table C-21   MenuItem Class Properties (VB 7.23)

CATEGORY	PROPERTY	DESCRIPTION	PROPERTY VALUES
Misc.	Checked	Indicates whether a check mark appears next to the text of the menu item	True **False**
	DefaultItem	Indicates whether the menu item is the default menu item	True **False**
	Enabled	Indicates whether the menu item is enabled	**True** False
	RadioCheck	Indicates whether the MenuItem, if checked, displays an option button instead of a check mark	True **False**
	Shortcut	Indicates the shortcut key associated with the menu item	Select from a list of keys (default is **None**)
	Text	Sets the text that displays for the menu item	Any text

Common MenuItem Class Methods and Events

Table C-22 summarizes the more common methods and events of the MenuItem class.

Table C-22   Common MenuItem Class Methods and Events (VB 7.23)

METHOD OR EVENT	DESCRIPTION
GetMainMenu method	Gets the MainMenu that contains this menu
MergeMenu method	Merges this MenuItem with another MenuItem
PerformClick method	Generates a Click event for the MenuItem, simulating a click by a user
PerformSelect method	Raises the Select event for this MenuItem
Popup event	Occurs before a MenuItem's list of MenuItems is displayed
Select event	Occurs when the user places the insertion point over a MenuItem

StatusBar Control Properties

Table C-23 summarizes the more common properties of the StatusBar control.

Table C-23   StatusBar Control Properties (VB 7.34)

CATEGORY	PROPERTY	DESCRIPTION	PROPERTY VALUES
Appearance	Panels	Collections of panels to display on the control	A collection of panels
	SizingGrip	Determines whether the status bar includes a sizing grip for the form on the lower right of the control	**True** False
Behavior	ShowPanels	Determines whether panels defined in the Panels property display	True **False**

StatusBar Panel Control Properties

Table C-24 summarizes the more common properties of the StatusBar Panel control.

Table C-24   StatusBar Panel Properties (VB 7.34)

CATEGORY	PROPERTY	DESCRIPTION	PROPERTY VALUES
Appearance	Alignment	Determines whether the information in the panel displays on the left, right, or center of the panel	**Left** Right Center
	AutoSize	If set to None, the panel remains the size set by its Width property; if set to Spring, the panel fills all remaining space on the StatusBar of which it is a part; if set to Contents, the panel is only as large as the information inside the panel	**None** Spring Contents
	BorderStyle	Determines the appearance of the border of the panel	None Raised **Sunken**
	Icon	Sets an icon to display in the panel	Any icon
Behavior	MinWidth	Sets the minimum width in pixels to which the panel can be resized	Any positive whole number (default is **10**)

PictureBox Control Properties

Table C-25 summarizes the more common properties of the PictureBox control.

Table C-25   PictureBox Control Properties (VB 7.38)

CATEGORY	PROPERTY	DESCRIPTION	PROPERTY VALUES
Appearance	Image	The image that displays in the control	Any image file with the file extensions of bmp, gif, jpg, jpeg, png, ico, emf, and wmf; any image matching those types also can be pasted into the control; default is **none**
Behavior	SizeMode	Determines how the control handles image placement and sizing	**Normal** StetchImage AutoSize CenterImage

FontDialog Control Properties

Table C-26 summarizes the more common properties of the FontDialog control.

Table C-26   FontDialog Control Properties (VB 7.41)

CATEGORY	PROPERTY	DESCRIPTION	PROPERTY VALUES
Misc	AllowScriptChange	Determines whether the user can change the character set of the font	**True** False
	AllowVectorFonts	Determines whether vector fonts can be selected	**True** False
	AllowVerticalFonts	Determines whether vertical fonts can be selected	**True** False
	FixedPitchOnly	Determines whether only fixed pitched fonts can be selected	**True** False
	Font	Defines the default font and font properties that are selected when the dialog box first displays	Select a default font from a font dialog box (default is the system default font)
	FontMustExist	Determines whether to report an error if the selected font does not exist	True **False**
	MaxSize	Indicates the maximum point size that can be selected (0 to disable)	Any positive whole number (**0** to disable)

(continued)

Table C-26   FontDialog Control Properties (VB 7.41) (continued)

CATEGORY	PROPERTY	DESCRIPTION	PROPERTY VALUES
	MinSize	Indicates the minimum point size that can be selected (0 to disable)	Any positive whole number (**0** to disable)
	ScriptsOnly	Determines whether to exclude nonstandard fonts such as Symbol character fonts	True **False**
	ShowApply	Determines whether to show the Apply button in the dialog box	True **False**
	ShowColor	Determines whether to show a color choice in the dialog box	True **False**
	ShowEffects	Determines whether to show the underline, strikethrough, and font color selections in the dialog box	**True** False
	ShowHelp	Determines whether to show the Help button in the dialog box	True **False**

Common FontDialog Control Methods and Events

Table C-27 summarizes the more common methods and events of the FontDialog control.

Table C-27   Common FontDialog Control Methods and Events (VB 7.56)

METHOD OR EVENT	DESCRIPTION
Apply event	Occurs when the user clicks the Apply button in the Font dialog box
HelpRequest event	Occurs when the user clicks the Help button in a common dialog box
ShowDialog method	Runs a common dialog box

MonthCalendar Control Properties

Table C-28 summarizes the more common properties of the MonthCalendar control.

Table C-28   MonthCalendar Control Properties (VB 10.45)

CATEGORY	PROPERTY	DESCRIPTION	PROPERTY VALUES
Appearance	CalendarDimensions:Height	The number of rows of months to display in the control	Any integer value from **1** to **12**
	CalendarDimensions:Width	The number of columns of months to display in the control	Any integer value from **1** to **12**

(continued)

Table C-28 **MonthCalendar Control Properties (VB 10.45)** *(continued)*

CATEGORY	PROPERTY	DESCRIPTION	PROPERTY VALUES
Behavior	FirstDayOfWeek	The first day of the week that displays in the left column of each month	**Default** Monday Tuesday Wednesday Thursday Friday Saturday Sunday
	MaxDate	The maximum date that the user can select	Choose a date from a drop-down calendar (**12/31/9998**)
	MaxSelectionCount	The maximum number of dates that the user can select at any time	Any integer value (**7**)
	MinDate	The minimum date that the user can select	Choose a date from a drop-down calendar (**1/1/1753**)
	ScrollChange	The scroll rate in number of months moved when the user clicks an arrow button on the control	Any positive integer value up to 20,000. The default is the number of months currently displayed.
	SelectionStart	The date marking the beginning of the currently selected range	Any valid date in the control
	SelectionEnd	The date marking the end of the currently selected range	Any valid date in the control
	ShowToday	Determines whether today's date displays at the bottom of control	**True** False
	ShowTodayCircle	Determines whether today's date is circled in the control	**True** False
	ShowWeekNumbers	Determines whether the week number (1 – 52) displays for each week in the calendar	True **False**
	TodaysDate	The current day	Choose a date from a drop-down calendar
Misc	AnnuallyBoldedDate	An array of recurring dates that the control bolds for every year	Select individual dates in a dialog box
	BoldedDate	An array of individual, non-recurring dates that the control bolds	Select individual dates in a dialog box
	MonthlyBoldedDates	An array of recurring dates that the control bolds for each month	Select individual dates in a dialog box

Common MonthCalendar Control Methods and Events

Table C-29 summarizes the more common methods and events of the MonthCalendar control.

Table C-29 Common MonthCalendar Control Methods and Events (N/A)

METHOD OR EVENT	DESCRIPTION
AddBoldedDate method	Adds a day that is displayed in bold
DateChanged event	Occurs when the date selected in the control changes
DateSelected event	Occurs when a date in the control is selected
RemoveBoldedDate method	Removes a date from the list of bolded dates
SetCalendarDimensions method	Sets the number of columns and rows of months that display in the control
SetDate method	Sets a date as the selected date in the control
SetSelectionRange method	Sets the selected dates in the control to a specified date range

PrintDialog Control Properties

Table C-30 summarizes the more common properties of the PrintDialog control.

Table C-30 PrintDialog Control Properties (VB 10.48)

CATEGORY	PROPERTY	DESCRIPTION	PROPERTY VALUES
Misc	AllowPrintToFile	Determines whether a Print to file check box displays on the Print dialog box	**True** False
	AllowSelection	Determines whether the Selection radio button displays on the dialog box, allowing the user to print just a selection from the document	True **False**
	AllowSomePages	Determines whether the Pages radio button displays on the dialog box, allowing the user to print just selected pages from the document	True **False**
	Document	A document control associated with the dialog box	The name of a document control
	PrintToFile	Reflects the state of the Print to file check box	True **False**
	ShowNetwork	Determines whether the Network button displays on the dialog box	**True** False

Common PrintDialog Control Methods and Events

Table C-31 summarizes the more common methods and events of the PrintDialog control.

Table C-31 Common PrintDialog Control Methods and Events (VB 10.51)

METHOD OR EVENT	DESCRIPTION
HelpRequest event	Occurs when the user clicks the Help button on a common dialog box
Reset method	Resets all options, including the last selected printer and page settings, to their default
ShowDialog method	Runs a common dialog box

PrintDocument Control Properties

Table C-32 summarizes the more common properties of the PrintDocument control.

Table C-32 PrintDocument Control Properties (VB 10.48)

CATEGORY	PROPERTY	DESCRIPTION	PROPERTY VALUES
Misc	DefaultPageSettings	Gets or sets page settings to use for all pages	Set several object properties. See Visual Basic .NET Help for PageSetting properties.
	DocumentName	Gets or sets the document name to display while the document prints	Any text value
	PrinterSettings	Gets or sets the printer settings for the current printer that prints the document	Set several object properties. See Visual Basic .NET Help for PageSetting properties.

Common PrintDocument Control Methods and Events

Table C-33 summarizes the more common methods and events of the PrintDocument control.

Table C-33 Common PrintDocument Control Methods and Events (VB 10.51)

METHOD OR EVENT	DESCRIPTION
Print method	Initiates printing of the document
BeginPrint event	Occurs when the Print method is called but before the first page prints
EndPrint event	Occurs when the last page of the document has printed on the printer
PrintPage event	Occurs when the output for the next page is needed

Web Form Properties

Table C-34 summarizes the more common properties of Web Form controls.

Table C-34 Web Form Properties (VB 11.34)

PROPERTY	DESCRIPTION	PROPERTY VALUES
Background	A background image that displays on the form	Choose an image from a dialog box
bgColor	The background color of the form	Choose a color from a dialog box
text	The text foreground color of text that is added to the form	Choose a color from a dialog box
title	The title that displays in the Web browser title bar when the page is active in a Web browser	Any text value

A P P E N D I X

D

General Forms of Common Visual Basic .NET Statements, Data Types, and Naming Conventions

Appendix D summarizes the common Visual Basic .NET statements presented in this book along with their general forms. The naming conventions for variables and controls used in this book also are included.

General Forms of Visual Basic .NET Statements

Table D-1 summarizes the general forms of Visual Basic .NET statements introduced in this book and the page number on which the general forms appear.

Table D-1   General Forms of Common Visual Basic .NET Statements

STATEMENT	GENERAL FORM	PAGE NUMBER
Assignment	1. Object = newvalue 2. Object.Property = newvalue	VB 3.59
Comment	1. ' comment 2. REM comment	VB 3.60
Constant Declaration	1. Const name As type = value 2. Const name = value	VB 4.36

Dim (array)	1. Dim arrayname(upperlimit) As datatype =
	    {initialvalue1, initialvalue2,…}
	2. Dim arrayname(upperlimit) As datatype
	3. Dim arrayname() As datatype =
	    {initialvalue1, initialvalue2…}
	4. Dim arrayname() As datatype
	
	where arrayname represents the array name and upperlimit represents the upper-bound value of the array. The upperlimit parameter can be repeated and separated by commas to define multidimensional arrays. Similarly, commas can be placed in the parentheses in forms 3 and 4 to define additional dimensions. For all arrays, the number of elements in the array is equal to upperlimit + 1, because the first element of all arrays has an index of 0.
		VB 7.45

Dim (Object)	1. Dim variablename As [class or Object] 2. Dim variablename As New [class or Object]	VB 6.38
Dim (simple)	1. Dim variablename As datatype = initialvalue 2. Dim variablename As datatype 3. Dim variablename	VB 4.43

Do Until	1. Do Until condition
	        statements
	    Loop
	2. Do
	        statements
	    Loop Until condition
		VB 6.43

Do While	1. Do While condition
	        statements
	    Loop
	2. Do
	        statements
	    Loop While condition
		VB 6.43

Table D-1 **General Forms of Common Visual Basic .NET Statements** *(continued)*

STATEMENT	GENERAL FORM	PAGE NUMBER
Exit	1. Exit Sub 2. Exit statement where statement is For, Do, Loop 3. Exit Function	VB 5.32, VB 6.56

For...Each	1. For Each item In collection
	     statements
	  Next element
	
	where item is of the object type of items in the
	collection and collection is the name of the collection.
		VB 6.62

For...Next	1. For k = initial value To limit value Step increment value
	     statements within For...Next loop
	  Next k
	or
	2. For k = initial value To limit value
	     statements within For...Next loop
	  Next k
	
	where k is a simple numeric variable called the loop
	variable, and the initial value, limit value, and increment
	value are numeric expressions.
		VB 6.53

Function	1. Function name(argument 1, ..., argument n)
	  As datatype
	    statements
	  End Function
	2. Private Function name(argument 1, ..., argument n)
	  As datatype
	    statements
	  End Function
	
	where the function name is a valid name following the
	conventions of variable naming.
		VB 7.52

Get	1. Get
	    statements
	  End Get
	
	where the Get statement occurs nested within a
	Property declaration.
		VB 9.27

(continued)

Table D-1 **General Forms of Common Visual Basic .NET Statements** *(continued)*

STATEMENT	GENERAL FORM	PAGE NUMBER

If…Then…Else	1. If condition Then clause Else clause
	2. If condition Then
	      clause 1
	      clause 2
	   Else
	      clause 3
	   End If
	3. If condition Then
	      clause
	   End If
	
	where condition is a relation that is either true or false and clause is a statement or series of statements; the Else keyword and subsequent clause are optional, as show in General form 3 above.
		VB 5.30

Imports	1. Imports namespace 2. Imports alias = namespace 3. Imports namespace.element 4. Imports alias = namespace.element where the namespace is a valid namespace in the current project or in a reference in the current project and where element is a valid class or other entity in the namespace.	VB 9.63
Inherits	1. Inherits classname where classname is another class in the current project or a class included in one of the references in the project.	VB 9.41
Option Strict	1. Option Strict On 2. Option Strict Off	VB 4.41

Property	1. [Public | Private | Protected] Property Name(argument 1, …, argument n) As datatype
	   Get and Set property procedures
	  End Property
	
	2. [Public | Private | Protected] [ReadOnly | WriteOnly] Property name() As datatype
	   Get and/or Set property procedures
	  End Property
	
	where at least one of the keywords, Public, Private, or Protected, is used and, in the second form, either the ReadOnly or WriteOnly keyword is used. The Property name is a valid name following the conventions of variable naming. All arguments must be passed by value (ByVal).
		VB 9.26

Return	1. Return 2. Return expression	VB 7.53

Table D-1 General Forms of Common Visual Basic .NET Statements (continued)

STATEMENT	GENERAL FORM	PAGE NUMBER

Select Case	Select Case testexpression
	    Case expressionlist
	      [statements]
	        .
	        .
	        .
	    Case Else
	      [statements]
	End Select
	
	where testexpression is a string or numeric variable or expression that is matched with the expressionlist in the corresponding Case clauses; and expressionlist is a numeric or string expression or a range of numeric or string expressions of the following form:
	1. expression, expression, . . . , expression
	2. expression To expression
	3. a relational expression where relation is
	   <, >, >=, <=, =, or <>
		VB 5.53

Set	1. Set (argument 1, ..., argument n)
	    statements
	  End Set
	
	where the Set statement occurs nested within a Property declaration.
		VB 9.30

Sub (simple)	1. Sub name(argument 1, ..., argument n)
	    statements
	  End Sub
	2. Private Sub name(argument 1, ..., argument n)
	    statements
	  End Sub
	
	where the sub procedure name is a valid name following the conventions of variable naming.
		VB 7.65

Throw	1. Throw exception	VB 10.23

(continued)

Table D-1   General Forms of Common Visual Basic .NET Statements (continued)

STATEMENT	GENERAL FORM	PAGE NUMBER

Try…Catch…Finally	1. Try
	    statements
	Catch [exception as datatype]
	    statements
	End Try
	
	2. Try
	    statements
	Catch [exception as datatype]
	    statements
	Finally
	    statements
	End Try
	
	where the statements following the Try statement include the statements being tested for exceptions. Only one Try clause and one Finally clause are allowed. Multiple Catch clauses are allowed if an exception object follows the Catch keyword. An Exit Try statement may be placed in either the Try clause or the Catch clause to cause the Try…Catch…Finally statement to exit.
		VB 10.22

While…End While	1. While condition statements End While	VB 6.45

Visual Basic .NET Data Types and Naming Convention

Table D-2 summarizes the Visual Basic .NET data types and the recommended naming convention for the three-character prefix preceding variable names of the corresponding data type.

Table D-2   Visual Basic .NET Data Types and Naming Convention

CATEGORY	DATA TYPE	DESCRIPTION	RANGE	PREFIX
Character	**Char**	16-bit (2 bytes) character	1 16-bit character	chr
	String	Sequence of 0 or more 16-bit characters	0 to 2,000,000,000 16-bit characters	str
Integral	**Short**	16-bit integer value	–32,768 to 32,767	shr
	Integer	32-bit (4 bytes) integer value	–2147483648 to 2147483647	int
	Long	64-bit (8 bytes) integer value	–9,223,372,036,854,775,808 to 9,223,372,036,854,775,807	lng
	Byte	8-bit (1 byte) unsigned integer value	0 to 255	byt

Table D-2   Visual Basic .NET Data Types and Naming Convention (continued)

CATEGORY	DATA TYPE	DESCRIPTION	RANGE	PREFIX
Nonintegral	**Decimal**	128-bit (16 bytes) fixed point	1.0e-28 to 7.9e28	dec
	Single	32-bit floating point	±1.5e-45 to ±3.4e38	sng
	Double	64-bit floating point	±5.0e-324 to ±1.7e308	dbl
Miscellaneous	**Boolean**	32-bit value	True or **False**	bln
	Date	64-bit signed integer – each increment represents 100 nanoseconds elapsed since the beginning of January 1 in the year 1	January 1, 0001:00:00:00 to December 31, 9999:23:59:59	dtm
	Object	32-bit number that represents the location of the object in memory	Any object	obj

Visual Basic .NET Control Naming Convention

Table D-3 summarizes the naming convention used in this book for naming controls. Use the three letters in the second column as a prefix to a meaningful name.

Table D-3   Control Naming Convention

CONTROL	PREFIX	CONTROL	PREFIX
CheckBox	chk	MainMenu	mnu
ContextMenu	cmu	MenuItem	mnu
ComboBox	cmb	NumericUpDown	nud
FontDialog	fod	PictureBox	pic
Form	frm	RadioButton	rad
GroupBox	grp	StatusBar	stb
Label	lbl	StatusBarPanel	sbp
ListView	lst (alternatively, lsv to distinguish from ListBox controls)	TextBox	txt

APPENDIX

E

The .NET Framework
Class Library Overview

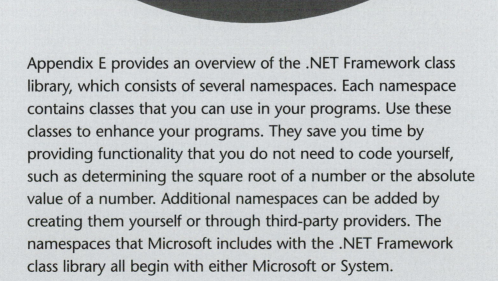

Appendix E provides an overview of the .NET Framework class library, which consists of several namespaces. Each namespace contains classes that you can use in your programs. Use these classes to enhance your programs. They save you time by providing functionality that you do not need to code yourself, such as determining the square root of a number or the absolute value of a number. Additional namespaces can be added by creating them yourself or through third-party providers. The namespaces that Microsoft includes with the .NET Framework class library all begin with either Microsoft or System.

Namespaces and Classes

The following tables provide the namespaces and classes that may be useful to you as a beginning programmer. The .NET Framework class library contains several more namespaces than those listed and most of the namespaces contain many more classes than listed. Each class presented may contain many methods and attributes. Use the Visual Basic .NET Help system to find more information about each class.

The example below shows the use of the System.Math.Cos() method in the Math class of the System namespace. The Cos() method determines the cosine of a given angle.

```
Dim dblCosine as Double
dblCosine = System.Math.Cos(90.0)
```

Microsoft.VisualBasic Namespace

The **Microsoft.VisualBasic Namespace** (Table E-1) contains classes that are useful mostly for backwards compatibility with older versions of Visual Basic.

Table E-1   Microsoft.VisualBasic Namespace

CLASS	DESCRIPTION
Collection	The Collection class provides a convenient way to refer to a related group of items as a single object. Methods such as Add and Remove are used to modify the collection.
Conversion	The Conversion class contains methods used to perform various conversion operations. For example, Int() is used to convert a Double value to an Integer.
DateAndTime	The DateAndTime class contains methods and properties used in date and time operations. For example, the DateAdd() method adds an interval of time to a specified date.
ErrObject	The ErrObject class contains properties and procedures used to identify and handle run-time errors using the Err object. This should be used only for backward compatibility with older versions of Visual Basic.
FileSystem	The FileSystem module contains the procedures used to perform file, directory or folder, and system operations. This should only be used for backward compatibility with older versions of Visual Basic. For example, the FileCopy() function can be used to copy a file from one folder to another.
Financial	The Financial module contains procedures used to perform financial operations. For example, the Pv() function is used to determine a present value of an annuity based on periodic, fixed payments to be paid in the future and a fixed interest rate.
Globals	The Globals module contains script engine functions. For example, the ScriptEngine and ScriptEngineMajor properties give the version of the Visual Basic .NET run-time engine that you are using.
Information	The Information module contains the procedures used to return, test for, or verify information. For example, the IsDate() function returns a Boolean value indicating whether an expression can be converted to a date.

Table E-1   Microsoft.VisualBasic Namespace (continued)

CLASS	DESCRIPTION
Interaction	The Interaction module contains procedures used to interact with objects, applications, and systems. This should be used only for backward compatibility with older versions of Visual Basic. For example, the Beep() function causes the speaker to emit a brief tone.
Strings	The Strings module contains procedures used to perform string operations. For example, the StrComp() function can be used to compare the contents of two strings.
VbMath	The VbMath module contains procedures used to perform mathematical operations. For example, the Rnd() function can be used to return a random number of type Single.

Microsoft.Win32 Namespace

The **Microsoft.Win32 namespace** (Table E-2) provides two types of classes: (1) those that handle events raised by the operating system and (2) those that manipulate the system registry.

Table E-2   Microsoft.Win32 Namespace

CLASS	DESCRIPTION
Registry	Supplies the base RegistryKeys that access values and subkeys in the registry.
RegistryKey	Represents a key level node in the Windows registry. Use this class to manipulate registry keys you may need in your application.
SystemEvents	Provides a set of global system events to callers. System events include shutdown notifications and changes to user preferences.

System Namespace

The **System Namespace** (Table E-3) contains fundamental classes and base classes. It provides services supporting data type conversion, mathematics, local and remote program invocation, and application environment management.

Table E-3   System Namespace

CLASS	DESCRIPTION
Console	Represents the standard input, output, and error streams for console applications. For example, the Console.Write() method writes an expression to a console window.
Convert	Converts a base data type to another base data type. For example, the Convert.ToDouble() method converts a specified value to a double-precision floating point number.

(continued)

Table E-3 System Namespace (continued)

CLASS	DESCRIPTION
Exception	Represents errors that occur during application execution. Two categories of exceptions exist under the base class Exception: (1) The predefined common language runtime exception classes derived from SystemException; (2) The user-defined application exception classes derived from ApplicationException. For example, the ToString() method creates and returns a string representation of the current exception.
Math	Provides constants and static methods for trigonometric, logarithmic, and other common mathematical functions. For example, the Cos() method returns the cosine of the specified angle.
Object	Supports all classes in the .NET Framework class library hierarchy and provides low-level services to derived classes. This is the ultimate superclass of all classes in the .NET Framework; it is the root of the type hierarchy.
Random	Represents a pseudo-random number generator, a device that produces a sequence of numbers that meets certain statistical requirements for randomness. For example, the Next() method returns a random number.
String	Represents an immutable series of characters. For example, the Format() method replaces each format specification in a specified String with the textual equivalent of a corresponding object's value.
TimeZone	Represents a time zone. For example, the CurrentTimeZone property gets the time zone of the current computer system.
Type	Represents type declarations: class types, interface types, array types, value types, and enumeration types. Use the Type class to create your own data types.
Version	Represents the version number for a common language runtime assembly. For example, the Major property gets the value of the major component of the version number for this instance.

System.Collections Namespace

The **System.Collections namespace** (Table E-4) contains interfaces and classes that define various collections of objects, such as lists, queues, bit arrays, hashtables, and dictionaries.

Table E-4 System.Collections Namespace

CLASS	DESCRIPTION
ArrayList	Implements an interface using an array whose size is increased dynamically as required. Use the Add() method to add new items to the array.
Comparer	Compares two objects for equivalence, where string comparisons are case-sensitive. For example, the Compare() method performs a case-sensitive comparison of two objects of the same type and returns a value indicating whether one is less than, equal to, or greater than the other.
HashTable	Represents a collection of key-and-value pairs that are organized based on the hash code of the key. Use the Add() method to add new items to the array.

Table E-4 System.Collections Namespace (continued)

CLASS	DESCRIPTION
Queue	Represents a first-in, first-out collection of objects. Use the EnQueue() and DeQueue() methods to add and remove objects from the queue.
SortedList	Represents a collection of key-and-value pairs that are sorted by the keys and are accessible by key and by index. Use the Add() method to add an item to the list. Use the GetByIndex() method to access an item by the sort key.
Stack	Represents a simple last-in-first-out collection of objects. Use the Push() and Pop() methods to add and remove items from the stack.

System.Data Namespace

The **System.Data namespace** (Table E-5) consists mostly of the classes that constitute the ADO.NET architecture. The ADO.NET architecture enables you to build components that efficiently manage data from multiple data sources.

Table E-5 System.Data Namespace

CLASS	DESCRIPTION
DataColumn	Represents a schema, or definition, of a column in a data table.
DataColumnCollection	Represents all of the DataColumns for a data table. Defines the schema of the table.
DataRow	Represents one row of data in a table.
DataRowCollection	Represents a collection of rows in a table.
DataRowView	Represents a customized view of a DataRow exposed as a fully featured Windows Forms control.
DataSet	Represents an in-memory cache of data.
DataTable	Represents one table of in-memory data.
DataTableCollection	Represents the collection of tables for the DataSet.
DataView	Represents a databindable, customized view of a DataTable for sorting, filtering, searching, editing, and navigation.
DataViewManager	Contains a default DataViewSettingCollection for each DataTable in a DataSet.
DataViewSetting	Represents the default settings for ApplyDefaultSort, DataViewManager, RowFilter, RowStateFilter, Sort, and Table for DataViews created from the DataViewManager.

System.Data.OleDb Namespace

The **System.Data.OleDb namespace** (Table E-6) is the OLE DB .NET Data Provider. A .NET data provider describes a collection of classes used to access a data source, such as a database, in the managed space. Using the OleDbDataAdapter, you can fill a memory-resident DataSet, which you can use to query and update the datasource.

Table E-6   System.Data.OleDb Namespace

CLASS	DESCRIPTION
OleDbCommand	Represents an SQL statement or stored procedure to execute against a data source.
OleDbCommandBuilder	Provides a means of automatically generating single-table commands used to reconcile changes made to a DataSet with the associated database.
OleDbConnection	Represents an open connection to a data source.
OleDbDataReader	Provides a way of reading a forward-only stream of data rows from a data source.
OleDbErrorCollection	Collects all errors generated by the OLE DB .NET Data Provider.
OleDbTransaction	Represents an SQL transaction to be made at a data source.

System.Drawing Namespace

The **System.Drawing namespace** (Table E-7) provides access to basic graphics functionality. More advanced functionality is provided in the System.Drawing.Drawing2D, System.Drawing.Imaging, and System.Drawing.Text namespaces. The Graphics class provides methods for drawing to the display device. Classes such as Rectangle and Point encapsulate primitives. The Pen class is used to draw lines and curves, while classes derived from the abstract class Brush are used to fill the interiors of shapes.

Table E-7   System.Drawing Namespace

CLASS	DESCRIPTION
Bitmap	Encapsulates a bitmap, which consists of the pixel data for a graphics image and its attributes. A Bitmap object is an object used to work with images defined by pixel data.
Brush	Classes derived from this abstract base class define objects used to fill the interiors of graphical shapes such as rectangles, ellipses, pies, polygons, and paths.
Font	Defines a particular format for text, including font face, size, and style attributes.
Graphics	Encapsulates a drawing surface.
Icon	Represents a Windows icon, which is a small bitmap image used to represent an object. Icons can be thought of as transparent bitmaps, although their size is determined by the system.

*Table E-7 **System.Drawing Namespace*** (continued)

CLASS	DESCRIPTION
Image	An abstract base class that provides functionality for Bitmap, Icon, and Metafile descended classes.
Pen	Defines an object used to draw lines and curves.

System.Drawing.Printing Namespace

The **System.Drawing.Printing namespace** (Table E-8) provides print-related services. Typically, you create a new instance of the PrintDocument class, set the properties that describe what to print, and call the Print method actually to print the document.

*Table E-8 **System.Drawing.Printing Namespace***

CLASS	DESCRIPTION
Margins	Specifies the margins of a printed page.
PageSettings	Specifies settings that apply to a single, printed page.
PaperSize	Specifies the size of a piece of paper.
PrintDocument	Defines a reusable object that sends output to a printer.
PrinterResolution	Represents the resolution supported by a printer.
PrinterSettings	Specifies information about how a document is printed, including the printer that prints it.
StandardPrintController	Specifies a print controller that sends information to a printer.

System.Drawing.Text Namespace

The **System.Drawing.Text namespace** (Table E-9) provides advanced typography functionality. Basic graphics functionality is provided by the System.Drawing namespace. The classes in this namespace allow users to create and use collections of fonts.

*Table E-9 **System.Drawing.Text Namespace***

CLASS	DESCRIPTION
FontCollection	Base class for installed and private font collections. Provides a method to get a list of the font families contained in the collection.
InstalledFontCollection	Represents the fonts installed on the system.

System.IO Namespace

The **System.IO namespace** (Table E-10) contains types that allow synchronous and asynchronous reading and writing on data streams and files.

Table E-10   System.IO Namespace

CLASS	DESCRIPTION
Directory	Exposes static methods for creating, moving, and enumerating through directories and subdirectories.
DirectoryInfo	Exposes instance methods for creating, moving, and enumerating through directories and subdirectories.
File	Provides static methods for the creation, copying, deletion, moving, and opening of files, and aids in the creation of FileStream objects. For example, the Copy() method copies an existing file to a new file.
FileInfo	Provides instance methods for the creation, copying, deletion, moving, and opening of files, and aids in the creation of FileStream objects. For example, the Name property gets the name of the file.
FileStream	Exposes a Stream around a file, supporting both synchronous and asynchronous read and write operations.
Path	Performs operations on String instances that contain file or directory path information. These operations are performed in a cross-platform manner. For example, the Combine() method combines two path strings.
Stream	Provides a generic view of a sequence of bytes.
StreamReader	Implements a TextReader that reads characters from a byte stream in a particular encoding.
StreamWriter	Implements a TextWriter for writing characters to a stream in a particular encoding.
StringReader	Implements a TextReader that reads from a string.
StringWriter	Writes information to a string. The information is stored in an underlying StringBuilder.
TextReader	Represents a reader that can read a sequential series of characters.
TextWriter	Represents a writer that can write a sequential series of characters.

System.Web Namespace

The **System.Web namespace** (Table E-11) supplies classes and interfaces that enable browser-server communication.

Table E-11   *System.Web Namespace*

CLASS	DESCRIPTION
HttpApplication	Defines the methods, properties, and events common to all application objects within a Web application. For example, the Session property gets the intrinsic session object that provides access to session data.
HttpApplicationState	Enables sharing of global information across multiple sessions and requests within a Web application. For example, the Item property gives you access to the state information regarding the user's session.
HttpBrowserCapabilities	Enables the server to gather information on the capabilities of the browser that is running on the client. For example, the JavaScript property gets a value indicating whether the client browser supports JavaScript.
HttpCookie	Provides a type-safe way to create and manipulate individual HTTP cookies. For example, the Name and Value properties give you the name and value of a cookie.
HttpCookieCollection	Provides a type-safe way to manipulate HTTP cookies. For example, the Add() method adds the specified cookie to the cookie collection.
HttpResponse	Encapsulates HTTP response information from a Web operation. For example, the Cookies property gets the response cookie collection.
HttpWriter	Provides a TextWriter object that is accessed through the intrinsic HttpResponse object. For example, the Write() method sends HTTP output to the client.

System.Web.Mail Namespace

The **System.Web.Mail namespace** (Table E-12) contains classes that enable you to construct and send messages. The mail message is delivered either through the SMTP mail service built into Microsoft Windows or through an arbitrary SMTP server.

Table E-12   *System.Web.Mail Namespace*

CLASS	DESCRIPTION
MailAttachment	Provides properties and methods for constructing an e-mail attachment. For example, the FileName property gets the name of the file attachment.
MailMessage	Provides properties and methods for constructing an e-mail message. For example, the Subject property gets or sets the subject line of the e-mail message.
SmtpMail	Provides properties and methods for sending messages. For example, the Send() method sends an email message.

System.Web.Services Namespace

The **System.Web.Services namespace** (Table E-13) consists of the classes that enable you to create XML Web services.

Table E-13   System.Web.Services Namespace

CLASS	DESCRIPTION
WebMethodAttribute	Adding this attribute to a method within an XML Web service created using ASP.NET makes the method callable from remote Web clients.
WebService	Defines the optional base class for XML Web services, which provides direct access to common ASP.NET objects, such as application and session state.
WebServiceAttribute	Used to add additional information to an XML Web service, such as a string describing its functionality.

System.Web.UI.WebControls Namespace

The **System.Web.UI.WebControls namespace** (Table E-14) is a collection of classes that allows you to create Web server controls on a Web page. Web server controls run on the server and include form controls such as buttons and text boxes. They also include special-purpose controls such as a calendar. Because Web server controls run on the server, you can control these elements programmatically. Web server controls are more abstract than HTML server controls.

Table E-14   System.Web.UI.WebControls Namespace

CATEGORY OR CLASS	DESCRIPTION
Controls	A category of classes that include all of the controls listed in the Web Forms tab of the Toolbox when creating a Web application. For example, the TextBox, Label, and Button controls are included.
WebControl	Serves as the base class that defines the methods, properties, and events common to all controls in the System.Web.UI.WebControls namespace.
Xml	Displays an XML document without formatting or using Extensible Stylesheet Language Transformations (XSLT).

System.Windows.Forms Namespace

The **System.Windows.Forms namespace** (Table E-15) contains classes for creating Windows-based applications that take full advantage of the rich user interface features available in the Microsoft Windows operating system.

Table E-15 System.Windows.Forms Namespace

CATEGORY OR CLASS	DESCRIPTION
Application	Provides shared methods and properties to manage an application, such as methods to start and stop an application, to process Windows messages, and properties to get information about an application.
Common Dialog Boxes	A category of classes that includes such classes as the SaveFileDialog, OpenFileDialog, FontDialog, and PrintDialog classes.
Components	A category of classes that includes the Tooltip class, Menu related classes, and Help classes.
Control	A high-level class from which the Controls and Form classes are derived.
Controls	A category of classes that includes all of the Windows Forms controls you see in the Toolbox window. For example, the TextBox, Label, and Button controls are included.
Form	Represents a window or dialog box that makes up an application's user interface.
Screen	Represents a display device or multiple display devices on a single system.
UserControl	Provides an empty control that can be used to create other controls.

System.Xml Namespace

The **System.Xml namespace** (Table E-16) provides standards-based support for processing XML.

Table E-16 System.Xml Namespace

CLASS	DESCRIPTION
XmlAttribute	Represents an attribute. Valid and default values for the attribute are defined in a DTD or schema.
XmlDocument	Represents an XML document.
XmlDocumentType	Represents the document type declaration.
XmlElement	Represents an element.
XmlNameTable	Table of atomized string objects.
XmlNode	Represents a single node in the XML document.
XmlNodeList	Represents an ordered collection of nodes.
XmlNodeReader	Represents a reader that provides fast, non-cached forward-only access to XML data in an XmlNode.
XmlReader	Represents a reader that provides fast, non-cached, forward-only access to XML data.
XmlText	Represents the text content of an element or attribute.
XmlTextReader	Represents a reader that provides fast, non-cached, forward-only access to XML data.

(continued)

Table E-16 System.Xml Namespace (continued)

CLASS	DESCRIPTION
XmlTextWriter	Represents a writer that provides a fast, non-cached, forward-only way of generating streams or files containing XML data that conforms to the W3C Extensible Markup Language (XML) 1.0 and the Namespaces in XML recommendations.
XmlWhitespace	Represents white space in element content.
XmlWriter	Represents a writer that provides a fast, non-cached, forward-only means of generating streams or files containing XML data that conforms to the W3C Extensible Markup Language (XML) 1.0 and the Namespaces in XML recommendations.

F

ASCII
Character Codes

Appendix F lists all 256 ASCII decimal codes and their
corresponding characters. The characters shown in Table F-1
on the next page for codes 128 to 255 represent the default
character set for a console application. These codes may differ
based on the selected typeface in which they are displayed.
Foreign character sets also may be represented by these
decimal codes.

ASCII Character Set

Table F-1 illustrates the ASCII character set. Decimal codes 0 to 31 are considered control characters and are not printable; thus the corresponding characters for these codes are blank. Code 32 is the space character.

Table F-1   ASCII Character Set

DECIMAL CODE	CHARACTER	DECIMAL CODE	CHARACTER	DECIMAL CODE	CHARACTER	DECIMAL CODE	CHARACTER	DECIMAL CODE	CHARACTER
0		51	3	102	f	153	Ö	204	╠
1		52	4	103	g	154	Ü	205	=
2		53	5	104	h	155	¢	206	╬
3		54	6	105	i	156	£	207	╧
4		55	7	106	j	157	¥	208	╨
5		56	8	107	k	158	₧	209	╤
6		57	9	108	l	159	ƒ	210	╥
7		58	:	109	m	160	á	211	╙
8		59	;	110	n	161	í	212	╘
9		60	<	111	o	162	ó	213	╒
10		61	=	112	p	163	ú	214	╓
11		62	>	113	q	164	ñ	215	╫
12		63	?	114	r	165	Ñ	216	╪
13		64	@	115	s	166	ª	217	┘
14		65	A	116	t	167	º	218	┌
15		66	B	117	u	168	¿	219	█
16		67	C	118	v	169	⌐	220	▄
17		68	D	119	w	170	¬	221	▌
18		69	E	120	x	171	½	222	▐
19		70	F	121	y	172	¼	223	▀
20		71	G	122	z	173	¡	224	∝
21		72	H	123	{	174	«	225	ß
22		73	I	124	¦	175	»	226	Γ
23		74	J	125	}	176	▒	227	Π
24		75	K	126	~	177	▓	228	Σ
25		76	L	127	⌂	178	▓	229	σ
26		77	M	128	Ç	179	│	230	µ
27		78	N	129	ü	180	┤	231	τ
28		79	O	130	é	181	╡	232	Φ
29		80	P	131	â	182	╢	233	θ
30	▲	81	Q	132	ä	183	╖	234	Ω
31	▼	82	R	133	à	184	╕	235	δ
32		83	S	134	å	185	╣	236	∞
33	!	84	T	135	ç	186	║	237	φ
34	"	85	U	136	ê	187	╗	238	∈
35	#	86	V	137	ë	188	╝	239	∩
36	$	87	W	138	è	189	╜	240	≡
37	%	88	X	139	ï	190	╛	241	±
38	&	89	Y	140	î	191	┐	242	≥
39	'	90	Z	141	ì	192	└	243	≤
40	(	91	[	142	Ä	193	┴	244	⌠
41	)	92	\	143	Å	194	┬	245	⌡
42	*	93	]	144	É	195	├	246	÷
43	+	94	^	145	æ	196	─	247	≈
44	,	95	_	146	Æ	197	┼	248	°
45	-	96	`	147	ô	198	╞	249	•
46	.	97	a	148	ö	199	╟	250	·
47	/	98	b	149	ò	200	╚	251	√
48	0	99	c	150	û	201	╔	252	ⁿ
49	1	100	d	151	ù	202	╩	253	²
50	2	101	e	152	ÿ	203	╦	254	■
								255	

Index